Greek Verbs Irregular and defective Their Forms Meaning and Quantity

William Veitch, Oxford at the Clarendon

Clarendon Press Series

GREEK VERBS

IRREGULAR AND DEFECTIVE

THEIR

FORMS MEANING AND QUANTITY

Embracing all the Tenses used by the Greek Writers, with References to the Passages in which they are found

BY

WILLIAM VEITCH, LL.D. EDIN.

NEW EDITION

Oxford

AT THE CLARENDON PRESS

M DCCC LXXXVII

PREFACE.

THIS book, on the *Irregular* and *Defective Greek Verbs*, is the result of much toilsome labour and anxious thought.

In the course of extensive and rather accurate reading of the Greek Authors, I had been accustomed to mark whatever occurred to me as rare or peculiar in form, quantity, and meaning. This often-enabled me to supply authority in cases where none had been previously given, and often to supply even tenses which had been denied to exist.

The chief peculiarities which distinguish this book from others on the same subject are the following:—

First, the history of the verb is more fully developed by being traced to a later period of the language, and the prose usage given commensurately with the poetic. I never could see the propriety of accepting parts and forms peculiar to the Anthology, but rejecting those which occur first in Aristotle, Polybius, Arrian, Dionysius of Halicarnassus, Lucian, etc. This fuller development will be of no slight advantage to the advanced scholar; and I have taken care to prevent its proving injurious to the less advanced—whose attention should be confined chiefly to what is strictly classical—by marking as late those parts and forms which are not found in the purer writers.

Second, I have enlarged considerably the list of verbs, and given authority for every part for which authority could be found, for the present as well as for the derivative tenses.

Third—and what I hold of capital importance—I have always given the parts in the simple form when I could find them, and in no instance have I given a compound without warning, or exhibiting its composition. The giving as simple forms those which the Greeks uniformly employed as compound, is a fault that deeply vitiates every book on the subject, and a fault of perhaps graver import than may on first thoughts be very obvious. It is easy to say that the compound infers the simple. But to what extent, and in what sense is this true? Legitimate analogical formation is one thing, usage is another. The Romans of the *classic* period said linquo, liqui, linquere, but re-lictus; tollo, tollere, but sustuli, sublatum; elicio, not lacio; inspicio, not specio, etc., etc.; and we say deceive, perceive, receive, but never *ceive;* preserve, observe, reserve, never, in this sense, the simple *serve*.

This might be followed out to great length, but it is enough for my purpose merely to indicate the line of investigation, and to suggest an analogous case in other languages, especially in our own in which we can feel more strongly and finely. From the frequent absence of simples in whole or in part, and from the analogy of other languages, is it not a natural and legitimate inference that the Greeks would have felt it as strange to hear certain of their compound verbs used in the simple form as we should do to hear some of ours? No doubt changes introduced by time, accident, use and wont, the absence of such combinations of circumstances as require the simple, the fact that compounds lose their more prominent distinctiveness and thus serve the purpose of simples, degradation from written or confinement to spoken speech, usurpation by other verbs identical or akin in meaning, loss of records, and other causes may go far towards accounting for certain curious phenomena in language; but let us have correct data from which to reason: let us have what the Greeks wrote. The investigation is an interesting one, and I should be glad if it were taken up by some person who has sufficient leisure, a mind of sufficient compass, and duly exercised by use to discern the things that differ.

I have uniformly used the best editions of the Greek Authors, and have thus been enabled to exhibit the Irregular and Defective Verbs somewhat more in accordance with the now approved Texts than has hitherto been done. Some books of considerable merit have been greatly marred by the use of uncritical editions. In cases of disputed readings, instead of arbitrating myself, I have given what in a book like this ought always to be given—the MSS. and Editors that support each reading; and have thus furnished the scholar with the proper data, the external grounds at least, for guiding his decision. All my references are the result of my own reading; I have not borrowed them from others, except in a few very late Authors, Philo for instance, Apollinaris, etc., and these I owe to Lobeck. To Buttmann and Matthiae I am much indebted. Buttmann on Epic diction has no equal; and Matthiae's list of Irregular Verbs in the third German edition of his Greek

Grammar (untranslated) is one of the best I have seen. I have also derived advantage from the Paris edition of Stephens' Thesaurus, and several useful hints from the works of Poppo, Krüger, and Ahrens.

Extreme care has been taken to secure accuracy in every respect, so essentially important in a work like this. But amid so many disturbing biases, so many risks of going wrong, it will be marvellous indeed if I have in all cases gone right. My eye may have slipped over errors, my judgment over graver faults.

In this second edition, I have corrected error and supplied defect by reading again the newest recensions of the classical, and extending my reading of the later writers. I have also tried so to arrange the vouchers as to shew the usage—general or confined to a class—of each part of the verb, as well as the defects and dialectic peculiarities. The book has thus been brought nearer to its aim—of being a trustworthy guide to the pupil and the teacher, and of some use perhaps also to the textualist and the advanced amateur scholar. I feel grateful to the Delegates of the Clarendon Press for their scholarly generosity in bringing out this book, so little fitted—however good and useful its aim—to engage the favour of the Trade.

1865.

The third edition is a severe revision of the second, with such additions and alterations as seemed to be necessary or useful. I gratefully acknowledge some important corrections and suggestions kindly communicated by the Dean of Christ Church.

1871.

In this fourth edition, besides a general revision, the references have been largely increased, Dialectic peculiarities more carefully noted, and a few verbs added noteworthy chiefly for considerable defect. I gladly accord due thanks to Dr. G. Curtius, Leipsic, and Dr. Pökel, Prenzlau, for kindly drawing my attention to some unseemly errors.

1879. W. V.

PRINCIPAL EDITIONS

TO WHICH REFERENCES ARE MADE.

Homer: Bekker, Spitzner, Dindorf, La Roche.
—— *Hymns*, *Batr.*: Francke, Baumeister, Draheim.
Hesiod: Goettling, Lennep, Schoem. Flach.
Pindar: Boeckh, Schneidew. Bergk, Mommsen, Christ.
Elegiac, Iamb. Lyr.* and Dithyramb. Poets: Bergk, Schneidew. Ahrens.
Poetae Scenici (Aesch. Soph. Eur. Aristoph.): Pors. Elms. Herm. Blomf. Linw. Dind. Franz; references uniformly to Dind. (5 ed.)
Comic Fragments (Com. or C. Fr.): Meineke.
Orphica: Hermann.
Anthology (Anthol. or Anth.): Jacobs, Tauchnitz, Meineke.
Theocritus: Meineke, Ziegler, Paley, Fritzsche.
Aratus: Bekker.
Manetho: Axt and Rigler, Koechly.
Lycophron: Bachm.
Callimachus: Ernest. Blomf. Meineke.
Ap. Rhodius: Wellauer, Merkel.
Nicander: Gottl. and Otto Schneider.
Babrius: Lachm. Lewis.
Dionys. Perieg.: Passow.
Oppian: Schneider.
Quint. Sm.: Tauchnitz, Koechly.
Nonnus: Graefe, Koechly.
Herodotus: Bekker, Gaisf. Dind. &c.
Hippocrates: Kühn, Littré, Erm.
Thucydides: Bekker, Poppo, Krüg.
Xenophon: L. Dind. Poppo, Bornem. Krüg. Sauppe, &c.
Attic Orat.: Bekk. Baiter and Sauppe, Maetzn. Dind. Scheibe, Francke.
Plato: Bekk. Bait. Orell. Winckel.
Aristotle: Bekker.
Theophrastus: Schneider, Wimmer.
Polybius: Bekker, L. Dind. Hultsch.
Diodor. Siculus: Tauchnitz, Bekker, L. Dind.
Dion. Halicarnas.: Reiske, Tauchnitz, Kiessling.
Plutarch *Vit.*: Bekk. Sintenis.
—— *Moral.*: Wyttenb. Dübner.
Arrian: Ellendt, Krüger.
Lucian: Bekk, Jacobitz, Dindorf, Fritzsche.
Pausanias: Siebel, Dind. Schubart.
Appian: Bekker, Mendelssohn.
Dio Cassius: Tauchnitz, Bekker, L. Dind.
Strabo: Kramer.
Alciphron: Wagner, Meineke.
Athenaeus: Dind. Tauchnitz.
Diog. Laertius: Tauchnitz.
Aelian: Schneider, Hercher.
Stobaeus: Tauchnitz, Gaisf. Meineke.
Chariton: D'Orville, Hercher.
Longus: Seiler, Hercher.
Epistologr. Graeci: Hercher.
Pseudo-Callisth.: Müller, Meusel.
&c. &c.

* Anacr. the genuine, Anacreont. the spurious Fr. of Anacreon.

GREEK VERBS

IRREGULAR AND DEFECTIVE.

('Αάω) Epic, *To injure mentally—infatuate*, **1 aor.** (ἄασα), ᾄᾰσας Il. 8, 237, ᾄᾰσε Matron, Athen. 4, 135, ᾄᾰσ' Od. 21, 296, -σε 297; Q. Sm. 13, 429, contr. ἆσε Od. 11, 61, ᾄᾱσαν, 10, 68; ἆσας Soph. Fr. 554; ἆσαι Aesch. Fr. 428: **1 aor pass.** ἀάσθην Il. 19, 136; H. Hym. 4, 253; Ap. Rh. 4, 412, ἀάσθης Hym. Cer. 258, ἀάσθη Il. 19, 113; subj. ἀασθῇ Hes. Op. 283 (Schaef. Goettl. Dind.); ἀασθείς Od. 21, 301; ἀάσθη Hym. Cer. 246; Ap. Rh. 4, 1080. **Mid.** ἄᾱται (ἀάεται) as act. Il. 19, 129: aor. ἀᾰσάμην intrans. *I erred*, Il. 9, 119. 19, 137 (ἀᾰσάμεσθα Q. Sm. 5, 422. 9, 509), ἀάσατο Il. 9, 537, ἀᾱσ- 11, 340, but trans. ᾄᾱσατο *misled, duped* (?) Il. 19, 95 (Vulg. Wolf, Heyne); and if correct ἀάσαντο *tore*, Fr. Incert. 39, 3 (Bergk), see below. **Vb.** ᾄᾰτος (-τός Buttm.) *hurtful*, Ap. Rh. 1, 459, with ἀ priv. ἀ-άᾰτος Od. 22, 5, ἀ-ᾱᾰ- Il. 14, 271, *inviolable*, ἄν-ᾱτος Aesch. Ag. 1211; Soph. O. C. 786.

At Il. 19, 95 quoted, Bekker, Spitzner, and Dindorf, instead of Ζῆν' ἄσατο the common reading, adopt Ζεὺς ἄσατο with Aristarchus. By this change the aor. mid. would lose its only instance of active force in *classic* Greek, unless Bergk's suggestion ἀάσαντο Fr. Inc. 39, 3, be correct for δάσαντο (Bekk.), see Apollodor. 3, 4, 4. We demur to this emendation of Bergk, both because we do not see the unsuitableness of the common reading, and because we never met with a decided case of ἀάω signifying *physical harm*. It certainly is not established by the quotation from Hesychius, ἀάσαντο, ἔβλαψαν, for, as far as documentary evidence goes, Hesych. may be merely defining his own notions of Epic usage; and even if he have a wider reference—to authors not now extant—it is still not decisive, for the equivalent ἔβλαψαν has notoriously a *double* aspect, φρένας βλάπτειν Il. 15, 724, as well as γούνατα 7, 271.

(**Ἀβακέω**) *To be speechless, know not* (βάζω), Epic, and only **aor.** ἀβάκησαν Od. 4, 249. The collateral **mid.** form ἀβακίζομαι is used in participle only, -ομένων Anacr. 74 (Bergk.) (ἄβᾰ-).

Ἀβολέω *To meet,* Orph. Arg. 472 if sound: fut. ἀβολήσω Ap. Rh. 3, 1145; Hesych.: in use chiefly **aor.** ἀβόλησα Callim. Fr. 455; Ap. Rh. 2, 770.

Ἀβροτάζω (ἀ(μ)βροτεῖν, ἁμαρτάνω) *To miss,* Epic, and only 1 **aor.** subj. ἀβροτάξομεν for -ωμεν, Il. 10, 65.

Ἁβρύνω (ῡ) *To make fine, adorn* (ἁβρός), only **pres.** Aesch. Ag. 919; late prose, Philostr. V. Soph. 2, 3: and **aor.** opt. ἁβρύναις Anth. (Leon. Tar.) 6, 281. **Mid.** ἁβρύνομαι *to pride oneself,* &c. Attic poet. Aesch. Ag. 1205; Soph. O. C. 1339; Eur. I. A. 858; Himer. Or. 5, 8. 13, 11: **imp.** ἡβρῡνόμην Attic prose, Xen. Ages. 9, 2; Pl. Apol. 20.

Ἀγάζω *To be greatly moved, feel displeasure, adore,* &c. Poet. and in **act.** only 2 sing. ἀγάζεις Soph. Fr. 797; and inf. ἀγάζειν Aesch. Supp. 1063. **Mid.** as act. ἀγάζονται (Hesych.); ἀγαζόμενοι Pind. N. 11, 6: **imp.** ἠγάζετο late, Orph. Arg. 64: **fut.** ἀγάσομαι, and **aor.** ἠγασάμην &c. are perhaps better referred to ἄγαμαι.

Ἀγαίομαι *To be indignant,* Epic, Ion. and only **pres.** -ομαι Archil. 25 (Bergk), -εται Hes. Op. 333; -όμενος Od. 20, 16; Ap. Rh. 1, 899; Her. 8, 69; late, *to admire,* Opp. Hal. 4, 138. (ᾰ.)

Ἀγαλλιάω *To rejoice,* unclassic, and **act.** rare, N. T. Rev. 19, 7 (Mss. A. C. Lach. Tisch.): **imp.** ἠγαλλίων Nicet. Eugen. 9, 285: **aor.** ἠγαλλίασα only Luc. 1, 47. Usu. **mid.** ἀγαλλιάομαι (classic ἀγάλλομαι) V. T. Jer. 49 (30), 4: **fut.** -ιάσομαι Esai. 35, 2; Herm. Past. 5, 1: **aor.** ἠγαλλιασάμην Ps. 15, 9; N. T. Joh. 8, 56; Orig. Ref. Haer. p. 243 (Miller): and in same sense **aor. pass.** ἠγαλλιάσθην Ps. 47, 12. 69, 5; -ασθῆναι N. T. Joh. 5, 35 (Vat. Griesb.), -αθῆναι (Sinait. Lach. Tisch.) For ἀγαλλιῶμεν Rev. 19, 7, some Mss. and edit. have **mid.** -ιώμεθα, and for ἠγαλλίασε Luc. 1, 47, Bretschneider would read **mid.** -άσατο on the ground that the το of the verb had been lost owing to the article τό immediately following. The best Mss. however present, and the best editors retain, the **aor. act.**

Ἀγάλλω *To adorn,* Pind. N. 5, 43; Eur. H. F. 379; Pl. Leg. 931; -λλῃ ibid.; -λλων Pind. Ol. 1, 86: **imp.** ἤγαλλον D. Cass. 47, 18. 57, 10. Fr. 57, 40 (Bekk.): **fut.** ἀγᾰλῶ Ar. Pax 399; Com. Fr. (Theop.) 2, 810: 1 **aor.** ἤγηλα D. Cass. 44, 48. 59, 3; subj. ἀγήλω Com. Fr. (Herm.) 2, 383; opt. ἀγήλαι Aristid. 10, 68 (D.), -ειεν D. Cass. 66, 2; inf. ἀγῆλαι Eur. Med. 1027: (**p. p.** ἤγαλμαι?): **aor. pass.** late ἀγαλθῆναι D. Cass. 51, 20. **Mid.** ἀγάλλομαι *am proud,* Il. 18, 132; Archil. 6 (Bergk); Eur. Bac.

1197; Ar. Pax 1298; Her. 4, 64; Thuc. 3, 82; Pl. Theaet. 176; imper. -λεο Archil. 66, 4: imp. ἠγαλλόμην Eur. Tr. 452; Her. 1, 143. 9, 109 (Bekk.); Thuc. 2, 44; Xen. Ages. 5, 3, ἀγαλλ- Or. Sib. 8, 476. We have never met perf. pass. except as a suggestion of D'Orville's, ἐξ-ηγαλμενος for the Mss. reading ἠγαιμένος Charit. p. 263, now read ἠγλαϊσμένος Anth. App. Epigr. 204. (ᾰ.)

At Her. 1, 143, Mss. and editors agree in the augmented form ἠγαλλ-, at 9, 109 they differ, ἀγαλλ- (Mss. Wessl. Schweigh. Gaisf. Stein), ἠγαλλ-' (Mss. Bekk. Dind. Krüg. Lhard. Bred.) The agreement of the Mss. in the first passage, and the general practice of Her. in by far the most of *analogous* verbs, favour the augmented form.

"Αγαμαι *To admire* (pres. and imp. like ἵσταμαι), Od. 6, 168. 23, 175; Eur. I. A. 28; Ar. Ach. 488; Her. 4, 46. 9, 79; Isocr. 5, 148; Pl. Menex. 249: imp. ἠγᾰμην Xen. Conv. 8, 8; Pl. Rep. 367: fut. Epic, and rare, ἀγᾰσομαι (σσ) Od. 4, 181; Opp. Hal. 2, 168: aor. mid. mostly Epic in classic Greek ἠγάσσατο Il. 3, 181, ἠγάσα- Callim. Apoll. 16; Anth. Pl. 4, 38; Opp. Hal. 2, 629, ἀγάσσ- Il. 3, 224; Q. Sm. 1, 353, ἀγάσ- Od. 18, 71; Opp. C. 3, 96; subj. -άσησθε Il. 14, 111; opt. -άσαιτο Ap. Rh. 1, 141; rare in *classic* prose Dem. 18, 204; freq. later, Plut. Mor. 30. 261. 595. Fab. Max. 18; (Eur.) Epist. 4; Themist. 10, 138. 11, 152 (Dind.); Galen 5, 289; Jos. Ant. 10, 10, 3 (Bekk.): usu. aor. pass. as mid. ἠγάσθην (not in Hom.) Hes. Fr. 206; Solon 33, 3 (Bergk); Pind. P. 4, 238; Eur. H. F. 845; Xen. Ages. 1, 8. Cyr. 6, 3, 36; Isocr. 4, 84; Pl. Parm. 135. Tim. 37; (Lys.) 2, 40; (Dem.) 60, 20; Luc. Charid. 16 (Jacob. Bekk. ἠρασθ- Dind.); Plut. Thes. 30. C. Gracch. 4. Popl. 17. Cat. Maj. 20 &c.; D. Hal. Ant. 2, 23; D. Cass. Fr. 43, 29 (Bekk.): (plp. ἤγαστο Hesych.): fut. p. rare and late ἀγασθήσομαι as mid. Themist. 27, 337. Vb. ἀγαστός Xen. An. 1, 9, 24. (ᾰγᾰμ-.) Hom. uses fut. ἀγάσσεσθαι Od. 4, 181, and sometimes aor. mid. ἀγάσαντο in the sense *regard with envy or anger*, Od. 8, 565. 23, 211, ἀγασσ- 23, 64 &c.; so Tryphiod. 272. The fut. is rare, in Hom. only once, for ἀγάσσεσθαι the old reading H. Hym. 3, 343, is now aor. -άσσασθαι, and ἀγάσσεαι formerly Od. 1, 389, was displaced by Wolf for νεμεσήσεαι (Eust. Schol.) which has been approved by perhaps every subsequent editor except Nitzsch. The *classic* usage of the Verb, then, seems to be: the pres. is employed by every class of writers, the fut. by Hom. only, the aor. mid. chiefly by the Epics, occurring in *classic* prose once only, Dem. quoted, never in Attic poetry, aor. pass. by Hes. Solon, Pind.

Eur. and Attic prose writers, but neither by Hom. nor the Comedians. We have traced the walk of this verb a little more particularly, because we have lately seen it marked as *poetical* only.

'Αγάομαι *To envy*, Epic (and only pres. and imp.), Hom. has ἀγᾶσθε Od. 5, 129, but usu. the lengthened forms ἀγάασθε Od. 5, 119; ἀγάασθαι 16, 203; part. ἀγώμενος Hes. Th. 619: imp. ἠγάασθε for -ᾶσθε (άεσθε) Od. 5, 122: for fut. and aor. see ἄγαμαι. Vb. ἀγητός Il. 5, 787. ἄγᾰασθε, but ἠγᾰασθε even in *thesis*, when a long precedes. At Od. 16, 203, ἀγάασθαι seems rather to mean *marvel at;* with seemingly a shade of *suspicion* or *awe* in ἀγώμενος Hes. Th. 619. Stein and Abicht read with some Mss. the Ionic form ἀγεόμενοι Her. 8, 69, for ἀγαιόμ-.

'Αγαπάζω *To shew regard, welcome,* Poet. Od. 16, 17; Opp. Hal. 1, 385, 3 pl. Dor. -άζοντι Pind. I. 5, 54; imper. -αζε Musae. 147; Epic inf. -αζέμεν Il. 24, 464; -άζων Eur. Ph. 1327 (trimet.): imp. ἀγᾰπαζον Ap. Rh. 4, 1291, ἀμφ- Od. 14, 381: 1 aor. in Dor. prose ἀγαπάξαι Callicr. Stob. 85, 18. **Mid.** ἀγαπάζομαι as act. imper. -άζεο Ap. Rh. 4, 416; -όμενοι Od. 7, 33. 21, 224: imp. Dor. ἀγαπάζοντο Pind. P. 4, 241. Mostly Epic and Lyric. (ᾰγᾰ-.) The collat. form ἀγαπάω is regular and pretty complete in act. and pass. but we think without mid. A Dor. inf. ἀγαπῆν occurs in Stob. Flor. 85, 17; and an Aeol. imp. ἠγάπευν Theocr. Epigr. 19.

'Αγγέλλω *To announce*, Soph. O. C. 1511; Ar. Lys. 1235; Her. 3, 140; Thuc. 7, 43, 3 pl. Dor. ἀγγέλλοντι, ἐπ- Pind. P. 4, 31; imper. ἄγγελλε Aesch. Ch. 658; Ar. Vesp. 409; Pl. Leg. 913, 3 pl. ἀγγελλόντων Attic so called, Il. 8, 517, δι- Pl. Leg. 784; ἀγγέλλων Od. 14, 123; Aesch. Ag. 30; Thuc. 7, 8, Dor. fem. ἀγγέλλοισα, δι- Pind. N. 5, 3: imp. ἤγγελλον Thuc. 7, 17; Xen. Cyr. 6, 2, 15, iter. ἀγγέλλεσκε, ἀπ- Il. 17, 409: fut. ἀγγελῶ Aesch. Pr. 943; Soph. O. C. 1429; Eur. Alc. 209; Ar. Thesm. 654; Thuc. 2, 85, ἀπ- Pind. P. 6, 18, Ion. ἀγγελέω Il. 9, 617; Her. 1, 43. 4, 14, Dor. ἀγγελιῶ, ἀν- Inscr. Heracl. 1, 70: 1 aor. ἤγγειλα Od. 23, 22; Soph. O. R. 604; Her. 8, 80; Antiph. 2, γ, 2; Pl. Phaed. 58, Dor. ἄγγηλα Inscr. Cret. 2556, 43 (Ahrens, ἀγγελ- 2 aor. Boeckh): p. ἤγγελκα Polyb. 35, 4, κατ- Lys. 25, 30, εἰσ- Lycurg. 1, περι- Dem. 21, 4: plp. ἠγγέλκει, ἀπ- Dem. 19, 23: p. p. ἤγγελμαι rare in Poet. Aesch. Ch. 774; Thuc. 8, 97; Pl. Charm. 153, ἐξ- Eur. Med. 1007: plp. ἠγγέλμην, 3 pl. -ελμένοι ἦσαν Xen. Hell. 6, 4, 16, Ion. 3 sing. ἄγγελτο if sound Her. 7, 37, see 2 aor.: 1 aor. ἠγγέλθην Eur. Hec. 591; Her. 6, 69; Thuc. 8, 1; Andoc. 2, 20; Xen. Hell. 1, 5, 16; Isae. 9, 3; Dem. 3, 5, ἀπ- Eur. Hec. 672; Antiph.

1, 11; Dem. 18, 284, ἐξαγγ- Her. 1, 21 (Gaisf. Dind. Stein), see below: **fut. p.** ἀγγελθήσομαι, ἀπ- Dem. 19, 324: **2 aor.** ἠγγέλην if correct, Eur. I. T. 932, the only instance in classic Greek (Mss. Matth. Passow, -έλθην Elms. Dind. Herm. Monk, &c.); often late, Plut. Ant. 68; Herodn. 3, 1; Polyaen. 2, 1, 9 (Mss. Woelf.), ἀπ-ηγγέλη Plut. Galb. 25; D. Hal. 9, 16. 20. 11, 23 (Kiessl.). 10, 20 (Vulg. -έλθη Kiessl.); Herodn. 3, 7, 1; (v. r. Her. 2, 121), δι- Ael. V. H. 9, 2, ἀν- V. T. Gen. 38, 24. Exod. 14, 5; N. T. 1 Pet. 1, 12, κατ- Act. 17, 13 &c.: **2. fut.** late ἀν-αγγελήσεται V. T. Ps. 21, 31, δι- 58, 13: **2 aor. act.** ἤγγελον perhaps late, often doubtful, D. Hal. 10, 20 (Vulg. -λλον Kiessl.); Polyaen. 4, 1, 21, κατ- Plut. Sert. 24; Herodn. 5, 2 (Bekk.), παρ- App. Civ. 1, 121 (Bekk.), unaugm. ἀγγελέτην Anth. (Agath. Schol.) 7, 614, doubtful in classic Greek, ἀπ-ήγγελον Her. 4, 153 (Mss. S. V. Gaisf. Schweigh. -ελλον Steph. Bekk. Dind. Krüg. Bred. Lhard. Stein), -ελον 7, 142 (Mss. Schweigh. Bekk. Krüg. -ελλον Ms. S. Ald. Gaisf. Dind. Bred. Stein), ἐξ-ήγγελε Lycurg. 85 (Vulg. Bekk. -ήγγελλε Mss. A. B., Bait. Saupp. Scheibe), εἰσ- Dem. 20, 79 (Wolf, Schaef. -ελλον Bekk. B. S. Dind. Voem.), see obs. **Mid.** ἀγγέλλομαι Poet. in *simple*, and only pres. Soph. Aj. 1376, ἐξ- Her. 6, 10, ἐπ- Thuc. 6, 88; Pl. Prot. 319: **imp.** ἠγγελλόμην, ἐπ- Soph. El. 1018; Her. 5, 98. 7, 1; Pl. Lach. 186: **fut.** (ἀγγελοῦμαι): **aor.** ἠγγειλάμην, ἐπ- Her. 6, 35; Pl. Gorg. 458: **2 aor.** very doubtful (ἀγγέλετο), ἄγγελτο if sound Her. 7, 37, is **pass.** and perhaps meant for **plp.** (Mss. S. V. Schaef. Gaisf. ἠγγέλλετο Bekk. Dind. Krüg. Bred.), ἐπ-αγγέλ- 3, 142 (Vulg. ἐπ-αγγέλλ- Ms. P. Gaisf. Stein, ἐπ-ηγγέλλ- Mss. V. S. Bekk. Krüg. Dind. &c.); ἐπ-αγγέλοιντο Xen. An. 5, 6, 26 (Mss. -έλλοιντο Mss. Krüg. -είλαντο Popp.), -έλοντο D. Sic. 11, 3 (Tauchn. -έλλοντο Bekk. Dind.); -ελόμενοι 11, 4. Fr. 30, 5 (Tauchn. -ελμένοι, -ελλόμενοι Bekk. Dind.) &c. &c. so doubtful are both **2 aorists** ἤγγελον, ἠγγελόμην, see v. r. Soph. O. R. 955; Thuc. 8, 86 &c.; Xen. An. 1, 4, 12. 3, 4, 14. 5, 6, 26 (Popp. Kühn.) **Vb.** κακ-αγγελτός Soph. Ant. 1286, ἀπ-αγγελτέον Aristot. Rhet. Alex. 31, 3. This verb in the Mss. of Her. is usu. with, often without augment. Gaisf. and Stein follow the Mss. ἀγγελ- 7, 37, ἐξ-αγγ- 1, 21. 5, 105. 118, ἐπ-αγγ- 3, 135. 142 &c. ἠγγ- 6, 69. 8, 80, ἐπ-ηγγ- 7, 1. 39 &c. but Bekk. Krüg. Bred. always ἠγγ-, and perhaps Dind. except once ἐξ-άγγ- 1, 21, seemingly by oversight.

In the later critical recensions, editors in accordance with the best Mss. have discarded almost entirely the **2 aor. act. mid.** and pass. for **1 aor.** and often **imp.** which, if the Mss. represent the usage, seems to have been sometimes used with apparently the force of an **aorist**. In Xen., Plato, and the Attic Poets, we think there is not left a trace of **2 aor.** except perhaps Eur. Hel. 448, ἀγγελεῖν, which, if correct, seems left to the sad choice of being either **2 aor.**, or **future** with ἄν. Gaisf. in his last ed. of Her. (1839) retains **2 aor. act.** we think in one place only, ἀπήγγελον 4, 153, Bekker and Krüg. at 7, 142, Dind. Bred. Lhardy **imp.** ἀπήγγελλον in both passages. In the orators, Bekker has left perhaps only one instance ἐξήγγελε Lycurg. 85, to which however, in the critical notes, he prefers ἐξήγγειλε, Bait. Saupp. Scheibe ἐξήγγελλε (Mss. A. B.): **2 aor. mid.** Gaisf. once and unaugm. ἄγγελτο (if not **plp.**) Her. 7, 37, but **imp.** ἠγγέλλετο (Bekk. Dind.), and Poppo, though retaining ἐπαγγέλοιντο Xen. An. 5, 6, 26, has nevertheless *stigmatized* it, and suggested ἐπηγγείλαντο from v. r. ὑπισχνοῦντο (Dind.): on the same grounds Krüger suggests **imp.** ἐπηγγέλλοντο, but gives in the text opt. -γέλλοιντο. Some foreigners, probably from want of Gaisford's last ed. of Her., have misrepresented the readings of that cautious, sound, and candid scholar.

'Αγείρω *To collect*, Aesch. Ch. 638; Dem. 8, 26, ξυν- Ar. Pl. 584; subj. ἀγείρῃς Alcm. 33 (Dind.); opt. ἀγείροι Od. 17, 362; Xen. Hier. 9, 9; imper. 3 pl. ἀγειρόντων Attic so called, Il. 2, 438; ἀγείρων Il. 11, 770; Her. 4, 35; Thuc. 2, 17; inf. ἀγείρειν Her. 4, 35, Dor. ἀγείρεν Theocr. 14, 40 (Mein. Words. -ρειν Ahr. &c.): **imp.** ἤγειρον Her. 1, 61, ἄγειρ- Ap. Rh. 2, 186: **fut.** (ἀγερῶ?): **aor.** ἤγειρα Il. 17, 222, ἄγειρ- Od. 14, 285; Hes. Op. 652; ἀγείρωσι Thuc. 6, 71; ἀγείραις Ap. Rh. 1, 893; inf. ἀγεῖραι Thuc. 1, 9; ἀγείρας Il. 9, 338; Soph. El. 695; Eur. Hec. 615; Thuc. 4, 105; Pl. Rep. 369, Dor. -είραις Pind. P. 9, 54: **p.** late συν-αγήγερκας Theodr. Prodr. 4, 467 (Herch.); -κώς Hesych.: **p. p.** ἀγηγερμένος App. Civ. 2, 134, συν- Phot. Hesych.: **plp.** ἀγήγερτο App. Mithr. 108, Epic 3 pl. ἀγηγέρατο Il. 4, 211; and late prose App. Hisp. 40: **aor.** ἠγέρθην Il. 1, 57, ἀγέρθη 22, 475, Epic 3 pl. ἤγερθεν Il. 1, 57. Od. 8, 24, ἄγερθεν Ap. Rh. 3, 356: **fut.** ἀγερθήσεται (Hesych.). **Mid.** ἀγείρομαι *gather for oneself*, Od. 13, 14; περι-αγειρόμενοι Pl. Rep. 621: **imp.** ἐσ-αγείρετο Il. 15, 240. 21, 417 (Bekk.): **fut.** ἀγεροῦνται reflex or **pass.** Orac. Sib. 1, 346: **1 aor.** ἠγειράμην, ἀγειράμενος Ap. Rh. 4, 1335; Q. Sm. 2, 559, ξυν-αγείρατο Od. 14, 323; late prose Ael. V. H. 4, 14: **2 aor.** ἀγέροντο Epic, and reflex *collected themselves, assembled*, Il. 18, 245. Od. 20, 277; ἀγερέσθαι Od. 2, 385 (Buttm. Bekk. -έρεσθαι Dind. Ameis); part. sync. ἀγρόμενος Il. 20, 166. Od. 20, 123. Late **pres.** ἀγέρομαι=ἀγείρ- Ap. Rh. 3, 895; Opp. Hal. 3, 378, ἀμφ- 3, 231; Theocr. 17, 94.

We have not observed the *simple* form of this verb in Comedy. The **1 aor. act.** seems to have been occasionally confounded with **1 aor.** of ἐγείρω. At Il. 5, 510, old editions have θυμὸν ἀγεῖραι, which late editors have properly changed to ἐγεῖραι; and μάχην ἤγειρας 13, 778, πόλεμον ἤγειραν Pl. Leg. 685, should also be referred to ἐγείρω. The **mid.** and **passive** in the *simple* form seem to be exclusively Epic in the *classic* period. The **2 aor. mid.** is always intrans., the **1 aor.** always trans. *simple* and comp.; ἐσαγείρατο λαός Od. 14, 248 (Vulg. Dind.) has been rightly altered to **imp.** ἐσαγείρετο by Bekker, and adopted by Faesi, Baeumlein, La Roche. Her. always augments this verb, ἤγειρ- 1, 61. 62, συν-ήγειρ- 4, 4. 163.

'Αγηλατέω, ἀγ- *To drive out as polluted* (ἄγος-ἐλαύνω), in the classic period, only **pres.** ἀγηλατέει Her. 5, 72: and **fut.** ἀγηλατήσειν Soph. O. R. 402. (ᾰ.)

'Αγίζω *To consecrate* (ἅγιος), Poet. and late prose, -ίζει Dio. H. 1, 57, -ίζουσι 4, 2; -ίζων Soph. O. C. 1495: **imp.** ἥγιζον *conveyed stealthily, filched,* Ar. Plut. 681: **aor. pass.** ἁγισθείς Pind. Ol. 3, 19. (ᾰ.)

'Αγῑνέω *To bring,* Epic and Ion. Od. 14, 105. 22, 198; Her. 3, 97, 3 pl. Ion. -εῦσι Callim. Apoll. 82; ἀγῑνεῖν Hes. Op. 676; Crates 1, 8 (Bergk), Ion. ἀγινέειν, ἀπ- Her. 3, 89, συν- Arr. Ind. 8, 10, Epic ἀγῑνέμεναι Od. 20, 213; ἀγινέων Her. 7, 25; and late, Arr. Ind. 8, 9: **imp.** ἠγίνεον Il. 18, 493, but ἀγίνεον 24, 784, κατ- Od. 10, 104; and always Her. ἀγίν- 3, 89. 93. 97. 7, 25, ἀπ-αγίν- 3, 92. 94, iter. ἀγίνεσκον Od. 17, 294, augm. ἠγίν- unus. and late Arat. 111 (Bekk.): fut. -ήσω H. Hym. 1, 57. 2, 71. 82: **pass. pres.** late ἀγινῆται Stob. (Hippod.) 43, 93; ἀγινέεσθαι Arr. Ind. 32, 7. **Mid.** ἀγινέομαι *cause to bring to oneself,* -εόμενος Her. 7, 33. ᾰ, ῑ always. ἠγίνεον Il. 18, 493, is trisyllabic, as ἠλάστεον 15, 21. ἀγίνεσκον from ἀγινέω, is analogous to καλέσκετο, πωλέσκετο.

'Αγκάζομαι *To lift in the arms,* Epic, and only **imp.** ἀγκάζοντο Il. 17, 722, ἠγκάζ- Nonn. 4, 203: (fut.?): and **aor.** late ἠγκάσσατο Nonn. 7, 318. 41, 199.

'Αγκαλέω Poet. for ἀνα-καλέω.

'Αγκαλίζομαι *To embrace,* Simonid. 7, 77 (Bergk); Plut. Mor. 638: (fut.): **aor.** ἠγκαλισάμην Anth. (Meleagr.) 12, 122; Maneth. 1, 45: with p. as mid. ἠγκαλισμένος Lycophr. 142, ὑπ- Eur. Heracl. 42: **pres. pass.** ἀγκαλιζόμενος Aesop 366 (Halm.) The comp. ἐν-αγκαλίζομαι is also **pass.** Diod. Sic. 3, 58, and **Mid.** Alciphr. 2, 4, 5 (Mein.); Plut. Camill. 5: **imp.** ἐν-ηγ- Alciphr. 3, 55, 8: **aor.** ἐν-αγκάλισαι Anth. 7, 476; -σάμενος N. T. Marc. 9, 36: with **p. p.** as **mid.** ἐν-ηγκαλισμένος Callistr. Descr. 146: and **plp.** ἐν-ηγκάλιστο 162 (Kayser), both missed by Lexicogr.

Ἄγκειμαι for ἀνά-κειμαι.

Ἀγκρεμάννυμι, see κρεμ-.

Ἀγλαΐζω *To make splendid, adorn,* Hippocr. 8, 368 (Lit.); Ael. N. A. 8, 28; Aristaen. 1, 1; Poet in Athen. 14, 16: **imp.** ἠγλάϊζον? Com. Fr. (Antiph.) 3, 148 (Mss.); Philostr. Apoll. 6, 248; Theoph. Epist. 15: **fut.** -αϊῶ, ἐπ- Ar. Eccl. 575: **aor.** ἠγλάϊσα Anth. 7, 321. 418; late prose Niceph. Rhet. 7, 9, ἀγλ- Theocr. Epigr. 1, 4; subj. ἀγλαΐσῃ, ἐπ- Com. Fr. (Ar.) 2, 1184; late prose ἀγλαΐσας Plut. Mor. 965: (**p.**): **p. p.** ἠγλάϊσται Ael. H. A. 17, 33; Philostr. Apoll. 1, 25; Anth. App. Epigr. 204; -ϊσμένος Com. Fr. (Eub.) 3, 268, ἐπ- (Cratin.) 2, 177: **aor.** late ἀπ-ηγλαΐσθη Agath. 2, 15. **Mid.** ἀγλαΐζομαι *adorn oneself, delight in,* Simon. Am. 7, 70 (B.); Pind. Ol. 1, 14: fut. ἀγλαϊεῖσθαι Il. 10, 331, ἐπ- 18, 133, the only tense *simple* or compd. used by Hom.

The **pres.** and **fut. mid.** are by some called **passive.** ἠγλάϊζεν **imp. act.** is used intrans. as **mid.** Antiph. Com. Fr. 3, 148, for which Meineke adopts Porson's suggestion ἐπηγλαΐζετο: but Hesychius's ἀγλαΐζει, θάλλει, if correct, seems against the change. This verb occurs neither in Trag. nor *classic* prose.

Ἀγνοέω *To know not,* Soph. Tr. 78. El. 1475; Isocr. 1, 17; Isae. 3, 29; Xen. Hell. 2, 3, 53; Epic subj. ἀγνοιῇσι Od. 24, 218; -οεῖν Antiph. 5, 44; Thuc. 2, 48; pt. -οῦντες Thuc. 1, 50, Ion. -εῦντες Her. 4, 156: **imp.** ἠγνόουν Isocr. 7, 21; Aeschin. 2, 136, Ion. -όεον Hippocr. 2, 226 (Lit.): **fut.** -ήσω Bacchyl. 31 (B.); Isocr. 12, 251; (Gorg.) Fr. 685; Dem. 32, 10. 54, 31; Pl. Alcib. (1), 133: **aor.** ἠγνόησα Thuc. 4, 96; Dem. 23, 155; subj. -ήσῃς Aesch. Eum. 134; -ήσειεν Isocr. 15, 220; -ήσας Xen. Mem. 4, 2, 29; Isae. 8, 4; Aeschin. 1, 83; -ῆσαι Isae. 11, 38, Epic ἠγνοίησα Il. 2, 807; Hes. Th. 551; Anth. 9, 548, iter. Ion. contr. ἀγνώσασκε Od. 23, 95: **p.** ἠγνόηκα Com. Fr. (Alex.) 3, 393. (Dion.) 3, 548; Hippocr. 4, 78; Aeschin. 3, 84; Dem. 23, 80: **plp.** -ήκειν Luc. Philops. 6: **p. p.** ἠγνόημαι Isocr. 15, 171; Pl. Leg. 797: **aor.** ἠγνοήθην Isocr. 5, 88; Dem. 18, 303: **fut. mid.** ἀγνοήσομαι as **pass.** Dem. 18, 249 (Bekk. B. S. Dind.); Luc. Jup. Trag. 5 (Mss. V. F.): but **fut. pass.** ἀγνοηθήσομαι Luc. quoted (Mss. A. C. M. Dind. Jacobitz); Dem. quoted (Vulg.). **Vb.** ἀγνοητέον Dioscor. Prooem. 1. Of this verb, Poets seem to have used only **pres. aor.** and rarely **perf. act.** Why **fut.-mid.** ἀγνοήσομαι should be said "to want classical authority" we know not, since it is vouched by the best Ms. and adopted by the best editors of Dem. 18, 249 (Ms. S. Bekk. Dind. Bait. Saupp.) Some lexicons err exceedingly in saying that the **fut. mid.** is more freq. than the **fut. act.** There is no ground for comparison, for in the only instance where the **mid.** occurs it is **passive.**

Ἄγνῡμι *To break*, Il. 12, 148; Achae. Fr. 24 (Wagn.), κατ- Thuc. 4, 11; Pl. Men. 79, and in comp. ἀγνύω, κατ- Com. Fr. 3, 254; Xen. Oec. 6, 5; Aristot. H. A. 9, 1, 21; Paus. 6, 20, 8, (ἄγω): **imp.** (ἦγον), Dor. ἆγε (if not from ἄγω *bring*) Bion 1, 82 (Vulg. ἆξε Mein.): **fut.** ἄξω, κατ- in tmesi Il. 8, 403; Com. Fr. 2, 559: **aor.** ἔαξα Il. 7, 270. Od. 5, 316; Theocr. 25, 256, κατ- Il. 13, 257; Ar. Vesp. 1435; Thuc. 3, 89; Pl. Crat. 389, and rare ἦξα Ep. Il. 23, 392, κατ- Hippocr. 5, 224; ἄξῃς Il. 23, 341, -ῃ 5, 161; ἄξαις Hes. Op. 434, -ειαν 440; imper. ἆξον Il. 6, 306; part. ἄξας Il. 16, 371; Eur. Hel. 1598; inf. ἆξαι Il. 21, 178; Ap. Rh. 3, 96, κατ- Eur. Sup. 508; Com. Fr. 2, 603: **p. p.** ἔαγμαι, κατ- Paus. 8, 46, 5; Luc. Tim. 10: **2 p.** in comp. ἔᾱγα, ἐπ- in tmesi *am broken*, Hes. Op. 534, κατ- Eur. Cycl. 684; Ar. Thesm. 403; Com. Fr. 3, 577; Pl. Gorg. 469; Dem. 54, 35, Ion. ἔηγα, κατ- Her. 7, 224; Hippocr. 3, 492 (Littré): **2 aor.** ἐάγην Il. 13, 162. 17, 607; Ap. Rh. 3, 954; Theocr. 22, 190, but Att. ἐᾱ́γην, κατ- Ar. Vesp. 1428. Ach. 944; Andoc. 1, 61; Lys. 3, 14, unaugm. ᾽ἄγην rare Il. 3, 367. 16, 801, ἄγεν Ep. 3. pl. 4, 214. Att. perhaps always ἐάγην, Ep. ἐάγην, only once ἐάγ- Il. 11, 559 in arsi, but *degraded* as *spurious* by Bekk. in 2 ed., by others retained; Batr. 238 (Mss. Draheim, ἐκλάσθη Vulg. 241.) **Vb.** κατ-ακτός Ar. Pax 1244.—ἄγεν 3 pl. for ἄγησαν, Il. 4, 214. See καταγνυμι.

The *simple* form is always poetic in the **act.** and mostly in the **pass.** voice, ἄγνῠται Eur. Hel. 410, περι- Il. 16, 78, κατ- Soph. Fr. 147; ἄγνῠτο Hes. Sc. 279; -ύμενος Il. 16, 769; Ap. Rh. 3, 1334; Her. 1, 185, never in Attic prose. We have never seen **pres.** ἄγω, and **imp.** only once, in the Dor. form ἆγε if correct, Bion 1, 82 (Mss. Vulg., Ziegl.), see above.

Ἀγνώσσω *To know not*, seems to be a late form, Musae. 249; Coluth. 186; Tzetz. A. Hom. 364; Nonn. 42, 163; Luc. Ep. Sat. 2, 25 (Jacobitz); -ων Coluth. 8; D. Per. 173. ἀγνώσασκε Od. 23, 95, seems rather to be an iter. Ion. form of ἠγνόησε.

Ἀγοράζω *To frequent the* ἀγορά, *to market, buy*, Her. 2, 35; Xen. Lac. 9, 4, Dor. -άσδω Theocr. 15, 16: **imp.** ἠγόραζον Her. 3, 139; Thuc. 6, 51; Dem. 19, 229: **fut.** -ᾰ́σω Ar. Lys. 633; Com. Fr. 3, 439; Charit. 1, 11, 3, Megar. -ᾰσῶ, -σοῦντες Ar. Ach. 750: **aor.** ἠγόρασα Com. Fr. (Sotad.) 3, 585; Xen. Hell. 7, 2, 18; Dem. 21, 149: **p.** ἠγόρακα C. Fr. (Menand.) 4, 182; ἠγορακώς Dem. 32, 14; Aristot. Oec. 2, 34, 5. 6; Polyb. 6, 17: **p. p.** ἠγορασμένα Isae. 8, 23, -μένος Com. Fr. (Men.) 4, 281, as **mid.** see below: **aor.** ἠγοράσθην always **pass.** (Dem.) 59, 46: **imp.** ἠγοράζετο Dem. 50, 25. **Mid.** -άζομαι *buy for oneself*, Xen.

An. 1, 3, 14: imp. (ἠγοράζετο): fut. (-άσομαι): aor. (ἠγορασάμην), subj. -άσωνται Dem. 50, 55: and as mid. p. p. ἠγοράσθαι Dem. 35, 19. ᾱγ-, but ᾰγ- Com. Fr. (Anon.) 4, 620.

Ἀγοράομαι *To harangue*, mostly Epic, -άασθε Il. 2, 337: inf. ἀγορᾶσθαι Theogn. 159: in Att. only imp. (ἠγοραόμην), ἠγορῶ Soph. Tr. 601 (trimeter), Epic 2 pl. -άασθε Il. 8, 230, -όωντο 4, 1; Ap. Rh. 3, 168; Q. Sm. 5, 432; Her. 6, 11, see below: fut. (ἀγορήσομαι): aor. unaugm. ἀγορήσατο Il. 9, 95. 18, 253. Od. 7, 185: 1 aor. p. ἀγορηθείς formerly Pind. I. 1, 51, has been altered by Pauw to εὐᾱγορηθείς Dor. for εὐηγ- which the sense and metre require.

Hom. has always the lengthd. forms ἀγοράασθε for -άεσθε, -ᾶσθε: so imp. ἠγοράασθε, 3 pl. ἠγορόωντο=άοντο, -ῶντο, Il. 4, 1; Her. 6, 11 (Gaisf. Bekk. Dind.), if correct, the only instance in prose, though Passow says it is frequent in Herodotus. Liddell and Scott have now corrected this error. ᾰγ- except Il. 2, 337, ᾱγ- in arsis.—The Epic form ἠγορόωντο in Her. is rather suspicious, unless it be granted that he *borrowed* it *unchanged* from Hom. see Il. 4, 1. It is not the *usage* of Her. to insert ο before ω contracted from αω: ὁρμέωντο 7, 88, ἐχρέωντο 1, 53. 4, 157 &c. ἐμηχανέωντο 7, 172 &c. &c. never -όωντο. Had ἀγοράομαι been an Ion. prose form and *peculiar* to the Ion. dialect, he would most probably have written ἀγορῶντο, -έωντο, or -έοντο, without augment; if common to the Attic and Ion. ἠγορῶντο, -έωντο, or -έοντο, with augm. The Herodotean form is ἀγορεύω, ἠγόρευον 1, 60. 3, 119 &c. &c. Mid. ἀγορεύσασθαι 9, 26. Dietsch, Abicht, Lhardy, accordingly read ἠγορεύοντο or -ευον, but if ἀγοράομαι is kept, ἀγορῶντο, Bredow ἠγορέοντο which occurs 2, 36. 4, 180. For the similar form κομόωσι 4, 191, Dind. Dietsch, Abicht, read -έουσι, Lhardy κομῶσι with Mss. S. V.

Ἀγορεύω *To harangue, proclaim*, Il. 1, 365; Eur. Elec. 1356; Antiph. 3, γ, 7; Xen. An. 5, 6, 27; Lys. 9, 10; Epic inf. -έμεναι, Od. 13, 327, -έμεν Il. 9, 369: imp. ἠγόρευον Soph. O. C. 838; Ar. Ach. 41; Her. 7, 10, 1. 9, 92; Xen. Hell. 6, 3, 7, ἀγόρ- Il. 1, 385, προ- Her. 1, 22 (Dind. Stein, προηγ- Bekk.): fut. -εύσω Il. 7, 361. Od. 1, 179. 3, 254. 4, 836. 12, 56; Hes. Op. 402; Alciphr. 3, 52, προσ- Pl. Theaet. 147, συν- Luc. pro Imag. 24: aor. ἠγόρευσα Luc. Pisc. 15, ἀγόρευσε Il. 8, 29, προ-ηγόρευσε Her. 1, 74. 125; Com. Fr. (Menand.) 4, 247, ἀπ- Dem. 40, 44. 55, 4, ἐξ- Longus 3, 30, Dor. ἀγόρευσεν Pind. P. 4, 156 (Bergk, ἀντ-αγόρ- Vulg.); ἀγορεύσῃς, ἀπ- Pl. Theaet. 200 (Bekk. Ast), -εύσῃ, κατ- Ar. Pax 107 (Dind. Bergk, -εύῃ Cob. Mein.); ἀγόρευσον Od. 1, 174. 4, 645, -εύσατε Il. 18, 142 (Vulg.); ἀγορεῦσαι Il. 12, 176. Od. 5, 183. 7, 241. 11, 381; Anth. 7, 377;

Her. 3, 74, προσ- Xen. Mem. 3, 2, 1; ἀγορεύσας, προσ- Lycurg. 9. 18; Dem.. 39, 38, συν- 19, 178: p. προ-ηγόρευκε (Dem.) 11, 20: p. p. προ-ηγορευμένα Xen. Mem. 1, 2, 35: aor. ἠγορεύθην, προσ- Aesch. Pr. 834, -εύθη Com. Fr. (Anaxil.) 3, 350. (Philem.) 4, 40; προσ-αγορευθῇ Dem. 40, 1, ἀνα- Xen. Ven. 1, 14: fut. mid. as pass. προ-αγορεύσεται Xen. M. Eq. 2, 7 (Vulg. -εύεται Dind. Sauppe): aor. ἀγορεύσασθαι Her. 9, 26. Vb. ἀγορευτέος, προσ- Pl. Phaed. 104.

We have drawn out this verb, not because of any irregularity, but because Cobet (Var. Lect. p. 36 &c.) maintains that it is used by classic writers in the pres. and imp. only, "praesentis tantum et imperfecti formam in usu esse," that its fut. and aor. &c. are ἐρῶ, εἶπον, and that "ἀγορεύσω, ἠγόρευσα, ἠγόρευκα et cognata omnia neque in simplici forma, neque in composita in antiquo sermone *Graeco* usitata fuisse, neque earum formarum exempla apud veteres extare, nisi forte in uno alteroque loco depravato." He bates a trifle in the case of προσαγορεύω, but adds "ceterarum (formarum) nec vola nec vestigium est." We think he has been misled by a too exclusive attention to a particular class of writers. But is it sound policy to allow a pragmatical section to give law on a matter which affects the liberties of the community, and on which other bodies are as well qualified to judge? The orator might from use and wont confine himself *professionally* to the pres. and imp., but is this to prevent poet, philosopher, and historian from freely using also the fut. aor. and perf. if it so pleased them? But even the orators seem sometimes to have leapt their limits—more freq., we think, than Cobet was aware when he was trying to define them. Nay, we think it probable that Aeschines himself, whom he rather confidently produces to vouch his views, wrote ἀνηγόρευσε, not -ρευε 3, 122, notwithstanding the proximity of ἀνεῖπε. See Pind. ὣς ἄρ' ἔειπεν. ἀκᾷ δ' ἀνταγόρευσεν καὶ Πελίας P. 4, 156 (Bergk.) The "sequiores," Cobet grants, used ἀγορεύσω, -ευσα, -ευκα, but "errant omnes, Sophistae, Rhetores, Magistri!" We have noted the following: ἀγορεύσω Alciphr. 3, 52; Philostr. Ap. 186, ἀπ- Plut. Lysand. 3. Nic. 21. Mor. 195, ἐξ- Luc. Navig. 11. Demon. 11; Orph. Arg. 1355, συν- Luc. Peregr. 13: aor. ἠγόρευσα D. Hal. 1, 65; Luc. Pisc. 15, ἀπ- Aristot. Oec. 2, 24; Plut. Mor. 228, προσ- Aristot. Polit. 1, 12, 3; Plut. Mar. 41; Polyb. 1, 8, 1, προ- D. Cass. 58, 12, ἀν- Plut. Mor. 240; Heliod. 4, 5, δι- Plut. C. Gracch. 16, ἐξ- Luc. Indoct. 25; D. Laert. Prooem. 4, 5: ἠγόρευκα Liban. Or. 7 (p. 319), ἀπ- Plut. Mor. 1096; Luc. D. Deor. 24, 2, προσ- Plut. Lycurg. 6; D. Sic. 1, 37: p. p. ἠγόρευται, ἀπ- App. Pun. 59; ἠγορευμένος, ἀπ- Aristot. Polit. 7, 17, 9; Joseph. Ant. 15, 4, 1: **aor.** ἠγορεύθην Strab. 3, 3, 5; προσαγορευθῇ Aristot. Polit. 7, 16, 18, ὑπ- Top. 6, 5, 2, ἀν- Plut. C. Gracch. 3. Mor. 176. 202. 768, προ- Heliod. 5, 23; App. Syr. 63 &c. &c.

Ἀγρέω *To take, catch*, Poet. and only **pres.** indic. and imperat. ἀγρεῖς Anth. 6, 304, -εῖ Sapph. Fr. 2, 14; Aesch. Ag. 126 (chor.); imper. ἄγρει Archil. Fr. 5, 3; so Hom. but only interjectionally, (*grip*), *come, come on*, Il. 5, 765. Od. 21, 176; Ap. Rh. 1, 487, ἀγρεῖτε Od. 20, 149. **Mid.** ἀγρέο Nic. Ther. 666, *now* for αἵρεο (Vulg.)

Ἀγριαίνω *To be wild* &c. is in *classic* authors rare, partial, and intrans. Pl. Rep. 493; D. Hal. 8, 50: **imp.** ἠγρ- Pl. Rep. 393: **fut.** -ἄνῶ 501: **aor.** late ἠγρίᾱνα trans. Dio Cass. 44, 47; subj. -ιάνῃς Ach. Tat. 2, 7; -άνας Ael. V. H. 2, 13. **Pass.** ἀγριαίνομαι rare and late D. Hal. 12, 6, 3, but ἐξ- Pl. Rep. 336; Aristot. H. An. 6, 18, 6: **imp.** ἠγριαίνοντο Plut. Ant. 58: **fut.** -ανθήσομαι V. T. Dan. 11, 11: **aor.** ἠγριάνθην D. Sic. Fr. Lib. 24, 1, 2, ἐξ- V. T. Dan. 8, 7 (Vat.), see below: for which *classic* authors use ἀγριοῦμαι Hippocr. 2, 64 (Lit.): **imp.** ἠγριούμην Eur. El. 1031: **p. p.** ἠγρίωμαι Soph. Ph. 1321; Eur. Or. 387. I. T. 348; Ar. Ran. 897; -ωμένος Pax 620; Xen. Cyr. 1, 4, 24, ἀπ- Soph. Ph. 226, ἐξ- Isocr. 9, 67: **aor.** late, ἠγριώθην Plut. Per. 34; Arr. Peripl. 4; App. Hisp. 46, but ἀπ- Pl. Polit. 274, ἐξ- D. Hal. 8, 57; V. T. Dan. 8, 7 (Alex. but -άνθην Vat.) The **act.** ἀγριόω again is rare, perhaps only ἀγριόωντα Opp. Cyn. 2, 49, and **aor.** ἠγρίωσε Eur. Or. 616; Joann. Ped. 7 (West.) In comp. however, as generally happens, the case differs somewhat: ἐξαγριῶ is used in **pres. act.** Pl. Leg. 935: **aor.** -ωσα Eur. Ph. 876; Her. 6, 123; and ἐξαγριαίνω in **pres. pass.** -αίνεσθαι Pl. Rep. 336. We therefore doubt the correctness of Phrynichus's statement ἀγριωθεὶς καὶ οὐκ ἀγριανθείς, καίτοι τὸ ἀγριαίνομαι καὶ ἀγριαίνεσθαι ἀττικῶς, at least in the *simple* verb.

Ἀγροικίζομαι *To be boorish*, **pres.** only classic Pl. Theaet. 146; Plut. Sull. 6: **fut.** (-ίσομαι): **aor.** -ισάμην Aristid. 39, 491.

Ἀγρώσσω *To catch*, Epic, only **pres.**, and only part. *classic*, ἀγρώσσεις Nonn. 16, 232, ἀγρώσσει Opp. H. 3, 339, -ουσι 3, 75. 543. 4, 532. 5, 522; Nonn. 48, 286; ἀγρώσσοιεν Opp. Cyn. 1, 129; ἀγρώσσων Od. 5, 53; Nic. Ther. 416; Lycophr. 499, -ουσα Callim. Ap. 59, -οντες Lycophr. 598; -ώσσειν Nonn. 16, 136. **Pass.** ἀγρώσσονται Opp. Hal. 3, 337. 415. 4, 565. We have seen no certain case of **mid.** ἀγρώσσοιο Opp. Cyn. 1. 129 (Vulg.) has been altered to ἀγρώσσοιεν (Bodin. Schneider); and **aor.** ἀγρώσσατο (Hesych.) is held spurious by Schmidt. This verb is handled defectively and faultily in the lexicons.

'Αγυρτάζω *To collect, beg,* Epic and only inf. -τάζειν Od. 19, 284.

Ἄγχω *To squeeze the throat,* Ar. Eccl. 640, -ομεν Dem. 54, 20; ἄγχοις Ar. Lys. 81; imper. ἄγχε Com. Fr. 2, 244; -ων Ar. Ran. 468, ἀπ- Od. 19, 230, ἄγχοντες (Dem.) 47, 59; -χειν Ar. Av. 1575: imp. ἦγχον Ar. Vesp. 1039, ἄγχ- Il. 3, 371: fut. ἄγξω Ar. Eccl. 638; Luc. D. Mort. 22, 1: aor. late ἦγξε Christ. Pat. 327; ἄγξειε Liban. Or. 13 (p. 205); inf. ἄγξαι Apocr. 4 Macc. 9, 17, but ἀπ-άγξαι Ar. Pax 795. Mid. *hang oneself,* rare ἄγχεσθαι Hippocr. 8, 468 (Littré). Pass. ἀγχόμενος Pind. N. 1, 46, -ένη (Dem.) 47, 59; Luc. Anach. 11. This verb is scarcely inflected beyond the fut. act. and pres. pass. occurring only once in Hom., never in Trag., and confined in classic prose to Dem. The only instance of mid. in the *simple* verb is Hippocr. 8, 468 quoted. ἀπ-άγχω is more used, and rather better developed, Od. 19, 230; Ar. Vesp. 686; late prose Polyb. 16, 34, 9; Plut. Mar. 27: imp. ἀπ-ῆγχον Jos. Ant. 12, 5, 4: fut. -άγξει Luc. Tox. 14 (Jacob. Bekk.): aor. -ῆγξα Ar. Pax 796; late prose Luc. Lex. 11. Mid. ἀπ-άγχομαι *strangle oneself,* Com. Fr. 3, 81; Hippocr. 4, 482; Andoc. 1, 125; Xen. Cyr. 3, 1, 25: imp. ἀπ-ήγχοντο Thuc. 3, 81, 2 sing. unaugm. ἀπ-άγχεο Archil. 67 (Bergk): fut. -άγξομαι Luc. Gall. 16; Charit. 1, 4: aor. -ηγξάμην Aesch. Supp. 465; Ar. Nub. 780; Theocr. 3, 9; Her. 2, 131. 7, 232; Xen. Hier. 7, 13; Luc. D. Mer. 2, 4. Philops. 29.

Ἄγω *To lead, bring,* Il. 9, 72; Pind. P. 9, 31; Aesch. Sept. 645; Soph. O. C. 183; Ar. Ran. 190; Her. 8, 65; Thuc. 2, 34; Pl. Gorg. 478, 3 pl. Dor. ἄγοντι Pind. P. 7, 13; Epic subj. ἄγησι Od. 6, 37; Epic inf. ἀγέμεν Il. 7, 420, Aeol. ἄγην Sapph. 1, 19; Dor. f. pt. ἄγοισα, παρ- Pind. N. 7, 23: imp. ἦγον Il. 7, 310; Aesch. Pers. 342; Soph. O. C. 927; Eur. I. T. 1352; Her. 1, 70; Thuc. 7, 29; Andoc. 3, 22; Lys. 3, 37; Xen. Hell. 4, 5, 3, Dor. ἆγον Pind. P. 9, 123; Theocr. 10, 2; Aesch. Pers. 863 (chor.); Eur. Ion 896 (chor.); Ar. Lys. 1255 (chor.), Poet. 'ἄγον Il. 7, 312; Pind. P. 5, 76, ξυν- Eur. Bacc. 563 (chor.), iter. ἄγεσκον Ap. Rh. 1, 849; Her. 1, 148: fut. ἄξω Il. 1, 139; Soph. O. C. 874; Ar. Pax 418; Her. 8, 60; Thuc. 4, 28; Pl. Rep. 466, Dor. 3 pl. ἄξοισι Pind. P. 6, 13: aor. rare ἦξα Hes. Op. 434. 440; Batr. 115. 119; Antiph. 5, 46, προσ- Thuc. 2, 97, see below; Epic imper. with vowel of 2 aor. ἄξετε Il. 3, 105. 24, 778 (v. r. -ατε). Od. 14, 414; inf. ἀξέμεναι Il. 23, 50, ἀξέμεν 23, 111. 24, 663: p. ἦχα Polyb. 3, 111; Stob. 70, 13, συν- Xen. Mem. 4, 2, 8, προ- Dem. 19, 18. 25, 8, later and perhaps unatt. ἀγήοχα Alex. Rhet.

p. 442; Dio Chrys. 32, 11 (Emper.); Jos. Jud. B. 1, 30, 1 (Bekk.), εἰσ- in Philip's *spurious* letter (Dem.) 18, 39, κατ- in a Pseph. ibid. 73, συν- Aristot. Oec. 2, 2, ἐξ- Polyb. 24, 3, παρ- Plut. Phoc. 17, προσ- Heliod. 9, 24: **plp.** ἀγηόχει Polyb. 30, 4: **p. p.** ἦγμαι Her. 2, 158; Pl. Leg. 781; Dem. 13, 15, παρ- Soph. Ant. 294, as **mid.** see below: **plp.** ἠγμένοι ἦσαν Thuc. 6, 100: **aor.** ἤχθην Her. 3, 145. 6, 30 (Bekk. ἄχ- Dind. Stein); Pl. Leg. 782, ἀπ- Antiph. 5, 85; ἀχθείς Hipponax 9: **fut.** ἀχθήσομαι Pl. Hipp. Maj. 292, προσ- Thuc. 4, 87, προ- Dem. 18, 269: and **fut. mid.** ἄξομαι **pass.** Aesch. Ag. 1632; Pl. Rep. 458, προσ- Thuc. 4, 115: **2 aor.** ἤγαγον Il. 6, 291; Simon. C. 120; Her. 8, 26; especially Att. Aesch. Pr. 465; Soph. Ph. 638; Ar. Eq. 743; Thuc. 5, 84; Pl. Tim. 30; Xen. Cyr. 6, 3, 8, Dor. ἄγ- Pind. Ol. 2, 51; Theocr. 15, 103; Soph. Tr. 858 (chor.), Poet. ἄγ- Il. 11, 112. 24, 764; Eur. I. T. 138 (Lyr.); subj. ἀγάγω Il. 2, 231; Ar. Av. 1078; Antiph. 6, 15; Pl. Rep. 415, Ep. -ωμι Il. 24, 717, 3 sing. -ῃσι 24, 155. 184: opt. ἀγάγοιμι rare Od. 17, 243. 21, 201, ἀπ- Eur. Hec. 950, ἀν- Xen. An. 2, 3, 21, ἐπ- Pl. Phaed. 106, συν- Her. 1, 196; ἀγαγεῖν Pind. P. 10, 6; Eur. Bac. 1355: Ar. Ach. 250; Her. 1, 5. 2, 162; Thuc. 2, 2: Lycurg. 91; Pl. Leg. 698, Dor. -αγέν Pind. P. 4, 56, -αγεῖν (Boeckh); -ών Il. 8, 490; Eur. Or. 65; Ar. Ach. 906; Her. 3, 85; Thuc. 4, 53. **Mid.** ἄγομαι *lead for oneself, marry*, Od. 10, 40. Il. 9, 146; Soph. Ph. 613; Eur. Or. 248; Her. 1, 34; Pl. Leg. 771; Xen. Lac. 1, 6: **imp.** ἠγόμην Od. 4, 10; Eur. Med. 1331; Ar. Eccl. 323; Her. 3, 137; Xen. Cyr. 5, 4, 39, Poet. ἀγόμ- Il. 7, 363: **fut.** ἄξομαι Od. 21, 214. 322; Soph. O. C. 1460; Eur. Hipp. 625; Her. 7, 8, προσ- Thuc. 3, 32, προ- Dem. 5, 14, as **pass.** see above: **1 aor.** (ἀξάμην) unattic and unaugm. ἄξασθε Il. 8, 505 (-εσθε Schol. Bekk. Dind. La R.), ἄξαντο 8, 545 (-οντο Bekk. Dind. La R.), ἐσ-άξαντο Her. 5, 34, προεσ- 1, 190 (Gaisf. Bekk. Dind. Krüg.), προσεσ- 8, 20 (Bekk. Dind.): **2 aor.** ἠγαγόμην Il. 22, 471. Od. 14, 211; Hes. Th. 508; Her. 2, 175. 6, 63. 9, 111; rather rare in Att. Eur. Or. 182. Andr. 104 (Dor. ἀγ- Dind.); Lys. 1, 6; Isocr. 19, 8, ἐπ- Thuc. 1, 104; Pl. Menex. 238; subj. ἀγάγηται Od. 6, 159; Xen. Eq. 4, 1, ἀγάγησθον Ar. Plut. 529; opt. -οιτο Pl. Rep. 574, προσ- Ar. Thesm. 849; ἀγαγέσθαι Il. 18, 87; Her. 1, 65; Thuc. 8, 21; ἀγαγόμενος Her. 1, 185. 2, 64, προσ- Thuc. 8, 106: and **p. p.** as **mid.** ἦγμαι late in *simple*, ἠγμένος *having married*, Jos. Ant. 18, 9, 5, but προσῆκται Isocr. 5, 20, προ- Dem. 54, 23: **plp.** ἦκτο Jos. Ant. 14, 12, ἠγμένοι ἦσαν Arr. An. 7, 4, 8. **Vb.** ἀκτός Plut. Gr. 7; ἀκτέος Hippocr. 5, 476; Andoc. 3, 40; Pl. Rep. 537; Dem. 8, 5.—Ep. inf.

ἀξέμεν, ἀξέμεναι seem used sometimes as **aor.** Il. 23, 50. 111 &c. ἄξοισι Dor. 3 pl. for -ουσι Pind. P. 6, 13, so ἀγαγέν Dor. inf. for -γεῖν, P. 4, 56 (Vulg. Bergk), ἄγεσκον Ion. **imp.** for ἦγον, Her. 1, 148, ἐσ-αγ- 1, 196. The Dor. συναγαγοχεῖα is not **plp.** but part.=-χυῖα Inscr. Ther. 2448. For ἀγεόμενος called Ion. for ἀγομ- Her. 3, 14 (Schweigh.), Wessl. reads ἡγεόμ-, Bekk. and Gaisf. ἡγεόμ-, Krüg. Dind. and Bredow, perhaps rightly, ἀγόμενος, and for ἀγέαται 2, 47 (Gaisf. Bekk. Krüg.), ἄγονται (Vulg. Dind. Stein, Abicht.) In Her. Gaisf. Stein &c. with the Mss. add or drop the augmt. ἦγον, ἄγον &c. ἄχθη, ἀπ-ήχθη; Bekk. Krüg. &c. with the majority of Mss. we think uniformly augment, excepting of course **1 aor. mid.** The **1 aor. act.** and **mid.** ἦξα, ἀξάμην are rare, the former scarcely the latter never occurring in Attic. ἦξαν Batr. 115 (Vulg. εἶλξαν Baumeist.): imper. ἄξατε Nonn. 44, 148. 48, 23; ἄξας Batr. 119; Hes. quoted; ἄξαι Antiph. 5, 46, προσῆξαν Thuc. 2, 97, doubted; but for προεξάξαντες 8, 25 (old edit.), now stands προεξάξαντες (Bekk. Popp. Krüg. L. Dind. προ-εξαΐξ- Ms. B.), so κατάξαντες Lycurg. 129 (old edit.), now τάξαντες (Mss. Bekk. B. Saupp.), ἀπῆξας Ar. Ran. 468, now ἀπῆξας (Dind.), and κατάξαντας Xen. Hell. 2, 2, 20 (some Mss. and edit.) has been altered from other Mss. to καθέντας by Breitb. Sauppe &c. and branded by L. Dind. as *barbarous* in *classic* Attic. Even in late Attic some editors have removed it for the **future**: ἀπάξωσι Arr. An. 5, 19 (Vulg. -ξουσι Ellendt, Krüg.), ἐξάξαντες Dio Cass. 38, 49 (Bekk. ἐξάξ- Dind.), still however κατάξωσι Dio. Hal. 6, 57, ἐπάξωμεν Plut. M. 713, προσ- 793. In the Ion. of Her. the only instance of **1 aor. act.** is συν-άξαντες 7, 60 (Mss. Gaisf.), συν-νάξαντες (Reiske, Bekk. Krüg. Dind.) from συν-νάσσω, approved by Schweigh.: **aor. mid.** (ἀξάμην) ἄξασθε Il. 8, 505, ἄξαντο 8, 545 (Wolf, Spitzn. but ἄξεσθε, ἄξοντο Schol. Bekk. Dind. La Roche), ἐσάξαντο Her. 5, 34, προεσ- 1, 190, προσ-εσ- 8, 20 (Bekk. Dind.), which three last, however, Bredow (Dial. Her. p. 351) would refer to σάσσω, not to ἄγω. This **aor. mid.** never occurs *certainly* in *early* Attic: thus ἄξασθαι Eur. Hipp. 625 (best Mss.) is opposed by **fut.** -εσθαι, and προαξώμεθα Dem. 5, 14 (Vulg.) is now -αξόμεθα (Mss. Bekk. Dind. Voem. &c.); sometimes in *late*, but scarcely in the new recensions, for προάξασθαι Dio Cass. 47, 34; Herodn. 1, 12, 4; Plut. Eum. 4; Philostr. Im. 788 (Vulg.), ἐπ- Plut. Marc. 29 (Vulg.), ὑπ- Paus. 9, 40, 4 (Siebel), have been displaced by **fut.** -άξεσθαι, -άξονται, in the recent edit. of Bekk. L. Dind. Kaiser, Schubart, and Sintenis. Besides *rarily* in Attic, the soundness of **1 aor. act.** προσῆξαν (Thuc. 2, 97) has been challenged on the ground that "it should answer to **imp.** προσεφέρετο." We doubt this. The cases differ, and the difference determines the *Tense.* The main object of Thuc. is to state the amount of *one* year's φόρος; and as this was statutory and fixed, he naturally views it as a *collective sum* and *one* payment —hence the **aor.** Whereas the δῶρα are, from the nature of the case, viewed as paid from time to time, as convenience or inclination might prompt—and hence **imp.** προσεφέρετο. So (Dem.) states the *fact* by ἐκεῖνοι μὲν Ἀθηναίοις φόρους ἤνεγκαν 11, 16, but the *wont* by φόρους ἡμῖν ἔφερον 7, 12, see 29, 47. προσήρκεσαν Badham's conject. (Adhort. 1869) we are inclined to think needless, at the same time an *addition* to classic prose. The compd. ἀνάγομαι in the sense *to set sail, put to sea,* Her. 7, 128; Antiph. 5, 25; Thuc. 1, 52: **imp.** ἀν-ήγετο Antiph. 5, 24, -ήγοντο Her. 6, 96; Thuc. 1, 48; Xen. Hell. 6, 2, 29: **fut.** -άξομαι Thuc. 6, 30. 32; Xen. An. 6, 1, 33; Dem. 50, 44: has **2 aor. mid.** ἀν-ηγαγόμην Thuc. 2, 92. 3, 79; Xen. Hell. 1, 1, 2: and in same sense **p. p.** ἀνῆγμαι Dem. 53, 5, -ῆκται Thuc. 6, 65; -ηγμένος Xen. An. 5, 7, 17; Plut. Tim. 11: **plp.** ἀν-ῆκτο Dem. 56, 9: **aor.** ἀν-ήχθην Her. 4, 152; Andoc. 2, 21; Xen. Hell. 1, 4, 8: **f. p.** ἀν-αχθήσομαι Aristot. Metaph. 10, 3, 4; Charit. 2, 9; Polyaen. 5, 22, 3.

Ἀγωνίζομαι *To contend,* Her. 8, 26; Antiph. 5, 3; Thuc. 4, 73; Lys. 9, 21; Isae. 1, 6: **imp.** ἠγων- Eur. Heracl. 795; Ar. Vesp. 1479; Her. 8, 87; Thuc. 1, 6; Xen. An. 4, 8, 27; Lys. 3, 44: **fut.** -ιοῦμαι Eur. Heracl. 992; Ar. Ach. 481; Thuc. 6, 78; Xen. Cyr. 6, 2, 22; Lys. 13, 88; Dem. 22, 38; D. Sic. 14, 25 (Bekk.); **passive** Dem. 21, 7, Ion. -ιεῦμαι, ἐν- Her. 3, 83, -ίσομαι D. Sic. 13, 21 (Vulg. Bekk., -ιοῦμαι L. Dind.): **aor.** ἠγωνισάμην Eur. Alc. 648; Ar. Eq. 614; Her. 1, 76; Andoc. 1, 17; Lys. 13, 60, Dor. ἀγωνισάμαν Anth. 11, 81; -ίσαιτο Thuc. 3, 38: **p.** ἠγώνισμαι **act.** Eur. Ion 939; Ar. Vesp. 993; Isocr. 18, 31; Isae. 10, 1, συν- 7, 10; Dem. 19, 60, and **pass.** Eur. Supp. 465; Pl. Tim. 81?; Dem. 24, 145; Plut. Cat. Maj. 14, 3 pl. Ion. ἀγωνίδαται Her. 9, 26: **plp.** ἠγωνισμένοι ἦσαν Isocr. 18, 1: **aor.** ἠγωνίσθην rare, and **pass.** Lys. 2, 34: **fut. p.** late ἀγωνισθήσεται Aristid. 39, 504 (Dind.) The **pres.** and **fut.** are sometimes **pass.** ἀγωνιζόμενος Dem. 24, 28: ἀγωνιεῖται 21, 7. **1 aor. act.** occurs in part. ἀγωνίσας Boeckh's Inscr. 1, 575. **Vb.** ἀγώνιστος, δυσ-κατ- D. Hal. Rhet. 8, 3, ἀγωνιστέον Xen. Cyr. 2, 3, 11. The **fut.** form ἀγωνίσομαι occurs actually in *late* writers only, and even in them less frequently than it was wont: ἀγωνισόμενος Dio. Hal. 3, 18 (*now* ἀγωνίζ- Kiessl.); Argum. Dem. 19; Jos. Jud. B. 3, 7, 15 (Bekk.); Porph. de Abst. 1, 31, but for -ίσομαι Alciphr. 1, 39 (Wagn.), -ιοῦμαι (Meinek.), -ισομένους Luc. Anach. 36 (Vulg.), -ιζομένους (Bekk. Dind. Jacob. 2 ed.) The Attics seem to have uniformly dropped σ in the fut. of verbs in -ιζω, excepting dissyllab., as κνίζω, -ίσω, κτίζω, -ίσω &c.

The collat. form ἀγωνιάω, *to contend, be anxious*, seems confined in classic auth. to pres. and aor. and in these to part. and inf. -ιῶν Isocr. 4, 91; Pl. Charm. 162; rare in Poet. -ιῶσα Com. Fr. 4, 438; inf. -ιᾶν Pl. Prot. 333: aor. ἀγωνιᾶσαι Com. Fr. 3, 607. It is rather better developed in later writers: ἀγωνιῶ Luc. D. Mer. 12, 4; Alciphr. 3, 59, -ιᾶτε D. Sic. 13, 52, -ιῶσι Aristot. Rhet. 1, 9, 21: imp. ἠγωνίων Ael. V. H. 2, 1; Polyb. 1, 10. 2, 6; D. Sic. 13, 81: fut. -ιάσω Porph. de Abst. 1, 54: aor. ἠγωνίᾱσα D. Sic. 14, 60; Plut. Caes. 46; Aristid. 12, 89 (Dind.): p. ἠγωνιᾱκώς, ὑπερ- (Dem.) 61, 28. For pres. indic. ἀγωνιῶ Lys. 26, 1 (Vulg.) now stands ἔγωγε (Bekk. B. Saupp. Scheib.) We have never seen either mid. or pass.

'Αδάξομαι, see ὀδάξω.

('Αδέω) *To be sated*, Homeric, aor. opt. ἀδήσειεν Od. 1, 134: p. part. ἀδηκώς Il. 10, 399 (ᾱ). Some aspirate ἁδησ-, ἁδηκ-.

'Αδηλέω *To be in the dark*, in act. only pres. and only in Soph. -οῦμεν O. C. 35. Pass. Ion. and Att. prose ἀδηλεῖται S. Emp. 79, 9. 319, 4; -λεῖσθαι 591, 25. 605, 15 (Bekk.); late ἀδηλουμένη Theophr. Fr. 30, -εύμενα Hippocr. 8, 18 (Lit.)

'Αδικέω *To injure*, Solon 4, 22; Eur. Ph. 958; Her. 2, 160; Antiph. 6, 7; Thuc. 3, 65; Isae. 11, 15; ἀδικεῖν Aesch. Eum. 85: imp. ἠδίκουν Ar. Nub. 1509; Antiph. 6, 9; Lys. 1, 38; Pl. Prot. 322, Ion. ἠδίκεον Her. 1, 121: fut. -ήσω Com. Fr. 3, 429; Xen. An. 2, 5, 3; Pl. Crit. 48: aor. ἠδίκησα H. H. Cer. 367; Her. 7, 35; Thuc. 3, 56: p. ἠδίκηκα Eur. Alc. 689; Antiph. 1, 23; Thuc. 3, 63; Lys. 9, 12, act. reg.: p. p. ἠδίκημαι Dem. 29, 50, -ηται Her. 3, 21; Antiph. 1, 31; -ημένος Eur. Med. 26; Antiph. 1, 21: plp. ἠδίκητο 6, 10; Dem. 29, 41: aor. -ήθην Antiph. 5, 88; Thuc. 3, 65; Pl. Rep. 344: fut. p. late -ηθήσομαι Aristid. 45, 63; Apollod. 1, 9, 23; Geop. 12, 10; (v. r. Dem. 20, 164. 21, 220. 23, 115): for which classic auth. always use fut. m. ἀδικήσομαι as pass. Eur. I. A. 1437; Thuc. 5, 56; Xen. Cyr. 3, 2, 18; Isocr. 2, 16; Pl. Gorg. 509; Aristot. Polit. 3, 13, 13; Dem. 20, 164. 21, 30. 220. 23, 115. Vb. ἀδικητέος Pl. Crit. 49.—ἀδικειμένος Ar. Ach. 914, is said to be Dor. for ἠδικημένος; Elms. proposed ἀδικείμενος Boeot. pres. which Meineke and *now* Dind. adopt, Fritzsche ἀδικεύμενος, and certainly the pres. of this verb is often used in the sense of the perf. Antiph. 4, δ, 9; Xen. An. (5, 7, 29). 7, 7, 31;

Pl. Rep. 359, &c. The Aeol. form ἀδικήει occurs Sapph. 1, 20. Twice in Dem. *some* of the Mss. present **fut. p.** -ηθήσομαι, and twice Reiske has adopted it, once with, and once without Ms. support. This verb scarcely occurs in Epic: **pres.** ἀδικεῖ Theocr. 11, 67; imperat. ἀδίκει 8, 64: 1 aor. ἀδικήσας H. Cer. 367, but neither in Il. Od. Hes. Theogn. Orph. nor Ap. Rh.

Ἄδω, ἁδῶ, see ἁνδάνω.

Ἄδω *To sing*, Att. for ἀείδω, Anacr. 45 (B.); Aesch. Ch. 1025; Eur. Cycl. 425; Ar. Eccl. 932; Pl. Phaed. 85; Dem. 19, 280: **imp.** ᾖδον Eur. Alc. 761; Com. Fr. 2, 638; Thuc. 2, 21; Dem. 54, 9, Dor. ᾆδ- Theocr. 14, 30: **fut.** ᾄσω Babr. F. 12, 18; rare, if correct, in good Att. Pl. Leg. 666; late prose Himer. Or. 1, 6; Menand. Rhet. 617; Nicol. Rhet. 11, 14; Aeneae Epist. 18, προσ- Ael. H. A. 6, 1, Dor. ᾀσῶ Theocr. 1, 145: generally **mid.** ᾄσομαι H. Hym. 6, 2. 32, 19; Theogn. 243; Ar. Vesp. 1233; Com. Fr. (Theoph.) 3, 629; Thuc. 2, 54; Pl. Leg. 664. Gorg. 502, Dor. ᾀσεῦμαι Theocr. 3, 38: **aor.** ᾖσα Ar. Nub. 1371; Pl. Tim. 21: (p. ᾖκα?): **p. p.** ᾖσμαι Com. Fr. 2, 638; late prose, Philostr. Ap. 1, 39; Himer. Or. 16, 2; ᾠσμένος Aristid. 5, 36 (D.): **aor.** ᾔσθην Xen. Cyr. 3, 3, 55; Pl. Lys. 205, ἐπ- Xen. Mem. 2, 6, 11: **pres.** ᾄδεσθαι Thuc. 2, 54; -όμενος Plut. Mor. 1144. **Mid.** ᾀδόμενοι late Dio Chrys. 23 (398): **fut.** ᾄσομαι see above: **aor.** δι-ᾄσασθαι Phryn. (Bekk. An. 37. 3.) **Vb.** ᾀστέος Pl. Rep. 390. See ἀείδω.—**Fut. act.** ᾄσουσι Pl. Leg. 666, is the reading of the Mss. and retained by Orell. Bait. Winck. and C. F. Herm. in their late editions: Porson suggested ᾄσουσι which some edit. have adopted. ᾄσεις Ar. Pax 1297 (R. Vulg.), but ᾄσει (Daw. Bekk. Dind.) ᾄσεται in some edit. of Eur. Med. 45, is a suggestion of Muretus for οἴσεται of the Mss. and adopted by Porson, Elms. Dind. &c., but Kirchhoff, Schöne, Nauck, and Witzschel retain οἴσεται.

Ἀεθλεύω *To contend*, Ep. and Ion. -εύουσι Opp. Hal. 3, 40; -εύωσι Il. 23, 737; Hes. Th. 435; -εύοιμεν Il. 23, 274; -εύειν 4, 389; Her. 5, 22; ἀεθλεύων Il. 24, 734 (Vulg. Wolf), but see below; Xenophanes 2, 21 (B.); Ap. Rh. 3, 480. 624. 778; Theocr. 24, 115: **fut.** -εύσω late, Q. Sm. 4, 113; Nonn. 37, 557. 42, 513: **aor.** ἀεθλεύσειε Musae. 197; -εύσας Nonn. 7, 97. —ἀεθλέω seems more Ion.: **imp.** unaugm. ἀέθλεε Anth. App. Epigr. 5, -λεον Her. 1, 67. 7, 212: **fut.** -ήσοντες Q. Sm. 4, 590 (Ms. A. Vulg. Lehrs, -εύσοντες Koechly). The contracted forms alone are used by the Attics: ἀθλεύω rare, -εύων Pl. Leg. 873; (in Hom. once only, Il. 24, 734 Mss. Bekk. Spitzn. Dind.; Ap. Rh. 2, 783; Or. Sib. 2, 38, -εύουσι Opp. Hal. 1, 37.

3, 596; -εύωσι 5, 198, see ἀεθλ- above): fut. ἀθλεύσω Aesch. Pr. 95; ἀθλεύσας Nonn. 9, 150. ἀθλέω Pl. Tim. 19; -εῖν Simon. C. 149; Aeschin. 2, 147: imp. ἤθλουν (Luc.) Asin. 11: fut. -ήσω Or. Sib. 2, 43; Artemidor. Onir. p. 112, 22: aor. ἤθλησα Soph. O. C. 564; Artemidor. Onir. p. 269, 2: pt. -ήσας Il. 7, 453. 15, 30, the only part of this form in Hom.; Eur. Supp. 317; Q. Sm. 6, 494: p. late ἠθληκότες Plut. Demetr. 5: (p. p. ἠθλημένων, κατ- Suid.) Mid. rare, aor. ἠθλησάμην, ἐν- Anth. 7, 117. Koechly has altered the Mss. reading ἀεθλήσοντες Q. Sm. 4, 590, to ἀεθλεύσ- on the ground of its being "the constant Epic form." But if the Epics used both the *open* and *contracted* forms of the pres. ἀεθλέω, ἀθλεύω, may they not have used also ἀεθλησ-, since they certainly have ἀθλησ-, and that too when ἀθλευσ- would have suited the metre equally well? Compare οἰνοχοεύω Od. 21, 142, the only form of the pres.: but the imp. οἰνοχόει Il. 1, 598: and aor. -οῆσαι Od. 15, 323. πολεύω pres. Od. 22, 223: but πολ- or πωλ-ήσεαι Il. 5, 350.

'Αείδω *To sing*, Poet. and Ion. Il. 1, 1; Solon 20, 3; Pind. Ol. 5, 10; Eur. Ion 92 (chor.). I. T. 1091 (chor.); rare in trimeters Eur. Fr. 188 (D.); Aesch. Ag. 16; Ion. prose Her. 2, 60; Hippocr. 7, 124; Epic subj. -δῃσι Od. 19, 519; opt. -δοιμι Il. 2, 598; inf. -δειν Od. 8, 45; Hes. Th. 34; Ar. Eq. 1266 (chor.), Ep. -δέμεναι Od. 8, 73, -δέμεν Theogn. 939, Lacon. -δην Alcm. 57 (B.), but -δεν 1, 3; Theocr. 7, 100: imp. ἤειδον Od. 8, 514, ἄειδ- Il. 1, 604; Pind. N. 5, 22; Theocr. 6, 4, ᾱ̓ει- in arsi Od. 17, 519; H. Hym. 18, 1; Pind. Fr. 30 &c.; Theocr. 18, 7: fut. ἀείσω Sapph. 64 (Ahr.); Hom. Epigr. 14, 1; Theogn. 4; Eur. H. F. 681 chor. (Mss. Vulg. Kirchh. 1 edit. Nauck, see below); Theocr. 22, 135 (Vulg. Mein. Ahr. Paley, -δω Ziegl. Fritz.); Callim. Apol. 30. Dian. 186. Del. 1; Anth. (Mnas.) 7, 192; Q. Sm. 3, 646; Opp. Cyn. 1, 80. 3, 83: and mid. ἀείσομαι Od. 22, 352; Theogn. 943; Pind. I. 7, 39 (Bergk, Momms.); Eur. Epigr. 3 (Bergk); Hom. H. 10, 1 (but ᾄσομ- 6, 2. 32, 19), δι- Theocr. 5, 22: aor. ἤεισα Callim. Epigr. 21, 4; Opp. Cyn. 3, 1, ᾱ̓ει- Simon. C. 53 (Bergk); Theocr. 9, 29, ἄει- Od. 21, 411; Theogn. 16; Anth. App. Epigr. 215; subj. ἀείσω Theocr. 1, 23; ἀείσετε, προσ- Hippocr. 6, 482; ἄεισον Od. 8, 492; Alcae. 63; Eur. Tr. 513 (chor.), -είσατε Hes. Th. 965; Ar. Thesm. 115 (chor.); ἀεῖσαι Od. 14, 464; Pind. Ol. 11, 24; Her. 1, 24; ἀείσας 1, 24. Mid. ἀείδομαι not found; unless ἀείδεο be sound H. Hym. 20, 1 (Mss. ἀείσεο Franke, Baum.): fut. ἀείσομαι see above: aor. only imper. Ep. ἀείσεο H. Hym. 17, 1 (ἀείδεο Vulg.); δι-αείσομαι Theocr. 5, 22, is called subj. by Ahrens for -αείσωμαι—we desiderate a more decisive example. Pass. only pres. ἀείδομαι

Pind P. 8, 25; ἀειδόμενος Her. 4, 35: and imp. ἄείδετο Pind. Ol. 10 (11), 76, ἠείδ- formerly 10, 70, has been discarded.—α is short except sometimes in arsi, ἀείδῃ Od. 17, 519; H. Hym. 18, 1. 27, 1; Opp. Hal. 5, 296.—Ep. inf. pres. ἀειδέμεναι Od. 8, 73. For ἀείσω Eur. H. F. 681 quoted, Elms. Dind. and now Kirchh. 2 ed. Nauck 3 ed. read pres. ἀείδω. ἀείσεο is perhaps an Epic 1 aor. with the termination of the 2 aor. Hom. H. 17, 1. ἀείσατο in some edit. of Pind. N. 4, 90, is an emend. of Pauw and Heyne for ἀείσεται of the Mss.; ἄεισέν ποτε was suggested by Herm. and adopted by Boeckh and Schneidewin; Kayser and Momms. retain the fut., so Bergk with seemingly a shade of doubt.

Ἀεικίζω *To abuse* (Epic for αἰκίζω), Il. 24, 54: imp. ἀείκιζον 24, 22: fut. ἀεικιῶ Il. 22, 256, but -ίσσω Q. Sm. 10, 401: aor. ἠείκισα, ἀεικίσσωσι Il. 16, 545: p. p. see αἰκίζω: aor. pass. ἀεικισθήμεναι Od. 18, 222: mid. as act. aor. ἀεικίσσωνται Q. Sm. 14, 43; -ισσαίμεθα Il. 16, 559; -ίσσασθαι 22, 404. (ᾰ.) See αἰκίζω, which Hom. has only in compos.

Ἀείρω *To raise*, Poet. and Ion. Aesch. Sept. 759 (chor.); Her. 2, 125; Hippocr. 8, 236, Dor. 3 pl. ἀείροντι, ἐπ- Pind. Ol. 9, 20; ἄειρε Il. 6, 264; ἀείρων Od. 11, 423: imp. ἤειρον Her. 2, 125, ἄειρ- Il. 19, 386; Ap. Rh. 1, 248: fut. ἀερῶ, contr. ἀρῶ Aesch. Pers. 795; Eur. Heracl. 322. I. T. 117. Tr. 1148, ἐξεπ-ᾱρεῖ Poet. Plut. M. 102: aor. ἤειρα Ap. Rh. 2, 1229; in tmesi Il. 10, 499. 24, 590, παρ- Archil. 94, ἐξ- Her. 6, 126, ἄειρ- Il. 23, 730; (ἀέρσῃ Panyas. Fr. 6); ἄειρον Theocr. 22, 65; ἀείρας Il. 12, 383; Soph. Ant. 418; Luc. D. Syr. 52, ἐπ-αείρας Her. 1, 87, Dor. ἀείραις Pind. Fr. 88: p. p. ἤερμαι, -μένος Ap. Rh. 2, 171: plp. ἄωρτο, for ἤερτο, Il. 3, 272; Theocr. 24, 43: aor. ἠέρθην Anth. 5, 299; Ap. Rh. 4, 1651, παρ- Il. 16, 341, ἀέρθ- Od. 19, 540; Ap. Rh. 4, 1757, Epic 3 pl. ἄερθεν for -θησαν, Il. 8, 74; subj. ἀερθῶ Eur. An. 848 (chor.); ἀερθεὶς Od. 8, 375. 12, 432; Pind. N. 7, 75. 8, 41; Aesch. Ag. 1525 (chor.); Her. 1, 165. 9, 52; Hippocr. 8, 122. 124 (Littré), see below. Mid. ἀείρομαι *raise oneself*, or *for oneself*, Soph. Tr. 216 (chor.); inf. -εσθαι Her. 4, 150; -όμενος 8, 140 (Mss. Stein, ἀντ- Bekk. Dind.), ἀπ- Il. 21, 563, ἀντ- Her. 7, 101. 209: imp. ἀειρόμην, 3 dual -έσθην Il. 23, 501: fut. (ἀερεῖται) contr. ἀρεῖται Eur. Hel. 1597: aor. ἀείραο Ap. Rh. 4, 746; Epic subj. ἀείρεται, συν- Il. 15, 680; ἀειράμενος Il. 23, 856. Od. 15, 106; Ion Fr. 3, 4 (Bergk); Her. 8, 94; ἀείρασθαι, ἀντ- 7, 212. Hom. never augments the *simple* verb except in tmesi, Her. varies: ἤειρον 2, 125, but ἀείροντο 8, 56 (Bekk. Dind. Abicht, Stein), which Bredow and Dietsch alter to ἠείροντο, Lhardy to ἀείρονται.

—Tragic usage: ἀείρω is used once only in trimeters, often in chor. and such parts only as are unsusceptible of augment: **pres.** ἀείρω Aesch. Sept. 759; imper. ἄειρε Eur. El. 873, -ετε Hec. 62; ἀείρειν Rhes. 25; ἀείρων Aesch. Pers. 660: **aor.** imper. ἀείρατε Eur. quoted (some Mss. and edit.); **part.** ἀείρας Soph. Ant. 418, the only instance in trimeters. **Mid.** ἀείρομαι Soph. Tr. 216 (chor.) **Pass.** ἀειρόμενος Eur. Alc. 450 (chor.): **aor.** subj. ἀερθῶ Eur. An. 848 (chor.); ἀερθεὶς Aesch. Ag. 1525 (chor.); Eur. Fr. 903 (chor.) ᾰ, late ᾱ in arsi, Opp. Cyn. 1, 347. 537. 2, 172. 216. 526. 4, 211.—We have never seen the open fut. ἀερῶ. Her. has usually the Ionic ἀείρω, and so, partly on theory, Dietsch, Abicht, Stein perhaps always, but ἐπ-αίρεις 7, 10 (7), ἦραν 9, 59, ἀπ- 6, 99, -αίρωσι 8, 57. 60, ἐπ-άρας 1, 90. 2, 162, ἐξ- 9, 79, ἐξ-ήρετο 6, 133, ἐπ-αρθῇς 1, 212, -αρθεὶς 1, 90. 5, 81. 91. 7, 38. 9, 49 (Mss. Gaisf. Bekk. Dind.) Hippocr. too, along with ἀείρω, has αἴρει 8, 368, αἴρειν 8, 144. 216, αἴρεται 8, 328, ἐπ- 8, 282, αἴρηται 8, 328, ἦρται, ἐπ- 8, 280 (Littré).

('Ακάζομαι) *To be reluctant*, Epic and only **part.** ἀκαζόμενος Od. 18, 135, -ομένη Il. 6, 458. H. Cer. 30; Q. Sm. 14, 29.

'Αελπτέω *To have no hope* (ἄελπτος), only part. Ep. and Ion. ἀελπτέοντες quadrasyll. Il. 7, 310; Her. 7, 168. Before Wolf, ἀελπέοντες stood in the Il.

'Αέξω *To increase*, Ep. and Ion. **pres.** only and **imp.** in classic auth. Il. 17, 226; Hes. Op. 6; Theogn. 1031; Simon. C. 84. 5; Pind. N. 2, 15; Soph. Aj. 226 (chor.); Eur. Hipp. 537 (chor.); once in Her. 3, 80: **imp.** never augm. in early Epic, ἄεξον Od. 17, 489. **Mid.** ἀέξεται *grows* Il. 18, 110; Hes. Op. 377; Pind. Fr. 203; Emped. 330; Aesch. Ch. 825 (chor. αὔξει Herm. and *now* Dind. 5 ed.): **imp.** ἀέξετο Il. 11, 84. Od. 22, 426; Hes. Th. 195, but ηὔξεν Callim. Jup. 55, -οντο Ap. Rh. 4, 1426.—Late forms, **fut.** ἀεξήσω Nonn. 12, 24: **aor.** ηέξησα 8, 104; Anth. App. Epigr. 299: **plp. p.** ηέξητο, ἀν- Nonn. 4, 427: **aor.** ἀεξήθην Anth. 9, 631; Nonn. 9, 168; -θείς Ap. Rh. 2, 511; Anth. 6, 171; Opp. Hal. 5, 464: **fut. m.** ἀεξήσεσθαι Ap. Rh. 3, 837. At Soph. Ant. 351, Dind. reads, from a suggestion of Döderl., ἀέξεται as act. for ἕξ- or ἄξ-εται of the Mss., but calls it 'incerta emendatio.' Franz suggested ὀχμάζεται, which Nauck adopts.

'Αεροβατέω *To tread the air &c.* Attic, and in classic auth. confined to **pres.** Ar. Nub. 225. 1503; -βατεῖν Pl. Apol. 19; -βατοῦντες (Luc.) Philop. 24: **aor.** ἀεροβατήσας (Luc.) Philop. 12.

'Αερομετρέω *To measure the air*, Attic prose, and only **inf.** -μετρεῖν Xen. Oec. 11, 3.

'Αέρρω Aeol. =ἀείρω *To raise*, Alcae. Fr. 78; Sapph. 91 (Bergk): aor. (ἤερσα), ἀέρσῃ Panyas. Fr. 6, 13 (Dübn.)

'Αερτάζω *To raise*, Poet.=ἀείρω, Anth. 9, 674; -άζων Callim. Fr. 19. 211; Orph. L. 222; -ειν 617: imp. ἠέρταζον Anth. 9, 12; Ap. Rh. 1, 738; Nonn. 48, 140: aor. ἀερτάσσειε Nonn. 43, 99; (from ἀερτάω) ἠέρτησεν Anth. 6, 223: p. p. ἠέρτημαι Anth. 5, 230; Opp. Cyn. 2, 99.—ἀερτάζω seems to be used only in pres. imp. and rarely in aor. (ἀερτάω) in aor. act. and p. pass. and both rather late.

('Αέω) *To breathe, rest, (sleep?)* Epic, and only aor. ἄεσα (ᾱ in arsi) Od. 19, 342, -σαμεν 3, 151, -σαν Ap. Rh. 4, 884, but (ᾰ in thesi) Od. 2, 490. 15, 188, contr. ἆσα, ἄσαμεν Od. 16, 367; inf. ἀέσαι 15, 40.

'Αζάνω *To dry*, only pres. pass. ἀζᾶνεται H. Hym. 4, 270. ἀζαίνω is late, and occurs only in aor. act. ἀζήνῃ Nic. Ther. 205, -ήνῃσι 368 (αὐήν- Schn.): and pres. pass. ἀζαίνεται 339 (Vulg. αὐαίνεται Schneid.), but the comp. κατ-αζαίνω occurs in iter. aor. κατ-αζήνασκε Od. 11, 587.

"Αζω Poet. *To dry*, only pres. act. Hes. Op. 587; Alcm. 123; Alcae. 39, 8; ἄζῃ Nic. Ther. 779 (Ott. Schneid.): and pass. ἄζηται Hes. Th. 99; -ομένη Il. 4, 487.—aor. ἀσθείη occurs only as a v. r. for ἀσηθείη Her. 3, 41.

"Αζω *To fear*, Poet. only part. ἄζοντα Soph. O. C. 134 (chor.) Generally ἄζομαι Dep. and only pres. Il. 6, 267; Alcm. 54; Eur. Heracl. 600. Alc. 326 (trimet.), ἄζεαι Ap. Rh. 3, 975, -εται Theogn. 1140; Aesch. Eum. 389. 1002 (chor.), -ονται Supp. 651 (chor.); Opp. Hal. 1, 187; ἀζοίμην Eur. Fr. 350, ἄζοιτο Theogn. 748; imper. ἄζεο Il. 5, 830; Theocr. 27, 14, ἄζευ Od. 17, 401; -όμενος Il. 1, 21; Hes. Th. 532; Theogn. 280; Soph. O. R. 155 (chor.); Theocr. 20 (25), 4: and imp. unaugm. ἄζετο Il. 14, 261; Ap. Rh. 3, 77, -οντο Q. Sm. 2, 66, but ἠζόμην if correct, Eur. Heracl. 1038 (Cob. Dind. 5 ed.). The Traged. use this verb in chor. only, except Eur. quoted.

'Αηθέσσω *To be unused*, Epic -έσσουσα Ap. Rh. 4, 38, -έσσοντες Nic. Alex. 378: imp. unaugm. ἀήθεσσον Il. 10, 493, but with σ dropped ἀήθεσον for the metre, Ap. Rh. 1, 1171, not ἀήθεσα aor. Though this view seems to be strengthened by the v. r. ἀήθεσκον in both passages, there is a strong probability in Ziegler's emendation ἀήθεον (Merkel), from ἀηθεῖν (Hesych.) (ᾰ.)

"Αημι (ᾰ) *To blow*, Epic unaugm. and inflected with η, ἄησι Hes. Op. 516; Opp. Hal. 1, 154, ἄητον Il. 9, 5, 3 pl. ἀεισι Hes. Th. 875; subj. ἀῇσι Opp. Hal. 3, 57. 67; imper. ἀήτω Ap. Rh. 4, 768; inf. ἀήμεναι Il. 23, 214. Od. 3, 176, ἀῆναι 3, 183; ἀέντος H. Hym. 6, 3, ἀέντι Theocr. 13, 29, ἀέντες Il. 5, 526, -των Od.

19, 440: **imp.** ἄη Od. 12, 325. 14, 458, δι-άη 5, 478. 19, 440 (Thiersch, Bekk.), -άει (Vulg. Dind. La Roche): **fut.** ἀήσει, δι- Hesych. **Mid.** κατ-αήσεται=καταπνεύσει Hesych. **Pass.** and **intrans.** ἄηται Pind. I. 4 (3), 9; Ap. Rh. 2, 81; ἀήμενος Od. 6, 131: **imp.** ἄητο Il. 21, 386; Hes. Sc. 8, ἄηντο Ap. Rh. 3, 288.—ἄεν Ap. Rh. 1, 605. 1228, is 3 sing. **imp.** of ἄω, which see. For ἀήσαντα Emped. 31, Stein reads ἀΐσσοντα. ἄημι is said to be *unattic;* ἄηται occurs in chor. however in the best Mss. and some of the best edit. of Aesch. Ch. 391 (Dind. *now*, 374 Franz, ἦται Pors.) ἄ.

'Αθανατίζω *To believe or make immortal*, perhaps only **pres. act.** Her. 4, 94; Aristot. Eth. Nic. 10, 7, 8 (Athen. 15, 52); -οντες Her. 4, 93. 5, 4: and **pass.** ἀθανατίζεται Polyb. 6, 54. The *simple* verb is Ion. and late Att. but the compd. ἀπ-αθανατίζειν is used by Pl. Charm. 156.

'Αθέλγω *To press out, drain* (Hesych.), if correct, has **pass.** ἀθέλγεται Hippocr. 5, 478 (Lit.): with **fut. m.** ἀθέλξεται as pass. Aretae. 48 (ed. Oxon.)

'Αθερίζω *To slight*, Epic and unaugm. Od. 8, 212; Anth. 12, 98: **imp.** ἀθέριζον Il. 1, 261: **fut.** -ίξω Ap. Rh. 3, 548 (Vulg. but -ίζω most Mss. Beck, Well. Merk.): **aor.** late ἀθέρισσα Ap. Rh. 2, 488, and -ιξα 2, 477; Orph. L. 675; Maneth. 2, 282: **aor. m.** ἀθερίσσατο Dion. Per. 997. (ᾰ.)

'Αθλέω, **-εύω**, see ἀεθλ-.

'Αθύρω Poet. *To play*, -ύρω Anth. 9, 505, -ύρεις Anth. Pl. 288; Opp. C. 2, 411, -ουσι Ap. Rh. 4, 950; Himer. Or. 3, 1; -ύρωμεν Or. 17, 7; -ύροι Ap. Rh. 3, 949; rare in Att., Eur. Fr. 325 (Dind.); -ύρων Il. 15, 364; H. Hym. 19, 15; Eur. Ion 53; -ύρειν Pind. I. 4, 39; very rare in prose Pl. Leg. 796; and late Philostr. Imag. 5; Himer. Ecl. 36, 13; Orat. 1, 5: **imp.** ἤθῡρε Opp. Hal. 5, 455; Dio Cass. 63, 26, unaugm. ἄθῡρε Pind. N. 3, 44; Opp. C. 4, 279. **Mid.** ἀθυρομένη Hym. Merc. 485. (ᾰ.)

Αἰάζω *To lament*, mostly Poet. Aesch. Pers. 922; Eur. Or. 80; Bion 1, 1. 6; Anth. App. Epigr. 200; -άζωμεν Eur. Tr. 146; -ων I. T. 227; Mosch. 4, 27; -ειν Soph. Aj. 432. 904; Eur. Med. 1347; rare in prose Aristot. Hist. An. 4, 9, 20. Gen. An. 5, 7, 24; D. Cass. 57, 5; Luc. Salt. 45: **fut.** -άξω Eur. H. F. 1054 (Herm. Dind. Kirchh. &c.); Orac. Sib. 7, 99: **aor.** rare, part. αἰάξας Anth. App. Epigr. 127, αἴξας (Mss.) **Mid.** αἰαζομένη (Hesych.) **Vb.** αἰακτός Aesch. Pers. 931, αἰαστής Nic. Fr. 74, 32. The Mss. and vulg. reading Eur. H. F. 1054 quoted, is **pres.** αἰάζετε. In prose this verb seems to occur first in Aristot. but not in classic Attic.

Αἰδέομαι *To fear, respect,* Dep. mid. and pass. Il. 6, 442; Pind. N. 5, 14; Aesch. Ag. 362; Soph. Aj. 1356; rare in comedy, Com. Fr. (Eubul.) 3, 236; Her. 1, 5; Antiph. 2, δ, 11; Pl. Leg. 886, -εῦμαι Solon 32, προ- Her. 3, 140, -έονται Pind. P. 9, 41; imper. αἰδεῖο Il. 24, 503. Od. 9, 269; -δεῖσθαι Il. 1, 23; Pl. Euth. 12; -ούμενος Aesch. Eum. 710; Pl. Phaedr. 254, Poet. αἴδομαι, imper. αἴδεο Il. 21, 74; -όμενος 1, 331; Aesch. Eum. 549 (chor.), see below: imp. αἰδέοντο Pind. P. 9, 41, προ- Her. 1, 61 (Bredow, Stein) see below, ᾐδοῦντο Aesch. Pers. 810; Eur. Alc. 823; Lys. 2, 12, ᾐδοίμην Luc. D. Deor. 6, 2, Poet. αἰδόμην Il. 21, 468: fut. αἰδέσομαι Il. 22, 124; Eur. Med. 326; Xen. Mem. 3, 5, 15, -έσσομαι Od. 14, 388: aor. m. ᾐδεσάμην mostly Poet. Od. 21, 28; Aesch. Ch. 108; Eur. Fr. 110 (Dind.), ᾐδεσσ- Coluth. 154; very rare in prose αἰδέσηται Dem. 23, 72. 37, 59. 38, 22, Epic -έσσεται Il. 22, 419, see below; imper. αἴδεσαι Soph. Aj. 506, Epic -εσσαι Il. 9, 640, -σάσθων (Dem.) 43, 57: p. ᾔδεσμαι, -μένος pass. *reconciled* Dem. 23, 77: aor. pass. ᾐδέσθην as mid. Lycurg. 142; Xen. An. 3, 2, 4, Ep. 3 pl. αἴδεσθεν for -θησαν, Il. 7, 93; αἰδεσθείη Pl. Rep. 566; imper. αἰδέσθητι Eur. Hec. 806, -θητε Od. 2, 65; -εσθεὶς Il. 17, 95; Pind. P. 4, 173; Aesch. Eum. 760; Soph. O. R. 647; Her. 7, 141. 9, 7; Pl. Rep. 393; Xen. An. 3, 2, 5: rare fut. αἰδεσθήσομαι and late in *simple,* Dio Cass. 45, 44; Galen 1, 62; Porph. ad Marcell. 20; Hierocl. in Aur. Carm. p. 59 (Mullach), but ἐπ- Eur. I. A. 900. Vb. αἰδεστός Plut. M. 67, -έον Eustath. αἰδεῖο imper. pres. contr. for αἰδέεο Il. 24, 503, but αἰδέο Theogn. 1331. αἰδήσομαι has, in good editions, given way to αἰδέσσομαι Od. 14, 388 (Wolf, Bekk. Dind. La Roche), yet Ermerins has ventured on editing αἰδήσεσθαι for ἡγήσ- Hippocr. 1, 3, rashly we think; αἰδέσσεται Il. 22, 419 (and some say -έσεται 9, 508) is subj. aor. for -έσσηται, -έσηται. The act. form is late, κατ-ῄδεσε Themist. 15, 191; -αιδέσαι Heliod. 4, 18, 24. 6, 9. The Ion. form προαιδεῖμαι occurs Her. 3, 140: imp. προηδέατο 1, 61 (Mss. Gaisf. Bekk. Krüg. Dietsch, Dind. &c.), προαιδ- (Bredow, Abicht, Stein.) Some say this is for Att. προῄδηντο, but then what is this? Others say more definitely, it is plp. pass. If so, it is *unique,* for the constant analogy of the verb is ε and σ in the perf. and aor. pass. -εσμαι, -έσθην, never -ημαι, -ήθην. We think it imperf. for προηδέοντο, or in stricter Ion. προαιδέοντο; for the general rule with Her. is not to augm. verbs beginning with αι. Besides, the imp. seems to suit the sense better. "Those cities contributed which *were previously wont to respect* them, and *were still feeling a touch of the old kindness.*" In good prose the aor. mid. occurs only in Dem.

and only in its *legal* sense *to pardon*, αἰδέσηται 37, 59. 38, 22; αἰδέσασθαι 43, 57; αἰδεσάσθων ibid. and, if the text be sound, *to fear so as to appease, appease by lowly submission* 23, 72, where for τινὰ some would read τὶς, but see 23, 77. Late prose authors occasionally use this **aor.** but in its usual sense of *fearing*, ᾐδέσατο Plut. Aem. Paul. 35; Apocr., Judith 9, 3; and now -σαντο Luc. Astrol. 7 (Bekk. for ᾔδεσαν Vulg. Dind.) The form αἴδομαι is poet. and only **pres.** and **imp.** αἴδεο imperat. Il. 21, 74; -όμενος 5, 531. 10, 237; rare in Att. and only in chor. Aesch. Supp. 362 (chor.). Eum. 549 (chor.); Eur. Ph. 1489 (chor.): **imp.** unaugm. αἴδετο Il. 21, 468. Od. 8, 86. Nor is it confined to "the early Poets:" -όμενος Ap. Rh. 1, 792. 3, 1023. 4, 796; Theocr. 26 (27), 68. 24, 68; Callim. Cer. 73; Orph. Arg. 1229; formerly in late prose, Plut. Symp. 3, 6, 4, but αἰδούμ- *now.*

Αἰθύσσω *To put in rapid motion, stir*, Poet. Soph. Fr. 486; Orph. Arg. 904. 972; Opp. Cyn. 2, 162 (δι- Pind. Ol. 7, 95, κατ- P. 5, 12, παρ- 1, 87); intrans. late Arat. Ph. 1034; Opp. C. 4, 159; Maneth. 2, 5: **imp.** αἴθυσσον, κατ- Pind. P. 4, 83, ᾔθυσσε Hesych.: (**fut.** -ύξω): **aor.** αἴθυξα, παρ- Pind. Ol. 11, 73; Ap. Rh. 2, 1253. **Pass.** αἰθύσσοιτο Nonn. 1, 31; αἰθυσσόμενας Sapph. 4 (Ahr.)

Αἴθω *To kindle, burn*, mostly Poet. and Ion. Theocr. 2, 24, αἴθει Eur. Rhes. 41 (Nauck); Anth. 12, 93, -ουσι Eur. Rhes. 95; subj. αἴθῃ Aesch. Ag. 1435; αἴθοιεν Her. 4, 145; αἴθειν Soph. Ph. 1033; rare in Att. prose Xen. An. 4, 7, 20; αἴθων Pind. P. 3, 58, fem. Dor. αἰθαίσας Ol. 7, 48 (as adj. Il. 4, 485 &c. Aesch. Sept. 448; Soph. Aj. 147; Eur. Rhes. 122; Pl. Rep. 559): **imp.** αἶθες Anth. 5, 300, αἶθε 15, 21, but ᾖθον intrans. Soph. Aj. 286. **Pass.** αἴθομαι *to blaze*, -εται Eur. Tr. 298 (Vulg. Dind. 2 ed. ἵσταται Nauck, Kirchh. Dind. 5 ed.); Her. 4, 61; Hippocr. 8, 352 (Littré); imper. αἰθέσθω Eur. I. A. 1471 (trimet.) Hom. only part. αἰθόμενος Il. 13, 320. Od. 7, 101; Pind. Ol. 1, 1; Eur. Tr. 1080 (chor.); Luc. Peregr. 7; inf. -εσθαι Eur. Bac. 624; Xen. An. 6, 3; 19. Cyr. 5, 1, 16: **imp.** αἴθετο Theocr. 7, 102; Ap. Rh. 3, 296; Nonn. Paraphr. 11, 21.

Αἰκάλλω *To fawn on*, only **pres.** and **imp.** and only in Dram. and late prose writers, αἰκάλλει Ar. Eq. 211. Thesm. 869, -ουσι Soph. O. R. 597 (L. and W. Dind. Hart.); Ael. H. A. 11, 3. 20; -ειν Polyb. 5, 36; -ων Eur. Andr. 630; Polyb. 16, 24, -ουσα Babr. 50, 14: **imp.** ᾔκαλλε Ar. Eq. 48; Philostr. Ap. 225.

Αἰκίζω *To plague*, in **act.** only **pres.** Soph. Aj. 403. Tr. 838; -ων Ant. 419. **Mid.** αἰκίζομαι *to harass, outrage*, Sim. Am. 1, 24? Aesch. Pr. 256; Soph. Aj. 65; Isocr. 4, 123: **imp.** ᾐκιζ- Soph.

Aj. 300; late prose, Apollod. 3, 5. 5: **fut.** *αἰκίσομαι* Anth. 12, 80, Attic *αἰκιοῦμαι, κατ-* Eur. Andr. 829: **aor.** *ᾐκισάμην* Xen. An. 3, 4, 5; Isae. 9, 17; Dem. 43, 72; *αἰκίσῃ* Soph. Aj. 111; *-ίσαιτο* Aristot. Rhet. 1, 12, 26: **p. p.** *ᾔκισμαι* as **mid.** Eur. Med. 1130, **pass.** *κατ-* Od. 19, 9, see below: **plp.** as **mid.** *ᾔκιστο* Plut. Caes. 29: but **aor.** *ᾐκίσθην* **pass.** Soph. Ant. 206; Andoc. 1, 138; Lys. 6, 27; Isocr. 4, 154.—**Pres.** *αἰκίζομαι* is sometimes **pass.** Sim. Am. quoted? Aesch. Pr. 168; (Pl.) Ax. 372: **imp.** *ᾐκίζοντο* (Hippocr.) Epist. 9, 408: and **perf.** *ᾔκισται, κατ-* Od. 16, 290. 19, 9; Eur. Med. 1130 quoted, if *ᾐκισμένην*, not *ᾐκισμένη*, be adopted; and late *ᾐκισμένον* Plut. M. 31; D. Sic. 18, 47; Polyaen. 8, 6.

Αἱματίζω *To draw, stain with, blood,* **pres.** in late Att. prose, Aristot. H. A. 4, 7, 6: **aor.** inf. *αἱματίσαι* Att. poetry, Aesch. Supp. 662 (chor.)—The collat. form *αἱμάσσω*, Att. *-άττω, -άξω, ᾕμαξα* Eur. Ion 274, Dor. *αἵμ-* Pind. I. 8, 50, is much more complete in act. and pass. and has also **mid.** *ᾑμάξαντο* Anth. 7, 10, missed or denied by Lexicogr. No part of the *simple* verb however occurs in *early* prose, often in *late*, Paus. 3, 16, 7; Luc. Syr. 8. Tyrann. 20, but *ἐξαιμάττων* Xen. Cyr. 7, 1, 29, *καθ-ῄμαξε* Pl. Phaedr. 254. *αἱματόω* is rare and poet. in **act.** Eur. Supp. 77. Andr. 260: **aor.** *-ῶσαι* Soph. Fr. 814: **pass.** *-οῦμαι* in prose and poetry, Aesch. Ag. 1656; Eur. Ph. 1149; Ar. Pax 1020; **p.** *ᾑματωμένος* Eur. Bac. 1135; Ar. Ran. 476; Thuc. 7, 84; Xen. Cyr. 1, 4, 10; *-ῶσθαι* Com. Fr. 3, 558.

Αἰνέω *To praise,* Il. 8, 9; Hes. Op. 824; Pind. Ol. 4, 15; Aesch. Eum. 737; Soph. Ph. 889; Her. 1, 137, Dor. 3 pl. *-έοντι* Alcm. 66 (B.), rare in Comed. and Att. prose, Monost. 506; Pl. Rep. 404; Plut. M. 177, generally *ἐπ-, παρ-αινέω*, see below: **imp.** *ᾔνουν* Eur. Hec. 1154, *αἴνεον* Her. 3, 73: **fut.** *αἰνέσω* Simon. Am. 7, 112 (Bergk); Pind. N. 7, 63; Aesch. Eum. 469; Eur. H. F. 1412, *συν-* Soph. El. 402, Epic and sometimes Pind. *αἰνήσω* Od. 16, 380; Theogn. 1080; Pind. N. 1, 72; Callim. Del. 189; Theocr. 27, 40: **aor.** *ᾔνεσα* Aesch. Fr. 322 (D. 5 ed.); Soph. Ph. 1398; Eur. Alc. 12, *αἴν-* Her. 5, 113, Ep. and Lyric *ᾔνησα* Il. 24, 30. 23, 552; Callim. Dian. 215; Ap. Rh. 4, 503; Philox. 3, 24 (Bergk); Archestr. Athen. 1, 52, *αἴνησα* Pind. Ol. 10, 100. P. 3, 13; *-ήσωσι* Od. 16, 403; *-ήσειε* Simon. C. 57 (Bergk), *-ήσαιτε* Opp. Hal. 1, 77; *αἰνήσας* Theogn. 969, Dor. *αἰνήσαις* Pind. Ol. 9, 14: **p.** *ᾔνεκα, ἐπ-* Isocr. 12, 207: **p. p.** *ᾔνημαι, ἐπ-* Isocr. 12, 233; Hippocr. 2, 334 (Lit.): **aor.** *ᾐνέθην, αἰνεθεὶς* Her. 5, 102. **Vb.** *αἰνετός* Anth. 7, 429, *-νητός* Pind. Nem. 8, 39, *αἰνετέον* late, but *ἐπ-αινετέον* Pl. Rep. 390.—Unaugm. in Pind. and Her.—No such form as *αἰνείω* occurs in Pind. now at least. —The *simple* verb is confined chiefly to Epic and Dramatic poetry, and Ionic prose: αἰνέω Her. 1, 137; -έων 1, 122. 6, 120: imp. αἴνεον 3, 73. 76. 8, 69: aor. αἴνεσε 5, 113; -έσας 1, 90: aor. pass. αἰνεθείς 5, 102: pres. p. αἰνεόμενος, 1, 98; twice only in good Att. prose, αἰνεῖς Pl. Rep. 404: αἰνείσθω Leg. 952. The Att. poets seem never to have used the fut. or aor. with η even in choral odes, and in the compd. never the fut. mid. except once ἐπαινέσεται Eur. Bac. 1195. Madvig however has suggested and Dindorf—rather doubtingly—adopted συναινέσονται Soph. Fr. 337. ἐπ-αινέω, παραινέω, συν-, συν-επ-, ὑπερ-επ- are freq. in good Attic prose, κατ-αινέω is rare, Thuc. 4, 122. Of these, however, ἐπαινέω and παραινέω alone have fut. mid. as well as fut. act., and in the same sense. See each in its place. αἰνέω and compds. never drop ς in the fut.

Αἴνημι *To praise*, Aeol. and Ep. for αἰνέω, only pres. Hes. Op. 683; and ἐπ-αίνημι Simon. C. 5, 19 (Bergk), quoted by Pl. Prot. 345.

Αἰνίζω Poet. *To praise*, only pres. and late in act. Anth. 11, 341. Mid. αἰνίζομαι Dep. only pres. Il. 13, 374. Od. 8, 487.

Αἰνίσσομαι *To speak darkly*, Dep. mid. Eur. Ion 430; Her. 5, 56, Attic -ίττομαι Ar. Pax 47 (Vulg. Br. Bekk. -ίσσομαι Dobr. Mein. Dind. 5 ed., as uttered by ἀνὴρ Ἰωνικός); Aeschin. 2, 108; Pl. Apol. 21: imp. ᾐνιττ- Pl. Charm. 162: fut. αἰνίξομαι Eur. Elec. 946: aor. ᾐνιξάμην Soph. Aj. 1158; Ar. Av. 970; Pl. Theaet. 152, αἰνίξ- Pind. P. 8, 40: p. ᾔνιγμαι pass. Theog. 681; Ar. Eq. 196; Aristot. Rhet. 3, 2, 12; Luc. V. H. 1, 2: aor. ᾐνίχθην pass. Pl. Gorg. 495. Vb. αἰνικτός Soph. O. R. 439. αἰνίττω in act. is late and rare Philostr. 6, 11 (245).

Αἴνῠμαι *To take*, Epic, Od. 14, 144; Simon. C. 5, 17 (Bergk); αἴνῠσο Nic. Al. 55. 148: imp. unaugm. αἰνύμην Il. 11, 580. 13, 550. 15, 459. Od. 21, 53; Hes. Sc. 149 (Wolf, Goettl.). Fr. 174; Ap. Rh. 4, 162; Callim. Fr. 238; Theocr. 24, 137; -ύμενος Od. 9, 429, -μένη Hym. Cer. 6; Ap. Rh. 4, 680, -ύμενοι Od. 9, 232, -εναι 22, 500, -μένους 9, 225.—Like δείκνῡμαι, but without augm.—ἀπο-αίνυμαι Poet. for ἀπαίν- *take from, have taken*, Il. 13, 262: imp. ἀποαίνυτο Od. 12, 419; but ἀπαινύμενος Il. 11, 582. 17, 85, as ἀπαίνυτο Il. 15, 595; Anth. 14. 3.

Αἰολέω *To variegate*, only inf. -ολεῖν Pl. Crat. 409.—αἰόλητο Ap. Rh. 3, 471 (some Mss. and edit.) is now ἐόλητο (Mss. Br. Well. Merk.)—αἰόλλω Ep. *To move quickly, to variegate*, is also very partially used, pres. αἰόλλῃ Od. 20, 27; -όλλει late Nic. Ther. 155: and pass. αἰόλλονται Hes. Sc. 399.—αἰόλλει Pind. P. 4, 233 (old edit.) is now ἐόλει (Boeckh, Bergk, &c.)

Αἰπολέω *To be a goatherd*, in act. only pres. -ολεῖν Com. Fr. 2, 430; -έων Theocr. 8, 85; late prose Aristid. 49, 384: and imp.

ἠπόλει Lys. Fr. 32, 2 (B. Saupp.): pass. αἰπολούμεναι *grazing*, Aesch. Eum. 196.

Αἱρέω *To take*, -ρεῖ Il. 3, 446; Soph. Ant. 606, -ρέει Her. 1, 132, -έουσι 8, 11, -οῦσι Thuc. 2, 68; Dor. inf. αἱρῆν, δι- (Pl.) Tim. Locr. 101: imp. ᾕρουν Il. 17, 463; Aesch. Sept. 1019; Soph. Tr. 240; Lys. 2, 4; Xen. Hell. 4, 5, 15, ᾕρεον Il. 24, 579, -ευν Hes. Sc. 302, Ion. αἵρεε Her. 5, 117, -εον 6, 31, iter. ἀπ-αιρέεσκον Her. 1, 186 (Ms. R. Ald. Stein, but see αἴρω): fut. αἱρήσω Il. 9, 28; Eur. Supp. 845; Her. 3, 151; Thuc. 6, 64; Pl. Rep. 410; Epic inf. -ησέμεν Il. 18, 260, perhaps late ἑλῶ, δι- Inscr. Ther. 2448, ἀν- D. Hal. A. R. 11, 18; Diod. Sic. 2, 25; ἐξ- D. Hal. 7, 56; Arr. Peripl. 11, καθ- Anth. Pl. 334; D. Hal. 9, 26: and late aor. εἷλα, ἀν-είλατε N. T. Act. 2, 23 (Mss. Gb. Lachm. Tisch.): 1 aor. ᾕρησα late, ἀν- Q. Sm. 4, 40; Polyaen. 7, 39; Pseud. Callisth. 1, 19. 2, 20. 3, 23: p. ᾕρηκα Aesch. Ag. 267; Thuc. 1, 61. 103; Xen. Hel. 4, 4, 19, Ion. ἀραίρηκα, -ηκώς Her. 4, 66, ἀν- 5, 102. 6, 36 (Bekk. Dind. Bred.), ἀν-αιρηκ- 4, 66. 6, 36 (Gaisf.): plp. ἀραιρήκεε Her. 3, 39 (Bekk. Dind. Bred.), αἱρήκεε (Gaisf. Baehr): p. p. ᾕρημαι Aesch. Ag. 1209; Soph. Ant. 493; Ar. Av. 1577; Thuc. 8, 82; Pl. Leg. 770; Dem. 20, 146, Dor. αἵρημαι, καθ- Sophr. 10 (Ahr.), Ion. ἀραίρημ- Her. 1, 185. 7, 118. 173 (Bekk. Gaisf. Stein): plp. ᾕρητο Thuc. 8, 82; Xen. An. 3, 2, 1, Ion. ἀραίρητο Her. 1, 191. 7, 83 (Bekk. Gaisf. Stein): aor. ᾑρέθην Aesch. Sept. 505; Soph. O. C. 1148; Ar. Av. 799; Thuc. 7, 31; Xen. An. 5, 9, 32, Ion. αἱρ- Her. 3, 55. 159: fut. αἱρεθήσομαι Her. 2, 13; Pl. Menex. 234: fut. mid. as pass. αἱρήσομαι, ἀφ- Eur. Tr. 1278, περι- Lys. 34, 4: 3 fut. rare ᾑρήσομαι Pl. Prot. 338, ἀφ- Eur. Tr. quoted (L. and W. Dind.): 2 aor. εἷλον Il. 10, 561; Pind. N. 3, 34; Soph. Ant. 655; Her. 8, 17; Antiph. 6, 38; Thuc. 1, 109; Pl. Leg. 698, ἕλον Il. 17, 321; Pind. I. 7, 14, iter. ἕλεσκε Il. 24, 752; subj. ἕλω Il. 7, 81; Soph. O. C. 814, -ῃ Il. 7, 77; Aesch. Eum. 356; Pl. Leg. 941, Ep. -ῃσι Il. 23, 345; ἕλοιμι Il. 22, 253; Soph. Ant. 747; Pl. Criti. 119; imper. ἑλέτω Od. 20, 52; Tyrt. 11, 30; ἑλεῖν Il. 8, 319; Soph. Ph. 347; Her. 1, 73; Pl. Conv. 182, ἑλέειν Il. 15, 558; ἑλών Il. 3, 72; Eur. Elec. 810; Xen. Mem. 1, 2, 49. Mid. αἱρέομαι *take for oneself, choose*, Aesch. Ch. 551; Ar. Nub. 990; Her. 8, 63; Thuc. 6, 80; Epic imper. ἀπο-αίρεο Il. 1, 275; part. Ion. αἱρεύμενοι Il. 16, 353, Aeol. αἰρεύμ- Hes. Op. 476 (Et. M. Flach): imp. ᾑρούμην Od. 21, 40; Thuc. 4, 26; Lys. 3, 9; Pl. Phil. 22, Ion. αἱρεύμην, ἐξ- Od. 14, 232, αἱρέετο Her. 1, 70. 5, 94: fut. αἱρήσομαι Il. 10, 235; Eur. Or. 307; Her. 5, 49; Pl. Phil. 22, as pass. see above, and late ἑλοῦμαι D. Hal. Ant. 4, 75;

Or. Sib. 8, 184, ἀφ- Timostr. Com. Fr. 4, 595; Anth. 9, 108; Polyb. 3, 29; Sext. Emp. 577, δι- D. Hal. Ant. 4, 60, ἐξ- Alciphr. 1, 9 (Meineke): 1 aor. rare, αἱρησάμην (Hesych.), ᾑρήσατο, ἐξ- Ar. Thesm. 761 (Vulg. ἐξαφείλετο Dind. 5 ed. διεχρήσ- Mein.); late subj. αἱρήσωνται Polyb. 38, 5 (Vulg. -ήσονται Bekk. Dind.), προ- Menand. Rhet. 1 (Spengel); αἱρησάμενος (Hesych.); Procop. Epist. 113; -ήσασθαι Hesych.: 2 aor. εἱλόμην Il. 16, 139; Pind. N. 10, 59; Soph. Tr. 734; Ar. Pax 1091; Her. 8, 113; Thuc. 3, 64; Andoc. 1, 57; Lys. 12, 54; Pl. Apol. 28, Dor. εἱλόμαν, ἀν- Ar. Ach. 810, Ion. εἵλεο, ἀφ- Il. 22, 18, and εἵλευ Her. 3, 52, ἑλόμ- Il. 19, 412; Alcae. 68; ἕλωμαι Il. 22, 119; Eur. I. A. 488; Her. 1, 181; Pl. Apol. 37; ἑλοίμην Il. 3, 66. Od. 24, 334; Eur. Alc. 464; Her. 3, 38; Pl. Rep. 347, ἑλοίατο, ὑφ- Ar. Nub. 1199; ἑλοῦ Soph. El. 345; Pl. Ion 542, ἑλεῦ Il. 13, 294 (Dind. ἕλ- Bekk.), ἑλέσθω 9, 139, ἑλέσθων Her. 8, 140; ἑλέσθαι Il. 10, 242; Soph. Ph. 365; Thuc. 3, 59; ἑλόμενος Aesch. Supp. 396; Eur. Hel. 294; Xen. An. 2, 2, 5: late εἱλάμην Anth. App. Epigr. 257; Polyb. 38, 1b (Bekk. -όμην Dind.), δι- Anth. 9, 56, ἀφ- Athen. 12, 65, ἐπαν- Polyb. 8, 14, παρ- 37, 1a (Bekk. -όμην Dind.): p. as mid. ᾕρημαι Ar. Av. 1577; Xen. An. 5, 6, 12; Pl. Rep. 620; Dem. 2, 16. 23, 214, προ- Isocr. 12, 24; Dem. 15, 34, ἀφ- 15, 3: plp. ᾕρηντο Thuc. 1, 62, ἀφ- Dem. 59, 13 (D.), ἀν- 6, 20, Ion. 3 pl. ἀραιρέατο, ἀν- Her. 6, 108 (Bekk. Krüg. Dind. ἀν-αιρ- Ms. Gaisf.) **Vb.** αἱρετός Her. 4, 201; Pl. Phil. 21, ἐξ- Il. 2, 227. αἱρετέος Pl. Tim. 75. ἑλετός Il. 9, 409.—εἵλατο Simon. C. 3 (5), 7 (Vulg.) is now εἵλετο (Herm. Bergk.)—**Fut. mid.** ἀφ-αιρήσει is trans. Soph. Ph. 376; Ar. Ach. 464, but **pass.** Eur. Tr. 1278, Ion. ἀπαιρήσεσθαι Her. 5, 35 (Mss. Schweig. Gaisf.), but ἀπαιρεθήσ- (Mss. Bekk. Dind. Krüg. Stein, Abicht), strengthened, we think, by the **pass.** form αἱρεθήσ- 2, 13, and by the **mid.** ἀπαιρήσεαι in a **middle** sense, 1, 71. 9, 82. διαιρήσεται Pl. Politic. 261 seems **pass.**, but ἀφελοῦνται Polyb. 3, 29 not necessarily so. The **perf.** and **plp.** with **middle** sense seem rare in poetry.

Αἴρω *To raise*, Aesch. Ch. 496; Soph. O. R. 914; Com. Fr. 3, 106; Pl. Crat. 410; αἴρωσι Thuc. 1, 90 (Vulg. ἄρ- Bekk. &c.); αἴρειν Andoc. 3, 41; Hom. only part. αἴροντας Il. 17, 724; Pl. Tim. 63: **imp.** ᾖρον Eur. Elec. 800; Pl. Crat. 423, iter. ἀπαίρεσκον Her. 1, 186 (Bekk. Dind. -έεσκον Stein, see αἱρέω): **fut.** ἀρῶ Soph. Aj. 75; Luc. Hist. Con. 14 (Dind. Fritzs.), ἐπ- Lys. 1, 36; Xen. Mem. 3, 6, 2, ἀπ- Pl. Crito 53 (but ἀρῶ Aesch. Pers. 795; Eur. I. T. 117. Supp. 772. Heracl. 322. Tr. 1148; Ar. Ran. 377; Anth. 5, 39 (Meineke), contr. from ἀερῶ of ἀείρω, which see): **aor.** ἦρα Aesch.

Ag. 47; Her. 9, 59; Thuc. 6, 18; subj. ἄρω (ᾱ) -ῃς Soph. Aj. 129, -ρῃ mid. (Dind. &c. *now*); "ἄρειας Aesch. Ch. 262, -ειεν Simon. Am. 7, 60 (Bergk); ἆρον Soph. Ph. 879; "ἄρας Tr. 795; Thuc. 2, 12, ἐπ- Her. 1, 90; ἆραι Callim. Cer. 35: **p.** ἦρκα Aristot. Incess. Anim. 11, 3; Dem. 25, 52, ἀπ- Thuc. 8, 100; Dem. 10, 23, ἐπ- Eur. Fr. 1027 (D.); Aristid. 46, 128: **plp.** ἤρκεσαν, ἀπ- Dem. 19, 150: **p. p.** ἦρμαι, -μένος Eur. Fr. 1027; Thuc. 7, 41, ἐπ-ῆρται 2, 11, as mid. see below: **plp.** ἦρτο Thuc. 1, 130: **aor.** ἤρθην Simon. C. 111; Aesch. Sept. 214; Thuc. 4, 42; Dem. 2, 8; even in Ion. Hippocr. 1, 737 (Erm.), ἐπ- 1, 479; ἐπ-αρθῇς Her. 1, 212 (-αερθ- Stein, Abicht); ἀρθείην Eur. Hip. 735; ἄρθητε Ar. Nub. 266; ἀρθῆναι Hippocr. 1, 249 (Erm.); ἀρθείς Il. 13, 63. Od. 5, 393; Soph. Ant. 111; Antiph. 2, 9, ἐπ- Her. 1, 90. 9, 49 (ἐπ-αερθ- Stein, Abicht): **fut.** ἀρθήσομαι Ar. Ach. 565; -θησόμενος D. Sic. 11, 61; -θήσεσθαι 12, 79; D. Cass. 37, 56: (**2 aor. act.** ἦρον not found; subj. ἐξ-ἄρῃ Ms. reading Athen. 1, 34 (Com. Fr. 2, 846) is now ἐξάγῃ (Dind. Meinek.); but opt. ἀντ-άροι late prose Agath. p. 209.)—**Vb.** ἀρτέον Com. Fr. (Alex.) 3, 498. **Mid.** αἴρομαι *lift for oneself, win,* Eur. El. 360; Thuc. 4, 60: **imp.** ἠρόμην Soph. Ant. 907: **fut.** ἀροῦμαι Soph. O. C. 460; Andoc. 1, 11; Pl. Leg. 969 (ἀροῦ—see ἀείρω), ἀρέομαι Pind. P. 1, 75: **p.** as **mid.** ἠρμέναι, see below: **1 aor.** ἠράμην Il. 14, 510; Theogn. 501; Pind. P. 3, 20; Eur. Heracl. 986; Com. Fr. (Plat.) 2, 653; Lys. 2, 14; Pl. Rep. 374, ἀρ- Pind. I. 6, 60; "ἄρωμαι Soph. Aj. 193; ἀραίμην Eur. Cycl. 474, -αιτο Or. 3; Ar. Ran. 1406; ἀράμενος Ar. Pax 763. Ran. 32; Antiph. 5, 63. 6, 16; Lycurg. 95; Dem. 18, 208. 21, 132; ἄρασθαι Com. Fr. (Aristophont.) 3, 357; Thuc. 6, 9: **2 aor.** Poet. unaugm. and referred by some to ἄρνυμαι, ἀρόμην (ᾰ) Il. 11, 625. 23, 592; "ἄρωμαι, -ρηαι Hes. Op. 632, -ηται Il. 12, 435; Pind. N. 9, 46; ἀροίμην Il. 18, 121; Xenophan. 2, 7; Aesch. Sept. 316; Soph. El. 34; ἀρέσθαι Il. 16, 88. Od. 22, 253; Soph. Aj. 245; Theocr. 17, 117; ἀρόμενος Aesch. Eum. 168: and as mid. **p. p.** ἠρμένοι Soph. El. 55; Strab. 3, 150; Philostr. Ap. 3, 115. 6, 273. ἦρα Ar. Ach. 913, is 2 sing. **1 aor. m.** Boeot. for ἤραο Xenophan. 5, 1, ἦρω. Hom. uses the indic. of both ἠράμην and ἀρόμην, but the other moods of the latter only, "ἄρωμαι, ἀροίμην, &c. The Attic poets seem to use ἠράμην alone in indic., but other moods (opt. inf.) of both indiscriminately. Eur. and the Comedians, we think, use **1 aor.** only. In prose perhaps uniformly ἠράμην and moods. Luc. however has ἀρέσθαι Conv. 42 (Jacobitz, Fritzs.), αἴρεσθαι (Dind.); and later Agath. has ἄροιτο p. 323. There seems to be no certain instance of **2 aor. act.** earlier than Agath. quoted, for ἐξάρῃ once Athen. (Nicoch.) 1, 34, has been displaced by ἐξάγῃ (Dind. Meinek.) The **act.** is exceedingly rare in Epic; but if our best edit. of Her. be correct, he uses parts of this verb more frequently than Lexicogr. allow, see ἀείρω. The initial α of **1 aor.** remains *long* in the *moods* 'ἄρω, 'ἄραιμι &c. because it is long by *compensation* before receiving the augm. ἆρα (for ἄρσα), with augm. ἦρα; but the lengthening of it in the **future** seems rather abnormal—Sophocles has avoided it. See ἀείρω.

Αἰσθάνομαι *To perceive* (rare αἴσθομαι, see below), Soph. El. 1477; Ar. Ran. 285; Thuc. 1, 33; Lys. 13, 81; opt. -νοίατο Ar. Pax 209: **imp.** ᾐσθαν- Thuc. 7, 69; Isocr. 15, 146: **fut.** αἰσθήσομαι Soph. Ph. 75; Ar. Ran. 634; Hippocr. 7, 284; Lys. 13, 19; Isocr. 1, 34; Dem. 43, 23: **p.** ᾔσθημαι Eur. Hip. 1403. Tr. 633; Thuc. 7, 66; Lys. 14, 43 (Scheib. Cob.); Pl. Phaed. 61: **2 aor.** ᾐσθόμην Aesch. Pr. 957; Soph. Ph. 445; Thuc. 5, 10; Lys. 1, 41; Pl. Tim. 66; Her. 7, 220 (Mss. Vulg. Bekk. Dind. Stein), but αἰσθ- Lhardy, Bred. Abicht &c. on the ground that Her. does not augm. verbs beginning with the diphthong αι, see αἴτεον, αἴνεον &c.; αἴσθωμαι Thuc. 6, 41; Isocr. 12, 111; -θόμενος Her. 3, 87; Thuc. 5, 3. Late writers use **1 aor. m.** subj. αἰσθήσηται Schol. Arat. 418 (B.): **aor. pass.** ᾐσθάνθην Schol. Aesch. Pr. 253; Schol. Ar. Ran. 644 (D.), and ᾐσθήϐην V. T. Job 40, 18, συν- Origen vol. 1, p. 222: **fut.** αἰσθανθήσομαι V. T. Esai. 49, 26, and αἰσθηθήσομαι 33, 11.—αἴσθομαι is rare, sometimes doubtful, in classic auth.; αἴσθεσθαι Thuc. 5, 26 (Mss. Bekk. Popp. Krüg. Classen). 7, 75 (2 Mss. Bekk. Boehme, Classen), προ- 2, 93 (2 Mss. Bekk. Classen). 3, 83 (2 Mss. Classen, -έσθαι Vulg. Stahl); αἴσθονται Isocr. 3, 5 (Mss. Urb. Bekk. B. Saupp. -θάνονται Vulg. Bens.), αἰσθόμεθα Pl. Rep. 608 (Mss. Bekk. Schneid. Or. B. W. εἰσόμεθα 2 Mss. Stallb.); often late, Himer. Or. 1, 10; Origen c. Cels. p. 420, 27; Clem. Alex. 2, 457, συν- 3, 519; Schol. Il. 17, 1, &c. **Vb.** αἰσθητός Pl. Meno 72.

Ar. has availed himself in trimeters of what is called the Ion. 3 pl. αἰσθανοίατο for -οιντο Pax 209; see also ἐργασαίατο Lys. 42 (D.). Av. 1147 &c.

'Αΐσθω (ἀΐω) *To breathe*, Epic and only **pr. p.** ἀΐσθων Il. 16, 468; Opp. H. 5, 311: and **imp.** unaugm. ἄϊσθε Il. 20, 403. (ᾰ.)

'Αΐσσω *To rush*, mostly Poet. Il. 17, 662; Hippocr. 5, 122. 8, 88. 358. 590, προεξ- Her. 9, 62 (trisyllabic *always* in Hom., *sometimes* in Trag. Soph. O. C. 1497. Tr. 843 (chor.); Eur. Tr. 156. Supp. 962 (chor.) &c. once in trimeters Hec. 31): **imp.** ἤϊσσον Il. 18, 506, ἀν- Hippocr. 3, 134, iter. ἀΐσσεσκον, παρ- Ap. Rh. 2, 276: **fut.** ἀΐξει Ap. Rh. 3, 1302 (Ms. G. Vulg. seemingly a false reading for subj. ἀΐξῃ Ms. L. Well. Merk.), but ὑπ-αΐξει

Il. 21, 126: aor. ἤϊξα Il. 21, 247. Od. 2, 154; Aesch. Pers. 470 trimet. (Pors. Well. Herm. ἦσσ' Dind.); rare in prose ἀΐξειεν Pl. Leg. 709, ἐπ-αΐξασα Theaet. 190; Aristot. H. An. 9, 44, 5, δι-ήϊξε Her. 4, 134 (Bekk. Dind. Stein), -ῇξε Gaisf., iter. ἀΐξασκε Il. 23, 369: aor. pass. ἠΐχθην as act. Il. 16, 404, ἀΐχθ- 24, 97. Mid. as act. ἀΐσσομαι Poet. Il. 6, 510, ἐπ- 23, 628; Hippocr. 7, 498 (Lit.): imp. ἀΐσσοντο Hym. Cer. 178; Hes. Th. 150; Orph. Arg. 519: fut. ἀΐξεσθαι, ἐπ- old reading which Bekker was inclined to recall Il. 23, 773: aor. rare, ἠιξάμην, ἀΐξασθαι Il. 22, 195, ἐπ- 23, 773, see fut.: and aor. pass. ἠΐχθην quoted.—Rarely trans. ἦξεν Soph. Aj. 40; hence ᾄσσεται pass. O. C. 1261. In Hom. (ᾱ) except ὑπᾰΐξει Il. 21, 126, Hes. and Ap. Rh. except ἀΐξῃ 3, 1302; in Trag. generally (ᾰ), Soph. has ᾱ once Tr. 843 (chor.); so Eur. Troad. 157. 1086 (chor.) See ᾄσσω, ᾄττω. Pierson (Moeris, 301) is inclined to remove the trisyllable forms from the Tragedians by slight alterations, and Blomf. from trimeters at least. Porson prefers granting a little licence to poets, and allows ἀΐσσω Eur. Hec. 31, ἀΐσσεις Iph. A. 12, ἤϊξε Aesch. Pers. 470, to stand, rather than alter them with Pierson to ἀνᾴσσω, ᾄσσεις, ἔπτηξ' or ἀπῇξ'. Elms. (Eur. Bac. 147) is still less stringent, and adds ἀΐσσω Supp. 962, and Herm., Ellendt, Seidler would add more. In trimeters however it occurs twice only, ἀΐσσω Eur. Hec. 31, ἤϊξε Aesch. Pers. 470 (Vulg. Pors. Bl. Well. Herm.), ἦσσι (Rob. Dind.) and rather approved by Blomf., Pors. (Add. in notas, p. 200.) Rare in prose, Hippocr. quoted, ἀν-αΐσσ- 2, 164, προεξαΐσσ- Her. 9, 62, διήϊξε 4, 134 (Bekk. Dind. Lhard. Krüg. Baehr) and approved by Bredow (Dial. Her. p. 174), but διῇξε (Vulg. Gaisf. &c.); Pl. Leg. Theaet. above; ἀναΐξας Xen. Ven. 6, 17 (Vulg.), but ἀνᾴξας (Dind. Saupp.) See ᾄσσω, ᾄττω.

*Αϊστόω *To destroy*, Aesch. Pr. 151: fut. -ώσω Her. 3, 69; Lycophr. 281, ἐξ- Aesch. Pr. 668 (-ώσοι Blomf. Dind.): aor. ἠΐστωσα Her. 3, 127; Orph. Arg. 667, Dor. ἀϊστ- Pind. P. 3, 37, ᾔστωσα Soph. Aj. 515 (trim.), but δι-ηίστ- Tr. 881 (chor.); ἀϊστώσειαν Od. 20, 79; ἀϊστώσας Aesch. Pr. 232: aor. pass. ἀϊστώθησαν Od. 10, 259; rare in Att. ἀϊστωθείη Pl. Prot. 321.

Αἰσυμνάω *To rule*, only pres. -υμνᾷ Eur. Med. 19.

Αἰσχύνω *To disfigure, disgrace*, Il. 24, 418; Tyrt. 10, 9; Pind. P. 4, 264; Soph. O. C. 929; rare in prose Hippocr. 6, 2; Xen. Eq. 1, 12; Lys. 1, 32; Isocr. 15, 251; Epic inf. -υνέμεν Il. 6, 209: imp. ᾔσχῡνε Il. 18, 27, αἴσχυνε, κατ- Pind. Ol. 10, 8, iter. αἰσχύνεσκε, κατ- Q. Sm. 14, 531: fut. -ῠνῶ Eur. Hipp. 719; Luc. Musc. enc. 9, αἰσχῠνεῖ, κατ- Aesch. Th. 546 (Herm. Weil) Dind. holds spurious, Ion. αἰσχῠνέω Her. 9, 53: aor.

ᾔσχῡνα Il. 23, 571; Soph. El. 1083; Eur. Hel. 721; Thuc. 4, 92; Lys. 1, 4; Pl. Rep. 495: p. late ᾐσχυγκέναι Dio Cass. 58, 16, -χυκα Draco p. 12, 15: plp. ᾐσχύγκει Dio Cass. 77, 16: p. p. Epic and rare ᾐσχυμμένος Il. 18, 180: aor. ᾐσχύνθην *felt ashamed,* Andoc. 1, 125; Pl. Leg. 819; Aeschin. 1, 42; -υνθεῖεν Thuc. 4, 126; -υνθείς Eur. Hipp. 1291; Her. 1, 10; Thuc. 3, 14; -υνθῆναι Isae. 9, 13, -θῆμεν Pind. N. 9, 27, see below: fut. αἰσχυνθήσομαι Com. Fr. (Philem.) 4, 53. (Diphil.) 4, 421, ἐπ- Aesch. Ag. 1373; Pl. Phaed. 85. **Mid.** αἰσχύνομαι Dep. pass. *feel ashamed, revere, respect,* Od. 21, 323; Soph. O. R. 1079; Ar. Fr. 487 (D.); Her. 1, 82; Thuc. 3, 82; Pl. Theaet. 183; Isocr. 16, 43; Isae. 1, 5: imp. ᾐσχυν- Ar. Plut. 981. 988; Isocr. 17, 14; Aeschin. 1, 26: fut. -ὕνοῦμαι Aesch. Ag. 856; Ar. Fr. 21 (D.); Pl. Tim. 49. Rep. 396; Aeschin. 1, 46: and rare in *simple* fut. p. αἰσχυνθήσομαι Philem. Diphil. quoted: p. late in this sense ᾔσχυνται V. T. 1 Reg. 27, 12, ἐν-ῄσχυνται Schol. Soph. Tr. 803: with aor. ᾐσχύνθην Xen. Hell. 4, 1, 30; Isocr. 12, 107; Eur. Hipp. 1291. Or. 802; Thuc. 3, 14; inf. αἰσχυνθῆμεν for -θῆναι, Pind. N. 9, 27: there seems to be no aor. of the mid. form. **Vb.** αἰσχυντέος Xen. Cyr. 4, 2, 40. The act. is rather rare in prose, αἰσχύνει Xen. Eq. 1, 12; -οιεν Isocr. 15, 251; -ύνειν Hippocr. 6, 6 (Lit.); -ύνων Luc. Imag. 11: fut. -υνέω Her. 9, 53: aor. -ῦνα Pl. Rep. 495; -ύνῃ Lys. 1, 32; -ῦναι Thuc. 4, 92; Pl. Menex. 246; -αντι ibid. In the *simple* verb the fut. m. -οῦμαι is much more frequent than fut. p. -υνθήσομαι, which in *simple* is scarcely used by classic authors, Philem. and Diphil. quoted, and late Heliod. 10, 18; but in the Septuag. and N. Test. it is frequent, and the only form used, -υνθήσομαι Esai. 1, 29. Jer. 2, 26; Apocr. Syr. 22, 25. 24, 22; N. T. 2 Cor. 10, 8. Phil. 1, 20. ἀπαισχύνομαι also is Dep. with fut. -οῦμαι Pl. Gorg. 494: and aor. -υνθῆναι ibid. 494. ἐπαισχύνομαι however seems to have the fut. always of the pass. form, -υνθήσομαι Aesch. Ag. 1373; Pl. Phaed. 85.—**Aor.** always of the pass. form, ᾐσχύνθην Thuc. 4, 126 &c.; Xen. Hell. 4, 1, 30, ἀπ- Pl. quoted, ἐπ- Pl. Soph. 247; Xen. Hell. 4, 1, 34, ὑπερ- Aeschin. 1, 33. 3, 151, late δι- Luc. Elect. 3 (Jacobitz.)

(**Αἰτιάζω**) *To accuse,* only pass. -άζομαι Xen. Hell. 1, 6, 5; -όμενοι, 1, 6, 12: and imp. late ᾐτιάζετο Dio Cass. 38, 10 (Bekk.)

Αἰτιάομαι *To blame,* Dep. Od. 1, 32; Soph. Ph. 385; Her. 4, 94; Antiph. 2, δ, 1. 6, 17; Isocr. 17, 48; Pl. Phaedr. 262, Ion. -ιῆται Hippocr. 6, 606 (Lit.): imp. ᾐτιώμην Antiph. 6, 24; Thuc. 5, 30; Lys. 7, 17; Isocr. 15, 243, Ep. ᾐτιόωντο Il. 11, 78, see below: fut. -ιάσομαι Ar. Nub. 1433; Thuc. 6, 77; Pl. Phaed. 85; Aeschin. 2, 24: aor. ᾐτιᾱσάμην Eur. Fr. 256 (D);

Antiph. 5, 25; Lys. 7, 40; Pl. Meno 93; Dem. 36, 16; -σαίμεθα Thuc. 1, 120; -ιᾱσάμενος Pl. Theaet. 150, Ion. -ιησάμενος Her. 4, 94; Hippocr. 6, 6 (Lit.): **p.** ᾐτίᾱμαι act. Dem. 19, 215, Ion. -ημαι (Hippocr.) Epist. 3, 784 (K. 9, 336 Lit.), **pass.** Thuc. 3, 61: **plp.** ᾐτίατο act. Xen. Mem. 1, 2, 64 (Dind.): **aor.** ᾐτιάθην always **pass.** Thuc. 8, 68; Xen. Hell. 2, 1, 32: **fut.** late αἰτιαθήσομαι Dio Cass. 37, 56. **Vb.** αἰτιατός Aristot. An. Post. 1, 9, 4, -έος Pl. Tim. 57. Lengthened Epic forms: αἰτιόωνται Od. 1, 32; opt. αἰτιόῳο Od. 20, 135, -όῳτο Il. 11, 654: inf. -ιάασθαι 13, 775: **imp.** ᾐτιάασθε Il. 16, 202, -όωντο 11, 78. In Hom. occur only **pres.** and **imp.** and only in the Epic form, in Traged. **pres.** and **aor.**, in Comed. only **pres.** and **future.** καταιτιάομαι has, we think, the **perf.** always **pass.**

Αἰτίζω *To ask, solicit*, a strengthened form of αἰτέω, Epic and only **pres.** Od. 20, 182; Callim. Dian. 32. Fr. 190; subj. -ίζῃ Od. 4, 651, once in Att. -ίζητε Ar. Pax 120 (Hexam.); -ίζειν Od. 17, 346; -ων 17, 222. 19, 273; Callim. Cer. 115; Anth. (Agath.) 10, 66: and **aor.** part. αἰτίσσας Anth 10, 66, missed or denied by Lexicogr.

Αἰχμαλωτίζω *To take captive*, is late, and very complete. We therefore should not have noticed it, had we not observed that all our Lexicogr. miss the **mid.** voice: -ίζομαι Jos. Jud. B. 4, 8, 1: **fut.** -ισόμενος 4, 2, 4: **aor.** ᾐχμαλωτίσαντο 1, 22, 1; -ισάμενος Diod. Sic. 13, 24: with **p. p.** ᾐχμαλωτισμένοι as **mid.** Jos. Jud. B. 4, 9, 8.

Ἀΐω *To hear*, Poet. Il. 15, 130; Pind. P. 1, 14; Aesch. Pers. 633; Ion. and late prose Hippocr. 7, 120 (Lit.); (Luc.) Philop. 1; ἀΐῃς Soph. Ph. 1410, ἀΐωσι Opp. Hal. 3, 272; ἀΐοιεν Il. 10, 189, ἀΐοιτε Opp. H. 5, 44; ἀΐειν Plut. M. 738; ἀΐων Il. 11, 532; Xenophan. 6, 5; Luc. Dom. 18, ἐπ- Her. 3, 29; Pl. Leg. 701, Aeol. ἀΐοισα Sapph. 1, 6: **imp.** ἄϊον Il. 10, 532; Pind. P. 3, 91; Eur. Med. 148, ἐπ- ἄϊον Fr. Achae. 8 (Wagn.), late ᾔϊον Maneth. 6, 113: **aor.** unatt. ἐπ-ήϊσε Her. 9, 93; Ap. Rh. 2, 195, -ήϊσαν 1, 1023. **Vb.** ἐπ-άϊστος Her. 2, 119. (ᾰ. ῐ.) In **pres.** ᾰ in Hom. Il. 15, 248. Od. 18, 11; in Attic poets ᾱ in trimeters, Soph. O. C. 304, ἐπ-ᾱΐω Aj. 1263; Ar. Nub. 650, in other metres ᾰ, Aesch. Supp. 59; Soph. O. C. 181; Aesch. Pers. 633; Eur. Rh. 546; Soph. Ph. 1410; Ar. Nub. 1166. Pax 1064; Com. Fr. 2, 398: in **imp.** ᾰ in Hom. ᾰ Il. 11, 463. 18, 222, ᾱ perhaps by ictus, Il. 10, 532. 21, 388, and always in Trag. Aesch. Pers. 874; Eur. Tr. 155. Ion 507. We doubt ῑ; at Hes. Op. 213, it depends on Spohn's doubtful reading ἄϊε for ἄκουε (Vulg.), and at Aesch. Eum. 844. 887, on arrangement.—Augments by *lengthening*, never by *changing* initial vowel, except late and in comp. The comp. ἐπ-αΐω Soph. Aj. 1263 (contr. ἐπᾴω Eur. Herc. F. 772) is freq. in prose, Her. 3, 29; Pl. Apol. 19. Charm. 170, &c.: **fut.** late -αΐσοντας Dion. de Avibus 2, 19, εἰσ- Orac. Sib. 1, 354 (Alex.): **aor.** ἐπ-ήϊσε Her. quoted.

'Αΐω *To breathe out,* (ἄημι) Epic and only **imp.** ἄϊον Il. 15, 252. (ᾱ, in arsi.) Some however refer this to the previous verb, *to note, know.*

Αἰωρέω *To hold aloft,* act. rare in classic auth. Pind. P. 1, 9; -ωρῇ Luc. Hist. Conv. 8; -ροίη Hippocr. 7, 522. 524; -ῶν Dem. 18, 260; later Plut. Brut. 37; Luc. Jup. Conf. 4: **imp.** ᾐώρει App. Civ. 2, 81: **aor.** ᾐώρησε Opp. C. 4, 216; Nonn. 1, 317. **Pass.** -οῦμαι Thuc. 7, 77, -εῦμαι Her. 7, 92; -ούμενος Soph. El. 1390, ξυν- Pl. Phaed. 112; -έεσθαι Hippocr. 3, 442, -εῖσθαι Xen. Ven. 4, 4: **imp.** ᾐωρεῦντο, ἀπ- Hes. Sc. 234, κατ- 225: **p. p.** ᾐώρηται Opp. Hal. 3, 532, -ηνται 2, 581, ἀπ- Aristot. Plant. 1, 4, 1, Ion. ἐπ-αιωρ- Aretae. Morb. Diut. 1, 50 (Ed. Oxon.): **plp.** ᾐώρητο Coluth. 108; Nonn. 19, 263. 24, 78, -ρηντο Orph. Arg. 1225: aor. αἰωρηθείς Her. 8, 100: with **fut. m.** αἰωρήσεσθαι Aristid. 46, 289 (D.): but **pass.** αἰωρηθήσεσθαι Dio Cass. 41, 1, ἀπ- Hippocr. 3, 468, ὑπερ- 4, 294. 382. 390 (Lit.), ἐπ- Dioscor. 5, 85. **Mid.** rare, aor. αἰωρησάμενος, προσ- D. Sic. 23, 9 (Bekk. 33, 7 Dind.). Our lexicons mislead by saying "**Pass.** with **fut. mid.**"

'Ακαχίζω *To grieve, afflict* (ἄχω, ἀκάχω, -έω), Epic Od. 16, 432: **imp.** ἀκάχιζε Q. Sm. 3, 112: **fut.** ἀκαχήσω H. Hym. 3, 286: **1 aor.** rare, ἀκάχησα Il. 23, 223; Opp. Hal. 4, 46; -ήσῃ Q. Sm. 1, 668: usu. **2 aor.** ἤκᾰχον Il. 16, 822. Od. 16, 427; H. Hym. 5, 56; Anth. 7, 1. 220; ἀκαχών Hes. Th. 868. **Mid.** ἀκαχίζομαι *to sorrow,* imper. -χίζεο Il. 6, 486, -χίζευ Od. 11, 486, later ἀκάχονται Q. Sm. 3, 224 (Mss. Koechl.): **imp.** ἀκάχοντο Q. Sm. 5, 652: **p. p.** ἀκάχημαι as **pres.** Od. 8, 314. 19, 95; imper. ἀκάχησο Ap. Rh. 4, 1324 (Merk.); ἀκάχησθαι Il. 19, 335. Od. 4, 806; **part.** accented as a **pres.** -ήμενος Il. 19, 312. 24, 550; Hes. Th. 99, and with a shifting of the quantity, ἀκηχέμενος Ap. Rh. 4, 1260, -χεμένη Il. 5, 364, -χέμεναι 18, 29: **2 aor.** ἀκαχόμην Od. 16, 342; ἀκαχοίμην Od. 1, 236, -οιτο Il. 13, 344; Ap. Rh. 2, 190; Theocr. 8, 91, -οίμεθα Il. 16, 16.—ἀκηχέδαται 3 pl. **perf.** for ἀκήχηνται, Il. 17, 637: **plp.** ἀκαχείατο, -ήατο (B.) 3 pl. for -χηντο, Il. 12, 179.—See also ἄχνυμαι, ἄχομαι. The **2 aor. act.** is *always* and *alone* augmented.

'Ακαχμένος, η, ον, (ἀκαγμένος redupl. **p. p.** part. of ἄκω?) Epic *sharpened,* Il. 14, 12; Hes. Sc. 135; Opp. Hal. 2, 465, -μένα Il. 12, 444.

'Ακέομαι *To heal*, Dep. (act. ἀκέω only Hippocr. 6, 294 (Lit. 2, 406 Erm.): aor. ἀκέσας, ἐξ- Pythag. Aur. C. 68) ἀκοῦμαι C. Fr. (Menandr.) 4, 287, if not fut., -εῖται Soph. Ant. 1027 (Vulg. Nauck), -έεται Democr. p. 178 (Mull.), -έονται, ἐξ- Il. 9, 507; but subj. ἀκῆται Soph. quoted (Wund. Dind.), -εώμεθα Il. 13, 115; ἀκοῦ Soph. Tr. 1035; -εῖσθαι Eur. Med. 199; Xen. Mem. 2, 7, 1; -ούμενος Pl. Phil. 30, Epic ἀκειόμενος Il. 16, 29; Pind. P. 9, 104: imp. ἀκέοντο Il. 22, 2; Ap. Rh. 2, 156: fut. late ἀκέσομαι Dio Cass. 38, 19; Aristid. 25, 312 (Vulg.), ἀκεσσ-, Musae. 199; Orac. ap. Aristid. 25, 312 quoted, unless ἀκεῖσθαι Pl. Rep. 364, ἐξ- Com. Fr. (Menandr.) 4, 287, be fut.: aor. ἠκεσάμην Il. 5, 901; Aristot. Physiog. 6, 56; Plut. M. 523; Paus. 8, 18, ἀκέσσατο Anth. 5, 291; ἀκέσσαιο Eur. Hec. 1067 (chor.); imper. ἄκεσσαι Il. 16, 523, ἀκέσασθε Od. 10, 69; ἀκεσάμενος Hippocr. 4, 368; Antiph. 4 (γ), 7; Aristot. H. An. 9, 39, 4; Luc. Conv. 47, ἀκεσσ- Plat. Epigr. 5 (B.); ἀκέσασθαι Her. 4, 90; Hippocr. 6, 588 (Lit.): aor. p. late ἠκέσθην pass. Paus. 2, 27, 3. 3, 19, 7: also pass. and late, pres. ἀκεῖται Aretae. C. M. 1, p. 70. Vb. ἀκεστός Il. 13, 115; Antiph. 5, 91. (ᾰ.)—ἀκέο 2 sing. imper. for ἀκέεο, Her. 3, 40, so λυπέο 8, 100, but ποιεῦ ibid.

'Ακηδέω *To neglect*, Poet. Mosch. 4, 81; imper. ἀκήδει Aesch. Pr. 508: imp. ἀκήδεον, -ήδεις Il. 23, 70: fut. late -ήσω Q. Sm. 10, 29: aor. ἀκήδεσα Il. 14, 427, later -ησα; subj. -ήσωσι Q. Sm. 10, 16; -δήσοι Soph. Ant. 414 (Bonitz, Dind., Nauck, ἀφειδ- Vulg.); -ήσας Q. Sm. 12, 376. Vb. ἀκήδεστος Il. 6, 60. (ᾰ.)

'Ακολασταίνω *To be licentious*, only pres. Com. Fr. (Mnesim.) 3, 569; Pl. Rep. 590. Phil. 12; Aristot. Eth. Nic. 2, 6, 19; and late Plut. Alcib. 36 &c.; Anth. 10, 56: imp. ἠκολαστ- Hesych. see ἐλασθαίνομεν: and fut. -ᾰνῶ Ar. Av. 1227. (ᾰ.) This verb occurs twice only in Com. poetry, Ar. and Mnesim. quoted; often in prose, but not earlier than Plato, and almost confined to inf. and part. pres.

'Ακοστήσας *Well fed* with barley (ἀκοστή), a defect aor. part. Il. 6, 506. (ᾰ.)

'Ακουάζω *To hear*, pres. act. only Hom. H. Merc. 423: and mid. ἀκουάζομαι as act. -άζεσθον Il. 4, 343, -άζεσθε Od. 13, 9; -άζωνται Od. 9, 7; (Hes.) Certam. p. 316, 6 (Goettl.); Ionic prose Hippocr. 7, 94 (Lit.)

'Ακούω *To hear*, Il. 2, 486; Pind. P. 1, 2; Aesch. Sept. 245; Soph. Aj. 16; Her. 1, 47 (Orac.). 3, 62; Antiph. 6, 14; Thuc. 6, 34, Dor. 3 pl. ἀκούοντι Pind. P. 5, 101; Epic inf. -έμεναι Od. 12, 193, -έμεν Il. 15, 129: imp. ἤκουον Il. 11, 768; Aesch. Pr. 448; Soph. Ph. 595; Ar. Lys. 390; Her. 2, 3; Antiph.

2, a, 9; Thuc. 8, 6; Dinarch. 3, 1; Dem. 54, 8, ἄκουον Il. 12, 442; Pind. N. 4, 77: fut. m. ἀκούσομαι Il. 15, 199; Aesch. Sept. 196; Soph. O. C. 988; Eur. Heracl. 718; Ar. Ran. 206. Ach. 335; Theocr. 29, 21; Her. 9, 79; Thuc. 7, 73; Andoc. 1, 47; Lys. 13, 2; Pl. Apol. 17; Dem. 14, 12: and late ἀκούσω Lycophr. 378. 1373; D. Hal. 5, 57; Dio Cass. 76, 4; Procop. Epist. 15 (Herch.); Anth. (Pallad.) 9, 397 &c.: aor. ἤκουσα Il. 22, 447; Soph. O. R. 95; Ar. Ach. 571; Her. 1, 48. 2, 3. 7, 102; Antiph. 6, 36; Thuc. 1, 22; Lys. 10, 2; Pl. Phaed. 57, ἄκ- Il. 24, 223; Pind. N. 2, 14, and Dor. ἄκουσα P. 9, 112; Theocr. 4, 6: p. Att. ἀκήκοα Aesch. Pr. 740; Ar. Nub. 738; Her. 1, 37. 8, 109; Antiph. 4, a, 7. 5, 81; Thuc. 6, 91; Lys. 1, 43; Isocr. 12, 187; Isae. 6, 64, Dor. ἄκουκα Plut. Agesil. 21. Mor. 191. 212: plp. ἀκηκόειν Her. always, 2, 52. 7, 208; Lycurg. 15; Pl. Crat. 384 (-όη Bekk. ἠκηκ- Schanz), παρ- Euthyd. 300, and ἠκηκόειν Ar. Pax 616. Vesp. 800 (Vulg. Bergk), see below; Hippocr. 7, 490; Xen. Cyr. 3, 2, 2. Oec. 15, 7 (-όη Saupp.). Hell. 5, 1, 26; (Dem.) 47, 57. 60, 29; late, Luc. Philop. 1. Halc. 2, ἀκηκοότες ἦσαν Isocr. 21, 20: p. p. late ἤκουσμαι D. Hal. Rhet. 11, 10; (Luc.) Philop. 4, and if correct, ἀκήκουσμαι Luc. Hist. Con. 49 (Jacob. Bekk. ἀκηκοέτω Dind. Fritzsche *now*, Cobet): plp. ἤκουστο quoted Demetr. Phal. 217, παρ- Joseph. Ant. 17, 10, 16: aor. ἠκούσθην Babr. F. 72. 76; Luc. Jud. Voc. 6; ἀκουσθείς Thuc. 3, 38; -ουσθῆναι Babr. F. 52; f. -ουσθήσομαι Pl. Rep. 507: and late as pass. f. m. ἐσ-ακούσεται Or. Sib. 2, 302. Mid. Poet. ἀκούομαι as act. rare, Archil. Fr. 69 (Pors. Schneid. Bergk): imp. ἀκουόμην rare Il. 4, 331: f. ἀκούσομαι see above: aor. rare ἠκουσάμην, subj. ἀκούσωμαι Procop. Epist. 66; opt. ἀκουσαίμαν Mosch. 3, 127, εἰσ- Rhet. V. 1, p. 615. Vb. ἀκουστός H. Merc. 512 if sound; Pl. Tim. 33, -έος Rep. 386. 532. Desider. ἀκουσείω, -ων Soph. Fr. 820.

Ὑπακούσεται Thuc. 6, 69, is held pass. by some. If so, it is the only instance in classic Greek, see Poppo, Krüger. ἤκουσμαι seems to have better authority than ἀκήκουσμαι, which however, if correct, disproves Buttmann's assertion "that the perf. pass. is formed without reduplication." There is not a single undoubted instance of first fut. ἀκούσω in the whole range of classic Greek, unless ἀκουσόντων Hyperid. Fun. Or. Col. 13, 3 (Bab.), 178 (Cobet) be correct, which we doubt, both because Hyperid. uses the classic form ἀκούσεσθαι Eux. p. 15, and because the pres. ἀκουόντων, a slight and easy change, suits the sense at least equally well. The copyist seems however to have meant the fut., for he has ἐγκωμιάσοντος in the *compared* clause. And if so, we cannot, with Cobet, condemn the fut. on the ground of its being "plane absurdum." "Nulla unquam," adds he, "fuit oratio neque erit, quae prodesse possit animis eorum qui eam *sint audituri*, id est quae prosit etiam *priusquam* audita sit." We think this an undue, and therefore an unfair, limitation of the phrase. The *hearing* of the things that were to benefit was surely future to his *present* utterance. Several late writers, from Lycophron onwards, use it freely, Anth. 9, 397; D. Hal. 5, 57; Menand. Rhet. 614; V. T. 2 Reg. 14, 16. Esai. 6, 9; N. T. Matt. 12, 19. 13, 14. Jo. 10, 16; Or. Sib. 4, 174. 8, 104. 206. 345; but even in late writers, the **mid.** seems to be the prevailing form. ἀκούω is not the only verb which takes, even in Attic Greek, the temporal as well as the syllabic augment in its **plp.**; in other words, augments occasionally at least, the reduplicated vowel, ὠρώρει Aesch. Ag. 653; Soph. O. C. 1622 (both trimeters), but ὀρώρει Ar. Pax 1287 (hexam.). In *Attic* prose, the correct theory would, perhaps, be always to augment it in accordance with occasional cases presented by the best Mss. e. g. ἀπ-ωλώλει Dem. 20, 79 (Ms. S. Dind. *now*). 19, 125 (most Mss. Bekk. Dind. Bait. Saupp. &c.) Herodian, an able grammarian, would write the **plp.** of ἀκούω always with η, ἠκηκόειν. But if the best Mss. and editors may be trusted, Herodotus seems never to have augmented the reduplication, the Attics to have augmented it, but certainly not "always." The form ἠκηκόη is called old Att. for -ειν, Ar. Pax 616 (Bekk. Dind.). Vesp. 800 (Dind. Meineke); Pl. Crat. 384 (Ms. T. Schanz), ἀκηκόη (Bekk. Or. B. W.).

In some edit. various forms of the **fut. act.** used to stand as follows: ἀκούσει Il. 7, 129, now ἀκούσαι, ἀκούσεις Alcae. Fr. 82 (85), now ἀκούσαις, so Aesch. Ag. 1406 (Blomf.), -ούεις (Mss. Dind. Herm.), ἀκούσετε Ar. Thesm. 1167 (Br.), now -σητε (Bekk. Dind.), so Dem. 18, 160 (Steph.). 25, 85 (some Mss.), now -σαιτε (Reisk. Bekk. &c.), ἀκούσομεν Ar. Ach. 295 (Mss. R. V.), -ωμεν (Elms. Bekk. Dind.), ὑπακούσοντες Thuc. 1, 140 (Vulg.), -σαντες (Mss. Haack, Bekk. Krüg. &c.), and ἀκούσετε Luc. Abdic. 26, ὑπακούσεις Navig. 11 (Vulg.) are now -ούσαιτε, -ούσει (Jacob. Dind.).

'Ακρᾰχολέω *To be passionate*, Att. prose, and only **part.** -οῦντα Pl. Leg. 731.

'Ακρῑβόω *To make accurate*, reg. but. **mid.** -οῦμαι late in *simple*, **fut.** -ώσομαι Joseph. Ant. 17, 2, 3: **aor.** ἠκριβώσατο Porph. V. Pythag. 11 (Nauck); Malal. p. 230, 14: and as **mid. p. p.** ἠκρίβωσαι p. 138, 3: **plp.** ἠκρίβωτο, ἀκριβῶς ᾔδει (Hesych.), all missed by Lexicogr. In *comp.* the **mid.** is classical, διακριβοῦμαι

Isocr. 4, 18; Pl. Theaet. 184: aor. -ιβωσώμεθα Isocr. Ep. 6, 8; -ώσασθαι Isae. 3, 39; Pl. Polit. 292.

'Ακροάομαι Dep. **Med.** *To hear, listen to*, Ar. Vesp. 562; Antiph. 5, 4; Thuc. 3, 37; Dem. 23, 78; -ώμενος Hippocr. 7, 252; Aristot. Rhet. 1, 1, 10; Aeschin. 3, 166: **imp.** ἠκροώμ- Andoc. 4, 8; Pl. Menex. 236: **fut.** -οάσομαι Andoc. 1, 105; Lys. 27, 7; Pl. Apol. 37; Isocr. 15, 21: **aor.** ἠκροᾱσάμην Ar. Ran. 315; Thuc. 6, 89; Lys. 16, 9; Pl. Ion 530; Dem. 43, 2; ἠκροᾶσο = -οῶ, C. Fr. 3, 50: **p.** ἠκρόᾱμαι Aristot. H. A. 4, 10, 11; Luc. D. Mer. 12, 2: **aor.** late and **pass.** ἀκροᾱθείς Aristid. 4, 30 (Vulg. ἀνακραθείς Reiske, Dind.); Joseph. Ant. 17, 5, 2 (Bekk). **Vb.** ἀκροατέος Ar. Av. 1228. In the classical period this verb seems nearly confined to comedy and Attic prose.—A poetic collateral form ἀκροάζομαι is found in Epicharmus 75; also Hippocr. 7, 70: **imp.** ἠκροάζετο Com. Fr. (Menand.) 4, 113, where Meineke however prefers with Steph. **aor.** ἠκροάσατο. For ἠκροᾶσο C. Fr. 3, 50, Cob. suggests ἠκρόᾱσο **plp.**

'Ακροβολίζω *To throw from a distance, skirmish*, in **act.** only **imp.** ἠκροβόλιζε Ant. Pal. 7, 546; Eustath. 5, 14. Usu. ἀκροβολίζομαι Dep. **mid.** and confined to prose, Xen. Cyr. 8, 8, 22; Luc. Tim. 45: **fut.** (-ιοῦμαι): **aor.** ἠκροβολισάμην Thuc. 3, 73. 4, 34; -ισάμενος Her. 8, 64. No **pass.** (?).

'Ακρωτηριάζω *To cut off the extremities*, Longin. 39, 4; Plut. Mor. 479; Polyb. 5, 54: **imp.** ἠκρωτ- Polyb. 1, 80; (Luc.) Amor. 24; Athen. (Clearch.) 12, 27: **aor.** ἠκρωτηρίασα Her. 3, 59; Strab. 17, 1, 46; Polyb. 8, 23; Diodor. 4, 10, 3: **p. p.** ἠκρωτηριασμένος Aristid. 13, 128 (Dind.); but. **act.** Dem. 18, 296: **aor.** -άσθην Plut. Alcib. 18. Nic. 13; Philostr. 7, 4 (Kayser): **mid.** -ασάμενος Xen. Hell. 6, 2, 36: and **p. p.** as **mid.** -ασμένος Dem. quoted.

'Αλαίνω (ᾰ) *To wander*, Tragic, and only **pres. act.** Aesch. Ag. 82; Eur. Tr. 1084; -αίνων I. T. 284. El. 204. Or. 532; (3 pl. Dor. ἠλαίνοντι Theocr. 7, 23, where once stood **mid.** ἠλαίνονται, see ἠλαίνω.)

'Αλαλάζω *To raise the war-cry*, Aesch. Fr. 55 (Dind.); late prose Plut. Luc. 32. Cat. Maj. 9; Arr. An. 1, 14, συν- Polyb. 18, 8: **imp.** ἠλαλ- Eur. Bac. 1133; Xen. An. 6, 5, 27, ἀν- 4, 3, 19, ἀλαλ- Nonn. 1, 242: **fut. mid.** -άξομαι Eur. Bac. 593: **act.** ἀλαλάξω late Arr. C. Alan. 25 (-άζω Herch.); V. T. Jer. 29, 3: **aor.** ἠλάλαξα Eur. Herc. F. 981; Com. Fr. (Anon.) 4, 676; Xen. An. 5, 2, 14 (Popp. Krüg.), ἀντ- Aesch. Pers. 399, ἐπ- Xen. Cyr. 7, 1, 26, unaugm. ἀλάλαξεν Pind. Ol. 7, 37; inf. -αλάξαι Soph. Ant. 133; part. ἀλαλάξαντες Xen. Cyr. 3, 2, 9; Luc. Nav. 36. **Mid.** ἀλαλαζομένη as **act.** Soph. Fr. 479 (Dind.): **imp.** ἠλαλάζετο

Arr. An. 5, 10, 3: fut. -άξομαι see above. For ἠλάλαξαν Xen. An. 5, 2, 14, L. Dind. and Cobet read ἠλέλιξαν. Xen. seems alone of classic prose writers to use this verb.

Ἀλάλκω *To ward off*, Epic, pres. late, Q. Sm. 7, 267 (Mss. Lehrs, Koechl.): fut. ἀλαλκήσω Ap. Rh. 2, 235: 2 aor. unaugm. ἄλαλκον Il. 23, 185; Hes. Th. 527; Pind. Ol. 10 (11), 105. N. 4, 60, but ἤλαλκε (Hesych.); subj. Ep. ἀλάλκῃσι Od. 10, 288 (Wolf, Bekk. Dind.); opt. ἀλάλκοις Od. 13, 319, ἀλάλκοι Il. 21, 138; Ap. Rh. 4, 872, ἀλάλκοιεν Il. 22, 196; ἄλαλκε Theogn. 13; ἀλαλκών Il. 9, 605; inf. Ep. ἀλαλκέμεναι Il. 17, 153, ἀλαλκέμεν Il. 19, 30 (Aristoph. Bekk.). Od. 3, 237, ἀπ- Theocr. 28, 20, ἀλαλκεῖν Il. 19, 30 (Dind. La. R.); Anth. (Antip. Sid.) 7, 8. For fut. ἀλαλκήσει Od. 10, 288 (Vulg.) Wolf, Bekk. Dind. and Ameis read subj. aor. ἀλάλκῃσιν. Bekk. *now* reads with Aristoph. ἀλαλκέμεν Il. 19, 30, for -αλκεῖν (Vulg. Dind. La Roche). ἀλάλκουσι Q. Sm. quoted, Lobeck (Tech. Verb. p. 60) would alter to ἀλέξουσι, but Koechly retains it.

Ἀλαλύκτημαι Ep. *To be troubled*, a reduplicated perf. pass. from ἀλυκτέω, with meaning of pres. Il. 10, 94. See ἀλυκτέω.

Ἀλάομαι *To wander*, mostly poet. ἀλῶμαι Aesch. Eum. 98, -ᾶται Solon 13, 43; Pind. Ol. 1, 58; Ar. Av. 942, -ώμεθα Soph. Aj. 23, -ᾶσθε Il. 10, 141, -ῶνται Dem. 19, 310, Ep. -όωνται Od. 3, 73; imper. Ep. ἀλόω (ἀλάεο, ἀλᾶο, ἀλῶ) Od. 5, 377; part. ἀλώμενος Od. 6, 206; Soph. O. C. 1363; Theocr. 13, 66; Her. 4, 97; Lys. 6, 30, -ωόμενος Q. Sm. 14, 63; ἀλᾶσθαι Aesch. Pr. 666; Eur. Med. 515; Thuc. 2, 102; Isocr. 4, 168: imp. ἠλώμην Od. 4, 91; Soph. O. C. 444; Eur. Ion 53; Ael. V. H. 4, 20; D. Sic. 5, 59; App. Civ. 1, 62. 4, 115, poet. ἀλᾶτο Il. 6, 201, Dor. ἄλῆτο, if correct, Bion 11 (8), 5 (Ahrens): fut. rather doubtful, ἀλήσεται, ἀπ- Hes. Sc. 409 (Vulg. so Goettl. in Text): but prefers aor. ἀπ-αλήσατο (3 Mss. Ranke): p. ἀλάλημαι as pres. Il. 23, 74. Od. 11, 167, -ησαι 15, 10, -ηται 20, 340; Hes. Op. 100; Bion 1, 20, -ησθε Od. 3, 72. 9, 253; imper. ἀλάλησο Od. 3, 313; ἀλάλησθαι 2, 370. 12, 284; Emped. 374 (Stein); ἀλαλήμενος with accent of pres. Od. 14, 122, -ημένη Anacreont. 56, 12 (Bergk): plp. as imp. ἀλάλητο Orph. Arg. 1264, -ηντο Eur. Andr. 307 (chor.); Ap. Rh. 1, 812: aor. ἠλήθην, poet. ἀλήθην Od. 14, 120, -ήθης 14, 362; sub. ἀληθῇ, ἐπ- 15, 401; part. ἀληθείς Od. 14, 380, ἐπ- 4, 81, Dor. ἀλᾱθείς Aesch. Supp. 870 (chor.); Theocr. 16, 51; in prose, rare and late ἀληθέντι (Heliod.) 10, 34 (Bekk.) In Att. poetry, the indic. pres. and imp. alone occur in trimeters, the perf. plp. and aor. pass. are almost exclusively Epic. In classic prose, occur only pres. indic. inf. and part. and these rather rarely.

(**Ἀλαόω**) *To blind*, rare, Epic and only **aor.** ἀλάωσε Od. 1, 69. 9, 516; Anth. 7, 601, ἐξ- Od. 9, 453; inf. -αῶσαι 504; -αώσας Opp. Cyn. 3, 228. In Hom. with gen. of the thing ὀφθαλμοῦ, but later with acc. of the person γενέτην Anth. quoted.

Ἀλαπάζω *To plunder*, Epic Il. 12, 67; Panyas. Fr. 5 (Dübn.): unaugm. **imp.** ἀλάπαζον Il. 11, 503: **fut.** ἀλαπάξω Il. 2, 367; Aesch. Ag. 130 chor. (Vulg.), ἐξ- Hes. Op. 189; Xen. An. 7, 1, 29; Ep. inf. -αξέμεν Callim. Dian. 251: **aor.** ἀλάπαξα Il. 11, 760; Theogn. 951; Anth. 7, 614. **Pass.** ἀλαπαζομένην Il. 24, 245: **aor.** late ἐξ-αλαπαχθῇ Or. Sib. 12, 305. For μοῖρ' ἀλαπάξει Aesch. Ag. quoted, Elms. reads (with Farn.) μοῖρα λαπάξει, which was adopted by Blomf. and now also by Herm. and Dindorf: compare λαπάξειν Sept. 47. 531. ἀλαπάζω is thus not Attic, except that Xen. l. c. uses the compd. ἐξαλ-.

Ἀλαστέω *To be wrathful*, Epic, and confined to **imp. fut.** and **aor. part.**: **imp.** ἠλάστεον trissyll. Il. 15, 21: **fut.** -ήσω: **aor. part.** ἀλαστήσας Il. 12, 163; Callim. Del. 239; Musae. 202; Maneth. 2, 183, ἐπ- Od. 1, 252; Ap. Rh. 3, 369. 557.

Ἀλγύνω (ῡ) *To vex*, poet. mostly Trag. Aesch. Sept. 358; Soph. O. R. 1067; Eur. Alc. 521; late Plut. Mor. 82; Maneth. 5, 101: **imp.** ἤλγυνον Aesch. Ch. 746, iter. ἀλγύνεσκε Q. Sm. 4, 416: **fut.** -υνῶ Soph. O. R. 332; Eur. Hipp. 1297; Com. Fr. (Eup.) 2, 457; and late Lycophr. 985: **aor.** ἤλγυνα Plut. Marcell. 25; opt. ἀλγύναις Soph. O. R. 446 (-νοις Elms.), -ύνειεν Tr. 458; inf. -ῦναι Eur. I. A. 326: **aor. pass.** ἠλγύνθην Aesch. Pr. 245; ἀλγυνθῶ Eur. Tr. 172; late prose Plotin. 26, 51: with **fut. mid.** ἀλγυνοῦμαι as **pass.** Soph. Ant. 230; Eur. Med. 622: but late **fut. p.** ἀλγυνθήσομαι, συν- Theodor. Stud. p. 210. Rare in prose, **act.** late ἀλγύνω Plut. Mor. 82: **aor.** ἤλγυνα Marcell. 25: **pass.** ἀλγυνόμενος Xen. Apol. 8; Plut. Lysand. 2.

• **Ἀλδαίνω** Poet. *To nourish*, Nic. Alex. 404; -δαίνειν Aesch. Sept. 557; -δαίνων Sept. 12. Pr. 539 (also ἀλδήσκω intrans. Il. 23, 599; Opp. Cyn. 1, 318, trans. Theocr. 17, 78): **2 aor.** Epic, ἤλδᾰνον Od. 18, 70. 24, 368: **1 aor.** late (ἤλδηνα), ἐν-αλδήνασα Nic. Alex. 409 (G. Schneid.), ἐν-αλδήσασα (Vulg.), iter. ἀλδήσασκε Orph. Lith. 364. **Pass.** ἀλδαίνηται Q. Sm. 9, 473. **Vb.** ἄν-αλτος *insatiable*, Od. 18, 114. For ἐναλδήνας, -ήσας Nic. Alex. 409, Otto Schneid. reads ἐνανθήσας with Ms. P.

Ἀλδήσκω, see preced.

(**Ἄλδω**), **pass.** -ομαι *To be healed*, seems late Q. Sm. 9, 475 (Spitzn. Koechl.), ἐν- Nic. Alex. 532. ἀλδομέναν in some edit. of Ar. N. 282, is a mere suggestion of Brunck for the Ms. and correct reading ἀρδ- (Dind. Bergk, Mein.). See ἄλθω.

Ἀλεγίζω *To care for*, Epic, Epigramm. and only **pres.** Il. 1,

160; Hes. Th. 171; Ap. Rh. 3, 193; late prose Ep. Phal. 29; ἀλεγίζειν Orph. Lith. 61; -ίζων Orph. Arg. 352. Lith. 38; Aretæ. C. Ac. Morb. 1 (83): and imp. unaugm. ἀλέγιζε Il. 11, 80; Ap. Rh. 1, 14; Nonn. 41, 332. **Pass.** ἀλεγιζόμενον Anth. 5, 18. The collateral ἀλέγω is also mostly Epic, and used only in pres. Il. 9, 504. 11, 389; Alcae. 58; Simon. C. 37, 10; Theocr. 15, 95; Opp. Hal. 2, 183; ἀλέγοι Nic. Ther. 5; ἀλέγων Od. 19, 154; Hes. Op. 251; Pind. Ol. 11, 15; once in Att. Aesch. Supp. 751 (chor.); -γειν Pind. I. 8, 47. **Pass.** ἀλέγονται Pind. Ol. 2, 78; subj. ἀλέγησθον Anth. App. 50, 6. ἀλεγύνω also is Epic, but scarcely so confined in its inflection, imper. ἀλέγυνε Hym. Merc. 476, ἀλεγύνετε Od. 1, 374; inf. -ύνειν 11, 186; part. -ύνων H. H. Merc. 361: imp. unaugm. ἀλέγῡνον Od. 13, 23; Ap. Rh. 2, 495: aor. ἀλέγῡνα Ap. Rh. 1, 394. **Mid.** aor. ἀλεγύνατο Emped. 433 (Stein) missed by Lexicogr.

'Αλεείνω Epic, *To avoid*, Od. 13, 148. Il. 11, 794; -νων Il. 16, 213; Hes. Op. 828; -είνειν Opp. H. 5, 78; late prose Luc. Dem. enc. 23; Agath. 2, 32: imp. unaugm. ἀλέεινον Il. 13, 356; intrans. *withdrew*, Ap. Rh. 3, 650: aor. late, inf. ἀλεεῖναι Maneth. 6, 736.

'Αλείφω *To anoint*, Ar. Ach. 1066; Com. Fr. (Crates) 2, 237; Her. 3, 8: imp. ἤλειφον Hipponax 41 (B); Plut. Themist. 3, ἐξ- Isocr. 21, 2, προσ- ἄλειφε Od. 10, 392: fut. ἀλείψω (V. T. Exod. 40, 13), ἐξ- Eur. I. A. 1486; Pl. Rep. 386: aor. ἤλειψα Il. 18, 350. Od. 19, 505; Ar. Pax 502, ἐξ- Andoc. 1, 103; Dem. 57, 63, ἄλειψα Od. 12, 177; -είψειε Pl. Lys. 217; -εῖψαι ibid.; Hippocr. 6, 452 (Lit.), ἐξ- Thuc. 3, 57: p. ἀλήλιφα, ἀπ- Dem. 52, 29 (Bekk. Dind. B. Saupp. ἀπ-αλήλειφα Ms. S, ἀπ-ήλειφα Ms. F.), ἐξ- Aristid. 33, 425 (Dind.): p. p. ἀλήλιμμαι (v. r. -λειμμαι) Thuc. 4, 68; Alciphr. 3, 28; Luc. Alex. 30, ὑπ- Xen. Oec. 10, 6, συν- Aristot. Meteor. 2, 7, 2, ἐξ- (Dem.) 25, 70, ἤλειμμαι late, see below: aor. ἠλείφθην Hippocr. 7, 606 (Lit.); Pl. Lys. 217, ἐξ- Æsch. Sept. 15; Eur. I. T. 698. Hel. 262: fut. ἀλειφθήσεται, ἐξ- (Dem.) 25, 73, κατ- (Hippocr.) Epist. 9, 320 (Lit.): 2 aor. ἠλίφην Joseph. Jud. B. 2, 8, 3 (Bekk.), ἐξ- Pl. Phaedr. 258 (Mss. Bekk. Stallb. Or. B. W.); Jos. Ant. 17, 12, 2, ἀπ- Dio Cass. 55, 13 (Bekk. L. Dind.). **Mid.** ἀλείφομαι *anoint myself*, Ar. Ach. 999; Com. Fr. (Cephis.) 2, 883. (Antiph.) 3, 81; Hippocr. 7, 276. 316; Xen. Occ. 10, 5: imp. ἠλειφόμην Simon. Am. 16; Archil. 31 (B.); Com. Fr. (Antiph.) 3, 117; Pl. Theaet. 144, ἐξ- Her. 7, 69: fut. -είψομαι Thuc. 4, 68: aor. ἠλειψάμην Ar. Nub. 836; Thuc. 1, 6, ἀλειψ- Il. 14, 171; -ψηται Hippocr. 8, 424; -ψαιτο 5, 284 (Lit.); -άμενος Il. 10, 577; Pl. Theaet. 144. **Vb.** ἀλειπτός late, but ἀν- ἐξ- Isocr. 5, 70; ἐξ-αλειπτέος Lys. 6, 8. The perf. forms ἀλήλιφα, ἀλήλιμμαι are now almost universally approved and adopted by late editors, though ἀλήλειφα, -ειμμαι are found in good Mss. and the latter edited hy Bekker, Aristot. H. A. 5, 19, 8, and by Sintenis, Plut. Marcel. 17, but -ιμμαι (Reisk. Bekk.), so ἀλήλιμμαι, -ιμμένος Mor. 148. 193 (Dübner), -ειπται has been discarded from Luc. also, for -ιπται Catapl. 24. Pisc. 36 (Mss. Jacob. Dind. Bekk.). The unreduplicated forms ἤλειφα, ἤλειμμαι seem scarcely to occur except in comp. and in inferior Mss. ἀπ-ηλειφέναι Dem. 52, 29 (Ms. F.), ἐξ- Aristid. 33, 425 (Vulg.), -αληλιφέναι (Ms. Θ. Dind.), ἠλειμμένος Geop. 7, 8, 9; V. T. Num. 3, 3, ἠλιμμ- (Alex.), ἐξ-ήλειπται Dem. 25, 70 (Vulg. Dobs., -αλήλιπται Bekk. Dind.), ἐξ-ήλιπται v. r. Luc. Pisc. 36 (Ms. F.) In Traged. this verb does not occur in the *simple* form: in Att. prose, the act. occurs only in aor. and only in Plato quoted, and part. ἀλείψαντες Demad. 17 (Bekk.) Hom. has only 1 aor. act. and mid. The 1 aor. pass. is by far the prevailing form, early and late. The only instance of 2 aor. in the *classical* period is ἐξ-αλιφῇ Pl. Phaedr. 258 (best Mss.), ἐξ-αλειφθῇ (Vulg.) Elsewhere he uses 1 aor. ἀλειφθέν twice Lys. 217, ἐπ- ibid., even ἐξ-αλειφθῇ without v. r. Theaet. 191, so that we have some misgiving about ἐξ-αλιφῇ though presented by Mss. Bodl. D G P. The perf. ἤλοιφα is not found, though we have ἀλοιφή the noun. We doubt however if the noun proves the actual existence of the perf. In *formation* we think analogy a sufficient guide without current usage.

'Αλέκω *To ward off*, Poet. late and doubtful in pres. Anth. 6, 245 (Mss. ἀλέγοις): fut. ἀλέξοντες, ἀπ- Bekk. Anecd. 415: 1 aor. ἤλεξα, opt. ἀπ-αλέξαι Aesch. Supp. 1052 (chor.); in tmesi Q. Sm. 6, 307: 2 aor. ἀλκαθεῖν only Trag. Aesch. Fr. 425; Soph. Fr. 827. **Mid.** *defend oneself*, fut. ἀλέξομαι Soph. O. R. 171; and *now* Xen. An. 7, 7, 3 (best Mss. Krüg. Dind. Kühn. Saupp.); -οίμην Soph. O. R. 539: aor. ἠλεξάμην, inf. ἀλέξασθαι Her. 7, 207; Hippocr. 6, 74 (Lit.); Xen. An. 1, 3, 6. 3, 4, 33. 5, 5, 21. Cyr. 1, 5, 13, ἀπ- Soph. Aj. 166. These forms are generally referred to ἀλέξω.

'Αλέξω *To ward off*, rare, inf. ἀλεξέμεν Il. 3, 9, -έμεναι Il. 1, 590. 11, 469; and, if sound, in a Spartan decree Thuc. 5, 77, -έξειν Pind. Ol. 13, 9; Xen. Cyr. 4, 3, 2, ἀπ- Poet. (Pl.) Alc. (2), 143. 148: fut. ἀλεξήσω Il. 9, 251; -ήσειν 20, 315. 21, 374, ἀπ- Od. 17, 364; -σων Il. 6, 109; Q. Sm. 10, 292: aor. (ἠλέξησα), ἀλεξήσειε Od. 3, 346, ἀπ-αλεξήσαιμι Il. 24, 371; ἀλεξῆσαι Opp. Hal. 5, 626; late prose ἀλεξήσας Apollod. 3, 12, 5; Euseb. adv. Hierocl. 69. **Mid.** ἀλέξομαι *defend oneself, ward off*, Xen. Mem. 4, 3, 11; -ώμεσθα Il. 11, 348, -ησθε Xen. An. 7, 3, 44; -ξευ Archil.

66; -όμενος Od. 9, 57; Her. 1, 211. 7, 225; Xen. An. 1, 9, 11: fut. ἀλεξήσομαι Her. 8, 81. 108 (Xen. An. 7, 7, 3?): aor. ἀλέξασθαι Il. 15, 565, see ἀλέκω.—The form ἀλεξήσασθαι though supported by all the Mss. Xen. An. 1, 3, 6, is rejected by the best editors for ἀλέξασθαι the reading of Castalio. Bornemann however has recalled the former, and Kühner follows him, but drops the *analogy* An. 7, 7, 3, and edits fut. ἀλεξόμεθα for ἀλεξησόμεθα. The forms in -ησω seem to be Ion. and too little in accordance with the usage of Xen. to be readily adopted even with Mss. For fut. ἀλαλκήσω, and 2 aor. ἄλαλκον, see ἀλάλκω. A pure form ἀλεξέω seems doubtful in pres. ἀλεξεῖν Pind. Ol. 13, 9 (several Mss. Vulg. Bergk) has been rejected by Boeckh, Hart. Momms. for ἀλέξειν.

Kühner and Jelf have said "fut. ἀλέξομαι is poet. only." Kühner however *now* defends it as a real fut. and the best supported reading Xen. An. 7, 7, 3, quoted.

Ἀλέομαι *To avoid*, Epic, contr. ἀλεῦμαι Theogn. 575, ἀλέονται Opp. Hal. 5, 432; (subj. -έηται Od. 4, 396, may be aor.); but opt. ἀλέοιντο Orph. Arg. 607, ἀλέοιο, ἐξ- Ap. Rh. 1, 490; ἀλευμένη Simon. (Amorg.) 7, 61 (Bergk): imp. ἀλέοντο in tmesi Il. 18, 586: aor. (ἠλεάμην), subj. ἀλέηται Od. 4, 396, -εώμεθα Il. 5, 34. 6, 226; opt. ἀλέαιτο Il. 20, 147. Od. 20, 368; imper. ἀλέασθε Od. 4, 774; inf. ἀλέασθαι Il. 13, 513. 23, 340. Od. 9, 411; Hes. Op. 446 (late prose Agath. 1, 15), ἐξ- Hes. Op. 105; Ar. Eq. 1080 (hexam.); Ap. Rh. 2, 319.

Opt. pres. ἀλέοιτο Il. 20, 147 (Vulg.) is now aor. -έαιτο (Bekk. Spitzn. La R. and *now* Dind.) ἀλεῦ read by Fritzsche, and approved by Rost, Aesch. Pr. 567, is an Ion. contraction for ἀλέου imper. of ἀλέομαι, but see ἀλεύω.

Ἀλεύω *To avert*, Poet. Aesch. Pr. 567; Paroem. Greg. Cypr. Cent. 1, 31. Diog. 2, 56; late prose Agath. 1, 15: fut. ἀλεύσω Soph. Fr. 825 (D.): aor. (ἤλευσα), ἄλευσον Aesch. Sept. 141. Supp. 528, -εύσατε Sept. 86. Mid. Epic ἀλεύομαι *to avoid*, Od. 24, 29; Hes. Op. 535; Ap. Rh. 4, 474; Mosch. 2, 77; imper. ὑπ-αλεύεο Hes. Op. 760: aor. ἠλευάμην Il. 13, 503. 17, 305; Ap. Rh. 4, 797, ἀλευ- Il. 11, 360. Od. 22, 260, 2 sing. ἀλεύαο Nonn. 33, 326; subj. -εύεται for -ηται, Od. 14, 400; and (ἠλευσάμην), subj. ἐξ-αλεύσωμαι Soph. Aj. 656 (Mss. Vulg. Lob.), but -αλύξωμαι (Hesych. Br. Nauck, Dind. *now*), see ἀλύσκω; imper. ἄλευαι Il. 22, 285; inf. ἀλεύασθαι Od. 12, 159; Hes. Op. 798; late prose Plut. Mor. 297; ἀλευάμενος Il. 20, 281; Theogn. 400. At Aesch. Pr. 567 quoted, Dind. has ἄλευ δᾶ by apocope—*singularis* apocope he grants—for ἄλευε, Weil ἄλευ' ἆ δᾶ, Herm. ἄλευε δᾶ. ἐξαλεύσωμαι

Soph. quoted, has good Mss. support, but is opposed by ἐξαλύξωμαι (Hesych.), approved by Wessel. Heath, Br. Herm. and *now* Dind. We do not however think it a valid objection against ἐξαλεύσωμαι "that the aoristic mid. forms of ἀλεύομαι occur elsewhere invariably without σ," ἠλευάμην, ἀλεύωμαι &c. These forms do, certainly, always occur elsewhere without σ, but then they are Epic, and never appear in Attic. We are therefore not sure that an Attic poet, neither quoting nor imitating nor accommodating an Epic poet, would have felt constrained (by *Attic usage*) to take the *Epic* mid. form instead of the form with σ, especially as Attic usage uniformly follows the σ formation in the act. ἀλεύσω, ἤλευσα. Besides, none of the v. r. point to the Epic form.

'Αλέω *To grind*, Ar. Nub. 1358; Hippocr. 8, 112 (Lit.); Aristot. Probl. 35, 3; Plut. M. 284, κατ- Her. 4, 172: imp. ἤλουν Com. Fr. (Pher.) 2, 254: fut. (ἀλέσω, Att. ἀλῶ Moeris, Suid.): aor. ἤλεσα, κατ- Strab. 260, Epic ἄλεσσα Od. 20, 109; ἀλέσαι Com. Fr. (Pher.) 2, 345; Hippocr. 7, 266 (Lit.); ἀλέσας 6, 454. 7, 170 (Lit.); Arr. An. 6, 23; Strab. 3, 3, 7; Herodn. 4, 7 (Bekk.): p. ἀλήλεκα Anth. (Nicarch.) 11, 251: p. p. ἀλήλεσμαι Her. 7, 23; Thuc. 4, 26 (Mss. Haack, Poppo, Krüg. &c.); D. Sic. 3, 14, ἀλήλεμαι Thuc. quoted (Mss. Bekk. Goell. Stahl); Com. Fr. (Amph.) 3, 303, and late ἤλεσμαι Dioscor. 1, 28: aor. late ἠλέσθην Dioscor. 1, 173; Geop. 7, 12, and if correct, ἠλήσθην Geop. 9, 19. Vb. ἀλεστέον late, Dioscor. 5, 95.—ἐπιαλῶ Ar. Nub. 1299, given by some as fut. of this verb, is fut. of ἐπιάλλω. Passow says that ἀληλεσμένος, though altered by Bekker to ἀληλεμένος Thuc. 4, 26, is still quite sure in Amphis (Athen. 14, 642). If the first line is made complete, ending with the participle, then ἀληλεσμένον is *undoubted*, because the form with σ is required by the metre; but if the first line is constituted defective, and the second complete, beginning with the participle, then is -εσμένος not only liable to doubt, but inadmissible, and the form without σ, ἀληλεμένον, absolutely demanded by the metre. Besides, it is the reading of all the Mss. In the *classical* period, the case, on the whole, seems to stand so: ἀληλεσμένος Her. 7, 23 (no v. r.); Thuc. 4, 26 (Mss. Haack, Popp. Krüg. &c.), -εμένος (Mss. Bekk. Goell. Cob. Stahl, &c.); Amphis, Athen. 14, 642 (all Mss. Meineke), -εσμένος (Casaub. Schweigh. Dind.); and later D. Sic. 3, 14; Arr. An. 6, 23, -εμένος Anon. Oec. 22. The strengthened form ἀλετρεύω is Epic and rare, Od. 7, 104; Hes. Fr. 26; -εύουσα Ap. Rh. 4, 1095: fut. late -εύσοντα Lycophr. 159.

'Αληθίζω *To speak truth*, rare and late in act. Plut. M. 230.

Mid. rare in classic Greek, and only pres. ἀληθίζομαι Her. 3, 72; -ίζεσθαι 1, 136; -ιζόμενος Dio Cass. 56, 41: aor. -ίσασθαι Alciphr. 3, 59 (Ms. Ven. Meineke). ἀληθεύω *to speak truth*, Hippocr. 2, 150; Xen. Pl.: fut. -εύσω Xen. An. 7, 7, 25; Aristot. Eth. N. 4, 13, 8: aor. ἠλήθευσα Xen. An. 5, 6, 18; -εύσαιμι Aesch. Sept. 562: p. -ευκα Aristot. Interp. 10, 14, has pass. ἀληθεύομαι *to be truly spoken, to accord with truth*, Aristot. Top. 5, 4, 2. 3 &c.: with fut. mid. -εύσεται as pass. N. Eth. 1, 11, 37. Top. 5, 5, 3. 5. Metaph. 10, 5, 10. 6, 17 (Bekk.)

Ἀλήθω *To grind*, usu. only pres. and rare, Hippocr. 6, 494 (Lit.); Theophr. C. P. 4, 12, 13; Anth. (Lucil.) 11, 154: imp. ἤληθον Babr. 131, 5 (Lach. Knoch); V. T. Num. 11, 8: aor. ἀλήσας Herodn. 4, 7, 5 (Vulg.) is now ἀλέσας (Bekk.): aor. p. ἠλήσθην Geop. 9, 19 (?). See ἀλέω. The collat. form ἀλίνω occurs only in pres. Soph. Fr. 826 (D.)

Ἀλῆναι, see εἴλω.

Ἀλησθύω, see ἀλυσθαίνω.

Ἀλητεύω *To wander about*, Ep. and Trag. and confined to pres. Od. 17, 501; inf. -εύειν 18, 114; part. -εύων 12, 330; Eur. El. 1113. Hipp. 1048: and fut. ἀλητεύσω Eur. Heracl. 515.

(Ἄλθω) and Ἀλθίσκω *To heal*, Hippocr. 1, 472 (Foes, 7, 52 Lit.), perhaps better -ήσκω (Galen, Rost, 2, 210 Ermerins): fut. late ἀλθήσω Nic. Ther. 587: aor. late ἤλθησα 496. Pass. ἄλθομαι, -ένη Q. Sm. 9, 475 (Mss. A. Vulg. ἀλδομ- Spitzn. Koechl.): imp. ἄλθετο Il. 5, 417: fut. ἀλθήσομαι, ἀπ- pass. Il. 8, 405: aor. ἀλθεσθῆναι, ξυν- Hippocr. 4, 126 (Lit.): aor. m. late ἠλθησάμην Poet. de Herb. 44. Epic except. pres. and aor. pass.—ἀλθεσθῆναι from ἄλθομαι, has analogy in ἀχθεσθῆναι from ἄχθομαι. A fut. m. ἀλθέξονται, as if from ἀλθέσσω, occurs in Aretae. 61, 30. Passow says "there is no example of pres. act. or pass." though ἀλθομένη is, we think, in every edit. of Q. Sm. quoted, except Koechly's (1850).

Ἀλιβδύω *To sink in the sea*, Poet. and late, Callim. Fr. 269: aor. ἀλιβδύσασα Lycophr. 351.

Ἁλίζω *To collect, assemble* (ἁλής), Her. 7, 12; Pl. Crat. 409: fut. (ἁλίσω, -ιῶ): aor. ἥλισα, ἁλίσας Eur. H. F. 412; Her. 1, 77; Nic. Damasc. Fr. 11 (L. Dind.); συν-ήλισαν Her. 1, 176, but συν-άλ- 1, 125 (Mss. Gaisf. Bekk. Krüg. Stein), συν-ηλ- (Dind. Bred.); συν-αλίσας Her. 1, 126; Xen. Cyr. 1, 4, 14; Arr. An. 5, 17: (perf.?): p. p. (ἥλισμαι), ἡλισμένην Anon. Stob. Flor. 28, 18 (Mein.), always unaugm. in Her. ἁλισμένος 4, 118. 7, 172; συν-αλίσθαι 5, 15: aor. ἡλίσθην, συν- Xen. An. 7, 3, 48;

Luc. Philops. 12; ἀλισθῇ Hippocr. 6, 168. 7, 280; Xen. An. 2, 4, 3; ἀλισθεῖεν Her. 1, 63; -ισθείς Emped. 150; Her. 5, 15; Hippocr. 7, 10. 282; -ισθῆναι Her. 1, 79; Aristot. Probl. 24, 9, 2: fut. ἀλισθήσομαι Aristot. Probl. 2, 28. (ᾱ) Eur. Heracl. 403. This verb is rare in Attic. ἁλίζεσθαι *may* be mid. Xen. An. 6, 3 (1), 3: imp. συν-ηλίζοντο Her. 1, 62. 5, 102. The perf. pass. is peculiarly Ion. and therefore not augmented by Her. ἤλισμ- however (Dind.) and 7, 172 (Abicht), but aor. συν-άλισε 1, 125, though supported by the Mss. should perhaps be altered to συν-ηλ- in accordance with συνήλισαν 1, 176, and συν-ηλίζοντο 1, 62. 5, 102. So, we observe, Dindorf and Abicht edit, and Bredow recommends: Lhardy suggests συν-αλίσας, an easy emendation. The collat. ἁλιάζω seems to occur only in the comp. συν-αλ-, and only in the Dor. aor. συν-ᾱλίαξε Ar. Lystr. 93.

(Ἀλινδέω, -ίνδω, ἀλίω) *To roll*, aor. ἠλίνδησε (Hesych.), ἤλῖσα, in comp. ἐξ-αλῖσας Ar. Nub. 32; Xen. Oec. 11, 18: p. ἤλῖκα, ἐξ- Ar. Nub. 33. Pass. ἀλινδοῦμαι Plut. M. 396; Luc. Dem. enc. 24, and poet. ἀλίνδομαι Anth. 7, 736; Nic. Ther. 156: aor. ἀλινδηθείς Nic. Ther. 204: p. ἠλινδημένος Dinarch. Fr. 10, 2 (B. Saupp.) Pass. forms mostly late.

Ἀλίνω, see ἀλήθω.

Ἀλιόω *To make fruitless*, (ᾰ) poet. and only fut. ἀλιώσω Soph. O. C. 704 (chor.): and aor. ἠλίωσα Tr. 258 (trimeter), ἀλ- Il. 16, 737. Od. 5, 104; Ap. Rh. 3, 1176. 4, 21. Mid. fut. as act. ἀλιώσεται *will destroy*, late Maxim. de Auspic. 582, but pass. or intrans. *will perish*, 512.

Ἁλίσκομαι *To be taken*, Pind. Ol. 8, 42; Aesch. Fr. 129 (D.); Soph. Aj. 648; Com. Fr. (Anax.) 3, 175; Her. 3, 154; Thuc. 8, 34; Lys. 13, 67: imp. ἡλισκόμην, never ἑαλ-, Antiph. 5, 11; Thuc. 1, 102; Her. 7, 181. so 2, 174 (Bekk. Dind.), ἁλισκ- (Schweigh. Gaisf.): fut. ἁλώσομαι Theogn. 236; Soph. O. C. 1065; Ar. Vesp. 893; Her. 7, 102; Antiph. 2, α, 8; Lys. 10, 22, -ώσει Pl. Gorg. 489, Ion. -ώσεαι Her. 1, 112: aor. ἁλῶσαι Hippocr. 6, 470 (Ms. H.), but corrected ἀναλῶσαι (same Ms. Littré): p. ἑάλωκα Aesch. Ag. 30; Her. 1, 191. 209; Thuc. 8, 23; Lys. 10, 25; Isae. 3, 5; Aeschin. 3, 251; Xen. Cyr. 7, 5, 33. An. 7, 1, 19; Pl. Apol. 38. Leg. 937, and ἥλωκα Com. Fr. (Antiph.) 3, 116. (Xenarch.) 3, 621; Her. 1, 70. 78. 83; Xen. An. 4, 2, 13. Cyr. 5, 5, 23; Dem. 21, 105. 227, Dor. ἅλωκα (ᾰ) Pind. P. 3, 57, 3 pl. -ώκαντι Plut. Lys. 14, 4: plp. ἡλώκειν Her. 1, 84. 8, 61; Xen. An. 5, 2, 15, ἑαλ- Plut. Lys. 14, 4: p. p. see ἀν-αλίσκω: aor. late in *simple* ἁλωθῆναι D. Sic. Fr. ex Lib. 21, 6 (Bekk.): 2 aor. ἑάλων Ar. Vesp. 355;

Hippocr. 7, 284; Thuc. 1, 128; Xen. Cyr. 3, 1, 4; Lys. 19, 4; Isae. 5, 12; Aeschin. 2, 12; Pl. Apol. 39, and ἧλων Od. 22, 230; Her. 1, 78. 3, 15, and always; Xen. An. 4, 5, 24. Hell. 5, 1, 27; (Pl.) Hip. Maj. 286; ἁλῶ Eur. Hipp. 420; Ar. Ach. 662, -ῷς Pl. Apol. 29, -ῷ Aesch. Sept. 257; Her. 1, 84. 4, 127 (Dind. &c. see below); Pl. Leg. 937, ἁλῶμεν Ar. Eccl. 287, ἁλῶσι Her. 2, 93; Pl. Leg. 937 &c.; ἁλοίην Il. 22, 253 (Bekk. Dind.); Antiph. 2, α, 8. 5, 59; Pl. Theaet. 179; ἁλούς Il. 2, 374. 5, 487; Soph. O. C. 764; Ar. Nub. 1079; Her. 5, 105; Xen. An. 5, 2, 8; ἁλῶναι Il. 21, 281; Soph. Ph. 1440; Ar. Thesm. 790; Antiph. 2, γ, 6; Thuc. 4, 100. **Vb.** ἁλωτός Thuc. 6, 77.—Active supplied by *αἱρέω*. ἁλώω, -ώῃ Epic **2 aor.** subj. for ἁλῶ, -ῷ, Il. 11, 405. 14, 81. 17, 506. Od. 18, 265; Her. 4, 127 (Bekk. ἁλῷ Dind. &c.) ἁλῴης opt. for ἁλοίης, Ap. Rh. 1, 491, ἁλῴη Od. 14, 183. 15, 300 (-οίη Dind. -ώῃ La R.), but at Il. 9, 592. 14, 81. 17, 506; Her. 4, 127 (Gaisf. Dietsch), it has been altered by Bekker to subj. ἁλώῃ, by Bredow, Dind. Stein and Abicht to ἁλῷ. ἁλώμεναι Epic inf. **2 aor.** for ἁλῶναι, Il. 21, 495. ᾰ in **pres.** Eur. Alc. 786, ᾱ in indic. **2 aor.** ἑάλων Ar. Vesp. 355, but ἑάλως Anth. 7, 114, ᾰ in the other moods, ἁλῶ, ἁλοίην, ἁλούς, ἁλῶναι, Il. 4, 291 &c. except ἁλῶναι Hipponax 74 (B.), ἁλόντε, which has ᾱ even in thesis, Il. 5, 487. ἑάλω dissyllab. Anth. 11, 155.—In Epic, this verb seems confined to **2 aor.** The **act.** forms ἁλίσκω, ἁλόω, are not found uncomp. except 3 sing. ἁλίσκει if sound, Prov. Diogen. Cent. 2, 66. 4, 45; and Hesych. In Her. and Xen. Mss. and edit. present both ἥλωκα and ἑάλωκα, the former prevailing in Her. the latter in Xen. In Thuc. Plato and, we think, the orators, except Dem. ἑάλωκα is the only form. Dem. as edited by Bekker, and B. Saupp. has both forms, ἥλωκα seven or eight times, 19, 179. 21, 105. 151. 227. 24, 77. 84 (105). 54, 33, ἑαλ- twice as often, 19, 169. 312. 341. 21, 11. 23, 28. 29. 30. 34. 35. 36. 38. 79. 95. 216. 219. 24, 112. 137. 25, 17. Dind. again, in his last edition (1855), gives uniformly ἥλωκα, and **aor.** ἥλων, except perhaps thrice ἑάλων 7, 37. 20, 79, seemingly by oversight. "ἥλωκα," Buttm. says, "belongs to the stricter Atticism." If this be correct in theory, we think it is not borne out by the *usage* of the stricter Attic prose writers at least. In fact, we find it most frequently in those authors that are least shy of an Ionic or a common form, Her. and Xen. quoted; ἡλωκώς Plut. Pyr. 18. Sol. 19. Cat. Min. 68. Ant. 39; D. Sic. Fr. 21. p. 4 (Bekk.) The compd. ἀναλίσκω, -αλόω would favour the opinion more. In Trag. the **perf.** occurs only once ἑάλωκεν Aesch. Ag. 30, the **aor.** never in indic. In Comed. the **perf.** occurs twice, and in the form ἥλωκα Com. Fr. quoted, indic. aor. ἑάλων rare Ar. quoted.

('Αλιταίνω only mid.) and 'Αλιτραίνω *To sin*, Epic Hes. Op. 241 (quoted Aeschin. 2, 158. 3, 135); Anth. (Jul.) 9, 763; Tryph. 269: **1 aor.** rare ἀλίτησα Orph. Arg. 647: **p.** ἠλίτηκα (Hesych.): **2 aor.** ἤλἴτον Il. 9, 375; Theogn. 1170; Callim. Dian. 255; Aesch. Eum. 269 (chor.); subj. ἀλίτῃ Pseud.-Phocyl. 208; opt. ἀλίτοιμι Aesch. Pr. 533 (chor.); -ιτών Eum. 316 (chor.); Opp. H. 5, 563. **Mid.** ἀλιταίνεται as **act.** (v. r. ἀλιτραίν-) only Hes. Op. 330, seems Epic subj.: **2 aor.** ἀλιτόμην Od. 5. 108; subj. ἀλίτωμαι Il. 24, 570, -ηται 19, 265; Ap. Rh. 2, 1028; inf. ἀλιτέσθαι Od. 4, 378; Ap. Rh. 2, 390: **p.** part. ἀλιτήμενος *sinning*, Od. 4, 807; Hes. Sc. 91. This verb is Epic and Epigramm. Of Attic poets, Aesch. alone uses it, but only **2 aor.** and only in chor.

'Αλίω, see ἀλινδέω.

('Αλκάθω) *To ward off*, only **2 aor.** inf. -ἄθεῖν Aesch. Fr. 425; Soph. Fr. 827 (D.) See ἀλέκω.

'Αλλάσσω *To change*, Emped. 72 (Stein); Eur. Phoen. 74; Hippocr. 2, 58, Att. -ττω Pl. Parm. 139: **fut.** -άξω Theogn. 21; Eur. Bacc. 1331, δι- Thuc. 8, 89: **aor.** ἤλλαξα Eur. Alc. 661; Plut. Mor. 212. 761, ἀπ- Her. 1, 16; Thuc. 1, 90, ἄλλαξα, ἐξ- Pind. I. 3, 18; ἀλλάξαιμι Aesch. Pr. 967; ἀλλάξας Luc. D. Deor. 4, 1; Apollod. 3, 4, 3, ἐπαλλάξας Il. 13, 359; ἀλλάξαι Soph. Ant. 945; Dion. Hal. Ant. 16, 1; Luc. Jup. Conf. 11; Apollod. 3, 4, 4: **p.** ἤλλαχα, ἀπ- Xen. Mem. 3, 13, 6; Dem. 18, 65, μετ- Hyperid. 4, 23, 11, δι- Com. Fr. (Dionys.) 3, 547: **p.p.** ἤλλαγμαι Com. Fr. (Antiph.) 3, 96; Anth. 9, 67; late prose Apollod. 3, 12, 6, but ἀπ- Her. 1, 60, δι- Aesch. Sept. 885; Pl. Menex. 244, and ἀπ-αλλ- Her. 2, 167 (Bekk. Dind. Stein): **plp.** ἤλλακτο Her. 2, 26; Luc. Tox. 30, ἀπ- Antiph. 1, 7: **1 aor.** ἠλλάχθην Anth. 7, 336, συν- Soph. Aj. 493, ἀπ- Her. 8, 18, ἀλλάχ- Eur. I. A. 797 (chor.); subj. δι-αλλαχθῆτε Ar. Lys. 900; Pl. Crat. 430; imper. ἀλλάχθητε Soph. Fr. 829; ἀλλαχθείς, δι- Andoc. 2, 26, κατ- Hyperid. Fr. 193: **f.** ἀλλαχθήσομαι, ἀπ- Eur. Med. 878; Ar. Av. 940: **2 aor.** ἠλλάγην Isae. 4, 13; Luc. Gall. 16, ἀπ- Aesch. Pr. 750; Her. 8, 84; Thuc. 2, 42, δι- Ar. Lys. 1161; Antiph. 6, 39: **fut.** ἀλλαγήσομαι Luc. Imag. 2, ἀπ- Her. 2, 120; Thuc. 4, 28; Pl. Rep. 445. **Mid.** ἀλλάσσομαι, -άττομαι *change one's own, barter*, Pl. Soph. 223: **imp.** ἠλλασσ- Eur. I. T. 292, ἠλλαττ- Com. Fr. (Philem.) 4, 23: **fut.** -άξομαι Dion. Hal. Ant. 19, 16 (Kiessl.); Luc. Tyr. 19, 7, ἀντ- Eur. Hel. 1088. Phoen. 1633: **aor.** ἠλλαξάμην Antiph. 5, 79; Thuc. 8, 82; Pl. Menex. 237; -ωμαι Eur. El. 103; *changed one's place, departed*, Dem. 55, 32; Aristid. 13, 95 (D.); *changed* (itself) Or. Sib. 5, 517; Dion. περιηγ- 392 (Passow): and **as mid. p. p.** ἐν-ήλλακται Soph. Aj. 208. **Vb.** ἀλλακτέον Plut. Mor. 53, ἀπ- Lys. 6, 8. See ἀπ-αλλάσσω. In Att. poetry the **1 aor. pass.** simple and compd. is used more frequently than **2 aor.** by Soph. and Eur. The **2 aor.** is always used by Aesch.; διηλλάχθητε Sept. 885, is merely a suggestion of Burney's for διήλλαχθε of the Mss. and editions; generally by Aristophanes; only once by Soph. ἀπαλλαγείς Ant. 423; thrice by Eur. ἀπ-ηλλάγην Andr. 592. Ph. 592. 1409. But though Tragic and Comic poets use both **aorists,** they never use **2 fut.** -γήσομαι, but always -χθήσομαι; whereas Her. and Attic prose writers use **2 fut.** -γήσομαι only: -χθήσομαι however is in late prose ἀπ- D. Hal. 7, 13, δι- Aristip. in Diog. L. 2, 82; Galen 10, 538. In prose, Her. has both **aor. pass.** in comp. but the first more frequently, ἀπ-ηλλάχθη 2, 152. 1, 170. 5, 65. 2, 2 (v. r. -γην), ἐξ- 5, 4 &c.: **2 aor.** ἀπαλλαγῆναι 8, 84, without v. r. (Schweigh. Bekk. Gaisf. &c.): **fut.** -αλλαγήσομαι 2, 120. Thuc. has always the **2** aor., Xen. almost always, but ἐπ-αλλαχθῇ Mem. 3, 8, 1; so Plato, but δι-αλλαχθῶμεν Crat. 430 (Epist. 335. 346); and the Orators, but δι-αλλαχθείς Andoc. 2, 26, κατ- Hyperid. Fr. 51 (B. Saupp.) It is therefore a mistake to say that "the Attic Historians, Plato, and the Orators use only the **2 aor.**," as well as that "Her. always uses the first."

Porson (Eur. Ph. 986) accounts for the frequent use of **1 aor.** in the Tragedians by their loving "rough and old forms." We think this, even with his own limitations, too strong a statement of the case. It appears, however, to be correct in regard to the following verbs and compds. whose **1 aor. pass.** is *alone* or preferably used by the Traged.: ἀγγέλλω, βρέχω, δέρκομαι, κλέπτω, κλίνω, κρύπτω, μάσσω, ῥίπτω, στερέω, τάσσω, τέρπω, but in others with some of their compds. it is difficult occasionally to see a preference; nay, sometimes a preference leans the other way: ἀπ-αλλάσσω, βλάπτω, ζεύγνυμι, θάπτω, μίγνυμι, πήγνυμι, πλέκω, πλήσσω, ῥήγνυμι, στρέφω, σφάζω, τήκω, τρέπω, τρέφω. The three Traged. have **2 aor.** ἀπ-ηλλάγην seemingly by choice, Aesch. Ag. 336; Soph. Ant. 422; Eur. Andr. 592, for here the metre admits ἀπ-ηλλάχθην. βλάπτω, 1 aor. ἀπο-βλαφθείς Soph. Aj. 941, not req.: **2 aor.** βλαβείς Aesch. Ag. 120, req. ζεύγνυμι, Aesch. has ζευχθείς Ag. 842, not required by the metre, ζυγείς Ch. 795, req. Soph. ἐζεύχθη Ant. 955, of choice, but ὑπ-εζύγην Aj. 24, also of choice, and ζυγείς Ph. 1025, ζυγῆναι O. R. 826, req. Eur. ἐζεύχθην Ion 949, ζευχθείς Supp. 877. Elec. 99, not req. ἐζύγη Supp. 822. I. A. 987, ζυγείς Med. 735. Supp. 220. Ph. 337, req., but ζυγεῖσα Fr. Aeg. 10, 2, by preference. θάπτω.

always **2 aor.** ταφείς Aesch. Sept. 1021; Eur. ταφείη Tr. 731, ταφείς Supp. 175. 545, ταφῆναι Ph. 776, never ἐθάφθην. μίγνυμι, μιχθῆναι Aesch. Supp. 295; Soph. O. R. 791, req. συν- Eur. Fr. 890 (D.), not req.: μιγῆναι Aesch. Pr. 738; Soph. O. R. 995; Eur. Ion 338, req. πήγνυμι, πηχθείς Eur. Cycl. 302, req.: παγείς Aesch. Eum. 190, of choice; Eur. Fr. Erecth. 4, 12, req. I. A. 395. πλέκω, πλεχθείς Aesch. Eum. 259: ἐμπλακείς Eur. Hip. 1236, req. συμ-πλακ- Soph. Fr. 548 (D.), of choice. πλήσσω, Aesch. never **1 aor.** πληχθείς, but **2 aor.** πληγείς Sept. 608. Fr. 129; so Soph. πληγείς Ant. 172. 819. Ph. 267; πληγῆναι O. C. 605; and Eur. πληγείς Supp. 934. Or. 497. Herc. F. 1393, never -χθείς, except ἐκ-πληχθεῖσα Tr. 183. ῥήγνυμι, always **2 aor.** ἐρράγην Aesch. Soph. Eur. στρέφω, ἐστρέφθην never in the Traged. though often in Hom.: **2 aor.** ἐστράφην, στραφείην Soph. Aj. 1117. Tr. 1134. Ant. 315, req., but O. C. 1648, not req. ἀπ-εστράφη Eur. Supp. 159. I. T. 1165. Hel. 77, req., but I. T. 1179, and ἀπο-στραφείς Or. 720, not req. σφάζω, **1 aor.** ἐσφάχθην occurs only once in Trag. σφαχθεῖσ' Eur. I. T. 177: often **2 aor.** ἐσφάγην, σφαγείς Eur. Tr. 619. Hec. 24. Ph. 933. I. T. 770, κατ-εσφάγη Rh. 810; -είς Tr. 483, of choice; σφαγῆναι Hec. 433. I. T. 598; σφαγείς 552. Cycl. 243, req., so κατ-εσφάγη Hel. 936. Cycl. 128; -σφαγείη Aesch. Eum. 102; Soph. O. R. 730; -σφαγείς Eur. Bac. 858, req. τήκω, **1 aor.** ἐτήχθην only once, συντηχθείς Eur. Supp. 1029, req.: **2 aor.** ἐτάκην, τακῇ Eur. Fr. 230, 4, of choice; τακείς Eur. Hel. 3, ἐν-τακείη Soph. Tr. 463, req. ἐκ- Aesch. Pr. 535. τρέπω, **1 aor.** ἐτρέφθην only once, Eur. Elec. 1046, req.: **2 aor.** ἐτράπην, τραπῇ Soph. O. C. 1537; τραπείς Aesch. Pers. 1027; Soph. Aj. 743; Eur. Med. 246; ἀνα-τραπῆναι Aesch. Sept. 1076, req. τρέφω, **1 aor.** ἐθρέφθην twice, Eur. Hec. 351. 600, req.: **2 aor.** ἐτράφην Aesch. Sept. 754; Soph. Aj. 557. Ant. 984; Eur. I. A. 575; τραφῆναι Soph. Fr. 911; Eur. Supp. 911. Bac. 295; τραφείς Soph. Aj. 1229. O. R. 1123. 1380. Ph. 3; Eur. Ion 693. Elec. 558. Or. 1340. I. A. 926. 1085. 1292, most, if not all, req., but Ion 263, of choice; φαίνω, **1 aor.** ἐφάνθην Aesch. Pers. 264; Soph. O. R. 525. 1485. Ant. 104, φάνθη Eur. H. F. 804, req.; φανθέν Soph. Tr. 743, not req.: **2 aor.** ἐφάνην Aesch. Eum. 320; Soph. Aj. 739. O. C. 77. 974. El. 154. 846. Ant. 457. Tr. 862; Eur. Hec. 112; subj. φανῶ; opt. -είην; imper. -άνηθι; φανείς; φανῆναι above fifty times in the three Tragedians, and always seemingly for the metre.

From this induction it would appear that, in some verbs, the Traged. used only the **1 aor.** or preferred it, or used it freely if the metre required—that in others they were guided by other reasons, use and wont, conventional meaning, peculiar liking, emphasis, harmony, or other causes too hidden for our search, or too fine for our perception.

Ἀλλέγω, see ἀνα-λ-.

Ἀλλογνοέω *To mistake for another* (νοέω), only aor. part. ἀλλογνώσας Ion. for -οήσας, Her. 1, 85.

Ἀλλοιόω *To make different*, reg.: with **fut. mid.** -ώσομαι as pass. Galen 3, 761: and **fut. pass.** -ωθήσομαι 3, 641. 9, 412. **Vb.** ἀλλοιωτός Aristot. Nat. Ausc. 3, 5. The **fut. mid.** has been missed by Lexicogr.

Ἄλλομαι *To leap*, Hym. Cer. 175; Ar. Lys. 82; Theocr. 3, 36; Thuc. 7, 45, ἐξ- Il. 5, 142, ἐσ- Her. 2, 66: **imp.** ἡλλόμην Xen. Cyr. 1, 4, 11; Plut. Brut. 31, ἐν- Aesch. Pers. 516, ἐξ- Ar. Vesp. 130, ἀλλ- Simon. (C.) 40, Aeol. ἀλλόμαν Sapph. 55 (B.): **fut.** ἁλοῦμαι (V. T. Esai. 35, 6), ὑπερ- Xen. Eq. 8, 4, ἐν- Plut. Mor. 1087, Dor. ἁλεῦμαι Theocr. 3, 25. 5, 144: **1 aor.** ἡλάμην Batr. 225. 249 (Baumeist.); Eur. Ion 1402; Ar. Ran. 244; rare in prose Luc. Indoct. 14. Fug. 2, ἐσ- Il. 12, 438. 16, 558; Xen. Cyr. 7, 4, 4; Ael. Fr. 50, ἀφ- Aesch. Pers. 305, ἐν- Soph. O. R. 1261, ἐξ- Xen. An. 7, 3, 33, Dor. ἁλάμαν Theocr. 23, 60; Anth. (Phan.) 6, 307; subj. ἅληται see **2 aor.**; ἁλάμενος rare, Ar. Av. 1395; Xen. An. 4, 2, 17 (Dind. Cob. v. r. Plut. Crass. 31); Synes. Epist. 57, καθ- Xen. Hell. 4, 5, 7 (Cob. Saupp. -όμενος Breitb. Dind.); ἅλασθαι rare if correct, Ael. Epist. 16 (Herch.), καθ- Luc. D. Mort. 14, 5 (Reitz, Jacob. -έσθαι Bekk. Dind.): **2 aor.** ἡλόμην indic. rare, often doubtful, Xen. Hell. 4, 4, 11 (Mss. Breitb. ἡλλ- Mss. Dind. Cob. Saupp.), ἐν- Aesch. Pers. 516 (Mss. Vulg. Schneid. &c. ἐνηλλ- Herm. Dind.), ἐξ- Soph. O. R. 1311 (Mss. Vulg. Schneidew. &c. ἐξηλλ- Herm. Dind.), ἆλσο Il. 16, 754, ἆλτο 5, 111, ἐπ- 21, 140; Pind. N. 6, 50, see below; subj. ἅληται Il. 21, 536, Epic ἅλεται Il. 11, 192. 207; opt. ἁλοίμην Anth. 7, 36; Xen. Mem. 1, 3, 9, εἰσ- Soph. Fr. 695 (D.), προ- Q. Sm. 4, 510, Dor. ἁλοίμαν Theocr. 5, 16; ἁλέσθαι Opp. Cyn. 1, 83, ἀφ- Ael. V. H. 6, 14 (-ασθαι Herch.), ἐν- Plut. Them. 10. Brut. 46, ἐξ- Mor. 341, καθ- Luc. D. Mort. 14, 5 (-ασθαι Reitz, Jacob.); ἁλόμενος Aesch. Eum. 368 chor. (Ven. 1. Herm. Dind. &c. ἀλλ- Med. &c.); Xen. An. 4, 2, 17 (Vulg. Krüg. Saupp. &c. ἁλάμ- Dind. Cob.); Luc. Peregr. 9. Apol. 4; Aesop 45 (Halm), ἀν- D. Hal. 8, 54, ἐξ- Plut. Mor. 984; Themist. 18, 221 (Cobet N. L. p. 454, calls this **2 aor.** pt. *barbarous*. We are anxious to know how he will *civilly* dispose of ἁλομένα Aesch. Eum. 368 quoted), Epic ἅλμενος Opp. Hal. 5, 666, and ἄλμενος, ἐπι- Il. 7, 15, ἐπ- Hes. Th. 855, κατεπ- Il. 11, 94; Opp. Cyn. 3, 120, ἐξ- Il. 17, 342; Opp. Hal. 2, 239, μετ- Bion 4, 6.

ἆλσο, ἆλτο (ἅλσο, ἅλτο Bekk. 2 edit.), ἄλμενος are, say the old grammarians, Epic syncopated 1 aor. forms, 2 aor. say the later, with *spiritus lenis* for ἄλ(ε)σο, ἄλ(ε)το, ἀλ(ό)μενος=ἥλου, ἥλετο. "α of the 1 aor. is said to be long, ἄλασθαι, as ἆραι, ἄρασθαι." The α in ἆραι, ἄρασθαι is certainly long, and should, on the same principle, be long also in ἄλασθαι, but we desiderate *actual* proof: ἀλάμενος Ar. Av. 1395, the only instance in poetry, is unfortunately not decisive. Theod. Kock scans it long ἀλάμ- (Ar. Av. 1864). For ἐνήλου Aesch. Pers. 516, Blomf. and now Dind. (Lex. Aesch.) read 1 aor. ἐνήλω; and for ἐξήλου Soph. O. R. 1311 (chor.), Elms. reads ἐξάλω, "inaudite δωρίζων" says Ellendt. It may be true that we have in our texts of the Tragedians no instance of this verb in the Doric form, yet in a Chorus, and amid Dorisms, Elmsley's ἐξάλω seems not so bold. Theocr. has 3 pers. ἐξάλατο 17, 100, how would he have written the 2d? Grammarians account for ἆλσο &c. with *lenis*, from "a consonant following the λ." How then did ἅλμα escape? It is more likely that it arose from a liking for *easy* utterance. See ἀθροίζω, ἀθρ-, ἔχω, ἕξω &c. &c.

Ἀλλοφρονέω *To think of other matters* &c. Ion. and only pres. -έει Hippocr. 7, 30 (Lit.); -έων Od. 10, 374; Theocr. 22, 129; Her. 7, 205: and aor. ἀλλοφρονῆσαι 5, 85. Bekker 2 ed. reads ἄλλο φρονέων Il. 23, 698, and Odd. quoted; so Ameis; but Dind. Spitzn. La Roche ἀλλοφρ-.

Ἀλ-λύω, see λύω.

Ἀλοάω *To thrash*, Ar. Fr. 544; Pl. Theag. 124, rarely ἀλ- Xen. Oec. 18, 3, Poet. ἀλοι- Theocr. 10, 48; imp. ἠλόα (Hesych.), Poet. ἀλοία Il. 9, 568, ἠλοία Babr. 98, 15: fut. -ήσω late Geop. 3, 11; V. T. Jer. 5, 17, ἀλ- Esai. 41, 15: aor. ἠλόησα Ar. Ran. 149; ἀλοῆσαι Plut. T. Gracch. 2; ἀλοήσας Synes. Epist. 108, but ἀλοάσας Com. Fr. (Pherecr.) 2, 278, κατ-ηλόησ- Aeschin. 2, 140, συν- Long. Past. 4, 29, Poet. and late prose ἠλοίησα Aesop 367 (Fur.), ἀπ- Il. 4, 522, συν- Theocr. 22, 128; Opp. Cyn. 1, 268; Athen. 524: p. p. ἠλόημαι Synes. Ep. 79 (Herch.), κατ- Com. Fr. (Eub.) 3, 211; ἠλοημένος Theophr. C. Pl. 4, 12, 9 (Mss. Urb. Wimm.), ἀπ- Dem. 42, 6; Luc. Icar. 15: aor. ἠλοήθην Polyb. 10, 12; Plut. M. 327; but ἀλοᾱθείς Theophr. C. Pl. 4, 6, 5 (Schneid.), -ηθείς (Wimm.), ἀλοιη- Nonn. 31, 7: fut. ἀλοηθήσονται Geop. 2, 26, ἀλ- V. T. Jer. 28, 33.

Ἀλοίω *To thrash*, aor. part. ἀλοίσας Epigr. (Diog. L.) 7, 31: p. p. as a v. r. ἤλοισται, κατ- Com. Fr. (Eub.) 3, 211.

Ἀλοκίζω (ἄλοξ) *To furrow*, Poet. defective, and rare, -ίζειν Ar. Vesp. 850: p. p. late ἠλοκισμένος Lycophr. 119. 381. 810 &c.; but κατὰ . . . . ἠλοκίσμεθα in tmesi Eur. Supp. 826.

(**Ἁλόω**), see ἁλίσκομαι, ἀναλόω.

(Ἀλυκτάζω Hesych.) *To be excited, distressed,* only **imp.** ἀλύκταζον Her. 9, 70. The form ἀλυκταίνειν is in Hesych.

Ἀλυκτέω *To be restless, anxious,* rare -τέει Hippocr. 8, 30 (Lit. Lind. ἀλύει Vulg. Erm.); aor. ἀλυκτήσας Hesych.: hence the Epic perf. ἀλαλύκτημαι Il. 10, 94.

Ἀλυσθαίνω and **Ἀλυσθμαίνω** *To be distressed,* only **pres.** and perhaps late, -σθαίνει (Hippocr.?); Nic. Ther. 427, -σθμαίνουσα Callim. Del. 212. Heringa suggested and Rost approves ἀλυσθαίνει Hippocr. 465, 10 (Foes) for ἀλησθύει (Mss. Vulg. Foes, Lind. 8, 268 Lit. 2, 713 Ermerins).

Ἀλυσκάζω *To avoid,* Poet., Il. 6, 443; Com. Fr. (Cratin.) 2, 99; -άζων Il. 5, 253. Od. 17, 581; Anth. 9, 371; Orph. Arg. 439: **1 aor.** ἀλυσκάσσειε Nonn. 42, 135. 48, 481. 630.—ἀλύσκασε Od. 22, 330 (Vulg.) is now ἀλύσκᾰνε from Cod. Harl. and Ap. Lex. (Wolf, Bekk. Dind. La R.)

Ἀλυσκάνω *To avoid,* Poet., only **imp.** ἀλύσκᾰνε Odd. 22, 330.

Ἀλύσκω *To avoid,* Poet. Ap. Rh. 4, 57, -σκει 2, 72; -σκων Od. 22, 363. 382: **fut.** ἀλύξω Od. 19, 558; Aesch. Pers. 94; Soph. El. 627. Ant. 488; -ξοι Od. 17, 547 (Bekk. Dind. -ξει La R. Ameis); -ειν Aesch. Ag. 1615, Ep. -έμεν Il. 10, 371 (Bekk. 2 ed.): and **fut. m.** -ύξομαι Hes. Op. 363: **aor.** ἤλυξα Od. 3, 297; Phryn. Fr. 5 (Wagn.), ἐξ- Eur. Bacc. 734, ἄλ- Od. 23, 328; Hes. Fr. 45, 4; Pind. P. 8, 16; -ύξω Od. 11, 113; Aesch. Pr. 587; ἀλύξας Aesch. Pers. 100 (chor.); Anth. P. 6, 217; -ύξαι Il. 8, 243; Theocr. 24, 69; Bion 10, 7: **1 aor. m. subj.** ἐξ-αλύξωμαι Soph. Aj. 656 (Hesych. Br. Herm. Dind. Wolf), perhaps the only instance, see ἀλεύω. In Prose, we have met with this verb only in Philostr. Her. 735 &c.

Ἀλύσσω *To be excited, distressed,* Ion. -σσων Il. 22, 70: **fut.** ἀλύξω Hippocr. 8, 16 (Lit.): **plp.** ἀλάλυκτο Q. Sm. 13, 499. 14, 24.

Ἀλύω *To be greatly moved by grief or joy,* mostly Poet. and only **pres.** Od. 18, 333; Eur. Hipp. 1182; Com. Fr. (Alex.) 3, 434; Soph. Phil. 174, ἀλ- (Ellendt); ἀλῠουσ- Il. 5, 352, -ῠων 24, 12, but -ύων Od. 9, 398; Aesch. Sept. 391: and **imp.** ἤλῠον Ap. Rh. 4, 1289. Occasionally in Ion. and late prose, Hippocr. 2, 708. 3, 122. 7, 384; Ael. V. H. 9, 25. 14, 12; Plut. Pyr. 16; Luc. D. Mar. 13, 1, ἀλ- Long. Past. 1, 28 (Seil.) In Hom. ῠ, except Od. 9, 398 ἀλῡων, at the end of a line; so Ap. Rh. 3, 866; Nic. Al. 317; and ἀλύει Opp. Hal. 4, 195; Emped. 445, in the fourth foot; in late Epic ῠ, in Attic ῡ.

Ἀλφάνω *To find, acquire,* Poet. only **pres.** Eur. Med. 298; Ar. Fr. 308; -άνῃ Com. Fr. (Eupol.) 2, 531: and **2 aor.** Epic ἦλφον Il. 21, 79; ἄλφοι Od. 15, 453. 17, 250, pl. -οιν for -οιεν 20, 383 (Bekk. Dind. La R.) This verb is rare: four times in Epic, once in Trag., twice in Comedy. A pres. ἀλφαίνω, and fut. ἀλφήσω, given by Passow, we have never seen, except -αίνει Hesych.; -αίνειν Et. Mag. 72, 39; ἐξ-αλφήσεις (Hesych.); also a pres. (ἄλφω), ἐξ-ἄλφεις, εὑρίσκεις (Hesych.)

Ἀλφιτοσῑτέω *To eat barley bread*, only pres. -σιτεῖ Xen. Cyr. 6, 2, 28.

Ἀλωπεκίζω *To play the fox*, rarely and partially used, -ίζειν Ar. Vesp. 1241; Zenob. Cent. 1, 70; imper. ἀλωπέκιζε Aesop 243 (Halm.)

Ἀμαθαίνω *To be untaught, ignorant*, only pres. and almost peculiar to Pl. -αίνῃ Leg. 863; -αίνειν 698; -αίνων Rep. 535; and late Aristid. 50, 411 (Dind.)

Ἀμᾰθύνω *To lay in the dust, destroy*, only pres. Il. 9, 593; Aesch. Eum. 937 (chor.); Opp. Hal. 2, 611; -ύνοι Theocr. 2, 26: and imp. or aor. ἠμάθῡνε Lycophr. 79, ἀμάθ- H. H. Merc. 140; Anth. (Paul. Sil.) 5, 281; Q. Sm. 11, 250. Pass. -ύνεται Q. Sm. 2, 334: imp. ἀμαθύνετο Apollinar. Ps. 87, 20.

Ἀμαλάπτω *To crush, destroy*, Poet. only aor. ἠμάλαψα Soph. Fr. 413 (D.); and late Lycophr. 34.

Ἁμαρτάνω *To err*, Simon. Am. 7, 111; Hipponax 83; Pind. Ol. 1, 64; Soph. O. R. 1149; Ar. Vesp. 515; Her. 1, 43; Antip. 2, β, 1; Thuc. 4, 61: imp. ἡμάρτανον Il. 10, 372. 24, 68. Od. 11, 511; Soph. O. C. 968; Her. 4, 140; Thuc. 1, 38; Pl. Phaedr. 242: fut. m. ἁμαρτήσομαι Od. 9, 512; Soph. El. 1207; Eur. Alc. 1099; Thuc. 4, 55; Xen. Mem. 3, 9, 12: and rare ἁμαρτήσω perhaps Dor. in *simple*, Chilon, Stob. Fl. 3, 79 (Mein.); and late Dio Cass. 59, 20; Galen 7, 653. 13, 755; Apocr. Syr. 24, 22; N. T. Matth. 18, 21, but δι- Hippocr. 9, 264, ἐξ- 2, 420 (Lit. 1, 335 Erm.): 1 aor. ἡμάρτησα usu. late, but ἁμαρτήσας (if correct) Emped. 372 (Stein); late V. T. 1 Reg. 19, 4; Anth. (Incert.) 7, 339; D. Sic. 2, 14 (Bekk.); Aristid. 45, 56; Ps. Calisth. 1, 9, ἀφ- Orph. Arg. 646: p. ἡμάρτηκα Soph. Ant. 926; Eur. Alc. 616; Ar. Plut. 961; Her. 9, 79; Thuc. 1, 38; Lys. 7, 1; Isocr. 15, 34, ἐξ- Antiph. 5, 91: p. p. ἡμάρτημαι Antiph. 5, 77; Thuc. 3, 56; -ῆσθαι Antiph. 5, 5; -ημένος Soph. O. C. 439; Eur. Tr. 1028; Com. Fr. (Menand.) 4, 274; Lys. 3, 10; Isocr. 12, 54. 14, 4: plp. ἡμάρτητο Thuc. 7, 18; Lys. 31, 20: aor. ἡμαρτήθην Thuc. 2, 65; Xen. An. 5, 8, 20; Vect. 4, 37: 2 aor. act. ἥμαρτον Theogn. 407; Aesch. Ag. 1194; Soph. Tr. 1136; Eur. Or. 596; Ar. Pax 668; Her. 5, 91; Antiph. 3, β, 7; Thuc. 2, 87; Pl. Rep. 340, ἀμ- Hom. always Il. 4, 491. 11, 233 &c.; Pind. N. 7, 37; -άρτω Her. 1, 207. 3, 35; Pl. Theaet. 146, -τῃ Il. 9, 501; Pl. Gorg. 489; -άρτοιμι Soph. Aj. 155, rare -άρτοιν C. Fr. (Cratin.) 2, 47, -τοις Xen. Cyr. 8, 3, 27 &c.; -αρτεῖν Od.

21, 155; Soph. Ph. 231; Thuc. 5, 7; -αρτών Il. 23, 857; Aesch. Supp. 915; Antiph. 3, β, 3; Pl. Leg. 690, Epic ἤμβροτον only *indic.* Od. 21, 425. 22, 154; Ap. Rh. 2, 623, -βροτες Il. 5, 287. 22, 279, -τε Od. 7, 292. 21, 421, 3 pl. -τον Il. 16, 336. **Vb.** ἀν-αμάρτητος Antiph. 3, δ, 8; ἐπεξ-αμαρτητέον Dem. 22, 6. Epic ἤμβροτον for ἤμαρτον seems to be formed by transposition, ἤμρα-, by change of vowel, ἤμρο-, then by the generation of β in pronouncing μρ, ἤμβρο-τον. The inf. ἀμβροτεῖν, we have never been able to find *simple* or *compd.* except in Hesychius, Aeol. -ῆν Inscr. Mityl. (Newton.)

Ἁμαρτέω, see ὁμαρτ-.

Ἀμαρύσσω *To sparkle, dart,* Epic and only **pres.** and **imp.** -ύσσει Opp. C. 2, 596; -ύσσων H. H. Merc. 278. 415: **imp.** ἀμάρυσσε Hes. Th. 827; and late Nonn. 5, 485. 15, 165. **Pass.** ἀμαρύσσεται Anth. (Mar. Schol.) 9, 668; Nonn. 33, 31: **imp.** ἀμαρύσσετο Ap. Rh. 4, 178. 1146; Non. 38, 307. 47, 422.

Ἁματροχάω *To run along with,* Epic and only part. -όωντα Od. 15, 451 (Vulg. Wolf &c.), but ἅμα τροχόωντα (Dind. Ameis), τρωχῶντα (Schol. Bekk. 2 ed. La Roche).

Ἀμαυρόω *To deprive of light,* rare in **act.** and late except **pres.** and perhaps aor. Solon Fr. 4, 35; Pind. Fr. 103; Eur. Hipp. 816; Com. Fr. (Monost.) 545; Hippocr. 2, 84. 4, 482. 8, 428 (Lit.); Xen. Cyn. 5, 4; **inf.** -οῦν Eur. Fr. 420 (Dind.); Xen. Ages. 11, 12; part. -οῦσα Luc. Cal. 1: fut. -ώσω Simon. C. 4, 5; Plut. Alcib. 6: **aor.** ἀμαύρωσε Pind. P. 12, 13. Ist. 4, 48 (Bergk, Momms.), ἠμαύρωσα Anth. (Leon. Tar.) 9, 24; Polyb. 20, 4; -ῶσαι 6, 15; -ώσας Luc. D. Mer. 4, 5: **p.** -ωκα Strab. 8, 1; Plut. M. 866. **Pass.** ἀμαυροῦμαι Hippocr. 5, 644. 6, 154 (Lit.); Aesch. Pers. 223 (μαυρ- Blomf. Dind.); Aristot. Eth. N. 10, 4, 9, and often late: **p.** ἠμαύρωται Aristot. Probl. 4, 25; -ωμένος Plut. Pericl. 11. Mor. 362: **aor.** ἀμαυρώθη unaugm. in Her. 9, 10; -θείη Hes. Op. 693; -θείς Anth. (Antip. Sid.) 7, 241. **Mid.** late, **aor.** ἀμαυρώσαιτο Aristaen. 1, 16, missed by Lexicogr., but ἀμαύρωσε (Ms. V.), -ρώθη (Herch.) The **pres. act.** seems alone to have been used in classic Attic. For ἀμαύρωσε Pind. quoted, Boeckh and Herm. read μαύρωσε.

Ἀμάω *To mow, gather,* in *simple* mostly Epic, ἀμᾷ Soph. Ant. 602; opt. ἀμῴς Theogn. 107, -ῷεν Od. 9, 135; ἀμώων Anth. 9, 362; Ap. Rh. 3, 1382, -ώοντας Theocr. 10, 51, Dor. ἀμάντεσσι Theocr. 10, 16, ἀμώντ- (Vulg.); rare in prose, ἀμᾶν Luc. Diss. con. Hes. 7, ἀμάαν Hes. Op. 392 (Vulg. Goettl.), -άειν (Koechly, Flach): **imp.** ἤμων Il. 18, 551, -μα Soph. Fr. 479 (D.): **fut.** ἀμήσω Hes. Op. 480; Her. 6, 28, ἐξ- Ar. Lys. 367: **aor.** ἤμησα Hes. Th. 181; Aesch. Ag. 1044; Anth. 9, 198; Opp. Hal. 4, 485; δι-ήμ- Eur. Elec. 1023, δι-άμησε Il. 3, 359; Q. Sm. 1,

620; subj. Dor. ἀμάσῃ Callim. Cer. 137, -ήσωσι Her. 3, 98 (Gaisf. Stein), see mid.; ἄμησον, ἀπ- Soph. Ph. 749; ἀμήσας Il. 24, 451. Od. 21, 301; Anth. 7, 241, ἀμήσας, ἐφ- Heliod. 2, 20 (Bekk.), Dor. ἀμάσας Theocr. 11, 73; ἀμῆσαι Ap. Rh. 4, 374, ἐξ- Aesch. Ag. 1655: (p. ἤμηκα?): p. p. ἤμημαι, ἐξ- Soph. Aj. 1179: aor. ἠμήθην late, ἀμηθείς Nic. Alex. 216. **Mid.** ἀμάομαι Hes. Th. 599. Op. 778; Eur. Fr. 423 (D.); Opp. Cyn. 2, 56; Q. Sm. 14, 199; Plut. Mor. 210, δι- Thuc. 4, 26: fut. ἀμήσομαι Ap. Rh. 1, 688, ἐξ- Eur. Cycl. 236, Dor. ἀμάτ- Soph. Fr. 550 (D.): aor. ἀμήσατο Ap. Rh. 1, 1305. 3, 859, ἐπ- Od. 5, 482, κατ- Il. 24, 165, Dor. ἀμάσ- Anth. 7, 446; ἀμήσηται Q. Sm. 13, 242, -ήσωνται Her. 3, 98 (Bekk. Dind.); ἀμησάμενος Od. 9, 247; Callim. Dian. 164; Anth. (Meleag.) 4, 1, 26; late prose Jos. Ant. 8, 13, 4 (B.), but ἐπ- Her. 8, 24; Xen. Oec. 19, 11, ἀντιπροσ- 17, 13; ἀμήσασθαι Ap. Rh. 4, 989.

Hom. and Hes. have in the *act.* form of the *simple* verb the initial ᾱ, and in arsi (except Od. 9, 135): ἀμ- Il. 24, 451. Od. 21, 301; Hes. Cert. p. 321, 19 (Goettl.). Op. 480, once in thesi between two *longs* Od. 9, 135, and ᾰ in comp. δι-ᾰμ. Il. 3, 359, but ἀπ-ᾱμ- Il. 18, 34; in mid. ᾰ and in thesi, ἄμ- Od. 9, 247; Hes. Th. 599. Op. 775, κατ- Il. 24, 165, ἐπ- 5, 482. The later Epics make in act. and mid. ᾱ in arsi, ᾰ in thesi (except Ap. Rh. 3, 859, ἀμ- between two *longs*): ἀμ- Theocr. 10, 16. 50; Ap. Rh. 1, 1183. 3, 1187. 1382; Anth. 9, 362, ἄμ- Theocr. 11, 73; Ap. Rh. 4, 374; Callim. Cer. 137; Anth. 7, 241; Nic. Ther. 684. 843. **Mid.** ἀμ- in arsi Ap. Rh. 1, 688. 4, 989; Q. Sm. 13, 242; Opp. Hal. 4, 420. Cyn. 2, 56; Or. Sib. 12, 87 (in thesi, between two *longs*, Ap. Rh. 3, 859); ἄμ- in thesi Ap. Rh. 1, 1305; Callim. Dian. 164; Anth. 7, 446. 4, 1, 26; Q. Sm. 14, 199, συνᾰμ- Ap. Rh. 3, 154. ᾰ in Attic, Soph. Ant. 602. Ph. 749; Eur. Cycl. 236; Ar. Lys. 367.

In the *simple* form, the Epics augmented the act. ἤμων, ἤμησα, but δι-ἄμησα (ἄμησεν H. Merc. 3, 357 Vulg. is now disallowed), never, we think, the mid. but ἀμήσατο, συν-ᾰμ-, and ἀμησ- by ictus, not ἠμ-. It would thus appear that Buttm. and Passow's doctrine regarding the "Homeric quantity and regularity of augm." holds good only in the *simple* and *active* form.

"Αμβᾰσε, see βαίνω.

'Αμβλακίσκω, see ἀμπλακ-.

'Αμβλίσκω *To miscarry*, Pl. Theaet. 149, and in comp. ἀμβλόω, ἐξ- Eur. Andr. 356; late prose, Athen. 1, 57: fut. late ἀμβλώσω Geop. 14, 14, ἐξ- Ael. N. A. 13, 27: aor. ἤμβλωσα Hippocr. 8, 68 (Lit.); Ael. V. H. 13, 6; Geop. 14, 14, ἐξ- Pl. Theaet. 150: p. ἤμβλωκα, ἐξ- Ar. Nub. 137: p. p. ἤμβλωμαι, ἐξ- 139: aor.

ἠμβλώθην Aristot. Gen. An. 4, 4, 43 (Bekk.), ἐξ- Apollodor. 3, 3, 3: 2 aor. act. late, ἐξ-ήμβλω Ael. Fr. 52; -αμβλῶναι Themist. 2, 33. Pres. pass. ἀμβλοῦνται Theophr. H. Pl. 4, 14, 6; Longin. 14, 3.

The *simple* form seems to occur only in pres. act. and pres. and aor. pass. The form ἀμβλύσκω is in Soph. Fr. 134; and ἀμβλυόω late, aor. -υώσῃ Geop. 18, 18: with κατ- only in p. p. ἠμβλυωμένον, κατ- Com. Fr. (Diph.) 4, 383.

'Αμβλύνω *To blunt*, Emped. 3 (Stein); Pind. in tmesi P. 1, 82; Hippocr. 6, 4 (Lit.); Aristot. de Sensu 5, 11; Theophr. H. P. 5, 3, 3; Plut. M. 31; Strab. 4, 6, 5: imp. ἤμβλ- Plut. Caes. 19: fut. -ὑνῶ Polyb. 15, 25, 8 (Dind.); Plut. M. 235, ἀπ- Aesch. Sept. 715: aor. ἤμβλῡνα Anth. 6, 67. 7, 243; Plut. Cat. Min. 12: p. p. ἤμβλυμμαι Galen 4, 374, ἀπ- Hom. Epigr. 12; Herodas 1, 4 (Bergk), ἤμβλυται? Sext. Emp. 230, 24, ἀπ- Plut. M. 785: aor. ἠμβλύνθην Anth. 6, 65; Galen 5, 465; Joseph. J. B. 7, 9, 1, ἀπ- Plut. Timol. 37: fut. ἀμβλυνθήσομαι, ἀπ- Aesch. Pr. 866: and fut. m. ἀμβλυνεῖται pass. Hippocr. 4, 464 (Lit.): pres. p. -ύνεται Aesch. Sept. 844; -ύνεσθαι Thuc. 2, 87.

'Αμβλυωπέω *To be dim-sighted*, only pres. and rare in classic authors, Hippocr. 2, 128; Xen. Cyn. 5, 27; -ωπῶν Com Fr. (Menand.) 4, 329; Plut. M. 53; Luc. Peregr. 45: imp. ἠμβλυώπουν V. T. 3 Reg. 14, 4 (Alex.).—ἀμβλυώττω also is rare in classic authors, and only pres. Pl. Rep. 508; Luc. Tim. 2, Ion. -ώσσει Hippocr. 7, 28, -ώσσουσι 7, 8. 8, 270 (Lit.); -ώττῃ Luc. D. Mar. 5, 2; -ώττοι Pl. Rep. 516. Hip. Min. 374; -ώττων Rep. 517; Luc. Tim. 27; Plut. M. 974; -ώττειν 979; Luc. Char. 7, Ion. -ώσσειν Hippocr. 6, 294: aor. late, ἀμβλυώσῃ Geop. 18, 18, seems to belong to ἀμβλυόω.

'Αμείβω *To change*, Eur. Or. 1504; Hippocr. 6, 482; Arr. An. 3, 4; -βειν Hippocr. 3, 280 (Lit.); Arr. Ind. 12, 8; -βων Il. 11, 547; Pind. N. 11, 42; Aesch. Ag. 729; rare in Attic prose Pl. Parm. 138. Soph. 224: imp. ἄμειβον Il. 14, 381 (Bekk.), late prose ἤμει- Diog. L. 4, 53; fut. -είψω Aesch. Pr. 23, ἐπ- Il. 6, 230; late prose Plut. Marcel. 19: aor. ἄμειψα Hym. Cer. 275; Ap. Rh. 3, 280, Dor. ἄμ- Pind. P. 5, 38, πεδ- for μετ- Ol. 12, 12, later ἤμειψ- Opp. Ven. 3, 82; late prose Ael. V. H. 3, 42; subj. ἀμείψω Ibycus 24 (Bergk); ἀμείψας Aesch. Pers. 69; Soph. Tr. 659; Hippocr. 6, 482; late, Plut. Lysand. 11; (Luc.) Amor. 7, but ἐξ- Xen. Ages. 2, 2; inf. ἀμεῖψαι Her. 5, 72: (perf.?): p. p. late ἤμειπται Galen 1, 210; Argum. to Ar. Nub. 6: plp. ἄμειπτο Nonn. 44, 241, may be syncop. imp.: 1 aor. ἠμείφθην late as pass. Anth. 7, 589. 638. 9, 304; D. Sic. Fr. p. 142. 13 (Bekk.); Dionys. de Av. 1, 21, see below: fut.

ἀμειφθήσεται Hesych.; Ephr. Syr. vol. 3, p. 337. **Mid.** ἀμείβομαι, *to make a return, answer,* Batr. 274; Pind. P. 6, 54; Aesch. Supp. 195; Her. 1, 38. 40. 120; -βεσθαι Xen. Mem. 3, 11, 12; -όμενος Od. 3, 148. 11, 81; Xen. Cyn. 9, 14; late Dem. Phal. 216; Aristid. 45, 61: **imp.** ἠμειβόμην Il. 1, 121. 4, 50. Od. 10, 71 &c. ἀμείβ- Il. 3, 171. 24, 200; Pind. P. 9, 39; so Her. always 1, 9. 35. 2, 173. 3, 14 &c.: **fut.** ἀμείψομαι Aesch. Ch. 965; Eur. Supp. 517; Plut. Cat. Min. 16; App. Hisp. 34; Aristid. 49, 380: **aor.** ἠμειψάμην Il. 23, 542; Soph. Ph. 378; Aristot. Eth. Nic. 9, 2, 5; Alciphr. 1, 33; Plut. M. 29; Ael. V. H. 12, 1; Dio Cass. 63, 5, ἀμειψ- Il. 4, 403; Her. 1, 37. 43. 2, 173. 4, 97. 5, 93, and always (Bekk. Krüg. Bred. Abicht, Stein), but ἠμειψ- 4, 97 (Mss. Gaisf. Dind. &c.); (Epic subj. -είψεται may have left, Od. 10, 328. Il. 9, 409): in same sense, but poet. and less freq. **aor. pass.** ἠμείφθην Babr. 12, 19; Opp. Cyn. 1, 19, ἀμείφ- Pind. P. 4, 102, ἀμ- Theocr. 7, 27, but ἀπ-ημείφθη Xen. An. 2, 5, 15, perhaps the only instance. **Vb.** δι-άμειπτος Sapph. 14 (B.). ἀμειπτέος?—In comedy and *classic* Attic prose, the mid. is scarcely ever used, ἀμειβόμενος *changing, leaving,* Pl. Apol. 37, never in the sense *to reply, answer,* except λόγοις ἀμείβου Com. Fr. (Monost.) 311. Late prose auth. follow, as usual, the poetic and Ion. prose usage. ἀντ-αμείβομαι *exchange, requite, answer,* is Dep. **mid.** and very much confined to poetry, esp. Attic, Archil. 65 (Bergk); Soph. O. C. 814: **imp.** ἀντ-ημειβ- Aesch. Sept. 1049, Dor. ἀντ-ᾱμειβ- Theocr. 24, 72, Ion. unaugm. ἀντ-ἀμ- Her. 9, 79: **fut.** ἀντ-αμείψομαι Eur. Tr. 915; Ar. Thesm. 722: **aor.** ἀντ-ημειψάμην, subj. -αμείψωνται Archil. 74, 7 (B.); imper. -άμειψαι Soph. Ph. 230; Eur. Phoen. 286. ἀπ-αμείβομαι, again, is Dep. **mid.** and **pass.** and much confined to Epic, -ειβόμενος Il. 20, 86: **imp.** ἀπ-αμείβετο Il. 20, 199. Od. 8, 400; Theocr. 8, 8, syncop. -ειπτο Anth. (Incert.) 14, 3, 2. 4, 2: **aor.** ἀπ-αμείψατο Callim. Cer. 63: and once in Attic prose **aor. pass.** ἀπ-ημείφθη as **mid.** Xen. An. 2, 5, 15. We have not met the **aorists** except in the passages quoted. It is a mistake in our lexicons to confine this verb to the **pass. aorist.** ἀντ-απαμείβομαι, only part. -όμενος Tyrt. Fr. 1, 4, 6 (B). μετ-αμείβω very rare in prose, Hippocr. 5, 318: **imp.** -άμειβε Mosch. 2, 52: **aor.** Dor. πεδ-άμειψαν Pind. Ol. 12, 12: **aor. pass.** late -αμειφθείς Dionys. de Av. 2, 4. **Mid.** -όμενοι Pind. N. 10, 55: **aor.** -ειψάμενος P. 3, 96.

'Αμείρω, see ἀμέρδω.

'Αμέλγω *To milk* (Ar. Eq. 326 has been altered), Her. 4, 2; Plut. Mor. 98. 956; Theocr. 5, 84, Dor. 2 sing. -έλγες 5, 85 (-γεις Ahr. Fritz. Ziegl.). 4, 3 (-γεις Ziegl. Ahr.); Philostr. Apoll.

3, 9, 101; imper. ἄμελγε Anth. 5, 295; Theocr. 11, 75: imp. ἤμελγον Od. 9, 238. 244. 308, but ἄμελγον Mosch. 3, 83, ἐν- Od. 9, 223: fut. ἀμέλξω Anth. 7, 623: aor. ἄμελξα Anth. 9, 645, ἤμελξα, ἐξ- Aesch. Ch. 898; subj. ἀμέλξω Her. 4, 2; Theocr. 23, 25; Bion 1, 48; ἀμέλξας Eur. Cycl. 389; Anth. 6, 239; Theocr. 1, 143: p.p. ἤμελγμαι Hippocr. 7, 334, ἐξ- Eur. Cycl. 209: pres. ἀμέλγεται Athen. (Ion) 10, 68; Aristot. Hist. An. 3, 20, 9. 21, 6; -γόμεναι Il. 4, 434: imp. ἠμέλγετο Aristot. Hist. An. 3, 20, 10, ἀμέλγ- Nonn. 12, 320. Mid. ἀμέλγομαι *To let milk, suckle,* Opp. Cyn. 1, 437, *to milk for oneself* ἀμέλγει Ar. Eq. 326 (ἀμέργει Kock, Dind.): imp. ἀμέλγετο Nonn. 26, 103: fut. προσ-αμέλξεται, Dor. ποτ-αμ- Theocr. 1, 26 (Vulg. -έλγεται Ahr. Ziegl. Mein. Fritz.)

Ἀμενηνόω *To weaken,* Epic and only aor. ἀμενήνωσε Il. 13, 562.

Ἀμέρδω and **ἀμείρω** *To deprive,* both Poet., ἀμέρδει Od. 19, 18; ἀμείρειν Pind. P. 6, 27: imp. ἄμερδε Il. 13, 340; Hes. Th. 698: fut. ἀμέρσω Orph. L. 167; Nonn. Metaphr. Joan. 16, 22; inf. Ep. -ερσέμεναι Q. Sm. 6, 243: 1 aor. ἤμερσα H. Cer. 312, ἄμ- Od. 8, 64, ἄμ- Pind. Ol. 12, 16; ἀμέρσας Simon. C. 115; Eur. Hec. 1027 (chor.); -έρσαι Il. 16, 53: aor. m. late ἀμερσάμενος see below, Anth. 15, 32. Pass. ἀμέρδομαι, -εαι Od. 21, 290, ἀμείρομαι, ἀπ- Hes. Th. 801 (Mss. Koechly, ἀπο-μείρ- Goettl.); Ap. Rh. 3, 785: aor. (ἠμέρθην), subj. ἀμερθῇς Il. 22, 58; rare and late in prose, ἀμερθῶσι Theophr. H. P. 9, 8, 2 (Mss. U. M. Wimm.), where used to stand act. ἀμέρσωσι; ἀμερθείς Orph. L. 73, ἀμερθέν Aretae. p. 191 (Adams.) Mid. ἀπ-αμείρεται *deprives,* quoted by Pl. Leg. 777 (and from him by Athen. 6, 87) from Od. 17, 322, where stands ἀπο-αίνυται: aor. late ἀμερσάμενος Anth. 15, 32.

Ἀμεύομαι Dep. *To change, excel* (ἀμείβομαι), Poet. and only fut. ἀμεύσεσθαι Pind. Fr. 300 (Boeckh, 263 Bergk): and aor. -εύσασθαι Pind. P. 1, 45; -σάμενος Euphor. Fr. p. 140.

Ἁμιλλάομαι *To strive,* Pind. N. 10, 31; Eur. Hipp. 971; Andoc. 4, 27; Pl. Lys. 208: imp. ἡμιλλώμην Eur. H. F. 960; Xen. Hell. 7, 2, 14: fut. -ήσομαι Ar. Pax 950; Pl. Rep. 349: p. ἡμίλλημαι act. Eur. Hel. 546, παρ- Polyb. 12, 11, but δι- pass. Luc. Paras. 58: aor. p. act. ἡμιλλήθην, subj. ἁμιλληθῶ Eur. H. F. 1255, Dor. -āθῶ Hel. 165 (chor.); Pl. Leg. 968; ἁμιλληθείς Eur. Supp. 195; Thuc. 6, 31, ἐξ- Eur. Hel. 387, but pass. ἁμιλληθέντα Eur. Fr. 809 (Dind.) quoted Aeschin. 1, 152, ἐξ-αμιλληθῇ Eur. Cycl. 628: later in *simple,* aor. m. ἡμιλλησάμην Plut. Arat. 3; Luc. Paras. 51; Dio Cass. 43, 23; Aristid. 13, 149, but ἐξ- Eur. Hel. 1471. Fr. 764 (Dind.) Vb. ἁμιλλητέον Isocr. 7, 73. The act. form ἁμιλλᾶν is in Hesych.

Ἀμμίγνῡμι for ἀνα-μιγ- Bacchyl. 27, 4 (B.)

Ἀμνάσω, see ἀναμιμνήσκω.

Ἀμνημονέω *To be unmindful, pass over*, common to the best Attic poet. and prose (but only **pres. imp. fut.** and **aor.**) Aesch. Eum. 24; Eur. Heracl. 638; Com. Fr. (Men.) 4, 268; Thuc. 5, 18; Isocr. 4, 144; Isae. 3, 79; Lycurg. 20: **imp.** ἠμνημ- (Dem.) 60, 31: **fut.** -ήσω Isocr. 12, 253: **aor.** ἠμνημόνησα Dem. 18, 285; -ήσας Isocr. 5, 72; inf. -ῆσαι Xen. Conv. 8, 1; Dem. 7, 19. No **mid.** nor **pass.** The form **ἀμνημονεύω** seems rather doubtful: -μονεῖν has been substituted for -μονεύειν Plut. M. 612: -μονῆσαι for -μονεῦσαι Luc. Hist. 18, but still -εύοντες Diog. L. 5, 72.

Ἀμνηστέω *To forget*, very rare, and only **pres. act.** Arat. 847, Dor. -αστέω Soph. El. 482 (chor.): and **pass.** ἀμνηστούμενα Thuc. 1, 20.

Ἀμπάλλω, see πάλλω.

Ἀμπαύω, ἀνα-π-, see παύω.

Ἀμ-πέμπω, ἀνα-π.

Ἀμπελουργέω *To prune, plunder*, only **pres.** -οῦσι Aeschin. 3, 166; and late Theophr. C. P. 3, 7, 5; Plut. Philop. 4; -οῦντες Luc. Hist. 39. **Pass.** ἀμπελουργουμένη Theophr. C. P. 3, 14, 1.

Ἀμπέχω *To have about, put about, clothe*, Simon. Am. 12; Aesch. Pers. 848; Soph. O. C. 314, ξυν- Aesch. Pr. 521, late **ἀμφέχω** Anth. (Apoll.) 7, 693, rare **ἀμπίσχω** Eur. Hip. 193. Sup. 165; Aristot. Polit. 7, 17, 3; Aretae. 78 (ed. Oxon.), κατ- Eur. Hel. 853: **imp.** (ἀμπεῖχον), Epic ἄμπεχον Od. 6, 225; Ap. Rh. 2, 1104; Opp. H. 5, 512, later ἄμφεχον Q. Sm. 3, 6. 5, 106; Or. Sib. 1, 36, and perhaps ἤμπισχον Eur. Ion 1159: **fut.** ἀμφέξω Eur. Cycl. 344: **2 aor.** ἤμπισχον Eur. Ion 1159 (?); Ar. Lys. 1156; Pl. Prot. 320. **Mid.** ἀμπέχομαι *to have round oneself, wear* Ar. Eccl. 374; Ach. 1024; Xen. Ven. 6, 17, ἀμπίσχομαι Eur. Hel. 422; and *now* Ar. Av. 1090 (Dind. 5 ed.); Philostr. V. Apoll. 8, and ἀμπισχνέομαι Ar. Av. 1090 (Vulg. Bergk, Meineke), -ισχέομαι (Mss. Br. Bekk. Dind. 2 ed.): **imp.** ἠμπειχόμην Pl. Phaed. 87; Luc. Peregr. 15, Epic ἀμφεχ- Ap. Rh. 1, 324 (Well. Merk.), ἀμπεχ- (Höltzlin) perhaps rightly, see ἄμπεχεν 2, 1104 (all Mss.): **fut.** ἀμφέξομαι Com. Fr. (Philet.) 3, 300: **2 aor.** ἠμπισχόμην Ar. Eccl. 540 (late Epic ἀμπισχ- Orph. Arg. 202), and ἠμπεσχόμην Ar. quoted (Bekk. Anecd. Meineke, Dind. 5 ed.); Eur. Med. 1159 (Vulg. Pors. Kirchh. ἠμπισχ- Elms. Dind. Nauck); Philostr. Ap. 333; subj. ἀμπίσχῃ Eur. I. A. 1439, if sound. For ἀμπίσχονται, -χνοῦνται Ar. Av. 1090, Br. Bekk. read -σχοῦνται as best supported by Mss. ἀμπίσχν- however has analogy in ὑπισχνέομαι. Monk, Kirchhoff, Hartung, &c. reject ἀμπίσχῃ Eur. I. A. 1439 (1417) as spurious, Dind. and Nauck retain it.

Ἀμπίσχω, **mid.** ἀμπίσχομαι, see preceding.

Ἀμπλακίσκω *To miss, err*, Theag. Stob. Flor. 1, 68 (Gaisf.), Dor. ἀμβλ- 1, 67 (so 1, 68 Meineke): **imp.** Dor. ἀμβλάκισκον Phynt. Stob. 74, 61: (fut.?): p. (ἠμπλάκηκας is Hartung's emend. for ἠμπόληκας Soph. Aj. 922 (978 D.): p. p. ἠμπλάκηται Aesch. Supp. 916: **2 aor.** ἤμπλᾰκον Simon. C. 119; Aesch. Ag. 1212; Soph. Ant. 910; Eur. Alc. 824, rare ἤμβλακον Archil. Fr. 73 (B.); ἀμπλάκω Soph. Ant. 554; ἀμπλακών Pind. Ol. 8, 67; Eur. An. 948, ἀμβ- Ibyc. 24 (B.); ἀμπλακεῖν Trag. Fr. Incert. 247 (Wagn.), perhaps wrongly attributed to Eur. by Trinc. and to Soph. by Brunck. **Vb.** ἀν-αμπλάκητος Aesch. Ag. 344 (D.) This verb is entirely Poetic, mostly Trag. ἀμπλακών Pl. Phaedr. 242, is a quotation from Ibycus. The **pres.** is very rare, the form ἀμπ- (Stob. 1, 68) doubtful, see above. Some to shorten the initial vowel, write the part. **2 aor.** ἀπλακών Eur. I. A. 124. Alc. 241 (Burn. Pors. Monk, Dind. Nauck). Neither **pres.** ἀμπλακέω, nor **fut.** ἀμπλακήσω given in lexicons, ever occur; they seem to have been assumed on ἠμπλάκηται.

(**Ἀμπνύω**) *To recover breath*, only in **aor.** and Epic (for ἀναπνέω Pl. Phaed. 112): **2 aor.** imper. ἄμπνῠε Il. 22, 222; late indic. ἄμπνῠεν Q. Sm. 9, 470, and -ῡε in arsi 1, 599. 10, 62 (Vulg.), but -ειε (Lob. Koechly): **2 aor. m.** syncop. ἄμπνῡτο for -ύετο as act. Il. 22, 475. Od. 24, 349: **1 aor. pass.** ἀμπνύνθην as act. Il. 5, 697; Q. Sm. 9, 430 (Struve, Lehrs, Koechl. Lob.), -ύσθην (Vulg.); -υνθῆναι Theocr. 25, 263.

Ἀμύζω *To suck*, only **pres.** Xen. An. 4, 5, 27, where late editors have μύζω, which see.

Ἀμυνάθω *To defend* (only in Attic poetry), -άθετε Ar. N. 1323; -άθειν Soph. O. C. 1015 (Herm.); Eur. An. 1080 (Mss.). I. A. 910 (Herm.) **Mid.** ἀμυνάθου Aesch. Eum. 438 (Herm.); -άθοιτο Eur. An. 722. Others hold these as *aorist* forms, and write ἀμυναθεῖν, -αθοῦ (Elm. Dind. Kirchh.)

Ἀμύνω *To ward off*, Il. 11, 588; Aesch. Ag. 102; Soph. O. C. 1128; Pl. Phil. 38; -ειν Pind. N. 9, 37; Her. 8, 87; Antiph. 4, δ, 1; Thuc. 1, 40, Epic -νέμεναι Il. 13, 464, -νέμεν 17, 273; -ων Anacr. 114; Antiph. 4, α, 7; Thuc. 3, 13; Lycurg. 48: **imp.** ἤμῡνον Lycurg. 78; (Pl.) Epist. 329. Ax. 369, ἄμ- Il. 15, 731: **fut.** Ion. ἀμῠνέω Her. 7, 168. 9, 60, but 3 pl. -νεῦσι if correct, 9, 6, Attic -νῶ Ar. Vesp. 383; Thuc. 6, 13; Pl. Rep. 474; -νεῖν Lycurg. 76: **aor.** ἤμῡνα Il. 9, 599; Soph. O. C. 429; Eur. I. A. 907. Rh. 400; Thuc. 6, 80, Dor. ἅμ- Pind. N. 1, 50, ἄμ- Il. 17, 615; subj. ἀμύνομεν, ἐπ- for -ωμεν Il. 13, 465; opt. ἀμύναι Il. 12, 334; inf. ἀμῦναι Il. 18, 450; Eur. Or. 556; Thuc. 7, 34; Pl. Phaedr. 276; ἀμύνας?: **2 aor.** ἠμύνᾰθον, see ἀμυνάθω. **Mid.** ἀμύνομαι *to repel*, Il. 17, 510; Pind. I. 7, 27; Aesch. Ag.

1381; Soph. O. C. 873; Eur. Heracl. 302; Her. 5, 101; Antiph. 2, α, 6; Pl. Soph. 246: **imp.** ἠμυνόμην (Il. 12, 179) Her. 3, 158; Antiph. 4, δ, 6; Thuc. 1, 137; Xen. Ag. 11, 3, ἀμ- Il. 13, 514: **fut.** ἀμυνοῦμαι Ar. Eq. 222; Thuc. 1, 144; Dem. 15, 24, -εῦμαι Her. 8, 143, -έομαι (Abicht): **aor.** ἠμυνάμην Soph. Tr. 278; Antiph. 2, β, 10; Lys. 3, 8; Isocr. 15, 2; Dem. 21, 75; opt. ἀμυναίμην Od. 12, 114; Com. Fr. (Cratin.) 2, 112; inf. -νασθαι (not *now* in Hom.) Soph. Fr. 833 (D.); Her. 8, 74; Thuc. 4, 34; Andoc. 3, 25; Lys. 4, 8; Dem. 19, 82. 21, 76. 23, 122; ἀμυνάμενος rare Dem. 21, 71; **2 aor.** ἠμυναθόμην, see ἀμυνάθω. **Pass.** rare, ἀμύνονται Pind. P. 11, 54; -έσθω Pl. Leg. 845. **Vb.** ἀμυντέος Soph. Ant. 677. **Perf. act. pass.** and **aor. pass.** occur not. Her. usu. leaves *liquid* fut. forms in εο, εου, *open*, ἀγγελλέοντα 4, 14, ἀμυνέοντες 9, 60, ὑπομενέουσι 4, 3. 7, 101. 9, 90 &c., suggesting ἀμυνέουσι as preferable to -νεῦσι 9, 6, quoted.

'Αμύσσω *To scratch, tear*, Aesch. Pers. 161; Her. 3, 108; Hippocr. 8, 252 (Lit.); Luc. Luct. 16, -ύττω Aristot. H. A. 9, 32, 8; Plut. M. 982, περι- (Pl.) Ax. 365: **imp.** ἄμυσσον Il. 19, 284; Theocr. 13, 71, ἤμυττον D. Hal. 15, 1: **fut.** ἀμύξω Il. 1, 243; late Attic prose (Aeschin.) Epist. 12, 10: **aor.** ἄμυξα Matron, Athen. 4, 135; Anth. 7, 218, late ἤμυξα Nonn. 40, 161. 47, 188; Long. Past. 1, 14; ἀμύξῃ in tmesi Theocr. 6, 14; ἀμύξας Opp. Hal. 2, 192, κατ- Com. Fr. (Phryn.) 2, 580: **aor. pass.** late ἀμυχθέν Anth. 11, 382; Athen. 10, 42; Geop. 18, 17: **fut. p.** late, ἀμυχθήσεται Aquila, Zach. 12, 3. **Mid.** ἀμύσσομαι *to tear oneself*, Anth. 5, 262; -σσηται Hippocr. 8, 176: **aor.** ἠμυξάμην, -άμεναι Anth. 7, 491, κατ-αμύξατο Il. 5, 425. **Pres. pass.** ἀμύσσεται Aesch. Pers. 115; subj. -σσηται Plut. M. 522. In early Attic prose this verb seems not to occur either simple or compd.

'Αμυστίζω *To drink deep*, only **pres.** Plut. M. 650: and **aor.** ἠμύστισα Eur. Cycl. 566 (Vulg. Dind. 5 ed.), -ικα (Dind. *formerly*.)

'Αμφαγαπάζω *To embrace, greet warmly*, Epic and only **pres.** -άζει Opp. Cyn. 2, 306: and **imp.** ἀμφαγάπαζον Od. 14, 381; Ap. Rh. 3, 258. 1167. **Mid. pres.** part. -όμενος as act. Il. 16, 192, -όμεναι H. Cer. 290. 436, late -άζεται Plotin. vol. 1, 203. The collat. form ἀμφ-αγαπάω is also Epic, and used only in **pres.** ἀμφαγαπᾷ Orac. Diodor. Ex. Vat. p. 11; part. -ῶντες Hes. Op. 58; late Tryphiod. 138: and **aor.** ἀμφαγάπησε H. Cer. 439.

('Αμφαγείρω) *To gather about*, Epic and only **2 aor. m.** -αγέροντο intrans. Il. 18, 37; Ap. Rh. 4, 1527: and late a shortened **pres.** ἀμφαγέρονται Theocr. 17, 94; Opp. Hal. 3, 231. 4, 130.

'Αμφαίνω, ἀνα-φαι-, see φαίνω.

'Αμφαραβέω *To rattle about*, Epic and only **aor.** -αράβησε Il. 21, 408. The collat. form ἀμφαραβίζω is Epic also, and occurs only in **imp.** ἀμφαράβιζον Hes. Sc. 64.

'Αμφαφάω Epic, *To feel all round, handle* (in **act.** late and rare except part.), -αφάεις Orph. L. 522; late Ion. prose -όωσι Aretae. Morb. diut. 2, 4, p. 55 (L. B.); part. Epic -αφόων Od. 8, 196; Anth. 9, 365; Ap. Rh. 2, 199, -όωσα Od. 4, 277; Anth. 2, 109, -όωντας Od. 19, 586: **imp.** iter. ἀμφαφάασκε Mosch. 2, 96. **Mid.** as **act.** -φάασθαι Il. 22, 373. Od. 8, 215. 19, 475; Orph. L. 187: **imp.** ἀμφαφόωντο Od. 15, 462.

'Αμφελίσσω *To fold round* (Poet. and late Ion.), **pres.** late, Aretae. Morb. Ac. 2, 4, p. 105 (L. B.): but **aor.** -ελίξαντες Eur. Andr. 425: and **mid.** -ελίξασθαι Pind. N. 1, 43, *to fold, fasten, their jaws*, &c. ἀμφιελίσσω in **pres.** seems late, Aretae. 996: but **aor.** ἀμφιελίξας Hippocr. 8, 340 (Lit.); Orph. Fr. 44.

('Αμφέρχομαι) *To come round*, Epic and only **aor.** ἀμφήλυθε Od. 6, 122. 12, 369.

'Αμφιάζω *To clothe*, (Plut. C. Gracch. 2, Ms. C. Blass, -έζω Bekk. Sint.): **imp.** ἠμφίαζε, ἀπ- Plut. M. 406: **fut.** ἀμφιᾰσω Alciphr. 3, 42; Geop. 3, 13: **aor.** ἠμφίασα Anth. 7, 368; Themist. 4, 58; ἀμφιάσας Polyaen. 1, 27: **p.** ἠμφιακώς, συν- Clearch. Athen. 6, 70: **p. p.** ἠμφιάσθαι may be **mid.** Stob. (Perict.) 85, 19. **Mid.** *to clothe oneself*, **fut.** ἀμφιάσομαι, μετ- Luc. Herm. 86 (Jacobitz, -έσομαι Dind. Fritzsche): **aor.** ἠμφιασάμην V. T. Job 29, 14, -ιάσατο Apollod. 2, 1, 2. 4, 10 (Bekk.); Themist. 16, 204; Pseudo-Callisth. 1, 26; -σάμενος Joseph. Ant. 10, 1, 3. Jud. B. 7, 5, 4, μετ-ημφιάσω Luc. Gall. 19 (Dind. -έσω Fritzsche): and as **mid.** **p. p.** ἠμφιασμένος, μετ- D. Sic. 16, 11. This form and its compds. are late: classic ἀμφιέννυμι.

'Αμφιάχω (ἰάχω) *To scream about*, only **part. perf.** irreg. ἀμφιαχυῖα Il. 2, 316.

'Αμφιγνοέω *To doubt*, Isocr. 2, 28; Pl. Gorg. 466: **imp.** ἠμφιγνόεον Xen. An. 2, 5, 33 (Vulg. Krüg. Popp. Saupp.), and ἠμφεγν- Xen. quoted (Dind. Cobet, Rehd.); Pl. Soph. 236. (Riv.) 135: **fut.** late -ήσω Synes. 1, B.: **aor.** ἠμφεγνόησα Pl. Polit. 291. Soph. 228: **aor. p.** ἀμφιγνοηθείς Xen. Hell. 6, 5, 26. Augments before, usu. before and after, prep. and is confined to prose: Soph. has once the form ἀμφινοῶ Ant. 376.

'Αμφιδαίω *To blaze, rage around*, Epic and only **perf.** ἀμφιδέδηε Il. 6, 329; Ap. Rh. 4, 397: and **plp.** ἀμφιδεδήει Hes. Sc. 62; in tmesi Il. 12, 35.

'Αμφιδῑνέω *To roll round*, Epic and only **pres. pass.** -δινεόμενοι late Aretae. 54, 8: and **p. p.** ἀμφιδεδίνηται Il. 23, 562. Od. 8, 405.

Ἀμφιδοκεύω *To spy about, watch for*, Epic and only **pres.** Orph. Arg. 930: and **imp.** -εδόκευε Bion 2 (4), 6; said to be in late prose Heliod. vol. 2, p. 306, where we have not found it.

Ἀμφιδονέω *To whirl round*, Epic and only **pres.** Anth. 9, 668: and **aor.** -εδόνησε Theocr. 13, 48 (Meineke).

(**Ἀμφιδύω**) *To put about* another, Poet. and late in **act. 1 aor.** ἀμφ-έδυσεν Schol. Ar. Thesm. 1044: but **fut. mid.** -δύσομαι Soph. Tr. 605.

Ἀμφιέννῡμι *To put about, clothe*, Pl. Prot. 321; Polyaen. 8, 33, late -ννύω Plut. Per. 9, and -έζω Plut. C. Gracch. 2, μεταμφ- Mor. 340 (Vulg. Dübn. -άζω Fritzsche): **fut.** ἀμφιέσω Od. 5, 167, Attic -ιῶ, προς- Ar. Eq. 891, ἀπ- Com. Fr. (Men.) 4, 171: **aor.** ἠμφίεσα Xen. Cyr. 1, 3, 17; ἀμφιέσω Ar. Pl. 936; -έσαιμι Od. 18, 361; -έσας 15, 369; Plut. Lucull. 19; -έσαι Hippocr. 7, 194: **p. p.** ἠμφίεσμαι Hipponax 3; Ar. Eccl. 879; Hippocr. 7, 456 (Lit.); Lys. 13, 40; Pl. Rep. 372: **plp.** ἠμφίεστο D. Laert. 6, 5, 7; Philostr. 4, 147: **aor.** late ἀμφι-εσθείς Herodn. 1, 10, 5. **Mid.** ἀμφιέννῡμαι *to clothe oneself*, Xen. Cyr. 8, 2, 21: **imp.** ἠμφιέννυτο, μετ- Heliod. 7, 27: **fut.** ἀμφιέσομαι Xen. Cyr. 4, 3, 20; Pl. Rep. 457: **aor.** Poet. ἀμφιεσάμην Od. 23, 142; Aesch. Epigr. 3, 4 (Bergk); -έσηται Opp. Hal. 2, 298; late prose ἠμφ- App. Civ. 2, 122, μετ- Luc. Gall. 19 (Fritzsche, Dind.); Herodn. 5, 5, 5. The *simple* is never used in prose. The **p. p.** form ἀμφιεῖμαι seems not to occur: it has probably been assumed on εἷμαι, ἐπιεῖμαι, καταεῖμαι. This verb has some peculiarities: it augments the preposition only; it drops, in Attic writers, the sibilant of the **fut. act.** though others of seemingly the same *affection* retain it, κατασβέσεις Ar. Lys. 375, ἐξαναζέσει Aesch. Pr. 370: it retains σ in the **mid. fut.** while it drops it in the **act.** This is for the *Uniformists*.

Ἀμφιζάνω *To sit about, settle on*, Epic and only **imp.** ἀμφίζᾰνε Il. 18, 25.

Ἀμφιθέω *To run about*, Epic and only **pres.** Od. 10, 413; Mosch. 2, 107.

Ἀμφικαλύπτω, see καλύπτω.

(**Ἀμφικεάζω**) *To cleave asunder*, Epic and only **aor. part.** -κεάσσας Od. 14, 12.

Ἀμφίκειμαι *To lie round*, Poet. and only **pres.** Pind. Fr. 69 (Bergk); -εῖσθαι Soph. Ant. 1292; -είμενος O. C. 1620.

(**Ἀμφιμάομαι**) *To rub, wipe*, Epic and only **aor.** -εμάσαντο Q. Sm. 9, 428; imperat. -ιμάσασθε Od. 20, 152.

Ἀμφινοέω *To doubt*, only **pres.** Soph. Ant. 376.

Ἀμφισβητέω *To dispute*, Antiph. 3, δ, 3; Lys. 4, 10; Isocr. 4, 20; **opt.** -οίην Pl. Euthyd. 296, 3 pl. -οῖεν Menex. 242, rare

-οίησαν Aristot. Polit. 3, 13, 1 (Bekk.); Ion. -ατέω Her. 4, 14 (Bekk. Dind. Stein). 9, 74 (Bekk. Gaisf. Dind. Stein) augments on prep. or double: **imp.** ἠμφισβήτουν Andoc. 1, 27; Lys. 1, 29; Isae. 11, 5; Dem. 19, 19. 32, 14. 48, 22. 29 (Bekk. Dind.), and ἠμφεσβ- Pl. Menex. 242; Dem. 39, 19. 44, 27 (Bekk. B. Saupp.): **fut.** -ήσω Antiph. 3, 1; Pl. Politic. 281; Isae. 4, 24: **aor.** ἠμφισβήτησα Isae. 2, 31. 3, 43. 11, 9; Isocr. 12, 193. 18, 52; Dem. 43, 55 (Bekk. Dind.), and ἠμφεσβ- Isocr. 13, 4 (Bekk. B. Saupp.); Pl. Gorg. 479; Dem. 27, 15. 33, 21. 43, 20 (Bekk. B. Saupp.): **p.** ἠμφισβήτηκα Isae. 7, 21, ἠμφεσβήτηκα Dem. 27, 23 (Bekk. B. S. ἠμφισ- Dind.): **aor.** ἠμφισβητήθην Isae. 8, 20. 44; Pl. Polit. 276; Dem. 38, 8 (Vulg. Bekk. B. S. Dind. ἠμφεσβ- Ms. S. pr. m.): **fut. m.** ἀμφισβητήσεται as pass. Pl. Theaet. 171: **pres. pt.** ἀμφισβητούμενα Thuc. 7, 18. **Vb.** ἀμφισβητητέον Aristot. Eth. Nic. 3, 7, 5. The best Mss. and the best editors differ on the augment of this verb: in Isocr. Benseler augments always, we think, the prep. only: so Dind. in Demosthenes, Bekk. B. Saupp. &c. vary: in Lys. and Isae. Scheibe with the Mss. augments prep. only, ἠμφισβ-, but leans to double aug. ἠμφεσβ-.

Ἀναβιβάζω, see βιβάζω.

Ἀναβιώσκομαι, see βιώσκομαι.

Ἀναβρύχω, see βρόχω.

Ἀναγιγνώσκω, **-γινώσκω**, *To know, make known, read, recite,* &c. (*common* in this sense), Ar. Eq. 1065; Her. 7, 10; Andoc. 1, 47; Xen. An. 5, 8, 6: **imp.** ἀνεγίγν- Pl. Phaed. 98; Dem. 18, 259: with **fut. m.** ἀναγνώσομαι Ar. Eq. 1011; Andoc. 1, 47; Lys. 19, 57; Pl. Leg. 755; Dem. 20, 27: **fut. act.** late, ἀναγνώσεις Herm. Past. Visio 2, 4 (Dressel): **1 aor.** see below: **p.** -έγνωκα Thuc. 3, 49; Isocr. 11, 1; Isae. 11, 6: **p. p.** -έγνωσμαι Isocr. 15, 67; Dinarch. 1, 25; Dem. 23, 53. 86; Luc. Necy. 20: **plp.** -έγνωστο Isocr. 12, 233: **aor.** -εγνώσθην Eur. Hel. 290; Her. 7, 236; Antiph. 5, 56; Pl. Parm. 127; Dem. 23, 172: **fut.** -ωσθήσομαι Lys. 17, 9; Isocr. 15, 1; Isae. 6, 7: **2 aor. act.** -έγνων Il. 13, 734; Antiph. 6, 38; Thuc. 7, 10; Isocr. 15, 93, 3 pl. ἀνέγνον for -ωσαν, Pind. I. 2, 23 (Schn. Ahr. Christ), -ων (Vulg. Bergk), see Pyth. 4, 120 &c.; -αγνῶ Ar. Nub. 19. Eq. 118; Dem. 18, 267; -γνωθι Andoc. 1, 13; Isae. 2, 13. 10, 10; Pl. Phaedr. 262; -ῶναι Her. 2, 91; Isocr. 12, 136; Pl. Rep. 368; -γνούς Xen. An. 1, 6, 4; Isae. 8, 34: but in the sense *make to know and feel up* to a desired point, *persuade,* this verb is almost peculiar to Ion. prose: **pres.** ἀναγινώσκεις Her. 7, 10: **1 aor.** -έγνωσα 1, 68. 87. 7, 144 &c.; -ῶσαι 8, 57; Hippocr. 4, 80 (Lit.); -ώσας

Her. 3, 61. 5, 106: (but **2 aor.** ἀν-έγνων *acknowledged*, 2, 91): **plp.** ἀνεγνωσμένοι ἦσαν *had been persuaded*, 8, 110: **aor.** -ώσθην 7, 7. 236: in this sense, rare in Attic, **pres. pass.** ἀναγινωσκόμενος Antiph. 2, β, 7, see δ, 7, where in a similar *phrase* he uses πεισθείς. In Ion. and Dor. poetry, this verb occurs in **2 aor.** only, Il. 13, 734. Od. 4, 250 &c.; Pind. Ol. 11, 1 &c.; Theocr. 24, 23; in Trag. once, **aor. pass.** Eur. quoted; and uncertain **2 aor. act.** Soph. O. R. 1348; more freq. in Comedy, **pres. 2 aor.** and **fut. m.** Ar. Eq. 1065. Ran. 52; Com. Fr. (Antiph.) 3, 112; Ar. Nub. 19. Eq. 1011; Com. Fr. (Alex.) 3, 444. The **1 aor.** ἀν-έγνωσα occurs in Ion. prose only, and only in the sense *persuade*. It is a mistake to exclude the meaning *persuade* entirely from Attic, and also a mistake to refuse it to the **pres.** in Ionic.

'Ανάγομαι, see ἄγω.

'Αναγορεύω *To proclaim*, in classic auth. scarcely used beyond the **pres.** Aeschin. 3, 3: and **imp.** ἀν-ηγόρευον Aeschin. 3, 122; (Plut. Lycurg. 26. Timol. 23): **fut.** -εύσω (Dem.?) 18, 120; Plut. Galb. 21: **aor.** -ηγόρευσα Hippocr. Epist. 9, 402 (Lit.); (Dem.?) 18, 54; Polyb. 18, 29, 9; Plut. Mor. 240. Publ. 10 &c.; Paus. 6, 13, 1; Heliod. 4, 5: (**p.** -ηγόρευκα): **p. p.** -ηγόρευται Plut. Demetr. 38. Mar. 45: **aor.** -εύθην (Xen.) Cyn. 1, 14; Polyaen. 8, 14; Plut. Mor. 176. 202. C. Gracch. 3. C. Marc. 12; Paus. 6, 14, 2: **fut.** -ευθήσομαι Paus. 6, 4, 11: classic, **2 aor.** ἀνεῖπον Thuc. 2, 2; Aeschin. 3, 122; Dem. 18, 58, Poet. -έειπον Pind. P. 1, 32. 10, 9: **aor. pass.** -ερρήθην Aeschin. 3, 45. 46. 47; Dem. 18, 120; (Plut. Demetr. 9): **fut.** -ρηθήσεται Aeschin. 3, 147. See ἀγορεύω.

'Αναθόρνυμι, -θρώσκω, see θρώσκω.

'Αναίνομαι *To refuse*, Il. 9, 116; Aesch. Supp. 801; Hippocr. 8, 282; Isae. 2, 27; Xen. Cyr. 2, 1, 31; Dem. 36, 31: **imp.** ἠναινόμην Il. 18, 450; H. Hym. 5, 330; Aesch. Ag. 300, ἀναιν- Il. 18, 500, late prose ἀνην- Agath. 1, 13. 2, 7: (**fut.**?): **aor.** ἠνηνάμην Hermes. Col. 2, 97 (Schneidw.); Arat. 103; Q. Sm. 5, 176, ἀπ- Il. 7, 185, and ἀνηνάμ- Il. 23, 204; late prose Alciphr. 3, 37, but ἀπ-ην- Aristid. 1, 5 (Dind.), Dor. ἀπ-ᾱνᾱν- Pind. N. 5, 33; **subj.** ἀνήνηται Il. 9, 510; **inf.** ἀνήνασθαι 7, 93; Eur. Med. 237; Ael. Fr. 47; ἀνηναμένη Callim. Del. 46, -ένα Anth. (Arch.) 7, 191, ἀπ- Aesch. Eum. 972. In classic prose, the **pres.** only is used, and rarely, though not so rarely as some teach, ἀναίνει Dem. 36, 31, -εται Isae. 2, 27, -ονται Hippocr. 8, 282 (Lit.); **opt.** -οιντο Xen. Cyr. 2, 1, 31; Pl. Phil. 57; -όμενος (Dem.) 61, 48; Plut. Lysand. 22; -νεσθαι Mar. 38; very rare in Comed. Com. Fr. (Plat.) 2, 678. (Men.)

4, 201. The pass. we think does not now occur: ἀνήνηται Il. and Theocr. quoted, is aor. subj.: plp. ἀνήνηντο Agath. 1, 13 (Vulg.) is now ἀνήνοντο (Ms. R. Niebuhr): and ἀπ-ανηνάσθην dual aor. mid. Hom. Epigr. 4, 10, has by oversight been taken for aor. pass.

'Αναισιμόω *To expend*, in Ionic does not augment: imp. ἀν-αισίμου Her. 1, 185: but Att. p. ἀν-ησίμωκας rare, Xen. Cyr. 2, 2, 15 (Mss. Dind. Sauppe, Breitb.), κατ-ησ- C. Fr. (Epin.) 4, 505: p. p. ἀν-αισίμωνται Her. 2, 134, but κατ-ησ- C. Fr. (Eubul.) 3, 211; ἀν-αισιμωμένος, προ- Her. 2, 11: plp. ἀν-αισίμωτο, προσ- Her. 5, 34: aor. ἀν-αισιμώθη 1, 179. 2, 125: imp. ἀν-αισιμοῦτο, 3, 90.

'Ανακοινόω, see κοινόω.

'Ανακράζω, see κράζω.

'Ανακύπτω *To pop up, emerge*, Pl. Phaed. 109: fut. -κύψω Aristot. H. A. 9, 34, 6; Luc. D. Mar. 3, 1; Chrys. 13, 435; opt. -κύψαι Pl. Euthyd. 302 (Bekk. Stallb. B. O. W. Herm.): and as act. fut. m. -κύψομαι Ar. Av. 146; -κύψοιτο as v. r. Pl. Euthyd. quoted (Steph. Heindorf): aor. -έκυψα Ar. Ran. 1068; Her. 5, 91; Xen. Oec. 11, 5: p. -κέκῡφα Eur. Cycl. 212; Xen. Eq. 7, 10. In classic auth. the fut. is exceedingly rare. Indeed the only instance simple or compd. that we have met is Pl. quoted, and there Mss. and edit. differ, some offering act. ἀνακύψαι τό, others mid. ἀνακύψοιτο. And though the weight of authority seems to favour the former, yet the fact of the only other classic instance of fut. being indisputably the mid. form, seems rather to countenance the latter—we are surprised that this has not been urged.

'Αναλέγω *To pick up*, Il. 11, 755, in tmesi; Aen. Tact. 38; Dio Cass. 53, 11: imp. ἀνέλεγον, Epic ἄλλεγον Il. 23, 253: fut. -έξω Ar. Av. 591; Aen. Tact. 38: aor. rare ἀν-έλεξα Luc. Gall. 4; Dio Cass. 37, 43, Epic ἄλλεξα Il. 21, 321. Pass. rare and doubtful -λεγόμενον Xen. An. 2, 1, 17. Mid. -λέγομαι *gather up for oneself, read*, Plut. Mor. 582; Aen. Tact. 38: imp. ἀν-ελέγετο Her. 3, 130: fut. -λέξομαι Luc. Dem. enc. 27; Galen 2, 880: aor. -ελεξάμην Callim. Epigr. 23; Anth. 9, 428. 12, 132; D. Hal. 1, 89; Luc. Pisc. 6; Galen 3, 601. The act. is rare, never in Trag. nor classic prose: the mid. again is frequent in late Attic, rare in Ionic prose, never in classic poetry.

'Αναλίσκω *To expend*, Eur. I. T. 337; Ar. Thesm. 1131. Fr. (Dait.) 15; Antiph. 6, 13; Thuc. 7, 48; Pl. Rep. 420; Dor. pt. -λίσκοισα Pind. P. 9, 25, and ἀνᾱλόω Aesch. Sept. 813; Eur. Med. 325; Ar. Pl. 248; Thuc. 2, 24; Dem. 50, 8: imp. ἀνήλισκον Xen. Cyr. 1, 2, 16; Isocr. 5, 96; Pl. Rep. 552, and ἀνάλουν Thuc. 8, 45, (but ἀνηλοῦντο 3, 81): **fut.** ἀνᾱλώσω Eur. Cycl. 308; Thuc. 6, 31; Pl. Rep. 568: aor. ἀνᾱλωσα Soph. Aj. 1049 (Dind. Nauck); Eur. Elec. 681; Thuc. 7, 83; Lycurg. 46 (Bekk. Scheibe), συν- Dem. 1, 11 (Bekk. συν- ανηλ- Dind.), and ἀνήλωσα Soph. Aj. quoted (Mss. Herm. Ellendt); Lys. 19, 18; Isae. 5, 35; Dem. 20, 10. 36, 39. 40, 36, rare and in comp. ἠνάλωσα, κατ- Isocr. 9, 60: p. ἀνάλωκα Thuc. 2, 64; Dem. 27, 38. 38, 25 (Bekk.), and ἀνήλωκα Xen. Cyr. 2, 4, 9; Lys. 26, 3; Isocr. 15, 158. 165; Isae. 8, 39; Dem. 3, 28. 27, 56. 40, 51 (Bekk. Dind.), 27, 38. 38, 25 quoted (Dind).: plp. ἀνηλώκει Xen. Cyr. 1, 4, 5; (Dem.) 7, 23, ἀναλ- Thuc. 6, 31: p. p. ἀνᾱλωμαι Eur. An. 1154; Hippocr. 2, 360 (K.), ἐξ- 7, 574 (Lit. 2, 455 Erm.); Isae. 5, 28. 29; D. Hal. 7, 49 (ἀνηλ- Kiessl.), and ἀνήλωμαι Hippocr. 7, 514. 588 (Lit.); Xen. Cyr. 6, 1, 14; Pl. Polit. 289; Dem. 27, 63. 50, 30, rare and in comp. ἠνάλωμαι, κατ- Isocr. 3, 31: plp. ἀνήλωτο Pl. Polit. 272, ἀνάλωτο, κατ- Hippocr. 1, 594 (Lit. 2, 30 Erm.): **aor.** ἀνᾱλώθην Eur. An. 455, ἀπ- Thuc. 7, 30, ὑπ- 3, 17, and ἀνηλώθην Lys. 26, 22; Dem. 48, 12. 50, 30, ἀπ-ανηλ- Thuc. 2, 13, rare ἠναλώθην, κατ- Hippocr. 5, 122. 126 (Lit. κατ-αναλ- Ald.); ἀναλωθείς Aesch. Ag. 570: fut. ἀναλωθήσομαι Eur. Hipp. 506; Dem. 22, 19; Dio Cass. 52, 28; Arr. An. 7, 17: and late **fut. m.** ἀναλώσεται as **pass.** Galen 15, 129: **pres.** ἀναλίσκεται Thuc. 8, 4; Pl. Rep. 573: **imp.** ἀνηλίσκετο Pl. Conv. 181; Dem. 50, 24. 25. **Mid.** *to expend, waste on oneself,* ἀναλίσκηται Pl. Gorg. 481: imp. ἀνηλοῦντο seems mid. *destroyed themselves,* Thuc. 3, 81: but **fut.** -ώσεται is **pass.** and late, Galen 15, 129. **Vb.** ἀνάλωτος Pl. Theaet. 179, -ωτέος Leg. 847. The tragedians and Thuc. seem to have preferred the unaugmented forms, yet ἀνήλωσε seems to be in all the Mss. Soph. Aj. 1049, and ἀνηλοῦντο Thuc. 3, 81, ἀπανηλώθη 2, 13; Xen. Plato and the orators the augmented; and late writers, though they prefer the latter, are far from consistent. Plutarch and Lucian have both forms, and Appian has even **imp.** ἀνάλισκον Civ. B. 3, 58. Hisp. 5, κατ-ανάλισκεν Plut. Philop. 4 (Ms. R. Sint. -ανήλ- Ms. U. Bekk.)

The form ἀναλόω occurs mostly in the older Attic: twice in Trag. ἀναλοῖ Aesch. Sept. 813, -οῖς Eur. Med. 325; three or four times in Comed. -αλῶν Ar. Eq. 915. Plut. 248, -αλοῦν Fr. 15, -άλουν ibid.; five or six times in Thuc. 2, 24. 6, 12, twice, 4, 48: **imp.** ἀνάλουν 8, 45, -αλοῦτο 1, 109, but -ηλοῦντο 3, 81 (Bekk. Krüg. Poppo, -ην always Stahl.); twice in Xen. ἀναλοῦν Hell. 6, 2, 13, -ούμενα Hier. 11, 1. But though most freq. in old Attic, it is not confined to it, ἀναλοῦν Com. Fr. (Arar.) 3, 275, ἀναλοῦται (Philem.) 4, 22; Hippocr. 2, 50. 7, 588 (Lit.)

παραναλούμενα Com. Fr. (Antiph.) 3, 90; and late Attic prose -οῦται Plut. M. 696, -οῦσθαι 877 &c.

Ἀναλύω, see λύω.

Ἀνα-μορμύρω *To seethe up*, only iter. imp. -ύρεσκε Od. 12, 238.

Ἀνανεόω *To renew*, act. late and rare, aor. ἀν-ενέωσα Malal. p. 141, 217, 225, 245, 267, &c. **Mid.** classic -εοῦμαι (Dem.) 18, 167; -οῦσθαι Thuc. 5, 23; Dem. 23, 121; -ούμενος Isocr. Epist. 7, 13: fut. -εώσομαι Polyb. 23, 7: aor. ἀν-ενεωσάμην Thuc. 5, 46; inf. ἀνανεώσασθαι Thuc. 5, 43; Isocr. 4, 43; Dem. 57, 32, poet. ἀννεώσασθαι Soph. Tr. 396.

Ἀναπίμπλημι, see πίμπλημι.

Ἀναπνέω, see ἀμπνύω.

Ἀνασκολοπίζω *To impale*, Luc. Jud. Vox. 12. Char. 14: fut. (-ίσω, -ιῶ): aor. -εσκολόπισα Her. 1, 128. 3, 159. 4, 43: p. p. -εσκολόπισμαι Luc. Catapl. 6. Peregr. 13: aor. -εσκολοπίσθην Luc. Pr. 10. Jup. Conf. 8; Herodn. 5, 2: fut. p. -ισθήσεται Luc. Char. 14. Prom. 7: and fut. m. -ιοῦμαι as pass. Her. 3, 132. 4, 43. This verb occurs only in Ionic and late Attic prose.

Ἀνάσσω *To rule* (ἄναξ), Epic and Trag. Il. 21, 86. Od. 4, 93; Soph. El. 841; ἀνάσσειν Il. 2, 108; Aesch. Ag. 415, Epic -ασσέμεν Il. 14, 85; Ap. Rh. 1, 719: imp. ἤνασσον Il. 10, 33. Od. 11, 276; Hes. Fr. 112; Eur. Andr. 940, ἄνασσ- Il. 1, 252. Od. 24, 30; Hes. Th. 1016; Eur. I. A. 282. 285 (chor.), Dor. ἄν- Pind. Ol. 6, 34, ἐάνασσ- Alcae. 64 (Bergk): fut. ἀνάξω Il. 19, 122. Od. 18, 115; Hes. Th. 491: rare aor. ἄναξεν Hes. Th. 837: mid. ἀνάσσομαι, -σσεσθαι Callim. Fr. 198?: aor. ἀνάξασθαι Od. 3, 245: pass. ἀνάσσονται Od. 4, 177; Soph. Phil. 140; Theocr. 17, 92; -σσόμενος Manetho 4, 607: imp. ἀνάσσετο Ap. Rh. 4, 266. The only comp. we have seen is συν-ανάσσειν Anth. App. Epigr. 336, 20.

Ἀναστρέφω *To turn up*, Soph. Ph. 449; Dem. 54, 8: fut. -ψω Eur. Bacc. 793: aor. -έστρεψα Thuc. 4, 43; -στρέψας Aesch. Pers. 333: perf. -έστροφα Com. Fr. 4, 549, &c. We notice this verb merely to draw attention to what we think a mistake in our best lexicons, "pass. with *fut. mid.*" The fut. is of the pass. form, ἀναστραφήσεσθαι Isocr. 5, 64; mid. -έψεσθαι we have not seen.

Ἀνατείνω *To stretch up*, Xen. Eq. 10, 4: fut. -τενῶ Ar. Lys. 129: aor. ἀν-έτεινα Xen. An. 3, 2, 33; -τείνας Cyr. 6, 1, 3, Dor. -τείναις Pind. I. 5 (6), 41, reg. in act.: p. p. ἀνατέταμαι Xen. Cyr. 7, 1, 4, as mid. see below. **Mid.** ἀνατείνομαι *stretch oneself, one's own, threaten*, Polyb. 2, 52. 5, 58: aor. -ετεινάμην Dem. 19, 153; Diod. Sic. 14, 3; Plut. Cleom. 10, Poet. ἀντειν- Simon. C. 8

(Bergk): with p. ἀνατεταμένος as mid. Xen. Cyr. 4, 1, 3: and aor. ἀν-ετάθην Polyb. 2, 52. 5, 55.

'Ανατέλλω, see τέλλω.

'Ανδάνω *To please*, Ion. and Poet. Od. 2, 114; Pind. P. 1, 29; Soph. Ant. 504; Eur. Rhes. 137. Or. 1607; Ar. Eq. 553; Hippocr. 2, 230 (Lit.); Plut. Mor. (Democr.) 82, 1; rare and late if correct, ἅδω Plut. Cim. et Lucull. 2 (Steph. Sint. ἀνδ- Reisk. συνᾳδ- Cor. Bekk.), ἀδῶ (Hesych.): imp. ἥνδᾰνον Il. 1, 24. 15, 674. Od. 10, 373; Solon 37; Her. 7, 172. 8, 29, ἑήνδ- Il. 24, 25. Od. 3, 143, and ἑάνδ- Her. 9, 5. 19 (Bekk. Dind. Stein, ἥνδ- Dietsch, Abicht): fut. ἁδήσω Her. 5, 39: p. rare, ἅδηκα Hippon. Fr. 100 (Bergk, ἅδ- Eustath.): 2 p. Epic ἕᾱδα Ap. Rh. 1, 867; (ἕᾱδε Theocr. 27, 22, Paley, Fritzs. 2 ed. ἀείδει Ziegl. 2 ed.); ἑᾱδότα Il. 9, 173. Od. 18, 422 (ἑαδ- Dind.); Ap. Rh. 2, 35. 4, 1127; Callim. Cer. 19: 2 aor. ἕᾰδον Her. 1, 151. 4, 201. 6, 106; Luc. Calumn. 3 (Vulg. Jacobitz, ἠδημόνει Cobet, Dind.), and ἅδον (ᾰ) Il. 13, 748; Hes. Th. 917; Theogn. 226, Epic εὔᾰδον Il. 14, 340. Od. 16, 28; Ap. Rh. 2, 501; Bion 3, 7; subj. ἅδῃ H. Hym. 1, 75; Her. 1, 133; ἅδοιμι Her. 9, 79, ἅδοι Od. 20, 327; Ap. Rh. 1, 828; ἁδεῖν Il. 3, 173; Solon 7; Soph. Ant. 89; Her. 3, 45, ἀδεῖν Pind. Ol. 3, 1 (Boeckh, Bergk); ἁδών Nem. 8, 38. Mid. ἀνδάνομαι as act. Anth. 10, 7: 2 aor. late ἁδέσθαι Pythag. Epist. 12 (Orell.); hither some have referred ἅσμενος as a syncopated and softened part. for ἁδόμενος, ἅδμενος, ἅσμ-, which it is perhaps better to assign to ἥδω. εὔαδον is softened from ἔϜαδον now edited by Bekker (2 ed.) Buttmann says that after the digamma disappeared the genuine Homeric forms were, without doubt, only ἑάνδανε, ἅνδανε, not ἑήνδανε, ἥνδανε, and the Herodotean ἥνδανον, not ἑάνδ-, after the analogy of ὥρων. We are not sure that it is quite fair to infer with Buttm. that because the aor. was ἔϜαδε, ἕαδε, ἅδε, the imp. must have been ἑάνδανε, ἅνδανε. Besides, we think both forms may be correct, and may have coexisted—the former the older representing its appearance at an earlier stage when the digamma was *agoing*, the latter when it had gone. Thus: old form Ϝανδάνω, imp. with digamma softened to ε, ἑάνδανον, contr. ἥνδανον, with syllabic augm. ἑήνδανον. Compare Ϝέλπομαι, ἐέλπετο, ἤλπετο Il. 25, 539. 17, 395 &c. (old reading.) Ϝέργω, ἐέργω, εἵργω, &c. In this way without, as we think, violating analogy, may be defended ἑήνδανε, ἥνδανε, as equally genuine and older than ἑάνδ-, ἅνδ-. In Her. ἥνδανε, ἑάνδ- have equal support, ἥνδ- 7, 172. 8, 29, ἑάνδ- 9, 5. 19, of which Buttm. and Bredow (Dial. Her. 314) maintain the former to be the true Ionic form, Dind. inclines to the latter—(Pref. to Her.)

Ἀνδραγαθίζομαι Dep. *To act the brave, good, man*, only pres. classic -ίζεται Thuc. 2, 63; -ίζεσθαι 3, 40: aor. ἀνδραγαθίσασθαι late, App. Civ. 5, 101. ἀνδραγαθέω Polyb. 14, 5, 8: imp. ἠνδραγάθουν Pseud. Callisth. 2, 16: has fut. -θήσω D. Sic. 23, 21 (Bekk.), not -θήσομαι given in lexicons: aor. -ήσωσι Polyb. 6, 39, 2; -ήσας Plut. Demosth. 22. Mor. 242; Polyb. 3, 71, 10: perf. ἠνδραγαθηκώς D. Sic. 14, 53: p. p. -γαθημένος Plut. Fab. 20. Mor. 195; -θῆσθαι Dio Cass. 49, 21.

Ἀνδραποδίζω *To enslave*, pres. rare and late, Alciphr. 3, 40: fut. -ιῶ Xen. Hell. 2, 2, 20: aor. ἠνδραπόδισα Her. 1, 151; Thuc. 1, 98: p. p. ἠνδραπόδισμαι Her. 6, 106. 8, 29; Isocr. 17, 14; Arr. An. 2, 15; but part. ἀνδραποδισμένος Her. 6, 119 (Mss. Schweigh. Gaisf. Stein, &c.), ἠνδραπ- (Bekk. Lhardy, Bred. Dind.), as mid. see below: aor. ἠνδραποδίσθην Lys. 2, 57; Isocr. 17, 49; Xen. Hell. 1, 6, 14; -θείς Her. 1, 156; fut. ἀνδραποδισθήσομαι Xen. Hell. 2, 2, 14; Ar. Ind. 28, ἐξ- D. Sic. 15, 51: and in Ion. fut. m. as pass. ἀνδραποδιεῦμαι Her. 6, 17, ἐξ- 6, 9, see mid. Mid. ἀνδραποδίζομαι Her. 3, 147; Andoc. 3, 21: imp. ἠνδρ- Her. 5, 27: fut. -ποδιεῦμαι, ἐξ- Her. 1, 66 (also pass. in simple and comp., see above): aor. ἠνδραποδίσαντο Her. 3, 59. 6, 18; Thuc. 4, 48; -ισάμενος Her. 4, 203, Dor. -ιξάμενος Epimen. in D. Laert. 1, 113; -ίξασθαι Disput. Mor. p. 548 (Mullach.): with p. p. in comp. προσ- εξ- ηνδραπόδισται Dem. 19, 112.

This verb seems entirely prosaic. Bekk. Lhardy, Bred. Dind. Krüg. augment p. part. ἠνδραποδισμένος Her. 6, 119, even against the Mss. on the ground that he uniformly augments the verb in every other place, see 1, 76. 151. 3, 59. 4, 204. 5, 27. 6, 18. 101. 106. 8, 29, ἐξ- 1, 161.

Ἀνδρόω *To change to a man*, late in act. ἤνδρωσαν Lycophr. 943; Anth. 7, 419; Plut. Mor. 490, is reg. in Attic; in Her. the pass. aor. is, in Mss. and nearly all editions, with and without augm. ἠνδρώθην 4, 155, but ἀνδρώθ- 3, 3; in Hippocr. ἠνδρ- 1, 614 (Erm.). 5, 356 (Lit.): and p. ἠνδρωμένος 4, 256, but ἐξ- ανδρ- Her. 2, 63 without *v. r.* Mid. aor. ἀνδρώσασθαι (Hesych.)

Ἀνέχω *To hold up*, Il. 23, 426; Soph. O. R. 174; Eur. Hip. 1293 (Mss. Monk, Kirchh. ἀπ- Mss. Nauck, Dind. 5 ed.); Her. 2, 29; Thuc. 1, 141; Epic subj. -έχῃσι Od. 19, 111 (Bekk.): imp. ἀν-εῖχον Thuc. 7, 48: fut. ἀνέξω rare, perhaps only Archil. Fr. 82 (Bergk); and late Luc. Hist. Con. 4; Orac. Sib. 5, 312; V. T. Haggai 1, 10; ἀνασχήσω also rare, Eur. I. A. 732; Her. 5, 106. 7, 14; late Att. prose Plut. Alcib. 30; Parthen. 9, 4: 2 aor. ἀνέσχον Il. 17, 310; Eur. Med. 482; Her. 8, 8; Xen. Hell. 1, 6, 28; Pl. Conv. 220, and Epic ἀνέσχεθον Il. 7, 412. Od. 9, 294; ἀνάσχω Soph. El. 636; -σχεῖν Il. 6, 257, -σχέμεν 24,

301; -σχών 18, 75; Soph. Tr. 204; Eur. Fr. 475 a; Theocr. 18, 57: **p.** ἀνέσχηκα late, Epist. Phal. 105, 2 (Herch.); Sext. Emp. 741: **p. p.** ἀνέσχημαι (?): **aor.** ἀνεσχέθην (?). **Mid.** ἀνέχομαι *to endure*, Od. 7, 32; Eur. Tr. 102; Ar. Vesp. 1337; Her. 1, 80; Antiph. 4, γ, 1; Pl. Leg. 708: **imp.** with double augm. ἠνειχόμην Aesch. Ag. 905; Soph. Ph. 411; Thuc. 5, 45; Lys. 3, 9; Dem. 30, 33. 50, 45: **fut.** ἀνέξομαι Il. 5, 895. Od. 19, 27; Aesch. Pers. 838; Soph. El. 1028; Eur. Hipp. 354; Com. Fr. (Men.) 4, 77; Isocr. 12, 140; Pl. Rep. 613; Dem. 18, 160; Poet. and less freq. ἀνασχήσομαι Aesch. Sept. 252; Ar. Ach. 299, syncop. ἀνσχήσ- Il. 5, 104: **2 aor.** with double augm. ἠνεσχόμην Aesch. Ag. 1274; Soph. Tr. 276; Eur. H. F. 1319; Ar. Nub. 1363; Her. 5, 48. 7, 159. 8, 26; Thuc. 3, 28; Andoc. 2, 15; Lys. 3, 3; Pl. Charm. 162; Dem. 19, 24. 96, syncop. ἠνσχ- Soph. Ant. 467 (Dind. 5 ed. ἂν ἐσχ- Erf. Herm.), rarer ἀνεσχ- Il. 18, 430; Aesch. Ch. 747; Eur. Hipp. 687 (both trimeters); Soph. Ant. 467 quoted (Wolf, Dind. in note, 5 ed.); Ar. Pax 347 (chor.); Her. 5, 89. 6, 112. 7, 139; Dem. 22, 68 (S. Bekk. Dind. ἠνεσχ- B. Saupp.); Luc. Astrol. 24, 2 sing. syncop. ἄνσχεο Il. 24, 518; imper. ἀνά- σχεο Il. 10, 321, ἄνσχεο 23, 587. **Vb.** ἀνασχετός Com. Fr. 2, 577, ἀνεκτός Il. 10, 118; Soph. Ant. 282, -έος O. C. 883. Her. presents three instances of double augm. ἠνέσχ-, and three of single, ἀνεσχ-, each without v. r., and what is rather curious, the instances of the former are all in sing. ἠνέσχετο, of the latter, all in pl. ἀνέσχοντο. That the Attic poets do not confine ἀνεσχόμην "to the chorus," but use it as well as ἠνεσχ- in trimeters, appears from Aesch. Ch. 747, more especially Eur. Hipp. 687, where ἠνεσχ- could not stand. Hom. Od. 19, 111, has 3 sing. **pres.** ἀνέχησί for -έχει, as if from ἀνέχημι, unless it be subj. for -ῃσι, which Bekker, Ameis and La Roche edit. The only instance we have met of the **pass.** v. is ἀνέχεται 4 Maccab. 1, 35 (Apel, Bekk. ἀντέχ- Gaisf.)

'Ανέωνται, see ἵημι, ἀφίημι.

'Ανήνοθε *sprung*, Epic **2 perf.** as **pres.** Od. 17, 270: as **aor.** Il. 11, 266. Formed by redupl. probably from root ἀνέθω.

'Ανθέω *To flourish* (ἄνθος) Hes. Op. 582; Pind. Ol. 13, 23; Aesch. Ch. 1009; Soph. Fr. 705; Hippocr. 2, 676 (Lit.), Ion. and Dor. 3 pl. ἀνθεῦσι Hes. Op. 227; Theocr. 27, 46; pt. ἄνθων Pl. Rep. 475, ἀνθοῦσα Isocr. 5, 10, Ion. and Dor. -εῦσα Her. 4, 1; Theocr. 5, 56: **imp.** ἤνθει Eur. Hec. 1210; Xen. Cyr. 6, 4, 1, Lacon. ἤνσει Ar. Lys. 1257: **fut.** ἀνθήσει Alcae. 83: **aor.** ἤνθησα H. Hym. 1, 139; Thuc. 1, 19; Dem. 2, 10, Dor. ἄνθ- Pind. P. 1, 66. I. 4 (3), 18 (Bergk); ἀνθῆσαι Od. 11, 320: **p.** ἤνθηκα Soph. Tr. 1089 &c.

(Ἀνθρακόω) *To burn to a cinder, blast,* Trag. and confined to **p. p.** ἠνθρακωμένος Aesch. Pr. 372; Eur. Cycl. 612. The comp. κατ-ανθρ- also has no **act.** but besides **p. p.** -ηνθρακώμεθα Eur. Cycl. 663; -ωμένος Soph. El. 58: and **aor.** -ηνθρακώθη Eur. I. A. 1602: it has **fut. m.** κατ-ανθρακώσομαι as act. Aesch. Fr. 280 (D.) ἀπ-ανθρακόω has **aor. act.** -ηνθράκωσεν Luc. D. Mort. 20, 4.

Ἀνῑάζω *To sorrow,* Poet. Il. 18, 300, ἀνῑ- Od. 22, 87, also *vex,* Od. 19, 323, -ῑάζουσι 4, 598; Opp. Hal. 2, 450; C. 3, 362: **imp.** ἀνίαζον Il. 23, 721, iter. ἀνῑάζεσκον Ap. Rh. 3, 1138: **aor.** ἠνῑᾶσα Anth. (Lucil.) 11, 254, overlooked by Lexicogr. (ῐ). See ἀνιάω.

Ἀνιάομαι, see ἰάομαι.

Ἀνιάω *To vex,* Soph. Ant. 550; Ar. Plut. 538. Eq. 349; Xen. Cyr. 5, 3, 7; Dem. 17, 17: **imp.** ἠνία Soph. Aj. 273; Pl. Gorg. 502: **fut.** ἀνιᾶσω Xen. An. 3, 3, 19; Plut. Sol. 12; Aristid. 45, 46, Ion. -ήσω Od. 19, 66; Anth. (Plato) 7, 100: **aor.** ἠνίᾱσα Andoc. 1, 50; Xen. Hell. 5, 4, 33, Ion. -ησα Phocyl. 16; ἀνιᾶσας Soph. Aj. 994; Ar. Pax 764, Ion. -ήσας Anth. 12, 153; Orph. Lith. 645, Dor. ἀνίασα Theocr. 2, 23: **p.** late ἠνίᾱκα Heliod. 7, 22. **Pass.** ἀνιῶμαι *to be grieved,* Od. 15, 335; Soph. Ph. 906; Ar. Lys. 593; Com. Fr. 2, 247. 3, 316; Xen. Mem. 3, 9, 8; Lys. 13, 43, Ion. -ιῆται (Hippocr.) Epist. 9, 384; opt. ἀνιῴμην Theogn. 668, 3 pl. Ion. ἀνιῴατο Her. 4, 130; -ιᾶσθαι 5, 93: **imp.** ἠνιῶντο Xen. Cyr. 6, 3, 10: as **pass. fut. mid.** ἀνιάσομαι Com. Fr. (Aristoph.) 2, 1148; Xen. Mem. 1, 1, 8; (Aeschin.) Epist. 8; Luc. D. Meretr. 8, 2, Ion. -ήσομαι, -ήσει Plat. Eleg. 8 (Bergk), Epic -ήσεαι Theogn. 991: **p.** ἠνίημαι Mosch. 4, 3: **aor.** ἠνιάθην Xen. Hell. 6, 4, 20, Ion. -ήθην Il. 2, 291. Od. 1, 133; Hippocr. 6, 392 (Lit.); Democr. p. 165 (Mullach): **fut.** late ἀνιαθήσεσθαι Galen 5, 51. **Mid. aor.** ἀνιάσασθαι Galen 3, 489, we think should be **fut.** -άσεσθαι. (ἄν- in **pres.** ᾱσ- in **fut.** &c. ῑ in Hom. and Trag. ῐ in Comed. except -ῑῶν Ar. Eq. 349, ῐ in others.)

Ἀνίημι, see ἀφίημι.

Ἀνῐμάω *To draw up,* in classic usage perhaps only **pres.** and **imp.** (later pretty complete with **fut. m.** as act.), Xen. Eq. 7, 2; Theophr. H. P. 4, 3, 5: **imp.** ἀνίμων Xen. An. 4, 2, 8: (**fut.** -ήσω?): **fut. m.** -ήσομαι Long. P. 1, 12 (Seil.): **aor.** ἀνίμησα Plut. Phoc. 18; Stob. (Hierocl.) 85, 21: **p. p.** ἀνίμημαι Luc. Pisc. 50: **aor.** ἀνιμήθην D. Laert. 1, 116; App. Mithr. 32. More usu. **mid.** ἀνιμῶμαι Aristot. Plant. 2, 6, 9; Luc. Alex. 14; Aretae. 77 (ed. Oxon.); Geop. 1, 13: **imp.** ἀνιμῶντο Polyaen. 4, 6, 8: **fut.** -ήσομαι Long. P. 1, 12 quoted: **aor.** -ησάμην Plut. Mor. 773; Luc. V. H. 2, 42; Long. P. 1, 12 (Seil.); App. Mithr. 71; Arr. Peripl. 8.

'Ανισόω *To make equal*, seems, in the classic period, to occur only in **pres. act.** ἀνισοῖ Xen. Cyr. 7, 5, 65 (Dind.); -ισων Pl. Polit. 289; -ισοῦν Aristot. Part. Anim. 3, 4, 19: and **aor. pass.** ἀνισωθείς Her. 7, 103. We notice it simply to supply a defect in all our Lexicons—the **aor. mid.** ἀνῑσώσαιτο Opp. H. 5, 37.

'Ανοίγνῡμι *To open*, Lys. 12, 10; Dem. 24, 209 (-ῡται Eur. Ion 923; -ύμενος Ar. Eq. 1326); ἀνοίγω Pind. P. 5, 88; Soph. Aj. 344; Her. 3, 117; Thuc. 4, 74; ἄνοιγε Aesch. Supp. 321; (Epic ἀναοίγω); later ἀνοιγνύω Dem. Phal. 122; Paus. 8, 41, 4: **imp.** ἀνέῳγον Il. 16, 221. 24, 228; Com. Fr. (Amips.) 2, 706; Her. 1, 187; Xen. An. 5, 5, 20, ὑπ- Dem. 32, 27, Epic ἀνῷγον Il. 14, 168, and rare ἤνοιγον Xen. Hell. 1, 1, 2. 6, 21; late, Paus. 4, 26, 8; Ach. Tat. 3, 17 (Vulg. ἀνέῳγ- Herch.); App. Civ. 2, 138, iter. ἀναοίγεσκον Il. 24, 455, late ἀνεῴγνυον App. Annib. 32. Civ. 4, 81, but -εῴγνυ Mithr. 44: **fut.** ἀνοίξω Ar. Pax 179; Polyaen. 5, 5, 1: **aor.** ἀνέῳξα Od. 10, 389 (Bekk. Ameis, La Roche); Ar. Vesp. 768; Thuc. 2, 2; Lys. 1, 14; Dem. 20, 53, rare ἤνοιξα Xen. Hell. 1, 5, 13; late, Apollod. 2, 5, 4; Charit. 1, 10, 2. 3, 4, 14; Or. Sib. 3, 500; Pseud.-Callisth. 1, 17; Polyaen. 3, 9, 45 (but ἀνέῳξα 5, 5, 1), Poet. ἀνῷξα Theocr. 14, 15, Ion. ἄνοιξα Her. 1, 68. 4, 143. 9, 118 (Gaisf. Bekk. Dind. Stein); ἀνοίξῃς Soph. O. C. 515; -οίξατε Aesch. Ch. 877: **p.** ἀνέῳχα Dem. 42, 30; Com. Fr. (Men.) 4, 133: **p. p.** ἀνέῳγμαι Eur. Hipp. 56; Hippocr. 5, 284; Thuc. 2, 4; Lys. 1, 24; Dem. 24, 208, Poet. ἀνῷγμαι Theocr. 14, 47, late ἤνοιγμαι Joseph. Ap. 2, 9, but δι- Hippocr. 5, 436 (Ms. G. Lit. ἀνέῳγ- Erm. 1, 689), ἠνεῳγμένος D. Sic. 23, 16 (Dind.); Heliod. 9, 9: **plp.** ἀνέῳκτο Xen. Hell. 5, 1, 14, late ἤνοικτο, δι- Heliod. 7, 15: **1 aor.** ἀνεῴχθην Eur. Ion 1563; ἀνοιχθῇ (Dem.) 44, 37; -θείη Pl. Phaed. 59, -θεῖεν Thuc. 4, 111; -οιχθῆναι Her. 2, 128; -θείς 4, 14; Antiph. 5, 54; Thuc. 4, 130; Pl. Conv. 216, late ἠνοίχθην Paus. 2, 35, 4; Pseud.-Callisth. 1, 19; V. T. Ps. 105, 17, ἀνωίχθη Nonn. 7, 317: **fut.** late ἀνοιχθήσομαι V. T. Esai. 60, 11; Galen 2, 473; Epict. Ench. 33, 13. **2 aor.** late ἠνοίγην (Luc.) Amor. 14; Pseud.-Callisth. 1, 19; Christ. Pat. 996: **2 fut.** ἀνοιγήσομαι late, V. T. Neh. 7, 3: **3 fut.** ἀνεῴξομαι Xen. Hell. 5, 1, 14 (Mss. Dind. Saupp. Breitb. Cob.); Dio Chrys. vol. 2, p. 329 (Dind.): **pres.** ἀνοίγεται Pl. Rep. 405, -νῦται Eur. Ion 923; -γεσθαι Thuc. 4, 104; -νύμενος Ar. Eq. 1326, -γόμενος Thuc. 4, 130: **imp.** ἀνεῴγοντο Thuc. 4, 111; Pl. Phaed. 59: **2 p.** ἀνέῳγα rarely act., ἀνέῳγε *opened*, (Hippocr.) Epist. 9, 394 (Lit.); Aristaen. 2, 22: **plp.** ἀνεῴγει Com. Fr. (Pher.) 2, 289 (Pors. Mein.);—usu. neuter, *stand open*, -ῴγασι Hippocr. 7, 558 (Lit.); Plut. Mor. 693; Luc. Gall. 30; D. Mort. 4, 1; Herodn. 4, 2, 7; Polyaen. 2, 28, which earlier Attic writers seem to have avoided, and used ἀνέῳγμαι instead: Dinarchus the orator is said, in Cramer's Anecd. 1, 52, to have been the only exception. **Mid.** *open for oneself, one's own,* rare and late, -οιγόμενος Plut. Mor. 339 (?): **aor.** ἀνοιξάμεναι Aristid. V. 2, 40 (Jebb.); -ασθαι suggested by Struve for ἀνωῖξαι Q. Sm. 12, 331. **Vb.** ἀνοικτέον Eur. Ion 1387. The less regular forms ἤνοιγον, ἤνοιξα are late, V. T. 1 Macc. 11, 2; Paus. 7, 19, 3; Clement. Epist. 43, except as nautical terms, *open out, gain the open sea,* in which sense exclusively Xen. uses them. Gaisf., with the Mss., edits ἀνῷξα Her. 1, 68, but ἄνοιξα 4, 143. 9, 118, Bekk. Dind. Bred. Lhardy uniformly ἄνοιξα, as it would seem that Her. perhaps never augments οι, ἀνέῳγες however 1, 187, but in an Inscr. Hippocr. augments it, ἀνέῳξε 6, 568 (Lit.) For the monstrous form ἀνωῖξαι Q. Sm. 12, 331, has been suggested, or substituted, ἀνοῖξαι (Pauw), ἀναπτύξαι (Koechly), ἀνοίξασθαι (Struve), called "inusitatum" by Koechly, rather hastily if Aristid. 2, 40, be sound. In late Greek, along with the classical forms ἀνέῳξε, ἀνέῳγμαι, ἀνεῴχθην, occur even with triple augm. ἠνέῳξε V. T. Gen. 8, 6; Joseph. Ap. 2, 9: ἠνέῳγμαι N. T. Rev. 10, 8; Heliodor. 9, 9; Polyaen. 8, 25 (Maasv. ἀνέῳγ- Woelffl.): ἠνεῴχθην Dio Cass. 44, 17 (Bekk. ἀνεῴχ- Dind.); V. T. Gen. 7, 11; N. T. Jo. 9, 10 (Vat. Sinait.) See Galen 4, 160. 478.

Ἀνορθόω *To set upright,* Xen. Hell. 4, 8, 12, (never augments the prep. in *classic* writers): **fut.** ἀνορθώσω Isocr. 6, 85: **aor.** ἀνώρθωσα Eur. Alc. 1138; Isocr. 5, 64; Aristid. 12, 84 (Dind.); -θωσον Soph. O. R. 51; -ώσας Thuc. 6, 88: (p.?): **plp.** late ἠνορθώκειν Liban. Epist. 959 (Wolf): **p. p.** ἀνώρθωμαι V. T. 2 Reg. 7, 16. 1 Par. 17, 14. 24; Liban. Decl. p. 800: **aor.** ἀνωρθώθην V. T. Ps. 19, 9. Ezek. 16, 7; N. T. Luc. 13, 13 (Vulg. Vat.), ἀνορθ- (Mss. Lachm. Tisch.): **imp. pass.** ἀνωρθοῦντο Eunap. Fr. 76 (L. Dind.) This verb never augments the prep. in *classic,* scarcely even in *late* Greek. The tendency to double augm. is confined to the double comp. ἐπ-ανορθόω, which, in classic Greek, always augments both verb and prep. **imp.** ἐπ-ηνώρθουν Isocr. 12, 200: **aor.** ἐπ-ηνώρθωσα (Lys.) 2, 70; Dinarch. 1, 96, συν-επ- (Dem.) 10, 34: **p. p.** ἐπ-ηνώρθωμαι Dem. 18, 311; Athen. (Macho) 578: **aor.** indic. late ἐπ-ανωρθώθη Apocr. 2 Macc. 5, 20; inf. ἐπ-ανορθωθῆναι Dem. 9, 76. **Mid. imp.** ἐπ-ηνωρθούμην Pl. Theaet. 143; Plut. Sert. 19; but later ἐπ-ανωρθ- Polyaen. 6, 4 (Woelffl.), see N. T. Luc. 13, 13, above: **aor.** ἐπ-ηνωρθωσάμην Isocr. 4, 165; Dem. 56, 43. (Dem.) 7, 18. **Vb.** ἐπ-ανορθωτέον Pl. Leg. 809. The Aldine reading Eur. Alc. 1138, is ἐξ-ανώρθωσας, not ἐξ-ην-. διορθόω, **aor.** δι-ώρθωσε Isocr. 9, 47, δι-ωρθωμένος

Plut. Alcib. 7 &c., not ἐδι-ώρθ-. κατορθόω, κατ-ώρθωσαν Thuc. 6, 33, not ἐκατ-ώρθ-.

'Αντᾰγορεύω *To speak against*, rare and only pres. -εύειν Ar. Ran. 1072: and Dor. aor. ἀντ-ᾱγόρευσε Pind. P. 4, 156 (Vulg. Boeckh, Momms. Christ), the rest supplied by ἀντιλέγω, ἀντερῶ, -είρηκα, &c.

'Αντάω *To meet*, Poet. and Ion. subj. ἀντᾷς H. Merc. 288; opt. ἀντῴη Soph. Tr. 902: imp. Ion. ἤντεον Il. 7, 423; Ap. Rh. 4, 845, for -αον: fut. ἀντήσω Il. 16, 423; Opp. Hal. 3, 71, Dor. -ᾱσω Eur. Tr. 212 (chor.): aor. ἤντησα Il. 6, 399. Od. 4, 327; Eur. Ion 802; Her. 1, 114. 2, 119, ἀπ- Thuc. 2, 20, Dor. ἄντᾱσα Soph. Ant. 982 (chor.), ὑπ- Pind. P. 8, 59; subj. ἀντήσῃς Eur. I. A. 150, Epic -ήσομεν Od. 16, 254; opt. ἀντήσειε Il. 7, 158; Maneth. 1, 24; part. ἀντήσας Aesch. Supp. 37; Soph. Aj. 533, Dor. -ᾱσαις Pind. Ol. 10, 42: p. ἀπ-ήντηκα Ar. Lys. 420; Dem. 18, 15. 125: p. p. -ήντημαι see foll. **Mid.** as act. ἀντᾶσθαι (Hesych.); usu. in comp. ἀπ-αντώμενα Polyb. 8, 8, branded by Luc. Lex. 25, as not Attic: fut. ἀπ-αντήσομαι Lys. 34, 8: aor. ἠντήσαντο Anth. (Rhian.) 12, 121; subj. συν-αντήσωνται Il. 17, 134: and as mid. p. p. ἀπ-ήντημαι Dio. Hal. 6, 88: aor. ἀπ-ηντήθη Polyb. 2, 7, see ἀπαντάω. **Vb.** ἀπ-αντητέον Pl. Theaet. 210. συν-αντήτην Epic 3 dual, imp. Od. 16, 333. ἀντάω uncomp. is rare, never in Comedy nor Attic prose.

'Αντεικάζω *To compare;* fut. m. -εικᾰσομαι Pl. Men. 80: aor. ἀντῄκᾰσα Ar. Vesp. 1311; sub. -εικάσω Pl. Men. 80.

'Αντευποιέω *To do good in turn*, Ar. Plut. 1029 (Vulg. W. Dind. Mein. ἀντ' εὖ ποιέω Bergk); Xen. An. 5, 5, 21 (Vulg. Krüg. Kühn. Saupp. ἀντ' εὖ ποι- L. Dind.); Pl. Gorg. 520 (Bekk. ἀντ' εὖ ποι- B. O. Winck.); Dem. 20, 141 (Vulg. Bekk. Bait. Saupp. but ἀντ' εὖ ποιέω W. Dind.): fut. -ήσω: aor. ἀντευποιήσωμεν Dem. 20, 124 (Bekk. Bait. Saupp. ἀντ' εὖ ποι- Dind.): p. ἀντευπεποίηκεν Dem. 20, 64 (Bekk. Bait. Saupp. ἀντ' εὖ πεποίηκεν Dind.) if right, the marvel vanishes.

'Αντιάζω *To meet*, &c. Soph. Elec. 1009; Eur. Andr. 572, ὑπ- Xen. Cyr. 5, 5, 9; subj. -άζωσι Pind. N. 1, 68; Her. 4, 118: imper. ἀντίαζε, ὑπ- Aesch. Pers. 834: imp. ἀντίαζον Her. 1, 166 (Mss. Vulg. Gaisf. Dind. Stein), ἠντ- (Bekk. Lhardy, Bred.), compare ὑπ-ηντ- 4, 121 (Mss. Gaisf. Bekk. Dind. Stein); Aesch. Pers. 407; Xen. An. 6, 5, 27; Luc. V. H. 1, 21. 37: fut. ἀντιᾰσω Od. 22, 28; Theogn. 552. 1308 (see ἀντιάω), Dor. -άξω Pind. Ol. 10 (11), 84: aor. ἠντίᾰσα Her. 4, 80. 9, 6; ἀντίᾰσον Eur. Supp. 272; -άσας Emped. 274; Aesch. Ag. 1557; Soph. El. 869; Her. 3, 45; and late prose, Ecphant. Stob. 48, 64 (-άξας Mein.), Dor.

-άσαις Pind. I. 6, 15, -άξαις, ὑπ-αντι- P. 8, 11; -ιάσαι N. 10, 20. This verb is Poet. and Ion. prose, late and rare in Attic prose, Plut. Dion. 45, but in comp. ὑπ- Xen. Cyr. 5, 5, 9. An. 6, 5, 27.

Ἀντιάω *To meet*, Poet. -άει Ap. Rh. 4, 1675, -ᾷ Opp. Cyn. 1, 536, Epic ἀντιόω Il. 12, 368; Opp. Hal. 1, 48; imper. -ιοώντων Il. 23, 643; inf. -ιάαν 13, 215; -ιόων 20, 125. Od. 1, 25, see below: imp. ἀντίαα Opp. Hal. 2, 334, iter. ἀντιάασκον Ap. Rh. 2, 100: fut. ἀντιάσω Od. 22, 28; Theogn. 552: aor. ἠντίᾰσα Callim. Epigr. 73, ὑπ-αντίασα Pind. P. 4, 135; subj. ἀντιάσῃσιν Ap. Rh. 3, 643, dual. -άσητον Il. 12, 356; opt. -σειας Od. 18, 147; Mosch. 2, 150, -σειε Il. 13, 290, -σαιμεν 7, 231; -άσας 1, 67. Mid. as act. rare ἀντιάομαι, Ep. opt. -ιόῳτο Ap. Rh. 1, 470; -άασθαι 2, 24: imp. ἀντιάασθε Il. 24, 62 (Vulg. Dind. La R.), ἠντι- (Bekk. 2 ed.) (ᾰ.) Some take ἀντιόω Il. 13, 752. Od. 1, 25 &c. for fut. lengthened on ἀντιῶ contr. from ἀντιάσω, for which see ἀντιάζω.

Ἀντιβολέω *To meet*, Ar. Nub. 155; Andoc. 1, 149; Lys. 4, 20; Isae. 9, 37: imp. ἠντιβόλουν Ar. Ach. 147 (Bekk. Dind. ἠντεβ- Cob. Mein.). Fr. 460; Lys. 1, 25. 29 (ἠντεβ- Cob. Frohb.); Dem. 37, 14: fut. -ήσω Od. 21, 306; Lys. 14, 16: aor. ἠντεβόλησα rare Ar. Fr. 101 (Mss. Dind.), Ep. always ἀντεβόλ- Il. 11, 809. 13, 210. Od. 24, 87. H. Merc. 143; Hes. Sc. 439; Pind. Ol. 13, 30; Ap. Rh. 2, 1121; Orph. Arg. 498 &c.; opt. -ήσαις rare form in Hom. Od. 4, 547. 13, 229: aor. pass. ἀντιβοληθείς Ar. Vesp. 560. ἀντιβόλησεν unaugm. Il. 11, 809 (Vulg.), and preferred by Buttm. Lexil. p. 122, on the ground of its being more in accordance with Homeric analogy, as the verb is a fixed compd., with augm. ἀντεβόλ- (Ms. Ven. Wolf, Bekk. Dind. La Roche.)

Ἀντιδικέω *To be a defendant*, Xen. Mem. 4, 4, 8: imp. ἠντιδίκει Lys. 6. 12 (ἠντεδ- Cob.), ἠντεδ- Dem. 39, 37. 40, 18 (Ms. S. Bekk. B. Saupp., ἠντιδ- Dind.): fut. ἀντιδικήσω Isae. 11, 9: aor. ἠντεδίκησα (Dem.) 47, 28 (Bekk. B. Saupp.), ἠντιδ- (Dind.)

Ἀντιλέγω *To speak against*, Ar. Ran. 1076; Her. 8, 77; Andoc. 1, 94; Xen. Hell. 3, 2, 18; Isocr. 15, 89; Pl. Euthyd. 285; Dem. 20, 62; inf. -λέγειν Euen. 1 (Bergk); Her. 8, 77; Lys. 8, 11; Isae. 10, 22: imp. ἀντέλεγον Ar. Fr. 407; Her. 9, 42; Thuc. 1, 28; Lys. 8, 11. 12, 25; Isocr. 12, 89; Isae. 6, 24: fut. -λέξω rare, Eur. Hipp. 993; Ar. Ran. 998; Lys. 8, 10. 11 (Scheibe); Xen. Conv. 2, 12; D. Hal. 10, 40: aor. ἀντέλεξα rare, and Poet. (?) Dio Cass. 68, 20; -έξας Dio. Hal. 9, 41; inf. -λέξαι Soph. O. R. 409; Ar. Nub. 1040. Lys. 806; Dio. Hal. 10, 40: pass. ἀντιλέγεται Xen. Hell. 6, 5, 37; -όμενος 3, 2, 30; -εσθαι Dem. 27, 15. Vb. ἀντιλεκτέος Eur. Heracl.

975. This verb seems not to occur in Epic; neither pres. nor imp. in Trag.; but freq. in prose and Comedy: fut. and aor. rare, and rather Poet. The usual fut. and aor. are: ἀντερῶ Aesch. Ag. 539; Eur. Hipp. 402. Med. 364; Ar. Eccl. 249. Ach. 702; Thuc. 1, 73; Andoc. 4, 25; Isocr. 12, 62. 18, 35; Aeschin. 2, 183; Pl. Rep. 580: aor. ἀντεῖπον Thuc. 1, 136. 4, 22; Lys. 19, 55; Isocr. 12, 215; subj. -είπῃ Ar. Eccl. 588, -είπητε Eur. Elec. 361; opt. -είποιμι Soph. El. 377, -είποι Eur. I. A. 1210 (Monk, Kirchh. Nauck, -ερεῖ Elms. Dind.); -ειπεῖν Aesch. Pr. 51; Soph. Ant. 1053; Andoc. 4, 34; Isocr. 18, 36; -ειπών Soph. Ant. 1232; Thuc. 8, 69: p. -ειρηκώς Soph. Ant. 47: fut. ἀντειρήσεται Soph. Tr. 1184. 1 aor. ἀντεῖπαν late, V. T. Jos. 17, 14. We have not seen the *indic.* ἀντεῖπον either in Trag. or Comedy.

(**'Αντιόω**), in use ἀντιόομαι Dep. *To oppose*, Ion. -εύμεθα Her. 9, 26; -εύμενοι 7, 139: imp. ἠντιοῦτο Her. 1, 76. 4, 3: with fut. m. ἀντιώσομαι Her. 7, 9. 102: but aor. p. ἠντιώθην as mid. Her. 7, 9. 10. 8, 100 (Bekk. Dind. Krüg. Stein), ἀντ- 7, 9 (Gaisf.); inf. ἀντιωθῆναι Aesch. Supp. 389; Her. 8, 100; -ωθείς 5, 100. See ἐν-αντιόομαι.

'Αντίχρη *It is sufficient* (χρή), impers. and only 1 aor. ἀντέχρησε Her. 7, 127. 187.

"Αντομαι *To meet, entreat*, Poet. Emped. 14 (Stein); Soph. O. C. 250; Eur. Alc. 1098; Ar. Thesm. 977 (chor.); Ap. Rh. 2, 1123; -εσθαι Il. 15, 698; -όμενος 11, 237; Pind. P. 2, 71: imp. ἠντόμην, -τεο Callim. Epigr. 31, -τετο Il. 22, 203, συν- Il. 21, 34. Od, 4, 367, but dual ἀντέσθην, συν- Il. 7, 22.

(**"Ανῡμι**) *To accomplish*, only imp. act. Dor. 1 pl. ἄνῡμες Theocr. 7, 10 (Vulg. Ahr. Ziegl. ἄνομες Meineke, Fritzs.). Pass. ἄνῡται pres. late, Opp. Hal. 3, 427 (Vulg.); Nic. Alex. 599 (G. and Otto Schneid. -εται G. Herm. Meineke): ἤνῡτο Od. 5, 243; Q. Sm. 9, 1, ᾶνυτο Theocr. 2, 92, -ετο (Mein.) (ᾱ seems to be always in arsi, ᾰ Nic. Al. 599, is in thesi.)

'Ανύω *To accomplish*, Il. 4, 56; Eur. Ph. 453; Ar. Ran. 606, ἐξ- Her. 7, 183, Attic ἀνύτω Soph. Ant. 805 (Dind.); Thuc. 2, 76; Xen. Cyr. 1, 6, 5, ξυν- Aesch. Ag. 1123: imp. ἤνῠον Her. 9, 66; Dem. 21, 104, and -ῠτον Soph. Tr. 319; Eur. Bac. 1100 (Dind. ἤν- Elms.); Pl. Conv. 217; Xen. Cyr. 5, 5, 22. 7, 3, 14 (Dind. Saupp. Hertl. -υον Vulg. Popp.), Dor. ᾶνυον Theocr. 21, 19: fut. ἀνύσω Soph. Aj. 607; Ar. Ran. 649; Artemid. Onir. 1, 51, and, according to some, ἀνύω Il. 4, 56 quoted, ἐξ- 11, 365. 20, 452: aor. ἤνῠσα Od. 24, 71; Aesch. Pers. 766; Soph. O. C. 454; Her. 1, 91, Dor. ᾶν- Theocr. 7, 6; -ύσειεν Od. 15, 294; Pl. Leg. 650; -ύσαι Thuc. 2, 97; ἀνύσας Ar. Nub.

635; Epic. ἤνυσσα Ap. Rh. 4, 413, ἄνυσσα Pind. P. 12, 11, ἄν- Anth. 5, 275; ἀνύσσας H. Merc. 337; Hes. Th. 954; -ύσσαι Ap. Rh. 1, 603: p. ἤνῠκα Pl. Polit. 264: p. p. ἤνυσμαι Polyb. 3, 44, δι- Xen. Cyr. 1, 4, 28; but ἠνυμένος if correct, Theod. Metoch. 2, p. 22 (Müll.), προ- D. Hal. Rhet. 5, 4: plp. ἤνυστο Luc. Herm. 3; Paus. 5, 1, 7: aor. ἠνύσθην D. Hal. Ant. 3, 6; Polyb. 32, 7, 17; Philostr. V. Apoll. 40; Heliod. 4, 6, ἐπ- Hes. Sc. 311: fut. ἀνυσθήσομαι Ael. V. H. 1, 21; Heliod. 3, 19. **Mid.** ἀνύομαι as act. Pind. P. 2, 49; -ύεσθαι Bion 7, 6, -ύτεσθαι Xen. An. 7, 7, 24 (D. Sauppe): imp. ἠνυτόμαν Aesch. Ag. 1159 (chor.): but fut. ἀνύσομαι (σσ) pass. (?) Od. 16, 373, act. -ύσεσθαι Xen. An. 7, 7, 24 quoted (Lion, Kühn.): aor. ἠνυσάμην Aesch. Pr. 700; Soph. Tr. 996; Ar. Plut. 196 (D.); rare in prose, Pl. Phaed. 69 (best Ms. Heind. Bekk. Stallb. Schanz, -ύσαμεν Mss. Herm. Wohlrab); (Hippocr.) Epist. 420 (Lit.); -ύσωμαι Aesch. Ch. 858; -ύσασθαι Xen. An. 7, 7, 24 quoted (Valken. Krüg. Schenkl); and late, Polyb. 9, 4, ἐξ- Strab. 10, 2, 25, unaugm. -ἀνύσαντο Eur. Bacc. 131 (chor.), Dor. ἀνυσάμαν Theocr. 5, 144. **Vb.** ἀνυστός Hippocr. 2, 142 (Erm.); Xen. An. 1, 8, 11, but ἀνῠτός Sext. Emp. 617 (B.), ἀν-ήνυστος Od. 16, 111, ἀν-ήνῠτος Soph. El. 166. For ἠνύσατο Her. 1, 91 (Mss. Schw. Gaisf.), Schaefer reads ἤνυσέ τε, and Bekk. Lhardy, Dind. Krüg. Stein approve and accept it. **Fut. m.** ἀνύσσεσθαι Od. 16, 373, is not, we think, *necessarily* pass. It may mean we *shall* never *accomplish* this *for ourselves, gain our object in this.* α and υ always short (Passow): if so, the following require correction, ἀνῡων Nonn. 21, 16 (Graef.), where have been suggested ἀλῡων (Wern. ἀλύω Koch, Meineke, ἐάσω Koechly); ἀνῦσαι Tryphiod. 126; ἀνῡσάμενοι Anth. Pal. 10, 12. The poets use both forms, more freq. ἀνύω; prose authors, again, prefer ἀνύτω, Thuc. and Plato perhaps always; so Xen. (Dind.), usu. (Vulg. Popp.). ἁνύω, ἁνύτω with aspirate, called Attic by Moeris, Herodn. &c., and so written by Porson Eur. Phoen. 463, Elms. Bac. 1098, and by Dind. *formerly* (4 edit.) uniformly in Sophocles, is not, we think, supported by the Mss. nor adopted by the generality of scholars: Dind. *now* always unaspirated ἀν-, ἠν- (5 edit.) ἀνύττω D. Laert. 1, 2, 16, and v. r. Pl. Soph. 261 &c. is a vicious form.

Ἄνω Poet. *To perform,* ἄνοις Aesch. Fr. 156 (Dobr. Herm. Dind.); ἄνοντος Ar. Vesp. 369; ἄνειν Pl. Crat. 415: **imp.** ἦνον Od. 3, 496; Eur. An. 1132. **Pass.** ἄνομαι Il. 10, 251; Pind. Ol. 8, 8 (best Mss. Boeckh, Bergk); Opp. Hal. 4, 528; ἄνηται 5, 442; ἄνοιτο Il. 18, 473; ἀνόμενος Aesch. Ch. 799; Ap. Rh. 2, 494; Opp. Cyn. 1, 111; Arat. 373 (B); Her. 7, 20, v. r.

ἀνύμ-: imp. ἤνετο Her. 1, 189. 8, 71 (Gaisf. Dind. Stein, Abicht, ἠνύετο Bekk. Krüg.), ἄνετο Theocr. 2, 92 (Meineke), perhaps needlessly, for ἄνυτο (Vulg.) ā usu. but in arsi, ă in thesi once in Hom. ἄνοιτο Il. 18, 473, ἄνοις Aesch. Fr. 156 (Dobr. Herm. Dind.). Ch. 799?; and late ἄνηται Opp. Hal. 5, 442.

'Ανώγω Poet. and Ion. *To order*, almost confined to 3 sing. -γει Il. 6, 439. 19, 102. Od. 5, 139. 357; Hes. Th. 549; Her. 7, 104, but 2 sing. -γεις Q. Sm. 13, 238, 3 dual -ώγετον Il. 4, 287, -γετε (Bentl. Bekk. 2 ed.), for subj. and opt. see **perf.**; (imper. ἄνωγε Eur. Or. 119; Callim. Fr. 440, -γέτω Od. 2, 195, -γετε 23, 132, *may* belong to **perf.**); part. -γων Lycophr. 572; -γειν Opp. Ven. 3, 194: **imp.** ἤνωγον Il. 9, 578. Od. 14, 237; Hom. H. 1, 105; Anth. App. Epigr 376; Ap. Rh. 4, 1594, ἄνωγ- Il. 5, 805. Od. 9, 331, -ωγε Her. 3, 81, is perhaps **perf.**: **fut.** ἀνώξω Od. 16, 404: **aor.** ἤνωξα Hes. Sc. 479; subj. -ώξομεν Ep. for -ωμεν, Il. 15, 295; inf. ἀνῶξαι Od. 10, 531: **2 p.** ἄνωγα as **pres.** and unaugm. Il. 14, 105; Soph. El. 1458; Eur. Cycl. 340. 701, -γας Il. 14, 262; Aesch. Eum. 902; Soph. Ph. 100, -γε Aesch. Pr. 947; Soph. O. R. 96; Her. 3, 81, pl. syncop. ἄνωγμεν H. H. 2, 350; subj. ἀνώγῃ Il. 9, 101. Od. 1, 316; Her. 7, 104; -γοιμι Il. 19, 206, -γοι Od. 8, 70; Theogn. 999, -γοιτε Od. 11, 356; imper. ἄνωγε Eur. Or. 119; inf. ἀνωγέμεν Il. 13, 56: **2 plp.** ἠνώγεα as **imp.** Od. 9, 44. 17, 55, 3 sing. ἠνώγει Il. 6, 170. 10, 394; Soph. O. C. 1598; Theocr. 24, 67; Ap. Rh. 4, 247, and ἀνώγει Il. 18, 176. Od. 2, 385.—The following are Poetic syncopated forms: ἄνωγμεν for -ώγαμεν, H. H. 2, 350, ἄνωχθι 2 sing. imper. Il. 23, 158; Aesch. Ch. 772; Eur. Alc. 1044, 3 sing. ἀνώχθω for -ωγέτω, Il. 11, 189, 2 pl. ἄνωχθε for -ώγετε, Od. 22, 437; Eur. Rhes. 987. **Imp.** ἠνώγεον trisyll. Il. 7, 394 (Mss. Vulg. La Roche), has been changed to **plp.** ἠνώγει(ν) (Spitzn. Bekk. Dind.)

'Αξιόω *To think worthy*, Soph. O. R. 944; Her. 4, 115; Antiph. 6, 8; Lys. 3, 4: **imp.** ἠξ- Soph. O. C. 953; Her. 3, 42; Antiph. 6, 34; Andoc. 1, 107: **fut.** -ώσω Her. 7, 16; Antiph. 5, 16: **aor.** ἠξίωσα Thuc. 2, 64; Isae. 3, 2: **perf.** ἠξίωκα Isocr. 18, 24:—reg. and noticed chiefly because we think our lexicons wrong in asserting the **mid.** to be in Attic prose. We think the **mid.** is nearly confined to Trag. and Ion. prose, ἀξιοῦμαι, -οῦσθαι Aesch. Ag. 370; Ion. ἀξιεῦμαι Her. 5, 106; ἀξιεύμενος 1, 199. 7, 16; ἀξιούμενος Aristot. Rhet. 2, 10, 11: but **fut.** ἀξιώσεται if correct, as **pass.** Soph. Ant. 637 (Musgr. Schn. Nauck, Dind.): with **fut. pass.** ἀξιωθήσομαι Isocr. 9, 6. 10, 43; Aristot. Polit. 2, 9, 27; Diod. Sic. Fr. B. 31, 11 (Bekk.): **aor.** ἠξιώσατο Aesch. Eum. 425: **imp.** late ἠξιοῦτο Dio Cass.

42, 35 (Bekk.) Vb. ἀξιωτέον Stob. 85 21, missed, by Lexicogr.

Ἀοιδιάω (ἀοιδή) Epic=ἀείδω, *To sing*, only pres. -ιάει Od. 10, 227; pt. -ιάουσ' 5, 61. Aor. ἀοίδησον if sound, Simon. C. 174 (Bergk), requires a pres. ἀοιδάω.

Ἀολλίζω *To bring together, assemble*, Epic, Anth. 9, 772; -ίζων 9, 649: aor. ἀόλλισσα Il. 6, 287; -ίσσας 6, 270; Ap. Rh. 1, 863: aor. pass. ἀολλίσθην *assembled*, Il. 19, 54; inf. Ep. -ισθήμεναι 15, 588. Pres. pass. ἀολλίζονται Callim. Del. 18. (ᾰ.)

Ἀπαγορεύω *To forbid, give up*, Ar. Ach. 169; Her. 7, 149; Antiph. 3, γ, 7; (Andoc.) 4, 9; Xen. Cyr. 1, 4, 13; Pl. Prot. 334: imp. ἀπηγόρ- Her. 3, 51. 4, 125; Xen. Cyr. 1, 4, 14; Isae. 2, 28; Dem. 37, 25: fut. -εύσω Plut. Mor. 195. Lysand. 3. Nici. 21, classic ἀπ-ερῶ Ar. Lys. 165; Thuc. 1, 29. 121; Xen. M. Eq. 3, 9, Ion. -ερέω Her. 7, 205: aor. ἀπηγόρευσα classic, but rare, Aristot. Oec. 2, 24, 4; Dem. 40, 44. 55, 4 (Dio Cass. 56, 27. 60, 5. 6. 17; Ael. Fr. 298; Plut. Mor. 77; Luc. Conv. 19); subj. -αγορεύσῃς Plat. Theaet. 200 (often late Plut. Mor. 124. 228. Alex. 42; Strab 12, 3, 11; Luc. Merc. Con. 26. Herm. 33); usu. ἀπ-εῖπον Aesch. Sept. 840; Soph. Tr. 789; Thuc. 7, 60; Pl. Rep. 337, &c.: 1 aor. rare in this comp. -εῖπα, -εῖπας Soph. Ant. 405; -είπας Her. 3, 153 (mid. not in classic Attic, ἀπειπάμην Her. 1, 59. 5, 56; Aristot. Eth. Nic. 8, 16, 4; Polyb. 33, 10, &c.): p. -ηγόρευκα Aristot. Physiog. 3, 8; Plut. Mor. 1096; Luc. D. Deor. 24, 2. Saturn. 3. (Asin.) 19; classic ἀπείρηκα Eur. Or. 91; Hippocr. 6, 210; Lys. 2, 52; Xen. An. 5, 1, 2; Pl. Phaed. 99; Isocr. Epist. 3, 4; Dem. 3, 8: plp. -ηγορεύκει D. Cass. 58, 8; Luc. D. Deor. 5, 2 (Fritz.), classic -ειρήκεσαν Xen. An. 6, 5, 30: p. p. -ηγόρευμαι Aristot. Polit. 7, 17, 9; D. Cass. 57, 15; Plut. Sol. 21; Joseph. Ant. 15, 4, 1; Heliod. 2, 33. 8, 7, classic -είρημαι Her. 6, 61; Aeschin. 3, 48; Pl. Rep. 396: plp. -ηγόρευτο Plut. Fab. 4; Heliod. 8, 6, classic -ειρήμην, -ητο Thuc. 5, 48: aor. -ηγορεύθην D. Cass. 56, 25, see Dem. Fr. 38, classic -ερρήθην Dem. Fr. 38: fut. ἀπορρηθήσομαι Lys. 22, 14. Vb. ἀπαγορευτέον Luc. Herm. 47.

Ἀπαλλάσσω *To set free, deliver*, Aesch. Ag. 1289; Soph. Ant. 596; Hippocr. 2, 156; Thuc. 8, 86, -άττω Pl. Gorg. 478: imp. ἀπήλλαττον Andoc. 1, 59: fut. -άξω Aesch. Pr. 773; Soph. Ant. 769; Her. 9, 106; Isocr. 5, 52; Isae. 11, 31: aor. -ήλλαξα Ar. Vesp. 1537; Her. 1, 16. 5, 63. 8, 68; Thuc. 1, 90; Isocr. 11, 5: p. -ήλλαχα Xen. Mem. 3, 13, 6; Dem. 18, 65; Liban. Or. 15 (p. 235): p. p. -ήλλαγμαι Soph. El. 783; Eur. Andr. 963; Antiph. 2, δ, 5; Thuc. 1, 122; -μένος Ar. Pax 1128; Isocr. 5, 49; Her. 1, 60, but ἀπ-αλ- 2, 144. 167 (Bekk. Dind. Stein), ἀπηλ- (Dietsch, Abicht): plp. -ήλλαξο Dem. 34, 31, -ήλλακτο Antiph. 1, 7; Thuc. 1, 138: **1 aor.** -ηλλάχθην Com. Fr. 2, 794; Hippocr. 1, 732 (Marc. Erm. -λάγη Vulg. Lit. 5, 228); Her. 8, 18, but ἀπ-αλ- 2, 152. 5, 65. 6, 40. 45, ἀπηλ- (Abicht); late Att. prose ἀπ-ηλλ- Diog. Laert. 2, 127; subj. ἀπ-αλλαχθῇ Soph. O. C. 786; Eur. Andr. 424; (Pl.) Epist. 7, 335; opt. -αλλαχθεῖτε Ar. Vesp. 484; imper. -άχθητι Eur. Cycl. 600, -άχθητον Ar. Plut. 66; -αχθείς Soph. Ant. 244; Eur. Hip. 1181; Ar. Vesp. 504; Com. Fr. (Theop.) 2, 794; Her. 1, 170; Arr. An. 7, 25; Diod. Sic. 20, 40; -αχθῆναι Plut. Mar. 35: **2 aor.** ἀπ-ηλλάγην Aesch. Pr. 750; Eur. Andr. 592; Com. Fr. (Anon.) 4, 696; Hippocr. 5, 206; Thuc. 2, 42; Andoc. 1, 68; Lys. 1, 17; Isocr. 3, 6; Xen. An. 1, 10, 8; Pl. Rep. 406; Aeschin. 1, 40. 53; Dem. 23, 169, and always in Att. prose; subj. -αλλαγῶ Aesch. Pr. 471; Ar. Eccl. 1100; Isae. 2, 30; Pl. Theaet. 168; -αλλαγείην Xen. Cyr. 6, 1, 45, -γεῖμεν Pl. Euth. 7, -γείητε Dem. 3, 33; -αλλάγηθι Com. Fr. 3, 462; Pl. Gorg. 491; -αλλαγείς Aesch. Ag. 336; Soph. Ant. 422; Eur. Ph. 592; Ar. Ach. 270; Andoc. 1, 66; Isocr. 8, 20; Pl. Phaed. 64; -γῆναι Com. Fr. (Polyz.) 2, 867; Xen. An. 5, 1, 13; Lys. 12, 45; Pl. Gorg. 458; Dem. 19, 314; rare in Ion. Her. 8, 84: **1 fut.** -αχθήσομαι Eur. Hip. 356; Ar. Av. 940; Dio. Hal. 7, 13: **2 fut.** -αγήσομαι Thuc. 4, 28; Pl. Leg. 642; Isocr. 4, 172. 189; Dem. 22, 37; D. Sic. 20, 40; rare in Ion. Her. 2, 120; Hippocr. 7, 174. 234: **3 fut.** ἀπ-ηλλάξει (Hesych.), -ξεται Dem. 20, 28 (Cobet, perhaps needlessly for ἀπ-αλλάξεται Mss. Bekk. Dind.). **Mid.** ἀπαλλάσσομαι *depart*, Aesch. Eum. 180; Eur. Med. 729; Phoen. 603; Her. 1, 199, -άττομαι Pl. Parm. 156: **imp.** Ion. ἀπ-αλλασσ- Her. 1, 82. 3, 25, &c. -ηλλαττ- Pl. Leg. 948: **fut.** ἀπαλλάξομαι Eur. Hel. 437; Ar. Ach. 757 (ἀπ-ηλλ- Cob. Dind.); Her. 7, 222; Thuc. 8, 83; Pl. Euth. 15; Dem. 20, 28: **aor.** ἀπηλλάξαντο Eur. Heracl. 317 (Mss. Vulg. Kirchh. Nauck, denied by Matth. and Poppo Thuc. 8, 2, ὑπ-ηλλ- Pflugk, Dind. 5 ed.); opt. -άξαιτο Plut. Cat. Min. 64 (Sint. Bekk.); Strab. 15, 1, 68, no v. r.; -άξασθαι Parthen. 5 (Ms. P. Westerm.); Aretae. 1, 7, see *simple* ἀλλαξάμενος Dem. 55, 32: in same sense **aor.** and **fut. pass.** ἀπ-ηλλάχθην: ἀπ-ηλλάγην: -αχθήσομαι: -αγήσομαι. **Vb.** ἀπ-αλλακτέον Lys. 6, 8; Pl. Parm. 163. Of this verb, Attic prose writers use neither **1 aor.** nor **1 fut. pass.** Aesch. has **2 aor. pass.** only, Soph. and Eur. have both first and second, but the first more frequently, not however for Porson's reason, for Soph. Ant. 422, and Eur. Andr. 592, would admit the first. Her. never augments the **imp.**: always the **1 aor. act.**: varies in the **p. p.** and **1 aor.**

pass. A desiderative form ἀπαλλαξείω occurs in part. -είοντες Thuc. 1, 95. 3, 84.

Ἀπαμείβομαι, see ἀμείβω.

Ἀπαντάω *To meet*, Eur. Ion 940; Ar. Pax 941; Thuc. 7, 31; Dem. 24, 193: **imp.** ἀπήντων Thuc. 4, 127; Lys. 2, 24, Dor. 3 sing. ἀπάντη Bion 4, 7 (Mein. Ziegl.): **fut. m.** -αντήσομαι; -εται Aeschin. 1, 164, -ονται Lys. 2, 32. 34, 8; -ήσεσθαι Thuc. 7, 80; Aeschin. 1, 174; (Dem.) 42, 14. 60, 20; -ησόμενος Thuc. 4, 77. 7, 2; Xen. Hell. 1, 6, 3, Dor. -ασεῖται Dius, Stob. 65, 16: **act.** -ήσω later, unless correct Hippocr. 3, 132 (Erm. 827 Foes, -σῃ Lit. 4, 264); (Aristot.) Rhet. ad Alex. 19, 4 (Bekk.); Polyb. 4, 26. 17, 7 (Bekk.); Plut. Syll. 20; Dio Cass. 42, 41; App. Civ. 1, 77. 3, 13; Diod. Sic. 18, 15; Aristid. 32, 422 (D.): **aor.** ἀπ-ήντησα Eur. Ph. 1392; Thuc. 2, 20; Lys. 1, 22: **p.** ἀπ-ήντηκα Ar. Lys. 420; Dem. 18, 15. 125: **plp.** -τήκει Arr. Anab. 6, 15, 5: **p. p.** late ἀπ-ήντημαι as **act.** Polyb. 2, 37; Dio. Hal. 6, 88. 8, 47: with **plp.** -ήντητο Sext. Emp. 106, 11: and **aor.** ἀπηντήθην as **act.** Polyb. 2, 7: so **pres.** as mid. ἀπαντώμεναι Polyaen. 7, 45; Polyb. 8, 8, branded by Luc. (Lex. 25) as not Attic: **imp.** ἀπηντᾶτο Polyaen. 1, 21. 5, 12. **Mid.** fut. -ήσομαι, see above: **aor.** late, imper. ἀπάντησαι V. T. Ruth 1, 16; -τήσασθαι D. Hal. 8, 68 (Vulg.) **Vb.** ἀπαντητέον Pl. Theaet. 210. **Fut. act.** ἀπαντήσω is not classic. ἀπαντήσων adopted by Matth. Eur. Supp. 772, from a suggestion of Markland for ἀπαντήσας, is against the Mss. and not required by the sense. With the exception of **fut.** -ήσομαι, the **mid.** and **pass.** are used by late writers only, and by them as **act.** συναντάω Xen. An. 7, 2, 5, has also **fut.** -ήσω late, V. T. Esai. 34, 14; Maneth. 4, 554; Jos. Jud. B. 4, 11, 2: but **aor.** -ήντησα Xen. An. 1, 8, 15: **p.** -ήντηκα Luc. Philop. 1: **p. p.** -ήντηται see **mid.**: **mid.** συν-αντῶνται (Hes. Th. 877, in some edit.); Polyb. 22, 7; Aristaen. 1, 12: **fut.** perhaps late, -ήσομαι V. T. Deut. 31, 29. Job 5, 14; (formerly Il. 17, 134); now **aor.** subj. -ήσωνται Il. 17, 134: late **p. p.** -ήντηται as **mid.** Herodn. 1, 17 (Vulg.), now συνήντα (Bekk.) At Hes. Th. 877, late editors, in accordance with some Mss, have preferred the form συν-άντωνται to -ῶνται, on the ground that "Epicorum est συνάντομαι, non συναντάω." συνάντομαι is, no doubt, the *usual* form, but if Hom. has the *pure* (ἀντάω) ἤντεον Il. 7, 423, and ἄντομαι; συναντάω Od. 16, 333, and συνάντομαι, we do not see why Hes. may not have the comp. συναντάομαι as well as -άντομαι, especially as Hom. has **aor.** συναντήσωνται Il. 17, 134. ὑπαντάω Eur. Sup. 398: **imp.** ὑπήντων Xen. Cyr. 3, 3, 2, Ion. -ήντεον Anth. Plan. 101: **fut.** -ήσω Joseph. Jud. B. 2, 15, 3, see **mid.**:

aor. -ήντησα Xen. Cyr. 3, 3, 2; -αντήσας Soph. Ph. 719, Dor. -άντᾱσε Pind. P. 8, 59. **Pass.?** **Mid.** -αντάομαι late, Herodn. 2, 5, 5. 5, 4, 5. 8, 1, 4: **fut.** -ήσομαι Joseph. Ant. 6, 6, 2. 9, 6, 3. 12, 4, 3; Sext. Emp. 644.

Ἀπατάω, *To deceive,* Theogn. 59; Thuc. 8, 98, Dor. 3 pl. ἀπατῶντι, ἐξ- Pind. Ol. 1, 29: **imp.** ἠπάτων Eur. El. 938; (Dem.) 47, 9, ἐξ- Av. Eq. 1224; Aeschin. 2, 123, iter. ἀπάτασκον, ἐξ- rare in Attic Ar. Pax 1070 (Hexam.): **fut.** -ήσω Od. 17, 139; Pl. Phaedr. 262: **aor.** ἠπάτησα Thuc. 5, 9; Pl. Rep. 573, Poet. ἀπατ- Il. 9, 344, Dor. ἀπάτᾱσα Soph. Tr. 500 (chor.): **p.** ἠπάτηκα Soph. Ph. 929; Her. 6, 80; Aristot. Rhet. 1, 15, 25: **p. p.** ἠπάτημαι Soph. Ph. 949; Eur. Andr. 435; Thuc. 5, 46: **aor.** ἠπατήθην Phocyl. 14; Thuc. 5, 85; Isae. 5, 14; Pl. Crit. 52; Dem. 44, 19, very complete, and reg. except **fut. m.** as pass. ἀπατήσομαι Pl. Phaedr. 262, ἐξ- Xen. An. 7, 3, 3: and **f. p.** ἀπατηθήσομαι Aristot. Anal. Pr. 2, 21, 9, ἐξ- Aeschin. 3, 168; Pl. Crat. 436. **Vb.** ἐξ-απατητέον Pl. Crit. 49. The orators very seldom use ἀπατῶ, see (Dem.) 47, 9; Lycurg. 86; Isae. 5, 14; Dem. 44, 19; Hyperid. Fr. 25 (Blass), though they freely use ἀπάτη and ἐξ-απατῶ.

(**Ἀπαυράω**) *To take away,* Poetic, imp. ἀπηύρων as **aor.** Il. 19, 89, ἀπηύρας 8, 237, -ηύρα 17, 125; Hes. Th. 423; Aesch. Pers. 949 (chor.); Eur. An. 1029 (chor.), pl. ἀπηύρων Il. 1, 430; and late Epic, Ap. Rh. 4, 916: allied in signif. **fut.** ἀπουρήσω Il. 22, 489 (Bekk. Dind. -ίσσω Vulg. Spitzn. La Roche): **1 aor. part.** ἀπούρας Il. 1, 356, Dor. -ούραις Pind. P. 4, 149. **Mid. aor.** ἀπηύρω Aesch. Pr. 28 trimet. (Vulg. Blomf.), -ηύρᾰτο (Od. 4, 646, before Wolf); part. ἀπουράμενοι Hes. Sc. 173, not pass. but *having taken* each *for himself* the life of the other—*deprived each other* of life. For ἀπηύρατο Od. 4, 646 (Vulg.), Wolf, Bekker, and Dind. adopt the v. r. ἀπηύρα, and for ἀπηύρω Aesch. Pr. 28 (Vulg.), Herm. with Ms. M. reads ἐπηύρω, Elms. Dind. and Weil ἐπηύρου. Ahrens tries very ingeniously to account for the seeming anomalous forms of this verb by supposing a digammated stem in ϝράω=ϝρύω, ἐρύω. ἀπούρας, ἀπουράμενος are thus softened from ἀπόϝρας, ἀποϝράμενος: and ἀπηύρας, -ηύρα, -ηύρατο are improperly written for ἀπεύρας (ἀπέϝρας), -εύρα, -εύρατο. There is, besides, an interchange of conjugations; ἀπηύρων, at least, is from -άω, and ἀπηύρω, -ηύρατο from -μι. Compare γαμέω, ἔγημα, ἐγημάμην.

Ἀπαφίσκω *To deceive,* Poet. Od. 11, 217; -ίσκων, ἐξ- Hes. Th. 537: **fut.** ἀπαφήσω Anth. 12, 26: **1 aor.** ἀπάφησα Q. Sm. 3, 502, ἐξ- H. Hym. 2, 198; Opp. Hal. 3, 94: **2 aor.** ἤπᾰφον Ap. Rh. 3, 130; Opp. Hal. 3, 483; Anth. 9, 739, παρα- in tmesi Od. 14,

488, παρ-ήπαφ- Il. 14, 360; Orph. Arg. 707; Theocr. 27, 11; subj. ἀπάφω Anth. Plan. 108, ἐξ- Od. 23, 79; ἀπαφών Opp. Hal. 3, 444, ἐξ- Eur. Ion 704 (chor.); Ap. R. 2, 1235; -οῦσα H. Hym. 4, 38: **2 aor.** m. opt. ἀπαφοίμην as **act.** Od. 23, 216, ἐξ- Il. 9, 376.

Ἀπεικάζω *To take a likeness*, Isocr. 1, 11: **imp.** ἀπ-είκαζον Pl. Leg. 857 (Mss. Vulg.), -ήκαζον (Mss. B. O. W. &c.): **fut.** m. -εικάσομαι Xen. Mem. 3, 11, 1: **fut. act.** -εικάσω later, Plut. Mor. 1135: **aor.** ἀπ-είκασα Pl. Theaet. 169. Gorg. 493 (B. O. W.), -ήκασα (Bekk.); Pl. Leg. 857 (Bait. O. Winck.); -εικάσαι Soph. Fr. 162; Dem. 21, 143: **p. p.** ἀπ-είκασμαι Pl. Crat. 420. Leg. 965: **aor.** ἀπ-εικασθείς Eur. El. 979; Pl. Rep. 511; -ασθῆναι Pl. Tim. 48: **fut.** -ασθήσομαι Themist. Or. 2, 33. **Vb.** ἀπεικαστέον Pl. Phaedr. 270. The best Mss. and editors differ on the augm. of the **imp.** and **aor.**, but they seem to agree in not augmenting the **perf.**, but see εἰκάζω. In lexicons this verb is handled defectively.

Ἀπειλέω (late Epic -λείω Musae. 131) *To threaten*, in Ionic varies in augm., Il. 1, 161; Ar. Ach. 328: **imp.** ἠπείλει Il. 15, 179; Theocr. 25, 75, ἠπείλουν Thuc. 8, 92, ἀπείλεον Il. 13, 220; Her. 3, 77, -λεε 4, 81. 6, 37. 75 (Mss. Reitz, Bekk. Krüg. Gaisf. Stein), ἠπ-ειλ- (Dind. Abicht, Bred.), Epic dual ἀπειλήτην Od. 11, 313: **fut.** -ήσω Il. 15, 212: **aor.** ἠπείλησεν Il. 1, 388; Her. 1, 214. 3, 124, ἐπ-ηπ- 1, 189. 6, 32 (Mss. Bekk. Gaisf. Krüg. Dind. Stein, Abicht); Thuc. 8, 84, ἀπείλ- Il. 2, 665. Od. 8, 383; Her. 6, 37 (Mss. Gaisf. Stein, Reiz): **p.** ἠπειληκώς D. Sic. 18, 8, 6: **p. p.** ἀπειλημένον Her. 2, 141: **aor.** (ἠπειλήθην), ἀπειληθείς Her. 1, 24. 8, 109. 9, 34; Pl. Leg. 823: **pres.** ἀπειλοῦμαι Xen. Conv. 4, 31. Mid. late, **aor.** ἠπειλησάμην Polyaen. 7, 35, 2; ἀπειλησώμεθα N. T. Act. 4, 17.

Ἀπέκιξαν *They scattered*, a def. **aor.** Ar. Ach. 869. (Root prob. κίκω=ἴκω.)

Ἀπεσσύα, see σεύω.

Ἀπεχθάνομαι *To be hated*, -άνεαι Od. 2, 202, -άνει Ar. Pl. 910; Pl. Apol. 24; -θάνηται Pl. Rep. 567, -ωνται Aeschin. 3, 172; -θάνοιτο Pl. Lys. 207; -εσθαι Rep. 378; -όμενος Antiph. 6, 11; Pl. Phaedr. 231; Aeschin. 3, 172, and late ἀπέχθομαι Theocr. 7, 45; Anth. 5, 177; Q. Sm. 5, 465; Plut. Marcell. 22; Luc. Tox. 51; Dio. Hal. 8, 29: **imp.** ἀπηχθανόμην Com. Fr. (Cratin.) 2, 36; Lys. 20, 8; Xen. An. 7, 7, 10: **fut.** ἀπεχθήσομαι Eur. Alc. 72; Her. 1, 89; Lys. 31, 13; Pl. Phil. 58: late reg. -εχθανεῖται Themist. 26, 322: **p.** ἀπήχθημαι, -θημένος Thuc. 1, 75; Xen. An. 7, 6, 34: **plp.** ἀπήχθησθε Thuc. 1, 76: **2 aor.** ἀπηχθόμην Il. 9, 300; Sapph. 41; Ar. Lys. 699; Thuc. 2. 63;

Dem. 33, 28; -έχθωμαι Il. 4, 53; Dem. 3, 21; -χθοίμην (Andoc.) 4, 10; -εχθέσθαι Il. 21, 83; Eur. Med. 290 (Elms. Dind. Nauck, Kirchh. 2 ed.); Pl. Rep. 343 (Ast.), -έχθεσθαι with accent of pres. Eur. quoted (Pors. Kirchh. 1 ed. &c.); Il. 21, 83 (Bekk.); Thuc. 1, 136; Isae. 3, 73; Pl. Rep. 343 (B. O. W.); -εχθόμενος Od. 18, 165; Pind. N. 10, 83; Pl. Rep. 321. There seems to be no good early authority for pres. ἀπέχθομαι. Of the Tragedians, Eur. alone has this verb, and only **2 aor.** and, if genuine, fut. ἀπεχθήσει Alc. 71 (Vulg.), but bracketed by Dind. Nauck, Kirchh. as spurious; ἀπέχθομαι Eur. Hipp. 1260 (Vulg.) has been altered to ἐπάχθομαι from Mss., but the inf. by being often accented on the antepenult ἀπέχθεσθαι, has led to the belief that it is pres. Il. 21, 83; Thuc. 1, 136; Isocr. Epist. 9, 12; Lys. 6, 53; Isae. 2, 30. Fr. 4 (Scheibe); Pl. Rep. 343 (Bekk. Popp. Krüg. B. S.), but ἀπεχθέσθαι always (Elms. Dind. Ast, Benseler.)

'Απιστέω *To disbelieve*, Soph. Aj. 940; Her. 3, 122. 4, 96; Antiph. 3, γ, 4; Thuc. 2, 35: **imp.** ἠπίστουν Pl. Theaet. 144, ἀπίστεον Od. 13, 339: **fut.** -ήσω Soph. Tr. 1183; Eur. Med. 927; Ar. Eccl. 775; Antiph. 5, 16; Pl. Rep. 500: **aor.** ἠπίστησα Her. 6, 108; Lys. 31, 21; Isocr. 17, 30. Epist. 2, 12; ἀπιστήσῃς Soph. Tr. 1224; -ήσειαν Isocr. 12, 73; -ῆσαι Aesch. Pr. 640; Thuc. 1, 91; -στήσας Pl. Apol. 29: **p.** ἠπίστηκα Pl. Soph. 258, &c., reg.: except **fut. m.** ἀπιστήσομαι **pass.** Pl. Rep. 450: **aor. pass.** late, ἀπιστηθείς Plut. Dion. et Brut. 5, see below: **fut. p.** late, ἀπιστηθήσομαι Diod. Sic. Fr. Lib. 32, 11 (Bekk.); D. Laert. 9, 11, 93. **Vb.** ἀπιστητέον Polyb. 4, 41, 8. ἀπιστέος v. r. Xen. An. 2, 6, 8, violates analogy (Poppo). Of the **pass.** form we have seen **pres.** and **imp.** only in classic authors, ἀπιστεῖται Pl. Charm. 168; -οῖτο Rep. 450; -ούμενος Rep. 502; -εῖσθαι Thuc. 7, 44: **imp.** ἠπιστεῖτο Thuc. 5, 68. ἠπιστήθη Her. 3, 15, seems better referred to ἐπίσταμαι.

'Αποδιδράσκω, see διδράσκω.

'Αποδίδωμι *To give back*, Her. 4, 119; Andoc. 3, 39; Isocr. 21, 3, like *simple* δίδωμι: **imp.** -εδίδουν Isocr. 10, 36; Pl. Polit. 273: **fut.** -δώσω Il. 7, 89; Ar. Av. 480; Her. 4, 9; Thuc. 2, 72; Andoc. 3, 34; Lys. 12, 60: **1 aor.** -έδωκα Il. 4, 478; Her. 3, 136; Pl. Gorg. 506; Isocr. 21, 16 &c.: **2 aor.** (-έδων), -έδομεν Pl. Leg. 813, -έδοσαν Isocr. 21, 17; Epic subj. -δῷσι Od. 8, 318; opt. -δοῖτε 22, 61; -δοῦναι Il. 3, 285; Her. 3, 147; Lycurg. 22, Epic δόμεναι, ἀπ- in tmesi Il. 1, 98. **Mid.** ἀποδίδομαι *give away, sell*, Isae. 6, 33; Lycurg. 23; Xen. An. 7, 2, 3: **imp.** -εδίδοντο Dem. 23, 205: **fut.** -δώσομαι Ar. Pax 1259; Aeschin. 1, 29, περι- Od. 23, 78: **2 aor.** ἀπεδόμην Ar. Ach. 542. Av. 17; Her. 1, 70; Thuc. 7, 87; Dem. 37, 17; subj. -δῶνται Xen. Mem. 3, 7, 6, but dual δώμεθον, περι- Il. 23, 485; δόσθαι, ἐκ- Pind. P. 4, 295: (1 aor. late ἀπο-δωκαμένη, *having given back*, Maneth. 5, 126.) Active rare in the sense *to sell*, ἀποδώσειν seems so used Eur. Cycl. 239, ἀπέδοσαν Thuc. 6, 62, where Bekker would prefer ἀπέδοντο, and ἀπόδος Ar. Ran. 1235 (Mss. Vulg. Bergk, Kock, -δου Mss. Dawes, Dind. Mein.); certain however later, Nicet. Chon. p. 574 (Bekk.). The Traged. seem to have confined themselves to the act. form of this verb, with the exception of one instance, ἀπέδοτο *hazarded*, Eur. Or. 652.

(Ἀποέρρω) *To sweep off*, Epic, only 1 aor. ἀπόερσε Il. 6, 348; subj. -οέρσῃ 21, 283; opt. -έρσειε 21, 329; -ερσον Nic. Th. 110. (ŏ in indic.; ō in subj. and opt. by arsis.)

Ἀποθνήσκω, see θνήσκω.

Ἀποκρίνω (ῑ) *To separate*, Com. Fr. (Pher.) 2, 261; Pl. Tim. 73: fut. (-ἴνῶ): aor. -έκρῑνα Pl. Leg. 946: p. (-κέκρῐκα): -κέκρῐμαι Her. 2, 36; Thuc. 1, 3; Pl. Rep. 407: aor. -εκρῐ́θην Archil. 89; Antiph. 4, δ, 8; Thuc. 4, 72; Pl. Leg. 961, Epic -εκρίνθην Il. 5, 12: fut. -κριθήσομαι Pl. Leg. 820. **Mid.** ἀποκρῖνομαι *to answer*, Ar. Pl. 17; Com. Fr. (Diph.) 4, 407; Antiph. 2, δ, 3. 6, 14; Xen. Cyr. 7, 2, 19; Pl. Rep. 351; Isae. 11, 6: imp. ἀπεκρινόμην Thuc. 7, 10; (Dem.) 7, 20: fut. -ἴνοῦμαι Ar. Nub. 1245; Pl. Gorg. 447; Dem. 8, 38; rare in Ion. Her. 8, 101 (Gaisf. Bekk.). 5, 49 (Gaisf.): aor. -εκρῑνάμην Eur. Bacc. 1272; Ar. Vesp. 1433; Thuc. 1, 28; Isocr. 19, 79; Pl. Gorg. 465: p. ἀποκέκρῐμαι act. Xen. An. 2, 1, 15; Pl. Prot. 358. Leg. 673; pass. Leg. 655. Men. 75: plp. ἀπεκέκρῐτο Gorg. 453: aor. ἀπεκρῐ́θην Com. Fr. (Pherecr.) 2, 275, if correct; Athen. (Macho) 13, 45; Theocr. 8, 74; (Pl.) Alcib. (2) 149; Luc. Demon. 26; (v. r. Xen. An. 2, 1, 22, see below); Polyb. 4, 30. 31. 15, 5. 25, 6 (Bekk.); Diod. Sic. 11, 28: late also in this sense fut. ἀποκρῐθήσομαι V. T. Ps. 119, 42; N. T. Matth. 25, 45. **Vb.** ἀποκριτέον *one must separate, reject*, Pl. Rep. 413; but *one must answer*, Alcib. (1) 114. ἀπεκρίθην in the sense of ἀπεκρῑνάμην *answered*, seems not to occur before Machon a Poet of the later Comedy, Athen. 8, 41. 13, 39 (unless ἀποκριθῶ be sound, Com. Fr. (Pherecr.) 2, 275); for Alcib. (1. 2) ascribed to Plato, is held to be spurious. For ἀπο- Hom. always, Her. usually, has ὑποκρίνομαι 1, 2. 78. 91. 164, &c., but ἀποκρίν- 8, 101 (Bekk. Dind. Gaisf.). 5, 49 (Gaisf.), ὑποκρ- (Bekk. Dind.) ἀπεκρίθη is in the best Mss. Xen. An. 2, 1, 22, and adopted by Kühner, but rendered doubtful by ἀπεκρίνατο in sect. 23: ἀπημείφθη quoted by Kühner is not a parallel, as Pind. has ἀμείφθη P. 4, 102. This verb is rare in poetry: once in Epic, ἀποκρινθείς Il. 5, 12, and Lyric -κριθείς Archil. 89 (Bergk), rare in Trag. aor. act.

ἀποκρίνας Soph. O. R. 640 (Mss. Vulg. Ell. Dind. 2 ed., dropped in 5 ed. Nauck); and **mid.** ἀπεκρίνω Eur. I. A. 1354; -κρίναιο Bac. 1272; imper. ἀπόκριναι I. A. 1133; more freq. in Comedy, **pres.** ἀποκρίνετε Com. Fr. (Pher.) 2, 261: **mid.** -όμενος Ar. Plut. 17; -εσθαι Ach. 632: **fut.** -οῦμαι Nub. 1245; Com. Fr. (Eup.) 2, 510. (Men.) 4, 144. 215: ἀπεκρινάμην Ar. Vesp. 964. 1433. Nub. 1244, &c.: ἀποκριθῶ, see above.

'Αποκρούω, see κρούω.

'Αποκρύπτω, see κρύπτω.

'Αποκτείνω *To kill*, Od. 22, 167; Aesch. Ag. 1250; Eur. Ph. 1620; Antiph. 4, α, 2; Pl. Rep. 573: **imp.** -έκτεινον Eur. Ion 1300; Thuc. 3, 81; Xen. Hist. 2, 3, 21: **fut.** -ενῶ Eur. Ph. 1621; Thuc. 4, 28; Lys. 1, 26, Ion. -κτενέω Her. 3, 30: **1 aor.** -έκτεινα Il. 9, 543; Eur. Med. 486; Ar. Av. 85; Her. 8, 38; Antiph. 1, 6. 2, β, 10; Thuc. 1, 30; Lys. 12, 34; Xen. An. 1, 2, 20: **p.** -έκτονα Lys. 10, 7; Isocr. 12, 66; Dem. 22, 2: **plp.** -εκτόνειν Dem. 19, 148, Ion. -εκτόνεε Her. 5, 67, rare and doubtful -εκτόνηκα in *classic* auth. Xen. Hier. 3, 8 (Vulg.); Pl. Ap. 38 (Vulg. but -έκτονα Mss. B V D &c. Stobae. Dind. Bekk. Stallb. &c.); Aristot. Soph. El. 33, 3: **plp.** -εκτονήκει Plut. Timol. 16 (Vulg.), and -έκταγκα Aristot. Pol. 7, 2, 11; Com. Fr. (Men.) 4, 173, later -έκτᾰκα Polyb. 11, 18, see κτείνω: **2 aor.** ἀπ-έκτᾰνον Epic only, Il. 6, 414. Od. 14, 271; Hes. Sc. 11; (Eur.) Rhes. 978; Anth. 11, 228; subj. -κτάνῃ Od. 12, 301, syncop. or from (κτῆμι) ἀπ-έκταν, ἀπέκταμεν Od. 23, 121; inf. ἀποκτάμεναι Il. 20, 165, abbrev. -άμεν Il. 5, 675: Epic also **2 aor. mid.** ἀπ-έκτατο as pass. or as we say *has got himself killed*, Il. 15, 437. 17, 472; -κτάμενος 4, 494. 23, 775; Q. Sm. 10, 3. **Pass.** late, ἀποκτείνεσθαι Palaeph. Incred. 7: **p.** ἀπ-εκταμμένος Apocr. 1 Macc. 5, 51; -εκτάνθαι Polyb. 7, 7; 2 Macc. 4, 36: **aor.** ἀπ-εκτάνθην Dio Cass. 65, 4. Fr. 43; 1 Macc. 2, 9; Dionys. de Av. 1, 3; N. T. Marc. 8, 31. Rev. 9, 18, &c., for which *classic* writers use τέθνηκα, ἔθανον, ἀποτέθνηκα, ἀπέθανον. The pass. form has been overlooked by Lexicogr. Collat. forms **ἀποκτίννῡμι**, -ῡσι Pl. Gorg. 469; Dem. 23, 163, -ῠμεν Pl. Gorg. 468, -ύᾱσι Xen. An. 6, 3, 5; Pl. Gorg. 466; Dem. 23, 142; -νύς Xen. Hell. 5, 3, 2; Pl. Crit. 48; -ῦναι Lys. 12, 7. 36; Xen. Hell. 5, 4, 32; Pl. Phaed. 58; Dem. 23, 74: **imp.** ἀπ-εκτίννῡσαν Xen. An. 6, 5, 28; (Lys.) 20, 9. **ἀποκτιννύω**, -ύουσι Xen. Hell. 4, 4, 2. 7, 4, 26 (Vulg. Breitb. Saupp. -ύασι Dind. *now*, Cob.); subj. -νύῃ Pl. Rep. 565; -νύοι Phaed. 62: **imp.** ἀπ-εκτίννῠον Xen. Hell. 5, 2, 43 (Breitb. Saupp., -ύσαν Dind. Cob.). **ἀποκτέννω** late, Anth. (Nicarch.) 11, 395; v. r. N. T. Matth. 23, 37. Luc. 13, 34: **Pass. imp.** ἀπ-εκτέννοντο V. T. Dan. 2, 13 (Gaisf. Tisch.)

Ἀπολαύω *To enjoy*, Ar. Vesp. 701; Thuc. 1, 70; Isocr. 5, 34; Dem. 23, 210; -ων Lys. 18, 19; Eur. Andr. 543; -ειν H. F. 1224; Isocr. 15, 105: **imp.** ἀπέλαυον Xen. Cyr. 5, 4, 34; Isocr. 1, 9, ἀπήλ- (Vulg. Bekk. ἀπέλ- Bens. Blass, L. Dind.): **fut. m.** ἀπολαύσομαι Ar. Av. 177; Isocr. 15, 305. Epist. 6, 12; Xen. Cyr. 7, 5, 81; Pl. Charm. 172; Luc. D. Deor. 10, 2; Themist. 1, 10: **fut. act.** ἀπολαύσω perhaps late (but Hyperid. Fun. Or. Col. 2, 147, if correct); Dio Hal. Ant. 6, 4. 15; Luc. Herm. 78; Plut. Pyr. 13. Mor. 776; Dio Cass. 43, 18. 52, 18; D. Sic. 2, 55; Herodn. 1, 6, 2 (Bekk.); Themist. 21, 247. 26, 330; Heliod. 7, 18; Joseph. Ant. 8, 11, 2, see below: **aor.** ἀπέλαυσα Eur. I. T. 526; Ar. Av. 1358; Her. 6, 86; Lys. 28, 6; Isocr. 16, 37. 19, 21; Dem. 48, 28: **p.** ἀπολέλαυκα Ar. Thesm. 1008; Com. Fr. (Pl.) 2, 671; Isocr. 15, 195. 19, 23; Aeschin. 1, 56: **p. p.** late, ἀπολέλαυται Philostr. Apoll. 6, 19, but -λελαυσμένος Plut. Mor. 1089. 1099: **aor.** ἀπελαύσθην late, -αυσθῆναι Phil. vol. 1, p. 37, 45. **Mid.** see below. **Vb.** ἀπολαυστός Plut. Arist. Cat. 4. The augm. with η seems late, and is disapproved by Herodian: ἀπήλαυον Schol. Aesch. Ag. 559; and Alciphr. 3, 53 (Vulg. but ἀπελ- Mein.): ἀπήλαυσα Ael. V. H. 12, 25 (ἀπελ- Herch.); Eunap. 131, 17; Schol. Aesch. Pr. 28; Dio. Hal. 1, 6. 2, 55. 76 (Ms. Urb. approved by Kiessl., ἀπέλ- Vulg.); Themist. 6, 76. 13, 167. 172. 16, 212 &c., ἀπελ- (Dind. always.) The earliest instance we know of **fut. act.** is ἀπολαύσομεν Hyperid. Or. Funebr. Col. 11, 142 (Bab.) This however we think a false reading for -σόμεθα, both because the classic writers invariably use the mid. form, and because the identical blunder occurs Pl. Charm. 172, where Par. E. alone of all the Mss. presents ἀπολαύσομεν, the rest, and all editions ἀπολαυσόμεθα. Cobet, strange to say, retains the Ms. reading because, says he, "utraque forma usu trita est." Each may be *trita*, but still keep to its *own walk*. **Aor. m.** ἀπελαυσάμην Ar. Av. 1358 (Br.) is a creation of Reiske's, and silently adopted by Brunck for ἀπέλαυσα the reading of the Mss. and all previous and subsequent editions; and inf. -λαύσασθαι, which used to stand Themist. Or. 9, 124, has been displaced by **fut.** -λαύσεσθαι (Dind.); but still in text subj. ἀπολαύσωμαι Aristaen. 2, 5 (Pauw, -σομαι ed. Samb. approved by Pauw, now -σαίμεν Hercher.) This verb is never in Epic; in Trag. Eur. only; oft in Comedy.

Ἀπόλλῡμι, -ύω, see ὄλλῡμι.

Ἀπολογέομαι Dep. *To make a defence*, Ar. Thesm. 188; Her. 7, 161; Antiph. 3, δ, 4; Thuc. 3, 62: **imp.** ἀπελογεῖτο Antiph. 2, β, 13; Thuc. 6, 29; Dem. 33, 32, Ion. -έετο Her. 6, 136:

fut. -ήσομαι Ar. Vesp. 949; Antiph. 1, 7; Thuc. 8, 85; Lys. 10, 6; Isocr. 18, 40: aor. ἀπελογησάμην Xen. An. 5, 6, 3; Lys. 22, 3; Dem. 34, 42; -σηται Thuc. 8, 109; -σάμενος 8, 68; Antiph. 5, 13; -σασθαι Eur. Bac. 41; Antiph. 5, 60; Lys. 9, 17: p. ἀπολελόγημαι act. Antiph. 5, 85; Andoc. 1, 33; Isocr. 12, 218, and pass. Andoc. 1, 70; Pl. Rep. 607: plp. ἀπελελόγητο act. Dio Cass. 40, 54: aor. ἀπελογήθην act. Antiph. 2, γ, 1 (Polyb. 23, 12); -ηθῆναι Antiph. 2, δ, 3; Com. Fr. (Alex.) 3, 388; -ηθείς Antiph. 3, γ, 2. 4, γ, 1, but pass. (?) Xen. Hell. 1, 4, 13: as 3 fut. ἀπολελογημένος ἔσομαι Andoc. 1, 72. Vb. ἀπολογητέον Antiph. 4, δ, 1. After the instances quoted of aor. pass. it is rather curious to find Cobet asserting "Attici omnes dicebant ἀπελογήσατο, deterrimus quisque sequiorum forma vitiosa ἀπελογήθη utitur" (Novae Lect. p. 307). An older than he has been more merciful, ἀπολογηθῆναι, ἀντὶ τοῦ ἀπολογήσασθαι· Ἄλεξις Ἀμπελουργῷ (Bekk. Anecd. p. 82). This verb is mostly prosaic, never in Epic, once in Trag.

'Απολογίζομαι *To reckon up, recount,* Dep. mid. Pl. Phil. 25: imp. ἀπελογ- Xen. Hell. 6, 1, 3; Aeschin. 3, 25: fut. -ιοῦμαι Dio Cass. Fr. 109 (Bekk.): aor. -ελογισάμην Pl. Soph. 261; Dem. 24, 108, Dor. -ιξάμην Inscr. vol. 2, p. 24 (Boeckh): p. -λελογισμένα pass. Xen. Oec. 9, 8, but act. ἀπολελόγισμαι Dio. Hal. ad Cn. Pomp. 1; Inscr. vol. 1, p. 157 (Boeckh), missed by Lexicogr. This verb is almost entirely prosaic; ἀπολογίζεται if correct Ar. Fr. 79 (Vulg. Dind. 2 ed.) is perhaps the only exception, but λογίζ- (Dind. 5 ed. with Dobree.) The act. -λογίζειν Ar. Fr. 185 (D.), and -γίζων Com. Fr. (Antiph.) 3, 70, have been altered to ἀπολοπίζειν, -ων by Fritzsche, Meineke, and now Dind. (5 edit.)

'Απομιμνήσκω, see μιμνήσκω.

'Απονοοῦμαι, see νοέω.

'Αποπατέω *To turn aside,* Com. Fr. (Crat.) 2, 48; Ar. Eccl. 351; Hippocr. 7, 100: fut. mid. -πατήσομαι Ar. Plut. 1184: but -πατήσω Hippocr. 7, 100 (Lit. 2, 237 Erm.); Galen 7, 790, ἐναπο- if correct, Com. Fr. (Polyz.) 2, 869, περιπατήσεις Com. Fr. (Antiph.) 3, 21; Xen. Conv. 9, 7, συμπεριπατ- Com. Fr. (Men.) 4, 104: aor. ἀπεπάτησα Hippocr. 2, 367 (Kühn); subj. -πατήσω 7, 114 (Lit.); Ar. Eccl. 354. Vb. ἀποπατητέον Ar. Eccl. 326. In Attic, πατέω and compds. have invariably, we think, fut. act. πατήσεις Ar. Eq. 166 &c., except ἀποπατέω which, in Attic, occurs once only in the fut., but indisputably in the mid. form ἀποπατησόμενοι Ar. quoted.

'Αποπειράω *To make trial of,* act. rare, (Luc.) Amor. 26: fut. -άσω Thuc. 6, 90: aor. -επείρᾱσα 4, 135. Mid. ἀποπειράομαι

Ar. Nub. 477; Andoc. 1, 105; Thuc. 4, 24: **imp.** -επειρᾶτο Her. 3, 119: fut. -άσομαι Ar. Ran. 648: but **aor. p.** as **mid.** -άθην Isocr. 18, 39; Aristot. H. An. 9, 32, 10, Ion. -ήθην Her. 2, 73. In classic Greek we think all the compds. take **aor. pass.** See πειράω.

Ἀποπῦρίζω (πῦρ) *To roast and eat*, Dor. 1 pl. -πυρίζομες Epicharm. 82 (Ahrens); -πυρίζων Hesych. πυρίζω *simple* seems not to occur.

Ἀπορέω *To be at a loss*, Soph. O. R. 485; Her. 1, 75. 191; Antiph. 2, δ, 1; Thuc. 6, 42; Isocr. 7, 9, Dor. 1 pl. ἀπορίομες Xen. Hell. 1, 1, 23: **imp.** ἠπόρουν Her. 3, 78; Lys. 19, 21; Pl. Prot. 321: **fut.** -ήσω Ar. Eccl. 664; Lys. 7, 23; Isocr. 8. 139: **aor.** ἠπόρησα Thuc. 1, 63; Isocr. 10, 12; ἀπορήσῃ Ar. Vesp. 590; -σειε Isocr. 5, 100: **p.** ἠπόρηκα Pl. Soph. 244, προ- Aristot. Met. 2, 1, 3: **p. p.** ἠπόρημαι Aristot. Pol. 3, 10, 5; (Luc.) Philop. 1, δι- Pl. Soph. 250, προ- Aristot. Phys. 4, 1, 2: **aor.** ἠπορήθην Pl. Leg. 799. **Mid.** and **pass.** as **mid.** ἀπορέομαι *to doubt*, or *be doubted*, &c. Xen. Lac. 13, 7; ἀπορῆται Com. Fr. (Antiph.) 3, 66; Ion. -εύμενος Her. 2, 121, -εόμενα **pass.** Hippocr. 1, 572 (Lit.); -έεσθαι Hippocr. 1, 242 (Erm.): **imp.** ἠπορούμην Lys. 3, 10: **fut.** -ήσομαι Aristot. Eth. Mag. 2, 3, 16; Sext. Emp. 479: **p.** ἠπόρημαι Eur. I. A. 537; **pass.** Aristot. Nat. Ausc. 4, 9, 3; Aristid. 26, 328 (Jebb, -ρησα Mss. Dind.); Sext. Emp. 479; ἠπορημένος Com. Fr. (Anon.) 4, 692, **pass.** (Luc.) Philop. 1, δι- Pl. Soph. 250: **aor.** ἠπορήθην Hippocr. 4, 212; Dem. 27, 53, **pass.** Pl. Leg. 799; Aristot. Eth. Mag. 2, 6, 45. Pol. 8, 6: **fut. p.** -ηθήσομαι, συν- Sext. Emp. 477 (Bekk.) This verb seems not to occur in Epic; rarely in Trag. **pres. act.** in Soph.; **pres. act.** and **perf. pass.** in Eur.: the **futures m.** and **p.** somehow appear rather late: **aor. mid.** simple or comp. we have not seen.

Ἀποστερέω *To rob, bereave*, Aesch. Pr. 777; Her. 6, 65; Antiph. 4, β, 7; Thuc. 1, 69; Pl. Leg. 721; Isae. 9, 23: **imp.** ἀπεστερ- Antiph. 5, 35. 62; Lys. 15, 5: **fut.** -ήσω Isae. 1, 18. 8, 43; Dem. 23, 135: **perf.** -εστέρηκα Soph. Ph. 1283; Her. 5, 106; Thuc. 7, 6; Isocr. 14, 35 &c.: **fut. mid.** -στερήσομαι as pass. Eur. H. F. 137; Thuc. 6, 91; Dem. 24, 210. 39, 11. 40, 10: and **fut. p.** -στερηθήσομαι Lys. 12, 70; Dem. 1, 22; Isocr. 7, 34 (Ms. U. Bekk. B. S. -στερήσομσι Vulg. Bensl. Blass.) ἀποστερεῖσθε Andoc. 1, 149, called **fut. m.** as if from -στέρομαι, may be **pres.** See στερέω.

Ἀποστρέφω *To turn away*, Aesch. Ag. 1306; Her. 4, 188; Dem. 19, 208: **fut.** -έψω Il. 10, 355; Soph. O. R. 1154; Xen. M. Eq. 1, 12; Pl. Soph. 239: **aor.** -έστρεψα Aesch. Ag.

850; Eur. Med. 1148; Her. 4, 52; Thuc. 5, 75; Isocr. 16, 20, iter. ἀποστρέψασκε Il. 22, 197; Epic subj. -στρέψῃσι Il. 15, 62 &c.: p. p. -έστραμμαι Her. 7, 160; Xen. Cyr. 6, 2, 17: plp. 3 pl. Ion. -εστράφατο Her. 1, 166. **Mid.** ἀποστρέφομαι *to turn oneself away, avoid,* Eur. I. T. 801; Pl. Rep. 515: fut. -στρέψομαι Xen. Cyr. 5, 5, 36; Plut. Mor. 387: aor. -εστρέψαντο late (unless sound Hermes. 83 Mss. Vulg., -ετρέψαντο Mss. Schneidew.); V. T. Osea 8, 3; 3 Macc. 3, 23: with p. p. -έστραμμαι Euen. 2, 5 (Bergk); Her. 7, 160; Luc. Calumn. 14: and aor. -εστράφην Eur. Supp. 159; Soph. O. C. 1272; Ar. Plut. 702; Xen. Cyr. 5, 5, 6; Dem. 18, 159: fut. p. late -στραφήσομαι Artemid. Onir. 1, 79; V. T. Num. 32, 22. Amos 1, 3. 6. 13, &c. The act. is occasionally intrans. ἀποστρέφειν Dinarch. 2, 23: aor. -στρέψας Xen. Hell. 3, 4, 12, iter. ἀποστρέψασκε Od. 11, 597. The aor. m. and fut. p. have been missed by Lexicogr.

'Αποστυγέω, see στυγέω.

'Απούρας, -ουράμενος, see ἀπαυράω.

'Αποχράω *To be sufficient,* seldom personal, in Att. contr. in η, ἀπόχρη Ar. Av. 1603, 3 pl. ἀποχρῶσι Her. 5, 31; ἀποχρῶν Com. Fr. (Pher.) 2, 327; (Pl.) Alc. (2) 145, -ῶσα Ar. Fr. 417, Dor. and Ion. -χρέω, 1 pers. in Epicharm. only, Fr. 114 (Ahr. see part. ἀποχρεώμενος Her. 1, 37): imp. -έχρη Pl. Phaedr. 275, -έχρα Her. 1, 66: fut. -χρήσει Pl. Polit. 279, -χρήσουσι Ar. Pl. 484: aor. ἀπέχρησε Her. 7, 196; Isocr. 4, 97. Pass. or mid. ἀποχράομαι *to be contented,* Dem. 17, 13, Ion. -έομαι, others -έωμαι Her. 1, 37, see 1, 34; -χρῆσθαι Thuc. 1, 68: imp. ἀπεχρᾶτο Aristot. Oec. 2, 21, 7; Her. 1, 102 (Aldin. &c. Gaisf. Bred. Stein, Abicht), but ἀπεχρῆτο (Ms. S. Bekk. Dind.), -εχρέετο (Schaef.), which Gaisf. Bekk. Dind. Lhardy have at 8, 14, -εχρῶντο Thuc. 3, 81 (Popp. Goell.); part. ἀποχρεώμενος Her. 1, 37 (Gaisf. Bekk. Dind. Stein, Lhardy), -εόμενος (Ms. S. Bredow, Dietsch, Abicht): aor. m. ἀπεχρήσαντο *used up, destroyed, killed,* only Ar. Fr. 328 (D.); ἀποχρήσασθε in usual sense, Thuc. 6, 17; -ασθαι Luc. Catapl. 2: p. ἀποκεχρημέναι Aristot. Oec. 2, 22. This verb is generally impers., and when pers. seldom goes beyond the 3 sing. and pl. ἀπόχρη Aesch. Ag. 1574; Isocr. 5, 28; Pl. Rep. 380, Ion. ἀποχρᾷ Her. 9, 79; inf. -χρῆν Com. Fr. (Antiph.) 3, 87; Dem. 4, 22; Luc. Hermot. 24; Aristid. 34, 443 (D.), Ion. -χρᾶν Her. 3, 138. 6, 137: imp. ἀπέχρη Isocr. 5, 72; Pl. Phaedr. 275, Ion. -έχρα Her. 1, 66: fut. ἀποχρήσειν Her. 8, 130: aor. ἀπέχρησε Isocr. 12, 79. Pass. or mid. imp. ἀπεχρέετο Her. 8, 14 (Bekk. Dind. -χρᾶτο Dietsch, Stein, Abicht, Bred.)

This compd. is not in Epic, once in Trag., rare in Comedy. In Her. Bredow, Abicht, &c. would always contract αε of this verb in α: ἀπεχρᾶτο, not -ῆτο, nor -έετο, and change α before ο, ω, into ε, -χράουσι, -έουσι, -χράονται, -χρέονται, -χραόμενος, -χρεόμενος, not -έωνται, -εώμενος; subj. -χράωνται, -έωνται. In the Mss. there appears an occasional tendency to slide into the contr. of αε in η for α, but whether by Her. or an innocent or learned copyist it is difficult to decide.

Ἅπτω *To fasten, kindle*, Eur. Or. 1543; Ar. Nub. 768; ἅπτειν Pl. Crat. 417, προτι- Il. 24, 110; pt. rare, ἅπτων, ἐξ- Il. 24, 51; Eur. Or. 383: **imp.** ἧπτον Ar. Nub. 57, ἐξ- Il. 22, 397, ἀν- Od. 12, 179, προσ- Pl. Rep. 400: **fut.** ἅψω Aesch. Ch. 868; Com. Fr. (Anax.) 3, 193, συν- Soph. Aj. 1317; Eur. Bac. 545; Xen. An. 1, 5, 16; ἀν- Orest. 1137: **aor.** ἧψα Simon. C. 99; Eur. Hel. 503; Ar. Ran. 505; Thuc. 2, 77, ἀν- Od. 3, 274, ὑπ- Her. 1, 176; ἅψωμεν Aesch. Eum. 307; ἅψαις, συν- Eur. Bac. 747; part. ἅψας Od. 21, 408; inf. ἅψαι Pind. I. 4, 43: **p. p.** ἧμμαι Eur. Hel. 107; Ar. Pl. 301; Thuc. 4, 100, ἐφ- Il. 7, 402, ἀν- Od. 12, 51, Ion. ἅμμ- Her. 1, 86, ἀπ- 2, 121, ἐπ- 8, 105: but plp. ἐφ-ῆπτο Il. 6, 241, συν-ῆπτο Her. 6, 93. 7, 158: **aor.** ἥφθην Thuc. 4, 133, Ion. ἅφ- Her. 1, 19, Epic ἑάφ- or ἐάφ- ἐπι in tmesi Il. 13, 543, referred by Curtius to ἕπομαι: **fut.** late ἁφθήσομαι, συν- Nicol. Rhet. 11, 14; Galen 3, 311, ἀνα- 7, 17: **2 aor.** ἥφην, ἁφῇ Aristot. Nat. Ausc. 8, 4, 8; ἁφῆναι D. Chrys. 36, p. 93 (Reiske). **Mid.** ἅπτομαι *to touch*, &c. Od. 10, 379; Pind. N. 8, 14; Soph. O. C. 1550; Ar. Eq. 1237; Her. 3, 109; Antiph. 6, 40; Thuc. 2, 50; Pl. Theaet. 189; ἁπτοίμην Pl. Lys. 208, Dor. ἁπτοίμαν, ἐφ- Pind. N. 8, 36: **imp.** ἡπτόμην Il. 8, 67. 11, 85. 20, 468; Thuc. 2, 17; Lys. 3, 37, Ion. ἁπτ- Her. 3, 137. 6, 70; Il. 2, 171 (Vulg. La Roche, ἡπτ- now Bekk.), but still καθαπτ- Il. 15, 127 (Bekk. La R.): **fut.** ἅψομαι Od. 19, 344; Soph. O. C. 830; Eur. An. 758; Her. 1, 198; Lys. 1, 36; Pl. Euthyd. 283: **aor.** ἡψάμην Il. 5, 799; Aesch. Ag. 1608; Eur. Med. 370; Thuc. 1, 97; Pl. Menex. 244, καθ- Solon 32, 3, Dor. -άμαν, ἐφ- Eur. Elec. 1225 (chor.), Ion. ἁψάμ- Il. 10, 377. 23, 666; Simon. (Am.) 1, 18; Her. 1, 19, ἐφ- Pind. P. 8, 60: with **p.** ἧμμαι Soph. Tr. 1009; Pl. Phaedr. 260; Dem. 21, 155. 51, 5. **Vb.** ἁπτός Pl. Rep. 525, ἁπτέος Com. Fr. (Alex.) 3, 498; Pl. Rep. 377.—In Epic, the act., especially the *simple* form, is very rare: Hom. aor. only ἅψας Od. 21, 408 quoted; in comp. προτιάπτω for προσ- Il. 24, 110, ἐξάπτων 24, 51: **imp.** ἐξῆπτεν 22, 397, ἀν- Od. 12, 179: **aor.** ἀνῆψεν 3, 274: **p. p.** ἐφῆπται Il. 2, 15. 32. 69. Od. 22, 41; ἀν-ήφθω 12, 162: ἐφῆπτο Il. 6, 241. Od. 22, 331:

mid. aor. 2 sing. subj. ἐφάψεαι Od. 5, 348. Hes. Theogn. Ap. Rh. Bion, Moschus, and Orpheus have not the **act.**: in prose, too, it is rare. Her. augments **aor. act.** and **plp. pass.**, but never, we think, the **imp.** and **aor. mid.**, nor the **perf.** and **aor. pass.** simple or compd.

'Απΰω *To emit a sound*, Pind. P. 2, 19; Aesch. Pr. 593. Pers. 124 (chor.); Ar. Eq. 1023 (trimet.), Epic ἠπ- Il. 14, 399. Od. 10, 83; ἀπύοι Soph. Aj. 887 (chor.); ἀπύων Pind. Ol. 5, 19, ἠπ- Mosch. 2, 124: **imp.** ἤπΰον Od. 9, 399; Ap. Rh. 4, 71, Dor. ἄπυ- Pind. Ol. 1, 72; Aesch. Sept. 206 chor. (Lachm. Dind. 5 ed.); Anth. (Leon. Tar.) 9, 99: **fut.** ἀπΰσω Eur. Bacc. 984 (chor.); Her. 2, 15 (Ald. Vulg. ἀπήσ- *now*): **aor.** ἤπῡσα Eur. Rhes. 776 (trimeter); subj. ἠπύσω Orph. Arg. 6; **imper.** 'ᾱπύσατε Eur. Supp. 800. **Mid.** ἀπυέσθω Inscr. Arcad. 2, (ᾱ). **Pres.** Ar. Eq. 1023 (trimeter) and ἤπυσα Eur. Rhes. quoted; it is therefore a mistake to say "this verb occurs only in the choral odes." (ᾱ, ῠ in **pres.** and **imp.**, but ἠπΰοντες Mosch. 2, 124, ἀνηπῠ- 98, ῡ in **fut.** and **aor.**)

'Απωθέω, see ὠθέω.

'Αρᾰβέω *To ring, rattle*, only **pres.** ἀρᾰβεῖ Epich. 9, 2 (Ahr.); pt. ἀραβεῦσαι Hes. Sc. 249: and **aor.** ἀράβησε Il. 17, 50. Od. 24, 525; Ap. Rh. 2, 281; Theocr. 22, 126.

'Αράομαι *To pray*, Dep. Il. 9, 240; Aesch. Sept. 633; Soph. Aj. 509; Ar. Thesm. 350; Plut. Crass, 16, ἐπ- Pl. Leg. 684, Ion ἀρέομαι Her. 3, 65; so Pind. P. 1, 75: **imp.** ἠρώμην, -ρῶ Od. 18, 176, -ρᾶτο Il. 10, 277; Aesch. Pr. 912; Soph. Ant. 428, -ῶντο Her. 8, 94, κατ- Hipponax 11 (B.): **fut.** ἀρᾶσομαι perhaps late in *simple* V. T. Num. 23, 8 (Alex.), ἐπ- Dem. 54, 38 (corr. S. Wolf, Bekk. Dind.), κατ- (Dem.) 25, 100, Ion. ἀρήσομαι Od. 2, 135: **aor. m.** ἠρᾱσάμην Soph. O. R. 1291; Eur. Hipp. 1168; Ap. Rh. 1, 1176 (unaugm. 'ἀράσαντο Sapph. 51 Bergk); rare in prose Andoc. 1, 31; late, Plut. Pelop. 20, but ἐπ- Isocr. 4, 156, κατ- Xen. An. 7, 7, 48; Lys. 6, 51; Dem. 22, 77, Ion. ἠρησάμην Il. 23, 144; Her. 3, 124; subj. -ήσομαι, for -ωμαι, Il. 9, 172; opt. -ησαίατο Od. 1, 164: **p.** in comp. ἐπ-ήρᾱμαι Dem. 18, 142, but **pass.** κατ-ηραμένος *accursed*, Plut. Lucull. 18; V. T. 4 Reg. 9, 34. N. T. Matth. 25, 41, with double augm. κεκατηρ- Num. 22, 6. Syr. 3, 16. Deut. 21, 23 (Vulg. Tisch. κεκαταραμ- Mai): **aor.** late κατηρᾱ́θην, -αραθείη V. T. Job 3, 5. 24, 18.—The Epic inf. ἀρήμεναι Od. 22, 322, is said by some to be a contraction for ἀραέμεναι = ἀρᾶν: Buttm. is inclined to think it an inf. **2 aor. pass.** for ἀρῆναι, from obsol. ἄρομαι. For **fut.** ἐπαράσεσθαι Dem. 54, 38 (Bekk. Dind.), several Mss. and Edit. have **aor.** -άσασθαι (B. S., &c.) **Vb.** ἀρᾱτός Soph. Ant. 972, -ητός Il. 17, 37.

(Initial ᾱ Epic, ᾰ Attic, second ᾱ before ς.) This verb in the *simple* form seems to occur once only in classic prose.

Ἀραρίσκω (ἄρω) *To fit*, Poetic, imp. ἀράρισκε Od. 14, 23; Theocr. 25, 103: fut. (ἀρῶ, Ion. ἄρσω Hesych.): **1 aor.** ἦρσα, ἐπ- Il. 14, 167, συν- Q. Sm. 3, 100, ἄρσε Od. 21, 45; imper. ἄρσον 2, 289, -ετε Ap. Rh. 2, 1062; ἄρσας Il. 1, 136: **p. p.** ἀρήρεμαι late in *simple*, ἀρηρέμενος accented as **pres.** Ap. Rh. 3, 833 (Merk. -εμένος Ms. G. Well.), -άμενος Opp. C. 2, 384; Q. Sm. 2, 265. 3, 632. 4, 149 and always; subj. προσ-αρήρεται, for -ηται, Hes. Op. 431: **plp.** ἠρήρειντο Ap. Rh. 3, 1398 (Merk.): **aor.** ἤρθην, 3 pl. ἄρθεν, for ἤρθησαν, Il. 16, 211: **2 p.** intrans. ἄρᾱρα Pind. N. 3, 64; Aesch. Pr. 60; Eur. Or. 1330. Andr. 255; -αρώς Pind. I. 2, 19; Eur. Elec. 948; *simple* late in prose ἄραρεν Luc. Pisc. 3. Catapl. 8; -ρώς Plut. Dion. 32; but προσαραρέναι Xen. Hell. 4, 7, 6, Ion. ἄρηρα Od. 5, 248 (Wolf, ἄρασσε Bekk. La R. Dind.); Anth. 6, 163; Opp. Hal. 3, 559, συν- H. Hym. 1, 164; subj. ἀρήρῃ Od. 5, 361; ἀρηρώς Il. 4, 134; Hes. Th. 608; Emped. 202; Theocr. 25, 113, ἐπ- (Hipp.) Epist. 9, 366 (Lit.): **plp.** ἀρήρειν Il. 10, 265. 16, 139. Od. 17, 4; Ap. Rh. 1, 957, and ἠρήρ- Il. 12, 56; Archil. 94: **2 aor.** redupl. ἤρᾰρον trans. and intrans. Il. 23, 712. Od. 4, 777. 5, 95, and ἄρᾰρ- Il. 16, 214; Soph. Elec. 147 (chor.); -άρῃ Il. 16, 212; -αρών Od. 5, 252; ἀρᾰρεῖν Simon. (C.) 41 (Bergk.) **Mid. fut.** ἄρσονται Lycophr. 995: **1 aor.** ἀρσάμενος act. Hes. Sc. 320: **2 aor.** late and **pass.** (ἠρᾰρόμην), opt. ἀρᾰροίατο Ap. Rh. 1, 369; but early if ἄρμενος be the syncop. part. of unredupl. (ἠρόμην) Il. 18, 600. Od. 5, 234. 254; Hes. Th. 639. Op. 407. 632; Pind. Ol. 8, 73. N. 3, 58; Hippocr. 3, 420 (Lit.); Theocr. 30, 9, ἅρμ- (Ahr.), rather than, as some say, part. of an unredupl. p. p. ἦρμαι. **Vb.** προσ-αρτέος Hippocr. 2, 678 (Lit.) ἀρᾰρυῖα **2 p.** part. Epic, for ἀρᾱρ-, Il. 5, 744. 12, 454. Od. 6, 70, but ἀρηρυῖα Hes. Th. 608. ἄρηρεν trans. Od. 5, 248 (Wolf), has been changed on Ms. authority to ἄρασσεν (Nitzsch, Bekk. Dind. La Roche).

Ἀράσσω *To strike* (ῥάσσω), Aesch. Pr. 58; Callim. Apoll. 3, ἀπ- Her. 5, 112, κατ- Aristot. Mund. 2, 13, ἀράττω Luc. Luct. 12; Dio. Hal. 1, 79: imp. ἤραττον Ar. Eccl. 977, -ασσον Soph. O. R. 1276, ἄρασσε Od. 5, 248, iter. ἀράσσεσκον Pind. P. 4, 226: **fut.** ἀραξῶ Dor. Theocr. 2, 159, in tmesi συν... ἀράξω Il. 23, 673, ἐξ- Ar. Thesm. 704: **aor.** ἤραξα Anth. 6, 217; Opp. Hal. 3, 558; Babr. 115, ἀπ- Il. 14, 497; Her. 8, 90, ἐξ- Ar. Eq. 641, κατ- Hipponax 38 (B.); Her. 9, 69; Dem. 23, 165, ἐπ- Pl. Prot. 314, ἄραξα Hes. Sc. 461, ξυν- in tmesi Il. 12, 384, ἀπο- 16, 324, Dor. ἅρ- Theocr. 2, 6; ἀράξητε, ἀπ- Thuc. 7, 63; -ειεν, ἐκ-

Simon. Am. 7, 17; ἀράξας Soph. Ant. 52; Eur. I. T. 1308; Lycophr. 15, ἐσ- Her. 4, 128: **p.p.** ἀρήρακται, συν- Hesych.: **aor. pass.** ἠράχθην, ἀραχθέν Soph. Ant. 973 (D.); Arr. An. 7, 19, 2, συν- Her. 7, 170, κατ- ηράχθη Thuc. 7, 6, συν-αράχθη in tmesi Od. 5, 426: **pres.** ἀράσσονται Ap. R. 4, 762; -σόμενος 2, 553; Her. 6, 44: **imp.** ἠράσσοντο Aesch. Pers. 460. **Mid. fut.** κατ-αράξεσθαι or καταρρ- **pass.** Plut. Caes. 44, missed by Lexicogr. This verb in *simple* does not occur in good Attic prose, and Her. has, we think, only **pres. pass.** ἀρασσόμενοι 6, 44.

Ἄρδω *To water*, Pind. Ol. 5, 12; Aesch. Pers. 806; Ar. Lys. 384; Her. 2, 18; Pl. Phaedr. 255; Xen. An. 2, 3, 13, Dor. 3 pl. -δοντι Pind. I. 6, 64: **imp.** ἦρδε Pl. Tim. 76, iter. ἄρδεσκε Her. 2, 13: **fut.** (ἄρσω): **aor.** ἦρσα Her. 5, 12; subj. ἄρσῃ 2, 14; ἄρσας H. Hym. 9, 3; Her. 2, 14. 5, 12. **Pass.** ἄρδομαι Her. 2, 13; Com. Fr. (Eubul.) 3, 266; Pl. Phaedr. 251; -ηται ibid.; -οιτο Tim. 77; -ομένη Ar. Nub. 282; (Pl.) Locr. 101, -όμενον Her. 1, 193. 7, 109; Pl. Tim. 78. Crat. 414. **Mid.** ἀρδόμενοι *drinking*, or **pass.** *watered*, H. Hym. 2, 85.—This verb, in Attic, seems to have only **pres.** and **imp. act.** and **pres. pass.** The collat. form **ἀρδεύω** is very rare in classic writers, perhaps only Aesch. Pr. 852; later Theophr. H. P. 7, 5, 2; Diod. Sic. 1, 34: **fut.** -εύσω Ael. H. A. 5, 52 (Schneid. ἐπ- Herch.); Geop. 3, 11; Or. Sib. 12, 120; Nonn. 42, 283: **aor.** ἤρδευσα Or. Sib. 9, 310; Diod. Sic. 2, 48; Geop. 10, 22: **aor. pass.** ἀρδευθῇ Aesop 166 (Halm): **pres. pass.** ἀρδεύεται Theophr. H. P. 4, 4, 3; -όμενα Aristot. H. A. 8, 19, 1, -ενοι Polyb. 10, 28. **Vb.** ἀρδευτέον Geop. 9, 11.

Ἀρέσκω *To please*, Bias 1, 1 (Bergk); Soph. Aj. 584; Ar. Ran. 103; Her. 1, 89; Thuc. 1, 128: **imp.** ἤρεσκον Soph. Aj. 1243; Her. 3, 142; Thuc. 6, 24; Lys. 12, 50; Isocr. 15, 96; Aeschin. 2, 161: **fut.** ἀρέσω Dem. 39, 33; (Pl. Leg. 702 Vulg.); Anth. 12, 248; Ap. Civ. 1, 12, ἀρέσσετε, συν- Ap. Rh. 3, 901: **aor.** ἤρεσα Soph. El. 409; Ar. Eq. 359; Her. 3, 63; Pl. Prot. 361, ἄρεσσα Ap. Rh. 3, 301; ἀρέσῃ Pl. Leg. 801; -σειεν Isocr. 2, 46; ἀρέσαι Il. 19, 138; Xen. Mem. 2, 3, 6: **p.** late ἀρήρεκα Sext. Emp. 852, 29: **aor. p.** ἠρέσθην active? -θείην Soph. Ant. 500, see below; late prose ἠρέσθη **pass.** Joseph. Ant. 12, 9, 6; ἀρεσθείς Paus. Cor. 2, 13, 8; Plotin. 1, 8; Geop. 5, 6. This **aor.** can be held active in Soph. quoted, only if ἀρεσθείην, the emendation of Hermann, be taken for -είη the reading of the Mss. and Dind. **Mid.** ἀρέσκομαι *to conciliate*, Xen. Mem. 4, 3, 16; Her. 1, 8. 9, 79; Plut. Mor. 4. Alex. 53: **imp.** ἠρέσκοντο Her. 6, 128: **fut.** ἀρέσομαι Aesch. Sup. 655, Poet. ἀρέσσ- Il. 4, 362. Od. 8, 402: **aor.** ἠρεσάμην, Poet. ἀρέσ- Hes. Sc. 255; ἐξ-αρέσηται (Dem.) 60, 25; ἀρεσάσθω Il. 19, 179, ἀρεσσ- Od. 8,

396; ἀρεσάμενος Dio. Hal. 1, 88; Parthen. 6, ἀρεσσ- Il. 9, 112; Theogn. 762; ἀρέσασθαι Jos. Jud. B. 1, 16, 7, ἐξ- (Dem.) 60, 26, which last, however, has no act. form, Epic ἀρεσσ-, ἀπ- Il. 19, 183. **Vb.** ἀρεστός Her. 1, 119. In classic prose the **mid.** is very rare, the **pass.** scarcely beyond the **pres.** ἀρέσκομαι Thuc. 1, 129; -ηται 1, 35; -όμενος Her. 3, 34; Thuc. 2, 68; -εσθαι 5, 4: ἠρέσκοντο Her. 4, 78. 9, 66; Thuc. 5, 37. 8, 84. **Perf. p.** ἤρεσμαι we have never seen, except in lexicons. In Her. Gaisf. always augm. this verb, except ἀρέσκετο 9, 66, though ἠρέσκ- is presented by several Mss. Bekk. Dind. Bred. Stein always augment.

'Αρετάω *To be fit, to prosper*, Epic and only 3 sing. ἀρετᾷ Od. 8, 329, and pl. ἀρετῶσι 19, 114. Occas. in very late prose, Philo, Procop. &c.

'Αρημένος *oppressed*, an Epic def. perf. p. Il. 18, 435. Od. 6, 2. (ā.) The derivation is uncertain. Thiersch says it is from root ϝαρε, whence βαρύς, βαρέ-ος, and bairan, bar (Goth.) to bear, bore, and with the strengthening α (ἀϝαρημένος, ἀαρημένος) ἀρημένος. Others suppose it may be abbreviated from βεβαρημένος by β as representing the digamma (ϝεϝαρημένος, βεβαρ-, as ϝρόδον, βρόδον, ῥόδ-) disappearing, ἀαρημένος, contr. ἀρημένος. We think Homeric usage against this. He has βεβαρηότες, -ηότα Od. 3, 139. 19, 122, when he might have used ἀρηότες. Besides, does β ever represent the digamma in Hom.?

'Αρθμέω (ἀρθμός) *To unite, join*, Epic, intrans. and only **aor.** ἀρθμήσαντε Il. 7, 302: and **pass.** ἀρθμηθέντες Ap. Rh. 1, 1344.

'Αριθμέω *To count*, Ar. Vesp. 333; Her. 2, 143; Thuc. 3, 20, Dor. 3 pl. ἀριθμεῦντι Theocr. 8, 16: **imp.** ἠρίθμει Od. 13, 218, but ἠρίθμεον trisyll. 10, 204, ἐξηρ- Her. 2, 143: **fut.** -ήσω Od. 4, 411; Pl. Theaet. 198: **aor.** ἠρίθμησα Ar. Eq. 570; Her. 7, 100, ἐξηρ- 7, 60; ἀριθμήσω Od. 13, 215; ἀριθμῆσαι Pind. N. 10, 46; Eur. Hel. 397; Pl. Theaet. 146; -ήσας Soph. Fr. 610 (Grot. ἐξ- Nauck, Dind. 5 ed.); Pl. Euthyd. 294: **p.** ἠρίθμηκα, ἀπ- (Dem.) 60, 12, complete and reg. in act. and **pass.**: **p. p.** rare ἠριθμημένος Eur. Hel. 729; Aristot. Nat. Ausc. 4, 14, 5, ἐξ- Her. 7, 185, κατ- Aristot. Topic. 1, 6, 1, see mid.: **aor.** -ήθην Her. 9, 32; Dem. 57, 13; Epic inf. -ηθήμεναι Il. 2, 124: Dor. **pres.** ἀριθμεῦνται Theocr. 17, 27. **Mid.** ἀριθμέομαι *to count to* or *for oneself*, Aristot. Met. 12, 6, 4. Nat. Ausc. 4, 14, 8: **imp.** ἠριθμοῦντο Thuc. 3, 20, Ion. -έοντο Her. 6, 111 (Bekk. Dind. ἀριθ- Gaisf. Stein): **aor.** ἠριθμησάμην Pl. Phaedr. 270; (Luc.) Amor. 50: but **fut.** ἀριθμήσομαι seemingly **pass.** Eur. Bac. 1318, ἐξ- Dio Cass. 79, 4 (B.), συν- Themist. 16, 203; V. T. Exod. 12, 4: with **fut. p.** -ηθήσομαι Galen 10, 68; V. T. Gen. 32, 12: **perf.** ἠριθμημένος as **act.** κατ-

Aristot. Topic. 1, 2, 1, ἐξ- Polyb. 9, 2, 1. In Her. Gaisf. always augments this verb simple and comp. except ἀριθμέοντο 6, 111, ἠριθ- (Bekk. Dind.) **Vb.** ἀριθμητός C. Fr. (Cratin.) 2, 102; Aristot. Nat. Ausc. 4, 14, 5.

'Αριστάω *To dine*, Xen. Oec. 11, 18; inf. -ιστᾶν Cyr. 3, 3, 40, Ion. -ιστῆν Hippocr. 2, 478. 7, 220 (Lit.): **imp.** ἠρίστ- Lys. 3, 11; **fut.** -ήσω Ar. Vesp. 435; Xen. Cyr. 5, 3, 35: **aor.** ἠρίστησα Ar. Av. 788; Xen. Cyr. 4, 1, 10; Dem. 54, 3; ἠρίστηκα Hippocr. 2, 482; Xen. Cyr. 4, 2, 39, in Comed. 1 pl. ἠρίσταμεν syncop. for -ήκαμεν, Com. Fr. (Theop.) 2, 799. (Ar.) 2, 1154; inf. ἠριστάναι Com. Fr. (Herm.) 2, 406: **plp.** ἠριστήκεσαν Xen. Cyr. 3, 2, 11, προ- Hippocr. 1, 305 (Erm.): **p. p.** ἠρίστηται impers. Ar. Ran. 376 (Dind.) Though the Comedians alone use the syncopated perf. they don't confine themselves to it, ἠριστηκότα Com. Fr. (Diph.) 4, 397, -ηκότες (Drom.) 3, 541, -ηκότων (Alex.) 3, 435, -ηκότας (Antiph.) 3, 126. (ᾱρ- Com. Fr. (Eupol.) 2, 525, later ἄρ- Anth. 11, 387.)

'Αριστοποιέομαι *To dine*, Dem. 23, 165; -εῖσθαι Thuc. 4, 30; Xen. Cyr. 3, 2, 11: **imp.** ἠριστοποιοῦντο Xen. An. 3, 3, 1; Dem. 50, 47: **fut.** ἀριστοποιήσομαι Thuc. 7, 39: **aor.** ἀριστοποιησάμενος Thuc. 8, 95: (**perf.**): **plp.** with double augm. ἠριστοπεποίηντο Xen. Hell. 4, 5, 8 (Vulg.), but ἠριστοποίηντο (Mss. Schn. Dind. Breitb. Saupp.): very rare in **pass.** sense ἀριστοποιούμενα Xen. Hell. 4, 5, 1.

'Αρκέω *To assist*, &c. Aesch. Pr. 621; Soph. El. 186; Hippocr. 3, 544; Antiph. 2, β, 2; Thuc. 6, 84; Pl. Theaet. 174; ἀρκῶν Xen. Cyr. 8, 2, 21, ἀρκέων, ἐξ- Pind. Ol. 5, 24: **imp.** ἤρκει Il. 13, 440; Aesch. Pers. 278; Thuc. 2, 47; Isae. 5, 5: **fut.** ἀρκέσω Il. 21, 131. Od. 16, 261; Cleob. 1, 2 (B.); Soph. Aj. 1242; Hippocr. 4, 282; Thuc. 1, 93; Pl. Rep. 466, ἀρκέσσω, ἐπ- Ap. R. 2, 1049: **aor.** ἤρκεσα Il. 20, 289; Simon. C. 101; Soph. O. R. 1209; Ar. Eccl. 828 (ἤρεσα Scal. Dind. 5 ed.); Her. 2, 115; Xen. Cyr. 1, 6, 45, ἀπ- Aesch. Pers. 474, Dor. ἆρκ- Pind. Ol. 9, 3; Epic inf. ἀρκέσσαι Ap. Rh. 2, 1124: **p. p.** late ἤρκεσται Stob. (Sthen. Locr.) 48, 63: **aor.** ἠρκέσθην Plut. Pelop. 35; -εσθείς Luc. Salt. 83. Philop. 29; Plut. Mor. 114: **fut. p.** ἀρκεσθήσομαι Dio. Hal. 6, 94; Stob. (Epict.) 5, 93; Dio Cass. 43, 18; Diod. Sic. 1, 8. 3, 11: but **pres. pass.** classic ἀρκέεσθαι Her. 9, 33, -εῖσθαι Hes. Fr. 181; Com. Fr. (Alex.) 3, 516; -εῖται (Pl.) Ax. 369 (Bekk. Stallb.), -οῦμαι Anth. (Incert.) 7, 157. **Vb.** ἀρκετός Athen. (Chrysip.) 3, 79. **Mid. aor.** ἠρκέσω Aesch. Eum. 213 (best Ms. Dind. 4 ed. ἤρκεσεν Weil, ἦκέ σοι Herm. Dind. 5 ed.) ἀρκέω unlike some others in εω never drops σ in the fut.

Ἁρμόζω *To fit*, Pind. P. 9, 117; Soph. Tr. 731; Hippocr. 1, 325 (Erm. 2, 368 Lit.); Aristot. Eth. Nic. 4, 5, 17, -όσδω, ἐφ- Theocr. 1, 53, -όσσω Hippocr. 3, 558 (Lit.), Att. -όττω (Andoc.) 4, 6; Isocr. 2, 34; Aeschin. 2, 96; Dor. pt. -όζοισα Pind. P. 9, 13: **imp.** ἥρμοζον Eur. Elec. 24; Hippocr. 1, 580 (Lit.), Dor. ἁρμ- Pind. N. 8, 11, ἥρμοττον Isocr. 7, 44; Pl. Soph. 262; Dem. 20, 66: **fut.** ἁρμόσω Soph. O. R. 902; Ar. Thesm. 263; Hippocr. 1, 61 (Erm.); Pl. Phaedr. 248: **aor.** ἥρμοσα Il. 17, 210; Pl. Crat. 405, Dor. ἅρμ- Pind. P. 3, 114; Anth. 7, 431, συν-άρμοξα N. 10, 12; -όσαιμι Soph. Tr. 687; pt. -όσας Solon 36, 17; Her. 9, 108, Dor. -όσαις Pind. N. 7, 98: **p.** ἥρμοκα Aristot. Poet. 24, 8; (Luc.) Ner. 6: **p. p.** ἥρμοσμαι Soph. Ant. 570; Eur. Ph. 116; Pl. Lach. 193, Dor. ἅρμοχμαι, -οκται Stob. (Ecphant.) 48, 64, see **mid.**: **aor.** ἡρμόσθην Pl. Phaed. 93. Tim. 41, Dor. ἁρμόχθην D. Laert. (Philol.) 8, 85: **fut.** ἁρμοσθήσομαι Soph. O. C. 908. **Vb.** ἁρμοστός Philem. (C. Fr.) 4, 4, ἁρμοστέος Geop. 20, 1, ξυν- Pl. Tim. 18. **Mid.** ἁρμόζομαι *to fit for oneself, engage to wife*, -όζεται Scythin. 1 (Bergk); -όζεο Od. 5, 162, -όζου Com. Fr. (Philem.) 4, 59; -εσθαι Aretae. de C. A. Morb. 1 (83), -όττομαι Pl. Rep. 349. 591: **fut.** late ἁρμόσομαι Galen 10, 971, μεθ- Synes. Epist. 133: **aor.** ἁρμοξάμην Dor. Alcm. 71 (B.), ξυν- (Pl.) Tim. Locr. 99, ἡρμοσάμην Her. 5, 32; ἁρμόσωμαι Com. Fr. (Heges.) 4, 479. (Mach.) 4, 497; Luc. Merc. Con. 30; -όσασθαι Harm. 1, συν- Pl. Tim. 53; ἁρμοσάμενος Her. 5, 47, ξυν- Pl. Polit. 309: **p. p.** as **mid.** Ion. ἅρμοσμαι Her. 3, 137 (**pass.** -οσμένος 2, 124. 148, συν- 1, 163), Att. ἥρμοσμ- Luc. Icar. 3, μεθ- Eur. Alc. 1157, περι- Ar. Eccl. 274. **Vb.** ἁρμοστέον see above. The Tragedians use the form -όζω, Plato and the Orators -όττω, the Comedians and Xen. vary: late editors however lean to -όττω in these also. In Herodotus, Mss. and edit. augment the **aor.**, never the **perf.**

Ἀρνέομαι Dep. *To deny*, Od. 1, 249; Aesch. Eum. 611; Soph. Fr. 109; Ar. Pl. 893; Her. 4, 68; Antiph. 6, 50; Isae. 4, 20; Dem. 23, 171; ἀρνούμενος Thuc. 8, 9, Ionic ἀρνεύμ- Hym. Merc. 390; Her. 2, 181. 6, 13, perhaps better ἀρνεόμ-: **imp.** ἠρνούμην Il. 19, 304; Xen. Hell. 7, 3, 7; Aeschin. 3, 175; Dem. 33, 29: **fut.** ἀρνήσομαι Aesch. Eum. 463; Soph. O. R. 571; Ar. Eccl. 365, ἀπ- Pl. Gorg. 461: **p.** ἤρνημαι Dem. 28, 24: **plp.** ἀπ-ηρνημέναι ἦσαν Joann. Ped. 8 (West.): **aor.** ἠρνήθην mostly Attic, Lycurg. 30; Dem. 29, 18; Anth. Pl. 205. 225, ἀπ- Soph. Tr. 480; ἀρνηθείην Dem. 21, 191, -εῖεν 9, 54; Hippocr. Epist. 9, 326 (Lit.); -ηθείς Thuc. 6, 60, ἀπ- Eur. Hipp. 1266; -ηθῆναι Lys. 4, 1; Isocr. 21, 21; Dem. 30, 27: and **mid.** ἠρνησάμην rather Epic and Ionic, Anth. (Incert.) 11, 272; Callim.

Cer. 75; Nonn. 4, 36; Maneth. 2, 308; rare in classic Attic Aeschin. 3, 224; Hyperid. Fr. 3, 140; and late, Dio. Hal. 9, 13; Dio Cass. 58, 19; Luc. D. Meretr. 7, 4, Poet. ἀρνησ- Anth. 7, 473; ἀρνήσῃ Eur. Ion 1026; Procop. Epist. 58; ἀρνησαίμην Aeschin. 2, 69, -νήσαιο Il. 14, 191, -σαιτο Tryphiod. 104; -ήσασθαι Il. 14, 212. Od. 21, 345; Orph. Lith. 162; Her. 3, 1; Hyperid. Fr. 3, 140; Aristot. Top. 8, 7; D. Laert. 2, 12, 5; -ησάμενος (Hippocr.) Epist. 9, 368 (Lit.); D. Laert. 2, 12, 4; Plut. Mor. 233; Dio Cass. 46, 30, ἐξ- Her. 3, 74: **fut.** ἀρνηθήσομαι, ἀπ- **pass.** Soph. Ph. 527; and late N. T. Luc. 12, 9, see below: **pres.** ἀρνουμένην also seems **pass.** Plut. Mor. 1072; ἀπ-αρνῆται Aristot. Anal. Pr. 1, 32, 9. **Vb.** ἀρνητέον Aristot. Top. 8, 7.

The *simple* **fut. p.** ἀρνηθήσομαι we have not met, but ἀπ-αρνηθήσ-is **pass.** Soph. quoted, and N. T. Luc. 12, 9, but **act.** V. T. Esai. 31, 7 (Alex.), where however the Vat. has **mid.** ἀπαρνήσονται (Tisch. Gaisf.) In Attic writers, the comp. ἀπ- ἐξ-αρνέομαι have, we think, only **aor. pass.** -ήθην Soph. Tr. 480; Eur. Hipp. 1266; Thuc. 6, 56; Pl. Phaedr. 256, ἐξ- Pl. Conv. 192. Leg. 949, but in Epic, Ionic, and late Attic, they have, contrary to what Lexicogr. teach, also **aor. mid.** ἀπηρνησάμην Callim. Del. 100. Cer. 75. 106; Ap. Rh. 3, 1133 (Well.); (Hippocr.) Epist. 9, 328 (Lit.); Dio Cass. 39, 30, ἐξ-αρνησάμενος Her. 3, 74; Dio. Hal. 10, 4. καταρνέομαι seems to occur only in **pres.** καταρνεῖ Soph. Ant. 442. In Epic poetry and Ionic prose the **aor. mid.** alone is used; in classic Attic, with the exception of one instance in Eur., two in Aeschines, and one in Hyperid. Fr. 30, 1 (3, 140), the **aor. pass.** Buttm. and Matth. wrongly confine the **aor. mid.** to poetry.

"Αρνῠμαι *To win*, Soph. Tr. 711. Ant. 903; Eur. Alc. 55, -υται Soph. Phil. 838; Eur. Andr. 696, -υνται Anth. (Mnas.) 7, 242; Aristot. Polit. 3, 16, 7; imper. ἄρνυσο Sapph. 75 (B.); Poet in Stobae. 2, 8; -ύμενος Il. 1, 159. 5, 553. Od. 1, 5; Eur. Hec. 1073; Pl. Leg. 813. 944. Rep. 346; Luc. Philops. 1. D. Syr. 48; -υσθαι Pl. Prot. 349: **imp.** unaugm. ἀρνύμην Il. 22, 160: **fut.** (supplied by αἴρομαι) ἀροῦμαι, **2 aor.** ἠρόμην.

'Αρόω *To plough*, Od. 9, 108; Tyrt. 5; Eur. Fr. 672 (D.); -όῃς Hes. Op. 479 (Goettl.), -όῳς (Lennep); ἀροῦν Theogn. 582, Ar. Plut. 525; Her. 4, 19; Xen. Oec. 16, 10; Pl. Phaedr. 276: **fut.** ἀρόσω Anth. 9, 729. 740; Geop. 3, 10: later **mid.** -όσομαι Theodor. Metoch. 76, p. 510 (Müll.): **aor.** ἤροσα Soph. O. R. 1497, περι- Plut. Mor. 820, ἄρ- Callim. Cer. 137; ἀρόσῃς Hes. Op. 485; Theophr. H. P. 8, 1, 6; ἀρόσειεν, περι- Plut. Popl. 16; ἀρόσαι Pind. N. 10, 26, -όσσαι Ap. Rh. 3, 497: **p. p.** ἀρήρομαι, -ομένος Il. 18, 548; Her. 4, 97: **plp.** ἀρήροτο Ap. Rh. 3, 1343:

aor. ἠρόθην Soph. O. R. 1485: pres. pass. ἀροῦται Dinarch. 1, 24; -οῦσθαι Soph. Fr. 298: imp. ἠροῦτο Hesych. Mid. ἀροῦσθαι Or. Sib. 5, 505 (Friedl.): fut. ἀρόσεται Thecd. Metoch. 76, 510. Epic forms: pres. inf. ἀρόμμεναι Hes. Op. 22 (Mss. Goettl. Lennep. -όμεναι and -ώμεναι other Mss.) Vb. ἀν-ήροτος Od. 9, 123; Aesch. Pr. 708.—ἀρόωσι 3 pl. pres. for ἀροῦσι, Od. 9, 108; Ap. Rh. 1, 796. ἀρόσσω, doubtful -ώσω, poet. fut. Anth. 7, 175: aor. -όσσα Ap. Rh. 3, 1053.

Ἁρπάζω *To seize*, Il. 5, 556; Aesch. Sept. 259; Her. 1, 4; Xen. Hell. 5, 2, 19; Dem. 53, 17; -άζητε Soph. Ant. 311; -άζειν Isae. 11, 16: imp. ἥρπαζον Her. 1, 106; Thuc. 1, 5: fut. ἁρπᾰσω Xen. Hipp. 4, 17; Anth. (Antiphil.) 7, 175, ἀν- Eur. Ion 1303, ξυν- I. A. 535; Luc. D. Deor. 8, δι- App. Lib. 55; Polyb. 4, 18, unatt. ἁρπάξω Il. 22, 310; Babr. 89; late prose Apollod. 2, 4, 7 (Bekk.): more freq. mid. -ᾰσομαι Xen. Cyr. 7, 2, 5; Ar. Pax 1118. Eccl. 866. Av. 1460, ξυν- Lys. 437, ὑφ- Nub. 490, δι- Pl. Rep. 336, ἀν- Her. 8, 28. 9, 59; Plut. Marcell. 6. Aristid. 17, and late ἁρπῶμαι V. T. Osea 5, 14, -ᾶται Ezek. 18, 7: aor. ἥρπασα Il. 13, 528; Aesch. Ag. 627; Eur. Or. 1634; Thuc. 6, 101; Her. 2, 156, Dor. ἅρπ- Pind. P. 3, 44. 9, 6; Bion 2, 10; -άσαι Soph. Aj. 2, unatt. ἥρπαξα Il. 12, 305. Od. 15, 174; ἁρπάξας Pind. N. 10, 67; Theocr. 17, 48: p. ἥρπᾰκα Ar. Plut. 372; Pl. Gorg. 481: p. p. ἥρπασμαι Xen. An. 1, 2, 27; Com. Fr. (Mnesim.) 3, 569, ἀν- Eur. Ph. 1079, late ἥρπαγμαι Paus. 3, 18, 7 (Vulg. -ασμαι Schub.); -άχθαι Strab. 13, 1, 11: plp. ἥρπαστο Eur. Elec. 1041: aor. ἡρπάσθην Pl. Phaedr. 229; -ασθείη Her. 7, 191; -ασθείς Eur. Hec. 513; Her. 1, 4; Thuc. 6, 104; -ασθῆναι Her. 1, 1, unatt. ἡρπάχθην, ἁρπαχθείς Her. 2, 90. 8, 115; Anth. 14, 95; Diod. Sic. 17, 74: fut. ἁρπασθήσομαι Luc. D. Mer. 9, 4 (Bekk. Jacob.), δι- Dem. 8, 55. 18, 213: 2 aor. late ἡρπάγην Lycophr. 505; Apollod. 1, 9, 19; Strab. 10, 4, 21, ἀν- Plut. Pyr. 7, δι- Polyb. 4, 79; Arr. An. 7, 13, 1: fut. late ἁρπαγήσομαι Joseph. J. Bell. 5, 10, 3; N. T. 1 Thess. 4, 17, ἐξ- Plut. Agis 19, δι- Oth. 3. Mid. fut. -άσομαι, see above: aor. late in *simple*, ἁρπασάμενος Luc. Tim. 22; Joseph. Ant. 5, 8 (Bekk.); Heliod. 4, 21; but ὑφαρπάσαιο Ar. Eccl. 921; διαρπάσασθαι Arr. An. 3, 18, 10, ἀν- Dio. Hal. 3, 5 (Kiessl.); and as if from (ἅρπημι) a poet. aor. ἁρπάμενος pass. Anth. 11, 59; Nonn. 40, 357, but act. in ὑφαρπαμένη Anth. 9, 619: and as mid. p. p. ἐξ-ηρπασμένοι Soph. O. C. 1016. Vb. ἁρπαστός late, -ακτός Hes. Op. 320. Lexicogr. have missed the aor. mid.—Epic, Ionic, and Doric writers use both the ς and γ formations -σω -ξω, -σα -ξα, -σμαι -γμαι &c.; the Attics invariably the former only. ἅρπαγμα, however,

Aeschin. 3, 222, for ἅρπασμα Pl. Leg. 906. In the best editions of Her. both formations of **1 aor. p.** have equal support, ἡρπάσθην 1, 1. 4. 7, 191 without v. r. -άχθην 2, 90. 7, 169. 8, 115; but as Her. has **fut.** -άσομαι, **aor.** -ασα ten or twelve times, uniformly without a v. r., and as good Mss. offer -άσθην twice for -άχθην of the edit. 2, 90. 7, 169, a doubt naturally arises about ἁρπαχθῆναι 8, 115, though supported by all the Mss., and a suspicion, at least, that Her. followed in this verb the analogy in use with the Attics.

'Αρρωδέω *To fear* (Att. ὀρρωδέω), is peculiar to Ionic, and therefore unaugm. ἀρρωδέω Her. 1, 111: **imp.** ἀρρώδεον 5, 35. 8, 74: **aor.** ἀρρώδησα, κατ- 6, 9: **p.** ἀρρώδηκα, κατ- 3, 145. 8, 75: **plp.** ἀρρωδήκεε, κατ- 8, 103.

'Αρτάω *To suspend*, reg. **fut.** -ήσω Anth (Diod.) 6, 245: **aor.** ἤρτησα Thuc. 4, 100; -ήσας Eur. Hipp. 1222; Thuc. 2, 76; -ῆσαι Eur. Andr. 811: **p.** ἤρτηκα, προσ- Arr. Epict. 1, 1, 14 (Müll.): **p. p.** ἤρτημαι Eur. Hipp. 857; Ar. Pax 1247; Her. 6, 109; Hippocr. 5, 308; Xen. Cyr. 6, 2, 32; Pl. Leg. 631; Dem. 9, 39; Dio. Hal. 2, 71, ἐξ- Thuc. 6, 96, 3 pl. Ion. ἀρτέαται Her. 1, 125: **plp.** ἤρτητο Her. 3, 19; Aristot. Fr. 151, see below: **aor.** -ήθην, προσ- Maneth. 4, 199. **Mid.** -άομαι *to suspend for oneself*, Eur. Tr. 1012; Ar. Pax 470: **fut.** intrans. *join*, ἐξ-αρτήσεται Xen. Cyr. 5, 4, 20: **aor.** late ἀρτήσαντο Orph. Arg. 1101; -ησάμενος Conon 35 (Westerm.), but ἐξ-ηρτήσασθε Eur. Tr. 129; Luc. Fug. 14: and in sense **p. p.** ἤρτηται, ἐξ- Ar. Eccl. 494; Dem. 9, 49: **plp.** ἤρτητο Ach. Tat. 1, 1, 12. See foll.

'Αρτέομαι *To prepare oneself* (ἄρτιος), Ion. Her. 7, 143: **imp.** ἀρτέετο 8, 97, -έοντο 5, 120, παρ- 8, 76: **p.** ἀν-άρτημαι 7, 8; -ημένος 1, 90. 6, 88: but **plp.** παρ-ήρτητο 9, 29, which Lhardy would alter to παράρτητο on the ground that in eight places where this verb occurs it is never augmented by Her.; and κατηρτημένον 3, 80, he would refer to καταρτᾶσθαι, or adopt Stephens' emendation -ηρτισμένον which many approve, and which Wm. Dindorf edits. Hippocr. however has κατήρτητο *was composed* 1, 192 (Erm.) Lexicogr. have improperly mixed up this verb with ἀρτᾶν *to hang, suspend*, and have called it the Ion. form. But ἀρτέει never occurs in **act.**, nor has **mid.** ἀρτέομαι ever the meaning *hang, suspend*. Besides, the verb with that meaning ἀρτάομαι is always augmented in Her. ἠρτημένος 5, 31: ἤρτητο 3, 19. 9, 68, except 3 pl. **perf.** ἀρτέαται 1, 125. At 6, 109 Mss. and edit. vary between ἤρτηται (F. a. b. c. old edit. Bekk. Lhardy, Dietsch, Stein, Abicht), and ἀρτ- (Mss. S. V. Wessel. Schweigh. Dind.).

'Αρτύνω *To prepare*, Epic, Od. 11, 366: **imp.** ἤρτυνον Il. 15, 303: **fut.** ἀρτυνέω Od. 1, 277. 2, 196; -έουσα H. Hym.

27, 15: ἤρτῡνα, ἀρτύνειας Ap. Rh. 3, 698; -ύνας Il. 12, 86. Od. 14, 469: aor. p. ἀρτύνθην Il. 11, 216, ἠρτ- (Bekk. 2 ed.): mid. ἀρτύνονται Opp. C. 4, 113: imp. ἠρτύνετο Il. 2, 55: aor. ἠρτῡναντο Od. 8, 53; Ap. Rh. 2, 67; Tryphiod. 50.

Ἀρτύω *To prepare*, Od. 4, 771; Com. Fr. 4, 460; Democr. Fr. 220 (Mullach); Geop. 7, 13; -ύοντες Aristot. Eth. Nic. 3, 13, 9; Theophr. Fr. 4, 3, 8; Plut. Mor. 137, ἐξ- Eur. Elec. 422; Thuc. 2, 17: imp. ἤρτυον Il. 18, 379; Joseph. B. Jud. 2, 21, 6, ἐξ- Thuc. 2, 3 (ῠ Hom. ῡ Att.): fut. ἀρτύσω Soph. Fr. 601; Anth. 12, 95; Athen. 4, 47, κατ- Soph. O. C. 71: aor. ἤρτῡσα Lycophr. 163; Her. 1, 12; -ῦσαι Com. Fr. (Cratin.) 2, 178; Polyb. 15, 25: p. ἤρτῡκα, κατ- Aesch. Eum. 473; Eur. Fr. 42 (D.); Poet in Galen 5, 418 (K.); Philostr. Ap. 215: p. p. ἤρτῡμαι Com. Fr. (Pher.) 2, 300. (Eupol.) 2, 564; Hippocr. 1, 604. 7, 168 (Lit.); Theophr. Odor. 51, ἐξ- Eur. Hip. 1186; Pl. Leg. 625: plp. ἐξ-ήρτυτο Her. 1, 61: aor. ἠρτύθην, -θείς Oribas. 4, 2, κατ-αρτυθείς Soph. Ant. 478, ἐξ- Thuc. 6, 31. Mid. in comp. ἐξ-αρτῡομαι Aesch. Pr. 908; Thuc. 2, 13: imp. -ηρτύοντο 2, 85: fut. -ύσονται Eur. Elec. 647; Thuc. 1, 121: aor. ἐξ-ηρτύσαντο 7, 65. In Hom. this verb has only pres. and imp. and is rarely used in comp. ἐπ-ήρτῠε Od. 8, 447: in Att. the *simple* form has neither pres. (excepting Com. Fr. quoted) nor imp. and rarely fut. aor. and p. p., but in comp. it is complete and reg. with ῡ throughout, ἐξ-αρτῡω Eur. Elec. 422: -ῡσω, κατ- Soph. O. C. 71: ἤρτῡκα, κατ- Aesch. Eum. 473; -ήρτῡμαι, -ηρτῡθην, -ῡσομαι, -ῡσάμην, ἐξ-αρτῡεται Eur. Heracl. 419, but κατ-αρτῠεται Solon 27, 11. As a prose form, it seems confined to Ion. and late Attic, ἀρτύοντες Plut. Mor. 137: ἤρτυσαν Her. 1, 12; -ῦσαι Polyb. 15, 25, but the comp. ἐξ- κατ- are in good Att. Thuc. 2, 3. 17, &c.; Pl. Meno 88. Leg. 625. 808. Critia. 117. Some Grammarians and Lexicogr. have maintained that the υ is short even in Attic, and appeal for proof to ἀρτύσω in a Fr. of Soph. Athen. 68 (Fr. 601, Dind.). The words are ἐγὼ μάγειρος ἀρτύσω σοφῶς, wanting a foot to complete the verse. But unless we know whether the missing foot stood at the beginning or the end, the line proves nothing. If it ended the line, υ is short, as -ύσω would form the fourth foot; if it began the line, -ύσω would form the fifth, and therefore *may* have υ long. Neither is καταρτύσων μολεῖν O. C. 71, decisive, owing to -ύσων occupying the fifth foot. It suggests, however, the *probability* that the defective line ended with ἀρτύσω σοφῶς. The fut. act. ἀρτῡσεις is indisputably long in Anth. (Meleag.) 12, 95, and mid. ἐξ-αρτῡσομαι Eur. Elec. 647, aor. ἤρτῡσα Lycophr. quoted, and p.p. ἤρτῡμαι Pherecratis, Eupolis and Eur. quoted. We may therefore easily dispense with the emendation ἀρτῦνῶ offered, both because it may not be needed, and should it be, there may be some demur about admitting into trimeters a form exclusively Epic.

'Αρύω *To draw water*, Anth. Plan. 333, ἐξ- Orph. Arg. 1119, and ἀρύτω Pl. Phaedr. 253: imp. ἤρυον Hes. Sc. 301: fut. (ἀρύσω): aor. ἤρυσα Com. Fr. (Pher.) 2, 323; ἀρύσας Ap. Rh. 3, 1015; Xen. Cyr. 1, 3, 9, ἀπ- Her. 4, 2: (p. ἤρυκα: p. p. ἤρυσμαι?): aor. ἠρύθην, ἀπ-αρυθείς Com. Fr. (Alex.) 3, 405, ἠρύσθην Hippocr. 7, 524. 526 (Lit.); Plut. Mor. 690. Mid. ἀρύομαι *to draw for oneself*, Ar. Nub. 272 (Mss. Bekk. Mein.); Anth. 9, 37; Ael. V. H. 1, 32. 13, 22; Paus. 10, 32, 7; Arr. An. 7, 11, 8; Apollod. 1, 7, 4, ἐσ- Hippocr. 8, 566, -ύτομαι Ar. Nub. and Aelian quoted (Suid. Br. Dind. Hercher); Com. Fr. (Pher.) 2, 316; Pl. Ion 534. Leg. 636, and rare Ion. ἀρύσσομαι Her. 6, 119 (Mss. F. S. Gaisf. Schweig. Dind. Abicht, Stein), but ἀρύομαι (Matthiae, Bekk. Krüg.): imp. ἀρυόμην Nonn. 12, 360. 42, 93, ἠρυ- Themist. 34, 39: fut. ἀρύσομαι Anth. 9, 230; Luc. D. Mar. 6 (Mss. Fritzs. Jacob.); Procop. Epist. 134: aor. ἠρυσάμην Christ. Pat. 1226; Plut. Mor. 516; Ael. V. H. 13, 23; Anton. Lib. 19 (ἀρ- Westerm.); ἀρυσαίμαν Eur. Hipp. 210 chor. (Dind. Kirchh. 2 ed. -μην Kirchh. 1 ed. Nauck), -ύσαιτο Aristot. Top. 6, 6, 18; imper. ἄρυσαι Anth. Pl. 9, 37. Epigr. incert. 100; ἀρύσασθαι Xen. Cyr. 1, 2, 8; ἀρυσάμενος Her. 8, 137; Ael. V. H. 1, 32; D. Hal. 2, 69; Luc. Herm. 59, Poet. ἀρυσσ- Hes. Op. 550; Anth. 11, 64, active, not, as some say, passive. Vb. ἀπ-αρυστέον Ar. Eq. 921. (ἀρύομαι occurs with ῠ, ἀρύου Anth. 9, 37; and later Nonn. 14, 46. 19, 244. 42, 93, &c., but only in *arsi*, for ἀρύοντο 12, 360. 15, 14.)

"Αρχω *To begin, command*, Il. 2, 805; Pind. P. 4, 230; Soph. El. 522; Her. 1, 120; Thuc. 5, 19; Xen. Hel. 3, 5, 10; -χειν Aesch. Ag. 1424: imp. ἦρχον Il. 3, 447; Soph. O. R. 591; Her. 1, 18, and always except p. p.; Thuc. 1, 20; Pl. Tim. 25, Dor. ἆρχ- Pind. Ol. 11, 51; Aesch. Pers. 856; Eur. I. A. 260 (chor.); Ar. Lys. 998: fut. ἄρξω Od. 4, 667; Aesch. Pr. 940; Her. 1, 120; Thuc. 1, 144; Lys. 12, 51: aor. ἦρξα Od. 14, 230; Aesch. Pers. 353; Ar. Pax 605; Her. 1, 14; Antiph. 4, β, 2; Andoc. 1, 90; Pl. Polit. 269: p. ἦρχα Psephism. Plut. Mor. 851; Inscr. 2, 828: p. ἦργμαι pass. in the sense *ruled over* we have not seen, see mid.: aor. ἤρχθην, ἀρχθῶσι Thuc. 2, 8; -χθῆναι 6, 18; Aristot. Pol. 7, 14, 6; ἀρχθείς 3, 4, 14: fut. ἀρχθήσομαι Aristot. Pol. 1, 13, 5; Dio Cass. 65, 10: and mid. ἄρξομαι sometimes pass. Pind. Ol. 8, 45; Aesch. Pers.

589; Her. 3, 83. 7, 159. 162. 9, 122; Lys. 28, 7; Pl. Tim. 34. Rep. 412, &c. **Mid.** ἄρχομαι *to begin*, H. Hym. 9, 8; Pind. N. 2, 3; Her. 4, 51; Thuc. 2, 1; -ηται Soph. Fr. 715; ἄρχοιτο Od. 8, 90: **imp.** ἠρχόμην Il. 9, 93; Her. 5, 28. 30; Andoc. 2, 9, ἀρχ- Pind. P. 4, 30; Her. 5, 51. 6, 75, κατ- 2, 45 (Mss. Gaisf. Stein, ἠρχ- Lhard. Bekk. Krüg. so Dind. except κατ-αρχ- 2, 45): **fut.** ἄρξομαι Il. 9, 97; Eur. I. A. 442; Her. 3, 83; Antiph. 6, 10; Xen. Cyr. 8, 8, 2, Dor. ἀρξεῦμαι Theocr. 7, 95: **aor.** ἠρξάμην Od. 23, 310; Aesch. Pr. 199; Soph. O. C. 625; Ar. Plut. 968; Her. 1, 95; Thuc. 6, 46; Lys. 18, 11; Pl. Prot. 338, Dor. ἀρξ- Simon. C. 46; Theocr. 6, 5. 8, 32: **p.** ἦργμαι as mid. Pl. Leg. 722. Hipp. Min. 364; ἠργμένος Hippocr. 1, 310 (Erm.); Pl. Leg. 771, Ion. ἄργμαι, -μένος Her. 1, 174 (ὑπαργμένα 7, 11, pass.?): **plp.** ἦρκτο App. Civ. 1, 28 (ὑπῆρκτο Antiph. 5, 58, pass.?) **Vb.** (ἀρκτός *ruled*), -έος *must be ruled*, or *begun*, Pl. Tim. 48; Dem. 22, 6.—ἀρχέμεναι Ep. inf. pres. Il. 20, 154. The collat. ἀρχεύω *to rule*, is Epic, and only in pres. ἀρχεύοι Ap. Rh. 1, 347; imper. ἄρχευ' Il. 2, 345; inf. -εύειν 5, 200.

(Ἄρω) *To fit*, see ἀραρίσκω.

Ἀσάω *To afflict*, (ᾰ) in act. only part. ἀσῶν Theogn. 593 (Bekk.), but ἀσῶ pass. (Bergk, Ziegl.). **Pass.** ἀσάομαι *to be grieved*, Theogn. 657; Hippocr. 6, 388. 8, 78 (Lit.); Aristot. H. A. 7, 4, 6; ἀσώμενος Theocr. 25, 240, Aeol. ἀσάμενος Alcae. Fr. 35 (Bergk): **imp.** ἠσᾶτο Hippocr. 5, 218: **fut. mid.** as pass. ἀσήσει (Hesych.): **aor.** ἠσήθην, ἀσηθῇς Theogn. 989; ἀσηθείη Her. 3, 41. This verb is, as Buttmann says, Dep. passive: there is no aor. mid. ἀσῶ Theogn. 657 sometimes quoted to vouch it, is no proof. The sense does not require an aorist, and the *form* forbids it.

(Ἀσελγέω) *To behave outrageously*, of which we have seen only **p.p.** ἠσελγημένα Dem. 21, 19: and late, **plp.** ἠσέλγητο Jos. Ant. 17, 5, 6 (Bekk.). The collat. ἀσελγαίνω is rather more freq. subj. -αίνῃ Dem. 21, 138, -αίνητε Dio Cass. 56, 5; -αίνων Andoc. 4, 7; Pl. Leg. 879; Dem. 21, 27; -αίνειν Pl. Conv. 190; Lys. 26, 5: **imp.** ἠσέλγαινον Dem. 21, 31. 54, 5; Luc. Bis. acc. 31: **fut.** -ᾰνῶ Dem. 24, 143: **aor.** late, ἀσελγᾶναι Dio Cass. 52, 31. The **pres.** seems to occur in subj. part. and inf. only.

Ἀσεπτέω *To act impiously*, only inf. -εῖν Soph. Ant. 1350.

Ἀσθμαίνω *To pant*, Poet. Ionic and late prose, and only **pres.** and **imp.** ἀσθμαίνεις Opp. Hal. 4, 14, -νει Hippocr. 7, 332. 8, 328; Aristot. Probl. 11, 60; Apocr. Syr. 34, 19; -αίνων Il. 5, 585. 10, 376. H. Hym. 2, 181; Pind. N. 3, 48; Orph. Lith. 89; Aesch. Eum. 651 (Dind. Weil); Aristot. Respir. 5, 6;

Plut. Mar. 26; Luc. Herm. 5. Rhet. 10: **imp.** ἤσθμαινον Luc. D. Mer. 5, 4.

'Ασμενέω *To feel glad*, only **imp.** ἠσμένει Dinarch. 1, 34. The collat. ἀσμενίζω is scarcely in classic, often in later Attic, ἀσμενίζομεν Luc. Amor. 27, -ίζουσι Plut. Mor. 101; often pt. -ίζων Polyb. 3, 97. 4, 11, 5: **aor.** ἠσμένισε (Aeschin.) Epist. 5, 1. **Mid. aor.** -ισαμένη Aesop 45 (Halm).

"Ασμενος, see ἀνδάνω.

'Ασπαίρω *To palpitate, struggle*, Aesch. Pers. 976; Opp. Hal. 2, 287; -αίρων Il. 12, 203; Eur. I. A. 1587; Her. 1, 111; Antiph. 2, δ, 5, the only instance in classic Att. prose: **imp.** ἤσπαιρον Il. 13, 571; Eur. Elec. 843; Her. 8, 5. 9, 120; Dio. Hal. 7, 25, iter. ἀσπαίρεσκον Q. Sm. 1, 350. 11, 104.

"ΑΙσσω *To rush*, Pind. N. 8, 40; Soph. Tr. 396; Com. Fr. (Eub.) 3, 242, ᾄττω Com. Fr. (Metag.) 2, 753; Pl. Theaet. 144; Dem. 25, 52, εἰσ- Ar. Nub. 996: **imp.** ᾖσσον Aesch. Pr. 676; Eur. Ph. 1382. 1466: **fut.** ᾄξω Eur. Hec. 1106; Ar. Nub. 1299: **aor.** ᾖξα Aesch. Pr. 837; Soph. O. C. 890; Eur. Elec. 844; (Dem.) 47, 53, εἰσ- Ar. Nub. 543, ἐξ- Plut. 733, Ion. ἤϊξε, δι- Her. 4, 134; ᾄξας Soph. O. R. 1074; Ar. Eq. 485; Isae. 4, 10. (Pl. has ἀΐξειεν Leg. 709, ἐπ-αΐξας Theaet. 190.) **Pass.** ᾄσσομαι Soph. O. C. 1261, ἀττ- Aristot. Prob. 16, 8, 3. See the poet. form ἀΐσσω. Some defend ἄσσω, ἄττω without iota subscr. ἄττει Arist. H. An. 9, 37, 12; Plut. Mor. 87; Dio Cass. 52, 16 (B. ᾄττ- L. Dind.), ἐξ-άττουσι Aristot. Probl. 30, 14, 6, δι- 2, 31, 2 (B.) This verb is rare in prose.

'Αστράπτω *To lighten, flash*, Il. 9, 237; Soph. O. C. 1067; Pl. Phaedr. 254. (Ep.) 1, 310; (Xen.) Ven. 6, 15: **imp.** ἤστραπτον Aesch. Pr. 356; Xen. An. 1, 8, 8, iter. ἀστράπτεσκεν Mosch. 2, 86: **fut.** -άψει Or. Sib. 6, 18; Nonn. 33, 376: **aor.** ἤστραψα Soph. Fr. 507; Opp. Cyn. 2, 23; Aristot. Anal. Post. 1, 4, 4. Rhet. 2, 19, 21; ἀστράψω Ar. Vesp. 626; -άψας Il. 17, 595: **pass.** late, unless **plp.** ἤστραπτο be correct Xen. Cyr. 6, 4, 1 (old reading, ἤστραπτε Popp. Dind. Saupp.): **aor.** ἠστράφθην very late. **Mid.** late, **aor.** subj. ἀστράψηται Aristid. 49, 391 (Vulg. ἀστράψῃ Reiske, Dind.), missed by all Lexicogr.

'Ασφαλίζω *To make sure, secure*, late, unless correct as a conjecture, Aesch. Supp. 146; Polyb. 18, 13: **imp.** ἠσφάλιζε Polyb. 1, 22; Theod. Prodr. 2, 201. **Mid.** -ίζομαι as **act.** Polyb. 6, 34: **fut.** -ίσομαι Diod. Sic. 20, 24 (Vulg. Bekk. -ιοῦμαι L. Dind.); Joseph. Ant. 13, 5, 11, -ιοῦμαι Jud. B. 2, 21, 4: **p.** ἠσφάλισμαι **act.** Polyb. 5, 43, but **pass.** 1, 42. 4, 65. 5, 59; Dio. Hal. 7, 44: **aor. m.** ἠσφαλισάμην Polyb. 2, 65. 4, 65. 5, 72; Diod. Sic. 14, 12; Geop. 10, 38; Joseph. Ant. 13, 5, 10;

V. T. and Apocr. always; N. T. Matth. 27, 66. Act. 16, 24: and as **mid. aor. pass.** ἠσφαλίσθην Polyb. 5, 7, 12, but if λίμνη (Bekk. Dind.) or λίμνη (Hultsch) be correct, it may be passive, as it seems to be in N. T. Matth. 27, 64 (Lachm. Tisch.). **Pres.** ἀσφαλίζεσθαι seems **pass.** Polyb. 4, 70. We have noticed this verb simply because it has been ill-handled by most of our Lexicogr.

Ἀσχαλάω *To be distressed, grieved,* Poet. -αλάᾳ lengthened 3 sing. Il. 2, 293. Od. 19, 159, for -αλᾷ Aesch. Pr. 764, ξυν- 161. 243 (Blomf. Herm. Weil.), which however *may* be: **fut.** for (ἀσχαλάσει, see below), but Ion. -ήσω Thales in Diog. Laert. 1, 1, 16, the only instance of the verb in prose. This verb is confined to **pres.** and **fut.** Hom. has always the lengthened forms -λάᾳ Od. quoted, 3 pl. -λόωσι Il. 24, 403; Ap. Rh. 2, 888; imper. ἀσχάλα Archil. 66; inf. ἀσχαλᾶν Eur. I. A. 920, -άαν Il. 2, 297; Mosch. 4, 71; part. -όων Il. 22, 412; Ap. Rh. 4, 108; Theocr. 25, 236; Bion 4 (2), 7 (Schaef. -άων Vulg. Mein. Ziegl.). The collat. form ἀσχάλλω has perhaps only **pres.** and **imp.** ἀσχάλλει Eur. Fr. 287 (Dind.), ἀσχάλλετε Dio Cass. 56, 6; subj. -λλῃς Od. 2, 193, -ωμεν Plut. Mor. 123; opt. -λοις Soph. O. R. 937; imper. ἄσχαλλε Theogn. 219; -ων Eur. Or. 785; Xen. Eq. 10, 6; often late, Plut. Mor. 465, &c.; Polyb. 11, 29; -ειν Dem. 21, 125; Polyb. 2, 64: **imp.** ἤσχαλλε Hes. Fr. 93, 3; Anacreont. 12, 14 (B.); Her. 3, 152. 9, 117; late Attic, Plut. Luc. 15. 24; Alciphr. 3, 19; Dio Cass. 48, 31. 51, 3; Herodn. 5, 5: **fut.** ἀσχαλεῖ Aesch. Pr. 764 (Herwerd. Dind. for -αλᾷ), so ξυν- 161. 243 (L. Dind.); ἀσχαλῶν, συν- 303, see above. Indic. **pres.** scarcely occurs in classic authors.

Ἀσχολέω *To engage, be engaged,* **act.** rare, Com. Fr. (Phil.) 4, 66; Aristot. Polit. 8, 3, 5; Luc. Zeux. 7; Himer. 14, 1: **fut.** -ήσω and **aor.** ησα very late, Greg. Naz. and Nyss. **Mid.** and **pass.** ἀσχολοῦμαι *engage oneself, be engaged,* Com. Fr. (Alex.) 3, 477. (Men.) 4, 315; Aristot. Eth. Nic. 10, 7, 6; Luc. Herm. 79: **imp.** ἠσχολεῖτο Com. Fr. (Alex.) 3, 503; Diod. Sic. 17, 94: with **fut. m.** -ήσομαι Marc. Ant. 12, 2; Aristid. 33, 423 (D.); Aesop 407 (Halm): and as **mid. fut. pass.** -ηθήσομαι Apocr. Sirach 39, 1: **perf.** ἠσχόλημαι D. Cass. 71, 10; Geop. 10, 2; Theod. Prod. 5, 336: **aor. m.** ἠσχολήσατο Galen 7, 657: and in same sense **aor. pass.** ἠσχολήθην, ἀσχοληθείς (Hippocr.) Epist. 9, 364 (Lit.); Luc. Macrob. 8; Diod. Sic. 4, 32. This verb, we think, does not occur in classic prose. The **fut.** and **aor. mid.** have been ignored by *all* our lexicons.

Ἀτάλλω *To skip, dance,* Poet. usu. Epic, only **pres.** -άλλων Hes. Op. 131; *make joyous, cherish,* Hom. Epigr. 4, 2; Soph.

Aj. 559, Dor. fem. -άλλοισα Pind. Fr. 198 (Bergk): and imp. ἄταλλε Il. 13, 27; Mosch. 2, 116. Pass. (-άλλομαι): imp. ἀτάλλετο H. Hym. 3, 400 (Vulg. Frank.). ᾰ, ᾱ in arsi Hes. Op. 131.

'Ατάομαι *To be injured*, Trag. Poet. and only pres. ἀτώμεσθα Soph. Aj. 269, -ῶνται Maneth. 5, 97; ἀτώμενος, ένη, -ους Soph. Aj. 384. Ant. 17. 314; Eur. Supp. 182. (ᾰτάο-.)

'Ατασθάλλω *To be insolent*, only part. -λων Od. 18, 57, -ουσα 19, 88. (ᾰ.)

'Ατέμβω Epic, *To harm*, only pres. Od. 2, 90; -ειν 20, 294. 21, 312, -έμεν (Bekk.). **Pass.** ἀτέμβομαι *to be bereft*, Il. 23, 445; -όμενος 23, 834. Od. 9, 42. 549. **Mid.** -ομαι *to blame*, subj. ἀτέμβηαι Ap. Rh. 2, 56; -οίμην 3, 99; -όμενος 3, 938; Q. Sm. 5, 147. 173. (ᾰ.)

'Ατέω *To be desperate*, Epic and Ion. only pres. ἀτέει if correct, Callim. Fr. 471; part. ἀτέων Il. 20, 332; Her. 7, 223. (ᾰ.)

'Ατίζω *To disregard*, Epic and Trag. Eur. Rhes. 252. 327; ἀτίζων Il. 20, 166; Aesch. Supp. 733; Eur. Alc. 1037. Supp. 19; ἀτίζειν Soph. O. C. 1153; Ap. Rh. 1, 478, usu. pres. only: but late **imp.** ἄτιζε Nicet. Eug. 3, 264: **fut.** ἀτίσεις Aesch. Fr. 103 (D.), Epic ἀτίσσ- Ap. Rh. 3, 181: **aor.** ἄτισε Hesych., ἄτισσε Ap. Rh. 2, 9, -σσαν 1, 615; ἀτίσῃς Aesch. Eum. 540; inf. ἀτίσσαι Ap. Rh. 4, 1100: **pass.** late prose ἀτιζόμενος Galen 18, 642. (ᾰ.)

'Ατῑμάζω, Od. 23, 116; Theogn. 821; Aesch. Supp. 912; Soph. Ant. 572; Lys. 31, 30; Isocr. 10, 58; Aeschin. 2, 8: **imp.** ἠτιμ- Lys. 16, 5; Dem. 40, 26, iter. ἀτιμάζεσκε Il. 9, 450, is reg. and complete in **act.** and **pass.** and used by every class of writers, by Hom. chiefly in Odyss. exactly as often as ἀτιμάω, but in **pres.** and **imp.** only: **fut.** -ᾰσω Aesch. Eum. 917; Soph. El. 1427; Pl. Rep. 465: **aor.** ἠτίμᾰσα Pl. Euthyd. 292 (Il. 1, 11, Mss. Bekk. 2 ed. La R., Ameis, -ησα Vulg. Spitzn. Dind.); subj. ἀτιμάσω Aesch. Pr. 783; Soph. O. C. 49; Eur. Heracl. 227; Ar. Nub. 1121; Com. Fr. (Phryn.) 2, 605; Isocr. 2, 14: **p.** ἠτίμακα Andoc. 4, 31; Pl. Polit. 266: **p. p.** ἠτίμασμαι Eur. Med. 20; Pl. Leg. 762, ἀπ- Aesch. Eum. 95: **aor.** ἠτιμάσθην, -ασθείς Pind. Fr. 100 (B.); Xen. An. 1, 1, 4; Pl. Leg. 931; Aeschin. 2, 121: **fut.** ἀτιμασθήσομαι Aesch. Ag. 1068 (Dind. Herm.); Soph. O. R. 1081. **Vb.** ἀτιμαστέον Pl. Phaedr. 266, -έη Hippocr. 3, 530. ἀτῑμόω is also reg. and complete in **act.** and **pass.**, but not Epic, freq. in Attic prose, especially the Orators, Aeschin. 3, 232: **fut.** -ώσω Aeschin. 1, 134; Dem. 21, 183: **aor.** ἠτίμωσα Aesch. Supp. 645; Ar. Pax 743; Andoc. 1, 106; Lys. 10, 22; Isae. 8, 41; Dem. 19, 257. 37, 24; Hyperid.

Eux. p. 15 (Schn.): p. ἠτίμωκα Dem. 21, 103: p. p. ἠτίμωμαι Eur. Hel. 455; Lys. 25, 24; Dem. 21, 91; (Her. 4, 66: plp. ἠτίμωτο Her. 7, 231): aor. ἠτιμώθην Aesch. Ch. 636; Andoc. 1, 33; Lys. 6, 25; Pl. Rep. 553; (Dem.) 59, 27: fut. ἀτιμωθήσομαι Aesch. Ag. 1068 (Vulg. Paley), see above; (Lys.) 20, 34; Isocr. 5, 64. 16, 49: 3 fut. ἠτιμώσομαι Dem. 19, 284, a form rare in verbs with the temporal augment: pres. ἀτιμοῦνται Antiph. 2, δ, 7. This verb is rare in Attic poetry and Ionic prose, Aesch. Eur. Ar. and Her. quoted. ἀτιμάω has in classic authors neither mid. nor pass. ἀτιμόω no mid., nor ἀτιμάζω, unless ἀτιμάζεσθαι N. T. Rom. 1, 24, be mid.

Ἀτῑμάω *To dishonour*, Od. 16, 307; Soph. Aj. 1129 (Schol. Herm. Dind. ἀτιζ- Elms. Nauck): imp. ἀτίμα Od. 21, 99, -μων 23, 28: fut. -ήσω Il. 8, 163; Hes. Op. 185: aor. ἠτίμησα Il. 1, 94. 2, 240; Mosch. 4, 6 (Mein.), Dor. ᾱσα Pind. P. 9, 80; ἀτιμήσῃ Callim. Dian. 260; ἀτιμήσειε Il. 6, 522, -ήσαιτε 14, 127; -ήσας Od. 20, 133. H. Hym. 1, 72; Callim. Dian. 261; -ῆσαι Od. 14, 57. Except in Epic, rare in poetry, Pind. and Soph. quoted: rare also in prose, pres. ἀτιμῶσι Xen. Rep. Ath. 1, 14 (v. r. ἀτιμοῦσι Dind. Saupp.): fut. ἀτιμήσει Stob. vol. 4. p. 105 (Meineke for ἔτι μισεῖ Dem. 18, 315 Mss. edit.), but -ήσομεν Hierocl. p. 44 (N.) is now -άσομεν p. 46 (Mullach): aor. ἠτίμησαν N. T. Marc. 12, 4 (Mss. B. D. Sin. Lachm.); ἀτιμήσαντες Plut. Mor. 1104: and p. ἠτιμήκασι Galen 1, 10; -ηκότι Plut. Cat. Maj. 15 (Ms. v. but -ωκότι Ms. V. Sint. Bekk.). Pass. late, -ᾶσθαι, aor. ἠτιμήθην Galen 5, 43. 44. Vb. ἀτιμητέον Isocr. 15, 175 (-μωτέον Cobet). (ᾰ, ῑ.)

Ἀτιτάλλω *To rear, tend*, Epic and Lyric, Od. 14, 41; Hipponax 86 (B.); Theocr. 15, 111; Epic inf. ἀτιταλλέμεναι Od. 11, 250; Hes. Th. 480: imp. ἀτίταλλον Il. 14, 202. Od. 19, 354; Pind. N. 3, 58; Ap. Rh. 4, 1739; Theocr. 17, 58; late prose, Themist. 20, 234 (v. r. ἠτίτ-): fut. (-ᾰλῶ): aor. ἀτίτηλα Il. 24, 60; Anth. 7, 334; Mosch. 2, 12. Pass. ἀτιταλλομένην Od. 15, 174: imp. ἀτιτάλλετο H. Merc. 400 (Baum.). Mid. aor. ἀτιτήλατο Opp. Cyn. 1, 271, missed by Lexicogr. (ᾰ.)

Ἀτίω *To slight*, Poet. and only 3 sing. pres. ἀτίει Theogn. 621, and pl. -ίουσι Orph. Lith. 62. Mid. late, aor. ἀτῑσατο Tzetz. P. Hom. 702, missed by Lexicogr. (ᾰ, ῐ, ῑσ-.)

Ἀτρεκέω *To be sure*, very rare, Aretae. Morb. Diut. 1, 9 (Vulg. now ἀτρεμέει): aor. ἀτρεκήσασα Eur. Fr. 317 (Dind.).

Ἀτρεμέω *To keep quiet, stationary*, Hippocr. 6, 102 (Lit.); Opp. H. 4, 643; subj. -έωσι Hes. Op. 539; -έοι Hippocr. 3, 458, late Attic ἀτρεμοῖεν Plut. Pyr. 12; -έειν Hippocr. 5, 402; -εῖν Aristot. Zenon. 3, 9; Luc. Herm. 35. Tox. 10; Plut. Mor.

134. Alcib. 38; ἀτρεμέων Opp. Hal. 2, 90, -ῶν Plut. Publ. 17; Arr. An. 7, 1, 4: **imp.** ἠτρέμουν Plut. Aristid. 18: **fut.** -ήσω Plut. Pomp. 58; App. Syr. 2: **aor.** ἠτρέμησα Her. 7, 8; -ήσῃ Hippocr. 6, 388; -ῆσαι Plut. Publ. 22; -ήσας Plut. Alcib. 34. Marcell. 3. **Pass.** or **mid.** ἀτρεμέεσθαι if correct, Theogn. 47 (Mss. Vulg.), see foll.

Ἀτρεμίζω *To keep quiet*, Theogn. 303; Hippocr. 6, 102. 282; -ίζων Her. 1, 185. 7, 18. 9, 74; rare in Attic, Antiph. 2, δ, 9. 3, β, 5. δ, 4. 5; (Pl.) Locr. 104; Themist. 26, 317; perhaps trans. Alex. ad Gent. p. 46: **imp.** ἠτρέμιζεν Hippocr. 5, 402 (Lit.): **fut.** -ιεῖν Her. 8, 68: **aor.** ἀτρεμίσῃ (Hippocr.) Epist. 9, 384; ἀτρεμίσας Hippocr. 6, 374 (Lit.) **Mid. fut.** -ιεῖσθαι Theogn. 47 (Bergk), -έεσθαι (Vulg.).

Ἄττω, see ᾄσσω.

Ἀτύζω *To terrify*, Epic and Lyr. Ap. Rh. 1, 465: **fut.** late, -ύξω Apollinar. Ps. 2, 9: **aor.** inf. ἀτύξαι Theocr. 1, 56. **Pass.** ἀτύζομαι Pind. P. 1, 13; Ap. Rh. 2, 635. 248; -όμενος Il. 18, 7. 21, 4. Od. 23, 42; Pind. Ol. 8, 39; Soph. El. 149 (chor.); Eur. Andr. 131 (chor.). Tr. 808 (chor.): **aor.** ἀτυχθείς Il. 6, 468; Ap. Rh. 1, 1286. (ᾰ.)

Ἀτυχέω *To be unfortunate*, Antiph. 2, δ, 9; Thuc. 1, 32; Com. Fr. 3, 593: **imp.** ἠτύχουν Com. Fr. 3, 522: **fut.** -ήσεις Ar. Nub. 427: **aor.** ἠτύχησα Antiph. 4, β, 6; Dem. 18, 263; -ῆσαι Her. 9, 111; Thuc. 2, 62; Pl. Leg. 807. Phaedr. 230, reg.: **p.** ἠτύχηκα Com. Fr. (Phil.) 4, 41; Himer. 4, 2; ἠτυχηκέναι Isocr. 5, 90; ἠτυχηκώς Lycurg. 41; Aeschin. 2, 100; Dem. 20, 53, &c.: **pass.** rare ἠτύχημαι Dem. 22, 17; Joseph. Ant. 16, 8, 6: **plp.** ἠτύχητο Dio. Hal. de Isocr. 9: **aor.** ἀτυχηθείς Dem. 18, 212. This verb seems not to occur in Epic nor Trag., rarely in Her., but often in Comedy and Attic prose.

Αὐαίνω *To dry*, Poet. and Ion. Solon 4, 36 (B.); Her. 2, 92; Hippocr. 6, 544 (Lit.), and αὑαίνω, varies in augm.: **imp.** ηὕαινε, καθ- (Luc.) Amor. 12 (D.), καθαύαιν- (Jacobitz): **fut.** αὐᾰνῶ Soph. El. 819, κατ- Archil. 61 (B.), καθ- Lycophr. 397, συν- Eur. Cycl. 463: **aor.** ηὗηνα, ἐξ- Her. 4, 173; subj. αὐήνωσι 1, 200; αὕηνον Nic. Fr. 70, 6; αὐῆναι Hippocr. 8, 206; -ήνας 7, 156; Her. 2, 77: but **aor. pass.** αὐάνθην, ἐξ- 4, 151, αὐάνθην, ἐπαφ- Ar. Ran. 1089 chor. (Ms. R. Suid. Bekk. ἐπαφηυ- Dind. ἀφηυ- Herm. Mein.); αὐανθῆναι Hippocr. 7, 498; αὐανθείς Od. 9, 321; Aesch. Ch. 260; Hippocr. 8, 32; Theophr. C. P. 5, 13, 4. H. P. 8, 11, 3: **fut. m.** as **pass.** αὐανοῦμαι Soph. Ph. 954: and **fut. p.** late in *simple*, αὐανθήσομαι Lycophr. 1424, but ἀφ-αυανθήσομαι Ar. Eccl. 146; late prose Oribas. 8, 25: **imp. pass.** ηὑαινόμην Ar. Fr. 514 (Dind.), αὐαιν- Xen. An. 2, 3, 16 (Popp.

Krüg. L. Dind. Saupp.) The **act.** form never occurs in good Att. prose, the **pass.** very rarely: **pres.** *ἀναίνοιτο* Xen. Oec. 16, 14; *ἀναίνεσθαι* 19, 11: **imp.** *ἀναίνετο* Xen. quoted. For *ἐξ-ηνήνε* Her. 4, 173, Bredow would read *ἐξ-αύηνε* in conformity with *ἐξ-ανάνθην* 4, 151: Abicht again uniformly augments, *-ηύηνε*, *-ηνάνθην*: Bekk. Dind. Stein *-ην*, *-αν*.

Αὐδάζω *To speak*, late in **act. fut.** *-άξω* Lycophr. 892: **aor.** *ηὔδαξα* Lycophr. 360; Anth. 6, 218: **aor. p.** *αὐδαχθεῖσα* Orph. Hym. 27, 9. **Mid.** (*αὐδάζομαι*) perhaps only **aor.** *ηὐδαξάμην* Her. 5, 51; Opp. Hal. 1, 127; Dion. Per. 22, *αὐδ-* Nic. Ther. 464; *-δάξασθαι* Her. 2, 57. For *ηὐδαξ-* Her. 5, 51, Bredow would read *αὐδαξ-* as more Herodotean, and so Abicht edits. This is difficult to decide. Gaisf. gives here no variant; and analogy gives us little help, both because verbs with initial *αυ* are few, and because in the Mss. these few shew both ways: *αὖδα*, *ηὖδα* Her. 2, 57; *ἐξ-ανάνθην* 4, 151, *ἐξηύηνε* 4, 173; *αὐξάνετο* 5, 92, *αὔξετο* 3, 39. 6, 63, **perf.** *αὔξηται* 1, 58, *ηὐξάνετο* 5, 92, *ηὔξετο* 3, 39. 6, 63, **plp.** *ηὔξηντο* 5, 78; *αὐτομόλεον* 1, 127, *αὐτομόλησε* 3, 160, *ηὐτομόλησε* ibid. *ἔν-αυε* 7, 231, no v. r.

Αὐδάω *To speak*, Poet. and Ion. Il. 14, 195. Od. 5, 89; Aesch. Sept. 1043; Soph. O. C. 864; Eur. Ph. 568; Ar. Ran. 369 (Dind.): **imp.** *ηὔδων* Il. 3, 203; Aesch. Sept. 591; Soph. O. R. 568; Eur. Andr. 619; Her. 2, 57 (Schweigh. Gaisf. Dind. Abicht, Stein), *αὔδ-* (Bekk. Bred. Lhardy, Krüg.), Epic dual *αὐδήτην*, *προσ-* Il. 11, 136, but always *-ηύδων* Od. 9, 345. 11, 56, *-ηύδα* Il. 4, 24. Od. 14, 79; Hes. Th. 169. Sc. 117. 445: **fut.** *αὐδήσω* Her. (Orac.) 1, 85; Soph. O. R. 846; (Theocr.) Epigr. 24 (Mein.), *προσ-* Soph. Aj. 855, Dor. *-άσω* Pind. Ol. 1, 7; Anth. 6, 304; Eur. Ion 886 (chor.), *ἐξ-* I. T. 181 (chor.), *-ᾱσοῦντι* Anth. Plan. 120: **aor.** *ηὔδησα* Soph. Tr. 171, Dor. *αὔδᾱσα* Pind. I. 6, 42; imper. *αὔδᾱσον* Soph. O. C. 204 (chor.); Eur. Ph. 124 (trimet. in melicis); **part.** *-ήσας* Il. 10, 47, Dor. *-άσαις* Pind. P. 4, 61, iter. *αὐδήσασκε* Il. 5, 786: **p.** *ηὔδηκα*, *ἀπ-* Hippocr. 8, 570 (Lit.); Luc. Luct. 24: **aor.** *ηὐδήθην*, *αὐδηθείς* Ap. Rh. 1, 624; Soph. Tr. 1106, Dor. *αὐδᾱθείς* Eur. Med. 174 (chor.): **fut.** late *αὐδηθήσομαι* Lycophr. 630. **Mid.** *αὐδάομαι* as **act.** Aesch. Eum. 380; Soph. Ph. 852; *-ώμενος* Ph. 130: **imp.** *ηὐδᾶτο* Soph. Aj. 772, Dor. *ηὐδώμαν*, *ἐπ-* Phil. 395 (chor.): **fut.** (*-ήσομαι*), Dor. *-ᾱσομαι* Pind. Ol. 2, 92: (**aor.** *ηὐδαξάμην* Her. 5, 51. 2, 55. 57, belongs to *αὐδάζω*, *-ομαι*.) An Epic **pres. pass.** *αὐδώωνται* occurs Opp. Hal. 1, 378. 776. Matthiae proposed, needlessly we think, to read *αὔδησον* for *αὔδασον* Eur. Ph. 124. Antigone has struck up the "Doric strain," and though her utterance here, as elsewhere, takes shape in a trimeter, she is still in *Doric mood.* αὔδασον occurs also in a trimeter ascribed to Aeschylus, Fr. 19 (Dind.), but too isolated to yield any safe inference.

This verb is almost exclusively Epic, Lyric, and Tragic. We think it occurs once only in prose, Her. 2, 57, and twice in comedy, αὐδῶ Ar. Ran. 369, **pass.** αὐδώμενος Com. Fr. (Alex.) 3, 492, comp. ἀπ-αυδῶ Ar. Ran. 369, -αυδᾷ Eq. 1072, πρωυδᾶν Av. 556. In *classic Attic* prose, we think it is entirely avoided, simple and comp. Hippocr. Theophrast. Luc. more freq. Plut. use ἀπαυδῶ, &c.

Αὐ-ερύω *To draw back*, augments not, and seems confined to **pres.** αὐ-ερύῃ Pind. Ol. 13, 81; -ύων Il. 8, 325; Anth. 5, 285: **imp.** αὐέρυον Il. 12, 261: and **aor.** αὐέρυσα Il. 1, 459. 2, 422; -ύσας Anth. 6, 96.

Αὐθαδίζομαι *To be self-willed*, Pl. Apol. 34, the only instance in classic Greek; Themist. 29, 346: **fut.** -ιοῦμαι, ἀπ- Philostr. Imag. 779: **aor.** late, -ισάμενος Themist. 34, 64, ἀπο- Plut. Mor. 250; -ίσασθαι 700.

Αὐλέω *To play on the flute* (αὐλός), reg. but unaugm. in Doric, Her. 1, 141: **imp.** αὔλει Theocr. 6, 43, ηὔλει Pl. Conv. 215: **fut.** αὐλήσω, 3 pl. Dor. -ησεῦντι Theocr. 7, 71: **aor.** αὔλησε Alcm. 82 (B.), ηὔλ- Ar. Vesp. 582; αὐλησάτω Epich. 86 (Ahr.). **Pass.** and **mid.** αὐλεῖται Eur. I. T. 367; -ούμενος Pl. Leg. 791; Plut. Mor. 1144: **imp.** ηὐλεῖτο Xen. Conv. 9, 3, -οῦντο Cyr. 4, 5, 7.

Αὐλίζομαι *To encamp*, usu. Dep. Eur. El. 304; Opp. Hal. 3, 237; Her. 9, 93; -ίζοιο Xen. Cyr. 4, 6, 10; -όμενος Od. 14, 412; Her. 9, 37; Thuc. 7, 4; -ίζεθαι Thuc. 6, 64: **imp.** ηὐλιζόμην Com. Fr. (Eup.) 2, 558; Xen. An. 7, 7, 6, Ion. αὐλ- Luc. D. Syr. 22 (Jacobitz), ηὐλ- (Dind. *now*): **fut.** (-ιοῦμαι?): **aor. m.** ηὐλισάμην Thuc. 4, 13. 6, 65. 71. 7, 3 and always; ἐν-αυλισάμενος Her. 9, 15: **p.** as **mid.** late ηὐλισμένος, κατ- Plut. Mor. 578: **plp.** ηὔλιστο Joseph. Jud. B. 1, 17, 5, ηὐλισμένοι ἦσαν Arr. An. 3, 29: **aor. p.** as **mid.** ηὐλίσθην Xen. An. 4, 1, 11. 3, 2. 5, 21 and always, κατ- Hipponax 63; Soph. Ph. 30; Eur. Rhes. 518, αὐλ- Anth. 9, 287; αὐλισθείς Her. 8, 9: fut. late αὐλισθήσομαι V. T. Ruth. 1, 16. Job 29, 19. Ps. 24, 13. Prov. 19, 23. Apocr. Sirach 24, 7. Tob. 6, 11 and always in Sept.; Or. Sib. 3, 789, ἐν- Hesych. **Vb.** αὐλιστέον Geop. 18, 3. **Act.** late in *simple*, αὐλίζων V. T. Jer. 38 (31), 9, but ἐν-αυλίζω Soph. Ph. 33, παρ- Eur. Ion 493 (chor.) **Fut. mid.** αὐλίσομαι, -ιοῦμαι, uniformly given to this verb by lexicons, we have never seen simple or comp. Thuc. and we think Luc. have always **aor mid.**; Xen. Polyb. and Arrian **aor. pass.**; Her. both; so Plutarch, but aor. m. oftener; in Att. poetry aor. pass. only, κατ- Soph. and Eur. quoted. Late as well as classic writers divide on these aorists: ηὐλίσαντο Dio. Hal. 9, 20. 26; Plut. Luc. 24. Cleom. 14. Tib. Gr. 16: aor. p. ηὐλίσθην Polyb. 2, 25. 5, 86. 8, 34 and always; Plut. Cam. 18; Arr. An. 1, 13. Ind. 23, 4. 40, 11, so in comp. ἀπ-αυλισθῆναι Dio. Hal. 8, 87. ἐν-ηυλισάμην Her. 9, 15; Thuc. 3, 91. 8, 33; Dio. Hal. 17, 4; Plut. Mor. 579. Sert. 11. Ant. 44: aor. p. ἐν-ηυλίσθην Xen. An. 7, 7, 8 (Vulg. Dind. Krüg.) ἐπηυλίσαντο Thuc. 3, 5. 4, 134; Luc. V. H. (1), 38. (2), 2; Plut. Ant. 44. Syll. 29. κατ-ηυλισάμην Plut. Themist. 30. Publ. 22. Tim. 12. Pyr. 27. Lys. 29: κατ-ηυλίσθην Xen. An. 7, 5, 15; Eur. Rhes. 518; Soph. Ph. 30; Polyb. 5, 8; Plut. Alex. 24. Themist. 30.

Αὐξάνω *To augment*, Pind. Fr. 130; Aesch. Pers. 756; Her. 7, 16; Pl. Tim. 41; intrans. *wax*, Aristot. Anal. Post. 1, 13, 3, so also later; and αὔξω trans. Hom. Epigr. 13, 3; Theogn. 823; Emped. 198; Pind. I. 3, 80; Soph. Tr. 117; Eur. H. F. 672; Hippocr. 6, 264; Thuc. 6, 40: imp. ηὔξανον (Eur.) Fr. 1117, 25 (D.), ηὖξον Com. Fr. (Athen.) 4, 557; Her. 9, 31; Pl. Rep. 569, both rare: fut. αὐξανῶ late, see below, classic αὐξήσω Thuc. 6, 18; Xen. Mem. 2, 7, 9; Pl. Rep. 468: aor. ηὔξησα Solon Fr. 11 (B.); Xen. Hell. 7, 1, 24; Isocr. 5, 120: p. ηὔξηκα Pl. Tim. 90; Plut. Sert. 25: p. p. ηὔξημαι Eur. Fr. 424 (D.); Hippocr. 4, 138; Pl. Rep. 371; Dem. 3, 29. 9, 21, αὐξ- Her. 1, 58: but plp. ηὔξηντο 5, 78 (Vulg. Bekk. Dind. Stein, αὐξ- Bred. Dietch, Abicht): aor. ηὐξήθην Emped. 61; Hippocr. 6, 512; Thuc. 6, 33; Pl. Criti. 121; -ηθείς Her. 4, 147; Dem. 23, 133: fut. αὐξηθήσομαι Aristot. Gen. An. 1, 18, 17; Dem. 56, 48: and as pass. fut. m. αὐξήσομαι Xen. Cyr. 6, 1, 12; Pl. Rep. 497. Mid. and pass. αὐξάνομαι *to grow*, Emped. 197; Eur. Med. 918; Ar. Av. 1065; Her. 5, 91; Pl. Phaed. 96, and αὔξομαι Mimnerm. 2; Pind. P. 8, 93; Soph. O. R. 173; Ar. Ach. 226; Her. 5, 91; Pl. Rep. 328: imp. ηὐξανόμην Ar. Vesp. 638; Pl. Polit. 273, αὐξ- Her. 5, 92, ηὐξόμην Hes. Th. 493; Eur. Hec. 20; Thuc. 1, 99, αὐξ- Her. 3, 39. 6, 63: fut. αὐξήσομαι Pl. Rep. 497: with p. ηὔξημαι Eur. I. A. 1248; Pl. Rep. 371; Dem. 9, 21: ηὐξήθην Pl. Conv. 210; Dem. 2, 5 &c. See ἀέξω. Vb. αὐξητέον Menand. Rhet. p. 193 (Spengl.) In the augmented tenses, Mss. and edit. of Her. vary between ηὐξ- and αὐξ-. The reg. fut. αὐξᾰνῶ occurs late, and is formed, some think, by a false analogy, as ν they say is not *characteristic*, V. T. Gen. 17, 6. 20. 48, 4. Lev. 26, 9: so aor. ηὔξηνα Syntip. p. 2 (Eberhard): aor. p. ηὐξήνθη Aesop 71 (Schaef. -ήθη Halm 374.) αὐξυνθείς (Halm 28) from a marginal correction by

Lachmann—if correct, the only instance of αὐξύνω we have seen. The only instance we have met with of the pure form αὐξέω is ηὔξουν Dio Cass. Fr. 89, 3 (Bekk.), and αὐξέεται Aretae. 42 (ed. Oxon.), αὐξοῦνται Plut. Mor. 724, mistakes perhaps for ηὔξον (so now L. Dind.), -ξεται, -ονται. Hes. Mimnerm. Soph. Thuc. always αὔξω, or αὔξομαι, and Pind. except αὐξάνοι Fr. 130 (Bergk): Aesch. once αὐξάνω, and once αὔξεται: Eur. αὐξάνω twice, -άνομαι once, αὔξω, -ομαι often: Her. αὐξάνω, -άνομαι, and αὔξομαι: Xen. αὔξω often, never -άνω, but αὐξάνομαι, αὔξομαι: Pl. αὐξάνω, αὔξω, -άνομαι, -ξομαι: Isocr. αὐξάνομαι, -ξομαι: Dem. αὔξω 3, 26, ἐπ-αυξάνω 3, 33, αὐξάνομαι 18, 161 (10, 34), ηὐξάνετο 18, 310: Ar. αὐξάνομαι, ηὐξανόμην, αὔξομαι: Com. Fr. αὔξω, -άνω, αὔξομαι.

'Αυτέω *To shout*, Poet. Aesch. Ch. 881; Eur. Ph. 1271; Ar. Lys. 717; Theocr. 24, 37: imp. ἄυτει Il. 11, 258. 20, 50; Ap. Rh. 4, 1702, ἀύτεεν Q. Sm. 3, 554, ἐπ-αύτεον Theocr. 22 (19), 91, Ion. ἀύτευν Il. 12, 160; Eur. Hipp. 167 (chor.): aor. late ἤύτησα Nonn. D. 11, 185. 33, 263, ἐπ- Q. Sm. 4, 262, ἀν- Opp. C. 4, 301. (ᾰ, ῡ.)

Αὐχέω *To boast*, Batr. 57; Aesch. Pr. 338; Eur. Alc. 95; Thuc. 2, 39; Her. 7, 103; -έοντες 2, 160: imp. ηὔχουν Aesch. Ag. 506; Eur. Heracl. 931; Luc. Alex. 42: fut. -ήσω Eur. Fr. 851; Anth. (Thall.) 7, 373. (Apoll.) 9, 791; Luc. D. Mort. 22, 2; Himer. Or. 3, 8: aor. *simple* late, ηὔχησα Anth. 15, 4; Apollod. 2, 4, 3, but κατ- Aesch. Pers. 352, ἐξ- Soph. Ph. 869, ἐπ- Ar. Av. 628. **Mid. aor.** αὐχήσασθαι (Hesych.). This verb seems not to proceed beyond the aor. and, in *simple*, is classic in pres. and imp. only. It occurs rarely in Epic, Lyric, and Comic poetry, Batr. 57; Com. Fr. (Cratin.) 2, 15; freq. in Aesch. and Eur., never (*simple*) in Sophocles. In *classic* prose, Her. and Thuc. alone and rarely use it.

Αὐχμάω *To be squalid*, only pt. αὐχμῶντες Theophr. H. P. 8, 10, 4; Plut. Mor. 187; Luc. Necyom. 4, αὐχμῶσα Luc. Apol. 6. Philops. 24, Epic -ώουσα Nonn. 37, 421, and αὐχμέω, -εῖς Od. 24, 250; Ar. Nub. 920, -εῖ Theophr. H. P. 4, 10, 7; -εῖν Ar. N. 442; Pl. Rep. 402; -ῶν Ar. Plut. 84: aor. αὐχμήσῃ Pl. Phaedr. 251; -ήσας Tim. 84.

Αὔω *To shout*, Poet. Aesch. Sept. 186; Timoth. 6 (B.): imp. unaugm. αὖον Il. 13, 477. 20, 48; Ap. Rh. 2, 566: fut. trisyll. ἀΰσω Eur. Ion 1446: aor. ἤϋσα Il. 18, 217. Od. 24, 530; Ap. Rh. 1, 383; in tmesi Soph. Tr. 565, Dor. 'ἄϋσ- Theocr. 13, 58, ἀντ-ᾱΰ- Pind. P. 4, 197 (B.), and unaugm. ἄϋσ- Il. 14, 147; Theocr. 8, 28; subj. ἀΰσῃς Soph. El. 830 (chor.); imper. ἀΰσατε Eur. Supp. 800 (chor.); ἀΰσας Il. 2, 334; Soph. O. R.

1260 (trimet.); ἀῦσαι Od. 9, 65. Diphthong resolved in **fut.** and **aor.** and ῡ: **pres.** and **imp.** never resolved, αὔω, αὖον, not ἀΰω, for ἀΰει Pind. I. 5 (6), 25 (Vulg. αὔει edit. Rom.) is now properly edited ἀΐει (Schol. Boeckh, Herm, Bergk). ἐπάῦσον occurs with ῠ Theocr. 23, 44, but the reading is probably corrupt. Mss. offer ὀπ-ασσον, ὀπαυσον &c. Briggs' emendation ἐπάπῦσον Dor. **aor.** of ἐπηπύω satisfies the sense, and is adopted by Meineke and Ziegler; but does it heal the metre? The **aor.** of ἀπύω is indisputably long Eur. Rhes. 776, and in no instance have we found either it or **fut.** decidedly short. Hermann very ingeniously changes ἐπ- of the common reading ἐπάῦσον into ἔτ', and preserves the quantity of υ by transposing ἄῦσον to the end of the line. Thus: for ἐπ | άῦσον· | ὦ φίλε, | κεῖσαι, he edits ἔτ' | ὦ φίλε, | κεῖσαι ἄῦσον—a considerable dislocation. Graefe saves the quantity by simply missing out ὦ, . . ἐπ' | άῦ | σον· φίλε, | κεῖσαι. We think neither way happy. κάπῦσον **aor.** of καπύω suits the metre, and, if it suit the sense, is perhaps as near the Mss. reading as other conjectures. Ahrens, we observe, reads ἐπαΐᾰσον. ᾰ Hom. ᾱ Pind. ἀντᾱῦσε P. 4, 197.

Αὔω *To kindle* (αῦ- La R.) Poet. and only **pres. act.** Od. 5, 490, Att. αὔω, ἀφ- Ar. Eq. 394: and **mid.** as **act.** αὔομαι Ar. Fr. 589 (D.); and late, Arat. 1035. Usu. ἐναύω Xen. Mem. 2, 2, 12; Dinarch. 2, 9: **imp.** unaugm. ἔναυον Her. 7, 231: **aor.** opt. ἐναύσει' Com. Fr. (Diph.) 4, 405 (Pors. Meineke); inf. ἐναῦσαι Plut. Phoc. 37; Stob. (Nicostr.) 70, 12. **Mid.** ἐναύονται Ael. Fr. 105; -αύεσθαι Com. Fr. (Cratin.) 2, 214; Plut. Num. 9: **fut.** ἐναυσόμενος Long. Past. 3, 6: **aor.** ἐναύσασθαι (Pl.) Ax. 371; -αυσάμενος Plut. Mor. 279; Luc. D. Mar. 2, 2. Tim. 6. Prom. 18. ἀφαύω is very rare, and seems confined to the **pres.**, occurring occasionally as a v. r. for ἀφεύω *to singe*, Ar. Pax 1144.

'Αφαγνίζω *To purify*, late in **act.** and **pass. fut.** -ιῶ V. T. Lev. 14, 52. Num. 31, 20: **aor.** -ήγνισα Paus. 2, 31, 11; inf. -αγνίσαι V. T. Lev. 14, 49: **aor. p.** -αγνισθῇ V. T. Num. 19, 12. 20: **fut.** -ισθήσεται 19, 19: **mid. fut.** ἀφαγνιούμενος Hippocr. 6, 364 (Mss. Lit. ἀπαγ- Vulg.): **aor.** ἀφ-αγνίσηται Eur. Alc. 1146; -ίσασθαι V. T. Num. 8, 21. The **mid.** only is classical.—Defectively handled in lexicons.

'Αφαιρέω, see αἱρέω.

'Αφάσσω *To feel, handle*, Her. 3, 69; Hippocr. 8, 120; Ap. Rh. 2, 710; Musae. 82: **imp.** ἄφασσε Ap. Rh. 4, 1522: **fut.** (-ᾰσω): **aor.** ἤφασα Her. 3, 69; ἄφασον ibid. **Mid.** ἀφάσσομαι, -όμενος Ap. Rh. 4, 181, and -σσάομαι: hence **aor.** ἀφασσήσῃ Hippocr. 7, 326 (Lit.), but ἀφασάμενος, παρ- Hippocr. 2, 720 (Erm. with Foes, Lind.) (ᾰ.)

'Αφαύω, see αὔω.

'Αφάω or **ἀφ-** *To handle*, Ion. and *simple* only in Epic part. ἀφόων Il. 6, 322 (Bekk.), ἀμφ-αφ- Od. 8, 196, but ἀφόων Anth. 11, 366, ἐπ-αφῶν Aesch. Pr. 849; rare in prose Pl. Crat. 404: imp. iter. ἀμφ-αφάασκε Mosch. 2, 95: fut. ἀφήσω, ἐπ- Hippocr. 8, 352 (Lit.); Alciphr. 1, 22: aor. ἤφησα, ἐπ- Hecatae. Fr. 360; Hippocr. 8, 342. **Mid.** trans. (ἀφάομαι), ἀμφ-αφάασθαι Il. 22, 373. Od. 8, 215; ἐπ-αφώμενος Mosch. 2, 50; Hippocr. 8, 346; Luc. D. Mer. 12, 3: imp. ἀφόωντο, ἀμφ- Od. 15, 462: aor. ἐπ-αφήσατο Anth. 5, 222; Nonn. 3, 285; -ήσῃ Hippocr. 8, 344; -ήσαιτο Hippocr. 8, 122 (Lit.); *simple* ἀφήσασθαι (Hesych.) (ᾰ.)

'Αφεύω, see εὔω.

'Αφέω, -ίω, see foll.

'Αφιέω *To dismiss*, -ιεῖς Dem. 24, 122 (Voem. -ίεις B. Saupp. -ίῃς Vulg. Bekk. Dind.), -ίει Hippocr. 7, 474, Ion. ἀπίει Her. 2, 96; imperat. ἀφίει Ar. Vesp. 428: imp. ἀφΐει Il. 11, 702 (-ίη Bekk. always now); Thuc. 4, 122. 8, 41; Xen. Cyr. 8, 3, 33. Hell. 6, 2, 28; Dem. 6, 20. 36, 16. 24 (Bekk. ἠφ- Dind.), Ion. ἀπ- Her. 4, 157, with double augm. ἠφίειν Pl. Euthyd. 293 (-ίην Bekk.), -ίει Hippocr. 5, 228 (Lit.); Thuc. 2, 49; Pl. Lys. 222. Lach. 183; Dem. 6, 20 (Dind.). 18, 218 (Bekk. Dind.), 3 pl. ἠφίουν rare and doubtful Isae. 6, 40, εἴων Scheibe (later occur ἀφέω, -εῖς N. T. Rev. 2, 20, and ἀφίω V. T. Eccl. 2, 18: imp. ἤφιε Marc. 11, 16, &c.); and some appearance of pres. subj. ἀφίῃ Pl. Parm. 156, -ίωσι Ar. Lys. 157; opt. ἀφίοιεν Xen. Hell. 6, 4, 3, -ίοιτε Pl. Apol. 29, see ἀφίημι. In Dem. Dind. edits *now* ἠφίει 6, 20. 36, 16. 24, and always, we think, in the act. form.

'Αφίημι *To let go*, Pind. P. 4, 149; Eur. Hec. 367; Isocr. 9, 21, -ίης Eur. Hipp. 1450; Pl. Phil. 50; Dem. 24, 122, -ίησι Eur. Hec. 1105; Hippocr. 1, 630, -ίεμεν Ar. Nub. 1426, ἀπ- Her. 2, 17, ἀφιᾶσι Andoc. 3, 18; subj. -ιῇ Pl. Rep. 520 (Bekk. Stallb. -ίῃ Bait. F. Herm.), -ιῆτε Xen. Hell. 2, 4, 16; imper. ἀφίετε Od. 22, 251; ἀφῑεῖσαι Od. 7, 126, -ῐέντες H. Hym. 2, 56; Pl. Leg. 761: imp. ἀφίην, -ίετε Dem. 23, 188 (Bekk. B. S.), -ίεσαν Thuc. 2, 76. 3, 111. 4, 48. 5, 21; Eur. Heracl. 821; Xen. An. 4, 5, 30. Cyr. 3, 3, 60. Hell. 7, 4, 39; Pl. Rep. 272; Aeschin. 3, 41; Dem. 21, 79 (Bekk.), and ἠφίην Pl. Euthyd. 293 (Bekk. -ίειν Vulg.), ἠφίει Thuc. 2, 49; Pl. Lys. 222, -ίη (Bekk.); Dem. 18, 218, -ίετε Dem. 23, 188 (Dind.). (Epist.) 3, 26 (Dind.), -ίεσαν Xen. Hell. 4, 6, 11; Dem. 21, 79 (Dind.), Ion. ἀπ- Her. 5, 42. 8, 52: fut. ἀφήσω Il. 2, 263; Soph. O. C. 857; Pl. Phil. 19, Ion. ἀπ- Her. 9, 18. 7, 193 (Dind. Dietsch, Abicht, ἀφ- Bekk. Gaisf. Stein): 1 aor. ἀφῆκα only indic. Soph.

Ant. 1085, -κας Soph. Ph. 1349. O. R. 1177; Eur. Hipp. 1324 (ἐφ- Dind.); Ar. Av. 91; Pl. Conv. 217; Dem. 50, 7, -ῆκε Il. 13, 410; Eur. Ion 47; Antiph. 2, α, 4; Pl. Leg. 885, -ήκαμεν Isae. 5, 1, -ήκατε Aeschin. 3, 85; Dinarch. 1, 57; Dem. 36, 10. 38, 18. 27, -ῆκαν Thuc. 7, 19; Xen. Hell. 1, 2, 18. 7, 2, 16; Dem. 36, 10, Ion. ἀπῆκ- Her. 3, 25. 75. 6, 30. 7, 121. 9, 18 &c., Epic ἀφέηκα Il. 23, 841: p. ἀφεῖκα Xen. An. 2, 3, 13; Dem. 56, 26, Dor. ἀφέωκα (Suid.): p. p. ἀφεῖμαι Soph. Ant. 1165; Eur. Med. 1002; Com. Fr. (Alex.) 3, 485; Pl. Leg. 635; Dem. 38, 8, 3 pl. ἀφέωνται for -εῖνται, late, N. T. Luc. 5, 23. 7, 48 (but ἀνέωνται Her. 2, 165, Mss. Bekk. Dind. Stein); imper. ἀφ-είσθω Thuc. 5, 91; Pl. Leg. 764; ἀφεῖσθαι Pl. Leg. 945; Dem. 37, 1; -ειμένος Thuc. 8, 33; Pl. Rep. 395; Aeschin. 3, 126: plp. ἀφεῖτο Pl. Criti. 116; Her. 8, 49 (Vulg.), ἀπ- (Bekk. Dind. Stein): aor. ἀφείθην Eur. Ph. 1377; Lys. 9, 8; Xen. Hell. 5, 4, 23; Pl. Leg. 781, unaugm. ἀφ-έθην (Hom.) Batr. 84, double augm. late ἠφείθην Plut. Syll. 28 (Bekk. Sint. ἀφ- Ms. C), Ion. ἀπείθ- Her. 6, 112. 7, 122; ἀφ-εθῆναι Thuc. 5, 65: fut. ἀφεθήσομαι Pl. Rep. 472; Lys. 12, 15; Dem. 19, 170; (Xen.) Ven. 7, 11: 2 aor. (ἀφῆν not used in sing. indic.), dual ἀφέτην Epic unaugm. Il. 11, 642, pl. ἀφεῖμεν Isae. 5, 29; Dem. 33, 12, ἀφεῖτε Dem. 3, 5 (Bekk.), ἀφεῖσαν Thuc. 5, 81. 7, 53; Xen. Hell. 1, 5, 19; Dem. 23, 205 (ἄφετε, ἄφεσαν), πρό-εσαν Od. 4, 681. 16, 328, once augm. παρὰ δ' εἶσαν Il. 24, 720, as always in Attic; subj. ἀφέω Hipponax 75 (B.), -έῃ Il. 16, 590, ἀφῶ Pl. Phil. 62; Plut. Mor. 726, -ῇς Soph. Aj. 496; Xen. Cyr. 5, 3, 26, -ῇ Soph. O. R. 198; Dem. 37, 59, Epic -ήῃ Il. 17, 63 (La R.), -ῶμεν Aeschin. 1, 73, -ῶσι Xen. Cyr. 1, 2, 8; opt. ἀφείην Il. 3, 317; Eur. Andr. 846; Dem. 53, 8; (Pl.) Epist. 349, pl. ἀφείητε Dem. 19, 71, and ἀφεῖτε Thuc. 1, 139, ἀφεῖεν Xen. Cyr. 1, 4, 11; ἄφες Aesch. Pr. 315; Ar. Eq. 1159; ἀφεῖναι Ar. Vesp. 595; Antiph. 2, δ, 11; Pl. Phil. 62; ἀφείς Eur. Alc. 794; Thuc. 8, 87, ἀπ- Her. 1, 77. **Mid.** ἀφίεμαι *to let go*, Thuc. 2, 60; Pl. Lach. 184, Ion. ἀπ- Her. 3, 101; -ίοιντο Antiph. 2, δ, 5: **imp.** ἀφίετο Od. 23, 240: **fut.** ἀφήσομαι Eur. Hel. 1629 (earlier ἐφήσ- Il. 23, 82): **2 aor.** ἀφείμην Xen. Hier. 7, 11; (πρό-ωμαι Plut. Them. 7); ἀφοῦ Soph. O. R. 1521, ἄφεσθε Ar. Eccl. 509; ἀφέσθαι Isocr. 6, 83; ἀφέμενος Pl. Rep. 354; Isocr. 9, 78: as **mid. p. p.** ἀφεῖσθαι if sound Dem. 23, 157; παρεῖνται 15, 15. **Vb.** ἀφετέος Pl. Euth. 15. (ῑ Att., ῐ Ep., but ῑ Od. 7, 126. 22, 251. 23, 240, in arsi.) For ἀνέωνται Her. 2, 165, Bredow would read ἀνεῖνται: ἀνεῖται occurs 2, 65. ἀφεῖτε 2 aor. opt. Thuc. 1, 139, Cobet would alter to ἀφείητε. ἀφίεσαν 3 pl. **imp.** act. is much better supported than ἠφίεσαν, but ἠφίετο (Dem.) 25, 47. In classic Greek, the **imp. act.** and **pass.** alone seem to augment the preposition.

'**Αφικνέομαι** *To come*, Aesch. Ag. 435 (chor.). Pers. 15 (chor.); Com. Fr. (Cratin.) 2, 132. 133; Ar. Eq. 975. Av. 1418; Thuc. 7, 33; Lys. 1, 23, Ion. ἀπικν- Her. 2, 41. 3, 82, but ἀφ- Heraclit. 18 (Byw.); subj. ἀφικνῇ Soph. O. C. 1531 (trimet.): **imp.** ἀφικνεῖτο Thuc. 3, 33; Lycurg. 21, Ion. ἀπικνέοντο Her. 4, 125: **fut.** ἀφίξομαι Il. 18, 270; Pind. P. 8, 54; Soph. O. R. 265; Pl. Leg. 744, 2 sing. Poet. ἀφίξεαι Od. 12, 39; Anan. 1 (B.), Ion. ἀπ- Her. 2, 29: **p.** ἀφῖγμαι Od. 6, 297; Aesch. Pr. 303; Soph. O. R. 920; Eur. Tr. 58; Ar. Plut. 265; Thuc. 4, 85; Isae. 2, 47; Pl. Phaed. 57, Ion. ἀπῖκται Her. 1, 193: **plp.** ἀφῖκτο Soph. O. C. 1590, Ion. 3 pl. ἀπίκατο Her. 8, 6, and ἀπιγμένοι ἦσαν 9, 118: **2 aor.** ἀφῖκόμην Il. 18, 395; Mimnerm. 9, 2; Aesch. Ag. 504; Soph. O. R. 1005; Eur. Alc. 26; Ar. Lys. 786 (ἀφῐκ- Pind. Ol. 9, 67); Thuc. 4, 129; Lys. 3, 34; Isocr. 11, 28. 17, 46, Ion. ἀπικ- Her. 2, 44. 8, 8, 2 sing. ἀπίκευ 1, 124, 3 pl. ἀπικέατο Her. 1, 15. 169 (Gaisf. Bekk. Krüg. -κοντο Dind. Dietch, Abicht, Stein); rare Dor. imper. ἀφίκευσο Theocr. 11, 42 (Junt, Schol. K. Ziegl. Fritzsche, -ίκευ τύ Vulg.) (ῐ, ῑ by augm.) **Pres.** and **imp.** not in Epic, rare in Traged. and, except once, only in chor., rare also in Comedy, but freq. in prose: other tenses common in all writers.

'**Αφρᾰδέω** *To be senseless*, Epic and only **pres.** ἀφραδέουσι Od. 7, 294; part. -έοντι Il. 9, 32.

'**Αφρέω** *To foam, cover with foam*, Ion. ἄφρεεν Ap. Rh. 1, 1327, 3 pl. ἄφρεον dissyll. Il. 11, 282.

'**Αφύσσω** Epic, *To draw, pour*, -σσων Il. 1, 598; Trag. Fr. (Ion) Euryt. 1; -σσειν late prose Philostr. Imag. 14: **imp.** ἄφυσσον Callim. Cer. 70: **fut.** ἀφύξω Il. 1, 171, Dor. -υξῶ Theocr. 7, 65: **aor.** ἀφύξῃ Op. Hal. 1, 769. **Mid.** ἀφύσσομαι *to draw for oneself*, Il. 23, 220; Anth. 9, 333. **Pass. imp.** ἠφύσσετο *was drawn*, Od. 23, 305. (ᾰ.)

'**Αφύω** (ῡ) *To draw*, **pres.** in comp. only, ἐξ-αφύοντες Od. 14, 95: **fut.** ἀφύσω (σσ) Anth. 5, 226: **aor.** ἤφῦσα Od. 9, 165, δια- in tmesi Il. 13, 508. 17, 315, ἄφυσσα Od. 2, 379; Eur. I. A. 1051 (chor.), ἤφυσσα, ἐξ- Opp. Hal. 1, 573; imper. -υσσον Od. 2, 349. **Mid. pres.** in comp. ὑπεξαφύονται Ap. Rh. 2, 983: **aor.** ἠφῦσάμην Od. 7, 286, and ἀφυσσάμην Il. 16, 230; -σσάμενοι Od. 4, 359, -μένη Ap. Rh. 4, 669, -μέναν Eur. Med. 836 (chor.); -ύσσασθαι Orph. L. 263; late prose -υσάμενος Polyaen. 8, 25, ἀρυσάμ- (Woelffl.) (ᾰ.)

'**Αχεύω** and '**Αχέω** *To be grieved*, Epic, only part. ἀχεύων Il. 23,

566; Hes. Op. 399, ἀχέων Il. 5, 399; Hes. Sc. 93; Ap. Rh. 3, 643; and late, inf. ἀχευέιν Q. Sm. 3, 643. (ᾰ.)

Ἀχέω *To sound*, Poet. trans. and intrans., Ionic with ᾰ (for ἠχέω) Hom. H. Cer. 479. Pan. 18 (Ilgen, Matth. Buttm.), ʼχέει (Mss. Franke, ἴει Baum.), but Dor. with ᾱ Pind. Fr. 53, 20; Eur. Supp. 72 (chor.); Theocr. 16, 96, ἀχεῦσι Epigr. 4, 10; imper. ἄχει Theocr. 2, 36: imp. ἄχει Alcae. 39 (Bergk); fut. ἀχήσω Eur. Ph. 1295 chor. (Elms. Dind. Nauck): aor. ἄχησα, ἀντ- Eur. Med. 428 (chor.), ἀχήσαμεν Ar. Ran. 210 (chor.), see below; subj. ἀχήσῃ Mosch. 5, 4; ἀχήσειεν Ar. Thesm. 328. **Mid.** ἀχέομαι *to sound, praise*, ἀχεῖται Pind. Fr. 45, 20 (Herm. Hart. ἀχεῖ τε 53 Bergk): fut. ἀχήσομαι H. H. Ven. 252 (Buttm. Lex. p. 181; Hesych., στοναχήσομαι Ms. Franke, στόμα χείσεται Mart. Baumeist.) In several places of the Tragedians and Ar. Elmsley, Dind. &c. would write ἀχέω Aesch. Sept. 868 (chor.); Soph. Tr. 642 (chor. also Herm. 1848), ἀχήσω see above, ἀχήσειε Ar. Thesm. 328, for Vulg. ἠχ- or ἰαχ-. The collat. ἠχέω is used in prose as well as poetry: ἠχεῖ Hes. Th. 42; Soph. Tr. 866; Hippocr. 2, 197. 225 (Erm.); Pl. Prot. 329; Arist. Probl. 11, 9, 1; Luc. Philops. 33; Plut. Coriol. 38: imp. ἤχεε Hes. Th. 835, -έεσκε Her. 4, 200: aor. ἤχησα H. Cer. 38; Hippocr. 3, 512 (Erm.), περι- Il. 7, 267; imper. ἀντ-ηχήσατε Eur. Alc. 423. **Mid.** ἠχεῖται Soph. O. C. 1500.

Ἄχθομαι *To be loaded*, hence *oppressed in spirit, displeased*, Il. 5, 361; Eur. Fr. 23 (D.); Com. Fr. (Eup.) 2, 442; Her. 3, 1. 80; Antiph. 5, 46; Aeschin. 3, 252; Pl. Men. 99: imp. ἠχθόμην Od. 15, 457; Hes. Th. 155; Eur. Alc. 815; Her. 9, 98; Thuc. 1, 92; Lys. 8, 4, ἄχθ- Callim. Cer. 32: fut. ἀχθέσομαι Ar. Nub. 1441; (Xen. Cyr. 8, 4, 10 Dind. Cob.); Pl. Rep. 603. Hipp. Maj. 292, v. r. ἀχθήσομαι (Steph.), not to be confounded with fut. pass. of ἄγω: p. p. late ἤχθημαι Lycophr. 827, ἀπ- Synes. Epist 95 (Herch.), if not rather to be referred to ἔχθω: aor. ἠχθέσθην Aesch. Pr. 390; Her. 2, 103; Thuc. 6, 15; Isocr. 12, 17; Aeschin. 1, 65: fut. p. as mid. ἀχθεσθήσομαι Andoc. 3, 21; Xen. Cyr. 8, 4, 10, (Hertl. Saupp.); Pl. Gorg. 506, συν- Aeschin. 3, 242. Pres. act. occurs late, ἀχθέει Aretae. 79 (ed. Oxon.); -έῃ 60: imp. ἤχθεε if sound, Hermes. Coloph. 2, 39: aor. ἀχθήσας (Hesych.), which gives some countenance to the fut. form ἀχθήσομαι occasionally found as a v. r. of ἀχθέσομαι. The fut. pass. seems to be perfectly good Attic, but prosaic: no aor. mid.

Ἀχλύω (ῡ) *To be dark*, Epic, pres. in comp. ἐπ- Ap. Rh. 4, 1480: aor. ἤχλῡσα Od. 12, 406; Anth. 7, 633; Ap. Rh. 3, 963, act. *darkened*, Q. Sm. 1, 598; Nonn. 4, 368: aor. p. late ἠχλύν- θην Q. Sm. 2, 550. 8, 446, though ἀχλύνω does not occur.

Ἄχνῠμαι *To be troubled,* Poet. Il. 18, 320; Archil. 89; Pind. P. 7, 16; Mosch. 4, 53: **imp.** ἀχνύ̆μην Il. 14, 38. Od. 11, 558; in Att. once only, Soph. Ant. 627 (chor.): **aor.** rare ἀχνυνθέντι Anth. 6, 343, missed by Lexicogr.

Ἄχομαι *To be grieved,* Epic and only pres. Od. 19, 129. 18, 256: and rare **aor.** ἤχθην, ἀχθέντες Trag. Fr. Diog. 4, 2 (Wagn. σαχθέντες Meineke). (ᾰ.)

Ἄω *To satiate,* Epic inf. ἄμεναι (ᾱ) for ἀέμ- Il. 21, 70: **fut.** ἄσω, -ειν Il. 11, 818: **aor.** ἆσα, subj. ἄσω Il. 18, 281; opt. ἄσαιμι 9, 489; imper. ἄᾰσον Q. Sm. 13, 236; inf. ἆσαι Il. 20, 78. **Mid.** ἄομαι, 3 sing. ἄᾰται, lengthened from ἆται, with **fut.** sig. Hes. Sc. 101: **fut.** ἄσομαι, ἄσεσθε Il. 24, 717, 3 sing. ἄᾰται lengthened, according to some, from ἆται (ἄσεται, ἄεται, ἆται, ἄᾰται), others make this a present from a similar process: **aor.** ἀσάμην, ἄσασθαι Il. 19, 307. **Vb.** (ἄ-ατος) ἆτος Il. 6, 203. ἄμεναι Ep. inf. **pres.** Il. 21, 70, is by some referred to (ἥμι). To this verb has been assigned ἑῶμεν (ἕωμεν) as a lengthened subj., with change of accent, for ὦμεν, cf. στέωμεν Il. 11, 348, φθέωσι Od. 24, 437. Spitzner derives it from a kindred form ἑάω *to satiate oneself.* It may however be 2 aor. of a form in μι (ἄημι), and its intrans. meaning, *satiate onself, get a glut of,* strengthens this view: it would then be 2 aor. subj. 1 pl. ἄ-ωμεν contr. ὦμεν, lengthened ἕωμεν, with change of spirit and accent ἑῶμεν; and ἄμεναι also intrans. will rank as its inf. with ᾱ by arsis. But it may be said the argument from the *meaning* is neutralised by the 1 aor. inf. ἆσαι being also used intrans. Il. 11, 574. 15, 317. 21, 168. 23, 157. In every instance however it is the same construction, χροὸς ἆσαι, χροὸς ἄμεναι, and the same expression except the last γόοιο ἆσαι, and, more especially, as ἆσαι is trans. *satiate* Il. 20, 78. 5, 289. 24, 211, and the other 1 aor. forms ἄσῃ, ἄσαιμι invariably so, there seem some grounds for suspecting that ἆσαι may somehow have crept in for ἆναι (ἄ-εναι) inf. 2 aor. as γηρᾶσαι for γηρᾶναι.

(**Ἄω**) *To blow,* and if correct (ἀέω) Epic, only imp. ἄεν Ap. Rh. 1, 605. 2, 1228, and δι-άει Od. 5, 478. 19, 440 (Vulg. Dind. La Roche) not **pres.** and given in its reg. form διάῃ Od. quoted (Thiersch, Bekk. Ameis). (ᾰ.) Hes. has **pres.** form ἄησι Op. 516, διάησι 517. 519 &c. See ἄημι.

Ἄωρτο Il. 3, 272, see ἀείρω.

Ἀωτέω *To sleep,* Epic and only pres. Il. 10, 159; Simon. C. 37, 5 (Bergk, Casaub. Gaisf.), -εῖτε Od. 10, 548.

B.

Βαδίζω *To go*, Eur. Ph. 544; Ar. Pl. 84; Hippocr. 6, 106; Antiph. 5, 24; Pl. Soph. 262: **imp.** ἐβάδιζον Hom. H. Merc. 210; Ar. Nub. 980; Pl. Parm. 126; Lys. 4, 7, βάδ- H. Merc. 320: **fut.** classic βαδιοῦμαι Ar. Thesm. 617; Isae. 9, 7; Pl. Conv. 190; Dinarch. 1, 49; Dem. 8, 72. 18, 263, late -ίσομαι Galen 4, 43: late also **fut. act.** βαδίσω Sopat. Rhet. p. 371; Or. Sib. 1, 353; Gl. (Ar. Plut. 495), δια- Dio Cass. 37, 53 (Bekk. Dind.), βαδιῶ Nicol. Soph. 12 (Speng.); Chron. Pasch. p. 286, 20, δια- (Luc.) Dem. enc. 1 (Ms. G. Jacob. Dind. -ίσω Vulg.): **aor.** ἐβάδισα Hippocr. 1, 610. 7, 274 (Lit.); (Pl.) Eryx. 392; Arr. An. 7, 3, 3; Dio Cass. 74, 1, δια- Thuc. 6, 101: **p.** βεβάδικα Aristot. Metaph. 8, 6, 9; Joseph. c. Ap. 2, 39. **Mid.** except **fut.** late δια-βαδίζοιτο Themist. 21, 253 (doubted by Dind.), missed by Lexicogr. **Vb.** βαδιστός Arr. Ind. 43, 10, βαδιστέον Soph. El. 1502; Aristot. Eth. Nic. 10, 10, 16, -έα Ar. Ach. 394. This verb is confined almost to Comedy and Attic prose. The **fut. m.** form βαδιοῦμαι is by far the prevailing one even in later Greek—the only form in Septuag. Plutarch, and the *genuine* Lucian.

Βάζω *To speak, utter*, Poet. Il. 9, 59; Pind. Fr. 134 (Bergk); Aesch. Ch. 882: **imp.** ἔβαζε Il. 16, 207; Eur. Rhes. 719: **fut.** βάξω, ἐκ- Aesch. Ag. 498: aor. ἔβαξα Hesych. (ἐμ-βαβάξαντες Hipponax 53 Schneider, ἐμβιβ- Schneidewin, Bergk): **p. p.** βέβακται Od. 8, 408.

Βαίνω *To go*, Il. 4, 443; Soph. O. C. 217; Eur. Hel. 661; Com. Fr. (Pher.) 2, 318; Pl. Tim. 62; βαίνῃ Theocr. 17, 42; βαίνοι H. Hym. Merc. 349; imper. βαῖνε Aesch. Supp. 832; Ar. Ach. 198; βαίνειν Aesch. Ag. 924; Pl. Leg. 670; -νων Simon. Am. 18; Aesch. Ch. 73; Thuc. 5, 70, -ουσα H. Merc. 28, fem. Dor. -οισα Pind. N. 10, 18, rare βάω, (βᾶτε Aesch. Supp. 191 may be **2 aor.** but) προβῶντες Com. Fr. (Cratin.) 2, 88, ἐκ- Thuc. 5, 77: **imp.** ἔβαινον Il. 5, 364. Od. 15, 145; Pind. I. 2, 2. Fr. 173 (Bergk); Athen. (Matron) 4, 136; late prose Luc. Prom. 6; Arr. Ind. 14, 6; Long. Past. 3, 13; Procop. Epist. 91 (for which, in *classic* Attic, ᾔειν), but Att. in comp. προ-έβαινον Soph. Ph. 285, εἰσ- Eur. H. F. 46, κατ- Ar. Av. 558, ἀν- Her. 7, 205; Lys. 24, 11; Xen. Cyr. 3, 3, 60; Pl. Apol. 40, ἀπ- Thuc. 4, 31; Xen. Hell. 1, 4, 18, συν- Ar. Ran. 807; Thuc. 7, 75; Pl. Leg. 830, Poet. βαῖνον Od. 3, 30. 7, 38; Pind. I. 2, 10; Athen. (Matron) 4, 13, iter. late βαίνεσκον Or. Sib. 1, 37, but μετ- ἐκ-

Her. 7, 41: **fut.** *βήσομαι* poet. in *simple* Il. 2, 339; Eur. Ion 76. I. T. 906; except late *βησόμενον* Themist. 21, 248 (D.), Dor. *βάσομαι* Aesch. Supp. 862 (chor.); Soph. Ph. 834 (chor.); Eur. Ion 689 (chor.), *ἀνα-* Pind. P. 2, 62, *βᾶσοῦμαι* Cleob. Epist. (Hercher), *-εῦμαι* Theocr. 2, 8. 4, 26, in Comedy *κατα-βήσομαι* Ar. Vesp. 979. Pax 725, *συμ-* Com. Fr. 3, 316, in classic prose *ἀπο-* Her. 8, 67; Thuc. 8, 75; Xen. Cyr. 1, 5, 13, *ἀνα-* Isocr. 12, 154, *δια-* Pl. Rep. 621, *παρα-* Isocr. 18, 34, *προ-* Xen. Hell. 6, 1, 14, *ἐκ-* Oec. 9, 8: **fut. act.** trans. *βήσω, ἐπι-* Il. 8, 197, *εἰσ-* Eur. I. T. 742, Dor. *βάσω, προ-* Pind. Ol. 8, 63, see below: **aor.** *ἔβησα* Theocr. 25, 213, in tmesi Od. 11, 4, *βῆσα* Il. 16, 810, Dor. *ἔβᾶσα* Eur. Med. 209 (chor.) *ἐπ-* Pind. I. 1, 39, see below: **p.** *βέβηκα* Il. 15, 90; Aesch. Ag. 37; Eur. Hel. 1524; Ar. Eccl. 913; Her. 7, 164; Pl. Tim. 55, Dor. *-ᾱκα* Pind. I. 4, 41; Aesch. Ag. 407 (chor.); Soph. Tr. 529 (chor.); Eur. Andr. 1026 (chor.), *ἐμ-* Pind. P. 10, 12, *βέβᾰα*, see below: **plp.** *ἐβεβήκειν* Il. 11, 296, *ξυν-* Thuc. 5, 37, *βεβήκ-* Il. 6, 495, *ἀνα-* Her. 1, 84. 7, 6, *παρα-* 7, 40 (Bekk. Dind., *παρ- εβ-* Stein): **p. p.** rare *βέβᾰμαι, ἀνα-* Xen. Hipp. 1, 4. 3, 4, *παρα-* Thuc. 1, 123, *ξυμ-* 8, 98, and, probably late, *βέβασμαι, παρα-* (Dem.) 17, 12. (Argum. to 22, 160): **aor. p.** rare *ἐβᾰθην, ξυν-* Thuc. 4, 30, *παρα-* 3, 67. 4, 23, *ἀν-* Xen. Eq. 3, 4, late *ἐβάσθην, παρ-* Phil. adv. Flacc. 986, and *ἐβάνθην, παρ-* Dio Cass. 39, 59. 48, 2, *συν-* 41, 53 (old edit.), but *παρ- συν-εβάθην* (Bekk. 1849): **pres.** *βαίνηται, κατα-* Xen. Eq. 11, 7; *βαινόμενος, ἀνα-* 1, 1, see below: **2 aor.** *ἔβην* Poet. in *simple* Il. 17, 112; Hes. Th. 194; Soph. O. R. 125; Eur. Andr. 401, *ξυν-* Ar. Nub. 67, *ἀν-* Thuc. 4, 115, *ἀπ-* 4, 39; Isocr. 14, 52, *κατ-* 4, 149, Poet. *βῆν* Il. 13, 297; Hes. Op. 153, Dor. *ἔβαν* Pind. Ol. 13, 97; Soph. Ph. 1216 (chor.), *ἔβα* Eur. H. F. 429 (chor.), Dual rare with augm. *ἐβήτην* Il. 6, 40, *ἀπ-* 21, 298, often *βήτην* 14, 281. Od. 8, 49, and *βάτην* Il. 9, 192. 19, 47. Od. 24, 361, *ἔβησαν* Il. 13, 332; Eur. Andr. 683, Dor. *ἔβᾶσαν* Eur. Hipp. 761 (chor.), *ἔβᾰσαν, ὑπερ-* Il. 12, 469, *ἔβαν* Il. 23, 58; Theogn. 1136; Pind. Ol. 2, 34, *βάν* Il. 20, 32; subj. (Epic *βέω, βήω, βείω*, see below) *βῶ* Eur. Alc. 864 (chor.), *βῶσι* Od. 14, 86, *ἀνα-* Xen. Cyr. 7, 5, 22, *ἀπο-* Pl. Leg. 878, *ἐκ- βῇ* Her. 2, 68; Thuc. 7, 14, Dor. 1 pl. *βᾶμες* Theocr. 15, 22; *βαίην* Il. 24, 246; Soph. O. R. 832; Eur. Rhes. 238; Ar. Av. 1396, *δια-* Xen. An. 7, 2, 27, *ξυμ- βαίημεν* Thuc. 4, 61, *ἐμ-* Xen. An. 5, 6, 12, sync. *βαῖμεν, ξυμ-* Eur. Ph. 590, *βαῖεν, ἐπι-* Il. 8, 512, *δια-* Xen. An. 7, 2, 12; *βῆθι* Anth. 6, 231, *μετα-* Od. 8, 492, *ἐκ-* Eur. I. T. 1086, *ἀνα-* Lys. 12, 24; Xen. Hell. 3, 2, 13, Dor. *βᾶθι* Soph. Ph. 1196 (chor.); Eur. Supp. 271 (chor.). Alc. 872 (chor.), *βήτω, ἐσ-* Eur. Tr. 1049, Dor. *βάτω* Soph. Aj. 1414

(Lyr.), see below; βῆναι Soph. Tr. 195; late prose Dio. Hal. in Dem. 26; Philostr. Apoll. 307, classic ἀνα- Lys. 14, 10; Pl. Rep. 519, ἐσ- Thuc. 3, 80, ἐκ- Xen. Hell. 7, 4, 3, Epic βήμεναι Od. 19, 296, ἐπι- Hes. Sc. 40, Dor. βᾶμεν Pind. P. 4, 39; βάς Il. 6, 65; Soph. Tr. 927; Her. 2, 47. 3, 148, ἐσ- Ar. Lys. 755, ἐπι- Pl. Leg. 864, ἀπο- Isocr. 9, 30, δια- 4, 164, κατα- Pind. N. 6, 51; Thuc. 2, 98, ἐμ- Lys. 2, 30: **2 p.** βέβᾰα, 3 pl. βεβά̆ᾱσι Il. 2, 134, Trag. contr. βεβᾶσι Aesch. Pers. 1002 (chor.); Eur. Tr. 835 (chor.); subj. βεβῶσι, ἐμ- Pl. Phaedr. 252; (βεβαίην; βέβᾰθι?); inf. Epic βεβάμεν Il. 17, 359, βεβάναι Eur. Heracl. 610 (chor.), ἀπο- Her. 5, 86, συμ- 3, 146; βεβαώς Il. 14, 477; Hes. Sc. 307, ἐμ- Il. 5, 199, ἐπεμ- Pind. N. 4, 29, and βεβώς Aesch. Eum. 76; Soph. Ant. 996; Eur. H. F. 965. Bac. 646, βεβῶσα Od. 20, 14, but βεβαυῖα Hom. Epigr. 15, 10, ἐν- Il. 24, 81; never we think in Comedy; and rare in prose, βεβῶτα Hippocr. 3, 282, ἐπι- ibid.; βεβῶτες Pl. Tim. 63, βεβῶτας, προδια- Xen. Hell. 7, 2, 3, βεβῶσαν Pl. Phaedr. 254: **plp.** (ἐβεβάειν), 3 pl. syncop. βέβᾰσαν Il. 17, 286, ἐμ- 2, 720. **Mid. fut.** -ήσομαι see above: **aor.** Epic ἐβησάμην, *moved myself, went*, -ήσαο H. Hym. 1, 141, -ήσατο 1, 49; Hes. Sc. 338, usu. ἐβησόμην Il. 14, 229. Od. 13, 75 (always Bekk. Dind. &c.), βησ- Il. 3, 262. 8, 389 (Bekk. Dind.); but ἀνα-βησάμενος *having made go, led up*, Od. 15, 475, ἐπ-εβήσατο Callim. L. Pal. 65, Ion. prose ξυμ-βήσηται Hippocr. 9, 28 (Mss. DHU. Lit.). **Vb.** βατός Xen. An. 4, 6, 17, ἀμ- Il. 6, 434, δια-βατέος Xen. An. 2, 4, 6. The **pass.** of the *simple* verb is rare, βαινόμεναι Her. 1, 192, βαίνεται Aristot. Metaph. 13, 6, 7; -εσθαι Hist. An. 5, 14, 26, usu. in comp.

βαίνω, especially in comp., has in some of its tenses a causative sense, *make to go*, or as we say *walk* a horse, or, familiarly, *walk* one out, down, &c.: **pres.** rare καταβαίνω Pind. P. 8, 78: **fut.** ἐπιβήσω Il. 8, 197; Epic inf. ἐπιβησέμεν Hes. Th. 396, εἰσβήσω Eur. I. T. 742, Dor. προβάσω Pind. Ol. 8, 63: **aor.** βῆσα Il. 16, 810, Dor. ἔβᾱσα Eur. Med. 209 (chor.), ἄμ-βᾱσε Pind. P. 4, 191, ἐπέβησα Il. 8, 129; Hes. Op. 580, Dor. -ᾱσε Pind. I. 1, 39, ἐξέβησα Eur. Hel. 1616, ἐν- Heracl. 845. Cycl. 467, εἰσ- Alc. 1055. Bac. 466 (trimet.); subj. βήσομεν Il. 1, 144, Dor. βάσομεν, for -ωμεν, Pind. Ol. 6, 24; in prose ἀνέβησα Her. 1, 80 (Mss. Bekk. Gaisf.), ἀπ- 5, 63. 6, 107. 8, 95, ἐν- 1, 46, very rare in Attic, ὑπερ-βησάτω Xen. Eq. 7, 2; and late ἐπιβήσειν Luc. D. Mort. 6, 4; but intrans. μεταβήσωμεν *let us digress*, Galen 11, 163, &c.: **fut. m.** ἐπιβήσομαι Hom. H. Merc. 166: **aor.** ἀναβησάμενοι Od. 15, 475, ἐπ- Callim. Pal. 65 &c. never **2 aor.** and **perf.** except in such phrases as ἐκβὰς πόδα Eur. Heracl. 802. We do not think that ἐπιβῆτον Od. 23, 52, ἐμβέβᾱκα Pind. P. 10, 12, are exceptions. In this sense however it is confined to poetry, and to Ionic and, with perhaps one exception, late Attic prose. βάτην 3 dual 2 aor. for ἐβήτην, Il. 1, 327, βάσαν, ὑπερ- 3 pl. Il. 12, 469, ἔβαν 2, 302. 10, 525; Pind. P. 4, 180; Aesch. Pers. 18 (chor.); Soph. Ant. 120 (chor.), βάν Il. 19, 241. 279; subj. βῆω, ὑπερ- βήῃ Il. 9, 501, ἐμ- 16, 94, βείω 6, 113, and (βέω), βέῃ 16, 852, βέωμεν, ἐπι- Her. 7, 50 (βῶμεν, παρα- Ar. Av. 461), pl. βείομεν, κατα- Il. 10, 97; but Dor. βᾶμες Theocr. 15, 22; imper. εἴσβα Eur. Ph. 193, ἔμβᾱ Eur. El. 113, ἐπί- Ion 167 (chor.); Theogn. 847, κατά- βᾱ for -βῆθι, (unless imper. of pres. ἐμβάω &c.) Ar. Vesp. 979, βᾶτε Aesch. Supp. 191 (trimet.); so Soph. O. C. 841 (chor.). 1547. Fr. 724 (trimet. D.); βήσεο, κατα- imper. 1 aor. m. Epic Il. 5, 109. καταβήσεται Hes. Th. 750, is a real fut. with its own proper force, and not a pres. Of this verb in *simple*, Attic prose authors use only pres. βαίνω Thuc. Xen. Pl. Dem. (ἔβαινον Luc. Arr. &c.): βήσομαι poetic: aor. ἔβησε Her. 1, 80, Vulg. is now ἀνέβησε (Mss. Bekk. Gaisf.): and p. βέβηκε Pl. Tim. 55; βεβηκώς (Her. 7, 164); Xen. An. 3, 2, 19; Pl. Tim. 62, syncop. βεβώς Phaedr. 254; βεβηκέναι Rep. 617. 2 aor. seems to occur very rarely, and only in Ionic and late Attic, βάς Her. 2, 47. 3, 148, but ἐμ-βάς Ar. Av. 202. 266, ἐπι- Thuc. 1, 137, ἐκ- Pl. Conv. 183; βῆναι Dio. Hal. in Dem. 26; Philostr. Apoll. 307, but ἐκ- Thuc. 1, 137; Pl. Rep. 614. The imp. fut. and aor. were supplied by ἀπέβαινον &c., εἶμι, and ᾖειν, see Thuc. 3, 26. 4, 104; Andoc. 1, 36. 45. 66; Thuc. 2, 36; Pl. Phaed. 100 &c. So in Comedy, βαίνω Com. Fr. 2, 494; Ar. Ach. 198 (but κατ-, συν-έβαινον, κατα-, συμ-βήσομαι): βέβηκε Com. Fr. 2, 15 (trimet.); Ar. Eccl. 913; -ηκώς Eq. 1039: (ξυν-, παρ- έβη, for) ἔβα in Aristoph. is Doric, either uttered by a Laconian, Lys. 106, or used allusively to some Tragic or Lyric Poet, Nub. 30. Av. 944; ξυμ-βῶ Ran. 175; προ- βῇς Com. Fr. 2, 60; βαίην Ar. Av. 1396, *simple* but Lyric, παρα-, προ- βαίην Lys. 236. Eccl. 161 (trimet.).

Βάλλω *To throw*, Il. 2, 376; Pind. P. 8, 57; Aesch. Ag. 1390; Soph. Ant. 1188; Ar. Nub. 401; Her. 8, 128; Xen. An. 3, 4, 49, Dor. 1 pl. βάλλομες Bion 7, 13; -λλων Il. 11, 723; Thuc. 7, 84: imp. ἔβαλλον Il. 3, 80; Aesch. Ag. 240; Her. 4, 156; Thuc. 4, 34; Pl. Crat. 420, βάλλ- Il. 18, 534: fut. βαλέω Ep. and Ion. Il. 8, 403; Simon. C. 5, 16, ἀπο- Her. 1, 71, Att. βαλῶ Aesch. Ag. 1172; Soph. Ph. 67; Ar. Ach. 283; (Il. 17, 451, but -έω Bekk.); Luc. Tim. 34, in classic prose, comp. ἀπο- Xen. Cyr. 8, 7, 23, κατα- 3, 3, 62; Pl. Euth. 277, ἐσ- Thuc. 2, 99, δια- Isocr. 11, 49; Pl. Euthyphr. 3, and only in

Ar. βαλλήσω Vesp. 222. 1491: aor. (ἐβάλλησα occurs not, ἔβαλα very late, ἐκβάλαι Malal. 3, p. 60): p. βέβληκα Aesch. Myrm. 132 (D.); Ar. Ach. 171; Xen. Cyr. 4, 6, 4, ἀπο- Her. 2, 131, ἐμ- Antiph. 2, β, 2; βεβλήκοι Il. 8, 270, ἐσ- Thuc. 2, 48: plp. βεβλήκει Il. 5, 661, ἐσ- εβ- Thuc. 3, 96, ἐξ- Aeschin. 2, 142: p. p. βέβλημαι, βέβληται Il. 5, 103, βέβληνται Pind. N. 1, 8, -ήαται Il. 11, 657; βεβλημένος Il. 11, 809; Eur. I. T. 49, παρα- Thuc. 7, 2; βεβλῆσθαι Pl. Phaedr. 264, δια- Thuc. 8, 109, Epic βεβόλησαι Ap. Rh. 4, 1318, -ηται 3, 893; βεβολημένος Il. 9, 9. Od. 10, 247; Ap. Rh. 1, 262; Orph. Arg. 36. 543; Maneth. 3, 117: plp. ἐβεβλήμην, ἐξ- Isocr. 18, 17, δι- Pl. Phaed. 68, βέβλητο Od. 12, 423, 3 pl. Ion. -βλήατο Il. 14, 28, περι- Her. 6, 25, see mid., Epic βεβολήατο Il. 9, 3: aor. ἐβλήθην Antiph. 3, β, 4; Thuc. 8, 84, ὑπ- Eur. Alc. 639; βληθείη Xen. Cyr. 8, 3, 31, ἐμ- Hippocr. 3, 536. 550; βληθῶσι Pl. Rep. 469, βληθῇς, δια- Eur. I. A. 1372; βληθήτω, ἐκ- Pl. Leg. 854; βληθείς Her. 1, 34. 43; Antiph. 3, β, 5; Xen. Cyr. 8, 3, 30, ἐκ- Eur. Elec. 289; βληθῆναι Xen. Cyr. 8, 3, 32: fut. βληθήσομαι Xen. Hell. 7, 5, 11, δια- Eur. Hec. 863. Heracl. 422; Lys. 26, 15, ἀνα- Isocr. 11, 25: 3 fut. βεβλήσομαι Eur. Or. 271. Bacc. 1314; *simple* late in prose Heliod. 2, 13, but δια- Dem. 16, 2. Proem. p. 1424, 8; pt. βεβλησόμενος rare and unclassic Philostr. Ap. 251: 2 aor. act. ἔβᾰλον Il. 13, 411; Pind. Ol. 7, 44; Aesch. Ag. 357; Soph. Ph. 1028; Ar. Pax 1274; Her. 6, 27; Antiph. 3, β, 3; Pl. Rep. 408, βάλ- Il. 11, 742; Hes. Sc. 384, κάββαλε (κατ-β-) Hes. Th. 189; Pind. Ol. 8, 39, iter. βάλεσκε, προ- Od. 5, 331; βάλησθα 12, 221; βάλοισθα Il. 15, 571; Dor. pt. fem. βαλοῖσα Theocr. 16, 11, Epic ἔβλην (βλῆμι), ξυμβλήτην *met*, Od. 21, 15; inf. -ήμεναι Il. 21, 578 (if not 2 aor. pass. for ἐβάλην). Mid. βάλλομαι *to throw oneself*, or *for oneself*, *cast in one's mind*, Pind. I. 6, 13; Pl. Leg. 779, 2 sing. Epic βάλλεαι Il. 9, 435; impr. βάλλεο 4, 39, βάλλευ Od. 12, 218: imp. ἐβαλλόμην Il. 10, 333; Eur. Fr. 392 (D.). Tr. 1137, ἀν- Her. 9, 8; Aeschin. 1, 63, περι- Thuc. 1, 8, προ- Xen. An. 6, 1, 25 (Dind.); Pl. Leg. 756, βαλλ- Pind. P. 4, 138, iter. βαλλέσκετο Her. 9, 74: fut. βαλοῦμαι late in *simple*, Or. Sib. 1, 208. 2, 230, προ- Ar. Ran. 201, ἐπι- Thuc. 6, 40, μετα- 8, 54, ὑπερ- Pl. Menex. 247; Dem. 19, 342, Ion. βαλεῦμαι, ἀμφι- Od. 22, 103, -έομαι, ὑπερ- Her. 7, 168, but pass. ἐκ-βαλοῦμαι Epict. Diss. 3, 24: 2 aor. ἐβαλόμην Il. 15, 566; Her. 1, 84; *simple* rare in Attic, Com. Fr. (Philem.) 4, 31; Pl. Leg. 961; Dem. 18, 87; (Pl.) Epist. 326; Dio. Hal. 3, 55, συν- Soph. O. C. 1151; Lys. 4, 10; Xen. An. 6, 6, 35. Hell. 6, 5, 5, ἀπ- Andoc. 3, 29, παρα- Ar. Ran. 269, περι- Eur. H. F. 334, ὑπερ- Soph. Tr. 584;

Ar. Pax 213, βαλ- Il. 11, 29; Pind. P. 1, 74; βάληται Od. 11, 428; -λοιο v. r. Pseud.-Phocyl. 185; Ion. imper. βάλεο, ἀνα- Pind. N. 7, 77, βάλευ Theogn. 1050; Her. 8, 68, Epic ἐβλήμην pass. Il. 11, 675, but ξύμ-βλητο mid. *he met*, 14, 39; subj. ξύμ-βληται Od. 7, 204, and βλήεται, for -ήηται, Od. 17, 472; opt. βλῆο Il. 13, 288 (Bekk.), -εῖο (Dind. La Roche); βλῆσθαι Il. 4, 115; -ήμενος Il. 11, 191. Od. 22, 18; Ap. Rh. 2, 1212: **fut.** ξυμ-βλήσεαι (for which some suggest -βλήεαι=ήηαι) *shall encounter*, Il. 20, 335: and as mid. p. p. ἐμ-βέβληται *put in, entered*, Dem. 40, 28, περι-βέβληται *threw, put about himself*, Pl. Conv. 216, Ion. 3 pl. -βλέαται Hippocr. 9, 80 (Lit.); -βεβλημένος Isocr. 4, 184, παρα- Thuc. 5, 113, συμ- Lycurg. 43, ἐμ- Dem. 40, 21: **plp.** περι-εβεβλήμην Xen. Hell. 7, 4, 22, 3 pl. Ion. -εβεβλήατο *threw themselves round, gained*, Her. 6, 25, -έατο (Stein, Abicht), see περιβάλλω. **Vb.** βλητός Callim. Cer. 101. μετα-βλητέος Hippocr. 1, 315 (Erm.), ἀπο- Pl. Rep. 387. The **1 aor. p.** ἐβλήθην does not occur in Epic, very rarely in Attic poetry: the fut. act. βαλῶ in the *simple* form is late in prose, βαλεῖτε Dio Chrys. Or. 34 (415), -οῦσι N. T. Matth. 13, 42 (Vat. -λλουσι Sin.), and the **1 aor.** seems scarcely to exist at all, ἐκ-βάλαι Malal. 3, p. 60. βλείης 2 sing. opt. Epicharm. 154, may be syncop. for βληθείης, or **2 aor. pass.** ἔβλην, for ἐβάλην. For ὑπερβαλλέειν Her. 3, 23, συμβαλλεόμενος 1, 68 &c., called Ion., Bekk. Dind. Krüg. read -βάλλειν, -λλόμενος, but **2 aor.** inf. βαλέειν 2, 111. 3, 12. 35, ἀπο- 3, 41. 8, 65, ἐμ- 4, 125, συμ- 2, 10. 3, 32 &c. (Bekk. Gaisf. Dind.), and ἐκβαλεῖν 5, 67, ἐμ- 9, 13, ἐσ- 6, 84, συμ- 9, 13 &c. (Bekk. Gaisf. and *always* Bred. Stein, Abicht); so Hom. βαλέειν Il. 2, 414. 10, 368 &c. βαλεῖν 13, 387. 14, 424. βέβληαι 2 sing. p. p. for -ησαι, Il. 5, 284, dissyll. or η shortened 11, 380, βεβλήαται for -ηνται, Il. 11, 657, but, if sound, sing. for -ηται, Hym. 1, 20 (Mss. Franke, νόμοι -ήαται Ilgen, Baum.); δια-βεβλῆσθε opt. Andoc. 2, 24.

Βαπτίζω, see βάπτω.

Βάπτω *To dip*, Od. 9, 392; Ar. Eccl. 216; Pl. Tim. 73: **imp.** βάπτε Ap. Rh. 1, 183: **fut.** βάψω *simple* late, Lycophr. 1121; Anth. 11, 408; Or. Sib. 7, 147; V. T. Lev. 4, 17 &c., but ἐμ- Ar. Pax 959: **aor.** ἔβαψα Aesch. Ch. 1011; Soph. Tr. 580; Eur. Or. 707; Her. 2, 47; Hippocr. 5, 234 (Lit.); Aristot. de Anim. 3, 12, 9; βάψω Ar. Ach. 112; -ειεν Eur. H. F. 929; βάψαι Pl. Rep. 429; βάψας Eur. Hec. 610; Ar. Fr. 16, ἀπο- Her. 4, 70: p. (βέβαφα?): **p. p.** βέβαμμαι Ar. Pax 1176; Mosch. 1, 29; -άφθαι Aristot. de Color. 1, 2; -αμμένος Her. 7, 67; (Plut. Mor. 954, μετα- Luc. Bis. acc. 8): **1 aor.** ἐβάφθην Anth. 6, 254, ἀπο- Ar. Fr. 366: **2 aor.** ἐβάφην, βαφῇ Pl. Rep.

429; βαφείς Tim. 83. Rep. 429; Hippocr. 5, 664 (Lit.), κατα- Luc. Imag. 16: **fut.** βαφήσομαι late, V. T. Lev. 11, 32; M. Ant. 8, 51. **Mid.** βάπτομαι Ar. Eq. 523, ἐμ- Xen. Cyr. 2, 2, 5: **fut.** βάψομαι Ar. Lys. 51; Com. Fr. (Menand.) 4, 178: **aor.** ἐβαψάμην Arat. 951; ἐμ-βάψαιτο Com. Fr. (Arched.) 4, 436; βαψάμενος Anth. 9, 326. **Aor. act.** Eur. Or. quoted, is intrans. *sank.* **Vb.** βαπτός Ar. Av. 287; Pl. Leg. 847. The **aor. pass.** of the collat. βαπτίζω seems to be used as **aor. mid.** intrans. ἐβαπτίσθη N. T. Luc. 11, 38: ἐβαπτίσατο V. T. 4 Reg. 5, 14; βαπτίσωνται N. T. Mark 7, 4.

Βᾰρέω *To load,* Luc. Soloec. 7; App. Hisp. 86; Athen. 5, 1: **imp.** ἐβάρει Charit. 4, 2, 1. 6, 1, 6: **fut.** βαρήσω Luc. D. Mort. 10, 4: **aor.** ἐβάρησα, ἐπ- App. Civ. 5, 107: **p.** βεβάρηκα Dio Cass. 78, 17; Aristid. 26, 329 (Vulg.), Epic βεβαρηώς Od. 19, 122; Ap. Rh. 4, 1526; and late prose Aristid. 26, 329 (Ms. L. Dind. -ηκότες old edit.): **p.p.** βεβάρηται Plut. Mor. 895; part. βεβαρημένος Theocr. 17, 61; Ap. Rh. 1, 1256; Anth. Plan. 98. 7, 290; Pl. Conv. 203; Aristot. Probl. 30, 1, 7 (from Od. 19, 122, where stands βεβαρηότα); Hierocl. 66 (Eberh.): **plp.** ἐβεβάρητο Galen 9, 71, βεβαρ- Orph. Arg. 247; Q. Sm. 2, 341: **aor.** ἐβαρήθην Dio. Hal. 1, 14; Artemid. Onir. 1, 77. **Mid. and pass.** βαρέεται Hippocr. 7, 578, -οῦνται M. Anton. 8, 44; -ούμενος Dio Cass. 46, 32: **fut. m.** as **pass.** ἐπι-βαρησόμενος Dio. Hal. 8, 73. missed by Lexicogr.—This verb is late, except **perf. act.** and **perf. pass.** See βαρύνω.

Βαρῡ́θω *To be oppressed,* Epic, Il. 16, 519; Hes. Op. 215; -θοιεν Ap. Rh. 2, 47; -θων 4, 621; Opp. Hal. 1, 366; Anth. 7, 481: **imp. iter.** βαρῡ́θεσκε Ap. Rh. 1, 43. **Pass.** βαρύθομαι late, Maxim. καταρχ. 212: **imp.** βαρύθοντο Q. Sm. 13, 6. (ᾰ.)

Βαρύνω *To load, annoy,* Pind. P. 1, 84; Hippocr. 2, 290. 7, 218; Xen. Cyr. 5, 5, 25; -ύνων Pl. Phaedr. 247: **imp.** ἐβάρῡνε Il. 11, 584. Od. 5, 321, βάρῡνε Il. 5, 664: **fut.** -ῠνῶ (Xen.) Apol. 9 (Dind.); Aristid. 30, 380 (D.); Galen 9, 447: **aor.** ἐβάρῡνα Plut. Mor. 127; Galen 9, 148; Anth. 9, 270 (?): **p.p.** βεβάρυμμαι, -υνται V. T. Nah. 2, 9; -ύνθαι Aristot. Physiog. 6, 10 (Bekk.); -υμένος (Hippocr.) Epist. 9, 374 (Lit. -ημένος Hercher): **aor.** ἐβαρύνθην Hippocr. 5, 674, Poet. 3 pl. βάρυνθεν Pind. N. 7, 43; βαρυνθῇ Pl. Phaedr. 248, -υνθῶσι Soph. Ph. 890; -θείς Il. 8, 308; Aesch. Ag. 1463; Soph. O. R. 781; Eur. Heracl. 204; Hippocr. 8, 32; Pl. Phaedr. 248; Plut. Mor. 895; D. Laert. 10, 1, 5: **fut.** βαρυνθήσομαι Soph. Fr. 627; Polyb. 5, 94; Galen 16, 191. Of the **act.** form, only **pres.** and **imp.** are *classic,* and confined to Epic, Lyric, and Attic prose: the **pass.** is classical, perf. excepted, and more generally used, especially pres. βαρύνομαι Il. 19, 165; (Simon. C.) 184 (Bergk); Aesch. Ag. 189. 836; Soph. Tr. 152. El. 820; Eur. Alc. 42. 385. I. T. 1228 &c.; rare in Comedy, Ar. Ach. 220; -ύνηται Xen. Eq. 8, 8; -νόμενοι Com. Fr. (Cratin.) 2, 110; Thuc. 2, 64; Xen. Mem. 2, 2, 5; -ύνεσθαι Thuc. 5, 7: imp. ἐβαρύνοντο Thuc. 2, 16. 8, 1. (ᾰ.)

Βάσκω Poet. *To go, come,* the *simple* in imper. only, βάσκε Il. 24, 144; Aesch. Pers. 662 (chor.), βάσκετε Ar. Thesm. 783 (chor.), but δια-βάσκει Av. 486 (anapest.); inf. Epic ἐπι-βασκέμεν =ειν, *cause to go, lead,* Il. 2, 234: imp. ἔβασκε (Hesych.), in comp. παρ-έβασκε Il. 11, 104.

Βαστάζω *To carry,* Pind. N. 8, 3; Soph. El. 1129; Eur. I. A. 36; Com. Fr. (Eup.) 2, 448; -άζων Od. 11, 594; -άζειν Simon. C. 168; Soph. Ant. 216; Eur. Alc. 41; Com. Fr. (Herm.) 2, 395; late prose Plut. Mor. 64: imp. ἐβάστ- Polyb. 8, 18: fut. βαστάσω Aesch. Pr. 1019; Soph. Aj. 920; late prose Pseud.-Callisth. 1, 42; Joseph. Ant. 15, 11, 2; Oribas. 10, 37, and -άξω Pseud.-Callisth. 1, 45; Maur. in Strateg. p. 83; Sym. Prov. 9, 12: aor. ἐβάστᾰσα Od. 21, 405; Aesch. Pr. 889 (chor.); Soph. Ph. 1127 (chor.); Ar. Thesm. 437 (chor.); βαστάσῃ Soph. Aj. 827 (trimet.); -άσαι Pind. I. 3, 8; late prose Alciphr. 3, 32; Plut. Mor. 317; Apollod. 3, 4, 3; (Luc.) Asin. 16, and late ἐβάσταξα Anth. App. Epigr. 324; Pseud.-Callisth. 1, 3: p. p. late βεβάστακται, ἐμ- (Luc.) Ocyp. 14: aor. late ἐβαστάχθην Diog. L. 4, 59; Athen. 2, 46: fut. -αχθήσομαι Pseud.-Callisth. 1, 42: 2 aor. late βασταγῆναι Artemidor. 2, 68, p. 249: pres. βαστάζονται Aristot. Rhet. 3, 12, 2. **Vb.** βαστακτός Anth. 12, 52. This verb never occurs in good prose, and is *classic* in the act. form only.

Βατέω *To go,* only pres. act. τὸ πατεῖν, βατεῖν Μακεδόνες καλοῦσι Plut. Mor. 292, βατέει, ἐμ- Nic. Ther. 147; ἐμ-βατέων 804; Anth. 7, 657: and mid. βατεῦνται Dor. Theocr. 1, 87: fut. βατήσονται, ἐμ- Lycophr. 642. (ᾰ.)

Βαΰζω *To bark, cry,* Com. Fr. (Crat.) 2, 17; Aesch. Ag. 449; Ar. Thesm. 173. 895; Heracl. Fr. 10 (Mullach); Luc. Merc. Cond. 34, Dor. βαΰσδω Theocr. 6, 10: aor. βαΰξας, κατα- Anth. 7, 408. **Vb.** δυσ-βάϋκτος Aesch. Pers. 574.

(**Βάω**) *To go,* occurs in subj. ἐπι-βῇ Inscr. Heracl. 1, 80; imper. ἔμ-βη Ar. Lys. 1303 (Ahr.) both Dor., βᾶτε however in an iambic trimet. Aesch. Supp. 191, all which are referred by others to 2 aor. of βαίνω; but pres. part. προβῶντες Com. Fr. (Cratin.) 2, 88 (Bekk. Anec. p. 371), and Dor. ἐκβῶντες Thuc. 5, 77, see βαίνω.

(Βδελυρεύομαι) *To behave abominably*, only fut. -εύσεται Dem. 17, 11.

Βδελύσσομαι, -ύττομαι *To abominate*, Dep. pass. in *classic* authors, Com. Fr. (Eup.) 2, 577; Ar. Nub. 1132. Av. 151; Hippocr. 7, 56; Pl. Rep. 605: imp. ἐβδελύττετο Ar. Plut. 700: fut. -ύξομαι Hippocr. 8, 96. 98 (Lit.): aor. ἐβδελύχθην act. Ar. Lys. 794; βδελυχθείη Plut. Mor. 753; βδελυχθείς Ar. Vesp. 792; Plut. Alex. 57: (aor. m. ἐβδελυξάμην late V. T. Lev. 20, 23; Joseph. J. Bell. 6, 2, 10; Chrys. V. 7, 351.) In late Greek occurs the act. (βδελύσσω), fut. -ύξω V. T. Lev. 20, 25: aor. ἐβδέλυξα Exod. 5, 21: p. p. ἐβδέλυγμαι act. Prov. 28, 9, and pass. Osae. 9, 10; N. T. Rev. 21, 8; Theodr. Prod. 1, 330, ἠβδελ- Paroem. (Apostol.) C. 4, 88: aor. ἐβδελύχθην pass. V. T. Ps. 52, 2: fut. -υχθήσομαι Apocr. Sir. 20, 8. Mid. βδελύσσομαι Amos 6, 8: fut. -ύξομαι Lev. 11, 11: aor. ἐβδελυξάμην Amos 5, 10.

Βδέω *To emit an offensive smell*, Ar. Plut. 703, βδεῖς Anth. 11, 415; βδέων Ar. Eq. 898; Hierocl. 237, -έουσα Ar. Plut. 693: fut. (βδέσω): aor. βδέσε Anth. 11, 242, and ἔβδευσα if correct, Hierocl. 233. 240. 241 (Eberh.) Pass. βδεόμενος Ar. Eq. 900. This verb is, luckily, very limited in its range. Epic, Trag. and genteel prose never name it, but Hierocles, and sometimes Galen professionally of course.

Βεβρώθω, see βιβρώσκω.

Βέομαι *I shall live*, Epic and only pres. with fut. meaning, Il. 15, 194, and βείομαι 22, 431 (βίομαι Hym. 2, 350), βέῃ Il. 16, 852. 24, 131.

Βήσσω *To cough*, Hippocr. 5, 378, Att. -ττω Com. Fr. (Philem.) 4, 42; Aristot. Probl. 10, 1; -ων Ar. Fr. 548 (D.); -ττειν Xen. Cyr. 2, 2, 5: imp. ἔβησσε Hippocr. 5, 324, -ττε Ar. Eccl. 56: fut. -ξω Hippocr. 8, 100: aor. ἔβηξα Hippocr. 5, 190; βήξῃ 8, 98; βῆξαι Her. 6, 107; βήξας 6, 107: aor. pass. ἐβήχθην, ἐκ- Galen 10, 341. Mid. βήσσεται as act. Hippocr. 7, 82 (Lit.): fut. βήξομαι, ἀπο- 8, 98. The mid. we think has been missed by Lexicogr.

Βιάζω *To force*, act. rare, Od. 12, 297: imp. ἐβίαζον Hippocr. 5, 96 (Lit.): aor. ἐβίασα Com. Fr. (Alcae.) 2, 833; late prose, Sopat. Rhet. vol. 8, p. 107 (Walz). Usu. βιάζομαι act. Il. 22, 229; Theogn. 547; Aesch. Pr. 1010; Soph. Ant. 663; Ar. Lys. 226: Hippocr. 6, 24; Her. 9, 41; Antiph. 3, β, 1; Thuc. 4, 9; Pl. Prot. 337, pass. Il. 11, 589; Aesch. Ag. 1510; Soph. Ant. 66; Ar. Thesm. 890; Hippocr. 2, 34 (Lit.); Antiph. 4, δ, 5; Thuc. 4, 10; Xen. Conv. 2, 26: imp. ἐβιαζόμην act. Ar. Lys. 396; Xen. An. 1, 3, 1; Isae. 3, 62, pass. Thuc. 5, 3, βιαζ- Il.

16, 102: **fut.** βιάσομαι act. Ar. Plut. 1092; Pl. Charm. 176. Phaed. 61. Leg. 627; Dem. 19, 238, βιῶμαι see below: and aor. ἐβιασάμην Com. Fr. (Crob.) 4, 567; Antiph. 2, α, 9; Thuc. 3, 55; Pl. Rep. 461, βιασσ- Opp. C. 3, 157: but ἐβιάσθην always pass. Pind. N. 9, 14; Soph. El. 575; Ar. Fr. Amph. 91 (D.); Thuc. 4, 44; Xen. Mem. 1, 2, 10; Pl. Rep. 413: **fut.** late βιασθήσομαι Charit. 2, 8; -θησόμενος Paus. 6, 5, 9: and perhaps **fut. mid.** βιᾶται as pass. Pl. Tim. 63 (?): **p.** βεβίασμαι usu. pass. Hippocr. 2, 54; Xen. Hell. 5, 2, 23, &c.; (Dem.) 10, 13, but act. Dem. 19, 206; Dio Cass. 46, 45. (ῐ.) **Vb.** βιαστέος Eur. Rhes. 584. The act. is very rare, never in Attic prose. In Attic writers βῐάσομαι, we fancy, should drop σ as well as βιβάσομαι; but we know of no instance, unless βιᾶται Pl. Tim. 63 be fut. and pass. If so, our Lexicogr. have overlooked both form and meaning.

(**Βῐάω**) Epic and Ion. *To force*, in act. only **perf.** βεβίηκε Il. 10, 172. 16, 22. Usu. βιάομαι act. Solon 13, 41; Theogn. 503; Simon. C. 76; Pind. N. 8, 34; Aesch. Ag. 385 (chor.); Her. 3, 80; Hippocr. 8, 328. 560 (Lit.), pass. Her. 1, 19; Hippocr. 7, 514; Ap. Rh. 4, 1236: **fut.** βιήσομαι act. Od. 21, 348; Emped. 16 (Stein), pass., Hippocr. 8, 280 (Lit.): **aor.** ἐβιήσατο Il. 11, 558; Her. 4, 43; Hippocr. 8, 556, βίησ- Il. 21, 451; Mosch. 4, 114; Epic subj. -ήσεαι Theogn. 1307; Dor. βιᾱσάμενοι Eleg. ap. Paus. 5, 23, 6: **p.** βεβίημαι act. Ap. Rh. 3, 1249; Opp. Hal. 1, 224, pass. Anth. 9, 546; Ap. Rh. 4, 1390: **aor.** ἐβιήθην pass. Her. 7, 83; but part. βιησθέν if correct, Hippocr. 8, 96 (Lit.) Epic forms: βιόωνται Od. 11, 503; Opp. Hal. 3, 284; opt. βιῴατο for βιῷντο, Il. 11, 467; βιωομένη Mosch. 2, 13 (Mein. Ahr.): βιόωντο Od. 23, 9.

Βιβάζω *To make go*, Com. Fr. (Alcae.) 2, 830; late prose Aristot. H. An. 6, 18, 28; Plut. Mor. 303, but κατα- Her. 1, 86, ἐσ- Thuc. 7, 60: **imp.** ἐβίβαζον, ἀπ- Her. 8, 76, ἐσ- Thuc. 7, 60: **fut.** βιβάσω, δια-βιβάσοντες Xen. An. 4, 8, 8. 5, 2, 10 (Popp. Krüg. Kühn. Saupp. &c.); -βιβάσειν Luc. Hipp. 2 (Dind.); Arr. Ind. 42, 7, and βιβῶ Soph. O. C. 381, προσ- Ar. Av. 425; Pl. Phaedr. 229, ἐμ- Xen. An. 5, 7, 7, δια- Pl. Leg. 900; Dem. 23, 157; and Xen. An. 4, 8, 8. 5, 2, 10 quoted (Dind. 1857, Cobet): **aor.** ἐβίβασα Aristot. Hist. An. 6, 18, 28, ἀν- Her. 1, 86. 3, 75; Xen. Hell. 4, 5, 3; Isae. 9, 30, ἀπ- Her. 8, 76; Pl. Gorg. 511, δι- Thuc. 1, 105: **p. p.** late, βε-βίβασται Sext. Emp. 252, 2: **aor.** rather late, βιβασθείς Aristot. H. A. 6, 23, 3; Geop. 16, 1: **fut.** late, διαβιβασθήσομαι Diod. Sic. 13, 81. **Mid.** in comp. **fut.** βιβάσομαι, ἀνα- Andoc. 1, 148 (Bekk. B. S.); Lys. 18, 24 (B. S. Scheibe); Luc. pro Imag. 24 (Dind.), and βιβῶμαι, ἀνα- Com. Fr. (Amips.) 2, 713; Aeschin. 2, 146; Dem. 19, 310: aor. ἐβιβασάμην, ἀπ- Her. 9, 32, ἀν- Thuc. 7, 35; Lys. 12, 24; Xen. Hell. 3, 4, 10; Isae. 11, 4; Pl. Apol. 18. (ῐ.) Vb. ἀνα-βιβαστέον Pl. Rep. 467.

Βιβάσθω *To step*, Epic and only part. βιβάσθων Il. 13, 809. 16, 534. (ῐ.)

Βιβάω *To step*, Poet. Hym. Merc. 225; part. βιβῶν Pind. Ol. 14, 17: imp. iter. ἐβίβασκε Hym. Ap. 133. (ῐ.) For βιβῶντα Il. 3, 22, βιβῶσα Od. 11, 539 (Mss. Vulg. La Roche), Bekk. Dind. Foesi, Ameis read -άντα, -ᾶσα, see foll.

Βίβημι Epic, *To go*, Dor. -āμι, 3 pl. βίβαντι Epigr. Lacon. (Ahr. Dor. D. p. 483); part. βιβάς Il. 13, 371; and 3, 22. Od. 11, 539 (Bekk. Dind. &c.), προ- Il. 13, 18. Od. 17, 27. (ῐ.)

Βιβρώσκω *To eat*, Babr. 108, 9, περι- Plut. Mor. 1059 (pass. -ώσκονται Hippocr. 6, 212 Lit.): fut. late βρώξω Lycophr. 678 (some Mss. and edit.): and m. late βρώσομαι Or. Sib. 7, 157; Philostr. p. 129: aor. late ἔβρωξα Anth. 11, 271, and ἔβρωσα, ἀν- Nic. Ther. 134: p. βέβρωκα Od. 22, 403; Soph. Tr. 1054; Xen. Hier. 1, 24; βεβρώκῃ Hippocr. 8, 350; -ώκοι Her. 1, 119; βεβρωκώς Il. 22, 94; Ar. Vesp. 462; Com. Fr. (Eup.) 2, 447; Hippocr. 6, 268. 7, 110 (Lit.); Aristot. Probl. 5, 7, 2, syncop. βεβρώς Soph. Ant. 1022: plp. ἐβεβρώκει Hippocr. 7, 236: p. p. βέβρωμαι Aesch. Ag. 1097; Hippocr. 5, 192. 6, 12, δια- Pl. Tim. 83, κατα- Her. 4, 199; Pl. Phaed. 110: plp. ἐβέβρωτο Hippocr. 5, 156: aor. ἐβρώθην Artemid. Onir. 5, 49; Apollod. 3, 4, 4; βρωθῇ Aristot. Probl. 22, 1, κατα- Her. 3, 16; βρωθείς Hippocr. 2, 300. 5, 322; Lycophr. 414. 1251; -θῆναι Artemid. Onir. 1, 67, δια- Hippocr. 6, 450: fut. late βρωθήσομαι Lycophr. 1421; Or. Sib. 7, 119; late prose Sext. Emp. 174, 18; Geop. 2, 18: 3 fut. βεβρώσομαι Od. 2, 203: 2 aor. Epic, ἔβρων Callim. Jup. 49, κατ- Hom. H. 1, 127. (ῐ.) Hesych. has the unredupl. βρώσκων, ἀνα-. The opt. βεβρώθοις Il. 4, 35, perhaps infers a pres. βεβρώθω. It may however be perf. from Theme βρώθω (βόρω, voro.) In fact βρώθειν, κατα- actually occurs Babr. 67, 18 (2 pt. Lewis.) A desiderat. form βρωσείοντες occurs Callim. Fr. 435. Vb. βρωτός Eur. Sup. 1110, -έος Luc. Paras. 9. The Attics seem to have used only perf. act. and pass.

Βίομαι, see βέομαι.

Βιόω *To live*. βιοῦσι Emped. 52 (Stein); Democr. p. 174 (Mull.); Luc. Pisc. 34. Philops. 25. adv. Indoct. 16; βιοῖ Com. Fr. (Mon.) 65; Aristot. H. An. 6, 23, 4. 7, 4, 10, δια- Pl. Leg. 730; βιοῦν Eur. Fr. 240 (Dind.); Com. Fr. (Mon.) 58; βιῶν Com. Fr. Mon. 656, -οῦντες Aeschin. 1, 5, -εῦντες (Phocyl.) 229:

imp. ἐβίουν Hippocr. 5, 236 (Lit.): **fut.** βιώσομαι Eur. Alc. 784; Ar. Eq. 699; Hippocr. 8, 484; Xen. Cyr. 5, 4, 34; Pl. Gorg. 481. Rep. 344; Aristot. Eth. N. 10, 7, 8; Luc. Herm. 6: later βιώσω Com. Fr. (Mon.) 270; App. Civ. 4, 119; Diog. Laert. 2, 68; Luc. Nav. 26 (Jacob. Bekk. -σῃ Dind.); and late Epic, Maneth. 4, 475, συν- Polyb. 32, 10 (Bekk. -σει L. Dind.); inf. βιωσέμεν Orph. Lith. 624: **1 aor.** rare ἐβίωσα Her. 1, 163. 2, 133; Hippocr. 4, 380; Com. Fr. (Anon.) 4, 669; Xen. Oec. 4, 18 (Vulg. L. Dind. Saupp. ἐπ-εβίω Cob.); Aristot. H. A. 5, 14, 15. 7, 4, 20; -ώσασα Hippocr. 5, 356, -ώσαντες Pl. Phaed. 113; later, Plut. Ant. 86; βιῶσαι Plut. Mor. 367, Luc. Macrob. 8, δια- Plut. Mor. 660, ἐγκατα- 783: **p.** βεβίωκα Hippocr. 2, 656; Andoc. 4, 39; Lys. 3, 6; Isocr. 15, 27; Aeschin. 1, 8. 2, 147: **plp.** ἐβεβιώκει D. Cass. 78, 4, 5; **p. p.** βεβίωταί σοι Dem. 22, 77. 24, 185, τούτῳ 22, 78; βίος βεβιωμένος Isocr. 15, 7, τὰ βεβιωμένα Dem. 22, 23: **fut.** late βιωθησόμενος Anton. 9, 30: **2 aor.** ἐβίων Hippocr. 5, 204 (Lit.); Isocr. 9, 71; Isae. 3, 1; Dem. 48, 5; (Pl.) Epist. 327, ἐπ- Thuc. 2, 65. 5, 26; Isae. 2, 15, ἀν- Andoc. 1, 125, retains long vowel ἐβίωσαν Isocr. 4, 151; Pl. Phaedr. 249; Aeschin. 1, 146; subj. βιῶ, δια- Pl. Rep. 365, βιῷ Pl. Leg. 872; opt. βιῴην Pl. Gorg. 512. Tim. 89, ἀνα- Ar. Ran. 177 (-οίην Cobet, Dind. 5 ed.); (βίωθι) -ώτω Il. 8, 429; βιῶναι Il. 10, 174; Soph. O. R. 1488; Com. Fr. (Menand.) 4, 135; Aeschin. 3, 174; Pl. Gorg. 512, δια- Eur. Fr. incert. 1039 (D.); βιούς Com. Fr. (Phryn.) 2, 592; Her. 9, 10; Thuc. 2, 53; Pl. Prot. 351, said to occur in masc. only, but βιοῦσ' Anth. App. Epigr. 262, is, and διαβιοῦσαι seems to be **aor.** Pl. Leg. 679, neut. βιοῦν, ἐπι- Pollux. **Mid.** βιόομαι *to live, gain a livelihood,* Her. 2, 177; Aristot. N. Eth. 10, 10, 11: fut. βιώσομαι see above, late Epic βώσομαι Ap. Rh. 1, 685: **aor.** ἐβιωσάμην trans. *caused to live,* Od. 8, 468; intrans. *lived* Anth. App. Epigr. 381; Hippocr. 9, 298 (Lit.), see βιώσκομαι. βιόμεσθα Hom. H. 2, 350, implies βίομαι, unless it be for βεόμεσθα which Wolf adopts. Ap. Rh. has **fut.** βώσεσθε for βιώσ- 1, 685. **Vb.** βιωτός Ar. Plut. 197, -έος Pl. Gorg. 500. In early writers, the **pres.** and **imp.** are rare: they use ζάω. From Aristot. onwards βιόω occurs often, βιοῦσι Luc. Pisc. 34, βιοῖ Aristot. Eth. Mag. 1, 4, 5. H. A. 5, 33, 5. 6, 22, 9; Com. Fr. (Diph.) 4, 424; Luc. V. A. 26. Philops. 25; βιοῦν Com. Fr. Mon. 58; Plut. Sert. Eum. 2; Luc. Nigr. 13, συμ- Aristot. Eth. N. 9, 3, 4; βιῶν Com. Fr. Mon. 656; Luc. Fugit. 5, so βιούντων Aeschin. 1, 5, ἐπιβιοῦντος Dem. 41, 18. 19. 55, 4, *seemingly* used aoristically. From the examples given above, Kühner's assertion appears to be too strong "that the **1 aor.** is found in the participle only, except ἐβίωσε Xen. Oec. 4, 18:" and W. Dind. is, we think, rash in expelling 1 aor. from Xen. If the part. is right in Plato, the indic. seems not far wrong in Xen. The Ionians used both aorists, why might not the Attics, Xen. especially, occasionally use the first?

Βῐώσκομαι *To recover life, revive,* intrans. Aristot. Meteor. 1, 14, 3, ἀνα- Pl. Conv. 203: aor. ἐβιωσάμην Hippocr. 1, 149; Anth. App. Epigr. 381; and late prose Liban. 1, 382: and 2 aor. act. ἀν-εβίων Andoc. 1, 125; Pl. Rep. 614. βιώσκομαι, ἀνα- is also trans. *restore to life*, Pl. Crit. 48: with aor. *simple* ἐβιωσάμην Od. 8, 468; Hippocr. 9, 298, and comp. ἀν- Pl. Phaed. 89. Late authors have pres. act. ἀνα-βιώσκει *restores to life*, Themist. 8, 115 (Dind.): fut. ἀναβιώσεις *will restore to life* Ael. H. A. 2, 29 (Schneid. -σει Oudend. Herch.): aor. ἀνεβίωσε Palaeph. 41, but intrans. Aristot. H. A. 7, 10, 3; Theophr. H. P. 4, 14, 12: aor. p. -ωθείς Philostr. Apoll. 186. Pres. βιώσκω occurs in an Epigr. in Joann. Comn. (Notices et Extraits de Mss. vol. 8, p. 183), ἀνα- Schol. Eur. Alc. 1; Themist. quoted.

Βλᾰ́βομαι *To be hurt*, only 3 pers. βλᾰ́βεται Il. 19, 82; Anacreont. 31, 26 (Bergk): for 2 aor. ἐβλᾰ́βην: and fut. βλαβήσομαι, see βλάπτω: a 2 aor. act. late ἔβλαβεν Q. Sm. 5, 509; βλαβών Quint. Sm. 11, 5.

Βλάπτω *To hurt*, Od. 21, 294; Tyrt. 12, 40; Aesch. Ch. 327; Eur. Cycl. 524; Ar. Av. 1642; Her. 2, 113; Antiph. 5, 2; Isocr. 12, 223: imp. ἔβλαπτον Hippocr. 1, 588; Thuc. 2, 51; Xen. An. 4, 8, 3, βλάπτ- Il. 15, 724 (B.): fut. βλάψω Eur. Heracl. 704. 1044; Hippocr. 2, 336; Thuc. 4, 98: aor. ἔβλαψα Il. 23, 782; Soph. O. R. 375; Ar. Ran. 1064; Thuc. 3, 40; Lys. 9, 14; Pl. Gorg. 511, βλάψ- Il. 23, 774; βλάψῃ- Aesch. Eum. 661: p. βέβλᾰφα Dem. 19, 180; Aristot. Rhet. 3, 16, 4, κατα- Lycurg. 19 (Sauppe, Rhed.), ἔβλαφα C. Inscrip. 1570: p. p. βέβλαμμαι Il. 16, 660; Hippocr. 8, 418. 494. 498; Isocr. 15, 33; Pl. Prot. 314: 1 aor. ἐβλάφθην Il. 23, 387. 6, 39; Antiph. 3, γ, 7; Thuc. 4, 73. 87; Pl. Leg. 844. 877; Mosch. 4, 76, ἀπο- Soph. Aj. 941: 3 fut. βεβλάψομαι Hippocr. 2, 256 (Lit.); Galen 3, 72: 2 aor. ἐβλᾰ́βην Hippocr. 5, 418. 460; Xen. Hell. 6, 5, 48; Pl. Apol. 38, 3 pl. Ep. ἔβλαβεν Il. 23, 461, and βλάβεν 545; Pind. N. 7, 18; -βῆναι Thuc. 1, 141; Ar. Pax 710; -βείς Aesch. Ag. 120: fut. βλαβήσομαι Isocr. 1, 25; Pl. Meno 77; opt. -ήσοιτο Plut. Philop. 3; -ησόμενος Mor. 23; D. Cass. 58, 28: and fut. m. as pass. βλάψομαι Thuc. 1, 81. 6, 64: but aor. as act. βλάψαντο late and rare, Q. Sm. 5, 466 (Koechl.) missed by Lexicogr. Buttmann unduly confined the reduplication in the perf. of verbs beginning with βλ to βλάπτω. See βλαστάνω, βλέπω, βλασφημέω, βεβλασφήμηκε Dem. 18, 10.

Βλαστάνω *To sprout*, Aesch. Sept. 594; Soph. O. C. 611; Ar. Av. 1479; Hippocr. 7, 518; Xen. Oec. 19, 2; Pl. Rep. 498; Dem. 53, 16, ἀνα- Pind. Fr. 182 (Schneid.), rare βλαστέω (if sound, Aesch. Ch. 589, but) Bion 3, 17 (Ursin. Ahr.); Theophr. C. P. 5, 4, 5. 2, 17, 4, ἀνα- Emped. 449 (Stein): **imp.** βλάστεον Ap. Rh. 4, 1425, ἐβλάστανε Themist. 22, 280, iter. βλαστάνεσκε Soph. Fr. 491: **fut.** βλαστήσω Trag. Fr. incert. 269 (Wagn.); Theophr. H. P. 2, 7, 2; Geop. 4, 5, ἀνα- Her. 3, 62: **1 aor.** ἐβλάστησα not in early Attic, Emped. 105. 244 (Stein); Hippocr. 7, 528. 546; Aristot. Mirab. 153 (B.); Theophr. H. P. 7, 4, 8; Himer. Or. 1, 9, 13; Porph. V. Pythag. 44, δι- Plut. Mor. 1003: **p.** βεβλάστηκα Hellanic. Fr. 2; Hippocr. 9, 182 (Lit.); Plut. Mor. 684, and ἐβλάστηκα Com. Fr. (Eup.) 2, 561; Eur. I. A. 595 (chor.): **plp.** ἐβεβλαστήκει Thuc. 3, 26; Luc. V. Hist. 1, 31: **2 aor.** ἔβλαστον Pind. N. 8, 7; Soph. El. 238; Eur. Fr. 432 (D.); Com. Fr. (Theop.) 2, 793; Ar. Av. 696, ἀν- Her. 7, 156, βλάστ- Pind. Ol. 7, 69: (late **aor. p.** βλαστηθείς Phil. vol. 1, p. 667.) **Mid.** βλαστουμένη Soph. Fr. 239 (D.): **fut.** late βλαστήσομαι Alex. Trall. 1, 6. βλαστάνω is occasionally trans. *make to sprout, bring forth*, Hippocr. 2, 25 (K.), παρα- Themist. 32, 360: **fut.** βλαστήσω Trag. Fr. incert. 269 (Wagn.): **1 aor.** ἐβλάστησα Ap. Rh. 1, 1131, ἐξ- Hippocr. 2, 17 (K.): **2 aor.** ἔβλαστον Eur. Fr. 430 (D.) In classic Attic prose, we have seen **pres.** and **plp.** only. A form in αω occurs late, βλαστῶντα Herm. Past. p. 57.

Βλέπω *To see*, Solon 11, 8; Aesch. Pers. 261; Soph. Tr. 594; Ar. Av. 176; Andoc. 1, 18; Isocr. 12, 188; Pl. Rep. 477; -ειν Pind. P. 8, 68; -ων Simon. Am. 19; Pind. N. 4, 39; Antiph. 4, γ, 1, -ουσα Soph. Tr. 313, Dor. -οισα (Theocr.) 20, 13: **imp.** ἔβλεπον Batr. 67; Aesch. Pr. 447; Soph. O. R. 1470; Pl. Leg. 743: **fut.** βλέψω perhaps late in *simple*, Orac. Sib. 1, 353. 8, 207; Aristid. 45, 46; V. T. Esai. 6, 9, ἀνα- Her. 2, 111; Ach. Tat. 6, 6, ἀντι- (Dem.) 25, 98 (Bekk. B. S. Dind.); Plut. Pomp. 69, ἀπο- Luc. Merc. Con. 15, see below: and βλέψομαι (Dem.) 25, 98, ἀνα- Eur. H. F. 563, προσ- Eur. I. A. 1192, ὑπο- Pl. Crit. 53, ἀπο- Luc. Som. 12. Rhet. 17. V. A. 10: **aor.** ἔβλεψα Soph. Fr. 517 (D.); Ar. Ran. 804; Thuc. 5, 98; Isocr. 12, 102; βλέψας Aesch. Pers. 802: **p.** βέβλεφα, ἀπο- Stob. (Antip.) 70, 13: **p. p.** βέβλεμμαι Athen. 9, 409: **aor.** ἐβλέφθην, προσ- Plut. Symp. 5, 7, 1. **Vb.** βλεπτός Soph. O. R. 1337, -έος Pl. Leg. 965. In *classic* authors, the **mid.** is confined to the **future**; for διαβλεψάμενος Pl. Phaed. 86 (old edit.) has been altered to διαβλέψας (best Mss. Bekk. B. Or. W.), but later occur pres. imp. and aor. ἀπο-βλεπόμενοι Luc. V. H. 2, 47: imp. ἀπ-εβλέπετο Malal. p. 126: aor. περι-βλέψαιτο Longin. 35, 3; ἀπο-βλεψάμενος Schol. Od. 12, 247, all missed by Lexicogr. περι-βλέπομαι Apocr. Sir. 9, 7: imp. περιεβλέπετο Polyb. 9, 17: fut. περιβλέψομαι V. T. Job 7, 8: aor. περι-βλεψάμενος Plut. Cat. Min. 37; Charit. 1, 4, 9 (D'Orv.); V. T. Exod. 2, 12; Jos. Ant. 17, 6, 7. ὑπο-βλέπομαι Niceph. Rhet. 7, 6: imp. ὑπ-εβλέποντο Luc. Conv. 6; App. Syr. 45; Procop. Epist. 152: fut. -βλέψονται Pl. Crit. 53: aor. -εβλέψατο Gorg. Rhet. p. 811, all missed, even the fut., by most of our Lexicogr. Pass. rare, βλέπεται Or. Sib. Fr. 1, 9; Plut. Mor. 1053, περι- Pl. Epigr. 8 (Bergk); subj. βλέπωμαι Luc. Fug. 19. Gall. 23, ἀπο- Ar. Eccl. 726; βλέποιτο Long. Past. 3, 15; βλεπόμενος Luc. D. Deor. 20, 10; Charit. 8, 6, ἀπο- Luc. Som. 11; βλέπεσθαι, περι- Eur. Phoen. 551, ἀπο- Luc. Nigr. 13. Fut. act. we think at least doubtful in the earlier Attics: βλέψω Eur. Hec. 585, seems subj. aor.: and ἀντιβλέψετε (Dem.) 25, 98, is opposed by ἀντιβλέψεσθε (Mss. F. V. Vulg. Dind. Oxf. 1848), which, one would suppose, is more likely to be the true reading, as the mid. form βλέψεσθε occurs a few lines before. Dind. however in his last edit. 1855, adopts ἀντιβλέψετε with Bekk. B. S. βλέψεις in some edit. of Sappho, Fr. 11, 7 (Brunck, Anal. 1, 57) is pretty evidently a late interpolation.

Βληχάομαι *To bleat*, Poet. Ar. Vesp. 570; -ώμενος Pax 535, and -έομαι, opt. βληχοῖντο Theocr. 16, 92, but -ῷντο (Briggs, Ahr.): imp. κατ-εβληχῶντο Theoc. 5, 42: aor. ἐβληχησάμην Long. Past. 3, 13; βληχήσαιντο Anth. 7, 657. βλήχομαι seems not to occur, for at Theocr. 16, 92, opt. βληχοῖντο, not βλήχοιντο, is the approved Ms. reading. This verb is rare: in Attic, pres. only.

Βλῑμάζω *To feel*, in act. only pres. Dor. -άσδομες Ar. Lys. 1164 (Br. Dind. -άττομες Vulg. Bekk. Bergk); βλιμάζων Ar. Av. 530; rare in prose Luc. Lex. 12; -άζειν Philostr. Imag. 429, 95: and imp. ἐβλίμ- Com. Fr. (Cratin.) 2, 183: aor. βλιμάξαι (Hesych.): pass. aor. ἐβλιμάσθη Hippocr. 5, 204 (Lit.).

Βλίσσω, -ττω *To take the honey*, Soph. Fr. 856 (D.); Ar. Eq. 794; Pl. Rep. 564; Aristot. H. An. 9, 40, 54: imp. ἔβλιττε Hesych: fut. (βλῐ́σω): aor. ἔβλῐσα Nonn. 5, 257, ἀπ-έβλισε Ar. Av. 498; βλίσειε Pl. Rep. 564: aor. m. ἀπεβλίσατο formerly Anth. 7, 34, has been altered to ἀπεπλάσατο (Jacobs). Pass. βλίττεται Aristot. H. A. 5, 22, 9. Vb. ἐκ-βλιστέος Hesych.

Βλύζω *To bubble*, Poet. and late prose, Orac. Paus. 5, 7, 3; Orph. Arg. 601; Anth. 7, 27; Max. καταρχ. 304; Philostr.

Apoll. 95. 132, ἀπο- Il. 9, 491, ἀνα- Aristot. Mirab. 113, βλύττω v. r. (Pl. Rep. 564), and βλύω Lycophr. 301, ἀνα- Hippocr. 6, 374 (Lit.), περι- Ap. Rh. 4, 788, ἐπι- 1238 &c.: imp. ἔβλῠον Nonn. Par. 2, 28, iter. βλύεσκε, ἀνα- Ap. Rh. 3, 223, βλύζεσκε, ἀνα- Q. Sm. 14, 496: fut. βλῡ́σω Anth. (incert.) 9, 819; (v. r. Pl. Rep. 564), (σσ) Nonn. Par. 7, 38: aor. ἔβλῡσα Ap. Rh. 4, 1446; Anth. 11, 24; Q. Sm. 1, 242, ἀνα- Aristot. Mund. 6, 32; Plut. Syl. 6: aor. pass. ἐβλύσθη late? Orac. Euseb. prep. ev. 5, 15. In pres. and imp. βλύω has ῠ, in fut. and aor. ῡ: but ἔβλῠσεν? Christ. Pat. 1083, ἀνα-βλῠσαι Plut. Syl. 6 (Sint. Bekk.).

Βλύττω, βλύω, see preced.

Βλώσκω *To go* (μλώσκω, μόλω), Poet. and late in *simple*, βλώσκων Nic. Ther. 450, κατα- Od. 16, 466; βλώσκειν, προ- Od. 21, 239, ἀπο- Ap. Rh. 3, 1143, Epic βλωσκέμεν Od. 19, 25: fut. (late βλώξω, κατα- Lycophr. 1068: and 1 aor. ἔβλωξα Lycophr. 1327): mid. μολοῦμαι in Trag. Aesch. Pr. 689; Soph. O. C. 1742; (Hippocr. 5, 698, seemingly corrupt): p. μέμβλωκα Od. 17, 190; Eur. Rh. 629; Callim. Fr. 124, παρ- Il. 4, 11. 24, 73: 2 aor. ἔμολον Pind. Ol. 14, 18; Aesch. Ch. 935. 937; Soph. El. 506. 1234; Ar. Lys. 984. Av. 404, unaugm. μόλον Pind. P. 3, 47, ἔκ-μολεν Il. 11, 604, προ- Od. 15, 468 (Hesych. has an aor. ἔβλω, ᾤχετο); subj. μόλω Soph. Ph. 479; Ar. Lys. 743, -λῃς Mimnerm. 12, 10; Aesch. Pr. 719; Soph. Ph. 1332, -λῃ Il. 24, 781; Aesch. Pers. 529, -λωμεν 230; μόλοιμι Eur. Hel. 246, μόλοι Pind. N. 3, 63; Aesch. Ag. 345; Soph. O. C. 70; Ar. Thesm. 1146; imper. μόλε Eur. An. 509; Ar. Thesm. 1155, προ- Il. 18, 392; μολεῖν Aesch. Pr. 236; Soph. O. C. 757; Eur. Alc. 107; μολών Il. 11, 173. Od. 3, 44; Aesch. Ag. 293; Soph. O. R. 35; Eur. Hipp. 661; Ar. Ran. 1232; late in prose ἐμόλετε Plut. Cleom. 38; except subj. μόλωσι Xen. An. 7, 1, 33; μολόντες Plut. Mor. 220. 225; μολεῖν Polyb. 30, 9. Late poets have pres. μολέω Anth. 12, 93: aor. μολήσας Tzetz. Anteh. 375. The pres. and perf. are Epic, excepting Eur. Rhes. quoted: the fut. seems confined to Tragedy: the 2 aor. is almost Poetic.

Βοάω *To shout*, (ᾰ) Il. 14, 394; Simon. C. 114; Aesch. Sept. 381; Soph. El. 295; Ar. Thesm. 507; Her. 3, 117; Thuc. 7, 48; Pl. Phaed. 114; opt. -ῷμι, ἐπι- Aesch. Supp. 675 (Turn. Wellau. now altered), Att. -ῴην Ar. Thesm. 506; Pl. Phaed. 101; contr. imper. βῶ, ἐπι- Aesch. Pers. 1054 (chor.): imp. ἐβόων Com. Fr. (Lysipp.) 2, 748; Thuc. 6, 28, βόων Hes. Sc. 243, iter. βοάασκεν Ap. Rh. 2, 588: fut. βοήσομαι Thuc. 7, 48; Pl. Apol. 30; Dem. 2, 29. 21, 138; Luc. D. Mar. 6, 3, ἀνα-

Eur. I. A. 465; Lycurg. 31, κατα- Ar. Eq. 286, Dor. βοάσομαι Ar. Nub. 1154 (chor.); Com. Fr. (Phryn.) 2, 598; Anth. App. Epigr. 200, ἀνα- Ar. Plut. 639 (chor.): late βοήσω Anth. 7, 32. 9, 100. Plan. 169; Ap. Rh. 3, 792; Or. Sib. 7, 111, κατα- Plut. Them. 7, δια- Herodn. 2, 2; V. T. Lev. 25, 10, Dor. -άσω? see below: **aor.** ἐβόησα Il. 11, 15. Od. 4, 281; Anacr. 100; Com. Fr. 3, 371 (chor.), ἀν- Antiph. 5, 69; Thuc. 1, 53; Isocr. 12, 264; Xen. Cyr. 7, 1, 38, ἐπ- Thuc. 5, 65, &c., 'βόησ- Soph. Tr. 772, βόησ- Il. 23, 847 (Bekk.); βοήσας Luc. Tim. 11, Dor. ἐβόασε in tmes. Eur. Tr. 522 (chor.), ἀντ- Bion 1, 38, βόασε Pind. P. 6, 36; Eur. Andr. 298 (chor.); pt. Dor. βοάσαις Pind. Ol. 8, 40; βοᾶσαι Aision ap. Aristot. Rhet. 3, 10, 7: **p.** late βεβοηκότες Philostr. V. Soph. 561: **p. p.** βεβόημαι Anth. 7, 138; Aristid. 7, 44 (D.), δια- (Pl.) Epist. 312, βεβόαμ- Anth. 15, 4: **plp.** ἐβεβόητο Paus. 6, 11, 2, δι- Luc. Peregr. 10: **aor.** ἐβοήθην, δι- Plut. Sol. 11. Timol. 5. **Mid.** βοάομαι rare in *simple*, βοάσθω may be mid. Eur. I. A. 438; βοᾶσθαι Hel. 1434; βοώμενος *shouting*, Ar. Vesp. 1228; Aratus 912, &c. ἐπι-βοᾶται Eur. Med. 168, in *classic* Attic prose only ἐπι- Thuc. 7, 69, δια- Dem. 26, 19; (Luc. Fug. 3); ἐπι-βοώμενος Thuc. 3, 59. 67. 7, 75. 8, 92; late Dio. Hal. 11, 49; Dio Cass. 39, 38; Luc. Tyr. 20. D. Mer. 12, 1; Themist. 6, 77: **imp.** ἐπ-εβοῶντο Dio Cass. 41, 9, -ᾶτο Luc. Necyom. 9: **fut.** βοήσομαι, -άσομαι see above: **aor.** βοησάμενος Dion. de Avibus 2, 19; βοήσατο Q. Sm. 10, 465 (Ms. A. Vulg. γοήσ- Pauw, Lehrs, Koechly); ἐπι-βοήσασθαι Plut. Syl. 6; Luc. D. Mar. 2, 4; Dio Cass. 59, 10; -σάμενος Ep. Phal. 132 (Herch.); Dio Cass. 39, 29. **Vb.** βοητός, περι- Thuc. 6, 31, -βωτος Euen. Ascal. 8 (Bergk.) Epic extended forms, βοάᾳ for βοάει, Il. 14, 394, βοόωσι for βοάουσι, Il. 17, 265, βοόων for -άων, Il. 15, 687. Epic and Ionic contr. forms: βῶται, ἐπι- Theocr. 12, 35: βώσομαι, ἐπι- Od. 1, 378. 2, 143. Il. 10, 463 (Vulg. Spitzn. La Roche, ἐπιδώσ- Aristarch. Bekk. and Dind. *now*), κατα-βώσ- Her. 6, 85: **aor. act.** ἔβωσα Hipponax 1 (B.), ἀν- Her. 1, 10. 3, 14. 155; βῶσον Com. Fr. (Cratin.) 2, 229, βωσάτω Ar. Pax 1155 (chor.); βῶσαι Her. 1, 146; βώσας Il. 12, 337; Her. 5, 1. 6, 105. 8, 92. 118, ἀμβώσας 1, 8. 3, 38. 7, 18: **p.** βεβωμένα Her. 3, 39: **aor.** ἐβώσθην Her. 6, 131. 8, 124: **aor. m.** ἐβώσατο Theocr. 17, 60, προσ- Her. 6, 35, ἐπ- 9, 23, &c. Her., we think, has always the contracted forms; Hom. has **aor.** ἐβόησα, rarely βόησα, only once -ῶσα, but always -ώσομαι. βοάσω Eur. Ion 1446 (chor.), ἀνα- Hel. 1108 (chor.), δια- Aesch. Pers. 637 (chor.) sometimes quoted as instances of Dor. fut. act. seem rather to be subj. **aor.** βοήσατο Q. Sm. 10, 465, has been altered to γοήσατο on perhaps insufficient grounds, "medio non usitato" (Koechly). That the mid. is used, *simple* and *compd.*, the quotations given above sufficiently prove. Koechly, on his alleged grounds of preference, had perhaps better reasons for quarrelling with aor. mid. βλάψαντο 5, 466, which, we think, is an unique instance of the *simple* aor. mid.

Βοηθέω *To assist*, Her. 1, 62; Antiph. 2, γ, 11; Isocr. 19, 15; Ion. imper. βωθεῖτε Anth. (Meleag.) 12, 84, is reg. in Attic: **imp.** ἐβοήθεον Her. 6, 103. 108. 138, ἐβώθ- (Dind.), -ήθουν Thuc. 7, 33; Lys. 31, 8: **fut.** -ήσω Andoc. 3, 26: **aor.** ἐβοήθησα Her. 7, 165 (ἐβώθ- D.); Lys. 31, 29; Dem. 22, 14; -ήσας Aesch. Supp. 613: **p.** -ηκα Thuc. 3, 97; Dem. 15, 3. 10, 18. **Pass.** rare, βοηθεῖται Plut. Mor. 687. 720, -οῦνται 689; -θεῖσθαι Apollod. 2, 8, 1 (B.): **p.** βεβοήθηται Antiph. 1, 31; βεβοηθημένος (Pl.) Epist. 347: **aor.** late ἐβοηθήθην V. T. Esai. 10, 3. 30, 2: with **fut. mid.** βοηθήσονται as pass. V. T. Dan. 11, 34. **Mid.** late, **fut.** βοηθήσομαι see above: **aor.** β ηθήσασθαι Galen 5, 29, both missed by Lexicogr. **Vb.** β ηθητέον Hippocr. 5, 316; Xen. Hell. 6, 5, 10. Her., according to Mss. and most edit., *generally* uses this verb in the Attic form βοηθέω, ἐβοήθεον, ἐβοήθησα, but occasionally in the Ionic, ἐβώθεε 9, 23, ἐπ- 8, 1. 14: ἐβώθησαν 8, 47, ἐπ- 8, 45; βωθήσας 8, 72; προ-βωθῆσαι 8, 144 (Gaisf. Bekk. Krüg. &c.), Stein always βοηθ-; Dind. and Abicht again edit, we think, in every case βωθέω, ἐβώθεε, ἐβώθησα, &c. "because in Ionic οη contract into ω." This reason would have been stronger had the verb been exclusively or even chiefly Ionic or poetic. On the contrary, it is very frequent in Attic, and prosaic, occurring once or twice in Tragedy, rarely even in Comedy, never, we think, in good Epic. It seems to us therefore as likely that Her. *meant* to use the Attic form, but was occasionally *surprised* into the Ionic. Hippocr. we think never has the contr. form βωθ-, but always βοηθέω, see 1, 598. 8, 402. 9, 208. 218. 234. 268, βοηθήσων (Epist.) 9, 420. In a Cretan Inscr. occurs fut. βοηθησίοντι (Bergm.)

(**Βολέω**)=**Βάλλω** *To throw, hit*, **p.p.** βεβόλημαι Ap. Rh. 4, 1318: **plp.** βεβόλητο Q. Sm. 7, 726, 3 pl. -ηντο 2, 585, -ήατο Il. 9, 3; -ημένος Il. 9, 9; Ap. Rh. 1, 262; Musae. 134: **aor.** late βοληθείς Or. Sib. 12, 75. In late Epic, the comp. ἀβολέω occurs in **fut.** -ήσομεν Ap. Rh. 3, 1145: and **aor.** ἀβόλησαν 2, 770; Callim. Fr. 455. (ᾰ.)

Βόλομαι Poet. (βούλομαι, volo) *To wish*, Il. 11, 319, βόλεσθε Od. 16, 387; Aeol. βολλόμενος Stob. Flor. (Dius) 65, 16 (Mein.): **imp.** ἐβόλοντο Od. 1, 234, Aeol. ἐβολλόμαν Theocr. 28, 15.

Βόσκω *To feed*, Od. 11, 365; Archil. 19; Soph. Fr. 518; Eur. Phoen. 396; Ar. Eq. 256; Her. 1, 44; Thuc. 7, 48: imp. ἔβοσκε Eur. Phoen. 405; Luc. Pseudol. 25; Philostr. 1, 5. 3, 111, βόσκε Il. 15, 548: fut. βοσκήσω Od. 17, 559; Ar. Eccl. 599: aor. late ἐβόσκησα Geop. 18, 7: aor. p. and fut. see below. Mid. and pass. βόσκομαι *to eat*, Od. 14, 104; Anacr. 75; Aesch. Ag. 118. Sept. 244; Ar. Av. 1099; Her. 9, 93; Pl. Rep. 586: imp. ἐβόσκετο H. Merc. 193; Eur. Bacc. 617; Luc. Peregr. 16, βόσκοντο Od. 12, 128, iter. βοσκέσκοντο Od. 12, 355: fut. βοσκήσομαι Serap. in Plut. Mor. 398; Or. Sib. 3, 788, Dor. -ησοῦμαι Theocr. 5, 103: aor. late ἐβοσκησάμην, κατ- Long. Past. 2, 16, ἐκ- Galen 1, 517: with aor. pass. ἐβοσκήθην Babr. 89, κατ- Pseud.-Callisth. 1, 32; Aesop 131 (Halm); βοσκηθείς Trag. Fr. (Incert.) 268 (Wagn.); Nic. Ther. 34; Hierocl. 128: and fut. βοσκηθήσομαι, κατα- trans. Geop. 2, 39, intrans. περι-βοσκηθ- 20, 22. Vb. βοσκητέος Ar. Av. 1359. βόσκεν Dor. inf. pres. Theocr. 4, 2 (Vulg. Meineke, -ειν Ahr. Ziegl. Fritzsche).

Βουκολιάζω, Dor. Βωκολιάσδω *To sing a pastoral song*, in act. only imp. βουκολίασδον Bion 5, 5: fut. -αξεῖς (see below). Mid. βουκολιάζεο Theocr. 9, 1, -άζευ 5, 60. 9, 5; Mosch. 3, 122 (132); -ασδώμεσθα Theocr. 7, 36: fut. βουκολιαξῇ 5, 44 (Ms. Vat. B. Valk. Gaisf. Mein. Ziegl. Ahr. &c. -εῖς Vulg.) Editors—even the same—vary between -άζω and -άσδω, βωκ- and βουκ-: Ahrens, Meineke, Ziegler, and Fritzsche always the latter.

Βουλεύω *To consult, counsel, plan*, reg. in act. Il. 10, 415; Aesch. Eum. 700; Antiph. 1, 26; Thuc. 8, 58; Epic subj. -ησθα Il. 9, 99; Epic. inf. -ευέμεν Od. 14, 491: imp. ἐβούλ- Her. 8, 49; Thuc. 5, 63, βούλ- Od. 1, 444: fut. -εύσω Il. 2, 379; Ar. Pax 692; Thuc. 8, 72; Epic inf. -ευσέμεν Od. 5, 179: aor. ἐβούλευσα Od. 5, 23; Aesch. Ag. 1627; Her. 3, 84, βούλ- Il. 9, 458; -εύσας Antiph. 4, α, 7; Pl. Apol. 32: p. βεβούλευκα Soph. O. R. 701; Isocr. 16, 43: p. p. βεβούλευται Aesch. Pr. 998; Her. 7, 10. 8, 100; Pl. Euth. 274; -ευμένον Epin. 982; Her. 4, 125, see mid.: plp. ἐβεβουλ- Her. 5, 92: aor. ἐβουλεύθην, -ευθῆναι Thuc. 1, 120; -ευθείς Pl. Rep. 442: fut. late ἐπι-βουλευθήσονται Dio Cass. 52, 33; Epist. Phal. 122 (Herch.): and fut. m. βουλεύσεται pass. Aesch. Sept. 198, ἐπι- Xen. Cyr. 5, 4, 34. Mid. βουλεύομαι *to deliberate*, &c. Soph. Ant. 772; Her. 7, 13; Antiph. 5, 72; Pl. Lach. 185: imp. ἐβουλ- Her. 3, 84; Thuc. 2, 4; Antiph. 1, 17; Dem. 48, 28: fut. -εύσομαι Aesch. Ag. 846; Thuc. 1, 43; Pl. Conv. 174: aor. ἐβουλευσάμην Soph. O. R. 537; Her. 1, 73; Antiph. 5, 71. 76; Xen. Cyr. 1, 4, 17, βουλευσ- Il. 2, 114: with p. βεβούλευμαι

Soph. El. 947; Eur. Med. 893; Her. 3, 134, -ευσαι Eur. Supp. 248; Aeschin. 3, 209, -ευται Xen. Cyr. 3, 1, 15, -εύμεθα Pl. Charm. 176, -ευνται Soph. El. 385; -εῦσθαι Aesch. Fr. 258; Thuc. 6, 8; Xen. An. 7, 6, 27; Isocr. 19, 1; Dem. 8, 3; -ευμένος Thuc. 1, 69; Dem. 18, 236: and late **aor.** ἐβουλεύθη Dio. Hal. Excerp. 15, 7; and ἐπιβουλευθῆναι Dio Cass. 59, 26 (Vulg. but ἐπιβουλεῦσαι Bekk. Dind.) **Vb.** βουλευτέον Thuc. 1, 72.

Βούλομαι (and **Βόλομαι**, which see) *To will, wish,* Il. 1, 117; Aesch. Pr. 929; Soph. O. C. 363; Ar. Nub. 78; Her. 2, 86; Antiph. 5, 80; Pl. Rep. 358, 2 sing. in Att. always βούλει Soph. Ant. 757; Ar. Ran. 3; Thuc. 6, 14, Ion. -λεαι Od. 18, 364; Her. 1, 11. 3, 53. 6, 69 &c.; subj. βουλῇ Ar. Eq. 850; Pl. Rep. 346, Epic -λεαι Hes. Op. 647 (Flach, Koechly), -ληαι (Goetll.), βούληται Ar. Ran. 381; Thuc. 4, 3, Epic -λεται Il. 1, 67; opt. -οίμην Od. 17, 187; Eur. Hec. 319, -οιντο Xen. An. 2, 3, 4, Ion. -οίατο Her. 1, 3 &c.; imper. βούλεο Theogn. 145: **imp.** ἐβουλόμην Il. 11, 79; Soph. Ph. 1239; Eur. H. F. 1305; Ar. Ran. 866; Her. 1, 165. 2, 120. 6, 66; Antiph. 4, δ, 4; Thuc. 3, 51; Xen. An. 1, 1, 1. Hell. 1, 7, 7; Lys. 3, 21. 13, 7; Dem. 1, 13. 4, 4 &c., βουλ- Il. 23, 682, and ἠβουλ- Eur. Hel. 752; Com. Fr. (Alex.) 3, 502; Isocr. 8, 10; Xen. Hell. 1, 1, 29 (Saupp. Breitb.). (Apol.) 11; Lys. 13, 6. 25, 14; Dem. 1, 15. 9, 61. 18, 101 &c.: **fut.** βουλήσομαι Hom. H. 2, 86; Aesch. Pr. 867; Her. 1, 127; Antiph. 6, 8; Thuc. 1, 22: (no mid. aor.): **p.** βεβούλημαι Dem. 18, 2: **aor.** ἐβουλήθην as mid. Eur. Hipp. 476; Antiph. 1, 13; Thuc. 1, 34; Xen. Hell. 2, 4, 8. 4, 4, 8 (Dind. Saupp.); Pl. Tim. 25; Lys. 14, 9; Isocr. 3, 39. 9, 65 (Bekk. B. S.); Isae. 5, 19; Dem. 19, 29. 23, 107 (Bekk. Dind. B. S.), ἠβουλ- Xen. Hipp. 3, 5 (D. Saupp.). Hell. 4, 4, 8 (Vulg.); Isocr. 5, 12 (Bekk. B. S. Bens.). 9, 65 (Bens.); Dem. 14, 15. 19, 43. 20, 114. 23, 202 (Bekk. B. S.); -ηθείς Soph. O. C. 732: **fut.** late, βουληθήσομαι Aristid. 24, 292 (Vulg. -λέσομαι Ms. T. Dind.); Galen 13, 636; **2 p.** poet. βέβουλα, προ- *prefer,* Il. 1, 113; Anth. 9, 445. **Vb.** βουλητός Pl. Leg. 733, -ητέος Aristot. Eth. Mag. 2, 11, 7. Ion. 3 pl. imp. ἐβουλέατο, for -λοντο, Her. 1, 4. 3, 143, ἐβούλοντο however is by far the prevailing form, 1, 165. 2, 120. 150. 5, 65. 7, 195. 229 (Schweigh. Bekk. Gaisf.) This verb never has double augm. ἠβουλ- in Hom. and Her.; rarely in the Tragedians, v. r. Soph. Ph. 1239, and once or so in Eur.; never in Aristoph., but once in Alexid. Com. Fr. 3, 502. In the Orators, Bekk. and B. Saupp. vary with the Mss. Benseler, again, ἠβ- always in Isocr., and W. Dind. always, we think, ἐβ- in Dem. (3 edit. 1855). In

Thuc. scarcely a trace is left of double augm. ἠβουλ- 2, 2. 2, 5. 6, 79 (Vulg.), ἐβουλ- (Popp. Krüg. and Bekk. *now*, 1846 Berlin), except 6, 79, where, perhaps from inadvertence, he still retains ἠβ-, and in Xen. the best Mss. and edit. differ. δύναμαι and μέλλω also take, besides the syllabic, the temporal augment—which see in their place.

Βρᾰδύνω (ῡ) *To make slow, delay*, Soph. Ph. 1400 (Ellendt)?; intrans. *to be slow*, Aesch. Supp. 730; Eur. Heracl. 733; Ar. Vesp. 230; Pl. Rep. 528. Polit. 277: **imp.** ἐβράδῡνον D. Hal. Ant. 9, 26; Luc. H. V. 1, 29; Ael. V. H. 3, 43: **fut.** -ύνῶ V. T. Deut. 7, 10: **aor.** ἐβράδῡνα Dio Chrys. Or. 40 (491); App. Civ. 1, 69; Luc. Char. 1; Dio Cass. 52, 37. 76, 7; Herodn. 3, 7, 4; Polyaen. Strat. 1, 48; βραδῦναι, ἐμ- Luc. Hip. 6: **p.** βεβράδῠκα?: **plp.** ἐβεβραδῠ́κειν Luc. Symp. 20. **Mid.** βραδύνομαι Aesch. Sept. 623 (Vulg. Herm. Weil, rejected by Dind.) **Pass.** βραδύνεται Soph. O. C. 1628. El. 1501. Classic authors seem to have used only **pres. act. mid.** and **pass.** Neither Soph. Ph. 1400, nor N. T. 2 Pet. 3, 9, are decisive instances of trans. meaning: V. T. Esai. 46, 13. is stronger.

Βράζω *To boil, shake*, Heliod. 5, 16, βράσσω Anth. 10, 1; Nic. Alex. 359, Att. -ττω Pl. Soph. 226; Ar. Fr. 267 (D.): **fut.** βρᾱ́σω, συνεκ- Lycophr. 898, ἐμ- Orig. Ref. Haeres. 4, 33 (Miller): **aor.** ἔβρᾰσα Anth. 6, 222; Nic. Alex. 25; Geop. 7, 15: **p. p.** βέβρασμαι Anth. 7, 288, ἐκ- Diod. Sic. 20, 112: **aor.** ἐβράσθην Aretae. Morb. Ac. 1, 5, ἀνα- Ap. Rh. 2, 566, ἐξ- Plut. Pyr. 15; Dio Cass. 48, 48; Diod. Sic. 20, 76. **Mid.** βράσσεται, ἐκ- Hippocr. 7, 166 (Lit.), where however some would make it pass. by reading θρόμβους for -ους, see also ἀποβράσσεται 7, 540. Ermerins reads act. form ἐκβράσσει 2, 313. **Vb.** βραστέον Geop. 3, 7.

(**Βράχω**) *To resound*, Epic and only **2 aor.** ἔβρᾰχε Il. 5, 863; Ap Rh. 2, 573; Callim. Del. 140, ἀν- Il. 19, 13, βράχε Il. 5, 838. 16, 468. 566. Od. 21, 49 (Bekk. ἔβρ- Vulg. Dind.); Hes. Sc. 423. Bekk. in his last edition (1858) writes βράχε always after a vowel.

Βρέμω *To roar*, Poet. and only **pres.** Il. 4, 425; Epich. 9 (Ahr.); Pind. P. 11, 30; Aesch. Sept. 378 (trim.). 84 (chor.); Soph. Ant. 592 (chor.); Hippocr. 7, 180; βρέμῃ Eur. Bac. 161 (chor.); -ειν Aesch. Eum. 979 (chor.); Eur. Heracl. 832 (trim.); -έμων Aesch. Pr. 424; Eur. Phoen. 112. H. F. 962. Tr. 83 (trim.). 520 (chor.): and **imp.** ἔβρεμον Ap. Rh. 2, 567; Non. 1, 231. **Mid.** βρέμομαι as act. Il. 14, 399; Pind. N. 11, 7; Aesch. Sept. 350 (chor.); Ar. Thesm. 998 (chor.) The Tragedians confine the usage of this word very much to chor.: ind. and inf. perhaps each once, part. thrice, in trimet. Eur. quoted.

Βρενθύομαι (ῠ) *To swagger*, only pres. Ar. Nub. 362. Pax 26. Lys. 887; -νόμενος Pl. Conv. 221; Luc. Tim. 54; -εσθαι Lex. 24: and late, imp. ἐβρενθύετο Liban. 15, p. 431.

Βρέχω *To wet*, Com. Fr. (Telecl.) 2, 376; Her. 1, 189; Xen. An. 3, 2, 22; Pl. Phaedr. 229, δια- Aesch. Fr. 318: imp. ἔβρεχον Philox. 5 (B.), βρέχε Pind. Ol. 7, 34: fut. late, βρέξω Or. Sib. 5, 377. 508. 10, 200, ἀνα- Oribas. 8, 39, ἀπο- Galen 6, 591: aor. ἔβρεξα Pl. Phaedr. 254; βρέξον Hippocr. 8, 192; βρέξαι Xen. An. 4, 3, 12; βρέξας Com. Fr. (Ax.) 3, 531; Aristot. Meteor. 2, 3, 36; Hippocr. 1, 576. 6, 632 (Lit.): p. p. βέβρεγμαι Pind. Ol. 6, 55; Com. Fr. (Eubul.) 3, 263; Hippocr. 2, 484. 8, 236 (Lit.); Aristot. Probl. 3, 1: aor. ἐβρέχθην Xen. An. 1, 4, 17; βρεχθῶ Aristot. Gen. An. 3, 2, 6, κατα- Ar. Nub. 267; βρεχθείς Eur. Elec. 362; Aristot. Probl. 21, 6; (Dem.) 55, 25; -ῆναι 55, 24: 2 aor. ἐβρᾰ́χην Anacreont. 31, 26 (Bergk); Hippocr. 8, 200 (Lit.); Aristot. Probl. 12, 3, 6: fut. late, βραχήσεται V. T. Esai. 34, 3. **Mid.** fut. βρέξεται, κατα- seemingly pass. occurs Hippocr. 2, 798 (Kühn), for which Littré reads inf. aor. act. καταβρέξαι (Mss. J. C. θ): aor. late ἀν-εβρέξατο Niceph. Rhet. 7, 11; ἐμ-βρέξαιο Nic. Alex. 237. **Vb.** βρεκτέον late Geop. 3, 8.

Βριάω *To make strong*, Epic -ᾰ́ει Hes. Op. 5. Th. 447; -ᾰ́οντα *be strong*, Hes. Op. 5; Opp. Hal. 5, 96. ῐ, ᾰ always, and only pres.

Βρίζω *To feel heavy, drowsy*, Poet. Aesch. Eum. 280; -ων Il. 4, 223; Aesch. Ag. 275. Ch. 897: aor. ἔβριξα Eur. Rhes. 825 (Vulg. Nauck, see βρίθω); βρίξον, ἀπο- Theocr. Epigr. 21; ἀποβρίξαντες Od. 9, 151.

Βρίθω (ῑ) *To be heavy, press*, Hom. H. 30, 9; Pind. N. 3, 40; Soph. Aj. 130; Pl. Phaedr. 247; (Hippocr.) Epist. 3, 370; Epic subj. βρίθησι Od. 19, 112 (others -θησι indic.): imp. βρῖθον Od. 9, 219: fut. βρίσω, -σέμεν H. H. Cer. 456 (Ruhnk. Frank. Baum. -νσέμεν Mss.), ἐπι-βρίσουσι Q. Sm. 10, 30: aor. ἔβρῑσα Il. 12, 346. 17, 512; Eur. Rhes. 825 (Vat. Kirchh. Dind. 5 ed.); Plut. Caes. 44. Lys. 12, βρῖσα Anth. 11, 91; βρίσῃ Hippocr. 6, 108. 112 (Lit.); Aristot. Probl. 16, 11, ἐπι- Il. 7, 343; βρίσειαν, ἐπι- Od. 24, 344; βρίσας Il. 17, 233. Od. 6, 159; Hippocr. 6, 112, Dor. βρίσαις, ἐπι- Pind. P. 3, 106, see below: p. βέβρῑθα Il. 16, 384; Pind. Fr. 100; Eur. Elec. 305; Hippocr. 8, 280; Plut. Mor. 349; Heliod. 5, 14, κατα- Hes. Op. 234: plp. βεβρίθει Od. 16, 474, ἐβεβ- Anth. 14, 120. Sometimes trans. *to weigh down*, βρίθειν Hes. Op. 466; late prose Themist. 20, 234; Aretae. Diut. Morb. 1, 48 (ed. Oxon.): aor. ἔβρῑσα Pind. N. 8, 18; βρίσας Od. 6, 159; Aesch. Pers. 346:

hence pass. βρίθεται Aesch. Fr. 114 (D.); Eur. Fr. 470 (D.), -ονται Bacchyl. 13, 12; -όμενος Il. 8, 307; Hes. Sc. 290; Aesch. Sept. 153; Com. Fr. (Pher.) 2, 350: aor. βριθῆναι Alciphr. 3, 67 (Wagn.) is uncertain, κριθῆναι (Mss.), πρισθῆναι (L. Dind.), ἐκρινηθῆναι (Boisson. Mein.) This verb seems not to occur in good Attic prose, except once in Plato.

Βρῑμάομαι *To be enraged,* (in *simple* aor. only) βριμώμενος, ἐμ- Aesch. Sept. 461: imp. late, ἐν-εβριμῶντο N. T. Mark 14, 5 (Vat. -οῦντο Sin.): fut. late, ἐμ-βριμήσεται Sym. Esai. 17, 13: aor. βριμήσαιο Ar. Eq. 855, ἐν-εβριμήσατο Luc. Necy. 20: aor. pass. as mid. ἐν-εβριμήθη N. T. Matth. 9, 30 (best Mss. Lach. Tisch. -ήσατο Vulg.): collat. imp. ἐβριμοῦντο Xen. Cyr. 4, 5, 9. Hesych. has aor. act. ἐμ-βριμῆσαι.

Βριμόομαι *To be enraged,* only imp. ἐβριμοῦντο Xen. Cyr. 4, 5, 9; N. T. Mark 14, 5 (Sin.), see preced.

Βρομέω Epic, *To buzz, roar,* Ap. Rh. 4, 787; subj. -έωσι Il. 16, 642; -έων Anth. 7, 278, -έουσα Orph. Arg. 1187: imp. βρόμεον Ap. Rh. 2, 597, iter. βρομέεσκον, περι- Ap. Rh. 4, 17.

·(Βροτόομαι) *To be stained with gore* (βρότος), Epic and only p. p. βεβροτωμένα Od. 11, 41; Q. Sm. 1, 717. A pt. act. βροτοῦσα occurs very late, Nicet. Eug. 5, 205 (Hercher).

(Βρόχω) *To swallow,* Poet. and in *simple,* only aor. ἔβροξε Anth. 9, 1; with its comp. κατα-βρόξειε Od. 4, 222, ἀνα- 12, 240; -ξασα Ap. Rh. 4, 826: 1 aor. pass. late, κατα-βροχθείς Lycophr. 55: 2 aor. ἀνα-βροχείς Od. 11, 586.—Hither, perhaps, rather than to ἀναβρυχάομαι, may be referred as 2 p. ἀνα-βέβροχεν the reading of Zenod. and *now* Bekker, for -βέβρῠχεν Il. 17, 54, *has drunk up,* viz. ὁ χῶρος.

Βρῠάζω *To teem, revel,* Poet. Aesch. Sup. 878; -άζων Timoth. 5 (Bergk); Orph. H. 33, 7. 53. 10; -άζειν Plut. Mor. (Epicur.) 1098: imp. ἐβρύαζον Dur. Sam. in Schol. Eur. Hec. 915: aor. comp. ἀν-εβρύαξαν Ar. Eq. 602: yet imp. mid. ἐβρυάζοντο: and fut. βρυάσομαι are given by Hesych. (ῠ.)

Βρύζω *To drink,* or *brew,* seems to have only imp. ἔβρυζε, if sound, Archil. 32 (Bergk): aor. βρύξαι (Hesych.).

Βρύκω (ῡ) *To grind the teeth, bite,* Hom. Epigr. 14, 13; Soph. Tr. 987 (chor.); Eur. Cycl. 359. 372 (chor.); Com. Fr. (Cratin.) 2, 43; Ar. Pax 1315, and βρύχω Anth. 15, 51; Hippocr. 8, 32. 84 (Lit.): imp. ἔβρῡκε Ar. Lys. 301, and ἔβρῡχε Com. Fr. (Stratt.) 2, 767, if sound: fut. βρύξω Hippocr. 8, 16; Lycophr. 545; Or. Sib. 8, 350: aor. ἔβρυξα Hippocr 5, 252 (Lit.); Anth. 7, 624, ἐπ- Com. Fr. (Arch.) 2, 725: p. late, unless to be referred to βρυχάομαι, βεβρῡχώς Opp. Hal. 2, 619; Q. Sm. 3, 146: 2 aor. ἔβρῠχε Anth. 9, 252, see below. Pass. βρύκομαι

Soph. Ph. 745: aor. βρυχθείς Anth. 9, 267. Generally βρύκω *bite*, βρύχω *gnash*, yet ἔβρῡχε *bit*, Anth. 9, 252. The change to ἔβρῡκε is easy, but their radical connection may as easily justify an occasional indiscriminate use. This verb is rare in Trag., never, we think, in Attic prose.

Βρῡχάομαι *To roar*, Soph. Tr. 805; Ar. Ran. 823; Hippocr. 2, 56 (Erm. Dietz); and late, Ael. H. A. 5, 51; Opp. C. 4, 161: imp. ἐβρυχῶντο Theocr. 25 (20), 137; Ael. Fr. 340, -ᾶτο Aesop F. 255 (Halm), βρυχ- Soph. Tr. 904: fut. very late (βρυχήσομαι, κατα- Eumath. 11, 445): p. βέβρῡχα Il. 17, 264; Soph. Tr. 1072; -βρύχῃ Il. 17, 264 (Bekk.); -βρυχώς 13, 393; late prose, Dio. Hal. 14, 18; Aristid. 15, 233: plp. ἐβεβρύχει Od. 12, 242: aor. m. ἐβρυχήσατο Dio Cass. 68, 24, βρυχήσ- Ap. Rh. 4, 19; Nonn. 38, 357; ἀνα-βρυχησάμενος Pl. Phaed. 117: with aor. p. as m. βρυχηθείς Soph. O. R. 1265. There are some traces of a form βρύχομαι, subj. -ωνται, if correct, Hippocr. 6, 360 (Lit. *gnash*, but see above 2, 56 Ermerins); part. -όμενος Q. Sm. 14, 484; Luc. D. Mar. 1, 4 (Jacobitz), but -ώμενος (Bekk. Dind.)

Βρύχω, see βρύκω.

Βρῠ́ω *To abound*, Il. 17, 56; Aesch. Ch. 64 (Med.); Eur. Bac. 107; (Pl.) Ax. 371; βρύῃ (Xen.) Ven. 5, 12; -ύων Aesch. Ag. 169; Soph. O. C. 16; Ar. Nub. 45; Aristot. Mund. 3, 1; βρύειν Aesch. Ch. 70: imp. ἔβρῠον Epigr. Athen. 2, 39; Diog. Laert. (Pherecyd.) 1, 122: fut. βρύσω Or. Sib. 6, 8; Hom. H. 5, 456 (Mss. Doederl. Voss, βρισ- Franke, Baum.), see βρίθω: aor. ἐξ-αμ-βρῦσαι Aesch. Eum. 912 (925) (Pauw. Herm. -βρόσαι Ms. Dind. 5 ed. but suggests -βρόξαι vel tale quid, metro postulante.) Occasionally trans. Anacreont. 44, 2 (Bergk); Phil. de Plant. 150; (Luc.) Trag. 117. This verb is scarcely in good Attic prose. (ῠ, ῡσ-.)

Βρωμάομαι *To roar*, Aristot. H. A. 6, 29, 6: aor. βρωμησάμενος Ar. Vesp. 618.

Βύζω, see foll.

Βῡνέω *To stop up*, imp. ἐβύνουν Ar. Pax 645, takes from βύω Aristot. H. A. 9, 50, 6. de Plant. 2, 9, 7 (βύονται 2, 9, 1): fut. βύσω, ἐπι- Com. Fr. (Cratin.) 2, 119, προ- Ar. Vesp. 250: aor. ἔβῡσα Luc. Char. 21; πρό-βυσον Ar. Vesp. 249; βύσας Hippocr. 7, 136 (Lit.), ἐπι- Ar. Pl. 379: p. p. βέβυσμαι, -μένος Od. 4, 134; Ar. Thesm. 506; Com. Fr. (Heg.) 4, 480; Hippocr. 8, 12; Alciphr. 3, 62; Luc. Peregr. 9, συμ- Ar. Vesp. 1110: plp. ἐβέβυστο Her. 6, 125, παρ-εν- Luc. Hist. Con. 22: aor. ἐβύσθην, παρ- Luc. Deor. Conc. 10, ξυμπαρ- Pisc. 12. Mid. in comp. δια-βυνέονται Her. 4, 71, παρα-βύεται Anth. 11, 210: aor. παρεβύσατο Luc. D. Mer. 12, 1; ἐπι-βυσάμενος Tim. 9. Herm. 81. Pass. δια-βύνεται Her. 2, 96, in accordance with which, Bredow and Abicht alter mid. διαβυνέονται to δια-βύνονται; Bekker, Dind. Stein retain -έονται. βύω pres. is rare, Aristot. H. A. 9, 50. de Plant. 2, 9, quoted. βυέω seems to lack authority, since ἐβύνουν has been accepted Ar. Pax 645 (Bekk. Dind.) for ἐβύουν (old edit.) Vb. βυστός, παρα- Aristot. Top. 8, 1, 17; Dem. 24, 47. (ῡ in fut. and aor. -βύεται Anth. (Lucill.) 11, 210, but in arsis.) The form (βύζω, -ύσω), pass. βύζεται is in late Ionic, Aretae. Morb. Ac. 2, 2; the adv. however βύζην *closely*, is in Thuc. 4, 8. βύζω *to hoot*, as the owl, is also late, fut. (βύξω): aor. ἔβυξα Dio Cass. 56, 29. 72, 24. βύκτης Od. 10, 20.

Βωθέω, see βοηθέω.

Γ.

Γᾱθέω, see γηθέω.

Γαίω *To be proud, exult*, Epic and only part. γαίων Il. 1, 405. 8, 51: but imp. iter. γαίεσκον (Hesych.)

Γᾰληνῐάω (γαλήνη) *To be calm*, only pres. pt. γαληνιῶν Alciphr. 1, 12, Poet. -ιόων Orph. Hym. 54, 11; Anth. (Incert.) 9, 208, -ιῶσα Alciphr. 3, 1, -ιόωσα Anth. (Rufin.) 5, 35; Opp. Cyn. 1, 115; -ηνιᾶν Themist. Or. 15, 195: and iter. imp. γαληνῐάασκε Mosch. 2, 115. The collat. forms γαληνιάζω, -νίζω are earlier, but neither in good Attic prose.

Γαμέω (ᾰ) *To marry*, of the man (*duco uxorem*) -μεῖ Eur. Or. 19; Ar. Ach. 49; Andoc. 1, 124; Aeschin. 3, 172, -μέει Her. 6, 71, -μοῦσι Pl. Rep. 613; -έειν Od. 15, 522, -εῖν Aesch. Pr. 909; Xen. Cyr. 8, 4, 17; -έων Od. 4, 208, -ῶν Aesch. Supp. 227: imp. ἐγᾰ́μουν Ar. Nub. 49, -μει Asius 1, 2 (Bergk); Isae. 6, 24; Hyperid. 3, 24, 4, -μεε Her. 3, 88: fut. (γαμέσω) γαμέω Il. 9, 388. 391; Her. 5, 16, Att. γαμῶ Aesch. Pr. 764; Soph. O. R. 1500; Xen. Cyr. 8, 4, 20; Luc. Tim. 52, late γαμήσω Anth. 11, 306; Plut. Mor. 386. 773; Luc. Rhet. 8. D. Mer. 7, 2; Diog. Laert. 3, 78; Long. Past. 4, 28: aor. ἔγημα Il. 14, 121. Od. 16, 34; Soph. Tr. 460; Ar. Nub. 46; Her. 3, 88; Isocr. 16, 31; Isae. 8, 7; Aeschin. 3, 172, γῆμα Il. 13, 433; Hes. Th. 960; γήμῃ Xen. Cyr. 5, 2, 8; γήμειε Hell. 4, 1, 9; γῆμον Her. 5, 39; γήμας Il. 11, 227; Eur. Phoen. 7; Andoc. 1, 128; Pl. Leg. 774; γῆμαι Od. 21, 72; Her. 5, 92; Thuc. 1, 128; Isae. 2, 18, Dor. ἔγᾱμεν Pind. N. 4, 65, γᾶμεν P. 3, 91; Theocr. 8, 93, later ἐγάμησα *gave to wife*, Com. Fr. (Men.) 4, 298; *took to wife*, Luc. Luct. 13. D. Deor. 5, 4; Diod. Sic. 2, 39: p. γεμάμηκα Ar. Lys. 595; Her. 6, 43; Pl.

Leg. 877; Dem. 39, 26: **plp.** ἐγεγαμήκει Thuc. 1, 126: **p. p.** γεγάμημαι of the woman, Xen. An. 4, 5, 24; (Aeschin.) Epist. 10, 6; Dem. 36, 32: **plp.** ἐγεγάμητο App. Civ. 4, 23: **aor.** late ἐγαμήθην Apollod. 2, 1, 3; Plut. Rom. 2; Dio. Hal. 11, 34; Strab. 10, 4, 20; Sext. Emp. 657; N. T. Marc. 10, 12 (Vulg.), and (ἐγαμέθην), γαμεθεῖσα if sound, Theocr. 8, 91 (Vulg. Ziegl. Fritzsche, hence γαμετή): **fut.** γαμηθήσομαι late, Charit. 5, 9; Dio Cass. 58, 3; Apollod. 2, 4, 7; Heliod. 5, 31. **Mid.** γαμέομαι *to marry*, of the woman (*nubo*) Od. 2, 113; Soph. El. 594; Eur. Ion 58; Her. 4, 117; Pl. Leg. 925: **fut.** γαμοῦμαι Eur. Phoen. 1673. Hel. 833; Ar. Thesm. 900; late prose γαμουμένη Athen. 12, 42; Epic γαμέσσομαι *provide a wife for*, Il. 9, 394 (Vulg. Dind. La R.), see below: late γαμήσομαι Plut. Eum. 3. Artax. 26: **aor.** ἐγημάμην Od. 16, 392; Anacr. 86; Eur. Tr. 474; Com. Fr. (Ar.) 2, 998; Her. 4, 117; Isae. 5, 5; Pl. Leg. 926; Dem. 30, 17; of the man, Com. Fr. (Antiph.) 3, 24. A desiderative form γαμησείω occurs in Alciphr. 1, 13, 2. **Vb.** γαμητέον (Eur.) Plut. Demetr. 14. Dio. Hal. Rhet. 2, 2; γαμετή *married, a wife*, Pl. Leg. 841.

If the anonymous author de Mulieribus &c. has quoted *exactly*, the **1 aor.** forms ἐγάμησα, ἐγαμήθην are as early as Ctesias, a contemporary of Xen., see Ctesias, Fr. de Rebus Assyr. 1, 5 (Müller.) ἐγάμησε of the woman, Trag. Fr. Adesp. 157 (Nauck), and ἐγημάμην of the male, Com. Fr. (Antiph.) 3, 24; -άμενος Apollod. 3, 12, 6. For γαμέσσεται Il. 9, 394, the only instance of this form, Bekker adopts, perhaps rightly, γε μάσσεται, the reading of Aristarchus. γαμοῦμαι **mid.** signifies *to give oneself*, or *one's own in marriage*: a woman γαμεῖται, *bestows herself*; a man γαμεῖται γυναῖκά τινι *bestows* a female *subject* or *relation in marriage*, Πηλεύς μοι γυναῖκα γαμέσσεται (if correct) *will bestow* on me *a wife*, one of *his subjects* Il. 9, 394; and if we may suppose that the Attics used it in this sense, it would favour the reading θυγατέρ' ἥν τ' ἐγήματο Eur. Med. 262, whom he *gave in marriage*, against ἥ τ' ἐγήματο *who married* him. The latter however is maintained by some of the ablest scholars, Elms. Matth. Hartung, Dind. and, perhaps, Porson, though he retained ἥν in the text, see note 264. If γαμοῦμαι *alone* is used of a man, it is in ridicule, as γαμεῖται ἕκαστος Luc. V. H. 1, 22; ἐγήματο Anacr. 86 (Bergk); Antiph. Com. Fr. quoted; see however Q. Sm. 1, 728; Apollod. 3, 12, 6.

Γᾰνάω Epic, *To be bright*, only part. in this sense, γανόωντα H. H. Cer. 10; Opp. Hal. 1, 659, -όωντες Il. 13, 265; Aretae. Diut. Morb. 1, 42 (ed. Oxon.), -όωσαι Il. 19, 359, lengthened on γανῶντα &c.; late, *to make bright*, γᾰνόωσι Arat. Phaen. 190. For γανᾷ 3 sing. pres. Aesch. Ag. 1392 (Vulg.), Dind. Herm. Paley &c. have adopted Porson's suggestion γάνει (Mss. γᾶν εἰ.)

Γανόω *To make bright, delight*, part. γανοῦντες Plut. Mor. 74; inf. γανοῦν 683: **aor.** ἐγάνωσα (Hesych.); part. γανώσας Anacreont. 48, 11 (Bergk), ἐπι- Com. Fr. (Alex.) 3, 470: **p. p.** γεγανωμένος Anacr. 13 (Bergk); Pl. Rep. 411; Themist. 33, 367: **aor.** ἐγανώθην Ar. Ach. 7; late prose, Plut. Mor. 370 (ᾰ.)

Γάνῡμαι *To rejoice*, Il. 20, 405; Aesch. Eum. 970 (chor.); Eur. Cycl. 504 (chor.); Ar. Vesp. 612; rare in prose Pl. Phaedr. 234; Luc. Imag. 4; Aretae. 112 (ed. Oxon.), see below: **imp.** ἐγᾰ́νυντο Q. Sm. 5, 652; Aristid. 27, 354 (D.): **fut.** Epic, γανύσσομαι Il. 14, 504: **p.** γεγάνῡμαι Anacreont. 35, 3 (B.) (ᾰ.)—This verb is scarcely in *classic* prose, Xen. Conv. 8, 30 being a quotation from Homer; more freq. in *late*, and sometimes with double ν, γάννυται Plut. Mor. 634; γαννύμενος Polyaen. 1, 18: ἐγανν- Heliod. 9, 1 (Bekk.) &c. A late form is γανύσκομαι Themist. 21, 254: **imp.** ἐγανύσκετο 2, 26; Epist. Socr. 18.

Γᾱρύω, see γηρύω.

Γαυρόω *To make proud*, in **act.** late, and only **aor.** ἐγαύρωσα Dio Cass. 55, 6 (Bekk.) Usu. γαυρόομαι, **pres.** alone classical, -οῦται Eur. Elec. 322, -οῦνται Xen. Hier. 2, 15; γαροῦ Eur. Fr. 22 (D.); Pseud-Phocyl. 53; -ούμενος Batr. 266; Eur. Or. 1532. Bac. 1144; late prose, Pseud.-Callisth. 3, 2: **imp.** ἐγαυρούμην Babr. 43, -οῦτο Dio Cass. 53, 27: **p. p.** late γεγαυρωμένος Apocr. Sap. 6, 2: **aor.** ἐγαυρώθην late, Dio Cass. 48, 20, but see below: **fut.** γαυρωθήσομαι V. T. Num. 23, 24. So ἐπι-γαυρόω Plut. Mor. 78: **fut.** -ώσω Dio Cass. 56, 3: **aor.** -εγαύρωσα 56, 41. **Pass.** ἐπι-γαυρούμενοι Plut. Oth. 17: **aor.** alone classic, ἐπιγαυρωθείς Xen. Cyr. 2, 4, 30; Plut. Mor. 760. ἐκ-γαυροῦμαι, -μενος is dep. and confined to **pres.** part. Eur. I. A. 101.

(**Γάω**) Poet. *To become*, **1 p.** Dor. (γέγᾱκα), inf. γεγάκειν, for -κέναι, Pind. Ol. 6, 49: **2 p.** (γέγᾰα), 2 pl. γεγάᾱτε Batr. 143, ἐκ- Hom. Epigr. 16, 3 (Vulg.) see below, γεγᾰ́ᾱσι Il. 4, 325. Od. 24, 84; (Hes.) Op. 108; Emped. 213; Ap. Rh. 3, 366; Pl. Crat. 410 is *quoted* from Hom. -γᾶσι Emped. 24: **plp.** 3 dual ἐκ-γεγᾰ́την Od. 10, 138; Ap. Rh. 1, 56; inf. Ep. γεγάμεν Pind. Ol. 9, 110, ἐκ- Il. 5, 248. 20, 106; part. Epic γεγαώς Maneth. 2, 421, ἐκ- Ap. Rh. 3, 364, γεγαυῖα 3, 535, ἐκ- Il. 3, 418. Od. 4, 219; Hes. Op. 256, neut. γεγαός?, -ῶτος?, -αῶτι Maneth. 6, 246, ἐκ- Il. 21, 185, γεγαῶτα Il. 9, 456. Od. 4, 144, -υῖαν Ap. Rh. 1, 719, dual γεγαῶτε Theocr. 22, 176, pl. -αῶτες Theocr. 17, 25; Maneth. 6, 694, -αυῖαι Hom. H. 3, 552, ἐκ- Hes. Th. 76, -ώτων?, -ῶσι?, -ῶτας Il. 2, 866; Ibyc. 16, Trag. γεγώς Soph. Aj. 472,

-ῶσα Eur. Andr. 434; rare in Comedy, Ar. Lys. 641; Com. Fr. (Antiph.) 3, 96; (Philem.) 4, 30. 47, neut. γεγώς?, -ῶτος?, -ῶτι?, -ῶτα Soph. Aj. 1013, -ῶσαν Eur. Med. 405, dual. -ῶτε Eur. Hel. 1685, pl. -ῶτες Med. 558; Com. Fr. (Mon.) 243, -ώτων Eur. Med. 490, -ῶσι Elec. 531, -ῶτας Soph. Fr. 94, 4 (D.) γεγάᾱτε Batr. 143, ἐκ- Hom. Epigr. 16, 3, are lengthened, Buttm. says, for the metre: Thiersch conjectures γεγάᾱσι, and Herm. has, from Suid., altered ἐκ-γεγάᾱτε to ἐκγεγάασθε, both which Franke adopts: γεγάασθε, ἐκγεγάασθε (Baum.) perhaps rightly. If so, they infer a **pres.** γεγάομαι, 2 pl. γεγάασθε, ἐκ- Batr. and Epigr. quoted. ἐκ-γεγάονται with fut. meaning, Hom. Il. 4, 197: ἐκ-γεγάαντο Anth. 15, 40, 20.

Γδουπέω, see δουπέω.

Γεγωνέω *To shout*, -ωνεῖ Anth. (Incert.) 7, 12; Aristot. de An. 2, 8, 7. Probl. 19, 2; -νῇ Solon 42; -είτω (Xen.) Ven. 6, 24; -ωνεῖν Il. 12, 337; Pind. P. 9, 3; Aesch. Pr. 787. 820; Eur. Hipp. 585. Rhes. 270; (Pl.) Hipp. Maj. 292; also (γεγώνω), subj. -ώνω Soph. O. C. 213; imperat. γέγωνε Aesch. Pr. 193; Soph. Phil. 238 (unless to be referred to p. γέγωνα), and γεγωνίσκω, -ίσκειν Aesch. Pr. 627; -ίσκων Eur. Elec. 809; Thuc. 7, 76: **imp.** ἐγεγώνει Il. 22, 34. Od. 21, 368; late prose Plut. Tit. Flam. 10, Epic -ώνευν Od. 17, 161, γεγω- 9, 47. 12, 370, and ἐγέγωνεν as **aor.** Il. 14, 469, ἐγεγώνισκον late prose, Dio Cass. 56, 14: **fut.** γεγωνήσω Eur. Ion 696; late prose Plut. Mor. 722: **aor.** γεγωνῆσαι Aesch. Pr. 990: **2 p.** γέγωνα, -ωνε Il. 24, 703. Od. 8, 305, -ώνασι Aristot. Probl. 11, 25, as **pres.** -ωνε Od. 5, 400. 6, 294; imper. γέγωνε Aesch. Pr. 193; Soph. Ph. 238; Eur. Or. 1220; γεγωνώς Il. 11, 275. 13, 149. 17, 247; inf. γεγωνέμεν Il. 8, 223. 11, 6. **Vb.** γεγωνητέον Pind. Ol. 2, 6.

Some do not admit **pres.** γεγώνω, and **imp.** ἐγέγωνον, unaugm. γέγων-, but assign the parts referable to those, viz. subj. γεγώνῳ Soph. O. C. 213, imper. γέγωνε Aesch. Pr. 193 &c. inf. γεγωνέμεν Il. 11, 6, to **perf.** γέγωνα with **pres.** as well as **perf.** sense. Of course they maintain γέγωνεν Il. 14, 469 (Vulg. H. Both.), against ἐγέγωνεν (Ms. Ven. Wolf, Spitzn. Bekk. Dind.) For ἐγεγώνει Il. 22, 34. 23, 425. Od. 21, 368, Bekk. *now* reads -ώνειν (2 ed. 1859.) γεγωνέω, and -ωνίσκω alone seem to occur in classic prose, and that rarely.

Γείνομαι, see γένω.

Γειτνιάω *To be near, a neighbour*, Aristot. Meteor. 1, 13, 11; (Hippocr.) Epist. 9, 394; Longin. 37; Plut. Sol. 23; -ιᾶν Aristot. Rhet. 1, 9, 30; Luc. Hist. Con. 55; -νιῶν Ar. Eccl. 327; Dem. 55, 3, **γειτονεύω** Xen. Vect. 1, 8, **γειτονέω** Aesch. Supp. 780; Pl. Leg. 842, are rare in *classic* Greek, and scarcely used beyond the pres.: but imp. ἐγειτνία Ael. V. H. 13, 12 (Herch.), -ίων Aesop 84 (Schaef.), -ίαζον (Halm 75), ἐγειτόνεον Anth. 7, 283, -όνουν Pl. Polit. 271: fut. γειτνιάσειν Galen 3, 690: aor. subj. -ιάσω Ael. H. A. 1, 37; γειτνιάσας Luc. Philopatr. 1. Mid. γειτονεύεται as act. Hippocr. 3, 480, -ονται, 4, 108 (Lit.)

Γελάω (ᾰ) *To laugh*, Hes. Th. 40; Theogn. 1113; Pind. I. 1, 68; Aesch. Eum. 560; Soph. Ant. 551; Ar. Ran. 43; Her. 4, 36; Pl. Rep. 457; γελᾶν Her. 1, 99, -λῆν (Hippocr.) Epist. 9, 338 (Lit.), Epic γελόω Od. 21, 105: imp. ἐγέλων Ar. Vesp. 1287; Com. Fr. (Antiph.) 3, 67; Lys. 1, 13; Xen. Cyr. 2, 2, 10. An. 5, 4, 34, Ep. γελώων Od. 20, 347: fut. γελᾰ́σομαι Pl. Ion 535. Phaedr. 252; Luc. Hist. 11; Plut. Mor. 145, προσ- Ar. Pax 600, κατα- Lys. 3, 9; γελασόμενος Xen. Conv. 1, 16; Luc. Sacr. 15; -άσεσθαι Luc. D. Mort. 20, 6: late γελᾱ́σω Anth. 5, 179. 11, 29; Anacreont. 38, 8 (Bergk); Athen. 14, 2; Synes. Epist. 156; Galen 10, 98, κατα- 5, 715; Stob. 23, 13, -άσσω Or. Sib. 1, 182: aor. ἐγέλασα Eur. I. T. 276; Ar. Eq. 696. Nub. 820; Pl. Lys. 207. Euthyd. 273, -ασσα Il. 21, 389; Theogn. 9; (Theocr.) 20, 1. 15 (Mss. Ahr. Fritzsche), Dor. -αξα (Vulg. Mein. Ziegl. Paley), Poet. γέλᾰσα Il. 23, 840; Eur. I. T. 1274 (chor.). Hel. 1349 (chor.), -ασσα Il. 2, 270. 15, 101. Od. 17, 542 (Bekk.); γελάσας Od. 2, 301; Her. 8, 114, -άσσας Il. 11, 378, Dor. -άσσαις Pind. P. 9, 38, Aeol. γελαίσαις Sapph. 2, 5: (p. ?): p. p. γεγέλασται, κατα- Luc. D. Mort. 1, 1: plp. ἐγεγέλαστο, κατ- Luc. Icar. 19: aor. ἐγελάσθην Dem. 2, 19; Plut. Mor. 47. 123; κατα-γελασθῇς Xen. Mem. 3, 7, 7; -θείς Thuc. 3, 83; Isocr. 5, 101; -θῆναι Pl. Euth. 3: fut. γελασθήσομαι Diog. Laert. (Pittac.) 1, 4, 4; (Luc.) Amor. 2, κατα- Luc. Indoct. 28. Jup. Trag. 18: pres. γελῶμαι Soph. Ant. 838. Vb. γελαστός Od. 8, 307, -έος late, Clem. Alex. 167. In (Hippocr.) Epist. 9, 336, Littré gives γελῇ, but γελᾷς 338. γελόω Epic, lengthened from γελῶ, Od. 21, 105; so γελόωντες 20, 374, and γελώοντες 18, 111: imp. γελώων 20, 347, see γελοιάω. For the Dor. part. γελεῦσα Theocr. 1, 36, -άοισα 1, 95. 96, -εῦντι 1, 89 (Vulg.), are now adopted γελᾶσα, -όωσα, -ᾶντι (Mss. Meineke, Ahr.), so Ziegler, Fritzsche, except that they retain -άοισα; Aeol. gen. γελαίσας Sapph. 2, 5: aor. part. γελάξας, -αις in some edit. of Pind. P. 9, 38, is a mere suggestion of Pauw and Heyne for γελάσσαις of the Mss. γελάσκω Anth. 7, 621, and the *desiderat.* γελασείω Pl. Phaed. 64, are confined to the pres.

Γελοιάω *To laugh*, Epic for γελάω, part. γελοίωντες Od. 20, 390 (Vulg. Dind.), -ώοντες (Bekk. La Roche): imp. γελοίων Od. 20, 347, -ώων (Bekk. La Roche): aor. part. γελοιήσασα Hom. H. Ven. 49.

Γέμω *To be full*, only pres. Soph. O. R. 4; Eur. H. F. 1245;

Ar. Pl. 811; Pl. Apol. 26; γέμων Aesch. Ag. 613; Thuc. 7, 25: and imp. ἔγεμον Isocr. 7, 51; Pl. Critias 117.

Γενειάζω *To get a beard*, scarcely in Attic, Anth. 12, 12; Dio. Hal. 1, 76, Dor. -άσδων Theocr. 11, 9: fut. (-ἄσω): p. γεγενειᾰκα Com. Fr. (Philem.) 4, 7, but γενειάω Hippocr. 7. 508 (Lit.); Ar. Eccl. 145; Xen. An. 2, 6, 28; Pl. Polit. 270; Luc. Cyn. 20: fut. (-άσω): aor. -ᾱσα, Ion. -ησα Od. 18, 176. 269. Also γενειάσκω, -ων Xen. Cyr. 4, 6, 5; -ειν Pl. Conv. 181.

Γεννάω *To beget*, Pl. Conv. 206: imp. ἐγέννων Pl. Conv. 191: fut. -ήσω Rep. 546, Dor. -άσω Eur. I. A. 1065 (chor.): aor. -ησα Pl. Tim. 92, Dor. -ᾱσα Aesch. Supp. 48 (chor.): p. -ηκα Pl. Leg. 889, &c. reg. except fut. m. γεννησόμενος pass. Diod. Sic. 19, 2 (Bekk.); Pseud-Callisth. 1, 4: but aor. as act. ἐγεννησάμην Pl. Tim. 34. Critias 113, &c.: so pres. γεννώμενος Pl. Leg. 784. Fut. mid. has been missed by Lexicogr.

Γέντο *He laid hold of*, an Epic aor. Il. 18, 476, some say for ἕλετο, viz. γ for the digamma, and ν for λ, (like ἦνθεν for ἦλθεν, Epicharm. 126); also γέντο for ἐγένετο, (Hes.) Th. 199.

(**Γένω** or **γείνω**) *To beget*, not used in act.: aor. mid. ἐγεινάμην Il. 15, 526; Hes. Th. 126; Simon. Am. 7, 57; Aesch. Eum. 736; Soph. O. R. 1020; Eur. Supp. 964, γειν- Il. 5, 800; Hes. Th. 185; Aesch. Supp. 581 (chor.); Callim. Ap. 103, γείνωνται, ἐγ- Il. 19, 26 (also intrans. in late poets, ἐγείνατο Or. Sib. 1. 9, γειν- Callim. Cer. 58. Del. 260; γεινάσθω Or. Sib. 1, 9); rather rare in prose, γεινάμενος, -η *a parent*, Her. 1, 120. 122. 4, 10. 6, 52; Xen. Mem. 1, 4, 7. (Apol.) 20; Aristot. H. A. 7, 2, 4; Ael. H. A. 10, 16; Dio. Hal. 2, 15; Luc. Calum. 1, ἐξ-εγείνατο Tragod. 4. Pass. γείνομαι Epic *to be born*, γεινόμενος Il. 20, 128. 24, 210. Od. 4, 208. 7, 198 (Vulg. Dind. La Roche); Hes. Th. 82. Op. 821; Solon 27, 4; Theocr. 17, 75; Luc. Jup. Conf. 1 (Jacobitz, but γιγνόμ- Dind. *now*): imp. γεινόμην Hes. Scut. 88; Il. 22, 477 (Vulg. Dind. La Roche γιγν- Bekk.); Theocr. 25, 124 (Vulg. Fritz. γίν- Ahr. Ziegl.) For γεινόμενος, imp. γεινόμεθα Il. Od. (Vulg. Dind. La Roche), Bekker, edits uniformly γιγνομ-. γείνεαι Od. 20, 202, is not pres. but subj. aor. for γείνηαι, and therefore no proof that the *pres.* is used actively. In classic prose, this verb seems to occur in aor. part. only; we have seen no part in comedy.

Γεραίρω *To honour*, Od. 14, 441; Pind. Ol. 3, 2; Anth. App. Epigr. 282; Ar. Thesm. 961 (chor.); Xen. Oec. 4, 8; (Dem.) 59, 78; Luc. Jup. Conf. 11; Dor. inf. -αίρεν Theocr. 7, 94: imp. ἐγέραιρον Eur. Elec. 712; Anth. App. Epigr. 282; Her. 5, 67; Xen. Cyr. 8, 1. 39, γερ- Il. 7, 321: fut. γερᾰρῶ Anth. App. Epigr. 393: 1 aor. ἐγέρηρα Anth. Pl. 4, 183; Orph. Arg. 507,

Dor. -ᾱρα Pind. Ol. 5, 5. N. 5, 8 (but imp. ἐγέραιρ- Momms.), γέρηρα Epigr. dedic. 892 (Kaibel); inf. γερῆραι Orph. Arg. 619: (2 aor. ἐγέρᾰρον: and mid. γεραίρομαι, we have never seen): but pass. γεγαίραμαι Eur. Supp. 553; Pl. Rep. 468; Arr. An. 4, 11; Dio. Hal. 2, 31; -όμενος Xen. Cyr. 8, 8, 4; -εσθαι Arr. Ind. 8, 5; Dio. Hal. 2, 23. The fut. and aor. seem to be poetic. The comp. ἐπιγεραίρω is confined to inf. pres. -ειν, and occurs only in Xen. Cyr. 8, 6, 11.

Γεύω *To give a taste of*, Plut. Mor. 982; γεύων Pl. Leg. 634: fut. γεύσω Com. Fr. (Anaxip.) 4, 460: aor. ἔγευσα Plut. Lycurg. et Num. 1; γεύσω Eur. Cycl. 149; γεύσας Com. Fr. (Theop.) 2, 819. (Eub.) 3, 264; Her. 7, 46; γεῦσαι Plut. Philop. 14, ἀνα- Ar. Nub. 523. Mid. γεύομαι *to taste*, Pind. I. 5, 20; Aesch. Fr. 3 (D.); Soph. Aj. 844; Her. 2, 18; (Dem.) 50, 26: imp. ἐγευόμην Soph. Ant. 1005: fut. γεύσομαι Il. 20, 258. 21, 61 (La R.); Com. Fr. (Antiph.) 3, 13; Her. 2, 39; Pl. Rep. 592; -σεσθαι Od. 17, 413. 21, 98: aor. ἐγευσάμην Pind. N. 6, 24; Aesch. Ag. 1222; Soph. Tr. 1101; Ar. Fr. 75 (D.); Her. 4, 147; Xen. An. 3, 1, 3; -σηται Pl. Leg. 844; -σαιο Alc. (1), 114, -αίατο Her. 2, 47; γεύσασθαι Od. 20, 181; -σάμενος Her. 1, 71; Thuc. 2, 50: p. as mid. γέγευμαι, -ευμένος Aesch. Fr. 238; Eur. Hip. 663; Pl. Leg. 762; Dinarch. 2, 3, unaugm. γεύμεθα Theocr. 14, 51, or rather pres. contr. for γευόμεθα: plp. ἐγέγευντο Thuc. 2, 70: aor. γευσθείς, κατα- Phot. Vb. γευστος Aristot. Pol. 8, 5, 20, ἄ-γευστος Xen. Mem. 2, 1, 23, γευστέος Pl. Rep. 537. Some hold γεύσεται Il. 21, 61, -σόμεθα 20, 258, subj. for -ηται, -ώμεθα; see Il. 24, 356, 357, &c. Aor. opt. γευσαίατο for -αιντο, Eur. I. A. 423 (trimet.)

Γηθέω *To rejoice*, γηθεῖ Il. 14, 140 (Wolf, Bekk. Spitzn. Dind. La R.), Dor. γᾱθεῖ Theocr. 1, 54, γηθοῦσι Maneth. 5, 295; imper. γηθείτω Q. Sm. 3, 608. 609; part. γηθούσῃ Aesch. Ch. 772 (Dind. 5 edit.), Dor. γᾱθεῦσαι Theocr. 9, 36, -εῦσι (Ahr.): imp. ἐγήθεον Il. 7, 127. 214; Anth. 2, 164; Q. Sm. 2, 630. 4, 17, ἐγάθεον Anth. (Antip. Sid.) 7, 425, γήθεον Q. Sm. 1, 72. 7, 646, γήθει Ap. Rh. 1, 436, ἐπ-εγήθει if correct, Aesch. Pr. 157 (Vulg.); Q. Sm. 2, 460. 12, 148. 439: fut. γηθήσω Hom. Epigr. 14, 21, -ήσεις Hom. H. 4, 279, -ήσει Il. 8, 378; Q. Sm. 3, 208; -ήσειν Il. 13, 416; Hes. Op. 476; Ap. Rh. 2, 442; Tryphiod. 246: aor. ἐγήθησεν Ap. Rh. 3, 925, in Hom. Hes. &c. always γήθησε Il. 10, 190. 17, 567; Hes. Th. 173; Theogn. 10; Ap. Rh. 4, 1126; Q. Sm. 1, 84. 5, 321, Dor. γάθ- Pind. P. 4, 122, γήθησαν Il. 24, 321. Od. 15, 165; Opp. Hal. 3, 565; Q. Sm. 7, 173; subj. γηθήσῃ Anth. 7, 26; opt. γηθήσαι Il. 1, 255, usu. -ήσειε Il. 9, 77. 13, 344; Opp. Hal. 5, 662; Q. Sm. 6, 17; part. -ήσας

Hes. Sc. 116; Ap. Rh. 4, 1369, ἐπι- Opp. Hal. 1, 570. 5, 633: **2 p.** as **pres.** in poetry and Attic prose, γέγηθα Eur. Hec. 279. Cycl. 465. Bac. 1197; Com. Fr. (Cratin.) 2, 107; Ar. Pax 335, -γηθας Soph. Ph. 1021; Orph. Hym. 2, 8, -γηθε Il. 8, 559. Od. 6, 106; Q. Sm. 3, 377; Eur. Hipp. 631. Or. 66; Ar. Eq. 1317; Pl. Leg. 671. 931. Phaedr. 251, -γήθᾱσι Joseph. J. Bell. 1, 33, 3, but Dor. γεγάθει with termination of **pres.** Epicharm. 75 (Ahr. Lorenz), γέγᾱθε as **perf.** Pind. N. 3, 33: **plp.** ἐγεγήθειν if correct, Aesch. Pr. 157 (Elms. emend. Bl. Herm. Dind. 5 ed.), γεγήθ- Il. 11, 683, Dor. γεγάθει Epicharm. 75, see **perf.**; γεγηθώς Soph. O. R. 368. El. 1231; Ap. Rh. 2, 707; Orph. Arg. 260. Hym. 47, 6; Pl. Phaedr. 258; Dem. 18, 291. 323; Luc. Somn. 14; Joseph. J. Bell. 1, 33, 7. γήθω is Epic and late, γήθει Orph. Hym. 78, 10; -ων 16, 10. 75, 4, -οῦσα 49, 7, &c. whence γέγηθα. **Mid.** γήθονται Sext. Emp. 567 (Bekk.); -όμενος Anth. 6, 261; Opp. Hal. 2, 262; Q. Sm. 14, 92; Theoph. Epist. 29. γηθέω is Poet. except the **perf.**: the **pres.** occurs in Attic once only, γηθούσῃ Aesch. Ch. 772 (Pauw, Blomf. Franz, Dind. *now*), γαθ- (Turn. Pors. Paley): the **aor.** is Epic and Lyric, γήθησαν (ἐγηθ- g h) Luc. Philopatr. 23, is a quotation from Hom.: **perf.** γέγηθα oft in poet. and prose, see above. There seems to be no doubt that the **pres.** was in use with the Epic and Pastoral poets: its use with the Attic poets depends on the soundness of Aesch. Ch. 772. Herm. begs the question when he says "the Attics did not use the **pres.**" The **imp.** ἐπ-εγήθει Aesch. Pr. 157 (Vulg. Paley, formerly Dind.) seems to favour the use of the **pres.** Elms. however, Blomf. Herm. and *now* Dind 5 ed. read **plp.** ἐγεγήθει, not on documentary evidence, but on the *Attic usage* of the **perf.** Herm. adds "and **plp.**" Of the **plp.** however, the only trace in *Attic* is their own emendation, and a v. r. in Mss. D. E.

Γη-πονέω, Dor. γᾱ-π- *To work the ground,* only inf. **pres.** -ονεῖν Eur. Rhes. 75.

Γηράσκω *To grow old,* Od. 7, 120; Simon. Am. 7, 86; Solon 18; Soph. O. R. 872; Eur. Supp. 967; Com. Fr. (Menand.) 4, 209; Xen. Vect. 1, 4; Aristot. P. Anim. 2, 5, 6, συν- Her. 3, 134; Isocr. 1, 7; -σκῃ Com. Fr. 3, 365; Pl. Theaet. 181; γηράσκειν Xen. Oec. 1, 22, Epic -έμεν Od. 4, 210; -σκων Il. 2, 663; Aesch. Pr. 981; Soph. El. 962; Ar. Lys. 594; Her. 3, 134; Pl. Lach. 189, and γηράω Com. Fr. (Mon.) 283. (Men.) 4, 212; (Theocr.) 23, 29; Xen. Cyr. 4, 1, 15; Aristot. Eth. Nic. 5, 10, κατ- Isae. 2, 22; Pl. Critias 112; inf. γηρᾶναι (γήρημι) see below: **imp.** γήρασκε Il. 17, 325, ἐγήρα Il. 7, 148. Od. 14, 67, κατ-

Her. 6, 72: fut. γηράσω, inf. -ᾱσέμεν Simon. C. 85, 9 (Bergk), -άσειν Pl. Rep. 393, κατα- Leg. 949: and γηράσομαι Critias Eleg. 7, 5 (Bergk), συγ- Eur. Fr. Incert. 1044 (D.), κατα- Com. Fr. (Eup.) 2, 577; Ar. Eq. 1308, ἐγ- Thuc. 6, 18: aor. ἐγήρᾱσα (κατ- Her. 2, 146; Pl. Theaet. 202); γηράσῃ Aristot. Plant. 1, 7, 1; inf. γηρᾶσαι Soran. Eph. p. 57 (Erm.); Xen. Mem. 3, 12, 8, -ᾶναι (L. Dind. Saupp.); γηράσας Her. 7, 114; Pl. Leg. 958, but act. *preserved to old age*, ἐγήρᾱσαν Aesch. Sup. 894; γηράσας Anth. (Philip. Thess.) 6, 94: p. γεγήρᾱκα *am old*, Soph. O. C. 727; Eur. Ion 1392; Aristot. Pol. 7, 16, 16, κατα- Isocr. 10, 1, ἐγκατα- Dinarch. 2, 3, παρα- Aeschin. 3, 251: **2 aor.** ἐγήρᾱν, according to Buttmann, Il. 17, 197; inf. Att. γηρᾶναι Aesch. Ch. 908; Soph. O. C. 870, -άναι (W. Dind.), κατα-γηράναι late prose Athen. 5, 190; part. γηράς Epic Il. 17, 197, but ὑπο-γηράντων Ael. H. A. 7, 17 (Schneid., pres. -ώντων Herch.), Ep. dat. pl. γηράντεσσι Hes. Op. 188, which some think the 1 aor. part. syncop. for γηράσας, γηρείς, -έντος Xenophanes 8. **Mid.** γηράσκομαι Hes. Fr. 163, late γηράομαι Epict. Stob. 9, 58: aor. γηράσασθαι, ἐν- Hesych. **Pass. aor.** ὑπερ-γηραθείς late, and rare, Pseud-Callisth. 1, 25. Lobeck rather inclines to write γηράναι with Schol. Aesch. Ch. 908, and Dind., but makes it inf. pres. from obsol. γήρημι, with the force of an aor.

Γηροτροφέω *To nourish in old age*, Isae. 1, 39; Dem. 24, 203: fut. -ήσω Pl. Menex. 248: aor. p. ἐγηροτροφήθην Lys. 13, 45; Lycurg. 144: with fut. m. γηροτροφήσομαι as pass. (Dem.) 60, 32, missed by Lexicogr.: pres. pass. γηροτροφούμενοι Isocr. 14, 48.

Γηρύω (ῡ) *To speak out*, Poet. Orph. Arg. 1275, Dor. γᾱρ- Pind. N. 6, 60; inf. γᾱρυέμεν N. 3, 32, and -ύεν for -ειν, Ol. 1, 3. P. 5, 72 (Bergk): imp. γᾱ́ρυον Pind. P. 4, 94: fut. (γηρύσω): aor. ἐγήρῡσα Ar. Pax 805: aor. p. ἐγηρύθην as act. see below. **Mid.** γηρύομαι as act. Hes. Op. 260; Aesch. Pr. 78 (in Trag. with aor. mid. and pass.), Dor. γᾱρύ- Theocr. 9, 7: imp. γηρύετο Hom. H. 3, 426: fut. γηρύσομαι Eur. Hipp. 213; Anth. 12, 137, γᾱρύσ- Pind. I. 1, 34: aor. ἐγηρύσω Eur. Elec. 1327; γηρύσαιτο Philet. 15 (Schneid.), Dor. γᾱρύσ- Theocr. 1, 136 (Vulg. Ahr. Ziegl. Fritzsche, δαρισ- Scalig. Mein.); γηρύσασθαι Orph. L. 60; Ap. Rh. 2, 845: and in act. sense also aor. p. ἐγηρύθην Aesch. Supp. 460. (ῡ) Orph. Arg. 434. 1275. Anth. 7, 201. Aesch. Pr. 78, (ῠ) Pind. Ol. 13, 50. Hes. Op. 260. Hom. H. 3, 426; ῡσ- always.

Γίγνομαι *To become, be*, Il. 2, 468. Od. 2, 320; Aesch. Pers. 708; Soph. O. C. 259; Ar. Eq. 180; Antiph. 2, β, 11; Thuc. 3. 42; Isocr. 7, 23, and γίνομαι Pind. P. 3, 12; Her. 8, 60;

Antiph. 3, β, 6; Lycurg. 126, see below: **imp.** ἐγίγν- Il. 13, 86; Soph. O. C. 272; Antiph. 5, 22; Thuc. 3, 12; Lys. 13, 8; Pl. Meno 89, γίγν- Il. 13, 684, ἐγίνετο Her. 8, 12; Antiph. 5, 21, -οντο Her. 1, 67 (Dind. Dietsch, Stein), -έατο (Gaisf. Bekk. Krüg.): **fut.** γενήσομαι Aesch. Eum. 66; Soph. Ph. 1067; Eur. Ion 981: Antiph. 2, γ, 10; Thuc. 6, 6, Dor. -ησοῦμαι Lysis Epist. ad Hipp. p. 53 (Orell.): **p.** γεγένημαι Simon. C. 69; Aesch. Ch. 379; Eur. Cycl. 637; Ar. Eq. 764; Antiph. 5, 9. 6, 50; Thuc. 4, 125; Pl. Rep. 411, Dor. γεγένā- Pind. Ol. 6, 53: **plp.** ἐγεγένητο Hippocr. 5, 184; Thuc. 7, 42; Xen. Hell. 6, 5, 16; Lys. 13, 5, γεγέν- Xen. Cyr. 3, 2, 24 (Breitb. Saupp.): **aor.** ἐγενήθην (Dor. and Ion.) Epicharm. (Phryn. p. 108); Archyt. (Gal. p. 674); Hippocr. 5, 356. 462 (Lit.); Anth. 5, 63. App. Epigr. 238; usu. late in Attic, Com. Fr. (Philem.) 4, 47; Polyb. 2, 67. 5, 22; D. Laert. 9, 7, 7, παρ- Machon in Athen. 13, 45; Dio. Hal. 4, 69; but γενηθεῖσα if correct, Lys. Fr. 22 (Scheibe): **fut.** γενηθήσομαι rare Pl. Parm. 141: **1 aor.** (ἐγενησάμην), of this the only trace seems to be ἢν . . γενήσῃ Eur. Aul. 1172 (Vulg. Kirchh. Nauck), but altered to fut. εἰ . . . γενήσει (Elms. Dind. Hartung, &c. see γένω, γείνω): **2 aor.** ἐγενόμην Il. 15, 653; Pind. I. 4, 14; Eur. Ion 926; Ar. Av. 477; Her. 8, 6; Antiph. 6, 32; Thuc. 1, 74; Lys. 9, 13; Pl. Conv. 173, Dor. -όμαν Aesch. Pers. 934 (chor.), γεν- Pind. N. 6, 22, 2 sing. Ion. γένεο Hes. Th. 657, γένευ Il. 5, 897, 3 pl. ἐγενέατο Her. 2, 166 (Bekk. Krüg. Dind.), ἐγένοντο (Dietsch, Abicht, Stein), γέν- Il. 11, 310; Phocyl. 3, 1; Ar. Av. 701 (anapaest.), iter. γενέσκετο Od. 11, 208; γενοίατο Il. 2, 340; Ar. Eq. 662; imper. γενεῦ Anacr. 2, 9 (B.): **2 p.** γέγονα Il. 19, 122; Aesch. Sept. 142; Eur. Ion 864. 1471; Ar. Eq. 218. Thesm. 746; Her. 1, 5; Antiph. 4, β, 1; Xen. Cyr. 1, 2, 13; Lys. 2, 10; Isocr. 12, 3; Pl. Phil. 26; subj. γέγονῃ Theogn. 300: **plp.** ἐγεγόνει Xen. Ag. 2, 28; Pl. Charm. 153; Lycurg. 21, Ion. -όνεε Her. 2, 2. 8, 27: Poet. γέγᾰα Il. 4, 325: **plp.** sync. dual γεγάτην, ἐκ- Od. 10, 138; Dor. γέγᾱκα, see (γάω).

ἔγεντο Hes. Th. 705; Sapph. 16; Theogn. 202; Pind. P. 3, 87; Theocr. 1, 88; Ap. Rh. 4, 1427, γέντο Hes. Th. 199; Emped. 207 (Stein); Mosch. 3, 29; Ap. Rh. 4, 225, **2 aor. m.** for ἐγένετο. The **aor. p.** ἐγενήθην is scarcely, if at all, used by the early Attics, for γενηθέντες Pl. Leg. 840 (Ms. V. Steph.) has been displaced by γεννηθέντες; and ἐξ-εγενήθη Phil. 62 (Steph. Bekk.) should perhaps be ἐξ-εγένετο (Heind. Stallb. B. O. W. Herm, &c.), though, in candour, we cannot say that its claim for reception is inferior to its **fut.** The **fut. pass.** γενηθήσομαι occurs only Pl. Parm. quoted, and is by some held doubtful:

Dind. thinks Schleiermacher's suggestion, γεγενήσομαι, is the right reading. Hom. Hes. and, we think, Her. never use p. p. γεγένημαι, but **2 p.** γέγονα: Thuc. again, seems not to have used γέγονα, and Plato to have used it far more frequently than γεγένημαι: generally, the Attic writers use both forms. The Epic forms ἐκγεγάασθε Hom. Epigr. 16, 3 Suid. Herm. (ἐκγεγάᾱτε Vulg.), lengthened from ἐκγεγᾶσθε, and ἐκ-γεγάονται which Suhle says is fut. for -γεγάσονται Hom. H. Ven. 197, if correct, imply a **pres. m.** γεγάομαι from p. γέγαα: see also ἐκγεγάαντο, -άοντο? Anth. 15, 40, 20, see (γάω). Hom. Hes. Pind. Thuc. Plato, the Tragedians, Aristoph. and generally Xen. use γίγνομαι; Her. and frequently late writers from Aristot. onwards have γῑνομαι; the Orators vary, but the latest edit. of Lys. generally, Isocr. and Dem. perhaps always, present γίγν-. Ion. opt. γενοίατο Il. 2, 340; Her. 1. 67. 2, 2; so Eur. Fr. 16 (trimet.)

Γιγνώσκω *To know*, Il. 11, 651; Simon. Am. 7, 114; Aesch. Pr. 377; Soph. O. R. 1325; Ar. Thesm. 620; Thuc. 2, 48; Antiph. 2, γ, 10 (Ms. N. Maetzn. Blass); Andoc. 4, 1; Pl. Phaed. 60, and γιν- Heraclit. 5 (Byw.); Her. 3, 81; Antiph. 1, 29. 4, δ, 9; Andoc. 3, 11, Dor. 3 pl. γινώσκοντι Epich. 5 (Ahr.); Pind. Ol. 6, 97: **imp.** ἐγίγν- Thuc. 6, 64; Lys. 12, 73 (Scheibe); Isocr. 21, 21; Isae. 5, 32 (Scheibe), γίγν- Il. 6, 191, ἐγίν- Her. 9, 2; Antiph. 5, 33; Andoc. 4, 29; Lys. 12, 73; Isae. 5, 32 quoted (Bekk. B. S.): **fut.** γνώσομαι Pind. Ol. 13, 3; Aesch. Supp. 57; Eur. Fr. 61; Ar. Plut. 1057, 2 sing. Ion. γνώσεαι Il. 2, 367; Theocr. 22, 63, γνώσῃ Il. 2, 365; Theocr. 26, 19, Att. -σει Aesch. Ag. 807; Soph. O. C. 852; Pl. Phil. 12, -σεται &c. Il. 8, 17; Eur. Bac. 859; Hippocr. 8, 438; Antiph. 6, 41; Thuc. 3, 37; Xen. Cyr. 4, 5, 20; Lys. 1, 39; Isocr. 8, 81; 3 pl. opt. -σοίατο Soph. O. R. 1274 (trimet.): rare if correct γνώσω, -σεις Hippocr. 3, 7 (Vulg. Kühn, but mid. γνώσῃ for -σει, Mss. Littré 8, 416); certain late, Isaac Porphyr. 287 (Hinck): **1 aor.** ἔγνωσα late, γνώσωσι Pseud-Callisth. 3, 22, and Ion. only in comp. ἀν-έγνωσα *I persuaded*, Her. 1, 68. 87 &c., see ἀναγιγν-: **p.** ἔγνωκα Pind. P. 4, 287; Aesch. Pr. 51; Soph. O. C. 96; Ar. Eq. 871; Her. 1, 207; Lys. 17, 6; Dem. 3, 10: **plp.** ἐγνώκειν Dem. 19, 154: **p. p.** ἔγνωσμαι Eur. H. F. 1287; Thuc. 3, 38; Lys. 1, 2; **plp.** ἐγνώσμην, κατ- Antiph. 5, 70; **aor.** ἐγνώσθην Eur. Elec. 852; Her. 4, 42; Antiph. 2, γ, 2; Thuc. 2, 65; Isae. 2, 33; Pl. Leg. 656, ἀνα- Her. 4, 154; γνωσθείς Aesch. Supp. 7: **fut.** γνωσθήσομαι Ar. Nub. 918; Thuc. 1, 124; Pl. Crat. 440; Isocr. 6, 106. 15, 7: **2 aor.** ἔγνων Il. 13, 72; Hes. Op. 218;

Pind. Ol. 7, 83; Aesch. Ag. 1106; Soph. Ant. 1004; Her. 8, 92; Antiph. 2, β, 3; Thuc. 7, 3; Isae. 2, 32, γνῶν Il. 4, 357; Hes. Th. 551, 3 dual γνώτην Od. 21, 36; subj. γνῶ, γνῷς &c. Il. 1, 411; Od. 22, 373; Ar. Ran. 1210. Pax 544; Antiph. 5, 46; Lys. 14, 4; opt. γνοίην Il. 5, 85; Soph. Tr. 1118; Ar. Vesp. 72; Antiph. 5, 72; Isocr. 11, 19 (-ῴην doubtful), γνοίημεν Pl. Leg. 918, γνοῖμεν Alcib. (1), 128, ξυγ- Soph. Ant. 926; γνοίητε Xen. Hell. 6, 3, 13; Isae. 4, 15, γνοίησαν Hippocr. 1, 622; Dem. 33, 15. 57, 12, γνοῖεν Il. 18, 125; Xen. Cyr. 8, 3, 49; Isae. 5, 31; γνῶθι Aesch. Sept. 652; Soph. O. C. 1025; Pl. Prot. 343, γνῶτε Il. 19, 84; γνῶναι Od. 13, 312; Soph. O.C. 137; Antiph. 2, α, 9; Thuc. 2, 40; Lys. 16, 7, Epic -ώμεναι Il. 21, 266; γνούς Soph. El. 731; Ar. Thesm. 171; Her. 4, 136; Thuc. 4, 28; Andoc. 1, 121: **1 aor. m.** late γνώσασθαι Maneth. 2, 51: **2** aor. opt. συγ-γνοῖτο Aesch. Supp. 216, the only instance we know of the **mid.** in Attic, except the **fut.**: in Ionic, **pres.** συγ-γινώσκομαι Her. 3, 99. 5, 94: **imp.** συν-εγινώσκετο 3, 53. 6, 61. **Vb.** γνωστός Xen. Cyr. 6, 3, 4, ἄ- γν- Od. 2, 175, γνωστέος Pl. Rep. 396, Poet. γνωτός Il. 7, 401; Soph. O. R. 396. Generally speaking, γιγνώσκω is since Wolf the prevailing form in Homer, Pind. (Boeckh, Schneidew. &c.) and the older Attics, γῑνώσκω in Pind. *now* however always (Bergk, Momms. Christ), and in Ionic and late prose from Aristotle downwards, Theocritus &c. The **1** aor. occurs in comp. ἀν-έγνωσα *persuaded*, Her. 1, 68: **2 aor.** ἔγνων 3 pl. for -ωσαν, Hym. Cer. 111; Pind. P. 9, 79, ἀν- I. 2, 23, and ἔγνον P. 4, 120, which Ahrens, Schneidewin, and Mommsen would read also in the other passages quoted; Epic subj. γνώω Od. 14, 118; Theocr. 25, 177, -ώῃς Il. 23, 487, -ώῃ 24, 688. Od. 17, 556, ἐπι- 24, 217, -ώωσι Il. 23, 610, ἐπι- Od. 18, 30, γνώομεν Od. 16, 304, for γνῶ, -ῷ, γνῶσι, γνῶμεν: opt. γνοῖμεν for -οίημεν, Pl. Alc. (1), 128, γνοῖεν for -ησαν, Il. 18, 125; Soph. Ph. 325; Dem. 41, 14, συγγνῴη Aesch. Supp. 215 (Turn. Well.) is accounted a false form for -οίη (Lob. Dind. Herm. Paley): **perf.** part. **p.** ἐγνωσμένους Dem. 18, 228, has been quoted as active, but the best Ms. has ἡμᾶς not ὑμᾶς, and this removes the *necessity* at least of taking it actively.

Γλάζω, *To utter song, sing*, poet. and only 2 sing. γλάζεις Pind. Fr. 97 (Bergk, 4 ed.).

Γλαυκιάω Epic, *To glare*, in early authors part. only, -ιόων Il. 20, 172; Hes. Sc. 430 (Q. Sm. 12, 408, -όωσα Maneth. 5, 250); but 3 pl. indic. -όωσι Opp. Cyn. 3, 70. 71; in prose, late and only Heliod. γλαυκιῶν 7, 10. (ῐ.)

Γλάφω Poet. *To scrape, hollow*, Hes. Sc. 432: **aor.** ἔγλαψε;

γλάψαι (Hesych.); in comp. δια-γλάψασα Od. 4, 438: and **m.** ἀπ-εγλαψάμην Com. Fr. (Anon.) 4, 628. (ᾰ.)

Γλίχομαι (ῐ) *To desire*, γλίχει Ar. Fr. 160 (D.), Ion. -χεαι Her. 7, 161, -εται Dem. 18, 207, -όμεθα Com. Fr. (Alex.) 3, 447; Her. 3, 72, -ονται Dem. 6, 11; -οίμην Isocr. 12, 64; γλίχου Anth. 9, 334; -χεσθαι Dem. 5, 23; -όμενος Com. Fr. (Antiph.) 3, 47; Her. 2, 102. 4, 152; Isocr. 6, 109; Dem. 19, 226: **imp.** ἐγλίχετο Dem. 5, 22, -οντο Thuc. 8, 15: aor. ἐγλιξάμην Com. Fr. (Plat.) 2, 695. This verb seems confined to Comedy and Prose.

Γλυκαίνω *To sweeten*, late in **act.** Dio. Hal. C. Verb. 12: **fut.** -ᾰνῶ Apocr. Sir. 12, 16: **aor.** ἐγλύκᾱνα Diog. Laert. 8, 70; V.T. Psal. 54, 15. Usu. **pass.** γλυκαίνομαι Soph. Fr. 239; Xen. Oec. 19, 19: **p.** γεγλύκασμαι Athen. 9, 384, but ἀπ-εγλύκασμ- Athen. (Diphil. Siph.) 2, 55: **aor.** ἐγλυκάνθην Mosch. 3, 112; Hippocr. 7, 160 (Lit.); Athen. (Callix.) 5, 30: **fut.** -ανθήσομαι Apocr. Sir. 49, 1. **Mid.** in comp. **1 aor.** as **act.** κατ-εγλυκάνατο, -ήνατο (Pors.) Com. Fr. (Chion.) 2, 6. (ῡ.)

Γλύφω (ῡ) *To grave*, Com. Fr. (Cratin.) 2, 213; Her. 7, 69; Pl. Hip. Min. 368: **imp,** ἔγλῠφον Hippocr. 3, 142; Ar. Nub. 879: **fut.** γλύψω V. T. Exod. 28, 9: **aor.** ἔγλυψα Anth. 9, 818; Strabo 9, 410, ἐν- Her. 2, 4, παρα- Hippocr. 3, 530 (Lit.): **p. p.** γέγλυμμαι Pl. Conv. 216 (best Mss. Herm. Stallb. *now*, &c.); Anth. 9, 752; Plut. Mor. 363; Athen. (Callix.) 5, 39, ἐγ- γέγ- Her. 2, 106. 124. 136. 138. 148; (Pl.) Eyrx. 400, κατα- Hippocr. 4, 386, δια- Ael. V.H. 3, 45; Diod. Sic. 1, 66, and ἔγλυμμαι Pl. Conv. quoted (some Mss. Bekk. Ast, B. O. W. &c.), ἐξ- Pl. Rep. 616 (no v. r.); Com. Fr. (Eup.) 2, 562, by preference seemingly, for the metre would allow ἐκ-γέγλυμ-, δι-έγλ- Athen. 3, 45: **plp.** ἐν-εγέγ- D. Cass. 42, 18: **1 aor.** ἐγλύφθην, γλυφθέν Anth. 6, 229, where **2 aor.** could not stand; Theophr. Fr. 2, 5, 32: **2 aor.** ἐγλῠ́φην Anth. App. Epigr. 66; Pseud-Callisth. 3, 22; Malal. 2, p. 50, δι- Ael. V. H. 14, 7. **Mid. aor.** ἐγλυψάμην Theocr. Epigr. 7; Plut. Syl. 3, ἐξ- Tib. Gr. 17. **Vb.** γλυπτός Anth. 6, 64. The form γλύπτω, we think, does not now occur: κροτοῦσα or κτυποῦσα is now read for γλύπτουσα, Eur. Tr. 1306. **1 aor. pass.** has been overlooked by Philologers.

Γνάμπτω *To bend*, Poet. -πτει Orph. L. 193; Opp. H. 5, 266, -πτουσι 5, 574, ἐπι- Il. 9, 514; γνάμπτων Anth. (Agath.) 11, 365, περι- Od. 9, 80, and γνάπτω (Hesych.): **fut.** γνάμψει Aesch. Pr. 995 (γνάψει Dind. Weil); Orph. L. 474; Lycophr. 1247: **aor.** γνάμψεν Ap. Rh. 2, 965. 3, 1350; in tmesi Il. 23, 731, ἐπ-έγν- 2, 14, ἀν-έγναμψαν Od. 14, 348 (ἔγναμψαν Il. 24, 274 Vulg. is now ἔκαμψαν); imper. γνάμψον Opp. C. 2, 370: **aor. p.**

ἐγνάμφθη (Hesych.), ἀν-εγνάμφθη Il. 3, 348. 7, 259. 17, 44. **Mid.** rare and late, **aor.** ἐπι-γνάμψαιο Nic. Alex. 363. **Pass.** γναμπτόμενοι Nic. Ther. 423: **imp.** ἐπ-εγνάμπτοντο Ap. Rh. 2, 591: **aor.** ἀν-εγνάμφθη Il. 3, 348, see above: **2 aor.** γναφῆναι (γνάπτω) Hesych.: the prose form κάμπτω has **perf. p.** This verb, we think, is entirely Poet. chiefly Epic, for γναμφθῆναι Thuc. 3, 58 (Duker) has no Ms. authority, and has, very properly, been left to wither. Bekk. Poppo, Goell. Krüg. Dind. have, in accordance with the Mss., edited the prose form καμφθῆναι.

Γοάω (ᾰ) *To bewail,* Epic in **act.** -ᾄει Opp. Hal. 3, 407; Mosch. 3, 88, 3 pl. -άουσι Ap. Rh. 3, 995, Dor. -άοντι Mosch. 3, 24; opt. γοόῳμεν Il. 24, 664 (Papyr. Bekk. Paley, γοάοιμεν Vulg. Dind. Ameis, La Roche), -άοιτε Anth. 5, 237, γοόῳεν Od. 24, 190 (Bekk. -άοιεν Vulg.); γοῶν Il. 18, 315. Od. 9, 467, γοόων Od. 19, 119, γοῶσα Theogn. 264, γοόωσα Il. 16, 857; inf. γοᾶν Aesch. Pers. 676 (Dind. Weil), Epic γοήμεναι Il. 14, 502: **imp.** γόων Od. 10, 567, iter. γοάασκεν Od. 8, 92, -άασκον Ap. Rh. 1, 293, γόασκε Hom. H. 4, 216: **fut.** γοήσομαι Il. 21, 124. 22, 353: late γοήσω Anth. 7, 638; Nonn. 2, 137. 29, 119: **1 aor.** ἐγόησα Anth. 7, 599. 611: **2 aor.** Epic, γόον Il. 6, 500. **Mid.** γοάομαι as **act.** Aesch. Pers. 1072; Eur. Tr. 289; Ar. Thesm. 1036; -άοισθε Mosch. 3, 3; γοώμενος Soph. Tr. 937, -ομένη Tr. 51; Lycophr. 972; in prose, only Xen. Cyr. 4, 6, 9: **imp.** γοᾶτο Soph. O. R. 1249 (trimet.): **fut.** γοήσομαι see **act.**: **aor.** γοήσατο Q. Sm. 10, 465 (Pauw, Koechly, βοήσατο Vulg.) **Pass.** γοᾶται Aesch. Ch. 632: **1 aor.** γοηθείς Anth. 7, 371. γοήμεναι Epic inf. for γοᾶν: iter. **imp.** γοάασκεν, γόασκ- see above. In prose, only Xen. quoted. The Attic poets never use the **active**, unless γοᾶν be correct Aesch. Pers. 676 (Dind. Weil, -γόεν Ms. Med.): of the **mid.** only **pres.** and **imp.**: of the **pass.** only **pres.**: the early Epics use the **active** only, with **fut. mid.** This verb seems not to contr. οη into ω, like βοάω, &c.

Γουνάζομαι *To grasp the knees, entreat,* unaugm. and proceeds not beyond the Epic **aor.** Il. 15, 665. Od. 11, 66; imper. -άζεο Il. 22, 345: **imp.** γουναζέσθην Il. 11, 130, -άζετο Ap. Rh. 1, 1133: **fut.** -άσομαι Il. 1, 427; Anth. 5, 2. 103: **aor.** γουνασάμεσθα Orph. Arg. 621; -άσσηαι Ap. Rh. 4, 747, -άσσωνται Orph. Arg. 946.

Γουνοῦμαι, Epic and Lyric, and only **pres.** and **imp.** Il. 21, 74; Od. 22, 312; Anacr. 1, 1. 2, 6; Anth. 7, 476; -ούμενος Il. 15, 660; Archil. 75: **imp.** denied, but γουνούμην Od. 11, 29, -νοῦντο Ap. Rh. 2, 1274.

Γράφω *To write,* Soph. Fr. 694 (D.); Ar. Ach. 31; Her. 7, 214; Antiph. 1, 30; Thuc. 1, 22; Isocr. 15, 56: **imp.** ἔγραφον

Ar. Ach. 144; Pl. Theaet. 143: fut. γράψω Eur. Phoen. 574; Her. 1, 95; Pl. Phaedr. 276: aor. ἔγραψα Solon 36, 18; Simon. C. 162; Pind. Ol. 3, 30; Eur. I. T. 585; Ar. Lys. 679; Her. 8, 22; Thuc. 1, 97; Pl. Phaedr. 278, γράψεν Il. 17, 599; part. γράψας 6, 169; Isocr. 10, 14; γράψαι Antiph. 5, 54: p. γέγρᾰφα Com. Fr. (Cratin.) 2, 90; Hippocr. 1, 620; Thuc. 5, 26; Isocr. 11, 1; Pl. Theaet. 166, and late γεγράφηκα Synes. Epist. 134; Archim. 48? v.r. Xen. An. 7, 8, 1; Aristid. 45, 68 (Vulg. γέγραφα Ms. L. Dind. παρασυγγεγράφηκας Dem. 56, 28. 34, is from -γραφέω): plp. ἐγεγράφει Dem. 18, 79 (D.): p. p. γέγραμμαι Pind. Ol. 11, 3; Aesch. Supp. 709; Eur. Supp. 433; Antiph. 4, δ, 7; Thuc. 2, 1; imper. γεγράφθω Pl. Leg. 745; late ἔγραμμαι Opp. Cyn. 3, 274: plp. ἐγέγραπτο Her. 3, 128; Xen. Mem. 1, 2, 64 (Dind. Saupp.), γέγρ- (Born. Kühn. &c.), 3 pl. ἐγεγράφατο D. Cass. 56, 32: 1 aor. ἐγράφθην, περι- Archim. Con. p. 48, 6; Galen 7, 489, δια- Dionys. 159, ἐν- Anth. 8, 147: 2 aor. ἐγράφην Her. 4, 91; Pl. Parm. 128; Dem. 24, 11; γράφῃ Pl. Phaedr. 275; γραφείς Thuc. 1, 133; Isocr. 5, 1; Pl. Polit. 295; γραφῆναι Pl. Lys. 209: fut. γραφήσομαι Com. Fr. (Nicom.) 4, 584; Hippocr. 2, 278 (Lit.); Aristid. 45, 59; Plut. Mor. 866, μετ-εγ- Ar. Eq. 1370, ἀντ- (Dem.) 25, 73, ἐγ- 59, 7: and as pass. fut. m. γράψομαι Galen 1, 36. 231 (Kühn); and v.r. Hippocr. 2, 304. 676. 4, 80 (Lit.) missed by Lexicogr. see mid.: 3 fut. γεγράψομαι Soph. O. R. 411; Theocr. 18, 47; Hippocr. 2, 304. 330. 676. 3, 70. 4, 108. 114. 174. 252, ἐγ- Ar. Eq. 1371. **Mid.** γράφομαι *write for myself, accuse,* Aesch. Ch. 450; Soph. Ph. 1325; Ar. Vesp. 576; Dem. 59, 52; -ηται Pl. Leg. 948, &c.: fut. γράψομαι Aesch. Supp. 991 (Ms. M. Well. Hart.); Ar. Pax 107; Dem. 19, 209: aor. ἐγραψάμην Ar. Vesp. 894. 907; Andoc. 1, 17; Isae. 3, 30; Pl. Apol. 26; -ψηται Thuc. 8, 67; -ψάμενος Ar. Nub. 1482; Isae. 11, 31; *got painted,* Her. 4, 88: p. p. as mid. γέγραμμαι Pl. Theaet. 210; Dinarch. 1, 101; Dem. 21, 130. 24, 189; -αμμένος Xen. Mem. 4, 8, 4. The act. also (γράφω) γράψω seems so used, Ar. Av. 1052; hence pass. γράφοιτο δίκη Nub. 758. **Vb.** γραπτός Eur. Fr. 764 (D.), -τέος Xen. Eq. 2, 1. Of this verb Hom. has only 1 aor. act.: no 2 aor. act. or mid. seems to occur: whereas 2 aor pass. alone occurs in *classic* authors, but in prose only, γράφεις Eur. I. A. 35, is 2 sing. indic. act. not part. 2 aor. pass. γεγραψόμενος Hippocr. 4, 80, if correct (v. r. γραψόμ-), is the only instance of the *participle* of the reduplicated fut. we ever met in a *classic* author, except διαπεπολεμησόμενον Thuc. 7, 25 (Vat. Bekk. Krüg. &c.), διαπολεμησόμ- (Vulg. Goell.) See πολεμέω.

Γρύζω *To grunt*, Aesch. Fr. 254 (D.); Ar. Plut. 454; Luc. Voc. 10: fut. γρύξεις Ar. Eq. 224 (Bekk. Bergk, Mein. but mid. -ει Elms. Dind.), in a different sense γρύσω, -ει Aristot. Probl. 4, 2, 5 (B.): and as active, mid. γρύξομαι Com. Fr. (Alcae.) 2, 831: aor. ἔγρυξα Pl. Euthyd. 301; subj. γρύξῃ Ar. Vesp. 374; γρῦξαι Isae. 8, 27; -ύξας Ar. Nub. 963, but γρύσαντος if correct, Teleclid. in Sext. Emp. 751 (B.) Vb. γρυκτός Ar. Lys. 656. For γρύξεις Ar. Eq. 294, Elms. and Dind. read mid. γρύξει, probably because γρύξομαι occurs in Alcaeus: the act. form is certain *late*, οὐ γρύξει κύων V. T. Exod. 11, 7; Apocr. Jud. 11, 19; and the collat. form γρῡλίζω has Dor. fut. act. -ιξεῖτε Ar. Ach. 746.

Δ.

(Δαέω) *To teach, learn*, see (δάω).

Δαιδάλλω *To deck curiously*, Poet. -δάλλουσι Opp. Cyn. 1, 335; in classic authors the act. occurs in pres. part. and inf. only, δαιδάλλων Il. 18, 479. Od. 23, 200; -άλλειν Pind. Ol. 5, 21: p.p. δεδαιδαλμένος Pind. Ol. 1, 29. 2, 53: aor. δαιδαλθείς N. 11, 18. A solitary fut. of a pure form (δαιδαλόω), δαιδαλωσέμεν occurs Pind. Ol. 1, 105.

Δαΐζω Poet. *To rend*, -ων Il. 11, 497; Ap. Rh. 3, 415; Aesch. Supp. 680 (chor.); -ΐζειν Tyrtae. 11, 17; Orph. L. 706, Epic -ιζέμεναι Il. 21, 33: imp. ἐδάϊζε Il. 21, 147, δάϊζε Orph. Fr. 12, 2: fut. δαΐξω Aesch. Ag. 207 (chor.); Nonn. 44, 158: aor. ἐδάϊξα Ap. Rh. 1, 1002. 2, 7; Opp. C. 4, 280; δαΐξαι Il. 2, 416. 16, 841; δαΐξας Aesch. Ch. 396 (chor.): p.p. δεδάϊγμαι, -άϊκται Opp. Hal. 5, 578; -ϊγμένος Il. 18, 236. 22, 72, and δεδαιγμένος Pind. P. 8, 87 (Herm. Hart. Schneidew.), δεδαγμ- (Bergk, Momms.): plp. δεδάϊκτο Nonn. 14, 387: aor. ἐδαΐχθην Anth. 8, 216; δαϊχθείς Pind. P. 6, 33; Ap. Rh. 4, 1400; Eur. I. T. 872 (chor.), and δαϊσθείς Eur. Heracl. 914 (chor. Ald.), but δαισθείς (Elms. Herm. Dind. Kirchh.) referred also to δαίω *burn*, and δαίνῡμι: pres. p. δαϊζόμενος Il. 14, 20: imp. ἐδαΐζετο 15, 629. Mid. so seems imp. δαΐζετο *began tearing*, Hym. Cer. 41, if so, missed by Lexicogr. Vb. δαϊκτός Orph. Arg. 979. δᾰΐζ- Il. 7, 247. 18, 27 &c., but δᾱ- in arsi, Il. 11, 497. This verb is Epic and Lyric: the Tragedians use it in chor. only.

Δαίνῡμι *To entertain*, imper. δαίνῡ Il. 9, 70: part. -ύντα Od. 4, 3, (δαινῦω): imp. δαίνῡ Il. 23, 29. Od. 3, 309, and δαίνῡεν Callim. Cer. 84: fut. δαίσω Il. 19, 299; Aesch. Eum. 305; Eur. I. A. 720: aor. ἔδαισα Eur. Or. 15; Her. 1, 162; δαίσας Pind. N. 1, 72: aor. p. δαισθείς Eur. Heracl. 914 (chor.)

Mid. δαίνῦμαι *feast, eat,* -ῦσαι Od. 21, 290, -ῦται Il. 15, 99; Soph. Tr. 1088; Opp. Hal. 2, 244; subj. δαινύῃ Od. 19, 328, see below; -ύσθω 21, 319, -υσθε 21, 89; -νυσθαι Her. 3, 18; -ύμενος Hipponax 35; Com. Fr. (Cratin.) 2, 95; Her. 2, 100; Opp. Hal. 1, 137, and δαίομαι Athen. (Matron) 4, 136?: imp. δαινῦμην Il. 23, 201. Od. 3, 66; Theocr. 13, 38; Ar. Pax 1280. 1282 (Hexam.), ἐδαίν- Soph. Tr. 771; Com. Fr. (Eub.) 3, 205; Opp. Hal. 1, 543; Her. 1, 211 (Bekk. Dind. Bred.), δαίν- (Gaisf.): fut. δαίσομαι Lycophr. 668 (δαΐσ- Maneth. 4, 615); Arr. An. 5, 3; Philostr. Ap. 208, μετα- Od. 18, 48: aor. ἐδαισάμην Archil. Fr. 99 (Bergk); Pind. P. 10, 31; Soph. Fr. 153 (D.), δαισ- Pind. P. 3, 93. N. 9, 24; subj. δαίσῃ Com. Fr. (Cratin. Min.) 3, 377, Epic δαίσομαι, μετα- Il. 23, 207; δαισάμενος Od. 18, 408; -σασθαι Soph. El. 543. **Vb.** ἄ-δαιτος Aesch. Ag. 151. Subj. δαινῦῃ Od. 19, 328, but δαινῦῃ even in *thesis* 8, 243, for which Ahrens would read δαινῦε' for -ῦεαι; ῡ in opt. δαινῦτο, δαινῦατο (for -ῦιτο, -υίαντο.) δαίνῡ 2 sing. imper. for -υθι Il. 9, 70, and 3 imp. for ἐδαίνῡ, Od. 3, 309, but δαίνῡ' 2 sing. imp. mid. for ἐδαίνυσο, -υνο, Il. 24, 63: δαινῦτο 3 sing. pres. opt. mid. for -ῦιτο, 24, 665, δαινῦατ' 3 pl. for -ῦιντο, Od. 18, 248. μεταδαίσομαι Il. 23, 207, seems subj. for -σωμαι. This verb is poetic, occasionally Ionic prose.

Δαίομαι *To divide, tear,* Pind. P. 3, 81; -όμενος Od. 17, 332: imp. δαίετο Od. 15, 140: fut. δᾶσομαι Il. 22, 354, ἀπο-δάσσ- 17, 231: aor. ἐδᾶσάμην Od. 14, 208; Ap. Rh. 1, 529, δι- Pind. Ol. 1, 51; Her. 8, 121, ἐδάσσ- Od. 6, 10; Hes. Th. 520, δάσσ- Il. 1, 368; Hes. Th. 112; δάσα- Opp. Hal. 1, 11, iter. δασάσκετο Il. 9, 333; δάσωνται Od. 17, 80; -σαίμεθα 2, 335; -σασθαι Il. 18, 511. 23, 21; Eur. Tr. 450; -σᾰμενος Her. 2, 4. 7, 121, δασσ- Od. 3, 66; Pind. Ol. 7, 75; rare in Attic, ἐδάσ- Xen. Oec. 7, 24. 25; δάσωνται Cyr. 4, 2, 43; δᾰσασθαι Plut. Rom. 17, ἀνα- Thuc. 5, 4; Plut. Agis 12; δασάμενος Rom. 27: and late p. p. δέδασται as mid. Q. Sm. 2, 57. **Pass.** δαίομαι *to be divided,* figur. in pres. *distracted,* Od. 1, 48, but ἀνα-δαιομένας *divided,* Orac. Her. 4, 159: p. δέδασμαι Il. 15, 189; Eur. H. F. 1329; Her. 2, 84; Stob. (Archt.) 1, 75 (Mein.), Epic δέδαιμαι, -αίαται Od. 1, 23 (but late δέδασται as mid. see above): aor. later, ἐδάσθην (Hesych.); ἀνα-δασθείς Plut. Agis 8; κατα-δασθῆναι Luc. Demon. 35 (Jacob.) **Vb.** ἀνά-δαστος Pl. Leg. 843. To this verb, rather than to δαίνυμι, some may be inclined to refer pres. δαίονται *divide for oneself, consume,* Athen. (Matron) 4, 136. The pres. and fut. seem to be poetic.

Δαίρω *To flay,* Ar. Nub. 442 (Bekk., δειρ- Dind.), see δείρω, δέρω. **1 aor.** δῆραι we have never met in any Greek.

(Δαίω) *To divide, entertain,* see δαίνυμι.

Δαίω *To kindle,* usu. Poet. δαίωσι Il. 20, 317; δαίων Aesch. Ch. 864. Ag. 496; but Hippocr. 6, 436 (Lit.); and, in a Byzant. decree, Dem. 18, 90: **imp.** ἔδαιε Hom. H. 2, 266; Ap. Rh. 4, 869, δαῖε Il. 9, 211. 18, 206: **p.** δέδαα late, δεδᾰυῖα Nonn. 6, 305: **p.p.** δέδαυμαι, -μένος Simon. (Am.) 30 (Bergk): **aor.** δαισθείς Eur. Heracl. 914 (chor.) has been referred hither by Elms. and Lobeck, see δαΐζω: **2 p.** δέδηα *blaze,* Il. 17, 253. 20, 18: **plp.** δεδήειν Il. 2, 93; Hes. Sc. 155, ἀμφι- 62. **Mid.** δαίομαι *to be on fire,* Od. 6, 132; Ar. Lys. 1284 (chor.); -όμενος Il. 8, 75; Theocr. 24, 52: **imp.** ἐδαίετο Soph. Tr. 765, δαίετο Il. 21, 343; Hes. Sc. 165: **2 aor.** (ἐδαόμην), subj. δάηται Il. 20, 316. 21, 375.—δεδαυμένος Callim. Epigr. 52 (Blomf. Mein.) is a conjecture of Bentley's for δεδαγμ-. This verb is almost entirely Poetic.

Δακνάζομαι *To be distressed,* Poet. and only **pres.** δακνάζου Aesch. Pers. 571 (chor.) **Act.** δακνάζω *to bite,* late -άζων Anth. 7, 504.

Δάκνω *To bite,* Hipponax 49, 6; Aesch. Sept. 399; Soph. Ant. 317; Ar. Vesp. 253; Her. 2, 95; Hippocr. 2, 414 (Lit.); Xen. An. 3, 2, 35; Pl. Rep. 474; Dem. 21, 89: **imp.** ἔδακνον Ar. Pl. 822: **fut.** δήξομαι Eur. Bac. 351; Ar. Ach. 325; Hippocr. 7, 336; Xen. Oec. 12, 16; (Dem.) 25, 96: late, δήξω Schol. Lycophr. 1006: **aor.** rare, ἔδηξε Paroem. C. 11, 82; δῆξον (Luc.) Asin. 9: **p.** δεδήχᾱσι (Hesych.); δεδηχώς Babr. 77 (Lachm.): **p.p.** δέδηγμαι Ar. Ach. 1; -μένος Aesch. Ch. 843; Eur. Rhes. 596; Xen. Conv. 4, 28; Pl. Conv. 217. 218: **aor.** ἐδήχθην Soph. Tr. 254; Ar. Ach. 18; Xen. Cyr. 1, 4, 13; δηχθῇ Aesch. Eum. 638; Hippocr. 7, 342; δηχθείη Eur. Med. 817; δηχθείς Eur. Hipp. 1303; Xen. Oec. 8, 1; Pl. Conv. 217, Dor. δαχ- Pind. Fr. 100, 8 (Bergk): **fut.** δηχθήσομαι Eur. Alc. 1100; Hippocr. 2, 578 (K.); Stob. (Teles.) 5, 67: **pres.** δάκνομαι Theogn. 910: **2 aor.** ἐδᾰ́κην late, Aretae. 60 (Ed. Oxon.): **2 aor. act.** ἔδᾰκον Batr. 181; Simon. C. 167; Ar. Eq. 1372; Her. 7, 16; (Dem.) 25, 96, δάκε Il. 5, 493; Hes. Th. 567; Demodoc. 4 (Bergk), redupl. δέδακε Anth. 12, 15; δάκω Eur. Phoen. 383, δάκῃς Cycl. 314, -κῃ Ar. Thesm. 530, -κωσι Luc. Philops. 40; δάκοιμι Eur. Med. 1345; Ar. Eq. 1010 (Br. Bekk. Kock); (Dem.) 25, 96; δακών Tyrtae. 11, 22; Aesch. Pr. 1009; Soph. Tr. 976; Ar. Nub. 1369; Xen. Mem. 2, 2, 7; δακεῖν Ar. Vesp. 374. Ach. 376. Aristot. Pt. Anim. 4, 11, 11, δακέειν Il. 17, 572. 18, 585: (a late **1 aor.** form ἔδακα, ἀντ- (Luc.) Ocyp. 27 (Dind.): **aor. mid.** ἐδηξάμην, δήξηται Hippocr. 2, 542 (Vulg. δήξεται Mss. Lind. Lit. Erm.); and late,

-ασθαι Herodn. 1, 15, 6, but -εσθαι (Bekk.) Of the pass. we hold the aor. not the perf. to be the more freq. Hom. seems to have only **2 aor. act.** : **fut. act.** and perhaps **1 aor.** are late: **aor. mid.** is doubtful. **Vb.** ἄ-δηκτος Hes. Op. 420.

Δακρῡχέω *To shed tears,* in early Epic has only part. -χέων Il. 9, 14; Aesch. Sept. 919 (chor.), -χέουσα Il. 22, 79; Ap. Rh. 1, 250, Aeol. -έοισα Callim. Cer. 80; but late occur **ind.** δακρυχέω Anth. (Meleag.) 12, 72, -έει 7, 600; -έειν Nonn. 19, 168: and **imp.** iter. δακρυχέεσκε Nonn. Metaphr. 20, 11.

Δακρύω (ῡ) *To weep,* Aesch. Ch. 81 (D.); Soph. El. 152; Ar. Ach. 690; Her. 1, 87. 3, 14; Andoc. 4, 39; Xen. Apol. 27; Isocr. 4, 168: **imp.** ἐδάκρῡον Xen. An. 1, 3. 2: **fut.** δακρῡ́σω Eur. Elec. 658; Alciphr. 1, 37: and late δακρῡ́σομαι Tryph. 404: **aor.** ἐδάκρῡσα Simon. (C.) 52 (Bergk); Eur. Bac. 1373; Ar. Av. 540; Her. 7, 45; Lys. 2, 40; Xen. Hell. 4, 2, 4. Cyr. 3, 1, 7, ἀπ- Ar. Vesp. 983, δάκρῡσα Od. 11, 55, 'δάκρ- Soph. Ph. 360 (trimet.); subj. -ύσω Aesch. Ag. 1490; Eur. Tr. 458; δακρῦσαι Eur. Hel. 948; Ar. Pax 611; Pl. Leg. 800; -ῡσας Il. 10, 377; Her. 1, 112; Pl. Phaed. 116: **p.** late δεδάκρῡκα Alciphr. 2, 3: **p.p.** δεδάκρῡμαι Epic, -κρυσαι Il. 16, 7, -κρυνται 22, 491. Od. 20, 204; and late prose δεδακρῡμένος (Pl.) Ax. 364; Plut. Public. 6. C. Gracch. 16; Luc. Icaromen. 13; Dio. Hal. 6, 81; Paus. 1, 21, 5; Aristaen. 1, 22, *bathed in tears*: **pres.** δακρύεται Eur. Hel. 1226. **Mid.** δακρύεσθαι as **act.** Aesch. Sept. 814 (Dind.): **fut.** late δακρῡ́σομαι Tryph. 404, quoted; **v. r.** Aesch. Sept. 814: late also **aor.** δακρῡ́σατο Tryph. 431, ἐδακρ- Nonn. 15, 381; unless δακρῡ́σασθαι be correct Aesch. Sept. 796 (Mss. Herm. for -ύεσθαι Mss. 814 Dind. Paley). **Vb.** ἀ-δάκρῡτος Il. 1, 415. ῡ except occasionally in late poets, δακρῠ́ω Christ. Pat. 356. 913, -ῠ́εις Theod. Prodr. 2, 300, δάκρῠε Anth. Pal. 9, 148. 12, 232, δακρῠ́σω Theod. Prodr. 1, 263. δακρῡ́σω called **fut.** Aesch. Ag. 1490; Soph. O. C. 1255; Theocr. 2, 64, seems rather subj. **aor.** Of the **pass.** the **pres.** δακρύεται Eur. Hel. 1226, and **perf.** δεδάκρυμαι quoted, are alone in use. The **pres. act.** is not used by the Epics; δακρύων Batr. 69, is the only instance we know: κλαίω is the Epic **pres.** Il. 1, 362. 24, 773, εἴβω, δακρῡχέων, &c. The **mid.** is Poet. but not in Hom. and in *classic* authors scarcely ventures beyond the **pres.** Our lexicons, we think, have entirely missed it.

Δαμάζω (δαμάω) *To tame,* mostly Poet. -άζεις Eur. Alc. 980, -άζει Aesch. Ch. 324; Anacreon 65 (B.); Nic. Ther. 363. Al. 5; V. T. Dan. 2, 40, Dor. -άσδει Theocr. 4, 55; δαμάζων Xen. Mem. 4, 3, 10 (see Hes. Th. 865; Pind. P. 11, 24), δαμάω in pres. is rare, and perhaps late, δαμόωσι Q. Sm. 5, 247, seems pres. (comp. -όωνται 249), see below: **imp.** ἐδάμαζον Eur. H.F. 374 (chor.): **fut.** δαμᾰ́σω, -άσει Anth. 6, 329; V.T. Dan. 2, 40, -άσσει Il. 22, 176; Ap. Rh. 3, 353. 4, 1654, and (δαμῶ), 3 sing. δαμᾷ Il. 1, 61, Ep. δαμάᾳ 22, 271, 3 pl. -όωσι 6, 368, by some called **pres.**: **aor.** ἐδᾰ́μᾰσα Pind. N. 7, 90, δάμασα Il. 16, 543. 22, 446; Hes. Th. 857; Pind. Ol. 10, 30; Soph. Ant. 827 (chor.), ἐδάμασσα Il. 5, 191. 16, 813; Hes. Th. 332; Pind. P. 2, 8; Eur. H.F. 381 (chor.), δάμασσα Il. 5, 106. Od. 14, 367; Pind. P. 8, 80; δαμάσσω Il. 16, 438, -άσῃ Od. 5, 468, -άσσῃ Il. 5, 138, -άσσομεν for -ωμεν, Il. 22, 176; δαμάσειεν Theocr. 22, 93; δάμασον Il. 9, 496, -ασσον 3, 352; δαμάσας Il. 19, 66; Eur. Phoen. 152; Com. Fr. (Plat.) 2, 672, -άσσας Od. 4, 244, Dor. -άσσαις Pind. Ol. 9, 92; δαμάσαι, -άσσαι Mosch. 2, 76; Opp. Hal. 1, 14 (δμῆσαι Hesych.): **p.** δεδαμακότες Stob. Flor. vol. 4, p. 273 (Mein.), (δέδμηκα?): **p. p.** δέδμημαι Il. 5, 878; -μημένος Il. 14, 482; Hes. Op. 116; Theogn. 177; Ap. Rh. 4, 1649: **plp.** δέδμητο Od. 3, 304; Ap. Rh. 1, 610, 3 pl. -μήατο Il. 3, 183, late δεδάμασμαι Nic. Al. 29; late prose Mythogr. p. 340 (Westerm.); Plut. Mor. 451: **plp.** δεδάμαστο Or. Sib. 5, 5: **aor.** ἐδαμάσθην Od. 8, 231, δαμάσθ- Il. 19, 9; subj. -ασθῇ Aesch. Sept. 338. 765; opt. -εῖεν Xen. Mem. 4, 1, 3; δαμασθείς Il. 22, 55; Simon. C. 151; Pind. Ol. 2, 20. P. 1, 73; Aesch. Pers. 279; Eur. Phoen. 563. Supp. 1011; -ασθῆναι Isocr. 7, 43, κατα- D. Cass. 50, 10, and ἐδμήθην Simon. (C.) 89 (Bergk); imper. δμηθήτω Il. 9, 158; δμηθῆναι Ap. Rh. 3, 469, -θήμεναι Opp. H. 5, 16; δμηθείς Il. 4, 99; Hes. Th. 1000; Lycophr. 441, ὑπο- Hes. Th. 327, Dor. (ἐδμᾱθ-), 3 pl. δμᾶθεν Pind. P. 8, 17; δμᾱθείς Aesch. Pers. 906 (chor.); Eur. Tr. 175 (chor.) Alc. 127 (chor.) I. T. 198. 230 (chor.): **3 fut.** δεδμήσομαι Hom. H. 2, 365: **2 aor.** ἐδᾰ́μην Il. 13, 812. 20, 94; Soph. El. 845 (chor.); Ar. Pax 584 (chor.), 'δάμη Aesch. Sept. 608 (trimet.), δάμη Il. 21, 383. Od. 3, 90; subj. Epic δαμείω Od. 18, 54, -είῃς Il. 3, 436, -ῇης (Bekk.), -είῃ 22, 246, -ῄῃ (Wolf, Bekk.), -είετε 7, 72, -ήετε (Bekk. La R.); opt. δαμείην Eur. Med. 647, -είη Il. 12, 403; Hes. Fr. 110; Soph. Tr. 432, 3 pl. -εῖεν Il. 3, 301; δαμείς Il. 22, 40; Hes. Op. 152; Sapph. 90; Pind. Ol. 1, 41; Aesch. Pr. 426. 861. Ag. 1495; Eur. Rhes. 764. Or. 845. I. A. 623; δαμῆναι Il. 15, 522. Od. 18, 156; Hes. Th. 464; Aesch. Ch. 367; Soph. Ph. 200, Epic δαμήμεναι Il. 10, 403; Ap. Rh. 3, 480. **Mid.** δαμάζομαι as act. Aesch. Supp. 884 (Vulg.); Eur. Fr. 683 (D.); Com. Fr. (Anax.) 3, 163. 175: **fut.** Epic δαμάσσεται Il. (11, 478 may be subj.) 21, 226; Opp. Hal. 4, 373: **aor.** δαμᾰ́σαντο Il. 10, 210; Q. Sm. 14, 138, δαμάσσ- Il. 5, 278, ἐδαμάσσατο Od. 9, 516; Pind. P. 3, 35; -αμασαίμην Od. 4, 637; -άσασθαι Il. 23, 655;

-ασσάμενος Od. 9, 454; late prose ἐδαμάσατο Galen 3, 3; Greg. Nyss. de hom. condit. 7, 3 (Forbes), but κατα-δαμασάμενος Thuc. 7, 81. (δᾰμ-.) Vb. δαμαστέον Geop. 16, 1, ἀ-δάμαστος Il. 9, 158, ἀ-δάμᾰτος Aesch. Ch. 54, ἄ-δμητος Il. 10, 293.

δάμεν Epic 3 pl. 2 aor. p. for ἐδάμησαν, Il. 8, 344; subj. δαμείω Od. 18, 54, -είετε Il. 7, 72 (Vulg. Dind. La Roche), -ήετε (Bekk.), δαμήῃς 2 sing. Il. 3, 436, -ήῃ 3 sing. 22, 246, for -μῇς, -μῇ; inf. δαμήμεναι Il. 10, 403. In classic authors δαμάω occurs rarely, if ever, in pres. act. δαμᾷ Il. 1, 61, may be fut. contr. from δαμάσει -άει -ᾷ, Epic -άᾳ 22, 271, -όωσι 6, 368, but δαμόωσι Q. Sm. 5, 247, δαμόωνται 5, 249, seem to be pres. Hom. has both aorists pass. in the double form ἐδαμάσθην, ἐδμήθην, 2 ἐδάμην: so Pind. -άσθην twice, Ol. 2, 20. P. 1, 73, -άθην once, P. 8, 17; 2 -άμην thrice, Ol. 1, 41. P. 3, 9. Fr. 203 (Bergk): so also the Traged. -άσθην Aesch. thrice, Pers. 279. Sept. 338. 765; Eur. thrice, H. F. 21. Supp. 1011. Phoen. 563, (-ήθην) always in chor. and always in the Dor. from -άθην Aesch. once, Pers. 906; Eur. four times, Alc. 127. Tr. 175. I. T. 198. 230; 2 ἐδάμην Aesch. eight, Sept. 608. Pr. 426. 602. 861. Ch. 367. Ag. 1451. 1495. 1519; Eur. four, Med. 648. Or. 845. Rh. 764. I. A. 623; Soph. four times and this form alone, El. 845. Tr. 432. Ph. 200. 335. It would thus appear that the 2 aor. ἐδάμην is rather the prevailing form in Pindar, and more than doubly so in the Tragedians. That the form ἐδμήθην is not Attic, is pretty plain from Eur. I. A. 623 (trimeter), where, in the fifth foot, he avoids δμηθείς, and uses δαμείς. The 2 aor. act. ἔδαμον, and perf. δέδμηκα, are confined, we think, to lexicons. In good prose, this verb is very rare: we have seen it in pres. act. only, and 1 aor. pass. -άσθην: perf. δεδαμασμένοι Isocr. 6, 65 (Steph.) is now ὡμαλισμένοι (Ms. Urb. Bekk. B. Saupp. Bens.)

Δαμαλίζω *To subdue*, only pres. δαμαλίζοι Pind. P. 5, 129 (162). **Mid.** δαμαλιζομένα Eur. Hipp. 231 (chor.) now approved for δαμαζομ-, but **pass.** δαμαλιζομέναν Pind. P. 11, 24 (39) now rejected for δαμαζομέναν. See δαμάζω.

Δαμνάω Poet. *To subdue*, -νᾷς Theogn. 1388, -νᾷ Od. 11, 221; imperat. δάμνα Sapph. 1, 3: imp. ἐδάμνα Il. 5, 391. 21, 270, δάμ- Il. 16, 103, iter. δάμνασκε Hom. H. 4, 251. **Mid.** δαμνάομαι trans. seems not quite certain, for δαμνᾷ Il. 14, 199, may equally well be 2 sing. of δάμναμαι, -ασαι, -ααι contr. -ᾷ, from δάμνημι, which see.

Δάμνημι *To subdue*, Poet. Il. 5, 893. 8, 390; Alcae. 92; Theogn. 173. **Mid.** δάμνᾰμαι as **act.** δαμνᾷ Il. 14, 199, but δάμνᾰσαι, ὑπο- Od. 16, 95, -νᾰται Od. 14, 488; Hes. Th. 122;

Archil. 85 (Bergk); Pind. Fr. 207; Aesch. Pr. 164 (chor.): **imp.** δάμνᾰτο Il. 11, 309, ἐδάμνᾰτο Q. Sm. 1, 243, κατ- H. Merc. 137. **Pass.** δάμναμαι Aesch. Supp. 904 (chor.); Opp. Hal. 23, 387; -άμενος Il. 13, 16; -νασθαι 8, 244: **imp.** ἐδαμνάμεθα Orph. Arg. 1092, δαμν- Il. 11, 309; Q. Sm. 3, 7: for **aor.** ἐδάμην, see δαμάζω.

Δανείζω *To lend money*, Pl. Leg. 742: **fut.** -είσω Dem. 35, 52, unclassic -ειῶ: **aor.** ἐδάνεισα Xen. Cyr. 3, 1, 34; Isae. 5, 40; Aeschin. 1, 100; Dem. 34, 23: **p.** -νεικα Aristot. Oec. 2, 13; Rhet. 2, 23, 23; Dem. 35, 52, complete and reg. in act. and pass.: **p.** δεδάνεισμαι Dem. 36, 5. 49, 53, see below: **aor.** ἐδανείσθην 33, 12. 35, 53; Xen. Hell. 2, 4, 28. **Mid.** δανείζομαι *to have lent to oneself, borrow*, Dem. 35, 22: **imp.** ἐδαν- 32, 4: **fut.** -είσομαι Dem. 32, 15 (Dind.), ἐπι- 35, 21: **aor.** ἐδανεισάμην Lys. 12, 59; Pl. Rep. 612; Dem. 34, 23. 35, 52. 48, 44: **p.** as **mid.** δεδάνεισμαι Xen. Hell. 6, 5, 19; Dem. 37, 53. 41, 9, προσ- Lys. 19, 26, προ- Hyperid. Fr. p. 348 (B. S.) **Vb.** δανειστέον Plut. Mor. 408. In very late Greek, along with the reg. **fut.** δανείσω, occurs the vicious form δανειῶ, -ειοῦσι V. T. Prov. 22, 7 (Vat. Alex.), -ειεῖς Deut. 15, 10. 28, 12 (Vat.), but -ιεῖς (Alex.), and 15, 6 (Vat.) &c.: so **mid.** δανειοῦμαι, -ειῇ 15, 6. 28, 12 (Vat. -ιῇ Alex.)

Δαπανάω *To expend*, Thuc. 7, 29; Xen. Cyr. 1, 2, 11: **imp.** ἐδαπάνων Xen. An. 1, 3, 3: **fut.** -ήσω Thuc. 1, 121, &c. (is pretty complete, but, in the *classic period*, with the irregularity of being Dep. pass.): **aor.** -ησα Isae. 5, 45: **p.** δεδαπάνηκα Lycurg. 139: **p. p.** -ημαι Her. 2, 125; Lys. 21, 5; Isocr. 2, 19; Diod. Sic. 1, 64: **plp.** ἐδεδαπάνητο, κατ- Her. 5, 34: **aor.** -ήθην Xen. Cyr. 2, 4, 11: **fut.** -ηθήσομαι Plut. Mor. 218; Athen. 4, 66. **Mid.** as Dep. pass. δαπανάομαι *to expend one's own*, Ar. Plut. 588; Andoc. 4, 32; Lys. 21, 3; Pl. Rep. 548, Ion 3 pl. -έωνται Her. 2, 37 (Gaisf. Bekk. Lhardy, -έονται Dind. Dietsch, Abicht, -ῶνται Stein): **imp.** ἐδαπανώμην Ar. Fr. 476 (D.); Lys. 25, 13: **fut.** (-ήσομαι): **p.** δεδαπάνημαι Isocr. 18, 63; Dem. 1, 27: **aor.** δαπανηθείς Isocr. 15, 225; Isae. 5, 43: but late, **aor. mid.** ἐδαπανησάμην Eunap. Hist. p. 99 (Bekk.) (δᾰπᾰν-.)

Δαρδάπτω *To tear*, is Poetic and confined, in classic authors, to **pres.** -δάπτει Ar. Ran. 66, -δάπτουσι Il. 11, 479. Od. 14, 92; Ar. Nub. 711: **imp.** late prose ἐδάρδαπτε Luc. Menip. 14: **aor.** (ἐδάρδαψα), δαρδάψῃ Opp. Hal. 4, 628: **p.** δεδάρδαφε (Hesych.)

Δαρθάνω *To sleep*, in *simple*, only **2 aor.** ἔδαρθον, Poet. ἔδρᾰθον Od. 20, 143; Coluth. 332. Usu. κατα-δαρθάνω Plut. Mor. 1026; -άνειν Pl. Phaed. 71. 72, ἐπικατα- Rep. 534, ἀπο- Ael. H. A. 3, 13: **p.** καταδεδαρθηκώς Pl. Conv. 219: **aor. pass.** κατεδάρθην, 3 pl.

-δαρθεν, for -θησαν, Ap. Rh. 2, 1227; -δαρθέντα Ar. Plut. 300 (Mss. Bekk. Bergk &c., but -δαρθόντα Pors. Dind.), -θέντες Philostr. 2, 36; (Luc.) Philop. 21, Poet. (κατεδράθην), subj. -δρᾰθῶ Od. 5, 471 (Vulg. Wolf), differing only in accent from subj. **2** aor. act. -δράθω (Bekk. Thiersch, Dind. La Roche): **2** aor. act. κατ-έδαρθον Com. Fr. (Ar.) 2, 1148; (Theocr.) 21, 39; Thuc. 6, 61; Lys. Fr. 54 (Scheibe); Pl. Apol. 40; Xen. Hell. 7, 2, 23; Luc. Merc. Con. 30, Poet. ἔδραθον Hom. always, Od. 20, 143, παρ- 20, 88, κατ- 23, 18; Theocr. 18, 9, 3 dual καδδρᾰθέτην (κατεδρ-) Od. 15, 494; subj. κατα-δράθω Od. 5, 471, -δάρθωμεν Ar. Thesm. 725, see above; -δάρθοι Xen. Ages. 9, 3; -δαρθεῖν Pl. Conv. 223; Ar. Nub. 38. Eccl. 628, ξυγκατα- 623, Poet. δραθέειν, παρα- Il. 14, 163; κατα-δαρθών Ar. Plut. 300 (Pors. Dind.), see above; Plut. Mor. 75. 264, -δαρθοῦσα Ar. Eccl. 37, ἐπικατα- Thuc. 4, 133. δαρθήσομαι we have never seen. Late prose authors sometimes present the Poet. form καταδραθών Char. 6, 7, καταδραθεῖσα 4, 1. W. Dindorf is quite decided on discarding the **1** aor. pass. of this verb, except in very late authors, such as the Scholiasts &c. (Thesaur. καταδαρθ-.)

Δατέομαι *To divide*, Il. 18, 264; Hes. Th. 606; Her. 1, 216; -εώμεθα Il. 9, 280; ἐν-δατούμενος Aesch. Sept. 578; Soph. Tr. 791; Eur. H. F. 218; -έεσθαι Democr. p. 177 (Mull.): **imp.** δατέοντο Il. 5, 158. 20, 394; Pind. Ol. 7, 55, and -εῦντο Il. 23, 121, only **pres.** and **imp.** unless δατέασθαι Hes. Op. 767, be inf. **1** aor.; but as such a form is against analogy, notwithstanding ἀλέασθαι, the reading should probably be **pres.** δατέεσθαι (Ms. Flor. D.), more especially as a **pres.** precedes it: for **fut.** δάσομαι: **aor.** ἐδασάμην, see δαίομαι. **Pass.** in comp. ἐν-δατεῖσθαι Soph. O. R. 205; δια-δατουμένης App. B. C. 1, 1.

(**Δάω**) *To teach, learn*, Epic **2** aor. ἔδᾰον *taught*, Theocr. 24, 128 (Vulg.); Ap. Rh. 4, 989, δάε 3, 529, *learned*, Pind. Fr. 143 (B.), redupl. δέδᾰε Od. 8, 448. 20, 72; Theocr. quoted (Ahr. Mein. Ziegl.): **2** p. δέδαα *have learned*, δεδάᾱσι Callim. Ap. 45; -αώς Od. 17, 519; (Hymn. Merc.?) 510; Ap. Rh. 2, 247, -αῶτε Emped. 120 (Stein); Ap. Rh. 1, 52: **plp.** δεδάει Orph. Arg. 127: **1** p. δεδάηκα Od. 8, 134. 146; Emped. 85 (Stein); Orph. Arg. 46; Her. 2, 165; -ηκώς Od. 2, 61; Hes. Fr. 215 (Marcksch.); Anacreont. 51, 12 (Bergk); late prose -ηκέναι Dio Chrys. 74, 15 (Emper.): **p. p.** δεδάημαι as **act.** -ημένος Hom. H. 3, 483; Ap. Rh. 1, 200; Theocr. 8, 4; δεδαῆσθαι Ap. Rh. 2, 1154: **2** aor. ἐδάην as **act.** Il. 3, 208; Tyrt. 11, 8; Crates 12 (Bergk); Aesch. Ag. 123 (chor.); Soph. El. 169 (chor.); Eur. Phoen. 819 (chor.); Hec. 76

(chor.); late Ion. prose Luc. D. Syr. 1; subj. δαῶ Il. 2, 299, Epic δαείω 16, 423. Od. 9, 280, δαῇς Heindorf's conjecture, Parmenid. quoted by Pl. Soph. 237. 258; opt. δαείην Ap. Rh. 2, 415, -είης Q. Sm. 11, 494, 3 pl. -εῖεν Ap. Rh. 1, 663; -ῆναι Od. 4, 493; Theogn. 969 (Bergk), Epic -ήμεναι Il. 6, 150. Od. 13, 335; δαείς H. Hym. 20, 5; Pind. Ol. 7, 53. 91; Solon Fr. 13, 50 (Bergk); Aesch. Ch. 603, προ- Od. 4, 396. **Mid.** (δάομαι) *to learn*, fut. δαήσομαι, -ήσεαι Od. 3, 187. 19, 325, -ήσεται Orph. L. 43, -ήσονται Ap. Rh. 4, 234: and as mid. p. p. δεδάημαι: **2** aor. ἐδάην, see above. **Vb.** ἀ-δάητος Hes. Th. 655. δαείω Epic **2** aor. subj. pass. for δαῶ, Il. 10, 425; inf. δαήμεναι Il. 21, 487, see above. From δέδαα comes a new pres. (δεδάομαι), hence inf. δεδάασθαι Od. 16, 316. This verb is not in Attic prose, excepting late, δεδαηκέναι Dio Chrys. quoted; in Attic poetry, only in chor.; rare in Ionic prose, Her. and Luc. Syr. quoted.

(**Δέᾰμαι**) Epic, *To appear*, δέατο a defect. imp. Od. 6, 242 (Wolf, Bekk. Dind. δόατο Vulg.) **Pres.** in Hesych. δέαται = δοκεῖ.

Δεδίσκομαι (**δείκνυμαι**) *To greet*, δεδισκόμενος Od. 15, 150. See δειδίσκομαι.

Δεδίσκομαι, δεδίσσομαι, -ίττομαι (**δίομαι**) *To frighten*, δεδίσκεαι Hom. H. Merc. 163, -ίττεται Luc. Bis acc. 7; Plut. Mor. 150. 724; -ίττωμαι (Dem.) Proem. 43; -ιττόμενος Pl. Phaedr. 245: **imp.** ἐδεδίσκετο Ar. Lys. 564: **fut.** δεδίξομαι Luc. Saturn. 4. Philops. 31: **aor.** ἐδεδιξάμην see below; -ίξαιτο Luc. Zeux. 4; -άμενος Dem. 19, 291; Plut. Cat. Min. 43. Also *to fear, feel timid*, δεδίσσομαι Hippocr. 2, 646 (διδίσσ- Lit. 8, 66, δεδίσσ- 2, 558 Erm.), δεδίττ- Aretae. 83 (Ed. Oxon.): **aor.** ἐδεδίξαντο Polyaen. 1, 12. The form δεδίσκομαι is very rare, δεδίσκεαι Hom. H. 3, 163 quoted, is an emendation of Pierson and Moer. for τιτύσκεαι of the Mss., but generally adopted. Maltby would discard this form in the sense *to frighten*, and read δεδίσσ-.

Δεδοίκω *To fear*, a Dor. pres. (or perf. with term. of pres.) Theocr. 15, 58.

Δεδοκημένος *watching*, a def. p. part. Epic Il. 15, 730; Hes. Sc. 214. See δοκέω.

Δεδόκειν Dor. inf. for -υκέναι Theocr. 1, 102.

Δεῖ *It is necessary*. See δέω *to want*.

Δείδεγμαι, see δείκνυμι.

Δειδίσκομαι *To greet, welcome*, Epic -όμενος Od. 3, 41: **imp.** δειδίσκετο Od. 18, 121. 20, 197; Ap. Rh. 1, 558.

Δειδίσσομαι Epic, *To frighten*, -ίσσεαι Il. 13, 810; imperat.

-ίσσεο 4, 184, -ισσέσθω 15, 196; rarely intrans. *fear, quail*, δειδίσσεσθαι Il. 2, 190; see Hippocr. 8, 66, διδισσ- (Lit.): imp. δειδίσσετο trans. *frightened*, in tmesi Il. 12, 52, *dreaded* Orph. Arg. 56: fut. δειδίξεται *will frighten*, Hes. Sc. 111; -ίξεσθαι Il. 20, 201. 432: aor. δειδίξασθαι Il. 18, 164; but late prose δειδισάμενος *dreaded*, Appian C. B. 5, 79: p. δείδιχθι Nic. Alex. 443; δειδίχθαι Maxim. Καταρχ. 149. See δεδίσκ-, δεδίσσ-.

Δείδω *To fear*, pres. perhaps Epic, and only 1 pers. sing. Il. 14, 44. Od. 12, 122; Ap. Rh. 3, 481; Q. Sm. 2, 46; δείδωσι v. r. Aristot. Pt. Anim. 4, 5, 16: (imp.?): fut. δείσεται Epic Il. 20, 130; -σεσθαι 15, 299; unless δείσει Xen. An. 7, 3, 26 (Dind.) be correct: late δείσω Q. Sm. 4, 36; Or. Sib. 12, 152; Aristid. 46, 168, κατα- Epist. Phal. 84: aor. ἔδεισα Il. 10, 240 (Bekk.); Simon. Am. 14, 2; Aesch. Sept. 203; Eur. Hec. 1138; Ar. Lys. 822; Her. 1, 153; Thuc. 1, 74; Lys. 14, 9; Xen. An. 6, 6, 7; Isocr. 9, 57, Epic ἔδδ- Il. 10, 240. 22, 19 (Vulg. Dind.) see below, δεῖσα Il. 8, 138; subj. δείσῃς Soph. El. 1309; Ar. Eccl. 586; Xen. An. 7, 3, 26, -σῃ Il. 24, 116; Pl. Theaet. 166, -ητε Il. 24, 779; Soph. O. R. 1414, -ωσι Isocr. 12, 133; opt. δείσαις ὑπο- Ap. Rh. 3, 435, δείσειε Il. 24, 672, -ειαν Thuc. 2, 15; imperat. δείσατε Ap. Rh. 4, 1042, ὑπο- Od. 2, 66; δείσας Il. 20, 62; Pind. P. 4, 112; Soph. Ant. 1005; Ar. Vesp. 109; Her. 1, 86. 4, 127; Antiph. 1, 27; Pl. Apol. 28, Dor. -σαις Pind. N. 5, 34; inf. δεῖσαι, κατα- (Dem.) Proem. 32: p. δέδοικα as pres. Theogn. 39; Ibycus 24 (B.); Aesch. Pers. 751; Soph. Tr. 306; Eur. Med. 37; Ar. Eq. 38; Thuc. 1, 81; Andoc. 3, 28; Isocr. 15, 215; Isae. 8. 34, Dor. -κω Theocr. 15, 58, -κας Soph. Tr. 457; Ar. Vesp. 628. Thesm. 202; Luc. Demon. 35; Philostr. Ap. 203, -κε Pl. Euth. 12; Dem. 28, 3, pl. rare -οίκαμεν Com. Fr. (Men.) 4, 230; (Luc.) Charid. 24, Dor. -αμες Theocr. 1, 16, -ατε Ar. Eccl. 181; Epist. Phal. 29 (Herch.), -ασι (Dem.) Epist. 3; Paus. 8, 54, 5, Epic δείδοικα Il. 1, 555. 21, 198; Callim. Epigr. 45; subj. rare δεδοίκωσι Hippocr. 4, 166 (Lit.); (opt.?): plp. as imp. ἐδεδοίκειν Xen. Cyr. 1, 3, 10; Pl. Charm. 175. Rep. 472, -εις Ar. Plut. 684; Luc. Icar. 3; App. Mithr. 58, -ει Lys. 12, 50; (Isocr.) 17, 14. 22, pl. ἐδεδοίκεσαν Thuc. 4, 27; Xen. An. 3, 5, 18; Polyaen. 2, 1, 6; inf. Poet. δεδοικέναι Eur. Supp. 548; Ar. Plut. 354. Vesp. 1091; and late prose (Pl.) Ax. 372; Polyaen. 8, 28; Apollod. 2, 5, 4; Luc. Ner. 4; Plut. Pyr. 16; T. Grach. 16; δεδοικώς Anacr. 44; Aesch. Eum. 699 (702); Eur. Phoen. 1594. Ion 624; Ar. Pax 607; rare in classic prose Her. 1, 107; Hippocr. 2, 76; Xen. Cyr. 6, 2, 15, -οικυῖα Pl. Phaedr. 254 (Ms. D. Bait. O. W. δεδιυῖα Bekk.); often late -κώς Plut. Tim. 20. Aem. P. 23.

Pelop. 27. 29. Cat. Maj. 21. Phil. 12 &c.; Luc. Par. 41; Diog. Epist. 45, -οικυῖα Herodn. 5, 7. For **2 p.** δέδια Il. 24, 663; Aesch. Pr. 902; Dem. 14, 4, Epic δειδ- Il. 21, 536, see δίω. In the **aorist**, Epic writers, at least most of our editions, double the δ after the augment: ἔδδεισα Il. 1, 33. 10, 240. 20, 61. 23, 425 &c.; Callim. Dian. 51; Ap. Rh. 3, 1293, and generally in comp. περίδδεισα for περιεδει- Il. 11, 508; περιδδείσας 15, 123. 21, 328. 23, 822. Ap. Rh. 4, 1650, ὑποδδείσαις Ap. Rh. 3, 435, ὑποδδείσας Il. 12, 413. 18, 199. 22, 282. Od. 9, 377. 10, 296; Ap. Rh. 4, 394, but ὑποδείσατε Od. 2, 66. This singularity has been attributed to the *digamma*. But, admitting the digamma, we think its operation too confined and freakish to be the true cause. It is dormant except in the **aorist**, and even there refuses to awake unless on special occasions, by a very near approach or actual contact, and not always even then. We would rather say that the lengthening of the ε is a *metrical exigency*, and, on the analogy of other short vowels similarly situated, does not require the doubling of the δ. When the vowel is in *arsis*, there is surely little need; for why should ε require two δs in ἔδδει|σεν ὑπέν|ερθε Il. 20, 61, and put up with one in δε̄ δεί|σαντες Od. 9, 236. τε̄ δεί|σῃ Il. 24, 116? And even in *thesis* there is no absolute necessity; for if Homer allowed himself to write the gen. of ἀνεψιός, ἀνεψ|ῐοῦ| Il. 15, 554, why might he not lengthen ε, similarly situated, in χαλε|πὴν ἐ|δείσατε Il. 13, 624, and τοὶ δ' ἔδ|εισαν Od. 10, 219, instead of ἐδδει-? It appears to us that in the first case the *stress* has been laid on the vowel, and left no trace; in the second, it has been laid on the consonant, and generated its like. But by the Poet, or the Editor? Are there metrical or rational grounds for the difference? We are inclined to think that Bekker is right in editing ἔδεισα, περιδεισ-, ὑποδεισ- always with single δ in his last edition (1859). The following examples may, by shewing the usage, serve to aid the easier comprehension of the case: no doubling of the δ (=digamma) beyond the **aor.** ὧδέ γ' ἐ|δείδιμεν Il. 6, 99, κεί|νου γὰρ ἐ|δει- Il. 5, 790, γὰρ κάλ' ἐ|δείδισαν 15, 652 (Bekk.), -ον καὶ ἐδείδισαν 7, 151, τίπτε σὺ| δείδοικ- Il. 12, 244, περὶ|δείδια, Il. 10, 93; where no trace of it appears even in the **aor.** τῶν δ' ἄρα| δεισάντ|ων. Od. 12, 203. 24, 534, ὑπŏ-|δείσατε| Od. 2, 66; where δ is doubled perhaps unnecessarily, ἔδδεισα Il. 1, 33, &c. &c., see above. The instances of δείδω in **pres.** beyond the 1 pers. sing. are rare, and by some thought doubtful, δείδετε Anth. Pal. 9, 147, δείδομεν Dio. Hal. Ant. 6, 32. The correction to δείδιτε, δέδιμεν is easy, and in Dio. Hal. has *now* been made, but the question is as easy, and not unreasonable—would later writers feel themselves restricted to exactly Homeric usage?

Perf. δέδοικα, plp. ἐδεδοίκειν seem confined to the indic. usually singular, part. and inf.; subj. δεδοίκωσι, however, Hippocr. 4, 166 (Mss. B. M. N. Lit.): δέδια, again, is used throughout, but less frequently, in indic. sing. perf. and plp.: of δέδοικα, good prose writers use 1 and 3 sing. the pl. is Poet.: of ἐδεδοίκειν they use 1 and 3 sing. and 3 pl.; δεδοικώς rarely; δεδοικέναι perhaps never (Pl.) Ax. 372. These are partially supplied by (δέδια), δέδιμεν, δέδιτε, δεδίασι; δεδιώς freq. Antiph. 2, δ, 1; Dem. 18, 263. 23, 126 &c. &c.; δεδιέναι Hippocr. 1222 (Foes); Thuc. 1, 136; Pl. Conv. 198 &c. See δίω. Cobet (Nov. Lect. p. 588) says "forma δείσομαι a Grammaticis ficta est, neque usquam in Graecorum libris legitur," and on this ground objects to L. Dindorf's reading δείσει Xen. An. 7, 3, 26, for δείσῃς (Vulg. Krüg. Saupp.) Hom. has this fut. twice indisputably: Cobet would, therefore, have taken safer ground if he had denied its being a prose form.

(Δειελιάω) *To take an afternoon meal*, Epic and only aor. part. δειελιήσας Od. 17, 599.

Δεικανάω *To shew* (*the hand*), Poet. pres. late, Arat. 209: imp. iter. δεικανάασκεν Theocr. 24, 56. Mid. δεικανάομαι *to welcome*, imp. 3 pl. Epic δεικανόωντο Il. 15, 86. Od. 24, 410, ἐδεικ- Ap. Rh. 1, 884. (ᾰ.)

Δείκνῡμι *To extend the hand, shew*, Pind. Fr. 108, 5; Soph. O. C. 1145; Eur. Heracl. 1048. Ion 1341; Ar. Av. 1080; Her. 2, 86 (Bekk. Dind.); Isocr. 4, 29; Isae. 11, 3; Pl. Rep. 514. 523; Xen. Oec. 20, 13, ἀπο- Antiph. 5, 59, and δεικνύω Hes. Op. 451; Com. Fr. (Men.) 4, 93. 245; Aeschin. 2, 71; Dem. 18, 76. 21, 169. 36, 47; Xen. Cyr. 6, 1, 7 (Popp. -υσι Dind. Saupp.), -ύουσι An. 6, 2, 2 (Krüg. Saupp. -ύασι Dind. Hug), προ- Her. 7, 37 (Bekk. Dind.), ἐν- Andoc. 2, 14, ἐπι- Isocr. 4, 4, ἀπο- Isae. 9, 31; imper. δείκνυε Hes. Op. 502; Pl. Phaedr. 228. 268 (Vulg.); Dem. 45, 45 (Bekk. Dind.), but δείκνῡ Pl. Rep. 523, ἐπι- Ar. Av. 666 (never -υθι), -ύτω Soph. O. C. 1532; Dem. 21, 28; δεικνύς Il. 13, 244; Her. 2, 78; Pl. Tim. 50; -ύων Xen. Mem. 1, 3, 1; Dem. 24, 35; δεικνύναι Theogn. 771; Her. 2, 148; Pl. Apol. 21; Dem. 2, 5, -ύειν Com. Fr. (Alex.) 3, 430; Dem. 2, 12. 24, 48; Luc. Prom. 11, ἐπι- Xen. Cyr. 8, 1, 21 (Dind. Saupp.): imp. ἐδείκνυν Xen. An. 4, 5, 33. Cyr. 8, 4, 35; Dem. 18, 213; δείκνυ Hes. Op. 526, ἐδείκνυον Her. 4, 150; Antiph. 5, 76; Aeschin. 3, 118; Dem. 18, 233. 34, 42, ἐπ- Lys. 6, 51, δείκν- Pind. P. 4, 220: fut. δείξω Od. 12, 25; Solon 10; Aesch. Eum. 662; Soph. Aj. 66; Her. 4, 79 (Bekk.); Thuc. 5, 9, Ion. δέξω see below: aor. ἔδειξα Od. 27, 147; Pind. P. 6, 46; Aesch. Pr. 482; Eur. Cycl. 9; Thuc. 4, 73; Lys. 12, 49; Pl. Tim. 41, δεῖξ- Od. 3, 174; Pind. Ol. 13, 75, Ion. ἔδεξα see below: p. δέδειχα Aristot. Top. 1, 18, 4; Com. Fr. (Alex.) 3, 517, ἀπο- 3, 503, ἐπι- (Dem.) 26, 16: p.p. δέδειγμαι Soph. Fr. 379 (D.); Xen. Cyr. 2, 3, 9; Pl. Leg. 896, Epic δείδεγμαι see mid.: plp. ἐδέδεικτο, ἀπ- Xen. Hell. 3, 2, 13, Ion. -εδέδεκτο Her. 3, 88, Epic δείδεκτο see mid.: aor. ἐδείχθην, ἐπ- Isocr. 4, 145, ἀπ- Pl. Prot. 359; but δειχθῇ Polit. 278; δειχθῆναι Antiph. 2, 1; -θείς Eur. Supp. 1209; Pl. Legg. 822: δειχθήσομαι Isocr. 5, 1. 12, 4; Dem. 21, 12: late 3 fut. δεδείξομαι Plut. Mor. 416; Galen 3, 419. 681. 9, 816, but δεδειγμένος ἔσται Antiph. 5, 80, ἀπο- Xen. An. 7, 1, 26. Ion. forms, fut. δέξω Her. 4, 179 (Bekk. Dind. Dietsch, Abicht), ἀπο- 3, 122. 5, 22: aor. ἔδεξα Her. 2, 30 (Dietsch, Abicht), ἀπ- 5, 22 (Bekk. Dind. Dietsch &c.): δέδεγμαι, ἀπο- 1, 153: ἐδέδεκτο, κατ- 7, 215: aor. ἐδέχθην, ἀπ- 6, 104; -θείς 1, 1: ἐδεξάμην, ἀπ- 1, 170. 7, 46. **Mid.** δείκνῠμαι Epic, *to hold out one's hand* &c., *to point, welcome*, Il. 23, 701. 9, 196, ἐν- Thuc. 4, 126: imp. ἐδείκνυτο, ἀπ- Her. 3, 82, ἐν- Pl. Charm. 162, ἐπ- Lycurg. 27: fut. δείξομαι, ἐν- Il. 19, 83; Eur. Bacc. 47; Pl. Euthyd. 278: aor. δείξατο H. Merc. 367, ἀπ-εδειξ- Xen. An. 5, 5, 3, ἐν- Pl. Apol. 32; Dem. 21, 145; δείξαιτο, ἐν- Eur. Alc. 154: p. δειδέχαται 3 pl. Od. 7, 72, ἐπι-δέδεικται Pl. Tim. 47, ἐν- Dem. 18, 10; (Hippocr.) Epist. 9, 400 (Lit.); D. Sic. 20, 93, missed by Lexicogr.: plp. δείδεκτο 3 sing. Il. 9, 224, δειδέχατο 3 pl. *greeted*, Il. 4, 4, ἀπο-δεδειγμένοι ἦσαν Xen. An. 5, 2, 9. **Vb.** δεικτέον Xen. Mem. 3, 5, 8. On the forms -υμι, -υω, Mss. and editors vary exceedingly: Hom. has only δεικνύς; Hes. δεικνύω always, unless δείκνυ Op. 526, be imp.; Her. δεικνύς 1, 114. 2, 78, and -ύων 3, 79. 3 pl. -ύουσι 3, 119, ἐπι- 4, 168, ἀπο- 5, 45, προ- 1, 209, and -ῦσι, ἀπο- 1, 171. 4, 8. 5, 45 (Bekk. Dind. -ύουσι 5, 45 Gaisf. Dietsch, Stein); Pind. has δείκνυεν P. 4, 200, but ἀπο-δεικνύμενοι N. 6, 49; so Her. ἀπο-δείκνυμι 2, 16. 18, ἀπ-εδείκνυσαν 2, 144. 9, 80, and προ-δεικνύει 7, 37, imp. ἐδείκνυε 4, 150, ἀπ- 1, 112, δι- 2, 162, but 3 pl. ἐδείκνυσαν, ἐπ- 1, 30, ἐδεικνύατο, ἐν-απ- Her. 9, 58. Tragedians and, we think, Aristophanes always -υμι; Plato almost always, Xen. varies more, but L. Dindorf in his last edition (1857–66) reads nearly always the form -υμι; the Orators also, in our best editions, vary much.

Educational books say "Forms from verbs in -ύω pres. and imp. indic. were used by earlier Attic writers only when the υ is followed by a long vowel or diphthong, as δεικνύει, but *not* δείκνυε." Mss. however and the most stringent editors present ἐδείκνυε Antiphon 5, 76; and ὤμνυον Thuc. 5, 19. 23. 24, ὤμνυε Lys. 19, 26.

Δειμαίνω *To fear*, Hom. H. 2, 226; Tyrt. 11, 3; Aesch. Pr. 41; Her. 8, 140; Pl. Rep. 330; -αίνοιμι Soph. O. C. 492; Mosch. 3, 55; -νων Ar. Vesp. 1042; Her. 3. 35; Pl. Leg. 933; Plut. Mor. 729; -νειν Aesch. Pers. 600; Pl. Leg. 790: imp. ἐδείμαινον Eur. Rhes. 933, iter. δειμαίνεσκε Q. Sm. 2, 439: fut. δειμᾰνεῖ in some editions of Aesch. Eum. 519, is an emendation of Abresch for δειμαίνει (Mss. Vulg. δειματοῖ Franz, δεῖ μένειν Dobr. and *now* Dind.) At Aesch. Eum. quoted, it means *to frighten*, and perhaps Pers. 600; Pl. Leg. 865: hence pass. δειμαίνοντο Q. Sm. 2, 499. In good Attic prose, Plato only.

Δεινόω, ἐκ- *To make dreadful, exaggerate*, Joseph. 17, 5, 5: in *simple*, only 1 aor. part. δεινώσας Thuc. 8, 74; and inf. δεινῶσαι Plut. Per. 28.

Δειπνέω *To sup*, Ar. Eccl. 683; Xen. Cyr. 3, 1, 37: imp. ἐδείπνεε Od. 17, 506; Hippocr. 1, 594, -νει Andoc. 1, 45; Pl. Conv. 217: fut. -ήσω Ar. Pax 1084; Xen. Cyr. 5, 3, 35, 3 pl. Dor. -ᾱσεῦντι Callim. L. P. 115 (Ernest. Bl.): and late -ήσομαι Plut. Mor. 225; Diod. Sic. 11, 9; Galen 10, 6: aor. ἐδείπνησα Com. Fr. (Antiph.) 3, 95; Hippocr. 5, 212; Pl. Conv. 203, δειπ- Od. 14, 111; -ήσωμεν Xen. An. 4, 6, 17; -ήσειαν Od. 9, 155; δειπνήσας 15, 79; Thuc. 3, 112: p. δεδείπνηκα Ar. Eccl. 1133; Hippocr. 5, 222; Xen. Cyr. 8, 4, 21: plp. ἐδεδειπνήκειν Antiph. 1, 18: Pl. Conv. 217, δεδειπ- Od. 17, 359. Syncop. forms δεδείπνᾰμεν Com. Fr. (Eubul.) 3, 248. (Alex.) 3, 429; δεδειπνάναι Com. Fr. (Pl.) 2, 663. (Ar.) 2, 1051. 1139 (Antiph.) 3, 79. (Eub.) 3, 248, for -ήκαμεν, -ηκέναι: p.p. δεδειπνημένος, παρα- Com. Fr. (Amph.) 3, 315. See ἀριστάω. This verb is once only in Trag. δειπνεῖν if sound, Eur. Fr. Incert. 688 (D.) δειπνίζω *to entertain*, Anth. 11, 394; Her. 7, 118; Xen. Mem. 1, 3, 7. Oec. 2, 5: has fut. δειπνιῶ Com. Fr. (Diph.) 4, 405: aor. ἐδείπνισα Her. 7, 118; Xen. Cyr. 4, 5, 5, Poet. δείπνισα Matron (Athen.) 4, 13; part. δειπνίσσας Od. 4, 535. 11, 411: p.p. late δεδειπνισμένος Plut. Mor. 92. This verb does not occur in Tragic poetry, occasionally in Comic, rare in Epic, only Od. quoted: rare also in Attic prose, only Xen. and late Luc. Ep. Sat. 22; Plut. quoted.

Δείρω *To flay*, a lengthened form of the more Attic δέρω, δείρουσι Her. 2, 39, ἀπο- 4, 64; imperat. δεῖρε Com. Fr. (Cratin.) 2, 224; Ar. Av. 365 (Dind. Bergk); (Luc.) Asin. 6; δείρειν Ar. Nub. 442 (Dind. Bergk): aor. ἔδειρα, ἀπ- Her. 5, 25; subj. δείρωσι, ἀπο- Her. 4, 61; δείρας, ἀπο- 4, 60. 64: pass. imp.

ἀπ-εδειρόμην Ar. Vesp. 1286: for p.p. and aor. see δέρω. In Ar. Bekk. reads δαῖρε, δαίρειν.

Δέκομαι *To receive*, Aeol. and Ionic prose for δεχ-, Sapph. 1, 22 (Bergk); Her. 9, 91; also Pind. Ol. 2, 63. P. 1, 98; imper. δέκευ Ol. 13, 68: imp. δέκετο Pind. I. 8 (7), 68, ἐδέκ- Her. 3, 135. 5, 18, -κοντο 6, 13. 8, 28.

Δέμω *To build*, pres. rare, part. δέμων Hom. H. 3, 87: imp. also rare, δέμον Od. 23, 192: fut. (δεμῶ?): aor. ἔδειμα Il. 21, 446; Ap. Rh. 4, 469; Her. 2, 124, δεῖμ- Ap. Rh. 3, 37; subj. δείμομεν, for -ωμεν, Il. 7, 337; δείμας Eur. Rhes. 232 (chor.); Her. 9, 10: p. (δέδμηκα?): p.p. δέδμημαι Il. 6, 249; Theocr. 17, 18; Her. 7, 200, Dor. -ᾱμαι Theocr. 15, 120: plp. ἐδέδμητο Il. 13, 683; Her. 7, 176, δέδ- Od. 14, 6. Mid. *to build for oneself*, aor. ἐδειμάμην Od. 6, 9; Eur. Fr. Dan. 22; Her. 4, 78; late Attic prose (Pl.) Ax. 370; Arr. 2, 5, 4; (Luc.) Amor. 36; Apollod. 2, 7, 2; Dio. Hal. 1, 55, δείμαθ' Od. 14, 8, dual δειμάσθην Opp. C. 4, 87. The pres. and imp. are confined to Ion. poetry, and are very rare. δέμοντα Hom. H. 3, 188, is an emendation of Barnes for νέμοντα. The verb scarcely occurs in Attic poetry, perhaps never in classic Attic prose, it is chiefly Ionic and late Attic. Fut. δεμῶ, p. δέδμηκα, 2 p. δέδομα we have never seen. A late form of p.p. δεδομημένος, as if from δομέω, occurs Arr. An. 7, 22; Aristid. 43, 555: aor. ἐδομήθησαν Hesych.: aor. mid. δομήσατο Lycophr. 48: redupl. fut. δεδομήσεται as act. Or. Sib. 3, 384.

Δενδίλλω *To glance at*, Epic and only part. -λλων Il. 9, 180; Ap. Rh. 3, 281.

Δεξιοῦμαι Dep. *To stretch out the right hand, entreat, greet*, Plut. Mor. 62; -ούμενος Eur. Rhes. 419; Xen. Hell. 7, 2, 9; -οῦσθαι Aristot. Mund. 1, 6; Luc. Alex. 41: imp. ἐδεξιοῦτο Ar. Plut. 753; Xen. Cyr. 6, 3, 15, 3 pl. Epic -όωντο Hom. H. 6 (5), 16; Ap. Rh. 2, 756. 3, 258: fut. -ώσομαι Aesch. Ag. 852; Soph. El. 976; Hyperid. Leosth. Col. 13, 13; Dio. Hal. 8, 45; Luc. Bis acc. 9; Herodn. 2, 13: aor. ἐδεξιωσάμην Lys. 2, 37; Xen. Cyr. 7, 5, 53: but ἐδεξιώθην pass. Pl. Rep. 468. δεδεξίωμαι we have not seen. Some assume, perhaps needlessly, a form δεξιάομαι for the Epic 3 pl. -όωντο.

Δερκιάομαι *To look*, a Poet. form of δέρκομαι and only 3 pl. pres. -ιόωνται Hes. Th. 911.

Δέρκομαι, Poet. *To see*, Dep. pass. and late, mid. Il. 11, 37; Emped. 81; Pind. P. 3, 85; Aesch. Pr. 843; Soph. El. 1116; Ar. Thesm. 700: imp. ἐδερκόμην Soph. El. 899; Eur. Elec. 867, προσ- Od. 20, 385, iter. δερκέσκετο Od. 5, 158: fut. late δέρξομαι Androm. Ther. 92 (Galen 6, 37): aor. m. late ἐδερξάμην Anth.

Pl. 166: aor. pass. ἐδέρχθην act. Aesch. Pr. 546, δέρχθη Soph. Aj. 425 (trimet. in chor.); imper. δέρχθητε Aesch. Pr. 93; δερχθείς Soph. Fr. 719 (D.): 2 aor. act. ἔδρᾰκον Od. 10, 197; Eur. Or. 1456 (chor.); Opp. Hal. 2, 538, ἀν- Il. 14, 436, δράκ- Hes. Sc. 262; δράκοι, δια- Il. 14, 344; δρακεῖν Aesch. Eum. 34. Ag. 602; -κών Eur. H. F. 951, late in comp. (with termination of 1 aor.) εἰσ-έδρᾰκα Orph. Arg. 133: 2 aor. m. rare, ἐδρακόμην Anth. 7, 224: 2 aor. pass. ἐδρᾰ́κην, -κείς Pind. P. 2, 20. N. 7, 3. Fr. 100 (Bergk): p. δέδορκα as pres. Il. 22, 95; Pind. Ol. 1, 94; Aesch. Sept. 104; Soph. Aj. 360; Eur. Andr. 545; δεδορκώς Od. 19, 446; Aesch. Ag. 1179; Soph. Tr. 747; Eur. Phoen. 377; late prose Aristot. Physiog. 3, 7; Plut. Mor. 15; Luc. Calumn. 10; Stob. (Nicostr.) 70, 12. Vb. in μονο-δέρκτης Eur. Cycl. 78. δέρκομαι and δέδορκα are also used intrans. Anth. 7, 21; Pind. Ol. 1, 94 &c. 1 aor. p. ἐδέρχθην seems confined to Trag.; 2 aor. (ἐδρᾰ́κην), δρακείς to Pind. This verb does not occur in early prose, occasionally in late, δέρκομαι (Luc.) D. Syr. 20, especially the perf. δέδορκα Plut. Mor. 15. 281; Luc. Calumn. 10. Herm. 20. Hist. Con. 37. Icar. 6; Galen 1, 5 (K). Late is found a pres. act. form ἐπιδέρκει Pseud.-Callisth. 1, 33, missed by Lexicogr.

Δέρω *To flay*, Com. Fr. (Anax.) 3, 181; Pl. Euthyd. 285; δέρων Ar. Ran. 619; δέρειν (Luc.) Asin. 6: imp. ἔδερον Il. 23, 167, δέρον Od. 8, 61: fut. δερῶ Ar. Eq. 370: aor. ἔδειρα Il. 2, 422; Dio. Hal. 7, 72, ἐξ- Eur. Elec. 824; Hyperid. Fr. 116, ἀπ- Luc. D. Deor. 16, 2; δείρας, ἐκ- Pl. Rep. 616; δεῖραι, ἐκ- Xen. An. 1, 2, 8: p.p. δέδαρμαι, -δάρθαι Solon Fr. 33 (Bergk); -δαρμένος Ar. Lys. 158, ἐκ- Her. 7, 70: 1 aor. ἐδάρθην, δαρθείς Com. Fr. (Nicoch.) 2, 844: 2 aor. ἐδᾰ́ρην Ael. Epist. 11; Luc. Lexiph. 2; δαρείς (Menand.) Mon. 422, ἐκ- Her. 7, 26, ἀπο- Xen. An. 3, 5, 9: fut. late δαρήσομαι N. T. Marc. 13, 9. Luc. 12, 47. Mid. late ἀνα-δέροιτο Philostr. V. Soph. 1, 25, 3, and ἀνα-δέρεσθον, a suggestion of Brunck, Ar. Ran. 1106 (Dind.) for -δέρετον (Mss., ἀνὰ δ' ἔρεσθον Bergk, Mein.) Vb. δρατός Il. 23, 169. δαρτός late, Galen. See δείρω.

Δεύω *To need, want*, Aeol. and Epic for δέω, pres. act. not used, aor. ἐδεύησα Od. 9, 540, see δέω. Mid. δεύομαι as act. 2 sing. -εαι Il. 23, 484, and -ῃ Od. 1, 254, -εται 7, 73, -ονται Q. Sm. 1, 459; -οιντο Callim. Ap. 50, -οίατο Il. 2, 128; -όμενος 3, 294; Lesb. Tit. 2189, Dor. -ομένα Eur. Tr. 276 (chor.): imp. ἐδεύεο Il. 17, 142, -εύετο 1, 468. 602. 4, 48, δεύοντο 2, 709: fut. δευήσεαι Od. 6, 192. 14, 510; -ήσεσθαι Il. 13, 786, ἐπι- Ap. Rh. 3, 717. Some say δεύω is softened from the digammated δέϝω.

Δεύω *To wet*, Il. 2, 471; Ar. Fr. 267 (D.); rare in prose -ων Hippocr. 6, 298. 420; -ειν 422. 8, 386: imp. ἔδευον Od. 8, 522, δεῦε Il. 23, 220, iter. δεύεσκον Od. 7, 260: fut. δεύσω Com. Fr. (Eub.) 3, 247: aor. ἔδευσα Soph. Aj. 376; Eur. Phoen. 674, κατ- Il. 9, 490; rare in prose, ἔδευσε Pl. Tim. 73; δεύσας Hippocr. 6, 448; δεῦσαι Xen. Oec. 10, 11: (p.?): p.p. δέδευμαι Eur. Fr. 470 (D.); Hippocr. 6, 422; Pl. Leg. 782; Xen. Cyr. 6, 2, 28: aor. ἐδεύθην Hippocr. 6, 412; Theophr. H. P. 9, 9, 1: pres. δεύεται Od. 6, 44: imp. δεύοντο Il. 23, 15. Mid. δεύεται Od. 5, 53?: fut. ἀνα-δεύσεται seemingly pass. Galen 10, 867, missed by Lexicogr. Quint. Sm. 4, 511, has 3 pl. 1 aor. δεύεσαν, which Lobeck would alter to δεύετον, but Koechly ἔδευσαν (1850). This verb is rare in prose: in good Attic, only aor. act. and p. pass.; in Epic, its walk extends not beyond pres. and imp. act., see above; (mid. δεύεται Od. 5, 53?), and pass. Od. 6, 44; Emped. 99; -οιτο Ap. Rh. 2, 974; -ομένη Opp. Hal. 3, 408: ἐδεύετο Ap. Rh. 3, 1138, δευ- Il. 17, 361; Ap. Rh. 1, 750, -οντο Il. 9, 570. 23, 15.

Δέχνυμαι Poet. *To receive*, late form for δέχομαι, Anth. (Antip.) 9, 553; imper. δέχνυσο Coluth. 159; Orph. L. 692, -υσθε L. 4: imp. ἐδέχνυτο Orph. Arg. 566.

Δέχομαι *To receive*, Il. 23, 647; Aesch. Ag. 1060; Soph. Ant. 1019; Ar. Ach. 199; Thuc. 1, 20; Pl. Critias 106, Ion. and Pind. δεκ- Her. 8, 137; Pind. P. 1, 98, see above: imp. ἐδεχ- Hym. Cer. 437; Soph. O. T. 1391; Thuc. 7, 44; Lycurg. 29: fut. δέξομαι Il. 22, 365; Pind. P. 9, 73; Aesch. Pr. 860 (Dind. Herm. Paley); Soph. O. C. 4; Her. 7, 102; Thuc. 4, 21; Pl. Phil. 24; δεξοίατ' Soph. O. C. 945 (trimet.): aor. ἐδεξάμην Il. 18, 238; Simon. Am. 7, 49; Solon 33; Pind. P. 1, 80; Aesch. Ag. 1537; Soph. Aj. 661; Her. 1, 70; Antiph. 1, 12; Lys. 18, 12; Thuc. 2, 36, δεξ- Il. 5, 158; Hes. Th. 184; Pind. Ol. 3, 27; δεξαίατο Soph. O. C. 44: p. δέδεγμαι Pind. P. 1, 100; Aesch. Eum. 894; Her. 9, 5; Thuc. 1, 9, 3 pl. δεδέχαται, ἀπο- Her. 2, 43. 65. 77, δέχαται see below; imper. δέδεξο Il. 5, 228, δέδεχθε H. Hym. 2, 360; δεδεγμένος Il. 11, 124; δεδέχθαι Pl. Phaedr. 256: aor. as mid. in comp. ἐδέχθην, δεχθείς, ὑπο- Eur. Heracl. 757, but pass. δεχθείς late in *simple*, Joseph. Ant. 18, 6, 4; Malal. p. 3, 2, εἰσ- Dem. 40, 14; Luc. Tox. 30. Merc. Cond. 10, προσ- Diod. Sic. 4, 26. 5, 58, ὑπο- App. Rom. 3, 2; Herodn. 1, 7, 2 (Bekk.): fut. late δεχθήσομαι pass. V. T. Lev. 19, 7, κατα- Dio Cass. 40, 40: 3 fut. δεδέξομαι act. Il. 5, 238; Anth. 5, 9; Or. Sib. 3, 351; Nonn. 46, 262. This reduplicated fut. seems to be Epic, for at Aesch. Pr. 866 (860 D.) now stands δὲ δέξεται (Dind. Herm. Paley), and for δεδέξεται Ar. Vesp. 1223

(Mss. R. V. Vulg. Br. Bekk), is now edited, rightly we think, δέξεται (Bergk, Hirschig, Richter &c.), compare 1225. 1243. Pax 144. Av. 1312 &c. &c. In no instance in fact, except the one recorded, do the Mss. offer a trace of δεδέξεται. Dind. 5 ed. omits it (Vesp. 1223) and with Dobree holds it a gloss. See δέκομαι. For δειδέχαται, δείδεκτο, δειδέχατο, δειδεγμένος, referred by some to this verb, see δείκνυμι. δέχαται Epic 3 pl. perf. without augm. for δέχνται, Il. 12, 147; part. δέγμενος *waiting*, Il. 18, 524: ἐδέγμην plp. *was expecting*, Od. 9, 513, δέκτο Ap. Rh. 1, 1242; but ἐδέγμην *received*, Anth. 7, 691, ἔδεκτο Od. 9, 353 (Bekk.); Pind. Ol. 2, 49; Anth. 7, 25, ὑπ- Hes. Th. 513, δέκτο Il. 15, 88; imper. δέξο Il. 19, 10, δέχθε Ap. Rh. 4, 1554; inf. δέχθαι Il. 1, 23; Eur. Rhes. 525. Of these Buttmann takes ἐδέγμην *received*, ἔδεκτο, δέκτο, δέξο, δέχθαι as syncop. aor., and assigns to the perf. and plp. those forms only which signify *to wait, expect*. Vb. δεκτέος Luc. Hermot. 74 (Jacob.), ἀπο- Xen. Oec. 7, 36.

Δέψω *To work, knead*, Ion. Her. 4, 64: fut. (-ήσω): aor. δεψήσας Od. 12, 48, as if from a pure form in -εω. Mid. aor. δέψηται, ἐκ- (Hesych.). Vb. ἀ-δέψητος Od. 20, 2.

Δέω *To bind*, Hes. Fr. 94, 3; Her. 4, 72; Pl. Crat. 403; δέοιμι Od. 8, 352; imper. δεῖτε Eur. Ion 1403; δεόντων Od. 12, 54 (Wolf, διδέντων Aristarch. Bekk. La R.); δεῖν H. Hym. 7, 12: imp. ἔδει Pl. Crat. 403; Dem. 24, 145, δέον Od. 22, 189; Hes. Sc. 291, ἐκ- Il. 23, 121: fut. δήσω Il. 21, 454; Ar. Eq. 367; Andoc. 4, 17; Xen. An. 5, 8, 24; Dem. 24, 144: aor. ἔδησα Il. 14, 73; Aesch. Eum. 641; Ar. Thesm. 1022; Her. 2, 122; Thuc. 8, 70, Poet. δῆσεν Il. 21, 30; Hes. Th. 502; Pind. P. 4, 71; imper. δήσατε Od. 12, 161, δησάντων 12, 50; Dor. pt. δήσαις Pind. P. 4, 234: p. δέδεκα Dem. 24, 207; and late (Dem.) Epist. 3 (1477); Anth. (Meleag.) 5, 96. 12, 132; Plut. Tit. 10, and δέδηκα Aeschin. 2, 134 (Bekk. B. Saupp. -εκα Franke, Weidner): plp. ἐδεδήκει Andoc. 4, 17 (Emper. B. Saupp. Blass, ἐδεδέκει Franke, ἐδεδοίκει Bekk.): p. p. δέδεμαι Theogn. 178; Pind. N. 11, 45; Eur. Rhes. 617. Hipp. 160; Hippocr. 4, 190; δεδεμένος Antiph. 5, 47; Thuc. 1, 93; Her. 3, 39, ἐπι- Hippocr. 4, 220 (Lit.), v. r. δεδεσμ- see below; imper. δεδέσθω Pl. Leg. 880; δεδέσθαι H. Cer. 456; Lys. 10, 16; Dem. 24, 103: plp. ἐδεδέμην Her. 9, 37; Andoc. 1, 48; Lys. 6, 23. 13, 55; Luc. D. Deor. 21, 2, δέδετο Il. 5, 387, δέδεντο Od. 10, 92, ἐδεδέατο Her. 1, 66. 5, 77: aor. ἐδέθην Her. 6, 2; Antiph. 5, 17; Lys. 13, 34; δεθῶ Pl. Meno 98; δεθείεν Dem. 24, 121; δεθείς Pind. N. 6, 35; Soph. Aj. 108; Eur. Hipp. 1237; Pl. Leg. 919; δεθῆναι Pl. Leg. 954: fut. δεθήσομαι Dem. 24, 126. 131.

190. 191, ἐπι- Hippocr. 3, 444 (Lit.): **3 fut.** δεδήσομαι Xen. Cyr. 4, 3, 18; Pl. Rep. 361; Alciphr. 3, 24; Luc. Catapl. 13. Tox. 35 (v. r. δεθησ- at both); but δεδέσομαι Aristid. 53 (Jebb, δεδήσ- Dind.). **Mid.** δέομαι trans. and Poet. in *simple*, *bind for oneself*, ἀνα-δέονται Her. 1, 195; imper. ὑπο-δεῖσθε Ar. Eccl. 269; ἀνα-δούμενοι Thuc. 1, 6. 50. 2, 90, ὑπο- Pl. Theaet. 193: **imp.** δέοντο Il. 18, 553, περιεδούμ- Pl. Leg. 830: **fut.** δήσομαι *simple*, perhaps late, Or. Sib. 12, 293, περι- Ar. Eccl. 122, ὑπο- Luc. Anach. 32, κατα- Theocr. 2, 158 (Ahrens, Fritzsche, Ziegl.) for -θύσομαι (Vulg. -έθυσα Mein.): **aor.** ἐδησάμην Il. 10, 22, ἀν- Thuc. 2, 92, Poet. ἐκ-δήσαντο Eur. Hipp. 761 (chor.), iter. δησάσκετο Il. 24, 15; κατα-δήσωνται Her. 3, 110; δησαίμην Il. 8, 26; δησάσθω, κατα- Hippocr. 8, 488; δήσασθαι Hes. Op. 542; δησάμενος Il. 17, 290; Ap. Rh. 2, 1013; Anth. 5, 255, ἀν- Pind. N. 11, 28, ἀνα- Thuc. 7, 74, ἐκ- Her. 4, 76: and **p. p.** ὑπο-δεδεμένος may be **mid.** Xen. An. 4, 5, 14, ἀνα- Polyb. 16, 6, 10: **plp.** δι-εδέδετο Luc. D. Mort. 12, 3. **Perf. act.** δέδηκα is best supported, Aeschin. quoted, only one Ms. has δέδεκα. The **p. p.** δέδεσμαι, v. r. Her. quoted, has very slender support, Cod. Fl.; and for ἐπιδεδεσμένος Hippocr. 3, 210 (Kühn), the Mss. give -δεδεμένος 4, 220. 268, προσ- 302 (Lit.) **Vb.** δετός, συν- Pl. Polit. 279, but ἀν-υπό-δητος Pl. Conv. 173; (Luc.) Asin. 16, but -δετος Luc. Philop. 21, δετέος, συν- Ar. Eccl. 785. At Luc. Tox. 35 occurs **fut.** part. δεδησόμενος, with v. r. δεθησ-, which we would decidedly prefer in an earlier writer; for we think the *part.* of the reduplicated **fut.** against Attic usage. The Attics used invariably, we think, the part. of the **fut. pass.** or the **fut. mid.** in a pass. sense. On this ground we object to Bekker's adoption of διαπεπολεμησόμενος Thuc. 7, 25, for διαπολεμησ- (Vulg.) δέω and compounds violate the general rule of dissyllable verbs in εω by contracting other concourses than εε, εει, as δέῃ, δῇ, συν- Pl. Rep. 462, δέον, δοῦν Plat. Crat. 419, ἀναδέων. -ῶν Ar. Plut. 589, κατ-έδεον, -έδουν Thuc. 6, 53, ἀνα-δοῦνται Pl. Rep. 465, συν- Polit. 310, περι-εδούμεθα Leg. 830, ἀνα-δούμενοι Sophron 97; Thuc. 2, 90, δια- Pl. Tim. 73; imper. περιδέον, -οῦ Ar. Eccl. 121, true, but Plato has also δέον Phaed. 99, and Dem. δέων 22, 68, δέουσι Dem. 51, 11, and late writers frequently.

Δέω *To need*, *lack*, Alcae. 102 (B.); Aesch. Pr. 1006; Lys. 17, 1; Isocr. 3, 34, δέεις, 11, 4, δεῖς Pl. Lys. 204; Dem. 37, 49, δέομεν Isocr. 4, 134. 14, 5, δέουσι Pl. Meno 92; Isocr. 4, 168. 12, 16. 14, 17; Dem. 24, 142. 53, 27: **imp.** ἔδεον Isocr. 7, 47; Xen. Hell. 4, 6, 11: **fut.** δεήσω Pl. Rep. 395: **aor.** ἐδέησα Lys. 3, 7. 30, 8; Isocr. 10, 36, once δῆσα Il. 18, 100 (Spitzn, Dind. La R.), ἔδησα (Bekk. *now*), Epic ἐδεύησα Od. 9, 540: **p.** δεδέηκα

Pl. Polit. 277. Mid. δέομαι, Epic δεύ- *to want, entreat,* Ar. Nub. 429; Her. 1, 8; Antiph. 1, 3. 5, 5; Thuc. 7, 63; Lys. 10, 21; Pl. Phaed. 87, δέει Ar. Thesm. 264; Pl. Parm. 126, δεῖ Ar. Lystr. 605, Epic δεύῃ Od. 1, 254, δεύεαι Il. 23, 484, δεῖται Aesch. Supp. 358; Soph. O. R. 1293; Ar. Av. 74; Antiph. 2, γ, 9; Pl. Rep. 465, δεόμεθα Eur. Rhes. 321; Ar. Pax 474; Thuc. 6, 80, δέονται Thuc. 1, 81; Pl. Theaet. 151; δέηται Crat. 406; δέοιντο Leg. 720, Ion. δεοίατο Her. 5, 73; δέεσθε 8, 22; -όμενος Pind. N. 7, 13: imp. ἐδεόμην Ar. Vesp. 850; Her. 3, 36; Andoc. 1, 49; Lys. 12, 11; Isocr. 17, 41, ἐδέου Her. 7, 161, ἐδεῖτο Eur. Heracl. 126; Ar. Plut. 980; Thuc. 7, 28; Dem. 29, 1. 18, 145, Ion. -έετο Her. 2, 30, Epic ἐδεύετο Il. 1, 602, ἐδέοντο Ar. Ach. 536; Her. 1, 196; Antiph. 6, 38; Thuc. 5, 36; Lys. 3, 19: fut. δεήσομαι Ar. Plut. 1160; Her. 8, 142; Antiph. 1, 21; Isocr. 14, 2; Isae. 5, 34; Pl. Rep. 348, Epic 2 sing. δευήσεαι Od. 6, 192; -ήσεσθαι Il. 13, 786: (aor. m. ἐδεησάμην, see below): p. δεδέημαι Xen. An. 7, 7, 14; Isae. 8, 22: aor. ἐδεήθην Ar. Plut. 986; Her. 4, 84; Thuc. 1, 27; Isocr. 4, 59; Pl. Rep. 380; δεηθῇς Soph. O. C. 1170; Pl. Gorg. 507; δεηθείην Ar. Plut. 977; Xen. Laced. 11, 2; Dem. 50, 56; -ηθείς Her. 9, 85: fut. late δεηθήσομαι Plut. Mor. 213; V. T. Job 9, 15; Aristid. 45, 42 (Dind.); Galen 1, 417. 13, 898; Aesop 123 (Tauchn. but pres. δεομ- Halm 304). For the Epic forms δεύομαι, ἐδεύετο, δευήσομαι, see δεύω. δέω is often used impersonally, δεῖ *it is necessary,* &c. Hom. only once, Il. 9, 337; Aesch. Eum. 826; Soph. Ph. 77; Antiph. 3, δ, 8; Thuc. 1, 71; δέῃ Eur. Rhes. 521; Ar. Nub. 493; Thuc. 1, 58; Pl. Rep. 333, but δῇ Ar. Ran. 265 (chor. Dind.); C. Fr. (Philet.) 3, 292; δέοι Thuc. 4, 4; Pl. Menex. 236; δεῖν Pl. Conv. 185; δέον Eur. I. A. 567: imp. ἔδει Soph. Ph. 292; Antiph. 6, 38; Thuc. 7, 8; Lys. 3, 1; Pl. Crat. 403, Ion. ἔδεε Her. 3, 45. 7, 9 (Bekk. Krüg. Dind. &c.). 8, 6 (Dind. Dietsch, Stein, ἔδει Bekk. Krüg.): fut. δεήσει Eur. Hipp. 941; Her. 6, 88; Thuc. 1, 81: ἐδέησε Thuc. 2, 77; Xen. Cyr. 3, 1, 27; δεήσῃ Her. 3, 155; Thuc. 6, 41; -σειε Pl. Leg. 814. δεῖσθαι, δεόμενον may be thought to have rather an appearance of impersonality at Pl. Meno 79; Her. 4, 11. δέεται, δέεσθαι, are sometimes uncontr. Xen. An. 7, 4, 8. 7, 7, 31 (most Mss. Krüg. δεῖται, δεῖσθαι 1 Ms. Dind. Popp. Saupp.); δέεσθαι Mem. 1, 6, 10. 2, 1, 30. 8, 1, προσ- 4, 8, 11; δέεται 3, 6, 14, προσ- 3, 6, 13. 14; ἐδέετο Hell. 6, 1, 18 (Mss. Buttm. Kühner, Breitb. &c. δεῖ-, ἐδεῖ- Mss. Lob. Popp. L. Dind. and *now* Saupp.) These instances, if correct, would seem to shew that Xen. *sometimes* did not avoid using certain forms *open* which are usually contracted in this verb: Isocr. also has the act. form *open* δέεις 11, 4. The aor. mid. we have never met, except ἐδεήσατο in the Argum. by Anton. Bongiovan. to Liban. Or. 13; and δεήσασθαι Emperius's unaccountable emendation adopted unaccountably by Westermann for fut. δεήσεσθαι Lys. 27, 14 (for which δεηθῆναι Kaiser, δεδεῆσθαι Cobet.)

Δηθύνω *To linger*, only pres. δηθύνησθα Od. 12, 121; δηθύνων Il. 6, 519; Ap. Rh. 2, 985; Anth. (Macεd.) 5, 223; -ύνειν Od. 17, 278; Ap. Rh. 2, 75: and imp. δήθυνε Il. 6, 503.

Δηϊόω *To waste*, Ionic, opt. δηιόῳμεν Od. 4, 226; δηϊόων Il. 18, 195. 23, 176; Ap. Rh. 4, 489; Q. Sm. 7, 554, Attic δηῶ, δηοῦτε Ar. Lys. 1146, δηοῦμεν Xen. Cyr. 3, 3, 18; so Hom. when the third syllable is long, part. δηῶν Il. 17, 65; Thuc. 4, 87: imp. Ion. ἐδηΐουν Her. 8, 33. 50 (Gaisf. Bekk. Dind. Stein, &c.), so 5, 89 (Mss. Stein), -ΐευν (Bred. Krüg. Abicht), but ἐδήευν (Ms. S. V. Bekk. Gaisf. Dind.), Attic ἐδήουν Thuc. 1, 65; Xen. Cyr. 5, 4, 23, δῄουν Il. 11, 71, iter. δηιάασκον Ap. Rh. 2, 142, see below: fut. δηώσω Il. 12, 227; Soph. O. C. 1319; Thuc. 2, 71; Xen. Cyr. 5, 4, 21: aor. ἐδήωσα Thuc. 1, 114; subj. δηώσῃ Il. 16, 650, -ωσιν 4, 416; Thuc. 2, 13; -ώσειαν Ap. Rh. 1, 244; part. δηώσας Il. 8, 534. 18, 83; Solon 13, 21; Xen. Hell. 2, 2, 9, Ion. δηϊώσας Her. 6, 135. 8, 121 (no v. r. Bekk. Gaisf. Dind.): p. late δεδήωκα Sopat. Rhet. p. 193: p. p. δεδηωμένος Luc. D. Mort. 10, 11: aor. Ion. ἐδηϊώθην Her. 7, 133 (Gaisf. Bekk. Dind.); δηωθείς Il. 4, 417; δηωθῆναι Ap. Rh. 1, 81. **Mid.** (δηόομαι), fut. as pass. δηώσεσθαι Ap. Rh. 2, 117: aor. as act. ἐδηωσάμην Opp. H. 5, 350; subj. δηώσωνται Q. Sm. 5, 374; -ώσασθαι 5, 567; late prose δηωσάμενος Joseph. Jud. B. 2, 13, 2 (Bekk.) For imp. pass. δηϊόωντο Il. 13, 675, we have analogy in ἀρόωσι, for ἀροῦσι from ἀρόω, but δηιάασκον Ap. Rh. quoted, points rather to (δηΐω, δηϊάω), imp. ἐδήϊον Ap. Rh. 3, 1374, iter. δηιάασκον Ap. Rh. 2, 142. See μηνίω, -ιάω. Her. seems to have used this verb, perhaps always, uncontracted. Hom. only in some forms of the pres. act. and imp. pass.: in Attic prose, it is confined to Thuc. and Xen.; in Attic poetry, to Soph. and Aristoph., and only once in each. We have noticed this verb, not because it is irregular, but because it has been ill handled by our Lexicogrs.

Δηλέομαι (δαΐω, *deleo*), Dep. mid. Poet. Ion. and Dor. *To injure, destroy*, -λῆται Stob. (Archyt.) 1, 70; Her. 4, 187; -έεσθαι 6, 36; -εύμενος Mimnerm. 7: imp. ἐδηλέοντο Her. 5, 83: fut. δηλήσομαι H. Merc. 541, -ήσεται Il. 14, 102; Orph. Arg. 352; Or. Sib. 3, 645: aor. ἐδηλησάμην Il. 1, 156; so Plut. Mor. 874 (from Her. 9, 63, see imp.), δηλησ- Il. 4, 236; Epic subj. δηλήσεαι 23, 428, -ήσεται Od. 8, 444; -σάμενος Her. 4, 115; late, Parthen. 29; -σασθαι Her. 7, 51; Theocr. 22, 189; late, Agath. Pref. p. 12: p. δεδήλημαι as pass. Her. 4, 198. 8, 100, perhaps act. Eur. Hipp. 175. **Act.** δηλέω formerly Xen. Oec. 10, 3, is a false reading, but preserved in the Latin *deleo*: **fut.** late δηλήσω Or. Sib. 7, 44: and **aor.** part. δηλήσας Or. Sib. 7, 28. Theocr. has usu. δᾱλέομαι, -εῖται 15, 48 (Ziegl. Ahr. Fritz. Mein. Paley), δαλεῖτο 22, 127 (Mein. Paley, δηλ- Ziegl. Ahr. Fritz.), δαλήσατο 9, 36.

Δήλομαι Dor. *To wish*, Heracl. Inscr. 1, 98; Theocr. 5, 27; subj. -ωμαι Plut. Mor. 219 (Apoph.); -όμενος Tim. Locr. 94; Stob. (Hippod.) 43, 94; δήλεσθαι Stob. Fl. (Archyt.) 1, 70 (Mein.): **fut.** (δηλήσομαι?): **aor.** δηλήσασθαι v. r. Stob. (Archyt.) quoted.

Δηλόω *To shew*, Soph. Aj. 355; Ar. Eccl. 7; Her. 2, 5; Antiph. 1, 30; Thuc. 1, 3: **imp.** ἐδήλουν Her. 2, 4; Thuc. 4, 68: **fut.** δηλώσω Soph. El. 29; Ar. Eccl. 3; Pl. Crit. 108; Isae. 11, 11: **aor.** ἐδήλωσα Aesch. Pers. 519; Antiph. 1, 30; Thuc. 2, 50; Isocr. 15, 5: **p.** δεδήλωκα Her. 2, 106; Thuc. 1, 9; Isocr. 15, 10: **p. p.** δεδήλωται Her. 5, 36; Thuc. 5, 1; imper. δεδηλώσθω Her. 2, 33: **aor.** ἐδηλώθην Antiph. 5, 70; -ωθῇ Her. 1, 159: **fut. pass.** δηλωθήσομαι Ar. Ran. 1303; Thuc. 1, 144: **3 fut.** δεδηλώσομαι Hippocr. 4, 190 (Lit.): and **mid.** δηλώσομαι pass. Soph. O. C. 581; but **act.** late Or. Sib. 1, 294. **Vb.** δηλωτέον Pl. Tim. 48. Herwerden suspects **fut. pass.** δηλωθήσεται Thuc. 1, 144, and would substitute **fut. mid.** δηλώσεται. He had better ascertain if the constitution of the line in Aristoph. Ran. quoted will stand the cure.

Δημοκρατέομαι (κρατέω) as pass. *To have a democratical constitution*, Ar. Eccl. 945; Her. 6, 43; Thuc. 8, 48; Isocr. 20, 20: **imp.** ἐδημοκρατεῖσθε Isocr. 16, 37; (Dem.) 17, 10: with **fut. m.** -ήσομαι Thuc. 8, 48; Lys. 34, 4; Dem. 24, 99; and Thuc. 8, 75 (Ms. G. Popp. Krüg. Stahl), but **fut. pass.** -ηθήσομαι (best Mss. A. B. E. F. &c. Bekk.): **p.** late δεδημοκρατημένη Dio Cass. 52, 13. Active form only by the Byzantine writers.

Δηόω, see δηιόω.

Δηριάω (ῐᾰ) Poet. *To contend*, part. δηριῶν Pind. N. 11, 26, -όων Ap. Rh. 1, 752; Opp. Cyn. 2, 247: **imp. iter.** δηριάασκες Q. Sm. 5, 443; Opp. Cyn. 1, 230. **Mid. Dep.** δηριάομαι, dual, -άασθον Il. 12, 421; imper. -αάσθων 21, 647; Ap. Rh. 2, 89, -όωνται 4, 1729; Opp. Hal. 2, 555. 4, 375; ἀμφι-δηριώμενος Simon. (Am.) 7, 118; -άασθαι Il. 16, 96: **imp.** δηριόωντο Od. 8, 78; Q. Sm. 4, 255. For **fut.** and **aor.** see foll.

(Δηρίω) Epic, *To contend*, **act.** late, **fut.** δηρίσω Lycophr. 1306:

aor. ἐδήρῑσα Theocr. 25, 82, δήρισ- Orph. Arg. 420; δηρίσω 410. **Mid.** δηρῑ́ομαι as act. Pind. Ol. 13, 44: fut. δηρῑ́σομαι Theocr. 22, 70: aor. δηρισάμην Od. 8, 76; Opp. Hal. 2, 627: and aor. pass. δηρίνθην as mid. Il. 16, 756; δηρινθῆναι Orph. L. 670; Ap. Rh. 2, 16, comp. ἰδρύω, ἰδρύνθην. **Vb.** ἀδήρῑτος Il. 17, 42, ἀμφι-δήρ- Thuc. 4, 134.

Δήω Epic, only **pres.** with **fut.** meaning, *I shall find*, δήεις Il. 13, 260; Anth. 7, 370; Orph. L. 607; Dion. Per. 483, δήομεν Od. 4, 544. 16, 44, δήετε Il. 9, 685, δήουσι Ap. Rh. 4, 591; subj. δήωμεν 4, 1336 (Vulg. Merk.); opt. δήοιμεν 4, 1460, which Wellauer reads at 4, 1336 also: **imp.** ἔδηεν Hesych.

Δηῶ, see δηιόω.

Διαιτάω *To arbitrate*, &c. Pind. Ol. 9, 66; Hippocr. 7, 30. 8, 236 (Lit.); Dem. 47, 12; Theocr. 12, 34: **imp.** διῄτων Dio. Hal. 2, 75; Galen 6, 332. 10, 678, but in comp. κατ-εδιῄτα (Dem.) 49, 19: **fut.** διαιτήσω Isae. 2, 30; Dem. 29, 58, κατα- 33, 16: **aor.** διῄτησα Isae. 2, 31; Plut. Pomp. 12; App. Civ. 5, 20; Strab. 2, 3, 8, but in comp. ἀπ-εδιῄτ- Isae. 12, 12; Dem. 40, 17. 30, 31, κατ-εδιῄτ- Isae. 12, 11; Dem. 21, 84. 96. 27, 51. 40, 17, μετ-εδιῄτ- Luc. D. Mort. 12, 3, late ἐδιαίτησα, ἀπ- Argum. Dem. 40, κατ- ibid., Dor. διαίτᾱσα Pind. P. 9, 68: **p.** δεδιῄτηκα Dem. 33, 31: **plp.** κατ-εδεδιῃτήκει 21, 85 (D.), κατα-δεδ- (Bekk.): **p. p.** (δεδιῄτημαι Thuc. 7, 77, see mid.), ἀπο- Dem. 21, 85. 96, κατα- 55, 31: **plp.** ἐδεδιῄτητο ἐξ- Thuc. 1, 132; Galen 6, 686. **Mid.** διαιτάομαι *to pass life*, Her. 1, 120. 5, 16, -έομαι Hippocr. 1, 574. 580 (Lit. Erm.); -ᾶσθαι Soph. O. C. 928; Andoc. 2, 10; Thuc. 2, 14; -ώμενος Thuc. 1, 6; Pl. Gorg. 449: **imp.** διῃτώμην Com. Fr. (Plat.) 2, 669; Lys. 1, 9. 32, 8; Isocr. 18, 49. 21, 2; Isae. 6, 21. 8, 9. 9, 27; Pl. Phaed. 61; Plut. Dion. 51; Dio Cass. 58, 1, Ion. διαιτώμην Her. 3, 65, -ᾶτο 3, 15. 4, 95. 121; Hippocr. 6, 514, διῃτέοντο (Luc.) D. Syr. 26 (Dind. διαιτ- Bekk. Jacob.): **fut.** διαιτήσομαι Hippocr. 6, 604; Lys. 16, 4; Pl. Rep. 372: **aor.** (in a different sense) κατ-εδιῃτησάμην (Dem.) 55, 2. 6. 34; sec 40, 18; Lys. 25, 16: with **p. p.** δεδιῄτημαι as mid. Thuc. 7, 77, κατα- Dem. 55, 31: and **aor.** διῃτήθην Thuc. 7, 87; Isae. 6, 15, but ἐξ-εδιῃτήθην Dio Cass. 48, 39 (Bekk.), Ion. διαιτήθην as mid. Her. 2, 112. **Vb.** διαιτητέον Hippocr. 1, 649 (K.) ἐδιαίτων, ἐδιαίτησα, ἀπ- Argum. (Dem.) 40, κατ- ibid., ἐδιαιτέοντο for διῄτων, διῄτησα &c., though given by Grammarians and Editors, are scarcely found in Mss. ἐξ-εδεδιαίτητο (Thuc. 1, 132 Ms. E). See Antiatt. 91, 18.

This verb seems never to be augmented in Her. In classic Attic, διαιτάω, in the *simple* form, has double augm. in the **perf.** and **plp.** only, δεδιῄτηκα, ἐδεδιῃτήκει, but late διῃτημένος Herodn.

6, 9, 5 (Bekk.); Galen 6, 249; Oribas. 2, 41; διῃτῆσθαι Galen 5, 32; even in Lys. Cobet edits ἐδιῃτώμην! 1, 9. 32, 8, for διῃτ- (Mss. edit.); in *comp. all* the augmented tenses have double augm. **imp.** κατ-εδιῄτα: **aor.** ἀπ-εδιῄτησα, κατ-, μετ-: ἐξεδιῃτήθην: but late συν-διῃτᾶτο Plut. Dion. 17; Themist. 32, 385; Aesop 346 (Halm); sometimes, also the classic rule is observed, διῄτησε 4 Macc. 2, 17, but ἐξ-εδιῄτησε 4, 19. The **mid.** does not follow a different law from the **act.**

Διακονέω (ᾱ) *To minister*, Ar. Av. 1323; Com. Fr. (Anax.) 3, 198; -ῶν Eur. Ion 396; Pl. Leg. 955; -εῖν Rep. 466 (Ion. διηκον-, see **fut.**): **imp.** ἐδιᾱκόνουν Com. Fr. (Alcae.) 2, 828; Eur. Cycl. 406 (Herm. Dind. Nauck, Kirchh. 2 ed.), διηκόνουν Eur. quoted (Mss. Vulg. Kirchh. 1 ed.); and later, see Luc. Philops. 35; Himer. Or. 14, 30; N. T. Matth. 4, 11: **fut.** διᾱκονήσω Com. Fr. (Cratet.) 2, 237; Pl. Gorg. 521, Ion. διηκ- Her. 4, 154: **aor.** indic. late διηκόνησα Aristid. 46, 198; but **inf.** διακονῆσαι Antiph. 1, 16: **p.** δεδιηκόνηκα Com. Fr. (Arched.) 4, 437, v. r. δεδιακ-: **p. p.** δεδιᾱκόνημαι Dem. 51, 7 (Bekk. Dind.): **aor.** ἐδιᾱκονήθην Dem. 50, 2: **3 fut.** δεδιακονήσεται Joseph. Ant. 18, 8, 7. **Mid.** διακονοῦμαι as act. Soph. Ph. 287; Ar. Ach. 1017; Pl. Leg. 763; Luc. D. Deor. 5, 2: **imp.** διηκονεῖτο Luc. Philops. 35; Dio Chrys. Or. 7 (112): **fut.** -ήσομαι Luc. Char. 1. D. Deor. 4, 4; Themist. 9, 124; Aristid. 45, 46; Ach. Tat. 2, 31: **aor.** διηκονησάμην Luc. Tyr. 22. Icar. 20; Stob. (Nicostr.) 74, 65. δεδιηκόνηκεν Arched. Com. Fr. quoted, is Valckenaer's emendation for δὲ διηκ-, but Ms. P. gives δεδιακόνηκεν the more Attic form. In this verb the Attics preferred the *initial* augment, and α unchanged; and on this ground Hermann altered διηκόνουν Eur. Cycl. quoted, to ἐδιᾱκ- which all but Kirchhoff, we think, have adopted. In 2 edit. however, he too now adopts it (1868).

Διαλέγω *To pick out, separate*, Ar. Lys. 720; Xen. Oec. 8, 9: **fut.** διαλέξω Dem. 20, 91: **aor.** διέλεξα Pl. Leg. 735. διαλέγομαι Dep. **mid.** and **pass.** *to discuss*, Archil. 80; Ar. Eccl. 930; Her. 1, 142; Pl. Apol. 33; Isae. 9, 20: **imp.** διελεγ- Her. 9, 112; Antiph. 6, 39; Thuc. 8, 93; Lys. 3, 31; Aeschin. 2, 125; Com. Fr. (Eub.) 3, 234: **fut.** διαλέξομαι Isocr. 12, 5. 112. 253; Isae. 7, 3; Aeschin. 2, 18: **aor.** διελεξάμην Epic, *pondered*, Il. 11, 407. 17, 97. 21, 562. 22, 385; Ar. Fr. 321 (D.); and late prose, *discussed*, Dio Cass. 38, 18. 56, 1; Aristid. 13, 144 (D.); Philostr. Ap. 156: **p.** διείλεγμαι Lys. 8, 15; Isocr. 5, 81; Pl. Theaet. 158; **pass.** Aristot. Topic. 8, 11, 1: **plp.** διείλεκτο Dem. 21, 119; but seemingly **pass.** Lys. 9, 5: **aor.** διελέχθην as **mid.** Her. 3, 51; Xen. Mem. 1, 6, 1; Isocr. 19, 37; Isae. 9, 20;

Pl. Parm. 126. Theaet. 142; Dem. 18, 252; -λεχθῶ Isocr. 3, 8; -λεχθείην Ar. Nub. 425. Plut. 1082; Hippocr. 5 446; Pl. Apol. 39; -θῆναι Xen. Cyr. 7, 5, 40; Isocr. 5, 14; -θείς 12, 38; Xen. Mem. 4, 4, 5: and fut. διαλεχθήσομαι Isocr. 9, 34; Dem. 18, 252; Plut. Mor. 236. 1082: 2 aor. rare διαλεγῆναι Aristot. Eth. M. 1, 29. Top. 7, 5, 2. 8, 3, 6 (Bekk.); Scym. Ch. Perieg. 7 (Mein.) Vb. διαλεκτέος Isocr. 12, 134; Pl. Lys. 211. This verb seems not to occur in Trag.: προδιαλέγομαι is Dep. pass. -λεχθείς Isocr. 12, 6; -χθῆναι 199.

Διαλύομαι, see λύω.

Διανοοῦμαι, see νοέω.

Διαπεραιόω *To take across*, unclassic in act. Plut. Sull. 27. διαπεραιοῦμαι *be conveyed across, pass through, over*, Thuc. 8, 32: has aor. pass. -επεραιώθην Soph. Aj. 730; Her. 2, 124. 5, 23; Luc. Phal. 2, 4; Plut. Demetr. 33: plp. διεπεπεραίωντο Thuc. 3, 23: and later aor. mid. -περαιώσασθαι (Pl.) Ax. 370.

Διαπονέω, with aor. mid. and pass. see πονέω.

Διασπουδάζω, see σπουδάζω.

Διατῑνάσσω *To shake in pieces*, pres. late, Alciphr. 2, 4 (but *simple* τινάσσω Il. 12, 298; Aesch. Pr. 917; Soph. Tr. 512; Ar. Ran. 328. 340): aor. ἐτίναξα Il. 20, 57; Sapph. 42, ἐξ- Hippocr. 5, 288, συν- Aristot. Mund. 4, 39, δι- Eur. I. T. 282; subj. in tmesi διὰ τινάξῃ Od. 5, 363; -τινάξαι Stob. 85, 21: p. p. late διατετινάχθαι Aesop 305 (Halm, but *simple* τετίνακται Hippocr. 6, 112 Ms. A. Lit.: and Epic aor. ἐτίναχθεν, for -θησαν, Il. 16, 348); -χθείς Plut. Cimon 16: fut. m. διατινάξεται reflex or pass. Eur. Bacc. 588, unnoticed by our Lexicogr.

Διαχλῐδάω (χλιδάω, χλίω), *To walk or live delicately, luxuriate*, only perf. -κεχλῐδώς Com. Fr. (Archipp.) 2, 728.

Διδάσκω *To teach*, Od. 1, 384; Aesch. Supp. 1061; Soph. El. 396; Ar. Av. 550; Her. 9, 31; Antiph. 5, 14. 6, 2; Lys. 14, 22; Pl. Conv. 185; imper. διδάσκετε Thuc. 4, 118; inf. -κειν Pl. Rep. 338, Epic -ασκέμεναι Il. 9, 442, -ασκέμεν 23, 308: imp. ἐδιδ- Simon. C. 148, 6; Her. 6, 138; Antiph. 6, 11; Thuc. 4, 83: fut. διδάξω Aesch. Supp. 519; Eur. Bacch. 287; Her. 7, 16; Antiph. 2, β, 9; Thuc. 5, 9; Lys. 9, 3: aor. ἐδίδαξα Il. 23, 307; Eur. Fr. 79 (D.); Ar. Nub. 382; Her. 3, 48; Antiph. 6, 49; Xen. An. 3, 4, 32; Isocr. 4, 47, δίδαξ- Il. 5, 51; Pind. N. 3, 55; -δάξω Pl. Euth. 297; -δάξαιμι Prot. 318; δίδαξον Aesch. Eum. 431; Pl. Euth. 6; -δάξας Thuc. 2, 93; Poet. (ἐδιδάσκησα), opt. διδασκήσαιμι Hom. H. Cer. 144; inf. διδασκῆσαι Hes. Op. 64, ἐκ-διδάσκησε Pind. P. 4, 217: p. δεδίδαχα Xen. Cyr. 1, 3, 18; Pl. Meno 85: p. p. δεδίδαγμαι Il. 11, 831; Her. 2, 69; Lycurg. 13; Pl. Phaedr. 269; imper. δεδιδάχθω Xen. Eq. 6, 9: aor. ἐδιδάχθην

Ar. Nub. 637; Her. 3, 81; Xen. Hell. 5, 4, 44; Dem. 20, 166; διδαχθῇς Theogn. 565, -χθῇ Aesch. Pr. 10; Ar. Thesm. 538; -δαχθῆναι Soph. El. 330; Antiph. 4, β, 8; -χθείς Solon 13, 51; Aesch. Eum. 276; Thuc. 8, 75: fut. late, διδαχθήσομαι Dio. Hal. 3, 70; Sext. Emp. 182, 6, ἀνα- Pseud.-Callisth. 2, 43: as pass. fut. mid. διδάξομαι Soph. Ant. 726; Ar. Nub. 127 &c. Others as mid. *learn.* **Mid.** διδάσκομαι *to educate, learn,* Pl. Prot. 325: fut. διδάξομαι Soph. Ant. 726; Eur. Andr. 739; Ar. Nub. 127; Pl. Rep. 421, Poet. 2 sing. -άξεαι quoted by Xen. Conv. 2, 4. Mem. 1, 2, 20, from Theogn. 35, where stands μαθήσεαι: aor. ἐδιδαξάμην Soph. Ant. 356; Ar. Nub. 783; Pl. Meno 93; Xen. Cyr. 1, 6, 2, Poet. 2 sing. διδάξαο Mosch. 3, 97; -ξάμενος Simon. C. 145; inf. διδάξασθαι Pind. Ol. 8, 59; Xen. Mem. 4, 4, 5. **Vb.** διδακτός Xen. Mem. 3, 9, 1, -τέος Pl. Euthyd. 273.

Δίδημι *To bind,* rare in prose, 3 pl. διδέασι Xen. An. 5, 8, 24; imper. διδέντων Od. 12, 54 (Bekk.): imp. 3 sing. δίδη for ἐδί- Il. 11, 105.

Διδόω *To give,* 2 sing. διδοῖς (-ως Bekk.) Il. 9, 164; Her, 8, 137, διδοῖσθα (-ῶσθα Bekk.) Il. 19, 270, διδοῖ Od. 17, 350; Mimnerm. 2, 16; Simon. Am. 7, 54 (δίδοι Bergk); Pind. I. 4, 33; Aesch. Supp. 1010; Her. 2, 48. 3, 119, ἐκ- 2, 29, 3 pl. διδοῦσι Il. 19, 265, and *always;* Theogn. 446. 591; Her. 2, 30. 89, and generally; Dio Cass. 65, 13: imperat. δίδου (δίδοε) Od. 3, 58; Eur. Or. 642; Her. 3, 140; Xen. Hell. 3, 4, 26, and δίδοι Pind. Ol. 7, 89. N. 5, 50; inf. διδοῦν Theogn. 1329, διδοῦναι only Il. 24, 425: imp. ἐδίδουν Ar. Eq. 678; Her. 6, 86; Andoc. 1, 101; Dem. 50, 10. 55, 27, παρ- Isocr. 17, 38, ἀπ- Dem. 33, 25, ἐδίδους Od. 19, 367 (-δως Bekk.); Xen. An. 5, 8, 4 (2 Mss. Born. Krüg. Dind.), ἀπ- Dem. 34, 26. 31, ἐδίδου Od. 11, 289 (Vulg. Dind. La Roche, -ίδω Bekk.); Hes. Th. 563; Theogn. 916; Pind. P. 9, 117; Her. 1, 208. 3, 128; Thuc. 8, 29; Xen. Cyr. 8, 2, 17; Isocr. 4, 94; Isae. 11, 2; Aeschin. 1, 102; Dem. 19, 166. 335. 50, 23, δίδου Il. 5, 165. 6, 192. 219 (Vulg. Dind. La Roche, δίδω Bekk.), 3 pl. ἐδίδουν Hes. Op. 139; Hippocr. 8, 446 (Lit.), ἀπ- 5, 126; D. Hal. 5, 6: fut. διδώσω Od. 13, 358. 24, 314. See δίδωμι. δίδοι 2 sing. imperat., though in Pind., Ahrens thinks not Doric (Dor. Dial. 314.) Bekker, in his last edition of Hom. (1859), writes the imp. always with long vowel, ἐδίδων, δίδω.

(Διδράσκω) *To run off,* only in comp. ἀπο-διδράσκω (Ion. -ήσκω) Ar. Lys. 719; Xen. Cyr. 1, 6, 40; Pl. Men. 97, δια- Thuc. 7, 85, ἐκ- Thuc. 6, 7, late, if at all, ἀποδράω (see Phrynichus p. 737): imp. ἀπ-εδίδρασκες Pl. Crit. 53, ἀπ-έδρων Apocr. Jud. 11, 16: fut. δράσομαι, ἀπο- Pl. Rep. 457; Dem. 9, 74 (act. late ἀποδράσει

Theod. Graec. Aff. p. 103, 8, Gaisf. συναποδράσοντας Zonaras Annal. vol. 2, p. 12), Ion. δρήσομαι, ἀπο-, &c. see below: **1 aor.** (ἔδρᾱσα), ἀπ- in classic authors occurs now only as a v. r. ἐξ-έδρασ' formerly Eur. I. T. 193, now ἐξ ἕδρας; ἀπο-δράσῃ Xen. Cyr. 1, 4, 13, now ἀποδρᾷ; but late ἀπ-έδρασεν Ael. V. H. 13, 27, -έδρα (Herch.); subj. ἀπο-δράσῃ Theophr. Char. 18 (Foss); opt. δια-δράσειε Heliod. 7, 24; ἀπο-δράσας Plut. Mor. 873; Joseph. Ant. 3, 2, 1 (Bekk.): **p.** δέδρᾱκα, δια- Ar. Ach. 601, ἀπο- Pl. Theaet. 203; Xen. Cyr. 4, 1, 10. An. 1, 4, 8: **plp.** ἀπο-δεδράκει 6, 4, 13 (Vulg. Krüg. Saupp.), ἀπ-εδεδρ- (L. Dind. Hug.): **2 aor.** ἔδρᾱν, ἀπ- Com. Fr. (Pher.) 2, 279; Ar. Fr. 431 (Dind.), ἀπ-έδρα Com. Fr. (Cratin.) 2, 62; Xen. An. 6, 6, 5; Pl. Prot. 310, ἀπ-έδρᾱμεν Ar. Fr. 431 (Dind.), ἐξ- Eur. Heracl. 14, ἀπ-έδρᾱσαν Thuc. 1, 128; Xen. Cyr. 5, 2, 36, syncop. ἀπ-έδρᾰν Soph. Aj. 167; Luc. Tox. 33 (Dind.), Ion. ἔδρην, ἀπ- Her. 4, 43; subj. -δρῶ Ar. Pax 234; Xen. Cyr. 1, 4, 13, -δρᾷ Thuc. 7, 86; Xen. Cyr. 1, 4, 13; Pl. Hipp. Maj. 295, -δρῶσι Xen. Cyr. 5, 1, 12; (Dem.) Epist. 3, 1478; opt. -δραίην, ἀπο- Theogn. 927; Xen. An. 2, 5, 7, -δρῴην Aristot. Oec. 2, 35 (Bekk.), -δραίημεν Xen. An. 6, 3, 16; imper. late -δρᾶθι V. T. Gen. 27, 43; δρᾶναι, (Hesych.), ἀπο- Thuc. 4, 46; Pl. Prot. 317; Isocr. 12, 93, ξυναπο- Ar. Ran. 81; -δράς Od. 17, 516; Ar. Eccl. 196. Av. 726; Andoc. 1, 125. 4, 17; Xen. An. 6, 3, 26; Lys. 6, 27, δια- Isocr. 18, 49; Her. 8, 75. 9, 58, all in comp. Ion. διδρήσκω also comp. ἀπο- Her. 9, 59, ἐκ- 3, 4. 9, 88: **imp.** -εδίδρησκον 2, 182: **fut.** δρήσομαι, ἀπο- 7, 210, δια- 8, 60: **p.** δέδρηκα, ἀπο- Hippocr. 8, 282 (Lit.): **2 aor.** ἔδρην, ἀπ- Her. 4, 43. 6, 2. 9, 37; inf. -δρῆναι 3, 45; but part. always δράς, ἀπο- 3, 148. 9, 118, δια- 8, 75, ἐκ- 4, 148. **Vb.** ἀ-δρηστος Her. 4, 142.

This verb seems to occur only twice in Trag. and only in **2 aor.** Soph. and Eur. quoted. We have never seen διδράσκω uncomp. except part. διδράσκων in Hesych. Of the pure **pres.** form διδράω, ἀπο- &c. we know no instance: συν-αποδρᾶν Herodn. 1, 10 (Vulg.) is now -δρᾶναι (Bekk.) The **1 aor.** does not *now* occur in classic Greek: ἀποδράσασα Andoc. 1, 125 (Vulg.), ἀποδρᾶσα (Bekk.), ἀποδράσας Lys. 6, 28 (old edit.) was altered by Reiske to ἀποδράς, which has been adopted by Bekker and every subsequent editor, ἀποδράσῃ Xen. Cyr. 1, 4, 13 (Vulg.), now ἀποδρᾷ (best Mss. Schneid. Popp. Dind.), ἐξέδρασ' Eur. I. T. 194 (Mss. Vulg. Musgr. Seidler), now ἐξ ἕδρας in every edit. &c. In recent editions of even late auth. the **2 aor.** has often been restored, ἀποδρώσωσι Dio Cass. 43, 38 (Vulg.), ἐκδρῶσι (Bekk. L. Dind.); ἐξέδρασεν 78, 34 (Vulg.), ἐξέδρα (Bekk.), ἀποδράσῃ Theophr. Char. 18 (Foss), ἀποδρᾷ (Dind.), ἀποδράσασα

Plut. Mor. 767 (Vulg.), ἀποδρᾶσα (Ms. E. Winck. Dübn.) &c. see above. **Mid. aor.** ἀποδράσασθαι, if correct, Philon. vol. 1, p. 551, 31, which should perhaps be altered to fut. -άσεσθαι Galen 9, 272, as διαδράσασθαι has been to -άσεσθαι Dio Cass. 43, 40. We have not seen the 3 pl. syncop. form ἀπ-έδρᾶν in *classic* prose.

Δίδωμι *To give*, Il. 23, 620; Aesch. Pr. 780; Eur. Ion 1286; Ar. Pax 424; Her. 3, 140; Lys. 4, 5; Pl. Charm. 163, δίδως Soph. Aj. 1354; Eur. Supp. 409; Ar. Pax 1262; Pl. Phaed. 100, δίδωσι Il. 20, 299; Archil. 16; Pind. P. 5, 65; Soph. O. C. 446; Ar. Plut. 278; Antiph. 1, 19; Thuc. 2, 101; Isae. 11, 2, δίδομεν Il. 2, 228; Ar. Eq. 69; Isae. 2, 5, δίδοτε Andoc. 2, 23; Xen. Cyr. 4, 6, 13 (5, 1, 1 Dind. Saupp.), διδόασι Ar. Vesp. 715; Antiph. 5, 34; Thuc. 1, 42; Isocr. 8, 135, διδοῦσι scarcely Attic, Com. Fr. (Antiph.) 3, 85?; subj. διδῶ, ἐπι- Xen. Cyr. 1, 4, 12, διδῷς Eur. Hel. 1257; Ar. Ach. 799; Pl. Prot. 310, διδῷ Theogn. 186; Eur. Or. 667; Ar. Av. 519; Pl. Leg. 691, διδῶσι Theogn. 45; Soph. Fr. 748; Antiph. 1, 23; opt. διδοίην Lys. 7, 6, -οίης Soph. O. C. 642, μετα- Theogn. 925, διδοίη Soph. O. C. 777; Her. 1, 86; Isae. 9, 24; Lys. 12, 14; Xen. Vect. 2, 6, -δῴη Plut. Lysandr. 9, -οίητε Plut. Alex. 302, -οῖτε Od. 11, 359, -οῖεν Aesch. Supp. 703; Andoc. 1, 90; Xen. An. 3, 2, 7; imper. δίδου see διδόω, δίδοθι occurs not, Epic δίδωθι Od. 3, 380, διδότω Pl. Leg. 916, δίδοτε Xen. Cyr. 4, 5, 47, διδόντων, ἀπο- Pl. Leg. 829, διδούς Il. 9, 699; Andoc. 2, 23; inf. διδόναι Her. 6, 62; Antiph. 6, 38; Thuc. 2, 97, Poet. διδόμεν Pind. N. 7, 97. I. 8, 60: **imp.** (ἐδίδων), ἐδίδως Od. 19, 367 (Bekk. Dind. -ους Ameis, La Roche); Xen. An. 5, 8, 4 (Vulg.), but ἐδίδους (Ms. A B. Born. Krüg. Saupp. and Dind. *now*), ἐδίδω Od. 11, 289 (Bekk. 2 ed. -δου Vulg. Dind. La Roche), δίδω Il. 5, 165. 6, 192. 219 (Bekk. -δου Dind. La Roche), 2 pl. ἐδίδοτε Com. Fr. (Sophil.) 3, 581, 3 pl. ἐδίδοσαν Her. 8, 9; Thuc. 7, 87; Pl. Critias 119, δίδοσαν Od. 17, 367, Epic ἔδιδον H. Cer. 437, δίδον 327, 3 pl. ἐδίδουν not Attic, see διδόω: **fut.** δώσω Il. 14, 268; Hes. Op. 57; Pind. P. 12, 32; Aesch. Supp. 733; Soph. Ant. 315; Eur. I. T. 744; Her. 8, 5; Antiph. 6, 36; Thuc. 7, 36; Lys. 10, 3; Pl. Phaedr. 236, Dor. δωσῶ Theocr. 5, 96; inf. δώσειν Simon. C. 173, Epic δωσέμεναι Il. 13, 369, δωσέμεν 10, 323. 22, 117 (Spitzn. Dind. La R. -ειν Bekk.), Epic διδώσω Od. 13, 358; inf. διδώσειν 24, 314: **1 aor.** ἔδωκα indic. only classic, Od. 9, 361; Solon 5; Soph. Ant. 902; Her. 1, 124; Antiph. 6, 15. 17; Pl. Rep. 612; Lys. 4, 13. 16, 14; Isae. 2, 42; Dem. 18, 179. 197. 22, 8, ἐξ- Lys. 16, 10, δῶκα Il. 4, 43, ἔδωκας Il. 21, 473; Hipponax 19 (B.); Soph. Tr.

201; Ar. Pax 963; Her. 3, 140; Xen. Cyr. 1, 3, 7; Dem. 32, 16, δῶκας Od. 4, 647, ἔδωκε Il. 11, 243; Hes. Th. 914; Pind. P. 2, 89; Aesch. Eum. 850; Eur. Cycl. 141; Ar. Eq. 1220; Her. 3, 160; Antiph. 6, 17; Thuc. 1, 58; Pl. Leg. 679, Poet. δῶκε Il. 5, 2; Hes. Op. 705; Pind. Ol. 1, 63, and 'δωκε Soph. Aj. 1303, ἐδώκαμεν Eur. Cycl. 296; Xen. An. 3, 2, 5. Hell. 6, 3, 6; Dem. 20, 139, προυδώκ- Eur. Heracl. 463, παρ- Her. 5, 91; Xen. Oec. 9, 9. 19, ἀπ- Com. Fr. (Alex.) 3, 479; Isae. 5, 28; (Dem.) 13, 3, ἐπ- Dem. 34, 38. 39, μετ- 23, 65, ἐδώκατε Com. Fr. (Alex.) 3, 479; Antiph. 5, 77; Dem. 20, 84. 85. 86. 97. 120. 21, 56. 57, 6, ἀπ- 21, 11, παρ- Xen. An. 7, 7, 10; Dem. 28, 8. 51, 8, προ- 23, 112, ἔδωκαν Il. 13, 303. 22, 379; Hes. Op. 92; Simon. (Am.) 7, 22; Theogn. 1057; Pind. N. 11, 39; Com. Fr. (Antiph.) 3, 88. (Anon.) 4, 670; Her. 1, 89; Xen. Mem. 1, 1, 9; Dem. 19, 190. 20, 70. 23, 200 (13, 23); Hyperid. 4, 14, 3, ἀπ- Lys. 19, 7, ἐξ- Eur. Heracl. 319, παρ- Med. 629; Ar. Nub. 969; Xen. Hell. 4, 4, 15; Isocr. 12, 106; Dem. 19, 94. 36, 14. 51, 8, προ- 20, 53, δῶκαν Hes. Op. 741; Pind. P. 4, 115; subj. late, if correct, ἀπο-δώκωσι Aesop 78 (Tauchn.): p. δέδωκα Pind. N. 2, 8; Aesch. Pr. 446; Soph. Ph. 664; Ar. Eq. 841; Her. 6, 56; Antiph. 6, 12; Lys. 10, 14; Xen. Cyr. 1, 4, 26; Isae. 8, 41; opt. δεδώκοιεν, παρα- Thuc. 7, 83: plp. ἐδεδώκει Xen. Cyr. 1, 4, 26; Isae. 3, 10; Dem. 3, 14. 37, 12, -κεε Her. 8, 67: p.p. δέδομαι Il. 5, 428; Aesch. Supp. 1041; Eur. Supp. 757; Her. 6, 57; Xen. Lac. 11, 6; Pl. Lys. 204; δεδόσθω Pl. Tim. 52; δεδόσθαι Her. 2, 141; -ομένος Thuc. 1, 26; Isocr. 5, 15: plp. ἐδέδοτο Thuc. 3, 109: aor. ἐδόθην Com. Fr. (Alex.) 3, 502; Her. 8, 136; Thuc. 3, 60; Pl. Leg. 829; subj. δοθῇς Com. Fr. (Theop.) 2, 804, δοθῇ (Dem.) 12, 14; opt. δοθείη in tmesi Od. 2, 78; Isae. 11, 40; δοθῆναι Eur. Fr. 771 (D.); Her. 9, 81; Xen. An. 1, 1, 8; δοθείς Aesch. Eum. 393; Eur. An. 15; Com. Fr. (Mon.) 752; Thuc. 5, 111: fut. δοθήσομαι Soph. Ph. 774; Eur. Phoen. 1650; Isae. 3, 39; (Dem.) 44, 63. 64. 59, 76, ἐκ- Isocr. 17, 9: 2 aor. act. (ἔδων) not in *indic.* sing. ἔδομεν Ar. Vesp. 586; Isocr. 17, 19, δόμεν Il. 17, 443, ἔδοτε Andoc. 2, 22; Lys. 19, 21; Aeschin. 3, 187, ἔδοσαν Od. 20, 78; Hes. Th. 141; Theogn. 272; Pind. N. 6, 10; Aesch. Ag. 1335; Ar. Vesp. 717; Her. 6, 108; Thuc. 4, 56; Lys. 12, 18; Pl. Conv. 220, δόσαν Od. 7, 242; Theogn. 463, Epic ἔδον Hes. Th. 30; and Dor. (Lacon. Inscr. 1511); subj. δῶ Od. 20, 296; Ar. Eq. 706. Pax 851; Andoc. 1, 113; Xen. Cyr. 8, 4, 16, δῷς Il. 7, 27; Ar. Eq. 710. Av. 978; Xen. Cyr. 4, 6, 14; Dem. 22, 7, δῷ Hes. Op. 354; Ar. Vesp. 583. Ran. 606; Antiph. 1, 24; Xen. Eq. 10, 16, δῶμεν Il. 23, 537. Od. 8, 389; Eur. Supp. 1231;

Ar. Pax 730. Thesm. 801; Pl. Leg. 702, δῶτε Xen. An. 7, 3, 17, δῶσι Il. 3, 66; Eur. Tr. 1267; Her. 6, 133, see below; opt. δοίην Od. 15, 449; Soph. O. R. 1161; Ar. Pax 1217; Her. 9, 111; Lys. 24, 1, δοίης Il. 16, 625. Od. 17, 455; Aesch. Sept. 260; Ar. Nub. 108; Xen. Cyr. 3, 1, 35, δοίη Il. 17, 127; Aesch. Ch. 889; Soph. O. C. 869; Ar. Ach. 966; Antiph. 1, 19; Pl. Conv. 196, δοίημεν Xen. Cyr. 5, 3, 2; Pl. Men. 96 (Vulg.); (Dem.) 10, 71, δοῖμεν Il. 13, 378; Pl. Rep. 607, δοίητε Her. 7, 135; Xen. Cyr. 4, 5, 47; Pl. Phaedr. 279, ἀπο- Isae. 7, 41, δοῖτε, ἀπο- Od. 22, 61; Pl. Tim. 20, δοίησαν Com. Fr. (Damox.) 4, 532, παρα- Xen. An. 2, 1, 10 (Mss. Krüg. Kühner, &c.), δοῖεν Il. 23, 650; Aesch. Sept. 418; Com. Fr. (Antiph.) 3, 89; Xen. An. 4, 8, 7, παρα- 2, 1, 10 (Mss. Popp. Saupp. Dind. *now*); δός Il. 5, 118; Hes. Op. 453; Aesch. Ch. 140; Soph. Aj. 483; Ar. Nub. 81; Xen. Cyr. 5, 1, 29, δότω Il. 18, 301; Eur. I. T. 735; Ar. Vesp. 935; Her. 1, 155; Pl. Leg. 929, δότε Il. 6, 476; Hes. Th. 104; Soph. O. C. 102; Pl. Lach. 187, δότωσαν Xen. Hier. 8, 4, δόντων Pl. Leg. 753; δοῦναι Il. 23, 593; Hes. Fr. 172; Pind. P. 4, 35; Soph. Ant. 303; Ar. Av. 347; Her. 6, 87; Antiph. 1, 12; Thuc. 5, 59, Poet. δόμεναι Il. 19, 138, δόμεν 9, 571; Hes. Op. 354; Theogn. 919; Pind. N. 8, 20; Ar. Av. 930 (Lyr.). 973 (hexam.); δούς Od. 15, 369; Aesch. Pr. 826; Soph. O. C. 855; Ar. Vesp. 52; Her. 3, 140; Thuc. 5, 45. **Mid.** δίδομαι in *simple* we have not seen except in tmesi, and not often in comp. except with ἀπό, ἐκ, περί, pres. ἐκ- δίδονται Her. 2, 47 (-δόαται Bekk.): **fut.** περι-δώσομαι Od. 23, 78, ἐκ- Hippocr. 7, 528 (Lit.), ἐπι- Hym. Merc. 383, περι- Il. 10, 463 (Bekk. Dind. -βώσομαι Wolf, Spitz. La R.): **2 aor.** ἔδοντο in tmesi, ἀπ'-... Her. 2, 39, ἐξ-έδου Eur. Med. 309, -έδοτο Dem. 41, 26; ἐπι-δώμεθα Il. 22, 254, 1 p. dual περι-δώμεθον rare Il. 23, 485; περί-δου Ar. Ach. 772. Nub. 644; ἐκ-δόσθαι Pind. P. 4, 295; Pl. Leg. 740, περι- Ar. Eq. 791, see ἀποδίδωμι. **Vb.** δοτέος Her. 8, 111; Pl. Phil. 32. For Attic 3 pl. pres. διδόᾱσι Hom. has always διδοῦσι Il. 19, 265. Od. 17, 450 &c.; Her. almost always, 2, 30. 4, 80, ἀπο- 3, 15, ἐκ- 4, 49 &c., but ἐκ-διδόασι 1, 93 (Bekk. Dind. Dietsch, -διδοῦσι Bred. Krüg. Abicht, Stein); and late, διδοῦσι Dio Cass. 65, 13, ἐκ-διδοῦσιν Arr. An. 6, 5, 7, but παρα-διδόασι 5, 25, 6, 1 pers. pl. rare and late διδόαμεν Joseph. Ant. 11, 5; Galen 11, 349, παρα- 13, 374; δίδωθι imper. for (δίδοθι) Od. 3, 380, Aeol. δίδοι Pind. Ol. 1, 85. 6, 104 &c.; διδοῦναι Epic for διδόναι, or from διδόω, Il. 24, 425: iter. **2 aor.** δόσκον Il. 14, 382; subj. (δώω, δώῃς) δώῃ Il. 6, 527. 7, 81. 16, 725, for δῷ, also δώῃσι for δώῃ, Il. 1, 324. 12, 275, δώωσι for δῶσι,

Il. 1, 137. 9, 278; Hes. Th. 222; Ap. Rh. 1, 1293, and δῷσι for δῷ, Od. 2, 144, δώομεν for δῶμεν, Il. 7, 299; inf. δόμεναι Il. 1, 116, and δόμεν 18, 458; also Dor. Thuc. 5, 77, ἀπο- ibid. in a Doric treaty; Ar. Lys. 1163, δοῦν Phoen. Coloph. 1, 20 (Schneidw.), μετα- Theogn. 104, for -δοῦναι. Opt. 1 pl. δοῖμεν for δοίημεν, Il. 13, 378. Od. 16, 386, and Attic, 3 pl. δοῖεν for δοίησαν, Il. 1, 18. 24, 686, also Attic, see above, and almost always, but the full form δοίησαν occurs Com. Fr. 4, 532, παρα- Xen. An. 2, 1, 10 (Mss. Krüg. Kühn. -οῖεν L. Dind. Saupp.) In late critical editions the form δῴην δῴης, δῴη for δοίην &c. is scarcely to be met with: **pres.** διδῴη Plut. Pyrrh. 14. Lysand. 9 (Sint. -οίη Bekk.): **2 aor.** δῴην Her. 9, 111 (Mss. Gaisf. δοίην Ms. S. Bekk. Krüg. Dind.), δῴης Xen. Cyr. 3, 1, 35 (old edit., δοίης Popp. Dind. Saupp.), δῴη Hes. Op. 357 (some Mss. and edit., δοίη Mss. Goettl., δώῃ Schoem.); Dem. 28, 17 (Mss. Bekk 1 edit. -δοίη 2 edit.); Luc. Cyn. 17 (Jacob. Bekk., δοίη Dind.), ἐκ- Plut. Mar. 10 (Sint. &c. -δοίη Schaef. Bekk.), δῴητε, ἀπο- Themist. 23, 283. (Lys.) 6, 19; Aristot. Metaph. 1, 8, 21, are perhaps the only instances in which it has not been changed by all modern editors either to subj. or to the common opt. form δοίη, which should probably be read at Lysias 6, 19 also in conformity with παραδοίη in section 21, below. In Hippocr. however δῴη is still read 1, 313 (Erm. 2, 318, Lit. v. r. δοίη); and Schanz seems inclined to replace it from the best Mss. in some passages of Plato (Phaedo 63.) Dor. inf. **pres.** δίδων Theocr. 29, 9 (Ahr. Fritzsche, Ziegl. διδῶν Vulg. Mein. Wordsw.) A late form of **1 aor.** is ἔδωσα, subj. δώσῃς Anth. App. Epigr. 204, ἐπι- Aristaen. 1, 5; opt. δώσαιμι Schol. Aesch. Pr. 292: and **1 aor. m.** (usually denied) occurs late ἀπο-δωκαμένη Maneth. 5, 126. Ahrens refers the aoristic forms in κα to the *second*, not to the *first* aor. (Conjug. in μι, p. 14.) See διδόω.

Διείρω *To pass or draw through*, Xen. Cyr. 8, 3, 10; Aeschin. 3, 166: **fut.** (-ερῶ and -έρσω): **aor.** διεῖρα, -εῖραι Hippocr. 7, 52 (Lit.); -είρας Luc. Alex. 26; Ael. V. H. 4, 28, and διέρσα; subj. -έρσῃς Hippocr. 4, 108 (Lit.); -έρσας 4, 296; inf. διέρσαι 4, 108: **p.** διεῖρκα, -ότες Xen. Cyr. 8, 3, 10.

Δίεμαι, see (δίημι.)

Δίζημαι Epic and Ion. *To seek*, (retains η) Anacr. 4, 2; Her. 7, 103; Theocr. 16, 68, δίζηαι Od. 11, 100, -ηται Her. 2, 38, -ήμεθα Theogn. 183; Ap. Rh. 4, 396, -ησθε Her. 5, 92, -ηνται Aesch. Supp. 821 (chor.); Her. 6, 52; inf. δίζησθαι Phocyl. 10 (B.); Theogn. 180 (Ms. A. Bergk, Ziegl.); Her. 2, 147. 7, 16; -ήμενος Il. 17, 221; Simon. Am. 29; Phocyl. 8 (B.); Theocr. 7, 61; Her. 2, 66. 7, 142. 166: **imp.** ἐδιζήμην Her. 3, 41;

Athen. (Phoen. Col.) 12, 530; Luc. D. Syr. 22 (Dind.), διζ- Callim. Jup. 16: fut. διζήσομαι Od. 16, 239; Lycophr. 682: aor. ἐδιζησάμην Heraclit. 80 (Byw.); Ael. Fr. 317; Plotin. 5, 5 (Kirchh.) Hesych. has aor. act. ἐδίζησα.

Δίζω *To consider*, only pres. Her. 1, 65 (Orac.): and imp. δίζε Il. 16, 713. Mid. δίζομαι *to seek*, &c. Nonn. Paraph. 8, 151, -ζεαι Theocr. 25 (20), 37, -εται Opp. Hal. 1, 334. 5, 585; Nonn. Paraph. 4, 135, -όμεθα Orph. Arg. 940, -ονται Callim. Epigr. 17; subj. δίζῃ 11, 1; -εο Anth. 11, 376; Nonn. 16, 154; -εσθαι Hes. Op. 603; Callim. Epigr. 11; -όμενος Orph. Arg. 1217; Opp. Hal. 1, 790: imp. ἐδίζετο Musae. 109, ἐπ- Mosch. 2, 28, δίζ- Bion 11, 2; Orph. Arg. 210; Nonn. 12, 104, δίζεο 16, 195. This verb seems to be entirely poetic. In Her. 1, 94. 95. 3, 41 &c.; Democr. Stob. Flor. 1, 40; (Luc.) D. Syr. 22, where it used to stand, the kindred form δίζημαι is found in one or more of the best Mss., and is now uniformly adopted by the best Editors.

Διηκονέω Ion. for διᾱκ-.

Δίημι for διίημι, *To send through, dilute*, perhaps does not occur, for διείς seems to be part. 2 aor. Com. Fr. (Sotad.) 3, 586; Hippocr. 4, 162 (Lit.); Pl. Tim. 77: so mid. as act. 2 aor. part. διέμενος Ar. Plut. 720; διέσθαι Hippocr. 1, 478 (K.)

(Δίημι) *To chase away*, only in comp. imp. unaugm. ἐν-δίεσαν Il. 18, 584. Mid. δίεμαι *to speed, flee*, Aesch. Pers. 700 (Herm. Dind. *now*), -ενται Il. 23, 475; Nic. Ther. 755; -ηται Ap. Rh. 2, 330; -εσθαι Il. 12, 304. See δίω.

Δικάζω *To judge, determine*, Il. 8, 431; Pind. Ol. 2, 59; Aesch. Ag. 1412; Her. 2, 137. 3, 31; Antiph. 1, 3; Thuc. 3, 58; Isocr. 15, 21; Epic inf. δικαζέμεν Il. 1, 542: imp. ἐδίκαζον Her. 1, 14; Pl. Criti. 119, δίκαζ- Il. 18, 506: fut. δικάσω Il. 23, 579; Ar. Eq. 1089. Vesp. 689. 801; Antiph. 5, 85; Isocr. 15, 173; Pl. Phaedr. 260. Rep. 433; Dem. 20, 118. 58, 25, -άσσω (Phocyl.) 11, Ion. δικῶ, inf. -κᾶν Her. 1, 97, but see mid.: aor. ἐδίκασα Eur. Or. 164; Her. 3, 14; Thuc. 5, 31; Pl. Leg. 877, δίκασα Od. 11, 547, -ασσα Il. 23, 574; δικάσσαι Theogn. 543: p. δεδίκᾰκα Athen. 12, 13: p.p. δεδίκασμαι Antiph. 5, 87; Lys. 21, 18; Pl. Rep. 614; (Dem.) 59, 125: aor. ἐδικάσθην Thuc. 1, 28; Pl. Rep. 614: fut. δικασθησόμενος Dio. Hal. Ant. 5, 61: 3 fut. δεδικάσομαι Luc. Bis acc. 14. Mid. δικάζομαι *to plead one's own case, go to law*, &c. Od. 11, 545; Antiph. 2, β, 12; Thuc. 3, 44. 5, 79; Dem. 33, 26: imp. ἐδικαζ- Lys. 1, 44; Dem. 21, 26: fut. δικᾰ́σομαι Ar. Nub. 1141; Her. 1, 96; Dem. 7, 8. 37, 37. 38, 16, ἐπι- Andoc. 1, 120, late -ῶμαι, ἐν- δικᾶται V. T. Lev. 19, 18: aor. ἐδικασάμην Lys. 12, 4; Isae. 3, 78; Dem.

33, 26, ἐπ- Andoc. 1, 120, Dor. ἐδικαξάμην Inscr. Heracl. 2, 26: with p. δεδίκασμαι Aristot. Rhet. 2, 23, 23; Dem. 37, 3: plp. ἐδεδίκαστο Dem. 33, 27: and aor. in comp. δια-δικασθῆναι Diog. Laert. 1, 4, 1; Dio Cass. 48, 12. The Attics seem never to have dropped the σ in the fut. of this verb, the Ionic and late writers did. What induced the Attics to spare the σ in δικάζω, and expel it from others in the same category, βιβάζω &c., we leave for Uniformists to tell.

Δικαιολογέω *To plead one's own cause,* rare and late in act. Luc. Tim. 11. Apol. 12. Mid. -οῦμαι as act. Lys. Fr. 34 (Scheibe); Aeschin. 2, 21: imp. -ούμην Luc. Alex. 55: fut. -ήσομαι Polyb. 4, 3, 12; Luc. Abd. 7: aor. -ησαίμην Luc. Prom. 4; -ησάμενος Joseph. Ant. 14, 3, 3: and as mid. aor. pass. -ηθῆναι Polyb. 31, 20, 8, missed by Lexicogr. The pres. mid. alone is classical.

Δικαιόω *To make right, judge,* hence *condemn, punish,* Pind. Fr. 146 (Bergk); Soph. O. R. 575; Her. 3, 142; Thuc. 1, 140, Ion. 3 pl. -εῦσι Her. 2, 47: imp. ἐδικαίουν Thuc. 4, 122, Ion. -καίευν Her. 3, 79. 6, 15: fut. δικαιώσω Her. 5, 92 (Orac.); Thuc. 5, 26; Polyb. 3, 31; Dio. Hal. Rhet. 8, 3; Dio Cass. 52, 26. Fr. 35, 2. 57, 47 (Bekk.): and mid. -ώσομαι Thuc. 3, 40: aor. ἐδικαίωσα Her. 3, 36; Thuc. 2, 71: (p.?): p.p. late, δεδικαίωμαι V. T. Gen. 38, 26: aor. ἐδικαιώθην Dio Cass. 49, 12; δικαιωθείς Aesch. Ag. 393; Dio. Hal. 10, 1: fut. late -ωθήσομαι V. T. Esai. 45, 25. Lexicographers err by giving fut. m. -ώσομαι as the *only* fut., or by giving it a preference over fut. act. Both fut. occur in the *same* author, and each without v. r. δικαιοῦνται Dio Cass. Fr. 17, 14 (Bekk.) seems mid.

(**Δίκω**) *To fling,* Poet. and only 2 aor. ἔδικον Pind. Ol. 10 (11), 72, ἀπ- Aesch. Ag. 1410, δίκον Pind. P. 9, 123; Eur. Phoen. 641 (chor.); imperat. δίκετε Eur. Bac. 600 (chor.), ἀπο-δίκε H. F. 1204 (chor.); δικών Aesch. Ch. 99; Eur. Or. 992. 1469. Pres. δίκει occurs late Aristaen. 2, 1: aor. δίξε, formerly Anth. 15, 27, has been altered to ἔκιξε.

Δινεύω Poet. *To turn round,* trans. and intrans. Eur. Phoen. 792 (chor.); Opp. Hal. 2, 93. 4, 672; -ύοι Il. 4, 541; -εύων 18, 543; Ap. Rh. 1, 215; Eur. Tr. 200 (chor.). Or. 837 (chor.): imp. ἐδίνευον Il. 18, 606, iter. δινεύεσκον Il. 24, 12; Ap. Rh. 4, 1456: aor. later, δινεύσας Ap. Rh. 3, 310; Philo, denied by our lexicons. Pass. or mid. δινεύομαι late, Arat. 455; Opp. Hal. 1, 376; -εύηται Orph. L. 705; -εύεσθαι Opp. Hal. 3, 60. The collat. δινέω is also trans. and intrans. and occasionally in prose, Aesch. Sept. 462; Hippocr. 6, 494, Aeol. 3 pl. δινεῦντι, ἐν-, Theocr. 15, 82; δινῶν (Luc.) Asin. 31; Dio. Hal. 1, 15: imp.

ἐδίνεον Il. 18, 494; Luc. Salt. 13, δίν- Od. 9, 384: fut. (-ήσω): aor. ἐδίνησα Nic. Alex. 188, Dor. δίνᾶσε Eur. Or. 1459 (chor.); Theocr. 24, 10; δινήσας Il. 23, 840; Aesch. Sept. 490, ἀπο- Her. 2, 14: p. p. δεδίνηται (Hesych.), ἀμφι- Il. 23, 562, ἐν- Hippocr. 5, 274: aor. ἐδινήθην, δινήθ- Il. 22, 165 (La R. περι-διν- Bekk.); δινηθῶσι Hym. Merc. 45; δινηθεὶς Od. 22, 85 (Vulg. Dind.); Eur. Rhes. 353; -θῆναι Od. 16, 63, Dor. ἐδινάθην Pind. P. 11, 38: and aor. mid. ἐδινήσαντο Nonn. 22, 9 (Koechly); imper. περι-δινήσασθε Anth. 7, 485: fut. -δινήσομαι Luc. Lex. 2, both missed by Lexicogr.: pres. δινεῖται, ἐπι- Od. 20, 218: imp. ἐδινεόμεσθα Od. 9, 153, dual δινείσθην Il. 17, 680. In classic prose, this verb is rare, and never in the act. form: mid. δινεῖσθαι Pl. Euthyd. 294: imp. ἐδινεῖτο Xen. An. 6, 1, 9: pass. δινούμενος Xen. Conv. 2, 8.

Δίνω (ῑ) Epic, *To turn round, thresh*, only pres. act. Hes. Op. 598: and pass. δινομένην Callim. Fr. 51. δινέμεν as inf. pres. Hes. quoted, is proved by the Lesbian form δίννω, and by ἀποδίνωντι in the Heracl. Inscr. 1, 54.

Διοικέω *To live apart, manage a house*, Xen. Vect. 4, 40; Isocr. 5, 150; Pl. Men. 91; -κεῖν Ar. Eccl. 306: imp. διῴκουν Thuc. 8, 21; Isocr. 7, 36; Isae. 11, 14, συν-διῴκ- 7, 9, see below: fut. -ήσω Pl. Men. 73: aor. διῴκησα Isocr. 1, 35; Dem. 20, 33: p. διῴκηκα Pl. Tim. 19; Dem. 27, 22, is reg. and, in classic authors, always augments after the prep., except that p. p. διῴκημαι Com. Fr. (Antiph.) 3, 106; Dem. 19, 22. 22, 74 has also double augm. δεδιῴκηται Com. Fr. (Antiph.) 3, 84; Machon (Athen.) 8, 26: plp. διῴκητο, προ- Dem. 23, 14: aor. διῳκήθη Luc. Necyom. 19: fut. -κηθήσεται Lys. 30, 35. Mid. διοικοῦμαι *to manage at will*, Dem. 44, 28; D. Hal. Rhet. 9, 7: fut. -ήσομαι Dem. 8, 13, but pass. Herodn. 8, 7, 6: aor. διῳκήσατο Aristot. Oec. 2, 24; Dem. 18, 247. 50, 11; App. Lyb. 113: with p. p. διῴκημαι as mid. Dem. 18, 178 (58, 30). In very late writers, occur ἐδιοίκουν, ἐδιῴκουν Malal. 4, p. 69. Unlike διαιτάω, this verb follows the same law in comp. as in *simple*. This double augm. occurs occasionally even in *early* Attic: ἀνέχομαι, ἠνειχόμην, ἠμπειχόμην, δεδιῄτηκα &c.

Διορίζω, see ὁρίζω.

Δῑφάω *To search, examine*, only pres. διφᾷ Callim. Fr. 32, -φᾶτε Fr. 165, Ion. διφέω Anth. 9, 559; διφῶν Il. 16, 747, -φῶσα Hes. Op. 374. Hesych. has aor. ἐξ-εδίφησε, ἐξ-εζήτησε.

Διψάω (ᾱ) *To thirst*, Od. 11, 584, Ion. -έω Archil. Fr. 68 (Bergk), late Epic διψώω Nonn. Par. 19, 29; Tryph. 548, contr. with η, as διψάει, -ῇ Pind. N. 3, 6; Pl. Rep. 439, διψῶσι Pl. Phil. 45, Aeol. δίψαισι Alcae. 39, 2; διψάῃ, -ῇ Pl. Gorg. 517; opt. διψῷ

Pl. Eryx. 401, but -ῴη Xen. Mem. 1, 3, 5. An. 4, 5, 27; **inf.** διψῆν Soph. Fr. 701 (D.); Ar. Nub. 441; Pl. Phil. 35; Her. 2, 24; διψῶν Pl. Gorg. 505, διψέων Archil. 68, διψώων Anth. (Agath. Schol.) 11, 57, -ψῶσα Pl. Rep. 439, -ψεῦσα Anth. (Incert.) 6, 21: **imp.** ἐδίψη Hippocr. 3, 36. 42 (Mss. Lit. 1, 202 Erm. -ει -α Vulg. Kühn 3, 469. 472), -ψων Luc. Hist. Con. 38: **fut.** διψήσω Xen. Mem. 2, 1, 17: **aor.** ἐδίψησα Pl. Rep. 562: **p.** δεδίψηκα Hippocr. 9, 80 (Lit.); Plut. Pomp. 73. **Mid.** -άομαι, subj. -ώμεθα Com. Fr. (Hermipp.) 2, 389. In late writers, this verb sometimes contr. with α, as διψᾷς Anth. (Philip.) Pl. 4, 137, διψᾷ (Pl.) Ax. 366; so Hippocr. 2, 365 (Erm. -ψῇ Lit. 7, 258); V. T. Prov. 25, 21; διψᾶν Galen 5, 837. 16, 302.

Δίω *To fear, flee, run*, **pres.** not used: **imp.** Epic δῖον Il. 22, 251 (Vulg. Dind. La R.), δίες (Bekk. 1859), δίε 5, 566; Ap. Rh. 4, 181: **2 perf.** δέδια Aesch. Pr. 182. 902 (chor.); Soph. O. C. 1467 (chor.); Dem. 14, 4; Luc. Prom. 5, 7. Pisc. 9. Navig. 30. D. Deor. 19, δέδιας late prose, Plut. Mor. 149 A; Luc. Jup. Conf. 9. Som. 22. Pisc. 24. Anach. 35. Luct. 16, δέδιε classic, but rare, Com. Fr. (Amph.) 3, 316. (Menand.) 4, 135; Hippocr. 8, 36; Dem. 4, 8; Luc. Prom. 13. Jup. Trag. 41, δεδίαμεν Thuc. 3, 53 (one Ms.); Isae. 5, 22 (Mss. and most edit., but) syncop. δέδιμεν Thuc. 3, 53. 56. 57; Isae. quoted (Scheibe), δεδίατε Epist. Phal. 88 (Vulg.), δέδιτε Thuc. 4, 126; and late, Luc. Pisc. 18; Arr. An. 5, 25; Epist. Phal. quoted (Hercher 141), δεδίασι Ar. Eq. 224; Isae. 8, 42; Isocr. 4, 116. 6, 67; Pl. Euth. 12; Dem. 14, 31; once in Hom. Il. 24, 663; subj. rare, and partial (δεδίω), -ίῃ Xen. Athen. 1, 11, -ωσι Isocr. 4, 156. 5, 70. 14, 36. 18, 43. 21, 8; opt. also rare, and partial, δεδιείην, -είη Pl. Phaedr. 251; imper. Poet. δέδῐθι Ar. Eq. 230. Vesp. 373; and late prose, Plut. Caes. 38; Luc. D. Deor. 5, 5, Bis acc. 8; Philostr. 5, 220 (δεδιέτω Stob. 79, 52?), in late poets δέδῑθι Babr. 75, 2, Epic δείδῐθι Il. 5, 827; Theogn. 1179, δείδῐθ' Od. 18, 63, late δείδῑθι Nic. Alex. 443, pl. δείδῐτε Il. 20, 366; inf. δεδιέναι Hippocr. 5, 414; Thuc. 1, 136; Lys. 7, 1; Isocr. 8, 7. 12, 48. 15, 141; Xen. Athen. 1, 11; Pl. Phaed. 88. Conv. 198. Rep. 386 &c., and always in his *genuine* works; Aeschin. 2, 106; Dem. 21, 201; later, Luc. Abd. 5. Tim. 2, &c.; Plut. Arist. 6. Pyr. 19. 29 &c., never in Attic poetry; Epic δειδίμεν Od. 9, 274. 10, 381, to be distinguished from δείδιμεν 1 pl. **perf.**; δεδιώς Hippocr. 2, 277 (Erm.); Antiph. 2, δ, 1. 4, δ, 11; Thuc. 6, 24. 7, 75. 8, 7; Xen. Hell. 1, 6, 12; Pl. Euth. 12; Lys. 3, 36. 30, 11; Isocr. 8, 138; Dem. 18, 263. 23, 129. 175 &c.; later, Aristot. Pol. 7, 1, 4; Luc. Icar. 22 &c.; twice in Comedy, Ar. Eccl. 643. Plut. 448, never in Trag., δεδιυῖα C. Fr. (Eubul.) 3, 271; Pl. Phaedr. 254

(Bekk.), Epic δειδιώς Il. 4, 431. Od. 14, 60. 18, 77; Hes. Sc. 248; Theogn. 764, δειδυῖα Ap. Rh. 3, 753: plp. ἐδεδίειν Hyperid. Lycophr. p. 25 (Schn.); Plut. Pomp. 8; Luc. Jup. Trag. 43, -εις Dem. 34, 27; Luc. Bis acc. 8, -ει Dem. 54, 23, pl. 1 pers. late ἐδεδίειμεν Themist. 18, 221, ἐδεδίεσαν Thuc. 4, 55. 5, 14 (v. r. 4, 117); Lys. 13, 27; Isocr. 7, 33; Xen. An. 5, 6, 36 (most Mss. and edit.), ἐδέδισαν (Cob. Stahl, so Isocr. quoted, Otto Schneid.) which occurs without v. r. Pl. Leg. 685, approved by Phryn. Lob. and Poppo: Epic δείδια Il. 13, 49; Panyas 6, 12, -ιας Od. 18, 80; Anth. 12, 138, -ιε Il. 18, 34. 24, 358, pl. δείδιμεν Il. 9, 230: plp. only pl. syncop. ἐδείδιμεν Il. 6, 99, ἐδείδισαν 7, 151, δείδ- 15, 652 (Dind. ἐδ- Bekk. La R.) **Mid.** Poet. δίομαι intrans. *to fear*, Aesch. Pers. 700, if correct (Mss. Dind. 2 ed.); but trans. *frighten, chase*, Opp. Ven. 1, 426 (Vulg.); subj. δίωμαι Od. 21, 370, δίηται Il. 7, 197. 16, 246. 22, 189. 456, δίωνται Il. 17, 110; opt. δίοιτο Od. 17, 317; inf. δίεσθαι Il. 12, 276. 18, 162. Od. 17, 398; Ap. Rh. 4, 498; διόμενος Aesch. Eum. 357. 385. Supp. 819 (chor.) For δίομαι Aesch. Pers. 700, Herm. Weil, and Dind. 5 ed. read δίεμαι. It thus appears that good Attic prose writers use of the **perf.** *indic.* **act.** the 1 and 3 sing. only, but all the persons of the pl. Matth. is therefore wrong in excluding δέδιε, and Lud. Dind. δέδιτε from Attic prose: of the **plp.** there occur in early Attic prose 2 and 3 sing. and 3 pl. See δείδω. δείδιε Il. 18, 34. 24, 358, perhaps 3 sing. **imp.** as if from (δειδίω), for though in form it may be 3 sing. of δείδια, the time is imp., and we find in later Epic ἐδείδιον, -ιες, -ιε Q. Sm. 10, 450; Nonn. 2, 608 &c.; even imper. δείδιε Q. Sm. 7, 298. 305, and δεδιέτω Pimpel. in Stob. Fl. 79, 52. Syncop. forms of **2 perf.** and **plp.** are generally used, δέδιμεν Thuc. 3, 56 (but δεδίαμεν Isae. 5, 22; v. r. in Ms. Reg. Thuc. 3, 53), and δείδιμεν Il. 9, 230, δέδιτε Thuc. 4, 126; δεδιείην Pl. Phaedr. 251; δέδῐθι Ar. Vesp. 373; Luc. D. Deor. 5, 5. D. Mer. 13, 4, and δείδῐθι Il. 14, 342, with elis. δείδιθ' Od. 18, 63, δείδιτε Il. 20, 366; inf. δειδίμεν Od. 10, 381; δειδυῖα Ap. Rh. 3, 753: **plp.** ἐδείδιμεν Il. 6, 99, ἐδείδισαν 5, 790, ἐδέδισαν Pl. Leg. 685, but ἐδεδίεσαν Thuc. 4, 55. 5, 14 (Mss. Bekk. Popp. Krüg.); Lys. 13, 27; Isocr. 7, 33; Xen. An. 5, 6, 36 (Krüg. Saupp. -δισαν Dind.); Hell. 4, 4, 16 (Mss. Saupp. Breitb. -δισαν Schneid. ὤκνουν Dind.), see above. Phrynichus approves decidedly of ἐδέδισαν; in several instances however ἐδεδίεσαν is the reading of all the Mss. The seemingly anomalous, we say not corrupt, form δεδιείην=δεδιοίην, derives some countenance from περιίειεν=περιίοιεν, in a Delphic Inscr. 1688 (Boeckh.) Late poets have imper. sometimes with ῑ in *arsis*, δέδῑθι Babr. 75, 2 (Lachm.), δείδῑθι Nic. Al. 443, which Otto Schneid. edits δείδιχθι (Ms. π), and would δέδιχθι in Babr. See δειδίσσομαι.

(Διωκάθω) *To pursue*, -ᾰ́θειν Eur. Fr. 364, 25; Pl. Euth. 15, others -αθεῖν 2 aor. (Elms. Dind.): imp. ἐδιώκαθον Ar. Vesp 1203; Pl. Gorg. 483, others 2 aor.; subj. -ᾰ́θω Ar. Nub. 1482; late part. -άθοντας, others 2 aor. -αθόντας Clem. Alex., a lengthened form of διώκω, which see.

Δῐώκω *To pursue*, Il. 22, 8; Archil. 63; Aesch. Ag. 394; Soph. El. 738; Ar. Thesm. 1066; Her. 4, 22; Antiph. 2, 2; Lys. 3, 36; Pl. Euthyphr. 3; imper. δίωκε Pind. Fr. 104; -κων N. 5, 24; Antiph. 5, 89; Thuc. 3, 24; -ώκειν Il. 21, 601; Pl. Phil. 67; Ar. Ach. 235; Ep. -έμεν Il. 5, 223, -έμεναι Od. 15, 278: imp. ἐδίωκον Il. 23, 424; Her. 6, 65; Thuc. 2, 91; Dem. 19, 293, dual διώκετον Il. 10, 364: fut. διώξω Sapph. 1, 21 (Bergk); Pind. Ol. 3, 45; I. 8 (7), 37; Ar. Eq. 968. Thesm. 1224 (Bekk. Bergk); Xen. An. 1, 4, 8. Cyr. 6, 3, 13; Dem. 38, 16, ἀπο- Ar. Nub. 1296 (Vulg. Bekk. Bergk, see mid.); Thuc. 6, 102 (best Mss. Popp. -ώξας Bekk. Krüg.); later, Plut. Ant. 48; Herodn. 5, 4, 10; Diod. Sic. 19, 108; Stob. 85, 19: and -ώξομαι Ar. Eq. 368; Thuc. 7, 85; Xen. Cyr. 1, 3, 14. 4, 1, 19. 4, 3, 18; Pl. Prot. 310. Theaet. 168; and Ar. Eq. 968. Thesm. 1224, ἀπο- Nub. 1296 quoted (Elms. Dind.); pass. Dio. Hal. Ant. 3, 20 (Kiessl.): aor. ἐδίωξα Her. 5, 92. 6, 104; Thuc. 6, 70; Antiph. 2, 6; Xen. Hell. 2, 4, 13: p. δεδίωχα Hyperid. Lyc. p. 29: p. p. late δεδιωγμένος N. T. Matth. 5, 10 (Vat. &c.), παρα- D. Hal. C. Verb. 20: aor. ἐδιώχθην Her. 5, 73; Antiph. 2, 3. 6; Babr. 95, 41; Paus. 10, 35, 5, κατ- Thuc. 3, 4. 8, 20, ἐπ- 3, 69: fut. late διωχθήσομαι Diod. Sic. 19, 95; Polyaen. Str. 2, 13: and as pass. fut. m. διώξεσθαι Dio. Hal. Ant. 3, 20: pres. διώκεται Thuc. 1, 136; Soph. El. 871; Ar. Ach. 700; Eur. Ion 1250; -ωκόμενος Il. 22, 168. Mid. διώκομαι as act. Aesch. Ch. 289: imp. διώκετο Il. 21, 602. Od. 18, 8; and late prose διωκόμενος Dio. Hal. Ant. 1, 87 (Mss. διοικ- Kiessl.): fut. διώξομαι, see above. Pass. διώκομαι *to be urged, pursued*, Soph. El. 871, διώκεται Thuc. 1, 136, -όμεσθα Eur. Heracl. 50, -εθα Ar. Ach. 700; -ώμενος Od. 13, 162; Ar. Ach. 216; Thuc. 2, 4; -ώκεσθαι Xen. Apol. 21, see above. Vb. διωκτός Soph. Fr. 870; Athen. (Chrysip.) 1, 8, -έος Her. 9, 58; Ar. Ach. 221; Pl. Tim. 80. In the Tragedians this verb is confined to the pres. act. mid. and pass. In Ar. mss. and most edit. present both forms of fut. -ώξω, -ώξομαι; Elms. and Dind. however uniformly read fut. mid. -ώξομαι Ach. 368, -ώξει 969. Thesm. 1224, ἀπο- Nub. 1296, for -ώξεις (Bekk. Bergk, &c.) The mid. fut. is not confined to classic writers, it is by far the prevailing form in the Septuag. Its pass. use by Dio. Hal. quoted, has been missed by Lexicogr.

Δυοπαλίζω (δονέω), *To shake, fling*, Epic, imp. ἐδυοπάλιζε Il. 4, 472: fut. -ίξω Od. 14, 512. Pass. δυοπαλίζεται Opp. Hal. 2, 295.

(**Δοάζω** Hesych.) Epic, only δοάσσατο *it seemed*, a def. 1 aor. m. Il. 14, 23. 16, 652; subj. δοάσσεται, for -ηται, Il. 23, 339.—δοάσσαι opt. aor. act. *he imagined*, Ap. Rh. 3, 955: and δοάσσατο indic. aor. m. *he doubted*, 3, 770, seem, in meaning, more allied to δοιάζω.

Δόατο Epic, *he appeared*, a def. imp. mid. Od. 6, 242, as a v. r. to δέατο.

Δοιάζω *To make double, hesitate about*, Epic iter. imp. δοιάζεσκον Ap. Rh. 3, 819: aor. ἐδοίασα (Hesych.), ἐπ- Ap. Rh. 3, 21: and mid. δοιάζοντο *they imagined*, Ap. Rh. 4, 576.—With this seems to be connected aor. act. (δόασσα), opt. δοάσσαι *he imagined*, Ap. Rh. 3, 955: and aor. m. δοάσσατο *he doubted*, Ap. Rh. 3, 770, see δοάζω.

Δοκέω (δόκω) *To seem, think*, Il. 7, 192; Solon 32; Heraclit. 5 (Byw.); Her. 2, 125, -κῶ Aesch. Pr. 289; Soph. O. C. 104; Ar. Pax 61; Antiph. 4, β, 1. 5, 65, -έει Il. 9, 625; Simon. Am. 1, 9, -εῖ Il. 12, 215; Thuc. 1, 128; subj. δοκῇ Andoc. 3, 41, δοκῶσι Antiph. 5, 80; opt. δοκέοιμι Theogn. 339, -κοῖμι Soph. O. R. 1470, -κέοι Her. 8, 19, -κοῖ Thuc. 2, 100; Pl. Rep. 438, -κοιμεν Thuc. 1, 122, and δοκοίην Antiph. 2, β, 4; Andoc. 1, 67; Isocr. 5, 98, -οίη Thuc. 4, 11, 3 pl. -κοίησαν very rare Aeschin. 2, 102, -οῖεν (Weidn. Franke in Note): imp. ἐδόκεον Her. 3, 65, -κουν Hom. H. Ven. 125; Antiph. 2, β, 10; Thuc. 1, 22; Lys. 7, 36, 'δόκουν Aesch. Pers. 188, ἐδόκεε Her. 1, 10, -κει Thuc. 2, 8 &c., Dor. 1 pl. ἐδοκεῦμες Theocr. 13, 1, δόκεον Ap. Rh. 4, 666, iter. late δοκέεσκον Anth. 5, 299: fut. δόξω Pind. N. 4, 37; Aesch. Ag. 415; Soph. Phil. 1372; Ar. Nub. 443; Her. 8, 80; Antiph. 3, β, 2; Lys. 8, 1; Isocr. 12, 90; Pl. Phaedr. 275, Dor. -ξῶ, -ξεῖτε Ar. Ach. 741 (δοκήσω usu. Poet. see below): aor. ἔδοξα H. Hymn. 3, 208; Pind. Ol. 5, 16; Aesch. Pers. 181; Eur. Hipp. 401; Her. 3, 19; Antiph. 2, α, 8; Thuc. 3, 82; subj. δόξω Pl. Rep. 509 &c.; δόξαιμι Ar. Eq. 1210; Pl. Apol. 34, -αις Phaedr. 275, -ειε Rep. 337, -αιμεν Polit. 280, -αιεν Xen. Cyr. 2, 1, 23, -ειαν (Dind. Saupp.): p. (δέδοχα?): plp. ἐδεδόχεσαν Dio Cass. 44, 26 (Bekk.): p. p. δέδογμαι Aesch. Supp. 601; Soph. Tr. 719; Ar. Vesp. 485; Her. 8, 100; Thuc. 3, 49; Pl. Crito 49; δεδόχθω Leg. 799: plp. ἐδέδοκτο Her. 5, 96 (Mss. Vulg. Dind. Stein, δέδοκ- Mss. Bekk. Gaisf. Abicht). 9, 74 (Mss. Dind. Abicht, δέδοκ- Mss.

Bekk. Gaisf. Stein); ἐδέδ- Pl. Menex. 244; Plut. Caes. 28: **aor.** ἐδόχθην, δοχθείς Polyb. 21, 8; Diod. Sic. 11, 50. 12, 55, κατα- Antiph. 2, β, 2. **Mid.**, see below. The forms from δοκέω are mostly Poet. **fut.** δοκήσω Aesch. Pr. 386; Eur. Heracl. 261 (trimet.); Ar. Nub. 562. Ran. 737 (chor.); Athen. (Archest.) 1, 52; Her. (only once) 4, 74, Dor. -ᾱσῶ Theocr. 1, 150 (Med. Vulg. Wordsw.), -ησῶ (Mss. Ahr. Mein. Ziegl. Fritzsche): ἐδόκησα Pind. Ol. 13, 56; Stesich. 42 (Bergk), δόκησε Od. 20, 93; -ήσας Eur. Supp. 129; Ar. Ran. 1485 (chor.); -άτω Aesch. Sept. 1036 (trimet.); late prose Joseph. 17, 6, 5: δεδόκηκε Aesch. Eum. 309 (chor.); late prose -ηκέναι Orig. Ref. Haer. p. 175 (Miller): (δεδόκημαι), -ησαι Eur. Med. 763 (chor.), -ηται Pind. N. 5, 19; Ar. Vesp. 726 (chor.); Her. 7, 16; (Hippocr.) Epist. 9, 402: ἐδοκήθην Anth. 8, 188; δοκηθείς Eur. Bac. 1390. Alc. 1161. Impers. δοκεῖ *it seems*, Thuc. 1, 3: ἐδόκει Antiph. 1, 16; Lys. 12, 14: δόξει Aesch. Pr. 259: ἔδοξε Her. 6, 86; Antiph. 1, 17; Thuc. 4, 15: δέδοκται Pl. Phaedr. 228; Her. 4, 68: **plp.** δέδοκτο 9, 74 (Gaisf. Bekk. Stein), ἐδέδοκτο (Dind. Dietsch); Paus. 9, 13, 4. So δοκήσει: ἐδόκησε Aesch. Sept. 1036: δεδόκηκε Aesch. Eum. 309: δεδόκηται Pind. N. 5, 19; Her. (once) 7, 16, where some would substitute δέδοκται, but Her. seems to have used both forms, see δοκήσει 4, 74 quoted; late prose δεδοκημένα Orig. Ref. Haer. 6, 21. 10, 6: δοκηθείς Agath. 1, 7. **Vb.** in ἀδόκητος Pind. N. 7, 31; Thuc. 7, 29. Hom. never has the short form (δόκω), δόξω, and of δοκέω only **pres.** and once **aor.** δόκησε: Soph. excepted, the Tragedians and Aristoph. use both formations, δόξω, -κήσω: ἔδοξα, -κησα: but δεδόκηκα only: of (δέδογμαι) only δέδοκται, δεδογμένος, and of (δεδόκημαι) only δεδόκησαι. But Aristoph., we think, never uses the long forms in trimeters, Aesch. and Eur. do, at least **fut.** and **aor. act.** The part. δεδοκημένος is Epic, and never used in the sense *determined*, *resolved*, but **act.** *watching*, *waiting*, and usually referred to δέχομαι. We have sometimes thought it might be referred to δοκέω, with the sense (*bethought*), *in earnest anxious thought*, hence *watching;* or that it belongs to the **mid.** form δοκέομαι *think for oneself*, *bethink oneself* in reference to the actions or intentions of another, *observe*, *watch*, &c., in which sense δοκεύμενοι occurs Orph. Arg. 1359, ἐδοκέοντο Opp. C. 4, 296; and that the Epics used δεδοκημένος as its **perf.** in this same **mid.** sense, Il. 15, 730; Hes. Sc. 214, and that other writers used indic. (δεδόκημαι), δεδόκησαι, -ηται (δεδοκημένος never), and δέδοκται, δεδογμένος as **pass.** *thought out*, *determined.* This is more direct than the derivation from δέχομαι, δέκομαι, δοκέομαι, and the meaning appears as legitimate, and not less natural.

In late Epic, δοκεύμενος signifies both *to seem*, Opp. Cyn. 4, 109, and *to watch*, Orph. Arg. 1359.

Δοκιμάζω *To examine, approve*, Her. 2, 38; Thuc. 6, 53; Xen. Mem. 2, 6, 6: imp. ἐδοκ- Isocr. 7, 53: fut. -άσω Synes. Epist. 99 (Herch.), ἀπο- Xen. Hipp. 1, 13, συν- Isocr. 2, 28, but Ion. δοκιμᾷ, ἀπο- Her. 1, 199, though called Attic, reg.: p. p. δεδοκίμασαι Lys. 32, 9; -ασμένος Xen. Mem. 3, 5, 20; Isae. 2, 39: aor. ἐδοκιμάσθην Andoc. 1, 85; Isae. 9, 29: fut. -ασθησόμενος Lys. 31, 1; Dem. 40, 34: with mid. δοκιμασώμεθα *choose*, Xen. Oec. 8, 10; δοκιμάσασθαι from Stob. Flor. (Menand.) 72, 2: pres. δοκιμάζηται App. Civ. 2, 124, may be mid. Vb. δοκιμαστέον Lys. 31, 25.

Δομέω, see δέμω.

Δονέω *To shake*, Il. 17, 55; Ar. Eccl. 954 (chor.); Her. 4, 2; δονέοι Pind. P. 4, 219; δονέων 1, 44, δονοῦσα Aesch. Fr. 321 (D.); δονεῖν Bacchyl. 20 (B.); late Attic prose, Luc. Anach. 20: imp. ἐδόνει Ael. N. A. 15, 21 (Herch.): fut. -ήσω Anacreont. 58 (Bergk): aor. ἐδόνησα Od. 22, 300; late Attic Alciphr. Fr. 6, 12 (Mein.) Pass. δονέονται Pind. P. 10, 39; Opp. Hal. 1, 476, -εῖται Ar. Av. 1183; late Attic prose, Plut. Mor. 1005; -ούμενος Themist. 1, 2, -εύμενος Bion 6, 5; Ap. Rh. 3, 1295: imp. ἐδονέετο Her. 7, 1, -εῖτο Hes. Sc. 237; App. Civ. 4, 52, δονέοντο Theocr. 7, 135; Ap. Rh. 1, 223: fut. mid. -ήσομαι as pass. Hom. H. 2, 92: p. δεδόνηται Opp. Hal. 2, 263; -ημένος Theocr. 24, 88: plp. ἐδεδόνητο Herodn. 7, 5, 8, δεδον- Theocr. 13, 65: aor. δονηθείς Pind. P. 6, 36 (Mss. Schneid. Bergk, Ahr.), -āθείς (Vulg. Boeckh.) This verb seems doubtful in classic prose; δονουμένους Xen. Conv. 2, 8 (Vulg.) is now edited, seemingly more correctly, δινουμ- (Steph. Dind. Mehl. &c.); Sauppe however retains δονουμ-.

Δουλόω *To enslave*, Aesch. Sept. 254: fut. -ώσω Soph. Tr. 257; Thuc. 3, 58 &c. reg.: p.p. δεδούλωμαι Her. 8, 101; Thuc. 1, 68. 4, 34; Pl. Menex. 240 &c.; but as mid. Thuc. 6, 82; D. Sic. 4, 28; Dio. Hal. 11, 35, κατα- Eur. I. A. 1269; Pl. Menex. 240: plp. ἐδεδουλ- Her. 1, 169. 7, 108, δεδουλ- 1, 95 (Bekk. Dind. ἐδεδ- Dietsch, Stein): aor. ἐδουλώθην 1, 174. 4, 93: and full mid. complement -οῦμαι Eur. Supp. 493; Thuc. 4, 92: fut. -ώσομαι Thuc. 7, 68. 75; Lys. 2, 21: aor. -ωσάμην Thuc. 5, 29. 6, 84; Pl. Menex. 239, κατ- Com. Fr. (Philem.) 4, 47.

Δουπέω *To sound heavily*, mostly Poet. Eur. Alc. 104 (chor.), and γδουπ-: imp. δούπ- Ap. Rh. 2, 1056, ἐγδούπει, ἐπ- Anth. 9, 662: fut. δουπήσω Anth. 9, 427: aor. ἐδούπησα Xen. An. 1, 8, 18; -ῆσαι Arr. Ann. 1, 6, 4, Poet. δούπησα Il. 5, 42. 17, 50 &c.,

and γδούπησα, ἐπι- in tmesi Il. 11, 45 (Bekk.): **2** aor. late ἔδουπον, κατ- Anth. 7, 637: **2** p. δέδουπα Anth. Plan. 94; δεδουπώς *fallen*, Il. 23, 679; Ap. Rh. 4, 557; Orph. Arg. 537. **Pass.** ἐδουπεῖτο Philostr. Her. 742: **1** aor. δουπήθησαν Anth. 9, 283. This verb scarcely occurs in prose. Dind. Hug bracket it, Xen. An. quoted, as an interpolation, Cobet drops it, Krüg. Kühner, Rhedantz, Sauppe, Skenkl retain it.

(Δοχμόω) *To turn, bend, double up*, Epic, act. late, aor. δόχμωσε Nonn. 42, 182 (251); but ἀπο-δοχμώσας Od. 9, 372: so mid. δοχμώσατο Nonn. 37, 254: pass. classic, but only aor. part. δοχμωθείς Hom. H. 3, 146; Hes. Sc. 389; late ἐδοχμώθησαν Nonn. 17, 348.

Δραίνω *To do, plan*, Epic and only pres. δραίνεις Il. 10, 96.

Δραμεῖν, see τρέχω.

Δρασκάζω *To run off*, only pres. and antiquated, Lys. 10, 17, explained by ἀποδιδράσκειν.

Δράσσω, -ττω, *To seize, grasp*, act. late Pollux 3, 155. Dep. δράσσομαι Her. 3, 13, δρατт- Themist. 1, 15; Phil. de Plant. 151: imp. 'δραττόμην Ar. Ran. 545 (chor.), ἐδρατт- Philostr. 2, 40, ἐδρασσ- Pseud.-Callisth. 3, 3: fut. δράξομαι Anth. Plan. 4, 275; Dionys. de Av. 3, 11; V. T. Num. 5, 26: aor. ἐδραξάμην Callim. Dian. 76; (Luc.) Asin. 25; -ξωνται Anth. (Demod.) 11, 238; δράξαιντο Callim. Dian. 92; -ασθαι Callim. Epigr. 1, 14; -άμενος Batr. 156; Theocr. 24, 28; Pl. Lys. 209; Plut. Alex. 74: p. δέδραγμαι, -αξαι Eur. Tr. 745, -ακται Plut. Mor. 1005; δεδραγμένος Il. 13, 393. 16, 486; Soph. Ant. 235 (Vulg. Schol. Nauck, πεφαργ- Dind.) The pres. imp. aor. part. and perf. seem alone to be used by classic authors.

(**Δράω**), see διδράσκω.

Δράω *To do*, Aesch. Eum. 162; Soph. Ph. 905; Ar. Plut. 414. Eq. 495; Antiph. 2, δ, 11; Thuc. 4, 19; Pl. Theaet. 151. Rep. 450; opt. δρῷμι Soph. Ph. 895, and -ῴην Eur. Or. 779, -ῴης Soph. Ant. 70, 3 sing. δρῷ Pl. Epin. 989, and δρῴη Soph. El. 258; Pl. Rep. 378, δρῴημεν Eur. Cycl. 132, δρῷμεν Soph. Phil. 1393; Ion. inf. δρῆν Hippocr. 3, 290: imp. ἔδρων Soph. O. R. 591; Ar. Pax 830; Antiph. 4, δ, 6; Thuc. 3, 55: fut. δράσω Aesch. Pr. 744; Eur. Hec. 876; Pl. Leg. 752: aor. ἔδρᾱσα Aesch. Eum. 723; Soph. Ant. 239; Ar. Vesp. 1002; Antiph. 3, β, 7; Thuc. 2, 49; Pl. Polit. 279, Epic -ησα Theogn. 954; δρᾶσαι Solon 37, 3; δράσας Antiph. 2, α, 7; Thuc. 3, 38, δρήσας Theogn. 954: p. δέδρᾱκα Soph. Ant. 536; Ar. Av. 325; Antiph. 3, δ, 5; Thuc. 8, 50: p.p. δέδρᾱμαι Ar. Pax 1039; -αμένος Eur. H. F. 169. El. 1106; late prose, Heliod. 10, 38 (Bekk.), seldom -ασμαι Thuc. 3, 54 (-αμαι some Mss. Herw. Stahl): aor.

ἐδράσθην, δρασθείς Thuc. 3, 38. 6, 53; and late, Herodn. 1, 13, 5 (Bekk.) Vb. δραστέος Soph. El. 1019; Pl. Leg. 626. -δρώωσι, παρα- Epic 3 pl. pres. for -δρῶσι, Od. 15, 324, ὑπο- 15, 333; opt. δρώοιμι for δρῷμι (δράοιμι) 15, 317. The fut. form δρᾶς (so pronounced by the Scythian) in Ar. Thesm. 1003, should probably be read δράσ' = δράσω, as κολύσ' for κολύσω, 1179, but δρᾶσ' (Mein.) δράσας aor. part. has ᾰ, Anth. 8, 192. Desiderat. δρασείω Ar. Pax 62; Soph. Aj. 326.

Δρέμω, see τρέχω.

Δρέπω *To pluck*, Pind. P. 1, 49; δρέπῃ Pl. Leg. 844; δρέπε, ἀπο- Hes. Op. 611; δρέπειν Eur. I. A. 1299; Her. 3, 110; Long. Past. 2, 4; δρέπων Eur. Elec. 778; Ar. Ran. 1300, κατα- Her. 8, 115, later and Poet. δρέπτω: imp. ἔδρεπον Eur. Ion 889, δρέπον Hom. H. Cer. 425, and δρέπτον Mosch. 2, 69: fut. (δρέψω): aor. ἔδρεψα Her. 2, 92; Pl. Tim. 91; δρέψαι, ἀπο- Pind. P. 9, 110; pt. δρέψασαι Hes. Th. 31 (Dind. Schoem. Flach), see mid.: aor. p. late ἐδρέφθην Philostr. Apoll. 334: 2 aor. act. ἔδρᾰπον, δρᾰπών Pind. P. 4, 130. Mid. δρέπομαι *to pluck for myself*, Pind. N. 2, 9; Bion 1, 22; Pl. Rep. 401, and later δρέπτομαι Anth. 10, 41: imp. δρεπόμην Hom. H. Cer. 429, Dor. ἐδρεπόμαν Anth. 12, 125: fut. δρέψομαι, ἀπο- Anth. 6, 303, Dor. δρεψεῦμαι, -εύμενος Theocr. 18, 40 (Vulg. Mein. -ούμ- Fritzs. Ahr. Ziegl.): aor. ἐδρεψάμην Anth. 7, 414, δρεψ- Orph. Arg. 1003; -ασθαι Hes. Th. 31 (Vulg. Goettl.); Aesch. Sept. 718; Theocr. 11, 27; -άμενος Od. 12, 357; late prose Dio. Hal. Ant. 1, 40; Stob. (Socr.) 410 (Gaisf.); Joseph. Jud. B. 4, 8, 4. Vb. ἄ-δρεπτος Aesch. Supp. 663.

Δρήσσω = δράω, *To do*, pres. act. and in comp. only, ὑπο-δρήσσων Ap. Rh. 3, 274; Coluth. 69.

Δρομάω *To run*, Poet. and only iter. imp. δρομάασκε Hes. Fr. 221, 2 (Goettl.): and p. δεδρόμηκα Babr. 60 (2 pt. Lewis), Dor. δεδρόμᾱκα, ὑπα- Sapph. Fr. 2, 10.

Δρύπτω *To tear*, Eur. Elec. 150 (chor.); late prose, Philostr. Apoll. 128; and in comp. δρῦφω, ἀπο-δρύφοι Il. 23, 187. 24, 21: fut. δρύψω, κατα- Anth. 5, 43: aor. δρύψα Il. 16, 324; Ap. Rh. 2, 109; subj. δρύψω, ἀπο- Od. 17, 480; Theocr. 25, 267, late prose, κατ-έδρυψα Niceph. Rhet. 1, 4; M. Anton. 6, 20: p.p. δεδρυμμένος ἀμφι- Q. Sm. 4, 396 (Koechl.): plp. δέδρυπτο Q. Sm. 14, 391: aor. ἐδρύφθην Babr. 36, 10 (Lewis, 2 pt.), δρύφθη in tmesi Od. 5, 426, περι- Il. 23, 395, ἀπ-έδρυφθεν, for -ησαν, Od. 5, 435, -εδρύφθησαν Q. Sm. 14, 577. Mid. δρύπτομαι *tear oneself*, Eur. Hec. 655; Xen. Cyr. 3, 3, 67: imp. ἐδρύπτοντο Hes. Sc. 243; Xen. Cyr. 3, 1, 13: aor. ἐδρυψάμην, δρυψ- Nonn.

2, 642; δρυψάμενος Od. 2, 153; late prose, Philostr. Imag. 825. Pass. δρυπτόμενος *torn*, Anth. 7, 2.

Δυάω *To afflict, distress* (δύη), only Epic 3 pl. δυόωσι Od. 20, 195: but p.p. δεδυημένη (Hesych.)

Δύναμαι *To be able*, Il. 3, 236; Hes. Op. 215; Aesch. Eum. 950; Soph. O. C. 136; Ar. Ran. 42; Her. 8, 29; Antiph. 1, 28. 5, 64; Thuc. 4, 95; Pl. Rep. 400; Epic 2 sing. subj. δύνηαι Il. 6, 229; Hes. Op. 350 (pres. and imp. as ἵσταμαι): imp. ἐδῠνάμην Il. 12, 417; Hes. Op. 134; Ar. Eccl. 316. 343; and always Her. 1, 26. 2, 29; Antiph. 6, 11; Thuc. 2, 52; Lys. 12, 85; Pl. Prot. 315, 2 sing. ἐδύνω (for ἐδύνασο late, Luc. D. Mort. 9, 1; Hippocr.? Epist. 3, 791 K. ἠδύν- Lit. 9, 344; Erm. 3, 584) Hom. H. 3, 405; Xen. An. 1, 6, 7, and ἠδυνάμην Hippocr. 1, 602, 4, 256. 8, 586 (Lit.); Thuc. 1, 4 (Bekk. Popp. Krüg.); Lys. 3, 33; Isocr. 5, 129; Dem. 18, 111. 33, 38 (Bekk. B. S.), 2 sing. (ἠδύνασο see above) ἠδύνω Com. Fr. (Philipp.) 4, 472, δυνάμην Il. 19, 136. 16, 509: fut. δυνήσομαι Il. 19, 163; Soph. Ph. 742; Eur. Elec. 337; Her. 8, 57; Thuc. 4, 60; Lys. 12, 45; Pl. Leg. 691, Dor. -ᾶσομαι Eur. Med. 862 (chor.), -ᾱσοῦμαι Stob. (Hippod.) 43, 93. (Archyt.) 46, 61. (Phint.) 74, 61: aor. m. poet. especially Epic, ἐδυνησάμην Il. 14, 33; Arat. 375, δυνησ- Il. 5, 621. 13, 510. 14, 423. Od. 17, 303 (Bekk.); Anth. 7, 148; subj. -ήσωνται if sound, Simon. (Am.) 1, 17; *classical* prose instances, and most of the *late* have now been corrected, δυνήσησθε Dem. 19, 323 (Reiske, now pres. -νησθε Mss. Bekk. B. S. Dind.); so Proem. 52, 10; -ήσασθε 56, 6 (Taylor, -ήσεσθαι Mss. Bekk. B. S. Dind.); but still -ήσωνται if correct, Pseud.-Callisth. 3, 29, -ήσηται Aen. Tact. 32 (Vulg. -ηνται Hertl. Herch.): p. δεδύνημαι Dinarch. 2, 14; Dem. 4, 30. 21, 81: aor. ἐδυνήθην Xen. Cyr. 3, 1, 30 (Dind. Saupp. Hertl. 3 edit. ἠδ- Popp. Hertl. 2 ed.). An. 3, 1, 35; Lys. 7, 2; Isae. 1, 25; Lycurg. 39; Dem. 21, 80, 'δυνήθ- Soph. Aj. 1067, Dor. -άθην Theocr. 11, 59, ἠδυν- Aesch. Pr. 206; Hippocr. 1, 480 (Erm.); Thuc. 4, 33 (Mss. Poppo, Krüg. Classen, Boehme). 7, 25 (Poppo, Goell. ἐδυν- Bekk. Krüg. Dind.); Lys. 3, 42; Isocr. 1, 5. 4, 102. 5, 129; Xen. Mem. 3, 13, 6. Cyr. 5, 4, 31 (Mss. Vulg. Popp. Kühn. Saupp. ἐδυν- Dind. 4 edit.); Dem. 19, 209. 30, 1 (Bekk. B. S. ἐδυν- Dind.), and more Ion. ἐδυνάσθην (not ἠδυν- except v. r. Her. 7, 106 Ms. S.; and late V. T. 2 Chron. 30, 3 &c.) Il. 23, 465 (Dind. δυν- Wolf, Bekk. La R.). Od. 5, 319 (Wolf, Dind. δυν- Bekk. La Roche); Pind. Ol. 1, 56; Her. 2, 19. 140. 7, 106; Hippocr. 4, 214 (Lit.); in Attic prose only Xen. Cyr. 1, 1, 5. 8, 2, 9. Mem. 1, 2, 24. Hell. 7, 3, 3 &c.; Soph. O. R. 1212 chor. (most Mss. Ellendt, -άθην Ms. B. Br.

Herm. Elms. Dind.); Eur. Ion 867 chor. (-ήθην Elms. Dind. Nauck); subj. δυνηθῶ Dem. 41, 2, -θῶσι Thuc. 1, 88, -ασθῶ Xen. Hell. 2, 3, 33. 6, 5, 40 &c: fut. p. as mid. late δυνηθήσομαι Dio Cass. 52, 37. 69, 4 (Bekk. but in the latter suggests δυνήσ- adopted in every case by L. Dind.); Ignat. Patr. Apost. p. 373 (no v. r.), the only instances we have met except V. T. 3 Reg. 3, 9 (Vat. δυνησ- Alex.); and Jer. 5, 22 (Alex. but δυνησ- Vat.), from which the fut. p. form in Dio Cass. (or Xiphilinus) quoted, seems to derive some support. Besides, the author is exceedingly fond of fut. pass. as well as of plp.: 3 fut. δεδυνήσομαι late, Sopat. p. 97 (Walz), the only instance. Vb. δυνατός Thuc. 2, 15.—δύνᾰσαι 2 sing. indic. pres. Il. 1, 393. Od. 4, 374; Pind. P. 4, 158; Soph. Aj. 1164 (chor.); Ar. Nub. 811. Plut. 574; Xen. An. 7, 7, 8. Mem. 2, 8, 6; Pl. Rep. 400; Dem. 21, 207, and always in *classic* prose, but in poetry and *late* prose, sometimes syncop. δύνῃ Pythag. Aur. Carm. 19; Ael. V. H. 13, 32; Polyb. 7, 11. 24 &c.; and, if correct, Soph. Phil. 798 (Mss.); Eur. Hec. 253. Andr. 239 (but some hold these subj.); Pors. however (Eur. Hec. 253) maintained, with the Atticists, δύνᾳ to be the more Attic form, compare Soph. Ph. 849, and O. R. 696 (Nauck), Herm. in his last edit. of Soph. Phil. (1839) decidedly inclines to it, Ellendt approves, and Dind. *now* adopts it Soph. Ph. 798; Eur. Hec. 253. Andr. 239 quoted (where Paley agrees); so Aesch. uses ἐπίστᾳ Eum. 86. 581 (Ion. ἐπίστῃ Theogn. 1085). δύνᾳ is also Dor. Theocr. 10, 2; to which some add Soph. Ph. 849 (chor.), see above; so ἐπίστᾳ Pind. P. 3, 80. If Porson be right, and perhaps he is, δύνᾳ is in Attic poet. 2 sing. indic.; δύνῃ subj. Ar. Eq. 491, and, when *indicative*, Ionic.—δυνέαται, ἐδυνέατο = δύνανται, -αντο, Her. 4, 30. 9, 70; δύνηαι 2 sing. subj. Epic Il. 6, 229.—δυνεώμεθα, -έωνται Ion. Her. 4, 97. 7, 163 (Gaisf. Bekk. Krüg. δυνώμεθα, -ωνται Dind. Dietsch, Stein). The Epics never augment with η, the Attic poets rarely, and only, we think, when compelled by the metre. In Bekker's Her. the syllab. augm. is, we think, uniformly ε, in Gaisf. frequently η, 4, 110. 185. 9, 70 &c.; so Stein in the two last. In some late critical editions of Attic prose authors, the *temporal* augm. is losing ground: W. Dind. has dropped it entirely in Dem., Scheibe in Isae., Franke in Aeschin., and Lud. Dind. is dropping it in Xen. (4 edit.), and Stahl in Thuc. Benseler however, in accordance with the Mss., edits uniformly ἠδυν- in Isocr. ῠ, but δῡναμένοιο by arsis, Od. 1, 276. 11, 414.

Δυνέω, ἐν- for ἐνδύνω, -έουσι Her. 3, 98 (Vulg. Gaisf. Bekk. Stein), but ἐνδύνουσι (Ms. S. Bred. Dind.)

Δύνω *To go into, set* (= δύομαι of δύω), Il. 17, 202; Hes. Sc.

151; Hippocr. 2, 42, ἐσ- Her. 2, 123, ὑπο- 4, 75; subj. δύνωσι Hes. Op. 616, rare in Attic δύνῃ Soph. Ph. 1331; δύνοντος Aesch. Supp. 255; Eur. Phoen. 1117; (Lycophr. 1277; Her. 3, 114. 9, 14); Xen. An. 2, 2, 3. 13. Hell. 1, 6, 21; (Aeschin.?) 1, 12; Dem. 15, 22 (Bekk. B. S. δύντος Dind.); δύνειν Callim. Epigr. 26, ὑπο- Her. 1, 155: imp. ἔδῡνον Il. 3, 339, ὑπ- Her. 6, 2, Poet. δῦνον Il. 11, 268; Orph. Arg. 539: 1 aor. late, ἔδῡνα Batr. 242. 256 (Draheim)? δύναντος Polyb. 9, 15; Ap. Hisp. 20; Ael. V. H. 4, 1 (Vulg. δύντος Scheff. Herch.); Paus. 2, 11, 7, εἰσ- Malal. p. 238: p. δέδῡκα Il. 9, 239, see δύω. **Mid.** δύνομαι as **act.** -όμενος Callim. Epigr. 19, 6. 21, 2 (Ernesti). For fut. δύσομαι, p. δέδῡκα, 2 aor. ἔδυν &c. see δύω, to which they properly belong. The form δύνω is rather Ionic. The Tragedians, to be sure, have used it in trimeters, and it still occurs twice or thrice in Attic prose, but we have never seen it simple or comp. in Comedy.

Δύπτω Poet. *To dip*, subj. -ῃσι Antim. Fr. 6 (Bergk 2 ed. dropt in 3); δύπτειν Theocr. 11, 60 (Herm. Mein.); δύπτων Lycophr. 715; Ap. Rh. 1, 1008: **aor.** ἔδυψα Lycophr. 164; δύψας Ap. Rh. 1, 1326.

Δύρομαι *To weep*, Trag.=ὀδυρ-, Soph. O. R. 1218 (chor.); Eur. Hec. 740 (trimet.); imperat. δύρεσθε Aesch. Pr. 271 (trimet.); -όμενος Aesch. Pers. 582 (chor.); Eur. Med. 159 (chor.) (ῡ.) **Vb.** πάν-δυρτος Aesch. Pers. 940.

Δυστυχέω *To be unlucky, unhappy*, Aesch. Pr. 345; Thuc. 6, 16. 7, 18: **imp.** ἐδυστύχει Her. 8, 105: **fut.** -ήσω Isocr. 19, 41: **aor.** ἐδυστύχησα Lys. 12, 98; Pl. Menex. 243, 'δυστ- Soph. O. R. 262 (trimet.): δεδυστύχηκα Pl. Lach. 183; Lys. 14, 41; Isocr 6, 85; Com. Fr. (Mon.) 4, 431: **aor. p.** ἐδυστυχήθην, δυστυχηθῇ Pl. Leg. 877; -θέντα *ill successes*, Lys. 2, 70. Verbs comp. with δυς augment before it, if they begin with a consonant, or a *long* vowel, as δυσ-κολαίνω, ἐδυσκόλαινον Pl. Phil. 26, δυσ-φορέω, ἐδυσφόρουν Xen. Cyr. 2, 2, 8, δυσ-χεραίνω, ἐδυσχέραινον Pl. Theaet. 169; Aeschin. 1, 54. 158: **aor.** ἐδυσχέρᾱνα Isocr. 12, 201, δυσωπέω, ἐδυσώπησα (Luc.) Asin. 38: ἐδυσωπούμην Pl. Phaedr. 242, δυσ-ωνέω, ἐδυσώνει Anth. 11, 169; but after it, if they begin with a *short* vowel, δυσ-αρεστέω, δυσ-ηρέστουν Polyb. 5, 107, 6 (Bekk. Dind. Hultsch); D. Sic. 18, 62.

Δύω *To enter, sink*, intrans. in *simple* only part. δύων Il. 21, 232. Od. 5, 272, trans. *cause to enter, put on another*, in this sense the *simple* **pres.** is found only once, δύοντες Theophr. H. P. 5, 4, 8, more freq. in comp. ἐν-δύουσι Her. 2, 42, κατα- Xen. Cyr. 6, 1, 37: **imp.** δύεν intrans. Bion 9, 6, ἔκ-δυε H. Ven. 165, trans. ἐν-έδυε Xen. Cyr. 6, 4, 3: **fut.** δῡ́σω intrans.

Or. Sib. 3, 420. 5, 121, ἀπο- in tmesi, trans. Il. 2, 261; Hes. Sc. 67; Ar. Thesm. 637, κατα- Xen. An. 7, 2, 13: 1 aor. trans. ἔδῡσα in tmesi Od. 14, 341, περί-δῡσε Il. 11, 100, *simple* rare in Attic, Com. Fr. (Timocl.) 3, 602; Pseud.-Callisth. 1, 31, ἐν- Ar. Thesm. 1044, κατ- Her. 8, 88, ἀπ- Pl. Charm. 154, περι- Hyperid. Fr. 291; δῦσον, ἀπο- Luc. D. Mort. 10, 8: p. δέδῡκα Il. 5, 811; inf. -υκέναι Pl. Phaed. 116, Dor. -υκεῖν Theocr. 1, 102 (Ahr. Ziegl. Fritz.); δεδυκώς, ἐν- Her. 7, 89 (rarely causative, ἀποδέδῡκε Xen. An. 5, 8, 23; Dio Cass. 45, 47): plp. ἐδεδύκειν ἐν- Xen. An. 5, 4, 13: p.p. δέδῠμαι, ἐν- Com. Fr. (Menand.) 4, 199; Anth. Pl. 4, 171; Hippocr. 6, 658, ἐκ- Lys. 10, 10; Dem. 54, 35, ἀπο- Lys. 10, 10: aor. ἐδῠ́θην, ἀπο-δῠθῇ Ar. Ran. 715, ἐκ- Com. Fr. (Alex.) 3, 414; Antiph. 2, β, 5: fut. δῠθήσομαι, ἀπο- Ar. Vesp. 1122; Luc. Herm. 39: 2 aor. act. ἔδῡν as mid. ἔδυ Il. 11, 63; Aesch. Ag. 217; Eur. Rhes. 569; Pl. Tim. 25, δῦ Il. 17, 210. 21, 118, ἐδύτην Il. 10, 254, ἔδῡμεν Soph. Fr. 336 (D.), ἔδῡτε Od. 24, 106, -ῡσαν Il. 18, 145, and ἔδυν Il. 11, 263, iter. δύσκεν Il. 8, 271, see below: 2 aor. p. rare, ἐδύην in διεκ-δυῆναι Hippocr. 1, 601, but this is probably a false reading for διεκδῦναι. **Mid.** δύομαι *to put on oneself, enter, go down*, Il. 5, 140; Simon. C. 63; Eur. Rhes. 529; Her. 4, 181; δύηται Pl. Soph. 235; imper. δύου Ar. Vesp. 148 &c.: imp. ἐδύετο Pl. Polit. 269, ἐξ- Il. 3, 114, δύ- 15, 345; Emped. 166: fut. δύσομαι Il. 7, 298. Od. 12, 383; Eur. Elec. 1271, δύσει Pl. Leg. 905, Epic δύσεαι Il. 9, 231: aor. ἐδῡσάμην, -ύσατο Il. 3, 328 (Wolf, -σετο Bekk. La R.); late Epic Ap. Rh. 4, 865, but δύσαντο Il. 23, 73 (Bekk. La R.); Nic. Alex. 302; Q. Sm. 5, 354. 8, 23, ὑπο- Ar. Vesp. 1159 (Vulg. Bekk. Richter), ἐκ- Her. 5, 106, ἀπ- Pl. Rep. 612 (Bekk. Stallb.); Lys. Fr. 75 (Scheibe), and Epic, especially Hom. (ἐδῡσόμην), ἐδύσετο Il. 3. 328. 21, 515 (rare later, Batr. 302; Ap. Rh. 1, 63), δύσ- Il. 7, 465 (Bekk. Spitzn. Dind. always); δυσαίατο 18, 376 (-οίατο Bekk.); imper. δύσεο Il. 19, 36. Od. 17, 276 (Wolf, Bekk. Dind.); Hes. Sc. 108; δυσόμενος Od. 1, 24; Hes. Op. 384. In this sense always 2 aor. ἔδυ, -ύτην, -ῡτε, -ῡσαν; subj. δύω Il. 22, 99, -ῃς 9, 604, -ῃ 11, 194; Pl. Crat. 413; opt. δῦη Od. 18, 348. 20, 286, ἀνα- 9, 377 (δυίη Thiersch), ἐκ-δῦμεν Il. 16, 99 (-νῖμ- Herm.); imper. δῦθι Il. 16, 64, -ἀπό-δῡθι Ar. Thesm. 214; Luc. Catapl. 24, δῦτε Il. 18, 140; inf. δῦναι Il. 10, 221; Soph. Aj. 1192; Eur. Elec. 190, ἀπο- Pl. Charm. 154, κατα- Xen. Cyr. 5, 5, 9, Epic δῡ́μεναι Il. 14, 63; Anth. 5, 255, δύς, κατα- Hes. Sc. 196; Aesch. Ag. 1123; Her. 8, 8, δῦσα Pl. Tim. 25, δύντες Soph. Ant. 1217. **Vb.** ἐν-δυτος Eur. Fr. 258, ἀπο-δυτέον Pl. Rep. 457. In pres. and imp. ῠ in Hom. Il. 21, 232. 15, 345, ῡ in Attic, and occasionally in late Epic, Ap. Rh.

1, 925; Eur. Rhes. 529; Com. Fr. (Pher.) 2, 258. (Phil.) 4, 68, and what is remarkable ῠ in perf. ἐκ-δέδῠκας Anth. (Rufin.) 5, 73, and in **2 aor.** subj. δῠ́ῃ Hes. Op. 728. May this be **2 aor. pass.**? If so, it has its proper *quantity*, and countenances the correctness of the inf. διεκ-δυῆναι quoted above from Hippocr. Besides, it has analogy in the **2 aor. pass.** ἐφύην, ἐρρύην, of φύω, ῥέω.

ὑπόδυθι Ar. Vesp. 1158, -δύσασθαι 1159, -υσάμενος 1168, have been altered by a late Editor to ὑποδοῦ, ὑποδήσασθαι, -δησάμενος, most unnecessarily, we think, especially in a comic writer. Ar. has said ὑποδυόμενος ὑπὸ τῶν κεραμίδων Vesp. 205: if therefore it is correct when applied to creeping under the roof of a house, we don't see how it may not legitimately express the *moving* of the foot *under* the *roof* of one's shoes. ὑποδῦσα θαλάσσης εὐρέα κόλπον Od. 4, 435, does not express going under the *bottom* of the sea, but only the surface, answering to the *upper leather* of a shoe. We are sorry to observe Dindorf giving in to this change: it is unworthy of him. ὑπόδυθι τὰς λακωνικάς seems to be explained by ἔνθες πόδ' 1161.

Δωρέω *To present*, fut. δωρήσω (Hom.) Fr. 7, 7: **aor.** ἐδώρησα Hes. Op. 82; Pind. Ol. 6, 78. Commonly Dep. δωρέομαι, -οῦμαι Soph. El. 458; Com. Fr. (Antiph.) 3, 3; Xen. An. 7, 3, 26, -έεται Her. 6, 125, -εῖται Xen. Cyr. 2, 1, 17: **imp.** ἐδωρούμεθα (Pl.) Alc. (2) 148, -εῖτο Plut. Mor. 761, Ion. -έετο Her. 3, 130: **fut.** δωρήσομαι Pind. Ol. 7, 3; Aesch. Pr. 778; Pl. Phaedr. 256: **aor.** ἐδωρησάμην Aesch. Pr. 251; Com. Fr. (Eup.) 2, 453; Her. 5, 37; Xen. Cyr. 8, 4, 24; Pl. Conv. 194; Charit. 8, 8, 10 (Herch.); subj. δωρήσῃ Xen. An. 7, 3, 20; opt. δωρήσαιτο Il. 10, 557; Pl. Rep. 394, -σαίατο, ἀντι- Eur. Hel. 159; -ήσασθαι Pl. Tim. 47: **p.** δεδώρημαι **act.** -ησαι Xen. Cyr. 5, 2, 8, -ηται Pl. Tim. 46. Leg. 672; -ῆσθαι Epist. 2, 314, and **pass.** -ηται Pl. Polit. 274; -ῆσθαι Tim. 47: **aor.** ἐδωρήθην always **pass.** Soph. Aj. 1029; Her. 8, 85; δωρηθέν Isocr. 4, 26; Pl. Tim. 47; -θῆναι Diod. Sic. 5, 49. **Vb.** δωρητός Il. 9, 526; Soph. O. R. 384. The **act.** v. is Poet. and confined to Epic, and Pindar: in Hom. the **aor. mid.** alone seems to occur.

E.

'Εάφθη or ἐαφ-, see ἅπτω.

'Εάω, ἐῶ *To let, leave alone*, Il. 8, 428; Aesch. Sept. 378; Soph. El. 632; Ar. Eq. 58; Her. 8, 69; Thuc. 3, 48; Isocr. 12, 227; Pl. Rep. 361; opt. ἐῷμι Od. 16, 85, ἐῷ 20, 12, Att. ἐῴην Pl. Gorg. 458, -ῴη Soph. Ph. 444; Xen. Cyr. 1, 5, 10; Dem. 53;

10, Epic εἰάω Il. 11, 550, augm. with ει: imp. εἴων Il. 18, 448; Thuc. 1, 28; Isae. 8, 26, ἔων Her. 9, 2, εἴα Od. 7, 41, ἔα Il. 5, 517; Her. 1, 17. 2, 18. 19, iter. ἔασκ- see below: fut. ἐάσω Il. 18, 296; Soph. O. R. 676; Eur. Andr. 875; Ar. Eccl. 239; Her. 6, 55; Antiph. 5, 90; Thuc. 1, 144; Lys. 3, 45: aor. εἴᾱσα Il. 11, 323. Od. 10, 166; Pind. Ol. 7, 61; Soph. Ant. 698; Thuc. 6, 41; Isocr. 5, 107, Poet. ἔᾱσα Il. 11, 437; Callim. Cer. 62; ἔασον Il. 8, 243; Aesch. Pr. 332; part. ἐάσας Her. 1, 90: p. εἴᾱκα Dem. 8, 37. 43, 78; Aristot. Metaph. 1, 9, 26: p. p. εἴᾱμαι Dem. 45, 22: aor. εἰάθην Isocr. 4, 97; Pl. Tim. 85; Aristot. Probl. 14, 2; (Dem.) 10, 8; Plut. Mor. 227, late εἰάσθ- Philo: fut. mid. ἐάσομαι pass. Eur. I. A. 331; Thuc. 1, 142: pres. ἐάσθω Soph. Tr. 329; ἐᾶσθαι O. C. 368; ἐώμενος Eur. I. T. 1344; Dem. 2, 16. Vb. ἐατέος Pl. Rep. 401. Pres. sing. ἐάᾳς Od. 12, 137, ἐάᾳ Il. 8, 414, lengthened with α, never with ο, so inf. ἐάαν Od. 8, 509, for ἐᾷς, -ᾷ, -ᾶν: iter. imp. ἔασκες Il. 19, 295, -σκε 2, 832. 11, 330. 24, 17, and εἴασκον Il. 5, 802, -ασκε 20, 408. Od. 22, 427, -ασχ' Il. 11, 125, not augmented, but from εἰάω. Forms in -σκον are scarcely ever augmented, except in cases of necessity, see ἐβίβασκε H. Apol. 133, but παρ-έβασκε Il. 11, 104, may be imp. of -βάσκω. (ᾰ in pres. and imp. only, except in late poets, for in fut. ἐάσουσι Od. 21, 233, ἐα- is scanned by syniz.) Her. never augments this verb. Littré edits inf. ἐῆν Hippocr. 8, 204 with Ms. G, in other places ἐᾷν 8, 184. 232; so Her. ἐᾶν 2, 175. 6, 23, and always.

Ἐγγυαλίζω *To put into the hand, bestow* (γύαλον), Poet. unaugm. Il. 2, 436; Pind. I. 8, 43: fut. -ίξω Il. 11, 192; Athen. (Hegem.) 15, 55; Ap. Rh. 2, 55; Orph. L. 169: aor. ἐγγυάλιξα Il. 11, 753; Hes. Th. 485; Ap. Rh. 1, 1181. 2, 180; Orph. L. 406. (ῠ ᾰ.)

Ἐγγυάω *To proffer, betroth*, Her. 6, 130; -υᾶν (Dem.) 59, 13; Plut. Aristid. 27: imp. ἐνεγύα Isae. 3, 45. 70 (Bekk. B. S.), ἠγγύα (Scheibe); Dem. 41, 6. 16 (Mss. Bekk. B. S.), ἠγγύα (Dind.), always in comp. κατ-ηγγ- Dem. 32, 29 (Mss. Bekk. B. S. Dind.), παρ- Soph. O. C. 94; Eur. Supp. 700; Xen. An. 4, 1, 17. 7, 1, 22; Polyb. 1, 76: fut. (ἐγγυήσω): aor. ἠγγύησα Eur. I. A. 703; Dem. 29, 47. 59, 79 (59, 62 Dind.); Dio Cass. 54, 31, κατ- Dem. 32, 30. 33, 10. 59, 40, παρ- Xen. Cyr. 3, 3, 69. An. 7, 3, 46, and ἐνεγύησα Isae. 3, 36. 52. 79. 9, 29 (ἠγγύ- Scheibe); (Dem.) 59, 62 (Bekk. B. S. ἠγγύ- Dind.); Dio Cass. 48, 54 (Bekk.); App. Lyb. 10; ἐγγυήσῃ Her. 6, 57: p. ἠγγύηκα Dio Cass. 38, 9; (Dem.) 59, 53 (corr. V. Dind.), ἐγγεγύηκ- (Ms. S. Bekk. B. S.); Isae. 3, 40, ἠγγύ- (Scheibe, see foll.): but plp. ἠγγυήκει Isae. 3, 58: p. p. ἐγγεγύημαι Pl. Leg. 923; Isae. 3, 73 (ἠγγυ- Scheibe); Dem. 33, 24 (Ms. S. Bekk. B. S.), ἠγγυ- (Dind.), as always in comp. ἐξ-ηγγ- 19, 169 (Bekk. Dind.), δι-ηγγ- Thuc. 3, 70: plp. ἐγγεγυήμην Dem. 33, 29 (Ms. Bekk. B. S., ἠγγυήμ- Dind.), ἐνεγεγυή- Isae. 3, 55 (Bekk. B. S.), ἠγγύ- (Scheibe): **aor.** ἠγγυήθην, ἐξ- Lys. 23, 11, κατ- (Dem.) 59, 49; ἐγγυηθείς, ἐξ- Andoc. 1, 44. **Mid.** ἐγγυάομαι, *to engage*, Ar. Plut. 1202; Pl. Prot. 336; Dem. 24, 41; -ᾶσθαι Her. 6, 130, Epic -άασθαι Od. 8, 351: **imp.** ἠγγυώμην Xen. An. 7, 4, 13; Lys. 13, 23; Pl. Phaed. 115; (Dem.) 59, 51, ἐνεγυ- Isae. 3, 70. 5, 18. 20, ἠγγυ- (Scheibe): **fut.** ἐγγυήσομαι Dem. 24, 46; Plut. Mor. 661, Dor. -άσομαι Pind. Ol. 11 (10), 16: **aor.** ἠγγυησάμην Andoc. 1, 44. 73; Dem. 22, 53. 33, 22. 27. 28. 53, 27 (Ms. S. Bekk. B. S. Dind.), δι-ηγγ- Isocr. 17, 14, and ἐνεγυησ- Isae. 3, 55. 5, 4 (ἠγγυ- Scheibe); Dem. 33, 29 (Bekk. B. S.), ἠγγυ- (Ms. S. Dind.) (ῡ.) In Isaeus, Scheibe now augments uniformly with η, so Dindorf in Dem., Bekk. and B. S. vary with the Mss. Compounds have always η, διηγγ- Isocr. 17, 14, ἐξ- Lys. 23, 11, κατ- Dem. 32, 30 &c., παρ- Soph. Eur. quoted; Xen. Hell. 4, 2, 19. There is therefore nothing remarkable in the aor. pass. being the only past tense that augments uniformly with initial η, ἠγγυήθην, seeing it is always a compound. The rather anomalous forms ἐνεγγύησα, ἐνεγγεγυήμην, ἐνεγγυησάμην with the unaugmented ἐγγυώμην, ἐγγυησάμην &c. have been wholly or almost discarded from late recensions; ἐνηγγύα App. Mithr. 102, ἐνηγγύησε ibid. 2, *now* ἠγγύα, ἠγγύησε (Bekk.), but still ἐνεγγύ- Dio. Hal. 3, 13. 4, 4. 28 (Kiessl.); Plut. Caes. 14. Cat. Min. 25. 31 (Sint.), but ἐνεγυ- (Bekk.). Artax. 27 (Bekk. Sint.): ἐνηγγυημένη App. Civ. 2, 14: ἐνεγγυήσατο Dio. Hal. 11, 28. This verb occurs in Hom. once only, and in the Epic inf. pres. mid. ἐγγυάασθαι Od 8, 351.

Ἐγείρω *To raise*, Il. 24, 344; Hes. Op. 20; Eur. Fr. 402 (Dind.); Ar. Plut. 541; Her. 4, 119; Thuc. 1, 121; Pl. Crat. 411; Ep. subj. ἐγείρομεν for -ωμεν, Il. 2, 440; ἔγειρε Pind. Ol. 9, 47; Aesch. Eum. 140; Soph. O. C. 1778: **imp.** ἤγειρον Ar. Pl. 740; Isocr. 16, 7; Pl. Crito 43, ἔγειρ- Il. 15, 594: **fut.** ἐγερῶ Plat. Eleg. 28 (Bergk); Plut. Mor. 462, ἐξ- Soph. Tr. 978; Xen. Hell. 6, 4, 36, ἐπ- Ar. Av. 84: **aor.** ἤγειρα Il. 17, 261; Aesch. Ag. 299; Com. Fr. (Menand.) 4, 208; Her. 1, 59; Pl. Polit. 272; Leg. 685, ἔγειρ- Od. 15, 45; Hes. Th. 713; Pind. N. 10, 21; Epic subj. ἐγείρομεν Il. 2, 440; ἐγεῖραι Il. 5, 510; Pind. P. 9, 104: **p.** late ἐγήγερκα Philostr. Epist. 16 (348); Orig. Ref. Haer. p. 195 (Miller): **plp.** ἐγηγέρκειν Dio Cass. 42, 48; Joseph. Ant. 17, 7, 4: **p. p.** ἐγήγερμαι Thuc. 7, 51; Himer. 5, 7, δι- (Hippocr.) Epist. 9, 340 (Lit.): **plp.** ἐγήγερτο Luc. Alex

19; Polyaen. 4, 18: aor. ἠγέρθην Polyaen. 1. 30, 4, ἐπ-ηγέρθ- Her. 7, 137, ἐξ- 1, 34. 209 (Bekk. Dietsch, Krüg. Stein); Xen. Cyr. 8, 7, 2, Epic ἔγερθεν, for -ησαν, Il. 23, 287 (ἄγερθ- La R.), ἐξ-εγέρθην Her. 1, 34. 209 quoted (Gaisf. Dind.); ἐγερθείη Hippocr. 1, 483 (Erm.); Xen. Vect. 4, 41; -θῆναι Her. 4, 9; -θείς Heraclit. 2 (Byw.); Pl. Tim. 52: **fut.** late ἐγερθήσομαι Babr. 49, 3: **2 p.** ἐγρήγορα *I am awake*, Ar. Lys. 306; Pl. Ion 532. Prot. 310. Theaet. 158; -ορώς Aesch. Eum. 685; Hippocr. 5, 310; Antiph. 5, 44; Xen. Cyr. 4, 5, 7. 7, 5, 20; Pl. Leg. 823; -ορέναι Hippocr. 5, 694; Pl. Phaed. 71: **plp.** ἐγρηγόρειν Ar. Pl. 744. Eccl. 32 (-όρη Pors. Dind.), -όρει Xen. Cyr. 1, 4, 20, ἐγρ- and ἠγρ- Com. Fr. (Men.) 4, 309. **Mid.** ἐγείρομαι *to rise*, Pl. Rep. 330; ἐγείροιτο Hippocr. 5, 384 (Lit.); -όμενος Od. 20, 100: fut. late ἐγερεῖσθαι *shall be raised*, Polyaen. 1, 30, 4, ἐξεγεροῦνται Or. Sib. 12 (14), 243 (Friedl.): **2 aor.** ἐγρόμην Epic in *simple*, Il. 2, 41. 15, 4. Od. 13, 187; Callim. Fr. 206, ἐξ- Theocr. 24, 21, ἠγρόμην, ἐξ- Ar. Ran. 51; Hippocr. 5, 204 (Lit.); subj. ἔγρωμαι, ἔγρῃ Ar. Vesp. 774, -ηται Hippocr. 8, 324, ἐξ- 6, 634; -ωνται, ἐπ- 6, 354; opt. ἔγροιτο Od. 6, 113; imper. Epic, ἔγρεο Il. 10, 159. Od. 23, 5; Orph. Arg. 541; Bion 1, 4, ἔγρεσθε Eur. Rhes. 532. 533 (chor.); Ap. Rh. 2, 884; ἐγρέσθαι Od. 13, 124 (Bekk. ἔγρ- Dind. La Roche), ἐξ- Pl. Conv. 223. Rep. 534; ἐγρόμενος Od. 10, 50; Ap. Rh. 4, 671; Pl. Lys. 204, ἐξ- Conv. 223: **2 p.** ἐγρήγορθα see below. **Vb.** ἐγερτός Aristot. Somn. 1, 12, ἀν-έγ- Gen. An. 5, 1, 11, ἐγερτέος Eur. Rhes. 690. For the rather startling **1 aor.** ἐγείρατο, and **plp.** ἐξήγερτο Hippocr. 3, 647. 545 (Kühn), we had happened to record as a *conjecture*, opt. ἐγείροιτο, and **2 aor.** ἐξήγρετο, which we are proud to say are now ascertained to be the Mss. readings, 5, 204. 384 (Lit.); ἐγείρατο however occurs late, Or. Sib. 3, 159, and ἤγερτο Joseph. Ant. 15, 11, 5. In Her. the Mss. preponderate in favour of the augment; Bekk. Lhardy, Bred. Krüg. always augment, Gaisf. thrice, but ἐξεγέρθη 1, 34. 209, and so, to our surprise, Dind.

Ἐγκωμιάζω *To praise*, Com. Fr. (Axion.) 3, 534; Isocr. 3, 7; Pl. Conv. 199: **imp.** ἐνεκωμ- Xen. Cyr. 5, 3, 3; Aeschin. 3, 86: **fut.** ἐγκωμιᾰσω Pl. Gorg. 518. 519; Isocr. 12, 111; Aeschin. 3, 241; Hyperid. Leosth. 15, 5: and **mid.** -ᾰσομαι Pl. Conv. 198. Rep. 581; Isocr. 5, 17. Epist. 7, 1; Aeschin. 1, 133: **aor.** ἐνεκωμίασα Isocr. 4, 159; Pl. Lach. 191; inf. -ιάσαι Conv. 214: **p.** 'γκεκωμίᾰκα Pl. Leg. 629. 754; Isocr. 7, 71. 15, 61: **p. p.** ἐγκεκωμίασμαι Pl. Conv. 177. Charm. 157. (Minos) 319; Isocr. 12, 81: **aor.** ἐγκωμιασθῇ Plut. Mor. 869; -ασθείς Her. 5, 5.

Ἐγρήγορα, see ἐγείρω.

Ἐγρηγοράω *To be awake*, Epic and only part. ἐγρηγορόων

waking, Od. 20, 6, late ἐγρηγορέω, -γοροῦσι Aristot. Probl. 4, 5; -γορῶν Themist. 26, 315.

Ἐγρήγορθα *I am awake*, Epic 2 p., of which occur 3 pl. ἐγρηγόρθᾰσι, for ἐγρηγόρᾱσι, Il. 10, 419; imper. ἐγρήγορθε, for -όρατε, 7, 371; inf. ἐγρήγορθαι or -όρθαι 10, 67. The rare collat. ἔγρω, see below.

Ἐγρήσσω *To be awake*, Epic and only pres. Od. 20, 33; Opp. Hal. 2, 659; late prose -σσωσι Aretae. Morb. ac. 1, 84 (ed. Oxon.); -σσων Il. 11, 551; Ap. Rh. 2, 308; -ήσσειν Hipponax 89.

Ἔγρω *To rouse, wake*, only imper. ἐγρέτω Athen. (Sopat.) 4, 77, ἔγρετε Eur. Rhes. 532 (Dind. 2 ed. ἔξιτε 5 ed. with Hart.) **Mid.** ἔγρομαι Eur. Fr. 775, 27 (D.); and late Epic, Opp. Hal. 5, 243, ἀν- Q. Sm. 5, 610; Opp. Hal. 2, 204: **imp.** ἔγρετο Opp. Cyn. 3, 421. See ἐγείρω.

Ἐγχρίμπτω *To bring near*, mostly Epic and Ion. Her. 3, 85; Opp. Hal. 2, 336; intrans. *approach*, subj. -ίμπτῃ Soph. El. 898, Poet. ἐνιχριμπ-: **fut.** (-χρίμψω): **aor.** ἐνέχριμψα, subj. ἐγχρίμψῃ Opp. Hal. 2, 71. 522, Poet. ἐνιχρίμψῃσι Ap. Rh. 4, 1512, -ητε 2, 398; ἐγχρίμψας Il. 23, 334; Her. 9, 98; Opp. Hal. 1, 720. ἐγχρίμπτομαι *to come near, approach*, Eur. Hipp. 218 (chor.); Her. 2, 93, and -ίπτομαι: **imp.** ἐνεχρίμπτετο 4, 113, ἐγχρίμπτ- Il. 17, 413: with **fut. mid.** ἐνιχρίμψεσθαι Ap. Rh. 4, 939: **aor.** ἐγχρίψαιντο Themist. 15, 192: and **aor. pass.** ἐγχριμφθήτω Il. 23, 338; ἐγχριμφθείς Il. 13, 146. ἐνιχριμφ- 17, 405; ἐγχριμφθῆναι Aesch. Supp. 790 (Vulg. -χριμφθῆν Dind. Weil.) This verb is rare in Tragedy, never, we think, in Comedy, nor classic Attic prose.

Ἑδνόω *To betroth* (ἕδνον), Poet. unaugm. **aor.** ἕδνωσε Theocr. 22, 147. **Mid.** -οῦμαι *to portion*, **fut.** ἑδνώσομαι Eur. Hel. 933 (Herm. Kirchh. Nauck, Paley): **aor.** ἑδνώσατο Q. Sm. 13, 510 (Koechl.); opt. ἐεδνώσαιτο Od. 2, 53, later *married*, ἑδνώσαιτο Anth. 7, 648. The Mss. reading Eur. Hel. 933 is ἑδάσομαι, ἑδνασ- (Ald. ἐκδώσομαι Elms. W. Dind. Fix, Hartung).

Ἑδριάω (ᾰ) *To sit*, Poet. ἅει Theocr. 17, 19; Epic part. ἑδριόων Ap. Rh. 3, 170; Orph. Arg. 807: **imp. iter.** ἑδριάασκε, ἐφ- Tzetz. Hom. 392. **Mid.** only in the Epic form ἑδριόωνται Hes. Th. 388; -ιάασθαι Od. 3, 35: **imp.** ἑδριόωντο Il. 10, 198. Od. 7, 98; Ap. Rh. 1, 530.

(**Ἕδω**) *To seat*, see (ἕζω) καθέζομαι.

Ἔδω *To eat*, usu. Epic in pres. and imp. Il. 6, 142. 15, 636. Od. 16, 431. 18, 280; Hes. Th. 640; Callim. Dian. 165; Anacreont. 14 (9), 25; rare in Attic, Eur. Cycl. 245 (trim.); Com. Fr. (Alcae.) 2, 832. (Eub.) 3, 219; rare also in prose, Hippocr. 1, 580 (Lit.); late Attic, Luc. Rhet. 11, Dor. 3 pl.

ἔδοντι Theocr. 5, 128; sub. ἔδω Od. 13, 419. 16, 389; opt. ἔδοιμι Il. 13, 322; Hes. Th. 525; Pseud-Phocyl. 156; Callim. Dian. 89; ἔδων Od. 10, 379. Il. 21, 465; Eur. quoted; Callim. Cer. 89; Ap. Rh. 1, 1289. 4, 265; inf. Epic is always ἔδμεναι Il. 13, 36. Od. 16, 84: imp. ἔδον Il. 15, 636. Od. 23, 9, iter. ἔδεσκον Il. 22, 501: fut. m. ἔδομαι Il. 18, 271. Od. 9, 369; Theocr. 3, 52; Ar. Nub. 121; Com. Fr. (Crat.) 2, 239; Pl. Rep. 373. Prot. 334; Plut. Mor. 996, κατ- Ar. Eccl. 595. Fr. 528 (D.); Com. Fr. (Antiph.) 3, 12. (Timcol.) 3, 600. (Men.) 4, 178, προσκατ- (Alex.) 3, 462, later ἐδοῦμαι, κατ- Dio. Hal. Ant. 1, 55 (Vulg. κατέδομ- Kiessl.), προ-κατ- Luc. Hes. 7 (-έδομαι Dind.): p. ἐδήδοκα Ar. Eq. 362; Com. Fr. (Alex.) 3, 462. 507, κατ- Aeschin. 1, 42. 106; opt. ἐδηδοκοίη Com. Fr. (Cratin.) 2, 179; ἐδηδοκώς Xen. An. 4, 8, 20, κατ- Aeschin. 1, 30: plp. ἐδηδόκει Luc. Gall. 4: p.p. ἐδήδεσμαι, κατ- Com. Fr. (Antiph.) 3, 87; Pl. Phaed. 110, and 3 sing. ἐδήδοται Od. 22, 56, κατ- Dio. Hal. Ant. 1, 55 (Vulg. -δεσται Kiessl.): aor. ἠδέσθην Hippocr. 1, 686 (Vulg.); Aristot. Probl. 13, 6, κατ- Com. Fr. (Plat.) 2, 627: 2 p. (ἔδηδα), ἐδηδώς Il. 17, 542, -δυῖαι Hom. H. 3, 560. Vb. ἐδεστός Pl. Tim. 72; Aristot. Pol. 7, 2, 15, -έος Pl. Crit. 47. Pres. and imp. mostly Epic, rare in prose. ἔδμεναι Epic and Lyric inf. pres. for ἐδέμεναι, ἔδειν, Il. 13, 36; Alcm. 100 (B.) Fut. ἐδοῦμαι, κατ- in late editions of Athenaeus, Com. Fragm. and Dio. Hal. has given way to κατέδομαι. See ἐσθίω.

'Εείδομαι, ἐέλδομαι, ἐέλπομαι, &c. see εἴδομαι, ἔλδομαι, ἔλπω &c.

(**'Εεργάθω**) *To shut out*, Epic for εἰργ- imp. ἐέργαθον Il. 5, 147. See ἐέργω.

'Εέργνυμι, see ἔργνυμι.

'Εέργω *To shut out*, Epic (and Ion.?) for ἔργω, εἴργω, Il. 13, 706. 23, 72 (B.). Od. 11, 503; Hes. Th. 751; Ap. Rh. 3, 427; Her. 8, 98 (old edit. Gaisf., ἔργει Mss. S. P. Wess. Bekk. Dind. Stein); subj. ἐέργῃ Il. 4, 131; ἐέργοι 18, 512 (Bekk. Dind.); ἔεργε Od. 12, 219: imp. ἔεργον Il. 8, 213: 2 aor. ἐέργαθον Il. 5, 147, called by some imp. of (ἐεργάθω): pass. ἐεργόμενοι Il. 13, 525; Ap. Rh. 3, 649?—also for ἔργω, and εἴργνυμι, *to shut in*, ἐέργει Il. 2, 617. 9, 404; Mosch. 4, 48, -εις Ap. Rh. 3, 427: imp. ἔεργον Od. 7, 88; Ap. Rh. 2, 201: aor. ἔερξε, κατ- H. Merc. 356: p.p. ἐεργμένος *closely compacted*, Il. 5, 89; Emped. 322: Ap. Rh. 2, 550: plp. Epic, ἐέρχατο (for -χντο= ἐεργμένοι ἦσαν) Od. 10, 241: pres. pass. ἐέργεται Ap. Rh. 4, 309; -όμενος Callim. Fr. 149; Opp. Hal. 1, 226. Gaisf. edits ἐέργει Her. 8, 98; but ἔργω, not ἐέργω nor εἴργω, seems to be the true Herodotean form, see 3, 48. 4, 164, ἀπ- 1, 72. 2, 99, δι- 1, 180, ἐξ- 3, 51, περι- 2, 148 &c. (Gaisf. Bekk. Dind. Stein.)

(Ἕζω) *To set, seat*, act. not used: εἷσα, εἵσομαι, εἱσάμην, see ἕω: Mid. usu. Poet. ἕζομαι *to seat oneself, sit*, Epic 2 sing. ἕζεαι Od. 10, 378 (Bekk. Dind.), -όμεσθα Soph. O. R. 32; subj. ἑζώμεσθα Eur. Elec. 109, Dor. ἑσδώμ- Theocr. 1, 21; imper. ἕζεο Il. 6, 354; Theocr. Epigr. 4, 13, Ion. ἕζευ Il. 24, 522; -εσθαι 18, 247; -όμενος Il. 14, 437; Soph. Aj. 249 (chor.); Eur. Phoen. 1517 (chor.); Ar. Ran. 682 (chor.). Pax 801 (chor.); Her. 4, 85: **imp.** unaugm. ἑζόμην as aor. Il. 1, 48. Od. 3, 389; Mimnerm. 9, 4; Pind. I. 6, 56; Theocr. 2, 113; Aesch. Eum. 3; Soph. O. C. 100; Eur. Ion 1202; Stob. (Phanocl.) 64, 14, see below: **aor. pass.** (ἥσθην), subj. ἑσθῶ Soph. O. C. 195 (Herm. Dind. 4 ed.), see below. Rare in prose, ἕζονται Luc. D. Syr. 31; imperat. ἕζεσθε Her. 8, 22: **imp.** ἑζόμην Her. 4, 165 (Gaisf. Bekk. Dind. Dietsch, ἱζ- Stein); Joseph. Ant. 18, 6, 6: for **fut.** ἑδοῦμαι, ἑδήσομαι &c. see καθέζομαι. For **aor. pass.** ἑσθῶ, Hermann's reading Soph. O. C. quoted, stands ἑστῶ (Nauck), ἦ 'σθῶ (old edit. Dind. doubtingly 5 ed. and suggests κλιθῶ), ἦ ἑσθῶ (Br.), ἦ στῶ (Reisig, Elms.), ἥσθω, ἡσθῶ (Mss.). καθεσθῶ (Gloss.) Phryn. Thom. Mag. and some late editors have objected to the **aor.** as a form of *bad mark*. Herm. however somewhat turns the point of this objection by maintaining that it does not, and was not intended to apply to poetic usage, but to the more common, more level, and less privileged style of writing. We know however of no *early* example of the *simple*, but there are several *late* of the comp. καθέσθην, see καθέζομαι.

Ἐθελοκακέω *To do evil advisedly*, Luc. Somn. 18: Ion. and unaugm. **imp.** ἐθελοκάκεον Her. 1, 127. 5, 78. 8, 85 (Mss. Bekk. Krüg. Stein, ἠθ- Dind.): **aor.** -ήσας Polyb. 5, 100; Luc. Apol. 8.

Ἐθέλω *To wish*, Il. 7, 364; Solon 4, 28; Simon. C. 88; Pind. Ol. 11, 9; Aesch. Pr. 1067 (chor.); Soph. El. 132. Ph. 145 (chor.); Eur. Ion 99 (chor.); Ar. Ran. 613 (trim.); Her. 9, 120; Antiph. 1, 15; Thuc. 4, 59; Pl. Rep. 370, Dor. 2 sing. -λησθα Theocr. 29, 4, 3 pl. -λοντι Pind. N. 7, 10; Bion 6, 4; Epic subj. -λωμι Il. 9, 397 (Bekk.), -ῃσθα 8, 471. Od. 12, 49; Emped. 28, -ῃσι Theogn. 139, ἐθέλητε Her. 4, 133; ἐθέλοιμι 9, 45; imper. ἔθελε Il. 2, 247; Dor. pt. ἐθελοίσας Pind. N. 3, 83: **imp.** ἤθελον Hes. Op. 136; Solon 33, 5; Pind. P. 3, 1; Aesch. Ch. 701; Soph. Aj. 88; Ar. Ach. 57; Her. 1, 16; Antiph. 6, 27; Thuc. 5, 15; Isae. 5, 32; Il. 14, 120, and ἔθελ- 6, 336; Theogn. 606; Pind. P. 9, 111, iter. ἐθέλεσκον Il. 13, 106; Her. 6, 12: **fut.** ἐθελήσω Il. 18, 262; Pind. Ol. 7, 20; Ar. Vesp. 291; Her. 1, 32; Antiph. 1, 16; Thuc. 6, 33; Xen. Hell. 3, 5, 3; Pl. Phil. 50: **aor.** ἠθέλησα Soph. O. R. 1348; Com. Fr. (Crito) 4, 538; Her. 2, 2; Antiph. 6, 24; Thuc. 4,

57; Lys. 2, 12; Dem. 2, 24, Poet. ἐθέλ- Il. 18, 396; App. Epigr. 223 (Her. 7, 168 Schäf. Gaisf. ἠθ- Bekk. Dind. Stein, Abicht); ἐθελήσῃ Aesch. Pr. 178; Pl. Phaedr. 257; opt. -ήσαις Pind. P. 1, 40; Pl. Gorg. 449. Lys. 206, but -σειας Polit. 272, -σειαν Isae. 8, 42; ἐθέλησον Pl. Gorg. 449: p. ἠθέληκα Aeschin. 2. 139; Xen. Cyr. 5, 2, 9; Dem. 47, 5: plp. ἠθελήκει Xen. Hell. 6, 5, 21. See θέλω. ἐθέλωμι Epic subj. pres. for ἐθέλω, Il. 1, 549. 9, 397. ἐθέλω alone is used in Hom. Hes. Theogn. and Pind. (Boeckh), but twice θέλων Ol. 2, 97. P. 10, 5 (Schn. Ahr. Bergk); in Ionic and Attic prose, Attic poetry, and in the later Epic and Bucolic writers, it is the prevailing form. In tragic trimeters, the pres. is of course admissible only under very limited conditions, not so in chor. Aesch. Ag. 1569; Soph. O. R. 1304 (Elms. Dind.), and comic trimeters, Ar. Plut. 375. 467. Lys. 134 &c. In Her. Bredow would always write ἐθέλω. Our editors however with the Mss., have both ἐθέλω 5, 19. 9, 120 &c. and θέλω 1, 59. 3, 65. 7, 10. 234 &c., but imp. always ἤθελον 1, 16. 97. 3, 52 &c. ἔθελ- 3, 146. 8, 80 (Vulg. Gaisf.) is ἤθελ- (Mss. F. K. Bekk. Dind. Stein), fut. ἐθελήσω 1, 206. 7, 10 &c. except δὲ θελήσει 1, 109 (Vulg. Gaisf. Bekk. δ' ἐθελ- Dind. Dietsch, Stein), aor. *indic.* perhaps always ἠθέλησα 1, 59. 2, 2. 7, 29. 9, 18 &c., ἐθελ- 7, 107. 164. 168 (Vulg. Gaisf. ἠθελ- Mss. F. S. Bekk. Dind. Stein); inf. ἐθελῆσαι 1, 3. 145. 7, 229. 230 &c., and θελῆσαι 1, 24. 2, 42 (Mss. Gaisf. Bekk. Stein &c.), where (1, 24) Dind. reads ἐθελ-, but 2, 42 θελῆσαι, why, we see not.

Ἐθίζω *To accustom*, Xen. Cyr. 1, 2, 10; Isocr. 12, 210, poet. εἰθ- Pythag. Aur. C. 9. 35, reg. but augm. with ει: fut. ἐθίσω, -ιῶ Xen. Cyr. 3, 3, 53: aor. εἴθισα Dem. 20, 68; Luc. Bis acc. 34: p. εἴθικα Xen. Hell. 6, 1, 15; Pl. Meno 70: p. p. εἴθισμαι Eur. I. A. 726; Ar. Eccl. 265; Hippocr. 4, 254; Thuc. 1, 77; Andoc. 3, 28; Iscor. 6, 2. 18, 34, 3 pl. εἰθίδαται Hippocr. 1, 307 (oldest Ms. Erm. εἰθισμένοι εἰσί Vulg. Lit. 2, 298): plp. εἴθιστο Hippocr. 2, 294; Xen. Ages. 11, 2; Isocr. 21, 11; (Dem.) 61, 14, ἤθιστ- (Ms. S.): aor. εἰθίσθην Ar. Vesp. 512; Pl. Leg. 681; ἐθισθῶ Hippocr. 1, 305 (Erm.): fut. later ἐθισθήσονται Dio. Hal. 4, 11; Aristid. 42, (518.) Vb. ἐθιστός Aristot. Eth. Nic. 1, 10, 1, -έος Isocr. 9, 7. εἴθιζον Plut. Lycurg. 12 (Vulg.) quoted by our lexicons as an instance of the act. used intrans. is now εἰθίζοντο (Bekk. Sint.) from Porphyry's ἠθίζοντο—the only case of augm. with η that we have seen, except ἤθισται (Dem.) 26, 18, ἠθισμένος 27, 64, and plp. ἤθιστο Dem. 61, 14 quoted (Ms. S.)

Ἔθω *To be accustomed*, Epic and only part. ἔθων Il. 9, 540. 16,

260: 2 p. εἴωθα *am accustomed*, Il. 5, 766; Eur. Supp. 576; Ar. Pax 730; Hippocr. 6, 242; Antiph. 6, 13; Thuc. 5, 9; Isocr. 5, 4; Pl. Apol. 17, Ionic ἔωθα Il. 8, 408; Her. 1, 133. 2, 91. 4, 134: plp. εἰώθειν Xen. An. 7, 8, 4; Pl. Conv. 213. Rep. 516, -ώθεσαν Thuc. 4, 130; Xen. Hell. 1, 3, 9, Ion. ἐώθεα Her. 4, 127, -θεε 4, 134. 6, 107, -θει Hom. H. 3, 305, -ώθεσαν Her. 1, 73. 3, 31; εἰωθώς Il. 15, 265; Soph. Ph. 938; Eur. Hec. 358; Ar. Pax 853; Hippocr. 2, 300; Thuc. 1, 67; Pl. Conv. 217, Ion. ἐωθ- Her. 3, 27. 31; εἰωθέναι Ar. Vesp. 94.

Εἴβω *To pour*, Poet. for λείβω, εἴβεις in tmesi Il. 16, 11, and εἴβει 19, 323; so opt. εἴβοι Od. 16, 332; and εἴβων Od. 11, 391: imp. εἶβον Od. 4, 153. 16, 219: so mid. εἰβόμενος Soph. Ant. 527 chor. (Tricl. Dind. λειβ- Ms. L. Nauck). Pass. or mid. intrans. εἴβεται *run, drop*, Ap. Rh. 2, 664; Opp. Hal. 2, 373; Bion 1, 9, κατ- Il. 15, 37: imp. εἴβετο Hes. Th. 910, κατ- Il. 24, 794. In every instance the dropping of the λ is required for the metre, except Ap. Rh. quoted.

(Εἰδέω, εἴδω, εἴδημι, ἴδω) (I.) *To see* with the bodily eye, pres. unused, unless εἴδομες be pres. Theocr. 2, 25?: usu. only 2 aor. εἶδον Il. 19, 292; Hes. Th. 589; Pind. P. 9, 98; Aesch. Ag. 247; Soph. El. 62; Ar. Pax 1184; Com. Fr. (Crat.) 2, 97; Her. 1, 68. 2, 148; Thuc. 2, 79; Lys. 1, 24; Pl. Phil. 65; later form εἶδα Orph. Arg. 119, usu. Epic ἴδον Il. 1, 262. Od. 12, 244; Hes. Th. 555; Mimnerm. 14, 2; Pind. P. 5, 84; Her. 2, 148 (Gaisf. εἰδ- Bekk. Dind. Stein), iter. ἴδεσκε Il. 3, 217; subj. ἴδω Il. 24, 555. Od. 16, 32; Soph. Aj. 530; Ar. Nub. 21; Her. 4, 119; Pl. Rep. 376, Epic ἴδωμι Il. 18, 63, ἴδῃς in Hom. if correct, only Od. 15, 76; Hym. 4, 278; Soph. Aj. 6; Ar. Ran. 644; Pl. Rep. 445 &c.; opt. ἴδοιμι Il. 6, 284; Soph. Ph. 1043; Ar. Eq. 1324 (D); Her. 2, 32; Thuc. 6, 34; Pl. Conv. 216; Xen. Cyr. 1, 1, 3; ἴδε, others ἰδέ Il. 17, 179; Aesch. Supp. 349 (chor.); Soph. Tr. 222 (chor.); Eur. Or. 1541 (chor.); Pl. Phaed. 72, ἴδετε Aesch. Ch. 406; Soph. Aj. 501; Eur. I. A. 593; ἰδεῖν Od. 11, 143; Soph. O. R. 824; Ar. Nub. 119; Her. 2, 32. 3, 65. 6, 137 &c.; Pl. Parm. 127, ἰδέειν Il. 23, 463; Her. 1, 32, περι- 1, 24 (Gaisf. Bekk. Dind. ἰδεῖν Bred. Stein, Abicht), Aeol. ἴδην Sapph. 101; ἰδών Il. 1, 148; Soph. El. 975; Ar. Ach. 5; Her. 2, 139; Antiph. 2, β, 6; Thuc. 3, 77; Pl. Phaed. 84: fut. Dor. ἰδησῶ (ῐ) Theocr. 3, 37. Mid. as act. 2 aor. εἰδόμην *I saw*, Il. 16, 278; Aesch. Pers. 179; Soph. Ph. 351; Eur. Hel. 122, Dor. -μαν Soph. O. R. 1217 (chor.); Eur. I. A. 254. 295 (chor.), in Attic prose, rare and in comp. προείδετο Dem. 19, 250; Strab. 12, 8, 11, Epic and Lyric ἰδόμην Il. 24, 484; Hes. Th. 451; Dor. ἰδόμαν Eur. I. T. 150 (chor.), εἰσ- Aesch. Pr. 427 (chor.);

subj. ἴδωμαι Il. 6, 365; Simon. (C.) 113 (Bergk 3 ed.); Ar. Vesp. 182 (R. V. Vulg. Bekk. Bergk, and *now* Dind. 5 ed. ἴδω Hirsch. Meineke), ἴδηαι Il. 8, 105, and ἴδῃ 3, 163. 4, 205, ἴδηται Il. 14, 416. 19, 151; Her. 2, 38, περι- Lys. 3, 47, προ- Com. Fr. (Dion.) 3, 547, προ- Xen. An. 6, 1, 8, ἰδώμεθα Od. 10, 44; Aesch. Eum. 142, ἐπ- Ar. Nub. 287 (chor.) see below, ἴδησθε Il. 15, 147, -ωνται Her. 1, 191. 2, 121. 4, 3; ἰδοίμην Il. 3, 453; Aesch. Pr. 896; Soph. Tr. 1004 (chor.); Her. 3, 148, ὑπ- Dem. 23, 3, ἰδοίατο Od. 1, 162; Her. 9, 51; ἰδοῦ Aesch. Ch. 231; Eur. Hec. 808; as exclamation, *lo!* ἰδού Soph. Ph. 776; Com. Fr. (Ar.) 2, 1134. (Phryn.) 2, 593; ἰδέσθαι Il. 9, 373; Pind. I. 4, 50; Aesch. Sept. 420 (chor.); Her. 2, 42. 135. 3, 6. 68; Hippocr. 3, 256 (Lit.); Plut. Themist. 13; Long. Past. 1, 13; Strab. 14, 2, 19, προ- Dem. 18, 301. 23, 134; ἰδόμενος (not in Hom.) Her. 1, 88. 207. 2, 32. 162, προ- *know beforehand*, Aeschin. 1, 165 (B. Saupp. Franke, Bens.); Dem. 19, 233 (Bekk. B. Saupp. Dind.); Luc. Tox. 39; Polyb. 27, 13 (Bekk.); Dio Cass. 52, 10 (Bekk.), ὑπ- 59, 23 Bekk.), and rare if correct, with augm. προ-ειδόμενος Thuc. 4, 64 (Vulg. Bekk. Popp. Krüg. &c., προ-ιδομ- L. Dind. Stahl); Polyaen 1, 36 (Vulg. προ-ιδ- Mss. M. P. Woelff.); Dio. Hal. 1, 65. 7, 42 (Vulg. προ-ιδ- Kiessl.); and Aeschin. 1, 165; Dem. 19, 233 (Vulg.) quoted. Compounds often belong, in *meaning*, to No. (II). Also in the **mid.** sense *make oneself appear, seem, resemble* &c. usu. Poet. εἴδομαι Il. 8, 559; Hes. Certam. p. 316, 10 (Goettl.); Mosch. 2, 155, προσ- Aesch. Ch. 178, ἐειδ- Theocr. 25, 58; εἰδόμενος Il. 13, 69; Aesch. Ag. 771 (chor.); Her. 6, 69. 7, 56, ἐειδ- Pind. N. 10, 15; Ap. Rh. 4, 221: fut. εἴσομαι, -σοιτο (Luc.) Ner. 2 (Kays. Jacob.): occasionally **2 aor.** εἰδόμην Hes. Fr. 169; Theocr. 13, 60: often **1 aor.** εἰσάμην Il. 20, 81; Hes. Th. 700; Ap. Rh. 2, 582; Mosch. 4, 94, ἐείσαο Il. 9, 645, -σω (La R.), -ατο 15, 415. Od. 5, 398; Ap. Rh. 4, 855; Callim. Cer. 44, -άσθην Il. 15, 544; opt. εἴσαιτο Il. 2, 215; (Luc.) Ner. 2 quoted (Dind. &c.); εἰσάμενος Il. 13, 45. 20, 224, ἐεισ- Il. 17, 326. 20, 82. Od. 6, 24. 11, 241; iter. εἰσάσκετο Il. 24, 607 (Bekk. ἰσάσκ- Dind. La R.)—εἴσαντο *they imagined*, Ap. Rh. 1, 718. (II.) *To see with the mind's eye, know*, imp. or 2 aor. εἶδον Pind. P. 2, 54; Soph. Aj. 1026; Dem. 4, 5. 6, 8; subj. ἴδῃς Com. Fr. (Men.) 4, 156: fut. εἴσομαι Il. 1, 548; Aesch. Ag. 489; Soph. O. R. 1517; Ar. Ach. 332; Hippocr. 1, 622 (Lit.); Thuc. 5, 26; Andoc. 2, 22; Lys. 14, 12; Isocr. 13, 3. 19, 2; Pl. Rep. 354, εἴσει Soph. O. C. 1149; Ar. Vesp. 774; Xen. Cyr. 7, 4, 12, -σεαι Il. 21, 292. Od. 2, 40, -σεσθε Isae. 10, 8; and more Ion. εἰδήσω Theogn. 814, -ήσεις Od. 7, 327. Hom. H. 3, 466; Her. 7, 234, -ήσει Hippocr. 7,

476. 8, 430, -ήσετε Hom. H. 2, 306; Attic prose, Isocr. 1, 44 (συν- 1, 16); Aristot. Top. 1, 18, 2. Eth. M. 1, 1, 3. 18; and perhaps later, (Aeschin.) Epist. 11, 8; Aen. Tact. 31; -ήσειν Il. 1, 546, Epic -ησέμεν Od. 6, 257: aor. εἴδησα Hippocr. 2, 436. 9, 230 (Lit.); Aristot. Probl. 19, 42. Eth. M. 1, 1, 3. 2, 10, 6; Theophr. Char. p. 1, ἐξ- Hippocr. 5, 352: p. εἴδηκα used to stand Aristot. Top. 1, 24, 484 (Sylb.): **2 p. as pres.** οἶδα Il. 5, 183; Archil. 42; Theogn. 491; Pind. Ol. 2, 56; Aesch. Pr. 504; Soph. O. R. 59; Eur. El. 299; Ar. Nub. 102; Her. 1, 209; Antiph. 1, 6. 11; Thuc. 6, 34; Isocr. 6, 60, see below; subj. εἰδῶ Il. 1, 515; Soph. O. C. 888; Her. 2, 114 (Bekk.); Xen. Oec. 11, 1, εἰδέω Od. 16, 236 (Vulg. Dind. La Roche, ἰδ- Bekk.); Her. quoted (Dind. Krüg. Stein), ἰδέω Il. 14, 235 (Bekk. Dind. La R.), εἰδῇς Theogn. 963, εἰδῇ Aeschin. 3, 47 &c. -ῶμεν Aesch. Ch. 890; Ar. Ran. 322; Pl. Theaet. 169, Epic εἴδομεν Il. 1, 363. Od. 3, 18, -δῆτε Thuc. 3, 67; Lys. 17, 8; Isae. 11, 38; Dem. 9, 65 (ἰδ- Bekk.), Epic εἴδετε Il. 8, 18. Od. 9, 17, εἰδῶσι Pl. Prot. 323; Isae. 3, 15, συν- Aeschin. 3, 34 &c.; opt. εἰδείην Il. 12, 229; Pind. Ol. 13, 46; Aesch. Supp. 289; Antiph. 1, 28; Lys. 23, 10, εἰδείης Theogn. 641; Her. 1, 206, -δείη Theogn. 770; Hes. Fr. 177, -δοίη Hippocr. 1, 624 (Lit. *v. r.* -δείη), εἰδείημεν Pl. Lach. 190 A, εἰδεῖμεν Rep. 581. Lach. 190 B, -είητε Andoc. 2, 19; Pl. Leg. 886; Isae. 8, 40, -δεῖτε Soph. O. R. 1046, -εῖεν Her. 9, 42 (v. r. -οῖεν); Xen. Cyr. 2, 2, 21. 8, 2, 11; Pl. Leg. 719, but -είησαν Her. 3, 61; Xen. Hell. 4, 2, 6; Dem. 34, 8 (Bekk. B. Saupp. Dind.); ἴσθι Od. 11, 224; Soph. Ph. 253; Ar. Nub. 39; Her. 7, 159. 8, 80; Pl. Conv. 208, ἴστω Il. 15, 36. Od. 16, 302; Soph. Ant. 184; Thuc. 1, 122, Boeot. ἴττω Ar. Ach. 860; Pl. Phaed. 62, late ἰδέτω Epist. Phal. 5 (Lennep, ἴστω Hercher); εἰδέναι Aesch. Ch. 690; Soph. Ant. 301; Ar. Vesp. 86; Her. 3, 21; Antiph. 1, 6; Thuc. 1. 52; Pl. Rep. 582, Epic ἴδμεναι Il. 13, 273; Theogn. 221, ἴδμεν Il. 11, 719, ἰδέμεν Pind. N. 7, 25; εἰδώς Il. 7, 278; Theogn. 193; Her. 8, 13; Antiph. 5, 65; Thuc. 6, 23, εἰδυῖα Il. 17, 5 &c.; Aesch. Pr. 441. 1076, but ἰδυῖα (ῐ) (only with πραπ-ίδεσσι) Il. 1, 608 &c.: **2 plp. as imp.** ᾔδειν Theogn. 667 (-δη Ms. A.); Eur. Tr. 650 if sound (ᾔδη Cob. Nauck, Dind. 5 ed.); Antiph. 2, β, 3; Lys. 1, 41; Xen. An. 3, 1, 20. Cyr. 1, 6, 43. Hell. 2, 3, 39; Pl. Phaed. 60; Aeschin. 2, 20; Dem. 30, 26 (W. Dind.); Lud. Dind. would now always, in good Attic, write ᾔδη not -ειν, see Xen. Mem. 4, 2, 24 (1862), ᾔδεις Ar. Thesm. 554 (-ησθ' Mein. Dind. 5 ed.); Anth. 12, 132; Antiph. 5, 15; Isae. 3, 41; Dem. 20, 160, -εισθα Eur. Cycl. 108 (Vulg. -ησθα Matth. Dind. 5 ed. Nauck 3 ed.); Pl. Euthyd. 277, -δει Soph. Ph. 1010; Antiph.

1, 8; Thuc. 7, 44; Isae. 3, 34; Eur. Ion 1361, but -ειν before a vowel 1187; so Il. 18, 404 (Bekk.); Ar. Vesp. 558; (Dem. 50, 44), but ᾔδει οὐδείς Thuc. 6, 27, old Attic 1 pers. ᾔδη Soph. Ant. 448. O. R. 433; Eur. Hipp. 405; Ar. Av. 511; Pl. Conv. 199. Rep. 337, Epic and Ion. ᾔδεα Il. 14, 71; Theogn. 853; Her. 2, 150, 2 sing. ᾔδης Soph. Ant. 447, ἐξ- Tr. 988 (Vulg. -ησθα in both *now* Dind. &c.), -ησθα Od. 19, 93; Eur. Elec. 926 (Dind.); Com. Fr. (Eup.) 2, 570; Pl. Meno 80. Rep. 337 (Soph. Ant. 447. Tr. 988 quoted), ᾔδη Il. 1, 70; Soph. Ph. 1010. O. R. 1525 (Dind. 2 ed., ᾔδει 5 ed.), and ᾔδην? Ar. Ach. 35 (Elms. -η Mein. -ει Dind.) and before a vowel Vesp. 635 (Richter, -ειν Dind. Mein.), Ion ᾔδεε Il. 17, 402 (Vulg. Dind. -δη Bekk.); Her. 2, 100. 9, 94 (συν- 7, 164. 8, 113), -εεν before a vowel Od. 23, 29, but ᾔδε' 13, 340, pl. ᾔδειμεν Aeschin. 3, 82 (ᾖσμεν Franke); Aristot. Anal. Post. 1, 31, 2; Ael. V. H. 10, 13, ᾔδειτε Dem. 55, 9, προ- Andoc. 2, 21, συν- Aeschin. 3, 175 (-ᾖστε Cobet, Franke), Ion. ᾐδέατε, συν- Her. 9, 58, ᾔδεσαν Theogn. 54; Her. 7, 175; Thuc. 2, 6; Lys. 12, 76; Isae. 7, 28; Dem. 18, 286, late ᾔδεισαν Strab. 15, 3, 23; V. T. Gen. 42, 23. Exod. 16, 15; N. T. Marc. 1, 34. Joh. 2, 9 &c. In 3 pl. of plp. ι is usually dropped, but δι-ηρπάκεισαν Dem. 29, 29 (Bekk. Dind. B. Saupp. 57, 63 Bekk. B. Saupp. -κεσαν Dind.), so παρεσκευάκεισαν 18, 234 (Bekk. B. Saupp. Dind. -εσαν Voem.) **Mid.** fut. εἴσομαι see above: **1 aor.** εἴσατο Dio Cass. Fr. 36, 27 (Bekk. εἰδείη L. Dind.): **2 aor.** in comp. προ-είδοντο *knew beforehand, foresaw*, Dem. 9, 68 &c. ὑπ- *suspected*, Eur. Ion 1023, see above, No. (I)—εἰδέω is not used in **pres.** indicative; at Il. 14, 235, it is subj. **2** aorist, ἰδέω (Bekk. La Roche.) **Fut. act.** εἴσω used to stand Appian B. C. 5, 39 *now* **mid.** εἴσονται (Bekk.)—2 sing. οἶδας Theogn. 491. 957; Hom. H. 3, 456. 467. Od. 1, 337 (Vulg. Dind. La Roche, ᾔδης Bekk.); Hipponax 89; Her. 3, 72; Hippocr. 2, 370; rare in Attic, Eur. Alc. 780; Com. Fr. (Philem.) 4, 14; Xen. Mem. 4, 6, 6 (Vulg. Kühn. Breitb. οἶσθα Dind. Saupp.); Luc. Catapl. 2; Pseud-Callisth. 2, 7, usu. οἶσθα Il. 1, 85. 7, 358. 15, 93. Od. 15, 20. 23, 60; Theogn. 375; Pind. P. 3, 80; Aesch. Pers. 479; Soph. O. R. 43; Eur. Tr. 293; Ar. Vesp. 4; Xen. Cyr. 1, 4, 28; Pl. Rep. 472, in Com. poetry, οἶσθας Com. Fr. (Cratin.) 2, 80. (Alex.) 3, 389. (Phil.) 4, 14. (Men.) 4, 174; Eur. Ion 999 (Dind. οἶσθ' Nauck, Kirchh.) Regular pl. forms rather rare, dual οἴδατον late, Epist. Socrat. 22, οἴδᾰμεν Her. 2, 17. 4, 46. 7, 214 &c.; Hippocr. 1, 622. 5, 196. 6, 120 (Lit.); Antiph. 2, 3; Xen. An. 2, 4, 6 (best Mss. Krüg. Shenkl, ἴσμεν Dind. Saupp. Hug); (Pl.) Alcib. (2) 141; (Dem.) 21, 82. 121; Aristot. Anal. Post. B. 8, 4, Hom. always ἴδμεν Il.

2, 486. Od. 17, 78; Hes. Th. 28 &c.; Her. generally 1, 6. 142. 178. 7, 170 &c., οἴδᾰτε Ar. Ach. 294 (Dind.); Anth. (Meleag.) 12, 81; Athen. 4, 53, κατ- Eur. Supp. 1044 (Mss. Kirchh. Nauck, -είδετε Elms. Dind.), οἴδᾱσι Her. 2, 43; Xen. Oec. 20, 14; Athen. 1, 45. 8, 68, συν- Lys. 11, 1, for which the Attics have from ἴσημι, usually the syncop. forms ἴστον Ar. Plut. 100, ἴσμεν Soph. Aj. 23; Ar. Nub. 693; Thuc. 1, 13; Isocr. 7, 13. 15, 106; Pl. Phaedr. 261, ἴστε Tyrt. 11, 7; Pind. I. 3, 15; Soph. O. R. 66; Ar. Pax 337; Antiph. 5, 73; Thuc. 7, 68; Pl. Rep. 328; Aeschin. 2, 14 (Il. 2, 485. Od. 7, 211), ἴσασι (Il. 6, 151. Od. 14, 89; Hes. Op. 814; Theogn. 598; Simon. C. 85, 11); Soph. Aj. 965; Ar. Eccl. 252; Antiph. 1, 29; Thuc. 4, 68; Lys. 4, 4; Isocr. 5, 42; Isae. 8, 17; so Hom. with ῐ, Il. 6, 151, but ῑ Il. 9, 36, Dor. ἴσαντι Pind. P. 3, 29; Theocr. 15, 64: imper. ἴσθι Od. 2, 356; Theogn. 31; Pind. Ol. 11, 11; Ar. Ran. 296; Her. 7, 14; Pl. Conv. 208, ἴσθ' Soph. Ant. 98, ἴστω Pind. Ol. 6, 8; Soph. Tr. 399; Xen. Cyr. 3, 3, 56, ἴστε Aesch. Pers. 211; Soph. Tr. 1107 &c. see above: in plp. the Poets especially dropped ι, as ᾔδεμεν for -ειμεν, Soph. O. R. 1232 (Elms. Dind.), ᾔδετε Eur. Bac. 1345, in prose ᾔδεσαν Her. 8, 78; Pl. Tim. 72; Xen. An. 4, 3, 10. 6, 5, 31; Isae. 3, 63. 7, 28; Dinarch. 1, 20; Dem. 57, 44; next ε, as ᾖσμεν for ᾔδεμεν, Aesch. Ag. 1099; Eur. Heracl. 658. Hec. 1112; Ar. Fr. 198; in prose, only Antiph. Fr. 7, 3; Aeschin. 3, 82 (Franke, Cobet), ᾖστε Soph. Fr. 317; in prose Dem. 49, 46 (Dind.), συν- Aeschin. 3, 175 (Franke, Cobet), ᾖσαν Aesch. Pr. 451; Eur. Cycl. 231. Rhes. 855, Epic ἴσαν Il. 18, 405. Od. 13, 170, dual ᾔστην Ar. Av. 19. Vb. ἰστέος Pl. Conv. 217.—2 sing. plp. ᾔδησθα Od. 19, 93; Soph. Ant. 447 (Cob. Dind. Nauck); Com. Fr. (Eup.) 2, 570; Pl. Meno 80. Euth. 15, and ᾔδεισθα Eur. Elec. 926. Cycl. 108 (Vulg. Kirchh. Nauck 2 ed. Dind. 4 ed. -ησθα Lob. Matth. Dind. 5 ed. Nauck 3 ed.); Pl. Euthyd. 277, for ᾔδης, ᾔδεις. In Plato, Schanz with the best Mss. leans to ᾔδεισθα against the precept of the old Grammarians ἀττικώτερον διὰ τοῦ η, ᾔδησθα. 3 sing. ᾔδειν before a vowel, Eur. Ion 1187; Ar. Pax 1182. Vesp. 558, and ᾔδην Vesp. 635 (Elms. Richter), even before a consonant Ach. 35 (Elms.) to which, we think, most scholars demur, -δη (Br. Bekk. Mein. -δει Vulg. Bergk, Dind. 5 ed., -ειν 4 ed.), ᾔδεεν Od. 23, 29 (Bekk. La Roche), and Il. 18, 404 (Vulg. Dind. La Roche, -ειν Bekk.)—ηείδης Il. 22, 280, ηείδη Od. 9, 206 (Bekk. Dind.), -δει (Eust. La Roche); Ap. Rh. 1, 984, Epic forms of plp.; but for ηείδεε Her. 1, 45 (Schaef. ᾔειδε Gaisf.), Bekker, Dind. Stein read ᾔδεε (Steph. Marg.)—ᾔδειν ἠείδειν, for ᾔδεσαν, Ap. Rh. 2, 65. 4, 1700, compare ἦν, for ἦσαν, Hes.

Th. 321. In Her. Gaisf. always writes plp. with augm. ᾔδεε &c. except συν-είδεε 8, 113 (Mss. S. P. F. -ῄδεε Vulg. Bekk. Bred. Dind. Krüg.) οἶδας 2 sing. perf. we might have said is rare in any class of writers. The only instance of it in Hom. is Od. 1, 337, where however Bekker reads ᾔδης. But yet it occurs twice in Theogn. 491. 957; twice in Hym. Merc. 456. 467; once in Eur. Alc. 780; Philem. Com. Fr. 4, 14. Strat. 4, 546. Phoenicid. 4, 510; twice in Her. 3, 72. 4, 157 (Orac.); Hippocr. 2, 370 (Lit.); and once in Xen. Mem. 4, 6, 6 (Mss. Kühn. Breitb. &c. οἶσθα Dind. *now*, Saupp.) It occurs occasionally also later, Aristot. Soph. El. 20, 3. 24, 2; Babr. 95, 14; Plut. Fab. 17. Pomp. 27; Dio. Hal. 16, 4; Himer. 5, 6; Luc. Catapl. 2. (Asin.) 11; Alciphr. 1, 29. 34. On the form οἶσθας scholars differ widely: some condemn it as barbarous, Bentley approved and Nauck has lately edited it in Eur. Alc. 780; so in Ion 999 (Dind. 5 ed.) Hirschig has altered ἴδωμαι Ar. Vesp. 182, to ἴδω ναί on the ground that the "mid. is not used in trimeters." This does not hold in the indic. opt. and imper. εἰδόμην *I saw*, Aesch. Pers. 179, κατ- Soph. El. 892 (trim.); εἰσ-ίδοιτο Soph. Tr. 151 (trim.); ἰδοῦ Aesch. Ch. 231. 247, ἴδεσθε 973. 980; Eur. Heracl. 29. Ion 1279 (trimet.); and even the subj. ἰδώμεθα is used by Aesch. in a trimeter Eum. 142, so Dionys. προ-ίδηται Com. Fr. 3, 547 (Dobr. Mein. προΐδη τε Mss.), and Ar. himself has ἐπ-ιδώμεθα Nub. 289, but in Lyric metre; we therefore question the propriety of disturbing, especially in a comic author, ἴδωμαι Vesp. 182, and think that Bergk has done wisely in retaining it. Dind. in his 4 edit. made the same alteration, without giving his reasons; but in his 5 edit. he has recalled ἴδωμαι. Buttmann, under ὁράω says "the mid. ὁρᾶσθαι, ἰδέσθαι in *simple*, is exclusively poetic." This is true of Attic classic prose, but as regards Ionic and *late* Attic prose, it is a considerable mistake; see the moods of εἰδόμην above.

Εἰκάζω *To assimilate*, Soph. O. R. 404; Eur. Tr. 165; Ar. Ran. 593; Her. 7, 49. 9, 17; Antiph. 5, 64. 66; Thuc. 5, 9, Aeol. εἰκάσδω Sapph. 104: **imp.** εἴκαζον Her. 4, 133; Xen. An. 1, 6, 11; Pl. Polit. 260; Luc. Hist. 14 (Mss. Vulg. Fritzsche, &c.), and ᾔκαζ- Eur. Heracl. 677; Ar. Eccl. 385; Thuc. 2, 54. 6, 92 (Bekk. Popp. Krüg.); Luc. quoted (Dind.): **fut.** εἰκάσω Aesch. Eum. 49; Paus. 10, 28. 31; Luc. Hist. Con. 60: **aor.** εἴκασα Her. 2, 104; Antiph. 5, 65; (Xen.) Apol. 15; Pl. Meno 80. Conv. 216; Luc. Char. 19 (Dind.); Soph. El. 662 (Mss. Vulg. Hart.), but ᾐκ- (Br. Dind. Nauck); so Aesch. Ch. 632 Supp. 288 (Herm. Dind.); Eur. Phoen. 420 (Dind. Kirchh.); Ar. Vesp. 1308. Eq. 1076. Nub. 350; Com. Fr. (Theop.) 2,

806; Luc. Scyth. 9 (D.); opt. εἰκάσσαις Theogn. 127: p. εἴκακα rare (Schol. Ar. Vesp. 151): p. p. εἴκασμαι Her. 2, 182. 3, 28; Xen. An. 5, 3, 12 (All); εἰκασμένος 5, 4, 12 (but ᾐκ- Kühn. Breitb. Shenkl); Pl. Crat. 439; (Dem.) 61, 24; Luc. Alex. 18 (Vulg. Fritzsche &c.), ᾔκ- Ar. Av. 807, ἐξ- Aesch. Ag. 1244. Sept. 445 (Herm. Dind.); Eur. Phoen. 162 (Pors. Dind. Kirchh. Nauck 3 ed., ἐξ-εικ Vulg. Nauck 2 ed.); Ar. Eq. 230; Luc. Alex. 18 (Dind.): plp. ἐξείκαστο Xen. Cyr. 1, 6, 39: aor. εἰκάσθην Thuc. 6, 31; Xen. Hell. 7, 5, 22: fut. εἰκασθήσομαι Ar. Ach. 782. **Mid. aor.** εἰκάσασθε, ἀν- C. Fr. (Cratin.) 2, 52. **Vb.** εἰκαστός Soph. Tr. 699, -έος, ἀπ- Pl. Phaedr. 270. The only verb that changes ει to η for augment. The compounds ἀντεικάζω, ἀπεικ- have fut. m. -άσομαι Pl. Meno 80; Xen. Mem. 3, 11, 1: but fut. act. ἀπ-εικάσει Plut. Mor. 1135. Her. Xen. Plut. and Luc. (except in Dindorf's ed.) seem never to augment this verb; in Thuc. and Plato the Mss. and edit. vary, but the leaning of recent editors, Stallb. excepted, is decidedly to augment: the same may be said of the Tragedians and Aristoph.

(**Εἰκάθω**) *To yield*, subj. εἰκάθω Soph. Ph. 1352. O. R. 650, εἰκάθῃ, παρ- Pl. Soph. 254; εἰκάθοιμι Ap. Rh. 3, 849, ὑπ- Soph. El. 361; Pl. Apol. 32; -άθειν Soph. El. 396. Ant. 1096; -άθων Tr. 1177, Epic -αθέων, ὑπ- Opp. Hal. 5, 500: imp. εἴκαθον Ap. Rh. 1, 505, ὑπο-εικ- Orph. Arg. 709, which Elms. Dind. and others take for **2 aor.** εἴκαθον; subj. εἰκάθω; inf. εἰκαθεῖν; εἰκαθών.

(**Εἴκω**) *To be like, appear*, imp. εἶκε *seemed likely, fitting*, Il. 18, 520 (hither some refer εἶκεν Ar. Av. 1298, *was like*, ᾖκεν Dind. 4 ed.), see perf.: fut. rare, εἴξω Ar. Nub. 1001: aor. εἶξα late and rare, part. εἴξας Sopat. Rhet. p. 208 (Walz): p. ἔοικα Od. 22, 348; Aesch. Ch. 926; Soph. Ph. 317; Eur. Hec. 813; Ar. Vesp. 1171; Pl. Apol. 21. Tim. 27, ἔοικας Il. 15, 90; Soph. El. 516; Eur. Hel. 793; Ar. Vesp. 1309; Her. 3, 71; Xen. Cyr. 1, 4, 9; Pl. Conv. 215, ἔοικε Il. 3, 170; Simon. Am. 7, 41; Pind. I. 1, 52; Soph. Ph. 911; Ar. Thesm. 382; Her. 1, 39 (Mss. Gaisf. Bekk. Lhardy), see below; Antiph. 2, β, 4; Andoc. 1, 137; Pl. Soph. 229, ἐοίκαμεν Pl. Lach. 193, ἐοίκατε Xen. Hell. 6, 3, 8; Pl. Theaet. 183, ἐοίκᾱσι Heraclit. 2 (Bywater); Andoc. 2, 15; Pl. Rep. 5, 84, Poet. ἔοιγμεν, εἴξασι, ἔϊκτον &c. see below, less freq. (εἶκα), εἶκας if correct, Alcm. 76 (Ahrens &c. but οἶκας 80 Bergk &c.), εἶκεν Ar. Av. 1298 (Br. see plp.), 3 pl. εἴξασι Eur. Hel. 497. I. A. 848; Ar. Nub. 341. 343. Av. 383; Com. Fr. (Pl.) 2, 664. (Eub.) 3, 250; rare in prose, Pl. Polit. 291. 305. Soph. 230; subj. ἐοίκω Xen. Conv. 6, 9; opt. ἐοίκοιμι Pl. Crat. 409; ἐοικέναι Ar. Vesp. 1142. Fr. 526; Pl. Parm. 132. Conv. 215.

Rep. 349. 611; Xen. An. 5, 8, 10. Cyr. 5, 1, 21, Attic Poet. εἰκέναι Eur. Fr. 167 (D.); Ar. Nub. 185, προσ- Eur. Bac. 1284; Ar. Eccl. 1161; ἐοικώς Il. 17, 323; Hes. Op. 235; Soph. Fr. 682 (D.); Thuc. 7, 71; Pl. Rep. 549; Xen. Cyr. 2, 3, 7, and εἰκώς Il. 21, 254; Aesch. Ag. 760; Soph. Aj. 824. Ph. 1373; Eur. Cycl. 376; Ar. Av. 697. Vesp. 1321; Pl. Leg. 647. Tim. 29, Ion. οἶκα Her. 4, 82, -ατε 5, 20. 7, 162, -ασι 5, 106; οἴκω 4, 180; οἰκώς 6, 125: plp. ἐῴκειν Il. 14, 474; Theocr. 7, 14; (Aeschin.) Epist. 10, 10; Luc. Nigr. 34, 3 pl. ἐῴκεσαν Thuc. 7, 75; Xen. Hell. 7, 5, 22, ἐοίκεσαν Hom. and only Il. 13, 102 (Vulg. Dind. La Roche, ἐῴκ- Bekk.), also ᾤκειν, προσ- Anth. 6, 353, Attic ᾔκειν Ar. Av. 1298 quoted above (Dawes, Bergk, Dind. 5 ed.)—Often impers. ἔοικε, *it seems, is fitting*, Il. 1, 119; Soph. O. R. 962; Ar. Plut. 76; Thuc. 1, 77, οἶκε Her. 5, 97; neut. p. εἰκός *fitting, reasonable*, Soph. Ant. 724; Ar. Pax 736; Thuc. 1, 10, Ion. οἰκός Her. 1, 155: plp. ἐῴκει Od. 24, 273. Contracted indic. forms dual and plural ἔοιγμεν 1 pl. perf. for ἐοίκαμεν, Soph. Aj. 1239; Eur. Heracl. 681. Cycl. 99, 3 pl. εἴξασι for εἴκ-(σ)ασι, Eur. Hel. 497; Ar. Nub. 341. 343. Av. 96. 383; Com. Fr. (Plat.) 2, 664; rare in prose, Pl. Polit. 305 &c. quoted, ἔϊκτον 3 dual Epic for ἐοίκατον, Od. 4, 27: plp. 3 dual ἐΐκτην Epic for ἐῳκείτην, Il. 1, 104. 23, 379; Hes. Sc. 390.

Similar pass. forms: perf. ᾔϊξαι, προσ- Eur. Alc. 1063, ᾔϊκται Nic. Ther. 658: plp. ᾔϊκτο Od. 20, 31 &c., ἔϊκτο Il. 23, 107, see εἴσκω. Part. in Hom. ἐοικώς Il. 2, 20. 5, 87. 17, 323 &c., εἰκώς only once, 21, 254, but fem. εἰκυῖα Il. 4, 78. 8, 305. Od. 7, 20, &c., εἰοικυῖα once, Il. 18, 418; with the Dramatists εἰκώς, εἰκέναι almost always, but ἐοικέναι Ar. Vesp. 1142. Fr. 526; ἐοικότες Soph. Fr. 682. Buttmann says the exclusive Ionic form is οἶκα, οἰκώς, οἰκός, and so Dind. and Stein uniformly edit in Her., and Bredow, p. 195, approves. This accords with the Mss. in the case of the part., but the indic. ἔοικε occurs often without v. r. 1, 39. 4, 31. 99. 132. 6, 64. 7, 18 (Gaisf. Bekk. Lhardy, Krüg.), ἔοικας 3, 71, v. r. ᾖκας but not pointing to ᾖκας.

Εἴκω *To yield, give way*, Il. 12, 48; Tyrt. 12, 42; Aesch. Pr. 320; Her. 2, 80; Thuc. 1, 84: imp. εἶκον Her. 8, 3; Thuc. 3, 11: fut. εἴξω Thuc. 1, 141, ὑπο- Il. 16, 305, ὑπ- Aesch. Ag. 1362; Her. 7, 160; Xen. Hell. 5, 4, 45: aor. εἶξα Il. 24, 718; Eur. Heracl. 367. Hel. 80; Her. 9, 63. 106; Thuc. 4, 126; Xen. Cyr. 3, 3, 8; Pl. Phaedr. 254, ἔειξ- Alcm. 31 (Bergk 3 ed.), iter. εἴξασκε Od. 5, 332; subj. εἴξῃ Il. 17, 230; opt. εἴξειε 22, 321; imper. εἶξον Pind. I. 1, 6: 2 aor. according to some, εἴκᾰθον Ap. Rh. 1, 505; subj. εἰκάθω Soph. O. R. 650; -θοιμι Ap. Rh. 3, 849; -θεῖν Soph. El. 396; -θών Tr. 1177, see εἰκάθω.

Vb. εἰκτέον late, Philo, but ὑπ- Pl. Crito 51.—εἴκωντι Dor. 3 pl. subj. for εἴκωσι, Thuc. 5, 77. ὑπείκω has fut. -είξω Aesch. Ag. 1362; Dem. 15, 24, Epic ὑποείξω Il. 15, 211: and mid. ὑπείξομαι Il. 1, 294. Od. 12, 117, ὑπο-είξ- Il. 23, 602: aor. mid. ὑπείξωμαι Ap. Rh. 4, 408, has been changed, on probable grounds, to act. ὑπείξω μή (Gerhard, Wellau. Merk.) The Attics use fut. act. alone, simple and comp.; Hom. has both act. and mid. but in comp. only; εἴξει Il. 17, 230 (Vind. and old edit.) has been altered to subj. εἴξῃ (Ven. Eustath. Heyn. Wolf, Bekk. Spitzn. Dind.)

Εἰλαπινάζω *To feast*, Poet. Od. 2, 57. 17, 536; Opp. Hal. 1, 468. 2, 177. 3, 219; 3 pl. Dor. -άζοισι Pind. P. 10, 40; -άζων Il. 14, 241: imp. εἰλαπίναζον Q. Sm. 6, 179. Only pres. and imp.

Εἰλέω, εἰλ- *To roll*, mostly Epic, Il. 2, 294; Hippocr. 8, 268 (Ms. Θ. Lit.), συν- Her. 4, 67, περι- Xen. An. 4, 5, 36, and εἰλ- Pl. Crat. 409; Geop. 12, 39; Ion. pt. εἰλεῦντα Od. 11, 573: imp. εἴλεον Od. 22, 460, εἴλει Il. 8, 215. Od. 12, 210; Ap. Rh. 2, 571. 4, 181 (Merk.), ἐείλ- Il. 18, 447, ἐόλει see plp.: fut. late, εἰλήσω Anth. 12, 208: and aor. εἵλησα Dioscor. 5, 102, εἵλ- V. T. 4 Reg. 2, 8; Geop. 10, 14; συνειλήσας Her. 3, 45: (p.): plp. ἐόλει Pind. P. 4, 233: p p. late, εἴλημαι, -ημένος Lycophr. 1202, but ἀπ- Her. 2, 141, ἐν- Artemid. Onir. 1, 13, ἐόλληται Hesych.: plp. εἴλητο Joseph. Ant. 12, 1, 8, Epic ἐόλητο Ap. Rh. 3, 471; Mosch. 1, 74 (Ahr.). 2, 74 (Mein.): aor. εἰλήθην, κατ- Her. 1, 190. 3, 146. 8, 27; εἰληθείς Hippocr. 7, 278 (Lit.), but εἰλ- 7, 592; Aristot. Mund. 4, 17; Arr. An. 6, 9, ἀπ- Her. 1, 24. 8, 109, ἀν- Thuc. 7, 81: fut. εἰληθήσονται, συν- Sext. Emp. 256, 6. Mid. (or pass.) εἰλοῦμαι Orph. H. 26, 9; Theocr. 1, 31; Geop. 1, 11, εἰλ- Ap. Rh. 4, 1271 (Merk.), εἰλέονται (Luc.) Astrol. 29, -εῦνται Opp. Hal. 1, 148, -οῦνται, ἀν- Aristot H. A. 9, 40, 57: imp. εἰλεῖτο Ap. Rh. 4, 1067 (Merk.), εἰλ- Mosch. 4, 104, εἰλεῦντο Il. 21, 8, εἰλέοντο Her. 8, 12, -οῦντο, συν- Xen. Hell, 7, 2, 8; εἰλεύμενος Her. 2, 76, εἰλούμ- Plut. Brut. 47, εἰλ- Luc. Icar. 19. D. Mort. 27, 9: aor. εἰλήσαντο, ἐν- Q. Sm. 14, 294. See εἴλω. To this verb Buttmann refers ἐόλει as imp. act. for εἴλει, Pind. P. 4, 233, and ἐόλητο plp. pass. for εἴλητο, Ap. Rh. 3, 471; Mosch. 2, 74 (Mss. Mein. Ziegl.), v. r. αἰόλει, αἰόλητο.

Εἰλίσσω *To roll*, Aesch. Pr. 1085; Ar. Ran. 1314; Her. 2, 38; (Luc.) Asin. 37 (Jacob.), Attic -ίττω rare, ἀν- Com. Fr. (Antid.) 3, 529; Pl. Phil. 15: fut. εἰλίξω Eur. Or. 171: aor. εἵλιξα Theocr. 22, 81; inf. -ίξαι Eur. Tr. 116; -ίξας Eur. Ph. 1178, -ίξασαι Her. 4, 34: p. p. εἵλιγμαι Eur. Fr. 385 (D.): plp. εἰλίγμην, 3 pl. -ιχατο Her. 7, 90, κατ- 7, 76: aor. later, εἰλίχθην Hesych.; εἰλιχθείς

Ap. Rh. 3, 655: **2 aor.** late, εἰλιγῆναι Malal. p. 47, 17. **Mid.** *roll oneself*, **aor.** εἰλιξάμενος Her. 2, 95 (Ms. S.), ἐν-ειλιξ- (Bekk. Lhardy, Bred. Krüg. Stein), ἐν-ελιξ- (Mss. Gaisf. Dind.)—εἴλιγμαι, -μην may belong to ἑλίσσω. This verb is Poet., Ionic, and late prose. The **aor.** form εἰλίσας, συνειλίσαντα Hippocr. 3, 148 (Kühn), has been discarded by Littré on the best Mss. authority for the **pres.** συνειλίσσοντα 4, 100, and we expect that the same Mss. will enable him to discard συνειλισθέντα 2, 438, for -ειλιχθέντα. They have, we *now* see, enabled him, but for συν-ειληθέντα 7, 180 (Mss. E. H. K. Θ. Mack.) See ἑλίσσω.

Εἴλλω, εἰλλ- for εἴλω, *To roll*, Ar. Nub. 761, ἐν- Thuc. 2, 76; εἴλλῃ, ἐξ- Dem. 37, 35 (Bekk.); ἀν-είλλεται Pl. Conv. 206; εἰλλόμενος Pl. Tim. 40. 76 &c. εἰλούμ- v. r. See εἴλω, ἴλλω.

Εἰλῠφάζω *To whirl up*, Epic Il. 20, 492: **imp.** εἰλύφαζον intrans. Hes. Sc. 275; also εἰλῠφάω, trans. and only **pres.** εἰλυφᾷ (Hesych.); Epic p. εἰλῠφόων Il. 11, 156; Hes. Th. 692; εἰλυφῶνται Hesych.

Εἰλύω *To roll, envelope, gather up*, Arat. Phaen. 432: **imp.** εἴλυε (Hesych.): **fut.** εἰλύσω Il. 21, 319: **aor.** εἴλῡσα, κατ- Ap. Rh. 3, 206: **p.p.** εἴλῡμαι Il. 5, 186. Od. 14, 479. Hom. H. 3, 245, κατ- Her. 2, 8: **plp.** εἴλῡτο Il. 16, 640: **aor.** εἰλύθην, -θείς rather doubtful, Theocr. 25, 246 (Vulg. Wüstm. εἰληθείς Mein. Ziegl. Ahr. with Vat. E), ἐξ-ειλυσθείς 24, 17 (Vulg. Mein. Wordsw. ἐξ-ειληθ- Ahr. Ziegl. Fritz.), δι-ειλυσθ- Ap. Rh. 4, 35; Nonn. 4, 364. **Mid.** εἰλύομαι *to move oneself by successive contractions, crawl*, εἰλῡόμενος Soph. Ph. 702: **imp.** εἰλῡόμην Soph. Ph. 291. See ἐλύω. (ῡ throughout, except in εἰλῠ́αται for -υνται, Od. 20, 352, εἰλῠομένων Com. Fr. (Metag.) 2, 753, and late εἰλῠ́οι Arat. Phaen. 432, -ῠ́εται Nic. Alex. 18; but εἴλῠσα quoted by Buttmann from Athen. 7, 293, has, we think, been given up. The latest recension presents ἅλις (Pors. emend.)

(**Εἴλω**) *To roll up, press together*, Epic. (εἴλομαι Il. 8, 215): **aor.** ἔλσα Il. 11, 413; Ap. Rh. 1, 1247; inf. ἔλσαι Il. 1, 409. 21, 225, ἐέλσαι 21, 295; ἔλσας Od. 7, 250; Callin. 1, 11 (Bergk), Aeol. ἔλσαις Pind. Ol. 11, 43: **p.p.** ἔελμαι Il. 24, 662; ἐελμένος 13, 524. 18, 287: **2 aor.** ἐάλην Il. 13, 408. 20, 278, and ’ἄλην, Epic 3 pl. ἄλεν 22, 12; ἀλῆναι 16, 714, and ἀλήμεναι 18, 76; ἀλείς 22, 308: **pres.** εἰλόμενος Il. 5, 203. 8, 215: **1 aor.** ἡλσάμην if correct Simon. Am. 17 (Bergk.)—εἴλω **pres. act.** seems not to occur: **1 aor.** εἶλα, συν-εῖλας (Hesych.): ἄλεν 3 pl. **2 aor.** for ἐάλησαν, Il. 22. 12, see εἰλέω.

Εἵμαρται, see μείρω.

Εἰμί *To be*, Il. 16, 722; Pind. N. 5, 1; Soph. O. C. 571; Ar. Eq. 34; Her. 6, 86; Antiph. 1, 11. 4, α, 5; Pl. Prot. 317;

Xen. Cyr. 8, 3, 45, εἶ Aesch. Eum. 722; Soph. O. R. 371; Ar. Ach. 109; Xen. An. 7, 3, 19; Pl. Conv. 173, Ion. εἷς (εἷς Bekk. La R.) Il. 21, 150; Archil. 107; Her. 3, 71, ἐστί Il. 3, 60; Hes. Th. 301; Thuc. 2, 35, 2 dual ἐστόν Il. 1, 259; Eur. I. T. 497, 3 dual ἐστόν Aesch. Ch. 207; Thuc. 3, 112, ἐσμέν Archil. 59 (εἰμέν Riemer); Aesch. Eum. 416; Ar. Ach. 507; Thuc. 3, 14; Pl. Rep. 378, ἐστέ Il. 2, 301; Tyrt. 11, 1; Soph. O. R. 947; Thuc. 2, 74; Pl. Tim. 22, εἰσί Il. 4, 7; Theogn. 163; Soph. O. C. 472; Ar. Nub. 341; Thuc. 2, 49, ἔασι Il. 10, 165; Xenophan. 7, 1; Theogn. 623 &c.; subj. ὦ Aesch. Pers. 692; Soph. Tr. 1107; Thuc. 4, 126; Xen. Cyr. 8, 7, 27, Epic ἔω, see below; opt. εἴην Il. 15, 82; Hes. Op. 271; Soph. O. R. 77; Ar. Eccl. 67; Pl. Prot. 317 &c., εἴητε Andoc. 2, 6; Lys. 1, 1, εἶτε Od. 21, 195, 3 pl. εἴησαν Her. 2, 6; Antiph. 2, α, 10; Thuc. 1, 9; Xen. An. 1, 1, 5; (Dem.) 47, 36, and εἶεν Il. 2, 372; Soph. Ph. 550; Ar. Pax 663; Her. 1, 170; Thuc. 3, 44; Pl. Rep. 515; imper. ἴσθι Theogn. 301; Aesch. Ag. 512; Soph. Ant. 71; Eur. Or. 1327; Isocr. 2, 24; Pl. Rep. 336, Epic ἔσσο Od. 13, 436 &c., ἔστωσαν Her. 1, 147; Thuc. 8, 18, ἔστων Od. 1, 273; Pl. Rep. 502, see below; inf. εἶναι Il. 2, 82; Soph. O. C. 60; Ar. Vesp. 82; Thuc. 3, 56; Pl. Phaed. 76, Epic ἔμεναι Il. 3, 42, ἔμμ- 7, 75, see below; ὤν Hom. H. 19, 32; Soph. Aj. 767; Ar. Ran. 80; Thuc. 4, 30; Isocr. 1, 42, Epic ἐών Il. 3, 46: imp. 1 pers. ἦν Il. 2, 96; Soph. Tr. 414; Ar. Plut. 29. 695; Antiph. 5, 23; Pl. Rep. 328, and ἦ Aesch. Ag. 1637; Soph. O. C. 973. O. R. 1123 (Dind. Wund. Nauck); Eur. Hec. 13, 284 (Nauck 3 ed.); Ar. Nub. 530 (Dind. 5 ed.). Av. 97. 1363 (Mein. Dind. 5 ed.); Pl. Conv. 173. Phaed. 61, 2 pers. ἦς (Pl.) Ax. 365, see below, ἦσθα Lys. 7, 20, 3 pers. ἦν Il. 5, 9; Soph. Tr. 9; Ar. Eq. 250; Thuc. 2, 3. 4, 84, Epic ἔον Il. 11, 762, 3 sing. ἔην 2, 219, Ion. ἔσκον Il. 7, 153, ἔσκε 16, 147; Pind. N. 5, 31; Aesch. Pers. 656 (chor.); Her. 6, 133, Dor. ἦσκε Alcm. 72, 3 pl. ἔσκον 4, 129. 9, 40. **Mid. imp.** ἤμην rare if correct, in classic Attic, 1 sing. Eur. Hel. 931 (Dind. 4 ed. Pflugk, Nauck, ἄρ' ἦν Mss. Herm. Kirchh. Dind. 5 ed.); Xen. Cyr. 6, 1, 9 (Vulg. Poppo, ἦν Dind. Saupp.); Lys. 7, 34 (Vulg. Bekk. εἴην Dobr. B. Saupp. εἰμι Scheibe); but Com. Fr. (Anon.) 4, 654; Epist. Phal. 16; Luc. D. Mort. 28, 2 (Jacob. Dind.). D. Mar. 2, 2 (Jacob. ἦν Dind.); Plut. Mor. 174, 180. 222. 225. Solon 28. Alex. 14. Pomp. 74, ἤμεθα N. T. Matth. 23, 30 (best Mss. Tisch. Lachm.). Act. 27, 37 (Mss. Lachm. Tisch.), and, if correct, Epic εἴατο Od. 20, 106 (Wolf, Dind. εἵατο Bekk. La Roche): **fut.** ἔσομαι Il. 6, 409; Ar. Ran. 500; Her. 1, 71; Antiph. 5, 90; Xen. Cyr. 8, 7, 27, Epic ἔσσ- Il. 4, 267; Pind. P. 3, 108, ἔσει Soph. Ant. 86; Ar. Eq. 164, ἔσεαι Theogn. 884; Her. 7, 14, ἔσσ- Il. 18, 95; Hes. Op. 310, syncop. 3 sing. ἔσται Il. 10, 41; Her. 8, 65; always in Attic, Soph. O. R. 420; Ar. Ach. 27; Antiph. 1, 8; Thuc. 3, 46; Pl. Prot. 318, Epic ἔσεται Il. 1, 211. Od. 21, 212, ἔσσ- Il. 4, 169; Ap. Rh. 2, 261; Aesch. Pers. 121 chor. (Vulg. Well. Herm. ᾄσεται Burn. Dind. Hart.), Epic and Dor. ἐσσοῦ- and ἐσσοῦμαι, ἐσσῇ Theocr. 10, 5, -εῖται Il. 2, 393. 13, 317; Hes. Op. 503; Theocr. 7, 67, ἀπ-εσσ- Od. 19, 302, Dor. prose ἐσεῖται Stob. (Hippod.) 102, 26, ἐσοῦνται Thuc. 5, 77; opt. ἐσοίμην Soph. O. R. 793, -οιτο Tr. 941; Her. 7, 226; Xen. Cyr. 7, 5, 52; ἐσόμενος 2, 3, 3, Epic ἐσσ- Il. 3, 460; Hes. Op. 56; ἔσεσθαι Hes. Th. 210; Soph. O. C. 390; Ar. Vesp. 400; Her. 7, 219; Antiph. 2, α, 7; Xen. An. 7, 7, 52, Epic ἔσσ- Il. 15, 292; Pind. Ol. 7, 68. **Vb.** ἐστέος, συν- Pl. Prot. 313.

Imp. mid. ἤμην seems doubtful in classic authors. Of the old Grammarians, some rejected, others received it with a caution. It occurs in some Mss. and editions of Soph. Tr. 24. Aj. 679, where now stand with general approval ἤμην, ἡμῖν; so in Eur. Hel. 931 (Choerobosc. Etym. Mag. Nauck), but altered to ἄρ' ἦν from Mss. by Herm. Kirchh. Paley, W. Dind. 5 ed.; in Xen. Cyr. 6, 1, 9, L. Dind. Breitb. and Sauppe read ἦν; in Lys. 7, 34, Dobree, Bait. Saupp. read εἴην, Westerm. ἦ μήν, Scheibe εἰμι; and for 3 pl. εἵατο Od. 20, 106 (Aristarch. Wolf, Dind.) εἵατο *they sat*, is adopted by Bekker, Ameis, La Roche &c. with Herodian. In late authors ἤμην is not unfrequent, Alciphr. 3, 13. 54; Long. 4, 28; Luc. D. Mort. 28, 2. (Asin.) 15. 46; Plut. Solon 28. Alex. 14. 29. Mor. 174. 180. 222. 225; Ach. Tat. 4, 1. 5, 1 (Herch.), παρ- Long. 2, 5, pl. very rare, see N. Test. quoted. In Luc. however, Fritzsche and Dind. often challenge it.

The following are some of the more striking dialectic forms and usages: 2 sing. εἷς (εἶς Bekk.) for εἶ, is Ionic Il. 21, 150; Her. 1, 207, ἐμέν for ἐσμέν, Soph. El. 21 (Schneid. &c.) is very doubtful, more certain Callim. Fr. 294; opt. 1 pl. εἶμεν for εἴημεν is not frequent, Eur. Hipp. 349 (trimet.). Alc. 921 (chor.); Pl. Theaet. 147. Rep. 558. Men. 86, not in Hom., εἶτε Od. 21, 195; and if correct, Soph. Ant. 215 (D.); Eur. Fr. 781, 56 (D.), seems not to occur in prose, but εἴησαν and εἶεν often, εἴησαν Her. 1, 2. 2, 6. 102. 3, 119. 4, 46; Antiph. 3, δ, 6; Thuc. 1, 9. 2, 72. 3, 22. 6, 96; Pl. Gorg. 492; Xen. An. 1, 1, 5. Conv. 5, 5, εἶεν Il. 2, 372; Aesch. Supp. 185; Her. 1, 63. 170. 3, 23. 4, 41; Thuc. 3, 44; Pl. Rep. 515; Xen. Cyr. 1, 2, 5, for εἰήτην dual sometimes εἴτην Pl. Tim. 31. Parm. 149 &c.;

imper. ἔστων 3 pl. less frequent than ἔστωσαν, Od. 1, 273; Pl. Leg. 759. Rep. 502; Xen. Cyr. 4, 6, 10. 8, 6, 11 (ἔστωσαν Bornem.), rarely ὄντων Pl. Leg. 879, 3 sing. ἤτω Rep. 361, has given way to ἔστω (Mss. C. Schneid.) or ἴτω (Neukirch, Bait. Or. W.), it occurs however Hippocr. 8, 340 (Lit. ἔστω C. H. θ, ἴνω D. J.); and late Aretae. 1, 2, p. 79; V. T. Ps. 103, 31. N. T. 1 Cor. 16, 22. Imp. 1 pers. ἦ for ἦν, Soph. O. R. 1123; Pl. Phaed. 61 &c. is perhaps old Attic, 2 pers. ἦς for ἦσθα, seems not Attic, Ar. Nub. 1029 (old edit.); Eur. I. A. 339, have been altered, but later οὐκ ἦς (Pl.) Ax. 365; (Luc.) Amor. 3 (Dind. &c.), dual ἤστον Pl. Euthyd. 294 (Bekk. -στην Bait.), ἤστην Il. 5, 10; Hes. Sc. 50; Eur. Hipp. 387; Ar. Av. 19. Eq. 983; Isae. 6, 6; Pl. Phaedr. 273. Euthyd. 271, rarely ἦτον Parm. 143, εἴτην, v. r. ἤτην, Phil. 41. Soph. 243, but plur. almost always ἦτε Il. 16, 557; Aesch. Ag. 542; Pl. Euthyd. 276, Ar. however has ἦστε Pax 821. Eccl. 1086 (Dind. Bekk. Mein.), παρ- Pl. Conv. 176, 3 pl. ἦν Hes. Th. 321; Poet ap. Aeschin. 3, 184; Soph. Tr. 520 (chor.); Ar. Lys. 1260 (chor.), ἐν- Eur. Ion 1146 (Xen. An. 1, 5, 7. Hell. 3, 1, 7. 7, 5, 17 &c. no proof), ἦ Pind. P. 4, 57?; ἦν always before its nom.

Chiefly Homeric and Ionic forms: 2 sing. ἐσσι Il. 1, 176, and εἶς 19, 217; Archil. 107; Her. 1, 207. 3, 71. 4, 80 &c. occasionally εἶ 3, 140 (Bekk. Dind., εἶς Stein, Abicht). 142 (Bekk. Dietsch, εἶς Dind. Stein, Abicht), 1 pl. εἰμεν Il. 8, 234; Hes. Sc. 351; Her. 7, 9. 9, 46, 3 pl. εἰσίν Il. 20, 183, and ἔασιν 7, 73; Hes. Th. 95; Xenophanes 7 (B); subj. ἔω Od. 9, 18, παρ- Her. 4, 98, εἴω, μετ- Il. 23, 47, ἦσιν 19, 202; Hes. Op. 294, ἔῃσι Il. 2, 366, μετ- 3, 109, ἔῃ 12, 300, ᾖ Her. 4, 66, 3 pl. ὦσι Od. 24, 491, usu. ἔωσιν Il. 9, 140. Od. 23, 119; so Her. 2, 39. 4, 66 &c. but ὦσι 2, 89 (Mss. Bekk. Gaisf. ἔωσι Dind. Bred. Stein); opt. εἴην Il. 13, 826, -ης 9, 57, -ησθα Theogn. 715, also ἔοις Il. 9, 284, ἔοι 14, 333, once Her. ἐν-έοι 7, 6, 2 pl. εἶτε Od. 21, 195; Soph. Ant. 215 (D.), εἶεν Il. 2, 372; Her. 1, 63. 170 &c. and εἴησαν 1, 2. 2, 102. 4, 46 &c. both also Attic; imper. ἔσσ' for ἔσσο, Od. 1, 302, ἔσο Plut. (Apophth. Lac.) 241, ἔστω Il. 22, 244; Hes. Op. 306, dual ἔστων 1, 338, pl. Od. 1, 273; inf. ἔμεναι Il. 8, 193, ἔμμ- 2, 249; Hes. Th. 610 (Sapph. 136; Pind. Ol. 1, 32 Bergk), ἔμεν Il. 19, 22; Hes. Th. 500, ἔμμ- Sapph. 2, 2; Pind. Ol. 5, 16; Soph. Ant. 623 (chor.), εἶναι Il. 21, 187; part in Hom. ἐών Il. 4, 231; Hes. Op. 514; Her. 1, 26. 2, 20, ἐοῦσα Il. 3, 159, ἐόν 11, 637 &c. Imp. ἦα Il. 5, 808. Od. 10, 156, ἔα Il. 4, 321; Her. 2, 19, apostr. ἔ' Od. 14, 222, ἔας Her. 1, 187, ἔον Il. 11, 762 (ἔην 1 pers. is now dropped). 23, 643, ἦσθα 23,

604; Theogn. 1314 (Dem. 18, 180. 45, 82), ἔησθα Il. 22, 435; Hes. Op. 314, 3 pers. ἦν Il. 4, 22; Her. 2, 102, ἔην Il. 12, 10. 24, 426; Hes. Th. 58; Her. 7, 143 &c. (Gaisf. but never Bekk.), ἦεν Il. 12, 9; Hes. Sc. 15, ἤην Il. 11, 808. Od. 23, 316, 2 pl. ἔατε Her. 4, 119. 5, 92 (ἔασαν, περι- 9, 31 Gaisf. περι-ῆσαν Bekk. Matth. Dind. Stein), ἦσαν Il. 3, 15; Hes. Th. 142; Her. 1, 13 &c. (Gaisf. Stein, ἔσαν Bekk. Dind.), ἔσαν Il. 4, 438; Hes. Th. 586; Pind. Ol. 2, 9. N. 9, 14; Her. 7, 219. 9, 16 (Bekk. Dind. ἦσ- Gaisf. Stein), ἔσσαν Pind. N. 9, 17, iter. ἔσκον Il. 7, 153, ἔσκε 3, 180, ἔσκον Her. 9, 40. Imp. mid. ἤμην rare, if correct, 3 pl. εἵατο Od. 20, 106 (Aristarch. Vulg. Dind. εἴατο Herodn. Bekk. Buttm. La R.): fut. ἔσομαι Il. 6, 409, ἔσσ- 4, 267, ἔσεαι 9, 605; Her. 8, 62, ἔσεται Il. 14, 480, ἔσσ- 4, 164, and ἔσται 4, 14 &c. even ἐσσεῖται 2, 393. 13, 317, ἀπ- Od. 19, 302, which (with ἐσσοῦμαι) is elsewhere Doric.

Doric forms: 1 pers. ἐμμί Theocr. 20, 32, rather Aeol. Sapph. 2, 15, (for Epicharm. 19, and Pind. N. 5, 1 &c. use εἰμί only), 2 pers. ἐσσί Epicharm. 130 (ἔσσ' 125 Ahr.); Pind. Ol. 6, 90. N. 10, 80; Theocr. 7, 43, 3 pers. ἐντί Theocr. 1, 17; Mosch. 5, 3 (Vulg. Mein. ἐστί Mss. A. B. &c. Ahr. Ziegl.), pl. εἰμές Theocr. 15, 73, ἦμες Cant. Lacon. Plut. Lycurg. 21, 16 (Bekk. Sint.); Theocr. 14, 29, Pind. εἰμέν P. 3, 60; Cant. Lacon. Plut. Lycurg. 21, 14, ἐντί Epicharm. 27. 92 &c.; Sophr. 52; Pind. N. 1, 24; Theocr. 11, 45; Ar. Ach. 902; Thuc. 5, 77; inf. ἦμεν Heracl. et Cret. Tit. 2555. 2558 &c.; Ar. Ach. 741 (Vulg. Dind. 4 ed.); Lacon. Decree Thuc. 5, 77 (some Mss. Ahr.); Theocr. 14, 6 (Ziegl. Fritz.), and εἶμεν Epicharm. 97; Lacon. Tit. 1335; Ar. Ach. 741. 771 Dind. 5 ed.); Arg. Treaty Thuc. 5, 77. 79 (Bekk. Krüg.); Theocr. 4, 9 (Ahr. Mein. Fritz.), also ἦμες Theocr. 14, 6 (Mein.), but condemned by Ahrens as an incorrect form of inf., and displaced by ἦμεν or εἶμεν 7, 129. 8, 73. 11, 79. 13, 3, ἤμεναι, εἴμ- Ar. Ach. 775, but Ahrens doubts whether this be Doric. The reading is certainly well supported, but, besides being unusual in Doric, it is made rather suspicious by the short form ἦμεν, εἶμεν being twice used by the same speaker 741. 771; Ahrens suggests εἶμεν, αὖ; Pind. has ἔμμεν P. 6, 42; Sapph. 34 (Bergk); so Soph. Ant. 623 (chor.), εἶμειν Rhod. Inscr. 2905, ἦμεν Cret. 3058; part. ἐών and ὤν, fem. οὖσα, ἐοῦσα Delph. Inscr. 1705, ἐοῖσα Pind. P. 4, 265; Theocr. 2, 64, εὖσα 2, 76 (Sapph. 27 Ahr. ἔσσα Bergk), παρ-εύσας 5, 26, ἐᾶσα Tim. Locr. 96. Ahrens, Meineke, and Ziegler formerly condemned the contr. masc. form. εὖντα Theocr. 2, 3, and approved the restitution of βαρυνεῦντα for βαρὺν εὖντα (Mss. Reiske), but in their last editions they have adopted εὔντα. A rare form ἔντες occurs Tab. Heracl. 1, 56, dat. ἔντασσι 69, 130, gen. παρ-έντων Alcm. 57 (Bergk, 64, 3 ed.) 'not from a noun εἱς,' says Ahrens, 'but probably from ἐών, ἔντος &c. after the analogy of κυών, κυνός:' imp. (ἦν, ἦσθα common), doubtful ἔης Theocr. 19, 8 (Vulg.), 3 sing. ἦς Theocr. 2, 90. 92. 124. 5, 10. 7, 1, and ἦν 2, 78. 4, 49. 20, 37 &c. Bion 8, 2. 7 (Mein. Ziegl.); Mosch. 2, 24. 50; so Pind. I. 1, 26. 2, 37. Ol. 8, 19 &c.

Εἶμι *I go,* usu. as fut. *shall go,* Il. 3, 410; Theogn. 1203; Aesch. Sept. 672. 700; Soph. Ph. 461; Ar. Pax 232; Antiph. 5, 62; Thuc. 2, 36, εἶς Hes. Op. 208, εἶσθα Il. 10, 450. Od. 19, 69, Attic εἶ Soph. Tr. 83; Ar. Av. 990, but ἄν-ει H. Cer. 403, εἶσι Il. 13, 796; Hes. Th. 972; Soph. O. R. 1458: Ar. Eccl. 933; Pl. Rep. 520, προσ- Thuc. 4, 85, ἴμεν Il. 17, 155; Aesch. Sept. 1068; Eur. Bac. 841: Ar. Vesp. 1250; Her. 9, 42; Thuc. 1, 82, ἴτε 1, 40, ἴασιν Il. 16, 160; Ar. Eccl. 615; Xen. Cyr. 8, 6, 2; Pl. Conv. 174, ἀπ- Her. 8, 60, ἐπ- Thuc. 4, 61; subj. ἴω Il. 18, 188; Theogn. 912; Soph. Ant. 315; Ar. Ran. 291; Pl. Conv. 174, ἐπ- Thuc. 4, 85, ἴῃς Il. 24, 295; Eur. Ion 1603; Ar. Av. 634, ἴῃσθα Il. 10, 67, ἴῃ Od. 8, 395; Thuc. 6, 79; Pl. Leg. 909 &c. Epic. ἴῃσι Il. 9, 701; ἴωμεν Batr. 280; Thuc. 6, 18; Pl. Rep. 543, Epic ἴομεν Il. 10, 126. Od. 23, 83 and always Hom.; Solon 2, 5, ἴητε Xen. An. 7, 3, 4, ἴωσι Il. 12, 239; Antiph. 5, 11; Thuc. 4, 42; opt. ἴοιμι Xen. Cyr. 5, 5, 1 (Vulg. Popp. Dind.), ἐπεξ- Antiph. 1, 11, and ἰοίην Xen. Conv. 4, 16, διεξ- Isocr. 5, 98. 6, 42, ἴοι Il. 14, 21; Pl. Rep. 415; Xen. Cyr. 3, 3, 27, ἴοιμεν, παρ- Ar. Lys. 151, προσ- 153, ἴοιεν Thuc. 7, 80; Pl. Rep. 360 &c., Epic 3 sing. ἰείη Il. 19, 209, and εἴη 24, 139; ἴθι Il. 3, 130; Aesch. Pers. 1038; Ar. Eq. 105; Her. 7, 234. 8, 57; Pl. Soph. 237, ἴτω Il. 12, 362; Soph. Ph. 120; Pl. Leg. 764, ἴτε 797; ἰέναι Il. 16, 87; Theogn. 352; Hes. Sc. 40; (in Trag.?); Ar. Av. 188; Her. 6, 134; Thuc. 7, 74; Pl. Conv. 174; ἰών Il. 7, 46; Soph. O. C. 618; Ar. Vesp. 99; Antiph. 2, β, 3; Pl. Euth. 273; Isocr. 4, 67: imp. ᾔειν 1 pers. rare, Luc. Herm. 25, προσ- Xen. Oec. 6, 15; Pl. Lys. 206; Dem. 34, 12, ἀπ- 45, 6 &c. ᾔεις, περι- Aeschin. 3, 164, ᾔεισθα, δι- Pl. Tim. 26, ᾔει Il. 10, 286. Od. 8, 290; Thuc. 3, 93; Andoc. 1, 36; Pl. Phaedr. 228, ᾔειτε, ἐξ- Andoc. 2, 8, and ᾖα Pl. Apol. 21. Charm. 153; Xen. Cyr. 5, 4, 10. 12, ᾖε Il. 12, 371, Epic and Ion. ᾔϊα only 1 and 3 sing. and pl. Od. 4, 433; Her. 1, 111. 4, 82, -ιε Il. 13, 602. Od. 8, 457; Her. 1, 119. 2, 26. 5, 51 &c. -ισαν Il. 17, 495. Od. 20, 7; Her. 1, 43. 2, 30 (Bekk.), see below: fut. Epic εἴσομαι Il. 14, 8. 24, 462: aor. Epic εἰσάμην Il. 5, 538, ἐεισ- 15, 415. 544. Od. 22, 89. **Vb.**

ἰτός Her. (orac.) 7, 140; Anth. 7, 480 (Lehrs), ἐξ-ιτός Hes. Th. 732, δυσπρόσ-ιτος Eur. I. A. 345, ἰτέος Thuc. 8, 2; Pl. Rep. 394, ἰτητέος Ar. Nub. 131, παρ- Thuc. 1, 72. See ἵεμαι.

The following are some of the more peculiar forms and usages: εἶς for εἶ perhaps does not occur in Attic, εἶσι as 3 pl. in old ed. Hes. Sc. 113, and Theogn. 716, has been altered to εἴσι; Dor. subj. εἴω Sophr. Fr. 2 (Ahr.); the opt. form ἰοίην seems in this verb very much confined to 1 pers., having 3 ἴοι Pl. Tim. 78. Phaed. 65. Some maintain that in this, and contracted verbs, -οίην alone was used in Attic prose—to which we demur; imper. εἶ for ἴθι in comp. only and poetic, ἔξει &c. Ar. Nub. 633, is perhaps the pres. as an *imperat.* fut., 3 pl. ἰόντων Thuc. 4, 118; Xen. An. 1, 4, 8; Pl. Leg. 956, and ἴτωσαν Eur. I. T. 1480; Pl. Leg. 765, ἐπεξ- 873, ἐπαν- Xen. Ven. 4, 5, rarely ἴτων Aesch. Eum. 32: the imp. form ᾖα is perhaps old Attic, Pl. Theaet. 180. Rep. 449; Dem. 45, 17, for 2 pers. ᾔεις Pl. has ᾔεισθα, δι- Tim. 26, ἐπεξ- Euthyphr. 4, and for 3 pers. ᾔει he has ᾔειν Criti. 117. Tim. 38, and ἀπ- even before a consonant 76; dual ᾔτην Pl. Euthyd. 294; pl. ᾖμεν, ᾖτε (are more frequent than ᾔειμεν, ᾔειτε), ᾖμεν Eur. Andr. 1102; Ar. Plut. 659; Pl. Rep. 328; Isae. 10, 18, προσ- Dem. 19, 17. 56, 11, ᾖτε Xen. An. 7, 7, 6, προσ- Eur. Cycl. 40, ἐξ- Dem. 23, 209 &c. indeed the full forms seem doubtful, ᾔειμεν Pl. Phaed. 59 (Ms. E. Steph. εἰσ- Ms. Bodl. Herm. -ᾖμεν Mss. Heind. Schanz &c.), ἐξ- Aeschin. 2, 97, παρ- 2, 108 (Vulg. -ᾖμεν Franke), ᾔειτε, ἀπ- Andoc. 1, 66, ἐξ- 2, 8, εἰσ- Aeschin. 3, 140 (Vulg. -ᾖτε Franke &c.), ᾔεσαν Xenophan. 3, 3 (ᾔισαν Renner), ᾖσαν Archil. 81 (Mein. Bergk), ἐπ- Od. 19, 445, μετ- Ar. Eq. 605, εἰσ- Com. Fr. (Callias) 2, 740 (ᾖσαν Her. 2, 163, Schweig. Gaisf. ᾔισαν Bekk. Dind.), but in Mss. and our editions of Attic prose authors almost always ᾔεσαν Thuc. 2, 3. 3, 22. 5, 17; Xen. Hell. 3, 2, 26. An. 6, 1, 11. Cyr. 4, 5, 55. Athen. 1, 18; Pl. Rep. 600. Lys. 206; Dem. 57, 15. 59, 48, ἀπ- Aeschin. 2, 111. 3, 76; Dem. 19, 154, προσ- 21, 23, συν- 23, 39 &c. all those however and all others, W. and L. Dindorf, Cobet, Voemel, Franke, &c. write, or would write ᾖσαν, ἀπ-ῇσαν, προσ-ῇσαν, συν-ῇσαν as the genuine Attic form—and say that though nearly obliterated by ignorant copyists, this form still occasionally shews in the best Mss. Under παρῇσαν, for instance, Dem. 1, 8, lurks, they allege, παρῇσαν, and so now they edit. If ᾔειν was not employed in, it seems to have at least partially followed, the inflection of the pluperf. ᾔε(ι)σαν would appear to be its legitimate 3 pl., and the *mistake*, if mistake it be, of retaining ε, appears as easily made and as great as our moved for mov'd, loved for lov'd, and fixed for fix'd, fixt. Judging from *appearances* one would be apt to suppose that the Ionians said (ἠίεσαν) ἤισαν, Poet. ᾖσαν, the Attics (ᾔεισαν), ᾔεσαν, Poet. and perhaps occasionally in prose ᾖσαν.

In Hom. 2 sing. εἶσθα Il. 10, 450. Od. 19, 69; subj. ἴῃσθα Il. 10, 67, 3 pers. ἴῃσιν 9, 701, pl. ἴομεν for -ωμεν, 2, 440; opt. ἴοι 14, 21, ἰείη 19, 209, and εἴη 24, 139. Od. 14, 496; inf. ἰέναι Il. 16, 87 &c. ἴμεναι Il. 20, 32 (Dind. La Roche). Od. 2, 298 (Dind. Kayser, ἰέναι Bekk.), Od. 8, 287, ἴμμ- Il. 20, 365 (Bekk.), ἴμεν Il. 10, 32 &c.; Pind. Ol. 6, 63 (rare ἴεμεν Dor. Stob. (Archyt.) 1, 71), rare ἶναι (ῐ) Strab. (Orac.) 9, 2, 23 (Kram.), ἐξ- Athen. (Machon) 13, 43: imp. ἤια Od. 10, 309; Her. 4, 82 (Xen. Cyr. 5, 4, 11 Popp. ᾖα Born. Dind.), and ἤιον Luc. D. Syr. 25, ἀν- Od. 10, 146, ἤιε Il. 7, 213; Her. 2, 26, ᾖε Il. 12, 371, κατ-ῄε Hes. Sc. 254 (Ranke, Flach, Rzach, -εῖε Vulg. Goettl. Schoem. Mss. differ), ᾔει Il. 13, 247. Od. 8, 290, and often ἴεν as aor. Il. 2, 872. Od. 16, 41. 155, 3 dual ἴτον Hes. Op. 199, ἴτην Il. 1, 347; so Hes. quoted (Lehrs, Koechl.), pl. ᾔομεν Od. 11, 22, ἤισαν Il. 10, 197; Her. 1, 43; Hippocr. 3, 212 (Soph. Tr. 514 chor. Br. Erf., ἴσαν Herm. Dind. &c.), ᾖσαν Her. 2, 163 (Schweigh. Gaisf. ἤισάν Bekk. Dind. Stein and always in Her., never ᾖσαν or ᾔεσαν), ἐπ- Od. 19, 445, μετ- Ar. Eq. 605, εἰσ- Com. Fr. 2, 740, ἴσαν Il. 3, 8; Hes. Th. 68; Soph. Tr. 514 (chor.); Eur. Bac. 421 chor. (Dind. 2 ed. Paley, ἴσα δ' Kirchh. Nauck, Dind. 5 ed.), and ἤιον, ἀν- Od. 10, 446, ἐκ- in tmesi 23, 370.

In Attic, εἶμι has almost always the sense of fut. ἐλεύσομαι *will go*, Aesch. Pr. 325; Thuc. 2, 36, also Her. ἀπ-ίασι 8, 60, even with ὅπως, as ὅπως ἔπεισι Thuc. 6, 18, εἰσ- Xen. An. 7, 3, 34; so opt. ἴοιεν, ἀπ- Xen. Hell. 5. 1, 34; also part. ἰόντες Thuc. 6, 63, ἐξ- Xen. Hell. 7, 5, 2; inf. ἰέναι ὑπεξ- Pl. Phaed. 103, but the *moods* are perhaps used oftener as pres. or aor. Even the pres. ἐπίασιν seems to have a pres. meaning Thuc. 4, 61, εἶσι doubtful in Aesch. Sept. 373 (Herm. Hart. εἰς Pors. Blomf. Linw. ὥστ' Dind. 5 ed.), more certain in late prose, συνίασι Strab. 3. 2, 2 &c. This Attic usage of pres. for fut. or pres. in a fut. sense, is no more marvellous than our own, *I go to-morrow by the coach, he comes on Friday week.* Hom. uses pres. both as pres. and fut., as pres. Il. 2, 87. Od. 4, 401, as fut. Il. 1, 426. Od. 17, 277.

(Εἴπω) ἔπω *To say*, pres. late Epic ἔπουσι Nic. Ther. 508. 738. Alex. 429. 490: 2 aor. εἶπον Od. 6, 223; Aesch. Eum. 638; Soph. Ant. 755; Ar. Ach. 579; Her. 8, 26; Antiph. 6, 23; Thuc. 3, 71; Pl. Rep. 331, εἶπες Od. 4, 204 (Wolf. Bekk. Dind. see below): Ar. Fr. 476 (D.); Pl. Euthyph. 11. 14. Rep. 338. Phaedr. 275 &c.; Dem. 18, 197 (Bekk. Dind.); Xen. Cyr. 1, 6,

16 (Popp. Breitb. Hertl. 2 ed. &c. -ας Dind. *now*, Saupp. Hertl. 3 ed.), εἶπε Il. 4, 22; Aesch. Ag. 125; Ar. Vesp. 44; Pl. Phaed. 59 &c. Epic, ἔειπον only indic. Il. 10, 445, ἔειπες Il. 1, 552. 4, 25. Od. 17, 406, ἔειπε Il. 15, 185; Pind. Ol. 4, 25, ἔειπον, προσ- Hes. Th. 749, iter εἴπεσκον Il. 3, 297; εἴπω Il. 9, 26; Aesch. Ch. 88; Soph. O. R. 329; Ar. Eq. 142; Her. 2, 105; Antiph. 5, 5; Andoc. 1, 51; Pl. Rep. 337, Epic εἴπωμι Od. 22, 392, -ησθα Il. 20, 250. Od. 11, 224, -ησι Il. 7, 87; εἴποιμι Od. 22, 262; Pind. N. 6, 65 (Vulg.); Soph. El. 413; Ar. Eq. 18; Pl. Rep. 400, -οις Il. 11, 791; Hes. Op. 721; Aesch. Ch. 847; Ar. Thesm. 549; Pl. Phil. 23, -οι Il. 17, 260; Ar. Av. 180; Antiph. 5, 50, -οιμεν Pl. Rep. 398, -οιτε Aeschin. 1, 74, -οιεν Pl. Leg. 709; imper. εἰπέ Il. 10, 384; Pind. P. 4, 100; Aesch. Ag. 121; Soph. Ant. 446; Eur. Hec. 986, and always in Tragedy; Ar. Ran. 39; Her. 5, 111; Xen. Cyr. 1, 4, 13, εἰπέτω Pl. Phaedr. 273. Lach. 194, προ- Hippocr. 4, 376 (Lit.), dual εἴπετον Pl. Protag. 330. Euthyd. 296, and -έτην Xen. Cyr. 3, 1, 42; Pl. Conv. 189, -ετον (Bekk.), pl. εἴπετε rare, we know only Pl. Prot. 357, but Epic ἔσπετε Il. 11, 218. 16, 112; Com. Fr. (Herm.) 2, 407 (hexam.); εἰπεῖν Il. 9, 102; Pind. Ol. 1, 52; Aesch. Ag. 367; Soph. O. R. 361; Ar. Eq. 608; Her. 1, 61. 2, 91 (Gaisf. Bekk.); Thuc. 4, 22, and always in Attic prose, Epic εἰπέμεναι Il. 7, 375; Solon 22, εἰπέμεν Il. 9, 688, Aeol. εἴπην Alcae. 50; Sapph. 28; εἰπών Il. 7, 1; Soph. O. C. 759; Ar. Plut. 670; Her. 1, 27 (Bekk. Gaisf. Stein, -ας Dind.); Antiph. 5, 75; Thuc. 2, 72; Isocr. 18, 2; Pl. Phil. 38, and perhaps always in classic Attic prose: 1 aor. εἶπα Her. 4, 44. 7, 11; Anth. 12, 130; rare in Attic, Com. Fr. (Alex.) 3, 383. Philem. 4, 52. (Athen.) 4, 558. (Euang.) 4, 572; Xen. Mem. 2, 2, 8; (Dem.) 47, 41; Polyb. 18, 7 (Bekk.), προσ- Eur. Cycl. 101, εἶπας Il. 1, 106. 108 (Heyn. Bekk. Dind. La R. with Aristarch.); Her. 7, 234; often in Attic, Aesch. Pr. 773. Pers. 798; Soph. Ph. 27. Aj. 1127. El. 407; Eur. Phoen. 915; Ar. Pax 131. Ach. 580. Lys. 595; Xen. An. 2, 5, 23 (Krüg. Dind.). Conv. 4, 56. Oec. 19, 14; Aeschin. 3, 163, Poet. ἔειπα Emped. 75 (Stein); Pind. N. 9, 33; Theocr. 22, 153 (Mein. Wordsw. Ahr.), -πας (not *now* in Hom.); Ap. Rh. 3, 1106 &c. pl. εἴπαμεν rare, Ar. Eccl. 75 (Ms. R. Vulg. Bekk. Bergk, -ομεν Mss. Dind. Mein.); Aristot. Nat. Ausc. 3, 2, 3. Top. 8, 10, 6 (v. r. -ομεν). Eth. N. 1, 11, 9. 12, 3 (Bekk., *now* -ομεν 3 edit.), εἴπατε rare and late in *simple*, Dio Cass. 59, 16; V. T. Gen. 44, 28. Esai. 28, 15, rare in comp. προ- Dem. 18, 80, προσ- App. Civ. 4, 10, συν- Aristid. 37 (471), εἶπαν Her. 1, 120. 4, 158. 5, 1. 18. 7, 27 &c.; rare, if certain, in Attic, Xen. Conv. 3, 2 (-ον Born. Dind. Saupp.). Hell. 3, 5, 24,

προσ- 4, 1, 31 (Breitenb. Saupp. but Dind. *now* -ον 3 edit.); Aristot. Eth. Eud. 7, 13, ἀπ- Dio. Hal. 11, 41, ἔειπαν Hes. Th. 24 (Goettl. Flach, v. r. -ον Koechly, Schoem.), late form εἴποσαν V. T. Ruth 4, 11; subj. εἴπω as above; opt. rare εἴπαιμι, εἴπαις if correct, Theocr. 15, 25 (Toup. Mein. Ahr. -ες Ziegl. Fritz.), εἴπαι Her. 3, 6. 4, 155. 9, 71 &c. (always Dind., εἴποι always Mss. Gaisf. Bekk. Stein), εἴπειεν (Dem.) 59, 70 (Bekk. B. Saupp. εἴποι Dind.), εἴπαιμεν Pl. Soph. 240, -οιμεν (Steph.), -αιεν (Dem.) 53, 24 (Bekk. B. Saupp. -οιεν Dind.); imper. εἶπον others εἰπόν Simon. (C.) 154 (B.); Pind. Ol. 6, 92; Theocr. 14, 11; Com. Fr. (Men.) 4, 297. (Euphr.) 4, 489. (Nicol.) 4, 579; Xen. Mem. 3, 6, 3; Pl. Men. 71, εἰπάτω Ar. Pax 660; Lys. 8, 3; Isae. 11, 3; Pl. Phil. 60; Xen. Athen. 3, 6; Dem. 20, 113, dual εἴπατον Ar. Av. 107. Ran. 1379; Pl. Euthyd. 294, pl. εἴπατε Od. 3, 427. 21, 198; Hes. Th. 108; Soph. O. C. 1115; Ar. Ach. 540; Thuc. 5, 85; Xen. An. 2, 1, 21; Pl. Lach. 187; Aeschin. 1, 70; Dinarch. 1, 43, late εἰπάτωσαν V. T. Ps. 39, 17; N. T. Act. 24, 20; Sext. Empir. 63, 26. 120, 10. 139, 29; Galen 1, 133; inf. εἶπαι Ion. Her. 1, 57. 3, 63. 4, 134. 6, 61 &c.; εἴπας Her. 1, 41. 3, 36. 65. 4, 98. 5, 20 &c.; Hippocr. 6, 170, rare and perhaps late in Attic, Com. Fr. (Philem.) 4, 14; Aristot. Top. 2, 2, 2. 4, 6, 12. 5, 2, 10 &c.; Theophr. Char. 7 (Foss); (Dem.) 59, 5, ἀντ- 59, 27, προσ- 50, 60 (Bekk. B. Saupp. -ών Dind.), προ- Com. Fr. (Dionys.) 3, 547, Dor. εἴπαις Pind. Ol. 8, 46. **Mid. pres.** ἔσπομαι late, Or. Sib. 2, 4: **1 aor.** (εἰπάμην) in tmesi, ἀπὸ δ' εἴπαο Callim. Dian. 174, ἀπ-είπατο Her. 1, 205, -άμεθα 9, 7, -αντο 6, 100; -είπασθαι 1, 59; -ειπάμενος 4, 125. 5, 56; Anth. (Alcid.) 5, 233. (P. Sil.) 234; and later Attic prose, ἀπ-είπατο Ael. V. H. 2, 42; Plut. Them. 23, -είπασθε Luc. D. Mort. 29; Aristid. 33, 415 (D.); -άμενος (Aeschin.) Epist. 10, 8; Arr. An. 3, 5, 2; -είπασθαι Aristot. Eth. N. 8, 16, 4; App. Civ. 3, 11; Polyb. 23, 9, διειπ- Aristot. Oec. 2, 30, συνειπ- Dio. Hal. Ant. 5, 48. 51. We however know no instance of this aor. mid. in *classic* Attic, and therefore demur to the soundness of Thom. Magister's doctrine 'ἀπειπάμην κάλλιον ἢ ἀπεῖπον.' The assertion of Matthiae, likewise, 'that the *Attics* have derived from εἶπα a **1 aor. mid.** ἀπειπάμην' should have been qualified by *later*, *less pure*, or some such expression: **2 aor.** ἀπ-ειπέσθαι occurs Joseph. Ant. 17, 3, 1 (Bekk.), the only instance we know.

1 pers. εἶπα is rare in Attic, εἶπας freq., but disputed in Hom. Wolf, with Schol. Ven. B., adopted εἶπες for -ας, Il. 1, 106. 108, and Spitzn. has followed him. Bekk. however, Heyne, Voss, and Dind. retain with Aristarch. εἶπας. Indeed, always in Il. and Od. Bekk. edits εἶπας, except -ες Od. 4, 204; Dind., again, has

εἶπες Il. 24, 744, and always in Od. except -ας 22, 46; La Roche εἶπας always except εἶπες Il. 24, 744, 1 pl. εἴπαμεν rare, see Ar. &c. quoted above, 3 pl. εἶπαν in Attic, is, if correct, confined to Xen. Bornemann decidedly approves and edits -ον, and so now L. Dind. (3 edit.); opt. εἴπαιμι &c. is very rare in Attic, so rare as to appear doubtful, and, if we may credit the Mss., never even in Herodotus, see above; the imperat. forms, again, εἰπάτω, εἴπατον, εἴπατε are more used by the Attics than the corresponding forms of the 2 aor.; inf. εἶπαι is not in Attic; part. εἴπας occasionally in later Com. poetry, but scarcely, if ever, in classic Attic prose. Kühner (Xen. Mem. 2, 2, 8) says 'the Attics avoided 1 pl. εἴπαμεν, but used freely εἴπατε.' Bekk. and Bergk have edited 1 pers., Ar. quoted above, and Aristot. Eth. Nic. 1, 11, 12. De An. 2, 11, 12, but εἴπατε *indic.* in *simple*, we should be glad to see in any *classic* writer. It occurs *late* certainly, V. T. Gen. 44, 28. Jer. 36, 15; Dio Cass. 59, 16, see above, but in classic Greek twice only, we think, and in comp. προ- Dem. 18, 80. As imperative however it is frequent in the classical period, εἴπατε Od. Soph. Thuc. Pl. quoted above, Ar. Lys. 1075, προσ- Pax 581. Ach. 891; Eur. Hipp. 1099. Alc. 610. Med. 895.—Aeol. inf. εἴπην Alcae. 50, digamm. ϝείπην 55 (Bergk, 45 Ahrens); see εἴπας Il. 1, 106, ϝεῖπας 1, 108 (Bekk.) With classical writers, the pres. is supplied by φημί, λέγω &c. the other parts by εἴρω (ῥέω), ἐρῶ, εἴρηκα, εἴρημαι, ἐρρήθην, Ion. εἰρέθην, rare ἐρρέθην, προ- Hippocr. 5, 196 (Littré), fut. ῥηθήσομαι, 3 fut. εἰρήσομαι.

(**Εἰργάθω**) *To shut out*, -άθειν Soph. El. 1271; Eur. Phoen. 1175; ἀπ-ειργάθῃ Soph. O. C. 862: **imp.** ἔργαθον Il. 11, 437, ἐέργ- 5, 147. **Mid. as act.** εἰργάθου, κατ- Aesch. Eum. 566. Some hold these to be **2 aor. act.** and **mid.** and accent εἰργαθεῖν, κατειργαθοῦ (Dind. &c.) A Poet. lengthened form for εἴργω.

Εἴργω *To shut in*, Theogn. 710 (Mss. but εἰργ- Ms. O, Bergk, Ziegl.); Antiph. 3, 2. 6, 46 (Bait. Saupp. εἴργ- Blass); Thuc. 3, 18 (Mss. P. Bekk. Krüg. εἴργ- Popp.), καθ- Luc. Amor. 39; Dio Hal. 11, 55, εἴργνυμι, καθ- Pl. Tim. 45 (-υται Com. Fr. (Cratin.) 2, 63), and εἰργνύω Andoc. 4, 27: **fut.** εἴρξω Eur. Elec. 1255; Thuc. 8, 74 (Bekk.); Dio. Cass. 39, 33 (Bekk. κατ- L. Dind.): **aor.** εἶρξα Eur. Bac. 443; Ar. Ach. 330; Antiph. 3, γ, 11; Thuc. 8, 92 (Bekk.); Dem. (12, 2). 21, 147, καθ- 3, 31. 18, 97, συγκαθ- Xen. Cyr. 6, 1, 36: **p. p.** εἶργμαι, -ένος Ar. Av. 1085; Xen. Hell. 5, 2, 31, καθ- 3, 2, 3, συγκαθ- Aeschin. 1, 182: **plp.** εἶρκτο Nic. Damasc. Fr. 8 (L. Dind.), καθ- Anth. Plan. 5, 384: **aor.** εἴρχθην, εἰρχθείς Lycurg. 112; εἰρχθῆναι (Dem.) 59, 66. **Vb.** εἱρκτή *a prison* Xen. Mem. 2, 1, 5. See ἔργω, ἔργνυμι.

Εἴργω *To shut out*, Hom. only Il. 23, 72 (ἐϝέργ- Bekk. *now*); Theogn. 1180; Aesch. Ag. 1333 (D.); Pind. N. 7, 6; Soph. Tr. 1257; Xen. Mem. 1, 2, 20; Dem. 23, 40; εἴργωσι Thuc. 1, 62: **imp.** εἶργον Soph. Ph. 569; Thuc. 3, 1: **fut.** εἴρξω Aesch. Sept. 503; Soph. Ph. 1406; Hippocr. 1, 4 (Erm.); Thuc. 1, 35; Aeschin. 2, 115, ἐξ- Ar. Ach. 825, ἀπ- Dem. 20, 5: **aor.** εἶρξα Luc. D. Mer. 10, 1, ἀπ- Thuc. 4, 37 (Bekk.); Arr. An. 3, 28, 8; εἶρξαι Soph. Aj. 753: **p. p.** εἶργμαι Democr. Stob. 406 (Gaisf.), ἀπ- Eur. Heracl. 877: **aor.** εἴρχθην Thuc. 5, 49 (Popp. Krüg. &c. εἵρχ- Bekk.); Dio Cass. 46, 48: **fut. m.** εἴρξομαι pass. or reflex, *shut oneself out, get oneself shut out*, Xen. An. 6, 6, 16; Aeschin. 3, 122: see **pres.** εἴργου *restrain yourself, keep off*, Soph. O. C. 836: some add as **2 aor. act.** εἴργαθον, εἰργάθω, εἰργαθεῖν Soph. El. 1271; Eur. Phoen. 1175: **2 aor. m.** as act. εἰργαθόμην, in κατ-ειργαθοῦ Aesch. Eum. 566, see ἔργω, εἰργάθω. **Vb.** late, εἰρκτέον Stob. (Hier.) 39, 36.

Εἰρέω *To say*, Epic only pres. part. fem. εἰρεῦσαι Hes. Th. 38, contr. for εἰρέουσαι: and **fut.** εἰρήσω, if correct, Hippocr. 7, 448 (Zwing. Lit. εἰρήσθω Vulg.)

Εἴρομαι *To ask*, Epic and Ion. for ἔρομαι, Il. 1, 553, 2 sing. εἴρεαι Il. 15, 247. 24, 390; subj. εἴρωμαι Od. 8, 549, -ηαι 1, 188, -ηται Od. 9, 503; Her. 4, 76, -ώμεθα Od. 16, 402; imper. εἴρεο Od. 1, 284; εἰρόμενος Il. 7, 127; Her. 1, 27; -εσθαι Od. 19, 95; Her. 8, 65, ἐπ- 1, 19: **imp.** εἰρόμην Her. 2, 44. 150, 2 sing. εἴρεο 1, 32, εἴρετο Il. 1, 513. Od. 20, 137; Pind. Ol. 6, 49; Her. 1, 30, -οντο Od. 11, 570: **fut.** εἰρήσομαι Od. 4, 61. 7, 237; εἰρησόμενος, ἐπ- Her. 1, 67. 4, 161. 6, 52 (Gaisf. Bekk. Dietsch, Stein), and now 1, 174 (Bekk. Lhardy, Stein, ἐπ-ερησ- Gaisf. Dind.): **aor.** late, if correct, προ-ειρησάμενος Galen 15, 111.—ἐπειρεόμενος Her. 3, 64 (Schweigh. Gaisf. &c.) is edited ἐπειρομ- by Bekk. Lhardy, Dind. Krüg. Stein with Mss. S. V. &c. See ἔρομαι.

Εἰρύω *To draw*, Epic and Ion. for ἐρύω, εἰρύμεναι Hes. Op. 818: **imp.** εἴρυον Mosch. 2, 14. 127, may belong to ἐρύω: **fut.** εἰρύσω Hippocr. 2, 176 (Erm.), διειρύσσ- Ap. Rh. 1, 687: **aor.** εἴρυσα Il. 11, 9; Her. 2, 136. 3, 30, -υσσα Il. 18, 165. Od. 8, 85, retains ει; subj. εἰρύσῃ Hippocr. 6, 166. 172, -ύσωσι 7, 16 (Lit.), ἀν-ειρύσσ- Mosch. 4, 116; εἴρυσον Soph. Tr. 1032 (chor.); εἰρύσαι Hippocr. 8, 108, ἐξ- Her. 1, 141, δι- 7, 24; εἰρύσας 4, 10, ἐπ-ειρύσσ- Ap. Rh. 3, 149 (Br. Well. -ύσ- Vulg. Merk.): **p. p.** εἴρυμαι, 3 pl. -ύαται Il. 14, 75; Hippocr. 5, 522; -υμέναι Il. 13, 682, and εἴρυσμαι, κατ- Od. 8, 151, ἀν- Arr. Ind. 35, 7: **plp.** εἰρύμην, -υντο Il. 18, 69, -ύατο 14, 30. 15, 654, and ἀν-ειρυσμέναι ἦσαν Arr. Ind. 33, 10: **aor.** εἰρύσθην Hippocr. 7, 178; -υσθείς 8, 84 (Lit.) **Mid.** εἰρύομαι *to draw to oneself, protect*, Il. 21, 588;

Hippocr. 8, 344. 352: fut. εἰρύσσομαι Il. 18, 276: aor. εἰρῠσάμην, -ῡσαο Il. 21, 230, -ῡσατο 4, 186, -ῠσατο H. Merc. 127, εἰρυσσ- 22, 306; retains ει, εἰρυσσαίμην Il. 8, 143. Od. 16, 459; εἰρύσσασθαι Il. 1, 216, -ύσασθαι Opp. Cyn. 1, 51; εἰρυσάμενος, ἐπ- Her. 4, 8, ἀν- Arr. Ind. 38: p. as mid. εἰρῡαται Il. 1, 239, -ύαται Od. 16, 463: plp. or syncop. aor. εἴρῡτο Od. 22, 90. Il. 16, 542. 24, 499, -υντο 12, 454, -ῡατο 22, 303; εἴρυσθαι Od. 3, 268. 23, 82. See ἐρύω.—ῠ in pres. fut. and aor. except in arsis, ῡ between two long syllables, as εἰρῡονται Ap. Rh. 4, 279, εἰρῡοιτο 4, 804, and in contracted forms and perf. pass. except perhaps one or two instances, as εἰρῡαται for -υνται, Il. 4, 248. Od. 6, 265.—εἰρῡμεναι inf. pres. Epic as from εἴρῡμι, Hes. Opp. 818 quoted. —εἰρῡαται, -ύαται (in arsis) 3 pl. pres.=εἴρυνται; imper. εἴρῡσο (in arsis) Ap. Rh. 4, 372; inf. εἴρυσθαι; 3 sing. imp. εἴρῡτο (in arsis), 3 pl. εἴρυντο may be also from εἴρῡμι; but some hold these as syncopated forms of pres. εἰρύομαι and imp. -υόμην, others as perf. and plp. or syncop. aor. in a mid. sense. See ἐρύω.

Εἴρω *To say*, Od. 11, 137. 13, 7, -έω Hes. Th. 58 (pres. not Attic): imp.?: fut. Ion. ἐρέω Il. 4, 39; Archil. 89; Hipponax 21; Pind. Ol. 8, 57; Her. 2, 38. 4, 118, and always; Hippocr. 7, 440. 490, -έει Il. 7, 91. Od. 3, 20, Attic ἐρῶ H. Cer. 406; Mimnerm. 7, 4; Aesch. Eum. 45; Soph. O. C. 811; Ar. Ran. 61; Antiph. 1, 6. 4, β, 3; Thuc. 6, 9; Lys. 8, 19; Isocr. 15, 178; Pl. Rep. 358, and εἰρήσω if correct Hippocr. 7, 448 (Zwing. Lit. 3, 525, Erm.): p. εἴρηκα Aesch. Pr. 821; Soph. Tr. 63; Ar. Ran. 558; Her. 1, 155; Antiph. 3, δ, 2; Thuc. 6, 87; Pl. Meno 80; Lys. 8, 16; plp. εἰρήκειν Aeschin. 1, 81; Dem. 21, 119. 34, 18; Plut. Mor. 184: p. p. εἴρημαι Il. 4, 363; Aesch. Eum. 710; Eur. Or. 1203; Ar. Lys. 13; Her. 8, 93; Antiph. 5, 5; Thuc. 1, 22; Pl. Conv. 219, 3 pl. Ion. εἰρέαται Her. 7, 81: plp. εἴρητο Il. 10, 540; Her. 8, 26; Thuc. 5, 21; Lys. 10, 9: aor. in Attic ἐρρήθην Xen. Cyr. 7, 5, 26; Pl. Rep. 504. Phil. 63; Aeschin. 2, 31. 118 (Mss. Bekk. &c.); Dem. 23, 16. 18, Ion. εἰρέθην Her. 4, 77. 156, and always (Bekk. Gaisf. Bred. Dind. Krüg.), rare ἐρρέθην, προ- Hippocr. 5, 196 (Lit.), ἐρρέθησαν Pl. Leg. 664 (Mss. ἐρρήθ- Bekk. B. O. W. Herm.), but in less pure Attic sometimes ἐρρέθ- Aristot. Categ. 9, 3; Plut. Quest. Conv. 7, 8, 1. 9, 14, 4, ἐρρήθ- however 4, 5, 1. 5, 3, 2, &c.; ῥηθείς Od. 18, 414; Soph. O. R. 1057; Pl. Leg. 861: fut. ῥηθήσομαι Thuc. 1, 73; Pl. Rep. 473; Isocr. 8, 73: 3 fut. εἰρήσομαι (always Hom. Pind. Attic Poets, and Her.) Il. 23, 795; Pind. I. 6, 59; Soph. O. R. 365; Eur. Hec. 825; Ar. Plut. 114, (ἀντ- Soph. Tr. 1184); Her. 4, 16; Hippocr. 1, 596

(Lit.); Thuc. 6, 34; Pl. Leg. 918. Rep. 473. **Mid.** as act. εἴρομαι pres. late, Nic. Ther. 359: **imp.** εἴρετο Il. 1, 513, -οντο Od. 11, 542: **fut.** ἐροῦμαι, ἀπ- Anth. 12, 120. **Pres. pass.** εἴρεται late, Arat. 172. 261. **Vb.** ῥητός Thuc. 1, 122, -έος Hippocr. 2, 127 (Erm.); Pl. Apol. 22. The **aor.** form εἰρέθην, ἐρρέθην has the short vowel ε in *indicative* only; subj. always ῥηθῶ Aeschin. 1, 31; Dem. 20, 87; ῥηθείς Her. 1, 91. 6, 86. 8, 115; Soph. El. 668; Thuc. 2, 5; ῥηθῆναι Her. 3, 9; Lys. 2, 54; Isocr. 12, 192; Pl. Crat. 419, see ῥέω. ῥηθήσομαι is used chiefly in inf. and part. but not confined to them, ῥηθήσεται Thuc. 1, 73; Xen. Hell. 6, 3, 7; Pl. Rep. 473. Leg. 957; Aristot. Categ. 8, 35. Rhet. 1, 12, 2; Luc. Merc. Con. 4, προσ- Pl. Polit. 259. 301. Rep. 479, ἀνα- Aeschin. 3, 147, pl. -ήσονται Aristot. Top. 5, 4; Hyperid. 4, 2, 5; Theophr. H. P. 1, 2, 4; Aen. Tact. 11, the only instances of pl. we ever met; part. -ησόμενος Thuc. 8, 66; Isocr. 5, 1. 14. 15. 140; 8, 63; Pl. Phaedr. 259 &c.; -ήσεσθαι Isocr. 4, 13. 8, 73. 12, 6. 24. 56. 258. 15, 55. 240. Epist. 1, 10; Pl. Phaed. 88. Conv. 189. Leg. 809 &c.; εἰρήσομαι in Attic is confined, we think, to 3 sing. *indic.* Aristides however has εἰρήσονται 51, 417; and Hippocr. inf. εἰρήσεσθαι 8, 28 (Lit.); and part. εἰρησόμενος, if correct, 3, 516 (Lit. v. r. ῥηθησόμενος strongly supported). 4, 238; Galen 15, 18; and late Attic Ael. N. A. 16, 36. We think the earlier Attics never used the **p. post-fut.** in the participle, and therefore demur to Bekker's substitution of διαπεπολεμησόμενον Thuc. 7 25 (Vat.), for διαπολεμησόμ- (Vulg.), see πολεμέω.

Εἴρω *To knit, join, simple* rare, Pind. N. 7, 77, ἀν- Ar. Ach 1006, περι- Her. 2, 96, δι- Xen. Cyr. 8, 3, 10; Aeschin. 3, 166, συν- Dem. 18, 308; ξυν-είρωμεν Pl. Polit. 267: **imp.** εἶρον, συν- Xen. Cyr. 7, 5, 6: **fut.** (ἔρσω, ἀν- if sound, Hesych.): **aor.** in comp. εἶρα, ἐξ- Ar. Eq. 378. Vesp. 423, and ἔρσα; δι-έρσῃς Hippocr. 4, 108 (Lit.); opt. παρ-είρειε Xen. Conv. 6, 2; δι-εῖραι Hippocr. 7, 52 (Lit.), but -έρσαι 4, 108 (-εῖραι in marg.); -είρας Aesch. Fr. 280 (D.), ἀν- Her. 3, 118, δι- Ael. V. H. 4, 28; Luc. Alex. 26, -έρσας Hippocr. 4, 296: **p.** in comp. εἶρκα, δι- Xen. Cyr. 8, 3, 10: **p. p.** εἶρμαι, εἰρμένος Callim. Fr. 140, Epic. ἐερμένος Od. 18, 296. Hom. H. 1, 104, Ion. ἑρμένος, ἐν- Her. 4, 190 (Mss. Vulg. Bekk. Gaisf. Dind.) which Bredow would write ἐν-ειρμ- (with Ms. M. P. K. F. Stein); so Aristot. ἐν-ειρμ- Plant. 1, 1, 15: **plp.** Epic, ἔερτο Od. 15, 460; Ap. Rh. 3, 868.—ἤειρε **imp.** or **aor.** Il. 10, 499, seems very irregular, unless we assume ἀείρω. See συνήορος.

Εἰρωτάω and -έω, Ion. for ἐρωτάω, *To ask*, εἰρωτᾷς Od. 4, 347. 17, 138; Her. 3, 14; subj. εἰρωτᾷ Theogn. 519; εἰρωτέων Her.

8, 26: imp. εἰρῶτα Od. 15, 423 (Bekk. La R.); Her. 1, 88, -τεον 4, 145, -τευν 1, 158. 3, 140 (Bekk. Dind. Stein, -εον Dietsch, Abicht.)—ἐρωτεόμενον Her. 1, 86 (Vulg. Gaisf.) is rightly edited εἰρωτ- by Bekk. Lhardy, Dind.

Εἶσα a defective aor. See (ἕω).

Ἐΐσκω *To liken, compare*, Epic Il. 5, 181; ἐΐσκοι Opp. Cyn. 1, 69; -σκειν Hes. Op. 62: imp. ἤϊσκον Il. 21, 332. Od. 4, 247, ἔϊσκον 9, 321; Theocr. 25, 140: p. p. ἤϊγμαι in comp. προσῄξαι *art like*, Eur. Alc. 1063: plp. ᾔκτο Od. 13, 288. 20, 31, ἔϊκτο Il. 23, 107; Ap. Rh. 2, 39; Mosch. 4, 110, referred also to εἴκω, ἔοικα: pres. ἐϊσκόμενος Nic. Ther. 421: imp. ἐΐσκετο Nonn. 4, 72.

(**Εἰσμάσσω**) *To thrust in* the hand, *to feel*, only mid. (-άσσομαι), aor. Ion. ἐσμᾰσάμενος Hippocr. 4, 198. 8, 148, Dor. ἐσεμάξατο Theocr. 17, 37. The Epic aor. ἐσεμάσσατο *touched, affected*, Il. 17, 564. 20, 425, seems to belong to μάω, μάομαι, μαίο-.

Εἴωθα, see ἔθω.

Ἐκβάω=ἐκβαίνω, occurs in this its original form, Thuc. 5, 77 (Doric treaty).

Ἐκκλησιάζω *To call an assembly*, Ar. Thesm. 84; Isocr. 7, 10 (augments before or after the prep.): imp. ἐξεκλησίαζον Xen. Hell. 5, 3, 16 (Vulg. Breitb. Saupp. ἠκκλ- Dind. 3 ed.); Lys. 13, 73. 76, and ἠκκλησ- Dem. 18, 265. 19, 60 (Ms. S. &c. Bekk. Dind. B. Saupp.), and, perhaps late, ἐκκλησίαζον Herodn. 2, 9, 6 (Bekk.); in Mss. however, Lys. 12, 73 (Bekk. ἐξεκλησ- Saupp. Scheibe, Westerm. ἠκκλησ- Frohb.): fut. ἐκκλησιάσω Ar. Eccl. 161; Thuc. 7, 2; Isocr. 8, 2: aor. ἐξεκλησίασα Thuc. 8, 93 (Bekk. Popp. Krüg. L. Dind.); Dem. 21, 193 (Ms. S. Bekk. B. Saupp.), ἠκκλησ- (W. Dind.) The form which doubles the preposition, as ἐξεκκλησίασα, though well supported, Thuc. 8, 93, is probably a mistake for ἐξεκλησ- which occurs in good Mss. and is now adopted by the best editors: it is certain however in late Greek, ἐξεκκλησίασεν Septuag. Num. 20, 10. 3 Reg. 8, 1 &c. The unaugmented imp. ἐκκλησίαζον Lys. 12, 73, quoted, seems more than doubtful, since at 13, 73. 76, occurs the augmented form ἐξεκλησίαζον (Mss. Bekk. Scheib. Cobet, ἠκκλ- Frohb.) Wm. Dindorf would, in classic Attic, uniformly augment with η, ἠκκλησίαζον, ἠκκλησίασα. This, no doubt, is more in accordance with strict rule, and is sometimes favoured by the best Mss.; but were the Attics always observant of *law*, and free from the bias of a false analogy? cf. ἐγκωμιάζω.

Ἐκκυκλέω *To wheel out*, act. late, fut. -ήσω Plut. Mor. 80: pass. ἐκκυκλούμενος *wheeled out, coming forth*, Ar. Thesm. 96: aor. ἐκκυκλήθητι Ar. Ach. 407: with fut. m. ἐκκυκλήσομαι 409.

'Εκλέγω, see λέγω *lay.*

'Εκμαίνω, see μαίνω.

'Εκτυπόω *To work in relief*, Dio. Hal. Rhet. 10, 17; Luc. Philops. 38; Plut. Mor. 902: **fut.** -ώσεις V. T. Exod. 28, 32: **aor.** -ετύπωσεν Xen. Equest. 1, 1: **p. act.**?: **p. p.** ἐκτετυπωμένος Pl. Conv. 193: **aor.**? **Mid.** ἐκτυποῦμαι Pl. Theaet. 206. Leg. 775; Luc. Jup. Tr. 33: **fut.** (-ώσομαι): with **aor. p.** as **mid.** ἐκτυπωθέντας Isocr. 13, 18, missed by Lexicogr.

(**'Εκχράω**) *To suffice*, Ionic impers. **fut.** ἐκχρήσει *it will suffice*, Her. 3, 137: **aor.** ἐξέχρησε 8, 70.

'Ελασσόω *To lessen, make inferior*, rare in **act.** Thuc. 3, 42, -ττόω Isocr. 4, 176. 8, 17; Polyb. 26, 3, 4; Plut. Mor. 687: **fut.** -ώσω: **aor.** ἠλάττωσα Aristot. Poet. 4, 13; Polyb. 16, 21; inf. ἐλαττῶσαι Lys. 13, 9: **p.** ἠλάττωκα Dio. Hal. C. V. 6; Diod. Sic. 1, 65: **p. p.** ἠλάττωμαι Polyb. 17, 4 (Bekk. 18, 4 Dind.): **aor.** ἠλασσώθην Thuc. 1, 77, ἠλαττ- (Dem.) 10, 33; Diod. Sic. 13, 13; -ωθείς Antiph. 5, 19: **fut.** -ωθήσομαι Thuc. 5, 34, -ττ- Dem. 21, 66: and **fut. m.** ἐλασσώσομαι as **pass.** Her. 6, 11; Thuc. 5, 104. 105; ἐλαττ- more **mid.** Aristid. 31, 395 (Dind.) All our lexicons, we think, miss the **mid.** form.

'Ελαύνω *To drive*, Il. 12, 62; Pind. I. 4, 6; Aesch. Eum. 421; Soph. O. R. 28; Ar. Nub. 29; Her. 1, 138 (Gaisf.); ἐλαύνῃς 8, 68; inf. -νειν 1, 79; Thuc. 1, 126; Epic inf. ἐλαυνέμεν Il. 23, 531, Poet. and rare ἐλάω Ap. Rh. 3, 411, ἐλάει Anth. 14, 14, ἐλᾷ Pind. N. 3, 74; ἔλα Aesch. Fr. 330; ἐλᾶν Xen. Hell. 2, 4, 32, Epic -άαν Il. 5, 366, see below: **imp.** ἤλαυνον Hom. H. 3, 75; Pind. P. 4, 228; Aesch. Eum. 604; Soph. O. R. 1139; Ar. Eccl. 39; Her. 2, 102; Thuc. 3, 49; Xen. An. 1, 5, 13, ἐξ- Il. 10, 499, ἐλ- Il. 23, 500 &c., ἐλαύνεσκον, ἀπ- Her. 7, 119, and ἔλαον, -ων rare and Poet. Il. 24, 696. Od. 4, 2, ἔλαεν Ap. Rh. 3, 872, augm. ἤλαε Opp. H. 5, 494, ἤλαον, ἀπ -Ar. Lys. 1001 (Brunck, Bekk. and formerly Dind.), but see **aor.** below, iter. ἐλάασκον (-άεσκον old reading) Ap. Rh. 1, 733. 2, 1071: **fut.** ἐλάσω Xen. An. 7, 7, 55 (Vulg. Popp. Krüg. Kühn. -λῶ Dind. Saupp.); Dio. Hal. Ant. 2, 36; Luc. Navig. 33; Geop. 13, 8, ἐξ- Hippocr. 6, 342. 7, 348. 428 (Lit.), ἀντιπροσ- Dio Cass. 46, 37 (Dind.), ἐλάσσω, παρ- Il. 23, 427, ξυν- Od. 18, 39, Epic ἐλάω Ap. Rh. 3, 411 (if not pres.), and ἐλόω Il. 13, 315. Od. 7, 319, Attic ἐλῶ Aesch. Eum. 75; Soph. Aj. 504; Ar. Ran. 203; Pl. Theag. 129; Her. 1, 207 and always (Bekk. Dind.); but Hippocr. see above: **aor.** ἤλασα Il. 5, 584; Hes. Th. 291; Tyrt. 11, 10; Pind. N. 10, 70; Aesch. Supp. 309; Eur. Elec. 1110; Her. 1, 59 (Bekk.); Thuc. 1, 126; Xen. Cyr. 4, 1, 7, Dor. 3 pl. ἤλααν, ἀπ- Ar. Lys. 1001 (Enger, Ahrens, and *now* Dind.), ἤλασσα, ἐξ- Il. 11, 562, ἔλασα 5, 80; Hes. Sc. 372; Pind. Ol. 10, 71, -ασσα Il. 18, 564, Dor. 1 pl. ἐλάσαμες Plut. Mor. 211, iter. ἐλάσασκε Il. 2, 199; Epic subj. ἐλάσσομεν, ξυν- Od. 18, 39, ἐλάσῃσθα, παρεξ- Il. 23, 344: p. ἐλήλακα Luc. V. H. 1, 42; Plut. Mor. 1131, ἀπ- Xen. Cyr. 4, 2, 10, ἐξ- Ar. Nub. 828: plp. ἐληλάκειν, ἐξ- Her. 5, 90: p. p. ἐλήλαμαι Il. 16, 518. Od. 7, 113; Hes. Th. 726; Tyrt. 12, 26; Aesch. Pers. 871; Soph. Aj. 275; Her. 1, 180. 9, 9, ἀπ- Pl. Menex. 238; (Dem.) 61, 49, unattic ἐλήλασμαι Hippocr. 8, 290. 426 (Lit.); and late Paus. 4, 26, 8 (Schub.), ἤλασμ- Aen. Tact. Excerp. 51 (Herch.): plp. ἠληλάμην Il. 5, 400; Hes. Sc. 143, ἐληλ- Il. 4, 135, ἀπ- Her. 7, 205, ἐληλέδατο, -άδατο Od. 7, 86 (others ἐρηρέδατο), late ἠλάσμην, συν- 2 Macc. 4, 26, see below: aor. ἠλάθην Aesch. Eum. 283; Eur. Heracl. 430; Apollod. 3, 10. 2, ἀπ-ηλ- Her. 3, 54, ἐξ- 7, 6. 4, 145. 5, 42 &c.; Ap. Rh. 4, 1760; Lys. 13, 13; Xen. Cyr. 6, 1, 15; ἐλαθείς Ar. Eccl. 4; Dio. Hal. 11, 33; ἠλάσθην, ἐλασθείς late Anacreont. 52 (Bergk); Anth. (Arch. Byz.) 7, 278; Diod. Sic. 20, 51 (Vulg. ἐλαθ- Bekk. Dind.), συν- Plut. Caes. 17; Gaisf. however and Stein edit ἀπ- ἐξ-ηλάσθην Her. 3, 54. 7, 6 &c.; fut. ἐλαθήσομαι, ἐξ- Dio. Hal. 4, 9, ἀπ- de Lys. 32; Aristid. 16, 244; (Argum. to Lys. 34.) **Mid.** *to drive for oneself*, ἐλαυνόμενος Il. 11, 674: fut. late? ἐλάσομαι, παρ- *will pass by*, Arr. An. 3, 30, but pass. ἐλάσονται *shall be driven away, get themselves driven*, Or. Sib. 1, 395: aor. ἠλασάμην Il. 11, 682; rare in prose, Pl. Gorg. 484; Plut. Lucull. 4, ἐλασσ- Orph. Hym. 44, 4, syncop. ἠλσάμ- Simon. Am. 17; Ibyc. 54 (Bergk); ἐλάσαιο Od. 20, 51, -αίατο Il. 10, 537; -ασσάμενος Od. 4, 637, ἐξ-ελασάμ- Polyb. 4, 75; ἐλάσασθαι Plut. Rom. 23, ἐξ- Thuc. 4, 35. 7, 5; Theocr. 24, 119. We have not seen the mid. in Attic poetry. **Vb.** ἐλατέος Xen. Eq. 2, 7, ἐλατός Aristot. Meteor. 4, 9, 18. 19, ἐξ-ήλατος Il. 12, 295, ἀν- Aristot. Meteor. 4, 9, 17.

ἐλάω Ap. Rh. 3, 411, pres. and imp. rare and Poet. ἐλάει Anth. 14, 14, ἐλᾷ Pind. N. 3, 74, ἐλάουσι Or. Sib. 3, 239 (ἐξ- Hes. Op. 224?); ἐλάοιεν Opp. C. 4, 72; imper. ἔλα Pind. I. 5 (4), 38; Eur. Fr. 779 (D.). H. F. 819; Anth. 7, 89; in Attic prose, only Xen. ἀπ- Cyr. 8, 3, 32; part. ἐλάων Hym. Merc. 342; Ap. Rh. 2, 80, εἰσ- Od. 10, 83, ἐλῶντα H. Merc. 355, Dor. ἐλᾶντα, παρ- Theocr. 5, 89, ἐλάουσα Nonn. Dion. 7, 139; Ep. inf. ἐλάαν Il. 8, 45 &c. Att. ἐλᾶν Com. Fr. (Canth.) 2, 835; Attic prose, only Xen. Hell. 2, 4, 32 (Mss. Dind. Breitb.): imp. ἔλων Il. 24, 696 &c. see above: fut. ἐλῶ Xen. Cyr. 1, 4, 20 (Dind. Popp. Saupp. -άσω best Mss. Bornem. Breitb.), ἐξ- Ar. Eq. 365 (Vulg. -ελξω Pors. Mein. Dind. 5 ed.), περι- Eq. 290, ἐλᾷς Eur. Bac.

1334, διεξ- Her. 5, 52, ἐλάσει 1, 77 (Vulg. Schaef. Schweig. Gaisf. but subj. -άσῃ Mss. M. F. a. c. Wessel. Bekk. Dind. Krüg.), ἐλᾷ Soph. O. R. 418 &c.; Xen. Eq. 3, 9; Dem. 21, 131, ἐλᾶτε Ar. Eq. 243, ἐλῶσι Eur. Alc. 951 &c.; Her. 1, 207; Xen. Eq. 3, 9, Epic ἐλόωσι see below; inf. ἐλᾶν Eur. Med. 70; Her. 7, 10; Pl. Theag. 129, Epic ἐλάαν Od. 5, 290; part. ἐλῶν Her. 2, 162; Xen. An. 1, 8, 10. Cyr. 6, 2, 17, ἐξ- Eur. Phoen. 607.—ἐλόωσι Epic 3 pl. pres. Opp. H. 5, 244; ἐλόωντες Opp. Hal. 2, 548; ἐλάαν pres. inf. Epic for ἐλᾶν Il. 13, 27: imp. ἀπ-ήλαον used by the Dorian Herald Ar. Lys. 1001 (Vulg. Bekk. Dind. 2 ed.), both Giese and Ahrens think corrupted from ἀπ-ήλααν (Dind. 5 ed.) 3 pl. aor. for ἀπ-ήλασαν the reading in Ms. Δ., compare ὅρμαον, for ὅρμησον, 1247: ἐλόωσι 3 pl. fut. for (ἐλάσουσι, -άουσι) ἐλῶσι Il. 13, 315; inf. ἐλάαν Od. 5, 290?: pass. pres. subj. ἐλάηται Opp. Hal. 2, 14: ἐληλάδατο, -έδατο (Bekk.) plp. Epic for ἐλήλαντο, Od. 7, 86: ἠλάσθην, if not ἐλήλασμαι, seems late, Paus. 4, 26, 8, συν- 2 Macc. 5, 5, see above. In Her. 3, 54. 4, 145. 7, 6 and always, Bekker, Bredow, Dindorf, Krüger adopt from certain Mss. perhaps rightly, ἀπ- ἐξ-ηλάθην not -άσθην, but Gaisford and Stein follow those Mss. which have the forms with ς, ἀπ- ἐξ-ηλάσθην. It would appear from this and many other verbs, that the elision of ς in the fut. was by no means peculiar to the Attic dialect: ἀτρεμίζω, fut. -ιεῖν Her. 8, 68, δικάζω, δικᾶν 1, 97, ἀποδοκιμάζω, -ιμᾷ 1, 199, διασκεδᾷς 8, 68, -σκεδᾶν 1, 79, θεσπιέειν 8, 135, καταγιεῖν 1, 86 &c. &c.

*Ἔλδομαι Epic, *To desire*, Il. 5, 481, -δεαι Pind. Ol. 1, 4, and ἐέλδομαι Il. 14, 276. Od. 15, 66; Hes. Op. 381, only pres.: and imp. ἐλδόμην Ap. Rh. 4, 546 (Facius, Herm. Merk.), ἐελδ- Od. 4, 162; Ap. Rh. 4, 546 (Vulg.); ἐλδόμενος Il. 23, 122, ἐελδ- 7, 7. Od. 14, 42. Pass. imper. ἐελδέσθω Il. 16, 494.

Ἐλεαίρω *To pity*, mostly Epic, Il. 2, 64. 7, 27; Mosch. 4, 72; Ar. Eq. 793 (hexam.): imp. unaugm. ἐλέαιρον Il. 21, 147. Od. 1, 19; Ap. Rh. 4, 1422, -αίρεσκον Il. 24, 23: aor. unaugm. ἐλέηρα Ap. Rh. 4, 1308.

Ἐλέγχω *To examine, confute*, Od. 21, 424; Tyrt. 10, 9; Pind. Ol. 8, 19; Soph. Ph. 338; Her. 2, 22; Antiph. 5, 84; Thuc. 6, 86; Pl. Charm. 166; imper. 'λεγχε Aesch. Ch. 919: imp. ἠλ- Soph. O. R. 783; Ar. Ran. 961; Her. 2, 115; Antiph. 2, γ, 5; Pl. Conv. 201: fut. ἐλέγξω Ar. Nub. 1043; Isocr. 6, 71; Pl. Apol. 29, ἐξ- Andoc. 3, 10: aor. ἤλεγξα Pind. P. 11, 49; Eur. Heracl. 404; ἐλέγξῃς Il. 9, 522; Pl. Rep. 539; inf. ἐλέγξαι Aesch. Ch. 851; Antiph. 6, 9; Lys. 7, 42: (p. ἐλήλεγχα?): p. p. ἐλήλεγμαι Antiph. 2, δ, 10; Pl. Leg. 805, ἐξ- Isocr. 10, 4, and, if correct, ἤλεγμαι, ἐξ- Lys. 6, 44 (Ms. S. Bekk. ἐξελήλεγ- Reiske,

B. Saupp. Scheibe): plp. ἐξ-ελήλεγκτο Dem. 32, 27 (Bekk. B. Saupp. Dind.): aor. ἠλέγχθην Eur. Hel. 885 (Vulg.); Antiph. 2, δ, 10; Pl. Gorg. 458; Dem. 36, 20, ἐξ- Thuc. 3, 64: fut. ἐλεγχθήσομαι Antiph. 2, δ, 10; Isae. 5, 3. 4, 10; Xen. Mem. 1, 7, 2. **Vb.** ἐλεγκτέον Pl. Leg. 905.—For ἐξήλεγμαι Lys. quoted, Reiske has ἐξελήλεγ-, so B. Saupp. Westerm. Scheibe: ἐξηλεγ- produced from Dem. 20, 131, as another instance, is no proof; the perf. there is from 'κλέγω, and in the best edit. is properly edited ἐξειλεγ-, and for the plp. form ἐξήλεγκτο 32, 27 (Vulg.), the approved reading is ἐξελήλεγκτο (Bekk. B. Saupp. Dind.)

Ἐλελίζω *To raise the war shout, to shout*, Eur. Phoen. 1514; Xen. An. 1, 8, 18: **aor.** ἠλέλιξα Xen. An. 5, 2, 14 (L. Dind. Saupp.); Dem. Phal. 98, ἐλέλ- Callim. Del. 137. **Mid.** ἐλελίζομαι *to bewail*, -ομένη Eur. Hel. 1111 (chor.); Ar. Av. 213 (chor.) See ἀλαλάζω.

Ἐλελίζω *To turn rapidly, whirl*, Epic and Lyric, Pind. Ol. 9, 13: **imp.** ἐλέλιζ- Nonn. 2, 525, ἠλέλ- Hesych.: **aor.** ἐλέλιξα Il. 8, 199. 17, 278. Batr. 286; Ap. Rh. 4, 351; Dor. part. -ίξαις Pind. N. 9, 19: **pass.** ἐλελίχθην Il. 22, 448, Epic 3 pl. -λιχθεν 6, 109. **Mid.** *to whirl, writhe oneself*, **1 aor.** ἐλελιξάμενος Il. 2, 316: **2 aor.** Epic, syncop. ἐλέλικτο Il. 11, 39; more as **pass.** 13, 558.

Ἐλεφαίρομαι *To deceive*, Od. 19, 565: **imp.** ἐλεφαίρετο Hes. Th. 330: **aor.** ἐλεφηράμενος Il. 23, 338. Hesych. has **act.** ἐλεφαίρειν, ἀπατᾶν: **aor.** ἐλεφῆραι, ἀπατῆσαι.

Ἐλῑνύω *To be quiet*, Poet. and Ion. Aesch. Pr. 53; Ar. Thesm. 598; Dem. (Orac.) 21, 53; Her. 1, 67; Hippocr. 2, 328. 4, 254. 5, 268 (Lit.); Plut. Mor. 275; Philostr. V. Apol. 2, 32: **imp.** in Epic and Ionic unaugm. ἐλίνῠον, ἐλίνῡ- Pind. Fr. 182 (Schneidw.); Her. 8, 71; Ap. Rh. 1, 862, ἠλίνῠ- App. Mithr. 43 (Bekk.), but iter. ἐλῑνύεσκον Ap. Rh. 1, 589: **fut.** ἐλινύσω Pind. N. 5, 1. I. 2, 46; Luc. Lex. 2: **aor.** ἐλίνῡσα Callim. Fr. 248; -ύσαιμι Aesch. Pr. 530 (chor.); -ῡσον Callim. Cer. 48; -ῦσαι Theocr. 10, 51; Anth. 5, 237; -ύσας Her. 7, 56; Ar. An. 3, 15, δι- Hippocr. 2, 318 (Lit.) Not used in classic Attic prose.—There is no necessity for writing ἐλινν-, as ι is long; and none for supposing a pres. ἐλινύσσω, or a fut. ἐλινῠ́σω Pind. quoted. (ῠ in pres. ῡ in fut. and aor.)

Ἑλίσσω *To roll*, Eur. H. F. 868; Com. Fr. (Strat.), 2, 787; Ap. Rh. 1, 463; Aristot. Part. Anim. 4, 8, 2, δι-εξ- Her. 4, 67 (Vulg. Gaisf. Dind. -ειλ- Bekk. Krüg. Stein), ἑλίττω Pl. Epin. 978 (Theaet. 194), ἐξ- Xen. Laced. 11, 9; imper. ἕλισσε Eur. Tr. 333; ἑλίσσων Hom. H. 8, 6; Pind. I. 8, 15; Soph. Ant. 231; Epic inf. ἑλισσέμεν Il. 23, 309: **imp.** ἕλισσε Eur. Or. 1432 (chor.), εἱλ- Callim. Fr. 242: fut. ἑλίξω Eur. Phoen. 711; Anth. 5, 275: aor. εἵλιξα Pl. Tim. 73; ἑλίξαι, ἐξ- Xen. Cyr. 8, 5, 15; ἑλίξας Il. 23, 466; Eur. Phoen. 1622, ἐξ- Xen. Hell. 4, 3, 18. Ages. 2, 11: p. p. εἵλιγμαι Hes. Th. 791 (but εἱλ- Fr. 201); Eur. Fr. 385 (Dind.), ἐν- Pl. Conv. 220, ἀν- (Aeschin.) Epist. 4, 3, περι- Paus. 6, 19, 5, and late ἐλήλιγμαι 10, 17, 6: plp. εἵλικτο Eur. H. F. 927, Ion. ἐπ-είλικτο Paus. 4, 26, 6: aor. εἱλίχθην Eur. I. T. 444, ἑλίχ- Anth. 5, 255; ἑλιχθείς Il. 12, 74; Plut. Mor. 224, περι- Pl. Phaed. 112. 113; ἑλιχθῆναι Galen 5, 582, ἀν- Aristot. Metaph. 11, 8, 13: fut. ἑλιχθήσεται, ἐξ- Aristot. Mechan. 24, 7: **2 fut.** late ἑλιγήσομαι V. T. Esai. 34, 4. **Mid.** ἑλίσσομαι *to roll, turn oneself*, H. Hym. 32, 3, -ισσόμενος Il. 21, 11. 23, 846: **imp.** ἑλίσσετο Od. 20, 24; Theocr. 24, 30, augm. εἱλ- Il. 12, 49, but ἐλλίσσ- (Bekk. Dind. from λίσσομαι): **fut.** ἑλίξεται Il. 17, 728 (La R.) seems to be subj.: **aor.** ἑλιξάμην, -άμενος Il. 12, 467. 17, 283, as **act.** 13, 204; Anth. 5, 275, ἐν- Hippocr. 8, 376; Anth. 12, 257; Her. 2, 95 (Vulg. Reitz, Schw. Gaisf. ἐκ-ειλιξ- Ms. S. Bekk. Dind. Stein), εἱλιξ- Nonn. 43, 65; ἑλίξασθαι, ἀμφ- Pind. N. 1, 43, εἱλιξ- Nonn. 43, 65; subj. ἑλίξεται for -ηται, see **fut.** **Vb.** ἑλικτός Soph. Tr. 12. See εἱλίσσω. Hom. has only ἑλίσσω, εἱλ- is augm.; the Tragedians ἑλίσσω and εἱλίσσω, Her. perhaps εἱλ- only, which again is exceedingly rare in Attic prose, ἀν-ειλίττων Pl. Phil. 15 (v. r. ἀν-ελ-), ἀν-είλιξις Polit. 270. 286.

Ἑλκέω *To draw*, Epic for ἕλκω, imp. ἕλκεον Il. 17, 395: fut. ἑλκήσω Il. 22, 336: **aor.** ἥλκησα Od. 11, 580, ἕλκ- (La R.): **aor. pass.** ἑλκηθείς Il. 22, 62.

Ἕλκω *To draw*, Il. 24, 52; Pind. P. 1, 52; Soph. Ant. 1233; Ar. Pax 470; Her. 7, 85; Pl. Rep. 533, later ἑλκύω Com. Fr. (Philem.) 4, 60, if correct (ἕλκε Grot. Mein.); Tzetz. Hist. 6, 621; imper. ἕλκε Aesch. Fr. 276, παρ- Od. 21, 111; Epic inf. ἑλκέμεναι Il. 10, 353, -κέμεν 2, 181; Hes. Op. 631, Aeol. -κην Sapph. 70: **imp.** εἷλκον Hom. H. Cer. 308; Aesch. Fr. 33; Soph. O. C. 927; Ar. Vesp. 793; Her. 7, 36; Thuc. 4, 14; Lys. 1, 12, Hom. ἕλκ- Il. 4, 213. Od. 21, 419 and always: **fut.** ἕλξω Aesch. Supp. 909; Eur. I. T. 1427; Ar. Plut. 955; Com. Fr. (Alex.) 3, 440; Aristot. Mechan. 18, 2; Dem. 21, 221, συν- Pl. Theaet. 181, καθ- Ar. Ran. 1398; Dem. 8, 74. Proem. 1455, 48, and ἑλκύσω Hippocr. 3, 422. 7, 558 (Lit.); rare and rather late in Attic, Com. Fr. (Philem.) 4, 58; Christ. Pat. 415; Geop. 15, 2, καθ- Luc. D. Deor. 21, 1, παρ- Apocr. Sir. 29, 5, ἀν- Aesop 4 (Tauchn.), ἐφ- Theod. Prod. 1, 278: **aor.** εἵλκυσα Batr. 233; always in Attic, Eur. Phoen. 987; Ar. Nub. 540; Com. Fr. (Antiph.) 3, 109; Hippocr. 6, 46; Pl. Rep. 560; Dem. 22, 59, ἀφ- Aesch. Eum. 184, ἀν- Thuc. 7, 1; subj. ἑλκύσῃ

Her. 2, 65; Pl. Theaet. 175; opt. ἑλκύσαις, δι- Ar. Plut. 1036; imper. ἕλκὔσον Pl. Parm. 135; inf. ἑλκύσαι Pind. N. 7, 103; Com. Fr. (Eup.) 2, 456; Ar. Pax 328; Her. 7, 167, ἀν- Thuc. 8, 11; ἑλκῦσας Eur. Cycl. 417; Her. 1, 179; Xen. Hell. 7, 1, 19, ἀν- Thuc. 6, 104, unattic and perhaps late εἷλξα Batr. 115, περι- Philostr. Her. p. 735, ἑλξ- Anth. 9, 370; Galen. 2, 30; subj. ἕλξω Append. Anacreont. 3, 5 (p. 857 Bergk, 1102, 3 ed.), ἕλξῃ Oribas. 7, 22; opt. ἕλξειε Plotin. 26, 72; imper. ἕλξατε Orph. Arg. 260: p. εἵλκὔκα (v. r. Dem. 22, 59) καθ- 5, 12: p.p. εἵλκυσμαι Eur. Rhes. 576; Hippocr. 8, 484, ἀν- Thuc. 3, 89, καθ- 6, 50, but unaugm. ἀν-ελκυσμένος Her. 9, 98 (Mss. Gaisf. Bekk. Dind. Krüg. Stein *now*, Lhardy doubtingly), ἀνειλκ- (Bred. Dietsch, Stein 2 ed. Abicht); so Hippocr. εἱλκυσμ- 8, 484 (Mss. C. F. I. Ald. Lit.): plp. εἵλκυστο Hippocr. 5, 178 (Lit.): aor. εἱλκύσθην Hippocr. 5, 152 (Lit.); ἑλκυσθῇ Her. 1, 140; Theophr. H. P. 5, 4, 5, ἐξ- Ar. Eccl. 689; -υσθῆναι Polyb. 15, 33, late εἵλχθην Ael. N. A. 4, 16; Diog. Laert. 6, 91; Philostr. V. Apoll. 359; Galen de Semin. 1, 6, 192; Plotin. 26, 76: fut. late ἑλχθήσεσθαι Galen 3, 533. 805, and ἑλκυσθήσομαι late in *simple*, Lycophr. 358, but ξυγκαθ- Aesch. Sept. 614. Mid. ἕλκομαι *to draw my own, or to myself*, Il. 17, 136; Hermesian. 2, 4; rare in prose Pherecyd. Fr. 33 (Müll.), ἐφ- Lys. 1, 13, προσ- Pl. Rep. 439; imper. ἕλκεο H. Hym. 7, 26: imp. ἑλκόμην Il. 1, 194. Od. 19, 506, ἐφ-ειλκ- Polyb. 25, 9; Plut. Pomp. 24: fut. late ἑλκυσόμενος, ἐφ- Oribas. 6, 10, ξυνεφ- Eustath. 3, 4, 4: aor. εἱλκυσάμην Anth. 7, 287, ἐφ- Hippocr. 9, 226; Aristid. 13, 120; ἀφ-ελκύσωμαι Ar. Ach. 1120; -υσάμενος Hippocr. 4, 106 (Lit.), προσ- Pl. Crat. 407, ἐφ- Plut. Pomp. 79; ἑλκύσασθαι Alex. 51, ἀν- Geop. Proem. 4: and more rarely εἵλξατο Galen 4, 534. Vb. ἑλκτέον Pl. Rep. 365, ἑλκυστέος, συν- Xen. Ages. 9, 4. The Attics scarcely used the pres. and fut. forms ἑλκύω, ἑλκῦσω, on the other hand, they avoided aor. εἷλξα, and used εἵλκὔσα. In old editions of Hom. the imp. of this verb used to have the augment, but late editors, in accordance with the precept of Aristarchus, have dropped it: in Her. again, all Mss. and editors agree in εἷλκε 7, 36, εἷλκον 1, 31. 2, 124. 6, 86. 7, 36. 40, varying between εἵλκετο 2, 125 (Mss. S. V. R. Ald. Bekk. Lhardy, Dind. Krüg. Stein) and ἑλκ- (Mss. F. Schweig. Gaisf.), but perf. ἀν-ελκυσμένος (all Mss. Gaisf. Bekk. &c.), which Bredow would alter to ἀν-ειλκ-, and Dietsch and others adopt. Besides, εἷλκε is read Hom. H. Merc. 116, εἷλκον Cer. 308; and always in Ap. Rh. 1, 533. 2, 668. 4, 888 &c. (Merk.) (ῠ). There is no sufficient authority for ῡ in fut. and aor. εἵλκῡσε old reading Od. 11, 580, has been altered to ἕλκησε (La Roche), ἥλκησε

(Bekk., see Galen 5, 342), ἑλκῦσαι Her. 7, 167, to ἑλκύσαι, ἑλκύσαντες Ap. Rh. 1, 955, to ἑκλύσαντες from Mss. and the Schol., and ἑλ-κύσει Opp. Hal. 5, 176, ἑλκῦσαι 3, 318, should be altered to -ύσσει, -ύσσαι.

Ἑλληνίζω *To speak Greek*, Xen. An. 7, 3, 25; Pl. Men. 82, is, in Mss. and most editions, usu. unaugm.: **imp.** ἑλλήνιζε Charit. 4, 5, ἡλλ- (Herch.); Dio Chrys. Or. 15 (239), ἡλλ- (Dind.): **fut.** (-ίσω, -ιῶ): **aor.** -ίσαι Dio Cass. 55, 3: **aor. pass.** ἑλληνίσθην Thuc. 2, 68 (Mss. Bekk. Arn.), ἡλλην- (Lob. Popp. Krüg. L. Dind.): but **p. p.** ἡλλήνισται late Joseph. Ant. 1, 6 (Bekk.) Similar verbs, we think, always augment, ἀττικίζω, ἠττίκιζον Dem. 58, 37, ἐκ-δεδωρίευνται Her. 8, 73, ἐλακωνομάνουν Ar. Av. 1281, ἐμήδιζον Her. 8, 30. 73. 9, 17: ἐμήδισε 8, 112. 9, 31. 87, ἐφιλίππιζον Dem. 58, 37.

Ἐλπίζω *To hope*, Emped. 46 (Stein); Aesch. Sept. 589; Her. 8, 60; Thuc. 3, 30; Andoc. 3, 27; Lys. 3, 2; Pl. Rep. 427: **imp.** ἤλπ- Her. 7, 168; Antiph. 2, α, 7; Thuc. 4, 43; Isocr. 7, 22, iter. late ἐπ-ελπίζεσκον Or. Sib. 1, 253: **fut.** ἐλπίσω late (in Aesch. Ch. 187 ἐλπίσω is subj., and -ίσει Dem. 19, 332 only a v. r.) Galen 10, 656; Dio Cass. 49, 34 (Vulg. ἐπ- Bekk. Dind.), -ιῶ V. T. Ps. 43, 7. 55, 4, -ιεῖς 90, 4, -ιεῖ 63, 11, ἀπ- Diod. Sic. 19, 50, -ιοῦμεν V. T. Ps. 39, 5, -ιοῦσι Esai. 11, 10. 42, 4 &c. &c.; quoted in N. T. Matth. 12, 21. Rom. 15, 12: **aor.** ἤλπισα Aesch. Pers. 746; Soph. Ph. 1175; Her. 8, 24; Thuc. 5, 7; Isocr. 5, 7: **p.** ἤλπικα Epist. Phal. 144 (Herch.); Zonar. p. 427, προ- Com. Fr. (Posid.) 4, 523: **plp.** ἠλπίκει Plut. Alcib. 17, -εσαν Herodn. 8, 5: **p. p.** ἠλπισμένος Dio. Hal. 5, 40: **aor.** ἐλπισθέν Soph. O. C. 1105. **Mid.** ἐλπιζόμενος *expecting*, App. Lyb. 115, missed by Lexicogr.

The early Greeks, it would appear, were chary in expressing confidence in the fut. We never met with ἐλπιῶ *simple* or *comp.* in any of their works. The equivalents are πληρωθήσεσθαι ἐλπίδος Pl. Rep. 494, ἐμπλησόμενος ἐλπίδος App. Syr. 7.

Ἔλπω Epic, *To cause to hope*, only 3 sing. ἔλπει Od. 2, 91. 13, 380; (Hesych. has ἐέλποιμεν): **2 p.** as pres. ἔολπα *I hope*, only indic. sing. Il. 22, 216. Od. 5, 379. H. Cer. 227; Hes. Op. 273; Ap. Rh. 2, 147; Mosch. 4, 55, -ας Il. 21, 583, -ε Od. 21 317: **2 plp.** as imp. ἐώλπειν usu. 3 sing. -ει Od. 21, 96; Ap. Rh. 3, 370; Theocr. 25, 115. **Mid.** ἔλπομαι *to hope*, Epic and Ion. Il. 13, 309. 18, 194; Pind. N. 6, 27; Theocr. 7, 31; Her. 2, 43. 6, 109, 2 sing. ἔλπεαι Il. 9, 40; Pind. Fr. 2, 9, Epic ἐέλπομαι Il. 13, 813; opt. ἐελποίμην 8, 196, ἐλπ- 21, 605; subj. ἔλπῃ Od. 6, 297; imper. ἔλπεο Il. 20, 201; Theogn. 47; ἐλπόμενος 18, 260; Her. 7, 218, ἐπ- Aesch. Ag. 1031 (chor.):

imp. ἠλπόμην augm. in Hom. only Od. 9, 419 (Wolf, Bekk. Dind. La R.); Pind. P. 4, 243; Anth. 7, 711. 8, 186; Orph. Arg. 1363; (Luc.) D. Syr. 22 (Dind.), ἐλπόμην Il. 12, 261. 17, 404. Od. 3, 275, and ἐελπ- Il. 12, 407. 13, 8; Orph. Arg. 536. Vb. ἄ-ελπτος Archil. 74, 1; Soph. Aj. 648, ἐπι- Archil. 74, 5.—ἐλπίζω is the Attic form.

(Ἐλσεῖν), see ἔρχομαι.

(Ἐλύθω), see ἔρχομαι.

(Ἐλύω) *To roll*, Epic and only **2 aor. pass.** ἐλύσθην *was rolled, compressed*, Il. 23, 393; ἐλυσθείς Od. 9, 433; Archil. Fr. 103 (Bergk); Ap. Rh. 1, 1034; Opp. Hal. 2, 89. See εἰλύω.

(Ἕλω), see εἴλω.

(Ἕλω) *To take*, see αἱρέω.

Ἐμβιβάζω, see βάζω.

Ἐμβριμάομαι, see βριμ-.

Ἐμέω *To vomit*, -έει Hippocr. 7, 10, ἐμοῦσι, κατ- Ar. Fr. 207 (D.); imper. ἔμει Com. Fr. (Phryn.) 2, 604; ἐμέων Il. 15, 11, -ῶν Aesch. Ag. 1599; ἐμεῖν Com. Fr. (Nicoph.) 2, 850; Pl. Phaedr. 268: **imp.** ἤμουν Ar. Fr. 130 (D.); Xen. An. 4, 8, 20, -εε Her. 7, 88: **fut.** Attic rare ἐμῶ, ἐνεξ- Com. Fr. (Polyz.) 2, 868, Ion. ἐμέσω Hippocr. 7, 28. 8, 16 (Lit.), ἐξ- D. Laert. 6, 2, 47, συνεξ- Geop. 19, 7: **mid.** ἐμοῦμαι Aesch. Eum. 730, and Ion. ἐμέομαι Hippocr. 2, 184. 6, 42 (ἐμέσεται Galen quotes): **aor.** ἤμεσα Hippocr. 2, 696. 7, 194 (Lit.); Luc. Herm. 11, ἐξ- Ar. Ach. 6, ἔμεσσα, ἀπ- Il. 14, 437; ἐμέσω Plut. Mor. 801, ἐξ- Ar. Ach. 586, ὑπερ- Hippocr. 7, 12; opt. ἐξ-εμέσειε Od. 12, 237. 437; ἐμέσας Aristot. Probl. 5, 7; inf. ἐμέσαι Her. 1, 133, ἐξ- Pl. Rep. 406; rare if correct, ἤμησα, ἐξ- Hes. Th. 497 (Vulg., ἐξ-ήμεσσα Herm. Goettl. Lennep, Flach), ὑπερ-ήμησ- Hippocr. 7, 10. 32 (Lit.), wrong, we think: **p.** rather late ἐμήμεκα Ael. H. A. 17, 37; Luc. Lexiph. 21, ἐξ- Aristid. 26, 322: but **plp.** ἐμημέκεε Hippocr. 5, 232 (Mss. Lit.), late ἐμεμέκει Diog. Laert. 6, 4, 7: **p. p.** ἐμήμεσμαι late, Ael. V. H. 13, 22 (Hercher): **aor.** ἐμεθῆναι Galen 7, 219, ἐξ- Oribas. 8, 6; συνεξ-εμεθείς 8, 4, but ἡμηθείς Schol. Od. 12, 439: **fut.** late ἐμεθήσεται, ἐξ- V. T. Job 20, 15. **Mid. aor.** subj. ἐμέσηται, if correct, Hippocr. 2, 494 (Lit.), see below. For the rare aor. form ἐξ-ήμησα in Hes. quoted, Passow suggested, and Herm. and Goettling adopted the Homeric -ήμεσσα. ἐξήμησε however may also in point of form, be from ἐξαμάω *to cut out*, a suitable sense enough, if that sense *suit the Myth*. Nor is it quite free from suspicion in Hippocrates, for though ὑπερ-εμήσῃ, -εμήσειε, -εμῆσαι, -εμήσας occur vol. 7, 10. 30. 32 (Lit.), yet we have ὑπερ-εμέσωσι twice without v. r. on p. 12, ἐμέσῃ 28. 86. 100, ἀπ- 110. 194. 288, ἐμεσάτω twice 60, ἐμέσαι

112 &c. In fact, the η occurs only in the comp. with ὑπέρ, and that, as we have seen, not constantly. But as ὑπέρ possesses no recognised *peculiar privilege* of lengthening, and as above thirty instances of aor. occur in the 2nd and 5th vols. of Littré's edition without a trace of η in the Mss., we cannot help thinking ὑπερήμησα a decided mistake for ὑπερήμεσα, and ought to be forthwith expelled. Dindorf, with we think less than his usual sifting caution, has allowed ὑπερήμησ- to pass unchallenged in Steph. Thes. At 2, 494 (Lit.) ἐμέσηται subj. aor. mid. has been challenged as an 'unauthorised form,' and the fut. ἐμέσεται proposed as the 'true form.' Ermerins 1, 353, reads ἐμέεται with Mss. A. C. The subj. however has Ms. support as well as the fut., and though not necessary in point of syntax after ὅκως μή, is yet perfectly legitimate, see Her. 6, 85 (Gaisf. Dind. Bekk.), Thuc. 1, 73. 4, 66; for ὑπελεύσηται which follows in the same construction, and may be suspiciously rare, we would suggest ὑπολύσηται as more appropriate, and less objectionable in form. See 3, 717 (K).

Ἐμπάζομαι *To care about*, Epic, Il. 16, 50; Opp. Hal. 1, 231, -άζεαι Od. 16, 422; imper. -άζεο Od. 1, 305: and imp. unaugm. ἐμπαζόμην Od. 2, 201; Bion 5, 9.

Ἐμπεδόω *To establish*, has imp. ἠμπέδουν Xen. Cyr. 8, 8, 2: but later aor. ἐνεπέδωσα Dio Cass. 60, 28 (Bekk. Dind.); ἐμπεδῶσαι Themist. 15, 190.

Ἐμποδίζω *To fetter*, *hinder*, Xen. Mem. 4, 3, 9: imp. ἐνεπόδ- Xen. Cyr. 2, 3, 10: fut. ἐμποδιῶ Isocr. Epist. 4, 11; Pl. Lys. 210, -ίσω late Geop. 2, 49, reg.: p. p. ἐμπεποδισμένος Aesch. Pr. 550: fut. late ἐμποδισθήσομαι Galen 10, 765; Oribas. 7, 23; Porphyr. de Abst. 1, 17: and as pass. fut. mid. -ποδίσεσθαι Stob. (Antip.) 67, 25, both missed by Lexicogr. **Mid.** ἐμποδίζεται Com. Fr. (Philem.) 4, 57.

Ἐμπολάω *To traffic*, *gain by*, Soph. Ant. 1037: imp. ἠμπόλα Ar. Vesp. 444, ἀπ- Eur. Tr. 973. Ion 1371: fut. ἐμπολήσω Soph. Ant. 1063: aor. ἐνεπόλησα Isae. 11, 43 (Dobr. B. Saupp. Scheibe), ἐνεπώλ- (Bekk.), but ἀπ-ημπόλ- Luc. Merc. Con. 24 (Fritz.); Apollod. 3, 6, 4, ἀπ-εμ- (Bekk.); ἐμπολήσας Soph. O. R. 1025; Ar. Pax 563: p. ἠμπόληκα Soph. Aj. 978; Ar. Pax 367, ἀπ-ημπ- Luc. Merc. Con. 24 quoted (Dind. Jacob.), but ἐμπεπόληκ- Catapl. 1 (Dind. Jacob.); -ηκώς Aesch. Eum. 631: p. p. ἠμπόλημαι Philostr. 7, 288, ἐξ- Soph. Ant. 1036, ἀπ- Luc. Merc. Con. 23, Ion. ἐμπολημένος, ἐξ- Her. 1, 1: aor. (ἠμπολήθην), ἐμποληθείς Soph. Tr. 250. **Mid.** *to amass by traffic*, only ἐμπολόωντο Od. 15, 456. The form ἐμπολέω is late, Tzetz. Hist. 1, 821 &c. ἀπ-εμπολεῖ D. Hal. Ant. 7, 63, ἀπ-εμπολεῖται Strab. 3, 2, 4.

Ἐμπορεύομαι, see πορεύομαι.

Ἐμπρήθω, ἐμπίπρημι, ἐμπιπράω, see πίμπρημι.

Ἐμφορέω, see φορέω.

Ἐν-αγκαλίζομαι, see ἀγκαλ-.

Ἐναίρω *To kill*, Poet. Il. 8, 296; Eur. Ion 191. 218 (chor.); ἔναιρε Il. 10, 481; -αίρων Il. 21, 26; Soph. Ph. 946; -ειν Il. 20, 96, -έμεν 13, 338: **imp.** ἔναιρεν Pind. N. 3, 47; Eur. Hipp. 1129 (chor.); Q. Sm. 1, 395: **1 aor.** rare and late ἔνηρα, κατ- Orph. Arg. 669: **2 aor.** ἤνᾰρον Eur. Andr. 1182 (chor.), κατ- Soph. Ant. 871 (chor.); Callim. Apol. 100, and ἔναρον Pind. N. 10, 15; Eur. Supp. 821 (hexam.); ἐναρεῖν, ἐξ- Hes. Sc. 329. **Mid.** ἐναίρομαι Epic as **act.** ἐναίρεο Od. 19, 263; -όμενος Il. 16, 92: **aor.** Epic ἐνηράμην 5, 59. Od. 24, 424; Hes. Th. 316, κατ- Od. 11, 519; Opp. Hal. 2, 505; Anth. App. Epigr. 306. **Pass.** ἐναίρομαι *to be destroyed*, Soph. O. C. 842: **imp.** ἠναιρ- Aesch. Sept. 811; -όμενος Orph. L. 229. 551.—ἐναιρέμεν Epic inf. pres. act. Il. 24, 244. **Act.** Epic and Trag. **Mid.** Epic. **Pass.** Trag. and late Epic. We have never seen *simple* or comp. in prose or Com. poetry. This verb seems rather allied to ἔνεροι than compounded of ἐν-αίρω (Buttm.) Hence augm. on initial syllable, **imp.** ἤναιρον, **2 aor.** with and without augm. ἤναρον, ἔναρ-, **1 aor. act.** and **mid.** always without, κατ-ένηρε, ἐνήρατο, κατ-ενήρ-, in which η is no augment, but the mere lengthened form of the penult, common to all *liquid* verbs.

Ἐναντιόομαι *To oppose*, Andoc. 3, 1; Pl. Apol. 31; Xen. Cyr. 4, 2, 39; Dem. 16, 24; -οῦσθαι Thuc. 4, 65; -ούμενος Soph. Ph. 643, Ion. -εύμενος Her. 7, 49: **imp.** ἠναντιούμην Her. 1, 76; Thuc. 6, 89; Andoc. 2, 4; Isocr. 19, 14: **fut.** ἐναντιώσομαι Aesch. Pr. 786; Eur. Alc. 152; Ar. Pax 1049; Hippocr. 6, 2. 7, 606; Thuc. 4, 85; Lys. 13, 17: **p.** ἠναντίωμαι Thuc. 2, 40; Pl. Apol. 40; Dinarch. 1, 61; Dem. 18, 293. 19, 205; Ar. Av. 385 (Br. Bekk. &c.), ἐνηντ- (Pors. Dind. Bergk, Mein.): **aor.** ἠναντιώθην Andoc. 1, 67; Xen. Mem. 4, 8, 5; Pl. Apol. 32. 40; -ωθῆναι Her. 7, 10 (4); Thuc. 1, 136: later **fut. p.** as **mid.** ἐναντιωθήσομαι Dio. Hal. 4, 51; Diod. Sic. 3, 6 (Vulg. Bekk. -ώσομαι Dind.); Luc. Navig. 32 (Vulg. Jacobitz), ἐναντία θησόμενος (Cobet, Dind. *now*, Fritzsche). **Vb.** ἐναντιωτέον Aristot. Top. 8, 9.—Dep. with **fut. m.** and **aor. pass.** in the classic period, later **fut. pass.** as **mid.**: **aor. mid.** we have not seen: and augments almost always prep. ἠν-αντ- instead of *simple* verb ἐν-ηντ-; but ἠνάντ- is inadmissible, Ar. Av. 385 quoted—metro repugnante.

'Εναρίζω *To slay, spoil,* Poet. -ίζοι Il. 1, 191 (Bekk. La Roche, see fut.); -ίζων Il. 21, 224; Hes. Sc. 194; but ἐξ-εναρίζεις, Il. 16, 850: imp. ἠνάριζον Aesch. Ag. 1644, ἐνάρ- Il. 16, 731, in anastrophe 12, 195: fut. ἐναρίξω, -ίξοι Il. 1, 191? (Wolf, -ίζοι Bekk. Dind.), -ίξει Or. Sib. 5, 133, ἐξ- Il. 20, 339 (Bekk. Dind. La Roche): aor. ἐνάριξα Il. 22, 323; Pind. N. 6, 52 (Bergk, Momms.), ἐξ-ενάρ- Hes. Th. 289; Ap. Rh. 1, 92; imper. ἐπ-ενάριξον Soph. O. C. 1733 chor. (Elms. Dind. &c. ἐνάριξ- Vulg.), later ἠνάριξα Lycophr. 486, and ἠνάρισα Anacr. Epigr. 100 (Bergk): p. p. ἠνάρισμαι, κατ- Soph. Aj. 26: aor. ἠναρίσθην, ἀπ- Hipponax 42, κατ- Aesch. Ch. 347 (chor.): pres. -ιζόμενος Soph. Tr. 94. Mid. late, fut. ἐναρίξεται trans. Or. Sib. 3, 468: aor. ἐναρίξατο Opp. Cyn. 2, 20; but -ίσασθαι, ὁπλίσασθαι (Hesych.) Lexicogr. have missed the mid.

'Ενασκέω *To work in, practise, train,* late, aor. -ήσας Plut. Alex. 17; intrans. Polyb. 1, 63: p.p. ἐνήσκημαι Joseph. 3, 7, 5: aor. -ησκήθη Anth. 11, 354: with fut. mid. ἐνασκήσεαι as pass. Luc. Auct. Vit. 3, missed by all Lexicogr.

'Εναύω, see αὔω.

'Ενδιάω *To stay in the open air, linger,* Poet. -ᾶει Anth. 5, 270; Opp. C. 4, 81; -ᾶουσα Anth. 5, 292: and imp. iter. ἐνδιάασκον Theocr. 22, 46, but trans. *keep, feed, in the open air,* Theocr. 16, 38. Mid. ἐνδιάονται Hom. H. 32, 6. (ῐᾰ.)

'Ενδοιάζω *To doubt,* Thuc. 1, 36; Plut. Sull. 9: aor. ἐνεδοίασα App. Mithr. 33; Plut. Mor. 11; Luc. Gall. 11: and ἐνδοιάζομαι Dio. Hal. Ant. 7, 59; Parthen. 9: imp. ἐνεδοιάζετο Luc. V. Hist. 2, 21. Conv. 9: aor. pass. ἐνεδοιάσθην passively Thuc. 1, 122; late, as act. Parthen. 9, 6 (Herch.): (v. r. aor. m. -άσασθαι ibid.)

('Ενέγκω), see φέρω.

'Ενεδρεύω *To waylay, lie in ambush,* Xen. Cyr. 6, 3, 30: imp. ἐνήδρευον 1, 6, 39: fut. ἐνεδρεύσω Plut. Ant. 63: aor. ἐνήδρευσα Thuc. 4, 67; Xen. Hell. 5, 1, 10: (p.?): p.p. ἐνηδρευμένος Luc. Calumn. 23: aor. ἐνηδρεύθην Dem. 28, 2; -δρευθῆναι Xen. Mem. 2, 1, 5: fut. m. as pass. ἐνεδρεύσοιντο *shall be caught, get themselves caught,* Xen. Hell. 7, 2, 18. Mid. aor. ἐνεδρευσάμενος *having placed himself in ambush,* Hell. 4, 4, 15: fut. -εύσομαι pass. see above.

('Ενέθω) 2 p. **ἐνήνοθα** *To sit, lie on,* only in comp. and Epic, ἐπενήνοθε Il. 10, 134. Od. 8, 365, κατενήν- H. Cer. 279; Hes. Sc. 269, παρενήν- Ap. Rh. 1, 664, all Epic, and used both as pres. and past. The early Epics used this verb of space *Il.* 2, 219. 10, 134. Od. 8, 365 &c., the later of time, *lie on, intervene,* Ap. Rh. 4, 276, but we should not from this feel warranted to infer that 'the later Epic writers appear to have misunderstood the Homeric acceptation of ἐπενήνοθα.' It has been said that 'the compound with κατά has the same meaning as the other (ἐπενήνοθα), and seems to have been assumed for the sake of the metre.' This is curiously incorrect. We venture to say that, on a careful examination, it will be found that the two compounds are in every instance purposely used in their *distinctive* meanings, and that—as in no instance is κατενήνοθε *demanded* on metrical grounds—it does not appear how it could be 'assumed for the sake of the metre.' It is joined with a plural κόμαι κατενήνοθεν H. Cer. 279.

'Ενέπω *To say*, Poet. Eur. Elec. 144 (chor.); Ap. Rh. 4, 985, -εις Nonn. D. 4, 47. 46, 38, -έπει Pind. N. 3, 75, -έπουσι Eur. I. A. 177 (chor.); Ap. Rh. 1, 26. 2, 905; Nic. Ther. 10, Dor. -έποισι Pind. N. 6, 61; subj. ἐνέπω Com. Fr. (Axion.) 3, 531 (lyr.); opt. ἐνέποιμι Od. 17, 561; Ap. Rh. 2, 1059, -οι Pind. Ol. 8, 82; Ap. Rh. 4, 1388; ἐνέπειν Eur. Rhes. 14 (chor.); ἐνέπων Il. 11, 643. Od. 24, 414; Hes. Op. 262, and ἐννέπω Aesch. Ag. 247; Soph. El. 1367; subj. -έπω Aesch. Supp. 930; -έποις Soph. Tr. 630; Hom. only imper. and imp. ἔννεπε Il. 2, 761. Od. 1, 1; Ap. Rh. 4, 2; Soph. O. C. 32, pl. ἐννέπετε Hes. Op. 2; part. ἐννέπων Hes. Op. 262; Pind. N. 7, 69; Soph. O. R. 1381, fem. Dor. ἐννέποισα Pind. I. 8, 46; ἐννέπειν Soph. Tr. 402, rare ἐνίπτω, -πτων, Pind. P. 4, 201; Aesch. Ag. 590, late ἐνίσπω Orph. Arg. 855, -ίσπει Dion. Per. 391, all Poet.: imp. ἔνεπον Pind. N. 1, 69, ἔννεπον Il. 8, 412. Hom. H. 19, 29; Pind. Ol. 1, 47. N. 10, 79; Theocr. 20, 2 (ἤνεπ- Pind. quoted, Bergk 3 ed., so προσήν- P. 4, 97. 9, 29): fut. ἐνίψω Il. 7, 447. Od. 2, 137, and ἐνισπήσω Od. 5, 98: 1 aor. late (ἔνιψα), subj. ἐνίψω (Theocr.) 27, 10. 38, ἐνίψῃ Nonn. Metaphr. Joan. 9, 22; ἐνίψαι 9, 23. Dion. 10, 201. 46, 44: 2 aor. ἔνισπον Il. 2, 80. 24, 388; ἐνίσπω 11, 839. Od. 9, 37; ἐνίσποιμι Il. 14, 107. Od. 4, 317; imper. ἐνίσπες Il. 11, 186. 14, 470. Od. 3, 101. 4, 314, and ἔνισπε 4, 642; Ap. Rh. 3, 1 (-ες Merk.); Theocr. 25, 34; Aesch. Supp. 603; ἐνισπεῖν Od. 4, 324; Hes. Th. 369 (Eur. Supp. 435), Epic -ισπέμεν Od. 3, 93 (Bekk.), -εῖν (Vulg. Dind. La R.) Vb. ἄ-σπετος Il. 11, 704. Soph. Tr. 961.—The Tragedians (Aesch. Soph. always) use ἐννέπω Aesch. Ag. 247. Ch. 550 &c.; Soph. O. C. 412. Aj. 764 &c.; Eur. Alc. 1154. Supp. 610 &c. never imperfect; ἐνέπω (single ν) in anapaests only and lyric passages, Eur. Hipp. 572. 580. Elec. 144 &c. never imperfect. Brunck would seem, therefore, to have erred in editing προυνέπω for προυνν- in a *trimeter*, and against the older Mss. Soph. Tr. 227. ἐνίπτω *say*, to be distinguished from ἐνίπτω *chide*.

'Ενέχω, see ἔχω.

'Ενήνοθα, see ἐνέθω.

'Ενθεῖν, ἦνθον, see ἔρχομαι.

'Ενθυμέομαι *To consider*, Aesch. Eum. 222; Hippocr. 1, 241. 278 (Erm.); Antiph. 5, 6; Thuc. 1, 120; Lys. 10, 30; -οίμεθα Simon. Am. 2: imp. ἐνεθῡμούμην Thuc. 7, 18; Isocr. 15, 6: fut. ἐνθῡμήσομαι Lys. 12, 45: (no mid. aor.): p. ἐντεθύμημαι Thuc. 1, 120; Xen. An. 3, 1, 43; but pass. Ar. Eccl. 262; Pl. Crat. 404: plp. ἐνετεθύμητο Lys. 12, 70, ἐντεθύμ- Joseph. Ant. 14, 13, 8: aor. ἐνεθυμήθην Ar. Ran. 40; Hippocr. 2, 142 (Erm.); Thuc. 2, 60; Xen. Hell. 4, 3, 13; Lys. 31, 27; Dem. 24, 122: fut. p. late ἐνθυμηθήσομαι as mid. Epist. Phal. 148 (Herch.); Epictet. Ench. 21; Philostr. V. Soph. 614; Aristid. 42 (525): the pres. part. ἐνθυμούμενος is used passively late, App. Civ. 5, 133, and, according to some, perf. ἐντεθύμ- Ar. and Pl. quoted. Vb. ἐνθυμητέον Epich. 127; Andoc. 1, 7. This verb is rare in poetry: once in Trag. -ουμένην Aesch. Eum. 222, occasionally in Comedy, Ar. quoted, and Nub. 820. Eccl. 138. ἐνθυμεῖσθε, if sound, Com. Fr. (Cratin. min.) 3, 374; -ούμενος (Pher.) 2, 338. (Herm.) 2, 399 &c. Act. ἐνθυμέω late, προ- Aen. Tact. 24, 18: aor. ἐνθυμήσας 37, 6.

'Ενίπτω, *say*, see ἐνέπω.

'Ενίπτω Poet. *To chide, reproach*, ἐνίπτοι Il. 24, 768; ἔνιπτε Il. 3, 438; ἐνίπτων Pind. P. 4, 201; Aesch. Ag. 590, ἐνίσσω, -ίσσων Il. 22, 497. 24, 238; Epic inf. -ισσέμεν Il. 15, 198: imp. ἔνισσον, -ομεν Od. 24, 161 (Wolf, Bekk. Dind.), late ἔνιπτον Nic. Ther. 347: 2 aor. (ἐνένιπτον v. r. Il. 15, 546 &c.) ἐνένισπον (v. r. Il. 23, 473 &c.) perhaps rather uncertain even late, Q. Sm. 2, 430. 4, 302. 5, 237 (Lehrs, ἐνένιπ- Koechly). 10, 26 (Lehrs, and, perhaps by mistake, Koechly), also ἐνένῑπον Il. 15, 546. 16, 626. 23, 473, and ἠνίπᾰπον 2, 245. Od. 20, 303. Werneke, Buttmann, Bekker, Spitzner discard from Hom. the forms ἐνένισπον, ἐνένιπτον. Q. Sm. has ἐνένισπον often, 2, 430. 5, 237 &c (Vulg. Lehrs), Koechly always ἐνένῑπον, except 10, 26, -ισπε perhaps unintentionally; Tryphiod. 419 (Wern.)

'Ενίσπω *say*, late in pres. Nic. Ther. 522; Dion. Per. 391; at Orph. Arg. 855, it may be subj. aor. See ἐνέπω.

'Ενίσσω, see ἐνίπτω.

'Εννέπω, see ἐνέπω.

'Εν-νοέω, see νοέω.

"Εννῡμι, ἐννύω, Poet. εἰνύω *To clothe another, simple* pres. not used, see ἀμφι- κατα-: fut. Epic ἕσσω Od. 16, 79. 17, 550. 557, but ἀμφι-έσω 5, 167, Attic προσαμφιῶ Ar. Eq. 891, ἀπαμφ- Com. Fr. (Men.) 4, 171: aor. ἕσα (σσ) Il. 5, 905. Od. 4, 253. 14, 320, and εἴνῦσα, κατα-είν- Il. 23, 135; imper. ἕσσον Il. 16, 670; ἕσσαι (Od. 14, 154); ἕσσας 14, 396, (ἕσα in comp. ἀμφι-έσαιμι Od. 18, 361; ἀμφι-έσᾶσα 15, 369.) Mid. ἕννῦμαι *to clothe oneself*, -υσθαι Od. 6, 28. 14, 522; ἐννύμεναι Orph. H. 43, 6: imp. ἐννύμην, -υτο Od. 10, 543. Hom. H. 4, 171; Theocr. 24, 138: fut. ἕσομαι (σσ), ἐφ- Ap. Rh. 1, 691, Ion. ἐπι-έσσ- Pind. N. 11, 16, ἐφ-εσσ- Ap. Rh. 1, 691: aor. ἑσάμην Il. 14, 178, Ion. or without elision of prep. ἐπι-εσάμ- Xen. Cyr. 6, 4, 6, ἑσσάμην Il. 14, 350; Pind. P. 4, 204, ἐπ-εσσ- Anth. 7, 446, ἐφ- Ap. Rh. 1, 1326, and ἐεσσάμ- Il. 10, 23: p. εἷμαι Od. 19, 72, εἷται 11, 191, and ἕσμαι, ἕσσαι Od. 24, 250, ἕσται Ion. ἐπί-εσται Her. 1, 47 (Orac.): plp. ἕσμην, ἕσσο Il. 3, 57. Od. 16, 199, ἕστο Il. 23, 67. Od. 24, 227, 3 dual ἕσθην Il. 18, 517, 3 pl. εἵατο Il. 18, 596, and ἐέσμ-, ἕεστο Il. 12, 464 (ἔϝεστο Bekk.). Hom. H. 4, 86; Ap. Rh. 3, 1225; εἱμένος Il. 20, 381. Od. 15, 331; Soph. O. C. 1701 (chor.); Eur. Tr. 496 (trimet.); Ion. κατα-ειμένος Od. 13. 351, ἐπι-ειμ- Il. 7, 164.—Epic and Ion. εἵνυμι, ἐπ-είνυσθαι Her. 4, 64; εἰνύω, κατα-είνυον Il. 23, 135 (Vulg.), where however Bekker, Dindorf, La Roche, after Aristarchus, read καταείνυσαν; but κατ-είνυον Opp. Hal. 2, 673. The perf. εἷμαι, εἷται, and 3 pl. plp. εἵατο for εἷντο, alone take the *temporal* augment. This verb seems to have been digammated (ϝέω) ϝέσσω, ϝεῖμαι, ϝείατο (Bekk. 1859), compare *vestio.* The *simple* verb is mostly Epic, twice only, we think, in Attic poetry, Soph. and Eur. quoted: the prose form is ἀμφιέννυμι.

Ἐνοχλέω *To harass*, Ar. Eccl. 303; Lys. 8, 4; Dem. 18, 4 (B.); Pl. Alcib. (1.) 104; -οχλῇ Xen. Mem. 3, 8, 2: imp. ἠνώχλεον Hippocr. 3, 94 (Lit.), -ουν Isocr. 5, 53; Xen. Cyr. 5, 3, 56; Aeschin. 1, 58; Dem. 48, 19: fut. ἐνοχλήσω Anth. 11, 126; Isocr. 15, 153; Dem. 58, 68; Luc. Tim. 34: ἠνώχλησα Dem. 19, 206. 43, 20; -ήσειε Isocr. 5, 59: p. ἠνώχληκα Dem. 21, 4: p. p. ἠνώχλημαι, παρ- Dem. 18, 50: aor. ἠνωχλήθην Hippocr. 5, 702 (Lit.); Artemid. Onir. 2, 3; V. T. 1 Reg. 30, 13: fut. late ἐνοχληθήσονται Geop. 14, 9; -θησόμενος Dio. Hal. 10, 3: and fut. m. ἐνοχλησόμενος as pass. Ap. Civ. 1, 36; Galen 3, 933 missed by Lexicogr. This verb is almost confined to prose, never in Trag., a few times in Comedy, but pres. only. The best Mss. present the forms with double augment, v. r. ἐνώχλουν, ἠνόχλουν Alciphr. 3, 53 (Vulg.), ἠνωχ- (Ven. Mein.), ἐνωχλεῖτο Aeschin. 3, 34 (Ms. c. d. k. l.), ἠνοχλ- (Vulg. B. Saupp.), ἠνωχλ- (Mss. Bekk. Franke) &c. The metre requires ἐννοχλέω Theocr. 29 (30), 36, and Hermann, Meineke, Ahrens, Ziegler so write it, ἐνοχλ- Fritzsche.

Ἐντέλλω *To enjoin*, Poet. in act. Soph. Fr. 252: aor. (ἐνέτειλα) ἔντειλεν Pind. Ol. 7, 40. Generally Dep. m. ἐντέλλομαι as act. Her. 4, 9. 94; Pl. Prot. 325: **imp.** ἐνετελλ- Her. 1, 90. 3, 16; Xen. Cyr. 5, 4, 2, Ion. 2 sing. ἐνετέλλεο Her. 1, 117: **fut.** late ἐντελοῦμαι Schol. Il. 24, 117; V. T. Esai. 13, 11: **aor.** ἐνετειλάμην Her. 1, 156; Xen. Cyr. 4, 2, 12; (Luc.) Philoptr. 13; -λωμαι Luc. D. Mort. 1, 2; -άμενος Her. 1, 117; -ασθαι 2, 121; Xen. An. 5, 1, 13: **p.** ἐντέταλμαι usu. pass. -ταλμένα Soph. Fr. 411 (Dind.); Eur. Phoen. 1648; Her. 6, 106; Xen. Cyr. 5, 5, 3; **act.** Polyb. 17, 2 (Bekk. 18 Dind.): **plp.** ἐντέταλτο **pass.** Her. 5, 2.

Ἐντροπαλίζομαι *To turn often back*, only part. -όμενος Il. 6, 496. 11, 547. 21, 492; late Epic Ap. Rh. 3, 1222; Q. Sm. 12, 583; and late prose Plut. Mor. 449.

Ἐντύω *To prepare* (ῠ), Poet. and unaugm. Theogn. 196; imper. ἔντῠε Anth. 10, 118, ἐπ- Il. 8, 374: **imp.** ἔντῠον Il. 5, 720; Pind. N. 9, 36; Mosch. 2, 164, but ἐντύνω has ῡ Anth. 9, 624; -ύνων Ap. Rh. 3, 737; Orph. Arg. 792; Opp. Hal. 4, 440: **imp.** ἔντῡνον Il. 9, 203. Od. 12, 183; Pind. P. 4, 181, iter. ἐντύνεσκε Ap. Rh. 3, 40: **fut.**- ῠνῶ Lycophr. 734: **aor.** ἔντῡνα, imper. ἐντύνατε Eur. Hipp. 1183 (trimet.); -ύνᾱσα Il. 14, 162. **Mid.** ἐντύνομαι Ap. Rh. 4, 1191; Opp. Hal. 1, 580, ἐπ- Od. 24, 89; -τύνοιτο Mosch. 2, 30 (Mein.); -τύνεσθε Callim. Ap. 8; -τυνόμενος Od. 17, 182: **imp.** ἐντύνοντο Il. 24, 124. Od. 16, 2: **aor.** ἐντῡνάμην, τῡνώμεθα Od. 17, 175, Epic 2 sing. -τύνεαι 6, 33; -τύναιο Ap. Rh. 3, 510, -αιτο 3, 293; -ασθαι Hes. Op. 632; Ap. Rh. 1, 1189; -άμενος Od. 12, 18; Ap. Rh. 1, 396. **Pass.** ἐντύνονται Ap. Rh. 1, 235. This verb is chiefly Epic, once only in Attic poetry, Eur. quoted.

Ἐνυπνιάζω *To dream*, rare in **act.** Aristot. H. A. 4, 10, 13; v. r. Hippocr. 1, 594 (Lit.) **Mid.** -άζομαι Hippocr. 1, 594; Plut. Brut. 24. Cat. maj. 23; V. T. Deut. 13, 5. Esai. 29, 8: **aor.** both ἐνυπνιασάμην Gen. 37, 9. Jud. 7, 13 (v. r. ἠν-), ἠνυπ- Jer. 23, 25 (v. r. ἐνυπ-): and ἐνυπνιάσθην Gen. 28, 12. 37, 5. 6. 41, 5. Dan. 2, 1, ἠνυπ- 3: but **fut.** -ασθήσομαι Joel 2, 28.

Ἐξακέσας, see ἀκέομαι.

Ἐξανδραποδίζω, see ἀνδραπ-.

Ἐξαπατάω *To deceive*, Her. 1, 90; Hippocr. 6, 496; Antiph. 5, 91; Xen. Cyr. 1, 5, 13, Dor. 3 pl. -απατῶντι Pind. Ol. 1, 29: **imp.** -ηπάτων Ar. Eq. 418, iter. -απάτασκον Pax 1070 (hexam.): **fut.** -ήσω Il. 9, 371; Lys. 4, 14: **aor.** -ηπάτησα Ar. Eccl. 949; Her. 9, 116; Pl. Meno 80, -απάτησα Il. 22, 299; -ήσας Andoc. 3, 33; -ῆσαι Od. 13, 277; Andoc. 3, 34: **p.** -ηπάτηκα Her. 6, 2; Pl. Prot. 342 &c. reg.: except **fut. mid.** -απατήσομαι as pass. Xen. An. 7, 3, 3: with **fut. p.** -απατηθήσομαι Pl. Crat. 436. Gorg. 499. **Mid.** ἐξαπατῶμαι seems doubtful, -ᾶται Hippocr. 1, 572 (Lit.

-απατᾷ Ermerins); Pl. Crat. 439 (2 Mss. Stallb., ἀπατᾷ Vulg. Bekk. B. O. W. Herm.); so Aristot. Probl. 29, 6 (Mss. Vulg. ἀπατᾷ Bekk.)

Ἐξαριθμέω, see ἀριθ-.

Ἐξαρνέομαι, see ἀρνέομαι.

Ἐξετάζω *To investigate*, Xen. Mem. 2, 2, 13; Pl. Prot. 333; Aeschin. 1, 195; -ετάζῃς Isocr. 5, 29; imper. ἐξέταζε Soph. Aj. 586; -άζειν Her. 3, 62; Isocr. 3, 17: imp. ἐξήταζον Thuc. 2, 7; Isocr. 15, 141: fut. ἐξετᾰ́σω Ar. Eccl. 729; Com. Fr. (Men.) 4, 151; Xen. Oec. 8, 10; Pl. Charm. 172. Apol. 29; Dem. 18, 11. 21, 21. 154, once only ἐξετῶ Isocr. 9, 34: aor. ἐξήτασα Ar. Thesm. 436; Aeschin. 1, 160; (Pl.) Epist. 13, 362 B, Dor. -ήταξα Theocr. 14, 28; subj. -άσω Soph. O. C. 211; Pl. Apol. 24; -άσαιμι Phaedr. 277, -άσειε Dem. 20, 18; -έτασον Dem. 18, 265; -άσαι Theogn. 1016; Com. Fr. (Men.) 4, 228; Thuc. 7, 33; -άσας (Dem.) 1469: p. ἐξήτακα Xen. Mem. 3, 6, 10. 11; Pl. Theaet. 154; Aeschin. 1, 92; Dem. 18, 172. (58, 19); Com. Fr. (Heges.) 4, 479. (Nicom.) 4, 583: p. p. -ήτασμαι Dem. 20, 49. 37, 46: aor. -ητάσθην Dem. 22, 66; -ασθῆναι Antiph. 5, 37; -ασθείς Pl. Crat. 436: fut. -ετασθήσομαι Dem. 2, 20; Luc. Jup. Tr. 42. Vb. ἐξεταστέον Pl. Rep. 599.—ἐξητασμένη is not act. (Dem.) Epist. 5 (1490.)—The preposition in this verb is not *inseparable*: pres. ἐτάζουσι Polus (Pythagor.) Stob. Fl. 9, 54: aor. ἥτασε Anth. 12, 135; ἐτάσῃς 7, 17; V. T. Gen. 12, 17, and often pres. fut. aor. act. and pass. and fut. pass. ἐτασθήσονται Apocr. Sap. 6, 7; ἠτάζετο Jambl. Dram. 12; even Plato in his Crat. 410, has ἐτάζει, ἐτάζον, though he seemingly uses the *simple* merely for an etymological illustration. How squares the elision of ς with Cobet's and J. Word.'s rule?

Ἐόληται, ἐόλητο, see εἰλέω.

Ἑορτάζω *To keep a festival*, Thuc. 3, 3; Arr. Cyn. 34; -τάζῃ Eur. I. T. 1458, Ion. ὁρτάζω Her. 2, 60: imp. ἑώρταζον Isocr. 19, 40, Ion. ὅρταζον Her. 9, 7: fut. late ἑορτᾰ́σω Alciphr. 3, 18; Luc. Mer. C. 16; Dio Cass. 47, 13; (Her.) V. Hom. 29: aor. ἑώρτᾰσα Dio Cass. 48, 34. 60, 17 (Bekk.); inf. ἑορτάσαι Ar. Ach. 1079; Pl. Rep. 458; ὁρτάσας Her. 7, 206: p. (ἑώρτᾰκα): plp. δι-εωρτᾰ́κει Dio Cass. 47, 20: aor. p. ἑωρτάσθην 56, 24, δι- 51, 21.

Ἐπαινέω *To approve*, Il. 4, 29; Aesch. Sept. 596; Soph. O. C. 665; Her. 6, 130; Antiph. 3, δ, 8; Thuc. 2, 35; Andoc. 3, 33; Xen. An. 3, 1, 45; Isocr. 11, 30 (Lacon. -αινίω Ar. Lys. 198, Aeol. -αίνημι Simonid. C. 5, 19), 3 pl. Dor. -έοντι Pind. P. 5, 107 (Bergk 3 ed.): imp. ἐπῄνεον Il. 4, 380; Eur. Or. 902; Isocr. 12, 264, -νει Pl. Rep. 582, Ion. ἐπαίνεε Her. 3, 34. 7, 116: fut. ἐπαινέσω Simon. Am. 7, 29 (Bergk); Aesch. Eum. 836;

Soph. El. 1044. 1057; Eur. Heracl. 300. Andr. 464. Cycl. 549; Xen. An. 1, 4, 16 (Dind. Krüg. Saupp. -σητε Popp.). 5, 5, 8; Pl. Conv. 214 (B. O. W. Stallb. -έσομαι Bekk.); Dem. 20, 143? -έσοι Pl. Leg. 719 (B. O. W. Herm. -έσαι Bekk.); later Aristot. Eth. M. 1, 32; Plut. Pomp. 71. Caes. 44; Luc. Herm. 42?; Lycophr. 1172; Epict. Ench. 54; Demetr. Phal. 295, Poet. -ήσω Theogn. 93 (v. r. -ήσῃ); Pind. P. 10, 69: and in same sense **mid.** -έσομαι Eur. Bac. 1195 (chor.); Isocr. 8, 140. 12, 109. Epist. 2, 21; Xen. Hell. 3, 2, 6; Pl. Rep. 379. 383. 426. Men. 236. Leg. 639. 688. Conv. 199; Dem. 2, 31. 19, 45. 21, 73. 58, 58; later Plut. Aristid. 12. Ages. 37. Pomp. 55. Cat. min. 59; Luc. D. Deor. 18. Somn. 7. 9. Prom. 15 &c.; Aristaen. 2, 2; Aristid. 42, 518; Demetr. Phal. 292: **aor.** ἐπῄνεσα Soph. Aj. 536; Ar. Ach. 485; Thuc. 1, 86; Isocr. 12, 265; Pl. Gorg. 471, Poet. -ήνησα Il. 18, 312; Theogn. 876; Pind. N. 5, 19; but Plut. Mor. 931; Dor. pt. -αινήσαις Pind. P. 4, 189: **p.** ἐπῄνεκα Isocr. 12, 261; Pl. Polit. 307, -ήνηκα (Suid.): but **p. p.** ἐπῄνημαι Hippocr. 2, 334 (Lit.); Isocr. 12, 233; Luc. Hist. 5, ἤπην- (Suid.): **aor.** ἐπηνέθην Thuc. 2, 25; Isocr. 12, 146; Luc. Somn. 8: **fut.** ἐπαινεθήσομαι Andoc. 2, 13; Pl. Rep. 474; (Dem.) 60, 15, later -ηθήσομαι Long. Past. 4. 4 (Seil. -εθήσ- Herch.) **Mid. aor.** late ἐπηνέσατο Ep. Phal. 147 (Herch.); inf. -ήσασθαι Themist. 16, 200 (D.) missed by Lexicogr. **Vb.** ἐπαινετέος Pl. Rep. 390. In Attic poetry **fut. act.**, with one exception, is the form in use; in Attic prose the **fut. mid.** prevails.

'Επανορθόω *To set upright*, Isocr. 1, 3; Lycurg. 7; Aeschin. 1, 3; Dem. 6, 34, always with double augment: **imp.** ἐπηνώρθουν Isocr. 12, 200: **fut.** -ώσω Thuc. 7, 77; Isocr. 6, 72: **aor.** ἐπηνώρθωσα Lys. 2, 70; Dinarch. 1, 96, συν- Dem. 10, 34, late ἐπ-αν- Eunap. Fr. 23 (L. Dind.): (p. a.): **p. p.** ἐπηνώρθωμαι Dem. 18, 311: **aor.** ἐπανορθωθῆναι Dem. 9, 76 (late, single augm. ἐπανωρθώθη 2 Macc. 5, 20): **fut.** -ορθωθήσομαι Aeschin. 3, 177; Dem. 6, 5: and **fut. m.** reflex or **pass.** ἐπανορθώσεται Isocr. 17, 15; Dio Cass. 73, 1. **Mid.** -ορθοῦμαι *right one's own*, Pl. Euth. 9: **imp.** ἐπηνωρθούμην Pl. Theaet. 143: **fut.** -ώσομαι Pl. Lach. 200; Dem. 15, 34; Plut. Them. 16; as reflex or **pass.** see Isocr. 17, 15; Dio Cass. 73, 1: **aor.** ἐπηνωρθωσάμην Isocr. 4, 165; Dem. 7, 18. 56, 43. **Vb.** ἐπανορθωτέα Pl. Leg. 809. This is the only comp. of ὀρθόω that doubles the augment. See ἀνορθόω.

'Επαυρέω and **'Επαυρίσκω** *To enjoy*, Epic and Lyric, both rare, -ρεῖ Hes. Op. 419, -ίσκουσι Theogn. 111: **2 aor.** Dor. ἐπαῦρον Pind. P. 3, 36; subj. ἐπαύρω, -ῃς Od. 18, 107, -ῃ Il. 13, 649; ἐπαυρεῖν Il. 15, 316. 23, 340, and ἐπαυρέμεν Il. 18, 302. Od.

17, 81. **Mid.** ἐπαυρίσκομαι *to reap good or ill, enjoy,* in poetry and prose, Il. 13, 733; Hippocr. 7, 488 (Lit.); Democr. p. 166 (Mull.); Themist. 21, 254, ἐπαύρομαι? -αύρεσθαι Ap. Rh. 1, 1275 (Well. Merk. but -έσθαι Ms. G.): **fut.** ἐπαυρήσομαι Il. 6, 353: **1 aor.** ἐπηυράμην Aristot. Eth. N. 8, 15, 11, ἐπαυρ- (Hippocr.) Epist. 9, 424 (Lit.); -αύρασθαι Hippocr. 4, 632 (Lit.): **2 aor.** ἐπηυρόμην Eur. Hel. 469, 2 sing. ἐπηύρου Aesch. Pr. 28, Dor. ἐπαύρεο Pind. N. 5, 49; subj. ἐπαύρηαι Il. 15, 17, -ωνται 1, 410; opt. ἐπαύροιτο Her. 7, 180; Themist. 23, 293; -όμενος Ap. Rh. 4, 964; Anth. 7, 376. 384; -έσθαι Eur. I. T. 529; Com. Fr. (Anon.) 4, 607. Rare in Attic prose ἐπαυρέσθαι Andoc. 2, 2; and late Dio Cass. 52, 12 (Bekk.); Ael. Fr. 86 (Herch.)

Ἐπείγω *To urge,* Il. 12, 452; Soph. O. C. 1540; Epic subj. ἐπείγετον Il. 10, 361; imper. ἔπειγε Od. 15, 445; Eur. Phoen. 1280; Ar. Thesm. 783; rare in prose -γει Hippocr. Epist. 9, 336. 342. 344 (Lit.); -γων Pl. Leg. 887; Luc. Jup. Tr. 41: **imp.** ἤπειγον Pind. Ol. 8, 47; Soph. Ph. 499, κατ- Thuc. 1, 61, Hom. always ἔπειγ- Od. 12, 205: **fut.** (ἐπείξω): **aor.** ἤπειξα perhaps late (Hippocr.) Epist. 9, 380 (Lit.); Alciphr. 2, 3; Plut. Pomp. 21, κατ- Sert. 19. Agis 19. Brut. 8: **p. p.** ἤπειγμαι Aristid. 15, 231; Galen 6, 177; Theod. Prod. 5, 317: **aor.** ἠπείχθην as mid. Thuc. 1, 80; Isocr. 4, 87; Pl. Leg. 887; ἐπείχθῃς Her. 8, 68. **Mid.** ἐπείγομαι *to haste,* Aesch. Ch. 660; Eur. Ion 1258; Ar. Ach. 1070; Her. 4, 139; Thuc. 3, 2; Pl. Rep. 517; -ωμαι (Pl.) Ax. 364; imper. ἐπείγου Soph. Fr. 690; Pl. Phaed. 116, ἐπειγέσθω Il. 2, 354; -όμενος Il. 23, 437; Pind. P. 4, 34; Her. 6, 112; Antiph. 5, 94; -εσθαι Eur. Alc. 1152; Pl. Leg. 965: **imp.** ἠπειγόμην Eur. Hipp. 1185; Her. 8, 18; Thuc. 4, 4. 5; Aeschin. 1, 96, ἐπειγ- Il. 5, 622; Hes. Sc. 21; Her. 4, 98 (Gaisf. Stein, ἠπειγ- Bekk. Dind. Dietsch): **fut.** ἐπείξομαι Aesch. Pr. 52; Ar. Eccl. 43; Aristot. Prob. 18, 6, 2. Occasionally as act. *urge on,* ἐπείγονται τὴν παρασκευὴν Thuc. 3, 2 &c.; -όμενοι Od. 2, 97. The act., again, is sometimes used as **mid.** ἔπειγε Soph. El. 1435; Ar. Pax 943 &c. **Vb.** ἐπεικτέον Pl. Leg. 687.—κατ-επείγω is more frequent in Attic prose, but confined, we think, in the classic period, to **pres.** Pl. Theaet. 187, and **imp. act.** κατ-ήπειγον Thuc. 1, 61: **mid.** κατεπείγομαι Alciphr. 3, 51; Polyb. 5, 37, 10.

Ἐπενήνοθε, see (ἐνέθω.)

Ἐπιβουλεύω *To plan against,* Soph. O. R. 618; Her. 3, 122; Antiph. 2, α, 2; Pl. Rep. 565: **imp.** ἐπεβούλ- Antiph. 5, 62; Thuc. 2, 5: **aor.** -εβούλευσα Antiph. 2, γ, 3: -ευκα Isocr. 18, 51: reg. except having **fut. mid.** -εύσομαι **pass.** Xen. Cyr. 5, 4, 34. 6, 1, 10: with **fut. pass.** -ευθήσομαι late Dio Cass. 52, 33; Epist.

Phal. 122 (Herch.): **aor. p.** -εβουλεύθην Antiph. 4, β, 5; Andoc. 1, 117; but -ευθῆναι as **act.** Dio Cass. 59, 26, which, though altered by Bekker and L. Dind. to **aor. act.** -εῦσαι, seems to derive some support from the *simple* form ἐβουλεύθην being used actively Dio Hal. Excerp. 15, 7 (15, 6, 7 Kiessl.) On the other hand, Dio Cass. uses ἐπεβουλεύθην passively 55, 18. 56, 40. 57, 19. 59, 16. 22. 27. 66, 16 and always, unless 59, 26 is to be excepted.

Ἐπιδέρκω, see δέρκομαι.

Ἐπι-έννυμι, see ἕννυμι.

Ἐπιθυμέω *To desire*, Aesch. Ag. 215; Hippocr. 2, 24 (Erm.); Thuc. 4, 108; Isae. 3, 8: **imp.** ἐπ-εθύμει Pl. Conv. 192, -μεε Her. 3, 120: **fut.** -ήσω Ar. Eccl. 804; Thuc. 4, 117: **aor.** ἐπ-εθύμησα Her. 1, 201; Andoc. 3, 3; Isocr. 15, 19 &c.: **act.** complete and reg. in Attic poetry, Ionic and Attic prose: of **pass.** we think the **pres.** alone classic Pl. Phil. 35: **aor.** -ηθείς late, Diod. Sic. Fr. 37, (40 Bekk.): no **mid.**, whereas ἐν- and προ-θυμ- have no **act.**

Ἐπιλέγω, see λέγω.

Ἐπιλογίζομαι *To think on, consider*, (Pl.) Ax. 365: **fut.** -ιοῦμαι (Pl.) Ax. 365: **aor.** in Attic -ελογισάμην Xen. Hell. 7, 5, 16 (Vulg. Breitb. Saupp. ὑπ- Schneid. Cob. L. Dind.); (Dem.) 44, 34: in Ion. -ελογίσθην Her. 7, 177 (though συλλογίσαιτο 2, 148, προσ- 5, 54): **p.** late -λελόγισμαι Dio. Hal. 3, 15. **Vb.** ἐπιλογιστέον Plut. Mor. 40.

Ἐπιμέλομαι *To care for*, Xen. Cyr. 1, 2, 3. 8, 8, 8; Isocr. 19, 49 (Bekk. B. Saupp. -οῦμαι Scheibe); Pl. Leg. 905 (Bekk. -οῦμαι B. O. W. Herm.); -λεσθαι Her. 1, 98; Xen. Cyr. 8, 1, 13 (Dind. Saupp.); -λόμενος Thuc. 7, 39; Xen. Mem. 2, 7, 8: **imp.** ἐπεμέλετο Her. 2, 174, -λοντο Thuc. 6, 54; Xen. An. 4, 2, 26; Pl. Gorg. 516; Lys. 14, 14, and ἐπιμελέομαι Eur. Phoen. 556; Ar. Vesp. 154; Lys. 7, 7; Isae. 11, 39; Pl. Prot. 325; -ελοῖτο Xen. Hell. 6, 1, 9 (Vulg. Saupp. Cob. -έλοιτο Dind. 3 ed.); -λεῖσθαι Antiph. 6, 12; Thuc. 4, 118. 6, 91; Andoc. 4, 1; Lys. 19, 18; Isae. 3, 69. 6, 20; Xen. An. 5, 3, 1. Hell. 1, 1, 22. 6, 2, 4 (Dind. Cob. Saupp.). Cyr. 8, 1, 13 (Popp. Saupp.); Isocr. 17, 3. 14, 19; -ούμενος Andoc. 4, 1: **imp.** ἐπεμελεῖτο Thuc. 7, 8; Xen. An. 1, 1, 5. Mem. 2, 9, 4 (-λετο Dind.); Lys. 13, 32; Isae. 1, 12; Lycurg. 44: whence **fut.** ἐπιμελήσομαι Her. 5, 29; Thuc. 3, 25; Xen. Cyr. 5, 4, 22; Pl. Rep. 460. 589. Gorg. 515. Leg. 766 and always; Lys. 21, 13; Isocr. 19, 35; Aeschin. 1, 10: (**aor. mid.** unclassic): **p.p.** ἐπιμεμέλημαι rare Thuc. 6, 41: **aor.** ἐπεμελήθην Lys. 6, 40; Isocr. 4, 38; Isae. 3, 71; Dem. 27, 19; -ηθῆναι Her. 8, 109; Thuc. 4, 2; Lys. 12, 85; -ηθείς

Thuc. 8, 68: fut. ἐπιμεληθήσομαι rare, if correct in classic authors, Xen. Mem. 2, 7, 8 (Mss. Vulg. Born. -λήσομαι Ms. E. Dind. Saupp. Kühn. Breitb.); Aeschin. 3, 27 (Mss. Bekk. -λήσομαι Mss. Bait. Saupp. Franke); later Plut. Mor. 776; Pseud.-Callisth. 1, 18; Dio. Hal. 1, 67 (Vulg. -λήσομαι Mss. A. C. Kiessl.): aor. m. late ἐπεμελησάμην (Diod. Sic. 2, 45, now -λομένην Bekk. L. Dind.); Galen 1, 21 (Kühn); and late Inscr. Boeckh. vol. 2, 2802, all act. Vb. ἐπιμελητέος Xen. Cyr. 7, 5, 70. The Herodotean form is ἐπιμέλομαι, -μέλεσθαι Her. 1, 98, imp. ἐπεμέλετο 2, 174 twice, -μελόμενος 2, 2 (Mss. K. F. &c. Schweigh. Gaisf. Bekk. Dind. -ούμενος Mss. S. d. Vulg.); Hippocr. has both forms, ἐπιμελῆται 3, 476 (Mss. Lit. -έεται Vulg.); -έεσθαι 3, 492. 9, 256 (Lit. &c.), but -όμενος 3, 522 (Mss. Lit. -εόμενος Vulg.) In Attic the *prevailing* form is -έομαι Xen. Plat. Orators: in the Poets it occurs very seldom, but in the pure form ἐπιμελούμεθα req. by the metre Eur. Phoen. 556 (Vulg. Pors. Herm. Kirchh.) which L. Dind. Nauck &c. doubt, and W. Dind. 5 ed. rejects, ἐπιμελοῦ Ar. Vesp. 154 (-έλου Dind.), both which are weak proofs, as their only strength is *accent*, imp. ἐπεμελεῖσθε Plut. 1117 (-έλεσθε Dind.); L. Dind. however in his last edition of Xen. has adopted -μέλομαι in many instances, and maintains that it ought to be adopted uniformly in Aristoph. also, Thuc. and Plato. It certainly is of more frequent occurrence than Lobeck in Buttmann seems to allow, unless he mean inf. -μέλεσθαι, which is very rare, but scarcely so rare as he seems to say, Her. 1, 98; Xen. Cyr. 4, 5, 46 (best Mss. Dind. Saupp.); Pl. Alc. (1) 121. 135; Polyb. 5, 47 (2 Mss. Bekk.); Euseb. Stob. 53, 16; Aristid. 1, 12 (Dind.); Themist. 1, 17 (Dind.) The fut. m. -λήσομαι is on unchallenged *documentary* evidence the earlier form, in fact -ληθήσομαι seems rather doubtful in classic Greek. At Xen. Mem. quoted, Dind. Saupp. and Breitb. edit, with Ms. E. fut. m. -λησόμενος, and Kühner approves: in every other instance Xen. has mid. Cyr. 5, 4, 22. An. 4, 3, 30, and συν-επιμελήσ- Mem. 2, 8, 3. On the other instance also, Aeschin. 3, 27, Mss. and editors are divided.

'Επινεύω, see νεύω.

'Επινοέω, see νοέω.

'Επιορκέω *To swear falsely*, Ar. Nub. 402; Xen. An. 7, 6, 18: fut. ἐπιορκήσω Il. 19, 188; Ar. Lys. 914; Aeschin. 1, 67; Dem. 47, 31; Aristot. Soph. El. 25, 2: and rare -ήσομαι, κατεπι- Dem. 54, 40 (Bekk. B. Saupp.): aor. ἐπιώρκησα Aeschin. 1, 115; Dem. 31, 9; -ήσας Ar. Ran. 102; Her. 4, 68; Lys. 32, 13; -ῆσαι Her. 4, 68; Xen. An. 2, 4, 7: p. ἐπιώρκηκα Xen. An. 3, 1, 22; Lycurg. 76; Her. 4, 68 (Ms. F. Bekk. Lhardy, Dind.

Krüg. Stein, -όρκηκα Schweig. Gaisf.) In the original sense simply *to swear to*, Solon ap. Lys. 10, 17. This verb, we think, does not occur in Trag.

Ἐπιπληρόω, see πληρόω.

Ἐπισκοπέω, see σκοπέω.

Ἐπίσταμαι *To know, understand*, Il. 13, 223. Od. 13, 207; Simon. Am. 24; Aesch. Eum. 667; Soph. Aj. 678; Ar. Eq. 715; Her. 3, 113; Antiph. 5, 67; Thuc. 2, 35; Lys. 9, 2; Pl. Euthyd. 296, Ion. 3 pl. -τέαται Her. 3, 2: **imp.** ἠπιστάμην Aesch. Pr. 265; Soph. O. C. 927; Eur. Or. 360; Ar. Eq. 462; Her. 3, 74. 8, 136 (Bekk.), see below; Antiph. 5, 74; Thuc. 6, 64; Lys. 10, 4; Isocr. 15, 27; Pl. Charm. 171, Epic ἐπιστ- Il. 5, 60. 17, 671, seldom ἠπιστ- Hom. Fr. 1; Callim. Cer. 112: **fut.** ἐπιστήσομαι Il. 21, 320; Soph. O. C. 290; Ar. Vesp. 1174; Pl. Men. 85; Aristot. Anal. Post. 1, 2, 3: **aor.** ἠπιστήθην Pl. Leg. 687; Xen. Oec. 2, 11; Her. 3, 15 (Mss. Gaisf. Dind. Dietsch, Stein), ἐπιστ- (Ms. S. Bekk. Krüg.) **Vb.** ἐπιστητός Pl. Theaet. 201, -έον late.—2 sing. ἐπίστασαι Aesch. Pr. 982; Soph. El. 629; Ar. Eq. 690; Pl. Phaedr. 230, sometimes ἐπίστᾳ Poet. Pind. P. 3, 80; Aesch. Eum. 86. 581, ἐπίστῃ Ion.? Theogn. 1085, and ἐπίστεαι, ἐξ- Her. 7, 135; subj. -ωμαι Xen. Cyr. 2, 3, 22, -ίστῃ Pl. Euthyd. 296, Ion. -έωμαι, 3 pl. -έωνται Her. 3, 134; Psephism. Dem. 18, 91; imper. ἐπίστασο Aesch. Pr. 840; Soph. O. R. 848. Ant. 305; Eur. Ion 650. An. 430; Ion. prose, Her. 7, 29, ἐξ- 7, 39 (Mss. Schweigh. Gaisf. Bekk. Bred. Stein &c.). 7, 209 (Wessel. Bekk. Bred. Stein), -ίσταο (Mss. Schweigh. Gaisf. and always Dind.), in Soph. more freq. ἐπίστω Tr. 182. Ph. 419. 567. O. R. 658 &c.; Attic prose Xen. Cyr. 3, 3, 32. Hell. 5, 4, 33: **imp.** 2 sing. ἠπίστασο Soph. El. 394. Aj. 1134, ἐξ- Dem. 19, 250, but ἠπίστω Eur. Herc. F. 344; Attic prose, Pl. Euthyd. 296. Ion 531; Xen. Hell. 3, 4, 9, Ion 3 pl. ἐπιστέατο Her. 2, 53. 3, 66. 8, 88 (Bekk. Krüg.), ἠπιστ- (Gaisf. Dind. Stein.). This verb in Bekker's and Krüger's edition of Her. is with and without, in Gaisford's generally with, augment: Dind. and Bredow, we think, invariably augment it. Lhardy, a fine and candid scholar, would write sing. ἠπιστάμην, -ατο, but the Ion. 3 pl. uniformly ἐπιστέατο without augm., so Bekk. edit. 1845, but still ἐπιστήθην 3, 15 (ἠπιστ- Gaisf. Lhardy, Stein), and with Stein now, imp. ἐπίστατο 9, 108 (ἠπ- Dind. Dietsch, Abicht.) **Vb.** ἐπιστητός Pl. Theaet. 201.

Ἐπιτάσσω, see τάσσω.

Ἐπιτέλλω, see τέλλω.

Ἐπιφράζω, see φράζω.

(**Ἔπω**) *To say*, see εἴπω, ἐνέπω.

Ἕπω *To be after, busy with*, Epic, the *simple*, except in tmesis, only in indic. ἕπει Od. 12, 209 (La R. Kayser, Ameis, ἔπι Vulg. Bekk. Dind.); part. pres. ἕποντα Il. 6, 321, unless perhaps 11, 483, ἀμφ- Ὀδυσῆα ... ἕπον, generally comp. ἀμφιέπω Il. 19, 392 (-φέπω Pind. Ol. 1, 12), διέπω H. Merc. 67; Theogn. 893; Her. 3, 53, ἐφ-έπω Il. 16, 724; Simon. C. 142, ἐπέπω Her. 7, 8 (1), περιέπω &c.: **imp.** εἶπον, διείπομεν Il. 11, 706, περι-εῖπεν Her. 2, 169; Xen. Mem. 2, 9, 5, Poet. ἕπον see above, ἀμφ- Il. 16, 124, δι- 2, 207, ἐφ- Pind. P. 6, 33, iter. ἕπεσκον, ἐφ- Od. 12, 330: **fut.** ἕψω, ἐφ- Il. 21, 588, περι- Xen. Cyr. 4, 4, 12; Luc. Tim. 12: **aor. p.** unaugm. περι-έφθησαν Her. 6, 15. 8, 27 (hither Curtius refers ἐάφθη, ἐάφ- Il. 13, 543. 14, 419): **2 aor. act.** ἕσπον (not ἕσ-) ἐπ-έσπον Il. 19, 294; Aesch. Pers. 552 (chor.), περι- Her. 6, 44; subj. ἐπί-σπῃς Il. 22, 39, -σπῃ 2, 359; opt. ἐπίσποι Od. 2, 250; μετα-σπών Il. 17, 190; ἐπι-σπεῖν 7, 52, περι- Her. 2, 64. **Mid.** ἕπομαι *to be after, follow*, Od. 15, 262; Hes. Th. 268; Pind. Ol. 2, 22; Soph. El. 28; Ar. Thesm. 116; Her. 1, 188. 9, 16; Thuc. 1, 42; Pl. Rep. 445; Ion. imper. ἕπεο Il. 18, 387; Her. 5, 18, ἕπευ Il. 13, 465, later Epic ἕσπομαι Hom. H. 29, 12; Pind. I. 5 (6), 17 (Pauw, Bergk 3 ed. Momms. Christ); Ap. Rh. 4, 1607; Dion. Per. 436; Opp. Hal. 1, 189. 2, 57. Cyn. 2, 435 &c.: **imp.** εἱπόμην Il. 23, 133; Eur. Hipp. 291; Ar. Thesm. 1219; Her. 1, 45; Xen. An. 4, 1, 6; Pl. Phaedr. 234, ἑπόμην Il. 15, 277; Hes. Sc. 277; Pind. N. 3, 39, and perhaps ἑσπ-: **fut.** ἕψομαι Il. 10, 108; Pind. Ol. 13, 42; Soph. El. 253; Eur. Hec. 346; Ar. Ach. 1232; Her. 8, 60; Xen. Cyr. 6, 3, 28; (Pl.) Epist. 312, but περι- by some held pass. Her. 2, 115. 7, 149: **1 aor.** see below: **2 aor.** ἑσπόμην Il. 11, 472; Hes. Th. 201; Simon. C. 147; Pind. Ol. 6, 72; Soph. Tr. 563; Eur. Tr. 946. Med. 1143; Ar. Vesp. 1087 (Vulg. Richt.); Her. 6, 90 (Bekk. Dind. &c. εἱπ- Stein); Pl. Polit. 280, ξυν- Thuc. 1, 60. 7, 57, Epic 2 sing. ἕσπεο Il. 10, 285, rare and in comp. ἑσπόμην, ἐπεσπ- Pind. P. 4, 133; subj. σπῶμαι in tmesi ἐπὶ δὲ- Od. 12, 349 (Bekk. *now*, 1858, see below), ἐπίσπῃ Soph. El. 967; Pl. Theaet. 192; ἑσποίμην Od. 19, 579. 21, 77 (σποί- Bekk. *now*), ἐπι- Her. 1, 32; Xen. An. 4, 1, 6; imper. Epic σπεῖο Il. 10, 285, for (σπέο) σποῦ, ἐπίσπου Pl. Theaet. 169, σπέσθω Il. 12, 350 (Bekk.), ἐπισπέσθε, συν- Pl. Critias 107; inf. σπέσθαι Il. 5, 423. Od. 4, 38. 22, 324 (Bekk. Dind.); Eur. Phoen. 426, ἐπι- Pl. Phaedr. 248; σπόμενος Il. 10, 246. 13, 570 (Bekk.); Pind. P. 4, 40, μετα- Il. 13, 567, ἐπι- Her. 3, 31. 7, 180; Thuc. 5, 11; Pl. Rep. 611. But the subj., opt. &c. *uncomp.* often retain the aspirated augment, δ' ἕσπωνται Od. 12, 349 (Wolf, Dind. La Roche), ἕσπηται Pind. Ol. 8, 11; ἅμ' ἑσποίμην Od. 19, 579 &c. (Wolf, Dind. La

Roche), ἕσποιτο Pind. Ol. 9, 83. P. 10, 17; imper. ἅμ' ἑσπέσθω Il. 12, 350. 363 (Wolf, Spitzn. Dind. La R.); γ' ἑσπόμενος Il. 10, 246 (Wolf, Spitzn. Dind.); Pind. I. 4, 36; Mosch. 2, 147; ἅμ' ἑσπέσθαι Il. 5, 423 (Wolf, Spitzn.). Od. 4, 38 (Wolf), Dind. Bäuml. La Roche with Heyne ἅμα σπέσθαι, so Bekker, who *now* in his 2 edit. of Il. and Od. (1858) drops the aspirated vowel invariably in subj. opt. imper. part. and inf.; always in comp. ἐπι-σπέσθαι Pl. Phaedr. 248; μετα-σπόμενος Il. 13, 567 (Wolf, Spitzn. Dind. &c.), ἐπι-σπόμ- Thuc. 3, 43. 5, 3; Pl. Rep. 611, not ἐφ-εσπ-: **1 aor.** ἐφεψάσθω Theocr. 9, 2 (Call. Vulg. Fritz.), ἐφ-αψάσθω (Med. Meineke), συν-αψάσθω (p. k. Ziegl. Ahr.), but later ἕψατο Hesych., συν-έψασθαι Anna Comn. p. 61. The **2 aor.** has given rise to much discussion, especially the introduction and retention of the *aspirate*. There seems to have been two forms, ἐσπόμην and ἑσπόμην, formed perhaps thus: ἕπομαι originally σέπομαι (Lat. sequor): **2 aor.** ἐσεπόμην, ε elided ἐσπόμην, subj. σπῶμαι; opt. σποίμην; σπέο; σπέσθαι; σπόμενος, like the act. ἕπω originally σέπω: **2 aor.** ἔσεπον, ἔσπον; subj. σπῶ, σποῖμι &c., so ἔχω, ἔχω (fut. ἕξω), originally σέχω: **2 aor.** ἔσεχον, ἔσχον; subj. σχῶ, σχοῖμι &c. ἑσπόμην, again, seems to have arisen from reduplication, σέπομαι, aor. ἐσεπόμην redupl. σεσεπόμην, ε elided σεσπόμ-, then with the usual substitution of the *spiritus asper* for σ, ἑσπόμην, and retained in the *moods* like other reduplications, ἕσπωμαι, ἑσποίμην, ἕσπου, ἑσπέσθαι, ἑσπόμενος; compare τέρπω, **2 aor. m.** ἐτάρπετο, redupl. τετάρπετο Il. 24, 513; subj. τεταρπώμεσθα 23, 10; τεταρπόμενος Od. 1, 310. See also κεύθω, πείθω, &c.

A trace of **pres. act.** (ἕσπω) ἕσπετε, perhaps=σέπω, σέπετε, σ transposed, but leaving its *aspiration* on the ε, occurs in a verse of Timon preserved in Diog. Laert. 9, 112; and perhaps Hom. H. 32, 1, where Lobeck defends the old reading ἕσπετε against ἔσπετε. **Pres. m.** ἕσπομαι, if not late, is rare; for though Wolf adopted it from Eustath. Od. 4, 826, the old reading ἔρχεται is maintained by Bekk. Dind. La Roche, and ἕσποντ' in some editions of Pind. Ol. 13, 42, is an emendation—seemingly unnecessary—of Bothe for the Ms. reading ἕψονται defended by Bergk, Schneidewin, and Kayser; ἕσπεσθαι however I. 5 (6), 17 (Pauw, Momms. Christ, Bergk 2, 3 edit., ἕψονται Bergk's conjecture 1 edit., σπέσθαι Mss.) The comp. περιέπω has **pass.** περιέπομαι *I am treated, handled,* **imp.** περιειπόμην Her. 7, 211; Xen. Hell. 3, 1, 16: **fut. m.** περιέψομαι **pass.**? Her. 2, 115. 7, 149: but **aor. p.** unaugm. περιέφθην Her. 6, 15. In Hom. ἕπω, ἕπομαι with, and without augm., in Her. Bekk. *now* always augments, Gaisford usually, but ἕποντο 1, 80. 172. 9, 15.

Ἐπώχατο, see ἔχω.

Ἔραμαι *To love*, Dep. (like ἵστἄμαι) Poet. for ἐράω, Il. 14, 328; Anacr. 46; Pind. P. 1, 57; Soph. O. C. 511 (chor.); Eur. Alc. 867 (chor.); Ar. Vesp. 751 (chor.); Dor. subj. ἔρᾱται Pind. P. 4, 92; opt. -αίμαν P. 11, 50: **imp.** ἠράμην, -ατο Hym. Cer. 129; Theogn. 1346; Pind. P. 3, 20; Theocr. 13, 6, Aeol. and Dor. 1 pers. -ἄμαν Sapph. 33 (Bergk), Aeol. 2 sing. ἄραο Sapph. 99 (ἄρασο Ahr.): **p.** late ἤρασμαι **act.** Parthen. 2, 2: **aor.** ἠράσθην **act.** Alcm. 33, 5, (Bergk 3 ed.); Soph. Aj. 967; Eur. Hipp. 1303; Ar. Nub. 1076; Her. 3, 31; Xen. An. 4, 6, 3; Pl. Conv. 213, ἀν-ηρ- Andoc. 1, 127; ἐρασθῆναι Isocr. 15, 318; ἐρασθείς Aesch. Pers. 826; Isocr. 12, 193: **fut.** ἐρασθήσομαι **act.** Aesch. Eum. 852; Luc. Luct. 13: also aor. m. Epic, ἠρᾰσάμην Il. 16, 182, ἠρασσ- 20, 223; Archil. 29, and ἐρασσ- Hes. Th. 915; Pind. P. 2, 27; -άμενος Bion 9, 8; Opp. Hal. 3, 404. **Vb.** ἐρᾰτός Il. 3, 64; Ar. Thesm. 993.—ἔρᾱται is Dor. subj. pres. for -ηται, Pind. P. 4, 92; so opt. ἐραίμᾱν P. 11, 50. For indic. ἐρᾶται, ἐράασθε, see ἐράω. ἐρᾶσαι (ἐράεσαι) Brunck's reading for ἔρασσαι Theocr. 1, 78 (Vulg. Wordsw. Ziegl. 1 ed.) is found in the Palat. Ms., and this countenances ἐρᾶται 2, 149 found also in the margin of same Ms., both of which Meineke and Fritzsche adopt: Ziegler now reads ἔρασσαι 1, 78, so Ahrens, but rejects the line as spurious. Attic Poets use **pres.** ἔραμαι in chor. only, but **aor.** -άσθην, and **fut.** -ασθήσομαι in trimet.

Ἐραστεύω *To love, desire*, only **aor.** inf. ἐραστεῦσαι and only Aesch. Pr. 893.

Ἐράω (ᾰ) *To love, desire*, Bion 9, 8; doubtful Pind. Ol. 1, 80. but Fr. 104, Ion. ἐρέω Archil. 25. 68 (Bergk), ἐρῶ Anacr. 3, 1; Ar. Fr. 273 (D); Soph. Ph. 660, ἐρᾷς Soph. Ant. 90; Xen. Conv. 8, 3, ἐρᾷ Aesch. Fr. 41; Soph. Ant. 220; Isocr. 8, 113; Pl. Phil. 35; subj. ἐρῶσι Lys. 3, 39; ἐράοι Opp. Hal. 3, 48, ἐρῴη Pl. Phaedr. 237; ἐρᾶν Aeschin. 1, 137; ἐρῶν Theogn. 1329: **imp.** ἤρων Eur. Fr. 161 (D); Ar. Ach. 146; Her. 9, 108; Pl. Lys. 222. **Pass.** ἐράομαι *to be loved*, indic. rare ἀντ-ερᾶται Xen. Conv. 8, 3; opt. ἐρῷο Xen. Hier. 11, 11; ἐρώμενος Pl. Rep. 403, -ένη Isocr. 8, 65, ὁ ἐρώμενος, ἡ ἐρωμένη *the beloved one*, &c. freq. Ar. Eq. 737; Xen. Conv. 8, 11. Mem. 1, 2, 29; Pl. Conv. 178; inf. ἐρᾶσθαι Aeschin. 1, 137; Plut. Brut. 29. Mor. 752, συν- Bion 9, 8 (Vulg.), συν-έρασθαι (Schaef. Herm.), so Meineke in Text, but in note recommends -αρέσθαι which Ahrens and Ziegler adopt: **aor.** late ἐρασθῆναι Luc. Philops. 15: **fut.** ἐρασθήσομαι Diog. Laert. 4, 34; Luc. Merc. Cond. 7; Themist. 26, 330. ἐράομαι is also Dep., 2 sing. ἐρᾶσαι Theocr. 1, 78, ἐρᾶται Sapph. 13 (Bergk); Theocr. 2, 149; Hippocr. 8, 360: **imp.** 2 pl.

ἐράασθε for ἐρᾶσθε (ἠράεσθε) Il. 16, 208: hither some refer p. ἤρασμαι Parthen. 2, 2: aor. ἠράσθην Alcman 33; Soph. Aj. 967; Isocr. 12, 193 &c.: fut. ἐρασθήσομαι Aesch. Eum. 852; Luc. D. Deor. 20, 15 &c.: aor. m. Epic, ἠρᾰσάμην &c. Il., and ἠρησ- Luc. D. Syr. 17, all act. see ἔραμαι. **Vb.** ἐραστός Pl. Conv. 204. In Her. both Mss. and edit. differ in the augment of this verb. Schaef. varies, Gaisf. and Bekk. *now* uniformly augment it.

Ἐράω *To pour*, only in comp. ἐξ-εράω, -ερᾷ Hippocr. 7, 578; imper. -έρα Dem. 36, 62; -ερῶν Com. Fr. (Pher.) 2, 318; -ερᾶν (Crat.) 2, 237: fut. (-εράσω): aor. -ήρᾱσα, ἐξ-εράσω Ar. Vesp. 993; -εράσῃς Hippocr. 7, 96; -εράσατε Ar. Ach. 341; συν-ερᾶσαι Isocr. 5, 138: aor. pass. ἐξ-ερᾱθεὶς Hippocr. 2, 782 (K.).

Ἐργάζομαι *To work*, Soph. Ant. 326; Ar. Ach. 461; Her. 2, 20; Xen. Hell. 3, 3, 7, rare and late pass. Dio. Hal. 8, 87; subj. -άζωμαι Hom. H. Cer. 139; Hes. Op. 312; opt. -οίμην Il. 24, 733; Antiph. 5, 92; -εσθαι Il. 18, 469. Od. 14, 272; Antiph. 5, 91; imper. ἐργάζευ Hes. Op. 299; -όμενος Thuc. 2, 72: imp. εἰργαζόμην Od. 3, 435; Hes. Op. 151; Ar. Nub. 880; Thuc. 3, 50, ἐργαζ- Od. 24, 210; Her. 1, 66. 2, 124 &c. and ἠργαζ- Hyperid. Eux. p. 16 (Schn.); C. Inscr. 162: fut. ἐργάσομαι Theogn. 1116; Soph. Ph. 66; Ar. Plut. 73; Her. 8, 79; Pl. Rep. 353, Dor. -αξοῦμαι Theocr. 10, 23, and -άξομαι Tab. Heracl. 1, 64, late ἐργῶμαι V. T. Gen. 29, 27. Exod. 20, 9. Job 33, 29. Jer. 22, 13. Apocr. Syr. 13, 4, and always in Septuag.: aor. εἰργασάμην Aesch. Sept. 845; Ar. Eccl. 134; Antiph. 5, 57; Lys. 2, 20; Pl. Rep. 450, Dor. -άμαν Pind. I. 2, 46, ἐργασάμην Her. 2, 115. 3, 15; Ephes. Inscr. 31, ἠργάσσατο Ross. Inscr. 3, 298, but ἐξ- ηργαξ- C. Inscr. 456; ἐργάσσαιο Hes. Op. 43, ἐργασαίατο Ar. Lys. 42: p. εἴργασμαι act. Aesch. Fr. 321 (D.); Soph. Ant. 1228; Ar. Plut. 1113; Antiph. 4, γ, 1. 5, 65. 6, 43; Thuc. 1, 137; Isae. 6, 20; Dem. 53, 3, ἔργασ- Her. 2, 121 (5). 3, 155. 9, 45, pass. εἴργασ- Aesch. Ag. 354. 1346; Soph. O. R. 1369; Eur. Or. 284; Ar. Ran. 1023; (ἐργ- Her. 7, 53); Thuc. 1, 93; Pl. Rep. 381: plp. εἰργάσμην act. Thuc. 6, 29; Dem. 54, 22, pass. Dem. 53, 18, ἐργασμ- Her. 1, 179, δι- 7, 10(3), act. κατ- 3, 157: aor. εἰργάσθην always pass. ἐν- Xen. Mem. 1, 4, 5, rare in Poet. συν- Anth. 9, 807, Ion ἐργάσθην, ἐξ- Her. 4, 179, κατ- 9, 35; opt. ἐργασθείη Pl. Polit. 281, 2 pl. δι-εργασθεῖτε Eur. Heracl. 174; ἐργασθεὶς Pl. Rep. 353, ἐξ- Isocr. 2, 7; -ασθῆναι, κατ- Her. 9, 108, ἀπ- Xen. Eq. 10, 5, ἐξ- Isocr. 5, 7: fut. ἐργασθήσομαι pass. Soph. Tr. 1218, κατ- Isocr. 5, 131, ἐξ- Epist. 6, 8. The act. form ἐργάζω is not in use, but the desider. ἐργασείω Soph. Ph. 1001. **Vb.** ἐργαστέος Aesch. Ch. 298; Eur. Med. 791. This verb in Bekker's Her. is, we think, never augmented, in

Gaisford's occasionally: Lhardy and Bredow would never augment it. Hom. seems to have used only **pres.** and **imp.**: the **aor. pass.** we think almost confined to prose.

(Ἔργ-) *do*, see ἔρδω.

(Ἐργάθω) see ἔργω *shut out.*

Ἔργνυμι *To enclose*, Ion. **pres.** in comp. ἐσ-έργ- Her. 2, 86, κατ- 4, 69 (Bekk.), ἐργνύω Hesych.: **imp.** Epic ἐέργνυν Od. 10, 238: **aor.** ἔερξε, κατ- Hym. Merc. 356.

Ἕργω *To shut in*, **pres.** in comp. περι-έργει Her. 2, 148: **fut.** ἕρξω, ἐφ- Tab. Heracl. 1, 83, in Attic ξυν- Soph. Aj. 593: **aor.** ἕρξα Her. 3, 136, κατ- 5, 63 (Bekk. Dind. Abicht, -εῖρξα Stein), Epic ἔρξα Od. 14, 411; in Attic, (καθ-έρξῃς Pl. Gorg. 461 Mss. Herm. Stallb.); part. ἕρξας Pl. Polit. 285, ξυν- Tim. 34. Rep. 461, περι- Thuc. 5, 11: **p. p.** ἔργμαι Hom. H. 3, 123, see below: **aor.** ἔρχθην Il. 21, 282; ἑρχθῇ Hippocr. 8, 26. 36; ἑρχθέν 8, 26 (Lit.); Opp. Hal. 1, 718: (**fut. m.** ἕρξομαι Soph. O. R. 890, called pass. see ἔργω.) **Vb.** see ἑρκτή Her. 4, 146, περί-ερκτος C. Fr. (Pher.) 2, 280.—ἔρχαται Epic 3 pl. **p. pass.** for ἔρχνται, Il. 16, 481: ἔρχατο Epic 3 pl. **plp.** 17, 354, ἐέρχ- Od. 10, 241. See ἐέργω. In Hom. this verb is written with the *lenis* even when signifying *to enclose*, and without augm. both in Hom. and Her.

Ἔργω *To shut out*, Ion. for εἴργω, Her. 8, 98, ἀπ- 1, 72. 2, 99, Epic ἀπο-έργ- Il. 8, 325. Od. 3, 296; ἔργων Her. 3, 48: **imp.** ἔργον, ἐξ- Her. 5, 22 (Bekk. Lhardy, Krüg. Dietsch, ἐξεῖργ- Gaisf. Dind. Stein): **aor.** ἔρξα, κατ- Her. 5, 63, κατ-εῖρξα (Mss. S P. Stein, see ἕργω); ἀπ-έρξαι 2, 124: **p. p.** ἔργμαι, ἀπ-εργμένος Her. 1, 154. 2, 99. 5, 64: to which some assign as **2 aor.** ἐργᾰθον Il. 11, 437, ἐέργ- 5, 147: and **mid.** ἐργαθόμην, κατεργαθοῦ trans. Aesch. Eum. 566 (-ειργ- Pors. Dind.): **fut.** ἔρξομαι *restrain myself, refrain*, Soph. O. R. 890, not pass. **Pres. pass.** ἔργομαι ἐξ- Her. 7, 96; ἔργεσθαι Her. 5, 57; ἐργόμενος 9, 108; Il. 17, 571 (Dind. &c.), ἐϝεργ- (Bekk. 2 edit.): **imp.** ἔργετο Her. 4, 164. 7, 197 (Bekk. Gaisf. Dind.) Her. seems not to have used εἴργω, εἵργω, εἴργνυμι with ι, nor the past tenses with augment. ἀπειργουσα, 9, 68, κατειργνῦσι 4, 69, ἐξεῖργον 5, 22, should be ἀπ- κατ- ἐξ-εργ- (Bekk. Lhardy, Bred. and in theory Dind. but ἐξ-εῖργ-, κατεῖρξ- Stein).

Ἔρδω and ἕρδω *To do, to sacrifice*, Poet. and Ion. Callin. 1, 21 (B.); Theogn. 675; Soph. O. C. 851; Her. 3, 80; subj. ἔρδω Od. 7, 202, ἕρδ- Simon. C. 5, 20; Her. 1, 119. 2, 121 (Bekk. Dind. ἕρδ- Stein); ἔρδοις Hes. Op. 362; ἔρδοι Il. 10, 503; Aesch. Ch. 513; Ar. Vesp. 1431; ἔρδε Il. 4, 29; ἔρδειν Od. 11, 132; Aesch. Ag. 933, ἕρδ- Solon 13, 67; Her. 8, 143; ἔρδων Od. 19,

92; Pind. Ol. 1, 64, ἔρδ- Theogn. 105: imp. ἔρδον Il. 11, 707, ἔρδ- Solon 35; Her. 9, 103, iter. ἔρδεσκε Od. 13, 350 (La R.); Her. 7, 33, ἔρδ- Il. 9, 540; so Ael. Fr. 325, see below: fut. (ἐργ-) ἔρξω Od. 11, 80; Hes. Op. 327 (Lenn.); Ap. Rh. 3, 728; Aesch. Pers. 1059; Soph. Ph. 1406; Ep. inf. ἐρξέμεν Od. 7, 294, ἐρξ- (La Roche): aor. ἔρξα Od. 23, 312; Aesch. Sept. 924. Ag. 1529 (chor. Dind.); Her. 5, 65. 7, 8; ἔρξῃς Il. 2, 364; ἔρξαιμι Od. 13, 147; Aesch. Eum. 467; ἔρξειεν Simon. Am. 7, 80; ἔρξον Il. 4, 37; ἔρξας Il. 5, 650; Aesch. Pers. 786; Soph. Ph. 117, ἔρξ- a Poet *quoted* Pl. Euth. 12; Schol. Od. 14, 411, ἀπ-έρξ- Her. 4, 62, Dor. ἔρξαις Pind. Ol. 10, 91; inf. ἔρξαι Theogn. 178; as imper. Od. 5, 342: **2 p.** ἔοργα Il. 22, 347; Her. 3, 127, 3 pl. ἔοργᾶν for -γασι Batr. 179; ἐοργώς Il. 9, 320: **2 plp.** ἐώργει Od. 4, 693. 14, 289 (εἰώργ- Bekk.), Ion. ἐόργεε Her. 1, 127. **Pass.** ἔρδομαι Pind. Ol. 8, 78, ἔρδ- Her. 4, 60, ἔρδ- (Stein). See ῥέζω. **Vb.** ἐρκτός Arr. Ind. 20, 11.—Iter. imp. ἔρδεσκον Il. 9, 540 (Wolf, Dind.), ἔρδ- Her. 7, 33, ἔρδ- (Stein).—ἔοργαν 3 pl. **2 perf.** for ἐόργᾱσι, Hom. Batr. 179. This verb seems never to be augmented except in **plp.** and only in Hom. ἦρξε Aesch. Ag. 1529, is **aor.** of ἄρχω; Dind. however *now* reads with Naber ἔρξε **aor.** of this verb (5 ed. 1868). Attic prose authors never use, they occasionally *quote* this verb, Xen. Mem. 1, 3, 3; Pl. Prot. 345. Alc. (2) 149. Euth. 12; see also Plut. Mor. 729.

Ἐρεείνω *To ask*, Epic and late prose, Il. 6, 145; Ap. Rh. 3, 1099; subj. -είνῃ H. Merc. 487; Plut. Mor. 288; -είνοι Od. 23, 86; ἐρέεινε 23, 365: **imp.** unaugm. ἐρέεινον Od. 4, 137; Ap. Rh. 3, 490; Com. Fr. (Theop.) 2, 802 (hexam.) **Mid.** as **act. imp.** ἐρεείνετο Od. 17, 305, ἐξ- Il. 10, 81.

Ἐρεθίζω *To excite, provoke*, Plut. Mor. 822: Anacreont. 18 (B.); Theocr. 5, 110, -ίσδω (Wordsw.); subj. -ίζω Od. 19, 45; imper. ἐρέθιζε Il. 1, 32; inf. -ίζειν Pl. Rep. 393; Xen. Ven. 10, 14, Epic ἐρεθιζέμεν Il. 4, 5; -ίζων 17, 658; Eur. Bac. 148. Rhes. 373 (chor.); Hippocr. 1, 424 (Erm.); Aeschin. 2, 177; (Pl.) Eryx. 392: **imp.** ἠρέθιζε Soph. Ant. 965 (chor.), ἐρέθ- Il. 5, 419; Telest. 4 (B.): **fut.** -ιῶ Hippocr. 4, 346 (Lit.); Polyb. Fr. Lib. 13, 4, -ίσω Galen 1, 385: **aor.** ἠρέθισα Dio. Hal. 3, 72; Themist. 23, 285; Synes. Epist. 159, unaugm. ἐρέθ- Aesch. Pr. 181 (chor. Turneb. Elms. Dind. ἠρέθ- Mss. Vulg. Herm.); ἐρεθίσας Her. 3, 146; and -ιξα, ἐρεθίξαι Anth. 12, 37: **p.** ἠρέθικα Aeschin. 2, 37: **p. p.** ἠρέθισμαι Eur. Med. 1119; Ar. Vesp. 1104; Hippocr. 3, 526; D. Hal. de Thuc. 44; (Luc.) Amor. 22: **plp.** ἠρέθιστο App. Civ. 5, 67: **aor.** ἠρεθίσθην, ἐρεθισθείς Her. 6, 40; Dio. Hal. 4, 57. **Vb.** ἐρεθιστέον Pl. Tim. 89.

Ἐρέθω *To provoke*, Epic, Od. 19, 517; Anth. 5, 256; subj.

-έθησι Il. 1, 519: imp. ἤρεθον Theocr. 21, 21; Mosch. 3, 85, iter. ἐρέθεσκον Ap. Rh. 3, 618.

Ἐρείδω *To prop*, Il. 16, 108; Aesch. Ag. 1003; Ar. Pax 25; Hippocr. 7, 178. 8, 390; Plut. Mar. 23. Mor. 515: imp. ἤρειδον Pind. Ol. 9, 32; Ar. Ran. 914; Philostr. Ap. 231, ἔρειδ- Il. 13, 131: fut. ἐρείσω Callim. Del. 234; Anth. 5, 301; Aristid. 15, 231: aor. ἤρεισε Soph. Ant. 1236; Pl. Tim. 91; Plut. Mor. 805, Poet. ἔρ- H. Hym. 1, 117; Ap. Rh. 1, 1198, in tmesi Il. 17, 48; subj. ἐρείσω Eur. Andr. 845, -σῃ Soph. Tr. 964 (D.); Hippocr. 4, 200 (Lit.); Plut. Mor. 368, -σωσι Aristot. Probl. 18, 1; opt. ἐρίσειε Hippocr. 4, 196; ἔρεισον Pind. P. 10, 51; Eur. Elec. 898. Heracl. 603, ἐρείσατε Soph. O. C. 1113; ἐρείσας Il. 22, 97. Od. 8, 473; Tyrt. 11, 31; Her. 6, 129; Pl. Phaedr. 254; Aristot. Mechan. 14; Plut. Num. 2. Brut. 52. Eum. 14. Crass. 19; Arr. An. 6, 9, 4, Dor. ἐρείσαις, ἀντ- Pind. P. 4, 37: p. ἤρεικα, συν- Hippocr. 6, 372 (Lit.), προσ- Polyb. 5, 60, and ἐρήρεικα, προσ- Plut. Aemil. Paul. 19: p. p. ἐρήρεισμαι Her. 4, 152; Hippocr. 4, 220. 312 (Lit.); Aristot. Mund. 3, 1; (Pl.) T. Locr. 97, 3 pl. ἐρηρέδαται Il. 23, 284, but ἐρήρεινται Ap. Rh. 2, 320, augm. on redupl. rare and late ἠρήρεισται Orph. Arg. 1142, and without redupl. (δι-ερεισμένη Ar. Eccl. 150 Br. has been altered) ἤρεισμαι perhaps late (Pl.) Locr. 98; Paus. 6, 25, 5; Diod. Sic. 4, 12, unless συν-ήρεισμ- be sound, Hippocr. 8, 270 (Mss. θ. Lit.), ἀπ- Polyb. 3, 66, act. 3, 109: plp. with reduplication augm. ἠρήρειστο Il. 4, 136; Anth. 5, 255; Ap. Rh. 2, 1105, ἠρήρειντο 3, 1398, Hom. ἐρηρέδατο Od. 7, 95 (some ἐληλέδατο, -άδατο): aor. ἠρείσθην, ἐρείσθην Il. 7, 145; ἐρεισθείς Il. 22, 225, συν- Eur. I. T. 457; ἐρεισθῆναι Plut. Cim. 13: 3 fut. ἐρηρείσεται Hippocr. 8, 292 (Ms. θ. Lit.) Mid. ἐρείδομαι *to lean*, intrans. Il. 14, 38; Aesch. Ag. 64; Hippocr. 4, 314 (Lit.); trans. Anth. 7, 457: imp. trans. ἠρειδόμην Ar. Nub. 1375: fut. ἐρείσομαι, ἀπ- Aristot. Probl. 6, 3; Plut. Mor. 775; Polyb. 15, 25: aor. ἠρεισάμην intrans. Hes. Sc. 362; Plut. Philop. 10. Eum. 7, ἀπ- Pl. Rep. 508, trans. Simon. (C.) 172 (Bergk); Hippocr. 3, 438. 4, 306, ἐρεισ- intrans. Il. 5, 309; trans. Anth. 6, 83: with p. p. ἐρήρεισμαι Her. quoted, ἀπ-ήρεισται Polyb. 3, 109: and aor. intrans. ἠρείσθην, ἐρείσθ- Il. quoted. Hom. augments the plp. only. The Vulg. reading Hippocr. 8, 292, is ἐνειρίσηται.—This verb is mostly poetic: in good Attic prose Pl. alone uses it.

Ἐρείκω *To tear, bruise*, Aesch. Pers. 1060; Hippocr. 8, 174; Pl. Crat. 426: imp. ἤρεικον Hes. Sc. 287; Aesch. Ag. 655: aor. ἤρειξα Ar. Fr. 88 (D.), κατ- Vesp. 649; ἐρείξας Hippocr. 7, 102. 354 (Lit.), and (from ἐρίκω?) ἤριξα, ἐρίξας, 8, 244 (Lit.)

v. r. ἐρείξ-), κατ- 246: p. p. ἐρήριγμαι Aristot. H. A. 8, 7; Hippocr. 7, 416 (Lit. ἐρήρισμ- some edit.). 8, 506 (no v. r.): ἠρείχθην Galen 6, 782; Oribas. 4, 8, ἠρίχθη (Hesych.): pres. ἐρεικόμενος Il. 13, 441: **2 aor. act.** ἤρῐκον intrans. Il. 17, 295; trans. Soph. Fr. 164 (D.), δι- Euphor. in Schol. Pind. N. 7, 39. **Mid.** in comp. κατ-ερείκεσθε Sapph. 62 (Bergk); -όμενοι Aesch. Pers. 538: **imp.** κατ-ηρείκοντο Her. 3, 66: **fut.** ἐρείξεται, ἀμφ- pass. (Hesych.): **aor.** in *simple*, late ἐρειξάμενος Porphyr. de abst. 2, 6.

Ἐρείπω *To throw down*, Il. 15, 356; Soph. Ant. 596; late prose Paus. 10, 32, 4?: **imp.** ἔρειπον Il. 12, 258, ἤρειπ- Her. 9, 70; Dio. Hal. 9, 56: **fut.** ἐρείψω Soph. O. C. 1373; Xen. Cyr. 7, 4, 1: **1 aor.** ἤρειψα Anth. Ap. Epigr. 214; Plut. Cim. 16. Mor. 327; ἐρείψῃ, ἐξ- Pind. P. 4, 264; ἐρεῖψαι Her. 1, 164: **p. p.** late ἤρειμμαι, but ἐρήρειπται, κατ- Plut. Mor. 849. 837, see below: **plp.** ἤρειπτο Plut. Brut. 42 (Coraes, Sint. but ἐρήριπτο Emper. Bekk. see below): and ἐρήριμμαι Arr. Ann. 1, 21, 6. 22, 1: **plp.** ἐρήριπτο 2, 22, 7, κατ- 1, 19, 2; Herodn. 8, 2, 4 (Bekk.), shortened ἐρέριπτο Il. 14, 15: **aor.** ἠρείφθην Arr. An. 1, 21, 4; ἐρειφθείς Soph. Aj. 309: **2 aor.** ἤριπον trans.? Simonid. C. 37, 3 (Bergk); and late Paus. 10, 32, 4, intrans. Il. 5, 47; Hes. Th. 858. Sc. 421; Opp. Hal. 1, 33; Theocr. 13, 50, ἐξ-ήρ- Hippocr. 3, 314, ἔριπον Il. 5, 68; ἐρίπῃσι 17, 522; -ιπών 8, 329: **mid.** ἠριπόμᾱν pass. Anth. 9, 152: **2 aor. p.** ἠρίπην, ἐριπέντι Pind. Ol. 2, 43 (best Mss. Boeckh, Bergk): **2 p.** ἐρήρῖπα, κατ- *have fallen*, Il. 14, 55. To this probably belongs **1 aor. m.** ἀν-ηρειψάμην *forced up, carried off*, Il. 20, 234. Od. 1, 241; Anth. App. Epigr. 51, 14 (late prose Themist. 37, 332), ἀν-ερειψ- Ap. Rh. 1, 214. Rare in good Attic prose, only Xen. quoted.—For **2 aor.** ἤριπον with trans. sense Her. 9, 70 (Schw. Gaisf. Stein), **imp.** ἤρειπον has been restored from Mss.; so Paus. 4, 25, 1 (Schubart); and the intrans. force preserved Q. Sm. 13, 452 (Koechly) by changing ὄλεθρον to -θρος; ἐριπόντες also Paus. 10, 32, 4, seems to admit of been changed to **pres.** ἐρείπ-. ἤρειπτο Plut. quoted, is the reading of Coraes for ἠρείπετο, ἠρίπετο of the Mss. The **plp.** is required, and Sintenis adopts it, but expresses a doubt whether ἐρήριπτο suggested by Emper. and received by Bekk. should not be preferred. If so, κατ-ερήρειπται, κατ-ερηρειμένος Plut. Mor. 849. 837 (Dübn.) should get a hint to follow suit.

Ἐρέπτω *To tear, eat*, Poet. and *simple* late in **act.** -ων Nonn. 40, 306: but **imp.** ὑπ-έρεπτε Il. 21, 271: **mid.** only part. ἐρεπτόμενος Il. 2, 776. Od. 19, 553. H. Merc. 107; Ar. Eq. 1295 (chor.); Opp. Hal. 1, 96. See ἐρέφω.

Ἐρέσσω *To strike, row,* Soph. Ph. 1135; Eur. Ion 161; ἔρεσσε Aesch. Pers. 1046. Sept. 855; inf. Epic ἐρεσσέμεναι Il. 9, 361; late Attic prose -σσων Plut. Mor. 1128; -σσειν App. Pun. 9, -έττω Anth. 14, 14; Ael. H. A. 14, 14; Luc. Char. 1: **imp.** ἔρεσσον Od. 12, 194, ἤρεττ- Long. 3, 21: **fut.** (ἐρέσω): **aor.** ἤρεσα Ap. Rh. 1, 1110, δι- Od. 12, 444, δι-ήρεσσα 14, 351 (Bekk.), ἔρεσσα, προ- Il. 1, 435. Od. 15, 497. ἐρεσσομένων Coluth. 209, is **mid.** unless ἐρετάων there means *oars,* as in Anth. 6, 4. **Pass.** ἐρέσσεται Aesch. Supp. 723: **imp.** ἠρέσσετο Pers. 422.

Ἐρεύγομαι *To cast forth, disgorge,* usu. Epic and Ion. Pind. P. 1, 21. Fr. 107 (Bergk); Hippocr. 7, 104. 180 (Lit.); Aristot. Probl. 10, 44; App. Mithr. 103, προσ- Il. 15, 621, ἐξ- Her. 1, 202; -όμενος Il. 16, 162: **imp.** ἐρεύγετο Od. 9, 374, ἠρεύγ- Hesych.: **fut.** ἐρεύξομαι Hippocr. 8, 100: **aor.** late ἠρευξάμην Or. Sib. 4, 81; Hierocl. 94 (Eberh.), ἐξ- V. T. Ps. 44, 1: **p.** ἔρευγμαι, ἐπαν-ερευγμένος Hippocr. 2, 64 (Vulg. Kühn), where however the **pres.** ἐπανερευγόμενος has by far the best Mss. support, and is adopted by Littré 2, 370: **pres. pass.** or **mid.** intrans. ἐρεύγεται Od. 5, 438; -όμενος Il. 17, 265: (**1 aor. act.** in comp. ἐξ-ερεῦξαι Dio. Hal. 2, 69 Vulg. ἐξ-ερῆσαι *now*): **2 aor.** ἤρῠγον Il. 20, 403; Aristot. Probl. 10, 44; Nic. Alex. 111, may belong to the Attic form ἐρυγγάνω, which see. This verb has the meaning *roar* in the **2 aor.** ἤρυγον, and *late* in the **pres.** 1 Macc. 3, 4: and **fut.** Oseae. 11, 10. Amos 3, 4. 8.

Ἐρεύθω *To make red,* Il. 11, 394; *become red,* Hippocr. 7, 132. 218 (Lit.); Luc. Ner. 7: **fut.** (ἐρεύσω v. r. Il. 18, 329): for which **aor.** ἐρεῦσαι Il. 18, 329: **2 aor. p.** opt. ἐρευθείην, ξυνεξ- Hippocr. 2, 176 (Lit.) **Pres.** ἐρεύθομαι Sapph. 93 (B.); Hippocr. 6, 390; -όμενος Theocr. 17, 127: **imp.** ἠρεύθετο Theocr. 30, 8 (newly found Ziegl. Fritz.), ἐρεύθ- Q. Sm. 1, 226. See ἐρυθαίνω.

Ἐρέφω *To cover,* Poet. Pind. I. 3, 72, and -έπτω: **imp.** ἤρεφον Pind. N. 6, 43 (Herm. Bergk, 4 ed.); Ar. Fr. 54, ἐρ- Pind. Ol. 1, 68, ἔρεπτον Pind. P. 4, 240; Opp. Cyn. 4, 262: **fut.** ἐρέψω Ar. Av. 1110: **aor.** ἤρεψα Dem. 19, 265, ἔρεψ- Il. 24, 450. Od. 23, 193; Pind. Ol. 13, 32; in tmesi Il. 1, 39; imper. ἔρεψον Soph. O. C. 473: **p. p.** late ἤρεπται Philostr. V. Apoll. 1, 25. **Mid.** ἐρέπτομαι *cover oneself,* or *for oneself,* Com. Fr. (Cratin.) 2, 72: **fut.** ἐρέψομαι Eur. Bac. 323, κατ- Ap. Rh. 2, 1073: **aor.** ἠρεψάμην Ap. Rh. 2, 159; Anth. 9, 363, κατ- Ar. Vesp. 1294. **Imp.** ἤρεφον Ar. Fr. 54 (D.), but Pind. ἔρεφον Ol. 1, 68: **aor.** unaugm. in Hom. and Pind. ἔρεψα Il. 1, 39. Od. 23, 193; Ol. 13, 32. ἤρεψα Dem. 19, 265, is the only instance of this verb in classic prose.

'Ερέχθω Epic, *To tear, torture* (ἐρείκω), only **pres. part. act.** ἐρέχθων Od. 5, 83: and **pass.** ἐρεχθομένη Hym. Ap. Pyth. 180; *tossed*, Il. 23, 317.

'Ερέω *To say*, would seem to be used especially in late Epic, ἐρέει **pres.** Nic. Ther. 484, ἐρεῖτε Epist. ad Diognet. 2 (Lindn.); subj. ἐρέω Nic. Ther. 636, ἐρέῃσιν Tzetz. P. H. 750; ἐρεοίην Liban. T. 1, 63; ἐρέειν, ἐξ- Anth. 11, 365: **imp.** ἤρεον Hippocr. 5, 88 (Lit.): **pass.** (εἴρεται Arat. 261.) See εἴρω.

'Ερέω *To ask*, Epic, ἐρέεις Anth. 14, 102, ἐρέουσι, ἐξ- Od. 14, 375; subj. ἐρείομεν for -έωμεν, Il. 1, 62; ἐρέοιμι Od. 11, 229; ἐρέων Il. 7, 128: **fut.** ἐρήσω late, Sopat. Rhet. vol. 8, p. 38 (Walz)?: **mid.** (ἐρέομαι) as **act.** διεξ-ερέεσθε Il. 10, 432; subj. ἐρέωμαι Od. 17, 509; ἐρέοιτο, ἐξ- 24, 238; inf. ἐρέεσθαι 6, 298; Hippocr. 1, 230: **imp.** ἐρέοντο Il. 1, 332: **fut.** ἐρήσομαι Ar. Nub. 1409; -ησόμενος Pax 105. ἐρείομεν Epic 1 pl. subj. for -έωμεν Il. quoted; imper. ἔρειο for ἐρέεο, ἐροῦ, Il. 11, 611.

'Ερητύω (ῠ) *To restrain*, Poet. and unaugm. -τύειν Il. 2, 75; Dor. ἐρᾱτύοι Soph. O. C. 164 (chor.): **imp.** ἐρήτυον Il. 2, 97. Od. 10, 442, iter. ἐρητύεσκε Q. Sm. 12, 370, -εσκον Ap. Rh. 1, 1301: **fut.** ἐρητύσω Ap. Rh. 1, 296; Orph. Lith. 223, κατ- Soph. Ph. 1416: **aor.** ἐρήτῡσα, -εις Il. 1, 192, -ύσαιμεν Ap. Rh. 2, 251; ἐρήτῡσον Eur. Ph. 1260 (trim.); -ύσας Panyas. Fr. 4, 11; iter. ἐρητύσασκε Il. 11, 567; Theocr. 25, 75: **aor. p.** ἐρήτῡθεν Aeol.=-ύθησαν, Il. 2, 211. **Mid.** as **act. imp.** ἐρητύοντο (λαόν) Il. 15, 723.—υ seems naturally short, long before σ, or a syllable long by nature or position, and in the Aeol. **aorist**: Hom. has it always short in ἐρήτυον, -υε, -ύεται. This verb seems not to occur in prose, and only twice in Attic poetry.

'Εριδαίνω (ῐ) *To contend*, Il. 2, 342; Luc. Pisc. 6; Athen. (Demetr. Byz.) 10, 77; imper. ἐρίδαινε Od. 21, 310; -δαινέμεν Od. 1, 79, -δαίνειν Callim. Dian. 262, and ἐριδμαίνω Il. 16, 260; Theocr. 12, 31: **imp.** ἠρῐ́δαινον Babr. 68, ἐρίδ- H. Merc. 313 (Schneidw. Baum.): **aor.** ἐρῐ́δηνα Ap. Rh. 1, 89: **mid.** ἐρῑδαίνομαι as **act.** -όμενος Q. Sm. 5, 105, missed by Lexicogr.: but **aor.** ἐρῑδήσασθαι (ῑ perhaps by arsis) Il. 23, 792, where the form with single δ is best supported (Wolf, Dind. La Roche, ἐριζήσ- however Bekk. 2 ed. with Schol. Vict.)—ἐριδμαίνω means also *to provoke*, and is scarcely used beyond the **pres.** -αίνουσι Theocr. 12, 31, Dor. -αίνοντι (Ziegl.); -αίνωσι Il. 16, 260; -αίνων Ap. Rh. 3, 94, -αίνουσαι Mosch. 2, 69; -αίνειν Q. Sm. 4, 551: **imp.** iter. ἐριδμαίνεσκε Nic. Alex. 407; Q. Sm. 4, 123.

'Ερίζω *To contend*, Od. 18, 38; Pind. N. 8, 22; Ar. Ach. 1114; Her. 5, 49; Pl. Prot. 337, Dor. 3 pl. -ίζοντι Pind. N. 5,

39; -ίζητον Il. 12, 423; -ίζοι Thuc. 5, 79; -ίζων Her. 7, 50; Isocr. 2, 39; ἐρίζειν Soph. El. 467; Ar. Ran. 1105; Dem. 2, 29, Epic -έμεναι Il. 21, 185, -έμεν 23, 404, Dor. ἐρίσδω Theocr. 1, 24. 7, 41: imp. ἤριζον Dem. 9, 11; Babr. 65, ἔρ- Il. 2, 555, iter. ἐρίζεσκον Od. 8, 225; Crates 4 (B.), Dor. ἔρισδεν Theocr. 6, 5, 1 pl. -σδομες 5, 67: fut. ἐρῐσω late? N. T. Matth. 12, 19, ἀντ- Nicet. Eug. 4, 354, δι- App. Civ. 5, 127, but Dor. ἐρίξω Pind. Fr. 189 (Bergk): aor. ἤρῐσα Hes. Th. 928; (Lys.) 2, 42; Luc. Indoct. 4, ἔρῐσα Pind. I. 8 (7), 27; -ίσωσι Od. 18, 277; ἐρίσσειε Il. 3, 223; ἐρίσαι Her. 4, 152; Ael. Fr. 110; -ίσας Her. 8, 55; Xen. Ages. 1, 5, Dor. ἤριξα Tab. Heracl. 2, 26: p. ἤρικα Polyb. 3, 91, συν-επ- Anth. 9, 709: p. p. ἐρήρισμαι as act. Hes. Fr. 219. Mid. ἐρίζομαι act. Il. 5, 172; Pind. Ol. 1, 95; -όμενος I. 5, 4: imp. ἐρίζετο Hes. Th. 534, ἠρίζοντο Aesop 274 (Tauchn. ἤριζον Halm 151): fut. ἐρίσ(σ)ομαι Od. 4, 80, if not aor. subj.: aor. (ἠρισάμην), Epic subj. ἐρίσσεται for -ηται, Od. 4, 80; δι-ερισάμενος Plut. Cat. maj. 15: and in sense p. ἐρήρισμαι Hes. quoted. Vb. ἐριστός Soph. El. 220.—Nicet. Eug. quoted has ῐ in fut. ἀντ-ερίσειν 4, 354.—ἐρίζοιτ' Pl. Lys. 207, is called pass., but why not act. for -οιτε?—ἐρίζοντι 3 pl. Dor. for -ουσι, Pind. N. 5, 39.—ἐρίξω fut. Nonn. 1, 502, has been altered to ἐρίζω by Graefe and Koechly; Eustath., however, Prooem. p. 11 (Schn.) quotes it from Pind. see above.—Rare in Attic poetry: once in Tragedy, thrice or so in Comedy, and confined to pres.: in good prose, it seems not to proceed beyond the aor.: the mid. is poetic.

Ἔρομαι *To ask*, 2 sing. ἔρεαι Hes. Certam. p. 314 (Goettl.), see below, Ion. εἴρομαι, which see: fut. ἐρήσομαι Soph. O. T. 1166; Eur. Or. 507; Ar. Nub. 1409; Com. Fr. (Antiph.) 3, 117; Xen. Oec. 15, 1; Lys. 8, 8; Pl. Prot. 355: 2 aor. ἠρόμην Anacr. 30; Eur. Ion 541; Ar. Pax 670; Thuc. 3, 113; Xen. An. 7, 2, 19; Isocr. 12, 20; Lys. 23, 8; Pl. Leg. 661; ἔρωμαι Od. 8, 133; Soph. Ph. 576; Ar. Nub. 345; Isocr. 12, 182; Pl. Rep. 538; Aeschin. 1, 187; ἐροίμην Od. 1, 135; Antiph. 5, 65; Thuc. 1, 90; Isae. 6, 53; Pl. Prot. 354; ἐροῦ Soph. El. 563; Eur. Or. 763; Ar. Av. 66; Pl. Gorg. 447, Epic ἔρειο Il. 11, 611; ἐρέσθαι Od. 3, 243; Eur. Andr. 602; Ar. Thesm. 135; Xen. Cyr. 8, 2, 15; Pl. Conv. 199; -όμενος Ar. Eq. 574; Thuc. 4, 40; Pl. Crat. 407; Isae. 8, 39. The pres. is very rare, and in most cases doubtful, for which ἐρωτάω, Epic and Ion. εἴρομαι, ἐρέω &c. are used. Scheibe reads pres. ἔρεσθαι Lys. 12, 24, with Ms. X, others aor. ἐρέσθαι.

Ἑρπύζω *To creep*, Poet. Il. 23, 225; Anth. Pal. 7, 22; Opp. Hal. 4, 295: imp. late εἵρπυζον Q. Sm. 13, 93: fut. ἑρπύσω, διεξ- Aristot. Mund. 6, 16 (Bekk.): aor. εἵρπυσα Ar. Vesp. 272; Anth. 12, 20; Babr. 118, usu. in comp. καθ- Ar. Ran. 485, παρ- Eccl. 398, Dor. -υξα Pempel. Stob. 79, 52. Very rare in prose ἑρπύσαντες Diog. Laert. 6, 40; Aretae. Morb. Diut. 2, 79 (ed. Oxon.); παρ-είρπυσεν Dio Cass. Fr. 63 (Bekk.); subj. ἐσ-ερπύσω Luc. D. Mort. 3, 2, ἑρπύσῃ, Ael. N. A. 2, 5 (Jacobs, Herch.), ἐξ- Aristot. H. A. 8, 14; ἐφ-ερπύσας Ael. Epist. 1. The Attics used the aor. only. ἐφερπῡσας Theocr. 22, 15 (Vulg.) with ῡ has been altered to ἐφερποίσας (Kiessl. Mein. Ziegl. Fritzsche, -ούσας Ahr.), ἐφερπῦσαι Ar. Plut. 675. The Greeks used the fut. form ἕρψω, rarely indeed ἑρπύσω, see Aristot. quoted.

Ἕρπω *To creep*, Poet. Il. 17, 447. Od. 18, 131; Pind. I. 4, 40; Aesch. Eum. 39; Soph. Ant. 618; Hippocr. 6, 480. 490; Dor. subj. ἕρπωμες Theocr. 15, 42; ἕρποι Hom. Epigr. 15, 6; Pind. N. 7, 68; ἕρπε Hym. Ven. 156; Aesch. Pr. 810; Eur. Med. 402, ἑρπέτω Ar. Lys. 130; Dor. fem. pt. ἕρποισα, ἐφ- Pind. Fr. 108, augm. ει: imp. εἷρπον Od. 12, 395; Pind. Fr. 57; Soph. O. C. 147; Ar. Fr. 18 (D.), περι- Ael. V. H. 13, 1: fut. rare ἕρψω, ἐφ- Aesch. Eum. 500, Dor. ἑρψῶ Theocr. 5, 45, -οῦμες 18, 40: aor. late εἷρψα Dio Chrys. Ep. p. 622, but ἧρψα, ἐξ- V. T. Ps. 104, 30 (classic εἵρπῠσα, see ἑρπύζω). Mid. ἕρπονται Aretae. 33 (ed. Oxon.), missed by Lexicogr. Vb. ἑρπετόν *creeping*, Ar. Av. 1069. Dor. dat. pl. pt. ἑρπόντεσσι Pind. Ol. 7, 52.

Ἔρρω *To go away, perish* (erro), Aesch. Ag. 419; Soph. El. 57; Eur. Ion 699; Ar. Eq. 527; Xen. Cyr. 6, 1, 3; Pl. Phil. 24; ἔρροι Soph. El. 249; Eur. H. F. 651. Med. 114 (chor.); ἔρρε Il. 8, 164; Ar. Plut. 604, ἐρρέτω Soph. Ph. 1200; ἔρρων Od. 4, 367; Aesch. Pers. 963; Pl. Leg. 677; ἔρρειν Aesch. Eum. 301; Pl. Leg. 677: fut. ἐρρήσω Hom. H. 3, 259; Ar. Lys. 1240. Pax 500: aor. ἤρρησα Ar. Ran. 1192, εἰσ- Eq. 4, ἀν- Com. Fr. (Eup.) 2, 517, εἰσ- Alciphr. 3, 55, and, according to some, ἔρσα, ἀπο- causative *forced away*, Il. 6, 348 &c., see ἀποέρρω: p. ἤρρηκα, εἰσ- Ar. Thesm. 1075. Imper. often in the sense *be gone, go to the mischief*, ἔρρε Il. 8, 164; Soph. O. C. 1383; Ar. Pl. 604, ἐρρέτω Il. 20, 349; Archil. 6 (B.); Soph. Ph. 1200, ἔρρετε Il. 24, 239; Ap. Rh. 3, 562; so opt. ἔρροις Eur. Alc. 734 (trim. Musgr. Monk, Dind. 4 ed. ἔρρων Dind. 5 ed. Kirchh.): and fut. οὐκ ἐρρήσετε Ar. Lys. 1240. Eustath. quotes ἔλλετε=ἔρρετε, from Callim., see Fr. 292.—Scarcely in prose beyond the pres. Xen. Plato quoted: imp. ἤρρον not found, though Elms. suggested περιῄρρεν for περιῄρχετ' Ar. Thesm. 504. The pres. seems to be used as imp. at least joined with it, ἀπέρρει καὶ προσεμειδία Niceph. 7, 23.

Ἐρυγγάνω (ᾰ) *To eruct, disgorge*, Attic for ἐρεύγομαι, Eur. Cycl.

523; Com. Fr. (Cratin.) 2, 43; Ion. and late Attic prose, Hippocr. 6, 618. 8, 384 (Lit.); Luc. Alex. 39: **2 aor.** ἤρῠγον Nic. Alex. 111 (*belched, roared* Il. 20, 403. 404; Theocr. 13, 58), ἐνήρ- Ar. Vesp. 913, κατ- 1151; ἀπ-ερῠγῇ Hippocr. 7, 104 (Lit.); ἐρῠγεῖν Aristot. Probl. 10, 44, ἀπ- 33, 5. **Mid.** ἐρυγγάνεται as act. Hippocr. 6, 616 (Lit.), intrans. *belch*, 6, 538: **fut.** ἐρεύξομαι see ἐρεύγω. **Pass.** ἐρυγγάνεται Hippocr. 6, 536. 618. The sense *roar* seems confined to the aor. but see ἐρεύγομαι. A pres. ἐρυγάω, -υγᾶν occurs late Geop. 17, 17.

Ἐρυθαίνω (ῠ) *To make red*, Poet. and late prose, Sext. Emp. 441 (Bekk.): aor. ἐρῠ́θηνα Ap. Rh. 1, 791. 4, 474; Orph. Arg. 230. **Pass.** ἐρυθαίνομαι *grow red, blush*, Bion 1, 35; Opp. H. 5, 271: **imp.** ἐρυθαίνετο Il. 10, 484. 21, 21; Anth. 12, 8, late ἠρυθ- Eustath. Macr. 3, 85. Rare and late in prose ἐρυθαίνεται Stob. (Arrian) vol. 4, p. 155 (Mein.)

Ἐρυθραίνω *To make red*, Theophr. H. P. 3, 15, 3; Perict. Stob. 85, 19. **Pass.** ἐρυθραίνομαι *to redden, blush*, Hippocr. 5, 636 (Lit.); Xen. Cyr. 1, 4, 4; Aristot. Eth. Nic. 4, 15; Plut. Mor. 894: **p.** ἠρυθρασμένη Dio Cass. 51, 12.

Ἐρυθριάω *To become red, to blush*, Hippocr. 7, 76 (Lit.); Com. Fr. (Antiph.) 3, 152; Pl. Lys. 204, Epic 3 pl. -ιόωσι Opp. Hal. 3, 25; -ιῶν Pl. Rep. 350; Com. Fr. (Men.) 4, 178, Epic -όων Musae. 161; -ιᾶν Aeschin. 1, 105; Com. Fr. (Men.) 4, 273; Luc. V. A. 10: **imp.** ἠρυθρίων Luc. Laps. 1; Aristaen. 1 13: **fut.** (-ᾱ́σω): **aor.** ἠρυθρίᾱσε Pl. Lys. 204. (Riv.) 134; Luc. Philops. 29; -άσειε Dem. 18, 128; -άσας Pl. Prot. 312; Xen. Oec. 8, 1; -ᾶσαι, ἀπ- Ar. Nub. 1216: p. in adv. ἀπ-ηρυθριακότως Com. Fr. (Apollod.) 4, 454. This verb in *simple* proceeds not beyond the aor. and is almost confined to Comedy and Attic prose.

Ἐρῡκᾰνάω *To restrain*, 3 pl. -ανόωσι Od. 1, 199 (Vulg. Dind. Ameis, La Roche); -όωσα Q. Sm. 12, 205, and ἐρῡκᾰ́νω both Epic, imper. ἐρύκανε, κατ- Il. 24, 218: **imp.** ἐρύκᾰνε Od. 10, 429, κατ- Orph. Arg. 650 (Voss. Schneid. -ύκακον Vulg.) Bekker, in his 2nd edit. of the Od. (1858), has expelled ἐρυκανόωσι 1, 199, from the text—and Düntzer approves. If he is right, the *pure* form is deprived of *classical* support.

Ἐρύκω (ῡ) *To hold back, impede*, usu. Poet. and Ion. Il. 10, 161; Hes. Th. 616; Emped. 23; Pind. Nem. 4, 33; Soph. Tr. 121; Eur. H. F. 317; Her. 5, 15 &c.; in classic Attic prose, only Xen. An. 3, 1, 25; Arist. H. An. 9, 37, 11; Polyb. Fr. incert. 111 (Bekk.); Dio. Hal. 8, 85, ἀπ- Xen. Mem. 2, 9, 2. Oec. 5, 6; **imper.** ἔρῡκε Il. 18, 126, -ετον Pind. Ol. 10 (11), 5; Epic. inf. ἐρυκέμεν Il. 21, 7: **imp.** ἔρῡκον Il. 16, 369; Emped

177, ἐξήρ- Soph. Ph. 423: **fut.** ἐρύξω Il. 21, 62. Od. 8, 317: **aor.** ἤρυξα Aesch. Sept. 1075, ἀπ- Xen. An. 5, 8, 25, ἔρυξα Il. 3, 113. Od. 17, 515; Epic subj. -ξομεν Il. 15, 297: **2 aor.** ἠρύκᾰκον Il. 5, 321, ἐρύκ- 15, 450; opt. ἐρῡκάκοι 7, 342; imper. ἐρύκακε 13, 751; ἐρῡκακέειν 5, 262 (rarely unredupl. and ῠ, ἐρύκοις Nic. Alex. 536, but ἐρύγοι Ms. P. Otto Schneid.), compare ἐνίπτω, **2 aor.** ἠνίπᾰπον. **Mid.** ἐρύκομαι *to hold oneself back*, intrans. Il. 23, 443. Od. 17, 17, ἀπ-ερύκου Soph. O. C. 169, -ύκεο Nic. Al. 608, trans. as **act.** Il. 12, 285, which some hold **passive**, but ἀπ-ερύκομαι **mid.** Theogn. 1207 (Vulg.) has been altered from the best Mss. to ἀπ-ερύκομεν. **Pass.** ἐρύκομαι Il. 12, 285, see above. Od. 4, 466; Soph. Ph. 1153; ἐρυκόμενοι Her. 9, 49. Rare in Attic prose, see above; never in Comedy: **fut.** and **2 aor.** Epic.

'Ερύω (ῠ) *To draw*, Epic Il. 22, 493; Mosch. 2, 83, rarely augm.: **imp.** ἔρῠον Il. 12, 258, ἤρ- Hes. Sc. 301, εἴρ- Mosch. 2, 14. 127, iter. ἐρύεσκε Nonn. 43, 50: **fut.** Ion. ἐρύω Il. 11, 454. 15, 351. 22, 67 (best Mss. Bekk. Spitzn. Dind.) where some take it as **pres.** for **fut.**, others adopt the full form ἐρύσω (Barnes, Clarke, Bothe), which occurs Opp. Hal. 5, 375; Nonn. 21, 268, ἐρύσσω Orph. Lith. 35; Nonn. 23, 298: **aor.** εἴρῠσα Od. 2, 389, Il. 16, 863, -υσσα 3, 373, ἔρῠσα Il. 5, 573, Od. 22, 193, ἔρυσσα Od. 11, 2, προ- Il. 1, 308, iter. ἐρύσασκε, ἐξ- 10, 490; subj. ἐρύσσῃς Il. 5, 110, ἐρύσῃ 17, 230, -ύσσῃ 5, 110, ἐρύσσομεν for -ωμεν, Il. 14, 76. 17, 635, ἐρύσωσι Hippocr. 7, 16 (Lit.) should perhaps be εἰρύσ- (v. r. εἰρ-, and εἴρ- six lines above, but see **aor. pass.**), -ύσσωσι Od. 17, 479; opt. ἐρύσαιμι Il. 8, 21; ἐρύσας 5, 836. 23, 21, Dor. -ύσαις Pind. N. 7, 67, -ύσσας Ap. Rh. 3, 913; Opp. Hal. 1, 265; ἐρύσαι Il. 17, 419, -ύσσαι 8, 23: **p.** εἴρυσται, κατ- Od. 8, 151; εἰρύσθαι, κατ- 14, 332, see below: aor. ἐρυσθείς Hippocr. 5, 234; παρ-ειρύσθη 3, 26 (Lit.) **Mid.** ἐρύομαι *to draw to oneself, protect, guard,* **imp.** ἐρύετο Il. 6, 403, but ἐρῡ́οντο 17, 277, ἠρυ- Philostr. Apoll. 4, 162: **fut.** ἐρῡ́σομαι, Epic -ύσσομαι Il. 10, 44. Od. 21, 125, and -ῡ́ομαι, inf. ἐρῡ́εσθαι Il. 9, 248. 14, 422: **aor.** ἐρῡ́σαντο Il. 1, 466. 7, 318; Hes. Fr. 234, but ἐρύσατο Od. 14, 279 (Wolf, Bekk. Dind. La R.). Il. 20, 450 (Bekk. 2 ed. La R.), ἐρύσσ- Il. 22, 367 (Wolf, Bekk. Dind. La R.). 20, 450 (Wolf, Dind.). Od. 14, 279 (Rost, Kühner); subj. ἐρῡ́σηται Ap. Rh. 1, 1204; opt. ἐρῡ́σαιο Il. 5, 456, 3 pl. ἐρυσαίατο 5, 298; ἐρῡ́σασθαι 22, 351, ἐρύσσ- 18, 174; ἐρυσσάμενος Il. 1, 190; Hes. Sc. 457; Pind. N. 9, 23: **p. p.** as **mid.** ἔρῡται *guards, watches,* Ap. Rh. 2, 1208; ἔρυσθαι Od. 5, 484. 9, 194 &c.; Mosch. 2, 73: **plp.** ἠρῡ́μην, ἔρῡσο Il. 22, 507, ἔρῡτο 4, 138. 23, 819; Hes. Sc. 415; Ap. Rh. 3, 1305; as aor. Il. 5, 23. 13, 555, ἔρυντο Ap. Rh. 1, 1083; Theocr. 25, 76, *keep back, ward off,* ἔρῦτο Il. 5, 538. 17, 518, εἴρῦτο Hes. Sc. 138, but ἔρὔτο pass. *was drawn in, kept,* Hes. Th. 304. Vb. ἐρυστός Soph. Aj. 730. Those forms which we have ranked as perf. and plp. may be, and indeed generally are, referred to the pres. and imp. contracted: as pres. ἔρῦται for ἐρύεται, ἔρυσθαι for ἐρύεσθαι: imp. ἔρῦσο for ἐρύεσο, ἔρῦτο for ἐρύετο &c. used sometimes as aor.; ἔρὔτο Hes. quoted, may on this view follow the analogy of verbs in μι, ἐδείκνὔτο &c. A rare if not the only instance of ῡ in the act. is τόξον ἐρύ̄ων *drawing*, Tzetz. Hom. 196. Buttmann has examined with his usual ability the *meanings* and *quantity* of ἐρύω, εἰρύω Lexil. p. 303; but, after all, we are inclined to think that the *quantity* of υ depends more on *place* in the verse than on *shades of meaning.* For the forms with ει, see εἰρύω.

Ἐρχατάω (ἔρχατος, ἔργω) *To shut in,* Epic, and only imp. pass. ἐρχατόωντο Od. 14, 15.

Ἔρχομαι *To go, come,* Il. 13, 256; Hes. Th. 751; Pind. N. 7, 69; Aesch. Supp. 254; Soph. Ph. 48; Ar. Thesm. 485; Her. 7, 102; Antiph. 6, 20; Thuc. 6, 36; Xen. Cyr. 1, 6, 4. Hell. 3, 2, 6; Pl. Rep. 424; Aeschin. 3, 19; Dem. 17, 10, Epic 2 sing. ἔρχεαι Il. 10, 385; Theogn. 1374, in Attic *indic.* chiefly; subj. rare ἔρχηται Il. 10, 185; Callim. Fr. 67; Hippocr. 7, 598 (Lit.); Pausan. 9, 39, 10, ἔρχησθον Od. 16, 170, ἐρχώμεθα Hierocl. 181 (Eberh.), ἔρχωνται Himer. Or. 15, 3, ἐξ- Hippocr. 8, 508 (Ms. C. Lit.), προσ- Isocr. Fr. 3, 7 (Bens.), ἐπ- Maneth. 6, 269, δι-έρχωμαι N. T. Joh. 4, 15 (Vat.); opt. rare ἔρχοιτο, ἐξ- Xen. Cyr. 4, 1, 1; imper. especially Epic ἔρχεο Il. 15, 54, ἔρχευ 23, 893; Theogn. 220 (Ms. A. Bergk, ἔρχου Vulg.); and late N. T. Luc. 7, 8. Rev. 6, 5 &c. ἔρχεσθον Il. 1, 322; Ar. Ach. 1144 (chor.), ἔρχεσθε Il. 9, 649; and late N. T. Joh. 1, 40; ἔρχεσθαι Il. 15, 161; Aesch. Ag. 917 (trimet.); Hippocr. 8, 546. Epist. 9, 418; Aristot. Meteor. 3, 3, 5; Plut. Philop. 2, ἀπ- Hippocr. 8, 42 (Lit.), ὑπ- Andoc. 4, 21; Dem. 23, 8, ξυν- (Pl.) Demod. 381; ἐρχόμενος Il. 3, 22. Od. 21, 39; Pind. P. 5, 14; Soph. Tr. 850 (chor.); Thuc. 6, 3 (some Mss. but ἐχόμ- Bekk. Popp. Krüg.); Pl. Conv. 174; Aristot. Mirab. 31; Plut. Mor. 518; Luc. Abdic. 23; Hierocl. 6, ἐπ- Aesch. Pr. 98 (chor.); Ar. Nub. 311 (chor.), διεξ- Hippocr. 2, 138, ἐπεξ- Antiph. 2, α, 2, ὑπ- Xen. Rep. Ath. 2, 14; Pl. Crit. 53, ἀπ- Lys. 16, 19 (Mss. Bekk. περι- Emper. Scheibe, Rauch. Westerm.), παρ- Od. 16, 357; Xen. An. 2, 4, 25 (Dind.): imp. ἠρχόμην rare and usu. late in *simple,* Hippocr. 5, 426. 9, 328 (Lit.); Arat. 102. 118; Babr. 46, 4; Luc. Jud. Voc. 4; Alciphr. 1, 22; Paus. 5, 8, 2; Strab. 3, 2, 6;

Argum. to Isocr. 8; often in Sept. Gen. 48, 7. Ezech. 9, 2; and N. T. Marc. 1, 45. Act. 9, 17 &c. (ἠρχόμεθα Pl. Leg. 685, is imp. of ἄρχομαι, see Conv. 210. Alcib. (1), 121, and ἠρχ- or προ-ηρχ- Xen. An. 1, 8, 17), δι- Pind. Ol. 9, 93, περι- Ar. Thesm. 504 (περι-ῄρρεν Elms. -έτρεχ' Hamak. Meineke), ἐπ- Thuc. 4, 120, προσ- 4, 121, ἀν- Hippocr. 5, 402, ὑπεξ- 5, 414 (Lit.) see below, more freq. later ἐξ- Aristot. de Plant. 2, 2, 4 (Bekk.), παρ- Alciphr. Fr. 6, 15 (Mein.), προ- Athen. 6, 108, περι- Ael. N. A. 2, 11, συν-Plut. Lycurg. 12. 31. Eum. 7, ἐπαν- Cim. 17. Sert. 25; Paus. 7, 26; Apollod. 2, 8, 3; D. Laert. 6, 59: fut. ἐλεύσομαι (ἐλεύθω obsol.) Il. 13, 753. Od. 16, 8; Ap. Rh. 3, 177; Ion. prose, Her. 6, 9. 8, 130; Hippocr. 7, 498. 612. 8, 38. 74 (Lit.), ἐξ- Her. 6, 106. 9, 37, κατ- 5, 125; occasionally in Attic poetry, Aesch. Pr. 854. Supp. 522; Soph. O. C. 1206. Tr. 595; not in Comedy; scarcely in *classic* Attic prose Lys. 22, 11 (Bekk. B. Saupp. Scheibe) doubted by Elms. Cobet, Frohberger; freq. later, Dio. Hal. 3, 15. 5, 31. 6, 65. 7, 68; App. Civ. 1, 89. 5, 123; Pseud-Callisth. 2, 14; Geop. 14, 3, εἰσ- Plut. Lucull. 16, ἐξ- Polyb. 4, 9, προσ- 21, 11, κατ- Arr. An. 6, 12, μετ- Luc. D. Mort. 5, 2. 18, 2 &c. Nav. 38, προ- Aristot. Plant. 2, 6, 5; Luc. D. Mort. 6, 4, ἐπ- Anach. 38, for which the earlier Attics generally use εἶμι, ἥξω, ἀφίξομαι; indeed the only exception in *classic Attic prose* is Lysias quoted, and here Elmsley thought it corrupt, as he did περιηρχόμην Ar. Thesm. 504. Elmsley was fine sometimes, we think to fastidiousness. His only ground of exception is *rareness in Attic*. But if we may believe the Mss. Lysias sometimes indulged himself with a *rarity*. Is it not as easy and as safe to suppose that he used a poetic or Ionic word as that a transcriber foisted it into the text? And why should Aristophanes scruple to use, if it so pleased him, the imperfect, which Thucydides had used before him?: **1** aor. rare and late, ἤλῠθα (Hes. Th. 660, is a false reading) Nonn. 37, 424, ἐπ-ήλυθα Anth. 14, 44, ἦλθα, ἀπ- N. T. Rev. 10, 9 (Mss. Lachm. Tisch.), ἤλθατε Matth. 25, 36, ἐξ- 26, 55, ἦλθαν Act. 12, 10, εἰσ- V. T. 2 Chron. 29, 17, προσ- N. T. Matth. 9, 28 (Vat.); imper. ἐλθάτω V. T. Esth. 5, 4, ἔλθατε Prov. 9, 5, δι- Amos 6, 2: **2** p. ἐλήλυθα Attic, Aesch. Pr. 943; Soph. O. C. 366. Ph. 141; Eur. Phoen. 286; Ar. Nub. 238; Her. 8, 68; Xen. Cyr. 1, 2, 15; Pl. Prot. 317. Leg. 900. Rep. 445; Lycurg. 33; Dem. 38, 3 (but ἐπ- Od. 4, 268), παρ- Thuc. 4, 86, 1 pl. ἐληλύθαμεν Isocr. 14, 51; Pl. Leg. 683, syncop. ἐλήλυμεν Com. Fr. (Cratin.) 2, 153; Achae. Fr. 22, ἐλήλυτε ibid. (Wagn.), -λύθασι Isocr. 13, 3. 14, 19; subj. ἐληλύθῃ, ὑπ- Hippocr. 2, 266 (Lit.); opt. rare ἐληλυθοίης, προ- Xen. Cyr. 2, 4, 17: **plp.** ἐληλύθειν Eupol. ap. Ar. Eq. 1306 (εἰλ- Mein.

Dind. 5 ed.), προσ- Thuc. 6, 65, διεξ- Dem. 21, 84, Ionic ἐληλύθεε Her. 5, 98. 8, 114, Epic **perf.** ἐλήλουθα, -ουθώς Il. 15, 81, and εἰλήλουθα 5, 204. 15, 131; Theocr. 25, 35, 1 pl. syncop. εἰλήλουθμεν Il. 9, 49. Od. 3, 81; -λουθώς 19, 28. 20, 360: **plp.** 3 sing. εἰληλούθει Il. 4, 520. 5, 44. 17, 350: **2 aor.** ἤλῠθον Epic and Pind. Il. 1, 152. 10, 28; Hes. Th. 668; Theogn. 711; Pind. N. 10, 79. P. 3, 99; Theocr. 12, 1. 22, 183; also Attic poet. especially in chor. Soph. Aj. 234; Eur. Or. 813. Phoen. 823. An. 302. Rhes. 263; Ar. Av. 952 (rare in trimeter, Eur. El. 598. Tr. 374. Rhes. 660), syncop. ἦλθον Il. 1, 207. Od. 4, 82; Hes. Th. 176; Pind. Ol. 1, 44. N. 6, 12; Aesch. Eum. 251; Soph. O. R. 447. El. 1235; Eur. Or. 1400. Hec. 506; Ar. Eccl. 381; always in *prose*, Her. 2, 115; Antiph. 1, 15; Thuc. 2, 56. 6, 82; Pl. Rep. 329; Lys. 12, 53; Isocr. 17, 42; subj. ἔλθω Il. 22, 113; Soph. O. C. 310; Ar. Pax 122; Her. 1, 209; Pl. Rep. 344, ἔλθῃσι Il. 5, 132; Hes. Fr. 80; opt. ἔλθοιμι Il. 5, 301. Od. 11, 501; Soph. Tr. 1189; Ar. Eq. 502; Antiph. 5, 34; Thuc. 6, 37; ἐλθέ Il. 23, 770; Soph. Ph. 1190; Eur. Cycl. 602; Ar. Ach. 673; Pl. Charm. 155; ἐλθών Il. 14, 8; Soph. O. C. 79; Ar. Nub. 89; Her. 2, 121; Thuc. 4, 83; Pl. Rep. 572, Dor. dat. pl. ἐλθόντεσσι Pind. P. 4, 30; ἐλθεῖν Il. 7, 160; Soph. O. R. 307; Ar. Av. 28; Her. 1, 27. 2, 32; Thuc. 2, 5, Epic ἐλθέμεναι Il. 1, 151, ἐλθέμεν 15, 146, Doric ἦνθον (not in Pind.) Epicharm. 126 (Ahrens); Callim. Lav. Pal. 8. Cer. 27; Theocr. 2, 118. 16, 9, Lacon. ἦλσον, ἔλσῃ Ar. Lys. 105; ἔλσοιμι 118; ἐλσών 1081; **aor. mid.** ἐλθοίμην rare and late, Batr. 179 (Mss. ἐλθυίην Franke, Baumeist. ἐρχοίμην Wolf): **1 aor. mid.** ἀπ-ελεύσασθαι occurs Charit. 1, 3 (D'Orville, but now -ελεύσεσθαι Lobeck, Hercher), ὑπ-ελεύσηται however is still in Hippocr. 2, 494 (Lit.) for which we would suggest ὑπολύσηται. But fut. ὑπε-λεύσεται is perhaps the true reading (Mss. C D, Erm. 1, 353.) **Vb.** μετ-ελευστέος Luc. Fugit. 22, ὑπ-ελθετέον Strab. 13, 3, 6 (Kram.)

Pres. ἔρχομαι is common in every class of writers, but for the *moods* ἔρχωμαι, ἐρχοίμην &c., and **imp.** ἠρχόμην the Attics usually employ ἴω, ἴοιμι, ἴθι, ἰών, ἰέναι: imp. ᾖα. More particularly, ἔρχωμαι rare, ἔρχεο, (-χου) -χευ often in Epic, we have not noticed in Attic; ἐρχοίμην rare in Attic, we have not seen or failed to note in Epic; ἐρχόμενος, ἔρχεσθαι often in Epic, occasionally in Attic: ἤλυθον and syncop. ἦλθον never drop the augment; the former confined to Indic. and almost always to the dactylic forms ἤλυθον, -ες, -ε; ἠλύθομεν however is the Mss. reading Hes. Th. 660 (Goettl.) not ἠλύθαμεν, which was first introduced into the text by Pasor, and adopted by some late editors. ἦνθον for ἦλθον seems to have been but partially used by the Dorians: Pind. never has it, and Timocr. Rhod. has ἐλθεῖν 1, 4 (Ahr.), ἦλθε Chilidonism. Puer. Rhod. 1. 3 pl. ἤλθοσαν for ἦλθον is a late form, often in Septuag.; Pseud.-Callisth. 2, 35: **2 perf.** in pl. is occasionally syncopated, ἐλήλυμεν, -λυτε for -ύθαμεν -ύθατε, Com. Fr. (Cratin.) 2, 153; Trag. Fr. (Achae.) 22. **Perf. pass.** διεληλύσθαι Xen. Cyr. 1, 4, 28 (old edit.) has been displaced by διηνύσθαι from Ms. Guelf.; another form however μετῆλθαι occurs in Peyron. Papyr. Aegypt. 1, p. 34. **Fut. pass.** ἐλευθησόμενα occurs late Paroem. Apostol. Cent. 18, 22.

For ἤρχετο, ἀν-ήρχετο, ὑπεξ-ήρχετο Hippocr. (Lit.) quoted, or Epidem. 7, Sect. 35. 45. 59, Ermerins reads ᾔει, ἀνῄει, ὑπεξῄει, 'because,' says he, 'the former was not in use when this book was written.' We think this a mistake, for διήρχετο is in Pind. Ol. 9, 93, and has never, as far as we know, been called in question. In Hippocr. there is no *variant* for ἤρχετο, ἀνήρχετο; for ὑπεξήρχετο, however, occurs ὑπεξέειν (Ms. C. for -ῄειν). But a question may arise whether this may not have been adopted by the Scribe merely because ἐξιέναι occurs two lines before. In Aristoph. Thesm. 504, Bekk. and Dind. retain περιήρχετ', Elms. suggested -ῄει or -ῆρρεν, Hamaker περιέτρεχ' approved by Bergk and adopted by Meineke; περιέρρει (περιρρέω) if suitable, seems fully as near the *draft*.

Ἐρωέω *To flow, move*, also *restrain, check*, Epic, -ωεῖ Od. 12, 75; imper. -ώει Il. 2, 179: **fut.** ἐρωήσω Il. 1, 303. 24, 101; Theocr. 22, 174; Q. Smyrn. 3, 520: **aor.** ἠρώησα Il. 23, 433; Callim. Del. 133; Theocr. 13, 74, but always ὑπ-ερώ- Il. 8, 122. 314; ἐρωήσαιτε *drive back*, Il. 13, 57 (so **fut.** ἐρωήσω Theocr. 22, 174: **aor.** ἠρώησε *forsook*, 13, 74, quoted).

Ἐρωτάω *To enquire*, Soph. El. 317; Antiph. 5, 64; Thuc. 1, 5; Lys. 12, 12: **imp.** ἠρώτων Hippocr. 5, 370; Antiph. 1, 16; Thuc. 7, 10 (Vulg. Göll.). 8, 92; Lys. 1, 25: **fut.** -ήσω Hippocr. 1, 606; Pl. Rep. 350; Isae. 11, 4: **aor.** ἠρώτησα Xen. Cyr. 4, 5, 21; -ήσας Soph. Tr. 403; Hippocr. 5, 370: **p.** ἠρώτηκα Pl. Phil. 18 &c. reg.—Epic and Ion. **εἰρωτάω** Od. 17, 138; Her. 3, 14: **imp.** εἰρώτα Od. 15, 423 (Bekk. Dind. La Roche); Her. 1, 88, 3 pl. εἰρώτεον 4, 145, -τευν 1, 158; without augm. but ἠρώτα Od. quoted (Wolf), and ἀν-ηρώτων Od. 4, 251 (Wolf, Bekk. Dind. La Roche), ἀν-ειρώτ- (Ameis, Kayser, Hentze with Eustath.), -ηρώτευν Theocr. 1, 81. Hom. has always the pres. form with ει, Her. always, except ἐρωτεώμενον 1, 86 (Vulg. Gaisf.), but εἰρωτ- (Bekk. Lhardy, Dind. Stein).

(**Ἐσθέω**) *To clothe*, perhaps only **perf.** and **plp. pass.** ἐσθημένος Her. 3, 129. 6, 112 (ἠσθ- Stein), ἠσθημένος Eur. Hel. 1539;

Ael. V. H. 9, 3; ἠσθῆσθαι Ael. H. A. 16, 34: pl. ἤσθητο Ael. V. H. 12, 32.

Ἐσθίω *To eat*, Il. 23, 182; Hipponax 85; Aesch. Fr. 246 (D.); Ar. Pax 1167; Her. 2, 35. 68; Pl. Theaet. 166; imper. ἔσθιε Od. 14, 80; ἐσθίειν Simon. Am. 7, 24; Soph. Fr. 596 (D.); Hippocr. 1, 584 (Lit.), Ep. -ιέμεν Od. 21, 69; ἐσθίων Her. 1, 133, also a pres. ἔσθω Il. 24, 415; Alcm. 33 (B. 3 ed.); Aesch. Ag. 1597; Com. Poet in Athen. 13, 596; Com. Fr. (Philip.) 4, 469; ἔσθειν Od. 5, 197, Ep. -θέμεναι Il. 24, 213. Od. 10, 373; rare and late in prose, Plut. Mor. 101. 829; Aretae. Morb. Diut. 2, 77 (ed. Oxon.); V. T. Lev. 17, 10; Apocr. Sir. 20, 16, also ἔδω Il. 5, 341. Od. 14, 81; Hes. Th. 640; Com. Fr. (Alcae.) 2, 832. (Eub.) 3, 219, Dor. 3 pl. ἔδοντι Theocr. 5, 128; in Trag. Eur. ἔδων Cycl. 245; Ion. and late prose, and rare, Hippocr. 1, 580 (Lit.); Luc. Rhet. 11: imp. ἤσθιον Od. 20, 19; Hes. Op. 147; Timocr. 1, 12 (B.); Eur. Cycl. 233; Ar. Eq. 606; Hippocr. 5, 222; Thuc. 3, 49; Xen. Ages. 9, 3, ἦσθον Od. 6, 249. 7, 177; Com. Fr. (Archip.) 2, 721 if sound, ἔδον Od. 23, 9, iter. ἔδεσκον Il. 22, 501: fut. ἔδομαι Il. 18, 271. 22. 509. Od. 9, 369; Ar. Nub. 121. Pax 1356; Pl. Rep. 373. Prot. 334; Luc. D. Deor. 4, 3 (ἐδοῦμαι? see below), and late φᾰγοῦμαι, if correct, V. T. Gen. 3, 2, and φάγομαι, -εσαι V. T. Gen. 3, 3; Esai. 1, 19; Or. Sib. 3, 790; 2 Macc. 7, 7; N. T. Luc. 17, 8; as pres. Apocr. Sir. 36, 23: p. ἐδήδοκα Ar. Eq. 362; Com. Fr. (Alex.) 3, 462; Xen. An. 4, 8, 20, ἀπ- Ar. Ran. 984, κατ- Aeschin. 1, 42: plp. ἐδηδόκειν Luc. Gall. 4: p. p. ἐδήδεσμαι, κατ- Pl. Phaed. 110; Com. Fr. (Antiph.) 3, 87, Epic ἐδήδομαι Od. 22, 56, but κατ-εδήδοται Dio. Hal. 1, 55 (Vulg. -εδήδεσται Kiessl.): aor. ἠδέσθην Hippocr. 1, 686 (K.); Aristot. Probl. 13, 6, κατ- Com. Fr. (Plat.) 2, 627, ἀπ- 2, 662: 2 p. Epic, ἔδηδα, -δώς Il. 17, 542, -δυῖα Hom. H. 3, 560: 2 aor. ἔφᾰγον Od. 15, 373; Ar. Thesm. 616; Xen. An. 4, 8, 20, φάγες Od. 9, 347, φάγε in tmesi Il. 2, 326 (Bekk.), φάγον Pind. Ol. 1, 51; subj. φάγῃ Soph. Fr. 149; Ar. Vesp. 194; Hippocr. 2, 264 (Lit.), -γῃσι Od. 8, 477; φάγοιμι Ar. Vesp. 511; Pl. Phaed. 81; imper. φάγε Ar. Vesp. 611; φαγεῖν Eur. Cycl. 336; Pl. Leg. 831, -έειν Od. 16, 429; Her. 2, 141 (-εῖν Stein, Abicht); Hippocr. 8, 610 (Lit.), φαγέμεν Od. 16, 143. 18, 3; φαγών Od. 4, 33; Simon. C. 169; Aesch. Supp. 226; Soph. Fr. 777 (D.); Ar. Eq. 806; Pl. Prot. 314. **Mid.** ἐσθίομαι as act. Hippocr. 5, 160 (Lit.); Theophr. H. P. 1, 6, 11, and late φάγομαι Apocr. Sir. 36, 23: fut. ἔδομαι see above: aor. late ἠδεσάμην, κατ-εδέσηται Galen 5, 752. ἐσθίομαι pass. is rare and confined to Epic and late prose, ἐσθίεται Od. 4, 318; -ίεσθαι Theophr. H. P. 1, 12, 4; Luc. Cyn. 11. **Vb.** ἐδεστός Soph.

Ant. 206, -έος Pl. Crit. 47.—φαγέω seems to have existed, hence opt. φαγέοις Pseud.-Phocyl. 157 (Vulg. φάγοις Vat. Mut. διάγοις Bergk): **fut.** φαγήσετε Liban. 3, 124, 6.—ἔδμεναι Epic inf. **pres.** for ἐδέμεναι, Od. 14, 42. In late recensions the **fut.** form ἐδοῦμαι has given way to ἔδομαι, κατέδεται Com. Fr. 3, 12. 600 (Athen. 338. 339), προσκατέδει Com. Fr. 3, 462 (Athen. 516, Dind.), κατεδοῦνται still, however, Dio. Hal. 1, 55 (Vulg. -δονται Kiessl.) φαγούμεθα also (Gen. 3, 2) is rendered doubtful, by the Alexandrian Ms. presenting φαγόμ-, and φάγεσθε occurring in the following verse. ἔσθω and ἐσθίω seem confined to **pres.** and **imp.**: of (φάγω) the **2 aor.** ἔφαγον alone is classic.

Ἔσπομαι *To say*, late Or. Sib. 2, 4. See imper. of (εἴπω) ἔπω.

Ἕσπομαι, see ἕπω.

Ἑσσόομαι, -οῦμαι (ἥσσων), *To be less, inferior, overcome*, Ion. unaugm. Her. 3, 106: **imp.** ἑσσούμην 1, 67. 7, 166. 8, 75: **p. p.** ἕσσωμαι 7, 10; -ωμένος 7, 9: **aor.** ἑσσώθην 2, 169. 3, 83; subj. -σωθέωμεν 4, 97. See ἡσσάω, ἡττ-.

Ἔσσυο, see σεύω.

Ἑστήκω, στήκω *To stand*, **pres.** rare and late, Posidip. Athen. 10, 4, στήκει N. T. Rom. 14, 4; στήκῃ, ἐν- Aretae. Morb. Ac. 2, 121 (ed. Oxon.): **fut.** ἑστήξω (Hom.) Epigr. 15, 14; Ar. Lys. 634; Pl. Conv. 220; Dem. 20, 37, καθ- Thuc. 3, 37, ἀφ- Xen. An. 2, 4, 5; Pl. Rep. 587: and -ήξομαι Eur. I. A. 675 (Mss. Vulg. Herm. Kirchh. Nauck); Com. Fr. (Heges.) 4, 480; Xen. Cyr. 6, 2, 17 (Vulg. Popp. &c., but **act.** ἑστήξει Dind. *now*, Saupp.). Ven. 10, 9 (Vulg. Dind. but **act.** -ξει Saupp.) **Pres. part.** συνεστηκουσῶν is the vulgar reading Hippocr. 1, 543 (Kühn), but Galen quoting the passage has **perf.** συνεστηκυιῶν adopted by Littré 2, 44. At Eur. I. A. 675, Elms. and W. Dind. read **fut. act.** ἑστήξεις for **mid.** ἑστήξῃ, or -ει of the Mss., and Lud. Dind. in his last edition of Xen. reads **act.** ἑστήξει for **mid.** ἑστήξεται, Cyr. 6, 2, 17; but retains **mid.** Ven. 10, 9. There is no doubt that the preponderance of authority is in favour of ἑστήξω as the earlier and more frequent form: at the same time, we think it not unlikely that the other might co-exist.

Ἑστιάω Ion. ἱστ- *To entertain*, Eur. Alc. 765; Pl. Conv. 175; Isae. 3, 80. 8, 20; Her. 2, 100 (Bekk. Gaisf.), ἱστ- (Dind. Stein): **imp.** εἱστίων Lys. 19, 27; Pl. Phaedr. 227, Ion. ἱστ- Her. 7, 135 (Bekk.): **fut.** ἑστιάσω Com. Fr. (Antiph.) 3, 36; (Luc.) Dem. enc. 26: **aor.** εἱστίᾱσα Xen. Cyr. 1, 3, 10; Isae. 8, 18; ἑστιᾶσαι Ar. Nub. 1212; Antiph. 1, 16: **p.** εἱστίᾱκα Pl. Gorg. 518; Dem. 21, 156: **p. p.** εἱστίᾱμαι Pl. Rep. 354, Ion. ἱστίημαι Her. 5, 20 (Bekk. Stein): **aor.** εἱστιάθην Pl. Phaedr. 247, συν- Dem. 19, 190. **Mid.** ἑστιάομαι intrans. *to feast*, Xen. Conv. 2, 3; Isae. 9, 21:

imp. εἱστιώμην Ar. Nub. 1354; Antiph. 1, 26; Dem. 19, 128: fut. ἑστιάσομαι, Pl. Theaet. 178; Luc. Conv. 2; later as pass. Aristid. 13, 124 (D.): and late fut. p. -αθήσομαι Schol. Ar. Ach. 977: also late aor. m. ἑστιάσασθαι Sext. Emp. 327, 28. In Her. Dind. and Bred. write uniformly ἱστ-, Gaisf. never, Bekk. and Lhardy write pres. ἑστ-, but augmented tenses ἱστ-.

Ἐσχατάω, or -όω *To be at the extremity*, Epic and only part. -όων Il. 10, 206; Theocr. 7, 77, -όωσα Il. 2, 508.

Ἐτάζω, see ἐξετάζω.

Ἑτοιμάζω *To prepare*, Eur. Supp. 454; Her. 6, 95; Thuc. 6, 34: imp. ἡτ- 6, 88: fut. -άσω 4, 46; C. Fr. (Antiph.) 3, 83 &c. reg. and complete: aor. ἑτοιμασάτω Il. 19, 197: p. p. ἡτοίμασμαι Thuc. 6, 64. 7, 62; and as mid. Xen. Cyr. 3, 3, 5; Dem. 23, 209; Diod. Sic. 1, 72 (Vulg. παρεσκεύασμ- Bekk. Dind.): pres. mid. -άζεται Thuc. 6, 17; imper. -άζεσθε Her. 9, 45: imp. ἡτοιμ- Thuc. 4, 77. 7, 31, ἑτοιμ-, προ- Her. 7, 22: aor. ἡτοιμασάμην Xen. Apol. 8, Ion. ἑτοιμάσαντο Od. 13, 184, προ-ετοιμάσατο Her. 8, 24; opt. ἑτοιμάσαιντο Thuc. 1, 58, poet. -ασσαίατο Il. 10, 571; -άσασθαι Thuc. 6, 22; -σάμενος Her. 8, 24.

Εὔαδε, see ἁνδάνω.

Εὐδαιμονέω *To be prosperous*, Soph. Ant. 506; Ar. Eq. 172; Pl. Leg. 636: fut. -ήσω Her. 1, 170; Eur. Med. 952; Isocr. 15, 85; Pl. Rep. 541: aor. ηὐδαιμόνησα Xen. Lac. 1, 2 (v. r. Thuc. 8, 24): but p. εὐδαιμόνηκα Aristot. Met. 8, 6, 8, else reg.

Εὐδοκιμέω *To be approved*, Her. 6, 63; Thuc. 2, 37; Pl. Prot. 315; Isocr. 9, 36, often without augm. εὐδ-, often with, ηὐδ-: imp. εὐδοκίμει Xen. Hell. 6, 1, 2; Aeschin. 2, 108, Ion. -ίμεε Her. 7, 227, ηὐδ- Pl. Gorg. 515: fut. -ήσω Cercid. 5 (B.); Isocr. 1, 21; Aeschin. 2, 130: aor. εὐδοκίμησα Her. 3, 131; Isocr. 12, 78; Lycurg. 82; Xen. Cyr. 7, 1, 46 (Vulg. Popp. ηὐδ- Dind. *now* 4 ed., Saupp.); Dem. 7, 20 (Mss. Bekk. &c. ηὐδ- Dind.): p. εὐδοκίμηκα Ar. Nub. 1031 (ηὐδ- Mein. Dind. 5 ed.); Pl. Criti. 108, ηὐδ- Luc. Paras. 32 (Dind.)

Εὕδω *To sleep*, Il. 14, 482; Alcm. 60; Pind. P. 1, 6; Aesch. Eum. 141; Soph. Aj. 291; Ar. Lys. 15; Her. 1, 34; Xen. Ven. 5, 11; εὕδειν Il. 2, 61, rare -έμεναι Od. 24, 255; subj. εὕδησθα Od. 8, 445: imp. εὗδον Il. 2, 2; Theocr. 2, 126; Eur. Bac. 683. Rhes. 763. 779 (Vulg. Kirchh. Nauck 2 ed.); Her. 3, 69, ηὗδ- Eur. Bac. Rhes. quoted (Elms. Dind. Paley, 683. 779 Nauck 3 ed.); Pl. Conv. 203, iter. εὕδεσκε Il. 22, 503: fut. εὑδήσω Aesch. Ag. 337: aor. καθ-ευδῆσαι Hippocr. 2, 451 (K.). Rare in prose, Her. 1, 209; Xen. quoted; Pl. Rep. 571. Leg. 823. Phaedr. 267; Plut. Ant. 36; Luc. D. Syr. 29: imp. εὗδον Her, 1, 211 (Gaisf. Bekk. Dind. Abicht, ηὗδ- Stein). 3, 69 (Bekk. Dind.

Abicht, ηὗδ- Gaisf. Dietsch, Stein); so Pl. Conv. 203 quoted. Vb. καθ-ευδητέον Pl. Phaedr. 259. See καθεύδω.

Εὐεργετέω *To do good,* Eur. Hel. 1020; Isocr. 12, 228; Pl. Crat. 428; -ετεῖν Aesch. Eum. 725; -ετῶν Soph. Ph. 670: imp. εὐηργέτουν Dio Cass. Fr. 9 (Bekk.); v. r. Xen. Ages. 4, 4, and εὐεργ- Xen. Apol. 26. Ages. 4, 4 (Dind. Breitb. Saupp.): fut. εὐεργετήσω Eur. Hel. 1298; Xen. Cyr. 3, 1, 34: aor. εὐηργέτησα Ar. Plut. 835; Lys. 9, 14; Dio. Hal. 2, 18, and εὐεργ- Isocr. 4, 56 (Bekk. B. Saupp. Bens.); Dinarch. 1, 16: p. εὐηργέτηκα Lycurg. 140; Luc. Abd. 18, and εὐεργ- Pl. Rep. 615; Isae. 4, 31; Dem. 20, 33 (Bekk. εὐηργ- Dind.): plp. εὐεργετήκει Xen. Ages. 2, 29 (Dind. Breitb. Saupp.): p. p. εὐηργέτημαι D. Cass. 56, 35; Luc. Abd. 14, εὐεργ- Xen. Mem. 2, 2, 3 (εὐηργ- Dind.); Isae. 7, 4; Pl. Crit. 43: plp. εὐεργέτηντο Dem. 20, 71 (Bekk. εὐηργ- Dind.): aor. εὐεργετηθείς Pl. Gorg. 250. Vb. εὐεργετητέον Xen. Mem. 2, 1, 28.—In Dem. Dind. always edits εὐηργ-, Bekk. always εὐεργ-, so B. Saupp.

Εὐκλεΐζω, see κληΐζω.

Εὐκρινέω *To separate well,* only inf. -ινεῖν Xen. Hell. 4, 2, 6.

'Εὐκτίμενος, see κτίζω.

Εὐλαβέομαι *To take care, beware,* Hippocr. 9, 360 (Lit.); -οῦνται Aristot. H. An. 4, 8, 12. Rhet. 1, 12, 6. Top. 8, 1, 12; Plut. Mor. 977; -βῶμαι Ar. Lys. 1277; Pl. Crat. 399; -βοῖο Phaed. 101; -λαβοῦ Aesch. Fr. 195; Soph. Tr. 1129; Isocr. 1, 32; Pl. Rep. 507, -λαβεῦ Cydias Fr. 1 (B.); -ούμενος Soph. O. R. 616; Eur. Supp. 325; Ar. Ach. 955; Pl. Rep. 372; -βεῖσθαι Ar. Lys. 1215; Pl. Charm. 155; -βέεσθαι Hippocr. 4, 502: imp. εὐλαβούμην Pl. Prot. 315; Aeschin. 1, 25, and ηὐλ- Aristot. Eth. N. 4, 13, 8 (B.); Eur. Or. 748. 1059 (Br. Pors. Dind. Nauck 3 ed. εὐλ- Herm. Kirchh. Nauck 2 ed. with Ald. Mss. V. a, &c.); Dem. 29, 1 (Dind. εὐλ- Bekk.): fut. εὐλαβήσομαι Pl. Rep. 410; Aeschin. 1, 38; Aristot. Eth. N. 4, 13, 8: with aor. p. εὐλαβήθην Dem. 28, 4, ηὐλ- (Dind.); so D. Sic. 13, 87; -θῶμεν Pl. Phaed. 89; -ήθητι Soph. O. R. 47: and fut. p. as mid. -βηθήσομαι Aristot. Eth. Mag. 1, 30 (-βήσομαι v. r.); Diog. Laert. 7, 116; Galen 5, 249; Porphr. de Abst. 43. Vb. εὐλαβητέον Hippocr. 8, 548; Pl. Rep. 424. The fut. pass. -βηθήσομαι, though scarcely classic, has better support than our lexicons allow. In the Septuag. and Apocr. we think it is the only form.

Εὐλογέω *To bless,* Eur. Ion 137; -λογεῖν Aesch. Ag. 580; Isocr. 11, 4; -γῶν Soph. Ph. 1314: imp. εὐλόγεις Eur. Fr. 349 (D.); Isocr. 12, 206, -γει Ar. Eccl. 454 (Vulg. Bekk. Bergk), ηὐλ- (Mein. Dind. 5 ed.); and late, Orat. tr. puer. 27: fut. -ήσω Eur. Hec. 465: aor. εὐλόγησα V. T. Gen. 2, 3. Jos. 14, 13, ηὐλ- Gen. 24, 1;

Dan. 4, 31; inf. εὐλογῆσαι Ar. Eq. 565: p. late εὐλόγηκα V. T. Gen. 17, 20: p. p. εὐλόγημαι V. T. Num. 24, 9, ηὐλ- (Alex.): aor. εὐλογηθείη Epist. Phal. 4: with fut. mid. εὐλογήσομαι as pass. Isocr. 9, 5 (Ms. Urb. V. Bekk. B. Saupp. Bens.): for fut. εὐλογηθήσομαι Isocr. quoted (Vulg.); and late V. T. Gen. 22, 18. Prov. 28, 20, and always: pres. -γούμενος Soph. O. C. 720; Isocr. 9, 6. Unless ηὐλόγει be right, Ar. Eccl. 454 (Mein. Dind. *now*), the augm. seems late: εὐλόγησα, οὐκ ηὐλ- (Suid.) The aor. m. ηὐλογήσατο we have seen only as a *v. r.* V. T. 1 Par. 29, 20. An Alexandrine form of 3 pl. opt. 1 aor. εὐλογήσαισαν occurs Tob. 3, 11 (Tisch.); but imper. -γησάτωσαν (Otto Fritzsche).

Εὐνάω *To put to bed, put to sleep*, fut. εὐνήσω Anth. 10, 12: aor. εὔνησα Od. 4, 440; Anth. 4, 3, 87; -ήσῃ Opp. Hal. 1, 161; Dor. -ᾶσειε, κατ- Soph. Ph. 699 (chor.); -ήσας Ap. Rh. 4, 87; Nonn. 13, 276; p. p. εὔνημαι Anth. 7, 397; aor. εὐνήθην Anth. 7, 78; -ηθῆναι Il. 14, 360. Od. 4, 334, συν- Her. 6, 107; -ηθείς Il. 2, 821. Od. 8, 292; Soph. Fr. 581 (trimet. Dind.), συν- Her. 6, 69, and, if sound, εὐνέθην, ξυν- Hippocr. 2, 833 (K.). Mid. εὐνάομαι *to sleep*, Soph. O. C. 1571 (chor.) to which may, perhaps, be assigned p. εὔνημαι: and aor. εὐνήθην. Twice in Trag. Soph. quoted, not in Comedy, nor, uncomp., in prose, except perhaps εὐνᾶσθαι Aretae. Morb. Ac. 2, 117 (ed. Oxon.) εὐνάζω Soph. O. R. 961, has rather a wider range, and in some editions appears with, and without augm.: fut. εὐνᾰσω Od. 4, 408; -άσειν Xen. Ven. 9, 3: aor. εὔνᾰσα Anth. 7, 25; Ap. Rh. 2, 856. 4, 1060; Eur. Rhes. 762 (Mss. Vulg. Kirchh. Nauck 2 ed.), ηὖν- (Dind. Nauck 3 ed.); εὐνάσῃ Aretae. Morb. Ac. 2, 107 (ed. Oxon.); εὔνᾰσον Soph. Tr. 1042. Pass. and mid. εὐνάζεται Hom. H. 4, 190; Eur. Med. 18; Hippocr. Epist. 9, 396, παρ- Od. 22, 37; -άζωμαι Luc. D. Syr. 25, -άζῃ Hes. Op. 339; -άζεσθαι Xen. Ven. 12, 2; -ζόμενος Luc. Cyn. 1: imp. εὐνάζετο Od. 20, 1, -οντο 23, 299; Ap. Rh. 2, 497, ηὐν- Themist. 26, 316: p. κατ-εύνασται Eur. Rhes. 611 (Kirchh. Nauck 2 ed.), -ηύνασται (Dind. Nauck 3 ed.): aor. εὐνάσθην Pind. P. 3, 25. Fr. 175 (Bergk), ηὐν- Eur. Ion 17. 1484 (Kirchh. Nauck, Dind.), ξυν-ηυν- Soph. O. R. 982 (Elms. Dind. *now*), but -ευνάσθην (Mss. Herm. Bergk, Nauck &c.), Epic 3 pl. κατ-εύνασθεν Il. 3, 448, συν- Pind. P. 4, 254; εὐνασθείς Soph. Tr. 1242; Xen. Ven. 9, 4: mid. aor. late, εὐνάσσαντο, ἐν- Nic. Fr. 33 (Gottl. Schn. 19 Otto Schn.)

Εὐνομέω *To enjoy good laws*, act. form only in pres. εὐνομοῦσα Pl. Leg. 927, where Ast suggests εὔνομος οὖσα. Pass. εὐνομοῦμαι *to be well governed*, Pl. Crit. 53. Rep. 605; Aeschin. 1, 5: p. εὐνομημένος Diog. Laert. (Epim.) 1, 113: aor. εὐνομήθην Her.

1. 66; Thuc. 1, 18: with **fut. mid.** εὐνομήσομαι as pass. Her. 1, 97; Pl. Rep. 380.

Εὑρίσκω *To find*, Od. 19, 158 (Wolf. Bekk. Dind.); Pind. P. 11, 52; Aesch. Eum. 989; Soph. El. 937; Com. Fr. (Alex.) 3, 501; Heraclit. 8 (Byw.); Her. 1, 5; Antiph. 5, 65; Lys. 8, 2; Pl. Ion 538, for augm. see below: **imp.** εὕρισκον Ar. Ran. 806; Her. 1, 68; Thuc. 1, 135; Xen. Hell. 5, 3, 23, ηὑρ- Pl. Gorg. 514 (best Mss. Stallb.); Ar. Ran. quoted (Mein. Dind. 5 ed.): **fut.** εὑρήσω Hom. H. Merc. 302; Theogn. 449; Pind. Ol. 13, 113; Aesch. Pr. 922; Soph. O. R. 441; Ar. Vesp. 1101; Her. 8, 60; Thuc. 3, 30; Isae. 1, 30; Pl. Leg. 968: **1 aor.** late, εὕρησα Maneth. 5, 137; Schol. Aesch. Pr. 59: **p.** εὕρηκα Soph. O. R. 546; Ar. Nub. 764; Her. 1, 44; Isocr. 2, 12; Pl. Lach. 186: **p. p.** εὕρημαι Aesch. Pers. 743; Soph. Tr. 1075; Eur. Bac. 203; Antiph. 5, 68; Xen. Cyr. 4, 2, 21, as mid. see below: **aor.** εὑρέθην Soph. Aj. 1135; Ar. Thesm. 521; Her. 9, 83; Antiph. 2, α, 4; Thuc. 6, 31: **fut.** εὑρεθήσομαι Soph. O. R. 108; Eur. I. A. 1105; Com. Fr. (Anon.) 4, 654; Hippocr. 1, 572 (Lit.); Isocr. 9, 41; Aeschin. 1, 166, and late εὑρηθήσ- Porphr. Antr. Nymph. 4; Geop. 13, 3, if not a mistake for εὑρεθ- see 13, 10: **2 aor. act.** εὗρον Il. 10, 34; Hes. Sc. 58; Pind. Ol. 12, 8; Soph. O. C. 1126; Ar. Lys. 72; Her. 8, 40; Antiph. 2, γ, 2; Thuc. 8, 66; Epic subj. εὕρησι Il. 12, 302; inf. Epic εὑρέμεναι Il. 2, 343, Aeol. εὕρην Sapph. 56 (B.) **Mid.** εὑρίσκομαι *to find for oneself*, Soph. El. 625; Xen. An. 7, 1, 31: **imp.** εὑρισκ- Pind. P. 1, 48: **fut.** εὑρήσομαι Her. 9, 6; -ησόμενος Aeschin. 3, 134; -ήσεσθαι Lys. 13, 9: **p.** εὕρημαι Aeschin. 3, 162; Dem. 23, 185. 55, 31; -ημένος 19, 17; Com. Fr. (Diph.) 4, 408: **2 aor.** εὑρόμην Il. 16, 472; Aesch. Pr. 267; Soph. Aj. 1023; Her. 9, 28; Thuc. 1, 58 (ηὑρ- Bekk.); Dem. 19, 69: and scarcely Attic εὑράμην Hes. Fr. 77 (Goettl. Flach, see below); Opp. Hal. 1, 508. 3, 363; Anth. 15, 7; Plut. Pomp. 80; Dio. Hal. 13, 11 (-ομ- Kiessl.); Dio Cass. 41, 42 (Bekk. -όμην L. Dind.), ἀν- Ap. Rh. 4, 1133; Com. Fr. (Tim.) 3, 592 (Mss. -όμην Dind. Mein.), with augm. ἐξ-ηύρατο (Menand.) 4, 115 (Mein. with Ms. A.) but seemingly favouring -ετο. **Vb.** εὑρετός Xen. Mem. 4, 7, 6, εὑρετέος Thuc. 3, 45, ἐξ- Ar. Nub. 728, εὑρητέος, ἐξ-ευρητ- now disallowed. At Pind. Fr. inc. 99, 11 (Bergk); and Dem. 19, 339 (450, 11) *now* occur εὑρόμενον, -ομένη, not -άμενον, -αμένη; and for εὑράμενος Hes. Fr. quoted, Lehm. Leutsch, Marksch. Schoem. read, with Fischer, εὑρόμ-. If they are right, the form with α is rendered doubtful in *classic* Greek.

The augment often occurs in editions by Elmsley, W. and L. Dindorf, Meineke &c., ηὕρισκον Soph. O. R. 68. Ph. 283

(Elms. Dind.); Ar. Ran. 806 (Mein. Dind. 5 ed.); Xen. Hell. 5, 3, 23 (Dind.); and often in late authors, Babr. 22; Polyb. 10, 7 (Bekk. Dind.), **pass.** ηὑρίσκετο Xen. An. 4, 4, 13 (Dind. 4 ed.): ηὗρον Thuc. 5, 42 (L. Dind.); Aesch. Pers. 474; Eur. Med. 553 (W. Dind. Nauck 3 ed.). Heracl. 957 (Elms. Dind. Nauck 3 ed.): ηὕρηκα 534; Soph. O. R. 546 (Elms. Dind.): ηὑρήκει Babr. 22: **p. p.** ηὕρηται Aesch. Pers. 743; Soph. Aj. 546; Eur. Bac. 203 (Elms. Dind.); ηὑρημένος Xen. Cyr. 2, 3, 14 (Dind. 4 ed.); Galen 13, 889, it is therefore a mistake to say that "the perf. is *never* written with ηυ:" **aor.** ηὑρέθην Soph. Aj. 1135; Ar. Thesm. 521 quoted; Eur. Andr. 219 (Dind.); Diod. Sic. 13, 90: **1 aor. m.** ηὕραο Anth. 9, 29: **2 aor.** ηὕροντο Aesch. Pr. 267 (Dind.); Thuc. 1, 58 (Bekk. Dind. Classen.) A **fut.** εὑρῶ occurs late Polem. 2, 40 (Orell.), and **1 aor.** εὕραμεν Pseud.-Callisth. 1, 39, as if from a liquid form εὕρω, to which also may be referred εὑράμην Hes. Fr. &c. above; and late Anth. Ap. Ep. 274; Paus. 7, 11, 1. 7, 17, 6. 8, 30, 4; Dio. Hal. 10, 48; Ael. V. H. 3, 17 &c. In Il. Od. and generally in Epic, **2 aor. act.** and **mid.** εὗρον, -όμην are alone used; ἐφευρίσκω however Od. 19, 158 (Vulg.) which Wolf, followed by Bekk. Dind. La Roche, altered perhaps correctly to ἔθ' εὑρίσκω (ἔνθ' εὑρ- Cod. Harl.) The **fut. pass.** form εὑρηθήσ- we have said is late.

Εὐτρεπίζω *To make* or *have ready*, Aesch. Ag. 1651; Hippocr. 6, 324, without augm. ευ, and with ηυ: **imp.** ηὐτρέπ- Himer. Or. 8, 1: **fut.** -ιῶ &c.: **p.p.** ηὐτρεπισμένος Eur. I. A. 1111; Ar. Plut. 626; Heliod. 10, 9; εὐτρεπίσθαι (Hippocr.) Epist. 9, 340 (Lit.), but εὐτρέπισται as **mid.** Dem. 18, 175 (Ms. S. Bait. Saupp. and Bekk. *now*), ηὐτρ- (Dind.): **plp.** ηὐτρέπιστο Luc. Am. 6 (Dind. εὐτ- Bekk.): **mid. pres.** εὐτρεπίζεται Themist. 2, 31: **imp.** εὐτρεπίζοντο Thuc. 4, 123 (all Mss. Bekk. Popp. Krüg. ηὐτρ- Stahl). 2, 18 (Ms. G. Popp. Krüg.), ηὐτρ- (Vulg. Bekk. Stahl); Dio. Hal. Ant. 2, 36; Pseud.-Callisth. 2, 19: **aor.** ηὐτρεπίσατο Nic. Damasc. 48, p. 34 (L. Dind.); εὐτρεπίσηται Dem. 23, 189: **p.** εὐτρέπισται see above: **plp.** ηὐτρέπιστο Heliod. 5, 13. **Vb.** εὐτρεπιστέον Hippocr. 6, 344.

Εὐτυχέω *To be fortunate*, Simon. Am. 7, 83; Pind. Ol. 7, 81; Soph. El. 945; Ar. Plut. 629; Thuc. 4, 62; -χῇς Aesch. Sept. 627; -οίης Aesch. Ch. 1063, -οῖμεν Supp. 1014; -τυχέειν Her. 1, 207; -τυχῶν Anth. 2, δ, 9, sometimes augm. ηυ, see below: **imp.** εὐτύχουν Soph. Fr. 94 (Vulg. Ellendt); Eur. Hec. 18. 1208. 1228 (Herm. Kirch. Nauck 2 ed.); Thuc. 4, 79 (Bekk. Popp.): **fut.** εὐτυχήσω Eur. Or. 1212: **aor.** εὐτύχησα Her. 7, 233; Eur. Or. 542 (Herm. Kirchh.); Xen. Hell. 3, 5, 12. An. 6,

3, 6 (Popp. &c.), and late -εσα Anth. App. Epigr. 9, 40; Dor. pt. -ήσαις Pind. I. 3, 1: p. εὐτύχηκα Isocr. 12, 7; Pl. Hipp. Maj. 285. Leg. 811; Dem. 19, 67 (Ms. S. Bekk. B. Saupp.): plp. εὐτυχήκειν Dem. 18, 18 (Ms. S. Bekk. B. Saupp.): p.p. εὐτύχημαι Thuc. 7, 77: aor. εὐτυχήθην late Herodn. 2, 14. Sometimes augm. ηὐτύχουν Aesch. Pers. 506; Soph. Fr. 94 (Dind. 5 ed.); Thuc. 4, 79 (L. Dind. Stahl); Eur. Hec. 18 (Ald. Pors. Dind. Paley, Nauck 3 ed.). 301 (Mss. Pors. Dind. Kirchh. Nauck). 1208. 1228 (Dind. Pors. Nauck 3 ed.): ηὐτύχησα Or. 542 (Vulg. Pors. Dind. Nauck 3 ed.); Xen. An. 6, 3, 6 (Dind. Breitb. Shenkl); Diod. Sic. 13, 22 (Bekk. Dind.): p. ηὐτύχηκα Xen. Cyr. 5, 2, 36 (Dind. 4 edit. Saupp.): plp. ηὐτυχήκειν Dem. 18, 18 (Dind.): p.p. ηὐτύχημαι Thuc. 7, 77 (Stahl.) On the augment. Mss. differ, and of course editors. In Eur. Herm. writes εὐ-, Dind. and now Nauck ηὐ-: in Xen. L. Dind. is now editing ηὐ-.

Εὐφραίνω *To cheer*, Xen. Men. 1, 6, 3; Com. Fr. (Arch.) 4, 436, Dor. 3 pl. -φραίνοισι Pind. Fr. 206; opt. -αίνοις Eur. Alc. 355, Epic ἐΰφ- Od. 20, 82; imper. εὔφραινε Theogn. 1033; Aesch. Supp. 515; Eur. Alc. 788; -αίνειν Eur. Alc. 237: imp. εὔφραινον Pl. Menex. 237, ηὔφ- Plut. Mor. 41: fut. εὐφρᾰνῶ Aesch. Ch. 742; Soph. O. C. 1353; Com. Fr. (Apoll.) 2, 881; Luc. Somn. 1; Philostr. 1, 46, Epic ἐϋφρᾰνέω Il. 7, 297, εὐφ- 5, 688; Theocr. 22, 178: aor. ηὔφρᾱνα Simon. (C.) 155, 12 (Bergk 3 ed.); Eur. Or. 217. 287 (Vulg. Pors. Dind. Kirchh. Nauck); Dio Cass. 43, 19 (B.), εὐφ- Pind. I. 7, 3; Eur. quoted (Herm. Witzsch.); Plut. Nic. 21. Oth. 2; -άναιμι Soph. Aj. 469; inf. εὐφρᾶναι Dem. 21, 202, Ion. εὔφρηνα Il. 24, 102; Theocr. 12, 8, ηὔφ- Opp. Hal. 3, 86; Epic ἐϋφρήνῃς Il. 7, 295; inf. -ῆναι 17, 28. **Pass.** εὐφραίνομαι *to rejoice*, Od. 2, 311; Soph. Aj. 280; Xen. Hier. 4, 6: imp. εὐφραινόμην Com. Fr. (Phil.) 4, 55, ηὐ- Xen. Cyr. 1, 4, 15 (Dind.). 2, 2, 5 (Dind. Hertl. Saupp.), εὐ- (Popp. 1, 4, 15 Hertl. Saupp.): with fut. m. εὐφρᾰνοῦμαι Xen. Conv. 7, 5, Ion. 2 sing. εὐφρανέαι Her. 4, 9, -έεαι (Bred. Abicht, Stein); -ούμενος Xen. Cyr. 1, 5, 9: and pass. εὐφρανθήσομαι Ar. Lys. 165; Aeschin. 1, 191: aor. εὐφράνθην Pind. Ol. 9, 62; Ar. Ach. 5 (Bekk. Bergk), ηὐφ- (Dind. Mein.); εὐφρανθῶσι Xen. Cyr. 1, 5, 9.

Εὐχετάομαι *To pray, profess*, Epic, pres. and imp. only, always in the lengthened forms, and unaugm. εὐχετάασθε Orph. Arg. 291, -όωνται Od. 12, 98: imp. εὐχετόωντο Il. 22, 394; Ap. Rh. 1, 231; opt. εὐχετοῴμην Od. 8, 467, -οῷτο Il. 12, 391, for -αοίμην, -άοιτο; inf. εὐχετάασθαι Il. 17, 19.

Εὔχομαι *To pray, boast*, Il. 6, 211. 8, 526; Hes. Th. 441;

Pind. Ol. 3, 2; Aesch. Ch. 540; Soph. Tr. 1190; Ar. Eccl. 171; Pl. Phaed. 117, προσ- Antiph. 6, 45; εὔχεσθαι Her. 1, 27; Thuc. 2, 43; Pl. Tim. 27; εὐχόμενος Antiph. 6, 45: imp. εὐχόμην Il. 3, 275; Pind. Ol. 6, 53; Eur. Elec. 809 (Kirchh. Nauck 2 ed. Witzsch.); Ar. Eccl. 141 (Bekk. Bergk); Her. 7, 54; Pl. Rep. 393. 394. Menex. 247; Xen. An. 1, 4, 7 (Popp. Krüg.), ηὐχ- Timocr. 1, 12 (B.); Aesch. Pers. 498 (D.); Eur. Or. 355 (Kirchh. Nauck, Dind.). Elec. 809 (Dind. Paley, Nauck 3 ed.); Ar. Eccl. 141 (Dind. Mein.); Com. Fr. (Eup.) 2, 466; Isae. 8, 16; Aeschin. 2, 118; Xen. Cyr. 3, 2, 15. An. 1, 4, 7 (Dind. 4 ed.); Pl. Alc. (2) 141, κατ- Soph. Tr. 764: fut. εὔξομαι Soph. Ph. 1032; Ar. Av. 623; Lys. 6, 4; Pl. Phaedr. 233, Epic 2 sing. ἐπεύξεαι Il. 11, 431: aor. εὐξάμην Il. 8, 254; Aesch. Ag. 933 (Blomf.). 963 (Pors. Herm. Blomf.), ηὐξ- (Dind.); Soph. Ph. 1019 (Herm.), ηὐξ- (Dind. Nauck); Eur. Phoen. 1373 (Herm.), ηὐξ- (Dind. Nauck), εὐξ- Ar. Av. 72 (Bekk.), ηὐξ- (Dind. Bergk, Mein.), εὐξ- Her. 4, 76; Pl. Phaed. 58; Xen. An. 4, 8, 25. Hell. 4, 4, 12 (Popp. Breitb. Saupp.), ηὐξ- (Dind.), ἐπ-ηυξ- H. Hymn. 2, 184; Epic subj. εὔξεαι Od. 3, 45; opt. εὐξαίμην Od. 12, 334, εὔξαιο Isocr. 5, 68, -αιτο Aesch. Ag. 1341; εὔξασθαι Pind. P. 3, 2; Her. 8, 64; -άμενος Thuc. 3, 58; Pl. Phaedr. 279: p. ηὖκται pass. and impers. Pl. Phaedr. 279; act. late V. T. Num. 6, 19: but plp. ηὔγμην act. Soph. Tr. 610, 3 sing. εὖκτο (syncop. aor. says Buttm.) Hom. Fr. 2, 15 (Franke): aor. late εὐχθεῖσα pass. Dio Cass. 48, 32. Vb. εὐκτός Eur. Ion 642; Xen. Mem. 1, 5, 5, -τέος, -έη, -έον Hippocr. 1, 85, if sound; and late, Epict. Ench. 77. Moeris held ηυ more Attic than ευ. Mss. however do not bear this out, and editors differ. Elmsley, W. and L. Dind. Meineke &c. favour ηυ, Lobeck, Herm. Blomf. Popp. Bekk. Ellendt &c. ευ. In Hom. Hes. Pind. Ap. Rh. and Her. never ηυ, but in later Epic ηὔχοντο Q. Sm. 6, 183 (Vulg. Koechl.), εὐχ- (Lehrs).

Εὕω *To roast*, Od. 2, 300; Hes. Op. 705 (Gaisf., but εὔω Goettl. Lenn. Schoem. Flach); and late Luc. Lexiph. 11: aor. εὗσα Od. 14, 75: p. p. εὖμαι, ἠφ-ευμένος Aesch. Fr. 321 (D. 5 ed.): aor. εὐθείς, ἀφ- (Suid.) This verb is written with the *lenis* εὔω by Goettl. and Lennep with some Mss. Hes. quoted, and v. r. Od. 2, 300. The *simple* form is Epic, and in act. goes not beyond the aor.: pass. εὑόμενοι Il. 9, 468. The comp. ἀφεύω is almost confined to Comedy, Ar. Eccl. 13. Pax 1144: aor. ἄφευσα (Simon. Am. 24 Bergk); Ar. Thesm. 590 (Vulg. Bekk. Bergk), -ηῦσα (Mein. Dind. 5 ed.); -εύσω 236: p. p. augm. on prep. ἠφευμένος Aesch. quoted: aor. -ευθείς (Suid.) We have never met with it in prose, though Buttmann says 'in prose usually ἀφεύω, ἀφεῦσα.' With ἐπί, it seems to occur once only, and late, ἐφεύσαις Nicand. Athen. 61 (Dind.); Nic. Fr. 79 (Otto Schneid. ἀφ- Fr. 9 Jo. Schneid.)

Εὐωχέω *To entertain, feast,* Her. 4, 73; Xen. Cyr. 5, 5, 42; -χῆτε Eur. Cycl. 346; -χεῖν Ar. Vesp. 342: **imp.** εὐώχουν Pl. Gorg. 522, Ion. -χεε Her. 1, 126: **fut.** -ήσω Theophr. Char. 7 (Foss); Plut. Mor. 785: **aor.** -ησα, subj. -ήσω Com. Fr. (Metag.) 2, 756. εὐωχέομαι *to eat, feast on,* Ar. Plut. 614; Her. 5, 8; Xen. Cyr. 6, 1, 10: **imp.** εὐωχοῦντο Xen. Cyr. 4, 5, 7 (Dind.): **fut.** -ήσομαι Ar. Eccl. 717; Com. Fr. (Alex.) 3, 489; Pl. Rep. 372; Luc. D. Deor. 26, 2: **aor.** rare, subj. εὐωχήσωνται Luc. Cron. 11: in same sense **p. p.** εὐώχημαι Hippocr. 8, 424 (Lit.); -ημένος Ar. Lys. 1224. Vesp. 1306 (Vulg. Mein. Dind. 4 ed.), ηὐωχ- (Dind. 5 ed.): with **aor.** εὐωχήθην Her. 1. 31; -θείς Ar. Eccl. 664; Pl. Leg. 666: and **fut. p.** εὐωχηθήσομαι (C. Inscr. 2336. v. r. Luc. D. Deor. 26, 2.) We have seen no trace of augment excepting ηὐωχ- Ar. Lys. Vesp. quoted (Dind. 5 ed.) The **aor. mid.** seems to have escaped the notice of Grammarians and Lexicogr. We never met with it except Luc. quoted, who uses it in exactly the same sense as Her. uses the **aor. pass.** ἔθυσάν τε καὶ εὐωχήθησαν Her. 1, 31. ὅπως θύσωσι καὶ εὐωχήσωνται without v. r. Luc. Cron. 11. To square this with his own notions, Cobet suggests **fut.** θύσουσι καὶ εὐωχήσονται.

Ἐφορμάω, see ὁρμάω.

Ἐχθαίρω *To hate,* usu. Poet. Od. 3, 215; Theogn. 297. 579; Aesch. Pr. 975; Soph. El. 1034; Ar. Ran. 1425, 3 pl. Dor. -αίροντι Theocr. 24, 29: **imp.** ἤχθαιρον Il. 17, 270; Eur. Supp. 879; Anth. 7, 648: **fut.** -ᾰρῶ: **aor.** ἤχθηρα Il. 20, 306; Hes. Th. 138; Aesch. Pers. 772; Soph. El. 1363; Dio Cass. 56, 38; Nic. Damasc. 53 (L. Dind.), Dor. -ᾱρα Timocr. in Plut. Them. 21. **Pass.** ἐχθαίρομαι *to be hated,* Aesch. Ch. 241; Soph. Aj. 458; opt. -ροίατο Aesch. Supp. 754: **imp.** ἠχθαίρετο Mosch. 6, 6: with **fut. m.** ἐχθαροῦμαι Soph. Ant. 93. **Mid.** as act. late ἐχθήρατο Nic. Alex. 618, ἀπ-εχθήρ- Q. Sm. 13, 255 (Vulg. Lehrs), -ηχθήρ- (Mss. Koechly.) **Vb.** ἐχθαρτέος *now* Soph. Aj. 679 (Mss. Dind. &c.)—Rare in prose, ἐχθαίρουσι (Hippocr.) Epist. 9, 378; Aristot. Eth. Nic. 10, 10, 12; Plut. Rom. 17: **imp.** ἤχθαιρε Dio Cass. 57, 1: **aor.** ἤχθηρα Dio Cass. 56, 38; Nicol. Dam. Fr. 21 (Feder.) Rather a better prose form is **ἐχθραίνω** Plut. Num. 5; Ael. H. A. 5, 2; but Babr. 59: **imp.** ἤχθραινον Xen. Ages. 11, 5: **aor.** late ἤχθρηνε Maxim. Καταρχ- 67, -ᾱναν 1 Macc. 11, 38. **Vb.** ἐχθραντέος late. Both verb and verbal used to occur in old editions of the Tragedians, the former at Soph. Ant. 93; Eur. Med. 555, the latter Soph. Aj. 679, but have been displaced in late recensions by ἐχθαίρω, ἐχθαρτέος from Mss. See Pors. Eur. Med. 559.

('Εχθοδοπέω) *To wrangle with,* Epic and only aor. inf. ἐχθοδοπῆσαι Il. 1, 518.

'Εχθέω, see foll.

"Εχθω *To hate,* Poet. and only **pres.** Aesch. Fr. 301 (D.); Soph. Ph. 510; Eur. Andr. 212; late Epic Callim. Del. 8. Fr. 118. **Pass.** ἔχθομαι Aesch. Ag. 417; -όμενος Od. 4, 502; -θεσθαι 756: **imp.** ἤχθετο Od. 14, 366; Eur. Hipp. 1402: **p.** late ἠχθημένος Lycophr. 827. There is some appearance of a form ἐχθέω, imper. ἔχθει Theogn. 1032 (Schneidew. Orell.), ὄχθει (Bergk, Emper.): **imp.** ἤχθεε Hermes. 2, 39 (Schneidew.), ἦχθεν (Dind.): **p. p.** ἠχθημένος quoted. See ἀπ-εχθάνομαι.

"Εχω *To have* (σέχω, ἔχω), Il. 3, 53; Pind. Ol. 6, 82; Aesch. Pr. 470; Soph. O. R. 277; Ar. Ach. 53; Her. 1, 71; Antiph. 6, 36; Thuc. 1, 4 1, ἔχεισθα Theogn. 1316; Sapph. 21 (Bergk), Dor. 3 pl. ἔχοντι Pind. P. 5, 82 (Bergk 3 ed.); ἔχῃσθα Il. 19, 180, -ῃσι Od. 20, 85; 3 pl. imper. ἐχόντων Her. 3, 155; Dor. pt. ἔχοισα Pind. P. 8, 4; Epic inf. ἐχέμεν Il. 13, 2; Theogn. 924; Hes. Sc. 369: **imp.** εἶχον Il. 7, 217; Hes. Sc. 132; Aesch. Ch. 351; Her. 1, 24; Antiph. 2, γ, 2; Thuc. 2, 22; Pl. Tim. 39, Aeol. ἦχον Sapph. 29 (B.), Epic ἔχον Il. 9, 1; Hes. Th. 466; Pind. Ol. 9, 61, iter. ἔχεσκον Il. 13, 257; Hes. Th. 533; Her. 6, 12: **fut.** ἕξω Il. 18, 274; Aesch. Sept. 67; Soph. O. C. 820; Ar. Ran. 339; Her. 3, 137; Antiph. 4, α, 4; Thuc. 4, 92; Isocr. 8, 137; Pl. Rep. 476; opt. ἕξοιμι Dem. 31, 2; ἕξειν Thuc. 3, 32, Ep. ἑξέμεν Il. 5, 473; Hes. Th. 394, and σχήσω Il. 17, 182; Pind. Fr. 217; Aesch. Eum. 695; Soph. Aj. 684; Ar. Ran. 188; Her. 9, 12; Thuc. 7, 62; Xen. An. 3, 5, 11, Epic 2 sing. σχήσεισθα Hom. H. Cer. 366; opt. σχήσοι Pind. P. 9, 116; Xen. Hell. 1, 1, 35; -σειν Solon 13, 66; Dem. 23, 128: **1 aor.** ἔσχησα (Inscr.; Or. Sib. &c.), see below: **p.** ἔσχηκα Pl. Leg. 765; Dem. 18, 99; Com. Fr. (Men.) 4, 154, μετ- Her. 3, 80, and Epic (ὄχωκα, for ὄκωχα) συν-οχωκώς Hom. once, Il. 2, 218: **p. p.** ἔσχημαι late in *simple,* Paus. 4, 21; Aq. Esai. 62, 4, ἀπ- Dem. 49, 65, κατ- Luc. D. Mort. 19, 1, and (ὦγμαι): **plp.** ἐπ-ώχατο Il. 12, 340: **aor.** ἐσχέθην Ion. and (late?) Attic, Arr. Ind. 37. An. 5, 7, συν- Hippocr. 2, 509 (K. 2, 378 Erm.), ἐπ- Callisth. Stob. 7, 65, περι- Luc. Peregr. 36; σχεθείς (Eur.?) Dan. 6, κατ- 27, ἐν- Plut. Philop. 6, κατα- Solon 21; σχεθῆναι Arr. An. 6, 11, 2; Pseud.-Callisth. 1, 6, περι- Paus. 4, 25, 3, συν- Athen. 12, 72: **fut.** late σχεθήσεται Galen 4, 221, ἐν- Plut. Mor. 980, κατα- Luc. Herm. 47, συν- Diog. Laert. 10, 117, ἐπι- Sext. Emp. 41, 16, περι- 451, 16: and **mid.** ἕξομαι as pass. Eur. Or. 516 (Mss. Ald. Nauck 2 ed. &c.), ἐνεξ- (2 Mss. Pors. Dind. Kirchh. Nauck

3 ed.); Aesch. Supp. 169; so Pl. Crito 52; Dem. 51, 11, συν- Epist. 3, 36 (B.): and σχήσομαι Il. 17, 639?: **2 aor. act.** ἔσχον Il. 17, 7; Pind. Ol. 2, 9; Aesch. Pers. 785; Soph. Ant. 225; Ar. Ran. 1035; Her. 3, 79; Thuc. 1, 112; Andoc. 1, 3; Isocr. 21, 16; Pl. Phil. 59; subj. σχῶ Il. 21, 309; Aesch. Fr. 280 (D.); Her. 4, 30; Pl. Leg. 958, in comp. ἀνα- Soph. El. 636, παράσχω Pl. Leg. 919; σχοίην Isocr. 1, 45; Pl. Apol. 34, ἐπι- Il. 14, 241, 3 pl. σχοῖεν Thuc. 6, 33, less freq. σχοίησαν Hyperid. Eux. p. 14, 25 (Schn.), and σχοῖμι, μετα- Soph. O. C. 1484, παρα- Eur. Hipp. 1111, κατα- Thuc. 6, 11, ἐπι- Pl. Phaedr. 257; σχές Soph. El. 1013; Eur. Hipp. 1354, ὑπο- Pl. Gorg. 497, occasionally σχέ in comp. πάρασχε Eur. Hec. 842 (Mss. Ald. Herm.), παράσχες (Pors. Dind. Kirchh.), see below; σχών Od. 4, 70; Soph. El. 551; Her. 4, 203; Antiph. 5, 67; Thuc. 5, 2, Dor. σχοῖσα, κατα- Pind. N. 10, 6; σχεῖν Il. 16, 520; Pind. P. 3, 89; Soph. O. R. 1461; Thuc. 4, 11; Pl. Leg. 648, Epic σχέμεν Il. 8, 254, Poet ἔσχεθον Il. 12, 184; Tyrt. 12, 22; Pind. Ol. 9, 88; Eur. Phoen. 408; Theocr. 22, 96, σχέθον Od. 10, 95; Pind. Fr. 65, κάσχεθε for κατά-σχ- Il. 11, 702; σχέθω Ar. Lys. 425, once in Doric prose κατα-σχεθῇ Epim. in Diog. Laert. 1, 113; σχέθοιμι Pind. I. 4, 54; Aesch. Eum. 857; Eur. Rhes. 602; σχέθε, -έτω Od. 8, 537; σχεθεῖν Aesch. Pr. 16, κατα- Soph. Ant. 1200, παρα- Ar. Eq. 320, Epic σχεθέειν Il. 23, 466, σχεθέμεν Pind. Ol. 1, 71; σχεθών Pind. P. 6, 19; Aesch. Ch. 832 (chor.). Others hold this form ἔσχεθον for imp. of a pres. σχέθω not used in indic.; subj. σχέθω &c., and accent the inf. σχέθειν, part. σχέθων. We hesitate to affirm that the "Homeric inf. σχεθέειν is *necessarily aorist*, and could *only* be produced from σχεθεῖν," see μάχοιτο Il. 5, 362. 16, 713, μαχέοιτο 1, 272. 344; ὄρσο Od. 7, 342, ὄρσεο Il. 3, 250 &c. **Mid.** ἔχομαι *to hold oneself, hold by, be near* &c. Il. 17, 559; Aesch. Sept. 97; Soph. O. C. 424; Ar. Pax 479; Her. 5, 49; Pl. Conv. 218: **imp.** εἰχόμην Pind. P. 4, 244; Eur. I. T. 1355; Her. 8, 11; Antiph. 5, 76; Thuc. 1, 49, ἐχ- Od. 5, 429, προὔχ- Od. 3, 8, iter. παρ-εχέσκετο formerly Od. 14, 521, is now edited παρεκέσκ- from παράκειμαι (Wolf, Bekk. Dind. La Roche): **fut.** ἕξομαι Il. 9, 102; Soph. O. R. 891; Eur. Hec. 398; Ar. Plut. 101; Thuc. 8, 3; Pl. Rep. 621, παρ- Antiph. 5, 30; **pass.** Eur. Dem. see above: and σχήσομαι Il. 9, 235; Her. (Orac.) 7, 220; Ar. Av. 1335; rare in Trag. ἀνασχήσει Aesch. Sept. 252, ἐξανα- Soph. Ph. 1355; in prose σχήσομαι Plut. Crass. 25; Pseud.-Callisth. 1, 6, παρα- Antiph. 5, 24; Lys. 9, 8; Hippocr. 6, 504 (Lit.), ἀπο- Dem. 33, 28: and in sense **p.** ἔσχημαι, παρ- Xen. An. 7, 6, 11; Isae. 4, 18. 31; Aeschin. 2, 181; Dem. 27, 49. 36, 35. 40, 54. 57, 29, Dor.

παρ- είσχ- Incr. Rhod. Del. Olb. (Ahr. Dor. Dial. p. 341. 574): **2 aor.** ἐσχόμην Il. 3, 84. Od. 17, 238 (σχό- Bekk.); Soph. O. R. 1387 (Dind. Nauck). Ant. 467 (Vulg. ἠνσχ- Dind. Nauck &c.); Her. 6, 85. 7, 169; late Attic prose Plut. Arist. 15. 17. Caes. 32, *classic* in comp. ἀνα, ἠν-έσχ- Aesch. Ag. 1274; Ar. Eq. 412; Thuc. 3, 28; Pl. Charm. 162, ἀπ- Thuc. 1, 20; Isocr. 16, 13, παρ- Eur. Fr. 882 (D.); Thuc. 7, 58; Pl. Phil. 59; Lys. 7, 23. 9, 9 (Ar. Thesm. 147) &c. ἐπ- Thuc. 7, 33 (Bekk. Goell.); subj. σχῶνται Od. 13, 151, ἀπό -σχ- Aesch. Supp. 756; Ar. Lys. 771, παράσχωμαι Pl. Leg. 642; σχοίμην Il. 2, 98, παρα- Eur. Andr. 55, ἀνα- Pl. Rep. 367; σχέο Il. 21, 379, σχοῦ, ἀνά-σχου Eur. Ion 947, -σχεσθον Pl. Euthyd. 278, σχέσθε Il. 22, 416, ἀνά-σχ- Ar. Ach. 296; σχέσθαι Od. 4, 422; Hes. Fr. 110; Eur. Rhes. 174, ἀπο- Pl. Leg. 872, παρα- Xen. Cyr. 1, 6, 22; Isae. 2, 38; σχόμενος Il. 12, 298, παρα- Thuc. 2, 41, ἐπι- Pl. Conv. 216; sometimes pass. ἔσχετο Il. 17, 696. Od. 4, 705; Her. 1, 31; Dio Cass. 50, 31, ἐν- Her. 7, 128; Pl. Lach. 183, σχέτο Il. 21, 345; σχομένη Od. 11, 279, κατα- Pind. P. 1, 10; rare in Attic, Pl. Phaedr. 244; occasionally doubtful κατ-έσχετο Eur. Hipp. 27 (Mss. most edit. κατείχ- Elms. Monk, Dind. Nauck 3 ed.), συν- Heracl. 634 (Vulg. συνείχ- Elms. Dind. Nauck); Pl. Soph. 250 (v. r. συνεχ-). Theaet. 165; also ἐσχεθόμην, προ- Theocr. 25, 254 (Meineke, Wordsw. Ahr.). **Vb.** ἑκτός late Diog. Laert. 3, 105, but ἀν-εκτ- Il. 11, 610, -έος Ar. Ach. 259, ἄ-σχετος, ἀά-σχ- Il. 16, 549. 5, 892, ἀνα-σχετός Thuc. 2, 21, ἀν-σχ- Od. 2, 63, ἐπισχετέος Pl. Phaedr. 272, ἀπο- Hippocr. 1, 323 (Erm.). In some editions of Her. ἔχω is occasionally unaugm. ἔχον 1, 102. 5, 73. 6, 95. 7, 61 &c. παρέχοντο 2, 148 (Schweigh. Schaef. &c.): Gaisf. Lhardy, Bredow, and *now* Bekk., we think, uniformly augment it, εἶχον, εἴχοντο &c. For ἐπέσχοντο Thuc. 7, 33 (Bekk.), Poppo reads ἐπέσχον τό, on the ground that Thuc. never uses the mid. form. It is little used by any writer, probably because the act. assumed a mid. sense. He uses however the mid. of other compounds, ἀπέσχοντο 1, 20 &c. παρεσχόμεθα 1, 74. 2, 41 &c.—A rare pres. form ἔχεισθα occurs Sapph. 21; Theogn. 1316 (Bekk., so Bergk, but prefers ἔχεσθα, ἔχοισθα Ms. A.); subj. ἔχῃσθα Il. 19, 180. The **1 aor.** ἔσχησα occurs on the Marmor. Farn.; and subj. σχήσῃσθα (or -εισθα fut.) Hom. H. Cer. 5, 366 (Ilgen, Matth.); σχήσειε Or. Sib. 9, 91 (Friedl.); Nonn. 17, 177 (Koechl.). ἔσχα a late form of **1 aor.**=ἔσχον is found in Inscr. **Aor. pass.** ἐσχέθην was scarcely used by the early Attics. ἐν-είχεε Her. 1, 118 (Mss. Gaisf. Bekk.), ἐνεῖχε (Steph. Dind. Stein): **2 aor.** ἐπισχέειν Her. 1, 32 (Gaisf.), -σχεῖν (Bekk. Stein), Epic σχεθέειν Il. 23, 466, σχεθέμεν Pind. P. 4, 75, inf. for σχεθεῖν; σχέ=σχές, though analogical, seems to occur once only, Orac. in Schol. Eur. Phoen. 638, and doubtful even there, for the Schol. Ar. Eq. 1256, quoting the passage, reads σχεῖν. It occurs however occasionally in comp. πάρασχε Eur. Hec. 842 (Mss. Herm. Pflugk.). Brunck held it barbarous, and substituted παράσχες, which Porson adopted, granting at the same time that πάρασχε is agreeable to analogy, but of rare occurrence; Pl. Prot. 348 πάρασχε (2 Mss.), -σχες (Mss. Bekk. &c.); Xen. Conv. 8, 4 (2 Mss., -εχε Mss. Born. Saupp. Dind.); κάτασχε Eur. H. F. 1210 (Mss.), κατάσχεθε (Elmsley's conjecture, Matth. Dind. Kirchh. &c.); μέτασχε Or. 1337 (some Mss.), -σχες (Mss. Pors. Herm. Dind. &c.)—εἴχοσαν Anth. 5, 209, ἔσχοσαν Scymn. 695, seem to be Alexandrine forms of 3 pl. imp. and 2 aor.

Ἐψιάομαι *To play with pebbles, amuse oneself*, Epic -ιόωνται Ap. Rh. 1, 459, ἐφ- Od. 19, 331; imper. ἑψιάάσθων Od. 17, 530; -ιάασθαι Od. 21, 429; Ap. Rh. 3, 950: imp. unaugm. ἑψιόωντο Callim. Cer. 39; Ap. Rh. 2, 811, ἐφ- Od. 19, 370: aor. ἑψιασάμην, ἀφ- Soph. Fr. 142. An act. form ἑψιέω or -όω occurs Aesch. Fr. 49 (D.) ἑψιοῦσα; but Lobeck (Rhemat. p. 154), restored ἐμψίουσα approved by Dind. 5 ed. In Callim. Meineke edits ἐψ-.

Ἕψω *To boil, cook* (ἑψέω rare and often doubtful, especially in Attic), Ar. Eccl. 845; Her. 3, 100; ἕψοι Pind. Ol, 1, 83; ἑψέτω Pl. Euthyd. 285; ἕψειν Xen. Cyr. 8, 2, 6: imp. ἧψον Ar. Ran. 505. Fr. 507. 548; Com. Fr. (Alcae.) 2, 831, ἕψεε Her. 1, 48 (Bekk. Gaisf. Lhardy), ἕψε (Bred.), ἧψε (Dind. Stein): fut. ἑψήσω Com. Fr. (Nicoch.) 2, 846. (Men.) 4, 145; Hippocr. 2, 246 (Lit.): and ἑψήσομαι see below: aor. ἥψησα Com. Fr. (Strat.) 2, 775; Ar. Fr. 109. 355 (Dind.); Hippocr. 1, 578 (Lit.); Luc. Gall. 14, ἕψησα Her. 1, 119 (Bekk. Gaisf. Lhardy, Bred.), ἥψ- (Ms. K. Dind. Stein, Dietsch); subj. ἑψήσῃ Pl. Euthyd. 301; ἕψησον Hippocr. 2, 522; -ῆσαι (Pl.) Eryx. 405 (also ἧψα, συνῆψας, if sound, Com. Fr. (Timocl.) 3, 606, see below): p. late ἕψηκα, with the *lenis*, Philo vol. 2, p. 245: p. p. ἥψημαι, -ῆσθαι Hippocr. 2, 254 (Lit. ἑψ- Vulg.); ἡψημένος Diod. Sic. 2, 9 (Bekk. Dind.); Aristot. Prob. 5, 36 (L. Dind. ἑψ- Mss. Bekk.); so Hippocr. ἑψημ- 8, 192 (Lit. ἡψ- Erm. 2, 628), ἀπ-εψ- Her. 1, 188 (Bekk. Gaisf. Dind. Stein, ἀπ-ηψ- Abicht), ἀφ- Plut. Conv. 692: aor. ἡψήθην V. T. 1 Reg. 2, 13; subj. ἑψηθῇ Her. 4, 61; Aristot. Probl. 21, 11; Plut. Mor. 690; ἑψηθείη, ἀφ- Athen. (Aristot.) 10, 34; ἑψηθῆναι, ξυν- Hippocr. 1, 616 (Lit.); ἑψηθείς Theophr. H. P. 3, 9, 2; Luc. V. Auct. 6; Galen 13, 399, ἀφ- Athen. 10, 34, late ἥφθην, ἑφθέντες Dioscor. Parab. 1, 148: fut. ἑψηθήσομαι Galen 13, 398. 893: ἑψόμενος Pind. N. 4, 82; Aristot. Pt. Anim. 2, 7, 16. Mid.

ἕψομαι Aesch. Fr. 321 (D.); -εσθαι Eur. Cycl. 404: fut. ἑψήσομαι Pl. Rep. 372: aor. ἡψήσατο Com. Fr. (Anon.) 4, 680, which Meineke would alter to ἐψησ- from ψάω. Vb. ἑφθός Eur. Cycl. 246. ἑψητός Xen. An. 2, 3, 14. ἑψητέον, ἐν- Aretae. Morb. Ac. 1, 84 (ed. Oxon.). The *classical* authority for ἑψέω depends almost entirely on the *accent*. ἑψῶ Ephipp. Com. Fr. 3, 338 (Ms. C.), ἕψω (Mein.), ἑψοῦσι Aristot. Mirab. c. 22, καθ- Xen. Eq. 9, 6, ἕψουσι, καθέψ- (Bekk. Dind.), but ἑψοῦσι Theophr. H. P. 4, 8, 12. 7, 4, 11 (Schneid. Wimmer); Geop. 5, 47; ἑψῇ Pl. Hipp. Maj. 290, ἕψῃ (Bekk. &c.); imper. ἕψεε Hippocr. 2, 518 (Mss. Lit.), ἕψε, so Ms. A, pointing to ἕψε which actually occurs without v. r. 7, 158. 160. 8, 174, ἑψέτω 8, 182; Pl. Euthyd. 285; ἑψεῖν 301 (Mss. Heind. Stallb. ἕψειν Bekk. B. O. W. &c.); so Hippocr. ἑψεῖν 7, 86. 196. 254. 8, 82. 92 &c. but ἕψειν 2, 32. 8, 174 (Lit.); ἑψῶν 7, 48. 266. 276 &c. (Lit.): imp. ἕψεε Her. 1, 48, ἧψε (Dind.), ἑψόμενος Hippocr. 7, 276 (Lit.), ἑψεῖσθαι Geop. 2, 35, καθ- (Luc.) Asin. 25 (Jacob.), -έψεσθαι (Dind.) who would expel the pure form ἑψέω entirely from the early writers. ἑψάω, if correct, is perhaps late, ἑψῶντες Diod. Sic. 1, 84, ἕψοντες (Bekk. Dind. from Euseb.); but ἑψῆν Hippocr. 8, 366 (Lit.) v. r. ἑψεῖν; ἐγκαθεψῶντα 2, 806 (K.), -έψοντα (Dind.). For aor. συνῆψας Com. Fr. 3, 606, quoted, Meineke, partly from Dindorf's conjecture, partly from his own, reads ἐν αἶσιν ἧψες imp. of the *simple*, adding that the aor. form ἧψας is 'quite unused.' We know no other instance (ἕψαντες Xen. An. 2, 1, 6 Vulg. has been altered), but it is countenanced so far by the *analogical* pass. aor. (ἥφθην), ἑφθέντες quoted from Dioscor.—ἕψω seems to have been also pronounced ἔψω, as our *heat* is by some pronounced '*eat*.

(῎Εω) *To be*, see εἰμί.

(῞Εω) *To clothe*, see ἕννυμι.

(῞Εω) *To send*, see ἱέω, ἵημι.

(῞Εω) *To seat*, *set*, in act. the aor. only, mostly Poet., not in Attic prose (fut. ἀν-έσω see below): εἷσα Il. 4, 392. 6, 189. Od. 8, 472; Hes. Th. 174; Soph. O. C. 713 (chor.); Her. 3, 61 (καθ-εῖσεν Eur. Phoen. 1188 trimet. is *now* καθ-ῖσεν Dind. Kirchh. &c.), ἕσσα, καθ- Pind. P. 5, 42 (Böckh, Momms.); opt. ἀν-έσαιμι Il. 14, 209; imper. εἷσον Od. 7, 163; inf. ἕσσαι in tmesi Pind. P. 4, 273, ἐφ- Od. 13, 274; part. ἕσας Od. 10, 361. 14, 280, ἀν- Il. 13, 657, εἵσας, ὑπ- Her. 3, 126. 6, 103. Mid. *to seat oneself*, *set for oneself*, *erect*, fut. εἵσομαι Ap. Rh. 2, 807; late prose Athen. (Demetr.) 4, 21; ἕσσεσθαι, ἐφ- Il. 9, 455: aor. ἑσσάμην Pind. P. 4, 204, ἐφ-έσσ- Od. 14, 295 (Bekk. *now*, with Rhian), καθ-έσσ- Anacr. 111 (B.); Pind. P. 5, 42 quoted (Hart. Bergk), ἑέσσ- Il. 10, 23. Od. 14, 529, ἐν-εεία- Ap. Rh. 4, 188; imper.

ἔσσαι, ἐφ- Od. 15, 277; ἑσσάμενος, ἐφ- 16, 443, and εἰσάμην Anth. (Anyt.) 7, 208; Theogn. 12; Callim. Iov. 67. Del. 309; Theocr. 17, 123; rare in Attic, Eur. I. T. 946 (ἐγκαθ- Hipp. 31, -καθ-ισ- Dind. 5 ed. Nauck); prose, Long. Past. 4, 39 (Seil.); Themist. 4, 54 (D.), late Epic ἑσ- Q. Sm. 2, 203; classic εἰσάμενος Her. 1, 66; Thuc. 3, 58 (Ms. Pal. Popp. Goell. L. Dind. ἑσσαμ- Mss. Bekk. Classen, ἑσαμ- Mss. approved by Krüg.); so Plut. εἰσάμ- Thes. 17. Pyr. 1 (Bekk. Sint.); εἶσασθαι Themist. 1, 8. Hither may be referred as p. p. ἧμαι as pres. *am set, sit;* see ἧμαι. The fut. ἀν-έσει Od. 18, 265, is usually considered a shortened form of ἀνήσει fut. of ἀνίημι. This we think doubtful: Düntzer reads opt. ἀνέσαι; La Roche suggests ἀνεῇ.

Ἑῶμεν, see ἄω *to satiate.*

Z.

Ζαμενέω *To be greatly excited,* Epic and only aor. ζαμένησε Hes. Th. 928.

Ζάω *To live,* Soph. O. R. 410; Eur. Or. 386, contracts αε into η, ζῇς Aesch. Eum. 603; Com. Fr. (Plat.) 2, 697; Andoc. 1, 99, ζῇ Soph. Ant. 457; Ar. Lys. 306; Heraclit. 25 (Byw.); Pl. Tim. 77; Xen. Cyr. 7, 3, 3, ζῶμεν Simon. Amorg. 1, 4; Soph. Ant. 214; Thuc. 3, 38, ζῆτε Ar. Av. 161; Pl. Leg. 771, ζῶσι Her. 2, 92. 4, 23. 103 (Gaisf. Stein, ζώουσι Bekk. Dind. Abicht); Xen. Mem. 2, 1, 10; subj. ζῶ Soph. El. 822; Xen. Cyr. 8, 5, 26, ζῆτε Pl. Conv. 192; opt. ζῴην Eur. Or. 1147; Ar. Nub. 1255; Xen. Conv. 4, 14, ζῴης Soph. El. 1090, -η Pl. Rep. 344, ζῷμεν Soph. O. C. 799, ζῷεν Pl. Menex. 248; imper. ζῆ Soph. Ant. 1169; Eur. I. T. 699. Fr. 823 (Dind.), and ζῆθι Anth. (Incert.) 10, 43. (Agath.) 11, 57; Com. Fr. (Mon.) 191; Pseud.-Callisth. 1, 8, ζήτω Pl. Leg. 952; inf. ζῆν Soph. O. C. 798; Ar. Plut. 552; Her. 5, 6; Thuc. 2, 43; Pl. Conv. 192; Isocr. 15, 147; Dem. 57, 31; Hom. only part. ζῶν Il. 1, 88; Soph. Ant. 210; Ar. Av. 754; Her. 2, 162 (Gaisf. Stein, ζώων Bekk. Dind.); Antiph. 1, 23; Pl. Phaed. 105: imp. ἔζαον, -ων Soph. El. 323; Eur. Alc. 295. 651 (Dind. Nauck); Ar. Ran. 1072; Luc. D. Mort. 27, 9, and (from ζῆμι) ἔζην only in 1 pers. sing. Dem. 24, 7, 2 sing. ἔζης (contr. from ἔζαες) Aesch. Ch. 360; Soph. Fr. 603 (D.); Andoc. 1, 99; Dem. 18, 263. 21, 134, ἔζη (ἔζαε) Aesch. Ch. 360; Soph. Aj. 1060; Ar. Pax 652; Pl. Rep. 406; Isae. 7, 14; Aeschin. 1, 102; Dem. 52, 15, pl. ἐζῶμεν (Pl.) Epist. 347, ἐζῆτε Xen. Cyr. 7, 2, 26, ἔζων Ar. Vesp. 709; Pl. Leg. 679: **fut.** ζήσω Epich. 149; Ar. Plut. 263. Fr. 498 (D.); Com. Fr. (Men.) 4, 345; Pl. Rep. 465. 591; Luc. Alex. 34, δια- Pl. Leg. 792: and **mid.** ζήσομαι Hippocr. 7, 536 (Lit.); (Dem.) 25, 82; Aristot. Pol. 7, 6, 7; Plut. Mor. 1082; Luc. Paras. 12; D. Laert. 6, 2, 44; Anth. (Antiph.) 7, 175: **aor.** ἔζησα Hippocr. 2, 112 (Lit.); Anth. (Meleag.) 7, 470; Plut. Mor. 785; Luc. Alex. 59; Dio Cass. 56, 3: **p.** ἔζηκα Aristot. Metaph. 8, 6, 8 (Bekk.); Plut. Mor. 1082; Polyb. 12, 25 h; Dio. Hal. Ant. 5, 68. For **aor.** and **perf.** the Attics commonly use ἐβίων, βεβίωκα. ἔζην Eur. Alc. 295. 651, has been altered from the best Mss. to ἔζων. **Fut.** ζήσω seems to have been the Attic form, though **mid.** ζήσομαι is earlier than some suppose. In the Septuag. the **mid.** is almost the constant form, in the N. T. the **act.**, we think, rather prevails.—The Epics, Ion. and Dor. use the collat. form. ζώω and ζόω; see the words.

Ζέννῡμι *To boil*, late for ζέω, only **pres. act.** ζέννυμεν Oribas. 5, 17; and **part. pass.** ζεννύμενον Alex. Aph. probl. 1, 104.—ζεννύω?

Ζεύγνῡμι *To join*, Aesch. Pers. 191, ὑπο- Pl. Polit. 309, 3 pl. ζευγνῦσι for -ύᾱσι Eur. El. 1323 (chor.); imper. ζεύγνῦτε Eur. Rhes. 33; -νύς Her. 1, 206. 4, 89; -ύναι 4, 83, συ-ζ- 189, μετα- Xen. Cyr. 6, 3, 21, see below, and ζευγνύω Her. 1, 205; Polyb. 5, 52; Anth. 12, 206; subj. ζευγνύῃ, κατα- Pind. P. 2, 11: **imp.** ἐζεύγνῡν, -ῡσαν Her. 7, 33. 36, ζεύγ- Il. 24, 783, and ζεύγνυον Il. 19, 393, ἐζεύγνῡε Her. 4, 89, ἐπ- 7, 36, ἀν- Xen. Cyr. 8, 5, 1. 28 (Vulg. Popp. Saupp. &c. ἀν-εζεύγνυ Dind. 4 edit.): **fut.** ζεύξω Pind. I. 1, 6; Aesch. Ag. 1640; Eur. Rhes. 772, ὑπο- Od. 15, 81, if sound: **aor.** ἔζευξα Od. 3, 478; Pind. P. 10, 65; Aesch. Pr. 462; Soph. Fr. 517; Eur. Ion 10; Ar. Pax 128; Her. 4, 87; Thuc. 1, 29; Isocr. 4, 89; Pl. Tim. 22, ζεῦξε Il. 24, 690; Hes. Fr. 93; Dor. f. pt. ζεύξαισα Pind. P. 4, 215: **perf.** late ἔζευχα, ἐπ- Philostr. V. Apoll. 2, 14, 64: **p. p.** ἔζευγμαι Eur. Fr. 598 (D.); Luc. Nav. 33, ἐν- Aesch. Pr. 108 (D.), συγκατ- Soph. Aj. 123, προσ- Eur. Alc. 482; Aristot. Mechan. 5, 10, ὑπο- Anth. (Alph. Mit.) 9, 526; ἐζευγμένος Il. 18, 276; Eur. Elec. 317; Her. 7, 34; Xen. An. 2, 4, 13; ἐζεῦχθαι Eur. Hel. 1654: **plp.** ἔζευκτο Her. 4, 85: **1 aor.** ἐζεύχθην Eur. Ion 949, κατ- Soph. Ant. 947, ζεύχ- 955 (chor.); -χθείς Aesch. Ag. 842; Eur. Elec. 99; in tmesi Pind. Ol. 3, 6; -χθῆναι Her. 7, 6; rare in *Attic prose*, Pl. Polit. 302; Arr. An. 5, 7. 5, 8, δια- Aristot. H. A. 7, 6, 1. Pol. 6, 4, 20; Alciphr. 1, 39, ἀπ- Babr. 37, ἐνι- Ap. Rh. 1, 686: **fut.** late, δια-ζευχθήσεται Galen 9, 938: **2 aor.** ἐζύγην Eur. Supp. 822. I. A. 907 &c.; Pl. Rep. 508; ζυγείς Pind. N. 7, 6; Aesch. Ch. 795, συν- Pl. Rep. 546, δια- Aeschin. 2, 179; ζυγῆναι Soph. O. R. 826. **Mid.** ζεύγνῦμαι trans. *join for oneself, to oneself, marry*, Eur. Alc. 428; perhaps also -νσθαι Od. 23, 245: **imp.** ζευγνύμην Il. 24, 281. Od. 3, 492: **fut.** ζεύξομαι Eur. Supp. 1229. Hec. 469: **aor.** ἐζευξάμην Ion 901. Tr. 671; ζευξάμενος Hom. H. 32, 9; Theogn. 952; Her. 3, 102; Luc. Hist. Con. 8; Heliod. 10, 29 (B.) The **mid.** in the *simple* form seems not to occur in good Attic prose, but διαζεύγνυσθαι Pl. Leg. 784, συνεζεύξατο Xen. Cyr. 6, 1, 51.—Epic **pres. inf.** forms, ζευγνύμεναι Il. 3, 260, ζευγνῦμεν 15, 120, and -ύμεν 16, 145, ῡ by ictus, therefore -ῦμεν is perhaps unnecessary: it is so read however by Wolf, Bekk. Dind. La Roche. **Vb.** ζευκτός Plut. Mor. 280.—Buttmann, strange to say, gives ἐζύγην as the only **pass. aor.** Eur. uses ζυγεῖσα of choice Fr. 4 (Dind.), ἀπ-εζύγην Med. 1017; so Aesch. Ch. 677, where ζευχθεῖσα, ἀπ-εζεύχθην might stand—a proof that the doctrine regarding the Tragedians "loving strong and rough forms of aorist" has been stated too strongly.

Ζέω *To boil*, Poet. ζείω trans. and intrans. Il. 21, 362; Aesch. Sept. 708; Her. 4, 181; Pl. Phaedr. 251; ζείων Ap. Rh. 1, 734; Callim. Dian. 60; Dor. f. pt. ζέοισα Pind. Ol. 1, 48, late ζέννυμι (-ύμενος Dioscor. 2, 77): **imp.** ἔζει Soph. O. C. 434, ἔζεε Il. 21, 365; Hes. Th. 695, ζέεν Ap. Rh. 4, 955: **fut.** ζέσω, ἐξανα- Aesch. Pr. 370: **aor.** ἔζεσα Her. 1, 59; Anth. 7, 385, ἐξ- Aesch. Sept. 709, ἐπ- Eur. Cycl. 392; Her. 7, 13, ζέσσα Il. 18, 349; Anth. 7, 208; ζέσῃ Hippocr. 7, 354; ζέσειε Pl. Tim. 70; **inf.** ζέσαι Com. Fr. (Anax.) 4, 463; ζέσας Eur. Cycl. 343; Pl. Tim. 85: **p. p.** ἔζεσμαι, ἀπ- Hippocr. 5, 324 (Lit.), later ζέζεσμαι, ἐκ- Geop. 10, 54, ἐξ-έζεσμ- (Niclas, perhaps rightly): **aor.** late ἐζέσθην Aretae. 93 (ed. Oxon.); Geop. 13, 1; Dioscor. 2, 102, ἀπο- 1, 3; Galen 10, 572, but ἀναζεθείς 13, 976 perhaps an error. **Vb.** ζεστός App. Hisp. 85.

Ζημιόω *To injure*, Eur. Ion 441; Com. Fr. (Antiph.) 3, 41; Thuc. 3, 43; Xen. Laced. 4, 6; ζημιοῦν Ar. Ach. 717; Her. 7, 35; Xen. Cyr. 6, 3, 27: **imp.** ἐζημ- Her. 3, 27; Lycurg. 65: **fut.** rare ζημιώσω Lys. 1, 48; Dem. 56, 4; Plut. Camill. 39; Dio Chrys. Or. 34 (414): **aor.** ἐζημίωσα Eur. Or. 578; Her. 9, 77; Antiph. 5, 47; Thuc. 2, 65; Lys. 9, 11; Isocr. 10, 7: **p.** ἐζημίωκα Dem. 21, 49: **p. p.** ἐζημίωσθε Dem. 22, 51; ἐζημιωμένος Isocr. 4, 116; Aristot. Rhet. 1, 12, 11: **plp.** ἐζημίωτο Dem. 31, 11: **aor.** ἐζημιώθην Andoc. 1, 134; Pl. Leg. 855; Lys. 9, 13; Isocr. 15, 160: **fut.** ζημιωθήσομαι Xen. Mem. 3, 9, 12; Lys. (6, 15). 8, 18. 29, 4; Isae. 1, 23. 10, 16; Dem. 23, 80; (Pl.) Hipparch. 226: and as often **fut. mid.** ζημιώσομαι **pass.** Her. 7, 39; Thuc. 3, 40 twice; Andoc. 1, 72; Isocr. 18, 37; Dem. 1,

27. 52, 11; (Pl.) Hipparch. 227; Dio. Hal. 10, 49; Luc. Hermot. 61; Xen. Mem. quoted (Dind.)

Ζητέω *To seek*, Batr. 25; Soph. O. R. 450; Her. 1, 32; Antiph. 5, 13. 6, 47; Pl. Charm. 165; imper. ζήτει Aesch. Pr. 776, Dor. ζᾱτῶ Epich. 127 (Ahr.); Bion 2, 5; Theocr. 21, 66: imp. ἐζήτουν Thuc. 6, 61; Lys. 8, 9, -εον Her. 1, 43, ζῆτ- Il. 14, 258, only here in Hom.; H. Merc. 22: fut. -ήσω Antiph. 2, δ, 11; Thuc. 3, 67; Pl. Phaed. 107: aor. ἐζήτησα Her. 3, 137; Antiph. 5, 68; Thuc. 3, 39; Isocr. 16, 14: p. ἐζήτηκα Dinarch. 2, 19 &c.: reg. except fut. m. ζητήσομαι as pass. late, Sext. Emp. 604 (Bekk.); Galen 1, 649, but act. ἐπιζητήσ- 9, 847: with fut. p. -ηθήσομαι Luc. Char. 23; Sext. Emp. 292 (B.): and aor. m. ζητησάμενος, ἀνα- Long. Past. Prol. 2, all missed by, we think, all Lexicogr. Vb. ζητητέος Pl. Rep. 401. The form in -εύω is poetic, Dor. ζᾱτεύει Alcm. 33 (B.); Ion. ζητεύῃς Hes. Op. 398; -εύων H. Apol. 215; -εύειν H. Merc. 392.

Ζόω *To live*, Poet. for ζάω, and rare, ζόειν Simon. (A.) 1, 17 (Bergk): imp. ζόεν Anth. 13, 21. Gaisf. reads ζόειν Her. 7, 46 (Ms. F.), Bekk. Dind. Stein ζώειν (Mss. M. P. K.) See Pors. Eur. Hec. 1090 (1108).

Ζώννῡμι *To gird*, παρα-ζωννύντα Pl. Rep. 553, and ζωννῡ́ω Hippocr. 8, 144 (Lit.): imp. ἐζώννῡες N. T. Joh. 21, 18: fut. ζώσω late, V. T. Exod. 29, 9. N. T. Joh. 21, 18: aor. ζῶσα Hes. Th. 573, ἔζωσα Ap. Rh. 1, 368; V. T. Ezec. 16, 10; imper. σύ-ζωσον Ar. Thesm. 255; ζώσας Od. 18, 76; Hippocr. 4, 122: p. ἔζωκα late, Anth. 9, 778; Paus. 8, 40, δι- Dio. Hal. 2, 5, ὑπ- Galen 9, 402: p. p. ἔζωσμαι Hippocr. 4, 134, ἐπ- Her. 2, 85, δι- Thuc. 1, 6 (-ζωμ- Stahl), περι- Ar. Av. 1148; Com. Fr. (Anax.) 3, 183, rare ἔζωμαι, περι- Athen. 14, 622: plp. ἔζωστο Plut. Ant. 4, but as mid. ὑπ-εζωσμένοι ἦσαν Her. 7, 69: aor. ἐζώσθην late, Nonn. Par. 5, 3, δι- Theophr. Fr. 6, 1, 22, ἀπο- Herodn. 2, 13, 12. 8, 8, 2. Mid. ζώννῠμαι *gird oneself*, Od. 24, 89: imp. ζωννῡ́μην Il. 10, 78, ἐζώννῠσο Nonn. Par. 21, 18, iter. ζωννύσκετο Il. 5, 857: fut. late ζώσομαι Theon. Rhet. 12, 51: aor. ζωσάμην Il. 14, 181. Od. 18, 67; Hes. Op. 345, ἐζωσ- Coluth. 207; Heliod. 8, 9, κατ- Eur. Bac. 698, ξυ-ζ- Ar. Thesm. 656, συ-ζ- Lys. 536 (Dind. but ξυ-ζ- Mein. Dind. 5 ed.), περι- Pax 687; Polyb. 30, 13: as mid. ὑπ-εζωσμένος Her. 7, 69 quoted. Vb. ζωστός Plut. Alex. 32. ζώννυνται Od. 24, 89, seems subjunctive. This verb is common in Epic, rare in prose, never, we think, in Trag. except κατ-εζώσαντο Eur. Bac. quoted, never in Comedy, except occasionally in comp.

Ζώω *To live*, Epic and Ion. for ζάω, (in Attic Poet. rare, never in trimet.) Il. 18, 61. Od. 24, 263; Pind. Ol. 2, 25. I. 3, 5;

Soph. El. 157 (chor.). O. C. 1213 (chor.). Fr. 520 chor. (D. 5 ed.); Ar. Av. 609 (anapaest.); Bion 1, 53; Anth. App. Epigr. 278; Her. 2, 36. 3, 22. 4, 22; Hippocr. 6, 482. 506. 8, 70 (Lit.); subj. ζώω Od. 3, 354; ζώοιμι Theogn. 1121, ζώοις Luc. D. Mort. 6, 5; ζώειν Il. 18, 91; Soph. O. C. 1212 (chor.); Her. 1, 31. 7, 46; Luc. D. Syr. 6, Epic -έμεναι Od. 7, 149, -έμεν 24, 436: imp. ἔζωον Od. 22, 245; Hes. Op. 112; Her. 4, 112, ζῶον Hes. Scut. 86, iter. ζώεσκον Hes. Op. 90; Bion 1, 30: fut. late ζώσω, ἐπανα- Dial. Herm. de Astrol. 1, 10, 42: aor. ἔζωσα, ἐπ- Her. 1, 120 (Mss. S. M. K. Gaisf. Krüg. Dietsch, Stein, ἐπ-έζησε Mss. F. a. Ald. Bekk. Dind.): p. ἔζωκα in Inscr. 3684. See ζάω. ζώω never occurs in classic Attic prose, and never in trimeter, in Attic poetry: in Her. Bekk. Bred. and Dind. decidedly prefer it, Gaisf. and Stein follow the Mss.

H.

Ἡβάω *To be at, or near, the age of puberty, be vigorous*, Anacr. 18; Aesch. Ag. 584; Eur. Bac. 190; Hippocr. 7, 450; Thuc. 3, 36, **ἡβάσκω** Eur. Alc. 1085; Hippocr. 1, 415 (Erm.); Xen. An. 4, 6, 1; subj. ἡβᾷ Eur. Or. 697, -ῶσι Aeschin. 3, 122?; opt. ἡβῷμι Il. 7, 133; ἡβῶν Il. 12, 382. Od. 23, 187; Aesch. Ch. 879; Ar. Ran. 1055; Pl. Leg. 763; Aeschin. 2, 142: imp. ἥβων Eur. H. F. 436; Ar. Vesp. 357: fut. Dor. ἡβάσω Anth. (Incert.) 7, 482, but ἐφ-ηβήσω Xen. Cyr. 6, 1, 12: aor. ἥβησα Eur. Alc. 654; Xen. Cyr. 8, 7, 6; Isae. 8, 31 (B. Saupp.); subj. ἡβήσῃ Od. 1, 41; Pl. Leg. 928, -ωσι Apol. 41; opt. -ήσειας Simon. C.? 183 (Bergk), -σειε Hes. Op. 132, -σαιμεν Isae. 1, 10; -ήσας Il. 5, 550; Eur. Heracl. 740; Isae. 10, 12; Aeschin. 1, 13; (Dem.) 46, 20; ἡβῆσαι (Dem.) 46, 24: p. ἥβηκα, παρ- Thuc. 2, 44, -ηκώς Her. 3, 53; Luc. Lexiph. 13: plp. παρ-ηβήκεε Her. 3, 53. ἡβώοιμι (-ώῳμι Düntzer) Epic opt. pres. lengthened on ἡβῷμι (-άοιμι) Il. 7, 157. 11, 670; ἡβώοντα 9, 446, -ώοντες 24, 604, -ώωσα Od. 5, 69.

Ἡγεμονεύω *To lead, command*, Il. 13, 53; Xen. Ages. 1, 3: imp. ἡγεμόνευον Il. 2, 645; Ar. Pax 1093; Her. 7, 99, Dor. ἁγεμ- Theocr. 11, 27: fut. -εύσω Od. 6, 261: aor. ἡγεμόνευσα Pl. Conv. 197, Dor. ἁγεμ- Pind. Ol. 9, 3: pass. -εύεσθαι Thuc. 3, 61, is reg. but not very complete, not in Trag., rare in Comedy, and, we think, without mid. The collat. ἡγεμονέω seems confined to pres. and used by Plato only, -ονεῖν Tim. 70; -ονοῦν 41.

Ἡγέομαι *To lead, think*, Od. 23, 134; Soph. Ant. 1167; Ar.

Pl. 27; Her. 2, 93; Antiph. 6, 8; Thuc. 2, 44, Dor. ἁγ- Alcm. 93 (B.); Eur. Phoen. 120 (chor.); ἡγεύμενος Her. 2, 93; Hippocr. 1, 612; Dor. imper. ἁγέο Anth. 12, 119, ὑφ- Theocr. 2, 101: imp. ἡγεόμην Il. 5, 211, -ούμην Aesch. Pers. 400; Antiph. 2, β, 9; Thuc. 3, 1; Lys. 1, 37; Pl. Phaedr. 244, Ion. -εύμην H. Cer. 181; Her. 2, 115, Dor. ἁγεῖτο Pind. P. 10, 45; Theocr. 11, 11: pass.? ἡγεόμενος Her. 3, 14 (Bekk.): fut. ἡγήσομαι Il. 14, 374; Soph. El. 1038; Ar. Pax 917; Thuc. 4, 20; Lys. 12, 35; Xen. Cyr. 2, 1, 13; Pl. Rep. 530: aor. ἡγησάμην Il. 12, 251; Aesch. Ch. 905; Ar. Nub. 1474 (Bekk. Bergk); Her. 1, 95; Antiph. 6, 35; Thuc. 1, 39; Lys. 3, 1; Pl. Leg. 635, Dor. ἁγησ-, εἰς- Epich. 66 (Ahr.): p. ἥγημαι usu. act. and as pres. Eur. Phoen. 550; Her. 1, 126. 2, 40. 72. 115; Pl. Tim. 19. Leg. 837. Hip. Min. 374 &c. Ion. 3 pl. -έαται Her. 1, 136, Dor. ἁγ- Pind. P. 4, 248; pass. Dem. 43, 66 (Dor. Orac.), δι-ηγ- Antiph. 1, 31, ἀπ- Her. 1, 207. 5, 62. 9, 26: plp. ἥγηντο act. Himer. Or. 13, 5: ἡγήθην *simple* if sound, rare and late, Polyaen. 2, 31, 4 (Murs. ᾠήθ- Woelffl.), but pass. περι- Pl. Leg. 770, ἀφ- Agath. 4, 30: fut. late ἡγηθήσεται pass. Orig. Ref. Haeres. p. 3 (Miller). Vb. ἡγητός, περι- C. Fr. (Antiph.) 3, 84, ἡγητέον Xen. Hell. 4, 7, 2. In Attic the perf. is rare, especially in poetry: in *classic* Greek we have not seen the *simple* aor. pass., the comp. only once. Some take ἡγεόμενον Her. 3, 14, quoted, as act. *leading, going first;* others read ἀγεόμενον (Mss. R. c.), ἡγεόμ- (Mss. M. V. S. &c.) Ion. for ἀγομ- (Dind. Abicht). Both ἡγεομ- and ἡγευμ- occur in Her. and Hippocr.

Ἡγερέθομαι *To be collected* (ἀγείρω), Epic and only 3 pl. -ονται Il. 3, 231; Hom. H. 1, 147; Or. Sib. 3, 166: and imp. ἡγερέθοντο Il. 23, 233. Od. 18, 41; Hes. Sc. 184; Orph. Arg. 114; Mosch. 2, 122; subj. -ωνται Opp. Hal. 3, 360; inf. -έθεσθαι Il. 10, 127 (Wolf, Bekk. Dind. La R. -έεσθαι Vulg. as from ἠγερέομαι).

Ἡδύνω (ῡ) *To make sweet,* Hippocr. 7, 78 (Lit.); Xen. Conv. 4. 8; Aristot. Meteor. 2, 3, 38, Dor. ἁδ- Epich. 82 (Ahr.): aor. ἥδῦνα, -ύνῃς Luc. Hist. Con. 10; -ῦναι Pl. Theaet. 175; ἡδύνας Hippocr. 8, 300; Com. Fr. (Diph.) 4, 385: p. p. ἥδυσμαι, -υσμένος Pl. Rep. 607; Aristot. Polit. 8, 5, 25. Probl. 20, 23, συν- Plut. Mor. 661: aor. ἡδύνθην, -υνθείς Com. Fr. (Antiph.) 3, 49, and ἡδύσθην, ὑπερ- Galen 4, 588. Vb. ἡδυντέον Com. Fr. (Alex.) 3, 470.

Ἥδω *To please,* Com. Fr. (Mon.) 38; (Pl.) Ax. 366; Sext. Emp. 7, 442, in act. rare, and perhaps rather late, except: imp. ἧδε Anacr. Fr. 148 (Vulg. Bergk 2 ed.): fut. ἥσω Liban. T. 4, 473: aor. ἧσα Anacr. quoted (Mss. A. C. Bergk 3 ed.); Com. Fr. (Ephipp.) 3, 326?; Ael. H. A. 10, 48. Mid. ἥδομαι *please oneself, delight in,* Simon. Am. 7, 90; Aesch. Eum. 312; Soph. Tr. 374; Ar. Pax 291; Her. 2, 68; Thuc. 1, 120; Xen. Cyr. 6, 2, 1; Lys. 21, 16: **imp.** ἥδετο Soph. Aj. 272; Xen. Cyr. 5, 4, 39: p. (ἧσμαι) perhaps in ἅσμενος with change of aspirate and accent for (ἡσμένος) Il. 14, 108; Pind. Ol. 13, 74; Soph. Tr. 18; Her. 8, 14. 106; Thuc. 3, 66, see below: **aor.** ἥσθην as **mid.** Soph. Ph. 715; Ar. Ach. 13; Her. 1, 56. 69; Thuc. 1, 129; Lys. 2, 26; Pl. Phaed. 97: **fut.** ἡσθήσομαι as **mid.** Soph. O. R. 453; Eur. Elec. 415; Hippocr. 6, 650; Xen. Cyr. 2, 1, 13; Isocr. 8, 5; Pl. Phaedr. 233, συν- Xen. An. 7, 7, 42; Isocr. 5, 131: **aor. mid.** ἥσατο rare and Epic, Od. 9, 353.—ἥδοντα *pleasures,* (Pl.) Ax. 366. ἧσται Sopat. Athen. 8, 26, has been referred to this verb, as p. p., but the passage seems to require it to be referred to ἧμαι *sit.*

Ἠερέθομαι *To be raised, elated, to flaunt* (ἀείρω), Poet. and only **pres.** -ονται Il. 2, 448. 21, 12; Ap. Rh. 3, 638; Opp. Hal. 1, 435: and **imp.** ἠερέθοντο Ap. Rh. 2, 1082. 3, 368.

Ἥκω *To come, am come,* Il. 5, 478 (Wolf, Spitzn. Dind.); Hipponax 13 (B.); Aesch. Pr. 284; Soph. O. C. 732; Ar. Ach. 37; Her. 3, 156. 7, 157 (1, 65 Orac.); Antiph. 2, β, 2; Thuc. 1, 137; Andoc. 1, 4; Lys. 12, 14; Isocr. 4, 3; Isae. 4, 24; subj. ἥκω Soph. Tr. 985, -κῃ Her. 7, 8; Pl. Rep. 540 &c.; ἥκοιμι Pl. Conv. 174, ἥκοι Soph. Aj. 186; Her. 3, 156; Pl. Leg. 952, -οιεν Her. 7, 203; Thuc. 6, 63; imper. ἧκε Soph. Aj. 1116; Ar. Pax 275; Xen. Cyr. 4, 5, 25, ἡκέτω Eur. Rhes. 337 &c.: **imp.** ἧκον *came, had come,* Aesch. Pr. 661; Soph. O. C. 738; Ar. Nub. 1383; Her. 1, 83; Antiph. 2, γ, 2; Thuc. 1, 91; Lys. 1, 11; Isocr. 14, 3: **fut.** ἥξω Sapph. 109 (B.); Aesch. Ch. 561; Soph. O. R. 1158; Eur. Andr. 738; Ar. Eq. 497; Her. 2, 29; Thuc. 3, 4; Isocr. 14, 43; Pl. Crit. 53, Dor. ἡξῶ Theocr. 15, 144; ἥξοι Her. 1, 127; Thuc. 4, 110; ἥξειν Antiph. 2, γ, 6: **aor.** ἧξα late, Paus. 2, 11, 5; Galen 10, 609: **pf.** late ἧκα Philostr. 115; Scymn. 62 (Mein.); V. T. Gen. 47, 4, Dor. 1 pl. ἥκαμες Plut. Mor. 225; ἡκώς Theod. Prodr. Catomyom. 39 (Herch.); ἡκέναι Nicet. Eug. 6, 97: **plp.** ἥκεσαν Joseph. Ant. 19, 1, 14. **Mid.** ἥκηται occurs Aretae. p. 92 (Adams): **imp.** ἡκόμην Musgrave's conjecture for ἠγόμην Eur. Fr. 206 (Dind.) is not *received:* **fut.** ἥξεται Marc. Ant. 2, 4; Or. Sib. 12, 199, the only instances we ever met.—Imper. ἧκε rare Soph. Aj. 1116; Ar. Pax 275. 845. Lys. 924; Xen. Cyr. 4, 5, 25, ἡκέτω Eur. Rhes. 337. The subj. opt. and imperf. seem to be used aoristically.—For this verb the old Poets generally use ἵκω. In Pind. ἥκω never occurs; in Hes. twice, Th. 669. Sc. 343; in Hom. twice, Il. 5, 478. Od. 13, 325 (Wolf, Heyne, Dind. Ameis.) In both places however

Bekk *now* (2 ed.) and La Roche write ἵκω in conformity with Il. 18, 406. Od. 15, 329. Kühner and Jelf seem to have foreseen and predicted this, for though ἥκω stands Il. 5, 478. Od. 13, 325, in all Mss. and, as far as we know, stood in all editions till 1858, they pronounced it several years previously *post-Homeric*. So too thought Choerob. and Eustath., but Buttmann held it to be a dialectic variety of ἵκω, and *Homeric*—Lobeck so far approves.

Ἠλαίνω *To wander, act foolishly*, Poet. and only **pres. act.** ἠλαίνοντι 3 pl. Dor. for -ουσι Theocr. 7, 23 (Junt. Mein. Ahr. Ziegl. Fritzsche), see mid.; -αίνων Callim. Dian. 251. **Mid.** ἠλαίνονται Theocr. 7, 23 (Vulg. Wordsw.) The Tragedians use ἀλαίνω.

Ἠλάσκω *To wander, flee*, only **pres.** -άσκουσι Il. 2, 470; Emped. 388 (Stein); part. -ουσαι Il. 13, 104, and ἠλασκάζω **pres.** -άζει Od. 9, 457 (ἠλυσκ- Bekk. Nauck); part. -άζων Il. 18, 281: and **imp.** ἠλάσκαζες Hom. H. 1, 142. Both Epic.

Ἡλιάζω *To sit in the court* Ἡλιαία, in **act.** only **fut.** -άξεις, if correct, Ar. Lys. 380 (Mss. Bekk. Bergk, but **mid.** -άξει Buttm. Dind.). **Mid.** ἡλιάζομαι Com. Fr. (Phryn.) 2, 605; Aristot. H. A. 9, 5, 7; -άζηται (Dem.) 24, 50: **fut.** -ἄσομαι, -ἄσει Ar. Vesp. 772, Dor. -άξει Lys. 380, see act.: **aor.** ἡλιάσασθαι Ar. Eq. 798.

Ἧμαι *To sit, simple* mostly Poet. Il. 18, 104. Od. 14, 41, ἧσαι Il. 15, 245; Aesch. Eum. 440, ἧσται Il. 19, 345; Aesch. Sept. 513; Eur. Alc. 604; Her. 9, 57, in comp. ἧται, κάθ-ηται Ar. Lys. 597; Pl. Apol. 35, ἥμεθα Il. 15, 740, ἧσθε Od. 2, 240; Com. Fr. (Cratin.) 2, 95 (hexam.), ἧνται Eur. Bac. 38; Callim. Fr. 122; Ap. Rh. 2, 1086, Epic εἵἄται Il. 10, 100; (Luc.) D. Syr. 31, Ion. ἕἄται Il. 3, 134, κατ- Her. 1, 199; subj. and opt. in comp. καθ-; imper. ἧσο Il. 3, 406. Od. 20, 262, ἥσθω, καθ- Aesch. Pr. 916, ἧσθε Ap. Rh. 4, 856; inf. ἧσθαι Il. 13, 253; Aesch. Ag. 862; ἥμενος Il. 5, 356; Hes. Op. 501; Pind. N. 10, 62; Aesch. Ag. 183; Eur. Andr. 699; Theocr. 1, 48, Dor. ἅμ- v. r. Pind. Ol. 10, 33: **imp.** or **plp.** ἥμην Il. 6, 336. Od. 11, 49; Soph. Tr. 24, ἧσο Eur. Rhes. 846, ἧστο Il. 23, 451; Hes. Sc. 214; Soph. Aj. 311; Eur. Supp. 664, καθ- Il. 1, 569; Eur. Bac. 1102; Ar. Ran. 778; Pl. Euthyd. 271, κατ- Her. 1, 46, and ἧτο in comp. καθ-ῆτο Dem. 18, 169, 'πικαθ-ῆτο Ar. Ran. 1046, and ἐκάθητο Ar. Av. 510; Thuc. 5, 6; Xen. Hell. 5, 2, 29, ἥμεθα Od. 3, 263, ἥμεσθα Eur. I. A. 88, ἧντο Il. 3, 153, Epic εἵἄτο 7, 61; Hes. Th. 622, Ion. ἕἄτο 7, 414, κατ- Her. 8, 73, dual ἥσθην Il. 8, 445, ἑήσ- Orph. Arg. 818. See ἕω, and κάθημαι.—καθῆατο Il. 11, 76 (Vulg.) is now καθείατο (Wolf, Bekk. Spitzn. Dind.)—ἧμαι in *simple* is Epic and Trag., once or twice in Ionic prose, ἧσται Her. and εἵαται

Luc. quoted: in Comedy and Attic prose, the comp. κάθημαι is the form in use.

'Ημί *I say*, as φημί (inquam), παῖ, ἠμί, παῖ Ar. Ran. 37, ἠσί Com. Fr. (Herm.) 2, 382; Sapph. 48 (Schneid. ἦσι Bergk 97), ἠτί Alcm. 139 (Bergk): **imp.** ἦν, ἦ colloquially, as ἦν δ' ἐγώ *said I*, Pl. Rep. 328, ἦ δ' ὅς, ἥ, *said he, she*, 327. Conv. 205, also ἦ δ' ὃς ὁ Γλαύκων Pl. Rep. 327, ἦ ῥ' Ἄμυκος Theocr. 22, 75, the Epics generally ἦ alone, as ἦ *he said*, Il. 1, 219, rarely in Hom. with nominative ἦ ῥα γυνή Il. 6, 390. 22, 77. Od. 3, 337. 22, 292. It is scarcely used beyond the 1 sing. pres. and 1 and 3 sing. imp. In Attic ἦν δ' ἐγώ &c. is generally in the middle or end of a sentence; Luc. however sometimes begins with it, ἦ δ' ὅς, σίγα, Philop. 22, ἦν δ' ἐγώ, ὀλίγοι 23.

Ἤμβλακον, see ἀμπλακίσκω.

'Ημύω (ῠ, late ῡ) *To bow, sink*, Poet. -ύει Il. 2, 148, -ύει, ἐπ- Opp. H. 1, 228, -ύουσι Nic. Al. 453, κατ-ημύουσι Ap. Rh. 3, 1400: **fut.** ἠμύσουσι act. Orac. Paus. 10, 9, 5 (Vulg. Schub. v. r. λήσουσι Herm.): **aor.** ἤμῡσα Il. 8, 308; Ap. Rh. 2, 582; rare in Attic Soph. Fr. 742 (D.); late ῠ Anth. 7, 88. 9, 262, κατ- 9, 309; opt. ἠμύσειε Il. 2, 373; part. -ύσασα Opp. Hal. 2, 307: **p.** in comp. ὑπ-εμνήμῡκε Il. 22, 491, formed by Attic reduplication, ἐμ-ήμυκε, with ν inserted, ἐμνήμυκε.

(**'Ηπάομαι**) *To mend, patch*, only inf. aor. ἠπήσασθαι Ar. Fr. 28 (D.); Galen 5, 812: and p. part. ἠπημένος pass. *patched*, late prose Aristid. 46, 307 (Dind.)

'Ηπιάω *To assuage, sooth* (ἤπιος), not used in *simple* except by Schol. and Old Lexicogr., but imp. pass. κατ-ηπιόωντο Il. 5, 417.

'Ηπύω, see ἀπύω.

'Ησθημένος, *clothed*, Eur. Hel. 1539, Ion. ἐσθημ- Her. 3, 129. See ἐσθέω.

'Ησσάω and ἡττ- *To conquer*, act. late, fut. ἡττήσω, opt. -ήσοιτε Theod. Prodr. 5, 174: **aor.** ἥττησα Polyb. 1, 75; Heracl. Incred. 16 (West.); Pseud.-Callisth. 1, 38. 3, 25; Joseph. Ant. 12, 7, 1: **p.** ἥττηκα Diod. Sic. 15, 87. **Pass.** ἡσσάομαι *to be inferior, conquered*, Soph. Fr. 674 (D.); Thuc. 3, 57, ἡττάομαι Pl. Phil. 12, Ion. ἑσσόομαι Her. 3, 106, see below; subj. ἡττᾶσθε Ar. Plut. 482; ἡττᾶσθαι Eq. 1230; Xen. Cyr. 5, 4, 32; Isae. 11, 21, ἡσσ- Eur. Rhes. 497; Thuc. 4, 64; ἡττώμενος Andoc. 3, 26; Pl. Prot. 352; Isocr. 9, 44, ἡσσ- Aesch. Sept. 516; Eur. Supp. 705: **imp.** ἡσσῶντο Eur. Supp. 683; Thuc. 1, 49, ἡττ- Xen. Hell. 5, 2, 5: with **fut. mid.** ἡττήσομαι as **pass.** Xen. An. 2, 3, 23; Lys. 28, 9: more freq. fut. p. ἡσσηθήσομαι Eur. Hipp. 727. 976, ἡττ- Lys. 20, 32; Xen. Cyr. 3, 3, 42. 44: **p.p.** ἥσσημαι Soph. Aj. 1242; Eur. Alc. 697. Fr. 283 (Dind.);

Thuc. 6, 91, ἡττ- Ar. Nub. 1102; Andoc. 3, 19; Pl. Euthyd. 300: plp. ἥττητο Dem. 19, 160. 24, 15: aor. ἡσσήθην Eur. Andr. 917; Thuc. 7, 25, ἡττ- Ar. Av. 70; Lys. 17, 5; Isocr. 8, 100; Pl. Menex. 243; Dem. 20, 146. **Vb.** ἡσσητέον Soph. Ant. 678, ἡττ- Ar. Lys. 450. Thuc. and, in late recensions, the Tragedians always have ἡσσάομαι, Ar., the Orators, and Plato ἡττ-, so Xen. (Popp. Dind.), but ἡσσημένον (Xen.) Apol. 19 (Bornem. Dind. Saupp.) Ion. ἑσσοῦμαι not augmented, **imp.** ἑσσοῦντο Her. 7, 166. 8, 75: **p.** ἕσσωται 7, 10; -ωμένος 7, 9. 8, 130: **aor.** ἑσσώθη 2, 169. 3, 45. 4, 162. 5, 102.

Ἡσυχάζω *To be at rest*, Thuc. 6, 38; in tragic poet. imper. ἡσῡχαζε Aesch. Pr. 344; Eur. H. F. 98, -άζετε Or. 1350; -άζων Soph. O. R. 620; Eur. Ion 601; Pl. Parm. 162; -άζειν Eur. Bac. 790; Thuc. 1, 120: **imp.** ἡσύχ- Thuc. 2, 81: **fut.** -ᾱσω Thuc. 1, 142. 143. 2, 84: and **mid.** -ᾱσομαι Luc. Gall. 1: **aor.** ἡσῡχασα Thuc. 8, 24; Anth. 5, 167; subj. -άσωσι Hippocr. 4, 326; but trans. *having put to rest*, ἡσυχάσας Pl. Rep. 572. The **mid.** form we have seen only in Luc. quoted, the **pass.** ἡσυχάζεται only in V. T. Job 37, 16.

Ἠχέω, see ἀχ-.

Θ.

Θαάσσω *To sit*, Epic (Attic θάσσω) θαάσσεις Hom. H. 3, 468, -άσσει Ap. Rh. 3, 659; Coluth. 343; inf. θαάσσειν Ap. Rh. 4, 1274, Epic -ασσέμεν Od. 3, 336; Hom. H. 3, 172; -αάσσων Ap. Rh. 2, 1026: **imp.** θάασσον Il. 9, 194. 15, 124.

Θᾱέομαι Dor. for θηέ- *To gaze at*, Poet. Pind. P. 8, 45: **imp.** θᾱεῖτο Theocr. 22, 200 (Vulg. Mein. Wordsw. θηεῖ- D. Junt. Ahr. Ziegl. Fritzsche): **aor.** imper. θάησαι Anth. App. Epigr. 213; -σάμεναι Pind. P. 9, 62 (Bergk, Momms.) **Vb.** θαητός Pind. Ol. 6, 2.

Θᾱκέω *To sit* (θᾶκος), Soph. Aj. 325. O. R. 20; Eur. Heracl. 239; imper. θάκει Soph. Aj. 1173; θᾱκῶν Aesch. Pr. 313; Soph. Tr. 23: **imp.** ἐθάκει Com. Fr. (Cratin.) 2, 146, θάκουν unaugm. Eur. Hec. 1153 (Mss. Pors. Dind. 2 ed. Kirchh. 1 ed. θάκους Herm. Nauck, Paley, Dind. 5 ed. Kirchh. 2 ed.) Dor.? and Ion. θωκέω, **pres.** only, θωκεῖτε Sophr. 41 (Ahr.); θωκέων Her. 2, 173.

Θᾰλέθω *To flourish, abound*, lengthened from θάλλω, and Poet. θαλέθει Ap. Rh. 2, 843, -ουσι Emped. 249; Q. Sm. 11, 96 (Koechly); -θοισι Ibyc. 1, 6; -έθων Od. 6, 63, -οντες Il. 9, 467. 23, 32; causat. *make to grow*, θαλέθουσι Theocr. 25, 16: **imp.**

iter. θαλέθεσκες Anth. 11, 374, -έθεσκε Mosch. 2, 67 (Mss. Ziegl. Meineke *now*).

Θαλέω (ᾰ, θᾱλέω is Dor.) *To flourish*, Ion. and late Epic, θᾰλέει Nonn. 16, 78, -έουσι Q. Sm. 11, 96 (Vulg.); θαλέοντα Hippocr. 6, 654 (Lit. v. r. θαλέθοντα): imp, iter. θαλέεσκε Mosch. 2, 67 (Ms. F. Mein. 1 ed. θαλέθεσκε Mss. Herm. Ziegl. Mein. 2 ed.) θᾱλέω Dor. See under θάλλω.

Θάλλω *To bloom, flourish*, Hes. Op. 236; Hom. H. Cer. 402; Archil. 100; Pind. Ol. 9, 16; Aesch. Supp. 858 (chor.); Soph. O. C. 700 (chor.); Eur. Ion 1436 (trimet.); Ar. Thesm. 1000 (chor.); Hippocr. 6, 248; Xen. Mem. 2, 1, 33; Pl. Conv. 203. Leg. 945; Dor. f. pt. -λλοισα Pind. P. 7, 19; also causative *produce*, Aesch. Pers. 616: **imp.** ἔθαλλον causative *made grow*, Pind. Ol. 3, 23; *grew*, Anth. 12, 256, and (θαλλέω) ἐθάλλεον if correct, see Plut. Mor. 110: **fut.** late θαλλήσω *will produce*, Alex. Aet. in Parthen. 14, 9, where Passow θηλήσω from θηλέω: **1 aor.** late ἀν-έθηλα Ael. H. A. 2, 25. 9, 21. V. H. 5, 3, 4: **2 aor.** rare and doubtful, θᾰ́λον Hom. H. 19, 33 (λάθε Ruhnk. κέλε Lobeck), but late prose ἀν-έθαλον V. T. Ps. 27, 7. Sap. 4, 4; N. T. Phil. 4, 10: **2 p.** τέθηλα as pres. Hes. Op. 227; Soph. Ph. 259; Luc. H. V. 2, 13; Dio. Hal. in Dem. 40, Dor. τέθᾱλα Pind. Fr. 106, 5 (Bergk); subj. τεθήλῃ Epigr. Pl. Phaedr. 264; Hippocr. 6, 654 (Lit.); τεθηλώς Od. 12, 103; Hippocr. 1, 626. 632 (Lit.), Dor. -ᾱλώς Pind. P. 11, 53, τεθηλυῖα Paus. 5, 13, 4, Epic -ᾰλυῖα Il. 9, 208; Hes. Th. 902; Simon. (C.) 102; τεθηλέναι Pl. Crat. 414; Arr. Ind. 40: **plp.** τεθήλειν as **imp.** Od. 5, 69, ἐτεθ- Philostr. Apoll. 311: **fut.** θᾰλήσομαι, ἀνα- Anth. 7, 281 (may be from θᾰλέω, late Epic Q. Sm. 11, 96). θηλέω, Dor. θᾱλ- is reg.: **imp.** ἐθήλεον Anth. App. Epigr. 207, θήλεον Od. 5, 73, Dor. ἐθᾱλ- Plut. Mor. 110 (Passow) for ἐθάλλ-, see above: **fut.** θηλήσω, ἀνα- Il. 1, 236: **aor.** ἐθήλησα, Dor. θᾱ́λησα Pind. N. 4, 88; θηλήσας Anth. 9, 363: **p. p.** τεθηλημένος Hippocr. 2, 11 (Kühn, but τεθήλῃ μέν Lit.), see above.

Θαλπιάω *To be warm*, is Epic and confined to pt. θαλπιόων Od. 19, 319, -όωντι Arat. 1073.

Θάλπω *To warm, flatter*, Ap. Rh. 4, 1542; Alciphr. 2, 2, 47; -πων Od. 21, 179: **fut.** θάλψω *denied*, but Alciphr. 2, 4, 74; Septuag. Job 39, 14; v. r. Nic. Alex. 411: **aor.** ἔθαλψα Soph. Tr. 1082 reg. and complete. θάλπεαι Ion. and Dor. 2 sing. **pass.** Theocr. 5, 31. No **mid.** we think, except θάλψομαι as **pass.** or **mid.** intrans. Alciphr. 3, 42, 17.

Θαμβαίνω, see θαυμαίνω.

Θανατόω *To put to death*, Xen. Hel. 2, 3, 15: **fut.** -ώσω Aesch. Pr. 1053; Her. 1, 113: **aor.** ἐθανάτωσα Antiph. 3, γ, 11;

Pl. Leg. 872: p. late τεθανατωκέναι Theod. Prodr. Catomyom. 300 (Herch.): p. p. τεθανατωμένος Polyb. 24, 4, 14: aor. p. ἐθανατώθη Hippocr. 3, 504; Xen. An. 2, 6, 4; Pl. Leg. 865: fut. θανατωθήσομαι late, V. T. Lev. 27, 29 &c.: reg. except. fut. mid. θανατώσοιτο pass. Xen. Cyr. 7, 5, 31, missed, we think, by Lexicogr.

(Θάνω) see θνήσκω.

Θάομαι (ᾱ) *To gaze at, admire,* Dor. subj. θάμεθα Sophr. 42; imper. θάεο Anth. Plan. 4, 306, θᾶσθε (Megar.) Ar. Ach. 770: fut. θᾱ́σομαι, and -οῦμαι, θασεῖσθε if correct, Callim. Cer. 3 (-σασθε Mein.); θᾱσόμεναι Theocr. 15, 23: aor. ἐθᾱσάμην, opt. θησαίατ' Od. 18, 191; imper. θᾶσαι Epich. 78; Sophr. 44; Theocr. 10, 41. 15, 65. Epigr. 16, 1; inf. θάσασθαι Theocr. 2, 72; θασάμενοι Tab. Heracl. 1, 70. This verb is poetic, and almost peculiar to the Doric dialect. Attic θεάομαι, Ion. θηέομαι, which see.

Θάομαι *To suckle,* see (θάω).

Θάπτω *To bury,* Aesch. Ch. 440; Eur. Alc. 834; Her. 2, 41; Thuc. 2, 34; Isae. 8, 22; Aeschin. 3, 244; subj. θάπτω Il. 21, 323; Pl. Phaed. 115; θάπτοι Od. 3, 285 &c.: imp. ἔθαπτον Soph. Ant. 402; Her. 9, 85; Thuc. 3, 109, θάπτ- Il. 23, 630; Hes. Sc. 472: fut. θάψω Aesch. Sept. 1052; Soph. Ant. 72; Her. 1, 119; θάψοι Isae. 2, 10; θάψων 8, 21; θάψειν 2, 25: aor. ἔθαψα Eur. Hel. 1166; Com. Fr. (Men.) 4, 164; Her. 1, 113. 117; Thuc. 5, 11; Xen. Cyr. 4, 6, 5; Isae. 2, 37; Dem. 18, 208, θάψ- Il. 24, 612; inf. θάψαι Aesch. Ch. 433: p. p. τέθαμμαι, -αψαι? Aesch. Ch. 366 (Mss. Vulg.), -θαπται Hom. Epigr. 3, 6; Isae. 6, 64; Xen. Hel. 2. 4, 19, 3 pl. Ion. τεθάφαται Her. 6, 103 (Bekk. Gaisf. Dind. Stein), τετάφ- (Ms. C. Bred. Dietsch, Classen); τεθαμμένος Xen. Hell. 2, 4, 33; Pl. Crat. 400; τεθάφθω Luc. D. Mar. 9, 1; τεθάφθαι Aesch. Ch. 366 (Ahr. Dind. Herm.); Lycurg. 113, τετάφ- Plut. Mor. 265. 296 (Dübn.): plp. ἐτέθαπτο Od. 11, 52; Her. 1, 113: 1 aor. Ion. and rare ἐθάφθην Simon. C. 168 (Bergk); θαφθῆναι Her. 2, 81; θαφθείς 7, 228: more freq. 2 aor. ἐτᾰ́φην Her. 3, 10. 9, 85; Thuc. 5, 74; ταφῶ Ar. Av. 396; ταφείην Eur. Tr. 731; Xen. An. 5, 7, 20; ταφῆναι Eur. Phoen. 776; Ar. Eccl. 592; Her. 3, 55; Lycurg. 115; ταφείς Aesch. Sept. 1021; Eur. Supp. 545; Thuc. 3, 58: fut. ταφήσομαι Eur. Alc. 56. 632. Tr. 446. 1193; Lys. 13, 45: 3 fut. τεθάψομαι Soph. Aj. 577. 1141; Eur. I. T. 1464; Luc. D. Mar. 9, 1. Vb. θαπτέον Soph. Aj. 1140. Perf. τέτᾰφα, given in lexicons, we have never seen.

(Θάπω or τάφω) θήπω Hesych. *To astonish,* chiefly Epic and Ion. p. τέθᾰφα, if correct, Com. Fr. (Crobyl.) 4, 566, Casaubon's emendation for τέθαιφε (Mss. τέθῠφε Mein.): 2 p. τέθηπα *am astonished*, Od. 6, 168; Her. 2, 156; Luc. Pisc. 34; Himer. Or. 7, 5; Themist. 4, 49ª. 6, 80; τεθηπώς Il. 21, 29; Emped. 81; Ap. Rh. 3, 215; Ael. V. H. 14, 47 (τέτηφε Hesych.): **plp.** ἐτεθήπειν Ael. Fr. 116; Luc. Peregr. 39. Scyth. 9, Epic ἐτεθήπεα Od. 6, 166: **2 aor.** ἔτᾰφον Aesch. Pers. 1000 (chor.); Callim. Dian. 103, τάφ- Pind. P. 4, 95; ταφών Il. 23, 101. Od. 16, 12. **2 aor.** Poet.: **1 perf.** doubtful: **2 perf.** Epic and Ion. but not in classic Attic prose, occasionally in late, Plut. Mor. 65; Luc. quoted; Philostr. 870; Dio Cass. 59, 27: ἐτεθήπεσαν Ael. H. A. 10, 48; App. Civ. 4, 14.

Θαρσύνω, see θρασύνω.

Θάσσω *To sit*, in Attic Poet. for θαάσσω, perhaps only **pres.** Eur. Or. 85, -εις Andr. 117; Ar. Thesm. 889, -ει Soph. O. R. 161, -ουσι Eur. Ion 415; θάσσων Bac. 622, -οντα Herc. F. 1214; θάσσειν 715. Hesych. has **aor. mid.** ἐθάσσατο.

Θαυμάζω *To wonder, admire*, Od. 4, 655; Pind. Fr. 99, 10; Aesch. Ag. 1199; Ar. Eq. 211; Antiph. 1, 5; Thuc. 6, 36; Lys. 2, 77, Ion. θωυμάζω Her. 1, 155. 8, 8, θωμ- in some edit.: **imp.** ἐθαύμαζον Eur. Elec. 84; Thuc. 1, 51; Pl. Conv. 206, θαύμ- Il. 10, 12; Ar. Pax 1291 (hexam.), Ion. ἐθώυμ- Her. 1, 68. 6, 1 &c. ἐθώμ- some edit., iter. θαυμάζεσκον Od. 19, 229; Theocr. 25, 186: **fut.** θαυμᾰσω doubtful in classic Attic, Xen. Cyr. 5, 2, 12 (Vulg. -άζουσι Mss. Popp. Dind. Saupp.), -άσετε Hell. 5, 1, 14 (-άσαιτε Dind. Breitb. Saupp.), -άσουσι Dinarch. 2, 15 (Maetzn. -άζουσι Mss. Bekk. B. Saupp.); but θαυμάσει Hippocr. 7, 530 (Lit.), -άσετε Galen 3, 77; and late Attic, Plut. Mor. 823; Ael. V. H. 8, 11 (Herch.); Himer. Or. 2, 3; (Luc.) Dem. enc. 43; Marc. Aur. 6, 25. 7, 26; Epist. Phal. 147 (Herch.); Dio Chrys. Or. 21 (273); Themist. 7, 98. 8, 120; Geop. 10, 89: **fut. m.** θαυμάσομαι Aesch. Pr. 476; Eur. I. T. 1318. Alc. 157; Pl. Parm. 129. Euth. 15; Xen. M. Eq. 9, 8; and late Plut. Cat. min. 59; Luc. D. Mort. 21, 2; Aristid. 43, 548; Philostr. Ap. 3, 66; V. T. Lev. 26, 32. Job 13, 10 and always, Epic -άσσομαι Il. 18, 467: **aor.** ἐθαύμασα Aesch. Sept. 771; Soph. Fr. 319; Eur. Elec. 516; Ar. Eq. 999; Thuc. 1, 138; Isocr. 4, 1; Xen. Mem. 1, 1, 1; Pl. Apol. 17, ἀπ- Od. 6, 49, ἐθώυμ- or ἐθώμ- Her. 8, 37, Poet. θαύμ- Hom. H. Merc. 414; Philox. 3, 23 (B.): **p.** τεθαύμακα Com. Fr. (Alex.) 3, 475; Xen. Mem. 1, 4, 2; Dem. 8, 4. 24, 159: **p. p.** τεθαύμασμαι Polyb. 4, 82: **aor.** ἐθαυμάσθην Xen. Ven. 1, 5; (Dem). 61, 43; θαυμασθῇ Thuc. 6, 12; -θεῖμεν Isocr. 15. 219: **fut.** θαυμασθήσομαι Thuc. 2, 41. 7, 56; Isocr. 6, 105; Com. Fr. (Anon.) 4, 690; late as **mid.** N. T. Rev. 17, 8 (Mss. Lach. Tisch. -άσονται Mss. Vulg. Sin.) **Vb.** θαυμαστός Hom. H. Cer. 10, -εός Eur. Hel. 85; Athen. 11, 508, θαυματός Hom. H. Merc. 80; Hes. Sc. 165; *now* Pind. P. 10, 30. **Mid.** late, θαυμάζονται Ael. V. H. 12, 30; Galen 1, 55 (Kühn): **fut.** -άσομαι classic, see above: **aor.** ἐθαυμασάμην Aesop 92 (Halm); Schol. Soph. O. R. 287; subj. θαυμασώμεθα Proclus in Pl. Parm. (Vulg. -αίμεθα Cousin, p. 959); opt. -άσαιτο Nicol. Rhet. 4 (Walz); Galen 6, 517; Joseph. Jud. B. 3, 5, 1: and, if correct, **aor. p.** ἐθαυμάσθην N. T. Rev. 13, 3 (Lach. ἐθαύμασεν Vulg. Sin. Tisch.): so **fut.** θαυμασθήσονται 17, 8, others -άσονται, see above. The **mid.** has been overlooked by all our lexicons. The Ionic form is variously θωϋμάζω, θωυμ-, θωμ-, **imp.** ἐθωΰμαζον, ἐθώυμαζον, ἐθώμ-. Gaisf. varies, Bekk. θώυμ-, ἐθώυμ-, Dind. leans to θώμ-, ἐθώμ-. Tischendorf (Rev. 17, 8) reads **fut. p.** θαυμασθήσονται as **mid.** *shall wonder*, but retains **aor.** ἐθαύμασεν (13, 3) in preference to ἐθαυμάσθη, on the ground that the *uncials* which form their endings are easily confused. Hesychius however explains ἀγασθείς by θαυμασθείς and ἐθάμβησεν by ἐθαυμάσθην (ἐθαύμασεν Schmidt), which, if correct, favours the reading ἐθαυμάσθη (Mss. A. C. Lach. Tregell.) against ἐθαύμασεν.

Θαυμαίνω *To admire*, Poet. **imp.** θαύμαινον H. Ven. 84 (Vulg. Baum. θάμβ- Ms. A. Herm.); Pind. Ol. 3, 32 (Boeckh, θάμβ- Bergk, Momms.): **fut.** Epic -ανέω Od. 8, 108. **Pass.** θαυμαίνονται Callicrat. Stob. Flor. 85, 17.

(Θάω) *To suckle*, Epic, of act. only **aor. inf.** θῆσαι Hesych. **Mid.** θάομαι *to milk*, contr. in η, inf. θῆσθαι Od. 4, 88: **aor.** ἐθησάμην *sucked*, Callim. Jov. 48 (Bl.), θησ- Il. 24, 58; Hym. Cer 236; Opp. Hal. 1, 661; but Hym. Apoll. 123, *suckled*.

Θεάομαι *To behold*, Soph. Tr. 1079; Ar. Eccl. 270 (Dind. 2 ed.); Her. 3, 32; Antiph. 3, γ, 7; Thuc. 5, 113, **pass.** late, Schol. Aesch. Sept. 50: **imp.** ἐθεᾶτο Thuc. 5, 7, Ion. -ῆτο Hippocr. 7, 490, -ᾶσθε Ar. Eccl. quoted (Dind. 5 ed. Bergk, Mein.), -εῶντο Pl. Charm. 154: **fut.** -άσομαι Eur. Hipp. 661; Com. Fr. (Plat.) 2, 679; Pl. Rep. 467. 545; Dem. 18, 144, Ion. -ήσομαι Her. 1, 8. 9, 25 (Bekk. Gaisf. Stein, θηήσ- Dind. Abicht): **aor.** ἐθεᾱσάμην Eur. H. F. 1131; Isocr. 4, 44; Pl. Conv. 221; Dem. 5, 7, ἐκ- Soph. O. R. 1253, Ion. ἐθεησ- Her. 7, 128: **p.** τεθέᾱμαι Ar. Nub. 370; Xen. Mem. 2, 1, 31; Pl. Polit. 264: **plp.** ἐτεθέαντο Dem. 21, 2: **aor. pass.** ἐθεᾱ́θην late and passively, Pseud.-Callisth. 2, 42. 3, 26; N. T. Marc. 16, 11; -αθῆναι Schol. Aesch. Pers. 26; Apoll. Tyan. Epist. 49; part. θεαθέν Schol. Aesch. Sept. 372; but in Thuc. 3, 38, is now read δρασθέν (best Mss. Bekk. Popp. Krüg. Dind.). **Vb.** θεατός Soph. Aj. 915, -έον Pl. Tim. 48. See θαέομαι, θηέομαι. The **act.** form θεάω is very late, imper. θέα, which Dindorf would alter to **mid.** θέασαι, Themist. 3, 44. 11, 146, but Hesych. has θέα, σκόπει: and Babr. **aor.** pt. θεήσασα 23, 8 (Lewis, 2 pt.)

Θείνω *To smite*, Poet. Aesch. Sept. 382; Opp. H. 5, 401; subj. θείνῃ Od. 18, 63, -ωσι Ap. Rh. 2, 81; imper. θεῖνε Aesch. Pr. 56; Eur. Rhes. 676, θείνετε Or. 1302; inf. Epic θεινέμεναι Od. 22, 443; θείνων Il. 17, 430; Eur. Rhes. 784; Theocr. 22, 108: imp. ἔθεινον Aesch. Pers. 418; Eur. H. F. 949: fut. θενῶ Ar. Ach. 564: 1 aor. ἔθεινα Il. 21, 491, θεῖνε Il. 16, 339; θείνας 20, 481: 2 aor. (ἔθενον), subj. θένω Ar. Lys. 821, -ῃς Eur. Rhes. 687; θένε Ar. Av. 54; θενεῖν Eur. Heracl. 271; θενών Pind. Ol. 7, 28 (Buttm. Bergk, Hart.); Ar. Eq. 640. Pass. θείνεται Aesch. Pers. 303; -όμενος Il. 10, 484; Eur. I. A. 220: imp. ἐθείνοντο Aesch. Sept. 959. Indic. 2 aor. seems not to occur. In Attic, the pres. form θένω is not found: θένει pres. Aesch. Sept. 382, is now edited θείνει from Mss.; inf. θένειν Eur. Heracl. 271, is now θενεῖν 2 aor.; θένε Ar. Av. 54, is imper. 2 aor. not pres.; and part. θένων Eur. Cycl. 7, is now θενών; but in Theocr. 22, 66, pres. θένων is still supported by Mss. Vulg. Ahr. Mein., aor. θενών (Kreussler, Fritz. and now Ziegl.).

Θέλγω *To stroke, charm*, mostly Poet. Il. 24, 343. Od. 5, 47; Sapph. 70; Pind. P. 1, 12; Eur. Hipp. 1274; Ael. N. A. 10, 14; Luc. Salt. 85; θέλγοις Theogn. 981; Aesch. Supp. 1056; θέλγων Pl. Conv. 197: imp. ἔθελγον Il. 21, 276; Soph. Tr. 710; late prose, Philostr. Apoll. 34, θέλγ- Il. 12, 255. 21, 604 (Bekk.), iter. θέλγεσκε Od. 3, 264: fut. θέλξω (Od.) 16, 298; Aesch. Pr. 174, -ξῶ Theocr. Epigr. 5, 3: aor. ἔθελξα Il. 15, 322; Gorgias Hel. Enc. 10 (Blass), θέλξα Pind. N. 4, 3; θέλξειεν Soph. Tr. 355; θέλξας Il. 13, 435; Aesch. Supp. 571: aor. pass. ἐθέλχθην Od. 10, 326, 3 pl. Epic ἔθελχθεν 18, 212; θελχθῇς Eur. I. A. 142; late prose -θείη Philostr. 290; -θῆναι Themist. 34, 60: fut. θελχθήσομαι Luc. Salt. 85. Vb. ἄ-θελκτος Lycophr. 1335. In classic prose, this verb occurs only in Pl. and Gorg. quoted.

Θέλω=ἐθέλω *To wish*, Solon 27, 12; Phocyl. 12; Simon. A. 7, 13 (Bergk); Aesch. Pr. 308. 343; Soph. Aj. 106; Ar. Eq. 713; Her. 7, 8; Antiph. 3, 8, 3; Xen. An. 3, 2, 16. Hell. 3, 4, 5 (Dind. Saupp.); Pl. Phaed. 77; subj. θέλω, Epic -ωμι Mosch. 2, 156, -λῃς Ar. Av. 929, -λῃ Nub. 801. Plut. 347; Hippocr. 2, 332 (Erm.); Xen. Cyr. 5, 4, 21; Dinarch. 2, 3, -λητε Pl. Phaed. 115, -λωσι Ar. Plut. 405; Antiph. 1, 20; Thuc. 5, 35. 7, 18; Xen. Cyr. 7, 1, 9; Aeschin. 3, 57; opt. θέλοιμι Aesch. Supp. 787, -λοις Pl. Rep. 581, -λοι Pind. Ol. 8, 85 (Bergk, Momms.); Aesch. Pr. 667; Ar. Ran. 533; Xen. An. 4, 4, 5, -οιμεν Thuc. 6, 34 &c.; imper. θέλε Eur. Fr. 174; Com. Fr. 3, 151; Isocr. 1, 24; θέλειν Soph. Ant. 669; Eur. Fr. 464; Her. 1, 59. 3, 145 after a vowel. 1, 164 after a cons. (Mss. Bekk.

Dind. Stein, ἐθελ- Bred. Abicht): **imp.** θέλεν Mosch. 2, 110, never ἔθελ-, for ἔθελε Her. 3, 146, ἔθελον 8, 80 (Vulg.) have been altered to ἤθ- of ἐθέλω (Mss. F. K. S. Bekk. Dind. Stein, Abicht): **fut.** θελήσω Ar. Ach. 318? ; Her. 1, 109 (Bekk. Gaisf. ἐθελ- Bred. Dind. Stein); Antiph. 5, 95; Xen. Mem. 1, 4, 18 (Dind. Saupp.). 2, 8, 2 (Breitb, Kühner); Lys. 20, 32: **aor.** (ἐθέλησα if correct Charit. 3, 7, elsewhere he has always ἠθέλ-), subj. θελήσῃ Aesch. Pr. 1028; Xen. Cyr. 2, 4, 19; Dem. 53, 8 (Bekk.), -ήσητε Dio. Hal. 4, 47; (Dem.) Proem. 1425, 10 (Bekk. 'θελ- B. Saupp.); θελήσαιμι Soph. O. C. 1133, -σειε Luc. Salt. 19 (Jacob.); θέλησον Aesch. Pr. 783; θελήσας Isae. 8, 11 (Mss. Bekk. Scheib. 'θελ- Bait.); Plut. Mor. 149; Herodn. 7, 11, 3; Luc. Tyr. 13 (ἐθέλ- Dind. *now*); θελῆσαι Her. 1, 24; Thuc. 5, 72 (Bekk. Popp. Krüg. ἐθέλ- L. Dind.); Luc. Tyr. 14; Merc. Con. 10 (ἐθέλ- Dind. *now*): **p.** late τεθέληκα Mosch. παθ. γυν. P. 14, 19; Sext. Emp. 682 (Bekk.); Orig. Ref. Haeres. 4, 15 (Miller): **plp.** ἐτεθελήκεσαν Dio Cass. 44, 26, but ἠθελήκ- (Bekk. L. Dind.), see 37, 23. 46, 47. 50. 79, 2. **Vb.** θελητός late V. T. Mal. 3, 12.—Epic subj. θέλωμι Mosch. 2, 156, Dor. part. θέλοισα Theocr. 11, 26. The *indic.* **imp.** is very rare, θέλει Mosch. 2, 110, θέλον Ap. Rh. 2, 960; the *indic.* **aor.** seems not to occur, at least we never could find sure instances of it, ἤθελον, ἠθέλησα belong to ἐθέλω. τεθέληκας Aeschin. 2, 139, has now given place to ἠθέληκας, but is found late, see above. θέλω is not used by Hom. unless ὅττι θέλοιεν be correct Od. 15, 317 (Bekk. 2 ed. La Roche), and Πηλεΐδη θέλ- Il. 1, 277 (La Roche), Hes. Theogn. nor Pind. according to Boeckh, but occasionally by later Epic and Bucolic writers, Hym. Apol. Del. 46. Cer. 160 (Baum. ἐθελ- Franke); Ap. Rh. 2, 960; Theocr. 8, 7. 25, 53. 23, 45; Bion 18, 1 &c. The Tragedians, again, use it alone in Iambic trimeters, while Lyric writers, and the Tragedians in lyric passages use θέλω and ἐθέλω interchangeably, Soph. El. 132; Eur. Ion 99. 1246 &c.; Sapph. 1, 17. 24; Anacr. 24, 2. 92, 1 (Bergk); Pind. always ἐθέλω (Boeckh, ἐθελ- and θελ- Bergk). Her. has both, θέλω 3, 65. 7, 234 &c. ἐθέλω 9, 120. 5, 19 &c., but **imp.** always ἤθελον 1, 16. 97 &c. (Bekk. Gaisf.), ἔθελ- 8, 80 (Vulg. Gaisf.), ἤθελ- (Mss. F. S. Bekk. Dind.): **fut.** ἐθελήσω 1, 206. 7, 10 &c. except δὲ θελήσει 1, 109 (Vulg. Gaisf. Bekk.), δ' ἐθελ- (Dind. Stein): **aor.** *indic.* perhaps always ἠθέλησα 1, 59. 2, 2 &c. ἐθελ- 7, 107. 164. 168 (Vulg. Gaisf. ἠθελ- Mss. F. S. Bekk. Dind.); inf. ἐθελῆσαι 1, 3. 145. 7, 229. 230 &c. and θελῆσαι 1, 24. 2, 42 (Mss. Gaisf. Bekk. Stein &c.), where (1, 24) Dind. reads ἐθελ- but (2, 42) θελῆσαι, why—we see not. Bredow would always read ἐθέλω in Her. In Attic prose θέλω is not frequent, and pretty much confined to the pres. θέλω Antiph. 3, δ, 3, θέλεις Xen. Hell. 3, 4, 5 &c.; subj. θέλω Thuc. 5, 35; Pl. Phaed. 115 &c.; opt. θέλοιμι Thuc. 2, 51. 6, 34; imper. θέλε Isocr. 1, 24; θέλων Xen. Cyr. 4, 5, 29; θέλειν Pl. Rep. 391: imp. never ἔθελ- always ἤθελ-: occasionally fut. θελήσω Xen. &c. and aor. in the oblique moods θελήσω &c. see above. In most cases after a vowel, perhaps always in Plato, except τοὺς θέλοντας Rep. 426; in Thuc. always, except δίκας θέλωσι 7, 18 (Bekk. Popp. Krüg. Stahl, ἐθέλ- L. Dind.); in Xen. usually after a vowel, but τοίνυν θέλεις Hell. 3, 4, 5; τὸν θέλοντα Cyr. 4, 5, 29 (Dind.); in the Orators almost always after a vowel, but μὲν θέλοντι Andoc. 4, 7; Lys. 19, 15; ἂν θέλῃ Lys. 1, 6; nearly always in Dem. now, we think, except θεὸς θέλῃ 25, 2 (Bekk. B. Saupp. Dind.); ἐθέλω is far more frequent, and is used after both vowels and consonants.

Θεραπεύω *To serve, court, heal,* Soph. Fr. 724; Eur. Bac. 81; Her. 1, 193: Pl. Gorg. 513; imper. -ευε Pind. I. 8, 8, -έτω Hippocr. 7, 176, -εύετε Ar. Vesp. 1054; -εύειν Hes. Op. 135; Soph. Ph. 149; Xen. Cyr. 7, 5, 36 &c.: imp. ἐθεράπ- Thuc. 6, 89; Isocr. 4, 111, θεράπ- Od. 13, 265: fut. -εύσω Eur. Phoen. 1686; Ar. Eq. 799; Hippocr. 1, 604. 6, 20 (Lit.); Thuc. 2, 51; Lys. 24, 6; Isocr. 19, 29; Dem. 23, 126: and as act. mid. θεραπεύσομαι Poet. Hom. H. 2, 212, but usu. pass. see below: aor. ἐθεράπευσα Ar. Thesm. 172; Thuc. 1, 137; Isocr. 19, 11, θερ- Pind. N. 8, 26: p. τεθεράπευκα Thuc. 4, 67: p. p. τεθεράπευμαι Pl. Epist. 1, 309. Leg. 763; Xen. Cyr. 7, 2, 15: aor. ἐθεραπεύθην Hippocr. 4, 374 (Lit.); Pl. Charm. 157, -εύσθην Hippocr. II. T. 5: fut. -ευθήσομαι late, Dioscor. 3, 119; Galen 10, 617; Geop. 2, 47, ξυν- Philostr. Ap. 270: and fut. m. -πεύσομαι pass. (Pl.) Alcib. (1), 135; -πεύσοιτο Antiph. 4, β, 4; Galen 10, 752; v. r. Xen. Cyr. 5, 4, 17 (-πεύοιτο Popp. Dind. Saupp.) Mid. as act. θεραπεύου Apocr. Sir. 18, 19: θεραπεύσομαι Hom. H. quoted: aor. late ἐθεραπεύσατο V. T. 2 Reg. 19, 24, but ἐθεράπευσε (Vat. Gaisf. Tischend.); subj. -εύσηται Nicostr. Stob. 74, 65, θεραπεύσαι (Halm, Mein.); inf. -εύσασθαι Galen 11, 295; -ευσάμενος 11, 341, missed by our Lexicogr. Vb. θεραπευτός Pl. Prot. 325, -έον Xen. Mem. 2, 1, 28.

Θερίζω *To perform the work of the hot season* (θέρος), *cut, mow,* Aesch. Supp. 636; Eur. Supp. 717; Ar. Av. 1697; Pl. Phaedr. 260; Theophr. H. P. 8, 2, 9; *to summer, pass the summer,* -ίζειν Xen. An. 3, 5, 15, Dor. inf. θερίδ-δειν Ar. Ach. 947 (Vulg. Bergk, -ίδδεν Br. Elms. Bekk. Dind.): imp. ἐθέριζον Ar. Av. 506; Pseud.-Callisth. 2, 16: fut. -ίσω Eustath. 5, 17 (Herch.), -ιῶ Aristot. H. An. 8, 19, 2; App. Lib. 100, (and -ίξω): aor.

ἐθέρισα Soph. Aj. 239, Gorg. Fr. 7, 3 (Bait. Saupp.), syncop. ἔθρισα Aesch. Ag. 536, ἀπ- Archil. 138; subj. θρίσσῃσι Opp. Hal. 3, 398, θεριξ- late, see ἐκ-θερίξω Anacreont. 9, 7 (Bergk); θερίσας Soph. Aj. 239; Her. 4, 42; -ίσαι Xen. Oec. 5, 9: p. p. τεθερισμένος Xen. Hell. 7, 2, 8: aor. ἐθερίσθην, θερισθῇ Soph. Fr. 587 (D.). **Mid.** aor. θερίσασθαι Ar. Plut. 515; but ἀπ-εθρισάμην Anth. Pal. 5, 237.

Θέρμω *To warm*, Epic, in act. only imper. θέρμετε Od. 8, 426; Ar. Ran. 1339 (hexam.). **Pass.** θέρμετ' subj. for -ηται Opp. Hal. 3, 522: imp. θέρμετο Il. 18, 348. Od. 8, 437; Ap. Rh. 3, 226. The collat. form θερμαίνω is more complete, and takes η in aor. ἐθέρμηνα Eur. Alc. 758; θερμήνῃς Ar. Ran. 844, -μήνῃ Il. 14, 7, but in less classic authors -μᾱνα Aristot. Gen. An. 1, 21, 11, δια- Probl. 4, 32, ἐξ- 4, 14: p. τεθέρμαγκε, ἐκ- Plut. Mor. 48 &c.

Θέρω *To warm*, Poet. act. rare, late, and only pres. part. θέρων Nic. Ther. 687: and imp. θέρον Ap. Rh. 4, 1312. **Pass.** and mid. θέρομαι *be warmed, warm oneself*, mostly Poet. Anth. Pal. 5, 6; θέρηται Il. 6, 331; θέρου Ar. Plut. 953; -εσθαι Od. 19, 64: fut. mid. θέρσομαι Od. 19, 507: 2 aor. pass. (ἐθέρην), subj. θερέω Od. 17, 23. In prose only pres. θέρηται Pl. Phil. 46; -εσθαι Luc. Lex. 2; -όμενος Aristot. Pt. Anim. 1, 5, 6 (B.); Archel. Plut. Mor. 954, late θερειόμενος Nic. Alex. 567: imp. late, ἐθερόμην Alciphr. 1, 23; Philostr. V. Apoll. 2, 18. 4, 155.

Θέσσασθαι *To pray, entreat*, a Poet. def. aor. mid. only 3 pl. θέσσαντο Pind. N. 5, 10; and part. θεσσάμενος Hes. Fr. 9; Archil. 11 (Bergk). Hesych. has pres. θέσσεσθαι; -όμενος. **Vb.** ἀπόθεστος Od. 17, 296?

Θέω *To run*, θέεις Il. 17, 75, θεῖς Ar. Vesp. 854, θέει Il. 22, 192, θεῖ Pl. Apol. 39, θέομεν Od. 8, 247; Ar. Eccl. 109, θεῖτε Ar. Lys. 550, θέουσι Il. 17, 727; Ar. Pax 839; Xen. Ven. 5, 14, Epic θείω Il. 10, 437; subj. θέω Il. 10, 63, θέῃσι and θείῃ Epic for θέῃ, Il. 22, 23. 6, 507, θέωσι Pl. Rep. 613; θέοιμεν Il. 19, 415, θέοιτε Ar. Eq. 1161; θέειν Il. 11, 617; Her. 8, 140, θεῖν Ar. Plut. 259, Epic θείειν Il. 10, 437 quoted; θέων Il. 8, 331, θέοντες Ar. Eq. 856; Pl. Rep. 417: imp. ἔθεον, ἔθεεν Il. 1, 483; Her. 1, 43, ἔθει Od. 12, 407; Thuc. 5, 10; Pl. Charm. 153, θέε Il. 20, 275; Hes. Sc. 224, ἔθεον Her. 1, 82; Thuc. 4, 67, θέον Il. 22, 161, iter. θέεσκον Il. 20, 229: fut. mid. θεύσομαι, ὑπο- Pind. P. 2, 84, Epic 2 sing. θεύσεαι Il. 23, 623, θεύσει Ar. Eq. 485, -σονται Av. 205, συν- Od. 20, 245, μετα- Xen. Ven. 6, 22; θευσόμενος Luc. Hist. Con. 8, ἀντι- Her. 5, 22, ἀπο- 8, 56; θεύσεσθαι Il. 11, 701: late θεύσω Lycophr. 1119. **Aor.** &c. supplied by τρέχω.—εω, εο, εον not contr., but εε always in Attic, except in some of the later writers, who occasionally leave εε of this verb open, ἔθεε Plut. Marc. 20; Herodn. 5, 6, 7, but παρ-έθει 5, 6, 8, ἔθεεν Diod. Sic. 16, 94 (Vulg.), but ἔθει (Bekk.), κατ-έθεεν Heliod. 2, 12 (Bekk.) This verb is rare in Tragedy: in *simple*, only Eur. Ion 1217, in comp. ὑπερ- Eur. Andr. 195. Fr. 232 (D.); and Aesch. Eum. 562: more frequent in Comedy: in *simple* eighteen or nineteen times in Aristoph.: in Attic prose, four or five times in Thuc., twelve or fourteen in Xen., and eighteen or nineteen in Plato's *genuine* works. In lexicons the *usage* is considerably understated.

Θεωρέω *To gaze, be a spectator* &c. Her. 8, 26; Pl. Rep. 467: **imp.** ἐθεώρουν Thuc. 3, 104; Isocr. 7, 46; Isae. 8, 16: **fut.** -ήσω Aesch. Pr. 302; Xen. An. 5, 3, 7: **aor.** -ώρησα, -ήσωμεν Pl. Rep. 372; Isocr. 8, 74; -ήσαιμεν 3, 17; -ήσας Her. 4, 76; Pl. Leg. 952: **p.** τεθεώρηκα Ar. Vesp. 1188; Isocr. 12, 21; Aeschin. 1, 65. 92: reg. except late **fut. mid.** θεωρήσεται as pass. Sext. Emp. 614, 30 (Bekk.); -ησομένη Ael. V. H. 7, 10: with **fut. p.** θεωρηθήσεται Sext. Emp. 348, 23 (Bekk.); Plotin. 12, 13, both missed by Lexicogrs. **Vb.** θεωρητέον Pl. Leg. 815.

Θήγω *To whet*, Il. 13, 475; Soph. Fr. 762 (D.), Dor. θάγ-; θήγων Il. 11, 416; Aesch. Ag. 1262; Eur. Phoen. 1380; Ar. Ran. 815, Dor. θάγ- Lys. 1256 (chor.); θήγειν Eur. Or. 1036; rare in prose, Xen. Cyr. 2, 1, 11. 13, 20. Mem. 3, 3, 7: **fut.** θήξω Eur. Cycl. 242: **aor.** ἔθηξα Philostr. Apoll. 333; θήξας Eur. Or. 51, Dor. θήξαις Pind. Ol. 11, 20: (**p. act.**: **aor. pass.**?): **p. p.** τέθηγμαι Aesch. Pr. 311; Soph. Aj. 584; Xen. Cyr. 1, 6, 41; Luc. Tim. 19. **Mid.** *sharpen one's own* weapon, **aor.** θηξάσθω Il. 2, 382; θηξάμενος Phanocl. 1, 8 (Schn.); late prose, Philostr. Imag. 13, 24. **Pres. pass.** θήγεσθαι Xen. Cyr. 1, 2, 10. He is the only *classic prose* author who uses the verb. **Vb.** θηκτός Aesch. Sept. 944.

Θηέομαι *To gaze*, Ion. θηοῖο Il. 24, 418; θηεύμενος Her. 7, 146; Ap. Rh. 4, 300; Theocr. 22, 36, Dor. θᾱέομαι Pind. P. 8, 45: **imp.** ἐθηεύμεσθα Od. 9, 218, ἐθηεῖτο Her. 4, 85. 7, 44, ἐθηεῦντο Her. 3, 136, θηεῖτο Od. 7, 133; Theocr. 25, 108, -εῦντο Il. 10, 524. Od. 17, 64; Mosch. 2, 49: **fut.** θηήσομαι Hes. Op. 482; Opp. Hal. 3, 304, -ήσεαι Her. 1, 8 (Dind. Abicht, θεησ- Bekk. Stein &c.): **aor.** θηησάμην Il. 22, 370. Od. 10, 180, ἐθηησ- Od. 8, 17 (Bekk. 2 ed.); Her. 3, 23. 24 (Schweigh. Dietsch &c.), but θεήσομαι, ἐθεησάμην uniformly in Her. we think (Bekk. Lhardy, with most Mss.), see θεάομαι. Her. seems, if we may trust the Mss., to have used two forms, θεάομαι, θηέομαι, both of which occur in pres. part. θεώμενος 6, 67. 7, 208, θηεύμενος 7, 44. 146.

8, 88, but **imp.** always ἐθηεῖτο 1, 68. 7, 56 &c., the **fut.**, again, always θεήσομαι 1, 8. 9, 25, and **aor.** ἐθεήσατο 7, 128, -αντο 6, 120, θεησάμενος 1, 59. 3, 25 &c., θεήσασθαι 1, 8. 9. 6, 120. 8, 24 &c. (Bekk. Lhardy, Dind.), so usually Gaisf. but occasionally θηησ- 1, 11, ἐθηησ- 4, 87, Dietsch and Abicht again θη- throughout, θηέομαι, θηησ-, ἐθηησ-. **Vb.** θηητός Hes. Th. 31.

Θηλέω, see θάλλω.

Θηλύνω *To make tender*, Anth. 10, 4; Plut. Mor. 999: **aor.** ἐθήλῡνα Eur. Fr. 362, 29 (D.), ἐξ- Strab. 5, 4, 13: **p.** τεθήλῠκα Aristot. Stob. vol. 4, p. 279 (rectius -υγκα Mein.): varies in **p. p.** τεθήλυσμαι Hippocr. 2, 60 (Mss. Lit. 1, 269 Erm. κατατεθ- Vulg.), ἐκ-τεθήλυσμ- 6, 202; Galen 10, 354, τεθήλυμμαι, ἐκ- Polyb. 37, 2 (Bekk. Dind.); ἐκ-τεθηλύνθαι 32, 2 (Bekk. Dind.), -ῡμαι, ἐκ- Diod. Sic. Fr. Lib. 30, 21 (Bekk. -υμμ- Dind. 30, 17); Luc. D. Deor. 5, 3 (Mss. Vulg. -υμμαι Reitz, Bekk. Dind., so κατα- Pisc. 31), -θήλυται Dio Cass. 50, 27 (Vulg. -υνται Bekk. Dind.): **aor.** ἐθηλύνθην Soph. Aj. 651; Synes. Epist. 146, ἐκ- Dio. Hal. 14, 12. **Mid.** *put on fine airs, coquet*, θηλύνετο Bion 2, 18; (Theocr.) 20, 14. Rare in Attic, Eur. Fr. quoted, and **pres. pass.** θηλυνόμενος Xen. Oec. 4, 2, the only instance in classic Attic prose.

Θήπω, see θάπω.

Θηράω *To hunt*, Aesch. Ag. 1194; Eur. I. A. 960; Xen. Mem. 3, 11, 6; opt. -ρῴη Cyr. 1, 4, 16: **imp.** ἐθήρων Soph. Ph. 958; Xen. Cyr. 1, 4, 11: **fut. aor.** &c. in Attic retain α, θηράσω Soph. Ph. 958; Eur. I. T. 1426; Xen. Cyr. 1, 4, 16. An 4, 5, 24. Mem. 3, 11, 7; Luc. Dips. 2, for **fut. m.** see **mid.**: **aor.** ἐθήρᾱσα, θηράσειεν Xen. Cyr. 1, 4, 10; θηρᾶσαι Aesch. Pers. 233; Xen. Cyr. 1, 4, 16; θηράσας Eur. Bac. 1215: **p.** τεθήρᾱκα Xen. Cyr. 2, 4, 16: **aor.** θηραθείς Aesch. Pr. 1072; -θῆναι D. Laert. 9, 11, 4: **fut.** θηραθήσομαι late, Geop. 12, 9. **Mid.** θηράομαι prop. *hunt for oneself*, Aesch. Pr. 109; Ar. Eq. 864; in prose, Her. 2, 77; Isocr. 10, 59; Xen. Ven. 11, 2; (Dem.) 61, 21: **imp.** ἐθηρ-, θηρώμεσθα in tmesi Soph. Ant. 433 (trimet.): **fut.** θηρᾱ́σομαι Eur. Bac. 228. I. T. 1324; Luc. Necyom. 21 (Fritzs. Jacob.): **aor.** ἐθηρᾱσάμην Soph. Ph. 1007; Eur. Hipp. 919; θηρήσαιο Athen. (Numen.) 7, 119, -ήσαιτο Orph. Arg. 644. **Vb.** θηρατέος Soph. Ph. 116, -ατός Polyb. 10, 47. So θηρεύω Od. 19, 465; Hipponax 22 (B.); Eur. Hipp. 956; Her. 4, 183; Antiph. 6, 18; Andoc. 1, 9; Pl. Gorg. 490; Poet. inf. θηρευέμεν Pind. N. 11, 47: **fut.** θηρεύσω Aesch. Pr. 858 (Herm. Weil); Pl. Theaet. 166: **aor.** ἐθήρευσα Pl. Euthyd. 290, θήρευ- Pind. P. 4, 90; -εύσας Her. 1, 200: **p.** τεθήρευκα Pl. Theaet. 200: **p. p.** rare τεθήρευμαι Com. Fr. (Lysipp.) 2, 746: **aor.** ἐθηρεύθην Aesch. Ch. 493; Her. 3, 102; Pl. Soph. 222. **Mid.** θηρεύομαι Eur.

Fr. 187 (D.); Com. Fr. (Anaxil.) 3, 348; Pl. Gorg. 464: fut. θηρεύσομαι Pl. Soph. 222; but pass. Themist. 22, 271: aor. ἐθηρευσάμην Pl. Euthyd. 290. Theaet. 197. Vb. θηρευτός Aristot. Polit. 7, 2, 15, θηρευτέον Polyb. 1, 35, 8. θηρεύω is more frequent in Attic prose than θηράω. Hipponax quoted seems to have shortened the diphthong -εῦει. θηριόω *to make wild, infuriate*, is very late in act., in pass. rare, and in classic authors pres. part. only, θηριούμενος Pl. Leg. 935; -οῦσθαι Com. Fr. (Eub.) 3, 254: p. late τεθηριωμένος Dioscor. 3, 11; Apocr. 2 Macc. 5, 11: aor. θηριωθῆναι Theophr. Char. 11 (19.)

Θιγγάνω *To touch*, Aesch. Ag. 432; Soph. O. C. 330; Hippocr. 6, 90; -ἄνων Com. Fr. (Pher.) 2, 254; late Attic prose Aristot. Part. An. 4, 10, 13. Gen. An. 1, 6, 3; Luc. Bis Acc. 1; Sext. Emp. 443 (Bekk.), and late θῖγω, θίγει Chr. Pat. 1109; Dor. part. θίγοισα Pind. P. 8, 24 (Schneid. Momms.) seems pres. but θιγοῖσα 2 aor. (Buttm. Bergk): imp. ἐθίγγᾰνε Pseud.-Callisth. 2, 36: fut. θίξω Herodian π. μ. λ. 22, 19 (Lehrs); Theognost. 140, προσθίξεις Eur. Heracl. 652 (Mss. Matth. Kirchh.): but mid. προσ-θίξει Eur. quoted (Elms. Dind. Nauck, Kirchh. 2 ed. &c.), because of θίξεται Hipp. 1086, see below: aor. p. late ἐθίχθην Sext. Emp. 435 &c. (Bekk.): 2 aor. act. ἔθῐγον Aesch. Ch. 949; Soph. Ant. 546; Eur. Alc. 108; late Attic prose Plut. Mor. 339. 665. 959. T. Gr. 17. Pelop. 28; Athen. 12, 72, Poet. θίγον Pind. I. 1, 18; Theocr. 1, 59; subj. θίγω Eur. Ion 560, -ῃς Alcm. 38; Mosch. 1, 29; Xen. Cyr. 1, 3, 5; Hippocr. 6, 300, -ῃ Soph. Tr. 715; Com. Fr. (Antiph.) 3, 30 (Jacobs, Mein.); Aristot. H. An. 6, 14, 6; Theophr. C. P. 4, 13, 3; θίγοιμι Eur. Alc. 345, θίγοις Hippocr. 8, 88; θιγεῖν Soph. O. C. 1133; Hippocr. 3, 272. 7, 386; Aristot. Metaph. 1, 7, 7; Plut. Alcib. 23, θιγέμεν Pind. N. 4, 35, Lacon. σιγῆν Ar. Lys. 1004; θιγών Soph. O. R. 760; Xen. Cyr. 5, 1, 16; Hippocr. 5, 184, Dor. f. θιγοῖσα Pind. P. 8, 24, see above: and 2 aor. mid. late θίγοιτο Themist. 4, 50. Vb. ἄ-θικτος Soph. O. C. 39. In classic Attic prose, this verb occurs rarely, and in 2 aor. only, θίγῃς, -ών Xen. quoted: pres. θιγγάνω Hippocr. 6, 90. 8, 350; and late, Aristot. Part. An. 4, 10, 13 &c.; Plut. Mor. 35. Rom. 21; Luc. Bis Acc. 1. Pass. θιγγανόμενος Aristot. H. A. 1, 16, 5. ἐπιθιγγάνω is confined to late prose, Theophr. Odor. 3, 11; Plut. T. Gr. 19, so συν-θιγγ- Themist. Or. 20, 235, προσθιγγάνω seems to be entirely poetic: fut. προσθίξεις Eur. quoted, corrected by Elmsley to mid. -θίξει from no Ms. authority, but because mid. θίξεται occurs Eur. Hipp. 1086. This to be sure gives an air of probability to the emendation, but it is somewhat weakened by τεθίξεται (Ms. A.) adopted by Kirchhoff in 1 ed. though θίξεται in 2. Hesych. has θίξεσθαι. Of the pres. θίγω, θίγει Chr. Pat. quoted is the only decided instance we ever met.

Θλάω *To bruise, break,* pres. rare and late, θλῶσα Galen 4, 83; θλᾶν 4, 113, indic. δια-θλῶσι Ael. N. A. 4, 21: imp. ἔθλα Babr. 125, συγκατ- Athen. (Mach.) 8, 41: fut. θλᾰ́σω Galen 4, 24, ἐν- Hippocr. 7, 276 (Lit.): aor. ἔθλᾰσα Od. 18, 97; Hes. Sc. 140, Epic θλάσσα Il. 5, 307: p. τεθλακότες late (if genuine) Herm. Past. p. 77, but συν-τέθλᾰκεν Theod. Prodr. Catomyom. 374: p. p. τέθλασμαι Theocr. 22, 45 (Mss. Vulg. Mein. Ahr. Ziegl. -αγμαι Vat. A. Br. Valck.); Dioscor. 5, 44, συν- Com. Fr. (Alex.) 3, 510: aor. ἐθλάσθην Hippocr. 6, 406 (Lit.); Aristot. Meteor. 4, 9, 12; Dio Cass. 57, 22 (21), συν- Aristot. Probl. 1, 38: fut. late θλασθησόμενος Galen 3, 851. 4, 61. Vb. θλαστός Ar. Fr. 345. p. p. ἐθλασμένος without redupl. occurs Athen. 15, 57.

Θλίβω (ῑ) *To press,* Ar. Pax 1239; Aristot. Probl. 24, 13; Plut. Mor. 141; θλίβων Dem. 18, 260; Luc. Nigr. 13: fut. θλίψω Or. Sib. 3, 182; Eustath. 5, 14 (Herch.), ἀπο- Eur. Cycl. 237 (Vulg. Herm. Kirchh. Nauck, ἀπολέψω Ruhnk. Dind. Nauck 3 ed.): aor. ἔθλιψα Pl. Tim. 60; Callim. Del. 35, θλίψε Opp. C. 4, 331; θλίψας Orph. Lith. 746: p. τέθλῐφα Polyb. 18, 7: p.p. τέθλιμμαι Aristot. Probl. 20, 23; Anth. 7, 472: aor. ἐθλίφθην Pl. Tim. 91, συν- ibid.: 2 aor. ἐθλῐ́βην Aristot. Probl. 20, 23; Dioscor. 3, 7; Geop. 6, 16, ἐκ- Hippocr. 2, 113 (Lind. Mack. ἐκφλιβῇ Kühn, Lit.); and late Plut. Cleom. 28 (Bekk. Sint.): fut. late θλῐβήσομαι Soran. Ephes. p. 41 (Ermerins); Herm. Past. p. 71; Eustath. 3, 4 (Herch.) · Mid. *to press, rub oneself,* fut. θλίψομαι Od. 17, 221. Buttmann mistakes in giving ἐθλίβην as the only pass. aor. ἐθλίφθην is classic: Aristot. has both forms θλιβείς, θλιφθῇ Probl. 20, 23. Schneider reads with Ms. Vat. πλευρῇσι θλῖβει Opp. Cyn. 2, 281: he might have preserved ῑ by reading πλευραῖς with Ms. Ven. The *simple* verb is not in Tragedy, unless θλιβομένης be *genuine,* Soph. Fr. Amph. 1, 1 (Br.) Dind. rejects it.

Θνήσκω *To be dying, die,* Od. 12, 22; Simon. Am. 1, 17; Aesch. Fr. 299; Soph. O. C. 611; Com. Fr. (Philem.) 4, 47; Hippocr. 5, 134 (Lit.); Antiph. 5, 48; Aristot. H. An. 9, 40, 24; -σκοι Pl. Phaed. 72; -έτω Pl. Leg. 946; -ων Thuc. 2, 53. 54; -ειν Hippocr. 5, 134, Dor. θνάσκω Pind. Ol. 2, 19; Aesch. Sept. 748 (chor.); Theocr. 1, 135, late if correct τεθνήσκω, προ- Aretae. 70, 5: imp. ἔθνησκον Soph. Tr. 708; Hippocr. 2, 630. 640. 642. 646. 5, 336; Thuc. 2, 48. 51, θνῇσκον Il. 1, 383; Hes. Op. 116: fut. (θανῶ, ἀπο- Ephr. Syr. vol. 3, p. 241, ἀπο-θνήξω Aesop 152, p. 92 Cor.) θανοῦμαι Simon. C. 85, 9 (Bergk); Soph. Ant. 462; Eur. Tr. 1056; Hippocr. 8, 70. 98. 356 (Mss

Lit.), in Comedy and Attic prose ἀπο- Ar. Eq. 68; Andoc. 1, 33; Pl. Gorg. 481; Xen. Cyr. 7, 1, 19; -θανοῖντο 7, 5, 34, Epic θανέομαι, -έεσθαι Il. 4, 12; Ap. Rh. 2, 626; Theocr. 22, 18, Ion. prose ἀπο- 2 sing. ἀπο-θανέαι Her. 4, 163, -έεαι (Stein), -έονται 4, 95; -έεσθαι Hippocr. 7, 218 (Lit.); but -εύμενος if correct, Her. 7, 134, see ἀμύνω: θνήξομαι only Anth. 9, 354; and Polyaen. Str. 5, 2, 22: also τεθνήξω once in Trag. Aesch. Ag. 1279; Ar. Ach. 590. Nub. 1436. Vesp. 654; Pl. Gorg. 469; -ξων Ar. Ach. 325: and perhaps late τεθνήξομαι unless genuine Lys. Fr. 112 (B. Saupp.); v. r. Ar. Ach. Nub. Vesp.; Pl. Gorg. quoted; Luc. Pisc. 10. Char. 8; Ael. H. A. 2, 46. V. H. 12, 29; Diog. Laert. 5, 20; Ach. Tat. 4, 1; Plut. Mor. 1082, Dor. -αξοῦμαι 219: 1 aor. late (ἐτέθνηξα), -θνήξαντα Niceph. Rhet. 7, 1, and (ἔθνηξα), subj. θνήξω Aesop 134 (Tauchn., but fut. m. τεθνήξομαι Halm 334): p. τέθνηκα Il. 18, 12; Aesch. Ch. 893; Soph. El. 1152; Ar. Thesm. 885; Her. 1, 124; Antiph. 3, γ, 10; Thuc. 2, 6; Pl. Apol. 41; Xen. An. 2, 5, 38; Lys. 13, 84, Dor. 1 pl. τεθνάκαμες Theocr. 2, 5, 3 pl. -ᾱκοντι Plut. Lycurg. 20; -ᾱκώς Pind. N. 7, 32: plp. ἐτεθνήκειν Antiph. 4, β, 3. 5, 70; Lys. 19, 48, Aeol. τεθνᾱκην Sapph. 2, 15, 3 pl. -ήκεσαν Thuc. 7, 85; Andoc. 1, 52, which occur also in the syncop. forms, 3 dual τέθνᾰτον Xen. An. 4, 1, 19, pl. τέθνᾰμεν Pl. Gorg. 492, τεθνᾶσι Il. 22, 52; Simon. C. 96; Aesch. Sept. 805; Soph. Aj. 99; Com. Fr. (Antiph.) 3, 29; Thuc. 3, 113; Lys. 13, 38. 89: plp. ἐτέθνᾰσαν Antiph. 5, 70; Andoc. 1, 59; Xen. Hell. 6, 4, 16, ἀπ- Od. 12, 393; opt. τεθναίην Il. 18, 98; Theogn. 343; Mimnerm. 1; Xen. Hell. 4, 3, 10. 7, 1, 32; Luc. Enc. 46; Alciphr. 1, 21, -ναῖεν Xen. Ages. 7, 5 (but subj. τεθνήκω Thuc. 8, 74); τέθνᾰθι Il. 22, 365, -ᾰτω 15, 496; Pl. Leg. 933; Dem. 9, 44; inf. τεθνηκέναι Soph. Aj. 479; Com. Fr. (Ant.) 3, 66; Lys. 13, 94, sync. τεθνᾰ́ναι Simon. Am. 3; Ar. Ran. 1012; Com. Fr. (Pl.) 2, 640; Her. 1, 31; Antiph. 5, 29; Thuc. 8, 92; Lys. 10, 28; Isocr. 10, 27. 53. 18, 53; Dinarch. 1, 40; Pl. Phaed. 67, and τεθνᾶναι Mimnerm. Fr. 2, 10 (Vulg. Bergk 2 ed., -άμεναι 3 ed.); Aesch. Ag. 539 (-άναι Herm. Weil, Dind. 5 ed.); Chr. Pat. 698 (but Ael. V. H. 3, 2, 3. 12, 3. 57, should perhaps be -άναι, and so now Hercher edits), Epic τεθνᾰ́μεν Il. 15, 497, τεθνᾰ́μεναι Il. 24, 225; Tyrt. 10, 1; Mimnerm. 2, 10 (Bergk 3 ed.); τεθνηκώς Theogn. 1230; Aesch. Ag. 869; Soph. Phil. 435; Antiph. 1, 3; Andoc. 4, 38; Thuc. 3, 98, Dor. -ᾱκώς Pind. N. 7, 32, τεθνηκυῖα Od. 4, 734 (Mss. Wolf, La R. Ameis, Düntz. Bekk. now, Hom. Blätt. p. 228); Hippon. 29 (Bergk); Eur. Or. 109; Plut. Ant. 85, Epic τεθνηυῖα Od. quoted (Mss. Thiersch, Dind. La R. Bekk. in ed.), τεθνηκός Pl. Phaed. 71; Aesch. 2, 34, syncop. τεθνεώς

Theogn. 1192; Ar. Av. 476; Her. 9, 120; Thuc. 3, 109; Andoc. 1, 119; Pl. Leg. 874, τεθνεῶσα Lys. 31, 22; Dem. 40, 27, neut. (τεθνεώς?) τεθνεός Her. 1, 112; Hippocr. 5, 212. 7, 350 (Lit.); Aristot. de gen. An. 1, 23, gen. τεθνεῶτος Od. 19, 331; Ar. Ran. 1028; Her. 5, 68; Antiph. 1, 4; Thuc. 5, 13; Lys. 1, 14; Isocr. 19, 3, neut. Pl. Tim. 85 (-εότος masc. Anth. App. Epigr. 14; Q. Sm. 7, 65 Vulg. -ἀότος Koechly), -εῶτι Antiph. 1, 4, -εῶτα Aesch. Ch. 682, -εῶτας Pl. Leg. 909, τὰ -εῶτα Phaed. 72, Hom. usu. τεθνηώς Il. 17, 161; Simon. C. 129, -ηῶτος Il. 6, 71; Hes. Sc. 454, and -ηότος Il. 17, 435. Od. 24, 56, Dor. -ἄότος Pind. N. 10, 74, fem. τεθνηυίης, κατα- Od. 11, 141, τεθνειώς is not favoured in Il. and Od. either by Wolf, Spitzn. or Bekk. Heyne, again, adopted it, and Buttm. allowed gen. -ειῶτος. It is more readily admitted in later Poets, Theocr. 25, 273; Ap. Rh. 3, 461; Q. Sm. 5, 502; Tryphiod. 178; Orph. Lith. 52: 2 aor. ἔθἄνον Poet. Ionic and late Attic prose, 1 pers. rare -ανον Anth. 7, 336. 349. 14, 32, Epic θάνον Od. 11, 412; Anth. 7, 167, ἔθανες Aesch. Sept. 961; Soph. Ant. 1268, θάνες Il. 22, 486, ἔθανε Il. 21, 610; Soph. O. C. 1706; Hippocr. 3, 116. 118. 5, 208. 214, and often (Lit.); Boeot. Inscr. 63 (Keil); Joseph. 17, 5, 7; in tmesi Her. 6, 114. 8, 89, θάνε Il. 2, 642; Pind. P. 11, 31, ἔθανον Simon. C. 97; Ar. Thesm. 865; Hippocr. 5, 240; Plut. Pelop. 1; Pseud.-Callisth. 2, 32, θάνον Od. 11, 389; Pind. P. 11, 31; Aesch. Pers. 490 (trimet.), in classic Attic prose ἀπ-έθανον, -ες &c. Antiph. 3, 1. 5, 21. 26; Thuc. 1, 134; Pl. Apol. 32; subj. θάνω Il. 11, 455; Eur. Tr. 904, θάνῃ Aesch. Ag. 1318, ἀπο- Pl. Gorg. 524, θάνῃς Soph. Ant. 546, θάνῃσι Il. 19, 228 &c. pl. θάνωμεν Od. 12, 156, Dor. -ωμες Mosch. 3. 105, θάνωσι Il. 7, 410; Aesch. Sept. 735; App. Civ. 1, 43; θάνοιμι Soph. O. C. 1306, ἀπο- Xen. Hell. 7, 3, 9, θάνοις Hes. Op. 378; Soph. El. 583; Eur. Med. 715, -οι Od. 15, 359; Soph. Aj. 533; Polyb. 9, 40, θάνοιεν Od. 22, 472, ἀπο- Pl. Men. 91; imper. rare, θάνε Il. 21, 106; Epist. Socrat. 14; θανεῖν Hom. once Il. 7, 52; Hes. Op. 175. 687; Pind. Ol. 1, 82; Aesch. Ag. 550; Soph. Ant. 72; Com. Fr. (Plat.) 2, 697. (Philem.) 4, 63; Hippocr. 5, 670. 8, 30; Plut. Sert. cum Eum. 2; Dio Cass. 63, 28; App. Civ. 2, 47; Anton. Lib. 19, θανέειν Il. 22, 426. Od. 1, 59. 4, 562. 5, 308 (ἀπο- Her. 1, 85), θανέμεν Pind. P. 4, 72, Aeol. θάνην, κατ-Alcae. 30; θανών Il. 23, 223. Od. 24, 93; Soph. Ph. 624; Ar. Ach. 893; Luc. D. Mort. 5, 2; Diog. Laert. 4, 21; Apollod. 3, 5, 5; Strab. 11, 8, 6; Sext. Emp. 445, ἀπο- Thuc. 3, 109, ἐν-Lys. 16, 15, Aeol. and Dor. θανοῖσα Theocr. 4, 38, κατ- Sapph. 68, ἀπο- Pind. Ol. 2, 25, Dor. dat. pl. θανόντεσσι Pind. Ol. 8, 77. It is said that τεθνεώς is never syncopated τεθνώς; but Herodian's expression "τεθνεὼς διῃρημένως" proves that τεθνώς was in use; indeed it actually occurs in the lately discovered Fab. of Babrius, τεθνώσας 45, 9; in an Epigram edited by Welcker, see Hermann's Opusc. 4, 313; (Luc.) Trag. 9 (Mss. Dind.); Eur. Supp. 273 hexamet. (Heath, Nauck), and Dind. with a "recte fortasse" rather approves, but edits with Reiske τεθνεώς. In earlier writers the fut. m. τεθνήξομαι has, since the days of R. Dawes, been rather yielding to the act. form τεθνήξω. At Pl. Gorg. 469, 3 sing. τεθνήξει is supported by, if not all, the best Mss. and τεθνήξομεν Aesch. Ag. 1279, τεθνήξων Ar. Ach. 325, by both Mss. and metre. τεθνήξει, again, 2 sing. mid. has all, or the best Mss. support, Ar. Ach. 590. Vesp. 654. Nub. 1436, and is so edited by Brunck, Bekk. Richter &c., but act. τεθνήξεις by Dawes, Elms. Dind. and even Bergk, who, to his credit we say it, is usually rather *conservative*. Did both forms co-exist, and were they so *indifferent* that Ar. could use either, as it might suit his fancy or convenience, or is mid. τεθνήξει a clerical blunder, involuntary or intentional, for τεθνήξεις, since Ar. has elsewhere certainly used the act. and was nowhere under any constraint to use the mid.? One would gather from Luc. Soloec. 7, that τεθνήξω was considered *high* Attic, ἀττικίζοντος δέ τινος καὶ τεθνήξει εἰπόντος ἐπὶ τοῦ τρίτου—. See Elmsley's note Ar. Ach. 590. In late authors τεθνήξομαι is the more frequent form, (Eur.) Epist. 4, 41 (D.); Plut. Mor. 865. 866; Luc. Tyrannic. 6. D. Mort. 6, 2. 4. 7, 1; Aristaen. 2, 1; Geop. 13, 3; Aesop 386 (Halm.) Bekker, in his Ar. Ach. 565. Vesp. 654, has the form τεθνήσει, which is so far countenanced by the act. τεθνήσειν Dio Cass. 51, 13, (Vulg. Bekk.), unless this be a vicious form of τεθνήξειν (L. Dind.) which occurs in part. τεθνήξων 58, 6. 78, 32 (Bekk.): θάνεται for -εῖται, late Or. Sib. 12, 91, κατα- 10, 36. Vb. θνητός Aesch. Pr. 800, θανετέον, ἀπο- Aristot. Eth. Nic. 3, 1, 8 (Bekk.)

In early Attic prose and Ion. of Her. the fut. and 2 aor. seem to occur only in comp. ἀποθανοῦμαι, ἀπέθανον, ἐν-, κατα-, προ-, συν- &c.: the perf. and plp., again, with every class of writers, are almost uniformly in *simple*, τέθνηκα, ἐτεθνήκειν. There are a few exceptions, though more than Buttmann and others are inclined to allow, κατατέθνηκα Il. 15, 664, συν- Ar. Ran. 868. 869; opt. κατατεθναίη Od. 4, 224; ἀποτεθνηῶτος Il. 22, 432, κατα- 16, 565. 23, 331. Od. 22, 448: plp. ἀπετέθνασαν Od. 12, 393; in prose προτεθνάναι Thuc. 2, 52; ἐκτεθνεῶτα Pl. Leg. 959, the only instances we know in good Attic, yet sufficient to prove Cobet's assertion "quae forma *numquam* componitur" to be too strong: more frequently in Hippocr. and later Attic, ἐκτέθνηκε Hippocr. 3,

252, ἐν- 8, 482 (Lit.), ἀπο- Plut. Mor. 178. 518; Ael. H. A. 4, 18. 2, 23; Dio. Hal. 4, 4; Charit. 4, 3; προτεθνηκώς Luc. Paras. 50, -νεώς Paus. 2, 18, 6: plp. προετεθνήκειν Dio Cass. 51, 12. 52, 17; Luc. Tox. 60, συν- D. Mort. 27, 3. The 1 pers. ἔθανον is of course rare, because the *conditions* are rare in which a man can tell the *fact* of his own death. Indeed, it must be told either by a *Ghost*, as ὣς θάνον "thus died I," says Agamemnon in the *Shades* Od. 11, 412; compare ἐπεὶ θάνον Simon. C. 122 (Bergk); ἔγωγ' ἔθανον Anth. 14, 32, ταφεὶς ἔθανον 7, 336; or *prophetically*, as προύθανον Eur. Heracl. 590; or *figuratively*, as ἀπέθανον ἰδών Ar. Ach. 15; or *hypothetically*, as ἂν ἀπέθανον, εἰ μή Pl. Apol. 32; Dem. 18, 209: 1 pers. ἔθανον in *simple* we have not seen in Attic. The Tragedians scarcely ever use ἀποθνήσκω, Eur. only once Fr. 582 (Aristoph. often pres. fut. and aor.), nor ἐκθνήσκω, Soph. only Tr. 568, and καταθνήσκω only in aor. and fut. and always in the syncopated forms κάτθανε, indic. rare, Aesch. Ag. 1553; Ap. Rh. 3, 796; Callim. Epigr. 21; subj. κατθάνω Eur. Or. 777, -άνῃς 308; -άνοι Eur. Alc. 143; -ανεῖν Aesch. Ag. 1364; Soph. Tr. 16; Eur. Ion 628; κατθανών Aesch. Ag. 873; Soph. Ant. 515; Eur. Hipp. 810: fut. κατθανοῦμαι Eur. H. F. 210. Or. 1061; (Ar. once aor. κατθανεῖν Ran. 1477); ὑπερθνήσκω only Eur. Andr. 499 &c.: and aor. -θανεῖν Alc. 155; -ανών Phoen. 1090; συνθνήσκω more freq. Aesch. Ag. 819; (Soph.) Ph. 1443; Eur. Supp. 1007. Or. 1075: fut. -θανοῦμαι Aesch. Ch. 979. Ag. 1139: aor. -έθανον Soph. Tr. 720. O. C. 1690 (Herm.); Eur. Med. 1210. Supp. 769: to which we add p. συν-τέθνηκε from Ar. Ran. 868. 869: and plp. συνετεθνήκει from Luc. D. Mort. 27, 3, because the lexicons confine this verb to Trag. Buttmann is rather mistaken in saying that "the feminine form τεθνεῶσα does not occur in prose, but that θανών, οἱ θανόντες as adjective occurs often." For τεθνεῶσα see Lys. 31, 22; Dem. 40, 27 quoted; and Theophr. Ign. 60; Aristid. 27, 351; Charit. 1, 5. 9. 14. 3, 3 (D'Orv.); θανών, οἱ θανόντες in *simple*, we have never seen in good Attic prose nor in Her., οἱ ἀποθανόντες is frequent Thuc. 2, 34; Pl. Rep. 468 &c., θανών, οἱ θανόντες in Poet. Od. 17, 115; Com. Fr. (Menand.) 4, 269. 270.

Θοάζω *To move rapidly, hurry*, Attic Poet. (θοός) trans. and intrans. Eur. Bac. 65. Tr. 307; hither some refer θοάζετε Soph. O. R. 2; and θοάζων Aesch. Supp. 595: imp. ἐθόαζον Eur. H. F. 383: fut. θοάσσω, if correct, Emped. 18 (48), -άξω (Mein., but -άζω Herm. Bekk. Stein).

Θοινάζω *To feast upon*, only imp. ἐθοίναζε Xen. Ages. 8, 7.

Θοινάω *To entertain, feast*, Poet. Eur. Ion 982: imp. ἐθοίνων *feasted on*, Hes. Sc. 212: aor. ἐθοίνησα Her. 1, 129 (2 Mss Bekk.

Gaisf. Dind. Stein, ἐθοίνισα others): p. p. as mid. τεθοίνᾱμαι Eur. Cycl. 377: so aor. θοινηθῆναι Od. 4, 36. Mid. θοινάομαι Eur. Fr. 790. Alc. 542; Com. Fr. (Cratin.) 2, 107: imp. ἐθοινᾶτο Athen. 12, 23: fut. θοινᾱ́σομαι Eur. Elec. 836. Cycl. 550, but -ήσομαι Stob. Ecl. Ph. 1, 41, 958; Or. Sib. 2, 158 (Mss. θρην- Friedl.), ἐκ- Aesch. Pr. 1025: aor. ἐθοινήσαντο Nonn. 5, 331, θοιν- Anth. 9, 244; Or. Sib. 2, 236: in sense p. τεθοίνᾱμαι Eur. Cycl. 377 (Dind. Nauck, Reiske's emendation for γε θοινᾶται): and aor. θοινηθῆναι Od. 4, 36 quoted.

(Θόρνῡμι, Θόρω) see θρώσκω.

Θρανεύω *To stretch on a θρᾶνος, to tan*, only fut. mid. and in pass. sense, θρᾱνεύσεται Ar. Eq. 369.

Θράσσω *To disturb*, Pind. I. 7, 39; Soph. Fr. 187 (D.), -ττω Pl. Theaet. 187: imp. ἔθραττον Synes. Epist. 4: aor. ἔθραξα Pl. Parm. 130; inf. θρᾶξαι Aesch. Pr. 628; Eur. Fr. 603: and, according to some, p. τέτρηχα as pres. intrans. *to be tumultuous*, Il. 7, 346; Anth. 7, 283: plp. τετρήχειν as imp. Il. 2, 95: aor. pass. ἐθράχθην Soph. Fr. 812 (D.): Dor. fut. m. θραξεῖται Hesych. Subj. aor. θράξῃς has the signification *break*, Anth. Plan. 255. Perf. τέτρηχα may as well be referred to ταράσσω.

Θρασύνω (ῡ) *To make bold*, in act. rare, and only pres. Aesch. Ag. 222; -οντες Thuc. 1, 142: aor. pass. θρασυνθῆναι Aesch. Supp. 772: in same sense aor. mid. ἐθρασῡ́ναντο rare, Isocr. 5, 23; Dio Cass. 56, 13; Arr. An. 4, 4, 2; -άμενος Isocr. 4, 12; Luc. Apol. 6; -ασθαι Dio Cass. 78, 17; Aristid. 8, 50: pres. θρασύνομαι *am bold, behave boldly*, freq. Thuc. 5, 104; Eur. Or. 607; Ar. Ach. 330; -ύνηται Aeschin. 3, 23; -ύνου Eur. Hec. 1183; -ύνεσθαι Aesch. Ag. 1188; Soph. Ph. 1387; -όμενος Pl. Leg. 879: imp. ἐθρασ- Himer. Or. 2, 10. The defects of this verb are supplied by the Ionic and old Attic θαρσύνω Od. 3, 361; Tyrt. 12, 19; Archil. 55; Her. 2, 141; intrans. Soph. El. 916, later Attic θαρρ- Xen. Cyr. 4, 2, 18 &c.: imp. ἐθαρσ- Thuc. 6, 72, θάρσῡνον Od. 9, 377, iter. θαρσύνεσκε Il. 4, 233: fut. -ῠνῶ Eur. Alc. 318: aor. θάρσυνα Il. 10, 190. (Od.) 13, 323; imper. θάρσυνον Il. 16, 242; -ῦναι Thuc. 2, 88.—Supplied also by the intrans. θαρσέω, -ρρέω.

Θραύω *To bruise*, Simon. C. 57; Aesch. Pers. 196; Pl. Crat. 426: imp. ἔθραυον Aesch. Pers. 416, iter. θραύεσκον Orph. Lith. 140: fut. θραύσω Ar. Av. 466; θραύσοι Pind. Ol. 6, 97: aor. ἔθραυσα Soph. El. 745; Eur. H. F. 780, κατα- Pl. Polit. 265: p. p. τέθραυσμαι Theophr. de Sens. 2, 11, συν- Xen. Ages. 2, 14, and τέθραυμαι, παρα- Pl. Leg. 757 (Mss. Bekk. B. O. W. Herm. -αυσμαι Vulg. Stallb.): plp. ἐτέθραυστο Plut. Caes. 19: aor ἐθραύσθην Soph. Ant. 476; Eur. Supp. 691; Strab. 15, 3, 7.

ἀπο- Ar. Nub. 997, κατα- Pl. Tim. 56: fut. late θραυσθήσεται Galen 10, 624. **Vb.** θραυστός Aristot. Part. An. 2, 6, 3; (Pl.) Locr. 99, ἡμι- Eur. H. F. 1096. Rare in classic prose, θραύειν Pl. quoted, θραύονται Pl. Phaedr. 248; -όμενος Her. 1, 174. θραύῃ (Xen.) Ven. 6, 1; -οντας Plut. Mor. 77; θραῦσαι Alcib. 23.

Θρέομαι *To utter, wail,* Trag. Poet. and only **pres.** -εῦμαι Aesch. Sept. 78 chor. (Herm.) -έομαι (Dind.); θρεόμενος Ch. 970 (chor.), -ένη Eur. Med. 51.

(Θρέφω) see τρέφω.

(Θρέχω) see τρέχω.

Θρηνέω *To mourn,* freq. in Trag. poet., in Comedy and good prose, confined, we think, to **pres. act.** Hes. Fr. 132; Aesch. Pers. 686; Soph. El. 94; Eur. Med. 1409; Ar. Av. 211; Plut. Mor. 78; -νοῖ Pl. Tim. 47; -εῖν Isocr. 8, 128; -ῶν Ar. Nub. 1260; Pl. Apol. 38; Isocr. 14, 47: **imp.** θρήνεον Od. 24, 61. Il. 24, 722 dissyl. (V. Bekk. La Roche), ἐθρήν- (Wolf, Dind.); Dio Cass. 65, 5; Plut. Mor. 113, -νευν Theocr. 7, 74: **fut.** -ήσω Aesch. Ag. 1541; Soph. Aj. 631: **aor.** ἐθρήνησα Pseud.-Callisth. 2, 23, θρήνησεν Mosch. 3, 39; θρηνῆσαι Eur. Tr. 111: **p. p.** τεθρήνηται Soph. Ph. 1401 (Dind. Nauck); Luc. Catapl. 20. **Mid.** θρηνεῖσθαι Aesch. Pr. 43, περι- Plut. Ant. 56: and **fut.** θρηνήσονται Or. Sib. 2, 158 (Friedl.), missed by Lexicogr. **Vb.** θρηνητέον Philostr. 410.

Θρίζω, see θερίζω.

Θροέω *To utter,* Poet. especially Trag. Aesch. Ag. 1137; Soph. Tr. 1232; Eur. Hipp. 213; rare in Comedy, -οεῖν Ar. Ran. 1276: **fut.** (-ήσω): **aor.** rare ἐθρόησα Soph. Aj. 947 (chor.) **Mid.** as **act.** θροούμενος Aesch. Eum. 510. **Pass.** in late poetry and prose, θροεῖσθε N. T. Matth. 24, 6: **aor.** ἐθροήθην Pseud.-Callisth. 3, 4; V. T. Cant. 5, 4; Nicet. Eugen. 2, 107. Rare in other poets, θροεῖ Anth. Plan. 4, 228; Luc. Tragod. 50; θροεῖν Lycophr. 1373; θροηθείς Theod. Prodr. 2, 296. On the contrary, the comp. διαθροέω is prosaic, διαθροούντων Xen. Hell. 1, 6, 4; -θροεῖν Dio Cass. 56, 46: **imp.** διεθρόει Thuc. 8, 91: **fut.** -ήσω: **aor.** δι-εθρόησα Thuc. 6, 46. **Pass.** late -οεῖται Dio Cass. 53, 19: **imp.** -εθροεῖτο 61, 8.

Θρυλλίζω or -ῡλίζω *To make a discordant note, jar, crush* (θρύλλ- or -ῦλος), Poet. Hom. H. 3, 488: **aor.** late θρῡλίξας Lycophr. 487: **aor. pass.** θρυλίχθη Il. 23, 396, which some refer to a form -ίσσω.

Θρύπτω *To break down, spoil,* Theocr. 17, 80; -τειν Pl. Crat. 426; -των Leg. 778, Dor. -οισα Locr. 103: **imp.** ἔθρυπτε Aesch. Ag. 1595; **fut.** late θρύψω Greg. Naz. p. 134: **aor.** ἔθρυψα, ἐν- Hippocr. 2, 713 (K.): **p. p.** τέθρυμμαι Hippocr. 6, 548 (Lit.);

Luc. Charid. 4, ἀπο- Pl. Rep. 495, δια- Xen. Mem. 1, 2, 25: **1 aor.** ἐθρύφθην Aristot. Probl. 11, 6 (Bekk.). De Anim. 2, 8, 5, ὑπ- Anth. 5, 294: **fut.** θρυφθήσομαι Arr. 4, 19, 2: **2 aor.** ἐτρύφην, δια-τρῠφέν Il. 3, 363, late ἐθρύβην Theod. Prod. 4, 327, συν- 325. **Mid.** θρύπτομαι *put on airs* &c. Pl. Leg. 777; Plut. Mor. 9, δια- Aesch. Pr. 891: **imp.** ἐθρύπτετο Pl. Phaedr. 228: **fut.** θρύψομαι Ar. Eq. 1163; Luc. Lap. 4. **Vb.** ἐν-θρυπτος Dem. 18, 260. The *simple* form seems not to occur in Tragedy, unless Soph. Fr. 708, be genuine. Dind. *now* has, we think, dropped it: Hartung retains it.

Θρώσκω *To leap*, Poet. Aesch. Ch. 846; Soph. Tr. 58; Theocr. 7, 25; Orph. Fr. 8, 18; Opp. Hal. 2, 135, ἐκ- Il. 10, 95, ἀνα- Her. 3, 64. 7, 18; subj. θρώσκωσι Il. 13, 589; θρώσκων 15, 470. 21, 126, ἀπο- Her. 3, 129: **imp.** ἔθρωσκον Hippocr. 9, 90, ἐξ- Aesch. Pers. 457, Epic θρῶσκον Il. 15, 314: **fut.** θοροῦμαι, ὑπερ- Aesch. Supp. 874, Epic -έομαι Il. 8, 179: **1 aor.** late ἔθρωξα, ἀνα- θρώξωσι Opp. Hal. 3, 293: **2 aor.** θόρον Il. 23, 509; Hes. Sc. 321, ἄν-θ- Ap. Rh. 3, 556, ἔθορε Opp. Cyn. 1, 520, ἐκ- δ' ἔθορεν Il. 7, 182, ἀνὰ δὲ...ἔθ- Eur. Or. 1416, ὑπερ- Solon Fr. 4, 29 (B.), ἀν- Apollod. 1, 3, 6; θόρωσι Od. 22, 303; θόρε, ἐκ- Soph. O. C. 234; θορών Il. 10, 528; Pind. P. 4, 36, ἀπο- Her. 1, 80; θορεῖν Opp. Hal. 3, 35, ἀνα- Xen. Lac. 2, 3, Ion. θορέειν, ὑπερ- Il. 12, 53; Her. 6, 134 (Bekk.): and perhaps **2 p.** τέθορα, τεθορυίης Canter's emendation of Antim. Fr. 70 (Dübn.) for τε θουρίης. θρώσκω seems trans. Aesch. Eum. 660, see also Fr. 13 (D.) Collat. form θορνύομαι, subj. -ύωνται Her. 3, 109, act. form in comp. late ἀνα-θορνύουσι Dio Cass. 63, 28 (L. Dind.), and late θόρνῦμαι Nic. Ther. 130: ἐθόρνυτο Hesych.; Euseb. Pr. Ev. p. 680, wrongly ascribed to Sophocl.

Θυίω *To rush*, Epic subj. θυΐωσι Hom. H. Merc. 560: **imp.** ἔθυιεν Hesych. &c. See θύω *to rage*.

Θῡμιάω *To burn incense, fumigate*, Pind. Fr. 99, 4 (Bergk); Her. 3, 112; late Attic prose, -ιᾶν Luc. Prom. 19: **imp.** ἐθυμίων Athen. 7, 34: **aor.** ἐθυμίᾱσα Hippocr. 7, 44 (Lit. 2, 205 Erm.); Philostr. 318, Ion. -ησα Her. 6, 97; -ήσας Hipponax 92 (B.): reg. but **aor. pass.** θυμιαθείς Dioscor. 1, 82, and θυμιασθείς, ὑπο- 1, 22: **fut.** θυμιαθήσεται Dioscor. 1, 83, ἐκ- Marc. Ant. 6, 4: and **fut. m.** θυμιήσεται **pass.?** Hippocr. 8, 272: **pres. pass.** θυμιᾶται Aristot. Meteor. 4, 9, 28, Ion. θυμιῆται Her. 4, 75, -ᾶται (Dietsch, Abicht); θυμιωμένων Pl. Tim. 66, the only part in classic Attic. **Mid. pres.** imper. θυμιήσθω Hippocr. 7, 342. 8, 318: **fut.** θυμιήσεται Hippocr. 8, 272 (Lit.) see above: **aor.** θυμιησαμένη Hippocr. 7, 322. 8, 322, ὑπο- 8, 276. Lexicons miss the mid.

Θυμόω *To enrage*, rare in act. and only aor. unless θυμῶντα (-οῦντα) V. T. 1 Esdr. 1, 52 (Gaisf.) be correct, which Fritzsche doubts, and recommends, perhaps rightly, θυμωθέντα offered by several Mss.: aor. ἐθύμωσα, -ῶσαι Eur. Supp. 581 (Vulg. Dind. -οῦσθαι Musgr. Kirchh. Nauck); V. T. Hosea 12, 14. Mid. and pass. with no difference of meaning, θυμοῦμαι *be enraged, rage*, Eur. I. T. 1478; Ar. Ran. 1006; Pl. Leg. 865; -οίμην Soph. El. 1278; Pl. Rep. 465; subj. -ῶται Xen. Eq. 1, 10; -μούμενον Antiph. 2, γ, 3; Thuc. 7, 68: fut. m. Poet. θυμώσομαι Aesch. Ag. 1069: and aor. (ἐθυμωσάμην), part. Dor. θυμωσαμένα Eur. Hel. 1343 (chor.): in same sense p. p. τεθυμῶσθαι Aesch. Fr. 369 (D.); Eur. Fr. 1063 (Dind. 5 ed.); Her. 3, 52; Xen. An. 2, 5, 13: and aor. ἐθυμώθην Her. 7, 39. 238, θυμώθη Batr. 241 (Franke); -ωθείς Soph. Fr. 514; Eur. Phoen. 461; Her. 5, 33; Pl. Leg. 931; Plut. Mor. 10 (often in V. T. ἐθυμώθην v. r. Gen. 6, 7, -ώθης 2 Reg. 19, 42, -ώθη Deut. 9, 8. Lev. 10, 16 &c.; N. T. Matth. 2, 16): fut. late θυμωθήσομαι V. T. Job 21, 4. Esai. 13, 13 &c. Lexicons overlook the mid. aor.

Θυνέω, θύνω, see θύω *to rage.*

Θυόω (**θύος**) *To make fragrant*, only p. pt. pass. τεθυωμένος Il. 14, 172; Hym. Hom. 2, 6; Callim. Lav. Pal. 61.

Θύω *To sacrifice*, (ῠ) Simon. Am. 20; Eur. I. T. 38; Com. Fr. (Pher.) 2, 261; Her. 6, 38; Thuc. 1, 126; subj. Dor. 3 pl. θύωντι Theocr. 4, 21; opt. θύοιεν Her. 2, 45; θῦε Soph. El. 632, θυέτω Theogn. 1146; θύων Od. 15, 260; Hom. H. Apol. 313; Soph. O. C. 1159; Her. 7, 191; Antiph. 1, 18. 6, 45; Isocr. 1, 13, Dor. θύοισα Pind. P. 3, 33; θύειν Eur. Elec. 1141; Her. 8, 55; Xen. Cyr. 8, 5, 26; Isocr. 1, 13: imp. ἔθυον Pind. Ol. 10, 57, ἔθῡον Aesch. Eum. 692; Her. 6, 67. 7, 191; Antiph. 1, 17; Thuc. 5, 50, θῦε Od. 15, 222, θύεσκε Hipponax 37: fut. θύσω Eur. Elec. 1141; Ar. Av. 894; Her. 2, 45; Pl. Leg. 909, Dor. θυσῶ Theocr. 2, 33: aor. ἔθυσα Od. 9, 231; Aesch. Ag. 1417; Soph. El. 576; Ar. Plut. 1180; Her. 6, 81; Thuc. 2, 71, θῦσε Od. 14, 446; -σαιεν Aeschin. 3, 111 (-ειεν Franke), -ειε Lycurg. 99; θῦσαι Il. 9, 219; θύσας Antiph. 1, 16: p. τέθυκα Ar. Lys. 1062; C. Fr. 3, 560; Isocr. 7, 10; Pl. Rep. 328: p. p. τέθυμαι, -ύσθαι Ar. Av. 1034; -υμένος Aesch. Eum. 341; Xen. Hell. 3, 5, 5: plp. ἐτέθυτο, see mid.: aor. ἐτύθην Aesch. Ch. 242; Her. 1, 216; Com. Fr. 4, 55; Aristot. Poet. 16, 6; (Dem.) Prooem. 54: fut. τυθήσομαι Diod. Sic. 16, 91; Luc. D. Deor. 4, 2: and seemingly pass. fut. m. θύσομαι Her. 7, 197. Mid. θύομαι *to sacrifice for oneself, take the auspices* &c. Aesch. Ag. 137; Her. 9, 10; Thuc. 5, 54; Xen. An. 5, 6, 27: imp. ἐθυ- Her. 7, 167; Xen. An. 5, 6, 28: fut. θύσομαι Eur. Heracl. 340, as pass. see above; Xen. Cyr. 6, 2, 40; προ-θῡσόμενος Ar. Thesm. 38: **aor.** ἐθῡσάμην Pl. Leg. 642; θυσάμενος Thuc. 4, 92; Isocr. 12, 92, ἐκ- Eur. Fr. 904 (Dind.); -ασθαι Her. 6, 91: with **p.** τέθῡμαι Xen. Hell. 5, 1, 18: **plp.** ἐτέθῡτο Antiph. 1, 17; Xen. Hell. 3, 1, 23. **Vb.** θυτέον Pl. Rep. 365. υ of the pres. and imp., though generally long, θύω Eur. H. F. 936; Ar. Plut. 1138, θῦε Od. 15, 222, is sometimes short, θῠοντα Od. 15, 260, ἔθῠε Pind. Ol. 10, 57, θῠεσκε Hippon. 36 (Bergk), θῠειν Eur. Elec. 1141, the only instance in Tragedy, if οὔ τι θύω Eur. Cycl. 334 (Herm. Dind. 5 ed.) be right for οὔτινι θῠω (Vulg. Dind. 2 ed. Nauck, Kirchh.); θῠω Ar. Ach. 792; Com. Fr. (Strat.) 4, 545, and late Poets, Theocr. 4, 21. In Theod. Prodr. 3, 96. 7, 421, the **perf.** τέθῡκα, τεθῡκότι is long; so τεθῡμένος 3, 83.—θύω and **mid.** θύομαι seem sometimes to differ little, Xen. An. 7, 6, 44. 3, 2, 9, but generally θύω expresses rather the mere *act*, θύομαι the *object* also.

Θύω (θυνέω) θύνω (ῡ) *To rage, rush*, Epic, θύει Il. 1, 342, -ουσι Hes. Th. 874, θύνει Pind. P. 10, 54, -νουσι Opp. Hal. 3, 63; imper. θῦνε Il. 5, 250; θύνων Il. 10, 524; Opp. Hal. 2, 564, θύων Il. 21, 234; Aesch. Ag. 1235: **imp.** ἔθῡον Ap. Rh. 3, 755, ἀν- Callim. Cer. 30, θῦον Il. 16, 699. Od. 11, 420; Hes. Th. 131, ἔθῡνον (Simon.C.?) 179 (Bergk), θῦνον Il. 2, 446. 5, 87; Orph. Arg. 633; Opp. Hal. 2, 677, ἐθύνεον Hes. Sc. 210. 286: **aor.** rare ἔθῡσα Anth. 13, 18; Callim. Fr. 82, ἐπι- Od. 16, 297, ἔθῡνα Anth. 6, 217?: **2 aor. m.** syncop. θῠμενος Athen. (Pratin.) 14, 617. Hither has been referred a **fut.** παρθύσει with ῠ, Anth. 12, 32. We believe the reading corrupt, and venture to suggest παρθέει pres. of παραθέω.—The form θυΐω occurs in **pres.** subj. only, θυΐωσι Hom. H. 3, 560, θυίῃσι Nic. Ther. 129 (Otto Schneid.), and **imp.** ἔθυιεν trisyll. Ap. Rh. 3, 755 quoted (Merk.)

Θωκέω, see θᾱκέω.

Θωρήσσω *To arm*, Poetic, and Ion. prose, -ήσσων Opp. Hal. 2, 678: **fut.** (-ήξω): **aor.** θώρηξα Il. 16, 155; Anth. 9, 140; subj. -ήξομεν for -ωμεν, Il. 2, 72; inf. -ῆξαι 2, 11; Hippocr. 4, 130; -ήξας Opp. Hal. 2, 512: **p.** τεθωρηκότα Ruf. Fr. p. 208. More freq. **mid.** *to arm oneself*, θωρήσσονται Hes. Th. 431, -ωνται (Goettl. Lenn. Schoem.); -οιτο Il. 10, 78; trans. Opp. Cyn. 1, 202; imper. θωρήσσεο Il. 19, 36; Anth. Plan. 94; inf. -εσθαι Il. 18, 167: **imp.** ἐθωρήσσοντο Od. 23, 369, θωρήσσ- Il. 8, 54; Ar. Pax 1286 (hexam.), 3 dual -ρήσσεσθον Il. 13, 301: **fut.** θωρήξομαι Il. 7, 101; Theogn. 413; Ar. Ach. 1135; Hippocr. 2, 229: **aor.** later ἐθωρηξάμην, θωρηξ- Opp. Hal. 3, 563; unless θωρήξομαι be Epic subj. Il. 8, 376; as **act.** θωρήξαιο Nic. Alex.

225: with aor. pass. as mid. θωρήχθησαν Il. 3, 340; Q. Sm. 9, 125; subj. -ηχθῶσι Hippocr. 2, 375; θωρηχθῆναι Il. 1, 226; -ηχθέντες 18, 277, Dor. -αχθείς Pind. Fr. 50 (Bergk). This verb has also the meaning *to drink, get drunk.* The Attic form is θωρακίζω Aristot. H. A. 6, 18, 3: aor. ἐθωράκισε Xen. Cyr. 6, 1, 29: p. p. τεθωρακισμένος Thuc. 2, 100; Com. Fr. (Ephipp.) 3, 332. Mid. -ίζομαι *arm oneself*, imp. ἐθωρακίζετο Xen. An. 2, 2, 14: aor. ἐθωρακίσαντο Pseud.-Callisth. 2, 16.

Θῶσθαι *To feast, revel,* Dor. Aesch. Fr. 44 (D.), θῶται, θῶνται Hesych.: fut. θωσούμεθα Epicharm. 167: aor. θώσασθαι Hesych.: p. τέθωσαι Phot.: aor. θωθῆναι Hesych.

Θωυμάζω, some θωμ- Ion. for θαυμάζω.

I.

Ἰαίνω *To warm,* Poet. Od. 15, 379; Alcm. 36 (Bergk 3 ed.); Pind. P. 2, 90; Theocr. 7, 29: imp. ἴαινον Hym. Cer. 435, iter. ἰαίνεσκον Q. Sm. 7, 340: aor. ἴηνα Od. 8, 426; ἰήνῃ Il. 24, 119; opt. ἰήνειεν Q. Sm. 10, 327, Dor. ἰάναιεν Pind. Ol. 7, 43: aor. pass. ἰάνθην Il. 23, 600. Od. 4, 549; ἰανθῇ 22, 59; ἰανθείς Pind. Ol. 2, 13: pres. ἰαίνομαι Od. 19, 537, -εται 6, 156; Theogn. 531: imp. ἰαίνετο Od. 10, 359, ἰαίν- 12, 175: subj. ἰαίνηται Hippocr. 8, 146, missed by Lexicogr. ἰαίνων is not now received Polyaen. 1, 1.—ῐ Od. 8, 426 &c., ῑ by *augm.* 10, 359, by *ictus* 22, 59; Anth. 12, 95 &c. Q. Sm. quoted; Opp. Hal. 3, 617.

Ἰακχάζω, ἰακχέω, see ἰαχ-.

Ἰάλλω (ῐ) *To send,* Poet. Od. 13, 142; Aesch. Ch. 45 (chor.); ἰάλλοις Theogn. 573; ἰάλλων Od. 10, 376: imp. ἴαλλον Il. 9, 91; Hes. Th. 269; Aesch. Pr. 659: fut. ἰᾰλῶ in ἐπ-ιαλῶ Ar. Nub. 1299: aor. ἴηλα Il. 15, 19, Dor. ἴᾱλα Sophr. 32 (Ahr.); ἰήλω Od. 2, 316; inf. ἰῆλαι 21, 241. ῑ sometimes by augm. ἐπ-ίηλεν Od. 22, 49. This verb seems to have been without, and with the *aspirate,* see passages quoted, and ἀπ-ιάλλην Lacon. inf. Thuc. 5, 77, ἐπ-ίηλεν Od. 22, 49, but ἱάλλω Eustath. 1403, 13, ἐφ-ιαλεῖς Ar. Vesp. 1348 (Bergk), -οῦμεν Pax 432, 'φιαλεῖς, -οῦμεν (Eustath.), φιαλ- (Dind. Mein. Richter).

Ἰάομαι *To heal,* Eur. Fr. 294 (D.), ἰᾶται Com. Fr. (Men.) 4, 240, ἰῆται Hippocr. 1, 459 (Erm.), Ion. 3 pl. ἰεῦνται, ἀν- Her. 7, 236; subj. ἰᾶται Pl. Charm. 164; opt. ἰῴμην Soph. Tr. 1210, ἰῷτο Pl. Charm. 164; imper. ἰῶ Aesch. Fr. 417 (D.); Her. 3,

53, ἰάσθω Ar. Av. 584; ἰᾶσθαι Pind. P. 3, 46; Soph. Fr. 98. 501 (D.); Thuc. 5, 65; Hippocr. 6, 316, but Ion. -ῆσθαι 6, 386; ἰώμενος Eur. Or. 650; Her. 3, 134; Pl. Rep. 346: **imp.** ἰᾶτο Il. 12, 2, -ῆτο Luc. D. Syr. 20, -ῶντο Her. 3, 132: **fut.** ἰάσομαι Eur. H. F. 1107; Ar. Plut. 1087; Pl. Gorg. 447; Isocr. 6, 101, Ion. ἰήσ- Od. 9, 525; Archil. 13; (Luc.) D. Syr. 20, ἐξ- Hippocr. 6, 150 (Lit.): **aor.** ἰᾱσάμην Eur. Fr. 1057 (Dind.); Pl. Phaed. 89; Xen. Cyr. 8, 2, 25, Ion. ἰησ- Il. 5, 904; Hippocr. 7, 174 (Lit.), ἐξ- Her. 3, 134. 132: **p. p.** late ἴᾱμαι **act.** V. T. 4 Reg. 2, 21, **pass.** N. T. Mar. 5, 29: **aor.** ἰάθην always **pass.** Andoc. 2, 9; Pl. Leg. 758; Anth. 6, 330, Ion. -ήθην Hippocr. 7, 172. 8, 24 (Lit.): and **fut.** ἰαθήσομαι (Luc.) Asin. 14; Geop. 12, 25; Galen 10, 377: and late **fut. m.** ἰάσεται as **pass.** Aristid. 47, 317. **Vb.** ἰητέος Hippocr. 6, 92 (Lit.), ἰατός Pl. Leg. 862. ι always long in Hom., varies in Attic and late Poets. An **act.** form (ἰάω) occurs late, **fut.** ἰάσω, ἰάσουσα Nicet. Eug. 3, 148: **aor.** ἰάσαμεν Galen 10, 352, missed by all Lexicogr. Her. has ἀνιεῦνται 7, 236, 3 pl. **pres.** as from Ion. ἀνιέομαι, but there is no need to ascribe to it a future meaning. The form however seems doubtful, at least it accords not with the forms of similar verbs as used by Her. With him verbs that have a vowel before the termination αω follow in their inflection the common form, see ἀνιᾶν, αἰτιᾶσθαι, βιᾶσθαι, βοᾶν, ἐᾶν, θεᾶσθαι, θυμιᾶν, ἰᾶσθαι &c. αἰτιῶνται 4, 94, βιώμενος 1, 19, βοῶσι 3, 117, ἀν-εβόων 3, 14, ἔων 7, 18. 143, ἰῶντο 3, 132 &c. &c. In accordance therefore with analogy, the correct Herodotean form would seem to be ἀνιῶνται, not -εῦνται. See ἀκέομαι.

Ἰαύω *To rest*, sleeping or awake, Poet. Il. 14, 213; Hym. Ven. 177; Eur. Rhes. 740 (chor.); ἰαύῃ Nic. Ther. 125; ἰαύοις 90; ἰαύων Il. 18, 259; Eur. Phoen. 1538 (chor.); Theocr. 3, 49; ἰαύειν Soph. Aj. 1204 (chor.); Theocr. 17, 133; Il. 19, 71, -έμεν (Bekk.): **imp.** ἴαυον Il. 9, 325. Od. 22, 464, iter. ἰαύεσκον 9, 184: **fut.** late ἰαύσω Lycophr. 101. 430: **aor.** ἴαυσα Hym. Cer. 264; ἰαύσῃς Hym. Merc. 288; Luc. Merc. Con. 11; inf. ἰαῦσαι Od. 11, 261; Q. Sm. 1, 670; ἰαύσας late prose, Themist. 26, 312. (ῐ always.) Used by the Tragedians only in **pres.** and only in chor.

Ἰαχέω *To shout*, Poet. Hom. H. 27, 7; Aesch. Sept. 868 (Herm. ἀχ- Dind.); Eur. H. F. 349 (Kirchh. Nauck, ἰακχ- Dind.), Ion. 3 pl. ἰαχεῦσι Callim. Del. 146, and ἰακχέω Eur. Heracl. 783. Hel. 1486. Or. 965 (Dind. ἰαχ- Nauck): **fut.** ἰαχήσω Eur. Phoen. 1523 (Pors. Herm. Klotz, Nauck). 1295 (Pors. Herm.), ἰακχ- (Klotz, ἀχήσ- Dind. Nauck): **aor.** ἰάκχησα Eur. Heracl. 752 (Dind.). Or. 826 (Dind. Pors. Herm.), ἰάχησα (Kirchh. Nauck), which occurs Hom. H. 5, 20. 28, 11; Ar. Ran. 217 chor. (Bekk. Bergk, Mein. Dind. 2 ed. ἄχησ- 5 ed.): aor. pass. ἰαχήθης? Eur. Hel. 1147, Hermann's emendation, and adopted by Paley for ἰαχῇ σῇ (Vulg. Kirchh. Nauck, Dind. doubtingly 5 ed.). ῐ, ᾰ usu. if not always.) In Attic poetry this verb is always in chor. Mss. and editors (Vulg. Kirchh. Nauck &c.) generally have ἰαχέω; but as α is usually short, Pors. Seidl. Herm. Dind. &c. write ἰακχέω when the second syllable requires to be long. In the Tragedians and Aristophanes, Elmsley and Dindorf would often read ἀχέω, -ήσω, -ησα for ἰαχέω &c. ἀχεῖν Aesch. Sept. 868, ἀχήσω Eur. Phoen. 1295. H. F. 1026, ἀχήσειεν Ar. Thesm. 328, all in chor. A collateral form ἰακχάζω occurs in Ion. and late writers, -χάζουσι Her. 8, 65; -χάζων Orph. Lith. 46: aor. -χάσας Long. 3, 11, but ἐπεξιάκχ- Aesch. Sept. 635. See foll.

Ἰάχω *To shout*, Poet. H. Hym. 27, 7 (Herm. Franke, -χεῖ Baum.); Eur. Elec. 707 chor. (Dind.); ἰάχων Il. 14, 421. Od. 10, 323: imp. ἴαχον Il. 18, 29; Hes. Th. 69; Eur. Elec. quoted (Elms. Nauck). Or. 1465 chor. (Vulg. Kirchh. Nauck, Dind. 2 ed. ἀντ-ίαχον 5 ed.); Anth. 6, 217, περι- Hes. Th. 678, iter. ἰάχεσκον Hes. Sc. 232: p. ἴαχα in comp. ἀμφιαχυῖα Il. 2, 316. ᾰ, ῐ unaugm. Od. 4, 454. Il. 4, 506, ῑ augm. Il. 18, 29. 20, 62. 21, 10.

Ἰδίω *To sweat* (ἶδος), Ar. Ran. 237. Pax 85, ἀν- Pl. Tim. 74 (ῑῐ): but imp. ἴδῐον Od. 20, 204: aor. ἴδῑσα Aristot. H. A. 3, 19, 8, ἐξ- ίδῑσε Ar. Av. 791.

Ἱδρόω (ῐ) *To sweat*, -οῦμεν Aristot. Probl. 2, 36 (-ῶμεν v. r.). 2, 42; but -ῴη Hippocr. 2, 34 (Lit.); ἱδροῦντι Xen. An. 1, 8, 1 (most Mss. Vulg. Popp. Krüg. Dind. -ῶντι Saupp. Schenkl, Rehdantz). Cyr. 1, 4, 28 (best Mss. Vulg. Popp. Dind. -ῶντι Saupp. Hertl. 3 ed.). Hell. 4, 5, 7 (most Mss. and edit.), -ῶντι (best Ms. Breitb. Dind. Saupp.): fut. ἱδρώσω Il. 2, 388: aor. ἵδρωσα Il. 4, 27; Hippocr. 5, 150; Xen. Cyr. 8, 1, 38: p. ἵδρωκα Luc. Merc. cond. 26: p. p. ἵδρωται Luc. Herm. 2.—In Epic and Ionic it contracts in ω instead of ου, οι, ἱδρῶσαι Il. 11, 598, but -ώουσ' (Bekk.); opt. ἱδρῴη Hippocr. 2, 34 (Lit.); and lengthens ο into ω, ἱδρώουσι Opp. Hal. 2, 450; ἱδρώουσα &c. Il. 11, 119, ἱδρώοντας Od. 4, 39; Ar. Pax 1283 (hexam. so ὑπνώοντας Il. 24, 344). Strong traces of this occur even in Attic, see Xen. above, and v. r. Aristot. quoted, and Theophr. Fr. 9, 7. 11. 36 &c. see ῥιγόω. An Ion. pres. form ἱδρώω however would seem to have existed, ἱδρώει Luc. D. Syr. 10, -ῴη Hippocr. quoted, -ώειν Luc. D. Syr. 17.

Ἱδρύω *To place, erect*, Plut. Mor. 474; ἱδρύῃ Pl. Tim. 66: imper. ἵδρῡε Il. 2, 191: imp. ἵδρῡον Ap. Rh. 4, 1550, καθ- Od.

20, 257: **fut.** ἱδρύσω Nic. Damasc. 52, p. 39 (L. Dind.), καθ- Eur. Bac. 1339: **aor.** ἵδρῦσα Il. 15, 142. Od. 3, 37; Her. 4, 124, Boeot. εἵδρ- Epigr. dedic. 895 (Kaibel); -ύσῃς Aesch. Eum. 862; imper. ἵδρῦσον Eur. Ion 1573; -ῦσαι Alc. 841; -ύσας Bac. 1070; Thuc. 4, 104: **p.** ἵδρῦκα, καθ- Aristot. de part. An. 3, 4, 6; Joseph. Jud. B. 2, 17, 3: **p. p.** ἵδρῦμαι Eur. Hipp. 639; Theocr. 17, 21; Her. 1, 69; Thuc. 2, 15; Pl. Rep. 429, Ion. 3 pl. ἱδρύαται, ἐν- Her. 2, 156; -ῦσθαι Aesch. Pers. 231; Soph. Tr. 68; Her. 2, 169; Thuc. 8, 40; -ῡμένος Aesch. Supp. 413; Her. 1, 75; Isocr. 12, 92, but -υσμένος, ἐν- (Hippocr.) Epist. 9, 396 (Lit.): **plp.** ἵδρῦτο Her. 1, 50; Aristot. Mund. 6, 9, -ύατο Her. 2, 182, and ἦν ἱδρῡμένος Ar. Plut. 1192: **aor.** ἱδρύθην Ar. Fr. 245 (D.); Thuc. 3, 72; Hippocr. 5, 150 (Lit.). 3, 146 (five Mss. -ύνθ- Vulg. Lit.); subj. -υθέωσιν Hippocr. 8, 314 (Mss. C. θ. Lit. -υνθῶ- Vulg.); -ῡθείς Her. 2, 118 (all). 4, 203 (most). 1, 172 (Bekk. Dind. Stein, -υνθ- Gaisf. Dietsch); Thuc. 1, 131; (Pl.) Ax. 365, καθ- Ar. Av. 45; ἱδρυθῆναι Her. 2, 44 (Gaisf. Bekk. Dind. Bred. -υνθ- Ald. &c.); Xen. Cyr. 8, 4, 10 (Born. Dind. -υνθ- Popp.), -ύσθην Diog. Laert. 4, 1, 3, and -ύνθην mostly Epic, and late, Il. 3, 78. 7, 56; Ap. Rh. 3, 1269. 4, 532. 723 (Well. Merk. -υθ- most Mss.); Hippocr. 3, 144. 146. 556 (Lit.); Plut. Marcel. 25 &c. (Bekk. Sint.), ἀφ- Anth. Plan. 260, ἐν- 10, 9, see below: **fut.** ἱδρυνθήσομαι Dio. Hal. Comp. verb. 6, ἱδρῡθ- Plotin. 9, 6, ἐν-ιδρῡθ- Dio Cass. 52, 35, καθ- Joseph. Ant. 13, 3, 2. **Mid.** ἱδρύομαι *erect for oneself* &c. Pl. Prot. 322: **imp.** -ύετο Eur. Ion 1134: **fut.** ἱδρύσομαι Eur. Heracl. 397; Ar. Plut. 1198; Aristid. 13, 111 (D.): **aor.** ἱδρῡσάμην Anacr. 104; Simon. C. 140; Eur. H. F. 49; Ar. Thesm. 109; Anth. Pal. (incert.) 6, 145; Her. 5, 82. 6, 105; Thuc. 6, 3; Pl. Tim. 38; late Epic Ap. Rh. 1, 959. 4, 1691; Orph. Lith. 129; imper. ἵδρυσαι Eur. I. T. 1453: **p.** ἵδρῡμαι as **mid.** Com. Fr. (Men.) 4, 127; Her. 2, 42; Pl. Conv. 195, καθ- Eur. Cycl. 318. **Vb.** ἱδρυτέον Ar. Pax 923.—In pres. and imp. ῡ in Attic, Eur. Heracl. 786. Ion 1134, ῠ in Epic, except Callim. Fr. 220 (Bl.): late poets shorten even the **aor.** ἐνιδρῠσατο Anth. 7, 109, but ἵδρῠσε Nonn. D. 4, 22, has been altered to ἵδρῠε (Herm. Graef. Koechly), and to ἵδρῡσ' Maneth. 3, 80 (Axt, Rigl. Koechly).

The **aor.** form ἱδρύνθην is not free from suspicion, for generally the best Mss. offer ἱδρύθην. -ύνθην is retained in Hom. by Wolf, Bekk. Dind. La Roche; in Ap. Rh. by Well. Merk.; in Theocr. by Mein. Ahrens, Wordsw.; occasionally in Her. by Gaisf., never by Bekk. Krüg. Dind.; in classic Attic there is *now* scarcely an instance of -ύνθην; Poppo (with Bekk. Krüg. Dind. Donalds.) is decidedly against it in Thuc., and we doubt if he would re-edit it in Xen. Cyr. 8, 4, 10: ἱδρύνθη however Hippocr. 3, 144. 146 (Lit.); Dio. Hal. 9, 47 (Vulg. -υθ- Kiessl.); -υνθείη Hippocr. 4, 118; -υνθῶσιν 8, 314 (Vulg. -υθέωσι Lit.); -υνθῆναι 3, 556 (Lit.); -υνθείς Hippocr. 1, 75 (Erm.); Aristot. Poet. 17, 6 (Bekk.); Plut. Rom. 1 &c. see above.

(Ἴδω) see εἴδω.

Ἵεμαι *To hasten* (mid. of ἵημι *send*), Od. 22, 304; Xen. Cyr. 4, 1, 17; imper. ἵεσθε Il. 12, 274; ἵεσθαι Her. 6, 134; Xen. An. 5, 7, 25; ἱέμενος Soph. Tr. 514; Xen. Cyr. 3, 2, 10, ἐσ- Od. 22, 470: imp. ἱέμην Soph. O. R. 1242; Ar. Eq. 625; Xen. An. 1, 8, 26. (ῐ Epic, ῑ Attic.) Some write ἵεμαι (mid. of εἶμι *go*): imp. ἱέμην.

Ἱέω *To send*, pres. partially in comp. ἀν-ιεῖς Il. 5, 880, μεθ- 6, 523 (Wolf, Spitzn. Dind. -ίῃς Bekk. 2 ed.), -εῖ 10, 121, but δι-ίει Hippocr. 5, 492 (Lit.), ἐξ- Her. 6, 20, καθ- Plut. Ant. 77, 3 pl. συν-ιοῦσι N. T. Matth. 13, 13; subj. and opt. in compds.; imper. ἵει Pind. Ol. 9, 11, παρ- P. 1, 86; Eur. Elec. 592 (in tmesi Il. 21, 338), καθ- Ar. Av. 387, ἀν- Pl. Crat. 420; inf. συν-ιεῖν Theogn. 565: imp. ἵειν, προ- Od. 9, 88. 12, 9 (Vulg. Dind. La Roche, -ίην Bekk. 2 ed.), ἵεις Ar. Vesp. 355, ἵει Il. 1, 479 (Wolf, Dind. &c. ἵη Bekk. 2 ed.); Hes. Fr. 4, ἀν-ίει Il. 15, 24. Od. 8, 359 (-ίη Bekk.); Her. 4, 152, ἠν-ίει Hippocr. 5, 414 (Lit.), καθ-ίει Plut. Ant. 77, 3 pl. ἵουν, ἠφ-ίουν Isae. 6, 40 (Vulg. εἴων Hirschig, Scheibe), iter. ἵεσκε, ἀν- Hes. Th. 157, προ- Q. Sm. 13, 8. The forms ἱεῖς, ἱεῖ are sometimes accented ἵεις, ἵει, and referred to ἵω, see Od. 4, 372; Her. 2, 70. See ἵημι.

Ἱζάνω *To seat, place*, also intrans. *sit*, Il. 10, 92 (ἰζἄνει Sapph. 2, 3); Hippocr. 6, 164 (Lit.); Thuc. 2, 76, προσ- Simon. Am. 7, 84; Aesch. Pr. 276. Sept. 696, καθ- Eum. 29; C. Fr. (Pher.) 2, 360. (Menand.) 4, 328; Isocr. 1, 52: imp. ἵζᾰνον Il. 23, 258. Od. 24, 209, ἀμφ- Il. 18, 25, ὑφ- Eur. Phoen. 1382. Buttmann and others therefore err in saying "*later* writers, from Aristot. onwards, have also a pres. ἱζάνω, καθιζάνω."

Ἵζω *To seat, establish* (Dor. ἵσδ-), Il. 24, 553; Aesch. Eum. 18; intrans. *sit*, Il. 13, 281; Aesch. Ag. 982; Eur. Hec. 1150; Ar. Ran. 199; Com. Fr. (Epicr.) 3, 366; rare in prose Her. 1, 198; Hippocr. 3, 470. 6, 570; Pl. Tim. 53, Dor. ἵσδει, ἐφ- Theocr. 5, 97; subj. ἵζῃ Hippocr. 6, 238 (Lit.); ἵζοι Aesch. Supp. 685; imper. ἵζε Od. 24, 394; Theogn. 34; Eur. Hec. 147. Ion 1258; ἵζων Soph. Ant. 1000; Ar. Eq. 403; Her. 5, 25, ἵζουσα Eur. Hel. 296, Dor. -οισα Pind. Ol. 10 (11), 38; ἵζειν Eur. Ion 1314; Her. 6, 57: imp. with augm. ἷζον Il. 2, 53. 18, 522 (Bekk.); Eur. Alc. 946 (but imperat. ἵζε), iter ἵζεσκον Od. 3, 409: late fut. ἱζήσω, ὑφ- Cyrill. Alex. T. 5, p. 412, but see καθ-ίζω: aor. late ἴζησα Dio Cass. 50, 2. 58, 5. 59, 25 (Bekk.); Philostr. V. Apoll. 2, 11; Heliod. 9, 4, συν- Plut. Mor. 665; Strab. 16, 2, 26 &c.: p. ἰζηκώς, ἐν- Galen 2, 691; Oribas. 7, 23, 40, συν- Galen 4, 191. 10, 472; Philostr. Imag. 844. **Mid.** ἴζομαι *to sit*, indic. rare, ἴζεαι Pind. Fr. 123, ἴζεται Mosch. 3, 62 (Mein. ἕζ- Ahr. Ziegl.); subj. -ηται Her. 1, 199; Hippocr. 4, 128. 162, ἐσ- Il. 13, 285, ἴζηνται Maneth. 2, 367; opt. -οιο Her. 7, 15, -οιτο Od. 22, 335; imper. ἴζου Aesch. Eum. 80; Eur. Andr. 1266, Ion. ἴζευ Il. 7, 115, ἰζέσθω Pl. Leg. 855, -εσθε Aesch. Supp. 224; inf. ἴζεσθαι Her, 5, 18. 7, 16. 120; Hippocr. 4, 82. 294. 352. 8, 334; Xen. Ven. 9, 14; part. ἰζόμενος Ar. Av. 742 (chor.); Her. 1, 199. 3, 65. 122. 9, 41; rare in Attic -ένη Pl. Tim. 25, Dor. -ένα Mosch. 3, 58 (Mein. ἑζ- Ahr. Ziegl.): **imp.** ἰζόμην Eur. Fr. incert. 853 (D.), ἴζεο Callim. Jov. 81 (ἕζ- Mein.), -ετο Her. 3, 140. 7, 44, -όμεθα 9, 26, -οντο Il. 3, 326. 19, 50; Her. 4, 146. 5, 18. 7, 140. 8, 67. 71. See καθίζω. In the trans. sense *to seat*, ἴζω seems never to occur in prose, and once only in *Attic* poetry, Aesch. Eum. 18, occasionally with an acc. *sit* on, θρόνον Aesch. Ag. 982; *sit* at, βωμόν Eur. Ion 1314. This verb is chiefly Poet. and Ion.: in Attic prose, Plato thrice, Xen. once: classic, only pres. and imp.

῞Ιημι *To send*, ἵης Soph. El. 596, ἵησι Il. 3, 12. Od. 11, 239; Xenophan. 1, 7; Aesch. Pr. 812; Soph. Ant. 1211; Eur. Hipp. 533; Com. Fr. (Cratin.) 2, 179; Ar. Nub. 397; Xen. An. 1, 5, 12, Dor. ἵητι, ἐφ- Pind. I. 2, 9, 3 pl. ἱεῖσι Il. 3, 152, ἀν- Her. 2, 36, ἐξ- 2, 87, ἐπ- 4, 30, Attic ἱᾶσι Pl. Phaedr. 259; Xen. Ven. 13, 16, ἀν- Thuc. 6, 86, μεθ- Pl. Tim. 81, ἀφ- Xen. Ven. 5, 14, Ion. ἀπ- Her. 2, 41 (Mss. Gaisf. Bekk. Dind. Dietsch, ἀπ-ιεῖσι Bred. Abicht, Stein, also 194 Mss. M. F. &c. Bekk. Dind. Dietsch.); subj. ἱῶ, μεθ- Pl. Phil. 62, ἱῇ, προ- H. Ven. 152, ἐφ- Pl. Rep. 388, Epic ἱῇσι Theogn. 94, μεθ- Il. 13, 234; opt. ἱείης, ἀν- Od. 2, 185; imper. προ- ἵει Od. 24, 519, ἀν- Plat. Crat. 420, but ξύν-ιε Theogn. 1240, ἵετε, ἐν- Il. 12, 441, ξυν- Archil. 50; ἱείς Solon 36, 10; Thuc. 3, 112: imp. (ἵην) sing. doubtful (but προ-ίην Od. 9, 88. 12, 9, ἵης, προ- Od. 24, 333 (Bekk. -ίειν, -ίεις La R.), ἵη Il. 1, 479 Bekk. 2 ed.), ἠφίην Pl. Euthyd. 293 (Mss. C. Bekk. approved by Schneid. Bait.). Lys. 222 (Bekk.) see below, 3 pl. ἵεσαν Hes. Sc. 278; Eur. Bac. 1099, syncop. ἵεν Il. 12, 33; Pind. I. 1, 25, in sing. the form ἵειν is better supported, ἠφίειν Pl. Euthyd. 293 quoted, 3 sing. ἵει Il. 1, 479 (see ἱέω); Eur. Med. 1187; Xen. Conv. 2, 22, ἠφίει Pl. Lys. 222. Lach. 183, iter. ἵεσκε, ἀν- Hes. Th. 157: fut. ἥσω Il. 17, 515; Aesch. Pers. 944; Soph. Aj. 630; Ar. Ran. 823, ἀφ- Pl. Conv. 175, ἀν- Rep. 498, Dor. ἡσῶ, ἡσεῖτε Ar. Ach. 747, and perhaps (ἕσω), ἀν-έσω Epic Od. 18, 265: **1 aor.** ἧκα *indic.* only, Il. 5, 125; Eur. Rhes. 927, ἕηκα, προ- Il. 8, 297, ἀν-ῆκας Il. 21, 396, παρ- Pl. Euth. 301, ἧκε Il. 13, 204; Hes. Th. 669; Aesch. Pr. 154; Soph. Tr. 567; Eur. Med. 1176; Pl. Rep. 336, 1 and 2 pl. rare ἐν-ήκαμεν Od. 12, 401, ἀφ- Isae. 5, 1, μεθ- App. Mithr. 62, συν- Aristid. 8, 47, ξυν-ήκατε Ar. Ach. 101, ἀφ- Dinarch. 1, 57; Aeschin. 3, 85; Dem. 36, 10. 38, 18. 27, often 3d ἧκαν Xen. An. 4, 5, 18, προ- Pind. Ol. 1, 65, ἐπ- Her. 7, 176, ἀφ- Thuc. 7, 19, παρ- 4, 38, καθ- Eur. Ion 1200; Pl. Tim. 77 &c., Epic ἕηκα in tmesi Il. 1, 48, ἀφ-έηκα &c. 21, 115, ἀν- Hes. Th. 495 (to which some add Epic (ἕσα) ἄνεσαν Il. 21, 537, παρὰ . . εἷσαν 24, 720; opt. ἀνέσαιμι Il. 14, 209, see ἕω *seat*): **p.** εἷκα in comp. παρ- Soph. Fr. 305 (D.); Eur. Hel. 1059; Dem. 8, 34, ἀφ- Xen. An. 2, 3, 13, ἀν- Dem. 56, 25: **p. p.** εἷμαι in comp. ἀφ-εῖται Soph. Ant. 1165; Isocr. 17, 11 &c., ἀν- Aesch. Sept. 413; Eur. Phoen. 947; Her. 2, 65; Pl. Leg. 637, ἐφ- denied, but Luc. Sat. 5. Tox. 37; ἀφ-είσθω Thuc. 5, 91; παρ-ειμένος Aesch. Pr. 819, καθ- Ar. Nub. 538; Pl. Criti. 118, ἀν- Thuc. 1, 6: **plp.** εἵμην, παρ-εῖτο Soph. El. 545, καθ- Thuc. 4, 103, ἀφ- Pl. Critias 117, Ion. ἀπ- Her. 8, 49, ἐφ- Luc. Sat. 5: **aor.** εἵθην, παρ- Il. 23, 868, ἀφ- Eur. Phoen. 1376, Ion. ἀπ- Her. 7, 122; subj. ἀν-εθῇ Pl. Polit. 270 &c.; παρ-εθῆναι Dem. 21 105: **fut.** ἑθήσομαι in comp. ἀν- Thuc. 8, 63: **2 aor. act.** ἧν in comp. ἀφ- &c. not in sing., dual κάθ-ετον H. Hym. 2, 309, ἀφ-έτην Il. 11, 642, pl. κάθ-εμεν Od. 9, 72, but ἀν-εῖμεν Ar. Vesp. 574; Thuc. 1, 76, ἀνεῖτε Soph. O. R. 1405, καθ-εῖσαν Eur. Bac. 695, ἀφ- Thuc. 7, 53, ἀν- Pl. Conv. 179, Epic ἕσαν, προ- Od. 8, 399, ἀν- Il. 21, 537; subj. ὧ, μεθ- Soph. Ph. 816, καθ- C. Fr. 2, 622, Epic εἱῶ, ἐφ- Il. 1, 567, ᾗ, ἀν- Pl. Rep. 411, Epic ἀν-ήῃ Il. 2, 34, ἧσι Il. 15, 359, μεθ-ῶμεν 10, 449; opt. εἵην Il. 3, 221 (Mss. La R. Ameis, ἵει Mss. Vulg. ἵῃ Bekk.), ἐφ- Il. 18, 124, ἐπ- Her. 3, 113; ἕς, προ- Il. 16, 38, συν- Pind. Fr. 81, ἀφ- Ar. Eq. 1159; εἷναι Ar. Ran. 133, κατ- Her. 7, 35, ἀν- Pl. Conv. 179, ἕμεν in the dialects, μεθ- Il. 1, 283. 15, 138, συν- Pind. P. 3, 80, ἕμεναι, ἐξ- Od. 11, 531; εἵς, ὑφ- Il. 1, 434, see ἀφίημι. **Mid.** ἵεμαι *to hasten, desire*, Od. 2, 327; Her. 2, 70; Pl. Phaedr. 241; ἱέμενος Od. 1, 6; Mimnerm. 16; ἵεσθαι, ἐφ- Antiph. 5, 79: **imp.** ἱέμην Ar. Eq. 625; Themist. 23, 298, ἵετο (ῑ) Il. 8, 301; Soph. O. R. 1242; Her. 9, 78, -έμεσθα Soph. Ant. 432, ἵεντο Hes. Sc. 251: **fut.** ἥσομαι in comp. ἐφ- Il. 23, 82, προ- Thuc. 6, 34; Lycurg. 126; Dem. 1, 12. 22, 37, ἐξαν- Eur. Andr. 718, Ion. and **pass.** μετήσεσθαι Her. 5, 35: **1 aor.** in comp. προσηκάμην rare, and only indic.? Eur. Elec. 622; Luc. Bis Acc. 20, προ-ήκω Dem. 32, 15, -ήκασθε 19, 78. 84, -ήκατο Plut. Publ. 5, προσ- Dio Cass. 59, 23; Plut. Mor. 153, -αντο Aristid. 37 (474);

for προηκάμενος Aeschin. 3, 130 (*v.r.* Bekk. Ed. Hal. 1815), προσκτησάμενος is the approved reading (Vulg. Bekk. Berol. 1823. B. Saupp. Franke): **2 aor.** εἵμην in comp. ἐφ-εῖτο Soph. Ph. 619, ἀν- Eur. Elec. 826, ἀφ- Xen. Hier. 7, 11, προ- Dem. 30, 14, Epic and Ion. ἕμην, ἕντο in tmesi Il. 9, 92. Od. 17, 99, σύν-ετο 4, 76 (B.); subj. ὧμαι, συν- Il. 15, 381, προ- Thuc. 1, 71; Dem. 16, 25. 21, 213; Plut. Them. 7; opt. εἵμην, παρ- Soph. O. C. 1666, ἀφ- Ar. Av. 627, and οἵμην, προ- Thuc. 1, 120; Pl. Gorg. 520; Dem. 21, 212. 18, 254, προει- (Bekk.); οὗ, ἀφ- Soph. O. R. 1521, Ion. ἔξ-εο Her. 5, 39; ἕσθαι, προσ- Ar. Vesp. 742; Dem. 9, 51, προ- Pl. Gorg. 520, εἰσ- Xen. Hell. 1, 3, 19; ἕμενος, προ- Thuc. 6, 78; Xen. An. 7, 7, 47; Isocr. 4, 164: **p. p.** as **mid.** προ-εῖνται Lys. 21, 12; Dem. 51, 5, παρ- 15, 15, but καθ-υφ-είμεθα 3, 8, we think **2 aor.**; προ-ειμένος Dem. 19, 161, καθ-υφ- Plut. Cic. 8: **plp.** καθ-υφ-εῖντο if not **2 aor.** Polyb. 3, 60; and προειμένος ἦν Dem. 36, 6. See ἀφίημι. **Vb.** ἑτός, ἑτέος, ἀν- Hyperid. Fr. 76; Pl. Conv. 217.—ἵειν 1 sing. **imp.**=ἵην, προ-ίειν Od. 9, 88. 10, 100. 12, 9 (-ίην Bekk.), ἠφ-ίειν Pl. Euth. 293 (-ίην Bekk.), ἵεν 3 pl. Epic for ἵεσαν, Il. 12, 33; Pind. I. 1, 25. ἕω, ἕῃς, ἕῃ, ἀφ-έῃ Il. 16, 590, and εἵω, ἐφείω Il. 1, 567, μεθ- 3, 414, subj. **2 aor.** Epic for ὧ, ᾗς &c., and 3 sing. ᾗῃ, ἀν-ήῃ for ἀνῇ 2, 34; inf. Epic ἱέμεναι, μεθ- Il. 13, 114, ἱέμεν Hes. Op. 596, μεθ- Il. 4, 351. ἕωνται Dor. 3 pl. **p. p.** for εἶνται, ἀν-έωνται Her. 2, 165 (Ms. F. Bekk. Dind. Stein), ἀφ- N. T. Luc. 5, 23; ἀνεῶσθαι Tab. Heracl. 2, 105. ἵοιμι opt. **pres. act.** ἀφ-ίοιτε Pl. Apol. 29, ἀφ-ίοιεν Xen. Hell. 6, 4, 3: and **2 aor. m.** οἵμην, προ-οῖντο Thuc. 1, 120; Xen. An. 1, 9, 10. Some refer **fut.** ἕσω, ἀν-έσω, **aor.** ἄν-εσαν, opt. ἀν-έσαιμι to ἕω, ἕζω, ἀν-έζω. 1 pers. ἵημι in *simple* we have not seen, but ἀφ-ίημι Pl. Euth. 9, παρ- Thuc. 6, 23; Pl. Conv. 214, μεθ- Soph. Ph. 818, Ion. μετ- Her. 1, 40 &c. ἵῃς rarely Soph. El. 566, ἵησι is frequent.

According to rule, ῐ in Epic, ῑ in Attic. It is often long, however, in Hom. by *ictus*, as ἵει Il. 3, 221, ἱεῖσαι Od. 12, 192, ἱέμεν Hes. Op. 596, ἱέμεναι Il. 22, 206, μεθ-ιέμεν 4, 351, ἐν-ίετε 12, 441, μεθ-ίετε 13, 116, ἱέμενος Od. 10, 529 &c. and short in Attic ἵησι Aesch. Sept. 310 (chor.), ἱεῖσα Eur. Hel. 188 (chor.), ἱέντα Aesch. Sept. 493, ἱείς Eur. I. T. 298, ἱεῖσα Hec. 338. I. A. 1101, the four last in trimeters, ἱεῖσαν Eur. Supp. 281 (dactyl). See also Com. Fr. (Anon.) 4, 652, ξυν-ίημι, Soph. El. 131 (dactyl); Ar. Av. 946; Com. Fr. (Strat.) 4, 545; but not "Ar. Plut. 75."

Ἰθύνω (ῡ) *To guide straight,* Poet. Il. 23, 317; Eur. Phoen. 179 (chor.); late prose Himer. Or. 17, 3, but κατ- Her. 2, 96;

Epic subj. -ομεν for -ωμ- Il. 8, 110. 11, 528, -ετε for -ητε, Od. 12, 82; ἰθύνοι Il. 24, 178; Aesch. Fr. 205 (D.); Eur. Hipp. 1227 (trimet.); imper. ἴθῦνε Hes. Op. 9; ἰθύνων Eur. Or. 1016 (chor.); late prose Ael. H. A. 13, 14; Plut. Mor. 984, ἰθύνουσαν *going straight*, Anth. 6, 328; -ύνειν Ap. Rh. 2, 897: imp. ἴθῦνον Od. 9, 78, iter. ἰθύνεσκε Q. Sm. 11, 101, -εσκον 2, 463: fut. ἰθυνοῦμεν (Hesych.): aor. ἴθῦνα Od. 23, 197; Himer. 31, 4, ἐξ- Hippocr. 4, 182; ἰθύνῃς Theocr. 5, 71 (Vulg. Mein.); -νειας Opp. Hal. 1, 77; inf. ἰθῦναι, κατ- Hippocr. 4, 292 (Lit.): p. p. ἰθυμμένος Dion. Per. 341, ἀπ-ίθυνται Hippocr. 3, 438, ἐξ- 426 (Lit.): aor. ἰθύνθην Il. 16, 475, ἐξ- Hippocr. 4, 182. 184 (Mss. Lit.) **Mid.** ἰθύνομαι as **act.** -όμενος Il. 6, 3: **imp.** ἰθύνετο Od. 5, 270. 22, 8; Hes. Sc. 324, -ύνοντο Ap. Rh. 2, 168: **aor.** late ἰθύνασθαι Q. Sm. 14, 500. (ῑ, ῐ once Anth. Plan. 4, 74.) Never in Comedy, nor *classic* Attic prose, occasionally in late Attic, once or twice in Her. in **pass.** ἰθύνεται 1, 194, -εσθαι 2, 177. Dind. in his last edition of Aeschylus, writes, with Ms. M., ηὔθυνεν Pers. 411. 773 for ἴθυνεν (Herm. Blomf.) In Eur. also, Theocr. &c. editors divide on ἰθυν- εὐθ-.

Ἰθύω (ῠ) *To rush straight*, Epic and Ion. Il. 11, 552; Pind. Fr. 219 (B.); -ύων Her. 7, 8: **aor.** ἴθῦσα Il. 15, 693; Her. 4, 122; subj. ἰθύσῃ Il. 12, 48; opt. ἰθύσειε Od. 11, 591; Her. 3, 39; inf. ἰθῦσαι Ap. Rh. 3, 1060; Her. 4, 134. υ of the **pres.** is always short, therefore ἐπῑθύουσι Il. 18, 175, ἐπῑθύει H. Merc. 475, must, some suppose, either be written ἐπιθύνουσι, ἐπιθύνει, or derived from ἐπι-θύω *rush*, and ῑ by arsis. ἰθύουσι still Opp. Hal. 2, 131. Cyn. 4, 68, ἰθύει 3, 500. 512 (Schneider, ἰθυν- Mss.).

Ἱκάνω (ᾰ) *To come*, Epic and Trag. Il. 18, 385. Od. 22, 231; Solon 13, 21; Aesch. Ag. 1337; Soph. Ant. 224. El. 1102; ἱκάνοις Theocr. 22, 60, -άνοι Il. 18, 465. Od. 19, 49; inf. ἱκάνειν Orph. Hym. 85, Epic ἱκανέμεν Od. 4, 139, -έμεναι Opp. C. 4, 387; ἱκάνων Pind. Ol. 3, 43: **imp.** ἵκᾱνον Il. 4, 210. Od. 19, 432; Hes. Th. 697; Theocr. 25, 211; Bion 4, 8. **Mid.** as **act.** ἱκάνομαι Epic Il. 10, 118. Od. 23, 108; Ap. Rh. 4, 85: **imp.** late ἱκάνοντο Anth. 15, 40, 38, the only instance we have seen —and seemingly with ᾰ. ῐ Epic and Trag., in **imp.** ῐ, ῑ by augm. Il. 6, 370; Od. 23, 93; Hes. Th. 681 &c. Never in Comedy or prose, and only **pres.** in Trag.

Ἱκετεύω *To come to as a* ἱκέτης, *supplicate*, in poetry and prose, Pind. Fr. 84, 7; Soph. O. R. 41; Eur. Or. 255; Ar. Thesm. 1002; Her. 6, 68; Andoc. 1, 149; Isae. 6, 57; Isocr. 14, 56; Pl. Phaed. 114; Dem. 57, 1: **imp.** ἱκέτευον Od. 11, 530; Hipponax 37; Com. Fr. (Strat.) 4, 546 (Pors.); Her. 1, 11; Thuc. 6, 19; Andoc. 1, 20; Xen. Cyr. 7, 4, 7; Lys. 1, 25. 29; Isocr.

14, 54: **fut.** rare -εύσω Eur. I. A. 462; Isocr. 7, 69. 14, 1; Lycurg. 143: **aor.** ἱκέτευσα Il. 16, 574. Od. 17, 573; Hes. Sc. 13; Eur. Med. 338. Heracl. 844; Thuc. 2, 47; Xen. Cyr. 4, 6, 9; Pl. Apol. 34; subj. -εύσω Eur. Or. 797, for -εύσῃς, Scyth. ἰκετεῦσι Ar. Thesm. 1002; -εύσας Pl. Leg. 730; -εῦσαι Eur. I. A. 462 (Mss.) now **fut.** -εύσειν: (p ?): **pass.** late, **aor.** ἱκετευθείς Joseph. Ant. 6, 2 (Bekk.) **Mid.** ἱκετεύομαι rare, Ar. Eccl. 915 chor. (Vulg. Bekk. Dind. -ομεν Herm. Mein.) **Vb.** ἱκετευτέος Luc. Merc. Cond. 38. (ῐ, but ῑ by augm. though never in Hom.) This verb is noticed for no irregularity, but because the **mid.** is missed by *some*, the **pass.** by *all* the lexicons. Besides, it has been treated too much as Poet. or Poet. and Ion. Hom. has only **imp.** and **aor.** indic.

Ἱκνέομαι *To come, come as a suppliant, implore*, Solon 4, 24; Simon. C. 38; Aesch. Ch. 376; Soph. Aj. 588; Ar. Eccl. 958. 966 (chor.); Her. 2, 36. 6, 57; Pittac. Diog. Laert. 1, 4, 10; rare in Attic prose Thuc. 1, 99; Aristot. Polit. 7, 14, 5 (Bekk.); ἱκνεύμεναι Od. 9, 128: **imp.** rare ἱκνεῖτο Soph. O. C. 970; late prose Dio Cass. Fr. 25, 5 (Bekk.), but ἀφ- Thuc. 3, 33; Lycurg. 21, Ion. ἱκνεύμεσθα Od. 24, 339: **fut.** ἵξομαι Poet. and Ion. Il. 6, 367. Od. 19, 20; Simon. Am. 1, 10; Aesch. Supp. 159; Soph. Aj. 1365; Eur. Ion 1037, ἵξεαι Hes. Op. 477; rare in prose, if correct, Her. 2, 29 (Ms. R. V. b. d. Ald. Schweigh. Bekk. Krüg. ἥξεις Mss. M. K. S. a. c. Gaisf. Dind. Stein &c.), ἀπ-ίξεαι 2, 29 (Gaisf. Bekk. Dind. Stein), ἀφ-ίξεται Pl. Leg. 744; ἐφ-ίξεσθαι Isocr. Epist. 4, 11; ἀφ-ιξόμενος Pl. Prot. 311, καθ- Plut. Caes. 39, Dor. ἰξοῦμαι Anth. (Glauc.) 9, 341: **p.** ἶγμαι Soph. Tr. 229, ἀφ- Thuc. 4, 85, ἐφ- Dem. 25, 101; ἰγμένος Soph. Ph. 494: **plp.** ἶκτο Hes. Th. 481; Anth. (Simonid. ?) 6, 217; Orph. 1187, or **2 aor.** syncop. ?: **2 aor.** ἱκόμην Il. 14, 260; Emped. 171; Aesch. Sept. 980; Soph. O. R. 318; Eur. Med. 484, Dor. -όμαν Pind. P. 4, 105; Aesch. Sept. 241 (chor.), ἵκεο Il. 9, 56, ἵκευ Od. 13, 4; Simon. C. 119; subj. ἵκωμαι Il. 5, 360; Pind. Ol. 6, 24, ἵκῃ Soph. Aj. 556, Epic ἵκηαι Il. 6, 143; Hes. Op. 468, -ηται Il. 6, 69; Soph. O. R. 76; Eur. Elec. 956; Pl. Phaedr. 276, dual ἵκησθον Hom. H. 2, 323, pl. -ώμεθα Od. 6, 296, -ησθε Il. 20, 24, -ωνται Il. 18, 213; ἱκοίμην Il. 9, 363; Soph. El. 315; Eur. Ion 1411, Dor. -οίμαν Eur. Bac. 403 (chor.); Theocr. 3, 13, -οιο Od. 19, 367; Theogn. 927, -οιτο Il. 13, 711; Soph. O. C. 308, -οίμεθα Il. 9, 141; Eur. Supp. 619, -οισθε Od. 11, 111; Ar. Lys. 1037; Theocr. 24, 9 (Mein.), -οιντο Ap. Rh. 2, 1174 (Well.), Ion. -οίατο Il. 18, 544; imper. ἵκεο Pind. N. 3, 3, ἵκου or -οῦ Anacr. 1, 4 (Bergk, ἥ κου 3 ed.); Soph. O. C. 741, ἱκέσθω Od. 15, 447, ἵκεσθε Il. 22, 417; ἱκέσθαι Il. 9, 22; Aesch. Sept. 286;

Soph. Ant. 165; Ar. Eccl. 959. 968 (chor.); ἱκόμενος Pind. Ol. 1, 10; Eur. Elec. 1157. Supp. 370, not in Hom., unless ἵκμενος Il. 1, 479 &c. be for ἱκόμενος; rare in prose ἵκετο Her. 1, 216, -οντο Thuc. 5, 40 (most Mss. Bekk. Popp.), but ἀφ- 2, 48. 4, 45; Pl. Prot. 318; ἵκηται Hippocr. 6, 348; Pl. Phaedr. 276; Luc. D. Syr. 29; Procop. Pers. p. 21, 247 &c.; ἱκοίμην Luc. Salt. 5, -οιτο D. Deor. 6, 4; ἱκόμενος Pittac. Diog. Laert. 1, 4, 10.—(ῐ naturally, sometimes ῑ in *aor.* by augm. ἱκέσθην Il. 14, 283, but ἱκ- 1, 328. 9, 185, ἵκετο Il. 11, 88; Hes. Th. 554, ἵκ- Il. 13, 837; Hes. Th. 685.) The sense *entreat*, which it seems to bear in pres. and fut. only, is confined almost to the Tragedians, ἱκνοῦμαι Aesch. Pers. 216; Soph. O. C. 275; Eur. Supp. 130; but Ar. Eccl. 958 (chor.): **fut.** ἵξομαι rare, Aesch. Supp. 159: **aor.** ἱκόμην *went to as a suppliant*, Il. 14, 260. 22, 122. Od. 9, 267 &c. The usual prose form is ἀφ-ικνέομαι, ἀφ-ίξομαι, ἀφ-ῖγμαι, ἀφ-ικόμην, except in the sense *to be suitable, fitting* &c. ἱκνέεται Her. 2, 36; ἱκνεύμενος 6, 84, -ούμενος Thuc. 1, 99; Plut. Mor. 6; in the sense *come*, see passages quoted under **2 aor.**, from which it would appear that Buttmann is rather strong in limiting the **2 aor.** to poetry. ἐφ-ικνέομαι less freq. Isocr. 4, 187; Pl. Phil. 46. Tim. 51: **fut.** -ίξεσθαι Isocr. Epist. 4, 11: ἐφ-ικόμην Isocr. 4, 113, Ion. ἐπ- Her. 7, 9; ἐφ-ίκοιτο Isocr. 9, 49; -ικέσθαι Xen. Cyr. 1, 1, 5; Isocr. 10, 13. 12, 227; Pl. Rep. 506. Hipp. M. 292, Ion. ἐπ-ικ- Her. 7, 35: ἐφ-ῖκται Dem. 25, 101; and καθ-ικνοῦμαι scarcely at all in early prose, Luc. D. Mar. 14, 3. D. Deor. 8, 1: καθ-ίξεται Plut. Caes. 39: καθ-ικόμην (Pl.) Ax. 369; Luc. Salt. 64. Bis Acc. 21 &c.

Ἵκω (ῑ) *To come*, mostly Epic, ἵκω Od. 17, 444, ἵκει Il. 18, 292. Od. 13, 248; Pind. Ol. 4, 11; Ar. Lys. 87; Epic subj. ἵκωμι Il. 9, 414, -κῃ 8, 509; ἷκαι 17, 399; ἵκειν Od. 13, 325; ἵκων Pind. P. 2, 36; Aesch. Fr. 5 (D.), Dor. εἵκω Epicharm. 19 (Ahrens): **imp.** ἷκον Il. 1, 317; Pind. P. 4, 126: **fut.** ἱξῶ in the Megar. Dial. Ar. Ach. 742: **mid.** ἵξομαι, see ἱκνέομαι: **1 aor.** ἷξα, ἵξατε Anth. 8, 170; Q. Sm. 12, 461 (Vulg. but ἷξον Spitzn. Lehrs, Koechl.): **2 aor.** ἷξον Il. 5, 773, ἷξες Hom. H. 2, 45 (Mss. Franke, Baum. ἷξας Vulg.), ἷξεν Il. 2, 667; Hes. Sc. 32. Fr. 82; Opp. Hal. 3, 392: **2 aor. m.** ἱκόμην, see ἱκνέομαι. **Pres. mid.** late ἵκεται (ῑ) Or. Sib. 9, 179, but ἵκονται (ῐ) 3, 802. ἵκοντα with ῐ Pind. P. 2, 36, has been altered in various ways by Boeckh, Bothe, Schneid. &c.; Momms. retains it, so Bergk with some doubt. ἵκω is not a prose form. ἀφίκει Hippocr. 1, 348 (Vulg. Kühn) is, we suspect, a false reading for ἀφήκει or ἀνήκ- (1 edit.) This has been *partially* confirmed by Littré, vol. 6, 32 (1849.) He reads ἐφήκει, and gives the variants so, ἀφήκει (A, Gal.) ἐφήκοι (H γ.) ἐφίκει (Zwing. in marg., Mack.), Ermerins adopts ἀφήκει 2, p. 79. At 3, 238, Littré retains ἀφίκειν (-ήκειν Mss. M. N.). 3, 242. 5, 224 (no v. r.) ἵκει Aristid. 49, 375, is a quotation from Il. 8, 192.

Ἱλάσκομαι *To propitiate*, Il. 6, 380; Pind. Ol. 7, 9; Ap. Rh. 1, 1139; Her. 5, 47; Luc. Gall. 22; -σκόμενος Her. 4, 7; -σκεσθαι Isocr. 10, 66; Xen. Oec. 5, 20 (Epic ἱλάομαι Il. 2, 550; -άεσθαι Ap. Rh. 4, 479, ἵλαμαι Hom. H. 21, 5; -ασο Plut. Sol. (Orac.) 9, and Attic ἱλέομαι Aesch. Supp. 118. 128 (chor.), ἱλεόομαι in prose Pl. Leg. 804; Luc. Salt. 17): imp. ἱλασκόμην Il. 1, 472; Her. 1, 50; Xen. Cyr. 3, 3, 22: fut. ἱλᾰ́σομαι Pl. Phaed. 95; Anth. App. Epigr. 47; late pass. V. T. 4 Reg. 5, 18, Epic -άσσομαι Od. 3, 419; Orac. Paus. 8, 42, 4, later -άξομαι Ap. Rh. 2, 808: aor. ἱλασᾰ́μην Luc. de Sacr. 12; Paus. 2, 7, 7, ἐξ-ιλασά- Com. Fr. (Men.) 4, 102; Xen. Cyr. 7, 2, 19, Epic -ασσ-; subj. ἱλάσσηαι Ap. Rh. 3, 1037, shortened -εαι Il. 1, 147, -άξησθε Or. Sib. 1, 167; ἱλασάμενος Her. 1, 67. 8, 112, ἀφ- Pl. Leg. 873, Epic ἱλασσ- Il. 1, 100; ἱλάξασθαι Ap. Rh. 1, 1093, and (ἱλεόομαι) ἱλεώσατο late, Dio Cass. 59, 27; -ώσωμαι Pseudo-Callisth. 1, 6; -ώσασθαι Dio Cass. 78, 34 (Bekk. -ώσεσθαι Dind.); ἐξ- Pseudo-Callisth. 1, 46; -σάμενος, 2, 40: aor. p. ἱλάσθην late in *simple*, N. T. Luc. 18, 13; but ἐξ-ιλασθέν Pl. Leg. 862: fut. late ἱλασθήσεται V. T. 4 Reg. 5, 18 (Alex.) ῑ, sometimes ῐ Il. 1, 100. 147; Theocr. Epigr. 13 &c. ῐ in ἱλάομαι and ἵλαμαι, but ῑ̔λασο by *ictus* Plut. Sol. (Orac.) 9, ῑ̔λασθαι Orph. Arg. 947 (Vulg.), ῑ perhaps in ἱλέομαι Aesch. Supp. quoted, and ἱλεῖσθαι Orph. Arg. quoted (Herm.) An act. fut. form ἐξ-ῑλᾰ́σουσι occurs late Or. Sib. 7, 30, and a pres. ἱλεοῦν Theod. Prodr. Catomyom. 203 (Hercher), aor. ἱλεώσητε Ael. Fr. 47, 16 (Hercher), missed by our Lexicogr. Vb. ἱλαστός, ἀν- Plut. Mor. 170, ἱλαστέον, ἐξ- Synes. Epist. 44 (Hercher) missed by Lexicogr.

Ἵλημι *To be propitious*, Epic, of pres. only imper. ἵληθι Od. 3, 380; Hom. H. 20, 8; Ap. Rh. 2, 693, and ἵλᾰθι Simon. C. 49; Callim. Dem. 139; Theocr. 15, 143; Ap. Rh. 4, 1014; Luc. Epigr. 22, ἵλᾰτε Ap. Rh. 4, 984; Maneth. 6, 754: perf. subj. ἱλήκω Od. 21, 365; opt. ἱλήκοιμι Hom. H. 1, 165; Ap. Rh. 2, 708; Coluth. 2, 50; Anth. 5, 73; late prose Alciphr. 3, 68; Heliod. 9, 25. 10, 16. (ῑ.)

Ἴλλω, for εἴλω or εἵλλω *To roll, press*, ἶλλε Ar. Nub. 762 (Ms. M. Br. εἶλλε Dind.); ἴλλων Nic. Ther. 478, ἐξ- Xen. Ven. 6, 15, ἀπ-ίλλει Lys. 10, 17; subj. ἐξίλλω Dem. 37, 35 (Dind. -είλλω Bekk.): aor. ἶλα, ὑπ-ίλας Eur. Fr. 544 (D.): mid. ἰλάμενος, περι- Ar. Ran. 1066 (Cob. Dind. περι-ειλ- Phot.) Pass. ἰλλόμενος Soph. Ant. 340 (chor.)—ἐπ-ιλλίζω Od. 18, 11.

Ἱμάσσω *To lash, strike* (ἱμάς): **fut.** -ᾰ́σω: **aor.** ἵμᾰσα Il. 11, 280. Od. 6, 316; Epic subj. -σσω Il. 15, 17, -άσσῃ Il. 2, 782; -άσσας Hes. Th. 857. **Pass.** ἱμασσόμενος Anth. 7, 696: **imp.** ἱμάσσετο Nonn. 42, 491. (ῐ.)

Ἱμείρω (Aeol. ἰμέρρω Sapph. 1, 27) *To desire*, (ῑ) Od. 10, 431; Solon 13, 7; Soph. Fr. 689 (D.); Eur. Fr. 660 (Dind.); Ar. Nub. 435; Theocr. 22, 145; -ρωσι Opp. Hal. 3, 647, -ροι 3, 48; -ρων Od. 10, 555; Hes. Th. 177; Soph. O. R. 59; rare in prose Pl. Crat. 418; (Hippocr.) Epist. 9, 428; Alciphr. 1, 22; -ρειν Aesch. Ag. 940: **imp.** ἵμειρον Aesch. Pers. 233. **Mid.** ἱμείρομαι as act. Od. 1, 59; Soph. O. R. 386; Eur. I. A. 486; Hippocr. 7, 558 (Lit.); Epic subj. -είρεται Od. 1, 41; -όμενος 5, 209: **imp.** ἱμείρετο Her. 3, 123, -οντο 6, 120: with **aor. mid.** ἱμειράμην, opt. -αιτο Il. 14, 163: and **aor. pass.** ἱμέρθην as mid. Her. 7, 44; -ερθείς Ap. Rh. 3, 117. **Vb.** ἱμερτός Il. 2, 751; Pind. P. 9, 75. **Act.** almost always poetic, **mid.** and **pass.** form in poetry and Ionic prose.

Ἰνδάλλομαι *To appear* (εἶδος, εἰδάλιμος), H. Ven. 178, -εται Il. 23, 460; Ar. Vesp. 188; Pl. Theaet. 189; Aristot. Mund. 6, 3: **imp.** ἰνδάλλετο Il. 17, 213: **aor. pass.** late, ἰνδαλθῇ Maxim. Καταρχ. 163; ἰνδαλθείς Lycophr. 961.

Ἰνέω or -άω *To void, purge*, (Hesych. Phot.): **fut. m.** ἰνήσεται Hippocr. 8, 112. 258 (Lit.): but **pass.**? 6, 318 (wrongly ἠνήσ- εἰνήσ- 2, 676. 132 Kühn): **aor.** ἰνάσατο Hesych., Ion. ἰνησ- ἀπεξ- Hesych. **Pass.** ἰνῶνται Hippocr. 6, 318 (Lit.); -ώμενος 6, 326: **fut. m.** as pass. see above: **aor.** ἰνηθείς Hesych.

Ἰπόω *To press, crush*, only **pres. act.** ἰποῦμεν C. Fr. (Cratin.) 2, 71; Hesych.: and **part. pass.** ἰπούμενος Aesch. Pr. 365; Ar. Eq. 924. Poetic, for at Dem. 1441, now stands ἠγμένος (Bekk. B. Saupp. Dind.) (ῑ.)

Ἱπποτροφέω *To maintain horses*, Dioscor. 4, 15; -οφῶν Hyperid. 3, 29, 6; Plut. Mor. 52; -οφεῖν Xen. Ages. 1, 23. M. Eq. 1, 11; Isocr. 16, 33: **fut.** -ήσω: **aor.** ἱπποτρόφησα Paus. 3, 8, 1: **p.** ἱπποτετρόφηκα Lycurg. 139, but ἱπποτρόφηκα Diog. Laert. 8, 51, καθ-ιπποτρόφηκα Isae. 5, 43. **Pres.** and **perf.** alone classic.

Ἵπτημι *To fly*, **pres.** in comp. late, if correct, διϊπτάντος Apocr. Sap. 5, 11, v. r. διαπτ-: **2 aor.** ἔπτην Batr. 210 (Franke), ἐξ- Hes. Op. 98, δι- Emped. 65 (Stein), ἐπ- Luc. V. H. 1, 28, Dor. ἔπτᾱν, προσ- Aesch. Pr. 555 (chor.), ἀν- Soph. Ant. 1307 (chor.); Eur. Med. 439 (chor.); subj. πτῇ, κατα- Luc. Prom. 4; πταίην Anth. 5, 152, ἀμ- Eur. Ion 796 (chor.), δια- Luc. Luct. 3; πτῆθι, ἀπο- Philostr. Epist. 11 (48 Boiss.); πτῆναι Anth. Plan. 108, ἀπο- Anth. 5, 212, ἐπι- Arr. An. 2, 3, 3, ἀνα- Alciphr. 2, 1, 5 (Mein.), πτάς, ἀνα- Aesch. Supp. 782? ἐπι- Anth. 11, 407, ἀπο- 12, 105, κατα- Ael. H. A. 17, 37, as ἔστην: 1 aor. in comp. and late περι-πτήσασα Or. Sib. 1, 245. Mid. ἵπτᾰμαι (as ἵσταμαι) Opp. Hal. 2, 536; Babr. 65, 4; Luc. Soloec. 7; Pseud.-Callisth. 1, 10, ἐφ- Mosch. 1, 16, περι- Aristot. H. A. 5, 9, 2: imp. ἱπτάμην Plut. Timol. 26; Or. Sib. 3, 163. 7, 70, ἀφ- Eur. I. A. 1608 if genuine, συμ-παρ- Luc. D. Deor. 20, 6; ἱπτάμενος (Mosch.) 3, 43, καθ- Luc. D. Deor. 20, 5: fut. πτήσομαι Anth. 5, 9. 12, 18; Or. Sib. 8, 342, ἐκ- Ar. Vesp. 208, ἐπι- Her. 7, 15, ἀνα- Aeschin. 3, 209; Pl. Leg. 905; Luc. Tim. 40: 1 aor. late, ἀπο-πτήσωνται Aristaen. 1, 3, for which we would suggest fut. -σονται; Hercher has -πτῶνται: 2 aor. ἐπτάμην Il. 13, 592; Eur. Hel. 18, παρ- Simon. Am. 13, 1, ἐσ- Her. 9, 100. 101, δι- Ar. Vesp. 1086 (R. V. Vulg. Bekk. Richter), Dor. ἐπτάμαν, ἀν- Soph. Aj. 693 (chor. Dind. Nauck), ἔπτατο Il. 13, 592, πτάτο 23, 880, ὑπέρ- 22, 275; (πτῶμαι), πτῆται Il. 15, 170, προσ- Xen. Mem. 3, 11, 5, πτῆσθε, ἀνα- Her. 4, 132, πτῶνται, ἀνα- Ar. Lys. 774 (hexam.); πτάσθαι, δια- Eur. Med. 1, ἀπο- Her. 7, 13; πτάμενος Il. 22, 362; Pind. Fr. 99, 4; Eur. Bac. 90. Ion 460 (chor.), ὑπερ- Alcm. 28, ἐπι- Alcae. 39; Xen. Cyr. 2, 4, 19 (Popp. Hertlein 2 ed. πτόμ- 3 ed.), ἀνα- Her. 2, 55, ἀμπτάμ- Eur. Andr. 1219 (chor.), ἀπο- Hes. Th. 284; Pl. Conv. 183. Rep. 469. ἔπτην and pres. ἵπταμαι in *simple* are late and rare, unless ἔπτη be genuine, Batr. 210, ἐξέπτη (Baum.) In *comp.* the former is poetic and late prose, the latter scarcely Attic, Eur. I. A. 1608, being held supposititious. Hirschig, Meineke, W. Dind. 5 ed. read with Brunck διέπτετο Ar. Vesp. 1086; L. Dind. Hertl. 3 ed. Sauppe ἐπιπτόμενος Xen. Cyr. 2, 4, 19, quoted.

Ἰσάζω, see (εἰδέω.)

Ἴσᾱμι (later form ἴσημι) *To know*, Dor. Epicharm. 98, 1 (Ahr.); Pind. P. 4, 248; Theocr. 5, 119, ἴσᾳς 14, 34, ἴσης (Vulg.), ἴσᾱτι Inscr. Brutt. 5773; Theocr. 15, 146, ἴσᾰμεν Pind. N. 7, 14, ἴσᾰτε Diog. Laert. (Periand.) 1, 99, ἴσαντι Epich. 26; Theocr. 15, 64; subj. ἰσᾶντι Inscr. Cret. 3053; (inf. ἰσάμεν); part. ἴσας, and Lesb. ἴσαις, if sound, Anth. (Nossis) 7, 718, dat. ἴσαντι Pind. P. 3, 29: imp. 3 pl. ἴσᾰν Il. 18, 405. Od. 4, 772, seems not Dor. but Epic=ᾔδεσαν. The form ἴσης &c. Theocr. 14, 34, has yielded to ἴσαις or ἴσᾳς from Mss. ῐ, but ῑ Theocr. 25, 27.

Ἴσημι, see εἰδέω and ἴσᾱμι.

Ἴσκω *To make like, take for*, Poet.=ἐΐσκω, only pres. ἴσκω Simon. C. 130 (Bergk); ἴσκοντες Il. 16, 41, ἴσκουσα Od. 4, 279: and imp. ἴσκε Od. 22, 31 &c. See ἐΐσκω. Later in the sense *speak, say*, ἴσκων Lycophr. 574: imp. ἴσκεν Ap. Rh. 2, 240. 4, 92, -κον 4, 1718; Theocr. 22, 167; to which some refer Od. 19, 203. 22, 31.

Ἱστάνω *To place, simple* late Orph. Arg. 904; Athen. 3, 83;

N. T. Rom. 3, 31, ἐφ- Polyb. 5, 35. 11, 2 (Bekk.); but *classic* in comp. if καθ-ιστᾰ́νειν be correct Isae. 2, 29 (Vulg. Bekk.); Lys. 25, 3. 26, 15. 28, 7 (Vulg. Bekk.), where however Bait. Saupp. and Scheibe have substituted καθιστάναι: **imp.** ἵστᾰνον, ἐφ- Plut. Mor. 233, συν- Polyb. 4, 82, δι- App. Hisp. 36, καθ- Diod. Sic. 15, 33. ἐφιστάνειν (Dem.) 26, 22 (Vulg.) is now ἐπιπέμπειν (Bekk. Dind. Bait. Saupp.)

Ἱστάω *To place*, rare, ἱστᾷ Her. 4, 103; Themist. 23, 292, ἱστῶσι Ctes. Frag. Pers. 6; Apocr. 1 Macc. 8, 1; subj. ἱστᾷς Ar. Fr. 445 (D.); imper. ἵστα, καθ- Il. 9, 202, and ἵστη 21, 313; ἱστᾶν Pl. Crat. 437; Themist. 20, 234; *to stop, staunch*, Dioscor. 4, 43: **imp.** ἵστα Her. 2, 106; Aesop 340 (Halm), κατ- Her. 6, 43, ἀν- Luc. Musc. enc. 7, συν- Polyb. 3, 43, καθ- Polyaen. 5, 33, 4 (Murs. καθῆκεν Woelff.) The Mss. and editors of Her. present both forms, ἱστᾷ 4, 103, and ἵστησι 2, 95, ὑπ- 5, 16, ἱστᾶσι 3, 24 (-ῶσι c. Ald.), imp. ἵστα 2, 106, κατ- 6, 43, and ἵστη 6, 61 (Bekk. Krüg.), ἀν- 1, 196, ἐν- 2, 102 (Gaisf. Bekk.). Bredow thinks ἵστησι, ἵστη the genuine Herodotean form, Dind. ἱστᾷ, ἵστα, and compds.

Ἵστημι *To make stand, place, raise*, Aesch. Ch. 885; Soph. El. 27; Ar. Av. 527; Pl. Crat. 437, καθ- Thuc. 1, 68, 3 pl. ἱστᾶσι Il. 13, 336; Her. 2, 65, καθ- Thuc. 8, 28; Xen. Cyr. 4, 5, 28; Pl. Rep. 410, Dor. -τᾶντι, ἐξ- (Pl.) Tim. Locr. 100, see below; ἱστῶ Pl. Rep. 361. Theaet. 157; (ἱσταίην), καθ-ισταῖμεν Xen. Vect. 2, 7; imper. ἵστατε Aeschin. 3, 156, see below; ἱστάναι Lys. 10, 18; Xen. Mem. 2, 9, 7, Dor. ἱστάμεν, παρακαθ- Stob. (Diotog.) 43, 95; ἱστας Xen. Cyr. 8, 2, 21: **imp.** ἵστην Ar. Vesp. 40; Her. 6, 61 (Bekk. Krüg. ἵστα Stein), ἀν- Il. 24, 515; Her. 1, 196, ἵστᾰσαν Il. 18, 346; Thuc. 5, 74. 6, 70, Epic iter. 3 sing. ἵστασκε Od. 19, 574: **fut.** στήσω Soph. O. C. 1342; Eur. Andr. 665; Xen. Cyr. 6, 3, 25; -ήσειν Od. 11, 314; Her. 4, 76, Dor. στᾱσῶ Theocr. 5, 54, ἀν- Soph. El. 138 chor. (and intrans. ἑστήξω *shall stand*, Hom. Epigr. 15, 14; Eur. I. A. 675 (Elms. Dind.); Ar. Lys. 634; Xen. Cyr. 6, 2, 17 (Dind. 4 ed. Saupp.); Pl. Conv. 220; Dem. 20, 37, καθ- Thuc. 3, 37. 102, ἀφ- Xen. An. 2, 4, 5; Pl. Rep. 587: and ἑστήξομαι Eur. I. A. 675 (Vulg. Kirchh. Nauck); Xen. Cyr. 6, 2, 17 (Popp. Hertl.). Ven. 10, 9; Com. Fr. (Hegesipp.) 4, 480 (from ἑστήκω or pf. ἕστηκα, see ἑστήκω): **aor.** ἔστησα Il. 1, 448; Soph. O. C. 1303; Her. 2, 121; Thuc. 2, 22; Lys. 2, 25; Pl. Phaed. 118, στῆσα Il. 4, 298. Od. 4, 582, Dor. ἔστᾱσα (Anacr. 104); Pind. P. 3, 53, ἀπ- Aesch. Ch. 416 (chor.), στᾶσα Pind. P. 9, 118, Epic 3 pl. ἔστᾰσαν for -ησαν, Il. 12, 56. Od. 3, 182 (late 2 sing. ἔστᾰσας Anth. 9, 714, ἔστᾰσε 708): **p.** ἕστηκα *I stand*, Il. 3, 231; Archil. 21; Aesch.

Ag. 1379; Soph. Aj. 815; Eur. Cycl. 681; Ar. Pax 1178; Her. 2, 26; Thuc. 5, 10; Isocr. 4, 180, Dor. -ᾱκα Aesch. Sept. 956 (chor.); Soph. Aj. 200 (chor.); Anth. (Anyte) 9, 314, παρ- Pind. P. 8, 71, 3 pl. ἑστάκαντι Theocr. 15, 82, late ἡστάκαμεν Apoll. Tyan. Epist. 62; ἑστήκῃ Od. 22, 469, ξυν- Pl. Tim. 78; -ήκοι, καθ- Leg. 759; ἑστηκὼς Pl. Meno 93, κατ- Her. 6, 140, συν- 8, 79, ἑστηκυῖα 2, 126; Pl. Leg. 802, -στηκός Pl. Soph. 249: **plp.** ἑστήκειν *stood*, -ήκη, ἀν- Pl. Prot. 335, 3 pers. -ήκει Il. 4, 329. 12, 446, and always; Com. Fr. (Men.) 4, 219; Hippocr. 1, 520 (Erm.), ἀν- Ar. Pl. 738, ξυν- Thuc. 1, 15. 4, 96, περι- 6, 61, προ- 8, 75 (Bekk. Popp. Krüg.), Ion. ἑστήκεε Her. 7, 152, κατ- 1, 81. 3, 90, συν- 4, 132, ἀπ- 5, 37 &c. and εἱστ- Hes. Sc. 269; Ap. Rh. 4, 1681; Asius 1, 4 (B.); especially Attic Eur. H. F. 925; Ar. Av. 513 (Bekk. Dind. Bergk); Thuc. 1, 89; Xen. Cyr. 8, 3, 9; Pl. Conv. 220; Dem. 19, 320. 37, 14, καθ- Antiph. 6, 13, περι- Thuc. 5, 73, ἀνθ- Dem. 9, 62, δι- 18, 18 &c. (syncopated forms of dual and pl. ἕστᾰτον, ἕστᾰμεν &c. see below), also ἕστᾰκα trans. Inscr. Ther. 2448, 1, 27, καθ- Hyperid. Eux. 38 (Linder, Bab.); Diod. Sic. Fr. Lib. 32, 11 (Dind. Bekk.), περι- (Pl.) Ax. 370, συν- Anth. 11, 139, μεθ- Longin. 16, 2, ἐφ- Polyb. 10, 21. 32, 9 (Bekk.): plp. ἑστᾰ́κει, ἐφ- Polyb. 10, 20 (Bekk.), καθ- Athen. 15, 697; Joseph. Vit. 17. (Dio. Hal. in Dem. 54, quotes p. καθέστᾰκεν from Dem. 9, 117, and Reiske has adopted it; the Mss., however, have **aor.** -ησεν which is taken by all other editors): **p. p.** rare, ἕστᾰμαι, δι-εσταμένος Pl. Tim. 81, καθ- Polyb. 10, 4; καθ-εστάσθαι 4, 84; 3 pl. Ion. κατεστέαται Her. 1, 196 (Schweigh. Gaisf.), but **p. act.** κατεστέᾱσι (Bekk. Bred. Dind. Krüg.) which occurs 1, 200. 2, 84. 4, 63 (Gaisf. Bekk. &c. -στᾶσι Stein): **aor.** ἐστᾰ́θην Od. 17, 463; Sapph. 53 (B.); Pind. P. 4, 84; Aesch. Pers. 206; Soph. O. R. 1463; Xen. Hell. 3, 1, 9. 5, 2, 43, κατ- Antiph. 6, 11; Lys. 13, 35, 3 pl. στάθεν for -θησαν Pind. N. 10, 66, ἐστάθ- Simon. C. 137; στᾰθῶ Aesch. Ch. 20; Isocr. 9, 74; στάθητι Pl. Phaedr. 236, -ητε Aesch. Sept. 33; στᾰθείς Pind. Ol. 9, 31; Soph. Aj. 1171; Eur. H. F. 529; Her. 3, 130; Thuc. 6, 55; Isocr. 5, 148, κατα- Archil. 66 (B. 3 ed.); Hippocr. 5, 308; Lys. 24, 9, συν- Pl. Leg. 685: **fut.** σταθήσομαι Andoc. 3, 34; Aeschin. 3, 103; Lycophr. 444: **2 aor.** ἔστην *I stood*, Il. 6, 43. Od. 10, 310; Solon 5; Aesch. Sept. 1016; Soph. Aj. 950; Com. Fr. (Pher.) 2, 298; Pl. Polit. 270, στῆν Il. 11, 744, dual στήτην 1, 332, ἀν- 305, δια- 6, Dor. ἔσταν Pind. N. 1, 19, μετ- Aesch. Supp. 538 (chor.), παρ- Eur. H. F. 439, 2 sing. ἔστας Anth. 7, 161, ἔστᾱ Pind. Ol. 9, 71. N. 1, 55, Epic 3 pl. ἔστᾰν Il. 1, 535; even in trimet. Eur. Phoen. 1246, ἀν- 824 (chor.) κατ- Pind. P. 4, 135, and στάν Il. 9, 193; Pind. I. 8, 58, iter. στάσκε

Il. 18, 160; στῶ Eur. Alc. 864; Ar. Ach. 176; Pl. Parm. 130, στῇ Pl. Apol. 28, ἀνα- Od. 18, 334, στῶμεν Thuc. 1, 33; σταίην Od. 1, 256; Soph. Tr. 656; Eur. Elec. 403; Pl. Leg. 895, 3 pl. σταῖεν, περι- Od. 20, 50, παρα- Od. 8, 218; Pl. Gorg. 452, very rare σταίησαν Il. 17, 733; στῆθι Il. 23, 97; Theogn. 1366; Soph. Tr. 1076; Ar. Vesp. 1150, Aeol. and Dor. στᾶθι Sapph. 29; Theocr. 23, 38, μετα- Soph. O. C. 163 (chor.), Poet. στᾶ, ἀπό-στα C. Fr. (Menand.) 4, 182; στῆναι Il. 21, 266; Soph. Ph. 277; Thuc. 5, 102, ἀν-στήμεναι Il. 10, 55; στάς Il. 16, 231; Eur. Elec. 840; Ar. Nub. 771; Pl. Phaedr. 247, see below. **Mid.** ἵστᾰμαι *to stand*, Il. 13, 271, ἵστασαι, παρ- 10, 279, ἵσταται Aesch. Sept. 564; Soph. Ph. 893; Ar. Eccl. 737; Her. 8, 68; Thuc. 1, 53; Pl. Ion 535, and trans. *set up for oneself*, Her. 7, 9; Xen. Hell. 2, 4, 14. Cyr. 8, 6, 18; imper. ἵστᾰσο intrans. Il. 17, 179; Hes. Sc. 449, ἀν- Eur. Hec. 499; Ar. Vesp. 998 &c.; Attic prose ἐξαν- Isocr. 1, 32, παρ- 1, 37, Poet. ἵσταο, παρ- Il. 10, 291 (Aristarch. Bekk. Faesi), ἵστω Soph. Ph. 893; Aj. 775; Ar. Eccl. 737, ἀν- Aesch. Eum. 133. 141: imp. ἵστατο *stood*, Il. 20, 68; Her. 1, 196, ἵσταντο *placed*, Xen. Hell. 7, 2, 15: fut. στήσομαι intrans. Il. 20, 90; Emped. 50; Eur. Hel. 1072; Ar. Lys. 232; (Dem.) 10, 10, Dor. στάσ- Pind. N. 5, 16; Theocr. 1, 112; Soph. Ph. 833 (chor.); Eur. I. A. 762 (chor.); στησόμενος Xen. Cyr. 1, 4, 23, ξυν- Pl. Tim. 54, κατα- pass.? Lys. 7, 41; Isocr. 7, 34; Dem. 1, 22; so Xen. An. 1, 3, 8, or reflex, *settle down, right themselves;* trans. Eur. Andr. 763; Ar. Thesm. 697; Her. 3, 84. 7, 236; Pl. Rep. 484, κατα- Thuc. 6, 83: aor. ἐστησάμην perhaps always trans. in classic auth. Her. 2, 35; Xen. Hell. 4, 2, 23; Pl. Rep. 554, στησ- Il. 1, 480. Od. 2, 431; Simon. C. 133 (Bergk), Aeol. and Dor. ἐστᾱσ- Alcae. 37; Theocr. 7, 150; στήσωμαι Hom. H. 1, 150; στησαίμην Ar. Pl. 453; -ήσασθαι Il. 6, 528; Xen. Ages. 11, 7; -άμενος Il. 18, 533. Od. 2, 94; Xen. Hell. 2, 4, 7; περι-στήσαντο *stood round*, Od. 12, 356. Il. 2, 410 (Vulg.) has been altered by Bekker to περίστησάν τε, which Dind. Ameis, La R. adopt, and ξυνιστησαμένῳ intrans. Luc. Philops. 18, has also been altered to fut. -ησομένῳ from Ms. A (Jacobitz, Bekk. Dind.); but στήσαντο intrans. Opp. C. 4, 128: **2 aor.** ἐστάμην we have never met, except perhaps ἔστατο, ἐκάθητο (Hesych.).

Epic inf. **pres.** ἱστάμεναι, παρ- Od. 7, 341, but ἀπιστάμεναι Her. 1, 76 (Mss. Wessl. Gaisf.) has been altered rightly, we think, to ἀπιστάναι by Bekk. Dind. Lhardy, with Ms. a. c. s., see ἀναπιμπλάναι 2, 129, without v. r. 3 pl. pres. in Her. is usu. ἱστᾶσι 2, 65. 5, 16 &c. but ἱστέασι, ἀν- 5, 71 (Gaisf. Bekk. Dind. -τᾶσι Bred. Dietsch, Abicht, Stein); ἔστᾰσαν 3 pl. 1 aor. for ἔστησαν, seems confined to Epic, Il. 12, 56. Od. 3, 182. It once stood in trimeter, Eur. Heracl. 937 (932), where now stands ἵστᾰσαν (Elms. Dind. Kirchh. Paley &c.) which has displaced ἕστᾰσαν at Il. 2, 525 also (Mss. Spitzn. Bekk. Dind.), and Od. 18, 307 &c. (Bekk. Dind.) This shortening seems to have some analogy to ἔπρεσε for -ησε (if correct) Hes. Th. 856, but it must be carefully distinguished from plp. ἕστᾰσαν, see Il. 2, 777. 12, 55. Od. 7, 89; Hes. Sc. 191.

The plp. occurs sometimes terminating in η, ἀν-εστήκη with v. r. -ήκειν Pl. Prot. 335. The augmented plp. εἱστ- is rejected in Hom. by Spitzn. Bekk. &c. with Aristarchus, and also in Her. It occurs, however, in Hes. and late Epic, Ap. Rh. Quint. Sm. and in Attic. ἵστη imper. pres. act. for ἵστᾰθι, Il. 21, 313; Archil. 43; Eur. Supp. 1230, καθ- Ar. Eccl. 743, and ἵστα, καθ- Il. 9, 202, προσ- Machon in Athen. 6, 243; ἵστω imper. mid. for ἵστᾰσο, Soph. Aj. 775. Ph. 893; Ar. Eccl. 737. Syncop. forms of p. and plp.: dual ἕστᾰτον Il. 23, 284, ἀφ- Pl. Parm. 161, pl. ἕστᾰμεν Od. 11, 466; Soph. O. C. 1017; Eur. Heracl. 145. I. A. 861; Pl. Gorg. 468, ἕστᾰτε Ar. Pax 383, προ- Her. 5, 49 (Bekk. -εστέατε Vulg.), ἀφ-έστατε Il. 4, 340; Dem. 8, 37, but ἕστητε Il. 4, 243. 246, unless wrongly accented for ἔστητε 2 aor. (La Roche, Düntzer), ἑστᾶσι Il. 12, 64; Hes. Th. 769; Mimnerm. 12, 10; Eur. Phoen. 1079; Pl. Rep. 436; Her. 1, 14. 51 &c. and ἑστέασι, κατ- 1, 200. 2, 84, ἀν- 3, 62, plp. dual ἑστάτην (Pl.) Epist. 7, 349, pl. ἕστᾰσαν Il. 12, 55; Soph. El. 723; Her. 4, 79; Thuc. 4, 56; Xen. Cyr. 8, 3, 10; Pl. Criti. 116; subj. only the forms in ω, ἑστῶ, ἑστῶμεν Pl. Gorg. 468, ἑστῶσι Dem. 20, 64, ἐφ- Eur. Bac. 319; opt. Poet. ἑσταίην, ἀφ- Od. 23, 101. 169; ἕστᾰθι 22, 489; Ar. Av. 206, ἑστάτω Tyrt. 11, 28; Soph. El. 50, ἕστατον Il. 23, 443, ἕστατε 20, 354; inf. ἑστᾰ́ναι Soph. Ant. 640; Antiph. 3, γ, 10. δ, 7; Pl. Parm. 132; Hippocr. 3, 324 (Lit.); Her. 1, 17 (Ms. m. Suid. Bekk. Dind. Bred.), so προ- 1, 69, συν- 1, 214, without v. r. but Gaisf. ἑστάμεναι 1, 17. 9, 27. 28 (Mss. S. B. V.) the Epic form Il. 10, 480. 13, 56, and ἑστάμεν 4, 342. Od. 21, 261, παρ- Hes. Th. 439, the full form ἑστηκέναι in *simple* seems late, Ael. V. H. 3, 18; Plotin. 24, 4 (Kirchh.), but ἀφ-εστηκέναι Aristot. Audib. 20; Dem. 19, 143. 51, 7; Paus. 1, 7, 2 &c., καθ- Hippocr. 8, 498, δι- D. Hal. C. Verb. 20; ἑστώς Aesch. Pers. 686; Soph. Aj. 87, -ῶσα Ar. Eccl. 64, -ός Pl. Soph. 249. Parm. 146. 156. Theaet. 183 (best Mss. Bekk. Bait. Or. W.), -ώς (Vulg. Stallb.), καθ- Thuc. 3, 9, περι- 4, 10 (v. r. -ώς), παρ- Ar. Eq. 564, gen. -ῶτος Soph. O. R. 565; Antiph. 3, γ, 10, Ion. ἑστεώς Her. 2, 38, -εῶσα 5, 92, -εός Hippocr. 4, 298 (Lit.), Epic ἑστηώς Hes. Th. 519,

-ῦῖα Ap. Rh. 4, 163, in Hom. and Pind. only ἑστᾰότος Il. 19, 79, -αότα 13, 261; Hes. Sc. 61; Pind. N. 5, 2, -αότε Il. 20, 245, -ᾰότες 13, 293, -αότων 18, 246, but Bekk. *now* ἑστεῶτα, -εῶτε Il. 13, 261. 20, 245 (2 ed.)—στέωμεν 1 pl. 2 aor. subj. Ion. for στῶμεν, Il. 11, 348, ἐξανα- Her. 4, 115, Epic στείομεν Il. 15, 297, περι-στείωσι Il. 17, 95, ἀπο-στέωσι Her. 3, 15, 2 sing. στήῃς Il. 17, 30, στήῃ 5, 598, ἀνα- Pind. P. 4, 155 (Herm. Boeckh), -αίῃ (Ahr. Bergk) for στῇς, στῇ; 3 dual παρ-στήετον Od. 18, 183; imper. στᾱ for στῆθι, Poet. and in comp. ἀνάστα late, N. T. Act. 12, 7. Ephes. 5, 14, ἄνστᾱ Theocr. 24, 36, παράστα Com. Fr. (Menand.) 4, 105, shortened ἄνᾰ Il. 6, 331. 9, 247. Od. 18, 13; Soph. Aj. 194 (chor.); Eur. Alc. 277. Tr. 98 (chor.) unless this be preposition so used. Epic inf. στήμεναι Il. 17, 167. Od. 5, 414, Dor. στᾶμεν Pind. P. 4, 2. ἱστέαται, ἀπ- Ion. 3 pl. pres. for -ανται Her. 2, 113: imp. ἱστέατο, ἐπαν- 4, 80, 3 pl. perf. ἑστέαται, κατ- for καθέστανται, Her. 1, 196 (Schweigh. Gaisf. but κατεστέασι perf. act. Bekk. Dind. with Ms. F.)—For ἐστᾰθην aor. pass. Callim. L. Pal. 83, Buttm. suggested ἑστᾰκῃ; Mein. edits ἕστᾱ θῆν; but Otto Schneider preserves the quantity by reading ἐστᾰ́θη. Vb. στατέον Pl. Rep. 503.

Ἱστιάω, see ἑστ-.

Ἱστορέω *To enquire*, Aesch. Eum. 455; Soph. Tr. 418; Aristot. Mirab. Ausc. 37; -έων Her. 1, 56. 2, 19: imp. ἱστόρεον 1, 122. 3, 77, is reg. but never in good Attic prose, freq. in Attic poetry, and in Ionic and *late* Attic prose, pass. rare -ούμενος Soph. Tr. 415; -έεσθαι Her. 1, 24, not mid. as some call it: perf. ἱστόρηται Aristot. Mund. 4, 25; -ημένα Her. 2, 44: aor. ἱστορηθείς Strab. 3, 2, 13, no mid.

Ἰσχᾰ́νω, -ανάω Epic *To check*, only pres. -άνει Il. 14, 387, -άᾳς Od. 15, 346, -ανᾰ́ᾳ Il. 17, 572, -όωσι 5, 89; ἴσχανε Od. 19, 42; -όων Il. 23, 300; Opp. Hal. 1, 287: and imp. ἴσχᾰνε Hym. H. 7, 13, ἰσχᾰνέτην Il. 17, 747, iter. ἰσχανάασκον Il. 15, 723: and mid. ἰσχανόωνται Od. 7, 161: ἰσχανόωντο Il. 12, 38; Ap. Rh. 2, 864. The pure form seems not to contract. ἰσχάνει Theophr. C. Pl. 4, 13, 6, seems a mistake for ἰσχναίνει.

Ἰσχναίνω *To make lean, dry*, Hippocr. 427, 14 (Foes); -αίνῃ Aesch. Pr. 380; -αίνειν Hippocr. 3, 468 (Lit.); Pl. Gorg. 521, Dor. 3 pl. ἰσχναίνοντι, κατ- Callim. Epigr. 48: fut. ἰσχνᾰνῶ, συν- Eur. I. A. 694: aor. ἴσχνᾱνα Aesch. Eum. 267; Ar. Ran. 941, προ- Aristot. Prob. 3, 23, Ion. ἴσχνηνα Her. 3, 24; Hippocr. 3, 316 (Lit.): p.p. ἰσχνημένον, κατ- Luc. Philopat. 20: aor. pass. ἰσχνάνθην Hippocr. 5, 662. 676 (Lit.); Aristot. De Coelo 2, 12, 11; Geop. 17, 1. Mid. fut. ἰσχνανοῦμαι, κατ- *consume away*, Aesch. Pr. 269. Vb. ἰσχναντέον, ἀπ- Aristot. Prob. 1, 50.

(Ἰσχνέομαι) see ὑπισχνέομαι.

Ἰσχῡρίζομαι *To contend, maintain,* Dep. mid. Antiph. 5, 76; Isae. 1, 18; Thuc. 3, 44: imp. ἰσχυρ- 7, 49: fut. ἰσχῡριοῦμαι Lys. 6, 35; Isocr. 17, 24: aor. ἰσχυρισάμην Thuc. 5, 26; Pl. Gorg. 489.—ἰσχυριζόμενος seemingly passive, Xen. Cyr. 6, 4, 18. Vb. ἰσχυριστέον Pl. Rep. 533.

Ἰσχύω (ῡ) *To be strong,* Pind. Fr. 39; Aesch. Eum. 621; Hippocr. 2, 38; Antiph. 5, 93; Thuc. 2, 87; Xen. Mem. 3, 12, 4: imp. ἴσχῡον Ar. Vesp. 357; Thuc. 1, 18; Dem. 18, 18: fut. ἰσχύσω Batr. 279; Aesch. Pr. 510; Xen. Athen. 1, 14; Aeschin. 1, 5: aor. ἴσχῡσα Soph. Aj. 502; Thuc. 1, 3; Isae. 11, 18: p. ἴσχῡκα Trag. Fr. (Aristo) 1, 12; Aeschin. 1, 165: aor. p. late ἰσχῡθείς, κατ- Diod. Sic. 15, 87. 20, 24. ῡ in Attic, ἰσχῡ́εις Soph. Aj. 1409; Com. Fr. (Pherecr.) 2, 359, in Pind. and late Poets ῠ sometimes, ἰσχῠ́ει Pind. Fr. 39, ἴσχῠε Anth. 5, 167, -ῠ́ετε 5, 212; ἰσχῠ́σει Theod. Prod. 1, 265. 2, 291; ἰσχῠ́σοι 8, 433; Nicet. Eug. 5, 39. 45.

Ἴσχω *To hold, restrain, have,* Il. 5, 90; Pind. P. 11, 29; Soph. Ph. 1094; Ar. Pax 949; Her. 1, 62. 5, 41; Thuc. 3, 58; Pl. Rep. 366; subj. ἴσχω Il. 20, 139; Pl. Phil. 37; opt. ἴσχοιμι Pl. Leg. 729; imper. ἴσχε Theogn. 365; Aesch. Ch. 1052; Com. Fr. (Antiph.) 3, 46; Eur. H. F. 624; ἴσχειν Il. 9, 352; Soph. Ant. 66; Her. 3, 111; Pl. Phaed. 102, Epic ἰσχέμεναι Od. 20, 330, ἰσχέμεν Il. 15, 456 (Bekk.). 17, 501; ἴσχων Od. 11, 82; Soph. O. C. 950; Her. 3, 77; Thuc. 7, 35: imp. ἴσχον Il. 15, 618, ἶσχ- (B.); Eur. Rhes. 687; Her. 1, 42. Mid. and pass. ἴσχομαι *restrain oneself, stay, remain,* Theogn. 384; Hippocr. 4, 216; Epic subj. ἴσχεαι, κατ- Il. 2, 233; ἴσχοιτο Hippocr. 2, 336 (Lit.); ἴσχεο Il. 2, 247; Bion 1, 97; ἰσχόμενος (pass. Isocr. 19, 11, σχόμ- Bens.), προ- act. Her. 3, 137; ἴσχεσθαι Od. 18, 347: imp. ἰσχόμην Il. 21, 366; Xen. An. 6, 3, 9, προ- Her. 1, 141: p. p. late ἴσχημαι, συν- Nicet. Ann. 7, p. 119.—Supplemented by ἔχω. The perf. ἴσχηκα Schol. Il. 5, 798, is not certain.

Ἴω *To send,* a form of ἵημι, in *simple* only 3 sing. ἴει Ap. Rh. 4, 634 (Mss. Wellau. Merk.); in comp. subj. προ-ίῃ Hym. Ven. 152, ἀφ-ίῃ Xen. Cyr. 8, 1, 6 (-είη Dind. 4 ed. Sauppe, see Popp.), -ίωσι Ar. Lys. 157; opt. ἀφ-ίοιτε Pl. Apol. 29, -ίοιεν Xen. Hell. 6, 4, 3; imper. ἴε Timoth. 13, 4 (B.), ξύνιε Theogn. 1240 (Bergk), -ίετε Com. Fr. (Cratin.) 2, 123; Ar. Pax 603: imp. ξύν-ιον Il. 1, 273 (Vulg. -ιεν for -ίεσαν, Spitzn. Bekk. Dind. Ameis, La R. with Aristarch.): p. p. Ion. (μετίω=μεθ-) μεμετιμένος Her. 6, 1 &c. The subj. ἀφίω, -ίωμεν, opt. ἀφίοιμι &c. Goettling p. 22, would accent ἀφιῶ, -ιῶμεν, ἀφιοῖμι &c. See ἱέω.

K.

Κάββαλε=κατ-έβαλε, Il. 8, 249; Ap. Rh. 4, 188.

Καγχάζω *To laugh loud*, late Anth. (Agath.) 6, 74; Athen. 10, 52, classic κᾰχάζω Soph. Aj. 199 chor. (Dind.); Ar. Eccl. 849 (trimet.); also later Anacreont. 31, 29 (Bergk.); Luc. D. Mer. 6, 3. (Amor.) 23 (Dind.): **fut.** (καγχᾱ́σω), καχᾱ́σω, Dor. καχαξῶ Theocr. 5, 142: **aor.** ἐκάγχᾰσα Anth. (Paul. Sil.) 5, 230, ἀν- Pl. Rep. 337; Luc. Pseudol. 7 (Jacobitz), ἐξ- Xen. Conv. 1, 16 (Vulg. Saupp. Mehler, -εκάχασα Dind. always); καγχάσας Babr. 99, ἀνα- Pl. Euthyd. 300.

Καγχαλάω Epic, *To rejoice*, -ᾶ̣ Opp. Cyn. 1, 507, 3 pl. -όωσι Il. 3, 43; Opp. H. 5, 236; Maneth. 5, 32; part. -ῶν Lycophr. 109, Epic -όων Il. 10, 565; Ap. Rh. 3, 124, -όωσα Od. 23, 59: **imp.** iter. καγχαλᾱ́ασκε Ap. Rh. 4, 996, -σκον Q. Sm. 8, 12.

(**Κάζω**) Poet. *To excel*, **act.** not in use. **Pass.** as **act. pres.** and imp. late, καζόμενος *excelling*, Nicet. Annal. p. 141: ἐκάζοντο p. 120: **perf.** (κέκασμαι) κέκασσαι Od. 19, 82, κέκασται Il. 20, 35; Emped. 347; Anth. 3, 18; Eur. Elec. 616 (trimet.); κεκάσθαι Il. 24, 546; Ap. Rh. 3, 1007; κεκασμένος Il. 4, 339; Hes. Th. 929; Ap. Rh. 4, 1585; Theocr. 7, 44 (Ms. M. Mein. Fritzs.); Aesch. Eum. 766 (trimet.); Ar. Eq. 685 (chor.), Dor. κεκαδμένος Pind. Ol. 1, 27: **plp.** ἐκέκαστο Il. 2, 530. Od. 19, 395; Ap. Rh. 2, 867, κέκαστο Il. 14, 124. Od. 7, 157, κεκάσμεθα Od. 24, 509. This word is poetic, for Plato, Rep. 334, rather *quotes* than *uses* it, see Od. 19, 305. See καίνυμαι, χάζω.

Καθαίρω *To purify*, Hippocr. 8, 54 (Lit.); Pl. Soph. 227; Aeschin. 2, 158; Dem. 54, 39; subj. -ωμεν Pl. Rep. 399, -ωσι Polit. 293; -αίρειν Od. 22, 439; Hipponax 4; Pl. Crat. 396; Xen. Oec. 20, 11; (Lys.) 6, 53; -αίρων Aesch. Ch. 74; Soph. Tr. 1061; Pl. Crat. 405. Tim. 72. Soph. 227: **imp.** ἐκάθαιρον, κἀκάθ- Ar. Vesp. 118, ἐξ- Il. 2, 153, κάθ- Od. 22, 453: **fut.** καθᾰρῶ Xen. Oec. 18, 6; Pl. Leg. 735 (Stallb.): **aor.** ἐκάθηρα Il. 16, 228; Theocr. 5, 119; Her. 1, 41. 44; Hippocr. 8, 106 (Lit.); Thuc. 3, 104; Xen. An. 5, 7, 35 (Ms. Vat. Popp. Krüg. Dind. Sauppe), κάθ- Il. 14, 171; -ήρῃ Pl. Rep. 567; -ήρειεν Leg. 735 &c.; (Luc.) Menip. 7; Plut. Pomp. 26. Brut. 39; Arr. An. 2, 4, 8, περι- Theophr. H. P. 9, 7, 4, and ἐκάθᾱρα Hippocr. 2, 418; Antiph. 6, 37; Xen. Oec. 18, 8 (Dind. Breitb. Kerst, Sauppe); Anab. 5, 7, 35 quoted (Vulg.); so Pl. Leg. 735 (Bekk. B. O. Winck. see **fut.**); Theophr. Ch. 16; Plut. Mor. 134; Diod. Sic. 4, 31, ἐκ- Dinarch. 2, 5; Dio. Hal. Rhet. 11,

9; Luc. V. A. 8. Fugit. 23, περι- Theophr. H. P. 4, 13, 5, ἀπο- Plut. Mor. 510, δια- Apollod. 3, 6, 7: (p. κεκάθαρκα late, Schol. Ar. Pax 753): p. p. κεκάθαρμαι Hippocr. 7, 322; Pl. Phaed. 69, ἐκ- Xen. Conv. 1, 4: 1 aor. ἐκαθάρθην Hippocr. 5, 204; Thuc. 3, 104; -αρθῇ Hippocr. 7, 322; Pl. Tim. 72; -θείη Hippocr. 7, 386; -αρθείς Her. 1, 43. 4, 71; Pl. Leg. 831; -αρθῆναι Dem. 23, 72: fut. -αρθήσομαι late, Galen 7, 222; Oribas. 7, 26: 2 aor. ἐκαθάρην, ἀποκαθαρῇ Arr. Ven. 27, 1, -αρθῇ (L. Dind.) **Mid.** καθαίρομαι *to clean oneself*, Aesch. Fr. 42 (D.): fut. καθαροῦμαι Hippocr. 7, 54; Pl. Crat. 396, pass. if correct, Hippocr. 7, 24. 330. 8, 338 (Lit. Lind. 2, 740 Erm. καθαιρ- Vulg.), ἀπο- Xen. Cyr. 2, 2, 27: aor. ἐκαθηράμην Hippocr. 2, 644. 5, 232; Philostr. Ap. 7, 32; καθήρηται Pl. Leg. 881; -ηράσθω 868; -ήρασθαι Aesch. Fr. 376 (D.); Pl. Phaedr. 243; -ηράμενος Pl. Leg. 865, Dor. καθᾱράμενος, ἀπο- (Pl.) Locr. 104. **Vb.** καθαρτέον Hippocr. 2, 129. In the best editions the aor. has nearly always η in Ionic (but καθᾶραι Hippocr. 2, 418 Lit.), and usually in Attic, varying there, and in late Greek, between η and α. Some, however, are inclined to write it always with η in classic Attic, as καθῆραι Antiph. 6, 37 (Saupp.), ἐκ-καθήρατε Dinarch. 2, 5 (Saupp.), καθήρῃς Xen. Oec. 18, 8 (Schneid.) quoted above. An act. 2 aor. seems not to occur—καθάρῃ so called by Stallb. Pl. Leg. 735, is assuredly not a decisive case—and the 2 aor. pass. only once, ἀπο-καθαρῇ, if sound, Arr. quoted; the 1 aor. pass. καθαρθῆναι is used by him An. 2, 4, 11 (Krüg.) Moeris, p. 101, says ἐκάθηρα Ἀττικῶς, ἐκάθᾱρα λέγουσιν Ἕλληνες.

Καθέζομαι *To sit down, be sitting*, Com. Fr. (Aristoph.) 2, 1145, in tmesi κατ' ἄρ' ἕζεαι Od. 10, 378, καθεζόμεθα Eur. Heracl. 33? -ονται Lys. 13, 37; (Pl.) Ax. 361; καθέζηται Thuc. 6, 49, -ώμεσθα Od. 1, 372, -ησθε Thuc. 7, 77; καθεζέσθω Hippocr. 7, 348 (Lit.); -εσθαι 8, 392 (Lit.); Andoc. 1, 38; -όμενος Thuc. 1, 24: imp. ἐκαθεζόμην Xen. An. 1, 5, 9. Cyr. 5, 3, 25; Aeschin. 1, 120. 123; often as aor. Thuc. 2, 18. 4, 110; Andoc. 1, 44; Pl. Euthyd. 272, Poet. καθεζόμην Il. 1, 536. 8, 51 &c.; Aesch. Eum. 6; Soph. Tr. 918; Ar. Lys. 1139: fut. (act. late, καθεδεῖν *will set, put down*, Synes. Prov. 2, 123, whence) mid. καθεδοῦμαι Ar. Ran. 200. Eccl. 617. Av. 727; Andoc. 1, 111; Pl. Theaet. 146; Dem. 5, 15. 9, 75, late καθεδήσομαι Diog. Laert. 2, 72: aor. late, ἐκαθέσθην Paus. 3, 22; Long. Past. 2, 38 (Seil.); Charit. 3, 2; Anth. 11, 392; Luc. Soloec. 11, rejects it: fut. καθεσθήσομαι, προ- Aeschin. 3, 167 (Vulg.) rather doubtful, προσκαθιζήσει (Lobeck, Bekk. B. Saupp. Franke). **Vb.** καθεστέον Com. Fr. (Pher.) 2, 360. The Doric form is καθέσδομ- Mosch. 3, 46 (Mein. καθέζ- Ahr. Ziegl.) Buttmann holds pres.

καθέζομαι suspicious, especially in early writers, and would substitute καθίζομαι. ἐκαθεζόμην he maintains to be, in Attic at all events, a pure aorist, not an imperfect. Instances in early authors, we grant, are rare; at the same time we think his remarks rather stringent. Od. 10, 378; Ar. in Com. Fr. 2, 1145; Lys. 13, 37; Hippocr. 8, 392 &c., to say nothing of Eur. quoted, are decided cases of pres., and, in point of form, derive support from the equally decided cases of imperfect, Xen. An. 1, 5, 9; Cyr. 5, 3, 25; (Dio. Hal. 3, 62; Pseudo-Callisth. 2, 16.) Late instances are not unfrequent, καθέζῃ, -εται, -ονται Plut. Mor. 45. 774; (Luc.) Asin. 20; Paus. 5, 11, 1.

Καθεύδω *To sleep*, Od. 8, 313; Anacr. 88; Aesch. Ag. 1357; Eur. Phoen. 634; Ar. Nub. 732; Her. 2, 95; Antiph. 2, δ, 8; Thuc. 4, 113; Pl. Crit. 43: imp. Attic ἐκάθευδον Hippocr. 5, 252; Xen. Oec. 7, 11; Lys. 1, 13. 23, and καθηῦδον Com. Fr. (Ar.) 2, 1059 (Mein.); Pl. Conv. 217. 219. 220, Epic καθεῦδον Il. 1, 611; Theocr. 20, 39, κάθ- (Ziegl. Fritz.); Ar. Av. 495 (anapaest, -ηῦδον Mein. Dind. 5 ed.): fut. καθευδήσω Xen. Cyr. 6, 2, 30; -ήσοιεν Hell. 5, 1, 20; -ήσων Ar. Eccl. 419; Lys. 1, 10; -ήσειν Com. Fr. (Men.) 4, 189: aor. subj. καθευδήσῃ (Luc.) Asin. 6; -ῆσαι Hippocr. 7, 198 (Lit.); -ησας Themist. 19, 229: p. late, καθευδηκέναι Epiphan. 1, p. 418. Vb. καθευδητέον Pl. Phaedr. 259. The Tragedians seem to have used only the pres. of this comp. The Mss. and editors of Herodotus present καθεύδει 2, 95, καθεύδουσι 4, 25, not κατεύ- which one would expect, and Bredow would write—and so, we now observe, Dietsch, Stein, and Abicht have lately edited.

(Καθέω) *To put, place down*, only 1 aor. act. and mid., and mostly Epic, καθεῖσε Il. 5, 36. 18, 389, κάθεσσαν Pind. P. 5, 42; subj. καθέσωσι Poet. quoted Thuc. 3, 104: mid. καθέσσατο Anacr. Epigr. 111 (Bergk), -έσσαντο Pind. P. 5, 42 (Vulg. Bergk) is in Boeckh's edition -εσσαν as above (Ms. Gu. Herm. Kays.), καθείσατο Musgrave's conjecture Eur. Hipp. 31 (Br. Monk) for ἐγκαθείσ- (Mss. A. C. Dind. 2 ed. Kirchh. &c.) and ἐγκαθίσ- (M. V. P. Ald. Dind. 5 ed.) Cobet calls καθέσωσιν *barbarum* for -έωσιν, and says "ἄγωνα καθεῖναι *recte dicitur*" (V. L. p. 447, 2 ed.) We venture to doubt if he is right in either assertion.

Κάθημαι *To sit*, Theogn. 1281; Archil. 87; Ar. Nub. 255; Pl. Phaed. 98; (Dem.) Epist. 2 (1472), κάθησαι Xen. Cyr. 3, 1, 6; Luc. Salt. 2, Ion. κάτησαι Her. 3, 134, κάθηται Ar. Lys. 597; Pl. Apol. 35; Dem. 9, 70, καθήμεθα Ar. Thesm. 886; Dem. 2, 23. 11, 17, κάθησθε Ar. Nub. 1201; Dem. 2, 24. 8, 53. 10, 1 &c. κάθηνται Ar. Fr. 722 (D.); Pl. Rep, 555; Dem. 47, 12, Ion. κατέαται Her. 2, 86; subj. καθῶμαι Eur. Hel. 1084, -ῆται Ar. Eq.

754, -ώμεθα Dem. 4, 44 (10, 3), -ῶνται (Dem.) 59, 67; opt. καθοίμην Pl. Theag. 130, -οῖτο Ar. Ran. 919, -ῆτο (Dobr.), -οίμεθα Lys. 149 (Br. Enger, Dind. 5 ed.), -ήμεθα (Ms. R. Bekk. Dind. ed. 1830, Bergk); imper. κάθησο Il. 2, 191; Eur. I. A. 627; Comic κάθου Com. Fr. (Ar.) 2, 1190. (Anax.) 3, 167. (Alex.) 3, 487. (Men.) 4, 317; and late prose V. T. Ps. 109, 1. N. T. Jac. 2, 3 &c., καθήσθω Aesch. Pr. 916, -ησθε Supp. 365; inf. καθῆσθαι Pind. Fr. 58; Soph. O. C. 1158; Eur. Heracl. 55; Thuc. 4, 124; καθήμενος Il. 14, 5; Aesch. Eum. 519; Soph. Fr. 380 (D.); Ar. Pax 266; Thuc. 2, 20, Ion. κατήμ- Her. 8, 73: imp. ἐκαθήμην Ar. Eccl. 152; Aeschin. 2, 89; Dem. 48, 31, ἐκάθητο Hom. H. 7, 14; Ar. Av. 510; Thuc. 5, 6; Xen. Cyr. 7, 3, 14; Aeschin. 1, 40, ἐκαθήμεθα Dio Cass. 72, 21, -θησθε Ar. Ach. 638, -θηντο Thuc. 3, 97; Lys. 13, 37; Pl. Prot. 315, Ion. ἐκατέατο Her. 3, 144. 8, 73 (Bekk. Gaisf. Dind.), and often—always in Tragedy—augmented after the preposition καθήμην (Pl.) Riv. 132, καθῆτο Dem. 18, 169. 217. 21, 206 (Ms. F. Bekk. Dind. ἐκάθ- Vulg. B. Saupp.), and καθῆστο Il. 1, 569; Eur. Bac. 1102. Phoen. 1466; Isae. 6, 19; Pl. Rep. 328; Her. 1, (45) 46. 3, 83 (Mss. Gaisf. but Ion. κατῆστο Bekk. Dind. Lhardy, Stein), καθήμεθα Soph. Ant. 411; Dem. 19, 155. 166, καθῆσθε Ar. Ach. 543; Dem. 25, 21, καθῆντο Ar. Eccl. 302; Thuc. 5, 58 (Bekk. Popp. ἐκάθ- Krüg.); Dem. 18, 30, Epic καθείατο Il. 11, 76, Ion. κατέατο Her. 9, 90 (Mss. Bekk. Gaisf. Dind. Bred.): fut. καθήσομαι, -ήσεσθε Eur. Fr. 952 (Dind. 5 ed. Nauck), which, if the Fragment be genuine, and the reading correct, is a solitary instance of the fut. in *classic* Greek. We have sometimes thought the reading should be pres. κάθησθ', or, if the fut. must be retained, τεθήσεσθ', or, perhaps better, καταστήσεσθ', see Dem. 1, 22. 59, 7. In late Greek, however, this fut. form occurs often, καθήσεσθε V. T. Lev. 8, 35. 1 Reg. 5, 7 &c. and N. T. Luc. 22, 30 (Mss. A. Q. Sin. Tisch. καθίσεσθε B5 Lachm.): the Attics used καθιζήσομαι Pl. Phaedr. 229. κάθῃ 2 sing. for κάθησαι, perhaps rather late Hyperid. Fr. 136 (Bekk. An. 100); Com. Fr. (Anon.) 4, 676. κάθησθε is pres., καθῆσθε imperf. Hom. and the Tragedians never augment this verb before the preposition, Aristoph. and prose authors augment either before or after. The simple ἧμαι is mostly poetic; κάθημαι is the prose form, and most assuredly not confined, as some teach, to "the 3 pers. κάθηται only."

Καθίζω *To set*, also *to sit*, Od. 2, 69; Soph. O. C. 21; Eur. H. F. 48; Ar. Vesp. 940; Thuc. 3, 75; Lys. 13, 24, Ion. κατίζω Her. 1, 181: imp. ἐκάθιζον Xen. Hell. 5, 4, 6; Dinarch. 2, 13, and καθῖζον Il. 3, 426. 8, 436. Od. 16, 408, and always (Bekk.

Dind. La R.), κάθιζ-, ἐκάθιζ- (Vulg. Wolf): **fut.** καθίσω Com. Fr. (Apoll.) 4, 451 (Xen. An. 2, 1, 4, some Mss. Kühner); Plut. Mor. 234, Ion. κατ- Her. 4, 190, Attic καθιῶ Xen. An. 2, 1, 4 quoted; Dem. 24, 25. 39, 11, παρα- Hippocr. 7, 608, Dor. καθιξῶ Bion 4, 16 (late καθιζήσω, see foll.): **aor.** ἐκάθῖσα Xen. Cyr. 6, 1, 23; Com. Fr. (Men.) 4, 102, κάθῖσα Il. 19, 280, and Attic καθῖσα Eur. Phoen. 1188; Ar. Ran. 911 (Bekk. Dind.); Thuc. 6, 66. 7, 82; -ίσῃ Dem. 21, 223, Ion. κατῖσα Her. 1, 88. 4, 79 (Bekk. Krüg. Lhardy), κάτισα (Gaisf. Dind.), but 4, 79 -ῖσα (Dind. -εῖσα Valck. Gaisf., in both Stein), late ἐκαθίζησα, subj. καθιζήσῃ Dio Cass. 37, 27 (B.); -ήσας 54, 30; Dor. -ίξῃ Theocr. 1, 51; Epic part. καθίσσας Il. 9, 488, Dor. καθίξας Theocr. 1, 12: **p.** late, κεκάθικα Diod. Sic. 17, 115; Epict. Diss. 2, 6, 23; Aesop 100 (Halm), but συγ- Aristot. Physiog. 3, 2: **aor. pass.** late καθιζηθείς Dio Cass. 63, 5. **Mid.** καθίζομαι *to sit*, Xen. Hell. 5, 4, 7; subj. -ίζηται Hippocr. 7, 100; Pl. Leg. 719; -ιζοίμην Ar. Eq. 750, -ίζοιτο Pl. Rep. 516; καθίζου Ar. Eq. 785; -ίζεσθαι Com. Fr. (Cratin.) 2, 231; Thuc. 1, 136 (Bekk. Popp. -έζεσθαι Krüg. Class.); -ιζόμενος Pl. Prot. 317: **imp.** ἐκαθίζ- Ar. Vesp. 824, ὑπ-εκ- Xen. Hell. 7, 2, 5, in tmesi κὰδ δὲ ἵζοντο Il. 19, 50: **fut** καθιζήσομαι Pl. Phaedr. 229, παρα- Lys. 207, προσκαθ- Aeschin. 3, 167, late καθίσομαι Plut. Mor. 583; N. T. Luc. 22, 30 (Lachm.), -ιοῦμαι V. T. Ps. 131, 12: **aor.** trans. ἐκαθισάμην (σσ) Callim. Dian. 233 (L. -εισ- Blomf. Mein.), καθισσ- Ap. Rh. 4, 278, καθίσατο Eur. Hipp. 31 (Nauck 3 ed., ἐγ- Dind. 5 ed. -είσατο Nauck 2 ed. Kirchh.), ἐπεκαθίσαντο Thuc. 4, 130 (Bekk. Popp.) which Poppo in note would write ἐπικαθ- but prefers ἐπικαθίσταντο, which Krüger approves, παρεκαθίσατο Dem. 33, 14; παρακαθισάμενος Lycurg. 241 (συμπαρα- Dem. 28, 15), but intrans. Xen. Cyr. 5, 5, 7. In late recensions of Demosthenes no such fut. act. form as καθεδεῖτε, for καθιεῖτε, occurs, see 24, 25. 39, 11: καθεδεῖτε is very late, see καθέζομαι. In late recensions of Homer and Herodotus, and usually in Attic, this verb has not the syllabic augment. The Tragedians seem not to use the **mid.** form, unless καθίσατο Eur. Hipp. 31 (Nauck 3 ed. ἐγκαθ- Dind. 5 ed.) be correct.

Καίνῦμαι Poet. *To excel, be adorned*, **imp.** ἐκαίνῦτο Od. 3, 282; Hes. Sc. 4; Ap. Rh. 1, 138; Mosch. 2, 92, ἀπ- Od. 8, 127. 219; Ap. Rh. 2, 783: **p.** (κάζομαι) κέκασμαι, -ασσαι Od. 19, 82, -ασται Il. 20, 35; Eur. Elec. 616 (trimet.), -μεθα Od. 24, 509; κεκάσθαι Il. 24, 546; Ap. Rh. 3, 1007; κεκασμένος Il. 4, 339; Hes. Th. 929; Ap. Rh. 2, 816; Aesch. Eum. 766 (trimet.); Ar. Eq. 685 (chor.), and Dor. κεκαδμένος Pind. Ol. 1, 27: **plp.** ἐκέκαστο Il. 16, 808. Od. 9, 509; Ap. Rh. 1, 153, κέκαστο Il. 14,

124. Od. 7, 157. See (κάζω). κεκάσθαι Pl. Rep. 334, is an accommodation of Od. 19, 395.

Καίνω *To kill*, Poet. Eur. Phoen. 44; subj. καίνω Callim. Dian. 12; καινέτω Soph. El. 820; καίνειν Aesch. Ch. 886; καίνων Aesch. Ag. 1562; Soph. O. C. 994; Timocr. 1, 9 (Ahr.); rare in prose Xen. Cyr. 4, 2, 24: **fut.** κᾰνῶ Eur. H. F. 1075: as **fut. perf.** κατα-κεκονότες ἔσεσθε Xen. 7, 6, 36: **2 aor.** ἔκᾰνον Aesch. Ch. 930; Soph. Ant. 1319; Eur. I. T. 1252; κάνοι Aesch. Sept. 630; κᾰνών Eur. H. F. 865; κανεῖν Theocr. 24, 91 (Mein. Ziegl. Ahr.), -ῆν (Vulg. Fritz.): **2 p.** κέκονα Soph. Fr. 896 (D.), κατα-κεκονότες Xen. An. 7, 6, 36 (Dind. 4 ed. Saupp. Rhed.), κατακεκανότες (Mss. A. B. Kühner, κατακανόντες Vulg. Popp. Krüg.) **Pass.** καίνεται Aesch. Sept. 347; -όμενος Eur. Cycl. 360 (Mss. Vulg. κλιν- *now*): **imp.** ἐκαινόμην I. T. 27. This verb, we think, does not occur in Epic, Comic, or Lyric, except Timocr. quoted: frequent in Tragedy: once only in prose. The prose form is usually κατα-καίνω **pres. imp. 2 aor.** and perhaps **2 perf.**, but, in the *classic* period, confined to Xen. Arrian also uses this verb κατακαίνουσι Ind. 11, 10; -αίνων An. 5, 24, 3; and Plut. -αίνειν Mor. 240: **imp.** -έκαινον Arr. An. 5, 17, 6: **aor.** -έκανεν An. 5, 18, 7 (Krüg.); -κάνοιεν Ind. 7, 3 (Herch.); -ανεῖν Ven. 25 (Saupp.) Defectively handled in lexicons.

Καίω *To burn, fire*, Il. 9, 77; Hes. Th. 557; Theogn. 1145; Aesch. Ag. 286 (Herm.); Soph. Fr. 480 (Dind. 2 ed. κάω Ellendt, ναίω Dind. 5 ed.); Eur. Cycl. 659 (Herm. Kirchh. Nauck, κάω Dind. 5 ed.); Her. 2, 39. 62; Hippocr. 6, 544, κατα- Thuc. 8, 39 (Bekk. Popp. Krüg.); so καιόμενος 2, 52, περι-καίονται Andoc. 2, 2, κάω Ar. Fr. 403; Pl. Tim. 58; see also Ar. Lys. 8; Com. Fr. (Alex.) 3, 452 (not contr. κῶ); Epic inf. καιέμεν Il. 14, 397: **imp.** ἔκαιον Od. 9, 553; Eur. Bac. 758 (Elms. Kirchh. ἔκᾱον Dind. 5 ed.); Xen. An. 1, 6, 1 (Popp. Krüg. Saupp. ἔκᾱον Dind. Cob.), καῖον Il. 21, 343, ἔκᾱον Com. Fr. (Phoen.) 4, 511; Xen. Hell. 5, 4, 41 &c., see also Thuc. 2, 49 (Bekk. Krüg. ἐκαι- Popp.): **fut.** καύσω Xen. Cyr. 5, 4, 21; Luc. Peregr. 5; Plut. Thes. 8; Anth. 9, 15, ἐπι- Com. Fr. (Plat.) 2, 681, κατα- Ar. Lys. 1218; Sopat. Athen. 4, 160: and καύσομαι rare, Ar. Plut. 1054, **pass.** or reflex καυσούμενος Galen 10, 656; N. T. 2 Pet. 3, 10. 12: **aor.** ἔκαυσα Ar. Pax 1088 (hexam.); in tmesi Her. 8, 33; Isae. 4, 19; Xen. Cyr. 3, 3, 33, ἀν- Eur. Cycl. 383 (trimet.), κατ- Thuc. 7, 25; καύσας 7, 80; καῦσαι Pl. Gorg. 456, Attic Poet. (ἔκεα) part. κέας Aesch. Ag. 849; Soph. El. 757 (Herm. Dind.), ἐκ- Eur. Rhes. 97 (trimet.); Ar. Pax 1132 (chor.), but ἀπο- Hippocr. 7, 422, Epic ἔκηα Il. 1, 40. 24, 34. Od. 19, 366 &c. (Bekk. Spitzn. Dind. La Roche, ἔκεια and -ηα Wolf,

Buttm.); Hippocr. 5, 216 (Lit.) if correct, the only prose instance we have seen, in tmesi κῆεν Il. 21, 349, late Epic κεῖαν Ap. Rh. 1, 588; subj. κήωμεν, Epic -ομεν Il. 7, 377. 396; opt. κήαι Il. 21, 336, -αιεν 24, 38, a rare form in Hom.; imper. κῆον Od. 21, 176; inf. κῆαι Od. 15, 97, κατα-κῆαι 11, 46, and κακκῆαι 11, 74; κήαντες Od. 9, 231, see below: **p.** in comp. κέκαυκα, κατα- Xen. Hell. 6, 5, 37, προσ- Com Fr. (Alex.) 3, 439: **p. p.** κέκαυμαι Eur. Cycl. 457; Hippocr. 6, 330. 442; Thuc. 4, 34, κατα- Andoc. 1, 108; Xen. Cyr. 7, 5, 23, ἐκ- Hippocr. 2, 54. 6, 192, but κέκαυσται if correct, 7, 242 (Lit.): **plp.** ἐκέκαυτο Eratosth. 1, 23 (Hiller); Dio Cass. 47, 18, ἀπ- Luc. Tox. 61: **1 aor.** ἐκαύθην Hippocr. 5, 146. 208; Artemid. Onir. 4, 43; -θείς Pind. N. 10, 35; Pl. Tim. 68, κατ- Thuc. 3, 74; Her. 1, 19. 4, 69. 6, 101, v. r. -σθην: **fut.** καυθήσομαι Hippocr. 7, 422; Luc. Peregr. 8, κατα- Ar. Nub. 1505; Xen. An. 7, 4, 15, ἐκ- Pl. Rep. 361: **2 aor.** unatt. ἐκάην Od. 12, 13, in tmesi Il. 9, 212; Hippocr. 5, 214, κατ- Her. 2, 180. 4, 79, δι- Hippocr. 6, 330 (Lit.); Plut. Oth. 6; Epic inf. καήμεναι Il. 23, 210, καῆναι Pseud.-Callisth. 3, 30, κατα- Her. 2, 107; καέντα Plut. Mor. 283, κατα- Her. 1, 51; Plut. Pyrrh. 3: **fut.** late καήσομαι Or. Sib. 3, 507; Apocr. Syr. 28, 23, κατα- N. T. 1 Cor. 3, 15, but συγκατα- Xanth. Fr. p. 41 (Müller): **pres.** καίεται Il. 20, 491; -όμενος 21, 361; Hes. Th. 694: **imp.** καίεο Od. 24, 67, καίετο Hes. Th. 861; Il. 10, 12, -οντο 1, 52, see below. **Mid.** *kindle for oneself*, **aor.** ἐκαυσάμην, ἀνα- Her. 1, 202. 8, 19, Epic κήαντο Il. 9, 88; -άμενος 9, 234. **Fut. mid.** καύσομαι seems not to occur in early prose except as a *v. r.* ἐκ-καυσόμενος Hippocr. 6, 302, and once only in poetry, Ar. quoted. See ῥοφέω. **Vb.** καυστός Eur. Cycl. 633, καυτ- (Kirchh. Nauck, Dind. 5 ed.), πυρί-καυτος Pl. Tim. 85, δια-καυτέον Geop. 17, 25.

It would appear that the Mss. of Hom. agree in giving **aor.** ἔκηα, ἔκηε, opt. κήαι, κήαιεν with η without *v. r.* but vary between η and ει in inf. κῆαι, κεῖαι, imper. κῆον, subj. κήομεν, κείομεν, **aor. m.** κήαντο, κείαντο &c. Bekk. Spitzn. Dind. write η, uniformly, with the approval of Matthiae and Lobeck, and for κατακειέμεν, -ηέμεν Il. 7, 408, Spitzner, Bekker and Dindorf give κατακαιέμεν with Eustathius. κήαντες (Mss.), κείαντες (Tricl.) used to stand Soph. El. quoted, but Br. and Herm. changed it rightly to κέαντες, see passages quoted from other Attic Poets. It is a mistake to say that "in the passive voice the **1 aor.** is the only tense in use by the Attics:" **pres. pass.** κάομαι Ar. Lys. 8, κάεται Ar. Vesp. 1372: **imp.** ἐκαίετο Thuc. 2, 49; Xen. Hell. 6, 4, 36; καϊόμενος Thuc. 2, 52; Pl. Phaedr. 115 &c. &c. and **perf.** κεκαυμένος Eur. Cycl. 457; Com. Fr. (Pl.) 2, 679; Thuc.

4, 34. καίω is Epic, Ionic, Doric, Lyric, and generally at least Trag. and Thuc. κάω is the prevailing, in some editions the only, form in Aristophanes, Isocrates, and Plato, varying more in Xenophon. L. Dindorf however in his last edition of Xen. seems to give κάω uniformly: so W. Dind. in the Tragedians (5 ed.) In late authors καίω is the more frequent form.

Καλέω *To call*, Il. 4, 204; Pind. P. 11, 8; Aesch. Eum. 287; Soph. Aj. 72; Ar. Av. 849; Her. 1, 131; Antiph. 5, 35; Thuc. 6, 4, Dor. 1 pl. καλέομες Epich. 51 (Ahr.), 3 pl. καλέοισι Pind. N. 9, 41; opt. καλέοι Her. 1, 11, -οίη Xen. Hell. 2, 1, 13; Epic inf. καλήμεναι Il. 10, 125; pt. καλεῦντες Od. 10, 255: **imp.** ἐκάλει Il. 22, 294; Pind. P. 4, 195, -λεε Her. 1, 120, -λουν Pl. Leg. 700, Poet. κάλεον Il. 10, 197, dissyll. Od. 8. 550, 'κάλεις Soph. O. R. 432, iter. καλέεσκον Il. 9, 562; Hes. Th. 207: **fut.** καλέσω Xen. Cyr. 2, 3, 22 (Mss. Born. Breitb. -λῶ Dind. Sauppe); Aeschin. 1, 67. 3, 202, if not subj. see below; Aristot. Eth. N. 2, 7, 10, συγ- Her. 3, 74, ἐγ- Dem. (17, 19) 19, 133. 23, 123, παρα- 8, 14 (18, 164. 165 Psephism), Hom. καλέω Il. 3, 383, Attic usually καλῶ Ar. Ach. 968. Nub. 1001; Xen. Conv. 1, 15; Pl. Charm. 155, ἐγ- Isocr. 17, 56; Dem. 55, 17: **aor.** ἐκάλεσα Pind. Ol. 1, 37; Eur. Hel. 348. H. F. 1179; Her. 6, 67; Pl. Rep. 477, Epic ἐκάλεσσα Od. 17, 379 (Wolf, Dind.); Pind. Ol. 6, 58, κάλεσσα Il. 16, 693, late ἐκάλησα Pseudo-Callisth. 3, 35 (but ἔκλησα Nicand. Fr. 22, ἐπι- Musae. 10, perhaps better referred to κλέω or κλῄζω); subj. καλέσω Soph. Ph. 1452; opt. -έσαιμι Pl. Conv. 174; part. καλέσας Il. 1, 402 &c.; Her. 2, 107; Pl. Charm. 155: **p.** κέκληκα Theogn. 1229; Ar. Pl. 260; Com. Fr. (Alex.) 3, 467; Pl. Rep. 580: **p. p.** κέκλημαι Il. 10, 259; Pind. Ol. 7, 76; Aesch. Eum. 417; Eur. Hipp. 2; Her. 1, 98; Thuc. 2, 37; Pl. Phaedr. 258 (and κεκάλεσμαι late if correct Suid. sub v. κλητή); opt. κεκλῇο Soph. Ph. 119, κεκλῄμεθα Ar. Lys. 253: **plp.** ἐκεκλήμην Her. 1, 119; Luc. Gall. 9, κέκλητ' Soph. Fr. 624 (opt. κεκλῇτ' Cob. Dind. 5 ed.), Ion. 3 pl. -ήατο Il. 10, 195: **aor.** ἐκλήθην Soph. O. R. 1359; Ar. Thesm. 862; Her. 1, 173; Hippocr. 1. 318 (Erm.); Antiph. 1, 23; Thuc. 6, 2; κληθείς Archil. 78 (and ἐκαλέσθην, προσ- Hippocr. 3, 614 Kühn, 5, 330 Lit., if the reading be sound, which Littré denies, and gives from Mss. προσεσκαλεύθη): **fut.** κληθήσομαι Pl. Leg. 681; Luc. Alex. 45 (v. r. Aesch. Pr. 840. Eur. Tr. 13), ἀντι- Xen. Conv. 1, 15, ἐσ- Paus. 5, 21: usu. **3 fut.** κεκλήσομαι Il. 3, 138; Archil. 24 (Bergk); Callim. Del. 269; always in Trag. Aesch. Pr. 840; Soph. O. R. 522 &c.; Eur. Ion 594 &c.; and Comedy, Ar. Vesp. 151. Av. 761; Com. Fr. (Anax.) 3, 191, προσ- Ar. Nub. 1277; κεκλήσοιτο Pl. Tim. 42; -ήσεσθαι 88: and **fut. m.** καλοῦμαι as **pass.** καλεῖ

Soph. El. 971. **Mid.** καλοῦμαι *summon to* or *for oneself*, to a *court or meeting*, Aesch. Ch. 201; Ar. Av. 1046; Pl. Leg. 914, ἐπι- Thuc. 3, 59; Ion. pt. καλεύμενος, προ- H. Merc. 241: **imp.** ἐκαλεῖτο, ἐξ- Od. 24, 1, -έοντο, ἐπ- Her. 7, 189, -οῦντο Thuc. 4, 48: **fut.** καλέσομαι *simple* uncontr. late (σσ) Nonn. 2, 235, ἐπι-καλέσομαι rare, Lycurg. 17. 143, ἐκ- Aeschin. 1, 174 (Bekk. B. Saupp. Franke); Themist. 9, 125; Geop. 13, 15, usu. contr. καλοῦμαι Ar. Eccl. 864. Nub. 1221; Xen. Conv. 5, 2, but **pass.** Soph. El. 971; Eur. Or. 1140: **aor.** ἐκαλεσάμην, καλέσαντο Il. 1, 270; Pind. Ol. 8, 32; subj. καλέσσεται for -ηται, προ- Il. 7, 39; καλεσάμενος Xen. An. 3, 3, 1; Pl. Leg. 937; καλέσασθαι Her. 7, 189; ἐπ-εκαλεσάμην Thuc. 1, 102, προσ- Isae. 6, 31; Dem. 34, 13. Epic ἐκαλέσσ- Il. 3, 161, καλέσσ- 15, 143, καλέσ- 1, 270: and late **p. p.** ἀνακέκλημαι V. T. Exod. 31, 2, προσ- 3, 18. Joel 2, 32. N. T. Act. 13, 2, ἐπι- 25, 12: plp. ἐκέκλητο, ἐξ- Polyb. 4, 57. **Vb.** κλητός Od. 17, 386, -έος Pl. Crat. 393.—Inf. Epic καλήμεναι Il. 10, 125, iter. imp. καλέεσκον 9, 562, κάλεσκον Ap. Rh. 4, 1514, **pass.** καλέσκετο Il. 15, 338, κεκλήαται 3 pl. **p. pass.** Epic for -ηνται, Ap. Rh. 1, 1128, Ion. κεκλέαται Her. 2, 164, but a late and corrupt form for κέκληται (Hippocr.) Epist. 3, 836 (K.), 3 pl. **plp.** κεκλήατο Il. 10, 195. **Fut.** καλέσω *simple* is rare. At Aeschin. 1, 67. 3, 202 (B. Saupp.) it may be subj. Franke and Weidner *now* however read in the former passage καλῶ, and in the latter, they and Bekker καλέσῃ, some Mss. and editors καλέσει, -έσοι. For ἐκκαλέσεσθαι also, Aeschin. 1, 174, Weidner, and now Franke (2 edit.) read -καλεῖσθαι; and we are inclined to think that Scheibe, in accordance with the strong current of Attic usage, will on the first opportunity alter ἐπικαλέσεται Lycurg. quoted, to ἐπικαλεῖται. Dind. however retains ἐγκαλέσει, -έσουσι, παρα-καλέσειν Dem. quoted.

Κάλημι *To call*, Aeol.=καλέω, Sapph. 1, 16 (Ahr.). The collateral form **καλίζομαι** seems to occur only in comp., and only in **pres.** and **imp.** indic. προκαλίζεται Opp. Hal. 2, 325. 329; **imper.** προκαλίζεο Od. 18, 20: **imp.** προκαλίζετο Il. 3, 19. 5, 807. Od. 8, 228.

Καλινδέομαι *To roll about, spend one's time*, -δεῖται Aristot. H. An. 9, 7, 2; -ούμενος Xen. An. 5, 2, 31; Isocr. 15, 30; Dem. 19, 199, ἐγ- Xen. Conv. 8, 32 (Vulg. Saupp.); -εῖσθαι Arr. Ven. 18, 2: **imp.** ἐκαλινδέετο Her. 3, 52, -εῖτο Xen. Cyr. 1, 4, 5, -οῦντο Thuc. 2, 52: **fut. m.** -ήσομαι?: **aor. pass.** late καλινδηθείς Synes. Epist. 32 (Herch.). This verb occurs in prose only, see κυλίνδω. Thuc. and Dem. have καλινδ- not κυλ-, likewise Her. but κατακυλισθῇ (-κυλίω) 5, 16, Isocr. usu. καλινδ-, but κυλ- 5, 81 (Ms. U. Bekk. B. Saupp.), and Xen. κυλινδ-, but καλινδ- An. 5, 2, 31, ἐκαλινδ- Cyr. 1, 4, 5, Pl. always κυλινδ-, with *v. r.* καλ- Theaet. 172. Phaed. 81 (Steph.).

Κᾰλύπτω *To hide*, Il. 17, 243; Hipponax 52; Aesch. Pr. 220; Soph. Ant. 1254; rare in prose, Xen. Eq. 12, 5; -τειν Lycurg. 89: **imp.** κάλυπτεν Il. 24, 20, ἐκαλ- Sapph. 19, περι- Xen. Cyr. 7, 3, 14: **fut.** καλύψω Il. 21, 321; Aesch. Sept. 1040; Soph. Aj. 916; Com. Fr. (Phil.) 4, 67: **aor.** ἐκάλυψα Il. 20, 444; Simon. C. 168; Aesch. Pers. 646; Eur. Supp. 766; Her. 2, 47, περι- Pl. Tim. 34, κάλ- Il. 23, 693; Hes. Op. 156, 'καλ- Eur. Bac. 12; -ύψῃ Il. 12, 281; -ύψαιμι Pind. N. 8, 38: (perf. late ἀπο-κεκάλυφα Origen vol. 3, p. 561): **p. p.** κεκάλυμμαι, -υμμένος Il. 16, 360; Pind. Ol. 5, 16; Xen. Cyr. 5, 1, 4, ἐγ- Andoc. 1, 17, ἐπι-κεκάλυπται Pl. Crat. 395: **plp.** κεκάλυπτο Il. 21, 549, ἐν-εκεκ- Pl. Phaed. 118: **aor.** ἐκαλύφθην, καλύφθ- Anth. 14, 53; -υφθείς Od. 4, 402; -υφθῆναι Eur. Supp. 531: **fut.** καλυφθήσομαι late in *simple*, Paus. 8, 11, 6; Aristid. 13, 130 (D.); Galen 3, 695, δια- Dem. 11, 13: **3 fut.** (κεκαλύψομαι?). **Mid.** καλύπτομαι *cover oneself, one's own*, Ar. Nub. 740: **fut.** καλύψομαι, ἐγ- Ael. H. A. 7, 12, συγ- Aristid. 45, 59: **aor.** ἐκαλυψάμην Hom. H. Ven. 183; Anth. App. Epigr. 127, καλυψ- Il. 14, 184; -άμενος Il. 3, 141. Od. 8, 92; Hes. Op. 198; Tyrt. 11, 24; rare in prose, Hippocr. 8, 322 (Mss. Lit.); and very late, Orig. Ref. Haer. p. 299 (Miller), but κατα- Her. 6, 67, ἐν- Aeschin. 2, 111; Pl. Phaed. 117; Isocr. 17, 18; Luc. D. Deor. 17, 1. **Vb.** καλυπτός Ar. Thesm. 890. συγ-καλυπτέος Aesch. Pr. 523; Geop. 16, 9. The *simple* form in **act.** is rare in prose, poetic in **mid.**; the comp. frequent in prose, ἀμφικαλύπτω however is Poet. chiefly Epic.

Κάμνω *To labour, be weary, sick*, Il. 19, 170; Eur. Andr. 816; Ar. Nub. 707; Hippocr. 6, 510; Xen. An. 3, 4, 47; subj. -νω Pl. Rep. 489; κάμνε Pind. P. 1, 90; -νων Her. 1, 197; Thuc. 2, 51; Isae. 8, 8; -νειν Aesch. Eum. 908; Thuc. 2, 41: **imp.** ἔκαμν- Il. 16, 106; Eur. Hel. 771; Her. 1, 118; Andoc. 1, 64; Dem. 50, 60, ἐξ- Thuc. 2, 51, κάμν- Il. 5, 797: **fut.** καμῶ doubtful (Hesych. has καμῶ, ἐργάσομαι, and καμεῖ Soph. Tr. 1215, *may* be 3 sing., usu. called 2 sing. of **mid.**) καμοῦμαι, -εῖ, -εῖται Il. 2, 389; Aesch. Eum. 881; Pl. Leg. 921, uncontr. -έεσθαι Ap. Rh. 3, 580: **p.** intrans. κέκμηκα Il. 6, 262; (Pl.) Eryx. 392, Dor. -ᾱκα Theocr. 1, 17 (Mein. Ahr.): **plp.** ἐκεκμήκεσαν Thuc. 3, 98; part. κεκμηκώς Soph. Fr. 268 (D.); Aesch. Supp. 158; Thuc. 6, 34; Pl. Leg. 927, Epic κεκμηώς Il. 23, 232, -ῶτι 6, 261, -ῶτα Od. 13, 282, -ηότα Ap. Rh. 3, 234, pl. -ηῶτες 3, 1341 &c. and κεκμηότας Il. 11, 802, -ηῶτας Thuc. 3, 59 (Vulg. Bekk. Krüg. Stahl), -ηκότας (2 Mss. Popp. Dind.) approved by Buttm. and Krüg.: **2 aor.**

ἔκᾰμον Il. 4, 244; Ar. Ach. 860; Her. 3, 16; Xen. Hell. 3, 3, 1. 5, 3, 19; Herodn. 3, 6, 3, κάμον Il. 8, 195. Od. 23, 189; Pind. P. 1, 78; subj. κάμω, -ῃς, -ῃ Il. 1, 168; Com. Fr. (Eup.) 2, 428; Her. 3, 99; Xen. Conv. 8, 18; Pl. Gorg. 470, Epic -ῃσι Il. 17, 658. Od. 14, 65, redupl. κεκάμω Il. 1, 168. 7, 5. 17, 658 (Vulg. Wolf, Spitzn. &c.), κε κάμω (Bekk. Dind. La Roche with Aristarch., thus doing entirely away with the reduplicated form); opt. κάμοιμι Il. 8, 22; Pind. Ol. 8, 29; Eur. Bac. 187; Ar. Lys. 541; Pl. Rep. 408; καμεῖν Aesch. Ag. 482, -έειν Ap. Rh. 1, 19; καμών Il. 23, 72; Pind. Ol. 2, 8; Aesch. Sept. 210; Soph. El. 532; Eur. H. F. 259; Andoc. 1, 120: **2 aor. mid.** Epic ἐκᾰμόμην *spend toil on, gain by*, Od. 9, 130; Ap. Rh. 2, 718, καμ- Il. 18, 341; Ap. Rh. 4, 1321. **Vb.** ἀπο-κμητέον Pl. Rep. 445.

Κάμπτω *To bend*, Ar. Thesm. 53; Xen. Eq. 1, 6; -των Aesch. Pr. 32; Soph. El. 744; Ar. Ach. 96; Her. 7, 58; Xen. Cyr. 7, 1, 6; -τειν Eur. Fr. 45 (D.); Xen. Eq. 7, 15: **imp.** ἔκαμπτον Eur. Bac. 1069; Com. Fr. (Cratin.) 2, 217; Plut. Mor. 496; D. Laert. 6, 48: **fut.** κάμψω, -ειν Il. 7, 118. 19, 72 (Epic -έμεν Bekk.); Soph. O. C. 91 (Mss. Elms. Dind. &c. -τειν Mss. Reis. Herm.), ξυγ-κάμψει Hippocr. 3, 424, ἀνα- Com. Fr. (Antiph.) 3, 6; Aristot. Meteor. 4, 9, 8, κατα- ibid.: **aor.** ἔκαμψα Od. 5, 453; Pind. P. 2, 51; Soph. O. C. 85; Com. Fr. (Cratet.) 2, 248, κατ- Eur. Tr. 1252; Pl. Tim. 36, συν- Phaed. 60; subj. -ψω Eur. Hec. 1079, -ψῃ Il. 4, 486; opt. κάμψαιμι Eur. Hipp. 87, -ειε Aesch. Pr. 396; Ar. Nub. 970; -ψον Soph. O. C. 19; inf. κάμψαι Eur. Supp. 748; Xen. Conv. 4, 6; κάμψας Ar. Nub. 178; Her. 4, 43: (**p.** κέκαμφα?): **p. p.** κέκαμμαι, -μψαι, -μπται Aristot. Probl. 15, 2; Nicol. Rhet. 12, 3; inf. κεκάμφθαι Hippocr. 4, 280 (Lit.); κεκαμμένος Aristot. Metaph. 4, 6, 11. 14, ἐπι- Hippocr. 1, 91 (K.), συγ- Xen. Eq. 7, 2: **aor.** ἐκάμφθην Pl. Menex. 244; inf. -φθῆναι Thuc. 3, 58; -φθείς Aesch. Pr. 513; Pl. Leg. 945: **fut.** late καμφθήσομαι Aristid. 13, 140; Dio Chrys. 77, 33; Galen 3, 147. 4, 387, ὑπο- Geop. 12, 19. **Mid.** κάμπτομαι *bend oneself* &c. κάμπτει Eur. I. T. 815 (Mss. Vulg. but act. κάμπτεις Blomf. Herm. Monk, Dind. Kirchh.): but aor. late κάμψηται Epist. Barn. p. 135 (Tisch.) **Vb.** καμπτός Pl. Tim. 44. See γνάμπτω.

Καναχίζω *To sound, ring*, Epic and only imp. κανάχιζε Il. 12, 36; Hes. Sc. 373; Q. Sm. 8, 55. (ᾰᾰ) The collat. κᾰνᾰχέω is Epic and Comic, -ουσι Com. Fr. (Cratin.) 2, 119; -ῶν 2, 162: **fut.** (-ήσω): **aor.** κανάχησε Od. 19, 469; Ap. Rh. 4, 907; Q. Sm. 3, 315.

Καπύω (ᾰῠ) *To breathe*, Epic and only **aor.** ἐκάπυσσα in tmesi Il. 22, 467, κάπ- Q. Sm. 6, 523.

Καρκαίρω *To quake*, Epic and only **imp.** κάρκαιρε Il. 20, 157.

Καρπόω (καρπός) *To produce fruit*, ἐκάρπωσα Aesch. Pers. 281; and late V. T. Deut. 26, 14. Lev. 2, 11. **Mid.** *to reap fruit*, -οῦμαι Thuc. 2, 38; Isae. 10, 19; Dem. 22, 67. 51, 13: **imp.** -ούμην Eur. Andr. 935; Her. 2, 168; Pl. Critia 118: **fut.** -ώσομαι Aesch. Pr. 851; Isocr. 4, 166: **aor.** -ωσάμην Pl. Conv. 187; Isae. 5, 35; Dem. 6, 21: with **p. p.** as **mid.** κεκάρπωμαι Xen. Cyr. 8, 7, 6; Dem. 27, 47. 29, 34.

Καρτύνω *To strengthen*, Epic for κρατύνω, usually confined to **aor. mid.** ἐκαρτύναντο Il. 11, 215. 12, 415; Theocr. 22, 80; Ap. Rh. 1, 510; once in prose D. Laert. (Thrasibul.) 1, 7, 9. **Act.** rare, **pres.** -ύνειν Pind. Ol. 13, 95: rare also **aor.** and late, καρτῦνας Stob. (Phanocl.) 64, 14; Ap. Rh. 2, 332; Opp. Hal. 2, 328.

Καταβρόχω, see βρόχω.

Καταγλωττίζω *To kiss wantonly, speak against*, **imp.** κατεγλώτ- Ar. Ach. 380: (**fut.** -ίσω, -ιῶ): **p. p.** κατεγλωττισμένος without redupl. Ar. Thesm. 131.

Κατάγνῡμι *To break*, Thuc. 4, 11; Pl. Phaedr. 265 (Soph. Fr. 147 (D.); Ar. Pax 703), and καταγνῡ́ω Hippocr. 7, 530; Xen. Oec. 6, 5; Com. Fr. (Eub.) 3, 254: **fut.** κατάξω Com. Fr. (Eup.) 2, 559: **aor.** κατέαξα Il. 13, 257; Ar. Vesp. 1435; Thuc. 3, 89; Xen. An. 4, 2, 20; Pl. Crat. 389, Ion. κατῆξα Hippocr. 5, 224 (Lit.); subj. κατάξῃ Ar. Ach. 932; Pl. Phaed. 86, *v. r.* -εάξῃ; imper. κάταξον Ar. Fr. 488; inf. κατᾶξαι Eur. Supp. 508; Com. Fr. (Phryn.) 2, 603; part. κατάξας Lys. 3, 42 (Dobr. Cobet, Scheibe), but κατεάξας (Mss. Bekk. B. Saupp.); Luc. Alex. 14: **p.** late κατεάγηκε if correct, Cinnam. p. 190: **p. p.** late κατέαγμαι Luc. Tim. 10; Paus. 8, 46, 5; Artemid. Onir. 5, 32: **1 aor.** late κατεάχθην V. T. Jer. 31, 25; -αχθείς Dio Chrys. 11, 339; but -αχθῆναι Aristot. Part. An. 1, 1, 16: **2 aor.** κατεᾱ́γην Ar. Vesp. 1428; Andoc. 1, 61; Lys. 3, 14; subj. καταγῇ Pl. Crat. 389; Hippocr. 4, 158 (Lit.), and if correct -εαγῇ 4, 172. 220, -ηγῇ 3, 428 (Lit. 1, 500 Erm.); opt. καταγείη Ar. Ach. 943, -εαγείη Hippocr. 4, 128 (Ms. H. Lit. -αγείη Vulg. Erm.); part. καταγείς Lys. 3, 40; Anth. Plan. 187; Hippocr. 4, 148. 154, sometimes κατεαγείς 4, 154. 172. 282. 346, and -ηγείς 4, 324 (Lit. καταγ- always Ermerins): **2 p.** κατέᾱγα *am broken*, Ar. Ach. 1180, Ion. κατέηγα Hippocr. 3, 428. 506, rare κάτηγα if correct, Hippocr. 3, 75 (Kühn); part. -ηγώς Phoen. Coloph. 6, 3, 4 (Schneidw.), -εᾱγώς Ar. Plut. 546; Pl. Gorg. 524, Ion. -εηγώς Her. 7, 224; Hippocr. 4, 130. 200. 278. 282 (Mss. Lit., but -εαγυῖα 3, 426. 4, 158); -εαγέναι Pl. Gorg. 469. In **2 aor.** ᾰ usu. in Epic, Anth. Pl. 187; Il. 17, 607. 3, 367, but ᾱ in arsis, Il. 11, 559; and

Attic, Ar. Ach. 944. Fr. 502 (D.): long in 2 perf.—ἄγνυμι had been digammated, hence aor. κατϜάξας, καϜϜάξ- (so κάππεσον &c.) softened κανάξαις 2 sing. opt. aor. for κατάξαις Hes. Op. 668. 693. This verb both in Mss. and edit. has often those forms augmented which usually have no augment: κατεάξαντες Lys. 3, 42 (all the Mss.); Ael. H. A. 10, 10, κατάξ- (Herch.); -εαγείς Hippocr. quoted; Lys. 3, 40 (some Mss.); and late, even fut. κατεάξει N.T. Matth. 12, 20: κατεάγνῦμαι Hippocr. 3, 244 (Kühn), κατάγν- Lit. 4, 278 rightly (with Chart.), wrongly however κατήγνυται 3, 556 (Mss. Lit.), and -ηγνύμενος 3, 506. 556, but κατάγνυται 3, 556. 558, ἀπ- 3, 558; and a still more curious form κατεάγοιντο Polyaen. 8, 7, 2, κατεάγν- (Woelffl. κατάγν- Ms. P.) For ἐξεάγεῖσα Ap. Rh. 4, 1686, Merkel reads ἐξᾶγ- with Guelph.

Καταδουλόω *To enslave*, act. reg. but rare, Thuc. 3, 70; Plut. Mor. 828: fut. -ώσω V. T. Jer. 15, 14: aor. -εδούλωσα Isocr. 9, 21; -λῶσαι Her. 6, 109: p. -λωκα C. Fr. (Menand.) 4, 169: p. p. καταδεδούλωμαι Pl. Conv. 219; Isocr. 4, 169; but mid. Eur. I. A. 1269; Pl. Rep. 351: so aor. -ωσάμην Lys. 12, 39; Isocr. 4, 67; Pl. Menex. 245: fut. -ώσομαι Lys. 34, 2. 8: pres. -δουλοῦμαι Her. 7, 51; Thuc. 3, 63; Pl. Gorg. 483; Isocr. 5, 53; Dem. 18, 72.

Καταείνυον, see ἕννυμι.

Καταζαίνω, see ἀζάνω.

Καταθνήσκω *To die*, is entirely Poet., -θνήσκει Orph. Lith. 407; -θνήσκων Il. 22, 355; -θνήσκειν Emped. 47 (Stein): fut. (always syncop.) κατθανοῦμαι Eur. Med. 1386. H. F. 210: aor. (always syncop.) κάτθανε Il. 21, 107; Ap. Rh. 3, 796; Callim. Epigr. 21; Bion 1, 31; Mosch. 3, 34; in Attic Aesch. Ag. 1553 (chor.); subj. κατθάνω Eur. Or. 777; κατθάνοι Alc. 143; -θανεῖν Aesch. Ag. 1364; Soph. Ant. 555; Eur. Andr. 1069; Ar. Ran. 1477; -θανών Epicharm. 146; Aesch. Ag. 873; Soph. Ant. 515; Eur. Or. 581: p. κατατέθνηκα Il. 15, 664; part. Epic -τεθνηώς Il. 22, 164. Od. 11, 84. We have never seen this verb in prose. The Attic Poets use fut. and aor. only: the Epics pres. and perf.

Καταιτιάομαι, see αἰτι-.

Καταιδέω, see αἰδέομαι.

Κατακαίνω, see καίνω.

Κατακτείνω, see κτείνω.

Καταλέω, see ἀλέω.

Καταλείπω, see λείπω.

Καταλύω, see λύω.

Καταναλίσκω *To expend*, imp. κατ-ανάλισκον Isocr. 1, 18, in some tenses augments occasionally the initial vowel of ἀναλ- as if a *simple:* aor. κατ-ηνάλωσα Isocr. 9, 60: aor. pass. κατ-ηναλώθην Hippocr. 9, 178. 180 (Lit.): p. p. κατ-ηνάλωμαι Isocr. 3, 31. See ἀναλίσκω.

Κατανέμω, see νέμω.

Κατανεύω, see νεύω.

Κατανοέω, see νοέω.

Καταράομαι, see ἀρά-.

Καταρρωδέω, see ἀρρωδέω.

Καταστρέφω, see στρέφω.

Καταφρονέω *To despise*, Her. 4, 134; Xen. Mem. 3, 12, 3; Isocr. 13, 8; Pl. Conv. 216 &c.; -νεῖν Thuc. 6, 34; -ῶν 2, 11: imp. κατ-εφρ- Xen. Hell. 4, 5, 12; Dem. 41, 2: fut. -ήσω Isocr. 11, 27: aor. -εφρόνησα Lys. 9, 17; Pl. Lach. 200; Aeschin. 1, 114; -ήσας Thuc. 6, 11: p. -πεφρόνηκα Andoc. 4, 16; Lys. 12, 84; Isocr. 5, 100. 12, 261: p. p. πεφρόνημαι Dem. 10, 6; -ημένος Isocr. 5, 137: aor. -εφρονήθην Isocr. 6, 108; Pl. Euthyd. 273: fut. p. -ηθήσομαι Isocr. 6, 95; Aeschin. 1, 176: and fut. m. as pass. -φρονήσομαι Pl. Hipp. Maj. 281. Vb. -φρονητέον Athen. 14, 20; Aristid. 45, 69. In Ion. this verb often means simply *to direct the mind to*, without the accessory notion of *despising*, Her. 1, 59. 66 &c.; Hippocr. 6, 390 (Lit.).

Καταχράω *To be sufficient, serve for*, Ion. and impers. in act. καταχρᾷ Her. 1, 164: imp. κατέχρα Her. 7, 70: fut. καταχρήσει 4, 118.

Καταψηφίζω, see ψηφίζω.

Κατενήνοθε, see (ἐνέθω).

Κατηπιάω, see ἠπιάω.

Κατισχναίνω, see ἰσχναίνω.

Κατορθόω *To put down straight, erect*, Eur. Hel. 1067; Thuc. 7, 47 &c. is reg. and introduced here simply because we think the mid. form has been missed by all our Lexicons: fut. κατορθώσεται may be pass. Hippocr. 3, 446 (Lit.): aor. -ορθώσηται 4, 156; -ωσάμενος 3, 436. 482; -ώσασθαι 3, 474: pres. -ορθοῦσθαι 4, 188, seems mid. see 8, 144.

Καττύω, and -σσύω (ῡ) *To stitch, patch*, Pl. Euthyd. 294; Athen. (Nicand.) 9, 9: fut. -ύσειν Alciphr. 3, 58: p. p. late κεκαττῡμένα Clem. Alex. 998, 43, ἐγ-κεκάττῡται Com. Fr. (Alex.) 3, 423. Mid. καττύομαι as act. Com. Fr. (Pher.) 2, 356: imp. παρ-εκαττύετο Ar. Plut. 663.

Καυάξαις, see κατάγνυμι.

Καυχάομαι *To exult*, -ῶμαι Theocr. 5, 77 (Ahr.), Ion. -έομαι (Vulg. Fritz. Ziegl.), -χᾷ Lycurg. Fr. 14, late -ᾶσαι N. T. Rom. 2, 17. 1 Cor. 4, 7; -ᾶσθαι Pind. Ol. 9, 38; Com. Fr. (Cratin.) 2, 72; -ώμενος (Phil.) 4, 40: imp. ἐκαυχώμην, ἐξ- Eur. Bacc. 31, ἐν- Aristot. de Plant. prol. 7: fut. καυχήσομαι, 2 sing. Ion. -ήσεαι

Her. 7, 39, -ήσεται Com. Fr. (Epicr.) 3, 369, -ήσεσθε Pseud.-Callisth. 2, 20: aor. ἐκαυχήσατο Athen. 14, 23; Aristot. Pol. 5, 10, 16; -ήσασθαι Com. Fr. (Eup.) 2, 473; Aristot. Polit. 5, 10, 16; (Aeschin.) Epist. 4, 5; Dio. Hal. 8, 30; subj. καυχήσῃ Babr. 96: p. late κεκαύχημαι N. T. 2 Cor. 7, 14. Scarcely in good Attic prose. The form καυχᾶσαι, though late, may represent early usage.

(Καφέω or κάπω) *To pant*, Epic part. 2 perf. κεκᾰφηώς Il. 5, 698; Anth. 9, 653; Opp. Hal. 3, 113.—Hesych. has κέκηφε, τέθνηκε.

Κᾰχάζω, see καγχάζω.

Καχλάζω and καγχλ-? *To dash, swell*, Aesch. Sept. 115 (chor.); late prose, Arr. An. 6, 4, 4; Diod. Sic. 3, 44; inf. -άζειν Arr. An. 5, 20; part. -άζων Theocr. 6, 12, fem. Dor. -άζοισαν Pind. Ol. 7, 2: imp. ἐκάχλαζον late, Philostr. 116, iter καχλάζεσκεν, ἐπι- Ap. Rh. 4, 944: aor. ἐκάχλασε, ἀν- Opp. Cyn. 1, 275. Only pres. and imp. in *simple*, and only in Poet. and late prose.

Κάω, see καίω.

Κεάζω *To split* (κέω, κείω), chiefly Epic, fut. κεάσσω Orph. Arg. 852: aor. κέᾰσα Od. 14, 418. 20, 161, κέασσ- Il. 16, 347, ἐκέασσ- Od. 5, 132. 7, 250; κεάσαιμι Od. 12, 388; inf. κεάσσαι 15, 322; Ap. Rh. 4, 392; Callim. Fr. 289; κεάσας Nic. Ther. 644, -άσσας 709 (κέδασσ- Otto Schneid.); Ap. Rh. 3, 378: p. p. κεκεασμένος Od. 18, 309: aor. κεάσθη Il. 16, 412, ἐκεάσ- Ap. Rh. 2, 104 (Merkel).

Κεδάννῡμι *To scatter* (κεδάω, -άζω), Epic=σκεδ- (part. pass. κεδαννύμενος Anth. 5, 276): aor. ἐκέδασσα Il. 17, 285; Opp. Hal. 1, 412; Ap. Rh. 3, 1360. 2, 1189, κέδασσα (Well.); inf. κεδάσσαι 2, 50: plp. pass. κεκέδαστο Ap. Rh. 2, 1112: aor. κεδάσθη Orph. Arg. 559, 3 pl. Epic ἐκέδασθεν Il. 15, 657 (Wolf, Bekk. Dind.); Ap. Rh. 2, 135 (Merk.), κέδασθ- (Vulg.); κεδασθείς Il. 15, 328.—κεδόωνται or σκεδ- 3 pl. pres. pass. Epic for κεδῶνται (κεδάονται) Ap. Rh. 4, 500, κεδᾶται Hesych. A collat. form κεδαίομαι, -αίῃ occurs Nic. Alex. 458; -όμενος Ap. Rh. 2, 626.

Κεῖμαι *To lie*, Od. 19, 516. Hom. Epigr. 3; Simon. C. 169; Pind. N. 7, 35. Fr. 222; Soph. Tr. 985; Eur. Hec. 28, Ion. (κέομαι), κεῖσαι Il. 19, 319; Aesch. Ch. 724; Soph. O. C. 1510; Eur. Fr. 908, Epic κεῖαι, κατά- Hom. H. Merc. 254, κεῖται Il. 6, 47; Hes. Th. 795; Aesch. Pers. 325; Eur. Med. 24; Ar. Ach. 584; Antiph. 5, 9; Thuc. 1, 36; Her. 1, 9 (Gaisf. Bekk. κέεται Dind. Stein), and Ion. κέεται Her. 4, 62; Hippocr. 2, 54 (Lit.), 3 dual κεῖσθον Eur. Phoen. 1698, κείμεθα Simon. C. 92; Soph. O. C. 248; Eur. Phoen. 1639; Thuc. 5, 108, κεῖσθε rare, πρό-κεισθε Eur. Tr. 1179, κεῖνται Aesch. Supp. 242; Antiph. 5, 14. 6, 2; Thuc. 2, 102; Pl. Menex. 242, Ion. κείαται Mimnerm. 11, 6 (Bergk); Ap. Rh. 4, 481, κατα- Il. 24, 527, κέαται Il. 11, 659; Archil. 170; Hippocr. 1,

248 (Erm.), ἀνα- Her. 1, 14, δια- 1, 105, ἐπι- 6, 58 &c. and κέονται Il. 22, 510. Od. 16, 232; Hippocr. 2, 22. 24 (Lit.); subj. rare (κέωμαι, -έῃ), κέηται Xen. Oec. 8, 19; Lycurg. 113; Pl. Soph. 257, κατα- Hippocr. 7, 206, συγ- Aristot. Metaph. 8, 10, 4, contr. κῆται only in Epic Il. 19, 32. and *now* 24, 554. Od. 2, 102. 19, 147 (Wolf, Bekk. Spitzn. Dind. La R. κεῖται Mss. Vulg. Buttm. and defended by Ahrens as an Epic subj. contr. for κείεται), δια-κέησθε Isocr. 15, 259, προσ-κέωνται Hippocr. 3, 438, κατα- Luc. V. Auct. 15; opt. κεοίμην, -οιτο Her. 1, 67; Isae. 6, 32; Pl. Rep. 477, κατα- Hippocr. 4, 122, ἐκ- Dem. 21, 103, προσ-κέοιντο Thuc. 4, 33; imper. κεῖσο Il. 21, 122, κείσθω Od. 15, 128; Soph. El. 362; Her. 2, 171; Pl. Leg. 926; κεῖσθαι Il. 8, 126; Eur. Hipp. 926; Her. 4, 22; Antiph. 5, 14; Pl. Rep. 534, but κέεσθαι Her. 2, 2; Hippocr. 2, 24. 118 (Lit.); κείμενος Il. 14, 10; Soph. Ant. 1174; Ar. Ran. 761; Her. 9, 100; Antiph. 5, 96; Thuc. 7, 85: imp. ἐκείμην &c. Il. 15, 388; Aesch. Ch. 964; Soph. El. 1134; Her. 7, 208; Thuc. 7, 4; Pl. Euthyd. 303, κείμην Od. 10, 54, Dor. κείμαν Theocr. 2, 86, ἐκει- Anth. 12, 140, κεῖσο Od. 24, 40, κεῖτο Il. 10, 77; Pind. P. 9, 83, ἔκειτο Il. 7, 156; Hes. Sc. 172; Thuc. 7, 4; Pl. Rep. 425, -έετο Her. 1, 196, 3 dual -είσθην Lys. 13, 37, pl. ἔκειντο Thuc. 2, 52, κεῖντο Il. 21, 426, Ion. ἐκέατο Her. 1, 167, κέατο Il. 13, 763; Hes. Sc. 241, Epic ἐκείατο Ap. Rh. 4, 1295, κείατο Il. 11, 162; Hes. Sc. 175, 3 sing. iter. κέσκετο Od. 21, 41, augm. παρεκέσκ- Od. 14, 521: fut. κείσομαι Il. 18, 121. Od. 22, 319; Aesch. Ch. 895; Soph. El. 245; Ar. Nub. 126; Pl. Rep. 451, Dor. κεισεῦμαι Theocr. 3, 53, 2 sing. Ion. κείσεαι Il. 18, 338, -σονται 22, 71: aor. (ἐκεισάμην), subj. κείσηται if correct, Hippocr. 3, 438 (Bosq. Lit. κείσεται Vulg.)—2 sing. pres. κεῖαι, κατάκειαι for -εισαι, Hom. H. 3, 254, but doubtful. The forms κεῖται, διάκειμαι, &c. occur sometimes as subj. for κέηται, δια-κέωμαι &c. In late recensions however most of them have been altered to the usual form; διάκειμαι Pl. Phaed. 84, may be indicative, see Thuc. 3, 53 &c. and for διάκεισθε Isocr. 15, 259 (Vulg.), Bekker, B. Saupp., and Benseler edit διακέησθε. κέαται, ἀνα-, ἐπι-, παρα- &c. 3 sing. occurs in the older editions of (Luc.) D. Syr. 6, 8. 27. 29 &c. but is certainly a false reading for κέεται, see Jacobitz and Dind. Even in Her. some of the Mss. occasionally offer κέαται sing. as 4, 62 (M. P.), κέεται (F. K. A.), ἀνακέαται 3, 31 (b. c. d. Gaisf.), -έεται (M. F. a. Bekk. Dind. Dietsch).

Κεινόω, see κενόω.

Κείρω *To shear* (Aeol. κέρρω), Il. 11, 560; Com. Fr. (Cratin.) 2, 38; Her. 4, 191; Theophr. C. P. 3, 23, 3, Dor. 3 pl. κείροντι Bion 1, 22 (Mein.); imper. κείρετε Od. 2, 143; κείρων Il. 21, 204;

Her. 9, 24; rare in Attic prose Thuc. 1, 64; κείρειν Pl. Rep. 470: imp. ἔκειρον Od. 11, 578; Soph. Aj. 55; Her. 6, 75. 99. 7, 131: fut. κερῶ Pl. Rep. 471; Babr. 51, Epic κερέω Il. 23, 146, and κέρσω, -οι Mosch. 2, 32 (Vulg. ἀμέργοι *now* Mein. Herm. Ahr.): aor. ἔκειρα Eur. Tr. 1173, κατ- Od. 23, 356, ἀπ- Anacr. 49; imper. κείρατε Pseud.-Callisth. 2, 39; κείρας Soph. Tr. 1196; Eur. Hel. 1124; Her. 5, 63; κεῖραι Pind. P. 9, 37, Epic ἔκερσα Ap. Rh. 2, 826, in tmesi Il. 13, 546, κέρσε Hes. Sc. 419, in tmesi Il. 10, 456; -σῃ Q. Sm. 11, 214; -σειε Aesch. Supp. 665 (chor.); κέρσας Il. 24, 450: p. κέκαρκα, περι- Luc. Conv. 32: plp. ἐκεκάρκει, ἀπ- Tox. 51: p. p. κέκαρμαι Theocr. 14, 46; Luc. Epigr. 34 (Jacob.), κέκαρσαι in tmesi Eur. Hec. 910; -μένος Archil. 36 (Bergk); Eur. Or. 458; Com. Fr. (Pher.) 2, 300; Ar. Ach. 849; Xen. Hell. 1, 7, 8; κεκάρθαι Her. 2, 36. 3, 8: plp. ἐκεκάρμην Luc. Lex. 5: 1 aor. ἐκέρθην, κερθείς Poet. Pind. P. 4, 82, καρθ- (Ms. C.): 2 aor. ἐκάρην, ἀμφ- Anth. 9, 56; subj. in *simple* καρῇ Her. 4, 127; καρείς Plut. Lys. 1; καρῆναι Luc. Soloec. 6. Mid. κείρομαι *to cut one's own hair*, Eur. Phoen. 322; Her. 3, 8. 4, 175: -όμενος Il. 23, 136: imp. κείροντο Od. 24, 46: fut. κεροῦμαι Eur. Tr. 1183; Callim. Apoll. 14, ἀπο- Pl. Phaed. 89: aor. ἐκειράμην Aesch. Ch. 189; Eur. Elec. 546; Aeschin. 3, 211, κειρ- Mosch. 3, 90 (Herm. Mein.), ἀπ-εκειρ- Il. 23, 141; Her. 6, 21; Isae. 4, 7; κείραιτο Aesch. Ch. 172; imper. κείρασθε Eur. H. F. 1390; κείρασθαι Il. 23, 46; -άμενος Bion 1, 81, Epic ἐκερσάμην, ἐκέρσω Callim. Fr. 311: -σάμενος Aesch. Pers. 952 (chor.) Vb. καρτός late Geop. 2, 6, 32. ἀπο-καρτέον Com. Fr. (Eup.) 2, 573. Neither of the aorists pass. seems to be of Attic usage.

Κείω *To wish to lie down, rest*, Od. 19, 340; κείουσι Arat. 1009; subj. κείομεν for -ωμεν, κατα- Od. 18, 419; imper. κείετε, κατα- 7, 188; and κέω in part. κέων Od. 7, 342, κείοντες Il. 14, 340, -ουσα Od. 23, 292; inf. κειέμεν Od. 8, 315. A desiderative to κεῖμαι *lie*; and to be distinguished from κείω *to split*, which has only pt. κείων Od. 14, 425.

Κεκᾰδήσω, Κέκᾰδον, see χάζω.

Κέκλομαι *To order*, Poet. and late in pres. Ap. Rh. 1, 716. 2, 693; Orph. Lith. 177; Opp. Hal. 3, 311: imp. or 2 aor. ἐκεκλόμην Hes. Sc. 341, and κεκλόμην Il. 16, 657: Ap. Rh. 4, 230; Pind. I. 6, 53 *called;* Dor. opt. κεκλοίμαν Aesch. Supp. 591 (chor.); κεκλόμενος Soph. O. R. 159 (chor.); but pass. Maneth. 2, 251. 3, 319. Hesych. has act. κέκλει, κελεύει. See κέλομαι.

Κελᾰδέω *To shout, sing*, Poet. Sapph. 4 (Vulg.); Pratin. 1, 3 (Bergk); Com. Fr. (Theop.) 2, 808; Eur. I. T. 1093 (chor.), -αδοῦσι (Luc.) Philop. 3, Dor. -ᾰδέοντι Pind. P. 2, 15; κελαδῇ

Stesich. 33 (B.); -αδεῖν Eur. Tr. 121 (chor.); Pind. Ol. 1, 9, and κελᾰ́δω, -άδει Sapph. quoted (Ahr. Bergk); part. κελᾰ́δων Il. 21, 16; Ap. Rh. 1, 501; Ar. Nub. 284 (chor.): imp. ἐκελάδουν Eur. Phoen. 1102 (trimet.); late prose Charit. 6, 2, 4, κελάδ- Eur. Elec. 716 (chor.): fut. κελαδήσω Terpand. Fr. 5 (Bergk); Pind. Ol. 2, 3; Eur. H. F. 694 (chor.): and mid. κελαδήσομαι Pind. Ol. 10 (11), 79: aor. κελάδησα Il. 23, 869; Pind. N. 4, 16; Aesch. Cho. 610 (chor.); Eur. Hel. 371 (chor.); Theocr. 22, 99, in tmesi Il. 8, 542; subj. -ήσῃ Eur. Ion 93 (chor.); Theocr. 18, 57; κελαδῆσαι Pind. P. 1, 58. This verb is almost always Epic and Lyric.

Κελᾰρύζω *To flow with a noise, gurgle*, Epic Il. 21, 261: imp. κελᾰ́ρυζε Il. 11, 813. Od. 5, 323; Theocr. 7, 137: fut. mid. κελαρύξομαι Or. Sib. 3, 440, -ύσομαι Hesych.: aor. κελᾰ́ρυξε Pind. Fr. 182[d] (Schneid.). Occasionally in late prose (Luc.) Philoptr. 3: imp. ἐκελ- (Hippocr.) Epist. 9, 350 (Lit.).

Κελευτῐάω *To cheer on*, a frequentative from κελεύω, and only pres. part. Epic κελευτιόων for -τιῶν Il. 13, 125.

Κελεύω *To order*, Il. 4, 286; Pind. N. 4, 80; Aesch. Eum. 674; Soph. O. R. 226; Ar. Av. 561; Her. 7, 102; Antiph. 1, 21; Thuc. 1, 129; Epic subj. κελεύομεν Il. 23, 659: imp. ἐκέλ- Il. 4, 380; Ar. Ran. 34; Her. 7, 88; Antiph. 1, 10; Thuc. 1, 126; Andoc. 1, 22; Lys. 12, 12; Pl. Conv. 220, κέλ- Il. 23, 767, 'κελ- Ar. Vesp. 501: fut. κελεύσω Il. 4, 322; Ar. Eccl. 261; Thuc. 3, 44; Epic inf. κελευσέμεναι Od. 4, 274, called aor. by Fäsi: aor. ἐκέλευσα Il. 5, 823; Pind. Ol. 6, 32; Soph. Ph. 544; Ar. Eq. 1047; Her. 8, 90; Antiph. 6, 15; Thuc. 2, 67; Lys. 12, 10; Xen. An. 1, 5, 8, κέλ- Pind. Ol. 6, 70; Il. 20, 4 (see fut.); -εύσαι Aesch. Eum. 618; κέλευσον Od. 7, 163: p. κεκέλευκα Lys. 1, 34; Luc. Demon. 44: p. p. κεκέλευσμαι Xen. Cyr. 8, 3, 14; Luc. D. Deor. 20, 8. Sacr. 11: plp. ἐκεκέλευστο D. Cass. 78, 4, 3, παρα-κεκέλευστο Her. 8, 93 (Bekk. Gaisf. παρ-εκεκέλ- Dind. Abicht, Stein, with S. V.): aor. ἐκελεύσθην Soph. O. C. 738; Eur. I. T. 937. Heracl. 501; Her. 7, 9; Thuc. 7, 70; Xen. Cyr. 4, 5, 21. Oec. 17, 2; Dio. Hal. 1, 48; 4 Macc. 9, 11, ἀντ- Thuc. 1, 139, but ἐκελεύθην if correct, Dio. Hal. 1, 84 (Vulg. -σθην Kiessl.); 4 Macc. quoted (Gaisf.): fut. late κελευσθησόμενος Dio Cass. 68, 9. **Mid.** rare in *simple*, κελεύομαι, aor. ἐκελευσάμην Hippocr. 7, 490 (Lit.)—διακελεύομαι is Dep. Her. 1, 42; Dem. 17, 12: imp. δι-εκελ- Thuc. 8, 97: with fut. -εύσομαι Her. 1, 36: and aor. -εκελευσάμην 9, 5, and, in the *classic* period, παρακελ-; ἐγκελεύω again, is classic, and -εύομαι late; but ἐπικελεύω and mid. -εύομαι are both classic. **Vb.** παρα-κελευστός Thuc. 6, 13. δια-κελευστέον Pl. Leg. 361. The

perf. and **aor. pass.** seem, at least in classic Greek, to have always σ. In fact, we have seen -εύθην only twice, never κε-κέλευμαι, though the noun κέλευμα, παρα-κέλευμα have, in some authors, as good support as κέλευσμα &c. We therefore doubt the statement of Lobeck "κεκέλευμαι et κεκέλευσμαι parem fere auctoritatem habent."

Κέλλω *To bring*, or *come, to land—as a ship*, Poet. and only fut. κέλσω Aesch. Supp. 330; Opp. Hal. 3, 221, ἐπι- Ap. Rh. 2, 352. 382: and aor. ἔκελσα Od. 12, 5; Soph. Tr. 804; Eur. Rhes. 898; Opp. Hal. 2, 632; late prose Dio. Hal. 14, 3, εἰσ- Ar. Thesm. 877; subj. κέλσω Eur. Hec. 1057; inf. κέλσαι Od. 10, 511; Aesch. Supp. 16; Eur. Hipp. 140; κέλσας Od. 9, 149; Aesch. Pr. 184; Eur. Elec. 139. Prose authors use ὀκέλλω.

Κέλομαι *To order*, usu. Poet. Il. 15, 138; Simon. C. 37, 15; Pind. P. 4, 159; Aesch. Ag. 1119; Eur. Hipp. 1283, Epic 2 sing. κέλεαι Il. 24, 434; κελοίμην Il. 9, 517; imper. κελέσθω Od. 3, 425, -εσθε Il. 9, 171; -εσθαι Od. 10, 299: **imp.** κελόμην Il. 1, 386; Anth. 14, 34, 2 sing. ἐκέλευ Theocr. 3, 11, κέλετο Il. 15, 119, Dor. κέντο Alcm. 141 (Bergk), κέλοντο Hes. Th. 33; Pind. Fr. 2, but κελόμεσθα is **pass.** Or. Sib. 8, 500: **fut.** κελήσομαι Od. 10, 296: 1 **aor.** ἐκελησάμην Epicharm. Fr. 48, κελησ- Pind. Ol. 13, 80. I. 6, 37: **2 aor.** redupl. κέκλετο (for κεκελ-) Il. 16, 421, augm. ἐκέκλ- Il. 11, 285; Hes. Sc. 341; Orph. Arg. 360; κεκλοίμαν Aesch. Supp. 591 (chor.); κεκλόμενος Hes. Th. 686; Ap. Rh. 1, 311 (**pass.** Maneth. 2, 251); Soph. O. R. 159 (chor.), ἀνα- H. Hym. 19, 5, Dor. κεκλομένα, ἐπι- Aesch. Supp. 41 (chor.), the only instances, we think, of aor. in Trag. κέλεαι 2 sing. trisyll. Il. 1, 74. Od. 5, 98 &c. but dissyl. Il. 24, 434. Od. 4, 812. 10, 337 (Wolf, Bekk. Dind.) where used to stand κέλῃ. Subj. κέλωμαι, and part. κελόμενος we have not seen. The **2 aor.** seems confined to indic. and part.—This verb, though mostly poetic, especially Epic, occurs occasionally in, perhaps, Doric prose, Pittac. Diog. Laert. 1, 4, 10; Plut. Mor. (Ages.) 211; Luc. V. A. (Heracl.) 14. Hesych. has **aor. act.** ἐκέλησεν, ἐκέλευσεν.

Κενόω, Ion. κειν- *To empty*, Eur. Med. 959; Hippocr. 6, 572; Pl. Conv. 197: **fut.** κενώσω Eur. Ion 447, Ion. κειν- Nic. Ther. 56: **aor.** ἐκένωσα Eur. Rhes. 914; opt. κεινώσειας Nic. Alex. 140, κενώσαι Aesch. Supp. 660; -ώσας Pers. 718; Pl. Rep. 560; inf. -ῶσαι Hippocr. 6, 568: **p.** -ωκα App. Civ. 5, 67: **p. p.** κεκένωνται Hippocr. 6, 378; -ωμένος Her. 4, 123 (Mss. Bekk. Gaisf. Stein), κεκεινωμ- (Dind. Bred. Dietsch): **aor.** -ώθην Thuc. 2, 51: **fut. p.** late κενωθήσεται Aretae. 89 (ed. Oxon.); Galen 4, 709, ἐκ- 1, 195: and **fut. mid.** as **pass.** κεινώσομαι Emped. Fr. 111

(Stein), ἐκ- Galen 3, 533, but act. 3, 341. Dind. and Bred. write p. p. κεκειν- because adj. κεινός, not κενός, κενεός, is the Herodotean form.

Κεντέω *To prick, goad*, Pind. P. 1, 28; Soph. Ant. 1030; Ar. Vesp. 1113; Pl. Gorg. 456: imp. ἐκεντ- Eur. Bac. 631: fut. -ήσω Soph. Aj. 1245: aor. ἐκέντησα Hippocr. 5, 234 (Lit.); Aristot. Hist. An. 5, 31, 2, Dor. κέντᾱσε (Theocr.) 19, 1; Epic inf. κένσαι (κέντω) Il. 23, 337: p. p. κεκέντημαι Hippocr. 3, 380 (K.): aor. ἐκεντήθην Aristot. de Spiritu 5, 7; Theophr. H. P. 9, 15, 3: fut. κεντηθήσομαι, συγ- Her. 6, 29: pres. κεντούμενος Thuc. 4, 47. Vb. κεστός Il. 14, 214. δια-κεντητέον Geop. 17, 19.

Κέομαι, see κεῖμαι.

Κερᾰΐζω *To attack* (κείρω), Il. 16, 752; Her. 1, 159; late Attic prose Ael. N. A. 6, 41; Parthen. 21; Epic inf. -ιζέμεν Od. 8, 516: imp. ἐκεράϊζον Her. 8, 91; Arr. An. 5, 17, 3, κερ- Il. 5, 557; Pind. P. 9, 21; Theocr. 25, 202: fut. (-ίσω), late -ίξω Or. Sib. 3, 466: aor. ἐκεράϊσα Her. 2, 115, and late κεράϊξα Nonn. 23, 21. Pass. κεραΐζομαι, -όμενος Il. 24, 245; rare in Attic Eur. Alc. 886 (chor.); Themist. 4, 57: imp. ἐκεραϊζ- Her. 8, 86.

Κεράννῡμι *To mix*, Pl. Tim. 41. Leg. 949; Com. Fr. (Apoll.) 4, 442, and -αννύω Com. Fr. (Alcae.) 2, 829. (Theoph.) 3, 627; Aristot. Meteor. 3, 2, 5; Hyperid. Fr. 72 (Blass); Plut. Mor. 451; Heliod. 10, 29, ἐγ- Com. Fr. (Eub.) 3, 248; subj. -ννύω, -ύωμεν Pl. Phil. 61: imp. ἐκεράννυν Luc. H. V. 1, 7, ἀν- Ar. Ran. 511: fut. late κεράσω Themist. 27, 340, κερῶ Hesych.: aor. ἐκέρᾰσα Hippocr. 1, 578 (Lit.), ἐν- Pl. Crat. 427, Poet. κέρασα Eur. Bac. 127 (chor.), Epic κέρασσα Od. 5, 93, ἐκέρ- Orph. Arg. 254; subj. κεράσσω Anacreont. 2, 4, κεράσῃ Com. Fr. (Antiph.) 3, 46; Pl. Soph. 262; -σειε Xenophanes 4 (B.); κέρασον Ar. Eccl. 1123; κεράσας Od. 10, 362; Com. Fr. (Ephipp.) 3, 329; Thuc. 6, 32; Pl. Phaedr. 265; inf. κεράσαι Com. Fr. (Eub.) 3, 245; Mosch. 3, 113; (Dem.) 21, 53 (Orac.), Ion. ἔκρησα rare in *simple*, κρήσας Hippocr. 7, 254 (Lit.); ἐπι-κρῆσαι Od. 7, 164: p. late, κεκέρᾰκα Niceph. Rhet. 3, 1; Eustath. 7, 3 (Herch.): p. p. κεκέρασμαι late, Opp. C. 3, 462; Anacreont. 16, 13 (Bergk); Aristot. Fr. 508; Dio. Hal. Comp. Verb. 24; Luc. D. Meretr. 4, 4; Polyaen. 8, 23, 1, classic κέκρᾱμαι Pind. P. 10, 41; Aesch. Pr. 116; Eur. Cycl. 557; Ar. Eq. 1187; Pl. Rep. 397; Aristot. Polit. 5, 8, 2; Dem. 24, 214, Ion. -ημαι Hippocr. 1, 600; -ημένος 2, 270 (Lit.); Her. 3, 106: plp. ἐκεκρᾱ́μην Sapph. 51 (Bergk); Pl. Polit. 272 (hither some refer Epic κεκράανται Od. 4, 616. 15, 116: plp. κεκράαντο 4, 132, others to κραίνω): aor. ἐκεράσθην

Xen. An. 5, 4, 29; Pl. Phil. 47. Tim. 85, συν- Leg. 889, and ἐκράθην Thuc. 6, 5; Eur. Ion 1016; Pl. Phaed. 86, συν- Soph. Tr. 661; Pl. Tim. 68, Ion. -ήθην Hippocr. 1, 616 (Lit.), συν- Her. 4, 152: fut. κραθήσομαι (Pl.) Ep. 7, 326, συγ- Eur. Ion 406. Mid. fut. late κεράσομαι, κατα- Eustath. 4, 25 (Herch.): aor. ἐκερασάμην (Pl.) Locr. 95, συν- Her. 7, 151; Pl. Tim. 80, Epic κερασσ- Od. 18, 423, ἐκερ- Nonn. 4, 237; κεράσαιο Nic. Ther. 601; -άσασθαι Luc. Imag. 7; -ασάμενος Luc. Hermot. 59 (as act.), ἐγ- Her. 5, 124, Pl. Politic. 268, κερασσάμενος Od. 7, 179; Ap. Rh. 4, 1128. Vb. ἄ-κρητος Il. 2, 341, κρατέον, συγ- Pl. Phil. 63. κεραννυτέον late Max. Tyr. 5, 4, 71. See foll.

Κεράω, -αίω *To mix*, Epic κερόωσι Arat. 780; Anth. 14, 133; imper. κέρᾱ Athen. (Com. Poet.) 2, 29, κέραιε Il. 9, 203; part. κερῶν Od. 24, 364, -όων Athen. (Antim.) 11, 33: imp. κέρων Ap. Rh. 1, 1185: for fut., aor. &c. see κεράννυμι. Mid. κεράομαι *to mix for oneself*, subj. κερῶνται Il. 4, 260 (Bekh. 2 ed. Ameis, κέρωνται Vulg. Dind. Spitzn. La Roche, as from κέραμαι, so δύναμαι, subj. δύνωνται); imper. κεράασθε, for κερᾶσθε, Od. 3, 332: imp. κερῶντο Od. 15, 500, and κερόωντο 8, 470. Pass. κεραιόμενος Nic. Alex. 178. 511. As baryton κέραμαι does not exist, and as Hom. has forms from the pure κεράομαι, κερῶνται not κέρωντ- is perhaps the correct form.

Κερδαίνω *To gain*, Ar. Av. 1591; Hippocr. 2, 405 (Erm.); Lys. 13, 84; Pl. Rep. 343; -αίνῃ Pl. Leg. 846; -αίνοιμεν Thuc. 5, 93; imper. κερδαίνετε Soph. Ant. 1037; -αίνειν Soph. Tr. 231; Ar. Plut. 520; Thuc. 3, 84; Isocr. 17, 36; -αίνων 1, 33: imp. ἐκέρδ- Eur. Supp. 708; Lys. 7, 32, ἀπ- Andoc. 1, 134: fut. Attic κερδᾰνῶ Aesch. Ag. 1301; Soph. O. R. 889; Eur. Or. 789; Ar. Nub. 259; Lys. 8, 20; Pl. Rep. 607, Ion. κερδανέω Her. 1, 35. 8, 60; and κερδήσω Anth. (Menecr. Smyrn.) 9, 390; Trag. Fr. (Mosch.) 14 (Wagn.); Niceph. Rhet. 3, 3: and mid, κερδήσομαι Her. 3, 72; Joseph. Ant. 19, 1, 18: aor. ἐκέρδᾱνα Pind. I. 5 (4), 27; and Attic, Soph. Fr. 499; Andoc. 1, 134; Xen. Cyr. 2, 2, 12; Dem. 9, 29. 32, 25, Ion. ἐκέρδηνα Hom. Epigr. 14, 6; Her. 8, 5, and ἐκέρδησα Her. 4, 152; Plut. Mor. 311; Ach. Tat. 5, 6; Galen 1, 14; Joseph. Ant. 10, 3, 1, ἀπο- Herodn. 6, 5: p. κεκέρδηκα late in *simple*, Orig. Ref. Haer. 9, 29, but προσ- Dem. 56, 30, later κεκέρδᾰκα Aristid. 29, 366 (D.); Ach. Tat. 5, 25; Epist. Phal. 81 (Herch.), and κεκέρδαγκα Ael. Epist. 14; Dio Cass. 53, 5, ἀπο- 43, 18 (Bekk. L. Dind.); Phot. Cod. 224. 388: p. p. κεκερδημένος Joseph. Ant. 18, 6, 5: aor. κερδανθείς Philodem. 22: fut. κερδηθήσονται N. T. 1 Petr. 3, 1 (-σωνται Vulg.). The Attics followed the *liquid* formation of this verb, fut. -ᾰνῶ, aor. -ᾱνα, except in perf. προσ-κεκερδήκασι Dem. 56, 30.

Κεύθω *To hide*, Poet. trans. and intrans. Od. 24, 474; Simon. C. 119; Aesch. Pr. 571; Soph. O. R. 1229; Eur. Supp. 295, κευθάνω see below; subj. κεύθῃ Il. 9, 313; κεῦθε Il. 16, 19. 18, 74: **imp.** ἔκευθεν Od. 23, 30; Hom. H. 5, 452, κεῦθεν Od. 19, 212 (Dind. Faesi, Nauck, ἔκευθεν Bekk. La R.): **fut.** κεύσω Od. 3, 187; Ap. Rh. 4, 1105, ἐπι- Aesch. Ag. 800: ἔκευσα, ἐπι-κεύσῃς Od. 15, 263: **2 p.** as **pres.** κέκευθα Il. 22, 118. Od. 3, 18; Simon. C. 97. 111 (Bergk); Aesch. Ch. 687; Soph. El. 1120; Eur. I. A. 112: **plp.** as **imp.** ἐκεκεύθειν Od. 9, 348, κεκεύθ- Hes. Th. 505: **p. p.** (κέκευται Hesych.); but κεκευθμένη Antim. Fr. 3 (Dübn.): **2 aor.** (ἔκῠθον), Epic κύθον Od. 3, 16; Eratosth. 1, 4 (Hiller); subj. redupl. κεκύθω Od. 6, 303. **Pass.** κεύθεται Ap. Rh. 4, 534, or **mid.** intrans. Opp. C. 3, 173. 179; subj. κεύθωμαι Il. 23, 244; κευθόμενος Tryphiod. 76; Maneth. 3, 127: **imp.** ἐκευθ- Nonn. 2, 304. This verb is Epic and Tragic; never, we think, in Comedy or prose. A collat. form κευθάνω occurs in **imp.** ἐκεύθανον Il. 3, 453, for which Düntzer suggests ἔκευθον ἄν. The **pres.** and **perf.** are used intrans. or passively of the dead only, *lie hid, buried,* Soph. O. R. 968; Aesch. Sept. 588 &c. κεκεύθει as **pres.** once stood in an Epigram of Simon. Anth. 7, 300 (106 Schneid. 126 Bergk), but nobody now thinks of founding on it a **pres.** κεκεύθω, since the true reading κέκευθε suggested by Stephanus in Thesaur. is found in the Cod. Pal.

Κέω, see κείω.

Κήδω (-έω) *To vex*, Epic in **act.** Il. 17, 550; Callim. Dian. 231: **imp.** ἔκηδε Il. 5, 404, iter. κήδεσκον Od. 23, 9: **fut.** κηδήσω Il. 24, 240: **aor.** (ἐκήδησα), ἀπο-κηδήσας Il. 23, 413 (but ἀ-κήδεσα 14, 427, see **mid.**): **2 p.** κέκηδα intrans. *I sorrow*, Tyrt. 12, 28 (Bergk). **Mid.** κήδομαι *to sorrow*, Il. 11, 665; Soph. El. 1327; Ar. Eq. 1342; Her. 1, 209; Thuc. 6, 84; Isocr. 4, 175; Pl. Crito 53; subj. -ωμαι Her. 3, 40; Pl. Gorg. 480; -οίμην Od. 3, 223; Pl. Rep. 412; κήδου Isocr. 2, 21, Dor. κᾶδευ Callim. Min. 140; κήδεσθαι Od. 19, 161; Thuc. 6, 14; Pl. Conv. 210; Dem. 8, 27; -όμενος Il. 7, 110; Soph. Aj. 203; Ar. Nub. 1410; Her. 6, 61; Lys. 13, 15; Isocr. 8, 39, Dor. κᾱδόμ- Pind. Ol. 6, 47: **imp.** ἐκηδόμην Her. 9, 45; Pl. Theaet. 143; Isocr. 7, 32, κηδ- Il. 1, 56, iter. κηδέσκετο Od. 22, 358: **fut.** (κηδήσομαι, ἀπο- Suid.), redupl. Epic κεκᾰδήσομαι Il. 8, 353: **aor.** (ἐκηδεσάμην), imper. κήδεσαι Aesch. Sept. 136 (chor.) like ἀκήδεσα Il. 14, 427 quoted.—**Fut.** κεκᾰδήσω, **2 aor.** κεκάδων are referred to χάζω. For κήδονται Her. 1, 209 (Gaisf. Bred. Dind. Stein) occurs κηδέαται (Bekk. Lhardy, Krüg.) The **act.** is exclusively Epic, for κήδεσαι Aesch.

Sept. 136, is imper. aor. mid. not inf. act. as our lexicons make it by writing κηδέσαι, but the mid. in pres. and imp. is used by every class of writers. The collat. κηδεύω seems confined to Tragedy and, perhaps, rather late prose, Aristot. Polit. 5, 7, 10. Fr. 83; κηδεύσειν Plut. Aristid. cum Cat. 6, aor. κηδεύσειεν (Dem.) 59, 81, κηδεῦσαι Ael. Fr. 48, κεκηδευμένος Joseph. 14, 7, 4, ἐκηδεύθη Plut. Alex. 56, -ευθείς Demad. 179, 9, -ευθῆναι Pseudo-Callisth. 1, 14. No mid.

Κηκίω *To gush forth*, Poet. Pind. Fr. 185 (Bergk *now*), ἀνα- Il. 13, 705: imp. ἐκήκῐε Ap. Rh. 1, 542 (Mss.), ἀν- Il. 7, 262, κήκῑον Od. 5, 455; Ap. Rh. 1, 542 (Well. Merk.), but Attic κηκῖον Soph. Ph. 784 chor. (Dind.) Pass. κηκῑομέναν Soph. Ph. 697 (chor.) ῐ Epic, ῑ Attic. The comp. ἀνακηκίω is also Poet. Il. 13, 705, imp. ἀνεκήκῑον Il. 7, 262: once however in prose, ἀνακηκίει Pl. Phaedr. 251, and in late Epic with trans. force, Ap. Rh. 4, 600, imp. Tryphiod. 322. ἀνακῑκύ̆ω is a suggestion of Schneider (Pind. Fr. quoted).

Κηρύσσω, -ττω *To proclaim*, Aesch. Cho. 1026; Eur. Her. 864; Her. 2, 134, -ύττω Ar. Ach. 623; Xen. Lac. 12, 6, Dor. κᾱρύσσ- Anth. 7, 431; κήρυσσε Soph. El. 606; -ύσσειν Il. 2, 51; -ύσσων 2, 438: imp. ἐκήρυσσον Il. 2, 444; Thuc. 1, 27, -υττον Andoc. 1, 112; Xen. Cyr. 4, 5, 42; Aeschin. 3, 154: fut. -ύξω Ar. Eccl. 684; Xen. An. 6, 6, 9, Dor. κᾱρύξω Eur. Ion 911 (chor.), -υξῶ Ar. Ach. 748: aor. ἐκήρυξα Her. 1, 194; Thuc. 4, 37; Xen. Cyr. 4, 2, 32, Dor. ἐκάρ- Pind. Ol. 5, 8, κάρ- I. 3, 12; inf. κηρῦξαι Soph. Aj. 1240; Thuc. 4, 68, Dor. καρ- Soph. Tr. 97 (chor.); part. κηρύξας Aesch. Ch. 124; Soph. Ant. 192; Pl. Leg. 917, Dor. κᾱρύξασα Eur. Hec. 179 (chor.); Pind. κᾱρύξαισα I. 4, 25: p. κεκήρῡχα, ἐπι- Dem. 19, 35: p. p. κεκήρυγμαι Eur. Fr. 1 (D.); Thuc. 4, 38: plp. κεκήρυκτο Ar. Ind. 15, 11: aor. ἐκηρύχθην Soph. O. R. 737; Thuc. 6, 50; Lys. 19, 63, ἀνα- Her. 6, 103: fut. -υχθήσομαι Xen. Cyr. 8, 4, 4; Aeschin. 3, 230: and as pass. fut. m. κηρύξεται Eur. Phoen. 1631 (old reading κηρύξατε): imp. ἐκηρύσσετο Antiph. 2, γ, 2. δ, 6. Mid. κηρύσσεται Soph. Fr. 68 (D.): aor. in comp. ὑπο-κηρυξάμενος Pl. Prot. 348; Aeschin. 3, 41, and late. This comp. ὑποκηρυσσ- seems to have no act. form, and mid. only in aor.

Κιγκράω, see κιρνάω.

Κιγχάνω, see κιχάνω.

Κίδνημι *To spread*, Poet. rare in act. and only in comp. ἐπι- Her. 7, 140 (Orac.). Mid. κίδνᾰμαι also Poet. Il. 23, 227; Pind. Fr. 106 (Bergk); Mimnerm. 2, 8 (B.); once in Trag. Eur. Hec. 916 chor. (Pors. Dind. σκίδν- Kirchh. Nauck); κιδνάμενος Anth. 7, 713: imp. ἐκίδνατο Il. 8, 1. 24, 695; Ap. Rh. 4, 183, κίδ- 2, 1079. Mss. divide on κίδν-, σκίδν- Eur. quoted: "anceps de hoc judicium" (Pors. 904).

Κικλήσκω *To call,* Poet. and late prose, only **pres.** Il. 11, 606; Hes. Th. 197; Aesch. Supp. 217; Soph. O. R. 209; Eur. Elec. 118. Ion 937; Com. Fr. (Stratt.) 2, 773; Ar. Nub. 565 (chor.); Aretae. C. et S. Morb. Ac. 2, 40 (ed. Oxon.), Dor. 3 pl. -σκοισι Pind. Fr. 64; subj. -ήσκω Aesch. Supp. 217, -ήσκωσι Callim. Dian. 154; imper. -ησκέτω Aesch. Eum. 507, -ήσκετε Aesch. Supp. 212; -ήσκειν Eur. Tr. 470, Epic -ησκέμεν Il. 9, 11; -ήσκων Il. 17, 532; Pind. P. 4, 119; Aesch. Ag. 1477: and **imp.** κίκλησκεν Epic Il. 2, 404. 7, 139. Od. 18, 6; Ap. Rh. 1, 230, ἐκίκλ- Aretae. C. et S. Morb. Ac. 2, 21 (ed. Oxon). **Mid. imp.** κικλήσκετο Il. 10, 300. **Pass.** κικλήσκομαι Batr. 27; Anth. App. Epigr. 289, -ήσκεται Od. 15, 403; Ap. Rh. 3, 200; Aesch. Fr. 324; Eur. Rhes. 279. Fr. 816 (Dind. 5 ed.), -ονται Ap. Rh. 4, 519: **imp.** ἐκικλήσκετο Aesch. Pers. 655 (chor.). Some of our lexicons miss the **mid.**

Κίκω, ἔκιξε, see κιχάνω.

Κινδυνεύω *To run a risk, dare,* Her. 2, 141; Thuc. 1, 39; Lys. 3, 38; Isae. 1, 6; -εύων Antiph. 2, γ, 3: **imp.** ἐκινδ- Isocr. 21, 19; Isae. 3, 62: **fut.** -εύσω Her. 8, 60; Thuc. 6, 78; Isocr. 3, 57: **aor.** ἐκινδύνευσα Thuc. 3, 74; Isocr. 10, 31; -εύσας Antiph. 5, 82: **p.** κεκινδύνευκα Lys. 3, 47 reg.: **p. p.** κεκινδυνευμένον Pind. N. 5, 14; Arr. An. 2, 7, 3, δια- Isocr. 11, 22: **aor.** κινδυνευθέντα Lys. 2, 54: **fut.** κινδυνευθήσεσθαι Dem. 30, 10: **3 fut.** κεκινδυνεύσεται Antiph. 5, 75, ἀπο- Thuc. 3, 39: **imp.** ἐκινδυνεύετο Thuc. 1, 73. **Fut. mid.** κινδυνεύσεσθαι we have seen only as a *variant,* Polyaen. 1, 28, but ἀπο-κινδυνεύσεται Dexipp. p. 23, 9 (Nieb.) It is a mistake to say "**pres. pass.** *alone* seems to have been used."

Κῑνέω *To move,* Aesch. Ch. 289; Soph. Ph. 866; Ar. Pax 491; Her. 3, 80; Thuc. 6, 36; κινῇ Solon 12; Aeol. imper. κίνη Sapph. 114: **imp.** ἐκίνουν Pl. Rep. 329, -νει Simon. Am. 28; Hippocr. 5, 214, -νεε Her. 5, 96: **fut.** -ήσω Eur. Or. 157; Her. 6, 134. 98 (Orac.); Pl. Tim. 57: **aor.** ἐκίνησα Pind. Fr. 220; Antiph. 5, 15; Thuc. 4, 89, κίν- Il. 23, 730, iter. κινήσασκε, ἀπο- Il. 11, 636: **p.** κεκίνηκα Dem. 45, 58; Luc. Eun. 2, &c.: **p. p.** κεκίνημαι Eur. Andr. 1227; Her. 2, 138; Pl. Leg. 908, -κινέαται Hipponax 62 (B.): **aor.** ἐκινήθην Hom. H. 28, 11; Her. 2, 156; Thuc. 3, 82, κινήθ- Il. 2, 144. 149, Epic 3 pl. ἐκίνηθεν Il. 16, 280: **fut. p.** κινηθήσομαι *shall be moved,* or reflex *shall move,* Ar. Ran. 796; Hippocr. 7, 332. 8, 484; Pl. Rep. 545; Aeschin. 3, 160; Dem. 19, 324: and **fut. m.** κινήσομαι in same sense Hippocr. 7, 90 (Lit.); Xen. Cyr. 1, 4, 19; Pl. Theaet. 182.

Tim. 57; Dem. 8, 37. 9, 51; Aristot. Metaph. 10, 6, 9; Plut. Mor. 1073, προσ- Ar. Lys. 227. Pax 902. **Mid.** κινοῦμαι intrans. *move, bestir oneself*, Simon. Am. 7, 75; Ar. Nub. 297; Pl. Leg. 816; -οῖτο Xen. An. 4, 5, 13; imper. κινεῦ Theocr. 15, 29; -ούμενοι Thuc. 7, 67: **fut.** -ήσομαι see above, with **fut. pass.** &c.: **p.** κεκίνησθε Dem. 9, 5?: **aor.** κινηθῆναι Xen. An. 6, 3, 8: but **aor. mid.** κινήσαντο trans. Opp. Cyn. 2, 582, missed by Lexicogr. **Vb.** κινητέος (Pl.) Riv. 134, -έον Pl. Leg. 738. (ῑ.) A Dor. form κινωμένα is in Tim. Locr. 95.

Κίνυμαι *To move oneself*, Epic and only **pres.** Ap. Rh. 1, 1308; -ύμενος Il. 10, 280. Od. 10, 556; Ap. Rh. 3, 971; Callim. Del. 143: and **imp.** κίνυντο Il. 4, 281; Ap. Rh. 4, 1174.

Κῑνύρομαι *To wail*, Poet. Aesch. Sept. 123 (Vulg. Herm. Weil); Ar. Eq. 11; Ap. Rh. 4, 1063; Callim. Ap. 20; late prose Ael. H. A. 5, 49; -όμενος Q. Sm. 7, 335; Opp. C. 3, 217: **imp.** κινύρεο Coluth. 215, -ύρετο Ap. Rh. 3, 664; Bion 1, 42: **aor.** κῑνύρατο Mosch. 3, 43 (Vulg. Mein. Ahr. Ziegl.), though our lexicons say "only **pres.** and **imp.**" (ῐῠ.) This verb is used chiefly in late Epic. For κινύρονται Aesch. Sept. 123, the sole instance in Tragedy, Dind. has *now* edited μῑνύρονται, moved perhaps by μινύρεσθαι Aesch. Ag. 16, and μινύρεται Soph. O. C. 671.

Κιρνάω, -νημι (Dor. κιγκράω, or κίγκρᾱμι, imper. κίγκρα Hesych., ἐγ-κίκρα Sophr. Fr. 2) *To mix*, κίρνης Plut. Cat. maj. 9, κιρνᾷ Her. 4, 52. 66, κίρνᾰμεν Pind. I. 6, 3, κιρνᾶσι Athen. (Theopomp.) 4, 31, ἐγ- Ar. Eccl. 841; imper. κιρνάτω, ἐγ- Pind. N. 9, 50, κίρνᾰτε Alcae. 45; inf. κιρνάμεν Pind. I. 5, 25, κιρνάναι Hippocr. 8, 244 (Lit.); Athen. 10, 426; part. κιρνάς Od. 16, 14; Ar. Fr. 555; Hippocr. 7, 256 (Lit.), Aeol. κίρναις Alcae. 27 (Ahr.), κιρνῶν Herodn. 8, 4, 9; κιρνᾶν Polyb. 4, 21: **imp.** ἐκίρνα Od. 7, 182. 10, 356, and (ἐκίρνην), κίρνη 14, 78. 16, 52, ἐκιρ- App. Mithr. 111. **Mid.** κίρνᾰμαι Pind. Fr. 162 (Bergk), ἀνα- Soph. Fr. 239 (D.); κίρνασθαι, ἀνα- Eur. Hipp. 254. **Pass.** κίρνᾰμαι Dio. Hal. in Dem. 41, ἐπι- Her. 1, 51, late -νάομαι, -ᾶται Athen. 11, 51; κιρναμένα Pind. N. 3, 78, -άμενος Euen. 2 (Bergk); Opp. H. 5, 275; Sext. Emp. 134, 5, ἀνα- (Pl.) Ax. 371; inf. κιρνᾶσθαι Aristot. Plant. 1, 2, 7; Athen. 10, 426, συγ- 11, 51: **imp.** ἐκίρνᾰτο in tmesi Com. Fr. (Anon.) 4, 676. The dropping of the γ in the comp. Dor. form (κίγκρᾱμι) ἐγ-κικρ- is analogous to πίμπρημι ἐμπίπρημι &c. Dor. dial. p. 346 (Ahrens).

Κῐχάνω (ᾰ) *To find*, Epic, Il. 19, 165; Archil. Fr. 54 (Bergk); imper. -άνετε Il. 23, 407; -άνειν Mosch. 2, 112, in Trag. κῐχάνω, rather κιγχάνω Solon 44; Aesch. Ch. 620; Soph. O. C. 1450; Eur. Hel. 597. Hipp. 1444 (also κίχημι): **imp.** ἐκῐχᾱνον Il. 3,

383, and (as from κίχημι) κῖχης Od. 24, 284 (Bekk. 2 ed., κίχεις La Roche, ἐκίχεις Vulg.), κίχημεν 16, 379 (Bekk. 2 ed. ἐκίχ- Vulg.), κιχήτην Il. 10, 376, called by some **2 aor.**; subj. κῖχω Soph. Aj. 657, κίχῃς Eur. Supp. 1069, -χῃσι Opp. Hal. 3, 433, Epic κιχείω Il. 1, 26; Bion 1, 43, -είομεν Il. 21, 128; opt. κιχείη Il. 2, 188. Od. 17, 476; inf. κιχήμεναι Il. 15, 274, and κιχῆναι Od. 16, 357; κιχείς Il. 16, 342: fut. κῑχήσομαι Il. 21, 605, -ήσεαι Od. 7, 53, -ήσεται Callim. Del. 95; Soph. O. C. 1487 &c.: late κῑχήσω, Epic inf. -ησέμεν Ap. Rh. 4, 1482: **1 aor.** late ἐκῖχησα Opp. Hal. 5, 116; -ήσας 2, 567; Musae. 149: **2 aor.** ἔκῐχον Od. 3, 169; Simon. C. 119; Pind. N. 10, 74; Eur. Bac. 903 (chor.), Epic κῐχον Il. 18, 153; Callin. 1, 15; Simon. C. 65; Pind. P. 9, 26; Opp. Hal. 4, 546; subj. κίχω Orph. Arg. 106, -χῃς Eur. Supp. 1069, κίχῃ Solon 13, 30; κίχοιμεν Orph. Arg. 1359; κιχών Od. 15, 157; Pind. P. 3, 43; κιχεῖν Theogn. 1300; Bacchyl. 29, 2 (B.): **mid.** κιχάνομαι as act. Il. 19, 289. 11, 441; Ap. Rh. 4, 760; -νόμενος Od. 9, 266, and (κίχημαι) κιχήμενος Il. 5, 187: **fut.** κιχήσομαι see above: **1 aor.** κιχήσαο H. Hym. 2, 62, -ατο Il. 10, 494. Od. 6, 51; Archil. Fr. 73 (Bergk), ἐκιχήσ- Q. Sm. 13, 172; and perhaps Epic subj. -χήσομαι for -σωμαι Il. 2, 258. **Vb.** ἀ-κίχητος Il. 17, 75; Aesch. Pr. 184. In the Tragedians κιχάνω always requires ῑ: and therefore late editors have substituted κιγχάνω, founding partly on Mss., partly on κιγχάνω in Hesych. and other Gramm., as in Soph. O. C. 1450 (Elms. Herm. Dind.) &c. κιχάνει still stands in some good editions of Aesch. Ch. 613 (622); but Franz found in the Med. Ms., the oldest and best, traces of an obliterated letter between ι and χ, which heightens the probability that κιγχάνει was the reading. To this verb some have referred ἔκιξε Simias in Ovo, Anth. 15, 27, ἀπέκιξαν Ar. Ach. 869, κίξατο Hesych. This verb is poetic, κιχάνω (Luc.) Philopatr. 3, is a quotation from Homer; and Susemihl, on perhaps too slender grounds, reads **2 aor.** inf. κιχεῖν Aristot. Polit. 4, 1, 4, for κοινωνεῖν 4, 1, 7 (Bekk., v. r. κινεῖν). In **pres.** and **imp.** ῐᾰ Epic, ῑᾰ Attic, in other forms κίχῃς &c. ῐ even in Attic.

Κίχρημι *To lend*, Dem. 53, 12 (κιχράω Liban. 4, p. 831): **fut.** χρήσω Her. 3, 58: **aor.** ἔχρησα Lys. 19, 24; Dem. 19, 170; χρήσῃς Dem. 53, 11; χρῆσον Ar. Ran. 1159. Thesm. 219. 250; Xen. Mem. 3, 11, 18; χρῆσαι Her. 3, 58. 6, 89; Lys. 19, 22; (Pl.) Demod. 384; χρήσας (Pl.) Demod. 384: **p.** κέχρηκα Com. Fr. (Men.) 4, 205. 247; Polyb. 29, 6c (Bekk.): **plp.** κεχρήκει App. C. B. 2, 29: **p. p.** κέχρημαι, δια- Dem. 27, 11. **Mid.** (κίχρᾰμαι) *to borrow*, -άμενος Plut. Mor. 534; and κιχράομαι, inf. κιχρᾶσθαι Theophr. Ch. 17, but κίχρασθαι (Foss, 30): **imp.** ἐκῑχρᾶμην Anth. 9, 584: aor. ἐχρησάμην Luc. Necyom. 16; imper. χρῆσαι Eur. Elec. 190; χρήσασθαι (Pl.) Demod. 384; -ησάμενος Batr. 186; Anth. 9, 13.

Κίω (ῐ) *To go*, Poet. and only pres. κίεις Anacr. 4; Aesch. Ch. 680 (trimet.); subj. κίῃς Od. 1, 311, and perhaps κίομεν for -ωμεν, Il. 21, 456, see imp.; κίοι Il. 11, 705; Aesch. Supp. 504, -οίτην Od. 15, 149. Il. 24, 285, -οιτε Od. 3, 347; κίε 7, 50; Aesch. Supp. 852. Pers. 1068; κιών Il. 16, 263, κιοῦσα Il. 9, 504. Od. 4, 736; κίειν Pl. Crat. 426: and imp. ἔκῐον, ἔκιες H. Hym. 2, 31, ἔκιε Od. 15, 147, κίε Il. 8, 337, 1 pl. κίομεν (if not subj. for κίωμεν) Il. 21, 456, ἔκιον Il. 12, 138; Hes. Op. 345, κίον Il. 23, 115, ἐκίαθον only in μετεκίαθον with ῑ in arsi, see μετακιάθω. κίοντες with ῑ, Il. 14, 340 (Ms. Ven. and some inferior editions) belongs not to this verb, but to κείω *wish to lie down*, and ought to be κείοντες (Bekk. Spitzn. Dind. La R.); so κείουσα for κί-, Od. 23, 292. Aeschylus alone of the Tragedians has this verb, and Plato uses it merely for an etymological purpose.

Κλαγγάνω, -αίνω, -γέω *To bark, scream*, Poet. and only pres. -γγάνει Soph. Fr. 782, -γγαίνεις Aesch. Eum. 131 (Mss. Vulg. Herm. -άνεις Dind.), -γγεῦντι 3 pl. Dor. Theocr. Epigr. 6. The comp. ἐπ-ανακλαγγάνω is used by Xen. Ven. 4, 5. 6, 23.

Κλάζω *To clang, scream*, mostly Poet. Aesch. Sept. 386; Eur. Ion 906; Opp. Hal. 4, 123; -ων Il. 16, 429; Soph. O. R. 966; Plut. Alex. 27: imp. κλάζον Theocr. 25, 72 (Reiske, Mein.): fut. κλάγξω Aesch. Pers. 947 (chor.): and mid. κεκλάγξομαι Ar. Vesp. 930: aor. ἔκλαγξα Il. 1, 46; Pind. P. 4, 23; Aesch. Ag. 201; Soph. Fr. 890 (D.); Eur. Ph. 1144; Pseud.-Callisth. 2, 16: p. as pres. κέκλαγγα (from κλάγγω, as λάμπω, λέλαμπα), subj. κεκλάγγω Ar. Vesp. 929 (Mss. Bekk. Mein. Dind. *now*); κεκλαγγώς, -γυῖα Xen. Cyn. 3, 9: 2 aor. ἔκλᾰγον Hom. H. 19, 14; Anth. 9, 571; Theocr. 17, 71, ἀν- Eur. I. A. 1062: 2 p. as pres. κέκληγα Epic, Opp. H. 5, 268; Orph. Lith. 45: plp. κεκλήγει Alcm. 47 (Schn. κέκλαγ' 7 Bergk 3 ed.); part. κεκληγώς Il. 2, 222. 11, 168; Hes. Sc. 99. Op. 449, late prose κεκλαγώς Plut. Timol. 26, but oblique cases (as if from κεκλήγων) κεκλήγοντες Epic Il. 12, 125. 17, 756. 759. Od. 12, 256. 14, 30 (Wolf, Spitzn. Dind. -ῶτες Bekk. Ameis, and in Od. La Roche), see below; Hes. Sc. 379, v. r. -ότες, -ῶτες, which last form Ap. Rh. uses 4, 876, and Bekker uniformly in Il. and Od. The form κεκληγότος, though occurring as a *v. r.* is rare in *Text*, perhaps only Orph. Lith. 374. Brunck and Bergk edit κεκλάγχω at Ar. Vesp. 929, implying κέκλαγχα; κεκλαγώς Plut. Timol. 26 (Vulg. Bekk. Sint.), for κεκλαγχώς says Lobeck.

(Κλᾴζω, κλᾴω) *To shut*, Dor. See κλῄω.

Κλαίω *To weep*, Il. 19, 300. Od. 8, 577; Archil. 20; Theogn. 1132; Soph. El. 283 (Herm. Nauck, κλά- *now* Dind.); Eur. Alc. 530 (Herm. Nauck, κλά- Dind.); Her. 4, 127; Andoc. 1, 48; Aeschin. 3, 207 (κλά- Bekk.); Pl. Leg. 792 (*v. r.* κλά-), Attic κλάω Aesch. Sept. 872. Ag. 18 (Pors. Dind. κλαί- Herm.); Soph. El. 283 (D.); Ar. Nub. 1415 &c.; Pl. Phil. 48, never contr. κλῶ; so κλάοιμι Ar. Av. 341, -οις Aesch. Supp. 925, κλαίοισθα Il. 24, 619, never κλῷμι nor κλῴην: imp. ἔκλαιον Od. 12, 309; Soph. O. C. 1621 (Herm. -λᾶον Dind.), κλαῖον Il. 17, 427. Od. 1, 363, ἔκλᾶε Isocr. 17, 18, 'κλαε Soph. Tr. 905 (Ell. κλᾶε Dind. 'κλαιε Herm.), iter. κλαίεσκον Il. 8, 364; rare in Attic poetry Aesch. Fr. 298 trimet. (Dind.); Her. 3, 119; (Luc.) D. Syr. 22: fut. κλαύσομαι Il. 22, 87. 20, 210; Eur. Cycl. 554; Ar. Nub. 58. Av. 342. Plut. 425 &c.; Com. Fr. (Eub.) 2, 513; (Dem.) 59, 38; always in Septuag.; κλαυσοῦμαι rare, Ar. Pax 1081 (hexam.); Dio Cass. Fr. 39, 8 (Bekk.): also rare κλαιήσω Dem. 21, 99. 37, 48. 54, 43 (Mss. Bekk. B. Saupp.), and κλᾱήσω 19, 310 (Bekk. B. Saupp. and *now* Dind. always in Dem.); Hyperid. Fr. p. 352 (B. Saupp.), and late κλαύσω Dio. Hal. 4, 70. Excerpt. 17, 8; (Theocr.) 23, 34 (Mss. Ahr. Wordsw. Fritzsche); Or. Sib. 1, 190. 7, 53; Maneth. 3, 143; N. T. always: aor. ἔκλαυσα Eur. Tr. 482; Theocr. 1, 72, κλαῦσε Od. 3, 261, ἀν-έκλαυσας Her. 3, 14; subj. κλαύσω Aesch. Sept. 828; Soph. El. 1122; Ar. Eq. 9; κλαύσειε, ἀπο- Soph. Ph. 693; κλαύσας Il. 24, 48; Plut. Alcib. 33; κλαῦσαι Soph. El. 285: p. (κέκλαυκα): p. p. κέκλαυμαι, -αυται Mosch. 4, 64; Anth. 7, 281; -αυμένος Aesch. Ch. 687; Soph. O. R. 1490, and later κέκλαυσμαι, -αυσται Plut. Mor. 115; -αυσμένος Lycophr. 273; and Anth. 7, 281, where in the same line occurs also -αυται without σ: aor. late ἐκλαύσθην Anth. App. Epigr. 341; κλαυσθείς Lycophr. 831; Joseph. Ant. 8, 11, 1: fut. late κλαυσθήσομαι V. T. Ps. 77, 64: **3 fut.** κε-κλαύσεται impers. Ar. Nub. 1436; but at Theogn. 1203, it is merely an emendation of Brunck for κεκλήσεται (Mss. Orell. Bergk): **2 aor. act.** ἔκλᾰον? see below. **Mid.** κλαίομαι as act. Aesch. Sept. 920 (κλάομ- Pors. Dind. 5 ed.), ἀνα- Soph. Ph. 939, μετα- Eur. Hec. 214, κατα- Elec. 155 (κλάομ- always Dind. 5 ed.), ἀπο-κλάομ- Ar. Vesp. 564: **fut.** κλαύσομαι, -σοῦμαι see above: **aor.** ἐκλαυσάμην trans. Soph. Tr. 153; Anth. 7, 412; Nicol. Rhet. 7, 1, ἀπο- Soph. O. R. 1467, ἀν- Anth. 9, 362; Antiph. 2, δ, 1; Dio. Hal. Ant. 3, 21. 5, 8. 6, 43: hence **perf.** κεκλαυμένος *bathed in tears*, Aesch. Ch. 457; Soph. O. R. 1490. **Vb.** κλαυτός Aesch. Sept. 333, ἄ-κλαυτ- Il. 22, 386, κλαυστός Soph. O. C. 1360, ἄ-κλαυστ- El. 912 (Vulg. Herm. Nauck, -αυτος Dind. 5 ed.)—In Tragedy κλαίω and κλάω, in Aristoph. κλάω prevails, in Attic prose κλαίω and κλάω, the latter gaining ground, compare editions by Pors. Elms. Herm. Bekk. Popp. Dind. Krüg. &c. κλαίοισθα Il. 24, 619. Theodr. Prod. has ᾰ in κλᾰ́ε 8, 393, Theocr. in ἔκλᾰεν 14, 32 (ἔκλαι' Fritzs.), so Hermes. in Athen. 597, if ἔκλαε δ' (Florent.) and 'Ικαρίου (Dind.) be the right reading. May this be **2 aor.**? Or. Sib. 1, 181, has even κλαίετ' (˘˘), κλάετ' (Dind.). Meineke suggests κλᾰ́ϊεν as the Aeol. form. κλαυσοῦμαι occurs only once in classic authors, Ar. Pax 1081 quoted, and there perhaps for the metre, -ούμεθα forming a dactyl. Dio. Hal. along with **fut. act.** κλαύσω quoted, has also **fut. m.** κλαύσομαι, ἀνα- 4, 33. In Attic prose this verb is much confined to the **pres. imperf.** and **fut.**

"Recte Cobetus," says Franke, "Tragicis νοσοῖμι et δοκοῖμι et similia concessit, non concessit Comicis et Scriptoribus Atticis." Aristoph. uses, to be sure, βοῴη Thesm. 506, ἀνα-βιῴην Ran. 178, δρῴη Thesm. 681, and βινοίη Ach. 1052, νοοίης Nub. 1381, αἰτοίη Eq. 513, ἀκολουθοίης Av. 340, but κλάοιμι 341, ἀπ-έλθοιμι Ach. 403, πλέοι Pax 699, δέοι Lys. 1132, ἀπο-δοίην Nub. 118, 755 &c. but ἐπί-δοιμι Ach. 1156 &c. &c. Prose δοκοίη Thuc. 6, 34. 8, 54, but δοκοῖ 2, 79. 100. 3, 16. ἐγχειροῖμ' ἂν Pl. Tim. 48, κοσμοῖ Lach. 196. νοοῖ Euthyd. 287. κατηγοροίη Menex. 244 (Bekk. Stallb.), but κατηγοροῖ Gorg. 251. ζητοίην Epist. 318, ζητοῖς Prot. 327 &c. &c.

Κλάω (˘) *To break*, Dio Cass. 71, 5; Paus. 6, 4, 2; κλᾶν, ἐνι- Il. 8, 408: **imp.** ἔκλων Paus. 6, 4, 1, κατ- Il. 20, 227; Her. 9, 62, ἀν- Thuc. 2, 76: **fut.** κλᾰ́σω Luc. D. Deor. 11, 1; Joseph. Ant. 10, 11, 3: **aor.** ἔκλᾰσα, κλάσε Od. 6, 128, κατ-έκλασσε Pind. P. 5, 34 (Bergk, 3 ed.); Pl. Phaed. 117, κλάσσε Theocr. 25, 147, δια- Il. 5, 216, ἐν-έκλ- Callim. Jov. 90: **p. p.** κέκλασμαι Hippocr. 3, 420 (Lit.); Aristot. Mechan. 25, 5, ἀνα- Com. Fr. 2, 812, προσ- Xen. Eq. 7, 6, συγ- Pl. Rep. 495: **plp.** κέκλαστο, ἐναπο- Thuc. 4, 34: **aor.** ἐκλάσθην Il. 11, 584; Hippocr. 7, 516; Plut. Mor. 758, κατ- Eur. Hipp. 766, ἐπι- Thuc. 3, 59. 67. 4, 37: **fut.** κλασθήσομαι Aristot. Meteor. 3, 3, 6, ἀνα- 3, 6, 6. Probl. 15, 12, 2: and **fut. m.** ἀνα-κλάσεται as pass. Galen 3, 147, and perhaps κατα-κλῶμαι, with elision, Babr. 91 (Lewis, 2 pt.): **2 aor. part.** (κλῆμι obsol.) κλάς, ἀπο- Anacr. 17 (Bergk); others take this for a syncop. **1 aor.** **Mid.** *to break one's own*, or *for oneself*, **fut.** as pass. see above: **aor.** κλάσσατο Anth. 7, 124, ἀπ-εκλάσατο 7, 506. **Fut. mid.** ἀνακλάσεται has been missed by Lexicogr.

Κλεΐζω, see κληΐζω.

Κλείω (old Att. κλῄω) *To shut*, Ar. Arch. 479 (Vulg. Dind. 2 ed. κλῄ- Mein. Dind. 5 ed.); Com. Fr. (Aristophon) 3, 359; Aeschin.

1, 10 (Mss. Bekk. B. Saupp. -ῄω Franke), κατα- Xen. Mem. 2, 1, 13, συγ- Aeschin. 1, 96: fut. κλείσω Or. Sib. 7, 85; late prose Himer. Or. 22, 7, but ἀπο- Xen. An. 4, 3, 20. 6, 6, 13, συγ- 7, 1, 12, and κλιῶ, κατα- Com. Fr. (Eup.) 2, 544: aor. ἔκλεισα Xen. An. 7, 1, 36; (Pl.) Epist. 7, 348, ἀπο- Isae. 6, 40; Xen. An. 7, 6, 24; ἐξ- Aeschin. 3, 74 (Bekk. B. S. -κλῃσα Franke, Weidner); κλείσαιτε Dem. 18, 32: p. κέκλεικα Theophr. Ch. 18 (Foss); Luc. Tox. 30, ἀπο- Strab. 4, 6, 3, δια- Polyb. 3, 60: plp. ἐκεκλείκειν App. Annib. 47: p. p. κέκλειμαι Her. 2, 121 (Bekk. Gaisf. -λῃϊμ- Dind. Stein); Dem. 19, 315. 25, 28, κατα- Ar. Plut. 206 (-ῃμαι Mein. Dind. 5 ed.); Isocr. 4, 34. 6, 40; Aeschin. 3, 87 (-ῃμαι Franke, Weidner), and -εισμαι Ar. Vesp. 198 (-ῃμαι Mein. Dind. 5 ed.); Com. Fr. (Alex.) 3, 426. (Men.) 4, 223; Hippocr. 5, 528 (Lit.); Xen. Cyr. 7, 5, 27 (Vulg. Popp. Born. -ειμαι L. Dind. 4 ed. Saupp.), ἀπο- Ar. Lys. 423 (-ῃμαι Mein. W. Dind. 5 ed.); Thuc. 3, 109 (Vulg. -ῃμαι Bekk. Popp. Krüg.), ἐγ- Aristot. Plant. 2, 2, 25 (Bekk.), κατα- Dio. Hal. 4, 52; κεκλεισμένος 3, 13, ἐγ-Pseud.-Callisth. ἐγ- 1, 17: plp. ἐκεκλείμην Xen. An. 6, 2, 8, ἀπ- Dem. 54, 11 (Bekk. Dind. -σμην Vulg. B. Saupp.), and with σ, συν-εκέκλειστο Andoc. 1, 48 (Bekk. Bait. -ῃτο Saupp.): aor. always ἐκλείσθην Dem. 23, 110; Dio. Hal. 4, 85; (Luc.) Syr. 10, ἀπ- Lys. 1, 17; Xen. An. 4, 3, 21, κατα- Ar. Nub. 404 (-ῄσθην Mein. Dind. 5 ed.); Dem. 22, 13: fut. κλεισθήσομαι late in *simple* Galen 3, 802, but συγ- Xen. Hell. 5, 2, 19: 3 fut. κεκλείσομαι Ar. Lys. 1072 (-ῄσομαι Dind. 5 ed. Mein.); Aristid. 30, 382, ἀπο- Themist. 15, 185. Mid. in comp. aor. κατα-κλεισάμενος reflex, *to shut himself up*, Xen. Cyr. 7, 2, 5, ἐγ- Hell. 6, 5, 9 (but trans. ἐγ-κλεισ- Luc. D. Meretr. 4, 3; αὐτοὺς ἀπο-κλῄ-σασθαι Thuc. 6, 101). See κλῃΐω, κλῄω. Vb. κλειστός Eur. Fr. 620 (D.), ἐγ-κλειστέος Geop. 19, 7. κεκλειμένου Her. 2, 121 (Mss. Bekk. Gaisf.) is in some editions κεκλῃϊμένου (Bred. Dind. Krüg. Abicht, Stein) perhaps rightly, at least more in accordance with the usage of Her. Nice scholars, Elmsley, Dindorf, Ellendt, &c. would banish κλείω with its derivatives and compounds from the Tragedians and Aristoph. at least, and read κλῄω instead as the old Attic form. It would appear however to be certain in Aristoph., Xenophon, the Orators and later, less certain in Plato. Meineke, Cobet, W. Dind. 5 ed. always write κλῄω in Aristoph., and L. Dind. would always in Attic, and the p. pass. without σ, κεκλειμένος, Attic -ῃμένος.

Κλείω *To celebrate*, see κλέω.

Κλέπτω *To steal*, Il. 1, 132; Solon 4, 13; Pind. P. 3, 29; Soph. Aj. 189; Ar. Ach. 525; Her. 1, 186; Antiph. 5, 38; Dor. f. pt. -τοισα Pind. Ol. 6, 36: imp. ἔκλεπτον Soph. Ph. 1272;

Ar. Eq. 420; Lys. 25, 19; Aeschin. 1, 110, iter. κλέπτεσκον Her. 2, 174; Anth. 11, 125: fut. κλέψω Ar. Eccl. 667; Xen. M. Eq. 4, 17; Luc. D. Deor. 7, 4; Lycophr. 1310; Anth. 12, 21, ἀπο- Hom. H. 3, 522, ἐκ- Soph. Ph. 55: and rare κλέψομαι Xen. Cyr. 7, 4, 13: aor. ἔκλεψα Il. 5, 268; Ar. Vesp. 238; Hippocr. 5, 226; Pl. Parm. 128, Poet. κλέψεν Pind. P. 4, 250, 'κλεψα Ar. Ran. 614; κλέψειας Soph. Aj. 1137, κλέψειεν Aesch. Ch. 854; κλέψας Archil. 103; Aesch. Pr. 8; Antiph. 2, γ, 4; Thuc. 1, 115, Dor. κλέψαις Pind. Ol. 1, 60: κέκλοφα Ar. Plut. 372; Pl. Leg. 941; Dem. 22, 49. 24, 120: p. p. κέκλεμμαι Soph. Ant. 681; Ar. Vesp. 57 (old reading κέκλαμ-); Aristot. Rhet. 3, 2, 10, ἐκ- Her. 2, 121, δια- Dem. 27, 12: 1 aor. ἐκλέφθην, κλεφθείς Eur. Or. 1580; Her. 5, 84: in Attic prose 2 aor. ἐκλάπην Xen. M. Eq. 4, 17; Pl. Rep. 413, ἐξ- Xen. Hell. 5, 4, 12, δια- Thuc. 7, 85; Polyb. 2, 62, 11. **Vb.** κλεπτός Ar. Vesp. 933, κλεπτέον Soph. Ph. 57. **2 aor. act.** ἔκλαπον we have never seen. The **pres.** and **imp. mid.** occur late, δια-κλέπτεται, -ετο V. T. 2 Reg. 19, 3, missed by Lexicogr.; but ὑπο-κλεπτόμενος Soph. El. 115, which however Pors. and Dind. hold spurious, others pass.

Κλέω *To celebrate,* Poet. Eur. Alc. 447 chor. (Elms. Dind. Monk. Nauck), I. A. 1045 (chor.), in **act.** Hom. always κλείω Od. 1, 338. 17, 418. Hym. 32, 19; so Hes. Th. 44. Op. 1; Stesich. 32 (Bergk); quoted by Ar. Pax 779 (chor.); κλείωμεν Ap. Rh. 2, 687: **imp.** ἔκλεον Ap. Rh. 3, 246, κλεῖον Orph. Lith. 193; Ap. Rh. 2, 163: **fut.** κλήσω Castor. 2 (B.): **aor.** ἔκλησε Athen. (Nicand. Col.) 2, 35. **Mid.** κλέομαι Eur. Fr. 370 (D.) **Pass.** Hom. κλέομαι Od. 13, 299; Pind. I. 5, 27; Soph. Tr. 639 chor. (Musgr. Dind. 5 ed. Nauck), but κλείομαι Ap. Rh. 1, 238; Orph. Lith. 278: **imp.** ἔκλεο for -έεο Il. 24, 202; Callim. Del. 40. **Vb.** κλειτός Il. 6, 227. κλέωα Dor. **pres. part. act.** for κλέουσα Ar. Lys. 1299. Kirchhoff retains κλείοντες Eur. Alc. 447; so Hermann, on what we think insufficient grounds: "in epico verbo sequendus epicorum usus. Syllaba eo loco anceps."

Κλῄζω *To celebrate, name* (Attic for κλεΐζω) Phryn. 1 (B.); Soph. O. R. 48; Ar. Av. 921. Thesm. 116; and late Orph. Arg. 16. Hym. 66, 10; Luc. Epigr. 11 (D.): **imp.** ἔκλῃζον Eur. H. F. 340: **fut.** κλῄσω Hom. H. 31, 18; Ap. Rh. 3, 993: **aor.** ἔκλῃσα, κλῇξα Orph. Arg. 1007; subj. κλῄσωμεν Eur. I. A. 1522; κλῇσον Ar. Av. 905, -ῄσατε 1745; κλῇσαι Hom. Epigr. 4, 9; Orph. Arg. 619: **p. p.** κεκλῃσμένος Eur. Ion 283 (Ald.) is now κεκλημένος (Mss. B. C. Dind. Kirchh. &c.) from καλέω. **Pres. pass.** κλῄζομαι Eur. Phoen. 10, κλῄζει Hel. 1441, κλῄζῃ Callim. Del.

276, κλῄζεται Soph. O. R. 1451. Tr. 659, -όμεθα Eur. Bac. 1180, -ῄζεσθε Ion 234; rare in prose (Pl.) Ax. 371, -ονται Xen. Cyr. 1, 2, 1 (Dind. Saupp. -ηΐζ- Popp. Born.): imp. ἐκληζόμην Aesch. Ag. 631; Soph. O. R. 1171; Eur. H. F. 493; and late (Luc.) Tragoed. 252.

Κληΐζω *To celebrate, call,* Ion. Hippocr. 3, 191 (and Dor. κλεΐζω late in pres.): fut. κληΐσω Aristid. 26, 328, Dor. κλεΐξω Pind. Ol. 1, 110: aor. (κλῇξα, see κλῄζω), Dor. εὐ-κλεΐξαι Pind. P. 9, 91; εὐ-κλεΐσας Tyrt. 12, 24: p. p. κεκλήϊσμαι Ap. Rh. 4, 618, and ἐκλήϊσμαι 4, 990: plp. ἐκληΐσμην 4, 267. Rare in prose, κληΐζεται (Pl.) Tim. Locr. 100; Arr. An. 7, 7, 3. 7, 13, 1; even Xen. Cyr. 1, 2, 1 if correct (Vulg. Popp. Born.), but κλῄζ- (Dind. Hertl. Saupp.) See κλῄζω.

Κληΐω *To shut,* Ion. περι- Her. 7, 198. 199, συγ- 4, 157; ἀπο-κληΐων Her. 4, 7, περι- 3, 116: imp. ἐκλήϊον, συν- Her. 7, 41: (fut. κληΐσω): aor. ἐκλήϊσα Od. 24, 166. Hom. H. 1, 6, ἐξ- Her. 1, 144, κλήϊσα Od. 21, 387; opt. κληΐσειε, ἐγ- Her. 4, 78; inf. κληΐσαι Od. 21, 382; κληΐσας, ἀπο- Her. 1, 37: p. p. κεκλήϊμαι Her. 2, 121 (Bred. Dind. Krüg.), ἀπο-, περι- 3, 117 (Gaisf. Bekk. Dind.), συγ- 7, 129 (Bekk. Bred. Dind.), but -ήισμαι (Gaisf.): plp. 3 pl. ἀπ-εκεκληΐατο Her. 9, 50 (Stein, Dind. Dial. Her.), ἀπο-κεκλέατο (Bekk. Gaisf.), -εκεκλέατο (Dind. in text): aor. ἀπ-εκληΐσθην Her. 3, 58; ἀπο-κληϊσθῇ 1, 165; -ισθείς 3, 55 (Bekk. Gaisf. Bred. Dind.), κατα-κληϊσθείς 2, 128 (Ms. M. Ald. Gaisf. Bred. Dind. Krüg.), -ηϊθείς (Bekk. with Ms. F.) Mid. fut. κληΐσσομαι Nonn. 2, 310 (Graefe, Koechly). Vb. κληϊστός Od. 2, 344. Bekker never doubles σ in the aor. holding ῐ with Buttmann. Lobeck says if it were long, κληΐω could not be contracted κλῄω. That a form κληΐζω, κλῄζω existed seems countenanced by Anth. 9, 62, κληζομένη τείχεσι, unless this be, as Dindorf thinks, a mistake for κληομ-, and by the Dor. (κλᾴζω), fut. κλᾳξῶ Theocr. 6, 32 &c. see κλῄω. Mss. and editors of Her. present κληΐω, -ῄω, -είω: the first seems the correct form. Bredow, Dindorf, and Krüger would, perhaps rightly, always write p. p. -ήϊμαι, aor. -ηΐσθην. Bekker has once κεκλεισμένος 2, 121, κεκλειμ- (Gaisf.), and once aor. -ηιθείς 2, 128, -ισθείς (Gaisf. &c. see above).

Κληρόω (κλῆρος) *To allot, choose by lot,* Isocr. 7, 22; Lycurg. 127; Dem. 39, 10: aor. ἐκλήρωσα Thuc. 6, 42, Dor. ἐκλάρωσα Pind. Ol. 8, 15: p. p. κεκλήρωμαι *have been allotted,* Eur. Tr. 240; *chosen by lot,* Dem. 24, 89, but as mid. *has acquired,* τίμην (Hippocr.) Epist. 9, 386 (Lit.); *possesses, has,* καρδίαν Ael. H. A. 5, 31: pres. mid. κληροῦμαι Aesch. Sept. 55; Pl. Leg. 741; Xen. Cyr. 1, 6, 46: imp. ἐκληρ- Lycurg. 88; Dem. 19, 1: fut.

κληρώσομαι Lys. 6, 4; Aeschin. 1, 188: aor. ἐκληρωσάμην Xen. Cyr. 4, 5, 55; Dem. 50, 7.

Κληρονομέω *To obtain by lot, succeed to,* Isocr. 1, 2; Isae. 4, 19; Aristot. Polit. 5, 8, 20; Dem. 19, 320: imp. ἐκληρ- Lycurg. 88: fut. -ήσω Isae. 4, 7 &c.: p. -ηκα Dem. 18, 312; -ηκώς Isae. 2, 35: reg. except fut. mid. κληρονομήσονται as pass. Luc. Tox. 22 (*v. r.* -ηθήσονται).

Κλῄω *To shut* (Attic for κληΐω, Dor. κλαΐω or κλᾴω, κλᾴζω, D. dial. p. 346, Ahr.), Eur. H. F. 997. Bac. 653 (Dind. Kirchh. Nauck): imp. ἔκλῃον Eur. Rhes. 304; Thuc. 7, 59 (Bekk. Krüg. Popp. Dind.): fut. κλῄσω Thuc. 4, 8, ἐκ- Eur. Or. 1127, συγ- Hipp. 498, ἀπο- Ar. Vesp. 775, Dor. κλᾳξῶ Theocr. 6, 32, -ᾳσῶ (Ahr.): aor. ἔκλῃσα Eur. Or. 1449; Thuc. 2, 4, ἀπ- Aesch. Pr. 670 (Dind. Hart.), ξυν- Thuc. 8, 67 (Bekk. Popp.); κλῇσαι Aesch. Pers. 723 (Dind. Herm.), ξυγ- Thuc. 5, 72; κλῄσας Pl. Rep. 560, ξυγ- Thuc. 4, 35, Dor. ἔκλᾳξα, ἐξ- Com. Fr. (Anon.) 4, 676; ἀπό-κλᾳξον Theocr. 15, 43; ἀπο-κλᾴξας 15, 77: p. κέκλῃκα, ἀπο- Ar. Av. 1262 (chor.): p. p. κέκλῃμαι Aesch. Supp. 956 (Dind. Herm.); Soph. Fr. 635 (D.); Eur. Hel. 977; Thuc. 5, 7, ἀπο- 3, 109. 4, 34 (Dor. κέκλᾳμαι Epich.): aor. ἐκλῄσθην, κατ- Thuc. 1, 117; ξυγ-κλῃσθέν 5, 72 (Bekk. Popp. &c.); ξυγ-κλῃσθῆναι 4, 67 (Popp. Krüg. Dind.), -ῃθῆναι (Bekk.), Dor. ἐκλᾴσθην, κατ- Theocr. 7, 84, κατ-εκλᾴχθ- is merely Valckenaer's conjecture, approved by Brunck. Mid. aor. περι-κλῄσασθαι Thuc. 7, 52, ἀπο- 6, 101, Dor. κατ-εκλᾴξατο Theocr. 18, 5. Vb. κλῃστός Thuc. 2, 17. "The Doric forms," says Ahrens, "are written with, and without ι subscr." Fut. κλασῶ or κλᾳσ- is well supported, Theocr. quoted. In Thucydides, Poppo, Krüger, and Dindorf always edit, perhaps rightly, the aor. pass. with σ, Bekker once without, -ῃθῆναι 4, 67.

Κλίνω (ῑ) *To bend,* Archil. 56; Soph. Aj. 131, ἀπο- H. Ven. 168; Pl. Polit. 309, Epic ἀγκλι- for ἀνα-κλ- Opp. Hal. 3, 565; κλίνῃσι Il. 19, 223; κλίνων Il. 23, 171; Aristot. Physiog. 6, 37; κλίνειν Com. Fr. (Anax.) 3, 176: imp. ἔκλ- Xen. Mem. 3, 5, 13, προσ- Od. 21, 165: fut. κλῐνῶ late in *simple,* Lycophr. 557; (Dem.) Prooem. 1450 (Bekk. Dind.); Theon. Rhet. 5, 31 (Walz), but ἐγκατα- Ar. Plut. 621: aor. ἔκλῑνα Il. 8, 435; Eur. Supp. 704, ἐξ- Xen. Cyr. 7, 3, 3, κλῖνα Il. 23, 510; κλῖνον Eur. Or. 311; κλίνας Il. 3, 427; Pl. Tim. 77, ἀγ-κλιν- for ἀνα-κλ- Il. 4. 113; κλῖναι Her. 9, 16: p. κέκλῐκα Polyb. 30, 10; Anth. 12, 213: p. p. κέκλῐμαι Il. 5, 709; Aesch. Pers. 930; Her. 4, 73; Xen. Eq. 5, 5, Epic. 3 pl. κεκλίαται Il. 16, 68: plp. ἐκέκλῐτο Il. 5, 356, κέκλ- 10, 472: aor. ἐκλῐ́θην Od. 19, 470; Pind. Ol. 1, 92; Soph. Tr. 101. 1226; Eur. Hipp. 212. Fr. 692 (Nauck); Her.

1, 211; Hippocr. 8, 312; Pl. Phaed. 109, ἐν- Xen. Conv. 3, 13, κατ- Com. Fr. (Soph.) 3, 581; Hippocr. 2, 682. 3, 40. 94. 140. 146 (Lit.); Xen. Hell. 4, 1, 30. Cyr. 8, 7, 4. Conv. 3, 13 (all or best Mss. Saupp. Mehler). Ven. 8, 3 (Dind.); Andoc. 1, 125 (Bekk.); Pl. Phaed. 117. Phaedr. 229; Hyperid. Eux. C. 31, συγκατ- Com. Fr. (Diod.) 3, 544, ἀπο- Dem. 55, 24, κλίνθην, ἐκλ- Epic and Poet. almost exclusively, Il. 10, 350. 3, 360; Hes. Th. 711; Archil. 34 (Bergk, Toup's emendation); Theocr. 3, 43, occasionally late prose, if correct, κατ- Ael. H. A. 2, 11 (-κλίνην Herch.), ἀπο-κλινθείς Plut. Rom. 2 (Sint. Bekk.). Galb. 27 (Sint. but -κλιθείς Steph. Bekk.): **fut.** κλιθήσομαι Or. Sib. 8, 77, κατα- Eur. Alc. 1090; Diod. Sic. Fr. Lib. 8, 19: **2 aor.** ἐκλῐνην (Eur. Fr. 692; Her. 9, 16, Herwerden's and Dind.'s suggestions), κατ- Ar. Lys. 906. 904. Vesp. 1211; Hippocr. 5, 444 (Lit.); Xen. Cyr. 5, 2, 15 (Dind. Saupp.); Pl. Conv. 213. Phaedr. 230. Rep. 372; and late Ael. H. A. 4, 31: **fut.** κλινήσομαι, κατα- Ar. Eq. 98; Pl. Conv. 222. **Mid.** κλίνομαι, ἀπο- *to lay oneself down, recline,* Her. 3, 104, κατα- Pl. Conv. 175. 203: **imp.** ἐκλίνοντο, κατ- Luc. D. Mar. 5, 1: **fut.** κλινοῦμαι, -ινεῖ, κατα- Ar. Lys. 910 (Br. Voss. -ίνει Dind. Mein.): **aor.** ἐκλινάμην, κλιν- Opp. Hal. 3, 488; -άμενος Od. 17, 340; late prose, κατα- Plut. Mor. 149: and seemingly **p. p.** κέκλιμαι: aor. ἐκλίθην &c. **Vb.** ἀπο-κλιτέον Aristot. Eth. N. 9, 2, 5. For **fut.** κλινεῖ Dem. 1450, 4 (Bekk. Dind.), Sauppe reads subj. κλίνῃ. **1 aor. pass.** with ν, ἐκλίνθην and compounds are not *now* admitted in *classic* prose. The only instance we know of **2 aor. p.** ἐκλῐνην *simple,* is κλίνηθι Herwerden's suggestion (adopted by Dind. 5 ed.) for κλίθητι Eur. Fr. 692, and κλινῆναι W. Dindorf's suggestion for κλῖναι Her. 9, 16, the necessity of which we do not see. Hippocr. has we think always **1 aor.** except once -ίνην 5, 444 (*v. r.* -ίθην). Epic writers and the Tragedians used **1 aor. p.** -ίθην, the Comedians almost always **2 aor.** -ίνην (in compos.): prose authors vary, Plato leaning to the second, Xen. to the first. Lud. Dindorf however in his last edition, adopts κατεκλίνη Hell. 4, 1, 30. Cyr. 8, 7, 4; -κλινείς 5, 2, 15. Cobet (V. Lect.) says, "Athenienses non aliter quam κατεκλίνη dicebant, et sequiores forma κατεκλίθην utuntur." Some of the best, sometimes all the Mss., and some of the best editors say otherwise.

Κλονέω *To move violently, drive,* Poet. in act. Il. 11, 526; Hes. Th. 935; Soph. Tr. 146; κλονέων Mimnerm. 14, 3; but Aretae. Morb. Ac. 2, 101 (ed. Oxon.): **imp.** ἐκλόνεον, συν- Il. 13, 722, iter. ἐκλονέεσκον, ἐπ- Ap. Rh. 3, 687: **fut.** κλονήσω only Ar. Eq. 361: (**p. a: p. p.**?): **aor.** κλονηθέν only in Ionic prose

Hippocr. 7, 532. **Mid.** κλονέονται *move themselves* &c. Ap. Rh. 2, 133; Hippocr. 7, 602; but **pass.** Il. 14, 59; Simon. Am. 1, 15; Pind. P. 9, 48; Soph. O. C. 1241; late prose Ael. H. A. 2, 44: **imp.** ἐκλονέοντο Hes. Sc. 317; **pass.** Luc. Asin. 47, κλον- Il. 5, 93: **fut.** κλονήσομαι reflex, or **pass.** only Hippocr. 7, 474 (Lit.).

Κλύω (ῠ) *To hear*, Poet. (but **pres.** not in Hom.) Hes. Op. 726; Pind. P. 1, 90; Aesch. Pr. 588; Soph. Aj. 871; Eur. Hipp. 585; Ar. Thesm. 1019; subj. κλύω Aesch. Ch. 771; Soph. El. 1238; (Eur. Supp. 436); opt. -οιμι Aesch. Pr. 313; Soph. Tr. 611; Eur. Supp. 570; late Epic Orph. Lith. 169; Theocr. 25, 191; imper. κλύε Emped. 264 (Stein); Aesch. Ch. 156; Soph. El. 675; Eur. Rhes. 384, κλύετε Aesch. Sept. 171; Ar. Plut. 601; κλύειν Aesch. Pers. 284; Soph. Tr. 290; Eur. Alc. 760; Ar. Av. 416. Ran. 1174; κλύων Aesch. Pers. 757; Soph. El. 655; Eur. Hec. 743; Ar. Av. 432; late Epic Orph. Hym. 3, 13: **imp.** ἔκλῠον Il. 10, 47; Soph. O. C. 1766; Eur. Phoen. 919; Ar. Pax 1283, κλύον Il. 15, 300; Hes. Th. 474: **p.** κέκλῠκα Epich.: **2 aor.** ἔκλυν (κλῦμι) only imper. κλῦθι Il. 1, 37; Archil. 75; Aesch. Ch. 332; Soph. Tr. 1115; Eur. Hipp. 872, κέκλῠθι Il. 10, 284; Ap. Rh. 783, κλῦτε Il. 2, 56; Solon 13, 2; Pind. Ol. 14, 4; Aesch. Ch. 399, Epic κέκλῦτε Il. 7, 67; Hes. Th. 644; Pind. P. 4, 13; Ap. Rh. 4, 1654: and perhaps **2 aor. mid.** κλῠ́μενος *renowned*, Theocr. 14, 26; Orph. Arg. 918. **Vb.** κλυτός Il. 2, 742. ῠ, except imper. κλῦθι, κλῦτε. **Imp.** ἔκλυον is used as aor. and, *inferentially* as pres. (*was wont to hear, ay heard*) *hears*, Il. 1, 218.

Κλώζω *To cluck, hiss*, rare, if at all, in classic writers, Alciphr. 3, 71: **imp.** ἐκλώζετε Dem. 21, 226 (Harpocr. Bekk. Dind.) where others read ἐκεκράγειτε (B. Saupp.). **Pass.** late, Aristid. 50, 403.

Κλώθω *To spin*, Her. 5, 12; late Attic Aristot. Mund. 7, 6; Luc. Fugit. 12. Jup. Conf. 19: **aor.** ἔκλωσα Nonn. 2, 678, ἐπ- Od. 3, 208; Eur. Or. 12; Anth. App. Epigr. 166; subj. ἐπι-κλώσῃς Pl. Theaet. 169: **p. p.** κέκλωσται Babr. 69 (2 pt. Lewis), ἐπι- Pl. Leg. 957: **aor.** κλωσθείς Leg. 960, ἐπι- Rep. 620. **Mid.** Dep. ἐπι-κλώσονται Od. 20, 196 (Vulg. -σωνται subj. aor. Bekk. Dind. &c.): **aor.** ἐκλωσάμην Anth. 7, 14, ἐπ- Il. 24, 525; Anth. 14, 124; subj. ἐπι-κλώσωνται Od. 20, 196, quoted. The **mid.** seems to be poetic.

Κναίω *To scrape*, **act.** late in *simple*, Apocr. Sirach. 38, 28 (Grabe's conjecture for καινιεῖ), ἀπο- Ar. Vesp. 681; Luc. Nigr. 8 (**pass.** ἀπο-δια- κναίομαι Eur. Med. 164; Pl. Rep. 406): **imp.** ἀπ-εκναίετε Ar. Eccl. 1087: **fut.** κναίσω, δια- Eur. Cycl. 486, Dor.

κναισῶ, 3 pl. κναισεῦντι, ἐκ- Theocr. 15, 88: aor. ἔκναισε, δι- Eur. Elec. 1307. I. A. 27, ἀπ- Pl. Rep. 406; subj. δια-κναίσῃ Ar. Ran. 1228 &c.: p. κέκναικα, δια- Com. Fr. (Pher.) 2, 327 (act. reg. pass. with σ): p. p. κεκναισμένος, δια- Ar. Nub. 120: aor. ἐκναίσθην, δι- Hippocr. 8, 132. 262 (Lit.), ἀπο- Dio Cass. 50, 33: fut. κναισθήσεται, δια- Ar. Pax 251.

Κνάω (as κναίω) *To scrape, rub*, κνᾷ Plut. Mor. 61, ἐπι-κνᾷς Ar. Av. 1586 (-ῇς Cob. Mein. Dind.); κνῶντες Babr. 94, 10 (Lewis 2 pt.); κνῶσαι Plut. Mor. 786; κνᾶν Her. 7, 239 (often contr. in η, as): imp. (ἔκναε) Epic κνῆ as aor. Il. 11, 639, if not really 2 aor. from (κνῆμι, ἔκνην): fut. κνήσω if correct, Hippocr. 5, 686 (Lit.): aor. ἔκνησα Pl. Conv. 185; Hippocr. 7, 226, κατ- Ar. Vesp. 965, ἐξ- Her. 7, 239: p. p. κέκνησμαι, κατα- Ar. Plut. 973 (Br. so Galen 13, 1022, but -κέκνισμαι Bekk. Dind. Bergk): aor. ἐκνήσθην, κατ- Ar. Eq. 771. Mid. κνάομαι *scratch oneself*, κνᾶται Plut. Pomp. 48; Galen 10, 979, but κνῆται Hippocr. 3, 490 (Lit. *v. r.* κνᾶ-); κνῆσθαι Pl. Gorg. 494, προσ- Xen. Mem. 1, 2, 30, κνᾶσθαι Plut. Mor. 89. 439; κνώμενοι Aristot. H. An. 9, 5, 8: fut. κνήσομαι Galen 10, 437: aor. ἐκνησάμην Luc. Bis Acc. 1; Galen 10, 980, προσ- Xen. Mem. 1, 2, 30, now altered, see above; κνήσαιο Pl. Conv. 185, is Luzac's conjecture, adopted by Bekker and Stallb., κνῆσαις (Stob. Ast, Otto Jahn), κινήσαις (Mss. Bait. Or. Winck.) We have failed, it may be from inadvertence, in finding a *sure* instance of fut. act. Pl. Theaet. 166, has ἀποκνήσειν, but we fear the sense requires this to be fut. of ἀποκνέω rather than of ἀποκνάω. The collat. form κνήθω is perhaps later, κνήθειν Anth. (Strat.) 12, 238, προσ-κνήθων a Poet in Plut. Mor. 462; and Aristot. in mid. and pass. H. A. 9, 1, 18. Probl. 31, 3.

Κνίζω *To scratch, tear*, Her. 7, 10; Theocr. 5, 122; Anth. 11, 73; Herodn. 4, 9; Himer. Orat. 22, 2; opt. -ίζοι Eur. Med. 568; -ίζων Hipponax 14 (B.); Opp. Hal. 2, 442: imp. ἔκν- Soph. O. R. 786; Eur. I. A. 330; Her. 6, 62. 7, 12; App. Hisp. 37, κνίζον Pind. N. 5, 32: fut. κνῐ́σω Ar. Ran. 1198: aor. ἔκνῐσα Pind. P. 11, 23. I. 5, 58 (Bergk); Ar. Vesp. 1286; Anth. 12, 126; late prose Alciphr. 1, 32; Plut. Mor. 65; Athen. 2, 36, and Dor. ἔκνιξα for the metre, Pind. I. 6, 50. P. 10, 60 (B.); subj. κνίσῃ P. 8, 32: p. p. κέκνισται Luc. D. Mer. 10, 4, κατα- Ar. Plut. 973 (Bekk. Dind. Bergk): aor. ἐκνίσθην Theocr. 4, 59; subj. κνισθῇς Eur. Andr. 209; κνισθῆναι Athen. (Macho) 13, 577: pres. κνίζομαι Eur. Med. 555; κνιζόμενος App. Lib. 10, Dor. -ιζομένα Pind. Ol. 6, 44: imp. ἐκνίζετο Themist. 21, 255. Mid. (κνίζομαι), aor. κνίξασθε, περι- Anth. 9, 226. See κνάω. κνίζω and compounds seem not to occur in *classic* Attic prose. The collat.

κνύω occurs only in pres. κνύειν Com. Fr. (Menand.) 4, 309: and imp. 'κνῦεν Ar. Thesm. 481.

Κνυζάω, -έω, *To whimper*, act. rare and late -υζεῖ Opp. Cyn. 1, 507. Mid. κνυζάομαι, -έομαι, -ῶνται Theocr. 2, 109 (Vulg.) -εῦνται (Mss. Ziegl. Fritzs. Mein.); -ᾶσθαι Soph. O. C. 1571 (Dind.), -εῖσθαι (Elms. Nauck); -ώμενος Fr. 646 (Blomf.), -ούμ- (Dind.); Ar. Vesp. 977; Lycophr. 608, -όμενος Ael. H. A. 11, 14 (Vulg. -ώμ- Hercher): imp. ἐκνυζᾶτο Theocr. 6, 30 (Mein.), -εῖτο (Fritz. Ziegl.): fut. -ήσεται Philostr. V. Ap. 3, 96. In our Lexicons, this verb in act. is vouched by Pollux and Suid. and the mid. is confined to the pres.

Κνώσσω *To sleep*, Poet. and only pres. -σσεις Simon C. 37 (B.); -σσων Od. 4, 809; Pind. Ol. 13, 71. P. 1, 8; Opp. Hal. 1, 31; Nic. Alex. 457; Maneth. 3, 95; -σσειν Anth. (Rhian) 12, 38: and imp. ἔκνωσσεν Anth. (Ant. Byz.) 9, 242.

Κοιλαίνω *To hollow*, Hippocr. 6, 418 (Lit.); Aristot. H. An. 9, 9, 4; Opp. Hal. 5, 214: fut. -ᾰνῶ: aor. ἐκοίλᾱνα Attic, Thuc. 4, 100; Luc. V. H. (2), 37, Ion. -ηνα Her. 2, 73; Anth. Pl. 4, 142, ἐγ- Her. 2, 73: p. p. κεκοίλαμμαι Etym. Mag., -ασμαι if correct, Hippocr. 9, 216 (Lit.): aor. ἐκοιλάνθην Hippocr. 5, 420 (Lit.), ἐγ- Theophr. H. P. 5, 2, 4. Mid. aor. κοιλήνατο Nonn. 12, 332, missed by Lexicogr.

Κοιμάω *To put to sleep*, Poet. especially in act. Soph. Ph. 650; imper. κοίμα Aesch. Eum. 832; κοιμῶν Aesch. Sept. 3. Ion. -έω (κοιμέονται Her. 2, 95); fut. κοιμήσω, κατα- Dio Cass. Fr. 36, 23 (Bekk.), and -άσω Anth. 7, 8. 12, 49, κατα- Soph. O. R. 870 chor. (Vulg. see aor.): aor. κοίμησα Od. 3, 397, in prose κατ-εκοίμ- Her. 8, 134; subj. Dor. κοιμάσῃ, κατα- Soph. O. R. 870 (chor.); κοίμησον Il. 14, 236; Aesch. Ag. 1247; -ήσας Il. 12, 281, in prose κατα- Pl. Conv. 223 (κοιμάσειε Eur. Hipp. 1387 Vulg. is now -μίσειε): pass. and mid. *to sleep*, p. p. κεκοίμημαι Athen. (Aeschr.) 8, 335; Anth. 7, 408; Luc. Tim. 6; trans. Gall. 6: aor. ἐκοιμήθην Eur. Andr. 390; Hippocr. 3, 114; Xen. An. 2, 1, 1; Luc. D. Mar. 2, 3, κοιμήθ- Od. 4, 430. 9, 559, Dor. ἐκοιμάθ- Soph. El. 509 (chor.); subj. κοιμηθῇ Pl. Rep. 571; -θείη Od. 4, 443; -θῆναι 14, 411; Pl. Rep. 621, ἐγκατα- Her. 8, 134; κοιμηθείς Od. 20, 4; Hippocr. 2, 478, ἀπο- Her. 8, 76: fut. κοιμηθήσομαι Alciphr. 1, 37, 3 (Mein.); Ach. Tat. 4, 16. 5, 14 (Vulg. see fut. mid.); Joseph. Ant. 11, 3, 2; (Luc.) Asin. 40 (Dind. &c.): and fut. mid. κοιμήσομαι Or. Sib. 3, 793; Luc. D. Deor. 4, 4. 5 (Jacobitz, Dind.); Alciphr. 1, 37, 1; Dio. Hal. 4, 64; Ach. Tat. 5, 15. 4, 16. 5, 14 (Herch.): aor. Epic κοιμησάμην Il. 1, 476. 11, 241. Od. 12, 32 (proverb ἐπὶ ὅλμου ἐκοιμήσω Greg. Cypr. Cent. 3, 52, Cod. Mosq.); subj. -ήσωνται Il. 10, 99;

pres. κοιμᾶται Od. 4, 403; Her. 1, 182, -ῶνται Xen. Cyr. 1, 2, 9, Ion. -έονται Her. 2, 95; -μῷτο 3, 68; -ώμενος Aesch. Ag. 2; Eur. Rhes. 439; Com. Fr. (Chion.) 2, 5; Pl. Conv. 203; -ᾶσθαι Ar. Eccl. 723; Com. Fr. (Timocl.) 3, 607; Pl. Phaedr. 252: **imp.** ἐκοιμᾶτο Hippocr. 3, 116, -ῶντο Xen. An. 4, 5, 14, κοιμ- Il. 6, 246; Pind. I. 8, 22. For **fut.** κατακοιμάσει Soph. O. R. 870 (Vulg.), some Mss. offer **aor.** subj. -άσῃ approved by Elms. adopted by Herm. and *now* by Dind. Hom. uses both **mid.** and **pass.** aorist, Attics the **pass.** only. We have seen the *simple* **act.** form neither in prose nor Comedy. The compounds ἀπο- ἐκ- ἐπι- παρα- συν- seem to have no **act.**

Κοινάω, see κοινόω.

Κοινολογέομαι *To confer*, Aristot. Polit. 2, 8, 13: **imp.** ἐκοινολογεῖτο Dem. 18, 137: **fut.** -ήσομαι Polyb. 22, 22; Polyaen. 3, 2: **aor.** ἐκοινολογησάμην Xen. Hell. 5, 4, 36; -ησάμενος Her. 6, 23; Thuc. 8, 98; Xen. Hell. 3, 1, 9; Polyb. 31, 13; Dio Cass. Fr. 93, 3 (Bekk.); Diod. Sic. 19, 46: **p.** as **mid.** κεκοινολόγημαι Dio Cass. 49, 41: with **plp.** ἐκεκοινολόγηντο Thuc. 7, 86: and **aor.** ἐκοινολογήθην in later usage Polyb. 2, 5. 10, 42. 15, 5. Classic writers use **aor. mid.**; Polyb. has **mid.** and **pass.** in same sense.

Κοινόω (Dor. -άω) *To make common, impart*, Pl. Leg. 952: **fut.** -ώσω Aesch. Ch. 673: **aor.** ἐκοίνωσα Thuc. 5, 38; Pl. Leg. 889; -ώσας Aesch. Supp. 369, Dor. -ᾶσα Pind. P. 4, 115: so **mid.** κοινοῦμαι Thuc. 8, 82, ἀνα- Her. 4, 48; imper. -κοίνεο Theogn. 73: **imp.** ἐκοινοῦντο Thuc. 8, 8, Dor. ἐκοινᾶτο, παρ- Pind. P. 4, 133: **fut.** -άσομαι Pind. N. 3, 12 (Boeckh, Schneid. Momms. Christ), -ώσομαι (Vulg. Bergk 2 ed., see below); Eur. Med. 499. Tr. 61; Artemid. Onir. 1, 80; -σοιτο Isae. 9, 25 (Cob. Scheib. -αιτο Mss. Bekk. B. S.); -ωσόμενος Dio. Hal. Ant. 5, 62: **aor.** ἐκοινωσάμην Isae. 11, 20; Xen. Hell. 7, 1, 27, ἀν-εκοιν- (D.), Poet. 'κοινωσ- Soph. Ant. 539; κοινωσαίμεθα Aesch. Ag. 1347; -άμενος Pl. Menex. 244; Isae. 11, 50: and **p. p.** as **mid.** κεκοίνωνται Eur. Fr. 496 (Dind.): **plp.** ἐκεκοίνωντο, ἀν- Xen. An. 5, 6, 36: but **aor.** ἐκοινώθην we think always **pass.** Eur. Andr. 38; Pl. Leg. 673. Tim. 59. For κοινάσομαι or -ώσομαι Pind. N. 3, 12, Bergk now (4 ed.) reads ex Schol. κοίν' ἀείσομαι. In some of our lexicons this verb is scarcely well handled.

Κοιτάζω *To put to bed*, **act.** very late, **aor.** κοιτάσαι Hesych. **Mid.** κοιτάζεσθαι Plut. Lysandr. 16; Polyb. 10, 15: **aor.** Dor. κοιτάξατο Pind. Ol. 13, 76.

Κολάζω *To punish*, Eur. Hel. 1172; Ar. Vesp. 258; Antiph. 3, δ, 8; Isocr. 4, 123; Xen. Cyr. 1, 2, 7; -λάζῃ Eur. Andr.

740; Pl. Leg. 741; κόλαζε Soph. O. R. 1147; Pl. Leg. 784; κολάζειν Soph. Aj. 1160; Antiph. 4, δ, 10; Thuc. 3, 46; -ων Pl. Leg. 867: **imp.** ἐκόλ- Xen. An. 2, 6, 9; Lys. 28, 3: **fut.** κολᾰ́σω Andoc. 1, 136; Lys. 31, 29 (B. Saupp. Scheibe); Isocr. 7, 42; Lycurg. 10; Xen. Cyr. 7, 5, 83. Athen. 1, 9; Pl. Leg. 714. Rep. 389. Crit. 120; Dem. 22, 39: less freq. **mid.** κολάσομαι, -ῶμαι, see below: **aor.** ἐκόλασα Antiph. 5, 77; Lys. 2, 16; Isocr. 1, 50; imper. κολάσατε Ar. Vesp. 927; Thuc. 3, 40; κολάσαι Ar. Thesm. 454; Antiph. 5, 94; Lycurg. 93: (perf.?): **p. p.** κεκόλασμαι Antiph. 3, δ, 8; Dem. 20, 139: **aor.** ἐκολάσθην Antiph. 3, δ, 8; Xen. Conv. 4, 48; κολασθήτωσαν Thuc. 3, 39, 5; -ασθῆναι 7, 68: **fut.** κολασθήσομαι Thuc. 3, 66; Xen. Cyr. 5, 2, 1; Luc. D. Mort. 30, 1. Prom. 20. **Mid.** κολάζομαι as **act.** Ar. Vesp. 406; Pl. Prot. 324; Luc. D. Mort. 30, 3: **fut.** κολᾰ́σομαι Com. Fr. (Theop.) 2, 801; Xen. An. 2, 5, 13 (Vulg. Krüg.). Hell. 1, 7, 19; Pl. Rep. 575; Luc. Jup. Conf. 18, and κολῶμαι, κολᾷ only Ar. Eq. 456; -ώμενος Vesp. 244: **aor.** ἐκολασάμην Thuc. 6, 78; Pl. Menex. 240. **Vb.** κολαστέος Pl. Gorg. 527. The quotations of **fut. act.** will show that Hemsterhuis and Porson were quite wrong in asserting that "the Attics use only the **mid. fut.** of this verb," and that Buttmann, Passow, and even Poppo are scarcely right in calling the **mid. fut.** 'usitatior' (Xen. Cyr. 7, 5, 83). The **p. pass.** in part. is frequent in the best prose. Besides Antiph. &c. quoted, see Xen. Hell. 5, 3, 27; Dem. 20, 139. 24, 116; Luc. Hermot. 86; κεκόλασται Plut. Mor. 585; κεκολάσθαι Aristot. Eth. N. 3, 15, 6; -ασμένος Eth. Eud. 3, 2, 1: **plp.** ἐκεκόλαστο Plut. Lycurg. 11. The **pres.** and **aor. mid.** are rather rare: the **fut. act.** is confined to prose, and never elided; the **fut. mid.** is in prose and Comedy, and, in the latter, elided or not, seemingly as suited or pleased the writer—a wholesome lesson this to rigid *uniformists*.

Κολούω *To cut short, maim*, Il. 20, 370; Eur. Fr. 93 (Dind.); -ούειν Her. 7, 10; Pl. Apol. 39; -ούων Her. 5, 92; Pl. Leg. 731: **imp.** ἐκολ- Her. 5, 92: **fut.** -ούσω Plut. Alcib. 34: **aor.** ἐκόλουσα Callim. Jov. 90; Theocr. 22, 196; Opp. Hal. 4, 484; Pl. Prot. 343; Aristot. Polit. 2, 12, 4: **p. p.** κεκόλουμαι Anth. 7, 234; Plut. Ages. 31, and -ουσμαι Dio Cass. Fr. 57, 24 (Bekk.): **aor.** ἐκολούθην Thuc. 7, 66 (Mss. Bekk. Popp. Krüg. -σθην Vulg.); Plut. Cat. maj. 26 (Bekk. Sint.); Galen 9, 529, and -ούσθην Aesch. Pers. 1035 (Blomf. Herm. Dind. -ούθην some Mss. Ald.); Theophr. H. P. 3, 7, 1. 7, 2. 4. C. P. 3, 19, 2; Dio Cass. 46, 19. 50, 34 (Bekk.): **fut.** κολουθήσομαι Galen 9, 529. The **aor.** with σ, -ούσθην is best supported Aesch. Pers.

1035, and without it -ούθην Thuc. 7, 66: the Mss. of Theophr. seem to favour -σθην (Wimmer.)

Κομίζω *To take care of, carry, bring,* Od. 24, 251; Soph. Aj. 544; Ar. Av. 410; Her. 4, 71; Thuc. 2, 85; Xen. Oec. 8, 12; κόμιζε Il. 6, 490; Pind. P. 8, 99; Aesch. Ch. 262; inf. -ίζειν Thuc. 4, 78, Epic -ιζέμεν Od. 23, 355: imp. ἐκόμ- Od. 17, 113; Her. 2, 175; Thuc. 7, 74, κομ- Pind. N. 3, 48: **fut.** κομίσω Anth. (Agath.) 6, 41; Apollod. 3, 12, 5; Longus 2, 30. 4, 17. 21 (Mss. Seiler, -ιῶ Hercher); Pl. Rep. 370 (Mss. Vulg. Schneid. B. O. Winck. Herm. -ιῶ Mss. Bekk. Stallb.); Ar. Plut. 768 (may be subj.), Attic -ιῶ Od. 15, 546; Ar. Eccl. 800. Thesm. 1198? Com. Fr. (Alex.) 3, 409; Her. 2, 121; Thuc. 1, 132; Dem. 19, 171, ἀπο- Xen. Cyr. 7, 3, 12: **aor.** ἐκόμισα Pind. N. 6, 30; Eur. Bac. 57; Her. 5, 98; Thuc. 5, 34; Pl. Phaedr. 242, ἐκόμισσα Il. 2, 875, κόμ- 2, 183 (Bekk.), Dor. ἐκόμιξα Pind. N. 2, 19, κομίσειεν Aesch. Ch. 344; -ίξαι Pind. P. 4, 159: **p.** κεκόμικα Her. 9, 115; Isae. 5, 44; Pl. Crito 45: **p. p.** κεκόμισμαι Dem. 18, 241: **aor.** ἐκομίσθην Her. 1, 31; Thuc. 5, 3; Xen. Hell. 5, 3, 19; Pl. Parm. 127, see **mid.**: **fut.** κομισθήσομαι Thuc. 1, 52; Dem. 18, 301. **Mid.** κομίζομαι *to carry oneself, return,* Aesch. Pr. 392; Her. 8, 110; *for oneself, bring off,* Soph. Aj. 63; Eur. I. T. 1362; Her. 2, 14; Thuc. 8, 103; Dem. 41, 11; and perhaps -ιζόμενος Od. 8, 451: **imp.** ἐκομιζ- Her. 4, 76. 8, 21; Isae. 3, 9; Aristot. Oec. 2, 17; Dem. 36, 20. 53, 20: **fut.** κομιοῦμαι Ar. Vesp. 690; Thuc. 1, 113; Lys. 12, 70; Isocr. 8, 22, Ion. -ιεῦμαι Her. 8, 62, -ιέαι 7, 49; (later -ίσομαι Aristot. Nat. Ausc. 2, 5, 4 (B.); Epist. Phal. 135 (Herch.); Justin Mart. 2, 7): **aor.** ἐκομισάμην Her. 6, 118; Thuc. 6, 103; Isocr. 9, 32; Isae. 3, 8, ἐκομίσσ- Od. 14, 316, κομίσ- Il. 1, 594, and κομίσσ- 8, 284; subj. -ίσωμαι Ar. Ach. 1031; Andoc. 3, 14; Dem. 16, 17; κομίσαιντο Pl. Rep. 615, ἀνα- Poet. ἀγ-κομ- Pind. P. 4, 9; imper. κόμισαι Eur. Tr. 588[d] (Ald. κοίμ- Dind.); -ίσασθαι Andoc. 1, 38; Dem. 16, 22; Xen. An. 5, 5, 20; -σάμενος 3, 2, 26; Isae. 1, 12: and in sense **p.** κεκόμισμαι Thuc. 8, 61; Isae. 5, 22; Dem. 18, 231. 20, 149. 21, 171. 41, 11, ἐσ- Ar. Vesp. 616, ἀνα- Xen. Cyn. 6, 1, 14: **aor.** ἐκομίσθην as **mid.** intrans. Thuc. 2, 33. 73: **fut.** -θήσομαι see Thuc. quoted, especially δια- Pl. Leg. 803. **Vb.** κομιστέος Aesch. Sept. 600 (Herm.), -ιστέον Pl. Rep. 413. Lexicons say "Her. uses the **fut.** and **aor.** **mid.** in the signification *come* or *go back,*" and quote as instances 6, 118. 8, 62. The first is certainly no proof, the second scarcely decisive.

Κομψεύω *To make fine* &c., rare in **act.** Soph. Ant. 324: **p. p.** κεκομψευμένος Pl. Phil. 56: but **mid.** κεκόμψευται Eur. I. A. 333; Pl. Phaedr. 227: with **aor.** ἐκομψευσάμην Pl. Rep. 489; Galen 10,

113: fut. -εύσομαι Aristid. 42 (517): pres. κομψεύομαι Hippocr. 4, 288; Pl. Crat. 400. Lach. 197.

Κονᾰβέω and -ίζω *To ring, rattle*, Epic, both late in pres. -αβεῖ Anth. (Cereal.) 11, 144, -ᾰβίζετε Orph. H. 38, 9: imp. κονάβιζε Il. 13, 498. 21, 255: aor. κονάβησε Il. 15, 648. Od. 17, 542. Hom. H. 3, 54; Hes. Th. 840.

Κονίω (-ίζω late) *To raise dust* &c. Poet. Il. 13, 820; Aesch. Sept. 60: fut. κονίσω Il. 14, 145: aor. ἐκόνῑσα Il. 21, 407, -ισσα Batr. 204 (Franke, Baum. v. r. -ισα); κονίσας Aesch. Pers. 163: p. p. κεκόνῑμαι Il. 21, 541; Hes. Op. 481; Ar. Eccl. 291; Anth. 6, 124; Luc. Tim. 45. D. Deor. 24, 1; Theocr. 1, 30 (some Mss. Br. Ziegl. Fritz. -ισμαι Mss. Vulg.) both doubtful: plp. κεκόνῑτο Il. 22, 405, later κεκόνιστο Anth. 9, 128. **Mid.** κονίομαι *to raise dust about oneself, roll oneself*, Aristot. H. A. 9, 49 B, 10; Paus. 10, 25, 4, and -ίζομαι Dionys. Av. 1, 8: **fut.** κονίσομαι Anth. Plan. 25, late prose -ῐοῦμαι Philo Vit. Mos. 3, and perhaps -ῑσομαι Galen 6, 162: **aor.** ἐκονισάμην Galen 6, 162; κόνῑσαι Ar. Eccl. 1176; -ισάμενος Luc. Anach. 31, -ισσάμ- Orph. Lith. 25; κονίσασθαι Themist. 21, 249, ἐγ- Xen. Conv. 3, 8. At Theocr. 1, 30, Wordsworth retains κεκονισμένος; Ziegler, Fritzsche in 2 ed. read κεκονιμένος; Ahrens κεκομημένος; Meineke *now* κεχροϊσμένος.

Κοννέω *To know*, Poet. and only pres. Aesch. Supp. 164, -εῖς 119 (Boisson. Dind. Herm.).

Κόπτω *To cut*, Aesch. Eum. 635; Eur. Elec. 838; Ar. Nub. 132; Hippocr. 6, 494; Xen. Eq. 1, 4; -των Od. 18, 28; Hipponax 83; Her. 6, 113; Thuc. 4, 90; -τειν Andoc. 1, 41: **imp.** ἔκοπτον Thuc. 8, 105, ἀν- Od. 21, 47, κόπτον 8, 274: **fut.** κόψω Hipponax 83; Ar. Ran. 460; Xen. Oec. 18, 5, ἀπο- An. 3, 4, 39; -κόψειν Il. 9, 241 (-ψέμεν Bekk.); Aeschin. 2, 76: **aor.** ἔκοψα Od. 10, 127 (in tmesi); Aesch. Ch. 423; Ar. Lys. 361; Her. 2, 94; Thuc. 2, 75, κόψ- Il. 13, 203: **p.** κέκοφα, ἐκ- Xen. Hell. 6, 5, 37, περι- Lys. 14, 42, συγ- Pl. Theaet. 169: **p. p.** κέκομμαι Aesch. Pers. 683; Com. Fr. (Strat.) 2, 768; Ar. Ach. 512; Her. 4, 71; Thuc. 4, 26: (1 **aor.** ἐκόφθην?): **3 fut.** κεκόψομαι, ἀπο- Ar. Nub. 1125, ἐκ- Ran. 1223, κατα- Xen. An. 1, 5, 16: **2 p.** as pres. act. (κέκοπα), κεκοπώς Epic, Il. 13, 60. Od. 18, 335: **2 aor. pass.** ἐκόπην, ἐξ- Ar. Nub. 24, περι- Thuc. 6, 27, ἀπ- Xen. An. 4, 2, 17; *in simple*, subj. κοπῇ Pl. Tim. 60; κοπεὶς Aesch. Ag. 1278; Ar. Ran. 723; Thuc. 8, 13, κατα- Her. 8, 92. 9, 89, ἐκ- Aeschin. 1, 172: **fut.** κοπήσομαι *simple* late, V. T. Jer. 16, 4; Galen 13, 759, but συν- Lys. 3, 34, κατα- Dio. Hal. Ant. 7, 5. **Mid.** κόπτομαι *strike for oneself, strike oneself for grief, bewail*, Ar. Lys. 396; Her. 2, 61. 121; Pl. Rep. 619: **imp.**

ἐκοπτ- Anth. 11, 159: **fut.** late? κόψομαι V. T. Jer. 22, 18, &c.; but seemingly **pass.** *shall be cut*, Or. Sib. 3, 651. 731: **aor.** ἐκοψάμην Her. 4, 166, ἐπ- Eur. Tr. 623, κοψ- Il. 22, 33. **Vb.** κοπτός Com. Fr. (Cratin.) 2, 211. See **act.** ἔκοψα κομμόν Aesch. Ch. 423, and **pass.** κέκοπται πέδον Pers. 683.

Κορέννῦμι, -έσκω, -έω *To satiate*, usu. Poet. **pres.** late κορεννύς Themist. 16, 213 (D.); Hexapl. Ps. 102, 5; κορέοις Nic. Alex. 195, κορέσκοις 360, -σκοι 415; -σκων 225: **imp.** κορέεσκε Anth. 5, 77: **fut.** κορέσω Her. 1, 212. 214; Anth. 14, 133; Orph. Lith. 266, -έσσω Anth. 14, 135, Epic κορέω Il. 13, 831. 17, 241 (Bekk. Spitzn. Dind.): **aor.** ἐκόρεσα, -εσσα Anth. 7, 204; subj. κορέσῃ Aesch. Pr. 165 (chor.), -έσσῃ Opp. Hal. 2, 180, -έσωμεν Ap. Rh. 3, 897; opt. κορέσαις, ὑπο- Theogn. 1158, κορέσσαι Theocr. 24, 136, κορέσειεν Il. 16, 747; Solon 13, 73; inf. κορέσαι Soph. Ph. 1156 (chor.), -έσσαι Lycophr. 1171: **p. p.** κεκόρεσμαι Anth. (Leon.) Plan. 190; Xen. Mem. 3, 11, 14; Plut. Demosth. 23; Luc. Nigr. 38, and Ion. κεκόρημαι Il. 18, 287. Od. 8, 98; Hes. Op. 593; Theogn. 751; Sapph. 48 (Bergk); Ar. Pax 1285 (Bekk. Dind.); Her. 3, 80: **aor.** always ἐκορέσθην Theogn. 1249; Ap. Rh. 4, 1449 (3 pl. -όρεσθεν, for -ησαν, Ar. Pax 1283-4, Epic parody), κορέσθ- Od. 4, 541. 10, 499; κορεσθείς Theogn. 1269; Eur. Hipp. 112 (late prose ἐκορέσθην Luc. D. Mer. 3, 2; Pseud.-Callisth. 1, 44; κορεσθῇ Ael. V. H. 4, 9; -εσθῆναι Luc. Amor. 17): **fut.** late κορεσθήσομαι Babr. 31, 19 (Lewis, 2 pt.); Hexapl. Ps. 21, 26 (Sym.): **3 fut.** late κεκορήσομαι Maxim. de Ausp. 117: **2 p.** as **pass.** and Epic κεκορηώς Od. 18, 372; Coluth. 119; Nonn. D. 5, 34. **Mid.** κορέννῦμαι **pres.** late, Orph. Lith. 726; Niceph. Rhet. 2, 3, and (κορέομαι); opt. -έοιτο reflexive, Nic. Alex. 263: **fut.** κορέσομαι Or. Sib. 3, 697: **aor.** ἐκορεσάμην, Poet. κορεσά- Orph. Lith. 558, ἐκορέσσ- Il. 11, 87, κορέσσ- 22, 427; Ap. Rh. 2, 307; κορέσωνται Il. 22, 509; Hes. Fr. 170; opt. 3 pl. κορεσαίατο Od. 14, 28; κορέσασθαι Il. 13, 635; Hes. Op. 368; Theocr. 8, 67; κορεσσάμενος Il. 19, 167; Hes. Op. 33; Ap. Rh. 2, 1227: and in sense κεκόρεσμαι, and -ημαι: ἐκορέσθην. **Vb.** ἀ-κόρητος Il. 20, 2; Ar. Nub. 44, -ετος Aesch. Ag. 1117, -εστος 756; Plut. Mar. 46, -έστερα Xen. Conv. 8, 15.—κεκορεσμένος seems the only participle used in *classic* Attic prose. Aristoph. has used the Ionic form κεκορημένοι Pax 1285, but in an Epic parody.

Κορθύνω (-θύω see **pass.**) *To raise up*, Epic, **aor.** κόρθῦνα Hes. Th. 853. **Pass.** κορθύνεται Ap. Rh. 2, 322, -ύεται (Merk.); so Nic. Ther. 426, κορθύεται Il. 9, 7.

Κορύσσω *To helmet, arm*, Poet. Opp. H. 5, 284. 286; -σων Il. 2, 273; Hes. Sc. 148; Pind. I. 8, 54; Eur. Rhes. 933; inf.

Epic κορυσσέμεν Pind. P. 8, 75: imp. Epic κόρυσσε Il. 21, 306, ἐκόρυσσε Nonn. 2, 5: aor. (ἐκόρυξα, see below): p. p. κεκορυθμένος Il. 17, 3; Eur. Andr. 279 (chor.). I. A. 1073 (chor.), κεκορυσμένος Hesych. **Mid.** κορύσσομαι reflexive, -ύσσεαι Il. 10, 37, -ύσσεται 4, 442; Simon. Am. 7, 105; Ap. Rh. 2, 71; Theocr. 25, 94; imper. κορύσσεο Ap. Rh. 4, 48; -σσόμενος act.? Opp. C. 4, 169: **imp.** κορύσσετο Il. 7, 206: **aor.** κορυσσάμενος Il. 19, 397, and if correct, later -ύξατο (Hippocr.) Epist. 1284 (Foes, 3, 597 Erm. -ύσατο Lit. 9, 372, -ύσσατο v. r.); -ύξασθαι Athen. 3, 127, see below. The 1 aor. act. ἐκόρυξα Theocr. 3, 5, and mid. ἐκορυξάμην (Hippocr.) Epist. p. 1284 &c.; Athen. 3, 127, referred to this verb, are probably corrupt forms for ἐκόρυψα, -άμην from κορύπτω *to butt;* indeed κορύψῃ is now the approved reading Theocr. 3, 5 (Mein. Ziegl. Ahr. Fritzsche), but Littré ἐκορύσατο Hippocr. quoted.

Κοτέω *To be angry*, Epic, Il. 14, 143; Hes. Op. 25; Ap. Rh. 4, 701; κοτεῖν, ἐγ- Aesch. Ch. 41; κοτέων Il. 10, 517; Hes. Th. 315 (and κοταίνω Aesch. Sept. 485 chor.): **imp.** κότεε Orph. Arg. 1370, ἐκότουν, ἐν- Soph. Fr. 871, iter. κοτέεσκε Orph. Arg. 537: aor. rare (ἐκότεσα); κοτέσασα H. Cer. 254: **2 p. as pres.** κεκοτηὼς Il. 21, 456. Od. 22, 477; Ap. Rh. 2, 89. **Mid.** as act. **imp.** κοτέοντο Il. 2, 223: **fut.** (or **aor.** subj. rather) κοτέσσομαι Il. 5, 747. 8, 391. (Od. 1, 101): **aor.** κοτέσσατο Il. 23, 383; Callim. Cer. 58; subj. -έσσεται for -έσσηται, see **fut.**; -εσσάμενος Il. 5, 177. Od. 5, 147. 19, 83; Q. Sm. 9, 304. 12, 169. This verb is purely Epic. The comp.? ἐγκοτέω, -εῖν occurs Aesch. Ch. 41 (chor.): **imp.** ἐνεκότουν Soph. Fr. 871 (D.)

Κουφίζω *To lighten*, Eur. Supp. 1047; Hippocr. 7, 146; Xen. Cyr. 6, 3, 24; -ίζων Hes. Op. 463; -ίζειν Soph. Ph. 735: **fut.** -ιῶ Soph. Ant. 43, Ar. Av. 1760: **aor.** ἐκούφ- Eur. Rhes. 281; Hippocr. 1, 228 (Erm.); -ίσας Soph. Tr. 1025; Thuc. 6, 34 &c. reg. **Mid.** late, and only **fut.** -ιοῦμαι as **pass.** Aristid. 46, 145: **fut. pass.** -ισθήσομαι classic, Eur. Med. 473. Lexicogr. have missed the **Mid.**

Κοχῦδέω (κοχύω ?) *To trickle*, Poet. κοχυδοῦντες Com. Fr. (Pher.) 2, 316: **imp.** iter. κοχύδεσκον Theocr. 2, 107 (Mss. Mein. Wordsw. Ahr. Ziegl.), κοχύεσκον (Vulg.) Collat. form (κοχύζω) κοκκύζω Com. Fr. (Stratt.) 2, 788.

Κραδάω, -αίνω *To shake, brandish*, in classic Greek scarcely beyond the **pres.** κρᾰδάουσι Opp. C. 4, 410; κρᾰδάων Epic Il. 7, 213. 13, 583. Od. 19, 438; κραδάοιεν, ἐπι- Opp. Cyn. 1, 91, κραδαίνοι Aesch. Pr. 1047 (chor.); -αίνων Ar. Ach. 965, -ουσα Eur. H. F. 1003: **aor.** late ἐκρᾰ́δᾱνα Plut. Ant. 37. **Pres.** κραδαινομένη Il. 13, 504; -νεσθαι Theophr. Fr. 8, 8: **imp.** ἐκραδαίνοντο Xen. Eph. 119: aor. ἐκραδάνθην, κρᾰδανθῇ Plut. Mor. 435; -θῆναι Plut. Alex. 74; -ανθείς Heliod. 10, 31.

Κράζω *To cry out*, **pres.** rare, Ar. Eq. 287; Aristot. H. A. 9, 1, 23; Theophr. Sign. 6, 4, 52 (Wimmer); Aesop 62 (Halm): **fut.** κεκράξομαι Com. Fr. (Eup.) 2, 428; Ar. Eq. 487. Ran. 265. Fr. 45, κατα- Eq. 287; late prose Plut. Phoc. 9; Sext. Emp. 557, 17: late κράξω Anth. 11, 141; Phil. Eleph. 362; N. T. Luc. 19, 40 (Vat. Tisch. Sin.): and κράξομαι, ἀνα- V. T. Joel 3, 16 (Alex.), ἀνακεκράξ- (Vat.): **1 aor.** rare and late, ἔκραξα V. T. Gen. 41, 55; N. T. Matth. 14, 30. Marc. 15, 14 &c.; Aesop 98 (Schaef. ἐκεκράγει Halm); κράξῃ Theophr. Sign. 6, 52. 53 (Wimm.); -ας Anth. 11, 211 (ἐκέκραξα V. T. Ps. 21, 6 &c.; 1 Macc. 11, 49): **2 aor.** ἔκρᾰγον (-άγετε some Mss. Dem. 21, 62, is a false reading), ἀν- Od. 14, 467; Pind. N. 7, 76; Antiph. 5, 44; Andoc. 1, 44; Xen. Cyr. 3, 3, 67. An. 5, 1, 14, ἐν- Ar. Plut. 428; Dem. 21, 215 (ἐκέκρᾰγον V. T. Esai. 6, 4): **2 p.** as **pres.** κέκρᾱγα Aesch. Pr. 743; Soph. Aj. 1236; Ar. Eq. 863; Hippocr. 8, 66; Aeschin. 3, 218; -γώς Xen. An. 7, 8, 15; Lys. 3, 15; Dem. 18, 132: **plp.** ἐκεκράγειν Com. Fr. (Antiph.) 3, 68. (Men.) 4, 118; Hippocr. 1, 661 (Erm.), 2 pl. ἐκεκράγετε Xen. Cyr. 1, 3, 10 (Dind. Saupp. -γειτε Vulg.), 3 ἐκεκράγεσαν Ar. Eq. 674; Luc. Anach. 23. Imper. κέκραχθι Ar. Vesp. 198; Luc. Tim. 53, so κέκραχθ' Ar. Ach. 335, pl. κεκράγετε Vesp. 415, for which some unnecessarily hold κέκραχθ' Ach. 335, a contracted form. **Pres.** κράζω, **fut. mid.** κεκράξομαι are rare; **fut. act.** κράξω, **1 aor.** ἔκραξα, and *simple* **2 aor.** ἔκρᾰγον seem not to occur in good Attic. The unredupl. **fut. mid.** κράξομαι is a v. r. N. T. Luc. 19, 40 (Ms. D.) Of **1 aor.** in Septuag. by far the prevailing form is the redupl. ἐκέκραξα, but ἀν-έκραξα: of **2 aor.** the only form ἐκέκρᾰγον, but ἀν-έκραγον: and always fut. κεκράξομαι: in N. T. the **aor.** is never redupl. In late Poets the **2 perf.** is sometimes short, κέκρᾰγεν Anth. 5, 87, κέκρᾰγ' Spitzner very happily, ἔκρᾰγεν **2 aor.** if admissible, would be easier still, ἐκεκρᾰγει, ἀν- Nicet. Eug. 6, 29. Collat. form κραυγάνομαι Her. 1, 111, κραγγάν- (Lob. Bred.)

Κραιαίνω *To accomplish*, Epic form of κραίνω, **imp.** κραίαινεν Il. 5, 508, ἐπ-εκραί- 2, 419. 3, 302: **aor.** ἐκρήηνα Hom. H. 4, 222; imper. κρήηνον Il. 1, 41, -ήνᾰτε Od. 3, 418; inf. κρηῆναι Il. 9, 101: **p. p.** 3 pl.? κεκράανται Od. 15, 116; Ap. Rh. 4, 193: **plp.** 3 pl.? κεκράαντο Od. 4, 132: **aor.** ἐκρᾱάνθην, 3 pl. -άανθεν Theocr. 25, 196. **Vb.** ἀκράαντος Il. 2, 138.

Κραίνω *To accomplish*, Poet. and Ion. prose, Od. 19, 567; Pind. Ol. 6, 81; Soph. Aj. 1050; Eur. Ion 464; Hippocr. 2, 528; κραίνῃ Aesch. Ag. 1424; κραίνειν Pind. P. 9, 66; -αίνων

Ol. 3, 11: imp. ἔκραινε Eur. Hel. 1318, iter. κραίνεσκε Orph. Arg. 477: fut. κρᾰνέω Emped. 25 (Stein); Ap. Rh. 4, 404, Attic κρανῶ Aesch. Ch. 1075; Eur. Supp. 375: aor. ἔκρᾱνα Aesch. Supp. 622; Eur. Ion 570, ἐπ- Soph. Ph. 1468, Epic ἔκρηνα, κρῆνον Od. 20, 115; κρῆναι 5, 170: p.p. 3 sing. κέκρανται Aesch. Supp. 943. Ch. 871, 3 pl. Eur. Hipp. 1255, where however Elms. Nauck, Kirchh. and now Dind. read συμφορά for -ραί, Epic κεκρᾱανται Od. 4, 616. 15, 116: plp. κεκράαντο 4, 132, referred also to κεράννυμι: aor. ἐκράνθην Pind. P. 4, 175; Aesch. Eum. 347; Eur. Supp. 814 (chor.): fut. κρανθήσομαι Aesch. Pr. 911: and fut. mid. pass. κρᾰνέεσθαι Il. 9, 626; and if correct, opt. κρᾰνοῖτο Aesch. Pr. 211 (Elms. and *now* Dind. Hart., κραίνοιτο Vulg. Herm. &c.): but aor. mid. as act. ἐπ-εκρήναντο Q. Sm. 14, 297, missed, we think, by Lexicogr. **Vb.** ἄκραντος Aesch. Ag. 249; Eur. I. T. 520.—Aesch. Ag. 1340, Dind. reads with the Mss. fut. ἐπικρᾱνεῖ with long penult.; Herm. holds this lengthening inadmissible, and alters the fut. to pres. ἐπικραίνει. From this Dind. (5 ed.) dissents, and retains fut. -ᾱνεῖ with a slight misgiving, "si scripsit Aeschylus, quod incertum est, ultimam syllabam produxit, quod perraro fit in hoc verborum genere." The same anomaly occurs in the fut. of αἴρω, and φαίνω, which see. We observe Burgess, Bergk, Mein. and now Dind. read φαίνω Ar. Eq. 300, for φᾱνῶ (Vulg. Bekk.) and we feel inclined to agree, not only because the lengthening of a liquid fut. seems a violent anomaly, and because Ar. has ἀποφᾰνῶ Nub. 1331, but because we think he shirks the use of ἀποφᾱνῶ in line 1334, by using ἀποδείξω in its stead—unless, to be sure, the latter is to be taken as a threat of demonstration.

Κρατέω *To rule*, Il. 5, 175; Pind. N. 4, 50; Aesch. Pr. 324; Soph. O. C. 68; Ar. Pax 680; Hippocr. 6, 504; Thuc. 4, 62; Xen. Mem. 2, 7, 2; Pl. Menex. 238; Isae. 8, 2; -τέειν Il. 1, 288, -τεῖν Antiph. 5, 26: imp. ἐκράτουν Thuc. 1, 50, -τει Pind. N. 5, 45; Lys. 13, 26, -τεε Her. 9, 42, κράτει Pind. P. 4, 245, iter. κρατέεσκον Anth. 5, 294, κράτεσκ- Pind. N. 3, 52: fut. -ήσω Aesch. Eum. 491; Her. 8, 15; Thuc. 6, 49; Pl. Leg. 781: aor. ἐκράτησα Pind. N. 10, 25; Soph. O. R. 1198; Her. 1, 92; Thuc. 2, 99; Isae. 5, 30, κρατ- Pind. N. 6, 35; pt. κρατήσας Simon. C. 155, 11, Dor. -ήσαις Pind. P. 10, 23: p. κεκράτηκα Aesch. Pers. 149; Thuc. 3, 30: reg. except fut. mid. κρατησόμεθα as pass. Aristid. 39, 501 (Dind.); read also by some Thuc. 4, 9 (Ms. G. Vulg. Haack): but fut. p. κρατηθήσ- (best Mss. Bekk. Popp. Goell. Krüg. Dind. &c.); Hippocr. 3, 482. **Mid.** aor. ἐπι-κρατησάμενος Galen 3, 467, missed by all Lexicogr., and we think fut. mid. also. Hom. seems to use pres. only.

Κράω, see *κεράννυμι.*

Κρέμᾰμαι *To hang, be suspended,* as ἵσταμαι, Anacr. 107; Theogn. 1371; Pind. Ol. 7, 25; Soph. Fr. 382; Com. Fr. (Herm.) 2, 403; Xen. An. 3, 2, 19, ἐπι- H. Hym. 2, 106; subj. κρέμωμαι, -ηται Hippocr. 4, 290 (Lit.); Arist. Rhet. 3, 14, 6; opt. κρεμαίμην, -αιο Ar. Nub. 870 (Bekk. Dind. Bergk), -αισθε Vesp. 298 (Dobr. Dind. Bergk, -οισθε Vulg. Bekk.); -άσθω Archil. 53; κρεμάμενος Her. 1, 66. 2, 121; Hippocr. 2, 118; Pl. Leg. 831; Xen. Conv. 8, 19; κρέμασθαι Com. Fr. 3, 41, ἀπο- Hippocr. 2, 152: **imp.** ἐκρεμᾰ́μην Com. Fr. (Pher.) 2, 300; Ar. Thesm. 1053; Xen. An. 4, 1, 2; Luc. Char. 17, 2 sing. ἐκρέμω Il. 15, 21, κρέμαντο Anth. Plan. 210: **fut.** κρεμήσομαι Ar. Vesp. 808; Luc. Fug. 31; Long. Past. 4, 9; Alciphr. 3. 21. The **act.** κρέμημι is given by Matthiae from Athen. 1, 46, where stands κρέμαντες, which, however, Schweigh. and Lobeck would alter to κρεμάσαντες, of κρεμάω.

Κρεμάννῡμι *To hang, suspend,* Theophr. C. P. 1, 7, 2; -αννύς Pl. Leg. 830, ἀνα- Tim. 90. Ion 536, later κρεμάω (Arist.) Hist. Mir. 6, and -μαννύω Aristot. H. A. 9, 6, 4; Theophr. C. P. 4, 3, 3; Themist. 26, 331: **fut.** κρεμᾰ́σω Com. Fr. (Alcae.) 2, 827; Or. Sib. 7, 25; Geop. 3, 6; V. T. Gen. 40, 19, Attic κρεμῶ, -ᾶς, -ᾶ Ar. Plut. 312, Epic κρεμόω Il. 7, 83: **aor.** ἐκρέμᾰσα Ar. Thesm. 1028; Arist. Oec. 2, 33; Anth. 6, 217; Paus. 3, 12, 8; Arr. An. 6, 30, ἀπ- Il. 23, 879, ὑπερ- Theogn. 206; Pind. Ol. 1, 57 (Vulg. Bergk 2 ed.), ἀν- H. Hym. 1, 8; Her. 5, 77. 9, 120; Aeschin. 3, 100, κρέμασε Pind. Ol. 1, 57 (Bergk 3 ed. Christ), in tmesi Od. 8, 67; κρεμάσας Il. 8, 19; Ar. Ran. 619, ἀγ-κρεμ- for ἀνα-κρ- Od. 1, 440; κρεμάσαι Ar. Ach. 58; Hippocr. 4, 86; Xen. An. 1, 2, 8, κατα- Her. 2, 121: **p. p.** late, imper. κεκρεμάσθω Archim. Tetrag. 131: **plp.** κεκρέμαστο, κατα- Diod. Sic. 18, 26: **aor.** ἐκρεμάσθην Ar. Thesm. 1053; Theocr. 23, 52; App. Civ. 1, 71; κρεμασθῇ Eur. Bac. 1240; -ασθείη Hipp. 1252; -ασθείς Xen. An. 7, 4, 17; Pl. Theaet. 175, ἀνα- Her. 9, 122, ἐπι- Thuc. 1, 18. 3, 40; -ασθῆναι, ἀνα- Her. 7, 26, ἐπι- Thuc. 2, 53: **fut.** κρεμασθήσομαι we have not seen. **Mid.** rare, **aor.** ἐκρεμασάμην Anth. 7, 473, κρεμασ- Opp. C. 4, 88; -άσωμαι, ἐκ- Anth. 5, 92, κρεμάσηται Hippocr. 12, 455 (ed. Chart. Ms. O. Gal. but κρέμηται Littré 4, 290); -άσαιο, ἐπεγ- Nic. Fr. 72 (O. Schn.); -άσασθαι Hes. Op. 629. **Vb.** κρεμαστός Soph. O. R. 1266. The form -αννύω seems scarcely classic, and κρεμάω in pres. still later, Pseud.-Aristot. quoted above; Dem. Phal. 216; Ael. H. A. 5, 3; Stob. (Nicol.) 123, 12; Geop. 10, 56. 13, 10; ἀπ-εκ-ρέμα (Luc.) Asin. 30 (Jacob. ἀπ-εκρήμνα Bekk. Dind.); κρεμᾶται Anacreont. 16, 17 (Bergk); κρεμᾶσθαι Antiph. Athen. 10, 88

(459) has been altered from Mss. to κρέμασθαι (Dind.); so Com. Fr. 3, 41 (Mein.) In Hippocr. however still stand κρεμᾶσθαι 1, 592 (Lit.). 2, 42 (Kühn, 2, 288 Lit.), προσ- 1, 463 (Kühn.) We doubt these, both because in the second and third citations one Ms. has κρέμασθαι, and in the fourth occurs ἐκκρεμάμενον not -ώμενον, and ἐκκρεμανῦντα seemingly a vicious form for -ννῦντα, 1, 464, tending to favour the belief that -ᾶσθαι is a wrong accentuation, and that the correct form in Hippocr. is the *classic* κρεμάννυμι, κρέμαμαι, see 2, 152. The form κατακεκραμμένον Hippocr. 3, 100 (Vulg.) called by some perf. pass. for -κεκρέμασμαι, as κεκέρασμαι, κέκραμαι, has been altered rightly by Littré (3, 490) to pres. κατα-κρεμάμενον, from eight Mss.

Κρέμημι, see κρέμαμαι.

Κρεοκοπέω *To cut flesh*, Poet. and only 3 pl. pres. -οῦσι Aesch. Pers. 463; and inf. -εῖν Eur. Cycl. 359. Late occurs the form κρεωκοπέω, and even in some edit. of Eur.

Κρέων *Ruling*, defect. part. Pind. N. 3, 10, Epic κρείων Il. 8, 31. 22, 48.

Κρήμνημι *To suspend* (κρημνός), Poet. imper. κρήμνη Eur. Fr. 918 (D.); κρημνάς Pind. P. 4, 25: imp. ἐκρήμνην late, App. Mithr. 97. Mid. κρήμνᾰμαι Aesch. Sept. 229; late prose, Athen. 13, 49, but κατα- Hippocr. 2, 220; imper. κρήμνασθε, ἐκ- Eur. H. F. 520; κατα-κρημνάμεναι Ar. Nub. 377: imp. ἐκρήμνατο Eur. El. 1217; late prose App. Civ. 1, 71 (Bekk.) The mid. is intrans. but ἐκ-κρημνάμεσθα as act. Eur. Ion 1613. This verb seems not to occur in Attic prose, occasionally in late and Ionic. κρημνάω also is very partially used, and late, κρημνᾷ (Luc.) Asin. 24; κρημνῶν Diog. Laert. 6, 50; κρημνᾶν Xen. Eph. 2, 13 (κρεμᾶν Passow): mid. κρημνᾶται, κατα- Dioscor. 4, 46: but imp. ἐκρημνῶντο, κατ- as early as Hom. H. 7, 39.

Κρίζω *To creak*, Poet. Com. Fr. (Men.) 4, 295; Boeot. inf. κριδδέμεν C. Fr. (Stratt.) 2, 781: 1 aor. ἔκριξα late prose, κρίξασαν Ael. H. A. 5, 50: 2 aor. κρῖκε Epic, Il. 16, 470, v. r. κρίγε (Herodn. Clark): 2 p. κεκρῖγότες Ar. Av. 1521.

Κρίνω (ῑ) *To judge*, Il. 5, 501; Aesch. Ag. 471; Soph. El. 339; Ar. Eq. 873; Her. 1, 30; Thuc. 5, 60: imp. ἔκρινον Hippocr. 1, 219 (Erm.); Thuc. 3, 43; Isocr. 16, 8; Aeschin. 2, 144: fut. κρῐνῶ Soph. Ant. 328; Ar. Ran. 1411; Thuc. 3, 57; Andoc. 1, 105; Pl. Phaedr. 237, Ionic κρῐνέω Heraclit. 26 (Byw.), δια- Il. 2, 387; Q. Sm. 6, 55: aor. ἔκρῖνα Od. 18, 264; Pind. N. 9, 35; Aesch. Pr. 485; Eur. Phoen. 1662; Ar. Ran. 1473; Her. 1, 120; Xen. Hell. 1, 7, 34; Pl. Rep. 578; κρίνας Il. 6, 188; Eur. Hec. 1249; Thuc. 4, 61; κρῖναι Soph. Tr. 970; Thuc. 1, 138; Pl. Apol. 35: p. κέκρῐκα Pl. Leg. 734;

Lys. 6, 54; Com. Fr. (Men.) 4, 260. (Nicol.) 4, 580: p. p. κέκρῐμαι Pind. Ol. 2, 30; Eur. Phoen. 1663; Her. 4, 64. 7, 16; (Andoc.) 4, 35; Pl. Gorg. 483; Dem. 6, 10; -ιμένος Il. 10, 417; Her. 3, 31; Lycurg. 52, 3 pl. Ion. κεκρίδαται, δια- Dio Cass. 42, 5: aor. ἐκρῐ́θην Eur. Hec. 644; Theocr. 8, 74; Her. 5, 22; Pl. Leg. 946, Poet. κρῐ́θ- Pind. P. 8, 84, Epic 3 pl. κρῐ́θεν 4, 168, ἔκρῐθεν Ap. Rh. 4, 1462, δι- Il. 2, 815; κρῐθῇ Aesch. Eum. 741; Her. 5, 5; Pl. Rep. 469; κριθεῖεν Thuc. 2, 40; κρῐθείς Pind. N. 7, 7; Soph. Ph. 1345; Isocr. 4, 46; κριθῆναι Andoc. 1, 44; Xen. Hell. 5, 4, 24, Dor. κριθῆμεν, δια- Thuc. 5, 79, Epic ἐκρίνθην, opt. 2 pl. κρινθεῖτε, δια- Il. 3, 102; κρινθείς Il. 13, 129. Od. 8, 48, δια- Il. 20, 141; inf. κρινθήμεναι Ap. Rh. 2, 148, δια- Il. 3, 98: fut. κριθήσομαι Aesch. Eum. 677; Antiph. 6, 37; Pl. Crat. 438; Lys. 13, 38; Aeschin. 3, 133. Mid. κρίνομαι *separate for oneself, choose, contend, interpret*, Il. 18, 209; Her. 3, 120: imp. ἐκρινόμην Ar. Nub. 66; Dem. 18, 249. 56, 47: fut. κρινοῦμαι Eur. Med. 609, δια- Dem. 32, 28 (Bekk. Dind.), Epic -έομαι, δια-κρινέεσθαι Od. 18, 149. 20, 180; Hom. H. 3, 438, not pass. we think; but κρινοῦμαι Pl. Gorg. 521, seems pass.: aor. ἐκρινάμην trans. Il. 5, 150. 9, 521, κριν- Hes. Th. 882; imper. κρινάσθων *let them select*, Od. 8, 36, not necessarily passive "*let be selected*" (and fut. διακρινέεσθαι Od. 18, 149 &c. quoted, is mid. intrans. *separate (themselves), decide their differences*): p. as mid. rare, and only in comp. δια-κεκρίμεθα Pl. Phil. 52, ἀνα- Dem. 53, 17. Vb. κριτός Il. 7, 434; -έον Pl. Gorg. 523. κρίθεν for ἐκρίθησαν, Pind. quoted. ἐκρίνθην is the pass. aor. form in Hom., δια-έκριθεν however Il. 2, 815, as always in Her. κριθῇ 5, 5 &c. Act. κρίνω in the sense *interpret*, Aesch. Ch. 542; Eur. Hec. 89; ἔκρινα Aesch. Pr. 485; Her. 1, 120. The mid. with *transitive* force is, we think, Epic. With this limitation, Buttmann's assertion that "this verb has a mid. voice only in the Epic language" seems correct.

Κροαίνω *To stamp, strike*, Epic, and only pres. part. -αίνων Il. 6, 507. 15, 264; Anacreont. 59, 6, -οντες Opp. Cyn. 1, 279; and late prose -αίνειν Philostr. Soph. 1, 25 (537), in allusion to Hom.

Κρούω *To beat*, Eur. Cycl. 328; -ων Soph. Fr. 938; Ar. Eccl. 317; Xen. Eq. 11, 4; -ειν Pl. Lys. 209: imp. ἔκρουον Pl. Theaet. 154, κρούεσκον, ἀνα- Ap. Rh. 4, 1650: fut. κρούσω Eur. Elec. 180: aor. ἔκρουσα Xen. An. 4, 5, 18; κρούσῃς Soph. Fr. 926, reg. in act.: p. κέκρουκα Prov. Diog. 3, 38, ἐκ- Pl. Phaedr. 228, προσ- Dem. 21, 206. 33, 7: p. p. κέκρουμαι, ἀπο- Ar. Ach. 459 (Bekk. Dind. Bergk); Xen. Hell. 7, 4, 26 (Dind. Saupp.), παρα- active, Dem. 6, 23 (best Ms. Bekk. Dind.), and -ουσμαι, παρα-

Dem. 24, 37 (Bekk. Dind.); D. Hal. 17, 4; Luc. Tyr. 1; but Luc. Tim. 57 (as mid.), so ἐκ- Ar. Fr. p. 169 (Bergk, 263 Dind.), ἀπο- Ar. Ach. 459 (Vulg. Elms.); and Xen. Hell. 7, 4, 26 quoted (old edit.): **plp.** ἐκέκρουστο, παρ- Pl. Theaet. 168: **aor.** always with σ, ἐκρούσθην late in *simple*, Eratosth. Catast. 32, 127, ἀπ- Thuc. 4, 107; Xen. Hell. 6, 4, 5, ἐξ- Thuc. 4, 102, παρ- Hippocr. 3, 148 (Lit.); Dem. 19, 86. **Mid.** κρούομαι *back a ship, row stern foremost*, Thuc. 3, 78: **imp.** ἐκρου- 1, 50: **fut.** κρούσομαι, ἀπο- Her. 8, 61, παρα- Dem. 18, 147. 276: **aor.** ἐκρουσάμην (πρύμναν) Thuc. 7, 40, δι- Her. 7, 169: and as **mid.** **p.** κέκρουμαι, παρα- Dem. 6, 23, and -ουσμαι Luc. Tim. 57. In this sense late writers use also the **act.** πρύμναν κρούειν Polyb. 16, 3, 8. **Vb.** κρουστέον Ar. Eccl. 988.

Κρύπτω *To conceal*, Il. 21, 239; Soph. El. 826; Ar. Thesm. 74; Heraclit. 11 (Byw.); Her. 1, 216; Antiph. 5, 53; Pl. Phil. 66, late κρῦβω, ἀπο- Diod. Sic. 3, 25, ἐγ- 1, 80, (Bekk.); Malal. p. 101, 21, and κρῦφω: **imp.** ἔκρυπτον Soph. Ant. 285; Eur. Hipp. 1209; Her. 1, 61; Xen. Hell. 3, 5, 10, iter. κρύπτεσκε H. Cer. 239, and κρύπτασκε Il. 8, 272, ἀπο- Hes. Th. 157, late ἔκρῦφον Anth. (Diod. Gr.) 7, 700; Q. Sm. 1, 393; Nonn. 23, 82, ἔκρυβον Conon. Narr. 50: **fut.** κρύψω Od. 17, 141; Aesch. Pr. 1018; Soph. Aj. 1012; Ar. Plut. 26; Paus. 4, 20, 2; Polyb. 1, 72; Himer. Or. 22, 7, ἀπο- Her. 7, 28, κατα- Pl. Rep. 460: **aor.** ἔκρυψα Hipponax 19; Aesch. Ag. 455; Soph. Ant. 25; Thuc. 1, 133, κρύψα Od. 14, 357 (Bekk. 2 ed.); Hes. Th. 482; Pind. Ol. 6, 31; subj. κρύψω Od. 13, 304, -ῃς Ar. Lys. 714; Thuc. 2, 34; opt. -ψαιμι Ar. Pl. 284, -ειας Eur. I. T. 1024 &c. -ειαν Pl. Rep. 548; inf. κρύψαι Il. 18, 397; Soph. Ph. 743; Her. 9, 80; -ψας Il. 14, 373; Eur. Ion 967; Her. 2, 86, Dor. -ψαις, κατα- Pind. N. 1, 31: **p.** κέκρῠφα Hippocr. 263, 51 (Foes, 1, 471 Kühn, but Littré κέκῡφα 8, 494 Ms. L., Ermerins 2, 809), συγ- Dio. Hal. C. Verb. 18: **p. p.** κέκρυμμαι, -υπται Eur. Ion 1351, -ύμμεθα Anth. 7, 506, 3 pl. Ion. κεκρῦφαται Hes. Th. 730; Hippocr. 8, 342, ἀπο- 7, 382 (Lit.); -υμμένος Od. 23, 110; Aesch. Pr. 501; Soph. O. R. 1398; Thuc. 3, 35; Isocr. 3, 52; κεκρύφθαι Pind. Ol. 7, 57; Ar. Lys. 119; Her. 3, 5: **plp.** κέκρυπτο Pind. Ol. 6, 54: **aor.** ἐκρύφθην Aesch. Ag. 387; Her. 2, 130; Thuc. 8, 50 (Poet. 3 pl. ἔκρυφθεν Eur. Hipp. 1247), κρύφθην Il. 13, 405; subj. dual κρυφθῆτον Eur. Hec. 897; κρυφθείς Soph. El. 837; Ar. Vesp. 351; Thuc. 2, 39; -φθῆναι Soph. O. C. 1546; Eur. Bac. 955: **fut.** κρυφθήσομαι perhaps late, Disput. Mor. p. 545 (Mullach): **3 fut.** κεκρύψομαι Hippocr. 8, 86. 98 (Lit.): **2 aor. act.** late ἔκρῠβον, περι- N. T. Luc. 1, 24; κατακρῠβών Plut. Mar. 38, ἐγκρυβοῦσα Apollod. 3, 13, 6: **2 aor. pass.**

ἐκρύβην late, Apollod. 3, 2; Aesop 127 (Halm); Geop. 12, 39; Babr. 60 (Lewis, 2 pt.); Hierocl. 264 (Eberh.); N. T. Joh. 8, 59; κρυβείς Pseud.-Callisth. 3, 33 (Soph. Aj. 1145, in some edit.), κατ- Alciphr. 3, 47, and ἐκρύφην, κρυφείς Soph. Aj. 1145 (Elms. Herm. Dind.), and late: **fut.** κρῠφήσομαι Eur. Supp. 543 (Elms. Hart. Dind. 5 ed. Nauck 3 ed.), but κρυβήσομαι (Mss. Dind. 2 ed. Kirchh. Nauck 2 ed.); and late, Plut. Mor. 576; Aesop 129 (Halm), ἀπο- Galen 3, 820: **pres. pass.** κρυπτόμενα Antiph. 2, γ, 8. **Mid.** κρύπτομαι *conceal oneself*, intrans. or *for oneself*, trans. also as **act.** Soph. Aj. 647; *simple* not in good prose, Nic. Damasc. 48, p. 35 (L. Dind.); (Luc.) Asin. 45; Herodn. 3, 4, 6, but ἀπο- Isocr. 15, 98; Pl. Prot. 327, ἐπι- Xen. An. 1, 1, 6; Pl. Lach. 196; Dem. 30, 34: **imp.** ἐκρύπτετο, ἀπ- Thuc. 2, 53; Isocr. 7, 35; Dem. 18, 156: **fut.** κρύψομαι Soph. Tr. 474; Eur. Bac. 955, in prose ἀπο- Isocr. 12, 100; Pl. Leg. 702; Dem. 6, 31. 13, 10. 19, 3, see below: **1 aor.** ἐκρυψάμην Soph. Aj. 246; Dem. 41, 17, ἀπ- Thuc. 7, 85; Pl. Euth. 11; Isae. 8, 20: **2 aor.** late, ἐκρῠβόμην, ἀπ- Apollod. 3, 2: and in sense **p.** κέκρυμμαι, ἀπο- Dem. 28, 3. **Vb.** κρυπτός Il. 14, 168, -έον Soph. Ant. 273. **Fut. act.** κρύψω seems rare in prose; at Xen. Cyr. 7, 3, 12, some hold it subj.; and **mid.** κρύψεται as **pass.** Hippocr. 2, 659 Kühn, has been altered to κεκρύψεται by Littré 8, 86, from Mss. CJθ. The forms with β are mostly late, ἐκρύβην in some editions Soph. Aj. 1145, opposed by ἐκρύφην the approved reading *now*, and κρυβήσομαι alone occur, and if sound only once in classic Greek. ἔκρυφθεν for -φθησαν, Eur. Hipp. 1247 (trimet.) a rare form in *Attic* poetry, so κατ-ένασθεν Ar. Vesp. 662 (Mss. R. V. Bekk. Dind.) **1 fut. pass.** κρυφθήσομαι of some lexicons we have never seen *in situ*, except in the passage quoted.

Κτάομαι *To acquire*, Eur. Supp. 950; Thuc. 2, 40, Ion. κτέομαι Her. 3, 98, -έονται (Dind. -έωνται Bekk. -ῶνται Stein); opt. κτῴμην Soph. Tr. 191: **imp.** ἐκτῶντο Lys. 12, 93; Isocr. 8, 101: **fut.** κτήσομαι Theogn. 200; Archil. 6 (B.); Aesch. Eum. 289; Soph. Tr. 471; Ar. Lys. 53; Pl. Rep. 417; opt. -ήσοιντο Thuc. 6, 30: **aor.** ἐκτησάμην Il. 9, 400; Aesch. Pers. 770; Soph. Ant. 924; Her. 1, 167; Thuc. 4, 98; Lys. 7, 5; Pl. Lach. 185, 2 sing. ἐκτήσω Od. 24, 193; Aesch. Pers. 755; Ar. Vesp. 685, Dor. ἔκτᾱσα Theocr. 5, 6, κτήσατο Od. 14, 4, Dor. dual -σάσθαν Pind. Ol. 9, 45 (Bergk, κτισσ- Momms. Christ): **p.** κέκτημαι as **pres.** *I possess*, Hes. Op. 437; Aesch. Supp. 336 (by some called passive); Soph. Fr. 779 (D.); Ar. Vesp. 615; Thuc. 6, 20; Andoc. 3, 38; Pl. Leg. 666, **pass.** Thuc. 7, 70; Pl. Leg. 965?; Luc. Fug. 20; Arr. 5, 26, 6. 7, 1, 4, προσ- Thuc. 2, 62, and rather Ion. ἔκτημαι active, Il. 9, 402; Simon. (Am.) 13, 2; Andoc. 3, 37; Her. 2, 44. 95, ἀν- Soph. Fr. 328, 3 pl. ἐκτέαται Her. 4, 23. 6, 52 &c. (Bekk. Gaisf.); -ημένος Aesch. Pr. 795; Pl. Leg. 954, προσ- Thuc. 2, 62 (Bekk. προσ-κεκ- Popp. &c.), ἐκτῆσθαι Pl. Phil. 58. Meno 97. Prot. 340. Rep. 464. 469. 505: plp. ἐκεκτήμην Andoc. 1, 74. 4, 41; Lys. 2, 17. 7, 32. 19, 27. 24, 11. 31, 14. 34, 3. Fr. 78 (Scheibe, 233 B. Saupp.); Isae. 6, 38, κεκτημ- Eur. I. A. 404 (Elms. Dind.), ἐκτημ- Her. 2, 108; Lys. 34, 3, quoted (B. Saupp.); and Andoc. 3, 37 (Bekk. B. Saupp. Blass); subj. (κεκτῶμαι, -ῇ) -ῆται Xen. Conv. 1, 8 (Saupp. Dind.); Pl. Leg. 936, κεκτῆσθε Isocr. 3, 49 &c.; opt. κεκτῴμην, -ῷο, -ῷτο Xen. Ages. 9, 7 (Schneid.), -ῆτο (Saupp. Dind. Breitb.), -ῴμεθα Eur. Heracl. 282, and κεκτήμην, -ῇο, -ῆτο Pl. Leg. 731. 742, -ήμεθα Rep. 505 (Bekk.): aor. ἐκτήθην always pass. Thuc. 1, 123. 2, 36; κτηθείς Eur. Hec. 449; D. Hal. Ant. 10, 27. 11, 40, κατα- Diod. Sic. 16, 56: fut. κτηθήσομαι late *shall be possessed*, V. T. Jer. 39, 43: but 3 fut. κεκτήσομαι *shall possess*, Aesch. Sept. 1017; Eur. Bac. 514; Com. Fr. (Cratet.) 2, 237; Pl. Gorg. 467, Epic 2 sing. -ήσεαι Emped. 225 (Stein); rare ἐκτήσομαι Pl. Lach. 192. **Vb.** κτητός Il. 9, 407, -έον Pl. Rep. 373. For 3 sing. imp. ἐκτέετο Her. 8, 112, Stein reads, and Lhardy and Bredow would read ἐκτᾶτο, Dind. has plp. ἔκτητο. Hom. uses the unreduplicated perf. ἐκτῆσθαι Il. 9, 402, and generally Her. 2, 44. 3, 100. 4, 23. 191. 6, 20. 52. 7, 5 &c. after vowel or consonant (so Plato freq. after a cons.), but κεκτημένος Her. 2, 173. 174. 7, 27; κέκτησο 7, 29, after a vowel. In Attic, ἔκτημαι is rare, except in Plato. Aesch. Pr. 795, has ἐκτημ- from constraint of metre, for he has κεκτημ- Supp. 336, where the metre would allow ἐκτημ-; so Soph. κεκτημ- Fr. 700; Eur. Or. 127. 489. Ph. 892. H. F. 468. Ion 322. Fr. 364, 19 (D.); Ar. Eccl. 1126; Com. Fr. (Antiph.) 3, 124. (Alex.) 3, 518. 520 &c. κτίζω however has ἔκτισμαι Eur. Fr. 362, 9, late κέκτισμ- Malal. p. 204. Ellendt (Lex. Soph.) seems to have overlooked Fr. 700, when he wrote "altera perfecti forma ἔκτημαι—apud Soph. jam *propter hiatum* non admittitur:" *Hiatus* in every case but this bars admission. The colloquial style of Plato admitted perhaps a little more freedom in dropping the κ.

Κτεᾰτίζω (κτέαρ) *To acquire*, Poet. and in act. only aor. κτεάτισσα Il. 16, 57. Od. 24, 207; Theocr. 17, 119; -τίσσας Od. 2, 102. 19, 147. **Mid.** κτεατίζεται Theocr. 17, 105: fut. -τίσσεται Maneth. 6, 677: aor. κτεατίσσατο Ap. Rh. 2, 788; κτεατίσσῃ, κατα- 4, 357: with p. as mid. ἐκτεάτισται H. Merc. 522.

Κτείνω *To kill*, Il. 21, 220; Soph. O. R. 813; Ar. Av. 1067; Her. 2, 66. 9, 22; Thuc. 3, 70, Aeol. κτέννω, ἀπο- Anth. 11,

395; Epic subj. κτείνωμι Od. 19, 490, κτείνῃ Pl. Leg. 865; κτεῖνε Her. 1, 85; -νων Pind. N. 3, 51; Her. 8, 38; Thuc. 7, 29, -ουσα Aesch. Pers. 794; κτείνειν Pl. Prot. 322 &c., Epic κτεινέμεναι Hes. Sc. 414: imp. ἔκτεινον Her. 3, 146; Thuc. 1, 50; Xen. An. 2, 5, 32, κτεῖν- Il. 18, 529; so Od. 14, 265. 17, 434 (Bekk. 2 ed.), ἔκτ- (Vulg. Dind. La R.), iter. κτείνεσκε Il. 24, 393: fut. κτενῶ (Il. 15, 65. 68?); Aesch. Ag. 1260; Ar. Fr. 533; Thuc. 3, 58. 66; Luc. Pisc. 3, Ion. κτενέω Il. 22, 13. 124. Od. 16, 404, ἀπο- Her. 3, 30, Epic κτᾰνέω Il. 18, 309, κατα- 6, 409: 1 aor. ἔκτεινα Il. 19, 296. Od. 12, 379; Pind. Ol. 2, 38; Aesch. Ch. 888; Soph. El. 561; Antiph. 5, 11; Thuc. 4, 74; Lys. 10, 11; Pl. Euth. 4, κτεῖν- Hes. Th. 982; Simon. C. 94; Pind. P. 4, 249; inf. κτεῖναι Soph. O. R. 641; Her. 2, 151; Lys. 1, 25; Pl. Leg. 866; κτείνας Il. 16, 292; Her. 2, 66; Thuc. 2, 102, Aeol. κτέννais Alcae. 33: p. ἔκταγκα, ἀπ- Aristot. Pol. 7, 2, 11; Com. Fr. (Men.) 4, 173, and ἔκτᾰκα, ἀπ- Polyb. 11, 18 (Mss. Vulg. Bekk. Dind.). 3, 86 (Mss. C. B. Vulg. -αγκα Bekk. Dind.), and ἐκτόνηκα, ἀπ- Aristot. Soph. 33, 3; rare and doubtful in *classic* authors, Xen. Hier. 3, 8 (but ἀπ-έκτονα Stob. &c. Dind. Saupp.); Pl. Apol. 38 Vulg. (but -εκτόνατε Mss. B. V. D. Bekk. Stallb. B. O. W.): plp. ἀπ-εκτονήκει Plut. Timol. 16 (Vulg. -ήκοι Mss. Sint. Bekk.), for which early writers use 2 p. ἔκτονα, ἐκτόνειν, ἀπ- see below: p.p. late, ἐκτάνθαι, ἀπ- Polyb. 7, 7: aor. ἐκτᾰθην Epic, and only 3 pl. ἔκτᾰθεν Od. 4, 537; Ap. Rh. 1, 1040; in tmesi Il. 11, 691, κατ- Il. 5, 558. 13, 780. Od. 3, 108, κτάθεν Q. Sm. 1, 812, and perhaps late, ἐκτάνθην, κτανθεὶς Anth. (incert.) 14, 32, ἀπ-εκτάνθην Dio Cass. (Xiphil.) 65, 4 (Bekk.); Apocr. 1 Macc. 2, 9 (κατεκτάνθη Schneidewin's conjecture, Hippon. 7, is certainly not certain): fut. κτανθήσεσθε late, Schol. Il. 14, 481: 2 p. as active, ἔκτονα, κατ- only once in Trag. Aesch. Eum. 587 (Mss. Dind. Franz, Herm.), ἀπ- Com. Fr. (Antiph.) 3, 106; Xen. An. 2, 1, 11. Hell. 2, 4, 21; Pl. Apol. 38. 39; Isocr. 12, 66; Lys. 10, 7; Dem. 22, 2; -τονέναι Lys. 10, 2: plp. ἀπ-εκτόνεσαν Dem. 19, 148, Ion. ἀπ-εκτόνεε Her. 5, 67: 2 aor. ἔκτᾰνον Poet. Il. 2, 701; Pind. Ol. 7, 29; Aesch. Eum. 96; Soph. O. R. 277, 'κταν- 844, κτάν- Il. 2, 701. 7, 155. 21, 236 (Bekk. 2 ed.); Ibycus 16 (B.); κτᾰνῃς Soph. O. R. 606; Eur. Hec. 278 &c.; κτᾰνοι Soph. O. R. 948; κτᾰνών Ant. 1263; Eur. Hec. 712; κτᾰνεῖν Aesch. Eum. 84; Soph. El. 536; Eur. Fr. 931; but Strab. 8, 28, and κατ-έκτανον Il. 23, 87; Soph. O. C. 975; Eur. Med. 505; Q. Sm. 1, 24; Plut. Mor. 189; -κτανεῖν Arr. Tact. 43 (Vulg. -κανεῖν Herch.); doubted in classic authors, Xen. An. 1, 9, 6 (most Mss. Kühn.). 4, 8, 25 (most Mss. Born. Kühn. and doubtingly Popp.). Ages. 2, 22 (Breitb.). Hier. 7, 12 (Saupp. 1 ed.

Breitb.), but in all those passages of Xen. Dindorf, Krüger, Saupp. 2 ed. and perhaps Bornemann and Poppo, either have written, or would now write κατέκανον, Poet. (κτῆμι) ἔκτᾰν, κατ- Il. 4, 319, ἔκτας Eur. Med. 1398 (Pors. Dind. 2 ed. ἔκανες Elms. Dind. 5 ed. Kirchh. Nauck), ἔκτᾰ Il. 12, 46; Soph. Tr. 38; Eur. H. F. 424, κατ- Aesch. Eum. 460, ἔκτᾰμεν Od. 12, 375, ἀπ- 23, 121, 3 pl. ἔκτᾰν Il. 10, 526. Od. 19, 276; subj. κτέωμεν Od. 22, 216 (Wolf, Bekk. Dind.); κτάμεναι Il. 5, 301. 17, 8, κακτάμ- Hes. Sc. 453, κτάμεν, ἀπο- Il. 5, 675, κατα- 15, 557; κτάς, κατα- Il. 22, 323; Aesch. Sept. 965; Eur. I. T. 715. **Mid. fut.** Epic, and as **pass.** κτανέεσθε, κατα- *shall be slain,* Il. 14, 481: **2 aor.** (ἐκτᾰ́μην) Poet. and **pass.** ἀπ-έκτᾰτο Il. 15, 437. 17, 472; κτάσθαι 15, 558; κτάμενος Il. 22, 75; Hes. Op. 541; Pind. Fr. 186 (Bergk); Aesch. Pers. 923 (chor.); Com. Fr. (Cratin.) 2, 72.—**2 aor.** ἔκτανον Poet. in the classic period, occurs occasionally in late prose, κτανεῖν Strab. 8, 3, 28 (Kram.), κατα- Arr. Tact. 15, 2 (Blanc. Müll. -κανεῖν Herch.); κατ-έκτανον Plut. Mor. 189 (Dübn.), and even in Xen., if some of the Mss. may be trusted, and these Breitb. and Kühner defend and follow, Ages. 2, 22. An. 1, 9, 6. 4, 8, 25. Of the **pass.** we have seen in *Attic* writers the **imp.** only, ἐκτείνοντο Thuc. 3, 81; later D. Cass. 47, 5; Plut. Lysand. 11; App. Mithr. 44; Paus. 10, 1, 2, see below. For the **pass.** forms they used θνήσκω, in prose more frequently ἀπο-: ἔθνησκον, and ἀπ-: **fut.** θανοῦμαι, in prose always ἀπο-: aor. ἔθανον, in prose always ἀπ-: p. τέθνηκα, and syncop. τέθνᾰτον, -ᾰμεν, -νᾶσι &c. &c. in Poet. and prose, and rarely compd. The Ionians said κτείνομαι Il. 14, 60; subj. -ώμεθα Il. 11, 668; imper. 3 pl. κτεινέσθων Her. 7, 10; -όμενος Il. 18, 99. Od. 22, 328; Her. 4, 3; and late, (Hippocr.) Epist. 9, 414; Plut. Mor. 757; V. T. Prov. 24, 11; -εσθαι Il. 5, 465: **imp.** ἐκτείνοντο Her. 6, 19, κτείνοντο Od. 11, 413. 24, 38: **fut.** as **pass.** κτανέομαι, κατα- Il. 14, 481: **aor.** (ἐκτάθην) -αθεν for -ησαν 11, 691. Od. 4, 537: and as **pass. aor. mid.** κτάσθαι Il. 15, 558; κτᾰ́μενος Il. 22, 75; scarcely in Attic, see above; ἀπ-έκτατο Il. 15, 437, see above. Our lexicons say "In prose the compds. ἀπο-, κατα-κτείνω are more common." This is true of ἀπο-; in regard to κατα- it is a capital mistake. Of classic Attic prose writers Xen. alone uses it, and even there, bating perhaps two or three cases, Mss. and editors divide on it and κατα-καίνω. The comp. ἀποκτείνω has in Attic poetry and prose, **fut.** -ενῶ: **1 aor.** -εινα: p. -έκτονα: but **2 aor.** ἀπ-έκτᾰνον, ἀπ-έκταν, and **mid.** ἀπ-έκτατο **pass.** are Epic only—ἀπέκτᾰνε, however, Eur. Rhes. 978. **Pass.** late ἀποκτείνεσθαι Palaeph. Incred. 7: p. ἀπ-εκταμμένος Apocr. 1 Macc. 5, 51, and -εκτονημένος Psell. Opusc. p. 107,

17; inf. -εκτάνθαι Polyb. 7, 7; 2 Macc. 4, 36: **1 aor.** -εκτάνθην 1 Macc. 2, 9; Dionys. de Av. 1, 3; N. T. Marc. 8, 31. Rev. 9, 18 &c.: **2 aor.** ἀπο-κτανῆναι Galen 13, 956. All our lexicons omit the pass. form.

Κτενίζω *To comb*, Hippocr. 6, 492; Dio. Hal. Comp. Verb. 208, 11: **imp.** ἐκτένιζ- Eur. Hipp. 1174: **fut.** (-ίσω, -ιῶ): **p.** ἐκτένισμαι Archil. 166 (Bergk); Simon. Am. 7, 65, δι- Philostr. 335 (redupl. κεκτενισμένος Xen. Lac. 13, 9, is a mere suggestion of Schneider for κεκριμένος): **aor.** late ἐκτενίσθην Hippiatr. p. 226. **Mid.** κτενίζομαι *comb one's own hair*, Her. 7, 208: **aor.** κτενίσησθε Ar. Fr. 501; opt. κτενίσαιντο Asius Fr. 13 (Marksch.)

Κτέννω, see κτείνω.

Κτερεΐζω *To bury with due honours*, Epic, Il. 23, 646; Epic inf. -ϊζέμεν 24, 657: has **fut.** -εΐξω Od. 2, 222: **aor.** ἐκτερέϊξα Ap. Rh. 2, 859, κτερ- Anth. 7, 163; -εΐξαι Od. 1, 291. But the form κτερίζω Poet. Eur. Hel. 1244; Soph. Ant. 204: has **fut.** -ιῶ Il. 11, 455: and **aor.** ἐκτέρισα Simon. C. 109 (Bergk); -ίσω Anth. 7, 180; -ίσαιεν Il. 24, 38, a rare form in Hom., but -ίσειεν Od. 3, 285.

Κτίζω *To found, make*, Emped. 124 (Stein); Her. 1, 170; Thuc. 5, 16; Pl. Prot. 322: **imp.** ἔκτιζον Thuc. 1, 12: **fut.** κτίσω Aesch. Ch. 1060; Her. 5, 42: **aor.** ἔκτισα Od. 11, 263; Aesch. Supp. 171; Her. 1, 167; Thuc. 4, 102; Isocr. 4, 35, ἔκτισσ- Pind. P. 1, 62; Aesch. Pers. 289 (chor.), κτίσσ- Il. 20, 216; Theocr. 28, 17, κτίσα Pind. P. 5, 89; Eur. Phoen. 682 (chor.); κτίσον Soph. Ant. 1101; κτίσας Aesch. Ch. 351; Thuc. 3, 61: **p.** κέκτικα Diod. Sic. Fr. 7, 3 (Bekk. ἔκτ- Dind.), but ἔκτικα 15, 13: and **p. p.** ἔκτισται Hippocr. 4, 194 (Lit.); ἐκτισμένος Eur. Fr. 362, 9 (D.); Her. 4, 46, late κεκτισμ- Malal. p. 204. 263, Epic κτίμενος as from (κτίω) Aesch. Ch. 806, in comp. ἐϋκτίμενος Il. 21, 433. Od. 4, 476; Hes. Sc. 81: **aor.** ἐκτίσθην Thuc. 1, 12; Pl. Hip. maj. 285, κτίσθ- Pind. Ol. 8, 37; κτισθῆναι Her. 8, 62; κτισθείς 1, 16, κτιθεῖσα Scym. 700 (Mein.), but perhaps not intended, see κτισθ- 833: **fut.** κτισθήσομαι Dio. Hal. Ant. 1, 56; Strab. vol. 3, p. 483 (Kram.): **pres. opt.** κτιζοίατο Aesch. Ch. 484. **Mid.** rare, **aor.** ἐκτίσσατο Pind. Ol. 10 (11), 25. Fr. 1, 4; Callim. Fr. 104. The **aor.** is very rare. The Doric dual κτισάσθαν Pind. Ol. 9, 45, has been altered by Boeckh, from Mss. and old editions, to κτησάσθαν (but κτισσ- Momms. Christ), and ἐκτίσαντο Eur. Phoen. 687 (Mss. Flor. Br. Beck &c.) is now ἐκτήσαντο (most Mss. Herm. Dind. &c. κτήσαντο Pors. Hart.), see κτάομαι. Our lexicons miss the **mid.** **Vb.** αὐτό-κτῐτος Aesch. Pr. 301.

Κτῐλόω (κτῖλος) *To tame*, seems to be used only in **aor. mid.**

ἐκτῖλώσαντο Her. 4, 113: and the form κτῖλεύω in pres. pass. -εύονται Pind. Fr. 223 (Bergk).

Κτίννῡμι -ύω *To kill*, both late in *simple*, and only pres. κτίννυμι App. C. B. 1, 71. 4, 35, but ἀπο- Xen. An. 6, 3, 5. Hell. 4, 4, 2 (Dind.); Pl. Polit. 298; Dem. 19, 259. 20, 158; κτιννύει Polyaen. 1, 25; Joseph. Ant. 17, 7, 7, ἀπο- Xen. Hell. 4, 4, 2 quoted (Saupp. Breitb.): and **imp.** ἐκτίννῡον late, Polyaen. 1, 23, but ἀπ-εκτίννυν Lys. 20, 9; Xen. An. 6, 5, 28, and -τίννυον Xen. Hell. 5, 2, 43 (Dind. Breitb. Saupp.), -υνε 7, 3, 8 (Breitb. Saupp. -υυ Dind. Cobet). **Pass.** κτιννύμενος App. C. B, 1, 2. Thus say Mss. and our editors. The old masters held -υμι the better Attic: -ύασιν ἀττικῶς, -ύουσι ἑλληνικῶς (Moer.), -ύουσι κοινόν (Thom. Mag.) κτέννω Aeol. Alcae. 26, Ahren's emend. for κταίνω (Eust.), and as a late form ἀποκτέννω Anth. 11, 395. Bekker, Dind. and Hultsch edit ἀποκτεινύναι Polyb. 2, 56.

Κτῠπέω *To sound*, mostly Poet. Il. 13, 140; Eur. Or. 1366; Ar. Ach. 1072; rare in prose, Pl. Rep. 396; Luc. Salt. 10; Philostr. 327: **imp.** ἐκτῠ́πουν Soph. Tr. 787; Eur. Med. 1180, -πεον Opp. C. 4, 247, κτύπεον Ap. Rh. 2, 83, iter. κτυπέεσκον Q. Sm. 9, 135: **1 aor.** ἐκτύπησα Eur. Phoen. 1181, κτύπ- Soph. O. C. 1606 (trimet.); Eur. Or. 1467 (chor.); late prose κτυπήσειεν Arr. Tact. 40: **aor. pass.** κτυπηθῆναι Philostr. 266: **2 aor.** ἔκτῠπον Il. 15, 377; Soph. O. C. 1456 (chor.); Ap. Rh. 2, 1257, κτύπε Il. 8, 75. 170. 17, 595, and always (Bekk.) **Mid.** κτυπέομαι as act. intrans. Ar. Thesm. 995, pass. Philostr. V. Apoll. 8, 14: **imp.** κτυπέοντο Q. Sm. 8, 449. After Homer κτυπέω is used also trans. *make resound*, ἐκτῠ́πει Eur. Rhes. 308: κτύπησε Or. 1467: ἔκτῠπον Hes. Sc. 61. (ῠ.) Rare in prose. Bekker now (2 ed.) writes uniformly κτύπε in Il. and Od., Dind. and La Roche ἔκτ-, except Il. 8, 170.

Κῠδάζω *To revile*, is reg. but defect. pres. only imper. κύδαζε Epich. 3 (Ahr.). **Pass.** κυδάζεται Soph. Aj. 722. **Mid.** κυδάζομαι Epich. 19, 6 (Ahr.); κῠδάζεσθαι Aesch. Fr. 91: **aor.** ἐκῠδάσσαο Ap. Rh. 1, 1337.

Κῡδᾰ́νω *To honour* (κῦδος), Epic, Il. 14, 73: **imp.** κύδᾰνον intrans. *vaunted*, 20, 42, ἐκύδ' (Bekk. La R.) Collat. form κῡδαίνω poet. and late prose, Il. 10, 69; Simon. C. 96 (Bergk); Pind. Ol. 10, 66; Plut. Tit. Flam. 13: **imp.** ἐκύδαινον Plut. C. Marc. 1, κύδαιν- Il. 5, 448; Q. Sm. 3, 127, iter. κυδαίνεσκον 2, 632; Orph. Arg. 62: **fut.** late κυδᾰνῶ Lycophr. 721. 929, περι- Or. Sib. 3, 575: **aor.** κύδηνα Il. 23, 793; -ῆναι Od. 16, 212, late prose ἐκύδηνε Themist. 11, 153, Dor. ἐκύδᾱνε Pind. P. 1, 31: **pass.** κυδαίνοιτο Anth. 7, 142. And Epic κῡδιάω pres. and imp. only, and these late, except. 3 pl. pres. and part. κυδῐάεις Coluth. 180,

-άει Anth. Plan. 339, but 3 pl. κυδιόωσι Hom. H. 30, 13; part. κυδιόων Il. 2, 579; Hes. Sc. 27, -όωντες Il. 21, 519: imp. iter. 3 pl. κυδιάασκον Ap. Rh. 4, 978; Q. Sm. 1, 391. 13, 418.

Κῠέω *To be pregnant*, Ar. Lys. 752; Pl. Theaet. 210. Conv. 206; -έων Il. 23, 266; Her. 6, 68; -εῖν Andoc. 1, 125; Lys. 13, 42 (B. Saupp. Scheibe. -ύειν Bekk.): imp. ἐκύουν Il. 19, 117; Ar. Lys. 745; Pl. Conv. 209: fut. κυήσω Hippocr. 8, 56. 414 (Lit.); Sext. Emp. 648, 14 (B.), ἀπο- Luc. Philop. 24: and mid. κυήσομαι Hippocr. 2, 717 (Kühn, 2, 614 Erm.), 1, 468 (Kühn, κυΐσκομαι Erm., in both Littré): aor. ἐκύησα Ar. Thesm. 641; Her. 5, 41; Hippocr. 5, 210. 212. 8, 416; Pl. Conv. 203; late *to beget*, Dio Cass. 66, 3: p. κεκύηκα Com. Fr. (Phil.) 4, 41; Sext. Emp. 81, 2; Dio Cass. 45, 1, ἐκ- Anth. 7, 385: p. p. late κεκύηται Porph. de Abst. 1, 54: aor. ἐκυήθην Plut. Mor. 567; Geop. 15, 2, ἐπ- Aristot. Gen. An. 4, 5, 3: fut. late κυηθησόμενος Galen 4, 326, προσ- Eustath. Philos. 3, 4, 3 (Herch.): pres. pt. κυούμενον Pl. Leg. 789. **Mid.** κυέομαι *bring forth*, Aristot. Gen. An. 4, 5, 4: aor. late ἐκυησάμην Himer. Or. 7, 4, κυησ- Opp. Cyn. 3, 22. See κύω.

Κυΐσκω *To conceive, bear*, Hippocr. 4, 554 (Lit.); Philostr. 1, 22; trans. *impregnate*, Himer. Or. 1, 7; *produce*, Pseud.-Callisth. 3, 6, ἀπο- Hippocr. 6, 618 (Lit. 3, 477 Erm.): imp. ἐκύϊσκον Paus. 5, 5, 2. **Mid.** κυΐσκομαι *to become pregnant, conceive*, Her. 2, 93. 4, 30; Hippocr. 8, 424. 488 (Lit.); Aristot. H. An. 6, 2, 31; Theophr. C. P. 1, 11, 2. 3, 24, 2; -ηται Hippocr. 8, 436. 490 (Lit.); -ομένη Pl. Theaet. 149: imp. ἐκυΐσκετο Hippocr. 5, 216 (Lit.). See κύω. Our Lex. err in confining the trans. meaning to Himerius, and giving Aelian as the earliest authority for ἀποκυΐσκω.

Κυκλόω *To encircle*, Pl. Crat. 408; -λῶν Com. Fr. 2, 380: fut. -ώσω Eur. Cycl. 462: aor. ἐκύκλωσε Pseud.-Callisth. 1, 10; pt. κυκλώσας Eur. I. A. 775, Dor. -ώσαις Pind. Ol. 10, 72: p. -ωκα Polyb. 3, 116: p. p. κεκύκλωμαι Thuc. 4, 32, see below: aor. ἐκυκλώθην Thuc. 5, 71; Pl. Critias 118: fut. κυκλωθήσομαι Dio. Hal. 3, 24 (Sylburg, Kiessl. -ώσομαι Vulg.); see also Polyaen. 5, 10, 3 (Vulg. -κλώσομαι Woelffl.): and as pass. fut. mid. κυκλώσομαι Dio. Hal. Ant. 3, 24 (Vulg.); see Polyaen. quoted. **Mid.** -οῦμαι Aesch. Sept. 121; Thuc. 4, 127: imp. ἐκυκλεῦντο Her. 8, 16 (Bekk. Dind. -εῦντο Reiske, Stein), -οῦντο 8, 10; Thuc. 7, 81, κυκλ- Eur. Bacc. 1066, in tmesi Aesch. Pers. 458 (trimet.): fut. -ώσομαι Callim. Dian. 170; Xen. Cyr. 6, 3, 20; Plut. Caes. 44; Polyaen. 1, 28; pass. Dio. Hal. Ant. 3, 24 (Vulg.); Polyaen. 5, 10, 3 (Woelffl.), see above: aor. ἐκυκλώσαντο Her. 9, 18; Dio Cass. 37, 4 (B.); Callim. Del. 250; Q. Sm. 8, 376;

-ώσωνται Opp. Hal. 2, 569; κύκλωσαι Ar. Av. 346; -σάμενος Her. 3, 157; Thuc. 5, 72 &c.: with p. p. as mid. κεκύκλωται, περι- Xen. An. 6, 3, 11, ἐγ- Ar. Vesp. 395; Dio Cass. 49, 37: and seemingly **aor.** κυκλωθείς Diod. Sic. 4, 24 (Bekk.); ἐγ-κυκλωθῆναι 4, 23. **Act.** rare.

Κυλίνδω *To roll*, Od. 1, 162; Pind. N. 4, 40; Aesch. Fr. 304; Soph. Ant. 590; Eur. Fr. 312 (Ar. Eq. 1249); Com. Fr. (Tel.) 2, 361. (Apoll. Car. 4, 441); κυλίνδων Plut. Pyrr. 30, κυλινδέω Com. Fr. (Nicoph.) 2, 851; prose Xen. An. 4, 7, 4 (Vulg. Krüg. Kühn. -δω Dind. Saupp.); Luc. Pseudol. 3 (Vulg. Bekk. -δω Dind.), κυλίω Com. Fr. (Anon.) 4, 618; Aristot. H. A. 5, 19, 18; Ael. H. A. 3, 16; Luc. Anach. 6; Dio. Hal. Comp. Verb. 20, προσ- Ar. Vesp. 202 (Vulg. Bekk. Bergk, Dind. 2 ed. -ισον 5 ed., Mein. see Aristot. Poet. 26. Pol. 6, 4, 13); ἀνα-κυλῖον Com. Fr. (Alex.) 3, 434, ἐγ- Hippocr. 8, 170: **imp.** ἐκύλινδον Orph. Arg. 681, -δουν Xen. An. 4, 2, 3. 20 (Vulg. Krüg. Popp. Saupp. -δον Dind. Cob. Schenkl); Aristid. 24, 302, ἐκύλῖον Theocr. 24, 18; Luc. Hist. Con. 3, ἐπ- D. Sic. 19, 19: **fut.** late κυλινδήσω Herod. Att. 1, 35; Anth. (Marcel.) App. Epigr. 50, 35, -κυλίσω, ἀπο- V. T. Gen. 29, 8. N. T. Marc. 16, 3: **aor.** ἐκύλῖσα Anth. 13, 12. App. Epigr. 15, 14; Trag. Fr. (Sosith.) 2, 20 (Wagn.); Theocr. 23, 52; Ael. H. A. 3, 22 (Schn.); Luc Hist. Con. 57, ἐξ- Pind. Fr. 3 (Bergk), εἰσ- Ar. Thesm. 651; Dor. pt. κυλίσαις, ἀμφι- Pind. N. 8, 23: **p. p.** κεκύλισμαι Paroem. Greg. Cypr. C. 4, 9; Luc. Hist. Con. 63; Athen. 480, κατα- Xen. Cyr. 5, 3, 1: **plp.** κεκύλιστο Nonn. 5, 47: **aor.** ἐκυλίσθην Aristot. Mechan. 24, 13, ἐξ- Il. 6, 42, κυλίσθ- 17, 99; κυλισθῇ, κατα- Her. 5, 16; κυλισθείς Soph. El. 50. Fr. 334, ἐκ- Xen. Mem. 1, 2, 22, late κυλινδηθείς Strab. 14, 2, 24; Heliod. 9, 8: **fut.** κυλισθήσομαι, ἐκ- Aesch. Pr. 87, ἀπο- Galen 3, 682. **Mid.** κυλινδεῖται Simon. Am. 7, 4; κυλῑόμενος Luc. Peregr. 44, in comp. κυλινδόμενος, προπρο- Il. 22, 221; ἐγκυλίεσθαι Theophr. H. P. 1, 6, 11: **imp.** ἐκυλινδούμην Ar. Av. 502 (Vulg. Bekk. Dind. 2 ed. Bergk, ἐκαλ- Cob. Mein. Dind. 5 ed.), -εῖτο Plut. Mor. 184?, προυκυλ- Dem. 19, 338 (Bekk. B. Saupp. προυκαλ- Dind.): **fut.** προ-κυλίσομαι App. Exc. Rom. 5 (Bekk.): **aor.** ἐγ-κυλίσασθαι Luc. Hip. 6. **Vb.** κυλιστός Com. Fr. (Alex.) 3, 26. (ῠ.) The **aor.** is sometimes written -ισσα—Theocr. 23, 52 (Ald. &c.); Opp. Hal. 2, 231—incorrectly, ι is long.

In classic authors, κυλίνδω, κυλινδέω are confined to the **pres.** and **imp. act. pass.** (or **mid.**) The former, according to the majority of Mss. and editions, is poet. and late prose, see above, and add κυλίνδει Pind. N. 4, 40; Plut. Pyrr. 30: **imp.** ἐκύλινδον Orph. Arg. 681; κυλίνδομαι Il. 11, 307; Alcae. 18, 2; Pind. Ol.

12, 6; Soph. Fr. 872 (D.); Ar. Eccl. 208; Paus. 10, 13, 2: ἐκυλίνδετο Il. 14, 411; Theocr. 7, 145, iter. κυλινδέσκοντο Pind. P. 4, 209; -δόμενος Il. 24, 165; Pind. P. 2, 23; Com. Fr. (Herm.) 2, 397; Ar. Nub. 375; Plut. Mor. 829; -δεσθαι Il. 11, 147. κυλινδέω again, is the prose form (most Mss. and edit.), rare in poetry, never in Epic, Lyric, or Tragic, but -δείτω Com. Fr. (Nicoph.) 2, 851, if correct; and Xenophon, who alone in classic prose has the **act.** κυλινδοῦσι, An. 4, 7, 4, δια- Aristot. H. An. 9, 8, 5; -δοῦντες Xen. An. 4, 2, 4; -δεῖν Luc. Pseudol. 3: ἐκυλίνδουν Xen. An. 4, 2, 20: κυλινδεῖται Simon. Am. 7, 4 (Bergk, -δεται v. r.); Isae. 5, 44; Pl. Rep. 479. Phaedr. 275, and always (except an occasional v. r. καλινδ-); Aristot. H. An. 7, 8, 7 (Bekk.); -δούμενος Xen. An. 5, 2, 31; Pl. Phaed. 82. Tim. 44 (Ion. -εύμενος Hippocr. 2, 38 Lit.), συγ- Xen. Conv. 8, 32 (Dind.); -δεῖσθαι Pl. Rep. 432, προ- Ar. Av. 501; Aristot. H. An. 9, 8, 3: ἐκυλινδούμην Ar. Av. 502; Xen. An. 4, 8, 28. So our best editions, except that Lud. Dindorf is now editing in Xen. uniformly κυλίνδω, καλινδέω, never κυλινδέω, and so W. Dindorf in Lucian, on the ground that "Veteres κυλίνδειν, et καλινδεῖν, non κυλινδεῖν dixerunt, quod librarii saepissime intulerunt ex more recentiorum." Of course he will require to alter Aristoph. Av. 501. 502, accordingly—and this he has now done in 5 ed. It is pretty clear that Homer, Pindar, and the Tragedians used the baryton κυλίνδω, but whether this, and the existence of the pure καλινδέω, prevented Aristoph. Xen. and Plato from using also the form κυλινδέω is just the question. See the collat. ἀλινδέω, καλινδέω.

Κυνέω *To kiss*, Poet. Eur. Alc. 183. Med. 1207; Ar. Ach. 1207; but Aristot. H. An. 6, 2, 24 (Bekk. κυέω v. r.): **imp.** κύνει Od. 4, 522, κύνεον 21, 224: **fut.** κυνήσω in tmesi Hipponax 32: **mid.** κυνήσομαι doubtful, Eur. Cycl. 172 (Vulg. ὠνήσομαι Tyrwh. Kirchh. Nauck, Dind. 5 ed.): late (κύσω) -σσων Babr. 54, 17 (Lewis, 2 pt.): **aor.** ἐκύνησα Athen. 9, 394, and in sense ἔκυσα Od. 23, 208; Eur. Cycl. 553; Ar. Av. 141; Anth. 12, 124; late prose, Alciphr. 3, 67; Luc. Alex. 41. 55, Epic, ἔκυσσα Il. 8, 371, κύσα Od. 14, 279. Il. 24, 478, -σσα Od. 24, 320. Instead of aor. mid. κυσάμεναι quoted by Buttmann from Athen. 9, 394, the edition of 1834 gives rightly, we think, **aor. act.** κυνήσασαι. κυνέω is not in classic prose, and rare in late, Aristot. H. A. 6, 2, 24. προσ-κυνέω is regular, and in both poetry and prose, Aesch. Pers. 499; Soph. O. R. 327; Eur. Or. 1507; Ar. Plut. 771; Her. 1, 134; Pl. Rep. 451; Aeschin. 2, 150: **imp.** προσ-εκύνεον Her. 3, 86: **fut.** -ήσω Pl. Rep. 469, in tmesi Hipponax 32 (Bergk); Plut. Them. 27. Alex. 51. Sull. 23: **fut.**

mid. προσ-κυνήσομαι given by lexicons as the *most frequent form* never occurs: **aor.** -εκύνησα Xen. Cyr. 5, 3, 18, but Poet. προσέκυσα Soph. Ph. 657; Ar. Eq. 640: **p.** late προσκεκύνηκα V. T. Exod. 32, 8; Plut. Alex. 54 (Ms. V. Vulg. -ησα P. C. M. Sint. Bekk.): **fut.** -κυνηθήσομαι late Pseud.-Callisth. 1, 33; Eustath. 3, 4, 3 (Herch.), not given by lexicons. Of this form Attic Poets use only **pres. act.** and **pass.** -νεῖσθαι Eur. Tr. 1021. **Vb.** προσκυνητέον Euseb. Prep. Evang. 3, 96b.

Κύπτω *To stoop*, Ar. Eq. 1354; Xen. Mem. 3, 9, 7: **imp.** ἔκυπτον Com. Fr. (Euphr.) 4, 487: **fut.** κύψω *simple* late, V. T. Ps. 9, 31, ὑπο- Aristid. 35, 451, ὑπερ- Hom. Epigr. 14, 22 (Vulg. -ψῃ Herm.); Or. Sib. 4, 60; ἀνα-κύψοι Pl. Euthyd. 302; -κύψειν Luc. D. Mar. 3, 1: and **mid.** κύψομαι, ἀνα- Ar. Av. 146: **aor.** ἔκυψα Archil. 35 (B.); Ar. Thesm. 664 (Bekk. διέκυψ- Dind. Bergk); Com. Fr. (Amph.) 3, 313; Her. 3, 14; Plut. Mar. 44, κατ- Il. 16, 611, ἀν- Xen. Oec. 11, 5; κύψειε Od. 11, 585; κύψας Il. 4, 468. 21, 69; Archil. 35: **p.** κέκῡφα Her. 4, 183; Hippocr. 8, 418; Pl. Rep. 586, ἀνα- Eur. Cycl. 212, Dor. 1 pl. κεκύφαμες, ἐπι- Ar. Lys. 1003. See ἀνακύπτω.

Κύρω (ῡ) *To meet, happen*, Poet. Parmen. 108; Ap. Rh. 2, 363; Anth. 9, 710; κύρων Eur. Hipp. 746 (Heath, Dind. 2 ed. ναίων Mss. Kirchh. Nauck, Dind. 5 ed.); Callim. Cer. 38: **imp.** ἔκῡρον Soph. O. C. 1159, κῦρον Il. 23, 821: **fut.** κύρσω Soph. O. C. 225 (chor.); Democr. Stob. Flor. 29, 88: **aor.** ἔκυρσα Aesch. Pers. 779; Eur. Ion 1105, ἐν- Il. 13, 145; κύρσῃ Theogn. 698; κύρσαιμι Soph. O. C. 1082, κύρσαιεν, ἐπι- Pind. P. 10, 21, κύρσειαν, συγ- Il. 23, 435; κῦρσαι Hes. Op. 691; κύρσας Il. 23, 428; Simon. C. 120, Dor. κύρσαις, ἐπι- Pind. Ol. 6, 7, Ion. and late prose, ἐν-έκυρσα Her. 3, 77. 4, 125; Arr. An. 2, 11. 5, 23; App. Civ. 4, 111. Annib. 37. **Mid.** κύρομαι as act. Il. 24, 530. κῡρέω is reg. Aesch. Pr. 330; Soph. Tr. 386; late Attic prose Polyb. 12, 15, but in Ionic ἐγ- Heraclit. 5 (Byw.): **imp.** 'κῦρουν Soph. El. 1331 (Dind.): **fut.** -ήσω Aesch. Ch. 707; Eur. Elec. 359; Her. 1, 112. 9, 88: **aor.** ἐκύρησα Archil. 18; Eur. Hec. 215; Mosch. 4, 68 (Vulg. Ahr.); Her. 1, 31. 7, 208 (Valken. Bekk. Dind.), ξυν- Hippocr. 2, 648, ἐν- Polyb. 33, 12, κύρησ- Pind. I. 6, 36; Anth. 13, 18; κυρήσῃς Soph. O. C. 1703; -ήσαις Aesch. Supp. 589 (chor.), -ήσειε, ξυγκ- Hippocr. 2, 350 (Lit.); κυρήσας Hes. Op. 755; Soph. O. R. 398; Eur. Phoen. 490; Her. 7, 158; κυρῆσαι Hom. Epigr. 6, 6; Eur. Ion 536; Her. 7, 158: **p.** κεκυρηκώς (Pl.) Alc. (2) 141, συγ- Dio. Sic. 3, 50; -ηκέναι 17, 106: **p. p.** rare συγ-κεκυρημένος Her. 9, 37. This verb seems to occur neither in Comedy nor classic Attic prose, with the doubtful exception of Pl. Alcib. (2) 141. κύρω is the usual Epic form, but with κυρήσας in Hes. and κυρῆσαι Hom. Epigr. quoted, we hesitate to follow Hermann in displacing ἐκυρήσαμεν Mosch. 4, 68 (Mss. Vulg. Ahr.) for ἐπεκύρσαμεν, on the ground that the former "non est epicorum" (Herm. B. et Mosch.) Meineke and Ziegler, we observe, adopt Hermann's emendation, and support it with ἐκύρσαμεν from Ms. C. We still demur.

Κύω (ῠ) *To be pregnant*, κύει Athen. (Call.) 454; Theogn. 1081; Her. 5, 92 (Orac.); Hippocr. 4, 546. 8, 416 (Lit.); Opp. Cyn. 1, 12; Aristot. H. An. 5, 14, 13; Xen. Cyn. 5, 13, -ουσι 7, 2 (Vulg. -υεῖ -νοῦσι Saupp.); κύουσα Eur. Fr. 206; Com. Fr. (Antiph.) 3, 26; Ar. Fr. 458 (D.); Xen. Cyr. 5, 4, 35 (-οῦσα now Dind. Saupp.); κύειν Andoc. 1, 125; Lys. 13, 42 (Bekk. -εῖν B. Saupp. Scheibe): **imp.** ἔκυε Ael. V. H. 5, 18 (Hercher): **aor.** ἔκῡσα trans. *impregnated*, Aesch. Fr. 41 (D.); Aristot. H. A. 6, 2, 24: **mid.** κῡσάμενος Hes. Th. 125. 405; Hom. H. 34, 4, ὑπο- Il. 6, 26. 20, 225. Od. 11, 254; Hes. Th. 308; but *brought forth*, Euphor. Fr. p. 150. ὑποκυσσ- is the old reading in Il. and Od.: even Wolf retained it Il. 20, 225. Od. 11, 254, but Bekk. Spitzn. Dind. La R. always -κῡσαμ-. It still stands with σσ, Hym. 32, 15 (Franke, Baum.), why we see not. In Attic prose, the leaning of editors is now decidedly to κυέω. See collat. forms κυέω, κυΐσκω, κυνέω.

Κωκύω (ῡ) *To lament*, Poet. Od. 8, 527, ἐπι- Soph. El. 283; κωκῡοι Ar. Eccl. 648; -ύειν Ran. 34; -ύων Bion 1, 23; late prose Luc. D. Mort. 10, 12: **imp.** ἐκώκῡον Il. 19, 284. Od. 19, 541; Mosch. 3, 47; late prose Luc. Tox. 15. Lap. 45, iter. κωκῡεσκον Q. Sm. 3, 460: **fut.** κωκῡσω Aesch. Ag. 1313; Q. Sm. 3, 484: and **mid.** κωκῡσομαι Ar. Lys. 1222: **aor.** κώκῡσα Il. 22, 407. Od. 24, 295; κωκῡσας Il. 18, 71; Soph. Ant. 1302; Achil. Tat. 3, 10; -ῦσαι Soph. Ant. 28. 204; late prose Plut. Mor. 357. **Mid.** κωκῡομαι as **act.** Anth. 7, 412: **aor.** κωκῡσαντο, περι- Q. Sm. 2, 591; but *simple* κωκυσαμένη Theod. Prodr. 7, 181. Before a consonant ῡ always, before a vowel ῠ generally, Od. quoted; Anth. 7, 558, but κωκῡοι Ar. Eccl. 648, and late authors κωκῡει Opp. Cyn. 1, 501, κωκῡουσα Bion 1, 23; Q. Sm. 3, 593. 779, κωκῡεσκεν 3, 460.

Κωλύω (ῡ) *To hinder*, Eur. I. T. 507; Ar. Lys. 607; Her. 2, 11; Xen. Mem. 2, 6, 26; Isae. 11, 28; -ύειν Thuc. 1, 53: **imp.** ἐκώλυον Thuc. 1, 118; Isocr. 21, 8, κώλ- Pind. P. 4, 33: **fut.** κωλῡσω Soph. Ph. 1241; Ar. Nub. 1449; Thuc. 2, 62; Lys. 13, 17: **aor.** ἐκώλῡσα Eur. Alc. 897; Thuc. 6, 80; Pl. Menex. 244; Aeschin. 1, 139: **p.** κεκώλῡκα Dinarch. 1, 101; Dem. 1, 22: **p. p.** κεκώλῡμαι Thuc. 2, 37; Aeschin. 2, 121: **aor.** ἐκωλύθην

Antiph. 3, γ, 6; Thuc. 2, 64; Pl. Leg. 920: **fut.** late κωλυθήσομαι Luc. H. V. 2, 25; Apocr. Sirach. 20, 2; Galen 1, 380: with **fut. mid.** κωλύσομαι rare and pass. Thuc. 1, 142. The **mid.** form we have not seen except κωλύου *restrain thyself*, Apocr. Sir. 18, 30, and **fut.** -ύσομαι **pass.** Thuc. quoted. **Vb.** κωλυτέον Xen. Hier. 8, 9. Before a vowel ῡ, κώλῡεν Pind. P. 4, 33, -ῡει Ar. Eq. 723, -ῡει Av. 463. Lys. 607. Pax 499 (Anapaest.), -ῡόμεσθα Eur. Ion 391, -ῡέτω Phoen. 990.

Κωμάζω *To revel*, Xen. Cyr. 7, 5, 15; -οιμι Theogn. 886; -αζε Pind. I. 7, 20; -άζειν Theogn. 1352; Com. Fr. (Alex.) 3, 499; Isae. 3, 14; -άζων Anacr. 17; Alcae. 56; Theogn. 1065; Pind. Ol. 9, 4; Eur. Alc. 815; Pl. Leg. 637; Lys. 3, 23, Dor. -άσδω Theocr. 3, 1: **imp.** ἐκώμαζον Lys. 14, 25, κώμαζ- Hes. Sc. 281: **fut.** κωμᾰσω Pind. N. 9, 1: **aor.** ἐκώμᾰσα Soph. Fr. 703 (D.); Eur. H. F. 180; Aristot. Fr. 517; Luc. Bis acc. 16, κώμ- Pind. N. 10, 35; part. κωμάσας Arr. An. 7, 25, Dor. κωμάσαις Pind. N. 11, 28; and imper. κωμάξατε N. 2, 24: **p.** κεκώμᾰκα Anth. 5, 112, ἐπ-εισ- Pl. Rep. 500. **Mid.** as **act. fut.** κωμᾰσομαι Pind. P. 9, 89; Anth. 5, 64. 9, 756; Plut. Alex. 75; Luc. Luct. 13, and Dor. κωμάξομαι Pind. I. 3, 90 (Schol. Herm. Bergk, Momms. Christ). In classic Attic prose, the **pres.** and **imp.** only seem to be used.

Λ.

Λαγχάνω *To obtain by lot*, Soph. Fr. 587. El. 751; Andoc. 1, 121; Isocr. 16, 2; Isae. 8, 1; Aeschin. 1, 62; -άνῃ Pl. Leg. 903; -άνειν Her. 6, 23 &c.: **imp.** ἐλάγχᾰνον Od. 20, 282; Her. 8, 117; Isocr. 18, 7; Isae. 7, 26, λάγχ- Od. 9, 160: **fut.** rare, λήξομαι Pl. Rep. 617; (Dem.) 55, 20, Ion. λάξομαι Her. 7, 144: (no **1 aor.**): **p.** εἴληχα Aesch. Sept. 423; Soph. Aj. 1058; Eur. El. 668; Theocr. 16, 84; Pl. Tim. 52; Isae. 7, 21; Dinarch. 1, 64; Dem. 21, 227: **plp.** εἰλήχει Pl. Phaed. 107; Poet. and Ion. λέλογχα Od. 11, 304; Hes. Th. 203; Sapph. 79; Pind. N. 1, 24; Eur. Tr. 282 (chor.); Her. 7, 53 (and late (Dem.) 21, 82; Aene. Tact. 18, 21; see Luc. Soloec. 7), ἐπι- Soph. O. C. 1235 (chor.): **plp.** ἐλελόγχει (Luc.) Amor. 18, λελόγχ- Theocr. 4, 40; also (λέλᾰχα) 3 pl. λελάχᾱσι Emped. 373 (Stein): **p. p.** εἴληγμαι, -μένος Eur. Tr. 296 (Heath, Seidl. Dind.); Isocr. 17, 22; Dem. 30, 34, rare and late λέλαγμαι, 3 pl. -άχαται Stob. (Perict.) 85, 19: **aor.** ἐλήχθην Lys. 17, 8; ληχθῆναι Isae. 9, 24; Dem. 54, 28; -χθείς Dem. 38, 20: **2 aor. act.** ἔλᾰχον Il. 10,

430; Hes. Th. 424; Pind. Ol. 10, 61; Aesch. Eum. 931; Soph. O. R. 1366; Ar. Pax 347; Her. 1, 167; Antiph. 6, 11; Thuc. 5, 21; Isae. 6, 46; Pl. Rep. 620, ἐλλ- Hom. H. 5, 87; Theocr. 25, 271, Ep. λάχον Il. 23, 862. 24, 400; Emped. 200; Pind. Ol. 6, 34; subj. λάχω &c. Il. 24, 76; Soph. O. C. 450; Ar. Pax 364; Thuc. 2, 44; Lys. 6, 4, Epic 3 sing. λάχησιν Il. 7, 171, redupl. λελάχω *cause to share*, only in Hom. λελάχητε Il. 23, 76, λελάχωσι 15, 350. 22, 343; λελάχοι Anth. Pal. (Incert.) 7, 341 means *get as a share, obtain*; λάχων Od. 5, 40; Aesch. Sept. 55; Soph. Fr. 267; Her. 6, 109; Thuc. 3, 50, Dor. fem. λαχοῖσα Pind. Ol. 14, 1; λαχεῖν Il. 7, 179; Soph. Aj. 825 (D.); Ar. Eq. 258; Isae. 3, 2; Pl. Leg. 669. **Vb.** ληκτέον Isae. 7, 23. The perf. in the Dor. form εἴλᾱχα Theocr. 16, 84, has given way to the better supported εἴληχα. λέλογχα is scarcely found in Attic prose. The genuineness of Dem. 21, 82 is doubtful, but λελόγχατε Dio. Hal. Ant. 4, 83, and plp. ἐλελόγχει (Luc.) Amor. 18, λελόγχ- Theocr. 4, 40. The 3 pl. p. is short in penult λελόγχᾰσιν Od. 11, 304 (Mss. Bekk. Dind. La R. &c.). Barnes preserved the ᾱ by eliding ι, λελόγχᾱσ' adopted by Wolf, but Eusth. found -ᾰσιν in all the Mss. It is short in Emped. also, λελόγχᾰσι πάντα 313 (Stein), where Barnes' emend. is inadmissible; so πεφύκᾰσι Od. 7, 114 (Herodn. Bekk. Ameis, La R.). The ει instead of the redupl. (εἴληχ-, for λέληχ-) seems a *liquidation* or dainty utterance of the initial λ, λέληχ- liquidated ἐέληχ- εἴληχ-.

Λάζομαι *To take*, Poet. and Ion. Hippocr. 6, 330. 8, 88. 108. 242; subj. -ηται 6, 330; opt. -οιτο 6, 330 (Lit.), 3 pl. -οίατο Il. 2, 418; λάζεο Orph. Lith. 170; Nic. Ther. 610; Theocr. 8, 84 (λάζου Attic, but only in imper. ἀντι- Eur. Or. 452), -ζευ Theocr. 15, 21, Dor. λάσδ- (Vulg.); λάζεσθαι Hippocr. 6, 276; λαζόμενος Ap. Rh. 3, 1394; Theocr. 18, 46 (Mss. Vulg. Ziegl. 1 ed. &c. -ζυμ- Mss. Br. Mein. Ahr. Fritz. Ziegl. 2 ed.), and Attic **λάζυμαι** Eur. Bacc. 503. Med. 956. Ion 1266 &c. also Hippocr. 7, 110. 8, 42. 278 (Lit.); -λάζυσθαι, ἀντι- Eur. Or. 753; λαζύμεναι Theocr. 18, 46 see above, προσ- Eur. Hec. 64: imp. ἐλάζετο Il. 5, 371, ἀν- Mosch. 2, 163, λάζ- Il. 4, 357. Od. 13, 254, -οντο Ap. Rh. 1, 911, ἐλάζυτο Hom. H. Merc. 316; Opp. Cyn. 2, 11, ἀντ- Eur. Med. 1216, see below. λάζομαι is the Epic form: indeed, in good editions of the Homeric Poems λάζυμαι is not found, except ἐλάζυτο H. Merc. 316 quoted, nor in Ap. Rh., nor Theocr. except λαζύμεναι 18, 46 (Br. Mein. Ahr. Ziegl. 2 ed.). λάζυμαι again, is the prevailing *Attic* form: Eur. has it six or eight times, λάζομαι scarcely once, except in imper. ἀντιλάζου (never λάζυσο) Or. 452, compare λάζευ Plut. Mor. (Poet. incert.) 456, λάζοισθ' Eur. Rhes. 877 (Vulg.) is now λάζυσθ' (Mss. B. C.

&c. Dind. Kirchh. &c.), ἀντιλάζομαι I. A. 1227 (Mss. Matth. Kirchh. 1 ed.), -υμαι (Markl. Herm. Dind. Monk, Nauck, Kirchh. 2 ed.), ἀντ-ελάζετ' Med. 1216 (Vulg.), -ελάζυτ' (Ms. C. Schol. Pors. Elms. Dind. Kirchh. &c.), and in Aristoph. λάζυσθε has better Mss. and editorial authority than λάζοισθε, Lys. 209 (Ms. R. Aug. Br. Bekk. Dind. Mein. Bergk). On this point Porson says "the Attics use λάζομαι but prefer λάζυμαι" Eur. Med. 1213 (suae edit.) Elmsley more specifically, "in Attic this form (λάζομαι) seems to occur in the imper. only." This is true and instructive. The Attics were influenced in their verbal forms by use and wont, caprice, &c. and sometimes wisely yielded to necessity just like peoples of other tongues. Hippocr. has both forms, see passages quoted. λάζευ and λάζεο, λασδ- (Vulg.) for λάζου, Theocr. 15, 21. 8, 84.

(Λάζω) *To lick*, only aor. part. λάξας Lycophr. 137.

Λαικάζω *To prostitute*, Ar. Thesm. 57: fut. λαικάσω, -άσεις Ar. Eq. 167 (Bekk. Bergk): but mid. -άσει (Cod. Ven. Dind. Mein.); so λαικάσομαι Com. Fr. (Cephis.) 2, 883, -άσει (Strat.) 4, 546, an ingenious and approved restitution by Coraes. This verb seems confined to Comedy.

Λαιμάττω *To swallow greedily*, only in Comedy, and only 3 pl. -ττουσι Ar. Eccl. 1178.

Λᾰκάζω *To shout*, Trag. and only pres. imper. λᾰκαζε Aesch. Supp. 872; inf. -ζειν Sept. 186.

Λᾰκέω Dor. for ληκέω, Theocr. 2, 24.

Λᾰλᾰγέω *To chatter, twitter*, Poet. Ion. and Dor. -λαγεῦσι Anth. (Marian.) 9, 668, 11, -λαγεῦντι Theocr. 5, 48; imper. λαλάγει Pind. Ol. 9, 40; pt. λαλαγεῦσα Anth. (Paul. Sil.) 6, 54, 9, -γεῦντες Theocr. 7, 139: aor. λαλαγῆσαι Pind. Ol. 2, 97.

Λαμβάνω *To take*, Pind. Ol. 1, 81; Aesch. Ch. 128; Soph. O. R. 1031; Ar. Eccl. 317; Her. 4, 79; Thuc. 7, 25; Isocr. 5, 31 Dor. 3 pl. -βάνοντι Epich. 25 (λαβέω, -ῶ only in Arcad. 149, 17): imp. ἐλάμβανον Eur. Bac. 1313; Her. 7, 187; Antiph. 6, 10; Thuc. 2, 43; Isocr. 21, 12, late 3 pl. -βάνοσαν V. T. Ezek. 22, 12: fut. (act. λήψω late, λήψεις if correct Archestr. 22, 13 (Bussem.), λήψετε Apocr. 1 Macc. 4, 18): but mid. λήψομαι Eur. Bac. 239; Ar. Eq. 1028; Antiph. 5, 58; Thuc. 3, 56; Lys. 10, 22; Isae. 6, 61; Pl. Phaed. 78; Xen. Hell. 5, 4, 7, late λήμψ- N. T. Act. 1, 8 (Vat. Sin.), Ion. λάμψομαι Her. 1, 199. 7, 39, Dor. λαψοῦμαι, -ῇ &c. Epich. Fr. 18; Theocr. 1, 4, and λαμψ- Ecl. (Stob.) 1, 20, 3, ἀπο- Archyt. Epist. 2 (Herch.): 1 aor. rare, ἔλαμψα, ἐξ- Bias in Diog. Laert. 1, 85; κατα-λήψῃ Theophr. Fr. 6, 3, 43, *now* λάμψῃ from λάμπω (Wimmer): p. εἴληφα Archil. 143; Soph. O. R. 643; Eur. Bac. 226;

Ar. Ran. 591; Hippocr. 8, 584; Antiph. 1, 7; Thuc. 8, 27; Lys. 12, 83; Isocr. 5, 21, Dor. -āφα Inscr. Phoc. 73, Ion. and Dor. λελάβηκα Her. 4, 79. 8, 122; Com. Fr. (Eup.) 2, 570, κατα- Epist. Pherecyd. p. 460 (Herch.), μετα- Archim. Aren. 127, 15: plp. εἰλήφειν, -φεσαν Thuc. 2, 88, -ήφει Isae. 7, 34; Xen. Cyr. 8, 4, 31; Dem. 40, 33, Ion. λελαβήκεε, κατα- Her. 3, 42: p. p. εἴλημμαι Xen. Conv. 3, 13, περι- Ar. Plut. 934, εἶληψαι Dem. 24, 49; Dinarch. 1, 103, -πται 2, 21; (Eur.) Fr. Dan. 57 (1117 Dind.), ἐπ- Soph. Ant. 732; εἰλημμένος Ar. Pl. 455. Lys. 832; Pl. Euthyd. 302; Dem. 18, 284, and Poet. λέλημμαι Aesch. Ag. 876; Soph. Fr. 794; Eur. Ion 1113. Bacc. 1102. Rhes. 74. Cycl. 433, δια- Ar. Eccl. 1090, Ion. and Dor. λέλαμμαι, ἀπο- Her. 9, 51, δια- 3, 117; inf. ἀνα-λελάφθαι Hippocr. 3, 308 (Mss. Lit. -άμφθαι Vulg. and Buttm. Gr. Gr. p. 231); λελάφθω Archim. Trag. 130, 39: plp. εἴληπτο, ἀν- Aeschin. 1, 58: aor. ἐλήφθην Soph. Tr. 808; Eur. Hipp. 955; Ar. Eq. 101; Thuc. 4, 38; Lys. 13, 66; Isocr. 19, 22; -φθῶσι Aesch. Ch. 557; Antiph. 5, 48, Dor. -άφθην Archim. Aren. p. 516, 134 &c., late ἐλήμφθην, ἀν- N. T. Marc. 16, 19 (Lach. Tisch. -ήφθην Vat.), Ion. ἐλάμφθην Her. 6, 92. 9, 119: fut. ληφθήσομαι Soph. Phil. 68; Eur. Med. 381; Thuc. 6, 91; Dem. 23, 156: 3 fut. late λελήψεται, κατα- Aristid. 54, 88 (D.), and εἰληφότες ἔσεσθε Lys. 27, 7. 30, 23: 2 aor. act. ἔλαβον Il. 17, 620; Pind. N. 3, 31; Soph. Ph. 1232; Ar. Pax 966; Her. 1, 34; Antiph. 5, 61; Thuc. 4, 9; Pl. Leg. 772; Dem. 32, 25, Epic. ἔλλαβ- Il. 11, 402. Od. 18, 88; Hes. Th. 179; Ap. Rh. 1, 1197, λάβ- Il. 2, 316; Pind. P. 4, 48, iter. λάβεσκον Hes. Fr. 96; Her. 4, 78 (Mss. Bekk. Gaisf.). 130 (Schaef. Bekk. Dind. Bred. Krüg. ἐλάβ- Schw. Gaisf.); subj. λάβω Soph. O. C. 828; Ar. Eccl. 353, -βῃς Soph. O. R. 461; Xen. Cyr. 1, 4, 13, -βῃ Il. 4, 230; Aesch. Eum. 556; Pl. Rep. 378, -βῃσι Il. 21, 24 &c., -βωσι Her. 3, 147; λάβοιμι Il. 15, 22; Aesch. Ag. 275; Ar. Pax 521 (rare and Trag. λάβοιν Eur. Fr. 362, 6), -βοι Her. 1, 75; Pl. Parm. 135 &c., -βοιεν Thuc. 2, 67; λαβέ Il. 1, 407; Pl. Rep. 511, 2 dual λάβετον Euth. 275 &c.; λαβεῖν Soph. Tr. 48; Her. 8, 90; Thuc. 5, 63; λαβών Il. 6, 45; Soph. El. 12; Ar. Ach. 81; Thuc. 2, 93; Isocr. 10, 19, Dor. fem. λαβοῖσα Callim. Lav. Pal. 93. **Mid.** λαμβάνομαι *lay hold of*, Eur. Heracl. 48; Andoc. 2, 15; Pl. Parm. 165, μετα- Her. 4, 45, late λάβεται Or. Sib. 9, 294: imp. ἐλαμβάνετο Her. 2, 121: fut. λήψομαι see above: (1 aor. εληψάμην rare, if correct ληψώμεθα Pseud.-Callisth. 1, 38, Ion. ἐλαμψ- uncertain, see below): 2 aor. ἐλαβόμην indic. *simple* rare, Ar. Plut. 690, -βοντο Xen. An. 1, 6, 10 (Vulg. Poppo, -βον Dind. Sauppe, Krüger), Epic ἐλλαβ- Od. 5, 325, λάβ- Batr. 46; λάβωμαι Soph. Ph. 761; Ar. Pax 508;

Hippocr. 7, 516; Pl. Conv. 218; -οίμην Eur. Cycl. 470; Pl. Leg. 637; λαβοῦ Rep. 491; -βόμενος Ar. Vesp. 1237; Her. 9, 76; Thuc. 3, 106; λαβέσθαι Soph. O. C. 374; Pl. Rep. 554, redupl. λελαβέσθαι Od. 4, 388: with p. ἐπ-ειλῆφθαι Pl. Crat. 396; and late κατ-ειλημμένος D. Sic. 17, 85. Vb. λαμπτέος, κατα- Her. 3, 127, ληπτός Pl. Rep. 529, -έον Phil. 34, κατα- Hippocr. 4, 280 (Lit.) For the augmented form ἐλάβεσκον Her. 4, 130 (Gaisf.), Bekker reads rightly λάβεσκον. p. p. εἴλημμαι always in Attic prose and Comedy, except διαλελημμένος Ar. Eccl. 1090 (in a psephisma), λέλημμαι always in Tragedy, except εἴληπται (Eur.?) Dan. 57, ἐπ-είλ- Soph. Ant. 732. For ἀνα-λελάμφθαι Hippocr. Offic. Med. 7 (Vulg.), Littré gives from ten Mss. and the Gloss. of Erot. -λελάφθαι 3, 308 (Lit.) Nevertheless, we think Buttm. may be right in maintaining -λελάμφθαι to be the genuine Ionic form, comparing λαμπτός. He might perhaps have strengthened his analogy by κεκάμφθαι 4, 280, ξυγ- 4, 322, with, in one case, the variant -άφθαι. In Xen. An. 7, 2, 14, the Mss. vary between fut. mid. συλλήψεται in pass. sense, and fut. pass. συλληφθήσεται. But though the former is offered by several of the best Mss., recommended by Larcher and Valckenaer, and received into the Text by Kühner (1852), the pass. use of this fut. mid. simple or compd. is against the uniform usage not only of Xen. but, we think, of all other writers. Of aor. mid. ἐλαμψάμην we have seen no sure instance. Matthiae quotes Her. 7, 157, but there occurs only fut. παραλαμψομένους: λάμψηται 8, 10 (Vulg.) is a wrong reading for fut. -ψεται (Mss. F. a. Schaef. Gaisf. Bekk. Stein), so ἀπολάμψαιτο 9, 38 (Mss. S. V.) for fut. -ψοιτο (Gaisf. Bekk. &c.), κατα- λαμψάμενον 6, 39 (Ms. S.) for -ψόμενον (Gaisf. Bekk. &c.), and λάμψασθαι 9, 108 (Ms. F.) for -ψεσθαι (Gaisf. Bekk. &c.), and παραλήψηται (for Vulg. παραλλάξεται -ηται) Hippocr. 6, 326 (Lit.) which depends, for at least its *extraneous* support, on Littré's "Je pense qu'il faut lire." ληψώμεθα, however, Pseudo-Callisth. 1, 38 (Müller, Meusel.).

(Λαμπετάω) *To shine*, Epic and only part. -τόων Il. 1, 104; Hes. Th. 110. Sc. 390; Ap. Rh. 3, 1362, -όωσα Orph. Lith. 89, -όωσαι 291.

Λάμπω *To shine*, Il. 13, 474; Solon 13, 23; Pind. Ol. 1, 23; Phryn. 2 (B.); Aesch. Ag. 774; Soph. O. R. 186; Eur. Ion 83; Ar. Eccl. 13; Her. 2, 44; Xen. Mem. 4, 7, 7: imp. ἔλαμπον Il. 22, 32; Anacr. 33; Soph. Ant. 1007; Pl. Phaedr. 250, λάμπε Hes. Sc. 71; Il. 12, 463, λάμφ' 11, 66, iter. λάμπεσκε Emped. 321 (Stein); Theocr. 24, 19: fut. λάμψω Soph. El. 66; Anth. 4, 2, 8, ἀνα- Plut. Alex. 30: aor. ἔλαμψα Soph. O. R. 473; Eur. Hel. 1477; Ar. Vesp. 62; Ap. Rh. 3, 371; Himer. Or. 14,

20; Plut. Timol. 3, ἐπ- Il. 17, 650; Pind. Fr. XI, 55 (Schneidw.); Her. 3, 135. 6, 118, ἐξ- 6, 82, ἀν- Xen. An. 5, 2, 24; λάμψη Theophr. Sig. 6, 3, 43; λάμψας Eur. Hel. 1131; Her. 6, 82; Aristot. Mund. 4, 18; (Pl.) Epist. 335: **p.** λέλαμπα Eur. Andr. 1025. Tr. 1295 (chor.): **aor. pass.** late λαμφθείς, περι- Joseph. Jud. B. 4, 10, 1: **fut.** λαμφθήσεται, ἐλ- Plotin. 30, 3. **Mid.** λάμπομαι as act. Hom. H. 31, 13; Eur. I. T. 1155; Ar. Ran. 293; -εσθαι Xen. An. 3, 1, 11; -όμενος Il. 17, 214; Plut. Mor. 343; (Luc.) Asin. 51: **imp.** ἐλάμπετο Il. 22, 134; Eur. Med. 1194, λάμπ- Il. 6, 319. 15, 608: **fut.** λάμψομαι, ἐλ- Her. 1, 80. 8, 74.—Eur. uses λάμπω transitively, *kindle up, make blaze,* Ph. 226. Hel. 1131. In good Attic prose this verb is confined to **pres.** and **imp.** active, and **pres. mid.**: **fut.** λάμψει Geop. 2, 5, 15: **aor.** λάμψας Her. 6, 82; (Pl.) Epist. 335; Polyb. 6, 43; Charit. 1, 9.

Λανθάνω *To lie hid, escape notice,* Pind. Fr. 53, 13 (Bergk); Aesch. Sup. 714; Soph. Ant. 9; Ar. Pax 618; Heraclit. 2 (Bywater); Her. 9, 47; Thuc. 7, 83; Pl. Crat. 393, Poet. ληθάνω and only 3 sing. in tmesi Od. 7, 221, and mostly Poet. λήθω Il. 23, 323. Od. 19, 91; Hes. Op. 268; Soph. O. R. 1325; Eur. Rhes. 810; Xen. Conv. 4, 48. Oec. 7, 31. Ages. 6, 5, Dor. λᾱθει Soph. El. 222 (chor.); inf. λᾱθέμεν Pind. Ol. 1, 64 (Mss. Schneid. Christ, Bergk, 3 ed. but see **2 p.**): **imp.** ἐλάνθᾰνον Il. 13, 721. Od. 8, 93; Soph. El. 914; Her. 1, 44; Thuc. 2, 76; Lys. 2, 77, λάνθ- H. Hym. 18, 9, ἔληθον Od. 19, 151; Soph. El. 1359, Dor. ἔλᾱθ- Pind. P. 3, 27, λῆθον Il. 15, 461, iter. λήθεσκεν Il. 24, 13: **fut.** λήσω Il. 23, 416; Soph. Tr. 455; Ar. Eccl. 98; Her. 8, 106; Antiph. 2, α, 7; Thuc. 8, 10; Lys. 4, 16; Isocr. 12, 139; Pl. Phaedr. 262; Dem. 23, 123, Dor. λᾱσῶ Theocr. 14, 9: **1 aor.** ἔλησα Poet. and late in *simple,* λήσειεν Nic. Al. 280, ἐπ-έλησεν *caused to forget,* Od. 20, 85, Dor. ἔλᾱσας in tmesi Alcae. 95 (Bergk): **p. p.** λέλησμαι (as mid. see below), late in pass. sense *is forgotten,* ἐπι-λελησμ- V. T. Esai. 23, 16. N. T. Luc. 12, 6: **1 aor.** (ἐλήσθην) *I forgot,* Dor. poet. inf. λασθῆμεν, for -ῆναι, Theocr. 2, 46, perhaps late in pass. sense ἐπ-ελήσθην V. T. Ps. 30, 13; Apocr. Sir. 13, 10 (Dor. if correct, ἐπιλασθέν Sylburg's conject. Pind. Fr. 98 (86), where Bergk reads σιγαθέν with Barnes): and late **fut.** ἐπι-λησθήσομαι V. T. Ps. 9, 19. Jer. 20, 11. 23, 40: but **3 fut.** λελήσομαι *will forget,* Eur. Alc. 198: **2 aor. act.** ἔλᾰθον Il. 17, 676; Simon. C. 150; Pind. Ol. 6, 36; Eur. Fr. 224 (Dind.); Ar. Eq. 116; Her. 9, 93; Thuc. 3, 112; Isocr. 8, 88, λάθον Il. 23, 388. 24, 331. Od. 13, 270, dual λαθέτην 22, 179, iter. late ἐξ-ελάθεσκε Or. Sib. 1, 44; **subj.** λάθω Eur. I. T. 995; Pl. Charm. 166; Dem. 45, 85, λάθῃ Aesch. Eum. 255; Soph. Ph. 156; Pl. Rep. 344, -θῃσι Il. 22, 191 &c. -θωσι Thuc. 1, 37; λάθοιμι Aesch. Supp. 988, -θοις Pl. Rep. 341, -θοι Il. 10, 468; Soph. O. R. 904; Eur. Med. 332; Pl. Leg. 747 &c., -θοιεν Thuc. 7, 56; -θεῖν Antiph. 5, 27; -θων 2, β, 3; Andoc. 3, 33, Epic redupl. λέλαθον, ἐκ- *caused to forget*, Il. 2, 600; *simple* λελάθῃ 15, 60; λελάθοιμι in usual sense Ap. Rh. 3, 779; and part. λελαθοῦσα Orph. Arg. 879, ἐκ- H. Ven. 40, but λελάθοντα, ἐκ- Theocr. 1, 63 seems **pres.**: **2 p.** λέληθα (not in Hom.) Simon. Am. 7, 9; Solon 13, 27; Soph. O. R. 415; Eur. Alc. 58; Ar. Thesm. 589; Her. 3, 2; Isocr. 9, 78; Isae. 3, 27; Dem. 23, 134, but as **mid.** *forget*, ἐπι- Her. 3, 46, Dor. λέλᾱθα, ἐπι- Pind. Ol. 10, 3; Plut. Mor. 232; inf. λελήθεναι Eur. Fr. 832, Dor. λελᾱθέμεν Pind. Ol. 1, 64 (Momms. Bergk, 4 ed.): **plp.** ἐλελήθειν *escaped observation*, Xen. Oec. 18, 9 (Dind. -ήθη Saupp.); Luc. Nigr. 4, Att. 2 sing. ἐλελήθης Ar. Eq. 822. 1044 (Br. Dind. Mein.), -ήθεις Luc. D. Deor. 8, -ήθη Ar. Nub. 380 (Br. Dind. 2 ed. Kock, Teufel), -ήθει (Bekk. Dind. 5 ed. Mein.); Pl. Lach. 183; Luc. D. Deor. 9, -ήθεε Her. 6, 79. 9, 22, -ήθεσαν Thuc. 8, 33, *forgot* Hippocr. 5, 208 (Lit.) **Mid.** λανθάνομαι *to forget*, Aristot. Poet. 17, ἐκ- Soph. O. C. 1005, ἐπι- Pl. Lach. 189, and usu. Poet. λήθομαι Il. 11, 790; Aesch. Ag. 39, Dor. λάθομαι Pind. Ol. 8, 72; Soph. El. 167 (chor.): **imp.** λανθανόμην Od. 12, 227, ἐπ-ελανθ- Pl. Prot. 309, ἐλήθετο Il. 5, 319, ἐπ- Her. 3, 75, λήθ- Il. 12, 393; Hes. Th. 547: **fut.** λήσομαι *will forget*, Od. 1, 308; Theogn. 2; Com. Fr. (Philem.) 4, 30, ἐπι- Lys. 6, 33, Dor. λᾱσεῦμαι Theocr. 4, 39, but *escape notice* λήσομαι Hippocr. 2, 170; Aristot. Anal. pr. 2, 19; Luc. Sacrif. 14; Dio. Hal. 3, 56; Diod. Sic. 14, 1; App. Syr. 8; Ap. Rh. 3, 737, unless here subj. for -ωμαι; but **pass.** *will be forgotten* Soph. El. 1249: **1 aor. mid.** late ἐλησάμην *escaped notice*, ἐλήσαο Nonn. 33, 149, ἐλήσατο, ἐπ- 48, 969; Q. Sm. 12, 468; λήσομαι subj. for -ωμαι? Ap. Rh. 3, 737; λησάμενος Q. Sm. 3, 99; Or. Sib. 12, 72, Dor. λᾱσαμένᾱ Mosch. 3, 61: **2 aor.** ἐλᾰθόμην Il. 13, 835 (Dind. Faesi, λάθ- Bekk. La Roche); Hes. Th. 547; Pind. P. 4, 41, λαθ- Il. 9, 537; -θωμαι Il. 10, 99; Tyrt. 12, 17; Eur. Hipp. 289; -οίμην Il. 10, 243, Dor. -οίμαν Soph. El. 1287 (chor.); Eur. Sup. 86 (chor.), -θοίατο Od. 10, 236; λαθέσθαι Il. 12, 235; Aesch. Sup. 731; Soph. Fr. 358 &c. (not in Comedy, nor *simple* in good prose, but ἐλάθοντο Plut. Caes. 38, classic ἐπ- Andoc. 1, 148; Pl. Apol. 17; Xen. Cyr. 1, 4, 28; Isocr. 12, 139, rarely ἐκ- (Pl.) Ax. 369; Plut. Cat. Min. 60; Apollod. 1, 8, 2. 9, 15), Epic redupl. λελάθοντο Il. 4, 127; Sapph. 93; opt. ἐκ-λελάθοιτο Od. 3, 224, but as **act.** λελάθ- Hes. Th. 471; imper. -θέσθω Il. 16, 200; inf. -θέσθαι 19,

136, ἐπι- Lys. 6, 33: and as mid. p. p. λέλησμαι Soph. El. 342; Eur. Phoen. 850; Pl. Phaedr. 252, Epic and Dor. λέλασμαι Il. 5, 834. 11, 313. Od. 24, 40; Theocr. 2, 158; inf. ἐπι-λελᾶσθαι Plut. Mor. 232: **plp.** ἐλέληστο, ἐπ- Xen. Cyr. 8, 3, 8: **1 aor.** ἐλάσθην, inf. λασθῆμεν Theocr. 2, 46: **2 aor.?** (ἐλήθην), δι-ελήθησαν Hippocr. 1, 417 (Kühn), see below: in same sense **3 fut.** λελήσομαι Eur. Alc. 198. **Vb.** ἄ-λαστος, or -ός, Il. 22, 261. 24, 105; Soph. O. C. 538, ἄ-ληστος, ἀλάθητος very late, Philo; Aesop 16, 17 (Schaefer.)—λήθει is sometimes used as λήθεται, if correct Anth. (Simon.?) 7, 25 (Cod. Pal. λήθη Vulg. Bergk 184, λῆγεν Suid. λήγει Pors. Schn.); so ἐπιλελῆθέναι Her. 3, 46, Dor. -λελᾶθ- Pind. Ol. 10 (11), 3, for -λελῆσθαι Opp. Hal. 5, 458. Instead of the approved reading λαθέμεν Pind. Ol. 1, 64 (103), some inferior Mss. and editions have **fut.** λασέμεν. We have found no satisfactory *classic* authority for the *simple* **1 aor.** ἔλησα. The best Mss. Thuc. 8, 10, offer for λήσωσι, **fut.** λήσουσι which is now the approved reading (Bekk. Popp. Krüg. Dind. Donalds.); and λήσαντα Xen. Cyr. 1, 6, 1, is rendered suspicious as well by the *v. r.* αὔσαντα, λύσαντα, as by its extreme rarity. The ablest editors have therefore generally agreed in substituting **fut.** λήσοντα (Herm. Popp. Bornem. Dind. Saupp. &c.), and λήσῃ Pl. Rep. 421. Alcib. (2) 138, δια-λήσῃ Isocr. 3, 16, have been changed to **fut.** λήσει, δια-λήσει; so also λήσῃ Dio. Hal. Ant. 6, 58 (Vulg.) now λήσει (Kiessl.) ἐπιλασθέν *forgotten*, in some edit. of Pind. Fr. 98 (86) is an emend. of Sylburg. διελήθησαν called **2 aor. pass.** Hippocr. quoted, we suspect to be a false reading for **plp.** διελελήθεσαν. ἐλελήθη, ἐπ-ελελήθη &c. Hippocr. 3, 66, 548 (K.), seem to be mistakes for -ήθεε or -ει. The compds. in the *active* form present λήθω, scarcely ever λανθάνω: διελάνθανεν Pl. Leg. 677, is the only classic instance we have remarked. The usual prose forms are ἐπι- seldom ἐκλανθάνομαι &c. The latter is poetic in the active, of which it has only **1** and **2 aor.** Hecker Comment. crit. de Anthol. Graec. p. 344, says "sed **aor.** ἐλησάμην num poetis in usu fuerit dubitare Cobetum video. Mihi nullum ejus exemplum ad manum est." We think the *Poets* were the only class that did use it: the instances quoted, Mosch. 3, 61; Nonn. 33, 149; Or. Sib. 12, 72, ἐπ- Quint. Sm. 12, 468; Nonn. 48, 969, have, as far as we know, never been challenged. ἐπιλήθω (ἐπιλανθάνω not in use) *cause to forget*, **pres.** and **fut.** late -λήθουσα Aretae. 2, 12 (ἐπίληθον adject. not ἐπιλῆθον part. is the approved reading Od. 4, 221 Wolf, Bekk. Dind.): **fut.** ἐπιλήσει Philostr. Epist. 68 (Kayser): but **aor.** ἐπέλησεν Od. 20, 85. **Mid.** ἐπιλήθομαι *forget*, Hes. Th. 102; Callim. Del. 233; Eur. Or. 66; Ar. Nub.

785; Ion. prose Her. 4, 43, Dor. -λᾶθομαι Soph. El. 146. 177 (chor.); Eur. Tr. 602 (chor.), in comedy and prose ἐπιλανθάνομαι Xen. Conv. 4, 62; Pl. Theaet. 153; Isocr. 4, 157; Com. Fr. (Mon.) 170: **imp.** ἐπελήθετο Od. 4, 455; Ion. prose Her. 3, 75, -ελανθανόμην Ar. Nub. 855; Her. 3, 147; Pl. Prot. 309: **fut.** -λήσομαι Il. 22, 387; in Attic Poet. only Com. Fr. (Philem.) 4, 6; but in prose Xen. Cyr. 5, 2, 11; Pl. Crat. 406; Lys. 6, 33; Aeschin. 1, 73: **1 aor.** late ἐπ-ελήσατο Nonn. 48, 969; Q. Sm. 12, 468: classic **2 aor.** ἐπελαθόμην Eur. Hel. 265; Ar. Ach. 473; Xen. Hell. 4, 3, 20; Isocr. 12, 139; Dem. 24, 86; subj. -λάθωμαι Andoc. 1, 148; Pl. Theaet. 206 &c.; in tmesi Il. 10, 99, &c. &c.: **p. p.** Attic ἐπιλέλησμαι as **mid.** Eur. I. A. 1232; Ar. Nub. 631; Pl. Phaedr. 235; Dem. 18, 182 (psephisma); Dor. inf. -λελᾶσθαι Plut. Mor. 232: **plp.** -ελελήσμην Xen. Cyr. 1, 3, 10; Pl. Theaet. 201: **2 p.** -λέληθα Ion. Her. 3, 46, Dor. -λέλᾱθα Pind. Ol. 11, 3, 1 pl. ἐπιλελάθαμες Plut. Mor. (Apophth.) 232. For the **p. plp. aor.** and **fut. pass.** in **pass.** sense, see above.

Λαπάζω, -σσω, -ττω *To empty, plunder* &c. Athen. 8, 64, -σσει Hippocr. 5, 628 (Lit.), (-ττονται Aristot. Prob. 23, 39): **imp.** ἐλάπασσε Hippocr. 5, 192: **fut.** λαπάξω Aesch. Sept. 47. 531; Galen 10, 893: **aor.** ἐλάπαξα Hippocr. 5, 176 (Lit.); Ael. H. A. 5, 39: **p. p.** λελάπαγμαι, -άχθω Aretae. 109, 34; -άχθαι Athen. 8, 64: **aor.** ἐλαπάχθην Hippocr. 5, 176 (Lit.); λαπάχθῃ 2, 478. Rare in Attic, never in classic prose.

Λάπτω *To lap, lick,* Aristot. H. A. 8, 6; Luc. V. H. 1, 23 (Bekk. Jacob.); Opp. H. 2, 618: **fut.** λάψω Il. 16, 161; Aristot. H. A. 8, 6, 1, ἀπο- Ar. Nub. 811: and **mid.** λάψομαι, ἐκ- Ar. Pax 885: **aor.** ἔλαψα late in *simple*, see Apollod. 3, 4, 4 (Bekk.), but ἐξ-έλαψα Ar. Ach. 1229; λάψαι Athen. 485: **p.** λέλᾰφα Ar. Fr. 492. **Mid. fut.** λάψομαι, ἐκ- see above: **aor.** λαψάμενος Com. Fr. (Pher.) 2, 294.

Λάσκω *To speak, say, gabble,* Poet. Eur. Andr. 671; -σκων Aesch. Ag. 865; Ar. Ach. 1046, Dor. λᾰκέω Theocr. 2, 24 (Ion. ληκέω): **imp.** ἔλασκον Aesch. Ag. 596; Eur. Elec. 1214, λάσκε Lycophr. 460, ἐλήκεον, ἐπ- Od. 8, 379: **fut.** λᾰκήσομαι Ar. Pax 381. 384: **1 aor.** ἐλᾰ́κησα indic. late, Hierocl. 176. 194 (Eberh.), see below; λᾰκήσῃς Ar. Pax 382, but δια-λᾰκήσασα Nub. 410 by license, or from Dor. διαλᾰκέω?: **2 aor.** ἔλᾰκον Aesch. Sept. 153; Soph. Tr. 824; Eur. Ion 776. Tr. 269; Ar. Plut. 39, Hom. always λᾰ́κε Il. 14, 25. 20, 277; Hes. Th. 694, λέλᾰκε Opp. Cyn. 2, 141; λᾰ́κοι Ar. Ran. 97; λᾰκεῖν Soph. Ant. 1094; Eur. Alc. 346: **2 p.** λέλᾱκα Aesch. Pr. 406; Eur. Hec. 678. Hipp. 55; Ar. Ach. 410, Epic λέληκα Hes. Op. 207; Simon. Am. 7,

15 (B.); Opp. Hal. 3, 247; also Aristot. H. An. 9, 32, 3; -ηκώς Il. 22, 141, but fem. λελᾰκυῖα Od. 12, 85: **2 aor. mid.** with Epic redupl. λελᾰ́κοντο H. Hym. Merc. 145. The pres. fut. 1 aor. and 2 p. with α, λέλᾱκα, are Attic: in Epic occur only 2 aor. act. and mid. and 2 p. with η, λέληκα. Rare in prose, but λέληκε Aristot. H. A. 9, 32; later **aor.** ἐλάκησε Geop. 13, 15; N. T. Act. 1, 18, and later.

Λαφύσσω *To devour*, Il. 11, 176; Opp. Hal. 2, 308; late prose Philostr. 3, 97. 4, 178; (Luc.) Asin. 27, Attic -ττω Athen. 8, 362: **imp.** 3 dual λαφύσσετον Il. 18, 583: **fut.** -ύξω Ael. Fr. 156: **aor.** ἐλάφυξα, inf. λαφύξαι Orph. Lith. 120; Q. Sm. 7, 490; Ael. H. A. 4, 45; Aretae. C. Morb. Ac. 2, 112 (ed. Oxon.) **Mid.** λαφύσσομαι Com. Fr. (Eup.) 2, 492; Luc. Tim. 17: (fut. λαφύξομαι Anth. 11, 379, altered to φυλαξ-): aor. λαφύξασθαι Lycophr. 321.—3 dual imp. λαφύσσετον for -ην Il. quoted.

Λᾰχαίνω *To dig*, -αίνων Opp. Hal. 5, 264: **imp.** ἐλᾰ́χαινε Mosch. 4, 96: **aor.** ἐλάχηνε Ap. Rh. 3, 222; Anth. (Paul. Sil.) 7, 609; λαχήνῃ Lycophr. 624 is Poet. and we think late in *simple* and compd. except ἀμφ-ελάχαινε Od. 24, 242.

Λάω *To see*, Epic and only part. λᾰ́ων Od. 19, 229; H. Hym. Merc. 360: and **imp.** λᾰ́ε Od. 19, 230.

Λάω, λῶ *To wish* (Dor. for θέλω), Ar. Lys. 981, λῇς Epich. 44. 94 &c.; Theocr. 8, 6; Ar. Lys. 95, λῇ Epich. 94; Ar. Lys. 1163, pl. λῶμες 1162 (-μεσθ' Mss.), λῆτε 1105 (Bekk. Dind. Ahr.), λῶντι Epich. 19; Theocr. 4, 14; subj. λῇς Theocr. 5, 21, λῇ Epich. 19; opt. λῴη Epich. 137 (λοίη Mss.), and doubtful λῷτε 58; inf. λῆν Thuc. 5, 77 (Poppo, Boehme); part. λῶντι Corcyr. Inscr. 1845; Epich. 19, 1.

Λεαίνω *To smooth*, Her. 4, 122; Xen. Mem. 1, 4, 6; Pl. Tim. 66, λειαίνω Solon 4, 35; and late Nic. Ther. 95; Geop. 4, 12, 13: **fut.** λεᾰνῶ Aristot. Part. An. 3, 14, 9, Ion. λειανέω Il. 15, 261: **aor.** ἐλέηνα, λεήναις Nic. Fr. 3, 15 (Gottl. Schneid. -ήνας Otto Schneid.); λεήνας Her. 1, 200. 8, 142, Attic -ᾱνα Aristot. Gen. An. 5, 8, 6; Aene. Tact. 31, 21; Philostr. Ap. 3, 139; Athen. 3, 79, Ion. ἐλείηνα, λειήν- Od. 8, 260; λειήνας Il. 4, 111; Hippocr. 8, 360. **Pass.** λεαίνομαι Pl. Polit. 270: **p. p.** λελεασμένος Galen 13, 989; Dioscor. 5, 85; Porph. de abst. 4, 7: **aor.** ἐλεάνθην, λεανθῇ Sext. Emp. 30, 30 (B.); Dioscor. 3, 106, Ion. λειανθέωσι Hippocr. 8, 346 (Lit. v. r. λεαν-); λεανθείς Dioscor. 3, 165, λειαν- Geop. 11, 13. **Mid.** λεαίνομαι *To smooth, rub oneself*, -αίνηται Stobae. (Muson.) 18, 38; -αίνεσθαι Plut. Mor. 410: **aor.** opt. λειήναιο Nic. Ther. 646. **Vb.** λεαντέον Dioscor. 5, 103.

Λέγω *To say, tell*, Hes. Th. 27; Anacr. 94; Pind. Ol. 8, 43; Aesch. Sept. 202; Soph. Ph. 1394; Ar. Eq. 22; Her. 1, 9;

Antiph. 6, 15; Thuc. 1, 129; Pl. Theaet. 198, Dor. 3 pl. λέγοντι Pind. Ol. 9, 49; 3 pl. imper. λεγόντων Her. 1, 89; Pl. Soph. 246: imp. ἔλεγον Od. 23, 308; Ar. Pax 213; Her. 8, 19; Antiph. 5, 42; Thuc. 1, 139; Lys. 8, 8, Epic λέγον Il. 2, 222?: fut. λέξω Emped. 130; Aesch. Ag. 859; Soph. El. 560; Her. 4, 14; Antiph. 6, 33; Thuc. 2, 48; Andoc. 3, 21; Lys. 8, 5. 26, 16; Isocr. 18, 35; Pl. Polit. 290; Isae. 10, 9. 2; Aeschin. 1, 156. 3, 17. 36. 57; Dem. 16, 3, Dor. 3 pl. λεξοῦντι Pind. Fr. 99, 10 (Bergk): aor. ἔλεξα Aesch. Eum. 114; Soph. O. R. 280; Ar. Eq. 654; Her. 1, 141; Antiph. 1, 15. 6, 21; Andoc. 1, 19. 113; Thuc. 4, 114; Xen. Hell. 1, 7, 16; λέξαιμι Lys. 8, 4; λέξον Hes. Cert. 320, 3 (Goettl.); λέξαι Anacr. 45; λέξας Pl. Soph. 217: p. λέλεχα Galen 16, 249 (Kühn, -λεγα, -λογα Hesych. classic εἴρηκα): p. p. λέλεγμαι Pind. N. 8, 20; Eur. Med. 354; Aesch. Eum. 675; Soph. Ph. 389; Ar. Ran. 1244; Her. 2, 21. 125; Pl. Leg. 732. 679. Tim. 89 (but δι-είλεγμαι mid. *discuss*, Pl. Prot. 313. Apol. 37: δι-είλεκτο Lys. 9, 5): aor. ἐλέχθην Soph. O. R. 1442; Her. 3, 80; Thuc. 6, 32; Pl. Phil. 24; -λεχθείς Aesch. Ch. 665 (but ἐπι-λεχθῇς active, *say further*, Aesch. Ag. 1498 Dind., λεχθῇ Herm., ἐπιλέξῃς Voss, Franz, δι- Her. 3, 51; Isocr. 19, 37): fut. λεχθήσομαι Mosch. Trag. Fr. 5 (Wagn.); Antiph. 3, γ, 4; Thuc. 5, 86; Pl. Tim. 67; Isocr. 12, 156: and fut. mid. as pass. λέξομαι Trag. Soph. O. C. 1186; Eur. H. F. 582. Hec. 906. I. T. 1047 &c. late prose, Aretae. 131 (ed. Oxon.): 3 fut. λελέξομαι Thuc. 3, 53; Pl. Rep. 457. Mid. (λέγομαι), subj. -ώμεθα Il. 2, 435. 13, 292: imper. λέγεο, ἐπι- Her. 7, 50: imp. ἐλέγετο, ἐπ- *said on, read*, Her. 1, 124: 2 aor. sync. προσ-έλεκτο *said to, addressed*, late Musae. 244, unless Od. 12, 34, may be taken in this sense: fut. λέξομαι Or. Sib. 3, 432: aor. ἐλέξω (Hesych.), προσ-ελέξατο Hes. Op. 499; Ap. Rh. 4, 833; Q. Sm. 1, 99. 10, 423, Dor. ποτ-ελέξ- Theocr. 1, 92, ἐπ- Her. 7, 239; Luc. Merc. Cond. 37; ἐπι-λεξάμενοι *chose*, Thuc. 7, 19, and ἐπι-λεξαμένα *mentioned*, Aesch. Supp. 49 (chor.), see aor. pass. Vb. λεκτός Soph. Ph. 633, -έος Xen. An. 5, 6, 6. This verb in the sense 'say, utter,' is said to be post-Homeric; but this meaning suits well Il. 2, 222, Ἀγαμέμνονι λέγ' ὀνείδεα, and Od. 23, 308 &c. quoted: κατείλοχε p. act. *he said*, Schol. Il. 14, 221: p. p. κατειλεγμένος *having been said, mentioned*, Themist. Or. 1, 22: 2 p. λέλεγα, λέλογα (Hesych. Phot.). Aor. ἔλεξα is notably rare in Plato and the Orators.

Λέγω *To lay, number, gather, choose*, Il. 23, 239; late prose, Pseud. D. Chrys. 37, 41, but ἐκ- Thuc. 4, 59; Epic subj. λέγομεν Od. 24, 72: imp. ἔλεγον, κατ- Thuc. 3, 75, Epic ἄλ-λεγον for ἀνα-λ- Il. 23, 253: fut. λέξω Od. 24, 224: aor. ἔλεξα *laid* (to rest) Il. 14, 252; λέξον 24, 635; Dor. pt. λέξαις *gathered*, Pind. P. 8, 53, usually comp. συν-έλεξα Ar. Ran. 1297; Her. 7, 8, ἐξ- Thuc. 8, 44, κατ- Xen. Hell. 3, 4, 15: p. εἴλοχα, συν- Dem. 21, 23; Dio Cass. 46, 26, and late εἴλεχα, ἐξ- Aristid. 49, 381: p. p. λέλεγμαι liquidated εἴλεγμαι, both in comp. unless εἰλεγμένας be correct Eur. Tr. 296 (Mss. Vulg. Kirchh. 1 ed. and not εἰλημ- Heath, Dind. Nauck, Kirchh. 2 ed., see Dem. 30, 34), προ-λελεγμ- Il. 13, 689; Ar. Vesp. 886; Theocr. 13, 18, ἀπο- Her. 7, 40. 41. 83, παρα- Ar. Eccl. 904, συν- Eccl. 58 (but συν-ειλ- for the metre, Av. 294); Her. 7, 26. 9, 41, ἐκ- Com. Fr. (Diph.) 4, 394; Xen. Hell. 1, 6, 16, ἐπι- Cyr. 3, 3, 41, more Attic εἴλεγμαι, συν- Ar. Av. 294; Thuc. 2, 10; Pl. Rep. 574 (as mid. Ax. 370), ἀπ- Xen. Hipp. 8, 12, ἐπ- Isocr. 4, 146, ἐξ- Dem. 23, 88 (as mid. Isocr. 9, 46; Dem. 20, 131), κατ- Lys. 9, 4. 16, 13; Dem. 39, 8, προεξειλ- Dem. 18, 234. 50, 9: 1 aor. ἐλέχθην Il. 3, 188, usu. comp. συν- Ar. Lys. 526; Her. 1, 97. 3, 130. 6, 39; Pl. Leg. 784. (Pl.) Epist. 348, ἐκ- Xen. Mem. 3, 5, 2; Pl. Leg. 864: fut. late λεχθήσοιντο, κατα- Dio Cass. 78, 28: more freq. in Attic, 2 aor. ἐλέγην, ξυν- Ar. Eccl. 116. 395; Her. 9, 27; Thuc. 6, 9; Pl. Phaed. 59; Isocr. 9, 56, κατ- Lys. 30, 8; Isae. 7, 5; Pl. Leg. 762. 943; Dem. 50, 7, ἐγ-κατα- Thuc. 1, 93: fut. λεγήσομαι, συλ- Aeschin. 3, 100, κατα- Themist. 16, 203, ἐγκατα- Luc. Catapl. 11. **Mid.** λέγομαι generally as act. *simple* poetic? Il. 8, 507. 13, 276 &c. ἐπι- Her. 6, 86: fut. λέξομαι *will lay myself* to rest, Od. 17, 102. 4, 413, συλ- 2, 292, κατα- 3, 353; Hes. Op. 523, Dor. λεξοῦμαι *will collect*, Callim. L. Pal. 116: aor. ἐλεξάμην, ἐλλεξ- Anth. App. Epigr. 114, λεξ- *selected*, Il. 21, 27; Pind. P. 4, 189, ἐξ-ελεξ- Eur. Supp. 341 (Vulg. Kirchh. 1 ed. -εδειξάμην Herm. Dind. Nauck, Kirchh. 2 ed.); Pl. Rep. 456, ἀπ- Her. 8, 101, ἐπ- 8, 22, ξυν- Thuc. 6, 71, ἐλεξ- *laid myself* to rest, Od. 4, 305, λεξ- Il. 14, 350, παρ-ελεξ- 6, 198; Pind. P. 2, 36, but δι- *laid out* in thought, *pondered*, Il. 17, 97 (unless rather to be referred to λέγω *say*); subj. λέξομαι for -ωμαι Od. 23, 172. Il. 4, 131, παρα- 14, 237; λεξαίμην Od. 3, 365, -αιτο 24, 108; -ασθαι Il. 2, 125: 2 aor. syncop. ἐλέγμην *I counted myself to* (by some called pass.) Od. 9, 335, 3 sing. λέκτο *counted for himself*, 4, 451, but *lay down*, 5, 487, ἔλεκτο 19, 50 &c.; Hes. Sc. 46, κατ- Il. 9, 662; imper. λέξο Il. 24, 650, and λέξεο Il. 9, 617, λέξε' Od. 10, 320 (Bekk. λέξο Aristarch. Dind. La R.); inf. λέχθαι, κατα- Od. 15, 394; part. -λέγμενος 22, 196: p. p. as mid. ἐξ-ειλεγμένος *having selected*, Isocr. 9, 46; Dem. 20, 131, late ἐπι-λέλεξαι *have chosen*, Heliod. 10, 7: aor. see ἐπι-λεχθῇς Aesch. Ag. 1498, under λέγω *say*. **Vb.** λεκτός Soph. O. R. 19, ἐκλεκτέος Pl. Rep. 456.—ἐλέγμην and in the sense *lay to rest* ἔλεξα, λέξομαι, ἐλεξάμην are Epic, and referred by Buttmann to λεχ- as their stem, whence λεχός, λεχώ &c. We are inclined to think with Heath, Dind. &c. that εἰληγμένας not εἰλεγ- is the true reading, Eur. Tr. 296. The female captives seem to be with stricter propriety called εἰληγμέναι the *allotted*, as objects of ἔλαχε in line 277, than εἰλεγμέναι.

Λειαίνω, see λεαίνω.

Λείβω *To pour*, Callim. Apol. 37; Aesch. Eum. 54; Eur. I. A. 650; Pl. Rep. 411; -ειν Hes. Op. 724; Aesch. Supp. 981; Il. 6, 266, -έμεν (Bekk.); -ων Il. 18, 32; Soph. O. C. 1251; Com. Fr. (Cratin.) 2, 157, liquidated εἴβω Poet. Il. 16, 11 in tmesi: **imp.** ἔλειβον Sapph. 51; Anth. 2, 1 (78), ἐπ- Od. 3, 341, λεῖβον Il. 13, 88, εἶβον Od. 4, 153, iter. λείβεσκον Q. Sm. 14, 103: **fut.** (λείψω?): **aor.** ἔλειψα, inf. λεῖψαι Il. 7, 481; λείψας Il. 24, 285; Orph. Arg. 319. **Mid.** λείβομαι as **act.** -ομένα Aesch. Pr. 400 chor. (Mss. Vulg.), εἰβομ- (Herm. Dind. *now*); so Soph. Ant. 527 chor. (Tricl. Dind.): **aor.** ἐλειψάμην Eur. Alc. 1015. **Pass.** λείβομαι *to stream, drop*, Eur. Andr. 532, λείβεαι Mosch. 4, 45, -εται Hes. Sc. 390, ἀπο- Od. 7, 107; -όμενος Eur. Phoen. 1522; Pl. Tim. 82: **imp.** ἐλείβετο Xen. Cyr. 6, 4, 3; Q. Sm. 14, 172. **Fut.** λείψω we have not seen.

Λεΐζομαι, see ληΐζ-.

Λείπω *To leave*, Il. 22, 483; Aesch. Supp. 507; Soph. O. R. 1232; Ar. Eq. 1251; Her. 2, 40; Xen. An. 1, 10, 13: **imp.** ἔλειπον Il. 19, 288; Aesch. Ag. 607; Soph. Tr. 234; Her. 8, 115, κατ- Thuc. 8, 73; Isae. 9, 11; Dem. 48, 6, λεῖπ- Il. 5, 157; Pind. Ol. 6, 45, iter. λείπεσκε, κατα- Her. 4, 78: **fut.** λείψω Il. 15, 136; Soph. Aj. 563; Eur. Or. 664, Lycurg. 76, ἐκ- Pind. Ol. 6, 51, κατα- Thuc. 3, 58, ἀπο- Pl. Rep. 509: **1 aor.** (scarcely Attic) ἔλειψα Anth. 8, 130; Opp. C. 4, 379; λείψειε Opp. Cyn. 2, 33; Maneth. 1, 153; ἀπό-λειψον Pseud.-Phocyl. 77 (Bergk); λείψας if genuine, the only instance in classic Attic, Com. Fr. (Antiph.) 3, 16; Anth. App. Epigr. 217. 238. 257, ἀπο- Hes. Th. 793 the earliest instance, if not from -λείβω; Pyth. Aur. Carm. 70 (Mullach); in prose rather late, ἔλειψε Pseud.-Callisth. 1, 44 (Meusel), ἐλείψαμεν, παρ- Polyb. 12, 15; Strab. 6, 3, 10; ἐκ-λείψωμεν Dio Cass. 38, 39 (Bekk. -λίπωμεν L. Dind.), ἐλλείψη Aristot. Pol. 1, 13, 12 (Bekk. 1 ed. -λείψει 2 ed.); λείψειε, ἀπο- Themist. Or. 25[d]; λείψας Luc. Paras. 42, κατα- D. Mer. 7, 3; Pseud.-Callisth. 1, 41; Joseph. Ant. 12, 9, 3: **2 p.** λέλοιπα Il. 1, 253; Soph. Tr. 327; Eur. I. T. 562; Isocr. 12, 76; Lycurg. 77; Dem. 22, 77, ἐκ- Aesch. Pers. 128, κατα- Ar. Lys. 736, ἀπο- Her. 4, 140, παρα- Andoc. 1, 70: **plp.** ἐλελοίπει Xen. Cyr. 2, 1, 21, ἐξ- Thuc. 5, 42, Ion. -οίπεε, ἐπ- Her. 3, 25, Dor. λελοίπη Theocr. 1, 139 (-πει Mein. Ziegl.): **p. p.** λέλειμμαι Il. 13, 256;

Hes. Op. 284; Pl. Tim. 61; Dinarch. 1, 109, 1 dual -είμμεθον Soph. El. 950 (Mss. Herm. Dind. Hart. Wolf); λελειμμένος Aesch. Ag. 517; Her. 2, 63; Thuc. 3, 67: plp. ἐλέλειπτο Il. 2, 700, κατ- Her. 7, 88 (Stein, Dind.), ὑπ- Thuc. 7, 33, λελείμμην Il. 22, 334, λέλειπτο 10, 256; Soph. Ant. 1202; Ap. Rh. 2, 272, κατα- Her. 1, 209 (Bekk. Krüg. Dind. κατ-ελ- Stein), and ἔλειπτο 1, 45. 824 &c. see λείβω, εἴβω: aor. ἐλείφθην Eur. Hel. 411; Her. 8, 44; Thuc. 3, 11, λείφ- Pind. Ol. 2, 43, Epic 3 pl. ἔλειφθεν Hom. H. Merc. 195; λειφθῇ Pl. Leg. 920; opt. -είη Conv. 191 &c.; inf. -φθῆναι Aesch. Pers. 344; Thuc. 6, 72; -θείς Antiph. 2, β, 9: fut. λειφθήσομαι Soph. Ph. 1071, περι- Ar. Nub. 725, κατα- Isocr. 15, 7. 17, 1, ἀπο- Aeschin. 3, 149: and fut. mid. λείψομαι as pass. or mid. intrans. Her. 7, 8. 48. 9, 56, ὑπο- Od. 17, 276, κατα- Xen. An. 5, 6, 12, ἀπο- 5, 4, 20: 3 fut. λελείψομαι Il. 24, 742; Eur. Hipp. 324; Xen. An. 2, 4, 5; -ψεσθαι Thuc. 5, 105, never in participle: 2 aor. act. ἔλἴπον Il. 2, 35 (Bekk.); Pind. I. 8, 57; Aesch. Pers. 985; Soph. El. 514; Her. 8, 35; Pl. Tim. 23; Dem. 24, 87, Epic ἔλλ- Ap. Rh. 2, 1032, λίπ- Il. 10, 406; Pind. Ol. 7, 59; Archil. 114, κἀλλιπ- Ar. Pax 1299 (pentam.); λίπω Il. 16, 453; Soph. Ph. 653; Com. Fr. (Antiph.) 3, 154; Pl. Leg. 924; -οιμι Il. 5, 685; Soph. O. R. 1247; Pl. Apol. 29; imper. λίπε Od. 15, 199, λιπέτω 3, 424; λιπεῖν Il. 12, 111; Soph. Aj. 653; Thuc. 4, 126, Epic -έειν Hes. Sc. 332, καλ- Od. 16, 296; λιπών Il. 9, 194; Soph. Tr. 47; Ar. Fr. 199 (D.); Thuc. 3, 11; Pl. Leg. 930, -οῦσα Eur. Hec. 934, Aeol. and Dor. -οῖσα Sapph. 84; Theocr. 2, 137: and 2 aor. pass. ἐλἴπην late (unless λίπεν Il. 16, 507, be taken as 3 pl. for -ησαν with Aristarch. Wolf, Spitzn. La Roche, for which λίπον aor. act. Zenodot. Bekk. Dind.); ἀπο-λιπῆναι Dio Cass. 37, 43 (Bekk. so L. Dind. but suggests -λείπεσθαι). **Mid.** λείπομαι *to leave oneself, remain*, pres. generally pass. but λείπεσθε Il. 23, 409, -ονται Od. 22, 250: imp. ἐλείπετο, ἀπ- Her. 7, 221, ὑπ- Thuc. 5, 61, and trans. *leave for oneself* (in which sense λείπομαι *simple* seems to be late λειπομένη δάκρυα Epigr. Sepulcr. 582 Kaibel, but) καταλείπομαι Xen. Mem. 1, 1, 8; Pl. Leg. 721, ὑπο- Eur. Hel. 293; Her. 6, 7; Thuc. 3, 84 if sound; Lys. 19, 23; Isocr. 9, 45: imp. ἐλειπ- Orph. Arg. 121 (Her. 7, 164 has been altered): 2 aor. ἐλιπόμην Eur. H. F. 169; Her. 1, 186. 2, 40. 136. 6, 109; Ap. Rh. 4, 452; Plut. Aem. Paul. 36, Attic prose κατ- Pl. Conv. 209. Rep. 599, ὑπ- Antiph. 5, 16; Dem. 28, 1; -λίπησθε Thuc. 1, 140, ἀπο-λίπῃ Pl. Charm. 176 (-λείπῃ Bekk.), but reflex or pass. *stayed, was left—inferior*, λιπόμην Il. 11, 693, -οντο Od. 8, 125; -ηται Il. 19, 235, -ησθε 23, 248; -οίμην 9, 437, -οιτο 3, 160; -έσθαι 5, 154; Her. 2, 136, ἀπ-ελιπόμην Lys. 20, 25 (Bekk. B. Saupp. -ελειπ- Steph. Scheibe, Westerm.); App. Civ. 2, 59: so fut. λείψομαι *will remain, be left* &c. Hes. Op. 198; Her. 7, 8. 48, ὑπο- Od. 17, 276. 19, 44, ἀπο- Pl. Charm. 176; Xen. An. 5, 4, 20; Anth. 12, 9, but *will leave for oneself*, ὑπο- Antiph. 3, δ, 9; Isocr. 21, 18: 1 aor. ἐλειψάμην (sometimes confounded with the mid. aor. of λείβω, see Eur. Alc. 1015) is very late, ἀπο-λειψάμενος Jos. Genes. Reg. 1, p. 3: late p. p. ὑπο-λελείμεθα (Eur.) Epist. 5. Vb. λειπτέον Pl. Rep. 400. ἔλλιπον for ἐλι- Ap. Rh. 2, 1032. ἐλίφθην, though in some Mss. and adopted by Ernesti, Callim. Cer. 93, is probably a mistake for -είφθην, which *now* is also the reading at Ap. Rh. 1, 1325, and Aristot. H. A. 5, 22, 12. ἐλείπετο trans. Her. 7, 164 (Vulg.) and ἐλίποντο as pass. 4, 84 (Mss. Vulg.). 7, 196 (Vulg.) are now ἐλίπετο trans., ελείποντο as pass. (Bekk. Dind.) Hom. has λιπέειν, καλ- inf. 2 aor. Od. 16, 296. ἔλειπτο Ap. Rh. quoted, is held by some a syncop. imp. aoristically used. L. Dindorf seems decided on expelling 1 aor. ἔλειψα from Polyb. Dio Cass. &c. We think his remarks too stringent, and inapplicable at least to the case in Strabo, see above. There is another case which we think they do not meet. Supposing that ἔλειψα had fallen rather into *conversational* use, it would be the more ready to come occasionally in the way, step in with unobtrusive familiarity, and find acceptance along with, perhaps before, its genteeler neighbour.

Λείχω *To lick*, Her. 4, 23. 172, ἀνα- 1, 74; -χωσι Aristot. H. An. 6, 37, 5; -ων Ar. Eq. 1285; -ειν Pax 855; Hippocr. 7, 48: imp. ἔλειχον, περι- Ar. Plut. 736: fut. late λείξω V. T. 3 Reg. 20, 19. Ps. 71, 9: aor. ἔλειξα Aesch. Eum. 106; Callim. Fr. 201; λείξας Ar. Eq. 103; λεῖξαι Trag. Fr. (Achae.) 9 (Wagn.); late prose Theophr. Sig. 15: 2 p. part. irreg. λελειχμώς Hes. Th. 826, or rather (the syncop. p. part. of λιχμάζω Hes. Sc. 235) λελιχμακώς, λελιχμώς, Epic λελειχμώς: aor. pass. late λειχθέν, ἐκ- Dioscor. 3, 44. This verb does not occur in classic Attic prose.

Λελίημαι, see λιλαίομαι.

Λεπτύνω *To make thin* &c. Hippocr. 5, 312; Aristot. H. A. 8, 10, 4: fut. -ῠνῶ V. T. Ps. 17 (18), 43: aor. ἐλέπτῡνα Hippocr. 5, 268 (Lit.): p. p. λελέπτυσμαι 4, 510. 6, 174 (Lit.); Aristot. H. An. 3, 2, 4, προ- Pl. Tim. 66; inf. -ύσθαι, κατα- Hippocr. 2, 26 (Lit. -ύνθαι Cob. Erm.), but λελεπτύνθαι Athen. 552: aor. ἐλεπτύνθην Hippocr. 4, 548 (Lit.); Diog. Laert. 7, 142, ἀπο- Pl. Tim. 83.

Λέπω *To peel*, Com. Fr. (Pl.) 2, 617. (Antiph.) 3, 75, ἐκ- Her. 2, 68; Aristot. H. A. 6, 2, 5 (B.): fut. λέψω, ἐκ- Ar. Av. 1108;

λέψειν, ἀπο- Eur. Cycl. 237, Epic -ψέμεν Il. 21, 455: aor. ἔλεψα Il. 1, 236, ἐπ- Hom. H. Merc. 109; ἐκ-λέψῃς Com. Fr. (Cratin.) 2, 82; ἀπο-λέψας Ar. Av. 673, prose ἐξ- Hippocr. 1, 420 (K.): p. p. λέλεμμαι, ἀπο- Epich. 109 (Ahr.): **2 aor.** ἐλάπην, ἐκ-λαπῆναι Ar. Fr. 211 (Dind.): **fut.** ἐκ-λαπήσεται Erotian. p. 148, ed. Franz. **Mid.** λέπομαι Com. Fr. (Alex.) 3, 404.

Λεύσσω *To see*, Poet. Il. 3, 110. 16, 127; Simon. C. 124; Pind. P. 4, 145; Aesch. Pr. 145; Soph. O. C. 705; Theocr. 22, 56: **imp.** ἔλευσσον Aesch. Pers. 710; Soph. Tr. 897, λεῦσσ- Od. 8, 200, iter. λεύσσεσκον Emped. 419 (Stein): **fut.** late, λεύσω Anth. 15, 7; Maneth. 6, 93: **aor.** ἔλευσα, λεύσῃ 4, 59. 5, 77. 6, 71, -σωσι 3, 352: **opt.** λεύσειεν 6, 620; λεύσας Or. Sib. 1, 235.

Λεύω *To stone*, Eur. Elec. 328; -ειν Thuc. 5, 60: **fut.** λεύσω, κατα- Ar. Ach. 285; Luc. Jup. Trag. 36: **aor.** ἔλευσα, κατ- Her. 9, 5; Thuc. 1, 106; Lycurg. 71; (Pl.) Epist. 8, 354; -λεύσας Dem. 19, 66: **1 aor. pass.** ἐλεύσθην, κατ- Xen. An. 5, 7, 2; λευσθῆναι Soph. O. C. 435; Eur. I. A. 1350, κατα- Xen. An. 1, 5, 14; λευσθείς (Hippocr.) Epist. 9, 412 (Lit.), κατα- Xen. Hell. 4, 3, 23: **fut.** λευσθήσεται Joseph. contra Ap. 2, 27, κατα- Aeschin. 1, 163.

(**Λέχω**), see λέγω *To lay*.

Λῄζω, see ληΐζω.

Λήθω, Poet. ληθάνω, see λανθάνω.

Ληΐζω *To plunder*, act. rare, and only **imp.** ἐλήϊζον Thuc. 3, 85 (most Mss. Popp. Böhm. -ηΐζοντο Bekk. Krüg. Classen, -ῄζ- Dind. Stahl). 4, 41 (Popp. Bekk. Krüg. Böhm. -ῃζον Dind. -ηΐζοντο Classen, -ῄζ- Stahl): hence **pass.** ληϊζόμενος *plundered*, Luc. Somn. 14 (ληζόμ- Bekk. Dind.): **p. p.** (λελήϊσμαι), Attic λέλησμαι Eur. Hel. 475; λελησμένος not -ημένος Eur. Med. 256. Tr. 373. Fr. 337 (Dind.): **aor.** ἐληΐσθην, ληϊσθείς Ap. Rh. 4, 400; Opp. H. 4, 157. **Mid.** ληΐζομαι as act. Hes. Op. 702; Simon. Am. 6 (Bergk); Her. 4, 112; Xen. Cyr. 3, 2, 1. An. 6, 6, 27. Hell. 5, 1, 1 &c. (Vulg. Popp. Krüg. Saupp. λῄζ- Dind. always); ληϊζόμενος Xen. An. 6, 1, 1, ληζόμ- Anth. (Tull. Sab.) 9, 410; Xen. An. quoted (Dind. Hug), Poet. λεϊζόμ- Anth. (incert.) 6, 169: **imp.** ἐληϊζόμην Lys. 20, 24 (Vulg. Bekk. B. Saupp. Scheibe, ἐληζ- Cobet), -ηΐζοντο Her. 4, 110; Thuc. 1, 5, 24; Xen. An. 4, 8, 23 (Bekk. Popp. Krüg. Saupp. -ῄζ- L. Dind. Hug); Dem. 23, 148 (Vulg. B. Saupp. -ῄζ- Dind. and *now* Bekk.): **fut.** ληΐσομαι (σσ) Od. 23, 357; Hes. Op. 322, -ίσεται Her. 6, 86 (Stobae. Gaisf. -ίσηται Bekk. Dind.): **aor.** ἐληϊσάμην Her. 3, 47; and still Andoc. 1, 101, Epic -ισσ- Opp. Hal. 1, 31, ληΐσσατο Il. 18, 28; Opp. Hal. 1, 730, Attic ἐλῄσατο

Eur. Tr. 866; subj. -ίσηται Her. 6, 86 (Bekk. Krüg. Dind.), Epic -ίσσεται Hes. Op. 322, see fut.; ληΐσσασθαι Her. 6, 86 (Orac.); ληϊσάμενος 4, 145. Vb. λεϊστός Il. 9, 408, ληϊστός 406. The act. ἐλήϊζον (ἔληζ-) Thuc. 3, 85, is supported by most of the Mss. and countenanced by the passive use of the *pres.* ληΐζομαι (λήζ-) Luc. quoted; and also read by some 4, 41 (Popp. Bekk. Krüg. Dind.). For fut. ληΐσεται Her. 6, 86 (Vulg. Gaisf.), Bekk. Krüg. and Dind. read subj. -ίσηται. Some able scholars seem inclined to edit the contr. form λήζ-, ἐλήζ- always in Attic writers.

(Ληκάω, -έω) *To sport*, aor. inf. ληκῆσαι Com. Fr. (Pher.) 2, 352. Pass. ληκούμεσθα Com. Fr. (Pher.) 2, 352; subj. ληκώμεθα Ar. Thesm. 493.

Ληκέω *To utter*, *sound* &c. Epic (for λάσκω) Dor. λᾱκεῖ Theocr. 2, 24: imp. ἐλήκεον, ἐπ- Od. 8, 379. Hesych. has aor. ἐλήκησα, ἐν-. See λάσκω.

Ληματιάω *To be resolute*, only -ιᾷς Ar. Ran. 494.

Λημάω *To be blear-eyed*, λημῶ Luc. Jup. Tr. 10, -ᾷς Ar. Nub. 327; Luc. Tim. 2; -ῶν Ar. Plut. 581; Luc. D. Mort. 9, 2.

Ληστεύω *To plunder*, -εύων Thuc. 4, 66; Dio Cass. Fr. 93, 4; Arr. An. 1, 3, 6; Luc. V. H. (2), 37; -εύειν Dem. 4, 23; Plut. Mar. 6; Arr. An. 7, 15, 2: imp. ἐλήστευον Thuc. 7, 18 (one good Ms. Bekk. Popp. Krüg. Dind. -εύοντο mid. Mss. Vulg.); Dio. Hal. 3, 45. 9, 60; Luc. Alex. 2: fut. -εύσω App. Lib. 116: aor. ἐλήστευσα Dio Cass. 76, 10. Pass. ληστεύομαι Thuc. 5, 14; Luc. Jup. Conf. 8: imp. ἐληστεύοντο Thuc. 4, 2: aor. ληστευθείς Diod. Sic. 2, 55; App. Numid. 5. This verb seems to have been very partially used; the mid. not at all, for which ληΐζομαι, λήζομαι.

Λιάζω *To bend*, *turn aside*, Epic, intrans. and act. form rare and late: imp. λίαζον Lycophr. 21: unless aor. λίασσε Aristarchus' reading for λίασθεν, Il. 23, 879 (Bekk. Dind. La Roche) be correct. Pass. λιάζομαι Il. 20, 420: imp. λιάζετο Il. 24, 96: aor. ἐλιάσθην Il. 15, 543; Emped. 9; Ap. Rh. 3, 1164; Eur. Hec. 100 (chor.), 3 pl. Epic λίασθεν Il. 23, 879 (Vulg. Spitzn. Faesi &c.); Ap. Rh. 4, 353; -ασθείς Il. 20, 418: plp. λελίαστο Mosch. 4, 118. Vb. ἀ-λίαστος Il. 12, 471.

(Λίγγω) *To twang* (λιγύς), only aor. λίγξε Il. 4, 125.

Λιθιάω *To suffer from stone*, and λιθο-φορέω *carry stones*, seem confined to the pres. λιθιᾷ Aristot. Probl. 10, 43; -ιᾶν Athen. (Machon) 578: -ιῶν Plut. Mor. 403; and Pl. Leg. 916 (Vulg. Bekk. Stallb. but λιθάω B. O. W.); -φορεῖν Thuc. 6, 98.

Λικμάω *To separate*, *winnow*, rare and defective, -μᾷ Xen. Oec. 18, 7; -μᾶν 18, 8; -ῶν Il. 5, 500; Xen. Oec. 18, 2, 6; Luc.

Bis Acc. 1. Anach. 25: fut. -ήσεις Xen. Oec. 18, 8: aor. subj. -ήσῃ Bacchyl. 49 (Bergk). Pass. λικμώμενος Plut. Mor. 701: p. p. λελικμημένος Joseph. Ant. 5, 9, 3: aor. -ηθείς Geop. 2, 25.

Λῐλαίομαι *To desire eagerly*, Epic, Il. 13, 253. Od. 15, 308, -εαι Il. 14, 331, -εται Od. 20, 27; imper. λιλαίεο 22, 349: imp. ἐλιλαιόμην Hes. Th. 665; Orph. Arg. 413, λιλαί- Il. 20, 76: p. (λιλέω, λελίλημαι), λελίημαι, -ησαι Theocr. 25, 196; -ημένος Il. 12, 106; Emped. 304; Ap. Rh. 1, 1164; Mosch. 4, 110; Orph. Arg. 640: plp. λελίητο Ap. Rh. 3, 1158; Orph. Arg. 1267.

Λιμπάνω *To leave*, only pres. and imp. (act. late in *simple*) κατα-λιμπάνουσι Thuc. 8, 17; ἀπο-λιμπάνοις Luc. Gall. 18; imper. κατα-λίμπανε Hippocr. 2, 516 (Lit.); κατα-λιμπάνειν (Pl.) Epist. 358: imp. ἐλίμπανε Arat. Phaen. 128 (Bekk.), -άνετε Jo. Chrys. in Matth. p. 387, ἐξ-ελίμπανον Eur. Elec. 909. Med. 800, κατ- Com. Fr. (Antiph.) 3, 18. Pass. λιμπάνεται Hippocr. 7, 602 (Lit.); ἀπο-λιμπανόμενοι Plut. Them. 10.

Λῑμώσσω *To hunger*, Anth. 6, 307, -ττω Babr. 45; Plut. Mor. 321; Alciphr. 1, 21; Luc. Luct. 9; Strab. 15, 2, 5: imp. ἐλίμωττε App. Mithr. 76: fut. mid. λιμώξεται Niceph. Rhet. 2, 3: aor. ἐλίμωξα Paroem. Apost. C. 10, 53; Niceph. Rhet. 2, 3. This verb is rarely used by early writers, and has therefore been slightly noticed in lexicons.

Λῐπαίνω *To make fat*, Athen. (Aspas.) 219; Eur. Hec. 454. Bac. 575 (chor.), ἐπι- Pind. Fr. 182 (Schneidw.): aor. ἐλίπᾱνα Com. Fr. (Axion.) 3, 532, and -ηνα Opp. Hal. 4, 357: p. λελίπασμαι Dion. Hal. Ant. Fr. 20, 1; Servill. Damocr. Incert. 83; Schol. Od. 19, 72: aor. λιπανθῆναι, ἐκ- Plut. Mar. 21. Mid. 1 aor. λῐπηνάμενος Anth. Plan. 4, 273. Pass. λιπαινόμενος Anth. 12, 192.

Λίπτω *To long, be eager for*, Poet. -τῃσι Nic. Ther. 126; -των Ap. Rh. 4, 813; Lycophr. 131: imp. ἔλιπτε Hesych.: p. part. pass. λελιμμένος as act. μάχης Aesch. Sept. 380.

Λίσσομαι *To supplicate*, usu. Poet. Il. 1, 174; Hipponax 64; Pind. Ol. 12, 1; Aesch. Supp. 748; Soph. El. 428; Eur. Hipp. 312; Ar. Pax 382, Epic 2 sing. -σσεαι Od. 4, 347, less freq. λῐ́τομαι Hom. H. 16, 5. 19, 48; Ar. Thesm. 313 (chor.); Anth. Pal. 5, 165; Orph. H. 41, 9. 82, 6; Opp. Cyn. 2, 367; -σσωμαι Il. 22, 418; Soph. O. C. 1560 (D.), -ηαι Od. 12, 53; -σσοιτο 6, 142; λίσσεο Il. 24, 467, -σσου Eur. Alc. 251; -εσθαι Od. 3, 19; Il. 10, 455; Her. 1, 24; -σσόμενος Il. 10, 118; Eur. Or. 1487; Her. 9, 91; Pl. Rep. 366, Dor. -τομέναν Ar. Thesm. 1040 (chor.): imp. ἐλισσόμην Eur. Andr. 972, -ετο Il. 1, 15, ἐλλ- 9, 585, λίσσ- 15, 660. 1, 15 (Bekk.); Pind. P. 4, 207, iter.

λισσέσκετο Il. 9, 451: fut. λίσομαι, λισσόμενος Bion 12, 3: 1 aor. ἐλῐσάμην (λλ) Od. 11, 35; Orph. Arg. 969; subj. λίσῃ Od. 10, 526; imper. λίσαι Il. 1, 394: 2 aor. (ἐλῐτόμην), λῐτοίμην Od. 14, 406; λῐτέσθαι Il. 16, 47. Rare in prose, λίσσεσθαι Her. 1, 24; -όμενοι 9, 91; Pl. Rep. 366; ἐλίσσετο Her. 6, 61; Luc. Syr. 18. **Vb.** πολύλλιστος Od. 5, 445, and late πολύλλῐτος Callim. Ap. 79. In Attic, pres. and imp. only. λῐ́τομαι and the aorists seem to be Epic chiefly. Kindred forms are λῐταίνω only pres. Eur. Elec. 1215; and λῐτᾰνεύω in poetry and prose, reg. but extending only to the aor.

Λιχμάζω, see foll.

Λιχμάω *To lick*, mostly Poet. -ῶσα Eur. Bac. 698; Opp. Cyn. 3, 168, Epic λιχμώωντες Q. Sm. 5, 40. 6, 200 (Koechly), and λιχμάζω Opp. Hal. 2, 172. 4, 115; Nic. Ther. 229: **imp.** λίχμαζον Hes. Sc. 235, iter. λιχμάζεσκε Mosch. 2, 94, ἐλίχμα, ἀπ- D. Hal. Ant. 1, 79: **aor.** λιχμῆσαι Or. Sib. 11, 139; in comp. subj. ἐπι-λιχμήσῃς Babr. 48: hither some refer p. part. λελειχμότες (v. r. λε-λιχμότες) Hes. Th. 826. **Mid.** λιχμάομαι Theocr. 24, 20; Opp. C. 3, 163; late prose, App. Mithr. 38; Philostr. Ap. 66, -μάζομαι in tmesi Opp. C. 2, 389: **imp.** ἐλιχμῶντο Ar. Vesp. 1033; App. Iber. 96: **fut.** (λιχμᾰ́σομαι Anth. (Nicarch.) 5, 38, has been altered) λιχμήσομαι late in *simple*, Joseph. Ant. 8, 15, 4, but ἀπο- *will lick off*, Il. 21, 123: **aor.** ἐλιχμήσατο Epigr. Diog. Laert. 8, 91; Ael. Fr. 82, περι- Luc. Prom. 10. See λείχω. **Act.** poet. except in comp. ἀπ-ελίχμα Dio. Hal. 1, 79: **mid.** occasionally in late prose.

Λογίζομαι *To count, consider*, Soph. Tr. 944; Ar. Ach. 31; Her. 2, 145; Thuc. 7, 77; Dem. 9, 20, but **pass.** or as we say *counts*, Her. 3, 95: **imp.** ἐλογιζ- Her. 8, 136; Thuc. 3, 82; Lys. 32, 20: **fut.** λογίσομαι late in this form, Niceph. Rhet. 7, 1 (Walz), Attic -ιοῦμαι Ar. Ran. 1263; Thuc. 6, 36; Lys. 32, 28; Lycurg. 67: **aor.** ἐλογισάμην Eur. Or. 555; Thuc. 6, 31; λόγισαι Ar. Vesp. 656, λογισάσθω, ἀντι- Antiph. 4, β, 6, λογίσασθε Dem. 34, 22; λογισάμενος Her. 7, 46; Pl. Men. 82: **p.** λελόγισμαι **act.** Lys. 32, 24; Dem. 28, 12; Luc. Abd. 27, and **pass.** Eur. I. A. 922; Pl. Phaedr. 246: **aor.** ἐλογίσθην always **pass.** Xen. Hell. 6, 1, 19; Pl. Tim. 34, except ἐπι-λογισθέντες Her. 7, 177, and perhaps συλ-λογίσθῃ Pl. Rep. 531: **fut.** late λογισθήσομαι Niceph. Rhet. 7, 22, κατα- Theoph. Epist. 12. **Vb.** ἀ-λόγιστος Pl. Apol. 37, λογιστέον Pl. Tim. 61. λελογισμένοι Eur. I. A. 922, is **act.** οἱ τοιοίδ' εἰσιν βροτῶν—*men of like bent* (*reckon*), *determine to live their day well and wisely;* and τὸ λελογισμένον 386, if viewed as a *function*, **pass.** if viewed as a function's product.

Λοέω *To bathe another*, Epic, **imp.** unaugm. λόεον Od. 4, 252:

fut. λοέσσω Nonn. 23, 294: aor. (ἐλόεσσα), opt. λοέσσαι Callim. Jov. 17; λοέσσας Il. 23, 282; inf. λοέσσαι Od. 19, 320. **Mid.** *to bathe oneself, bathe*, fut. λοέσσομαι Od. 6, 221; Anth. 9, 618: aor. λοέσσατο Od. 6, 227; Ap. Rh. 3, 1203, ἐλοέσσω Callim. Cer. 17, λο- (Mein.); λοεσσάμενος Il. 10, 577. Od. 8, 427; Hes. Op. 522. See λόω.

Λοιδορέω *To rail at*, Aesch. Eum. 206; Her. 3, 145; Thuc. 3, 62; Lys. 9, 18; Aeschin. 2, 78: imp. ἐλοιδόρουν Lys. 8, 5; Pl. Rep. 551: fut. -ήσω Dem. 40, 48: aor. ἐλοιδόρησα Eur. Med. 873; Andoc. 1, 67; Isocr. 10, 45; -ήσαιμι Thuc. 6, 89; -ῆσαι Pind. Ol. 9, 37, reg. in act.: p. λελοιδόρηκα Pl. Phaedr. 241; Dem. 57, 34: p. p. λελοιδόρημαι, -ημένος Xen. Hell. 5, 4, 29: aor. pass. ἐλοιδορήθην, -θείς Pl. Phaedr. 275. Gorg. 457; Aristot. Polit. 1, 2, 9, as mid. see below. **Mid.** λοιδοροῦμαι *to rail at each other*, or as act. Ar. Ran. 857; Her. 4, 184; Xen. Conv. 6, 8. 9; Dem. 21, 200: imp. ἐλοιδ- Antiph. 2, α, 4; Xen. Cyr. 1, 4, 9: fut. λοιδορήσομαι Ar. Eq. 1400; Xen. Cyr. 1, 4, 9; Aeschin. 3, 207; Dem. 21, 138: aor. ἐλοιδορησάμην Alciphr. 3, 62; App. Lib. 131 (B.); subj. earlier λοιδορήσηται Isae. 6, 59; Ael. Epist. 16; -ήσασθαι Isocr. 7, 49; Charit. 1, 4, 12; -ησάμενος Luc. Somn. 4; Dio Cass. Fr. 104, 4 (B.): and as mid. aor. pass. ἐλοιδορήθην Dem. 21, 132; λοιδορηθῶσι Dem. 9, 54; -ηθείς αὐτοῖς *having railed at them*, Dem. 54, 5, δια- 21, 86. The Tragedians used neither mid. nor pass. Vb. λοιδορητέον Max. Tyr. 3, 3.

Λουέω *To bathe*, Epic as λοέω, only imp. ἐλούεον, Hom. H. Cer. 289.

Λούω *To bathe*, pres. very rare, λούει Bion 1, 84; Her. 6, 52; λούειν Hippocr. 7, 34; Pl. Phaed. 115: imp. ἔλουε Luc. Necy. 7 (Vulg. Bekk. ἔλου Dind.), ἐξ- Babr. 72, 8: fut. λούσω Callim. Del. 95, Dor. λουσῶ Theocr. 5, 146: aor. ἔλουσα Anacr. 48; Soph. Ant. 901; Eur. Tr. 1152; Ar. Lys. 19, λοῦσ- Il. 16, 679. Od. 10, 364; Simon. C. 106; opt. λούσειεν Aesch. Sept. 739, in tmesi Il. 18, 345; subj. λούσω Eur. Hec. 613, in tmesi Il. 14, 7; λοῦσον Il. 16, 669; Com. Fr. (Men.) 4, 83; λοῦσαι Il. 24, 582; λούσας Od. 5, 264; Com. Fr. (Magn.) 2, 10; Her. 2, 86; Luc. Luct. 11: p. p. λέλουμαι, -ένος Il. 5, 6, or as mid. λέλουται Ar. Pax 868; -ουμένος Av. 140; Her. 1, 126; Pl. Conv. 174. Phaed. 116, late -ουσμαι Cyrill. Hieros. Cat. 3, 2, 35; V. T. Cant. 5, 12 (Vat. -ουμαι Alex.): aor. ἐλούθην Hippocr. 2, 633 (K.), late -ούσθην pass. Lycophr. 446. **Mid.** λούομαι *to bathe oneself*, Anth. 14, 25; λούονται Her. 4, 75 (best Mss. Stein, λοῦνται Bekk. Dind.), λοῦνται 1, 198. 2, 37 (Stein, Bekk. Dind.); Xen. Cyr. 1, 3, 11; λούεται Luc. Philops. 19 (Vulg. Bekk. Jacob.

λοῦται Dind.); subj. -ωμαι Com. Fr. (Anon.) 4, 675; λούεσθαι Il. 6, 508; Hippocr. 5, 244; Lys. 1, 9 (Bekk. B. S. Scheibe, Westerm. -οῦσθαι Cobet, so Od. 6, 216; Her. 3, 124; Pl. Leg. 942); λουόμενος Her. 3, 23 (Mss. Bekk. Krüg. Dietsch &c. λούμ- Dind.); Xen. Mem. 3, 13, 3 (Vulg. Saupp. 1 ed. Kühner, λούμ- Dind. Saupp. 2 ed.). Hell. 7, 2, 22 (Vulg. Breitb. Saupp. λούμ- Dind.): **imp.** ἐλούετο Athen. (Ptol. Everg.) 10, 52, ἐλοῦντο Xen. Cyr. 4, 5, 4; so Her. 3, 125: **fut.** λούσομαι Ar. Nub. 837; Pl. Phaed. 116, ἀπο- Od. 6, 219: **aor.** ἐλουσάμην Ar. Plut. 85; Eur. Alc. 160; Hippocr. 5, 248; Pl. Phaed. 116, λουσ- Il. 10, 576; subj. -σησθε Com. Fr. (Anax.) 3, 197, -σωνται Her. 1, 198; opt. -σαιτο Od. 24, 254; -σασθε 23, 131; -σάμενος Simon. C. 143; Ar. Plut. 615; Her. 5, 20; Xen. Conv. 1, 7; -σασθαι Il. 23, 41. Od. 8, 449; Her. 5, 20; Xen. Cyr. 8, 7, 4: **p. p.** as **mid.** λέλουμαι: **aor.** ἐλούθην see above. **Vb.** ἄ-λουτος Her. 2, 64; Eur. Elec. 1107, λουτέον Geop. 16, 19, -στέον Galen 10, 554. See λόω. In Attic, and also in Her. the **pres.** and **imp.** generally drop ε and ο in their terminations, as ἔλου, ἐλοῦμεν, λοῦμαι, λοῦται, λοῦσθαι for ἔλουε, ἐλούομεν &c. unless they should be referred to λόω. On these forms Mss. and editors differ. Lud. Dind. and Cobet in Xen., and W. Dind. in Her. and Luc., edit now invariably the short forms ἔλου, λοῦται, λούμεθα, λοῦσθαι, λούμενος, for ἔλουε, λούεται, λουόμεθα, λούεσθαι, λουόμενος. How far this is right, we think rather a nice question. From analogy we should think it likely that there would be a severe and a less severe Atticism, a glib and a grave. To say that λούμενος &c. is in all cases right, and λουόμενος &c. wrong, because in a particular instance one or even all the Mss. preserve it, is vicious reasoning. It assumes undeviating uniformity, and keeps out of view that a *nicer* form may in some cases be owing entirely to a *nicer* copyist. See λόω.

Λοχάω *To lie in ambush, waylay*, Soph. Ant. 1075; Eur. El. 225; Plut. Ant. 46; Polyb. 3, 40; Luc. Herod. 5; Sext. Emp. 231, 19, Epic 3 pl. -όωσι Od. 13, 425, but λοχῶσι 14, 181; -όωντες 4, 847: **imp.** ἐλόχα Joseph. Ant. 14, 15, 8: **fut.** -ήσω Luc. D. Mar. 6, 2; Joseph. Ant. 14, 15, 3: and in Hom. **mid.** -ήσομαι as **act.** Od. 4, 670, see **mid.**: **aor.** ἐλόχησα Her. 5, 121. 6, 138; Ap. Rh. 1, 1252; λοχήσας Od. 22, 53; Eur. Alc. 846; Her. 6, 87; Thuc. 1, 65. 3, 94; often late Paus. 1, 6, 5. 4, 16, 5; Luc. D. Mar. 14, 1; λοχῆσαι Il. 18, 520. **Mid.** as **act.** **fut.** λοχήσομαι Od. 4, 670: **aor.** ἐλοχησάμην Ap. Rh. 2, 967; -ησάμενος Od. 13, 268; Anth. 7, 717: **p.** λελοχημένοι *having placed themselves in ambush*, Ap. Rh. 3, 7. 168, -ημένος Epist. Phal. 122 (Herch.). The **act.** is frequent in *late*, rare in *early*

Attic prose. Indeed, we think Thuc. quoted the only instance. The mid. is Epic. No part seems to be used passively.

Λόω *To bathe*, act. Poet. λόει Schol. in Athen. 695; inf. λοῦν Hippocr. in Galen: imp. λόε Od. 10, 361 (ἔλου Luc. Necy. 7, Dind.), ἀπ-έλου Ar. Vesp. 118, ἐλοῦμεν Plut. 657, λόον Hom. H. 1, 120. **Mid.** λόομαι, λόει, κατα- Ar. Nub. 838, λοῦται Xen. Cyr. 1, 3, 11 (Vulg. Popp. Dind. v. r. λούετ-), λοῦνται Her. 1, 198; λόεσθαι Hes. Op. 749, λοῦσθαι Od. 6, 216; Her. 3, 124; Hippocr. 7, 74 (Lit.); Pl. Leg. 942; (Dem.) 50, 35 (Bekk. Dind.); λούμενος Ar. Plut. 658; Xen. Hell. 7, 2, 22. Mem. 3, 13, 3 (Dind. λουόμ- Vulg. Breitb. Kühner): imp. ἐλούμην Com. Fr. (Men.) 4, 178, ἐλοῦτο Her. 3, 125, ἐλοῦντο Xen. Cyr. 4, 5, 4 (Popp. Dind. Saupp. v. r. -ούοντο), Dor. λῶντο Callim. Min. 72, and λώοντο 73. See λούω.

Λὕγίζω *To bend, twist*, Theocr. 1, 97 (Fritz, Ahr.); Luc. Anach. 1; Philostr. Imag. 102: imp. ἐλύγ- Philostr. Ap. 4, 180: fut. -ίσω, ιῶ, Dor. -ιξῶ Theocr. 1, 97 (Vulg. Mein. Ziegl.): aor. -ισα Ar. Vesp. 1487: p. p. λελυγισμένος Hippocr. 4, 348 (Lit.); Anth. 11, 20: aor. ἐλυγίσθην Epist. Phal. 147 (Herch.), Dor. -ίχθην Theocr. 1, 98. 23, 54. Rare in Attic poet. Ar. quoted, and pass. -ίζεται Soph. Tr. 779; Com. Fr. (Eup.) 2, 566; and in good Attic prose only -ιζόμενος Pl. Rep. 405.

Λῡμαίνω *To abuse, maltreat*, in act. rare and late, aor. subj. λυμάνῃ Herm. Past. 4, 2; inf. λυμᾶναι 4, 1; λυμήναντα Liban. 4, 350. Usu. λυμαίνομαι as act. Soph. O. C. 855; Ar. Av. 100; Her. 6, 12; Thuc. 5, 103; Isocr. 8, 46, ἀπο- Il. 1, 313, but pass. Antiph. 5, 63; Lys. 28, 14: imp. ἐλυμαιν- Hippocr. 1, 624 (Lit.); Lys. 13, 64; Isocr. 8, 99, ἀπ- Il. 1, 314: fut. λυμανοῦμαι Xen. Cyr. 6, 3, 24; Isocr. 11, 49; Dem. 24, 1; Com. Fr. (Mach.) 4, 496, but pass. late *shall be marred*, Galen 5, 830: aor. mid. ἐλυμηνάμην Eur. Hel. 1099; Her. 8, 28; Hippocr. 4, 116; Isocr. 1, 6; Isae. 6, 18; Dem. 55, 11: p. p. λελύμασμαι act., 3 sing. λελύμανται Dem. 9, 36. 21, 173; -ασμένος Xen. Hell. 7, 5, 18; Dinarch. 1, 29; Dem. 19, 105 (Bekk.), and pass. λελυμάνθαι Dem. 20, 142; -μασμένος Paus. 7, 5, 2. 10, 15, 3; (Dem.?) Proem. p. 1429, δια- Her. 9, 112: plp. ἐλελύμαντο pass. Dio Cass. 39, 11: aor. ἐλυμάνθην pass. Aesch. Ch. 290, δι- Eur. Hipp. 1350; (Dem.) Epist. 1, 1466: 3 fut. as act. λελυμασμένος ἔσοιτο Xen. Hell. 7, 5, 18: pres. λυμαίνεσθε Lys. 28, 14; -νόμενος Antiph. 5, 63. **Vb.** δοριλύμαντος Aesch. Fr. 128.

Λῡπέω *To vex*, Soph. El. 355; Hippocr. 7, 384; Xen. Cyr. 7, 1, 16; λύπῃς Hes. Op. 401; λυπέων Her. 8, 144, λυπῶν Xen. Cyr. 3, 3, 50, -εῦσα Her. 7, 190, -ποῦν Thuc. 2, 61; -πεῖν

1, 71 &c.: imp. ἐλύπουν Thuc. 7, 87; Lys. 12, 56, -πεε Her. 9, 61, -πει Pl. Euthyd. 297: fut. -ήσω Soph. Aj. 1139; Isocr. 4, 185: p. λελύπηκα Dem. 24, 175, act. reg. **Pass.** λυποῦμαι *to sorrow*, Eur. Med. 286; Thuc. 2, 64; -ώμεθα Soph. Aj. 1086; Ion. opt. -οίατο Her. 1, 99; -ούμενος Soph. El. 1170; Ar. Plut. 1010: imp. ἐλυπ- Thuc. 2, 65: p. λελύπημαι Eur. Ion 1311; Plut. Aem. P. 10: aor. ἐλυπήθην Soph. O. C. 816; Isocr. 1, 47; Dem. 37, 10; -ηθῇς Aesch. Fr. 321; Pl. Phil. 52: fut. λυπηθήσομαι Aristot. Eth. Eud. 3, 5, 7; Luc. D. Mer. 8, 2; Dio Cass. 36, 47 (B.); Diog. Laert. 7, 118, συλ- Her. 6, 39: Attic, fut. mid. λυπήσομαι as pass. Eur. Med. 474; Com. Fr. (Men.) 4, 234; Chilo in Diog. Laert. 1, 69; Aristot. Eth. Nic. 4, 2, 25; Luc. Nigr. 9, συλ- Pl. Rep. 462. **Vb.** λυπητέον Xen. Apol. 27.

Λύω *To loose, release*, Od. 7, 74; Soph. O. R. 1034; Ar. Ach. 173; Her. 4, 139; Thuc. 1, 123; Pl. Phil. 20; λύοι Pind. I. 8, 45; λύε Il. 10, 480; λύων 23, 62; Thuc. 1, 53, Poet. ἀλ-λυ- Od. 24, 145: imp. ἔλῡεν Il. 23, 513, ἔλῠον Od. 7, 6; Xen. An. 4, 2, 25, λῦε Il. 10, 498. 11, 620. 17, 524, iter. in tmesi ἀνα-λύεσκε Ap. Rh. 3, 822, ἀλ-λύεσκεν (ἀνα-λυ-) Od. 2, 105: fut. λύσω Il. 1, 29; Aesch. Pr. 873; Soph. El. 939; Ar. Lys. 684; Her. 8, 108; Thuc. 1, 123; Pl. Rep. 592: aor. ἔλῡσα Il. 18, 244; Pind. Ol. 4, 23; Aesch. Ag. 876; Soph. El. 755; Her. 3, 31; Thuc. 6, 60, λῦσ- Il. 8, 433; Hes. Th. 501; Pind. P. 4, 291; Epic subj. λύσομεν, ἀπο- Il. 10, 449: p. λέλῠκα Isocr. 12, 96; Dem. 8, 39, ἀπο- Ar. Vesp. 992; λελυκώς Thuc. 1, 67, κατα- Athen. (Mach.) 13, 44; λελυκέναι Thuc. 7, 18: p. p. λέλῠμαι Il. 2, 135; Aesch. Pers. 592; Ar. Eccl. 377; Her. 4, 140; Thuc. 1, 87; Xen. Cyr. 1, 1, 4, as mid. see below; Epic opt. λελῦντο (-ύοιντο) Od. 18, 238 (Bekk. Dind. -ῦτο Wolf, La R.): plp. ἐλελῠμην Antiph. 5, 13, -έλῠτο Eur. Bacc. 697; Hippocr. 5, 222, -έλυντο Od. 22, 186: aor. ἐλῠθην Aesch. Pers. 594; Eur. Hel. 860; Her. 2, 135; Thuc. 2, 103; Pl. Lach. 191, λύθη Il. 8, 315, λύθεν for -ησαν, Il. 16, 805; Emped. 53; λῠθῶ Ar. Thesm. 1205. 1207; Pl. Tim. 38; λυθείην Rep. 515, -είησαν Xen. An. 3, 4, 35 &c.: fut. λῠθήσομαι Isocr. 12, 116; Pl. Tim. 41; Dem. 20, 58. 24, 73, ἀπο- Hippocr. 8, 484, κατα- Thuc. 3, 115; Pl. Leg. 714; Dem. 38, 22: 3 fut. λελύσομαι Dem. 14, 2, ἀπο- Xen. Cyr. 6, 2, 37: 2 aor. mid. as pass. ἐλῠμην Il. 21, 80 (Bekk. 2 ed.), λῠτο 21, 114; Opp. Hal. 2, 71, but λῦτο by *ictus* Il. 24, 1 (Wolf, Ahr. &c. λῦτο Bekk. Spitzn. Dind.), λύντο 7, 16, ὑπ-έλυντο 16, 341 (syncop. from ἐλῠόμην?). **Mid.** λύομαι *loose for oneself, ransom*, λυώμεθα Il. 23, 7; λυόμενος Pl. Tim. 22; λύεται, ἐκ- Soph. Tr. 21, κατα- Andoc. 3, 17, δια- Isocr. 15, 16; -λύεσθαι

Thuc. 1, 145: imp. λυόμην Od. 9, 463, λῦοντο Il. 17, 318: fut. λύσομαι Il. 10, 378, κατα- Her. 9, 11, ἀνα- H. Hym. 3, 258; Dem. 14, 34; λύσοιτο, ἀνα- Xen. Hell. 7, 5, 18; λυσόμενος Il. 1, 13; Antiph. 5, 20; -σεσθαι Lys. 19, 25. 26, 24 (B. S. Scheibe), see below: aor. ἐλῦσάμην Il. 14, 214; Pind. I. 8, 52; Aesch. Supp. 1066; Com. Fr. (Ant.) 3, 156; Her. 8, 120; Antiph. 5, 63; Lys. 19, 59; Isae. 5, 44; -σασθαι Il. 24, 175; Antiph. 5, 63; -σάμενος Ar. Vesp. 1353; Xen. An. 7, 8, 6; Pl. Menex. 243: and p. p. as mid. λέλυμαι, -υσαι Dem. 36, 45; Aristot. Rhet. 2, 23, 23, δια- Isocr. 14, 27; -λυμένος Dem. 53, 7, κατα- Thuc. 6, 36. Vb. λυτός Pl. Tim. 41, -έον Gorg. 480. Some read λῦτο Il. 24, 1, as imp. for λύετο, others λῦτο as 2 aor. lengthened by arsis, so ἀπο-λύμενα Opp. Cyn. 3, 128. λελῦτο perf. opt. for λελύοιτο, Od. 18, 238 (Wolf, &c.), λέλῦτο (Buttm.), -ῦντο (Bekk. Dind.). The fut. mid. λύσομαι, κατα- Xen. Cyr. 1, 6, 9 (Vulg. Breitb.) seems pass. or rather reflexive *will break down* (but act. *break off*, Dio. Hal. 3, 60), see δια- Thuc. 2, 12, ἐπι- Lys. 25, 33, κατα- intrans. Her. 9, 11; so aor. κατελυσάμεθα *dissolve*, Aristid. 29, 370 (D.); Christ. Pat. 505; -σάμενος intrans. Her. 9, 11; but trans. -σάμενοι τὰς ἔχθρας 7, 146; and καταλυσαίμαν Eur. Med. 146, is not necessarily pass.: remove the comma usually placed after it, and its activity will be more apparent. In pres. and imp. ῠ in Homer, ῡ in Attic: in fut. and aor. act. and mid. ῡ always, in perf. and plp. act. and pass. and aor. pass. ῠ. The unique instance of ῡ in p. pass. ἐκλελῡμένος in Posidipp. Athen. 377, has, by a simple and happy emendation, been altered by Meineke to ἐκλελεγμένος Com. Fr. 4, 523. Late, however, occur λελῡμένη Theod. Prodr. 3, 503, ἐκ-λελῡμ- 4, 231. 5, 213; and λύσεο (v. r. λύεο) if sound Opp. C. 2, 368, should be imper. p. p. for λελύσεο.

Λῶ Dor. for θέλω, see λάω.

Λωβάομαι *To abuse, insult*, Simon. Am. 7, 109; -ᾶται Soph. Tr. 1031; Her. 3, 154; Pl. Crito 47, Dor. -ῆται Herodas 3 (Bergk), Ion. -έομαι Hippocr. 4, 158 (Lit.): imp. ἐλωβᾶτο Ar. Eq. 1408; Themist. 21, 255, Dor. -ῆτο Sophr. 66: fut. λωβήσομαι Pl. Crito 47, Dor. λωβᾱσεῖσθε Theocr. 5, 109 (Ahr. Fritz.): aor. ἐλωβησάμην Lys. 26, 9; D. Hal. 15, 2; Theocr. 16, 89, λωβησ- Il. 13, 623; subj. -ήσῃ Pseud.-Phocyl. 38, -ήσησθε in some edit. Theocr. 5, 109 (Wordsw. Mein.), see fut.; opt. -ήσαιο Il. 1, 232. 2, 242; -ησάμενος Her. 3, 154. 156; -ήσασθαι Alciphr. 3, 45; Dio. Hal. Ant. 7, 9: p. λελώβημαι pass. Her. 3, 155; Pl. Rep. 495: plp. λελώβητο Arr. An. 6, 29, 10 (Krüg.): aor. ἐλωβήθην pass. Pl. Gorg. 473, ἀπ- Soph. Aj. 217, ἐξ- Ph. 330. The act. form is late, fut. λωβήσει Or. Sib. 9, 71: aor. λώβησον Pseud.-

Phocyl. 38 (Vulg. -ήσῃ mid. Mss. Bergk); κατ-ελώβησαν Polyb. 15, 33. Vb. λωβητός Il. 24, 531; Soph. Ph. 607, Dor. -ᾱτός 1103 (chor.). λωβεύω *mock*, Epic and only pres. Od. 23, 15. 26.

M.

(Μάθω) see μανθάνω.

Μαιεύω *To act as midwife, deliverer*, act. very late. **Pass.** only aor. ἐμαιεύθη Philostr. Ap. 4, 174; μαιευθέντα Pl. Theaet. 150. Usu. mid. μαιεύομαι Pl. Theaet. 149. 157; Luc. D. Deor. 26, 2; -εύεσθαι Pl. Theaet. 150; -όμενος: fut. -εύσομαι Ar. Lys. 695; Dio Chrys. vol. 2, p. 344 (D.): aor. μαιεύσαντο Callim. Jov. 35 (Bl. μαιώσ- Mein.); -εύσασθαι Philostr. Ap. 1, 5; Galen 5, 221. The later form (μαιόω) seems to follow much the same tract, aor. pass. ἐμαιώθην Nonn. 2, 498; -ωθείς Apollod. 1, 4, 2: fut. μαιωθήσονται V. T. Job 26, 5. **Mid.** μαιοῦμαι Plut. Mor. 999: imp. ἐμαιοῦτο Luc. D. Deor. 16, 2: fut. -ώσομαι Luc. D. Deor. 8: aor. ἐμαιωσάμην Themist. 4, 59; Nonn. 5, 60, μαι- 8, 186; Anth. (Leon. Tar.) 9, 80; Coluth. 180; and Callim. Jov. 35 quoted (Meineke).

Μαιμάω *To desire eagerly, rage*, Poet. μαιμᾷ Aesch. Supp. 895 (chor.), μαιμῶσι Il. 13, 78, Epic -ώωσι 13, 75; so part. μαιμώων Il. 15, 742; Theocr. 25, 253, μαιμῶσα Soph. Aj. 50 (trimet.), Epic -ώωσα Il. 5, 661, -ώοντα Her. 8, 77 (Orac.); Orph. Arg. 419; μαιμᾶν Aristot. Rhet. 3, 11, 3: aor. μαίμησε Il. 5, 670; Orph. Lith. 133. **Mid.** late, imp. Epic, μαιμώωντο Dionys. Per. 1156, -οντο (Cod. Pal.) ᾱ in ἀνα-μαιμάει Il. 20, 490.

Μαίνω *To madden*, pres. rare in *simple*, Orph. H. 71, 6, but ἐκ- Eur. Hipp. 1229; Ar. Eccl. 965; Hippocr. 1, 8 (Erm.): aor. ἔμηνα Eur. Ion 520; Ar. Thesm. 561; Xen. Hell. 3, 4, 8 (intrans. Epist. Phal. 13, if correct), ἐξ- Eur. Bac. 36; ἐκ-μῆναι Soph. Tr. 1142, and late -μᾶναι Ael. H. A. 2, 11, -ῆναι (Herch.): p. late μεμάνηκα, ἐπι- Cyrill. Alex. 1, 181; Epic part. μεμᾰνηότι *maddened*, Or. Sib. 9, 317: p. p. rare, μεμάνημαι Theocr. 10, 31; Or. Sib. 3, 39: 2 aor. ἐμάνην Eur. Bac. 1296; Her. 3, 30. 38, ἐπ- Ar. Vesp. 1469; subj. μανῶμεν Pl. Leg. 672; μανῆναι Her. 6, 84; μανείς Soph. Aj. 726; Her. 2, 173; Xen. An. 2, 5, 10; Isocr. 7, 73; Isae. 6, 9; Dem. 21, 69: 2 fut. late, μανήσομαι Anth. 11, 216; Diog. Laert. 7, 118; Or. Sib. 7, 102: 2 p. μέμηνα *am mad*, Alcm. 68 (B.); Soph. El. 879; Eur. Bac. 359; (Hippocr.) Epist. 9, 352; Epist. Phal. 147 (Herch.); -ήνοι Luc. Philops. 5; -ηνώς Aesch. Pr. 977; Lys. Fr. 88, 1; Alciphr.

1, 18; Luc. Amor. 27; Plut. Nic. 13; Herodn. 1, 9, 5, and often late. **Mid.** μαίνομαι *to rave, rage,* Il. 5, 185; Aesch. Ag. 1064; Soph. Tr. 446; Ar. Pax 54; Her. 1, 109; Hippocr. 8, 468; Dem. 8, 25. 9, 9. 34, 14; -οίμην Eur. I. A. 1256; Dem. 21, 208, -οιτο Dem. 19, 138; -όμενος Il. 5, 831; Pind. P. 2, 26; Aesch. Sept. 343; Dem. 16, 23; -εσθαι Isocr. 8, 41; Isae. 5, 8: **imp.** ἐμαίνετο Eur. Phoen. 1172; Her. 9, 34; Antiph. 2, β, 5; Hyperid. 2, 6, 2, μαίν- Il. 15, 605: **fut.** μᾰνοῦμαι rare Her. 1, 109; Synes. Epist. 72: **aor.** Epic, ἐμηνᾰ́μην, -ήναο Bion 1, 61, μήνατο Theocr. 20, 34, ἐπ-εμήν- Il. 6, 160; late prose (Luc.) Syr. 21; μηνάμενος Anth. 9, 35.

Μαίομαι *To feel after, desire* (μάω), Ap. Rh. 4, 1556; -εσθαι Od. 14, 356; -όμενος 13, 367; Hes. Op. 532; Pind. Ol. 8, 5; Aesch. Ch. 786 (chor.); Soph. Fr. 658 (D.): **imp.** ἐμαίετο Soph. Aj. 287, ἐπ- Il. 8, 392: **fut.** Epic, μᾰ́σομαι (σσ) Il. 9, 394 (Bekk. with Aristarch. γαμέσσ- Vulg.), ἐπι-μάσσ- 4, 190; Soph. Fr. 53: **aor.** Epic μᾰ́σασθαι in tmesi Od. 11, 591, ἐσ-εμάσσατο Il. 17, 564. 20, 425, ἐπ- Od. 13, 429; Ap. Rh. 4, 18, Dor. ἐσ-εμάξατο Theocr. 17, 37; ἐσ-μασάμενος Hippocr. 4, 198 (Lit.), ἐπι- μασσ- Od. 9, 446. This verb seems to occur once only in prose, μαίεσθαι Pl. Crat. 421. **Vb.** ἐπί-μαστος Od. 20, 377.

Μᾰλᾰκίζω *To make soft, effeminate,* act. rare and late. **Mid.** μαλακίζομαι *to become effeminate,* Dem. 9, 35; Aristot. H. A. 8, 26; -ίζηται Thuc. 6, 29; Xen. Cyr. 2, 3, 3; -ίζοιτο 3, 3, 41; -όμενος An. 5, 8, 14; -εσθαι Thuc. 3, 37: **aor. mid.** ἐμαλακίσατο Xen. Apol. 33; -σάμενος Cyr. 4, 2, 21: oftener in same sense **aor. pass.** ἐμαλακίσθην Thuc. 2, 42; Luc. Tyrannic. 14; subj. -ισθῆτε Thuc. 5, 9; -ῆναι 2, 43. 5, 72. 7, 68; -ισθείς 3, 40. 7, 77; Pl. Soph. 267; Dem. 24, 175: **fut.** μαλακισθήσεσθαι Dio Cass. 38, 18.

Μᾱλοφορέω, see μηλοφ-.

Μανθάνω *To learn* (μήθω), Soph. Tr. 472; Ar. Ran. 65; Her. 1, 39; Thuc. 6, 39; -ανε Aesch. Fr. 92; -άνων Pind. P. 3, 80; Aesch. Ag. 615: **imp.** ἐμάνθανον Soph. Ant. 532; Ar. Eq. 1238; Her. 7, 208; Pl. Menex. 236: **fut.** (μαθήσω, -ήσετε late if correct, Galen 1, 105. 13, 450): **mid.** classic μᾰθήσομαι Theogn. 35; Aesch. Pr. 926; Soph. O. C. 1527; Ar. Nub. 130; Her. 9, 11; Lys. 13, 4; Isae. 11, 15; Pl. Phil. 53, Dor. μᾰθεῦμαι Theocr. 11, 60 (Vulg. Ziegl. μεμᾰθ- Mein. Fritz. μᾱσεῦμ- Ahr.): (no **1 aor.**): **p.** μεμάθηκα Anacr. 74; Ar. Nub. 1148; Her. 2, 51; Isocr. 12, 108; Lycurg. 36; Pl. Euth. 9: **plp.** ἐμεμαθήκη (v. r. -ειν) Pl. Euth. 14, 3 sing. -θήκει Meno 86, μεμαθ- Hippocr. 1, 592 (Lit.): **p. p.** μεμάθημαι see below: **2 aor.** ἔμᾰθον Pind. N. 7, 18; Aesch. Pers. 108; Soph. O. R. 494; Eur. Hec. 703;

Ar. Eccl. 242; Her. 1, 80; Thuc. 2, 87; Isocr. 15, 252, Epic ἔμμαθ- Od. 18, 362, μάθ- Il. 6, 444; Pind. P. 8, 12; Bion 7, 1; subj. opt. imper. freq.; inf. -εῖν Theogn. 578; Soph. O. C. 22; Antiph. 3, δ, 1; Pl. Rep. 337, -έειν Her. 1, 10 (Bekk. Dind. Dietsch, -εῖν Abicht, Stein); μαθών Eur. Alc. 754; Thuc. 1, 42, -οῦσα Soph. Aj. 294, Dor. -οῖσα Theocr. 2, 162. **Pass.** in classic authors only **pres.** μανθάνομαι and rare, -νηται Pl. Tim. 87; -όμενα Meno 88: **p.** late μεμαθημέναι as **act.** or as we say colloquially *having been learned*, Aesop F. 23, p. 92 (Schaef. 421 Tauchn.) the only instance we have seen. **Vb.** μαθητός Pl. Prot. 319, -έον Leg. 818, κατα- Hippocr. 1, 606 (Erm.). Ahrens edits μᾰσεῦμαι Theocr. 11, 60, Dor. for μήσομαι from (μηθ) root of μανθάνω; Meineke the redupl. μεμᾰθεῦμαι, and (μᾰθοῦμαι) μαθῇ Mosch. 1, 6.

Μαντεύω *To prophesy*, late in **act.** Arr. Ind. 11, 5; Himer. Or. 23, 23; Xen. Eph. 5, 4 (-εύεται Herch.), προ- Plut. Cat. maj. 23: **aor.** ἐμάντευσα Himer. Or. 14, 34. **Mid.** classic μαντεύομαι as **act.** Il. 2, 300; Aesch. Eum. 33; Soph. Aj. 746; Her. 4, 67. 8, 134; Thuc. 5, 18; Pl. Leg. 694: **imp.** ἐμαντ- Her. 8, 36; Pl. Rep. 431, μαντ- Od. 15, 255: **fut.** -εύσομαι Od. 17, 154; Pind. Ol. 6, 38; Aesch. Sept. 406; Eur. Ion 365; Hippocr. 9, 8; Her. 1, 65 (Orac.); Luc. Alex. 19; -σόμενος Her. 1, 46: **aor.** ἐμαντευσάμην Aeschin. 3, 107; Pl. Apol. 21, προ- Eur. Fr. 485; Her. 3, 125, μαντευ- Pind. Ol. 7, 31: **p.** μεμάντευμαι **act.** Pind. P. 4, 163; Pl. Phil. 67, but μεμαντευμένα **pass.** Her. 5, 45; and late Paus. 7, 21, 1; Heliod. Aeth. 7, 1: **aor.** ἐμαντεύθην **pass.** Her. 5, 114; Heliod. 7, 1. **Vb.** μαντευτέον Eur. Ion 373; Pl. Phil. 64.

Μαπέειν, see μάρπτω.

Μᾰραίνω *To make wither*, Aesch. Pr. 597; Soph. Aj. 714; Pl. Rep. 609: **fut.** μαρᾰνῶ Anth. (App. Epigr.) 149: **aor.** ἐμάρᾱνα Hom. H. Merc. 140; Soph. O. R. 1328; Isocr. 1, 6: and **mid.** as **act.** ἐμαρηνάμην Anth. P. p. 967 (Jacobs): **p. p.** μεμάραμμαι Plut. Pomp. 31, and μεμάρασμαι Luc. Anach. 25; Ael. H. A. 1, 18: **plp.** μεμάραντο Q. Sm. 9, 371: **aor.** ἐμαράνθην Il. 9, 212; Bion 1, 76; Plut. Nic. 13; Paus. 2, 34, 2: **fut.** μαρανθήσομαι Galen 7, 691; N. T. Jac. 1, 11: **pres.** -αίνεται Aesch. Eum. 280; Luc. de Dom. 9; -αίνεσθαι Her. 2, 24; Themist. 26, 325: **imp.** ἐμαρ- Thuc. 2, 49. **Vb.** ἀ-μάραντος Luc. de Dom. 9. In the aor. of this verb the Attics retain α.

Μαργαίνω *To rage*, Epic, -αίνουσι Opp. H. 5, 365; -αίνειν Il. 5, 882; -νοντι Opp. Hal. 1, 38; Coluth. 197, -οῦσα Democr. Plut. Mor. 129; Opp. Hal. 3, 491, μαργάω Poet. and only part. -ῶν Aesch. Sept. 380; Soph. Fr. 722; Callim. Fr. 456, -ῶσα Eur.

Hec. 1128, Ion. -έων, κατα- Her. 8, 125: and μαργόομαι pass. -ούμενος Pind. N. 9, 19: p. μεμαργωμένος Aesch. Supp. 758. **Mid. aor.** ἐμαργήναντο Hesych.

Μαρμαίρω *To flash, gleam,* Poet. and late prose, Alcae. 15, 1 (Bergk); Eur. Fr. 231 (D.); Plut. Caes. 6; Alciphr. 3, 67, Dor. 3 pl. -ροισι Bacchyl. 27, 8 (B.); subj. -μαίρῃ Orph. Fr. 7, 22; Hom. and Hes. only part. -μαίρων Il. 13, 22. 801. 23, 27 &c. not in Od., -ουσα Hes. Th. 699; so Trag. Aesch. Sept. 401, -ων Eur. Ion 888. I. A. 1154, except Fr. 231, quoted: **imp.** ἐμάρμαιρον Athen. (Sophr.) 6, 16; Luc. D. Mer. 13, 3, μάρμ- Mosch. 2, 85, iter. μαρμαίρεσκον Q. Sm. 1, 150. For ἐμάρμαιρον Sophr. quoted, Ahrens reads ἐγάργαιρον Sophr. Fr. 59 (Dor. dial. 471). This verb is confined to **pres.** and **imp.** and not used in classic prose.

Μάρνᾰμαι *To fight,* Poet. inflected like ἵσταμαι, and only **pres.** Anth. 11, 63, -ᾰσαι Pind. N. 10, 86, -αται Il. 4, 513; Pind. Ol. 5, 15, -άμεθα Hes. Th. 647; Theogn. 888, -ανται Eur. Med. 249; Opp. Hal. 1, 16; subj. μάρνωμαι Hes. Sc. 110; opt. -αίμην Od. 11, 513 (Bekk.); imper. μάρνᾰο Il. 15, 475, -άσθω Pind. I. 5, 54; μαρνάμενος Il. 3, 307; Tyrt. 12, 33; Pind. P. 8, 43; Eur. Phoen. 1574 (chor.); μάρνασθαι Il. 5, 33; Eur. Tr. 726 (trimet.): and **imp.** ἐμαρνάμην Anacreont. 12, 11 (Bergk), -ᾰο Od. 22, 228, -ατο Il. 12, 40, μάρν- 11, 498, ἐμαρνάσθην 7, 301; Hes. Sc. 238, -άμεσθα Eur. Phoen. 1142. I. T. 1376, μαρνάμεθα Od. 3, 108, -αντο Il. 13, 169. 17, 403; Hes. Th. 629. Bekker and Dindorf read μαρναίμεθα Od. 11, 513, for -οίμεθα (Vulg. La Roche). There is no necessity for μάρναται Pind. N. 5, 47, being either, as some say, subj. or long in the penult.

Μάρπτω *To seize,* Poet. Eur. Hipp. 1188; Orph. Arg. 1116; Opp. Cyn. 2, 201; Epic subj. -πτῃσι Il. 8, 405: **imp.** ἔμαρπτε Il. 23, 62, μάρπτε 14, 228; Emped. 282: **fut.** μάρψω Il. 15, 137; Aesch. Eum. 597; Eur. Ion 158: **1 aor.** ἔμαρψα Od. 24, 390; Archil. 59; Pind. Ol. 6, 14; Soph. Aj. 444 (trimet.). O. C. 1682 (chor.); Eur. Bac. 1172. Rhes. 681 (chor.); subj. μάρψω Eur. Alc. 847, -ψῃ Il. 21, 564; Ar. Eq. 197 (hexam.), -ωσι Opp. Hal. 2, 134; inf. μάρψαι Il. 22, 201; Eur. Hec. 1061 (chor.); μάρψας Od. 10, 116; Lycophr. 311, Dor. -ψαις Pind. N. 1, 45: **2 aor.** Epic, ἐμέμαρπον if correct, Hes. Sc. 245 (Schoem. probante Rank. μέμαρπ- some Mss. Lennep, Flach, so Goettl. but approving ἔμαρψ-), and ἔμᾰπον, inf. μαπέειν 231. 304; opt. redupl. μεμάποιεν 252, v. r. μεμάρπ-, μάρπ-: **2 p.** Epic μέμαρπε, ἀμφι- Q. Sm. 3, 614 (Rhod. Spitzn. Koechly, -αρφε Vulg.); μεμαρπώς Hes. Op. 204; Ap. Rh. 1, 756. 4, 432. 1663: **plp.** μεμάρπει Hes. Sc. 245 quoted (Dind. e conject.

Herm.), see **2 aor.** **Pass.** μαρπτομένη Callim. Dian. 195.—Q. Sm. has **1 perf.** ἀμφιμέμαρφε 3, 614 (Mss. Vulg.), for which Rhod. Spitzn. Lobeck and Koechly approve and edit **2 p.** -μέμαρπε.

Μαρτῠρέω *To bear witness*, Simon. C. 4, 7; Aesch. Ag. 494; Soph. O. C. 1265; Com. Fr. (Apoll.) 4, 454; Her. 8, 94; Antiph. 4, 8, 8 Xen. Mem. 1, 2, 21; pt. -εῦντας Alcae. 102: **imp.** ἐμαρτ- Antiph. 2, γ, 2; Lys. 20, 18; Isae. 11, 25: **fut.** -ήσω Pind. Ol. 6, 21; Soph. Ant. 515; Antiph. 2, α, 9; Isae. 9, 30; Pl. Apol. 21: **aor.** ἐμαρτύρησα Com. Fr. (Amips.) 2, 706; Isae. 1, 11; Aeschin. 1, 88; Dem. 29, 33; subj. -ήσῃς Pl. Rep. 340; -ῆσαι Pind. I. 5, 48, -ήσειε Soph. O. R. 1032; Isocr. 21, 14; -ησον Aesch. Eum. 609; inf. -ῆσαι Antiph. 2, δ, 7: **p.** μεμαρτύρηκα Andoc. 1, 19; Lys. 7, 11; Isae. 2, 17: **p. p.** μεμαρτύρηται Antiph. 5, 31; Andoc. 1, 113; Lys. 13, 66; Isae. 3, 55: **aor.** ἐμαρτυρήθην Isae. 3, 11; (Dem.) 45, 40, δι- Lys. 23, 13; -ηθείς, κατα- Antiph. 2, δ, 7: **fut.** μαρτυρηθήσομαι Isae. 8, 13; Dem. 19, 40: and **fut. mid.** μαρτυρήσομαι as **pass.** Xen. Mem. 4, 8, 10. Apol. 26; Dem. 57, 37. **Mid.** μαρτυροῦμαι Luc. Sacrif. 10; Sext. Emp. 260, 15: **imp.** see below: (**fut.** -ήσομαι belongs to **pass.**): **aor.** μαρτυρησάμενος, ἐκ- Isae. 3, 25: with **p.** μεμαρτύρημαι late V. T. Gen. 43, 2. But μαρτῠρομαι Dep. *call witnesses, shew*, Alcm. p. 832 (Bergk 3 ed.); Aesch. Eum. 643; Soph. O. C. 813; Ar. Ach. 926; Antiph. 1, 29; Thuc. 6, 80: **imp.** ἐμαρτῠρου Pl. Gorg. 473: **fut.** late μαρτυροῦμαι, δια- V. T. Exod. 18, 20. Jer. 39, 44: **aor.** ἐμαρτῡράμεθα Pl. Phil. 47. Her. has μαρτυρόμενος 1, 44, ἐπιμαρτυρόμεθα 5, 92, but ἐπεμαρτυρέοντο 5, 93 (Vulg. Gaisf. Bekk. Dind. Stein), -ύροντο (Bred. Dietsch, Abicht).

Μάσσω *To knead*, Soph. Fr. 149 (D.); Hippocr. 1, 385 (Erm.), -ττω Com. Fr. (Eup.) 2, 566; Xen. Cyr. 8, 2, 6: **imp.** ἔματτε Ar. Plut. 305: **fut.** μάξω Ar. Lys. 601, ἀνα- Od. 19, 92: **aor.** ἔμαξα, προσ- Ar. Eq. 815; inf. μᾶξαι Com. Fr. (Pher.) 2, 345; μάξας Pl. Rep. 372: **p.** μέμᾰχα Ar. Eq. 55: **p. p.** μέμαγμαι Archil. 3 (B.); Com. Fr. (Metag.) 2, 753; Ar. Eq. 57; Thuc. 4, 16: **1 aor.** ἐμάχθην *simple* late, μαχθείη Aretae. 148 (ed. Oxon.), προσμαχθέν Soph. Tr. 1053: **2 aor.** ἐμᾰγην, ἐκ-μαγῇ Pl. Theaet, 191; -μαγῆναι ibid. **Mid.** μάττομαι *knead for oneself*, Ar. Nub. 788, ἀπο- Eq. 819: **imp.** ἐμάττετο, ἀν- Ar. Nub. 676: **fut.** μάξομαι, ἐν- Callim. Dian. 124: **aor.** ἐμαξάμην Her. 1, 200, ἀν- Ael. Fr. 21, μαξ- Anth. 5, 296, ἀπο- Ar. Ran. 1040, ἐν-εμαξ- Opp. Hal. 2, 502; Nic. Ther. 767, Dor. ποτεμάξατο Theocr. 3, 29 (best Mss. Ahr. Ziegl. Fritzsche, ποτιμαξαμένῳ Schneid. and *now* Meineke, -άμενον Vulg. Wordsw.) **act.** or **mid.** **intrans.** according to the reading, not pass.: and as mid. p. p. μέμακται, ἐκ- Dio. Hal. in Dem. 13; Luc. Indoct. 21. Often comp. ἀπο-εκ-. We have observed the mid. neither in Tragedy nor *classic* Attic prose. See μαίομαι.

Μαστῑάω *To scourge*, Epic and only part. μαστιόων Hes. Sc. 431.

Μαστῑγέω *To lash*, only pres. part. -έων Her. 1, 114, which Dind. would write μαστιγῶν, see foll.

Μαστῑγόω *To lash*, Ar. Thesm. 1125; -γοίην Aeschin. 2, 157 (Mss. B. Saupp. Franke, -γοιμι Bekk.); -γοῦν Her. 3, 16; Isocr. 17, 15; -ῑγῶν Epich. 19, 12 (Ahr.): imp. ἐμαστιγοῦν Aeschin. 1, 59: fut. -ώσω Xen. Cyr. 1, 4, 13: aor. -γωσάτω Xen. Cyr. 1, 4, 9; -ώσας Her. 3, 154: aor. p. -ωθείς Her. 3, 16; Pl. Leg. 854; Lys. 1, 18: reg. except fut. mid. μαστῑγώσομαι pass. Pl. Rep. 361; Philostr. Ap. 193: late fut. pass. -ιγωθήσομαι V. T. Ps. 72, 5. Hesych. has aor. mid. ἐκ-μαστιγώσηται, see ἐκ-δέψηται. Vb. μαστῑγωτέος Ar. Ran. 633. In contract. verbs, the Attic Comic and prose authors seem to have used the opt. 1 pers. -οίην &c. in preference to -οιμι.

Μαστίζω *To lash*, pres. late, not 'obsolete,' Nonn. 2, 645; Dor. opt. -ίσδοιεν Theocr. 7, 108; -ίζων Nic. Ther. 476; Musae. 297; -ίζειν Aretae. C. Morb. Ac. 1, 90 (ed. Oxon.); N. T. Act. 22, 25: imp. ἐμάστιζον Plut. Alex. 42: fut. μαστίξω Nonn. 2, 274: classic aor. μάστιξα Il. 5, 366. Od. 6, 82; subj. -ίξω Anth. App. Epigr. 121; opt. -ειεν Luc. Tim. 23; μάστιξον Com. Fr. (Alex.) 3, 443; (Hippocr.) Epist. 9, 312 (Lit.); μαστίξας Com. Fr. (Eup.) 2, 452; Plut. Sull. 29; -ίξαι Luc. pro Imag. 24: aor. pass. μαστιχθείς Anth. 9, 348. νόον μαστίζετο Nonn. 33, 198, may be pass. μαστίω is Epic, imp. μάστιε Il. 17, 622; Hes. Sc. 466: ἐμάστ- Nonn. 1, 179. Mid. μαστίεται *lashes his sides*, Il. 20, 171.

Μάχομαι *To fight*, Il. 7, 352; Ar. Eq. 767; Her. 8, 24; Xen. An. 6, 1, 8; Isocr. 20, 1; Pl. Rep. 556, -χει Aesch. Pr. 1010, -χεαι Il. 17, 471, Epic -έομαι see opt. &c. below; subj. -ωμαι Il. 5, 227; Soph. Fr. 205 (D.); Thuc. 6, 100; Xen. An. 6, 3, 13; -οίμην Il. 12, 324; Her. 7, 104, -οιο Od. 18, 31, -οιτο Il. 5, 457; Eur. Fr. 362, 26 (D.); Com. Fr. (Cratin.) 2, 43; Pl. Rep. 439, Ep. -έοιτο Il. 1, 272 &c. -χοιντο Eur. Heracl. 172; Pl. Rep. 471, -οίατο Il. 4, 348, but -έοιντο 1, 344, -εοίατ' (Hoffm. Düntz.); imper. μαχέσθων Her. 9, 48; Epic pt. -εούμενος Od. 11, 403, -ειόμενος 17, 471: imp. ἐμαχ- Il. 12, 152. 13, 700; Simon. C. 91; Her. 1, 127; Thuc. 1, 49; Lys. 2, 68, μαχ- Il. 1, 267. 271 (Bekk.), iter. μαχέσκετο Il. 7, 140: fut. μαχέσομαι Ion. Her. 4, 127. 7, 102. 209 (δια- 9, 48 Bekk.); and late Plut. Mor. 215. 225; Dio. Hal. 3, 58 (Vulg. -ήσ- Kiessl.); App. Pun. 60, and Epic μαχέομαι -έονται Il. 2, 366 (Wolf, Bekk. Dind.), but -εῖται Il. 20, 26; Aesch. Supp. 740; Soph. O. C. 837; Eur. Heracl. 689; Ar. Vesp. 667; Thuc. 3, 40; Pl. Lach. 193; Xen. An. 2, 1, 12; Lycurg. 47, also (Epic, and late prose) μαχήσομαι Il. 18, 265. 21, 498 &c.; Solon 2, 5 (B.); Com. Fr. (Mon.) 45; Dio. Hal. 3, 63. 8, 12; Plut. Cam. 40. F. Max. 5. Mor. 225. 309: aor. ἐμαχεσάμην Ar. Vesp. 1383; Her. 9, 48; Xen. An. 1, 7, 17; Isocr. 10, 53; subj. -σωμαι, δια- Her. 9, 48 (Stein, -σομαι Bekk. Dind.), ἀνα- D. Cass. 42, 18; -σαίμην, -σαιο Il. 6, 329, -σαιτο 24, 439; Ar. Vesp. 1195, -σαιντο Xen. Oec. 8, 5; -σάμενος Her. 1, 103; Thuc. 5, 34; Pl. Menex. 241; Xen. Cyr. 4, 1, 16, συμ- 7, 1, 14 (Popp. Dind. Saupp.); -σασθαι Il. 3, 20; Theogn. 687; Her. 1, 82, Epic μαχησ- Il. 2, 377. Od. 2, 245; -ησαίμην Il. 13, 118 (Wolf, Bekk. Dind. μαχεσσ- Spitzn. &c.); -ησάμενος Il. 3, 393; -ήσασθαι 5, 483. Od. 2, 245; late prose -ησαμ- Paus. 1, 27, 1 (Vulg. -εσ- Schub.), ἀνα- Diod. Sic. 19, 93 (-εσ- Bekk. Dind.), δι- Plut. Mor. 81: p. p. μεμάχημαι Thuc. 7, 43; Lys. 7, 41; Isocr. 6, 54, δια- Pl. Leg. 647 (μεμάχεσμαι, συμ- Xen. Cyr. 7, 1, 14 Vulg. Zeune, Schneid. is disallowed by Buttmann and Matthiae, and now edited συμμαχεσαμένων Popp. Born. Dind. Saupp.): plp. ἐμεμάχητο Philostr. Ap. 62: aor. late, μαχεσθῆναι Paus. 5, 4, 9; -εσθείς Plut. Mor. 970: fut. late, -εσθήσομαι Schol. Aesch. Sept. 672. Vb. μαχητός Od. 12, 119, ἀ-μάχετος Aesch. Sept. 85, μαχετέον Pl. Soph. 249, -ητέον v. r., δια-μαχητ- 241.—μαχεούμενος, -ειόμενος pres. part. Epic, Od. 24, 113. 17, 471, not in Il. μαχέοιντο Il. 1, 344, ἐκλελάθοιντο Od. 22, 444, are, we think, the only instances in Hom. of 3 pl. opt. not being in the Ionic form -οίατο (γιγνοίατο, γενοίατο, βιῴατο &c.); Bekk. Dind. La R. retain it, Hoffm. Koechly, Ameis edit. οίατ', Thiersch suggested fut. -έονται, Porson subj. -έωνται. In Hom. Wolf, Bekker, and Dindorf prefer, with Aristarchus, the fut. and aor. forms -ήσομαι, -ησάμην, to -έσσομαι, -εσσάμην; and μαχησαίμεθα Theocr. 19 (22), 74 (Mss. Ziegl.) has preferable support to μαχεσσ- (Vulg. Fritzs. Paley), for which fut. Dor. μαχησεύμεσθ' (Mein. 3 ed.). In Herodotus, Bekk. Krüg. Bred. and Dind. read, or approve μάχομαι, -όμενος 7, 104. 225. 239. 9, 67. 75, Gaisford -εόμενος: fut. -έσομαι 4, 125. 127. 7, 102. 209. 8, 26. 9, 48 &c. (Bekk. Krüg. &c.): aor. -εσάμην 1, 18. 95. 7, 103, ἐν- 9, 7 (2) &c. (Bekk. Krüg. Bred. Dind.), -έσομαι and -ήσομαι, -εσάμην and -ησάμην (Schweigh. Gaisf. &c.), -ήσομαι, -εσάμην Stein now always). Hom. never augments the aorist of this verb; and the Tragedians seem to have pres. and fut. only: subj. aor. we have not seen except διαμαχεσώμεθα Stein's reading Her. 9, 48, and ἀνα- Dio Cass. quoted.

(Μάω, μένω) *To desire eagerly*, Poet. and in act. only 2 p. as pres. (μέμᾱα sing. not used, μέμαεν Theocr. 20 (25), 64 Vulg. is now μέμονεν Mein. Fritzsche, Ziegl. 2 ed. -όνει Herm. Ziegl. 1 ed.), dual syncop. μέμᾰτον Il. 10, 433, pl. μέμᾰμεν 9, 641, μέμᾰτε 7, 160, μεμάᾱσι 10, 208: and 2 plp. as imp. (μεμάειν) 3 pl. μέμᾰσαν 13, 337; imperat. μεμᾰ́τω Il. 20, 355; μεμᾰώς 10, 339; Hes. Sc. 414, -ᾰυῖα Il. 15, 172, but μεμᾱώς 16, 754, usu. -ᾱῶτος 8, 118; Pind. N. 1, 43, but μεμᾱότα Theocr. 20 (25), 105, -ᾱότες Il. 2, 818 (for μέμονα, μεμόνειν, see μένω, and μέμονα). **Mid.** μάομαι as act. Sapph. 115 (Ahr.), espec. Dor. μῶται Epich., μῶνται Euphor.; opt. μῷτο Stob. Flor. (Diotog. Pythag.) 5, 69; imper. μῶσο rather than μώεο Epich. 121 (Dind. Ahr.), see Xen. Mem. 2, 1, 20; inf. μῶσθαι Theogn. 771, see Pl. Crat. 406; μώμενος Soph. O. C. 836 (chor.), μωμένη Tr. 1136 (trimet.), Dor. -μένα Aesch. Ch. 45. 441 (chor.): aor. ἐμώσατο Hesych. **Vb.** ἐπίμαστος Od. 20, 377. The common reading Theocr. 25, 64, is μέμαεν, approved by Valckenaer. All the Mss. however agree in the form μέμονεν variously represented -ονε, -οινε, -οκνε, -ηνε, but as the perf. is used as pres. and a past tense required, Hermann has given plp. μεμόνει, which Ahrens and Paley adopt as the true reading: Fritzsche, again, Ziegler 2 ed. and Meineke retain the perf. μέμονεν with an *aoristic* meaning.

Μεγᾰλίζομαι *To bear oneself high*, Epic and only pres. Od. 23, 174; imperat. -ίζεο Il. 10, 69.

Μέδομαι *To be concerned about*, Epic (Il. 9, 622); Orph. Arg. 90; subj. -δηαι Od. 11, 110, -δήται 19, 321, -ώμεθα Il. 5, 718; opt. 3 pl. -οίατο Il. 9, 622; μεδέσθω 2, 384; -εσθαι 18, 245: imp. μέδοντο Il. 24, 2: fut. μεδήσομαι only Il. 9, 650. We have not met μεδόμενος.

Μέδω, -έω (μέδημι) *To rule*, Poet. μέδεις Alcae. 5. 49 (Bergk, but Ahrens pt. see below); Soph. Ant. 1119 (chor.). Fr. 341 (quoted Ar. Ran. 665), μέδει Emped. 88, late 3 pl. μεδέουσι Q. Sm. 5, 525; part. sing. μέδων only Od. 1, 72, and fem. μέδουσα Orph. H. 74, 3, μεδούσης Lycophr. 1178, pl. μέδοντες often, Il. 16, 164. Od. 8, 11 &c. and μεδέων Il. 16, 234; Pind. Ol. 7, 88; Melanip. 6 (B.), μεδέουσα Hom. H. 10, 4; Hes. Th. 54; Eur. Hipp. 167. Or. 1690 (chor.); late prose, Aristid. 46, 192, -έοντι Eur. Fr. (incert.) 904 (D.), -εῦντι Callim. Fr. 95 (Blomf.), -έοντα Hom. H. Merc. 2; Orph. Fr. 1, 16, Aeol. part. μέδεις Alcae. 2. 40 (Ahr.). The part. has generally the force of a noun, *Ruler*.

Μεθίημι *To send away*, Soph. Ph. 818, Ion. μετίημι Her. 1, 40, μεθίης Il. 6, 523. Od. 4, 372 (Bekk. -ιεῖς, -ίεις Dind. Ameis, La R.), μεθίησι Hippocr. 8, 310, μεθιεῖ Il. 10, 121 (Bekk. Dind.),

-ίει Hippocr. 7, 572, Ion. μετίει Her. 2, 70. 6, 37 (Bekk. Gaisf. -ιεῖ Schaef.), -ἵεμεν Il. 14, 364, -ἵετε Il. 12, 409, 3 pl. Attic μεθιᾶσι Xen. Mem. 2, 1, 33; Pl. Tim. 81, Ion. μετιεῖσι Her. 1, 133; subj. μεθ-ιῶ Pl. Phil. 62, Epic -ίῃσι Il. 13, 234; imper. -ίετε Il. 4, 234; μεθιείς Il. 6, 330; Xen. Cyr. 4, 3, 9, μετ- Her. 1, 24; inf. μεθιέναι Aesch. Pers. 690; Ar. Av. 1085; Pl. Rep. 450, Epic μεθιέμεναι Il. 13, 114, -ιέμεν 4, 351: imp. μεθίη Il. 15, 716. 21, 72 (Bekk. always *now*), -ίει (Vulg. Dind. La R.); Eur. Bac. 1071, 3 pl. μέθιεν for -ίεσαν, Od. 21, 377, iter. μεθίεσκεν Ap. Rh. 4, 799: fut. μεθήσω Il. 11, 841; Hes. Op. 209; Aesch. Ch. 823; Eur. Hipp. 356; Xen. An. 7, 4, 10; Pl. Phil. 23, Ion. μετ- Her. 3, 143; inf. -ήσειν Eur. Med. 751, Epic -ησέμεναι Od. 16, 377, -ησέμεν Il. 20, 361: 1 aor. μεθῆκα Od. 5, 460; Aesch. Ag. 1385; Soph. O. C. 906; Ar. Eccl. 534; Hippocr. 7, 570; Pl. Tim. 78, Ion. μετ- Her. 5, 120, Epic μεθέηκα Il. 23, 434, and late μεθῆσα, part. -ήσας Coluth. 127: (the unusual perf. μεμέθεικα Anacr. 78 or 74, is merely an emendation of Bergk's, and withdrawn in 2 ed.): p. p. μεθεῖμαι Aesch. Sept. 79 (Herm. Weil); Pl. Phil. 62, Ion. with augm. on prep. μεμέτιμαι, -τιμένος Her. 5, 108. 6, 1. 7, 229; imper. μεθείσθω Pl. Soph. 267, Ion. μετ- Her. 4, 98: aor. Ion. μετείθη Her. 1, 114: and fut. mid. as pass. μετήσομαι *shall be sent*, Her. 5, 35, but μεθήσομαι *shall leave, quit*, Eur. Hipp. 326. Heracl. 266. Tr. 464; Ar. Vesp. 416; late prose Dion. Hal. Ant. 1, 86; Plut. Cat. min. 15: 2 aor. mostly Poet. (sing. μέθην &c. not used) μεθεῖμεν Pl. Phil. 62, -εῖτε Eur. Andr. 1017, -εῖσαν Ion 233; subj. -θῶ Soph. Phil. 816; Eur. Ph. 276, Ep. -είω Il. 3, 414, -θῇς Soph. Phil. 1300, -θῇ Eur. Alc. 849; Hippocr. 7, 570. 572, -θήῃ Od. 5, 471 (Bekk. La R. -είῃ Vulg. Dind.), -θῶμεν Il. 10, 449; Aesch. Pr. 262 &c.; opt. -θείην Soph. Phil. 1302; Eur. Alc. 1111, -είης Ar. Lys. 976, -είη Il. 13, 118; Eur. Med. 177; μέθες Soph. El. 448; Eur. Hipp. 333; Ar. Eccl. 958, Ion. μετ- Her. 1, 37. 39, dual μέθετον Eur. Ph. 584, -θετε Hipp. 1372 (chor.); μεθείς Aesch. Pers. 699; Soph. Phil. 975; Eur. Tr. 777; Ar. Lys. 485; Pl. Phil. 16, Ion. μετ- Her. 1, 33. 9, 62; μεθεῖναι Soph. Aj. 250; Eur. Tr. 780; Pl. Phil. 50, Epic -έμεν Il. 15, 138: 2 aor. mid. μεθεῖτο Soph. Tr. 197; subj. dual μεθῆσθον Ar. Ran. 1380, pl. μεθῆσθε Ar. Vesp. 434; opt. μεθείμην Eur. I. Aul. 310, μεθεῖο Med. 736 (Lasc. Pors. Elm. Dind.); μέθεσθε Soph. O. C. 1437; μεθέσθαι Aesch. Supp. 849; Soph. El. 1277; late prose μεθέμενος Plut. Mor. 97. **Vb.** μεθετέον Pl. Tim. 55. The 2 aor. act. is seldom, we doubt if the mid. be, in *classic* Attic prose. ῑ in Attic, ῐ in Epic, but μεθίετε Il. 4, 234, -ῑέμεν 351, -ῑέμεναι 13, 114, in arsis; so imp. μεθίη Il. 15, 716. 16, 762. 21, 72, or by augm. as some say, but 3 pl.

μεθΐεν Od. 21, 377, in thesis, or, as some say, by dropping the augment.

Μεθύσκω *To intoxicate*, pres. rare -ύσκων Pl. Leg. 649; Aristot. Meteor. 4, 9, 29; Anth. (incert.) 11, 8; Plut. Mor. 704: fut. late μεθύσω V. T. Jer. 38, 14: aor. ἐμέθυσα Poet. -υσσα Nonn. 7, 337. 47, 61; -ύσωμεν Luc. V. H. 2, 46; -υσον Anth. 12, 74; inf. μεθύσαι Com. Fr. (Alex.) 3, 481, -ύσσαι Anth. 5, 261; -ύσας (Luc.) D. Syr. 22, κατα- Her. 1, 106; Pl. Gorg. 471: p. p. μεμέθυσμαι Athen. (Hedyl.) 4, 78; Anth. 11, 26; Luc. D. Mer. 3, 1: aor. ἐμεθύσθην Eur. Cycl. 538; Ar. Vesp. 1252; Heraclit. 73 (Byw.); Hippocr. 6, 636; Xen. Hell. 5, 4, 5; Pl. Conv. 214, ὑπερ- Her. 2, 121: fut. μεθυσθήσομαι late, Luc. Luct. 13; Diog. Laert. 7, 118.—μεθύσθην Alcae. 20. 35, 4 (Bergk) is Aeol. inf. for -σθῆναι. μεθύσκομαι *become, get intoxicated*, Com. Fr. (Antiph.) 3, 61; Xen. Cyr. 1, 3, 11; -κόμενος Her. 1, 133; -ύσκεσθαι Her. 1, 202; Pl. Conv. 176, in which sense the act. form μεθύσκω occurs Hippocr. 3, 12: imp. ἐμεθύσκετο Xen. Cyr. 4, 5, 8.

Μεθύω *To be intoxicated*, Theogn. 478; Com. Fr. (Alex.) 3, 428; Pl. Lys. 222; -ύωμεν Eur. Cycl. 535; -ύων Il. 17, 390; Pind. Fr. 105 (Bergk); Eur. Cycl. 671; Ar. Pax 537; Antiph. 5, 26; Pl. Leg. 640; -ύειν Soph. Fr. 697 (D.); Com. Fr. (Anax.) 3, 183; Pl. Conv. 215; -ύων Dem. 54, 7: imp. ἐμέθυον Com. Fr. (Phil.) 4, 62; Luc. V. H. 1, 8, 'μέθ- Ar. Vesp. 1322: aor. ἐμέθυσα rare and late, μεθύσας Nonn. 28, 211; Plut. Mor. 239.

(Μειδάω) *To smile*, Epic, and in use aor. only, μείδησε Il. 15, 47. Od. 5, 180; Hes. Sc. 115; Orph. Fr. 16, 4, -ησαν Ap. Rh. 3, 100; μειδήσας Il. 1, 596; Anth. (Meleag.) 12, 126; Babr. 94, 6; μειδῆσαι H. Cer. 204. The pres. in use is μειδιάω in prose and poetry, -άει Hom. H. 10, 3; Anth. 10, 6, Epic, -ιάᾳ for -ιᾷ, Opp. Hal. 3, 228; Q. Sm. 9, 476, μειδιᾶν Pl. Parm. 130; μειδιάων Hom. H. 7, 14, -ιῶν Ar. Thesm. 513; Luc. Merc. Con. 11; Plut. Mor. 176; Ael. V. H. 8, 13, Epic -όων Il. 23, 786; Theocr. 7, 20, -ιόον Anacr. Fr. 124 (Bergk): imp. ἐμειδία (Hippocr.) Epist. 9, 352; Luc. D. Mer. 3, 2, iter. μειδιάασκε Q. Sm. 9, 117: fut. μειδιάσω (Heraclit.) epist. 5 (Byw.): aor. ἐμειδίασα Plut. Mor. 172. Crass. 19; Luc. Jup. Conf. 4; -άσω Merc. Con. 30; μειδιάσας Pl. Phaed. 86; Batr. 56, Aeol. fem. -ιάσαισα Sapph. 1, 14 (Bergk); inf. μειδιᾶσαι Apollod. 1, 5, 3. Of this form Hom. has in Il. only the Epic part. pres. μειδιόων Il. 7, 212, -όωσα 21, 491. In the Hymns occur μειδιάει 10, 3; -ιάων 7, 14; in Batrach. aor. μειδιάσας 56, trisyllab.

(Μείρω, μόρω, μορέω) *To divide, share*, Poet. and in act. only 2 aor. ἔμμορον, 1 pers. late, ἐξ- Nic. Ther. 791, ἔμμορες Ap. Rh. 3, 4. 4, 62, ἔμμορε (perhaps) Il. 1, 278; Dion. Per. 239: and

2 p. ἔμμορα *gained a share,* only 3 pers. ἔμμορε Il. 15, 189. Od. 11, 338; Hes. Op. 347; Theogn. 234, 3 pl. Dor. ἐμμόραντι in Hesych: **1 p.** late, μεμόρηκε Nic. Alex. 213. **Mid.** and **pass.** μείρομαι *to obtain,* Poet. in pres. μείρεο Il. 9, 616 (Vulg. Dind. La R.), *degraded* as spurious (Bekk. 2 ed.), μείρεται, ἀπο- *distributes,* Hes. Op. 578, but pass. Th. 801, v. r. ἀπ-αμ-: **p. p.** εἵμαρται (from σμείρω?) impers. *it is allotted, fated,* Pl. Phaedr. 255, Dor. ἔμβραται (Hesych.); εἱμαρμένος, -η, -ον Callin. 1, 12; Aesch. Ag. 913; Com. Fr. (Phil.) 4, 47. (Men.) 4, 135; Antiph. 1, 21; Pl. Prot. 320. Leg. 918. Menex. 243, -ένα Theogn. 1033; Aesch. Ag. 913; Soph. Tr. 169, Dor. ἐμβραμένα (Et. Mag.), -ένους Pl. Phaed. 113; inf. εἱμάρθαι App. Civ. 2, 4, καθ- Luc. Philop. 14: **plp.** εἵμαρτο *it was fated,* Il. 21, 281; Hes. Th. 894; Dem. 18, 195, late μέμαρμαι, -μένον Agath. 1, 1, 8, and μεμόρηται Ap. Rh. 1, 646; μεμορημένος Nic. Alex. 229; Anth. 7, 466, also μεμορμένος Ap. Rh. 3, 1130; Lycophr. 430; Anth. 7, 700; Plut. Mar. 39; inf. μεμόρθαι Schol. Il. 10, 67: **plp.** μεμόρητο Ap. Rh. 1, 973. Pl. Locr. 95, has a 3 sing. **p. p.** μεμόρακται, an error perhaps for -ᾱται, unless from a form μοράζω: **pres. pass.** μειρομένη *divided, maimed,* Arat. 657 (B). **Vb.** εἱμαρτός Plut. Alex. 30. Some perhaps may be inclined to explain the **p. p.** εἵμαρμαι by a form σμείρω (Sanscr. *smri*): original form σέσμαρμαι, then the first σ becoming a mere aspirate ἕσμαρμαι, the next, the second becoming an ι, εἱμ-. So σίστημι, ἵστ-.

Μελετάω *To care for, practise,* Pind. Ol. 6, 37; Soph. O. C. 171; Her. 6, 105; Antiph. 3, β, 3; Thuc. 6, 11, reg.: **fut.** -ήσω Thuc. 1, 80. 121: later -ήσομαι Luc. Soloec. 6; Aristid. 27, 353; Philostr. Soph. 1, 529, but in the sense *exercise oneself, declaim.* **1 aor. act.** ἐμελέτησα *practised,* H. Merc. 557; Hippocr. 6, 10; *took exercise* Aristid. 27, 358; *declaimed* Philostr. Soph. 1, 529.

Μελίζω *To sing, play,* Dio. Hal. de vi Dem. 50, Dor. -ίσδω Mosch. 3, 120 (Mein.); subj. -σδω (Theocr.) 20, 28; Bion 6, 5. 10; imper. -ίσδετε Mosch. 3, 15: inf. -ίζειν Aesch. Ag. 1176, -ιζέμεν Pind. N. 11, 18: **fut.** μελίξομαι Mosch. 3, 52. Usu. **mid.** -ίζομαι Anth. 7, 189, Dor. -ίσδομαι Alcm. 98 (B); Theocr. 1, 2; Anth. (Leon.) Plan. 307, 2 sing. -ίσδεαι Mosch. 3, 121 (Mein.): **imp.** ἐμελιζόμην, -ίζετο Nonn. 8, 14, Dor. 2 sing. μελίσδεο Mosch. 3, 59, μελίζετο Nonn. 5, 96: **fut.** -ίξομαι see **act.** For μελίσδεις Mosch. 3, 120 (Vulg. Meineke), Ahr. and Ziegl. read **mid.** μελίσδῃ. This verb is confined to **pres. act.** and **pres. imp.** and **fut. mid.**: Poetic, occasionally *late* prose, Dio. Hal. quoted. μελίζω *to dismember, joint,* has **fut.** -ιῶ V. T. Lev. 1, 6: **aor.** ἐμέλισα Dio. Hal. Ant. 7, 72: **p. p.** μεμελισμένα Opp. Cyn. 3, 159.

Μέλλω *To be about, intend, delay*, Il. 14, 125; Pind. P. 9, 52; Aesch. Pr. 625. 627; Soph. Ant. 939; Ar. Ran. 77; Her. 9, 17; Antiph. 1, 7; Thuc. 6, 20: imp. ἔμελλον Il. 6, 52; Hes. Th. 468. 490. 552; Soph. Aj. 443; Ar. Eq. 267; Her. 2, 43; Antiph. 2, γ, 5; Thuc. 2, 71; Xen. Cyr. 8, 1, 12; Isocr. 4, 83 (Mss. most edit.); Pl. Phaed. 75. Crat. 418, and perhaps always; Dem. 9, 64 (Bekk. Dind.), and ἤμελλον Hes. Th. 888; Theogn. 906; Ar. Eccl. 597. Ran. 1038; Isocr. 12, 231 (Bekk. B. Saupp. Scheibe). 13, 1 (Scheibe, ἔμελλ- Bekk. B. Saupp.); Aeschin. 3, 164; Dem. 21, 191. 27, 57. 29, 9 (Bekk. B. Saupp. ἔμελλ- Dind. always), Epic μέλλον Il. 17, 278, iter. μέλλεσκον Theocr. 25 (20), 240; Mosch. 2, 109: fut. μελλήσω Thuc. 5, 98; Dem. 6, 15; (Pl.) Epist. 7, 326 (Bekk. Stallb.): aor. ἐμέλλησα Thuc. 3, 55; Xen. Hell. 5, 4, 65. Cyr. 1, 3, 15. 3, 1, 34 (Popp., always Dind. Saupp.); Isocr. 4, 97 (Bekk.); Dinarch. 1, 49, rare ἠμέλλ- Theogn. 259 (Bergk); Xen. Hell. 7, 4, 16. 26 (Schn. Breitb. &c.). **Pass.** μέλλεται *to be delayed*, Thuc. 5, 111; Xen. An. 3, 1, 47: fut. μελλήσομαι late, Procop. Goth. 2, p. 464: p. μεμελλημένος Galen 8, 269. Vb. μελλητέον Eur. Phoen. 1279. In Attic Poetry pres. and imp. only. Augment η never in Homer, the Tragedians, Herodotus, nor perhaps Thucydides and Plato, rare in Aristophanes, twice in Xenophon (Schaef. Schneid. Breitb.), and a few times in the Orators, in the *imperfect*. Here however especially, the best Mss. and editors vary and differ: in Isocrates, Bekker and B. Saupp. with Mss. give ἔμελλ-, ἤμελλ-; Scheibe, favoured mostly by Ms. Urb. edits always ἤμελλ-; in Demosthenes, Bekker, B. Saupp. with the best Mss. ἔμελλ-, ἤμελλ-, Dind. ἔμελλ- always, we think, *now*; ἔμελλ- Isaeus and Lycurgus perhaps always. There seems no foundation for Buttmann, Kühner, Jelf &c. confining the **1 aor.** to the meaning *have delayed*, see Thuc. 1, 134. 3, 55. 92. 5, 116. 8, 23; Isocr. 4, 97. 6, 44.

Μέλπω *To sing, celebrate*, Poet. Lasus 1 (B.); Eur. Tr. 407; imper. μέλπε Ar. Thesm. 961; Opp. Cyn. 1, 35; -πων Il. 1, 474; Eur. Ion 906; Ar. Thesm. 970; Epic inf. -έμεν Pind. Fr. 53, 11 (Bergk): imp. ἔμελπον Eur. Tr. 547; Mosch. 3, 81: fut. μέλψω Eur. Alc. 446 (chor.); Ar. Thesm. 989 (chor); Bion 2, 4; Anth. Pl. 1, 8: aor. ἔμελψα Aesch. Ag. 244; subj. μέλψω Ar. Thesm. 974 (chor.); -ψας Aesch. Ag. 1445: no perf. **Mid.** μέλπομαι Dep. Hes. Th. 66; Pind. P. 3, 78; Eur. Phoen. 788; -όμενος Theocr. 8, 83, -ομένῃσι Il. 16, 182; μέλπεσθαι 7, 241: imp. ἐμέλπετο Od. 4, 17, Dor. -ελπόμαν Eur. Tr. 553 (chor.), μέλποντο Eur. Andr. 1039 (chor.): but fut. μέλψομαι pass. Anth. 9, 521, but act. ἀνα- Apollinar. Ps. 77, 4: aor. μελψάμενος act.

Anth. (Leon.) 7, 19, ἀνα- Pseudo-Callisth. 1, 46, missed by Lexicogr.

Μέλω *To concern, be a care to,* also *to care for,* in personal form rare and mostly Poet. Il. 20, 21. Od. 9, 20; Anacr. 93; Solon 13, 48; Pind. Ol. 10, 14; Eur. H. F. 772; Anth. 10, 10; Pl. Leg. 835; Plut. Sull. 7; Epist. Phal. 13; subj. μέλω Eur. Andr. 850; μέλοι Supp. 939; μελέτω Il. 24, 152, 3 pl. μελόντων 18, 463; μέλειν Soph. El. 342; Thuc. 1, 141, Epic μελέμεν Od. 18, 421; μέλων Pind. Fr. 132 (Bergk); Eur. Tr. 842, -ουσα Soph. O. C. 1433: **imp.** ἔμελε Od. 16, 465; Ar. Eccl. 459; Her. 8, 72; Isocr. 15, 146; Dem. 5, 22, μέλε Od. 5, 6: **fut.** μελήσω, -ήσεις Theogn. 245, usu. 3 sing. and pl. Il. 5, 228. 430; Eur. Elec. 1342; Ar. Lys. 538; Xen. Cyr. 2, 1, 15; Epic inf. -ησέμεν Il. 10, 51: **aor.** late as *personal,* ἐμέλησα Aristid. 25, 318 (Vulg. ἐμελλ- Mss. Dind.), -ησε Luc. Salt. 27, see below: **1 p.** late as *personal,* μεμέληκας Aristaen. 1, 10, see below, but with *neut.* nom. μεμέληκε Isocr. 15, 133: **2 p.** Epic and Lyric μέμηλε as pres. Il. 2, 25; Hes. Op. 238, -ηλας as **perf.** Hom. H. 3, 437, -ήλῃ Il. 4, 353: **2 plp.** μεμήλει Il. 2, 614, ἐμεμ- Or. Sib. 1, 89; μεμηλώς *caring, eager for,* Il. 5, 708. 13, 469, Dor. μεμᾱλώς *dear,* Pind. Ol. 1, 89 (Vulg. Bergk 3 ed.) **Vb.** μελητέον Pl. Rep. 365. **Mid.** μέλομαι Poet. (in prose ἐπι-μέλ-, μετα-) as **act.** -λεται Theogn. 296; Callim. L. Pall. 138, -λόμεσθα Eur. Hipp. 60, -λονται Heracl. 354; Ap. Rh. 2, 376; -ληται Opp. Hal. 3, 260; -οίμην Callim. Del. 98, -οιτο Soph. El. 1436; μελέσθω Od. 10, 505; Aesch. Supp. 367, μέλεσθε Sept. 177; Eur. Hipp. 109; -λόμενοι Aesch. Sept. 178; Eur. Heracl. 96 (impers. μέλεται Theocr. 1, 53; -έσθω Aesch. Eum. 61; Soph. El. 74; μέλεσθαι Eur. Phoen. 759; -ομέναν *desired,* Eur. Phoen. 1303 chor.): **imp.** ἐμέλοντο Ap. Rh. 1, 967, μέλ- 4, 491, μετ-εμελ- Thuc. 5, 14: **fut.** μελήσομαι rare Il. 1, 523, μετα- Xen. Mem. 2, 6, 23, ἐπι- Thuc. 3, 25: **p. p.** as pres. μεμέληται late in *simple,* unless correct Hom. H. 1, 20 (Herm. Schneidew. for βεβλήαται Vulg.); Opp. Cyn. 1, 349. 436, -ήμεθα Anth. 10, 17; -ημένος 5, 153 (Salm. Mein.); Theocr. 26, 36; Opp. Hal. 4, 101, ἐπι- Thuc. 6, 41, Epic **p. p.** μέμβλεται Il. 19, 343 (but in late Epic from pres. μέμβλομαι, -βλεται Opp. Hal. 2, 152, 2 pl. μέμβλεσθε Ap. Rh. 2, 217, μέμβλονται Opp. Hal. 4, 77: **imp.** ἐμέμβλετο Opp. C. 4, 284): **plp.** μεμέλησο Anth. 5, 220, μεμέλητο Theocr. 17, 46; Or. Sib. 1, 94, -ληντο Nonn. 24, 98, Epic μέμβλετο Il. 21, 516: **aor.** μεληθείς **act.** *having cared for?* Soph. Aj. 1184, but **pass.** Anth. 5, 201, μετ-εμελήθη Polyb. 8, 25; Pseud.-Callisth. 2, 41: **fut.** ἐπι-μεληθησόμενος Xen. Mem. 2, 7, 8; Aeschin. 3, 27 (both doubtful, -μελησ- L. Dind. Breitb. Saupp. Franke); later Dio. Hal.

Ant. 1, 67, (-μελησ- Kiessl.) &c. Impersonal μέλει *it is a care*, Il. 24, 683; Aesch. Pr. 938; Ar. Ran. 224; Pl. Theaet. 172; μέλῃ Aesch. Ch. 780; Pl. Rep. 469; μέλοι Aesch. Ag. 974; Xen. Cyr. 4, 3, 7; μελέτω Od. 1, 305; Pl. Lys. 211; μέλον Pl. Apol. 24; μέλειν Soph. El. 1446; Thuc. 1, 141: **imp.** ἔμελε Ar. Eccl. 641; Her. 6, 101; Isocr. 15, 146; Dem. 35, 31. 43, 38: **fut.** μελήσει Eur. Heracl. 713; Ar. Thesm. 240; Her. 8, 65; Pl. Leg. 923; -ήσειν Her. 8, 19: **aor.** ἐμέλησε Ar. Lys. 502; Hippocr. 6, 16; Andoc. 1, 23; Lys. 14, 9; -ησάτω Aesch. Pr. 332; -ῆσαι Isocr. 12, 131: **p.** μεμέληκε Pl. Crat. 428; -ηκέναι Xen. Oec. 2, 16; Pl. Lach. 187; -ηκός Prot. 339: **plp.** ἐμεμελήκει Xen. Cyr. 8, 3, 25. The **mid.** form μέλομαι does not occur in classic prose; occasionally in *late*, in the sense *to be an object of care, to be cared for*, μελόμεθα (Hippocr.) Epist. 9, 428 (Lit.), μέλονται Joseph. Jud. B. 5, 2, 2: **fut.** μελησόμεθα (Hippocr.) Epist. 9, 428.

Μέμβλεται, -βλετο, see μέλω.

Μεμνόμενος, see μιμνήσκω.

Μέμονα (μένω, μένος) *I desire*, a Poet. and Ion. perf. used as a **pres.** Il. 5, 482, -ονας 14, 88; Ap. Rh. 3, 434; Aesch. Sept. 686 (ch.), -μονε Il. 16, 435; Eur. I. T. 655 (chor.), ἐμ-μέμ- Soph. Tr. 982, ἐπι- Ph. 515 (chor.); μεμονέναι Her. 6, 84: **plp.** μεμόνει Theocr. 25, 64 (Herm. Ziegl. 1 ed. Paley), but **p.** μέμονεν as **aor.** (Mein. Ziegl. 2 ed. Fritzsch.) μέμονα seems allied to μέμαα, as γέγονα to γέγαα. See μάω.

Μέμφομαι *To blame*, Theogn. 797. 873; Pind. P. 11, 53; Aesch. Supp. 136; Soph. Fr. 734 (D.); Ar. Plut. 10; Her. 1, 91; Thuc. 4, 61; Isocr. 7, 72, ἐπι- Il. 1, 65: **imp.** ἐμεμφ- Batr. 70; Xen. An. 2, 6, 30; Pl. Theag. 123, μεμφ- (Theocr.) 19, 5: **fut.** μέμψομαι Hes. Op. 186; Pind. N. 7, 64; Aesch. Sept. 652; Soph. Tr. 470; Ar. Ran. 1258; Her. 9, 6; Pl. Leg. 910: **aor.** ἐμεμψάμην Mimnerm. 14, 5 (Bergk); Soph. O. R. 337; Eur. Phoen. 772; Thuc. 1, 143. 3, 61; Pl. Phaedr. 234; Lys. 2, 1; Isocr. 16, 19; Dem. 55, 7; subj. -ψωμαι Aesch. Pr. 1073; Eur. Med. 215; Thuc. 2, 60; opt. -ψαίμην Aesch. Pr. 63; Soph. Ant. 1157; Eur. El. 903; Ar. Thesm. 830; Thuc. 2, 64; Pl. Rep. 487; Isae. 1, 9; Aeschin. 1, 41; -άμενος Her. 2, 24; Isocr. 15, 87; Dem. 18, 94; -ασθαι Eur. Hipp. 695; Ar. Vesp. 1016; Her. 8, 106; Thuc. 3, 37; Xen. Cyr. 7, 5, 42; Isocr. 15, 251; Lys. 8, 1; Dem. 19, 38: and in same sense **aor. pass.** ἐμέμφθην Pind. I. 2, 20; Eur. Hipp. 1402. Hel. 463. 637. Fr. 199 (Dind.); rare in Attic prose, μεμφθῇ Thuc. 4, 85; μεμφθείς Eur. Hel. 31; Her. 1, 77. 3, 13. 4, 180. 7, 146 (κατα- Pind. N. 11, 30), **pass.** Plut. Agis 21; μεμφθῆναι Hippocr. 6, 466; Stob. 9, 45: **fut.**

μεμφθήσομαι Com. Fr. (Men.) 4, 337. **Vb.** μεμπτός Thuc. 7, 15, -τή Pl. Leg. 716, but -τός fem. and **act.** Soph. Tr. 446, -τέος late, Plotin. 42, 7 (Kirchhoff.) This verb in the *simple* form occurs first in Hes. and Theogn. but ἐπι-μέμφομαι is in both Il. 1, 93. 2, 225, and Od. 16, 97. Pind. has **aor. pass.** only, Her. **mid.** and **pass.** The Attics use **mid.** except Eur. and Thuc. who have both; the latter however **aor. pass.** once only. In late authors the **aor. pass.** seems to be used passively, but **act.** Anton. Lib. Transf. 16. Buttm. narrows rather unduly the usage of **aor. pass.** by confining it to the "Ionics and Tragedians." **Aor.** part. **act.** μέμψας occurs in Aesop 132 (Tauchn.), and μεμφόμενος **pass.** in Diog. Laert. 6, 47.

Μενοινάω (μένος) *To desire earnestly*, Poetic, Ion. -νέω see **imp.** Epic -νώω Il. 13, 79, -οινᾷς Il. 14, 264. Od. 4, 480; Eur. Cycl. 448, -οινᾷ Od. 17, 355. Hom. Epigr. 12, 4; Orph. Arg. 285; Soph. Aj. 341, Epic -οινάᾳ Il. 19, 164; subj. Epic, and rather anomalous, μενοινήῃσι Il. 15, 82 (Aristarch. Bekk. Dind. La R., -ήσειε Herm. Spitzn.); -νῶν Il. 15, 293; Pind. P. 1, 43; Ar. Vesp. 1080, Epic -ώων Ap. Rh. 4, 1255: **imp.** ἐμενοίνα Hes. Sc. 368, μεν- Il. 13, 214. Od. 18, 283, 3 pl. Ion. μενοίνεον Il. 12, 59: **fut.** (-ήσει Orph. Lith. 85, Vulg.): **aor.** μενοίνησεν Od. 2, 36; subj. -ήσωσι Il. 10, 101; opt. -ήσαι Orph. Lith. 85, -ήσειε Od. 2, 248 (Wolf, Bekk. Dind.). Il. 15, 82 (Herm. Spitzn. see above). This verb is Poetic, chiefly Epic. Attic poets use **pres.** only, and rarely. The subj. form μενοινήῃσι seems anomalous. But if Homer occasionally contracts αε into η, συλαέτην, -ήτην Il. 13, 202 &c. and perhaps ὅρηαι from -άεαι, Od. 14, 343, the way seems smoothed for contracting, as the Dorians did, άῃ into ῄ, μενοινάῃσι, -νῇσι, extended -νήῃσι, as in **pres.** μενοινάω, -νῶ, -νώω. It would familiarise the *monster* a trifle to read μενοινᾶῃσι: α so circumstanced is long in the indic. μενοινᾶᾳ Il. 19, 164. *Reflex assimilation* may have something to do with it. Perhaps some would refer it to a form in -εω.

Μένω *To remain, await*, Il. 14, 367; Pind. N. 6, 4; Aesch. Eum. 894; Soph. Ant. 563; Ar. Vesp. 969; Her. 1, 199; Thuc. 6, 77, Dor. 3 pl. -νοντι Pind. N. 3, 4; Epic subj. μένῃσι Il. 22, 93; imper. μενόντων Il. 23, 160; inf. μένειν Ar. Pax 341; Thuc. 1, 28; Il. 10, 65, but Ep. μενέμεν 5, 486: **imp.** ἔμενον Il. 13, 836; Her. 1, 169; Thuc. 4, 14; Pl. Euth. 11, Poet. μένον Il. 15, 406; Pind. Ol. 9, 90, iter. μένεσκον Il. 19, 42; Her. 4, 42: fut. Ion. μενέω Il. 19, 308; Her. 4, 119. 8, 62, Attic μενῶ Aesch. Sept. 436; Soph. Ph. 810; Ar. Ach. 564; Thuc. 1, 71; Isocr. 12, 238; Pl. Leg. 833, Dor. 3 pl. μενεῦντι Callim. Lav. Pall. 120: **aor.** ἔμεινα Il. 15, 656; Pind. P. 3, 16; Eur. Hipp.

1322; Her. 3, 59; Antiph. 5, 69; Thuc. 4, 6; Pl. Leg. 685, μεῖνε Il. 14, 119: p. μεμένηκα Dem. 18, 321; Luc. Pisc. 44, ἐμ- Thuc. 1, 5; Isocr. 6, 1: **2 p.** rare, μέμονα Eur. I. A. 1495, which however some refer to the def. form *am eager*. **Vb.** μενετός Thuc. 1, 142, -έον Pl. Rep. 328, late -ητέον Dio. Hal. Ant. 7, 27 (Vulg. -ετέον Kiessl.).

Μερίζω *To divide*, Pl. Polit. 292; Dem. 56, 49, Dor. -ίσδω Bion 2 (15), 31: **imp.** ἐμερ- Polyb. 11, 28, 9: **fut.** -ιῶ Pl. Parm. 131: **aor.** ἐμέρῐσα Com. Fr. (Nicom.) 4, 584; Polyb. 2, 5, 6; Himer. Or. 21, 11, Dor -ιξα (Pl.) Tim. Locr. 99: **p. p.** μεμέρισμαι Pl. Parm. 144; Dem. 15, 5, as **mid.** see below: **aor.** ἐμερίσθην Xen. An. 5, 1, 9 (Dind.); Pl. Tim. 56: **fut.** late μερισθήσομαι Plotin. 22, 4. 26, 8: and **mid.** -ιοῦμαι as **pass.** Aristot. Part. Anim. 3, 3, 3. **Mid.** μερίζομαι *divide for oneself, get, claim a share*, (Pl.) Epist. 358; Himer. 2, 18; imper. -ίζευ (Theocr.) 21, 31: **fut.** -ίσομαι Sopat. Rhet. p. 306, -ιοῦμαι V. T. Prov. 14, 18, as **pass.** see above: **aor.** ἐμερισάμην Pl. Polit. 261; Isae. 9, 24; Dem. 34, 18. 35, μερισ- Opp. C. 2, 609: and as **mid. p. p.** μεμέρισμαι (Dem.) 47, 34.

Μερμηρίζω *To ponder, devise*, Epic, Il. 20, 17. Od. 20, 38. 41; -ίζων (Hippocr.) Epist. 9, 352: **imp.** μερμήριζον Il. 12, 199, ἐμερμ- (Hippocr.) Epist. 9, 366: **fut.** -ίξω Od. 16, 261: **aor.** μερμήριξα Il. 5, 671; inf. -ίξαι Od. 16, 256; -ίξας 11, 204; Callim. Epigr. 9, and ἐμερμήρισα, ἀπο- Ar. Vesp. 5; Dio Cass. 55, 14. Rare in prose, (Hippocr.) quoted; Luc. Bis Acc. 2, in imitation of Homer.

(**Μετᾰ-κιάθω**) *To follow after*, Epic and only **imp.** μετ-εκίᾰθον Il. 18, 581; Ap. Rh. 1, 90. 3, 802; Callim. Dian. 46, called by some **2 aor.** (ῐᾰ.)

Μετᾰμέλει *It repents one* (like *simple* μέλει), Ar. Plut. 358; Pl. Apol. 38; -μέλῃ if sound, Aesch. Eum. 771, see below; -μέλειν Thuc. 2, 61: **imp.** μετέμελεν Thuc. 3, 4: **fut.** -ήσει Her. 3, 36; Xen. Hell. 1, 7, 27; -ήσειν Ar. Pax 1315: **aor.** -ησε Her. 7, 54; Antiph. 5, 91; Pl. Gorg. 471; Isocr. 15, 19; subj. -ήσῃ Andoc. 1, 149; opt. -ήσειε Isocr. 18, 64; -ησάτω Lys. 30, 30; -ῆσαι Xen. Cyr. 5, 1, 22. Occasionally with a neuter subject, Her. 9, 1; Ar. Nub. 1114; even μεταμέλῃ πόνος, if genuine, the only instance of the verb in Trag. Aesch. Eum. 771 (Dind. Weil reject it). **Mid.** personal and *indic.* late μεταμελομαι Plut. Mor. 178; -όμενος Xen. Cyr. 4, 6, 5; -λεσθαι (Pl.) Dem. 382; Plut. Timol. 6 (Bekk. Sint. *now*). Demosth. 21; Epist. Phal. 76, rare and late -λέομαι if sound, -λοῦνται Plut. Mor. 5; -λέεσθαι (Hippocr.) Epist. 9, 420 (Lit.); subj. -λῆται Her. 3, 36 (Gaisf. Bekk.), but -μέληται (Krüg. Dind. Bred. Stein); -εῖσθαι v. r.

Plut. Timol. 6: **imp.** *μετεμελόμην* Thuc. 7, 50. 8, 92; Plut. Mor. 196, late *-ούμην* Schol. Ar. Pax 363: **fut.** *-λησόμενον* Xen. Mem. 2, 6, 23, not pass. but *what will repent them, cause sorrow after:* **p. p.** late *-μεμέλημαι* Apocr. 1 Macc. 11, 10: **aor.** late, *μετεμελήθην* Polyb. 8, 25; Plut. Alex. 30. Cato Min. 7; Pseud.-Callisth. 2, 41; Geop. 5, 10: **fut.** late *-ηθήσομαι* Schol. Eur. Phoen. 899; V. T. Ezec. 14, 22. *μεταμέλεσθαι* (Pl.) Dem. 382, does not appear necessarily impers. **Mid.** form not in poetry, nor the orators.

Μεταμφιάζω, see *ἀμφιάζω*.

Μετα-τροπᾰλίζομαι *To turn oneself about*, only **imp.** 2 sing. *-λίζεο* Il. 20, 190. The *simple* form we have seen in Hesych. only, *τροπαλίζει, στρέφει.*

Μετᾰχειρίζω *To have in hand, manage*, **act.** rare, Eur. Fr. incert. 904 (Dind.); Thuc. 4, 18. 6, 16: **imp.** (*μετεχειρ-*: **fut.** *-ιῶ*): **aor.** *-εχείρισα* Her. 3, 142; Thuc. 1, 13. 7, 87: **p.** *ἐγκεχείρικα* Dem. 19, 180. Usually **mid.** *-χειρίζομαι* as act. Xen. Mem. 1, 4, 17; Pl. Men. 81; *-όμενοι* Antiph. 1, 20; Isocr. 12, 87: **imp.** *μετεχειρ-* Pl. Epin. 988: **fut.** *-ιοῦμαι* Lys. 24, 10; Pl. Rep. 410: **aor.** *-εχειρισάμην* Pl. Rep. 408; *-χειρίσαιο* Ar. Eq. 345; *-ασθαι* Her. 2, 121; *-άμενος* Isocr. 12, 73: **p.** as mid. *-κεχείρισμαι* Pl. Tim. 20. Leg. 670: and seemingly **aor. p.** as **mid.** *-χειρισθῆναι* rare Pl. Phaedr. 277; *ἐγ-χειρισθείς* Luc. Prom. 3. **Vb.** *-χειριστέον* (Aristot.) Rhet. Alex. 39, 3; Geop. 7, 18. The *simple* *χειρίζω* seems to be unclassic.

Μήδομαι *To devise* (*μῆδος*), Dep. **mid.** and Poet. Il. 21, 413; Pind. Ol. 1, 106; Aesch. Ag. 1102; *-οίμην* Od. 5, 189; *-όμενος* Ar. Av. 689; Ap. Rh. 4, 578: **imp.** *ἐμηδόμην* Simon. C. 140 (Bergk 2 ed.); Hom. H. 3, 46; Orph. Arg. 892, *μηδ-* Il. 7, 478, and always; Hes. Sc. 34: **fut.** *μήσομαι* Soph. Tr. 973; Eur. Hipp. 592; Callim. Del. 127, 2 sing. *μήσεαι* Od. 11, 474; Anth. App. Epigr. 134, *-εται* Eur. H. F. 1076: **aor.** *ἐμησάμην* Od. 3, 194; Simon. C. 137; Pind. Ol. 1, 31; Aesch. Pr. 477; Soph. Ph. 1139; late prose (Luc.) Astr. 6, 21, *μησ-* Il. 6, 157; Hes. Th. 166; Aesch. Ch. 605 (chor.); Eur. Phoen. 799 (chor.), 2 sing. *μήσαο* Il. 14, 253; Ap. Rh. 4, 739; *-σωμαι* Aesch. Sept. 1057; *-σάμενος* Alcm. p. 832 (Bergk); Soph. Ph. 1114. This verb occurs only once or twice in comedy, never in *classic* prose. Indeed Luc. quoted is the only prose instance we have met. *μήδεσθαι* Plut. Mor. 407, is now *κήδεσθαι* (Dübn. &c.)

Μηκάομαι *To bleat, cry*, **pres.** *μηκᾶται* Schol. in Nicand. Alex. 214, in comp. *ὑπο-μηκῶνται* Aesch. Fr. Edon. 51 (Vulg.) *-μῡκ-* (58 Herm. 55 Dind.): **2 aor.** (*ἔμᾰκον*) *μᾰκών* Il. 16, 469. Od. 18, 98: **2 p.** as **pres.** (*μέμηκα*) *μεμηκώς* Il. 10, 362, fem. shortened, μεμᾰκυῖα 4, 435: hence, or from a new pres. imp. ἐμέμηκον Od. 9, 439 (Wolf, Dind. La R.), μέμηκ- (Bekk.) The pres. even in comp. seems doubtful; ὑπομῡκῶνται is best supported Aesch. quoted.

Μηλοφορέω *To carry apples*, only Dor. imp. ἐμᾶλοφόρει Theocr. Epigr. 2.

Μηνίω *To be wroth* (μῆνις), Od. 17, 14; Soph. O. C. 1274; Her. 9, 7, Dor. μᾶν- Simon. C. 50; Eur. Hipp. 1146 (chor.); imper. μήνῐε Il. 1, 422; -ίων Eur. Rhes. 494; D. Hal. Ant. 12, 12: imp. ἐμήνῐον Il. 1, 247; Her. 5, 84; Plut. Mor. 777, μήνῑεν Il. 2, 769: fut. (μηνίσω), ἀπο-μηνίσει Od. 16, 378, late -ιῶ, -ιεῖ V. T. Ps. 102, 9: aor. ἐμήνῑσα Aristot. Anal. Post. 2, 13, 18. Rhet. 2, 24, 6; Athen. 6, 91; -ίσας Il. 5, 178; Soph. Ant. 1177; Plut. Mor. 775; Apollod. 1, 9, 24; Diod. Sic. 15, 49; -ῖσαι Her. 7, 229; Ael. Fr. 74; App. Mithr. 102. Mid. μηνῑεται Aesch. Eum. 101. Vb. ἀμήνῑτος Aesch. Ag. 649. The form μηνιάω is late, -ιῶν Dio. Hal. Rhet. 9, 16 (-ίων Ant. 12, 12); Ael. H. A. 6, 17 -ίων (Herch.), Epic 3 pl. -ιόωσι Ap. Rh. 2, 247. In pres. and imp. ῐ usu. in Hom., so Eur. Hipp. 1146. Rhes. 494, but ῑ Il. 2, 769 by arsis, also Aesch. Eum. quoted, ῑ always in fut. and aor. This verb seems to occur neither in Comedy, nor *classic* Attic prose.

Μηνύω *To declare*, H. Merc. 254; Soph. O. R. 102; Antiph. 2, α, 5; Thuc. 6, 74; Lys. 12, 48, κατα- Her. 6, 29. 7, 30, Dor. μᾱν- Pind. N. 9, 4; Bacchyl. 22 (B.) (Attic ῡ throughout, Epic and Pind. ῠ in pres. and imp., ῡ in fut. aor. &c.): imp. ἐμήνυε Antiph. 5, 54, Dor. μάνῠε Pind. Ol. 6, 52: fut. μηνῡσω Eur. Ion 750; Her. 2, 121; Andoc. 1, 15; Pl. Polit. 264, κατα- Aesch. Pr. 175: aor. ἐμήνῡσα Andoc. 1, 28; Lys. 6, 23; -ύσῃς Eur. Hipp. 520, -σωσι Thuc. 8, 39; -ύσαιμι H. Merc. 364, -ειας Eur. El. 620; μήνῡσον Ar. Ach. 206, Dor. μάν- Eur. Hec. 193. 194 (chor.); -ῦσαι Phoen. 1218; Antiph. 5, 68; Thuc. 6, 60; -ύσας Soph. O. R. 1384; Her. 1, 23: p. μεμήνῡκα Andoc. 1, 22; Pl. Menex. 239: p. p. μεμήνῡται Andoc. 1, 10; -μηνῦσθαι Thuc. 6, 57; -υμένος 6, 53: plp. ἐμεμήνῡτο 6, 61: aor. ἐμηνύθην Andoc. 1, 59; Pl. Criti. 108: fut. late μηνυθήσομαι Galen 3, 403. Mid. late, aor. μηνῠσαιτο Theod. Prod. 8, 339, missed by Lexicogr. Late, υ seems also short in fut. and aor. μηνῠσω, ἀντι- Nicet. Eug. 8, 276; μήνῠσε Epigr. D. Laert. 9, 7, 11; μηνῠσας Theod. Prodr. 5, 513.

Μηρύομαι *To draw, take in*, Anth. 10, 5; Luc. Herm. 47, Dor. μᾱρύ- Theocr. 1, 29: imp. μηρύοντο Ap. Rh. 4, 889, ἐξ-εμηρ- Xen. An. 6, 5, 22: aor. ἐμηρῡσάμην Soph. Fr. 699, μηρῡσ- Od. 12, 170; Orph. Arg. 638; -ύσασθαι Hes. Op. 538 (late prose μηρύσαιο Aretae. S. Ac. Morb. 1, 4 (ed. Oxon); ἐξ-εμηρύσατο Polyb. 3, 53.) At Theocr. 1, 29, it is intrans. *draws itself, creeps, winds,* or pass. *is drawn.* The *simple* form seems not to be used in *classic* prose. The act. form (μηρύω Suid.), p. μεμήρυκε occurs, with some Ms. support, in Hippocr. 9, 192 (Lit.); 3, 241 (Ermerins), unnoticed by Lexicogr.

Μητῐάω, Epic -ῐόω *To plan* (μῆτις), -όωσι Il. 10, 208; -ιόων 20, 153, and μητίω: but only in imp. μήτῑον (ῑ in arsi) Orph. Arg. 1341, iter. μητῐ́ασκον Ap. Rh. 4, 7. **Mid.** μητῐάομαι, Epic 2 pl. -ᾰ́ασθε Il. 22, 174, -όωνται Q. Sm. 12, 249; inf. -άασθαι Ap. Rh. 3, 506, συμ- Il. 10, 197: imp. μητιόωντο Il. 12, 17; Pind. μητῐ́ομαι P. 2, 92: fut. -ῑ́σομαι Il. 15, 349: aor. ἐμητῑσάμην Od. 12, 373, μητῑσ- Parmen. 131; Opp. Hal. 2, 483; subj. -ῑ́σομαι for -σωμαι, Il. 3, 416; opt. -ῑσαίμην Od. 18, 27; -ῑ́σασθαι Il. 10, 48. Od. 9, 262. Before Wolf -ίσσομαι. ῑ in fut. and aor. ῐ in pres. mid. Pind. quoted, ῑ in imp. act. *in arsi,* Orph. Arg. 1341. We should be glad of fact or analogy in proof of "ι is long by nature."

Μηχᾰνάω *To devise,* act. Poet. rare, and only pres. pt. Epic -νόων Od. 18, 143; and inf. -χανᾶν Soph. Aj. 1037: p. p. μεμηχάνημαι Soph. Tr. 586; Her. 1, 98. 2, 95. 5, 90; Pl. Tim. 54; Isocr. 3, 6, προσ- Aesch. Sept. 541. 643, see below: plp. ἐμεμηχάνητο Her. 8, 71; Antiph. 5, 55: aor. ἐμηχανήθην Hippocr. 9, 88 (Lit.); and late, μηχανηθείς Dio. Hal. Exc. 11 (14); Joseph. Ant. 18, 2, 4. Usu. mid. μηχανάομαι Od. 3, 207; Aesch. Ag. 965; Eur. Bac. 805; Ar. Ach. 445; Her. 6, 62; Antiph. 6, 9; Thuc. 5, 45; Pl. Rep. 519; opt. -νῷτο Pl. Leg. 965 (Bekk. Stallb.), Ion. 3 pl. -νῴατο Her. 6, 46: imp. ἐμηχανώμην Soph. Ph. 295; Ar. Pax 621; Her. 8, 106; Thuc. 7, 25; Pl. Tim. 74: fut. -ήσομαι Aesch. Sept. 1038; Her. 5, 30; Pl. Leg. 965: aor. ἐμηχανησάμην Eur. Med. 1014; Ar. Thesm. 16; Her. 1, 48; Antiph. 5, 25; Thuc. 4, 47; Isae. 10, 17, Dor. ἐμᾱχανᾱσ- Tim. Locr. 99: and p. as mid. μεμηχάνημαι Pl. Tim. 47. Leg. 904; Isae. 11, 36; Aeschin. 2, 131; -ημένος Xen. Hier. 11, 4; Dem. 45, 24, more freq. pass., see above. **Vb.** μηχανητέον Pl. Leg. 798. (ᾰᾰ).—Epic forms, μηχανόωντες Od. 18, 143: mid. -όωνται 3, 207, -άασθε 20, 370; subj. -ᾱ́ᾱται Hes. Op. 241 (Goettl. Lennep, indic. Schoem. Koechly); opt. -όῳτο Od. 16, 196: imp. μηχανόωντο Il. 8, 177. In Mss. and edit. of Her. the 3 pl. imp. varies in form: ἐμηχανῶντο 6, 133, -έωντο 7, 172 (Gaisf. Bekk.) -έοντο 8, 7 (Dind. Stein, Abicht always, and here Gaisf. Bekk.), but ἐμηχανέατο 5, 63, Lhardy with Matth. Krüg. and Dind. maintains to be a vicious form unauthorised by example or analogy, and confidently suggests ἐμηχανῶντο, Matth.

ἐμηχανώατο or plp. ἐμεμηχανέατο, Dind. reads -έοντο, for though -έατο is often for -οντο, and plp. -ηντο, it is never for -άοντο, -έοντο of contract verbs. Bredow defends ἐμηχανέατο by the analogy of ὡρμέατο 1, 83. 158 &c. which he takes, of course, for imp. ὡρμέοντο, Lhardy, Matth. &c. for plp. ὥρμηντο.

Μῐαίνω *To stain*, Eur. H. F. 1232; Opp. H. 5, 418; -αίνῃ Pl. Leg. 868; -αίνων Aesch. Ag. 209; -αίνειν Soph. Ant. 1044; Antiph. 2, α, 10; Pl. Tim. 69: imp. ἐμίαινον Lys. 12, 99: fut. μιᾰνῶ Antiph. 2, β, 11: aor. ἐμίηνα Ion. Hippocr. 6, 112 (Lit.); Opp. Hal. 3, 162; μιήνῃ Il. 4, 141; Anth. 7, 162; and late -ῆναι App. Civ. 2, 104; Plut. Mor. 725, Attic ἐμίᾱνα (Pind. N. 3, 16); late prose, Philostr. Ap. 210; μιάνῃ (Eur.) I. A. 1595; μιάναιμι Eur. Hel. 1000, -άνειε Soph. Fr. 91; -άνας Solon 32 (Bergk); late prose, Luc. Phal. 1, 12; Alciphr. 1, 8: p. late μεμίαγκα, -κώς Plut. T. Gracch. 21: p. p. μεμίασμαι Hippocr. 2, 127 (Erm.); Thuc. 2, 102; Pl. Phaed. 81; Ap. Rh. 4, 716; Plut. Aristid. 20; Herodn. 1, 15, 7. 8, 5, 7, and late μεμίαμμαι Dio Cass. 51, 22 (Bekk. L. Dind.); Epist. Phal. 121 (Herch.): aor. ἐμιάνθην, μιάν- Il. 16, 795. 23, 732; -ανθῆναι Eur. Ion 1118; -ανθείς Aesch. Ch. 859; Soph. O. C. 1374; Pl. Leg. 873: fut. μιανθήσομαι Pl. Rep. 621: pres. -αίνεσθαι Il. 16, 797: imp. ἐμιαιν- 17, 439. Mid. pres. in comp. ἐκ-μιαίνομαι Ar. Ran. 753: but aor. in *simple* ἐμιήνατο Nonn. 45, 288, missed by Lexicogr. Vb. ἀμίαντος Aesch. Pers. 578. (ῐ.) μιάνθην Epic 3 pl. 1 aor. pass. for μίανθεν shortened form of ἐμιάνθησαν, Il. 4, 146, others for dual μιανθήτην. Of neither perhaps have we sure examples, for the metre requires ἔγνον not -ων Pind. P. 4, 120 (Bergk &c.) and permits it (9, 79. I. 2, 23; Hym. Cer. 111) and is so edited by Schneidewin and Ahrens. But though such syncopated 3 plurals shorten the last syllable, as ἔστᾰν for -ησαν, τίθεν for -θησαν &c. yet there appears some analogy for retaining the long vowel, in the Doric ἦν for ἦσαν, Ar. Lys. 1260; Epich. 30. 31, ἐνῆν 52 (Ahr.) Buttmann says it is from an aor. whose 3 sing. is ἐμίαντο, 3 dual ἐμιάν-σθην, then μιάνθην. Have we example or analogy of this? Ahrens thinks that the proper analogical form μίανθεν may be admitted on the ground that a *short* syllable may stand for a *long* before the *Bucolic caesura.* Some of the late Attic prose writers use the Ionic form of aor. ἐμίηνα Plut. Mor. 725; App. Civ. 2, 104, but καταμιάνητε Lyb. 85 (Bekk.) The Septuagint uniformly, we think, -ίανα.

Μῐγάζομαι *To mingle, embrace*, Epic and only part. -αζόμενος Od. 8, 271; Orph. Arg. 345.

Μίγνῡμι *To mix*, Pl. Leg. 691; (Dem.) Epist. 1, 1465; imper. μίγνῡ Pl. Phil. 63; μιγνῦναι 59; Hippocr. 2, 261 (Erm.); Xen.

Oec. 20, 3, παρα- Hippocr. 8, 502 (Lit.), μιγνύμεν Simon. C. 31; μιγνύς Pind. Fr. 107 (B.); Ar. Eq. 1399; Pl. Rep. 488, ἐπι- Thuc. 1, 2, μιγνύω Com. Fr. (Damox.) 4, 532; Aristot. H. A. 9, 40, 50; Theophr. Lith. 53, παρα- Hippocr. 8, 340 (Lit.), συμ- Xen. Mem. 3, 14, 5 (Breitb. Saupp.), συμπαρα- Ar. Plut. 719, ἀνα- Plut. Mor. 638, and μίσγω Soph. Fr. 265; Aristot. H. A. 6, 23, 6, συμ- Her. 9, 51, προσ- Thuc. 6, 104; imper. σύμ-μισγε Theogn. 1165; μίσγειν Theophr. H. P. 8, 8, 1, προσ- Her. 4, 46, ξυμ- Pl. Leg. 678, Epic μισγέμεναι Od. 20, 203; μίσγων Pl. Tim. 41, συμ- H. Merc. 81; Her. 1, 123: imp. ἐμίγνυν, συν- Xen. Cyr. 8, 1, 46 (Vulg. Popp. Saupp. and always *now* Dind.), (ἐ)μίγνυον Pind. N. 4, 21, προσ- Xen. Cyr. 3, 3, 60, συν- 7, 1, 26 (Vulg. Popp. Saupp. -υν Dind.); Plut. Rom. 11, ἔμισγον Od. 1, 110; Pl. Tim. 41, συν- Her. 5, 112, μῖσγ- Il. 3, 270: fut. μίξω Soph. O. C. 1047; Pl. Phil. 64, μετα- Od. 22, 221: aor. ἔμιξα Archil. 86; Pind. I. 7, 25; Aesch. Ch. 546; Pl. Phaedr. 240, συν- H. Hym. Ven. 250, μῖξα Pind. P. 4, 213; Opp. Hal. 3, 402; inf. μῖξαι Il. 15, 510; Dor. pt. μίξαις, ἐπι- Pind. N. 3, 61: p. μέμιχα Galen 13, 865, συμ- Dio Cass. 67, 11; Polyb. 38, 5; Epist. Phal. 77: plp. ἐμεμίχειν Galen 13, 784, συν- Dio Cass. 47, 45: p. p. μέμιγμαι Simon. C. 5, 7; Pind. Ol. 1, 91; Aesch. Sept. 940; Soph. El. 1485; Com. Fr. (Stratt.) 2, 784; Pl. Prot. 346; Aristot. Metaph. 7, 2, 3, Ion. 3 pl. μεμίχαται, ἀνα- Her. 1, 146; μεμιγμένον ἐστίν Od. 8, 196 &c.; -μένοι Il. 10, 424; Emped. 259; Xen. Cyr. 1, 3, 10: plp. ἐμέμικτο Il. 4, 438; Aristot. Nat. Ausc. 1, 4, 12: 1 aor. ἐμίχθην Il. 10, 457; Her. 2, 181, ξυν- Thuc. 2, 31, ἀν- Dem. 54, 8, μίχθη Il. 20, 374; Hes. Fr. 77; Pind. Ol. 9, 59, Poet. 3 pl. ἔμιχθεν N. 2, 22. I. 2, 29, in tmesi Il. 23, 687; μιχθῇ Her. 1, 199, ξυμ- Pl. Phil. 47; μιχθῆναι Aesch. Supp. 295; Soph. O. R. 791; Her. 1, 199. 4, 9; Xen. Cyr. 8, 7, 25, Ep. -ήμεναι Il. 11, 438; μιχθείς Hes. Th. 288; Pind. Ol. 6, 29; Com. Fr. (Anax.) 3, 193; Pl. Leg. 837. Phil. 46: fut. μιχθήσομαι late in *simple*, Palaeph. 14; Dio Cass. 55, 13; Galen 1, 327. 10, 399, but ἀνα- Aeschin. 1, 166: 2 aor. ἐμίγην Il. 15, 33; Her. 2, 131, μίγη Il. 6, 25; Hes. Sc. 36, Poet. 3 pl. μίγεν Od. 9, 91; Pind. P. 9, 68, ἔμιγεν Hes. Cert. 317, 7; Ion. subj. μιγῇς Od. 5, 378, μιγέωσι Il. 2, 475; Hippocr. 8, 62; -είην Od. 15, 315; inf. Epic μιγήμεναι Hes. Th. 306; Il. 15, 409, but μιγῆναι 19, 176; Aesch. Pr. 738; Soph. O. R. 995; Eur. Ion 338; μιγείς Hes. Th. 53; Pind. P. 9, 84; Com. Fr. (Crat.) 2, 147; Ar. Av. 698; Hippocr. 7, 180; Pl. Rep. 490, ξυμ- Her. 8, 38; Thuc. 8, 103: fut. μῐγήσομαι Il. 10, 365; Paroem. Zenob. Cent. 2, 68; Nonn. 2, 147; Alciphr. 3, 1; Apollod. 3, 5, 7: 3 fut. μεμίξομαι Hes. Op. 177; Aesch. Pers. 1052 (Vulg.), ἀνα- Anacr.

77 (Bergk); Hippocr. 7, 498 (Lit.), ἀμ-μεμ- Aesch. Pers. quoted (Herm. Dind. now). **Mid.** μίγνῦμαι *mix oneself with, join* &c. Hippocr. 8, 424; Pl. Phaed. 113. Conv. 203, and μίσγομαι Pind. Fr. 184, ἐπι- Il. 10, 548; 2 sing. Epic subj. μίσγεαι Il. 2, 232; -γεσθαι Her. 5, 6: **imp.** ἐμίγνυντο Pind. P. 2, 45, ἐπ- Thuc. 2, 1, ἐμισγέσθην Il. 14, 295, -γετο Od. 15, 430; Her. 1, 61, μίσγ- Il. 18, 216, iter. μισγέσκετο Od. 18, 325, rare with augm. ἐμισγ- Od. 20, 7, see below: **fut.** μίξομαι Od. 6, 136. 24, 314, συμ- Her. 8, 77 (Orac.); Theogn. 1245, called pass.: **aor.** perhaps late μίξαιο Androm. Ther. 125; μιξάμενος Anth. (Incert.) 7, 44; Nic. Ther. 603; Theophr. C. P. 3, 22, 3: **2 aor.** sync. μίγμενος trans. Nic. Alex. 574; intrans. ἔμικτο Od. 1, 433; Ap. Rh. 3, 1163, μῖκτο Il. 11, 354. 16, 813 (Bekk. μίκτο Dind. La R.); so Ap. Rh. 3, 1223, called by some a syncop. plp. **Vb.** μικτός Pl. Phil. 27, -έος Tim. 48. Iterative forms are seldom augmented, perhaps never in prose, but εἴασκον Il. 5, 802, ἔφασκον 13, 100, -κε Od. 13, 173, 1 and 2 pl. very rare νικάσκομεν Od. 11, 512 (Bekk. Dind.), ἐφάσκετε 22, 35, ἀνεμορμύρεσκε 12, 238, ἀναμ- (Dind. and Bekk. 2 ed. La R.), παρεκέσκετο 14, 521, παρέβασκε Il. 11, 104; but for ἐλάβεσκον Her. 4, 130 (Mss. Vulg. Schweigh. Gaisf.), Schaef. Bekk. Krüg. Dind. λάβεσκον which occurs without v. r. 4, 78, ἐσεπέμπεσκον 1, 100 (Mss. Schweigh. Gaisf.), ἐσπέμπ- (Bekk. Krüg. Dind.) with ἐκπέμπεσκε ibid. (Mss. Gaisf. Bekk. Krüg. Dind. &c.) It would thus appear to be rather a mistake to confine the iter. form entirely to the "sing. and 3 pl.," as well as to assert that "in the *latest* editions of Homer and Herodotus ἐμισγέσκοντο and ἐλάβεσκον are the only iter. forms that retain the augment" (Rost's Gr. Gram. p. 322. 2 ed. 1859). The form μίσγω alone occurs in Hom. Hes. Theognis, Her. Theocr. Ap. Rh., once in Trag. Soph., not in Comedy, freq. in Thuc. occas. in Xen. and Plato, and not seldom in less classic writers, Aristot. Theophr. Luc. Dio. Hal. Diod. Sic. &c. μίγνυμι, ἐμίγνυν were preferred especially by the earlier Attics to -ύω, -υον. The latter, except of course subj. and opt. is never in the Traged. nor Thuc., nor *now*, we think, in Plato, and only once in Aristoph. but frequent along with -υμι in the Mss. and edit. of Xen. Lud. Dind. however has in his last edit. of Xen. displaced -ύω, except -ύων Mem. 3, 14, 5, and adopted -υμι. We demur to this, because forms in -ύω had been *kything* in the Old Comedy, Com. Fr. (Pher.) 2, 324, and were coming more into use with writers of the Middle, Aristophanes, Amphis &c. contemporaries of Xen., and went on increasing in classic prose and the Later Comedy. We therefore think that in Xenophon's time both forms were in use, and that though -υμι was

the more freq., it may be the more approved form, yet that an author felt at perfect liberty to use -ύω, whether to meet a metrical exigency, to please a fancy, or simply to vary his diction. ὀμνύων is demanded by the metre Alex. Com. Fr. 3, 437, ὀμνύοντος Antiph. 3, 149, ὀμνύοντι Amphis 3, 319, ὀμνύουσι Alex. 3, 458, as well as συμπαραμιγνύων Ar. Plut. 719, occurring along with the rival form ὑπομνύμενον 725.

Μῑμέομαι *To imitate*, Hom. H. 1, 163; Aesch. Ch. 564; Eur. Ion 451; Her. 2, 104; Thuc. 2, 37; Pl. Crat. 423, but **pass.** Rep. 604; imper. μίμεο Simon C. 29: **imp.** ἐμιμεῖτο Xen. Conv. 2, 22, -έετο Her. 4, 166: **fut.** μιμήσομαι Eur. Rhes. 211; Ar. Plut. 306; Isocr. 11, 40; Pl. Rep. 539, Dor. -ᾱ́σομαι Ecph. Stob. 48, 64: **aor.** ἐμιμησάμην, -ήσω Dem. 22, 7, Ion. -ήσαο Her. 3, 32, -σαντο 1, 176; -ήσαιτο Pind. P. 12, 21; Pl. Soph. 267; -ησαίμεθα Isocr. 11, 20; -σασθαι Andoc. 1, 141; Isocr. 6, 83; -σάμενος Ar. Vesp. 1019; Lys. 2, 61; Pl. Crat. 423: **p.** μεμίμημαι Her. 2, 169; Pl. Menex. 238. Phil. 40, but **pass.** Ar. Lys. 159; Her. 2, 78. 86. 132; Pl. Crat. 425, Dor. -ᾱμαι **act.** Ecph. Stob. 48, 64: **aor.** always **pass.** ἐμιμήθην Pl. Leg. 668: **fut.** μιμηθήσομαι **pass.** Pl. Rep. 599. **Vb.** μιμητέον Pl. Rep. 396. ῐ only in very late poets, Orac. Sib. 2, 146; Greg. Naz. The Traged. have only **pres.** and **fut.**

Μιμνάζω *To wait*, Poet. and only **pres.** intrans. Il. 2, 392; Opp. Hal. 1, 145; Anth. 4, 4, 6, trans. *await*, Hom. H. 9, 6: and **imp.** μίμναζε Opp. H. 5, 463.

Μιμνήσκω *To cause to remember, remind, simple* Poet. in **act.** Od. 14, 169, ὑπο- Aesch. Pers. 989; Pl. Rep. 427, ἀνα- Thuc. 2, 89; Andoc. 1, 31; μίμνησκε Od. 14, 169; Theogn. 1123; Dor. μιμνάσκων, ὑπο- Theocr. 21, 50: **fut.** μνήσω Il. 15, 31. Od. 12, 38, ἀνα- Soph. O. R. 1133, ὑπο- Her. 9, 6; Pl. Phil. 67. Lach. 181; Dem. 22, 15, Dor. ἀ-μνάσει (ἀνα-) Pind. P. 4, 54: **aor.** ἔμνησα Od. 3, 103; Eur. Alc. 878 (chor.), ἀν- Isocr. 12, 130, ὑπ- Thuc. 2, 60; Pl. Phaed. 88; Dem. 19, 25, Dor. ἔμνᾱσα Pind. P. 11, 13, ὑπ- Soph. Ph. 1169 (chor.); μνήσῃ Od. 14, 170, ὑπο- Thuc. 2, 60; (ἀνα-) ἀ-μνάσειεν Pind. P. 1, 47; μνησάτω, ὑπο- Andoc. 1, 70; μνήσας Il. 1, 407, ἀνα- Her. 6, 21: **p. p.** as **pres. mid.** μέμνημαι *I remember*, Il. 9, 527; Aesch. Ag. 830; Eur. H. F. 1122; Ar. Pax 1060; Antiph. 3, δ, 10; Thuc. 2, 8; Dem. 21, 143, Dor. -ᾱμαι Pind. Ol. 6, 11; Eur. Elec. 188 (chor.); Theocr. 5, 118; Epim. in Diog. Laert. 1, 113, μέμνησαι Il. 23, 648; Pl. Rep. 350, Epic -νηαι Il. 21, 442, -νῃ Od. 24, 115, Dor. μέμνᾳ Theocr. 5, 116 (Ziegl. Fritz.), see below; -νῆσθαι Il. 19, 231; Her. 6, 94; Thuc. 6, 12, Dor. νᾶσθαι Pind. Ol. 6, 92; -ημένος Od. 4, 151; Hes. Op. 641; Her. 3, 147; Thuc. 7, 63,

-āμένος Pind. N. 7, 80: plp. ἐμεμνήμην Lys. 18, 18, Dor. -αντο Pind. I. 8, 27, see mid.: so aor. ἐμνήσθην *remembered*, Soph. El. 373; Eur. Or. 579; Ar. Eq. 1277; Callim. Epigr. 2, 2; Her. 9, 46; Pl. Phil. 59; Isocr. 10, 14, 'μνήσθην Ar. Av. 1632, Dor. -άσθην Pind. N. 9, 10; Eur. El. 745 (chor.); subj. μνησθῶ Soph. Ph. 310; Lys. 21, 9, μνησθῇς Her. 7, 159 &c.; -θείην Isocr. 12, 92; Xen. Hell. 6, 5, 48; μνήσθητι Xen. Cyr. 1, 6, 16, -ητε Antiph. 6, 41; -θείς Thuc. 6, 68; Her. 3, 32; μνησθῆναι 9, 45; Od. 4, 118, the only instance in Hom. of aor. pass. in the *simple* form: fut. μνησθήσομαι Eur. Med. 933; Thuc. 3, 90; Lys. 3, 45; Isocr. 8, 81; Aeschin. 1, 106. 170. 193. 2, 76. 167. 3, 84; Dem. 15, 22: **3 fut.** μεμνήσομαι *will bear in mind*, Il. 22, 390; Eur. Hipp. 1461; Her. 8, 62; Pl. Polit. 285; Lys. 6, 42; Isocr. 12, 259; Aeschin. 2, 11. **Mid.** μιμνήσκομαι *remember*, *mention*, Od. 15, 54; Theocr. 25, 173; (Pl.) Ax. 368 (ἀνα- Andoc. 1, 46); Dio. Hal. Ant. 1, 13; Plut. Mor. 653; μιμνήσκεο Il. 22, 268; -νησκόμενος Thuc. 6, 60, and Epic μνάομαι Od. 16, 77; μνώμενος (Theocr.) Epigr. 15, 4, μνωόμ- Od. 4, 106: imp. μιμνήσκοντο Il. 13, 722, and ἐμνώοντο Il. 2, 686, μνώοντο Il. 11, 71. 16, 697. 771: fut. μνήσομαι poet. Il. 2, 724. Od. 7, 192, μνήσει Eur. I. A. 667, Epic μνήσεαι Theogn. 100, but ἐπι-μνήσομαι Her. 1, 5. 177. 2, 101; Paus. 5, 25, ἀπο- Thuc. 1, 137, ἀνα- Hippocr. 1, 175 (Erm.); Dinarch. 1, 37: aor. ἐμνησάμην poet. Il. 24, 602; Soph. O. R. 564, μνησ- Il. 4, 222, 14, 441, Dor. μνᾱσαμ- Aesch. Supp. 51, ἐπ-εμνᾱσ- Ch. 623 (chor.), iter. μνησάσκετο Il. 11, 566; subj. μνήσῃ Od. 8, 462, μνησώμεθα Il. 19, 148; Simon. C. 104 (Bergk); μνησαίμην Tyrt. 12, 1 (Bergk), -αιτο Od. 4, 527, 3 pl. -αίατο 7, 138; μνῆσαι Il. 10, 509; Callin. 2 (B.); -σάμενος Il. 19, 314; μνήσασθαι Od. 7, 217; in prose rare, Her. 7, 39; and late (Luc.) D. Syr. 39: as mid. p. p. μέμνημαι Il. 9, 527; Her. 8, 22; Thuc. 5, 26; Pl. Leg. 633; Xen. An. 5, 8, 25, &c.: plp. ἐμεμνήμην Her. 4, 164; Thuc. 2, 21; Xen. Cyr. 2, 1, 10; Isocr. 12, 35, Ion. 3 pl. -έατο Her. 2, 104, μεμνή- Il. 17, 364: aor. ἐμνήσθην Thuc. 1, 10; Lys. 1, 19; μνησθῶ Soph. Ph. 310, -σθέω, ἐπι- Her. 2, 3, see above: fut. μνησθήσομαι *will mention*, Her. 6, 19; Thuc. 3, 90; Isocr. 15, 259. Epist. 9, 12; Dem. 15, 22. 18, 11, ἀνα- 19, 283, ἐπι- Her. 2, 3; Dem. 19, 276, see above: **3 fut.** μεμνήσομαι Il. 22, 390; Xen. Cyr. 8, 6, 6; Pl. Leg. 783, see above. **Vb.** ἄ-μναστος Theocr. 16, 42, μνηστέον Hippocr. 2, 157, ἐπι- Pl. Tim. 90. Epic lengthened forms, μνώοντο, ἐμνώοντο imp. 3 pl. for ἐμνῶντο, Il. 11, 71. 2, 686; so part. μνωόμενος Od. 4, 106; imper. μνώεο Ap. Rh. 1, 896. μέμνηαι for -ησαι, 2 sing. perf. Il. 21, 442, contr. μέμνῃ 15, 18; Theocr. 21, 41, μεμνέαται for -νηνται, Democr. p. 196 (Mull.); subj. μεμνώμεθα

Od. 14, 168; Soph. O. R. 49 (Elms. Dind.); Pl. Phil. 31, Ion. -εώμεθα Her. 7, 47 (Bekk. Krüg. -νώμ- Dind. Stein); opt. μεμνῄμην Il. 24, 745, -ῇτο Ar. Plut. 991; Pl. Rep. 518, also μεμνῷο Xen. An. 1, 7, 5 (Schneid. Krüg. -ῇο Dind. Saupp. -οιο Mss. Kühner), -ῷτο Xen. Cyr. 1, 6, 3 (-ῇτο Saupp. Dind. *now*), Ion. -έῳτο Il. 23, 361 (Dind. La R. -ῇτο Bekk. *now*), ᾠμεθα Soph. O. R. 49 quoted (Eustath. Nauck &c.), and μεμναίατ' for -αιντο, Pind. Fr. 71 (Bergk, Hart.) quoted in Etym. M. and Cram. Anecd. as δωρικώτερον διὰ τοῦ αι; imper. μέμνεο Ion. for -νησο, Her 5, 105; Orph. Lith. 603, 3 Dor. μεμνάσθω Pind. N. 11, 15: **plp.** ἐμεμνέατο for -ηντο, Her. 2, 104, Dor. -μναντο Pind. I. 8, 26. μεμνόμενος Archil. 9, 2 (Bergk) is a mere conjecture of Scaliger, adopted however by Grotius and Gaisf. for μεμφόμενος (Vulg.) which Bergk in his 2 and 3 ed. retains, but suggests μελπόμενος, or μεμβλόμ-. **Pres.** μιμνήσκω and **fut.** μνήσω in *simple* are Epic. Hom. and the Traged. use both **aor. pass.** and **mid.**, the Comedians and prose writers seem never to use the **mid. aor.** simple or comp. The only exception we have met is μνήσασθαι Her. 7, 39; (Luc.) D. Syr. quoted. ἀπομιμνήσκομαι has no **act.** form, and **fut. mid.** ἀπομνήσεσθαι only Thuc. 1, 137: **aor.** ἀπεμνήσαντο Il. 24, 428; Hes. Th. 503; imper. ἀπόμνησαι Eur. Alc. 299: (**p.** -μέμνημαι: **aor.** -εμνήσθην we have not seen.)

Krüger thinks that Thuc. (1, 137) probably wrote ἀπομεμνήσεσθαι, on the ground that the Attics do not use the **fut.** of the mid. form. No doubt they usually employ μνησθήσομαι and μεμνήσομαι, but the approved reading Eur. I. Aul. 667 is μνήσει **fut. mid.** not μνήσῃ subj. **aor.** And though the *simple* μνήσομαι is poetic, that is no bar to a comp. being used in prose: it is a common occurrence. Besides, μνήσομαι is the prevailing **fut.** form in Her. ἐπι-μνήσ- 1, 5. 177. 2, 101 (ἀνα- Hippocr. 2, 650. 5, 98, ἐπι- App. Prooem. 13; (Luc.) D. Syr. 36), and this we think strengthens the probability that it may have been used in the old Attic prose of Thuc. Nor is its *uniqueness* decisive against it, for Thuc. alone of Attic prose authors uses the **aor. pass.** ἐμέμφθην (common in Ion. and Eur.), and only once, μεμφθῇ 4, 85, though he has **aor. mid.** ἐμεμψάμην five or six times. Luc. pro Imag. 9. Char. 1, has 3 **fut.** in part. μεμνησόμενος, which classic writers, we think, avoided, see πολεμέω.

Μίμνω *To remain, await,* trans. and intrans. Poet. and only **pres.** Il. 13, 747; Hes. Op. 520; Aesch. Ag. 154; Soph. Aj. 601; Eur. Ion 513: and **imp.** ἔμιμνον Il. 9, 662; Hes. Op. 97; Theogn. 907; Eur. Andr. 961, μίμ- Il. 15, 689, iter. μίμνεσκεν Orph .Lith. 108. Rare and late in prose, Aretae. C. et S. Diut. Morb. 1, 33 (ed. Oxon.); (Luc.) D. Syr. 29.

Μῐνῠ́θω *To make less*, Poet. and Ion. prose, Il. 20, 242; Hes. Op. 6; *to grow less*, Il. 17, 738; Hes. Op. 244; Aesch. Eum. 374 (chor.); Soph. O. C. 686 (chor.); Hippocr. 4, 360 (Lit.), and -υθέω?: imp. ἐμῐ́νῠθει Hippocr. 3, 330 (Lit.), ἐμίνυθε (Erm. Pref. 3 vol. p. 4), μίνῠθον Q. Sm. 3, 406, iter. μινύθεσκον Od. 14, 17: fut. μινυθήσω Hippocr. 4, 388 (Lit.): aor. ἐμινύθησα 3, 322: p. μεμινύθηκα 4, 348 (Lit.): aor. pass. ἐμινύθη 3, 219 (Kühn) seems a false reading for imp. act. ἐμίνυθε (Erm.), or -ύθει (Mss. C E F G H I K) which also Galen reads and Littré adopts at 3, 63 (Kühn) for ἐμινύθη (Vulg.), and παρα-μινυθέωσι 2, 642 (Kühn) may in form and sense be subj. pres. act. The collat. form μινυθίζω, aor. ἐμινύθισα trans. Hippocr. 2, 154 (K.)

Μῐνῠ́ρομαι *To warble, hum*, Poet. and only pres. μινύρεται Soph. O. C. 671; -ύρεο Callim. L. Pal. 119; -ύρεσθαι Aesch. Ag. 16; -υρομένη Ar. Eccl. 880. The earlier μῐνῠρίζω is occas. used in prose, Aristot. H. An. 9, 32, 3; imper. μινύριζε Il. 5, 889; -ίζων Ar. Av. 14, 14; Pl. Rep. 411: imp. μινύριζον Od. 4, 719: and late, aor. subj. -ίσωσι Plut. Mor. 56.

Μίσγω, see μίγνυμι.

Μῑσέω *To hate*, Anacr. 74; Pind. P. 4, 284; Aesch. Pr. 1068; Soph. Ant. 495; Antiph. 2, β, 6; Thuc. 2, 61; Isocr. 15, 122: imp. ἐμίσουν Soph. Aj. 1347; Xen. Cyr. 8, 8, 12; Lys. 3, 31: fut. -ήσω Pl. Theaet. 168; Isocr. 11, 49; Dem. 10, 19: aor. ἐμίσησα Eur. Or. 619; Isocr. 5, 77; (Dem.) 12, 4, μίσ- Il. 17, 272: p. μεμίσηκα Ar. Ach. 300; Pl. Phil. 44: plp. μεμισήκει Babr. 111: p. p. late except pt. μεμίσημαι Herodn. 8, 5, 6; Alciphr. 1, 32; -σημένος Isocr. 5, 137; Dio Cass. 52, 4; V. T. Esai. 60, 15: aor. ἐμισήθην Isocr. 8, 100. 15, 219; -ηθείς Aesch. Pr. 45; Soph. Aj. 818; Her. 2, 119; Isocr. 8, 47: fut. μισηθήσομαι late Dio Cass. 52, 39; Aristid. 52, 426; V. T. Eccl. 8, 1; Apocr. Syr. 9, 18: classic, fut. mid. μισήσομαι as pass. Eur. Tr. 659. Ion 597. 611; Trag. Fr. 159 (Wagn.); Babr. 13; Philostr. Ap. 251, or *get myself hated*: pres. -οῦμαι Thuc. 2, 64. Vb. μισητός Pl. Phil. 49, -έος Xen. Conv. 8, 20. (ῑ.)

Μισθόω *To hire out*, Isae. 6, 36; Dem. 21, 155: fut. -ώσω Dem. 27, 42: aor. ἐμίσθωσα Her. 2, 180; Lys. 7, 10; Dem. 29, 29; -θωσον Ar. Lys. 958; -ώσας Dem. 18, 21: p. μεμίσθωκα Lys. 17, 5; Dem. 21, 80: p. p. μεμίσθωμαι Her. 9, 38; Pl. Leg. 800; Xen. Cyr. 6, 2, 10: aor. ἐμισθώθην Xen. An. 1, 3, 1; Isae. 6, 36; Dem. 18, 284. Mid. -οῦμαι *hire in*, -οῦται Dem. 18, 149, -οῦνται Xen. Cyr. 6, 2, 20; Her. 5, 62, but -εῦνται 3, 131; -οῖτο Ar. Av. 1152: imp. ἐμισθοῦντο Her. 1, 68. 9, 34; Thuc. 4, 76; Isae. 6, 37: fut. -ώσομαι Ar. Vesp. 52; opt. -ώσοιτο Dem. 27, 40: aor. ἐμισθωσάμην Lys. 3, 24; Aeschin. 1, 13. 162; Dem. 36,

13; -σάμενος Thuc. 6, 90; -ώσασθαι Her. 1, 24: and as mid. p. p. μεμίσθωμαι Lys. 17, 8; Isae. 6, 39; Dem. 45, 79. 48, 44; Com. Fr. (Phil.) 4, 64: and plp. ἐμεμίσθωτο Lys. 3, 11; Dem. 36, 9. 45, 29.

Μιστῠλάομαι, or μυστῐλ- *To ladle out*, Ar. Eq. 827: imp. -ᾶτο Luc. Lex. 5: p. μεμιστύλημαι Ar. Plut. 627, but pass. Eq. 1168.

Μνάομαι, *To remember*, see μιμνήσκω.

Μνάομαι *To court, desire*, contr. μνῶμαι Od. 1, 248. 16, 77; late prose, Luc. Pseudol. 28; Herodn. 7, 9, 11 (Bekk.), but προ- Soph. O. C. 1075; Pl. Theaet. 151: μνάσθω Od. 16, 391; μνώμενοι Od. 13, 378; Her. 1, 205; Heliod. 3, 14; Plut. Tib. Gracch. 1; μνᾶσθαι Od. 14, 91: imp. μνώμην Od. 24, 125, ἐμνᾶτο Her. 1, 205; late prose, Plut. Demetr. 31, but προὐμνᾶτο Xen. An. 7, 3, 18, ἐμνῶντο Hom. H. 4, 24, unaugm. μνώμεθα Od. 24, 125, iter. μνάσκετο 20, 290: aor. ἐμνήσατο Com. Fr. (Eup.) 2, 575; προ-μνησαμένη Xen. Mem. 2, 6, 36. Lengthened forms, μνάᾳ 2 sing. pres. for μνᾷ (μνάῃ) Od. 16, 431; inf. μνάασθαι 1, 39; part. μνεώμενος Her. 1, 96 (μνώμ- Stein): imp. ἐμνάασθε, ὑπ- Od. 22, 38, μνώοντο 11, 288, ἐμνώ- (Theocr.) 27, 22. Vb. (μνηστός), -στή Il. 6, 246.

Μνημονεύω *To remember, mention*, Epicharm. 1; Aesch. Pers. 783; Soph. Aj. 1273; Her. 1, 36; Isocr. 1, 47; Isae. 3, 16; Dem. 5, 10, δια- Antiph. 5, 54: imp. ἐμνημ- Aeschin. 2, 76: fut. -εύσω Ar. Eccl. 264; Isocr. 12, 136: aor. ἐμνημόνευσα Soph. Fr. 779; Pl. Rep. 544, ἀπ- Her. 5, 65: does not redouble in p. ἐμνημόνευκα Joseph. Ap. 1, 1, ἀπ-εμνημ- Pl. Leg. 672. Phaed. 103: p. p. ἐμνημόνευται, δι- Pl. Critias 117: aor. ἐμνημονεύθην Isocr. 12, 192: fut. μνημονευθήσομαι Isocr. 12, 128. 199; Dem. 18, 231: with fut. mid. μνημονεύσεται as pass. Eur. Heracl. 334: pres. p. -ευόμενα Thuc. 1, 23: imp. ἐμνημ- 2, 47. Mid. aor. ἐμνημονευσάμην *mentioned*, Galen 15, 20, missed by all Lexicogr. Vb. μνημονευτός Aristot. Rhet. 1, 11, -τέον Pl. Rep. 441.

Μνήσκομαι *To remember*, only pres. Anacr. 94 (Vulg. Bergk) who suggests μήσεται, Franke μνήσεται perhaps unnecessarily. Pres. act. occurs in comp. ὑπομνήσκουσα Orph. Hym. 77, 6.

Μνηστεύω *To woo*, Od. 18, 277; Theogn. 1112; Eur. I. A. 847; Pl. Leg. 773, Dor. μναστ- Theocr. 22, 155 (Mein.): imp. μνήστευον Hes. Fr. 41 (Goettl. Schoem.), ἐμνήστ- Xen. Hell. 6, 4, 37: fut. -εύσω Isocr. 10, 39: aor. ἐμνήστευσα, -εύσας Od. 4, 684; -εῦσαι Isocr. 10, 20, Dor. μναστ- Theocr. 18, 6: reg. except redupl. p. μεμνηστευκώς Diod. Sic. 18, 23: p. p. μεμνήστευμαι V. T. Deut. 22, 28; Artemidor. Oneir. 2, 12, but ἐμνήστ- N. T. Luc. 1, 27. 2, 5, as mid. see below: aor. ἐμνηστεύθην, Dor. ἐμναστ-

Eur. I. T. 208 (chor.), ὑπ-εμνηστ- Aristot. Polit. 5, 4, 7: pres. μνηστεύεσθαι Isocr. 10, 39. Mid. μνηστεύομαι late, Apollod. 2, 5, 12; Nonn. 7, 118: imp. -εύοντο Luc. Bis Acc. 27 (Bekk. Jacob.); Plut. Mor. 775: aor. -ευσάμην Plut. Lysand. 30; Luc. Mer. Con. 23, ὑπο- Aristot. Polit. 5, 4, 7: and p. as mid. μεμνηστευμένος (Luc.) Asin. 26.

Μνώομαι, see μιμνήσκω, μνάομαι.

Μολέω *To go*, late if correct, imper. μολεῖτε Anth. 12, 93; μολοῦντες Or. Sib. 1, 85; Anth. (Christodor.) 2, 128; Christ. Pat. 215: 1 aor. late, μολήσας Tzetz. Anteh. 375: classic, 2 aor. and usu. Poet. ἔμολον Pind. Ol. 14, 16; Aesch. Ch. 935; Soph. El. 506; Ar. Lys. 984, μολ- Pind. P. 3, 47, ἐκ- Il. 11, 604; subj. μόλω Soph. Ph. 477, μόλῃ Il. 24, 781; Pind. P. 4, 77; Soph. Aj. 688, dual μόλητον Eur. Phoen. 585, but μόλωσι Xen. An. 7, 1, 33; -οιμι Soph. O. C. 70; μόλε Eur. Or. 176 (chor.); Ar. Lys. 1263 (chor.); -λεῖν Soph. O. C. 757; Eur. Bac. 838; late prose Polyb. 30, 9; -λών Il. 6, 286. Od. 3, 44; Soph. O. R. 35; Ar. Ran. 1232; late prose Plut. Mor. 220. 225: fut. μολοῦμαι Trag. Soph. O. C. 1742; -λεῖσθαι Aesch. Pr. 689. See βλώσκω. For μολοῦντες pres. part. Or. Sib. &c. some would edit -όντες 2 aor.

Μόργνῡμι *To wipe*, late, and in *simple*, only aor. mid. μόρξαντο Q. Sm. 4, 270. 374, but ἀπ-εμορξάμην Ar. Ach. 706; Anth. 6, 217. See ὀμόργνῡμι.

Μορμολύττομαι *To scare, fear* (μορμών), Xen. Conv. 4, 27; Pl. Gorg. 473; -τηται Crito 46; -τεσθαι Ar. Av. 1245; -όμενος (Pl.) Ax. 364: imp. ἐμορμολύττετο Com. Fr. (Crat.) 2, 235 (Mein.): aor. μορμολυξάμενος Galen 10, 106, missed by Lexicogr.

(Μορύσσω) *To soil, pollute*, later *mix*, Epic, late and aor. in act. ἐμόρυξα, -ύξαις Nic. Alex. 144: and classic p. p. μεμορυγμένος Od. 13, 435 (Wolf, Dind. -υχμ- Bekk. La R.); Opp. Cyn. 3, 39; Q. Sm. 5, 450; Nic. Alex. 318. 375, -υχμ- (Otto Schn.)

Μουσίζω *To sing*, Dor. -ίσδω Theocr. 8, 38; -ίσδων 11, 81, only pres. act.: and mid. as act. μουσίζομαι, -ιζόμενος Eur. Cycl. 489.

Μῡέω *To initiate*, μυῶν Andoc. 1, 132; μυεῖν Pl. Epist. 333: imp. ἐμύει Philostr. Apoll. 5, 19 (202): fut. -ήσω (Dem.) 59, 21; Luc. Fugit. 8; Philostr. Apoll. 4, 156: aor. ἐμύησ- Plut. Mor. 607; Anth. 9 162; -ῆσαι (Dem.) 59, 21; -ήσας (Hippocr.) Epist. 9, 420 (Lit.): p. μεμύηκα Heliod. 3, 14. Pass. more freq. -έεται Her. 8, 65 (Dind. Stein) -εῖται (Bekk.); -ούμενος Pl. Phaedr. 250: p. μεμύημαι Ar. Ran. 456; Her. 2, 51; Pl. Gorg. 497, -ησθε Andoc. 1, 31: aor. ἐμυήθην Ar. Plut. 845 (Br. Mein. ἐνεμ-

Bekk. Bergk, Dind.); Com. Fr. 3, 626; (Hippocr.) Epist. 9, 314 (Lit.); Philostr. Apoll. 292; -ηθῇ Dem. 59, 21; μυηθείην Pl. Conv. 209 &c.: **fut.** -ηθήσομαι Alciphr. 2, 4, 21: and as **pass. fut. mid.** μυήσομαι Philostr. Apoll. 4, 156, but seemingly **act.** Euseb. adv. Hierocl. 30 (Kayser in text, but μυῆσαι in Annot. crit.), both missed by Lexicogr.

Μύζω *To suck*, Xen. An. 4, 5, 27 (Suid. Dind. Popp. Krüg.); Hippocr. 8, 592 (Lit.), and μυζέω, 7, 252, later μυζάω, ἐκ- D. Cass. 51, 14; Ael. H. A. 3, 39: **imp.** ἔμυζε Hippocr. 8, 594: **aor.** ἐμύζησα, μυζήσας Opp. Hal. 2, 407, ἐκ- Il. 4, 218; Luc. Tim. 8: ἐμυζήθην, ἀπ- Themist. 22, 282. ἀμύζω stands in some editions of Xen. An. 4, 5, 27. This verb must be distinguished from μύζω *to mutter, grumble*, Aesch. Eum. 117; Ar. Thesm. 231; Hippocr. 7, 84. 252: **imp.** ἔμυζε 5, 206: **fut.** μύξω Diog. Laert. 10, 118: **aor.** ἔμυξα Com. Fr. (Men.) 4, 92, ἐπ- Il. 8, 457, ἔμυσα Hippocr. 3, 546 (Kühn); (μύσας Plut. Pomp. 60, if not from μύω). **Mid. aor.** ἐμύξατο (Hesych.), ἀπ-εμ- Nic. Al. 482.

Μῡθέω *To speak, tell*, Poet. rare and perhaps late in **act.** Stob. (Democr.) 98, 61; part. μυθεῦσαι for -οῦσαι Eur. I. A. 790 chor. (Kirchh. Nauck, μυθεύσουσι Dind. 5 ed.): **aor.** μυθήσας Phot. Usu. μῡθέομαι Dep. mid. Il. 7, 76, Dor. -εῦμαι Theocr. 10, 21, 2 sing. μυθεῖαι for -έεαι Od. 8, 180, and by dropping ε, μυθέαι Od. 2, 202, -θεῖσθε Aesch. Supp. 277; μυθεῖσθαι Tyrt. 4, 7; -θούμενος Soph. Aj. 1162, -θεύμενος Simon. Am. 7, 18: **imp.** ἐμῡθεόμην Od. 12, 451, μῡθ- Od. 4, 152, dual -θείσθην 3, 140, μυθεῦντο Ap. Rh. 1, 458, iter. μῡθέσκοντο Il. 18, 289: **fut.** -θήσομαι Od. 11, 328; Soph. Aj. 865, -θήσεαι Od. 19, 500: **aor.** μυθήσατο Il. 17, 200; Theocr. 2, 154; Epic subj. -θήσομαι Il. 2, 488; -σαίμην Il. 3, 235. Od. 21, 193; Pind. P. 4, 298; imper. -ήσασθε Il. 6, 376; -ήσασθαι Il. 11, 201. Neither in Comedy nor Attic prose: παρα-μυθοῦμαι is in both. The later form μυθεύω occurs in Eur. but not in classic prose. The Lexicons have overlooked the **mid.** μυθεύονται Strab. 5, 3, 2: **aor.** ἐμυθεύσαντο Plut. Mor. 894, μυθεύσ- Tzetz. Antihom. 74, both without v. r.

Μῡθίζω *To say, tell*, late in this form, -ίζων Maneth. 1, 238, Dor. fem. -ίζοισα (Theocr. 20, 11; inf. -ίσδεν 10, 58; Lacon. μυσίδδω, -ιδδε Ar. Lys. 94; -σίδδειν 1076: **aor.** μυσίξαι 981. **Mid.** μυθίζομαι Stob. (Perict.) 85, 19; -ίζοιτο Orph. Arg. 192.

Μῡκάομαι *To bellow* (μύ, μύκω) Eur. H. F. 870; Ar. Vesp. 1488, παρα- Aesch. Pr. 1082; μυκώμενος Od. 10, 413; Pl. Rep. 396: **imp.** ἐμυκᾶτο Ar. Ran. 562; Pl. Rep. 615: **fut.** μυκήσομαι Anth. 9, 730; Luc. Phal. (1), 11: **aor.** ἐμυκήσαντο Theocr. 16, 37; Paus. 9, 19, 4; Dio Cass. 51, 17, μυκήσ- Theocr. 26, 20;

Mosch. 2, 97, Dor. μυκάσ- Theocr. 22, 75 (Vulg. Mein. -ησ- Ahr. Ziegl. Fritzsche); -ησάμενος Ar. Nub. 292; Philostr. Apoll. 4, 162: **2 p.** μέμῡκα Hes. Op. 508; Aesch. Supp. 351 (chor.), in tmesi Il. 24, 420, ἀμφι- Od. 10, 227; μεμῡκώς Il. 18, 580. 21, 237: **plp.** μεμύκειν Od. 12, 395 (Bekk. 2 ed. La Roche), ἐμεμύκ- (Vulg. Dind.): **2 aor.** Epic μύκον Il. 5, 749, in tmesi 20, 260. The **act.** form seems to be late, **fut.** μῡκήσω Or. Sib. 8, 349: **aor.** μῡκήσας Anth. (Dioscor.) 6, 220. **Mid.** μύκομαι, -ομενάων Or. Sib. 2, 9. In good Attic prose the **pres.** and **imp.** alone occur and rarely.

Μῡλῐάω *To grind, gnash the teeth,* Epic and only pt. μῡλῐόωντες Hes. Op. 530. ῡ by ictus, for in μύλη and compds. ῠ.

Μύρω *To run, flow,* Poet. and in **act.** only **imp.** μῦρον for ἔμῡρ- Hes. Sc. 132. **Mid.** μύρομαι *flow with tears, lament,* Il. 19, 213; subj. -ρηαι Theocr. 16, 31; μύρεο Bion 1, 68; Mosch. 3, 14; -όμενος Il. 23, 14. Od. 19, 119; Theogn. 730; -ύρεσθαι Ap. Rh. 4, 666: **imp.** μύροντο Il. 19, 6, -ετο Hes. Op. 206: **aor.** ἐμύρατο Mosch. 3, 91, μύρ- 3, 37; Anth. App. Epigr. 251; -ύρασθαι Mosch. 3, 73.

Μῠσάζω *To abhor,* act. late, Aquil. 1 Reg. 25, 26, -άττω Hesych. In classic use only mid. -άττομαι, as Dep. pass. Hippocr. 2, 260 (K. -άσσ- Lit. 7, 72); Xen. Cyr. 1, 3, 5; Anth. 3, 6, 2: **imp.** ἐμυσαττ- Luc. Prom. 4: **fut.** -αχθήσομαι **act.** Luc. D. Mer. 11, 3: aor. ἐμυσάχθην act. Themist. 19, 226; subj. μυσαχθῇς Luc. Somn. 8; -θείς Eur. Med. 1149; Luc. Bis Acc. 21.

Μύσσω, -ττω *To wipe, gull,* Hesych.; act. *in use* in comp. only, προ-μύσσω Hippocr. 9, 256, ἀπο-μύσσω Anth. 11, 268, -ττω Pl. Rep. 343: **aor.** ἀπο-μύξῃ Diog. Laert. 6, 44: **plp. p.** ἐμέμυκτο, ἀπ- Com. Fr. (Men.) 4, 215. **Mid.** μύσσομαι *to wipe one's nose,* Hippocr. 6, 606 (Lit.), κατα- Her. 4, 71, ἀπο-μύττ- Xen. Cyr. 1, 2, 16: **imp.** ἀπ-εμυττ- Com. Fr. (Cratin.) 2, 209; Xen. Conv. 1, 15: **aor.** μυξάμενος, ἀπο- Ar. Eq. 910. The mid. in the *simple* form has been overlooked by all Lexicographers. ἀπεμέμυκτο Com. Fr. quoted, is Burmann's approved emendation for ἀμέμικτ'.

Μύω *To shut the lips or eyes,* Soph. Fr. 754; Callim. Dian. 95; Pl. Soph. 239; Aristot. Pt. Anim. 4, 11, 8, κατα- Athen. (Hedyl.) 8, 34; μύων Nicand. Fr. 74, 56: **fut.** μύσω late, Lycophr. 988; Niceph. 7, 15: **aor.** ἔμῡσα Hippocr. 5, 234 (Lit.), μύσαν Il. 24, 637, ἔμῡ- late; μύσῃ Pl. Theaet. 164, μύσωσι Aristot. Meteor. 4, 3, 20; μύσας Soph. Ant. 421; Eur. Med. 1183; Ar. Vesp. 988; Pl. Theaet. 164; Luc. Merc. Con. 21; Plut. Pomp. 60? see μύζω: **p.** μέμῡκα *am shut,* in tmesi Il. 24, 420; Hippocr. 8, 14. 64 (Lit.); Aristot. Probl. 11, 2; -υκώς Anth. App. Epigr.

48, συμ- Pl. Phaedr. 251. The aorist is occasionally long in late Poets, ἔμῡσε in *arsi* Anth. 7, 630. 9, 558, κατα- Batr. 191, unless it should be written -υσσ-. In Attic, υ is said to be short in pres. μῠ́ω. It is difficult to get a direct crucial instance. μῠ́ωψ is short in Anth. 6, 233; Tryph. 352, but μῡ- Nic. Ther. 417, in *arsi*.

Μωμάομαι *To blame*, μωμᾷ Ar. Av. 171, Ion -έομαι, -εῦνται Theogn. 369; -εύμενος 169: fut. μωμήσομαι Il. 3, 412; Simon. Am. 7, 113 (Bergk); Theogn. 1079; Callim. Dian. 222; Inscr. in Plut. Mor. 346: aor. ἐμωμησάμην Aesch. Ag. 277, μωμησ- Q. Sm. 12, 563, μωμᾶσατο Theocr. 9, 24; opt. μωμήσαιτο Theogn. 875; Luc. D. Deor. 20, 2; -ήσασθαι Hist. con. 33. Pass. rare, aor. μωμηθῇ *be blamed*, N. T. 2 Cor. 6, 3. Vb. μωμητός Aesch. Sept. 508. The collat. μωμεύω we have seen in the pr. subj. only μωμεύῃ Od. 6, 274; and inf. -εύειν Hes. Op. 756.

N.

Ναιετάω *To dwell, inhabit*, Poet. trans. and intrans. and only pres. Od. 9, 21, -ετάεις Opp. Hal. 1, 411, -ετάει Hes. Th. 775, -άουσι Il. 4, 45; -άων Od. 17, 523; Emped. 235; Simon. C. 84; Pind. N. 4, 85, παρα- Soph. Tr. 635 (chor.); -άειν Ap. Rh. 3, 680: and iter. imp. ναιετάασκον Il. 2, 841. 11, 673. Od. 15, 385; Ap. Rh. 1, 68. 3, 977. This verb usually maintains its forms uncontracted, ναιετάει, -άουσι, -άων &c., but ναιετῶν Soph. Ant. 1123 chor. (Dind. &c.) In the imp. -άασκον it has the regular lengthening, and in the fem. part. the irregular, ναιετάωσα Od. 1, 404, εὐ- Il. 2, 648, but ναιετάουσα Hom. H. 18, 6, and now Od. and Il. quoted (Bekk. 2 ed.), -όωσα (La Roche).

Ναίω (νάω) *To inhabit, settle*, Poet. Il. 16, 235; Hes. Op. 391; Simon. C. 164; Emped. 353; Pind. P. 12, 3; Aesch. Pr. 809; Soph. O. R. 414; Eur. I. T. 66, Dor. 3 pl. ναίοισι Pind. P. 12, 26; ναίων Il. 6, 15; Soph. Ph. 1105; rare in Comedy, Ar. Ran. 324 (chor.); Com. Fr. (Alex.) 3, 393 (hexam.), Dor. fem. ναίοισα Theocr. 2, 71; ναίειν Anacr. 112; Soph. O. C. 812; so Il. 18, 87; but -έμεν 15, 190, -έμεναι Od. 15, 240: imp. ἔναιον Il. 2, 824; Simon. C. 98; Pind. P. 3, 63; Aesch. Pr. 452, ναῖον Il. 5, 710. 9, 484; Hes. Sc. 473; Simon. C. 48, iter. ναίεσκε Il. 16, 719; Hes. Fr. 81: fut. mid. νάσσομαι Epic, Ap. Rh. 2, 747: aor. ἔνασσα *caused to dwell, placed*, Hom. H. 2, 120; Pind. P. 5, 71, κατ- Hes. Th. 329. Op. 168, νάσσα Od. 4, 174; ἀπο-νάσσωσι Il. 16, 86 (Wolf, Spitzn. Dind. La R. -δάσσωσι Bekk. 2 ed.): p. p. late νένασμαι Anth. Ap. Epigr. 51, 8; -ασμένος Dion. Per.

264: aor. ἐνάσθην (Soph.?) Fr. 795 (hexam.), νάσθην Il. 14, 119, ἀπ-ενάσθην Eur. Med. 166 (chor.), κατ- Phoen. 207 (chor.), κατ-ένασθεν for -ησαν, Ar. Vesp. 662 (anapaest.): aor. mid. ἐνασσάμην *took up my abode*, νάσσατο Hes. Op. 639, ἀπ-ενασσ- Il. 2, 629, *emigrated*, so Od. 15, 254, ἐσ- Hermes. Col. 2, 31, but νάσσατο as aor. act. *settled, stationed*, Ap. Rh. 4, 275, ἀπ-ενάσσ- Eur. I. T. 1260 (chor.); κατα- νασσαμένη Aesch. Eum. 929 (chor.); later ναιήσαντο Dion. Per. 349, νηήσ- (Passow); fut. very late ἐν-νάσσεται Ap. Rh. 4, 1751, ἀπο- Apollinar. Ps. 51, 9. ἀπο-κατα-ναίω are also poetic, and confined entirely or almost to aor. act. mid. and pass.

Νάσσω, -ττω *To stuff, compress*, Stob. (Epictet.) 121, 29: imp. ἔναττον Athen. (Hippol.) 130: fut. (νάξει, ἐρείσει Hesych.): aor. ἔναξα Od. 21, 122, κατ- Her. 7, 36: p. p. νένασμαι Ar. Eccl. 840 (Vulg. Mein. Dind. 4 ed.); Theocr. 9, 9; Alciphr. 3, 47, and νέναγμαι Hippocr. 7, 520 (Lit. -ασμαι Lind.); Ar. Eccl. quoted (Dind. 5 ed.); Arr. An. 6, 24, 4 (Krüg. Sint.): plp. νένακτο Joseph. Jud. B. 1, 17, 6. Vb. ναστός, νακτός late.

Ναυπηγέω *To build ships*, rare in act. Ar. Plut. 513: (Pl.) Alc. 1, 107: imp. ἐναυπήγουν Polyb. 1, 36 (Mss. Vulg. suspected by Schweigh. -οῦντο mid. Bekk. Dind.): p. p. νεναυπηγημένος Aristot. Eth. Eud. 7, 14, 5: aor. -ήθην Thuc. 1, 13 (Bekk.): Xen. Hell. 1, 3, 17; Arr. An. 6, 15, 1. Usu. mid. -οῦμαι *build ships for oneself*, Ar. Eq. 916; Aeschin. 3, 30; Ion. part. -εύμενος Her. 2, 96. 6, 46; inf. -πηγέεσθαι 1, 27, -εῖσθαι Andoc. 3, 14: imp. ἐναυπηγ- Thuc. 1, 31; Xen. Hell. 2, 1, 10. 5, 4, 34; and *now* Polyb. 1, 36 quoted: fut. -γήσομαι Dem. 17, 28: aor. -ησάμην Andoc. 3, 7; Isocr. 9, 47; -ήσωνται Her. 2, 96; -ησάμενος Thuc. 6, 90: and as mid. p. p. νεναυπηγημένος Diod. Sic. 20, 16.

Ναυστολέω *To convey by ship, steer* &c. Eur. Or. 741; Ar. Av. 1229; Luc. Lex. 2; *sail, voyage*, Soph. Ph. 245: imp. ἐναυστ- Soph. Ph. 279: fut. -ήσω Eur. Supp. 474: aor. ἐναυστόλησα I. T. 103; subj. -ήσω Hec. 1260; Alciphr. 2, 4: p. νεναυστόληκα, συν- Soph. Ph. 550: aor. p. late ναυστοληθείς Diod. Sic. 4, 13: fut. mid. ναυστολήσομαι as pass. *shall sail, be shipped off*, Eur. Tr. 1048. Pres. ναυστολούμενα pass. Eur. Fr. 495 (D). Not, we think, in classic prose.

Ναυτιάω *To be sea-sick* seems confined to pres. Ar. Thesm. 882; Pl. Leg. 639; Themist. 26, 315: imp. ἐναυτίων Luc. Nec. 4: and aor. ἐναυτίασα Galen. 16, 665.

Ναυτίλλομαι *To sail*, only pres. Soph. Ant. 717; Eur. Fr. 791 (D.); Her. 1, 202. 2, 5; Himer. Or. 21, 7; subj. -ληται Aristot. H. An. 9, 37, 29; Ap. Rh. 3, 61, shortened -λεται Od. 4, 672; -λοιντο Ap. Rh. 1, 918; -λεσθαι Od. 14, 246; Pl. Rep.

551; -λόμενος Her. 2, 178. 3, 6; Luc. Hist. 62. Tox. 4. Fug. 13: and imp. ἐναυτιλλόμην Her. 1, 163, ναυτιλλ- Ap. Rh. 4, 299: and aor. ναυτίλασθαι Dio Cass. 56, 3. Not in Comedy, and only once in *classic* Attic prose.

(Νάω) *To dwell*, see ναίω.

Νάω *To flow*, only pres. Il. 21, 197. Od. 6, 292; -άῃ Epigr. in Pl. Phaedr. 264: and imp. (with ᾱ) νᾶον Callim. Dian. 224; Ap. Rh. 3, 224 (Mss. Well. Merk.). 1, 1146 (Well.), and ναῖον Od. 9, 222 (Bekk.); Ap. Rh. 1, 1146 (Ms. G. Merk.) **Mid.** or pass. νάόμεναι Nicand. Fr. 2, 58 (Goettl. Schn.), ναιόμ- (Otto Schn. 74, 58, in note); with Alex. 515. νᾶον once stood Od. 9, 222, but Wolf, Bekker, Dindorf and La Roche adopt ναῖον the reading of Aristarchus, and thus preserve ᾰ in Homer. The approved reading now (Ar. Ran. 146) is ἀείνων, once ἀεὶ νῶν. Callim. has ᾱ of imp. in *thesis*, Ap. Rh. in *arsis*—twice in Wellauer's edition, once in Merkel's.

Νεᾱνῐεύομαι *To behave like a youth, thoughtlessly, wantonly* (νεᾱνίας), Dep. Ar. Fr. 653 (D.); Pl. Gorg. 482; Isocr. 20, 17: fut. -εύσομαι Dem. 19, 242: aor. ἐνεανιευσάμην Dem. 19, 194. 21, 69: with p. νενεανιευμένος pass. Dem. 21, 18: and late aor. νεανιευθείς Plut. Mar. 29. The collat. νεᾱνισκεύομαι is rare, and only pres. -εύεται Com. Fr. (Eup.) 2, 434 &c.; -εσθαι Xen. Cyr. 1, 2, 15; -όμενος Plut. Mor. 12. νεάζω Poetic, late prose, and perhaps only pres. Aesch. Supp. 104; -άζων Soph. O. C. 374; Eur. Phoen. 713; Com. Fr. (Men.) 4, 276; late prose -άζειν Alciphr. 1, 28 &c.

Νεάω and νεόω *To make new* (νέος), both very partially used, the former in pres. and aor. act. only, νεᾶν Ar. Nub. 1117; late prose Theophr. C. P. 3, 20, 1. 7: aor. ἐνέασα, νεάσωσι 3, 20, 8: and pass. νεωμένη Hes. Op. 462; the latter in aor. act. only, νέωσον Aesch. Supp. 534 (chor.), late prose -ώσατε V. T. Jer. 4, 3: and mid. ἐνεώσατο Anth. App. Epigr. 147. νεοχμόω too is very limited in its inflections, and prosaic, but perhaps not used above once in classic Attic, Her. 4, 201; Aristot. Mund. 7; Dio. Hal. Ant. 5, 74; aor. ἐνεόχμωσα Her. 5, 19; Thuc. 1, 12; Dio. Hal. 1, 89.

Νεικέω *To chide*, Il. 1, 521, 3 pl. -κεῦσι 20, 254, Epic -κείω Il. 4, 359; Hes. Op. 332 (Lennep, Koechl.), -κείουσι Theocr. 1, 35; subj. 3 sing. -κέῃ Od. 17, 189, -κείῃσι Il. 1, 579; νεικέων Her. 9, 55, Epic, -είων Hes. Th. 208; -είειν Il. 2, 277: imp. ἐνείκεον Il. 18, 498, -κεε Her. 8, 125, νείκεον Il. 12, 268, νείκεε 2, 224, νείκειον Od. 22, 26, iter. νεικείεσκον Il. 4, 241: fut. νεικέσω Il. 10, 115: aor. ἐνείκεσα Il. 3, 59, νείκεσα 10, 158, -εσσα 7, 161. The iter. form νεικέσκομεν Od. 11, 512 (Vulg.) has been altered to νῑκάσκομεν (Wolf, Bekk. Dind. La Roche). Mostly Epic, but νεικέων Her. 9, 55; imp. ἐνείκεε 8, 125.

Νείσσομαι, see νίσσομαι.

Νείφω, see νίφω.

Νεμέθω *To feed* (νέμω), Epic, and in act. late νεμέθων Nic. Ther. 430. **Mid.** νεμέθονται, ἐν- Opp. Hal. 1, 611: **imp.** νεμέθοντο Il. 11, 635.

Νεμεσάω *To take ill, blame,* Il. 4, 413; Hes. Op. 741; Theocr. 27, 63, rare in prose Pl. Leg. 927: Aristot. Rhet. 2, 6, 19; Plut. Mor. 780; Dio. Hal. 1, 67. 10, 47, Epic -σσάω Od. 23, 213; Hes. Op. 756: **imp.** ἐνεμέσων Plut. Sull. 6, -έσσων Il. 13, 16: **fut.** -σήσω Aristot. Rhet. 2, 9, 8; Opp. Hal. 4, 582: **aor.** ἐνεμέσησα Dem. 20, 161; Plut. Mar. 39; (Luc.) Amor. 25, νεμέσ- Il. 4, 507. Od. 21, 285, Dor. -ᾱσα Pind. I. 1, 3; -σήσητε (Hippocr.) 9, 326. **Mid.** νεμεσάομαι Epic and late prose, Dio. Hal. 8, 50, -εσσ- Il. 13, 119; Od. 4, 158. 195: **fut.** -ήσομαι Il. 10, 129. 195, -σήσεαι Il. 10, 115. Od. 1, 158: **aor.** (ἐνεμεσησάμην) Epic and rare, subj. Epic νεμεσήσεται Od. 19, 121; νεμεσσήσαιτο Od. 1, 228: usu. **aor. pass.** as **mid.** ἐνεμεσήθη Plut. Cat. min. 38, Epic νεμεσσήθη Od. 1, 119, 3 pl. -έσσηθεν Il. 2, 223; subj. -εσσηθῶμεν 24, 53, -θέωμεν (La R.), -θείομεν (Bekk. 2 ed.); imper. -εσσήθητε Il. 16, 544; -εσσηθείς Il. 15, 211.—νεμέσασκον of our lexicons has escaped us.

Νεμεσίζομαι *To be wroth, dread,* Dep. Epic, and only **pres.** Il. 2, 296; Orph. Fr. 11, 4; Coluth. 358: and **imp.** νεμεσίζετο Od. 1, 263.

Νέμω *To distribute, pasture, consider,* Od. 6, 188; Pind. Ol. 10, 13; Aesch. Supp. 505; Soph. El. 598; Ar. Av. 384; Her. 4, 191; Thuc. 1, 71; Isocr. 3, 15: **imp.** ἔνεμον Eur. H. F. 462; Her. 1, 32; Thuc. 8, 70; Pl. Prot. 320, νέμον Od. 8, 470. 15, 140: **fut.** νεμῶ Soph. Aj. 513, ἀπο- Pl. Phil. 65, late νεμήσω Long. Past. 2, 23 (Seiler); (Eur.) Epist. 5, 56 (D.): **aor.** ἔνειμα Od. 14, 210; Simon. C. 142; Aesch. Eum. 401; Soph. O. C. 1396; Her. 3, 39; Antiph. 5, 10; Thuc. 6, 88; Dem. 20, 141, νεῖμα Il. 3, 274; Pind. I. 2, 22; Soph. Aj. 1201 (chor.): **p.** νενέμηκα, δια- Xen. Cyr. 4, 5, 45, ἀπο- Luc. Prom. 9: **p. p.** νενέμημαι Pl. Parm. 144. Leg. 760; νενεμήσθω Soph. 267; -ημένος Xen. An. 7, 3, 21; Pl. Tim. 53: **aor.** ἐνεμήθην Pl. Leg. 849; Dem. 59, 104. 36, 38 (Mss. A v. S ex correct. Dind.), δι-ενεμήθ- Xen. Hell. 7, 4, 27; Pl. Leg. 835; Dinarch. 1, 24, but ἐνεμέθην Dem. 36, 38 quoted (Vulg. Bekk. B. S.); Aeschin. 2, 175 (Mss. Benseler, -ήθην Mss. Ald. τμηθῆναι Wolf, Valken. B. S. Franke): **fut.** late νεμηθήσεσθαι Plut. Ag. 14; -σόμενος Galen 2, 404. 3, 709: **pres. opt.** νέμοιτο Il. 2, 780. **Mid.** νέμομαι *allot to oneself, inhabit, feed* &c. Il. 20, 8; Pind. Ol. 2, 66; Aesch. Pr. 411;

Soph. Ph. 709; Ar. Av. 310; Her. 8, 106; Thuc. 1, 10, 2 sing. -μεαι Od. 9, 449; subj. -μηαι Il. 20, 185: imp. ἐνεμομ- Il. 2, 531; Theogn. 56; Ar. Av. 330; Her. 3, 133; Thuc. 3, 68; Dem. 40, 14: fut. νεμοῦμαι Thuc. 4, 64; Dem. 21, 203, ἐκ- Soph. Aj. 369, Ion. νεμέομαι, ἀνα- Her. 1, 173, late νεμήσομαι Dio. Hal. 8, 71; Plut. Crass. 14. Ant. 55, ἐπι- Caes. 19, pass. δια-νεμήσεσθαι App. Civ. 4, 3: aor. ἐνειμάμην Lys. 16, 10; Isae. 7, 5; Pl. Leg. 771; Dem. 36, 10. 19. 48, 33; -άμενος Thuc. 8, 21, unattic ἐνεμησάμην Athen. (Clearch.) 12, 58, ὑπο- Hippocr. 1, 520 (K.): as mid. p. p. νενεμημένος Dem. 47, 35? προσ-νενέμησθε 2, 29. 13, 20, see below. **Vb.** δια-νεμητέον Xen. Oec. 7, 36. ἐπινέμομαι is dep. mid. and later pass. Aesch. Ag. 485: imp. ἐπ-ενέμετο Her. 5, 101: fut. -ήσομαι Plut. Caes. 19: aor. -ενειμάμην Thuc. 2, 54; imper. -νειμαι Pind. Ol. 9, 6: late aor. pass. -ενεμήθην as mid. Diod. Sic. 14, 54. So κατα-νέμομαι Isocr. 14, 20: aor. κατενειμάμην Thuc. 2, 17: p. κατανενέμημαι *have divided or wasted,* Isocr. 14, 7: aor. κατ-ενεμήθην *I wasted,* Plut. Pericl. 34. Artax. 23; Athen. 15, 677 (also pass. κατα-νενεμῆσθαι *have been divided,* Aristot. Pol. 7, 12, 1: κατα-νεμηθείς Pl. Leg. 848). νώμ' for νώμαε Pind. I. 2, 22 (old edit.) written νῶμ' by Damm, and called **2 p.** (pret. med.) for νένωμ', by others imp. of a form νώμω on what authority we know not, has been altered to νεῖμ' by Herm. Boeckh, Bergk, on the ground that ᾰ from the contraction of αε could not be elided.

Νέομαι *To go, come,* or as fut. *will go,* Poet. Il. 3, 257. 23, 150; Pind. P. 4, 102, contr. νεῦμαι Il. 18, 136; Epigr. 15, 11, 2 sing. νεῖαι Od. 11, 114. 12, 141, νεῖται 12, 188, and νεῖτ' 4, 633, νεύμεθα Ap. Rh. 2, 1153; Theocr. 18, 56, νέεσθε Ap. Rh. 3, 306, and νεῖσθε 3, 373; Eur. Alc. 737. νέονται Od. 20, 156; subj. νέηαι Il. 1, 32, -ηται Od. 1, 205 &c.; opt. νεοίμην Il. 14, 335, -οίμεθα Od. 3, 170, -οίατο Il. 18, 377; imper. νεῖο Leon. Tar. 70, νεέσθω Il. 23, 662, -έσθων 3, 74; inf. νεῖσθαι Od. 15, 88; Pind. P. 4, 247; Ap. Rh. 3, 431; Soph. Ant. 33, usu. νέεσθαι in Hom. Il. 2, 84. 9, 42. 14, 221. Od. 3, 60. 4, 8 &c.; Hes. Op. 554; Theocr. 16, 28; Ap. Rh. 1, 708. 2, 12. 3, 646 &c.; νεόμενος Eur. Elec. 723 (chor.), νεύμ- Anth. 9, 96: imp. νεόμην Od. 17, 148; Theocr. 25, 207, νέοντο Il. 5, 907; Pind. N. 4, 77, ἐνέοντο Ap. Rh. 4, 315: and perhaps aor. νησαμένη, ὑπο- Hippocr. 9, 192 (Lit. -νεμησαμ- Vulg. 279, 43 Foes.) νέομαι occurs once in prose, νέονται Xen. Cyr. 4, 1, 11 (Ms. Vat. Schn. Popp. Dind.) A fut. act. νησοῦντι Dor. for νήσουσι, occurs Sophr. Fr. 19 (Ahr.) if correct; and late a pres. νέει Aretae. C. Morb. Ac. 2, 118 (ed. Oxon.) A lengthened form νηέομαι occurs late in fut. νηήσεται Opp. Hal. 2, 216, unless this be from νηέω *to heap up.* See νήχομαι.

Νεόω, see νεάω.

Νευστάζω, see νυστάζω.

Νεύω *To bend, nod*, Eur. Fr. 152 (D.); Ar. Pax 883; Aristot. Mund. 7, 6; Theophr. H. P. 4, 9, 1; -οιεν Od. 18, 237; Hes. Op. 473; -ων Il. 13, 133; Soph. Ant. 441; Her. 2, 48; Thuc. 4, 100; Pl. Leg. 945: imp. ἔνευον Il. 11, 42, νεῦον Od. 9, 468: fut. νεύσω Od. 16, 283; Hippocr. 5, 196, ἀνα- Luc. Saturn. 1, 1, ἀπο- Polyb. 5, 46, Dor. νευσεῖς Theocr. 7, 109; Epic inf. νευσέμεν, κατα- Q. Sm. 2, 149: fut. mid. -εύσομαι only in comp. see below: aor. ἔνευσα Eur. Hec. 545; Ar. Thesm. 507; Pl. Phaed. 117, κατ- Il. 4, 267; Pind. N. 1, 14, νεῦσα always Hom. Il. 8, 246. 9, 223. Od. 17, 330 &c.; H. Merc. 395; Pind. I. 8, 46; so Ap. Rh. 2, 949. 3, 441, but κατ-ένευσα Il. 9, 19 &c.; νεύσῃ Eur. Alc. 978; νεύσαις Theocr. 7, 109; νεῦσον Pind. P. 1, 71; Soph. Ph. 484: p. νένευκα Antim. Fr. 39 (Dübn.); Anth. 7, 142; Arist. Probl. 7, 5, 4; -κώς Eur. I. A. 1581; Theocr. 22, 203; Luc. Somn. 13. D. Deor. 17, 2, προ- Pl. Euthyd. 274: plp. ἐνενεύκειν Polyb. 9, 5: (p. p. νένευμαι: aor. ἐνεύθην?) Vb. νευστός? The comp. ἀνανεύω has fut. mid. -νεύσομαι Pl. Rep. 350: but -εύσω Luc. Saturn. 1, 1. So κατα-νεύω, fut. mid. -νεύσομαι Il. 1, 524; Pl. Rep. 350: late -νεύσω Q. Sm. 2, 149: aor. καννεύσας for κατανεύ- Od. 15, 464; κατᾱνεύων in arsis, Od. 9, 490. ἐπινεύω also has both fut. but late -νεύσω Luc. Saturn. 1, 4 (Jacob.): -νεύσομαι Aristaen. 2, 1.

Νεφέω, νέφω *To be clouded, lower*, only in comp. συν-νεφεῖ Eur. Fr. 329 (Wagn. -νέφει 332 Dind.); Ar. Av. 1502, -νέφει (Cob. Mein. Dind. 5 ed.); prose, Aristot. Rhet. 2, 19, 24; -νεφοῦσα Eur. El. 1078, -νέφουσα (Cob. Nauck, Dind. 5 ed.); -νεφεῖν Plut. Mor. 641: fut. late -νεφήσει Sym. Job 37, 21: 2 p. συν-νένοφε Ar. Fr. 142 (D.); late prose Dio Cass. 55, 11; -νενοφώς Ar. Fr. 349; late prose Philostr. 508.

Νέω *To swim*, Pind. Fr. 203 (Bergk 2 ed., 136 Schneidw. Herm. Momms.), νεῖ Pl. Rep. 453, νέουσι Aristot. Part. An. 4, 13, 9; νέειν Her. 8, 89, νεῖν Epich. 26 (Ahr.); Ar. Fr. 654; Thuc. 7, 30; Xen. An. 5, 7, 25; Pl. Leg. 689; but uncontr. νέων Od. 5, 344; Com. Fr. (Alex.) 3, 413; Pl. Rep. 529: imp. ἔνεον Ar. Eq. 321, ἐσ- Thuc. 4, 26, Epic ἔννεον Il. 21, 11: fut. νευσούμενος Xen. An. 4, 3, 12 (Mss. Ald. Popp. Krüg. -σόμενος Hesych. Dind. Saupp.): aor. ἔνευσα, ἐξ- Eur. Cycl. 577; Thuc. 2, 90; inf. -νεῦσαι Pind. Ol. 13, 114; Eur. Hipp. 470, δια- Pl. Parm. 137: p. νένευκα, δια- Pl. Rep. 441. Vb. νευστέον Pl. Rep. 453. Hither has been referred as a "probable reading," aor. mid. νησαμένη, ὑπο- Hippocr. 9, 192 (Lit. for -νενησ- 279, 43 Foes.) νέω *to swim*, however, never takes -ήσω, -ησα, always -εύσομαι, -ευσα, and νέομαι *to go* &c. seems to yield as good a meaning.

Νέω (νάω Phot.) *To heap up*, pres. in comp. ἐπι-νέουσι Her. 4, 62; περι-νέειν 6, 80: **fut.** νήσω (Suid.): **aor.** ἔνησα Eur. Cycl. 387 (Reisk. Herm. Dind. 2 ed. Nauck 2 ed. ἔστρωσεν Pierson, Dind. 5 ed. Nauck 3 ed.), συν- Her. 1, 34; νήσας Eur. H. F. 243; Ar. Lys. 269; Thuc. 2, 52, συν- Her. 1, 86. 7, 107: **p. p.** νένημαι Xen. An. 5, 4, 27; Arr. An. 6, 26, 4, ἐπι- Ar. Eccl. 838 (Dind. 5 ed.), ξυν- Thuc. 7, 87, and νένησμαι Ar. Nub. 1203 (-νημαι Dind. would now); Luc. Peregr. 35, ἐπι- Ar. Eccl. quoted (Vulg. Dind. 4 ed. Mein.), συν- Com. Fr. (Alex.) 3, 495: **plp.** ἐνένηστο Ael. V. H. 5, 6: **aor.** late ἐνήθην, ἐπ- Herodn. 4, 2, 10, and ἐνήσθην Arr. An. 7, 3, 2. **Mid.** *heap up for oneself*, **aor.** ἐνησάμην, ἐνήσω, ἀπ- Eur. Fr. 281; νησώμεθα Polyaen. 8, 65, missed by Lexicogr.; νησάμενος, ἀπο- Eur. Ion 875, but ὑπο- Hippocr. 9, 192 (Lit.) we think should be rather referred to νέομαι *to go*. **Vb.** νητός Od. 2, 338. See νηέω.—συν-νενέαται 3 pl. Ion. for. -νηνται, Her. 2, 135. 4, 62. For ἔστησεν Eur. Cycl. 387 (Mss. Kirchh.), Reiske suggested, and Herm. Nauck 2 ed. &c. adopted ἔνησεν: so Dindorf, but in 5 ed. he and Nauck in 3 ed. read ἔστρωσεν with Pierson.

Νέω, νήθω *To spin*, νεῖ Hes. Op. 777; νήθειν Pl. Polit. 289: **imp.** iter. νήθεσκες Anth. 14, 134: **fut.** νήσω Ar. Lys. 519; Com. Fr. (Men.) 4, 298: **aor.** ἔνησα Batr. 183; Soph. Fr. 391, ἐπ- Il. 20, 128: p. p. late νένησμαι Phil. de Verm. Ser. 34, ἐπι- (Luc.) Philop. 14: **aor.** ἐνήθην Pl. Polit. 282: **mid.** Epic as **act. aor.** νήσαντο Od. 7, 198. **Vb.** νητός. Aelian H. A. 7, 12, has 3 pl. νῶσι which implies νάω, or a peculiarity of contraction in ω for ου; so νῶντα, νήθοντα Hesych.; see also νῶσαι Eup. Com. Fr. 2, 556, which Meineke has altered to νῆσαι.

Νέω, νηέομαι, *To go, come*, see νέομαι.

Νηέω *To heap up*, Epic and Ion. **imp.** νήεον Il. 23, 163; Ap. Rh. 1, 403, ἐνή- Il. 23, 169 (Bekk. 2 ed. νή- La R.): **aor.** νήησα Od. 19, 64; Ap. Rh. 3, 1208; Opp. Hal. 4, 496; part. νηήσας Il. 9, 358; Her. 1, 50 (Gaisf. Bekk. νήσ- Dind. Dietsch, Stein); νηῆσαι Od. 15, 322, περι- Her. 2, 107 (-νῆσαι Dind. Stein &c.) **Mid.** aor. ἐνηήσαντο Opp. Hal. 4, 500, νηήσ- Ap. Rh. 1, 364; Q. Sm. 5, 619; imper. -ησάσθω, Il. 9, 137; inf. -ήσασθαι 9, 279: but fut. νηήσεται as **pass.** Opp. Hal. 2, 216.

Νήθω *To spin*, see νέω.

Νηνέω *To heap up*, Epic and only **imp.** in comp. ἐπ-ενήνεον Il. 7, 428. 431, παρ-ενήν- Od. 1, 147. 16, 51 (Wolf, Spitzn. Dind. La Roche, but ἐπ-παρ-ενήεον Bekk. 2 edit.); Ap. Rh. 1, 1123; Q. Sm. 4, 135. 10, 462 (Vulg. but παρ-ενήεον Koechl. 2 edit.),

The *simple* νήνεον once Il. 23, 139, is now read νήεον (Wolf, Bekk. Spitzn. Dind. La Roche) and which Bekker *now* reads in the compds. also, ἐπ-παρ-ενήεον uniformly in Il. and Od. (2 ed.), and Koechly in Q. Sm. (2 ed.) If they are right, and perhaps they are, νήνεον would seem to be a late form, and its only unchallenged voucher Ap. Rh. 1, 1123. The middle ν seems called in for a *rest*, or represents, it may be, a *nasal*.

Νήφω, Dor. νάφ- *To be sober*, seems in good authors confined to pres. Theogn. 478; Com. Fr. (Bato) 4, 499; Hippocr. 6, 192; Pl. Leg. 918; Dor. imper. νᾶφε Epich. 119 (Ahr.); νήφειν Archil. 5, 4; Pl. Conv. 213; usu. part. νήφων Soph. O. C. 100; Ar. Lys. 1232; Her. 1, 133; Xen. Cyr. 7, 5, 20; Isocr. 8, 13; Pl. Critias 121. Rep. 396. Leg. 773 &c.: imp. ἐξ-ενήφομεν Athen. 4, 5: fut. νήψω, ἐκ- trans. Apocr. Sir. 34, 2: aor. νήψατε Or. Sib. 1, 154; νήψας Ael. (Orac.) Fr. 103, -αντες Joseph. Ant. 11, 3, 3; but trans. ἔνηψε, ἐξ- Aretae. Morb. Ac. 2, 114 (ed. Oxon.) The trans. usage has been overlooked by Lexicogr.

Νήχω *To swim*, Dor. νάχω, mostly Epic νήχει Nic. Al. 590; -χων 168; Epic inf. νηχέμεναι Od. 5, 375: imp. νῆχον Od. 5, 399. 7, 280; Hes. Sc. 317; Ap. Rh. 4, 915, Dor. ἔνᾶχε, προσ- Theocr. 21, 18: fut. νήξει Ael. H. A. 9, 25? Usu. νήχομαι Dep. mid. Orph. L. 517; Opp. Hal. 2, 153. 4, 39; -όμενος Od. 7, 276. 14, 352; Mosch. 2, 47; -εσθαι Alcae. 107 (Bergk): imp. νήχοντο (Soph.) Fr. 179; Opp. H. 5, 489, Dor. ἐνάχετο, ἐπ- (Theocr.) 23, 61: fut. νήξομαι Od. 5, 364; Musae. 208, συν- Ar. Eccl. 1104 (Vulg. -είρξομαι Bergk, Dind. 5 ed. Mein.), ἐκ- Aristot. Mund. 6, 16, προσ- Luc. Navig. 15, and late νηχήσομαι Or. Sib. 2, 209. 12, 343: aor. ἐνηξάμην Dio. Per. 141; Lycophr. 76; Anth. 9, 36; Aristid. 16, 238 (D.), προσ- Callim. Del. 47, ἀπ- Polyb. 16, 3; Arr. An. 2, 22, 5. This verb occurs also in late prose, rare, if at all, in act. νήχειν Paus. 10, 20, 4 (Vulg. νεῖν best Mss. 10, 20, 7 Schub.) Mid. freq. νήχομαι Democr. 3, 12 (Mull.); Luc. D. Mar. 12, 2; Ael. N. A. 3, 11; Plut. Mor. 1063; Arr. Ind. 6, 3: imp. ἐνηχόμην Plut. Mor. 161; Luc. D. Mar. 15, 2. V. H. 1, 30: fut. νήξομαι Galen 3, 7: aor. νήξασθαι Luc. Dom. 1; Arr. An. 2, 4, 7: with p. νενῆχθαι, ἐκ- Athen. 7, 98.—Buttmann says "νήχομαι is used in late prose as Dep. mid." This is true, but apt to mislead. The pres. and fut. mid. are in Hom., and the aor. as well as other parts are as frequent in late poetry as prose.

Νίζω *To wash*, Epich. 118 (Ahr.); νίζε Il. 11, 830, -έτω Ion 2 (Bergk); νίζων in tmesi Il. 7, 425; Eur. I. T. 1338; νίζειν Od. 19, 374; Theocr. 16, 62, κατα- Hippocr. 6, 432, and νίπτω *simple* later in act. Com. Fr. (Mon.) 543; Anth. 11, 428; Epictet.

Diss. 1, 19, 4; Plut. Thes. 10, see mid.: imp. νίζον Il. 11, 830. Od. 1, 112, ἔνιζον, ἐξαπ- 19, 387: fut. νίψω Od. 19, 376; Her. (Orac.) 6, 19; Eur. I. T. 255: aor. ἔνιψα Il. 16, 229 (Bekk. 2 ed.); Eur. Supp. 765, νίψεν Il. 10, 575. Od. 19, 505; Eur. Andr. 286 chor. (Herm. Dind. &c.); νίψω Eur. I. T. 1230; νίψειε Ap. Rh. 4, 588, ἐκ- (Pl.) Epist. 352; νίψον Od. 19, 358; νίψαι Soph. O. R. 1228; Eur. I. T. 1191: p. p. νένιμμαι Il. 24, 419, Theocr. 15, 32, ἀπο- Ar. Vesp. 1217. Eccl. 419, ἐκ- Com. Fr. (Eub.) 3, 231: aor. ἐνίφθην, κατ- Hippocr. 1, 218 (K.), ἐπ- Theophr. C. P. 5, 9, 13: 2 aor. (ἐνίφην?): but fut. νιφήσομαι late V. T. Lev. 15, 12. Mid. νίζομαι *wash oneself*, ἐν-απο- Her. 1, 138, δια- Hippocr. 8, 204. 206 (Lit.), and νίπτομαι 8, 116 (Lit.), ἀπο- Od. 18, 179: imp. νίζετο Od. 6, 224, ἀπ-ενίζ- Il. 10, 572; Com. Fr. (Drom.) 3, 541, ἐνίπτετο Eustath. Philos. 1, 8: fut. νίψομαι Ap. Rh. 4, 541, ἀπο- Ar. Av. 1163; Com. Fr. (Antiph.) 3, 21, ἐκ- Dem. 18, 140: aor. ἐνιψάμην Paus. 9, 18, 4, νίψατο Il. 16, 230; Hes. Fr. 76 (Goettl.); Eur. Bac. 767 (trimet.), ἀπ-ενίψ- Callim. Lav. P. 5; νιψάσθω Hippocr. 8, 218: νιψάμενος Il. 24, 305. Od. 12, 336; Hes. Op. 739; Her. 2, 111; Hippocr. 8, 130 (Lit.), ἀπο- Pl. Conv. 223; νίψασθαι Od. 4, 54. 17, 93: and seemingly p. p. νενίμμεθα, ἀπο- Ar. Vesp. 1217. Vb. ἄ-νιπτος Il. 6, 266, δυσέκ- Pl. Rep. 378. The *simple* verb seems not to occur in *classic* prose, but comp. ἀπο-νίζω Pl. Conv. 175 (mid. ἐναπο- Her. 1, 138. 2, 172, imp. ἐναπ-ενιζ- 2, 172): fut. νίψουσι 6, 19, but in an Orac.: fut. mid. ἐκ-νίψει Dem. 18, 140 (Dind. -ψῃ Bekk.): ἀπονιψάμενος Pl. Conv. 223; but *simple* νίπτομαι Hippocr. 8, 116; Strab. vol. 3, p. 567 (Kram.); νιψάσθω Hippocr. 8, 218; -άμενος 8, 130 (Lit.). In late prose act. νίπτω Plut. Thes. 10; N. T. John 13, 6: ἔνιψα 13, 14; νίψαι V. T. Gen. 43, 23: νένιπται Lev. 15, 11: νιφήσεται 15, 12. Mid. νίπτομαι Plut. Mor. 142; V. T. Exod. 30, 18. N. T. Mat. 15, 2: imp. ἐνίπτοντο V. T. Exod. 38, 27: νίψομαι 30, 19: ἐνιψάμην Plut. Mar. 26; V. T. Jud. 19, 21. N. T. John 9, 15.

Νῑκάω *To conquer*, -κῶ Simon. C. 152; Eur. H. F. 342; Ar. N. 894, -ᾷς Il. 2, 370; Ar. Eq. 277; Her. 1, 40, -κᾷ Il. 1, 576; Aesch. Ag. 574; Soph. Ant. 795; Pl. Rep. 588 &c., and νίκημι Theocr. 7, 40; subj. νικῶ Eur. Heracl. 253; Pl. Menex. 247; opt. νικάοιμι (-ῷμι and -οίην), -ικῷ Pl. Leg. 658, -ῴη Tyrt. 12, 4; Xen. Hell. 6, 5, 6, -ῷεν 4, 3, 1; Pl. Conv. 179, Her. 9, 69; νικῶν Her. 9, 68, dat. pl. νικῶσι Xen. Cyr. 8, 2, 27, Dor. νικώντεσσι Pind. Ol. 7, 10: imp. ἐνίκων Il. 9, 130; Eur. Phoen. 1143; Ar. Lys. 1254; Her. 6, 18; Pl. Menex. 242, νίκ- Il. 15, 284, ἐνίκα 18, 252; Soph. Ant. 274; Her. 8, 9; Thuc. 3, 8, νίκα Od. 13, 261, Dor. νίκη Pind. N. 5, 5, Iter. νικάσκομεν Od. 11, 512: fut.

νικήσω Aesch. Eum. 722; Ar. Eq. 364; Pl. Theag. 128, -ήσεις Her. 1, 71; Ar. Eq. 904, Dor. -ᾱσεῖς Theocr. 8, 10, -ήσετε Thuc. 7, 66; -ήσειν Ar. Ach. 651, Dor. -ασεῖν Theocr. 8, 7, Ep. -ησέμεν Il. 7, 192: mid. late νικήσεσθε Hierocl. 205 (Eberh.), Dor. νικαξοῦμαι, -καξῇ if correct, Theocr. 21, 32 (Vulg. Ziegl. νυσταξῇ Ameis, Fritzsche): aor. ἐνίκησα Il. 3, 439; Simon. C. 155, 7; Soph. Ant. 233; Her. 1, 74; Thuc. 2, 54, νίκ- Od. 11, 545, Dor. ἐνίκᾱσα Pind. I. 8, 65, νίκασα Simon. C. 53; νικήσας Il. 3, 404; Eur. Tr. 1209; Pl. Rep. 557, Dor. -άσαις Pind. Ol. 5, 8. P. 9, 73. N. 10, 24; νικῆσαι Il. 21, 501; Pl. Lach. 191, Dor. -ᾶσαι Pind. N. 10, 48: p. νενίκηκα Her. 1, 82; Thuc. 2, 89; Andoc. 3, 18; Isae. 6, 60: p. p. νενίκημαι Aesch. Eum. 795, Dor. -κᾱμαι Pind. N. 9, 2; -ημένος Her. 1, 40. 8, 109: aor. ἐνικήθην Xen. Hell. 4, 5, 2; -ηθῇς Ar. N. 1087, -ηθῇ Her. 9, 26, -ηθῶσι Thuc. 1, 50; -κηθεὶς Il. 23, 663; Her. 1, 130; Thuc. 2, 69. **Mid.** see **fut.** above—overlooked by Lexicogr.

Νίπτω, see νίζω.

Νίσσομαι *To go, come,* and as fut. Poet. Od. 10, 42; Hes. Op. 237 (Goettl. νείσσ- Lennep); Pind. Ol. 3, 34 (Boeckh). N. 5, 37; Eur. Cycl. 43, ἐπι- Soph. O. C. 689: imp. νίσσοντο Il. 12, 119; Hes. Sc. 469; Ap. Rh. 2, 824, ἐνίσσετο, μετ- Il. 16, 779: **fut.** νίσομαι Il. 23, 76; Pind. Ol. 3, 34 quoted (Bergk, Momms.); Eur. Phoen. 1234 (Ald. &c. νείσ- Pors. νίσσ- Dind. Herm. Kirchh. Nauck), περι-νισομ- Phocyl. 11, 1, ποτι-νίσομ- Pind. Ol. 6, 99, μετα-νίσεαι P. 5, 8, ἀπο-νίσομ- Theogn. 528; Ap. Rh. 3, 899 (Well. -νίσσ- Merk.): aor. *simple* late (ἐνῑσάμην) νίσηται Maneth. 3, 412 (A. Rigl. νίσσ- Holst. Koechly), but κατ-ενίσατο Hermesian. 2, 65 (Schneidew.) In classic authors this verb is now written almost uniformly νίσσομαι, fut. νίσομαι. In late recensions of Homer there is no trace of the forms νείσσ-, νείσ-, nor in Hesiod, except that Lennep retains νείσσονται Op. 237, for νίσσ- (Goettl. Schoem. Koechly), nor in the Tragedians except νείσεσθε Eur. Phoen. 1234 (Pors. νίσσ- Dind. Herm. Kirchh. Nauck), περινείσεται Alc. 449 (Musgr. Matth. περινίσσ- Monk, Dind. Kirchh. Prinz). In Ap. Rh. also, the forms νείσσ-, νείσ- (Vulg.) have been altered to νίσσ-, νίσ-, ἀπονισ- 3, 899 (Wellau. Merkel). The Mss. vary, but the old Grammarians and Lexicographers seem to have preferred what is now the established usage. Later however still νείσσομαι Anth. 5, 189 (even νεισομ- 6, 265), **fut.** νείσομαι Anth. 7, 566.

Νίφω, νείφ- *To snow, cover with snow,* Epic inf. νειφέμεν Il. 12, 280 (Bekk. Baüml. νῑφ- Wolf, Dind. La R.); νίφει Ar. Ach. 1141; νίφῃ Xen. Ven. 8, 1; νιφέτω Luc. Icar. 26; νίφων Pind. I. 7, 5: **imp.** ἔνῑφε Babr. 45, and ἔνειφε, ὑπ- Thuc. 4, 103 (Bekk.

Popp. Krüg. Dind. &c. -ένιφεν Vulg. Stahl): **fut.** νίψω Poet in Plut. Mor. 949, κατα- Luc. Lex. 15: **aor.** ἔνιψα, κατ- Ar. Ach. 138; Dio. Hal. Ant. 12, 8. **Pass.** νίφομαι Her. 4, 31; -όμενος Aesch. Sept. 213; Ar. Ach. 1075; Xen. Hell. 2, 4, 3, νειφόμ- Simon. C. 117 (B.); Plut. Mar. 23. Lucull. 11 &c. (Sint. Bekk.), ὑπο- Thuc. 3, 23: **aor.** ἐνίφθησαν Dio. Hal. Ant. 12, 8 (Vulg. ἐλύθησαν Kiessl.); Phot. We have never seen **2 aor.** except in lexicons: νιφέμεν, say they, is inf. aor. **2**, for νιφεῖν, Il. 12, 280. We are sorry we cannot give them the benefit of a doubt. Bekker writes νείφῃ Ar. Vesp. 773, Epic νίφῃσι Hes. Cert. p. 324, 29.

Νοέω *To think, mark,* Il. 22, 235; Her. 3, 81, νοῶ Simon. C. 85, 8; Pind. N. 10, 86; Soph. Ph. 1176; Ar. Pax 661; Pl. Crat. 407; νοοίης Ar. N. 1381, νοοῖ Pl. Euthyd. 287; νοεῦντες Hes. Op. 261; Her. 8, 3, reg. in Attic: **imp.** νόει Od. 6, 67, ἐνόει H. Hym. 3, 213, Hippocr. 1, 537 (Erm.); Pl. Rep. 524, -όεε Her. 8, 103: **fut.** -ήσω Il. 9, 104; Pl. Rep. 524: **aor.** ἐνόησα Il. 17, 486; Xen. An. 3, 4, 44, νόησ- Il. 8, 91; Hes. Th. 838; νοῆσαι Solon 16; Pind. Ol. 13, 48; Pl. Conv. 182; νοήσας Eur. Phoen. 1407: **p.** -ηκα Com. Fr. (Stratt.) 2, 779; Pl. Phaedr. 229: **p. p.** -ημαι (Pl.) Epist. 343: **aor.** -ήθην Pl. Leg. 692; Luc. Alex. 4: **fut.** νοηθήσομαι Sext. Emp. 97, 12. 372, 20; Galen 4, 348. 10, 155: **mid.** νοούμενος Soph. O. R. 1487: **aor.** νοήσατο Il. 10, 501, προυνοησάμην Eur. Hipp. 399. 685; Ar. Eq. 421; Antiph. 5, 43. **Vb.** νοητός Pl. Tim. 48, -έον Epin. 991.

In Ionic the **aor. perf.** and **plp.** contracting οη into ω, become ἔνωσα, ἐν-νώσας Her. 1, 86: νώσατο Ap. Rh. 4, 1409; νωσάμενος Theogn. 1298; Callim. Fr. 345; Theocr. 25, 263; νώσασθαι late Dor. prose Stob. 85, 19: **p.** νένωκα, ἐν- Her. 3, 6: **p. p.** νένωται as **act.** *he purposed,* Soph. Fr. 191; νενωμένος Anacr. 10 (Bergk); Her. 9, 53: **plp.** ἐνένωτο as **act.** Her. 1, 77 (Mss. Gaisf. Lhardy, Stein &c.), ἐν-νένωτο (Bekk. Dind.), δι-ενένωντο 7, 206, ἐν-νένωντο ibid. (Bekk. Dind.), ἐνένων- (Lhardy, Stein) on the ground that Her. usually augments plp. and uses νοέεσθαι, ἐννοέειν, never ἐννοέεσθαι: but **aor.** uncontr. ἐνοήθην, ἐπ- 3, 122. 6, 115 (Vulg. Gaisf. Bekk. Lhardy, Krüg. Stein), but -ώθην (Dind. Abicht.)

νοοῦμαι as **act.** Soph. O. R. 1487, is usually Dep. **pass.** in its compounds, ἀπο-, δια-, ἐν-, ἐπι-, μετα-, προ-: ἀπονοοῦμαι Plut. Sol. 31: **p.** -νενοημένος Isocr. 8, 93; Dem. 19, 69. 43, 41: **aor.** -ενοήθην perhaps always, Xen. Hell. 6, 4, 23; Plut. Cat. min. 63; Diod. Sic. 17, 84, but συν-απονοήσασθαι Diod. Sic. 15, 40. διανοοῦμαι Her. 6, 86; Antiph. 4, γ, 4; Pl. Phil. 43: **imp.** δι-ενοεῖτο

Thuc. 1, 93: fut. -νοήσομαι rare Pl. Leg. 793: -νοηθήσομαι 837. 890: p. -νενόημαι Hippocr. 6, 466; Thuc. 4, 72; Xen. Mem. 3, 6, 2, pass. Hippocr. 9, 270 (Lit.): plp. -ενενοήμην Pl. Euthyd. 295: aor. -ενοήθην Antiph. 2, γ, 3; Thuc. 4, 13; Pl. Phaed. 99; Isocr. 21, 11; Dem. 35, 19 &c.; -ηθῆναι Her. 2, 126; διανοηθείς Antiph. 4, δ, 4; Isae. 1, 11; Aeschin. 3, 91, but διανοηθέν pass. Pl. Leg. 654: late aor. mid. διενοήσατο Diod. Sic. 20, 3. ἐννοοῦμαι Eur. Med. 900; -οῶνται Xen. An. 3, 1, 41: aor. ἐνενοήθης (as act.) Apoll. Tyan. Epist. 100; ἐννοήθητι Plut. Mor. 114; ἐννοηθείς Pl. Tim. 61. Leg. 859; and in some editions of Eur. Med. 882, but pass. Luc. Salt. 36: fut. -ηθήσεται late, Aquil. Gen. 11, 6. ἐπινοοῦμαι, (-ενοούμην v. r. Isocr. Epist. 3, 2): aor. mid. late ἐπενοήσατο (Luc.) Astr. 17 (-ωσ- Dind.); Diod. Sic. 17, 65. Fr. (Lib. 30, 20 Dind.): *classic* aor. pass. ἐπενοήθην as mid. Her. 3, 122. 6, 115; (Luc.) Amor. 31 (Jacob. Dind.), but pass. Hippocr. 4, 184 (Lit.); Luc. D. Conc. 13; Diod. Sic. 11, 42: fut. -ηθήσεται pass. Sext. Emp. 434, 6 (B.): with p. ἐπινενόηται pass. Luc. Anach. 21. Alex. 21; Diod. Sic. 17, 53. κατανοέω, act. complete, Her. Thuc. Plato: mid. we have not seen: pass. rare -ούμενος Pl. Tim. 90: aor. -ηθῆναι pass. Aristot. Mirab. Ausc. 86. μετανοέω, mid. -οῦμαι? : but aor. pass. μετανοηθείς as act. late Diod. Sic. 18, 72. προνοοῦμαι Thuc. 6, 9; Xen. An. 7, 7, 33: fut. -νοήσομαι (Dem.) Proem. 43; Dio. Hal. 8, 90; Aristid. 37 (467); Pseud.-Callisth. 1, 18: aor. προυνοησάμην Eur. Hipp. 399. 685; Ar. Eq. 421; rare in classic prose Antiph. 5, 43; Paus. 4, 20; Diod. Sic. Fr. Lib. 40, 1 (Bekk.); Diog. Laert. 6, 2, 3: more frequent aor. pass. -ήθην as mid. Hippocr. 6, 612; Lys. 3, 29. 37. 42; Isocr. 12, 80; Isae. 2, 46; Pl. Crat. 395; Dem. 23, 135; Polyb. 4, 61, 4, but pass. late Galen 2, 632. 6, 179; Sext. Emp. 469, 3: p. προνενοῆσθαι as mid. Polyb. 6, 48; Diod. Sic. 12, 69, and πεπρονοῆσθαι 17, 23 (Bekk. Dind.) These compounds have been badly handled by our Lexicogr.

Νομίζω *To think,* Aesch. Pers. 169; Soph. O. R. 39; Eur. Med. 493; Ar. Vesp. 1067; Her. 2, 92; Antiph. 5, 36; Thuc. 1, 77; Isocr. 5, 139: imp. ἐνόμιζον Her. 1, 8; Thuc. 1, 93; Lys. 8, 5: fut. Attic νομιῶ Ar. Av. 571; Thuc. 5, 111; Xen. Cyr. 1, 6, 11; Isocr. 14, 2, Ion. 1 pl. νομιέομεν Her. 2, 17 (Dind. -ιεῦμεν Abicht, -ιοῦμεν Bekk. Stein), late -ίσω Procop. Epist. 12 (Herch.); App. Pun. 8, 64 (Schweigh. -ίζων Bekk.); Long. 1, 1: aor. ἐνόμῐσα Eur. Bac. 431; Ar. Lys. 464; Her. 1, 34; Antiph. 2, α, 8; Thuc. 5, 1; Pl. Prot. 322, νόμισα Pind. I. 5 (4), 2; -ισον Soph. Fr. 441: p. νενόμικα Com. Fr. (Axion.) 3, 534; Her. 1, 173; Lycurg. 75: p. p. νενόμισμαι Eur. Med. 170; Her. 1, 138; Antiph. 4, α, 1; Thuc. 7, 86; Pl. Gorg. 520, Ion. 3 pl. νενομίδαται Dio Cass. 51, 23; Dor. inf. νενομίχθαι Stob. (Sthenid.) 48, 63: plp. νενόμιστο Ar. Nub. 962 (anapaest.): aor. ἐνομίσθην Her. 1, 140; Thuc. 4, 24; Pl. Conv. 182; -θείς Eur. Bac. 71; Soph. Fr. 107 (D.): fut. νομισθήσομαι Pl. Soph. 240; Dem. 54, 15: and as pass. fut. mid. νομιοῦμαι Hippocr. 6, 352 (Lit.) **Vb.** νομιστέον Pl. Soph. 230.

Νοσφίζω *To separate, deprive, kill,* act. Poet. but not *early* Epic, Anth. 5, 293; Dion. Per. 25, ἀπο- Soph. O. R. 480: fut. -ιῶ Soph. Ph. 1427; Eur. Alc. 43: aor. ἐνόσφισα Pind. N. 6, 62; Aesch. Sept. 982; Eur. Rhes. 56; late Epic Ap. Rh. 2, 793; ἀπο-νοσφίσσειεν Hom. H. 5, 158; νοσφίσας Soph. Ph. 684; Eur. Hel. 641: p. p. -ισμένος: aor. -ίσθην see foll. **Mid.** νοσφίζομαι *separate for oneself, appropriate, deprive,* Eur. Supp. 153, *separate oneself, abandon,* Od. 23, 98; Soph. O. R. 693, *turn away, depart,* Il. 2, 81: fut. Epic -ίσσομαι Ap. Rh. 4, 1108: aor. usu. Epic ἐνοσφισάμην N. T. Act. 5, 2, νοσφ- Od. 11, 425. 19, 339, -ισσ- 4, 263; -ίσασθαι Xen. Cyr. 4, 2, 42; -ισάμενος Plut. Demosth. 4: Cat. min. 45: in same sense trans. and intrans. aor. pass. ἐνοσφίσθην Archil. 96 (Bergk); Aesch. Ch. 491; -ισθείς Od. 11, 73; H. Cer. 92; Theogn. 94: and p. νενοσφισμένος trans. Plut. Mor. 809. Lucull. 37; Strab. 2, 3, 5.

Νύσσω *To push, thrust,* Attic -ττω Ar. Plut. 784; Plut. Mor. 464; νύσσων Il. 13, 147. 16, 704; Hes. Sc. 62; Plut. Aem. Paul. 20, -ττων Plut. Mor. 84; Luc. Merc. Cond. 21: imp. ἔνυττον Luc. Pseudol. 27: fut. νύξουσι Or. Sib. 8, 296, -εις Theocr. 21, 50 (Vulg.); νεύξοις Ael. N. An. 8, 26 (Schneid. see foll.): now aor. ἔνυξας Theocr. 21, 50 quoted; Luc. Ep. Sat. 38; Themist. 2, 33, νύξε Il. 16, 346; νύξῃς Anth. (Plan.) 248; νεύξειας Ael. N. An. 8, 26 quoted (Herch.); νύξας Od. 14, 485; Ar. Nub. 321; Theocr. 21, 51; Luc. Herm. 71; Plut. Mor. 79. Cleom. 37; D. Laert. 6, 53: (p.): p. p. νενυγμένος Galen 10, 221. 13, 420; Oribas. 10, 34: 1 aor. ἐνύχθην, νυχθῆναι Diog. L. 2, 10, 5; Galen 10, 390; -χθείς Diog. L. 2, 10, 5: 2 aor. ἐνύγην Christ. Pat. 1083, κατ- Pseud.-Callisth. 1, 14; νυγῇ Galen 10, 391; νυγείς Plut. Mor. 901. **Act.** alone classic, but not in prose.

Νυστάζω *To sleep, feel drowsy,* Ar. Av. 638; Hippocr. 5, 390 (Lit.); Pl. Ion 532: fut. late (νυστάσω) -άξω V. T. Esai. 5, 27: aor. ἐνύστασα Anth. 12, 135; νύστασον, κατα- Com. Fr. (Alex.) 3, 515; νυστάσαι Com. Fr. (Dion.) 3, 549, and ἐνύσταξα Theophr. Char. 7 (Foss), ἐπι- Plut. Brut. 36; Luc. Bis Acc. 2. νευστάζω Epic and only part. -άζων Il. 20, 162. Od. 18, 154; Theocr. 25, 260; Bion 5, 3; Opp. Cyn. 2, 467.

Νωμάω *To distribute, direct, wield*, a collat. form of νέμω, is Poet. Od. 21, 400; Aesch. Ag. 781; Soph. Fr. 678; imper. νώμα Pind. P. 1, 86; νωμῶν Pind. P. 8, 47; Her. 4, 128; Themist 14, 181: **imp.** ἐνώμα Il. 5, 594; Orph. Arg. 817, νώμα Il. 15, 677, iter. νώμασκε Mosch. 4, 108: **fut.** νωμήσω Ap. Rh. 4, 1006, ἀμφι- Aesch. Fr. 305 (D.), Dor. 3 pl. νωμάσοισι Pind. P. 4, 18: **aor.** ἐνώμησα, Hom. always νώμ- Il. 1, 471. 9, 176. Od. 21, 272; Dor. pt. νωμάσας Pind. I. 1, 15. **Mid.** νωμᾶται intrans. *moves*, Bacchyl. 47 (B.): **aor.** trans. -ήσασθαι Q. Sm. 3, 439, missed by Lexicogr. This verb was not in use with Attic prose writers; Plato merely mentions it as synonymous with σκοπέω: τὸ νωμᾶν καὶ τὸ σκοπεῖν ταὐτόν Crat. 411.

Νωτίζω *To turn the back*, in Tragedy only, and confined to aor. ἐνώτισε Eur. Phoen. 654 (chor.), -ισαν Andr. 1141 (trimet.), ἀπ- Soph. Fr. 638; νωτίσαι Aesch. Ag. 286 (trimet.); Soph. O. R. 192 (chor.): but **imp.** in comp. ἀπ-ενώτιζον Eur. Bac. 763.

Ξ.

Ξενόομαι **Mid.** *To receive kindly, entertain*, Aesch. Supp. 927, Ion. ξειν- Ap. Rh. 1, 849: **fut.** ξενώσομαι late as mid. Lycophr. 92, as pass. see below. **Pass.** ξενόομαι Eur. Hip. 1085; Xen. An. 7, 8, 6. 8: with **fut. mid.** -ώσομαι as pass. Soph. Ph. 303: **p. p.** ἐξενωμένος Soph. Tr. 65; Eur. Ion 820; Lys. 6, 48; Xen. Hel. 4, 1, 34: **aor.** ἐξενώθην Aesch. Ch. 702; Eur. Alc. 68; Xen. Hel. 4, 1, 29; Pl. Leg. 953, Ion. ἐξειν- Her. 6, 21; ξενωθείς Pind. P. 4, 299. **Act.** ξενόω occurs late, ἐξένωσας Heliod. 6, 7 (Bekk.), ἐξείνωσαν, ἀπ- Opp. Hal. 1, 272.

Ξέω *To scrape, smooth*, Pl. Theag. 124: **imp.** ἔξεον Od. 23, 199: **fut.** ξέσω (Hesych.): **aor.** ἔξεσα Il. 5, 81 (Vulg. La R. ξέσ- Bekk. 2 ed.); Sophr. 73 (Ahr.); Anth. (Plan.) 4, 160; Ap. Rh. 1, 1119; Hippocr. 7, 276, περι- Theocr. 22, 50, ἐπι- Hippocr. 7, 276 (Lit.), ξέσα Il. 5, 81 quoted (Bekk. 2 ed.); Anth. (Simon.?) Plan. 60, Epic ξέσσα Od. 5, 245. 21, 44: **p.** (ἔξηκα Cram. An. vol. 4, 196): **p. p.** ἔξεσμαι Ar. Fr. 684 (D.), ἀπ- Hippocr. 7, 430 (Lit.), κατ- Aristot. Mirab. Ausc. 100, συν- Dio. Hal. Comp. Verb. 22: **aor.** late ξεσθῆναι Geop. 10, 65, κατα- Plut. Mor. 953. **Vb.** ξεστός Od. 18, 33.

Ξηραίνω *To dry*, Hippocr. 6, 508; Xen. An. 2, 3, 15: **fut.** ξηρᾰνῶ Eur. Cycl. 575; Aene. Tact. 31, 10; Geop. 3, 10: **aor.** ἐξήρᾱνα Hippocr. 8, 59; ξηράνῃ, ἀγ- Il. 21, 347; ξηρᾶναι Hippocr.

5, 104. 8, 244, ἀπο- Her. 2, 99 (Mss. Bekk. Gaisf. Dind. Dietsch, -ῆναι Bred. Abicht, Stein); Thuc. 7, 12; ξηράνας 1, 109, Ion. ἐξήρηνα, ἀν- Her. 7, 109; ξηρῆναι Hippocr. 5, 476: p. p. ἐξήρασμαι Com. Fr. (Antiph.) 3, 125; Hippocr. 6, 322. 588 (Lit.), ἀπ- Her. 1, 186. 7, 109, and ἐξήραμμαι Theophr. C. P. 5, 14, 6, ἀπ- Com. Fr. (Alex.) 3, 440, and late, if correct, -αμαι, -αμένος, προ- Dioscor. 5, 86: **aor.** ἐξηράνθην Il. 21, 348; Hippocr. 5, 228; Pl. Phil. 31: **fut.** late ξηρανθήσομαι Galen 1, 516; Geop. 3, 5. 10, 67; V. T. Job 18, 16: and **fut. mid.** as **pass.** ξηρανοῦμαι Hippocr. 6, 236 (Lit.); Aristot. Meteor. 2, 3, 5 (v. r. -ανθήσεται). 2, 3, 6. **Vb.** ξηραντέον Aristot. Probl. 37, 3, 7. The form ἐξήραμαι, προαπεξ- Hippocr. 2, 188 (Kühn), and later, is perhaps a mistake. It has *now*, we observe, been altered by Littré in Hippocr. vol. 6, 172, to -εξήρασμαι from Mss. Ε Η Θ (1849), ἀν-εξήρασμ- 6, 586. The Attics appear to have written the aorist uniformly with α, -ᾱνα, the Ionians with η and α, -ρηνα, -ρᾱνα. ἀγξηράνῃ Il. 21, 347, by elision and assimilation for ἀνα-ξηρ-.

Ξῠλίζομαι *To gather wood*, Dep. and only **pres.** part. *classic* ξυλιζόμενος Xen. An. 2, 4, 11; Plut. Artax. 25; -ίζεσθαι 25: **aor.** -ισάμενος Alciphr. 1, 1.

Ξῠράω *To shear, clip*, late, Plut. Apophth. 180; (Luc. Cynic. 14), ξῠρέω Soph. Aj. 786; Her. 2, 65; Pl. Rep. 341, rare ξύρω: **imp.** ἔξυρον Luc. Pseudol. 27: **fut.** -ήσω V. T. Esai. 7, 20: **aor.** ἐξύρησα Her. 5, 35; Hippocr. 6, 212; Diod. Sic. 1, 83; ἔξῡρα, ξύρας Hippocr. 7, 118 (Lit.); and late Tzetz. Hist. 9, 231: **p. p.** ἐξύρημαι Ar. Thesm. 191; Her. 2, 36; Luc. Mer. C. 1, ὑπ- Archil. 58: **fut.** late ξυρηθήσομαι V. T. Lev. 13, 33. **Mid.** ξυράομαι late? Diod. Sic. 1, 84; Diog. Laert. 7, 166, classic -έομαι, -έονται Her. 2, 36. 66 (Abicht, -εῦνται Dind. so Bekk. 36, -ῶνται in both, Stein); -ούμενος Com. Fr. (Alex.) 3, 508, and ξύρομαι late Plut. Mor. 352; Luc. Peregr. 17: **fut.** late ξυρήσομαι V. T. Num. 6, 9; Joseph. Jud. B. 2, 15, 1: **aor.** late ἐξυρησάμην Luc. D. Mer. 12, 5; Pseud.-Callisth. 1, 3; V. T. Jud. 16, 22, ἐξῡράμην Plut. Mor. 336; (Luc.) D. Syr. 55.

Ξύω *To polish*, Sophron Fr. 94; Hippocr. 7, 180; Aristot. Probl. 31, 5: **imp.** ξῦον Od. 22, 456: **aor.** ἔξῡσα Il. 14, 179; Hippocr. 7, 38 (Lit.); ξύσας, ἀπο- Il. 9, 446; Anth. 15, 37, but ῠ in ἐγξῦσαι Eur. Fr. 300 (Nauck, Dind. 5 ed. -ξύσῃ Vulg. Matth.), ἀνα- Antiph. 5, 45: **p. p.** ἔξυσμαι Galen. 13, 544, περι- Hippocr. 8, 372 (Lit.), δι- Aristot. Physiog. 3, 10, seemingly as **mid.** ἀπ- Alciphr. 3, 40: **aor.** ἐξύσθην Aristot. H. A. 6, 16; Theophr. C. P. 5, 6, 13, ἐπι- Pl. Rep. 405. **Mid.** ξύομαι *to smooth, shave oneself*, or *for*—Aristot. H. A. 6, 28: **imp.** ἐξυόμην Luc. Lex. 5: **aor.**

ἐξυσάμην Xen. Cyr. 6, 2, 32: and in sense p. p. ἔξυσμαι, ἀπ- Alciphr. 3, 40. Vb. ξυστός Her. 2, 71. The prevalence of ῡ in all tenses has induced some to suggest ἐγξέσῃ for -ύσῃ Eur. Fr. quoted (Wagn. 26); δι-έξῦσεν Nonn. Dion. 39, 321 (Vulg.) has also been altered to διέξεσεν (Graefe, Koechly).

O.

'Οαρίζω *To converse as lovers*, Epic, Hom. H. 23, 3; in prose, perhaps only Luc. -ίζειν Paras. 43, Epic -ιζέμεναι Il. 22, 127, but -ίζειν Hym. Merc. 170: imp. ὀάριζον Il. 6, 516. 22, 128; Q. Sm. 2, 113, iter. contr. ὠρίζεσκον Hom. H. Merc. 58, very rare in iter. forms in -σκον.

'Ογκόω *To swell*, Eur. Heracl. 195; late prose Plut. Mor. 616: **fut.** -ώσω Alex. Aetol. in Parthen. Erot. 14, 33: **aor.** ὤγκωσα Eur. Andr. 320; Ar. Vesp. 1024; late prose Longin. 28, 2: **p. p.** ὤγκωμαι Eur. Elec. 381. Fr. 822 (Dind.); Xen. Mem. 1, 2, 25: **plp.** ὤγκωτο, ἐξ- Her. 6, 125 (Vulg. Bekk. Dind. Stein), -όγκ- Ms. S. Gaisf.): **aor.** ὠγκώθην Soph. Fr. 679; Eur. Ion 388. **Mid.** intrans. **fut.** ὀγκώσομαι Ar. Ran. 703, ἐξ- Eur. Hipp. 938, called by some **pass.**: **aor.** ὠγκωσάμην Athen. 9, 403, ἐξ- 7, 290. A rare form ἐξογκέω Hippocr. 4, 248 (Lit.)

'Οδ- and **ἀδ-άξω, -ξάω, -ξέω** *To smart from a bite*, ἀδαξῶντα Hippocr. 8, 58 (Lit.): **imp.** ὤδαξον Xen. Conv. 4, 28 (Vulg. L. Dind. Saupp.), -ξουν (Born.): **fut. mid.** ὀδαξήσομαι as **pass.** Hippocr. 8, 330: **p. p.** ὤδαγμαι (Soph.) Fr. 708: **pres. pass.** ὀδαξᾶται Hippocr. 8, 214 (Lit.); Ael. H. A. 7, 35. **Mid.** ὀδάξομαι as **act.** Hippocr. 2, 833. 8, 338: **aor.** ὠδαξάμην Anth. 9, 86. ὀδάξομαι is used passively Hippocr. 1, 449 (Kühn, 2, 761 Erm. but act. Lit. 8, 568, retaining μυκτῆρας), and the form ἀδάξομαι 2, 842 (K. see 8, 352 Lit.); also ὀδαξάομαι Ael. H. A. 7, 35, and -έομαι, -ούμενος Dioscor. 2, 150 (Sprengel): **fut.** ὀδαξήσομαι Hippocr. 8, 830 quoted. The Mss. differ widely in the forms of this verb, see Born. Xen. Conv. 4, 28. **p. p.** ὤδαγμαι pointing to a form (ὀδάζω) L. and W. Dindorf hold spurious.

'Οδάω *To put on the way, export, sell* (ὁδός), Poet. and only **aor. act.** ὅδησον Eur. Cycl. 133; ὁδῆσαι 98: and **pass.** ὁδηθείης 12.

'Οδμάω, ὀσμ- *To smell*, **act.** late Galen 4, 487. **Mid.** ὀδμάομαι Hippocr. 8, 282 (Lit. 2, 722 Erm.), ὀσμ- Soph. Fr. 186 (D.); Heraclitus Ap. Plut. Mor. 943; Aristot. H. An. 5, 5, 12. de anima 2, 9, 9; Theophr. Sens. 21: **imp.** ὠσμᾶτο Hierocl. 126: **fut.** (-ήσεται v. r. Nic. Ther. 47): **aor.** ὀδμήσαιτο Nic. Ther. 47 (v. r. -σηται); ὀδμησάμενος Anth. 11, 240: and as **mid. aor. pass.** ὀδμηθῇ Hippocr. 7, 292 (Lit. 2, 386 Erm.) missed by Lexicogr.

Ὁδοποιέω, see foll.

Ὁδοιπορέω *To be a wayfarer*, Soph. El. 1099; Xen. An. 5, 1, 14, varies in augm.: **imp.** ὡδοιπόρεις Soph. Aj. 1230, -ρουν Aristid. 27, 356, -ρεον Her. 4, 110. 116 (ὁδοιπ- Stein): **fut.** -ήσω Hippocr. 4, 250 (Lit.): **aor.** ὡδοιπόρησε Hippocr. 6, 276; ὁδοιπορήσῃ Soph. O. C. 849: **p.** ὁδοιπεπόρηκα Com. Fr. (Philip.) 4, 471: but **plp.** ὡδοιπορήκεσαν, δι- Her. 8, 129 (Wess. Bekk. Krüg. Dind. δι-οδοιπ- Schaef. Gaisf. Stein): **p. p.** ὡδοιπόρηται Luc. Herm. 2. So ὁδοποιέω *make a way*, **imp.** ὡδοποίουν Xen. An. 4, 8, 8; Dem. 55, 11: **fut.** -ήσω &c.: **p.** with double augm. ὡδοπεποίηκα: **plp.** ὡδοπεποιήκειν Arr. An. 1, 26, 1 (Ellendt, Krüg.): **p. p.** ὡδοπεποιημένη Xen. An. 5, 3, 1 (Popp. Krüg. Kühn.); Arr. An. 3, 13, 2, and ὡδοποι- Xen. An. quoted (Dind. Saupp.). Hell. 5, 4, 39; App. B. Hann. 52, προωδοποι- Luc. Lex. 22 (Jacob. Bekk.); Aristot. Part. An. 2, 4, 4 (B.), but προωδοπεποι- Polit. 2, 9, 11 (B.); Luc. quoted (Dind.)

Ὀδῠνάω *To pain*, Eur. Hipp. 247; Ar. Lys. 164; Aristot. Probl. 5, 40, 5 (B.); Plut. Mor. 603: **fut.** ὀδυνήσω Ar. Eccl. 928; Joseph. Ant. 6, 7, 4 (Dor. -άσω Soph. Fr. 146 corrupt?): **aor.** ὠδύνησα Hippocr. 9, 34 (Lit.); ὀδυνήσας Galen 1, 359; -ῆσαι 10, 853. **Pass.** ὀδυνάομαι *suffer pain*, Soph. El. 804; Ar. Plut. 722; Hippocr. 7, 70 (Lit.); Pl. Phaedr. 251. Rep. 515, -έομαι Aretae. C. et S. Diut. Morb. 2, 63 (ed. Oxon.); **pt.** κὠδυνωμένη, καὶ ὀδυν- Soph. El. 804: **imp.** ὠδυνᾶτο Hippocr. 5, 206; Aeschin. 1, 58: with **fut. mid.** ὀδυνήσομαι Com. Fr. (Men.) 4, 164; Stob. (Teles.) 5, 67; Synes. Epist. 105; Galen 1, 247. 10, 387: and late **fut. p.** ὀδυνηθήσομαι Galen 1, 248. 10, 851; V. T. Zach. 9, 5: **aor.** ὠδυνήθην Ar. Ach. 3. Ran. 650; Hippocr. 5, 150 (Lit.): **fut.** -ηθήσομαι quoted. **Act.**, we think, not in classic prose, **pass.** rarely. Our Lexicogr. seem to have missed the **fut. mid.**

Ὀδύρομαι *To lament*, in classic Greek **Dep. mid.** Il. 22, 424; Solon 13, 35; Soph. Aj. 383, -ύρει Eur. Supp. 770, -ύρεαι Od. 8, 577; rare in Comedy, Com. Fr. (Apoll.) 4, 452; Andoc. 1, 48; Pl. Rep. 329; Xen. Cyr. 7, 3, 14; Isocr. 4, 169; Epic subj. ὀδύρεται Od. 4, 740; imper. ὀδύρεο Il. 24, 549: **imp.** ὠδύροντο Il. 24, 166; Dem. 53, 7. 58, 2; Dio. Hal. 8, 59; Nic. Damasc. Fr. 8 (L. Dind.), ὀδύρ- Il. 22, 79, iter. ὀδυρέσκετο Her. 3, 119: **fut.** ὀδυροῦμαι Isocr. 18, 35 (Cor. B. Saupp. Bens.); Dem. 21, 186. 38, 19; Luc. D. Mort. 23, 2:

aor. ὠδῡράμην Isocr. 12, 8; Dion. Hal. Ant. 18, 15 (Kiessl.); Ap. Rh. 1, 1066; Theocr. 1, 75, ἀν- Xen. Cyr. 5, 1, 6. 7, 3, 9; ὀδῡράμενος Il. 24, 48; Isocr. 15, 65; -ασθαι Dem. 21, 95: and late ὠδύρθην pass. κατ-οδυρθείς Plut. Mor. 117. Vb. ὀδυρτός Ar. Ach. 1226, -έον late. Collat. tragic form δύρομαι Soph. O. R. 1218 (chor.); Eur. Hec. 740 (trimet.); δυρομένα Med. 159 chor. (Dind. Kirchh. Paley &c.); δύρεσθε Aesch. Pr. 271 (trimet.); δυρόμενοι Pers. 582 (chor.) For ταῦτ' ὀδύρομαι Eur. Andr. 397 (Vulg. Herm. Dind. &c.) Porson suggested ταῦτα δύρομαι, on the ground that "the third and fourth foot of a (tragic) senarius never form one word." Paley retains the common reading ταῦτ' ὀδύρ-, and adds "Porson is not followed by the more recent critics." But he is followed by Hartung, Nauck in his 1, 2, and 3, and by Kirchhoff in his 2 edit. Paley then refers us to a note on Bacch. 1123, where he adduces five or six "similar instances of want of caesura," not one of which meets Porson's objection—"the *third* and *fourth* foot in one word." We don't say Porson is right, we say he is not refuted. "The *fourth* and *fifth* foot formed by one word" is assuredly no rarity in Eur.

(Ὀδύσσομαι) *To be angry,* Poet. p. p. ὀδώδυσμαι Od. 5, 423: aor. ὠδύσθην Hesych.: so aor. mid. ὠδύσαο Od. 1, 62, -σατο Il. 18, 292. Od. 5, 340, -σαντο Soph. Fr. 408, Epic -σσατο Hes. Th. 617, ὀδύσαντο Il. 6, 138; -σσάμενος 8, 37; but trans. ὠδύσατο *he enraged,* Hom. Epigr. 6, 8.

Ὄζω *To smell,* Aesch. Ag. 1310; Com. Fr. (Eup.) 2, 280; Ar. Eccl. 524; rare in prose Hippocr. 5, 680. 7, 280; Xen. Conv. 2, 3. 4. Ven. 5, 1. 7; Aristot. Probl. 4, 12, 1. 12, 3, 4. 12, 5; ὄζειν Her. 3, 23; Xen. Conv. 2, 4; Pl. Hipp. maj. 299; (Lys.) 6, 1, Dor. and Aeol. ὄσδω Theocr. 1, 149, 3 pl. ὄσδοντι 5, 52: imp. ὦζε Com. Fr. (Cratet.) 2, 234, Dor. ὦσδε Theocr. 7, 143: fut. ὀζήσω Ar. Vesp. 1059, Ion. ὀζέσω Hippocr. 8, 424. 488; Geop. 12, 29: aor. ὤζησα Ar. Fr. 538 (D.), Ion. ὤζεσα Hippocr. 1, 468 (K.). 8, 488 (Lit.): p. ὤζηκα Phot.: 2 p. as pres. ὄδωδα Anth. 7, 30; late prose, Plut. Mor. 916; Artemid. Onir. 1, 67; Aristaen. 1, 12; ὀδωδώς Alciphr. 3, 59, ὠδωδ- metri grat. Athen. (Epigr.) 2, 9: plp. ὀδώδειν Od. 9, 210; App. Hisp. 97 (Bekk.), and ὠδώδειν Anth. 13, 29; late prose Plut. Alex. 20. Dem. et Ant. 3. Mid. ὀζόμενος as ὄζων, Hippocr. 2, 117 (K.), ὀσδόμ- Xenophanes Fr. 1, 6 (Bergk, ὀζόμ- Herm. Renner).

Ὄθομαι *To care about,* Epic and only pres. Il. 1, 181, -εται 15, 107. 182; Ap. Rh. 3, 94: unless ὄθετ' be imp. Il. 5, 403; Callim. Fr. 316.

Οἰᾱκίζω *To steer, manage* (οἴαξ), only part. and only in Ion. and late prose, Ion. οἰηκ- Her. 1, 171, but οἰακ- Heraclit. 28 Byw.); Aristot. Eth. Nic. 10, 1; Polyb. 3, 43. 8, 8. **Pass.** οἰᾱκίζεσθαι Strab. 17, 3, 7; -ιζόμενος Diod. Sic. 18, 59.

Οἰᾱκοστροφέω *To turn the helm, govern*, pres. late: imp. unaugm. οἰᾱκοστρόφουν Aesch. Pers. 767 (Vulg. Herm.), but ᾠακοστ- (Pors. Dind.)

Οἴγνῡμι *To open*, Poet. Anth. 9, 356, ὑπ- Ar. Eccl. 15, δι- 852, ἀν- Dem. 24, 209, and οἴγω Hes. Op. 819; Aesch. Pr. 611; Eur. H. F. 332; Ar. Ran. 1274, δι- Hippocr. 5, 446 (Lit.), ἀν- Thuc. 4, 74: fut. οἴξω Eur. Cycl. 502: aor. ᾦξα Il. 24, 457, ἀν- Theocr. 14, 15, usu. in Epic ὤϊξα Il. 6, 298. 24, 446. Od. 3, 392. 23, 370 &c.; Ap. Rh. 3, 645; (Theocr.) 23, 53; Hippocr. 5, 144 (Mss. Lit. v. r. ᾦξα), ἔῳξα (Hesych.), always unaugm. in Her. ἄν-οιξα 1, 68. 4, 143 &c.; part. οἴξας Il. 6, 89; Eur. Alc. 547: p. p. ἔῳγμαι, ἀν- Thuc. 2, 4; Lys. 12, 16: plp. ἔῳκτο, ἀν- Xen. Hell. 5, 1, 14: aor. subj. οἰχθῇ Aristot. H. An. 10, 7, 5; part. οἰχθείς Pind. N. 1, 41, ἀν- Thuc. 4, 67, δι- Pl. Conv. 215: **3 fut.** ἀν-εῴξεται Xen. Hell. 5, 1, 14 (Dind.), see ἀν-οίγνυμι. **Pass.** οἴγνῡται Aretae. C. et S. Ac. Morb. 2, 72 (ed. Oxon.): **imp.** ἐῳγνῡ́μην, ὑπαν- Com. Fr. (Ephipp.) 3, 327, Epic ὠιγνύμην Il. 2, 809, and οἰγόμην Ap. Rh. 2, 574, ἐῴγοντο, ἀν- Thuc. 4, 111. **Vb.** ἀν-οικτέον Eur. Ion 1387. See ἀνοίγνυμι. οἴγω is the more common form. Double augm. seems to occur in comp. only. In prose, the compounds ἀνα-, δια- are frequent, Thuc. 4, 74. 5, 10; Xen. An. 5, 5, 20; Isocr. 17, 23; Lys. 12, 10; Pl. Prot. 310; Dem. 24, 209; Aristot. H. A. 9, 7, 5; Theophr. H. P. 4, 7, 8. οἰγνύω is rare and late, -ύει (Hesych.), ἀν-οιγνύουσι Galen de Usu. part. 7, 14, 569. Her. never augments the aor. ἄν-οιξα 1, 68. 4, 143. 9, 118, but imp. ἀν-έῳγες 1, 187, in an Inscr. however, and Hippocr. has ὤϊξα 5, 144 (Lit.)

Οἶδα *To know*, see (εἰδέω, εἴδω).

Οἰδάω *To swell*, Plut. Mor. 734, οἰδέω Her. 3, 76. 127; Hippocr. 7, 272; Pl. Gorg. 518; Aristot. Probl. 4, 3, ἀν- Her. 7, 39 (Gaisf. Bekk. Stein); οἰδοῦσα Ar. Ran. 940, οἰδᾰ́νω Il. 9, 554; Ap. Rh. 1, 478; Ar. Pax 1166 (chor.), -αίνω Arat. 909; late prose Ael. H. A. 3, 18 (Schn. -άνω Herch.); Themist. 8, 111 (Her. 3, 127 Vulg. -έω Gaisf. Bekk. &c.): imp. ᾤδεον Od. 5, 455; Hippocr. 5, 186, iter. οἰδαίνεσκον Ap. Rh. 3, 383: fut. οἰδήσω, -σοντος Hippocr. 3, 431 (Kühn, *now* aor. -σαντος Lit. 5, 76; Erm. 1, 467, from Mss.): aor. ᾤδησα Hippocr. 5, 84. 168; Pl. Phaedr. 251, ᾤδηνα Androm. Senior. 29, 98, ἀν- Q. Sm. 14, 470 (Tychsen, Herm. Koechly); οἰδήσας Theocr. 22, 101; Aristot. Prob. 9, 4, 2, οἰδῆσαν, ἀν- Eur. Hipp. 1210: p. ᾤδηκα, Dor.

3 pl. -δήκαντι Theocr. 1, 43, ᾤδηκε, ἀν- Hippocr. 2, 246 (Lit.); ᾠδηκώς Plut. Mor. 831; Luc. Philops. 11, ἐξ- Eur. Cycl. 227, ἀν- Aristot. H. An. 9, 40, 22: plp. ᾠδήκει Aristid. 24, 305, δι- Luc. Menipp. 18. **Mid.** intrans. or pass. οἰδάνομαι Il. 9, 646, late οἰδέομαι Heliod. 2, 9: but aor. as act. οἰδήσαντο, ἀν- Q. Sm. 9, 345; and ἀν-οιδήνασθαι 14, 470 (Mss. A. Vulg. but act. -οιδῆναι Tychs. Herm. Koechly), see above. οἰδάνω is trans. Il. quoted, intrans. Ar. Pax 1166, where once οἰδαίνω improperly stood.

The forms οἰδάω, οἰδαίνω seem to be late. Buttmann's assertion that the "formation in -ήσω is the only one for all four forms" would appear to be not quite correct. Kühner and Jelf quote from Eur. Hipp. 1210, ἀνοίδησαν as an instance, we presume, of οι unaugm. in Attic. The only admissible reading there however is neut. part. ἀνοιδῆσαν, which alters the case.

'Οϊζύω *To wail, be miserable*, Epic, (ῠ) Il. 3, 408, but (ῡ) Ap. Rh. 4, 1324. 1374: imp. ὀϊζύομεν Il. 14, 89: aor. part. ὀϊζύσας Od. 4, 152. 23, 307. Only **pres. imp.** and **aor.** In **pres.** υ only before a *long* -ύει, -ύων Ap. Rh. quoted, in aor. ῡ.

Οἰκέω *To inhabit, live*, Od. 6, 204; Pind. N. 7, 9; Aesch. Eum. 758; Soph. O. R. 414; Ar. Nub. 138; Her. 8, 73; Antiph. 5, 78; Thuc. 3, 37, Dor. 3 pl. οἰκέοισι Pind. P. 10, 43; Aeol. inf. οἴκην, ξυν- Sapph. 27 (Ahr.), Poet. οἰκείω Hes. Th. 330; Theocr. 12, 28 (Ahr. Fritz. Ziegl.): **imp.** ᾤκεον Il. 14, 116; Hes. Fr. 216, Attic ᾤκουν Hipponax 47; Pind. P. 3, 34; Soph. O. R. 990; Thuc. 3, 72; Andoc. 1, 146; Isocr. 7, 22, Ion. οἴκεον Her. 1, 57: **fut.** -ήσω Hom. H. 2, 344; Aesch. Eum. 654; Eur. Ion 791; Her. 7, 176; Thuc. 5, 42; Pl. Phaed. 69: **aor.** ᾤκησα Pind. N. 3, 14; Eur. Hel. 928; Ar. Vesp. 391; Thuc. 5, 1; Lys. 12, 4, Ion. οἰκ- Her. 2, 154. 4, 105: **p.** ᾤκηκα Soph. El. 1101; Luc. Philops. 34, κατ- Pl. Leg. 666: **plp.** ᾠκήκειν, κατ- Criti. 112: **p.p.** ᾤκημαι Xen. Vect. 1, 6 (-ισμαι Dind. Saupp.), Ion. οἰκ- Her. 7, 22. 122, as **mid.** see below: Ion. **plp.** οἴκητο Her. 1, 193: **aor.** ᾠκήθην Dem. 9, 26, Epic 3 pl. ᾤκηθεν for -θησαν, *were housed, settled*, Il. 2, 668; οἰκηθείη Xen. Mem. 4, 4, 16: **fut. mid.** as **pass.** οἰκήσομαι Thuc. 8, 67; Pl. Rep. 520; Isocr. 12, 133; Aeschin. 1, 22; Aristot. Pol. 2, 1, 3. 3, 14, 1; (Dem.) 58, 62, as **mid.** see foll. **Mid.** trans. *inhabit, manage for oneself*, **fut.** οἰκήσομαι *simple* late Menand. Rhet. 103, but δι- Dem. 8, 13: **aor.** late in *simple* οἰκησάμενος Aristid. 13, 103, but δι-ῳκήσατο Dem. 18, 247; προδι-οικήσασθαι Aeschin. 1, 146: and as **mid. p.p.** (ᾤκημαι) Ion. 3 pl. οἰκέαται Her. 1, 142; οἰκημένος 1, 27. 5, 73, Attic κατ-ῳκημ- Thuc. 1, 120, δι-ῳκημ- Dem. 18, 178. The **aor. mid.** has been missed by Lexicogr. and the **fut.** in **trans.** sense. Her. never augments this verb, but Hippocr.

has imp. ᾤκει 2, 666, and with double augment ἐῴκεον (Hippocr.) Epist. 9, 406 (Lit.), but ᾤκεον (Ms. I. Ermerins.)

Οἰκίζω *To found, settle,* Eur. I. A. 670; Ar. Av. 149; Her. 7, 143; Thuc. 1, 13; Pl. Rep. 420: imp. ᾤκιζον Pl. Rep. 453: fut. οἰκιῶ Thuc. 1, 100. 6, 23; Luc. Nav. 38: aor. ᾤκισα Eur. Heracl. 613; Ar. Av. 1515; Thuc. 1, 98; Isocr. 15, 254, ἀπ- Od. 12, 135, ᾤκισσα Pind. I. 8, 20, Ion. οἴκ- Her. 3, 91. 5, 42: p. late ᾤκικα, συν- Strab. 12, 3, 10: plp. ᾠκίκειν App. Civ. 2, 26. Hisp. 100: p. p. ᾤκισμαι Eur. Hec. 2; Pl. Rep. 427, Ion. οἴκισ- Her. 4, 12: aor. ᾠκίσθην Thuc. 6, 5; Pl. Tim. 72, Ion. ἐν-οικίσθ- Her. 1, 68: fut. οἰκισθήσομαι Dem. 5, 10; App. Civ. 2, 139, κατ- Thuc. 2, 17: and as pass. fut. mid. οἰκιεῖται Xen. Hell. 1, 6, 32 (Vulg. Saupp. Dind. 2 ed., οἰκεῖται Schneid. Dind. 3 ed. Breitnb.) Mid. οἰκίζομαι *found for oneself, inhabit, migrate, settle,* Pl. Phaed. 114. Leg. 708: imp. ᾠκιζ- ἀν- Thuc. 1, 58: fut. οἰκιοῦμαι Eur. Heracl. 46: aor. ᾠκισάμην Anth. 7, 75; κατ-οικισάμενος Thuc. 2, 102; Isocr. 19, 23. 24, ἀν- Thuc. 1, 58, ἐν- 6, 2; D. Hal. 1, 22: with p. p. ᾤκισται *inhabits,* Eur. Tr. 435, εἰσ- *migrated,* Ar. Pax 260, ἐξ- *emigrated,* 197. Dindorf in his 2 edit. recalled fut. mid. οἰκιεῖται in pass. sense Xen. Hell. 1, 6, 32, but in the 3 edit. he has resumed οἰκεῖται (Schneid. &c.) pres. pass. of οἰκέω. Breitenbach retains οἰκεῖται, but as the sense, says he, seems to require a fut. he suggests οἰκήσει intrans. in preference to mid. οἰκιεῖται because "nunquam significat *incoletur.*" This is what we call a petitio principii. In our Lexicons this word is ill handled.

Οἰκοδομέω *To build a house, rear,* reg. but in Her. unaugm. Her. 2, 121; Andoc. 3, 12; Thuc. 1, 93: imp. ᾠκοδόμει Xen. Cyr. 7, 5, 11, οἰκοδόμεε Her. 1, 186, ᾠκοδόμουν Thuc. 8, 90, οἰκοδόμεον Her. 8, 71: aor. ᾠκοδόμησε Xen. Hell. 5, 2, 4, οἰκοδ- Her. 2, 127. 153: p. ᾠκοδόμηκε Anth. 11, 312; Aristot. Metaph. 8, 6, 9; Dem. 21, 158: p. p. ᾠκοδόμηται Thuc. 7, 29; late Attic οἰκ- Aen. Tact. Exc. 57 (Herch.); and Ion. Her. 1, 181. 2, 149, 3 pl. -μέαται 4, 185: aor. ᾠκοδομήθην Thuc. 6, 100; Dem. 22, 68: fut. -ηθήσεται Lys. 12, 63: aor. mid. ᾠκοδομησάμεθα Andoc. 3, 7, οἰκοδ- Her. 3, 10 &c. So οἰκοφθορέω, mostly confined to Ionic prose, and always unaugm., see Her. 8, 142. 144. 5, 29. 1, 196; even Dio. Hal. de Thuc. jud. 14.

Οἰκουρέω *To keep the house, guard,* only pres. in classic authors, Aesch. Ag. 809; Soph. O. C. 343; Pl. Rep. 451: imp. later, and unaugm. οἰκούρει Plut. Camill. 11, ὑπ- Pomp. 42, οἰκούρουν Camill. 28.

Οἰκοφθορέω, see οἰκοδομέω.

Οἰκτείρω *To pity,* Il. 23, 548; Anacr. 114; Simon. C. 113;

Aesch. Ag. 1321; Soph. Aj. 652; Antiph. 3, 2, reg. in classic Auth. but οἰκτῖρετε for -ειρ- Anth. (Posidip.) 7, 267: imp. ᾤκτειρε Stesich. 18 (Bergk), Ion. οἴκ- Her. 3, 52: fut. -ερῶ Aesch. Fr. 196 (D.): aor. ᾤκτειρα Il. 11, 814; Aesch. Pr. 352; Soph. Tr. 464; Xen. Cyr. 5, 4, 32; οἰκτείρας Aesch. Ag. 1241; Her. 7, 38; -τεῖραι 3, 119; Antiph. 1, 25: no p. act.: no 2 aor.: nor mid. v.: and pass. confined to pres. οἰκτείρονται Xen. Oec. 7, 40: and imp. ᾠκτείρετο Soph. El. 1412.—R. Prinz is editing in Eur. οἰκτίρω for -είρω. Though a form in -έω seems not to exist, we find late fut. οἰκτειρήσω V. T. Jer. 13, 14; N. T. Rom. 9, 15; Joseph. Macc. 5; Schol. Od. 4, 740; Schol. Aesch. Supp. 209: aor. ᾠκτείρησα Schol. Aesch. Pr. 353; Nicet. Ann. 7, 5, κατ- Joseph. Ant. 8, 13, 3: aor. pass. -ηθῆναι Schol. Aesch. Pr. 637.

Οἰκτίζω *To pity, lament*, pres. in *simple* we have not seen except late, Heliod. 4, 9, but κατ-οικτίζεις Aesch. Eum. 122: fut. Attic οἰκτιῶ, -ιεῖς Aesch. Pr. 68, κατ- Supp. 903; Soph. O. C. 384; Eur. Heracl. 152 (Elms. Dind. Kirchh. -ίσειν Mss. Brod. &c. -ίσει Ald.): aor. ᾤκτισα Aesch. Supp. 639; Soph. Tr. 897; Eur. Hec. 720 (Pors. Dind. Paley); rare in prose Xen. Apol. 4, συν- Cyr. 4, 6, 5; οἰκτίσειε Aristot. Mund. 1, 4: (p. act.: p. p.?): aor. ᾠκτίσθην, κατ- Eur. I. A. 686. Mid. as act. οἰκτίζομαι Aesch. Supp. 1032; Eur. I. T. 486. Tr. 155; rare in prose Dinarch. 1, 110; Ael. Fr. 63; Heliod. 9, 11: imp. ᾠκτίζοντο Thuc. 2, 51; Plut. Mor. 566, Ion. οἰκτίζ-, κατ- Her. 3, 156, as mid. *bewailed himself*: aor. ᾠκτισάμην Aesch. Eum. 515; Eur. Supp. 280. Hel. 1053 (Hec. 720 Vulg. Nauck, see above); late prose Plut. Eum. 7, οἰκ- (Mss. P M V); -σάμενος App. Annib. 46; Epist. Phal. 20, κατ- Her. 2, 121 (3).

Οἰμάω *To rush, dart*, Epic and only fut. -ήσουσι Her. 1, 62 (Orac.): and aor. οἴμησε never augm. Il. 22, 140. Od. 24, 538; Q. Sm. 1, 592; -ήσας Opp. Hal. 2, 119.

Οἰμώζω *To lament*, Hom. Epigr. 14, 20; Tyrt. Fr. 7 (Bergk); Soph. O. C. 820; Ar. Ran. 257; Hippocr. 7, 294. 6, 354; Dio. Hal. 4, 85; Luc. D. Mort. 10, 11, ἀπ- Aesch. Ch. 1014; Soph. Ant. 1224: imp. ᾤμωζον Ar. Lys. 516, οἰμώζεσκε, ἀν- Q. Sm. 14, 281: fut. οἰμώξομαι Attic, Com. Fr. (Eup.) 2, 551; Ar. Plut. 111. Av. 1207. Pax 466; Com. Fr. (Alex.) 3, 430. (Men.) 4, 120 &c.; Xen. Hell. 2, 3, 56; Dem. 35, 40: later οἰμώξω Anth. (Agath.) 5, 302; Orac. Sib. 5, 296. 476; late prose Plut. Apophth. 182; Long. P. 3, 19 (Seil.): aor. ᾤμωξα Il. 18, 35; Aesch. Ag. 1599; Soph. Tr. 932; Ar. Ran. 743, ἀπ- Antiph. 5, 41; οἰμώξειεν Il. 7, 125; Her. 7, 159: p. p. unaugm. οἴμωγμαι, -μένος Eur. Bacc. 1286 (Vulg. Kirchh. 1 ed. ᾕμαγ- 2 ed. with Musgr. Nauck), but ᾠμ- (Elms. Dind. Paley): aor. οἰμωχθείς

Theogn. 1204. **Vb.** οἰμωκτός Ar. Ach. 1157 (Mss. Bekk.) rejected by Pors. Dind. &c. This verb occurs rarely in early Attic prose, and only, we think, in **fut. mid.**, for οἰμώξοιτο has displaced οἰμώξειεν Xen. Hell. 2, 3, 56 (Mss. Schneid. Dind. Saupp. &c.) An **aor. m.** occurs late ἀπ-οιμώξασθαι Eustath. Opusc. p. 305, 85.

Οἰνίζομαι *To buy, fetch wine,* Il. 8. 506: **imp.** unaugm. οἰνιζόμην 546: aor. late οἰνισάμενοι Luc. V. H. 1, 9.

Οἰνοχοεύω Epic and **pres.** only, see foll.

Οἰνοχοέω *To pour wine,* Com. Fr. (Pher.) 2, 282; Xen. Cyr. 1, 3, 8; -οοῦσα Sapph. 5, -οεῦσα (Bergk); Hom. always -χοεύω in pres. Od. 21, 142; -εύων 1, 143; -εύειν Il. 2, 127. 20, 234: **imp.** unaugm. οἰνοχόει Il. 1, 598. Od. 15, 141 (Bekk. Spitzn. Dind. La R. with Aristarch. ᾠνοχ- Vulg.), ᾠνοχ- Anacr. 32; Nic. Damasc. 64 (L. Dind.), and with double augm. ἐῳνοχόει Il. 4, 3. Od. 20, 255: **fut.** -ήσω Xen. Cyr. 1, 3, 9; Nic. Damasc. 64: **aor.** οἰνοχοῆσαι Od. 15, 323; Sapph. 32 (Mss. Schn.), -όησαι (51 Bergk, 32 Ahr.) which Athen. makes ᾠνοχόησεν 10, 25, οἰνοχ- (Schweigh.) Hom. has **pres.** -εύω, never -έω: the **imp.** again, and aor. always from -έω: compare ἀεθλεύω, **aor.** ἄθλησα.

Οἰνόω *To intoxicate,* in **act.** only **aor.** οἰνῶσαι Critias 2, 28 (Bergk). **Pass.** οἰνόομαι *to be in wine,* Plut. Mor. 672: **p. p.** οἰνωμένος Soph. Tr. 268 (Mss. Herm. Ellendt, Bergk); Eur. Bacc. 687, ἐξ- 814 (Vulg. Kirchh. 1 ed.); Com. Fr. (Cratin.) 2, 211 (or Pollux 6, 21); Her. 5, 18; Aristot. Mirab. 101. Rhet. 2, 12, 8 (Bekk.); and late Plut. Mor. 1. 712; Diod. Sic. 1, 57, others ᾠνωμ- as more Attic, Aesch. Supp. 409 (Ms. med. Pors. Elms. Dind. Herm.); Soph. Tr. quoted (Elms. Dind. Nauck); Eur. Bacc. quoted (Elms. Nauck, and *now* Dind. Paley, Kirchh. 2 ed.); Cratin. Com. Fr. quoted (Mein.), δι-ῳνωμένος Pl. Leg. 775, κατ-ῳνωμ- 815, *v. r.* δι-κατ-οινω-: **aor.** οἰνωθείς Od. 19, 11; Soph. Fr. 668; Anth. 7, 444: **fut.** late οἰνωθήσομαι Diog. Laert. 7, 118.

Οἴομαι *To think,* Od. 10, 193 (Epic ὀΐομ- see below); Aesch. Ch. 758; Soph. O. C. 28; Ar. Nub. 1342; rare in prose, Thuc. 2, 60. 6, 36. 40; Xen. Mem. 2, 3, 10 (οἶμ- L. Dind.). Oec. 3, 9; Pl. Leg. 798. Conv. 173; Lys. 22, 11; Isae. 2, 41; Dem. 1, 16. 22, 42. 23, 115. 126 (Bekk. B. S. &c. οἶμ- Dind. always *now*), more freq. οἶμαι (not in Hom. see below) Aesch. Ag. 321; Soph. O. C. 498. El. 932 &c.; Ar. Thesm. 27. Av. 75 &c.; Antiph. 5, 57; Thuc. 1, 10. 2, 54. 4, 64. 6, 92; Xen. An. 2, 1, 16. Cyr. 1, 3, 11 &c.; Pl. Rep. 400 &c.; Isocr. 4, 84 &c.; Isae. 3, 77; Dem. 1, 27. 4, 15. 5, 3. 22, 40 &c. (Bekk. B. S. and always Dind.), 2 sing. οἴει Ar. Ran. 54; Pl. Apol. 26, rare

Dor. οἴη Soph. Fr. 23: imp. ᾠόμην Aesch. Pr. 268; Soph. Ant. 453; Ar. Vesp. 791. 1138. Nub. 1472; scarcely now in classic prose, (Aeschin.) Epist. 11, 1; (Dem.) Proem. 1457 (Mss. Bekk. B. S. ᾤμην Dind.); Luc. Abd. 3. Amor. 53 (Jacob. Bekk. ᾤμ- Dind.); v. r. Xen. Cyr. 4, 5, 30. 6, 9, and ᾤμην Ar. Nub. 373. Plut. 834; perhaps always in good prose, Antiph. 3, γ, 1; Thuc. 1, 143; Xen. Mem. 4, 2, 23. 24. 4, 4, 12; Pl. Phaedr. 235; Lys. 1, 10. 3, 10. 8, 11; Isocr. 4, 187; Isae. 3, 25; Aeschin. 2, 95; Dem. 18, 28. 19, 215. 40, 13 &c.: fut. οἰήσομαι Pl. Leg. 891. Rep. 397; Lys. 30, 8; Dem. 56, 48 (Bekk. Dind.): late aor. mid.: aor. pass. as mid. ᾠήθην Hippocr. 1, 600 (Lit.); Antiph. 1, 8; Thuc. 4, 130; Xen. An. 4, 7, 22; Isocr. 7, 6; Isae. 11, 15; Aeschin. 1, 83; subj. οἰηθῇς Ar. Eq. 860, -θῇ Pl. Theaet. 178 &c.; opt. -είην Isocr. 12, 23, 1 pl. -θείημεν Xen. Mem. 1, 5, 1 (-θεῖμεν L. Dind.), and -θεῖμεν Pl. Legg. 712 (Bekk.), -θείημεν (Bait. Or. Winckl.); -ήθητι Com. Fr. 4, 101; -ηθείς Eur. I. A. 986: fut. late οἰηθήσεται as mid. Galen 1, 208 (K.): and late aor. mid. ᾠησάμην Arat. 896; late prose Porphyr. Abst. 2, 24 &c. see below. Vb. ἀν-ώιστος Il. 21, 39, οἰητέον Aristot. Pol. 1, 8, 11. The Epic and Attic poets never use fut. οἰήσομαι, nor aor. ᾠήθην except once subj. οἰηθῇς Ar. Eq. 860, and once part. οἰηθεῖσα Eur. I. A. 986. The act. form οἴω occurs only in 1 pers. sing. pres. Il. 5, 252. 19, 71; Hes. Sc. 111, and is often, οἴομαι almost always, resolved by Epic poets thus ὀΐω (ῑ) Il. 1, 59; Ap. Rh. 3, 28, ὀΐομαι (ῑ) Il. 5, 644; Ap. Rh. 4, 197 (but οἴομ- Od. 10, 193), ὀΐεαι Il. 1, 561. Od. 10, 380, ὀΐεται Od. 17, 586. 19, 312, ὀϊόμεθα 21, 322. 22, 165, ὀΐεσθε Ap. Rh. 2, 342; but οἴοιτο Od. 17, 580. 22, 12; ὀϊόμενος Il. 15, 728. Od. 2, 351. 22, 210; Ap. Rh. 1, 1037, but οἰόμ- Callim. Epigr. 7: imp. ὠΐετο Od. 10, 248, ὀΐ- Hym. 2, 164: fut. (ὀΐσομαι only as v. r. unless ὀΐσσεαι, ὀΐσεται be fut. Opp. Hal. 1, 432. 4, 368): aor. ὀΐσατο (ῑ) in Hom. never augm. Od. 9, 213. 19, 390, later ὠΐσ- Coluth. 370; Arat. 1006; ὀϊσάμενος Od. 15, 443; Coluth. 258, ὠϊσάμην (ῐ) Mosch. 2, 8; Ap. Rh. 1, 291; Q. Sm. 2, 19; ὀΐσασθαι Orph. Lith. 562. 563; ὀϊσάμενος late prose Polyb. 3, 94 (Bekk.), ὀϊσσάμ- Opp. C. 4, 228; Polyb. quoted (Dind. Hultsch): aor. pass. ὠΐσθην Od. 16, 475, -θη 4, 453; ὀϊσθείς only Il. 9, 453. The act. form ὀΐω has sometimes ῐ, Il. 11, 609. 13, 153. 23, 467 &c.; Q. Sm. 4, 28. οἰῶ Ar. Lys. 81. 156. 998. 1256 (best Mss. Dind. Enger, Bergk), οἴω (Br. &c.) is commonly identified with this verb. It is, perhaps, an exclamation rather peculiar to the Laconians, something like our *ho yo!* It occurs also in a Fr. of Coraliscus. In Hom. the aor. mid. is *now* never written with σσ, ὀΐσσ-; in Ap. Rh. Mss. and edit. differ, but Wellau. and Merkel uniformly -ισσ-

with Mss. Laur. Guelf.; but in Q. Sm. now -ισα- (Koechly); so in Arat. (Bekk). The Attics usually contracted **pres.** οἴομαι into οἶμαι, and in prose, perhaps always **imp.** ᾠόμην into ᾤμην but both in 1 sing. only. Hom. never uses the syncop. οἶμαι, and rarely the contr. οἴομαι Od. 10, 193; οἴοιτο 17, 580. 22, 12, which two last Doederl. would alter to ὀΐοιτο, unaware of the first which we think their support; (οἰόμενος Callim. Epigr. 7, 2.) From this it appears that Buttmann's assertion that "the Epics always separate the diphthong in the **mid.** ὀΐομαι" is wrong, and that our Lexicogr. are not quite right in confining the contr. form to the opt. οἴοιτο.

(**Οἰόω**) *To leave alone*, Epic and only **aor. pass.** unaugm. οἰώθην Il. 6, 1. 11, 401, -ησαν Q. Sm. 6, 527.

Οἰστράω *To goad, harass*, also *be harassed*, Com. Fr. (Men.) 4, 158; Pl. Phaedr. 251; Aristot. H. An. 19, 11, later οἰστρέω Ach. Tat. 2, 37, -τρεῖ Theocr. 6, 28 (Vulg. Ahr. Ziegl.), but -τρῇ Dor. for -άει (Herm. Mein.); see -εῖσθαι Ael. N. A. 15, 9, -ᾶσθαι (Herch.); -ούμενος (Luc.) Asin. 33: **fut.** -ήσω Athen. (Theod.) 7, 302; Geop. 17, 2: **aor.** unaugm. οἴστρησα Eur. Bac. 32 (Ald. Herm. Kirchh. 1 ed.), but ᾤστ- (Pors. Elms. Dind. Paley, Nauck, Kirchh. 2 ed.); οἰστρήσας Aesch. Pr. 836: **p. p.** late οἰστρημένος Lycophr. 818; Ael. N. A. 16, 36: **aor.** οἰστρηθείς Soph. Tr. 653 (Vulg. Nauck, στρωθείς Musgr. Dind.); Opp. Hal. 2, 352; Ael. N. A. 4, 6.

Οἴχομαι *To go, be a going* (and perhaps -έομαι, only **pres.** -εῦμαι Anth. 7, 273), usu. as **perf.** *to be on the road, gone*, Il. 23, 577; Pind. N. 10, 78; Aesch. Eum. 117; Soph. O. C. 894; Ar. Ach. 221; Her. 2, 29; Antiph. 2, δ, 4; Thuc. 7, 12, 2 sing. Ion. οἴχεαι Her. 2, 115; imper. οἴχεο, ἐπ- Theogn. 353: **imp.** ᾠχόμην as plp. and aor. Il. 1, 366. Od. 16, 24; Hes. Sc. 91; Mimnerm. 11, 7; Pind. N. 7, 40; Soph. Ph. 273; Antiph. 2, γ, 2. 5, 13; Thuc. 6, 61; Lys. 1, 14; Xen. An. 4, 3, 30. 5, 35, Ion. οἰχομ- Her. 1, 48. 5, 43. 6, 97 &c.: **fut.** οἰχήσομαι Com. Fr. (Plat.) 2, 635; Ar. Vesp. 51; Hippocr. 6, 20; Andoc. 1, 4; Lys. 10, 20; Isae. 2, 43; Pl. Theaet. 203: **p.** οἴχωκα Soph. Aj. 896 (Mss. Herm. Bergk, ᾠχ- Dind. Nauck); Anth. App. Epigr. 34; Her. 9, 98, παρ- Il. 10, 252 (Bekk. *now*), ᾤχωκα Aesch. Pers. 13 (Ald. Blomf. Dind. οἴχ- Ms. Schn. Herm.); Soph. Fr. 227 (D.), Epic and late prose ᾤχηκα, παρ- Il. 10, 252 quoted (Wolf, Dind. Faesi, -οίχωκα Bekk. -ῴχωκα Aristarch. La Roche, Franke); Dio. Hal. 11, 5; Nicol. Rhet. 11, 1; Heliod. 6, 1; Sext. Emp. 500, 26: **plp.** Ion. οἰχώκεε Her. 1, 189. 5, 20. 7, 164. 8, 126 &c. late prose παρ-ῳχήκει Polyb. 8, 29: **p. p.** οἴχημαι Anth. 7, 273 (Mss. -εῦμαι Jac.), δι-οίχ- Her. 4, 136, and ᾤχημαι, παρ- Plut.

Camill. 14.; Sext. Emp. 164, 14; Hippocr. 1, 15 (Vulg. Kühn, but παρ-οιχόμενος Ms. A. Littré 6, 16), so παρῳχημένος Xen. An. 2, 4, 1 (some Mss. Popp. Kühner, but -οιχόμενος Vulg. Krüg. and *now* L. Dind. 4 ed. Saupp.); in good Attic, therefore, the perf. pass. seems doubtful. Vb. οἰχητέον Alciphr. 3, 42.—To this verb, and to ἐποίγνυμι, has been referred ἐπώχατο or ἐπῴχ- Il. 12, 340. We would rather, with Buttmann, refer it to ἐπ-έχω, perf. act. redupl. -όχωκα for -όκωχα, p. p. -ωγμαι, plp. -ώγμην, 3 pl. -ωγντο, Ion. -ώχατο, ἐπ- *were held to, shut.* The formation is legitimate, and the sense afforded suits the passage best. The act. οἴχω is Dor. and rare, imper. οἶχε Plut. Pyrrh. 28. The collat. οἰχνέω is Poet. and confined to pres. -χνῶ Soph. El. 166, -νεῖ Aj. 564, Epic 3 pl. -νεῦσι Od. 3, 322; οἰχνέοντες Pind. P. 5, 86; -νεῖν Soph. El. 313: and iter. imp. οἴχνεσκον Il. 5, 790.

Οἴω *To think*, see οἴομαι.

(**Οἴω**) *To bring*, see φέρω.

Οἰωνίζομαι *To take an augury from birds*, Com. Fr. (Epin.) 4, 506; -όμενος Xen. Cyr. 1, 6, 1: imp. unaugm. οἰωνίζοντο Xen. Hell. 1, 4, 12. 5, 4, 17; App. Annib. 18: fut. late -ιοῦμαι V. T. Lev. 19, 26: aor. οἰωνισάμην 3 Reg. 21, 33; opt. οἰωνίσαιτο (Dem.) 25, 80; -άμενος Aristot. Pol. 5, 4, 5; Plut. Mor. 676; -ασθαι Aristid. 27, 356, μετ- Dinarch. 1, 92.

Ὀκέλλω *To run ashore*, intrans. and trans. Xen. An. 7, 5, 12, ἐξ- Her. 7, 182; -λοι Ar. Ach. 1159: imp. ὤκελλον Her. 8, 84: aor. ὤκειλα Eur. I. T. 1379; Thuc. 2, 91, ἐπ- Her. 7, 182; -είλας Thuc. 4, 11; -εῖλαι 4, 12. Only once in Trag. and Comedy.

(**Ὀκρῐάω**) *To make rough, enrage*, only pass. and only imp. Epic ὀκρῐόωντο Od. 18, 33: and p. p. ὠκριωμένος late Lycophr. 545.

Ὀκχέω, see ὀχέω.

Ὀλέκω, see ὄλλυμι.

Ὀλισθάνω *To slip*, Soph. Fr. 963; Xen. An. 3, 5, 11 (Pors. Popp. Krüg. Dind.); Pl. Crat. 427; Hippocr. 3, 460. 4, 100. 260. 292 &c. (Mss. Lit.), ἀπ- Thuc. 7, 65, ἐξ- Eur. Phoen. 1383 (Ms. C. Pors. Herm. Dind. Kirchh.); Ar. Eq. 491, and -αίνω rare if correct in early Auth. δι-ολισθαίνει Pl. Lys. 216 (B. O. W. Stallb.); Hippocr. 6, 290 (Lit.), ἀπ- 2, 262 (Lit. *v. r.* -άνω), later ὀλισθαίνει Opp. Hal. 2, 378; Aristot. Prob. 24, 1. 25, 11 (Bekk. *v. r.* -άνει), ἀπ- Hist. An. 7, 3; ὀλισθαίνων Polyb. 3, 55 (Bekk. -θάν- Dind. Hultsch); Plut. Mor. 90. 392; Ap. Rh. 1, 377: imp. ὠλίσθανον Com. Fr. (Anon.) 4, 673; Orph. Arg. 271; Anth. 7, 233: fut. late ὀλισθήσω V. T. Prov. 14, 19; Nonn. 36, 458: 1 aor. unattic, ὠλίσθησα Demod. 5 (Bergk); Anth. 9, 125; Opp.

C. 4, 451; but Apollod. 2, 5, 4. 3, 2; Strab. vol. 3, p. 476 (Kram.), δι- Hippocr. 4, 274: p. unattic, ὠλίσθηκα Hippocr. 4, 246. 276. 308. 314 &c. (Lit.); Diod. Sic. 4, 79: plp. ὠλισθήκει Philostr. Apoll. 3, 129: **2 aor.** ὄλισθε Hom. always, Il. 20, 470. 23, 774; Theocr. 25, 230, ὤλισθον mostly Poet. Soph. El. 746; Anth. 11, 316; Ar. Ran. 690 (ἐξ- Eccl. 286); also Ion. and late prose, Hippocr. 4, 100. 302. 306 (Lit.); Philostr. Apoll. 4, 142; Plut. Brut. 39, ἐν- Cim. 16, περι- Marcell. 15, ἀπ- Alciphr. 3, 11. Of the form ὀλισθαίνω a few traces still linger in uncritical editions of the earlier authors, or as a *v. r.* ἐξολισθαίνοι Eur. Phoen. 1383 (Vulg. -άνοι Pors. Dind.); -αίνειν Ar. Eq. 489 (Br. -άνειν Bekk. Dind.); Pl. Crat. 427; at Lys. 216 however διολισθαίνει is still in the text even of B. O. W. Stallb. &c. The most and best Mss. of Hippocr. have ὀλισθάνω (Lit.), but still in text ἀπολισθαίνειν 2, 262, *v. r.* -άνειν &c. The reg. **aor.** ὠλίσθηνα or -ανα occurs late Nic. Al. 89; as *v. r.* Xen. An. 3, 5, 11. The **pres.** -αίνω is trans. *make slip*, Nilus Sent. 50; ὠλισθήκει Philostr. Apoll. 3, 129. ὀλισθράζω occurs Epich. 19 (Ahr.). ὀλισθέω **pres.** seems not to exist; ὀλισθοῦσι Ar. Ran. 690, called by some a **pres.** is too evidently dat. pl. of the **2 aor.** part.

Ὄλλῡμι *To destroy, lose,* Poet. Soph. Ant. 673; Eur. Or. 1302; ὀλλύς Il. 4, 451. 8, 472 (prose ἀπ-όλλῡμι Her. 9, 48, -ύασι Thuc. 7, 51 (Bekk. Stahl). 8, 10; Pl. Rep. 421, -ῦσι Her. 4, 69; Pl. Leg. 706), and ὀλλῠ́ω only **pres.** in *simple* and rare, Archil. 27 (Bergk); Com. Fr. (Anon.) 4, 687; imper. ὄλλῠε Archil. 27 (prose ἀπ- Hippocr. 1, 111 (Erm.); Thuc. 4, 25. 7, 51 (most Mss.); Xen. Cyr. 4, 5, 20 (Hertl. Saupp. -υμι Dind.); Pl. Gorg. 496; Isocr. 5, 52. 12, 226. 228, προσαπ- Her. 1, 207. 6, 138, δια- Pl. Crito 47 best Mss.): **imp.** ὤλλυν, -ῠσαν Aesch. Pers. 461; Soph. O. C. 394 (prose ἀπ- Isocr. 12, 219; Pl. Rep. 562, and ἀπ-ώλλῠον Hippocr. 7, 576; Andoc. 1, 41. 58. 114; Isocr. 11, 8. 21, 12; Dem. 9, 31): **fut.** Epic ὀλέσω Od. 13, 399; Hes. Op. 180; Anth. App. Epigr. 134, once in Her. προσαπ- 2, 121 (Wessel. Gaisf. Bekk. but -έει Dind. -έσῃ Stein, Abicht), rare in Attic, ἀπ- Com. Fr. (Plat.) 2, 621; later App. Civ. 1, 10; Pseudo-Callisth. 3, 13; Charit. 1, 10. 2, 5 (D'Orv. -λεῖ Herch.); Long. Past. 3, 25; (Luc.) Asin. 33; Geop. 2, 25, Epic ὀλέσσω Il. 12, 250. Od. 2, 49, Ion. ὀλέω, -έεις, -έει, ἀπ- Her. 1, 34. 8, 60; -έοντες 6, 91 (Gaisf. Bekk. Dind. Dietsch &c.), -εῦντες 9, 18 (S. V. Gaisf. Dietsch, Dind. better -έοντες F. Bekk. Abicht, Stein), Attic ὀλῶ, -εῖς, -εῖ Tyrt. 3; Soph. O. R. 448; Eur. Hipp. 440; in tmesi Ar. Plut. 65; Aristot. Fr. 501, ἀπ- Theogn. 36; Pl. Meno 95; Isae. 11, 31; Dem. 33, 10: **aor.** ὤλεσα Il. 22, 107; Hes. Op. 163; Simon. C. 138; Aesch. Sept. 1056; Soph. El. 270;

in tmesi Her. 3, 36, ἀπ- Xen. Hell. 1, 1, 7, Epic and Lyric ὄλεσα Od. 23, 319; Eur. Ph. 663 (chor. Herm. Nauck, Kirchh. Dind. 5 ed), -σσα Od. 21, 284; Theogn. 831; Pind. P. 11, 33, iter. ὀλέσκεν in tmesi Il. 8, 270 (Bekk. Dind. -εσσεν Vulg. Spitzn. Franke, La R.); subj. -έσω, -ῃς Il. 1, 559; Tyrt. 12, 34 &c., opt. -έσαιμι, -έσειε Il. 8, 358; Eur. Med. 1389, -έσειαν Aesch. Sept. 567; ὀλέσσας Il. 19, 60; Soph. Aj. 390 (chor.), ὀλέσας Aesch. Pers. 534, Dor. ὀλέσαις Pind. Ol. 1, 79: p. ὀλώλεκα, ἐξ- Ar. Plut. 867, ἀπ- Her. 1, 45; Antiph. 5, 91; Thuc. 2, 65; Lys. 19, 8: plp. ὀλωλέκει, ἀπ- Dem. 19, 260, ἀπωλ- (Dind.): **2 p.** ὄλωλα *am undone*, Il. 16, 521; Aesch. Pers. 1015; Soph. Ph. 76, ἀπ- Her. 2, 181; Antiph. 5, 66; Pl. Euthyd. 300: plp. ὀλώλειν Il. 10, 187, ἀπ- Her. 3, 119; Isae. 6, 37; Thuc. 4, 133 (Bekk. Popp. Krüg. -ωλώλ- Dind. Scheib.); Dem. 18, 49. 20, 79. 39, 33 (Bekk. -ωλώλ- Dind.), and -ολώλη Pl. Apol. 31, but ἀπ-ωλώλειν Antiph. 5, 70 (Bekk. B. S. Maetzn.); Aeschin. 1, 95. 2, 92 (Mss. B. S. Frank. &c. -ολώλ- Bekk.); Dem. 19, 125 (Bekk. B. S. Dind.); Thuc. 7, 27 (Krüg. Dind. -ολώλ- Bekk. Popp.): p. p. late ὀλώλεσμαι: aor. late ὠλέσθην, ἀπ- V. T. Ps. 82, 18; Aesop 67 (Tauchn.): fut. late, ἀπ-ολεσθησόμενος Galen 9, 728. **Mid.** ὄλλῠμαι *to perish*, Il. 20, 21; Soph. O. R. 179; Ar. Av. 1070, ἀπ- Antiph. 5, 35; Andoc. 1, 49: imp. ὠλλύμην Eur. Alc. 633, Dor. -ύμαν Hec. 914 (chor.), -υτο Soph. El. 927, ἀπ- Her. 2, 120; Antiph. 2, β, 3: fut. ὀλέομαι, -έεσθε Il. 21, 133, (ἀπ-ολεόμεθα Her. 9, 42, -έεται 8, 57, -εομένης 8, 69, but -εύμενοι if correct, 7, 209, see ἀμύνω), but ὄλουμαι, -εῖται Il. 2, 325; Theogn. 867; Aesch. Ch. 888; Soph. Ant. 59; Eur. Med. 788; in tmesi Ar. Nub. 792. 1440, ἀπ- Thuc. 8, 55; Andoc. 1, 66: (1 aor. as act. late, ὠλέσατο Ps. Callisth. 1, 2, Ms. L): **2 aor.** ὠλόμην Il. 13, 772; Aesch. Eum. 565; Soph. Ant. 517; Eur. Alc. 718, ἀπ- Antiph. 5, 3; Pl. Rep. 469, ὀλ- Od. 11, 197; Eur. Or. 199 (chor.), -όμαν I. T. 152; Ar. Pax 1013 (chor.); ὄληαι Il. 3, 417, -ηται 20, 303; ὀλοίατο Aesch. Sept. 552, ἀπ- Od. 9, 554; ὀλόμενος Aesch. Pers. 1075, Epic οὐλ- Il. 1, 2. Od. 10, 394; Aesch. Pr. 397 (chor.); Eur. Phoen. 1528 (chor.), iter. ὀλέσκετο, ἀπ- Od. 11, 586. For ὀλέεσκεν Ion. imp. implying ὀλέω, Il. 19, 135 (Wolf, Spitzn.), Bekker, Dind. La R. read ὀλέκεσκεν from ὀλέκω; ὀλέεσκες however occurs Q. Sm. 2, 414 (Koechly) which some may think strengthens the reading in Homer. ὤλεσκον with augm. is late, Or. Sib. 1, 108. ὀλομέναν part. 2 aor. as adj. *pernicious*, *fatal*, Eur. Phoen. 1029 (chor.), and usually οὐλόμ- properly Epic, Il. 14, 84; Tyrt. 7, 2; Theogn. 156; Pind. P. 4, 293; but Aesch. Pr. 399 (chor.); Eur. Phoen. 1527 (chor.) In strict Attic, instances of fut. with σ are rare, διολέσω Eur. Hel. 888, may perhaps be subj. but ὀλέσεις Ar. Av. 1506 (Mss. Bekk. ὀλεῖς Bergk, Mein. Dind. 5 ed., ὀλεῖ Dind. 2 ed.), ἀπολέσω Com. Fr. (Plat.) 2, 621. 633 (Mein. -λῶ, -λεσας Hanov.) Collat. form ὀλέκω properly Epic, Il. 18, 172; Emped. 64; Soph. Ant. 1285 (chor.); Opp. Hal. 2, 660: imp. ὄλεκον Il. 11, 150; Theocr. 22, 108, iter. ὀλέκεσκεν *now* Il. 19, 135 (Bekk. Dind. La R.) **Mid.** ὀλέκομαι *perish*, ὀλέκει Aesch. Pr. 563 (chor.), -κονται Il. 16, 17: imp. unaugm. in Hom. ὀλέκοντο Il. 1, 10, but ὠλεκόμαν Dor. Soph. Tr. 1013 (chor.) This verb is poetic in *simple*, except late, fut. ὀλεῖ V. T. Prov. 1, 32: aor. ὤλεσα Arr. Peripl. 3 (Gesn. ὤνησ- Herch.); subj. ὀλέσητε V. T. Jer. 38, 2; opt. ὀλέσαισαν (sic) Job 18, 11. 20, 10: **2** p. ὄλωλα Jer. 38, 2. **Mid.** ὄλλῡται *perishes*, Prov. 11, 7: fut. ὀλεῖται Prov. 25, 19, -οῦνται 13, 2: **2** aor. ὤλετο Job 4, 11, -οντο Jer. 29, 11. In classic prose ἀπόλλυμι. ὀλλῦσαι Il. 8, 449, is part. pres. not inf. aor.

Ὀλολύζω *To shout*, ὀλόλυζε Od. 22, 411; -ζειν Ar. Pax 97; Dem. 18, 260: imp. ὠλόλυζον Com. Fr. (Men.) 4, 166: fut. ὀλολύξομαι Eur. Elec. 691; Or. Sib. 1, 163: act. ὀλολύξω late V. T. Esai. 16, 7. 65, 14. Amos 8, 3: aor. ὠλόλυξα Eur. Bac. 689; late prose Heliod. 3, 5, ἀν- Simon. (C.) 148 (Bergk); Aesch. Ag. 587; Soph. El. 750; Eur. Med. 1173 ἐπ- Ar. Av. 782, unaugm. in Epic ὀλόλ- Od. 3, 450. 4, 767. Hom. H. 1, 119. 2, 267; Ap. Rh. 3, 1218; Theocr. 17, 64; imper. ὀλολύξατε Aesch. Eum. 1043. 1047; Ar. Eq. 1327; inf. ὀλολύξαι Dem. 18, 259: aor. mid. ὠλολύξατο, ἐπ- Aesch. Ag. 1236.

Ὀλοφύρομαι *To bewail*, Dep. Il. 16, 450; Tyrt. 12, 27; Pind. Fr. 84, 17; Soph. El. 148 (chor.); Eur. Rhes. 896 (chor.); Her. 2, 141; Thuc. 2, 44: imp. ὀλοφύρετο Ap. Rh. 1, 250, ἀπ-ωλ- Xen. Hell. 1, 1, 27: fut. ὀλοφῡροῦμαι Lys. 29, 4: aor. ὠλοφῡράμην (Lys.) 2, 37. 61, ἀν- Thuc. 8, 81; Pl. Prot. 327, Epic unaugm. ὀλοφῡρ- Il. 8, 245. Od. 11, 418; Ap. Rh. 4, 29; Bion 1, 62; ὀλοφύρασθαι Thuc. 7, 30: aor. pass. ὀλοφυρθείς Thuc. 6, 78 as mid. (Schol. Bauer &c.), as pass. (Port. Elms. and seemingly Popp. Krüg.) Poppo in reference to the meaning of aor. p. ὀλοφυρθείς Thuc. 6, 78, says cautiously, "as this verb both in Thuc. and other authors is Dep. mid. one confidently expects the aor. p. with pass. meaning," and refers to Rost's Gr. Gram. 113, 6. Rost there says that "the **1** aor. pass. of Dep. mid. verbs is *always* pass." This is too strong: ἄγαμαι, ἀπολογέομαι, ἀρνέομαι &c. have in classic Auth. both aor. mid. and pass. as mid., and μέμφομαι has in Thuc. himself, ἐμεμψάμην 3, 61. 2, 64, and in same sense ἐμέμφθην 4, 85.

Ὁμᾰλίζω *To level, smooth*, Xen. Oec. 18, 5; Aristot. Pol. 2, 7, 8: fut. -ίσω late V. T. Symm. Job 3, 10, -ιῶ Esai. 45, 2: aor.

-ισα Esai. 28, 25: p. p. ὡμαλισμένος Isocr. 6, 65: aor. ὡμαλίσθην Aristot. Pol. 2, 7, 3: fut. ὁμαλισθησόμενος Aristot. Pol. 2, 6, 10: and earlier fut. mid. as pass. -ιεῖται Xen. Oec. 18, 5.

'Ομαρτέω *To be together, accompany*, mostly Poet. -τεῖ Eur. Bac. 923, -τέει Hippocr. 7, 94 (Lit.); Opp. Cyn. 2, 223; imper. -άρτει Theogn. 1165; -τέων Il. 24, 438; -τεῖν Aesch. Eum. 338: imp. ὡμάρτουν Aesch. Pr. 678; Soph. O. C. 1647, Ion. -τευν Ap. Rh. 1, 579, 3 dual ὁμαρτήτην for -είτην Il. 13, 584 (Vulg. Wolf, Spitzn.), see below: fut. ὁμαρτήσω Hes. Op. 196; Ap. Rh. 1, 305; Eur. Phoen. 1616; late prose, Philostr. Ap. 96 (Kayser): 1 aor. ὡμάρτησα Hes. Th. 201; Orph. Arg. 1219; opt. ὁμαρτήσειεν Od. 13, 87 (ἁμ- La R.); -ήσας 21, 188 (ἁμ- La R.); Theocr. 25, 192: 2 aor. ὅμαρτεν Orph. Arg. 513. For ὁμαρτήτην Il. 13, 584 (Vulg.) called Ion. imp. for -είτην, Bekker, Fäsi, Dind. La R. read with Aristarch. adv. ὁμαρτήδην. This verb is mostly confined to Epic and Tragic writers. We have not seen it in Comedy, nor good Attic prose.

'Ομῑχέω *To make water*, Hes. Op. 727; Diog. Laert. 8, 17; aor. (ὀμίχω) ὧμιξεν Hipponax 55 (Bergk.)

Ὄμνῡμι *To swear*, Pind. P. 4, 166; Aesch. Sept. 529; Soph. Tr. 1188; Eur. Hipp. 1026; Ar. Thesm. 274; Andoc. 1, 91; Xen. An. 6, 6, 17; Pl. Phaedr. 236; Dem. 23, 68; ὄμνῦθι Il. 23, 585, Att. ὄμνῦ Soph. Tr. 1185; Eur. Med. 746, 3 pl. ὀμνύντων Thuc. 5, 47; ὀμνύναι Her. 4, 68; Xen. Hell. 1, 3, 11; Isocr. 15, 21; Isae. 2, 39; Dem. 54, 39, ὀμνῡ́ω Com. Fr. (Pher.) 2, 324. (Antiph.) 3, 149; Her. 4, 172. 5, 7; Xen. An. 6, 1, 31. 7, 6, 18; Lycurg. 76; Dem. 23, 5. 54, 41, ἀπ- Pind. N. 7, 70; ὄμνυε Theocr. 27, 35, -έτω Il. 19, 175; ὀμνύων Dem. 54, 40. 57, 56, and ὀμόω pres. only in part. ὀμοῦντες if correct, Her. 1, 153 (Vulg. Gaisf. -νύντες Bekk. Dind. Stein): imp. ὤμνυν Ar. Eccl. 823, Av. 520 (Br. Dind. Bergk); Andoc. 1, 90; Lys. 25, 27; Dem. 17, 10, ἀπ- Od. 2, 377; Ar. Eq. 424, and ὤμνῠον Il. 14, 278; Epicharm. 71 (Ahr.); Thuc. 5, 19. 23. 24; Lys. 19, 26; Dem. 19, 292. 21, 119: fut. ὀμοῦμαι, -εῖ, -εῖται &c. Il. 1, 233; Hes. Op. 194; Ar. Lys. 193; Xen. Hell. 1, 3, 11; Dem. 39, 3, Dor. 1 pl. ὀμιώμεθα Ar. Lys. 183 (Vulg. Bekk. Bergk, ὀμιόμ- Elms. Dind. Mein.): fut. act. late, ὀμόσω Anth. 12, 201; Plut. Cic. 23; App. Civ. 1, 30; Dio Chrys. Or. 56 (568); Diog. Laert. 1, 9; Geop. 12, 28: and mid. ὀμόσομαι, ἐπ- (Luc. Philopatr. 5): aor. ὤμοσα Od. 4, 253; Soph. Ph. 623; Ar. Nub. 825; Her. 1, 165; Antiph. 5, 85; Thuc. 3, 59; Lys. 12, 10; Pl. Leg. 683, Epic ὤμοσσα Il. 20, 313, ὄμοσσα 10, 328, ὄμοσα 19, 113; Dor. pt. ὀμόσσαις Pind. Ol. 6, 20: p. ὀμώμοκα Eur. Hipp. 612; Ar. Ran. 1471; Andoc. 1, 90; Lys. 10, 32; Isae. 2, 47;

Dem. 9, 34, ἀντ- Antiph. 1, 8: plp. ὀμωμόκει Xen. Hell. 5, 1, 35 (Vulg.) ὠμωμ- (Dind. Breitb.), ὀμωμ- Dem. 9, 15. 19, 318 (Bekk.), ὠμωμ- (Dind. Saupp.), συν-ομωμ- Dio Cass. 64, 51 (Bekk.), συν-ωμωμ- (L. Dind.), συν-ωμοκ- (Vulg.): p. p. ὀμώμοται (Aesch. Ag. 1290); Dem. 20, 159, ξυν- Ar. Lys. 1007, ὀμώμονται Andoc. 1, 98, and ὀμώμοσται Eur. Rhes. 816 (Mss. Vulg. Kirchh. Nauck, -οται Buttm. Dind. Matth.); Aristot. Rhet. 1, 15, 27; ὀμωμοσμένος Dem. 7, 10. 22, 4; Aristot. Rhet. 1, 15, 33, but later ὠμοσμένος Dio. Hal. 10, 22 (Vulg. ὀμωμοσ- Kiessl.); App. Lib. 83 (ὀμωμοσ- Mendels.), συν-ωμοσ- Joseph. Ant. 15, 8, 3: aor. ὠμόθην Isae. 2, 40, ὑπ- Dem. 48, 25, and ὠμόσθην Xen. Hell. 7, 4, 10 (-όθην Dind. Cob.), ὑπ- Hyperid. Fr. 204 (Blass): fut. ὀμοσθήσομαι Andoc. 3, 34. **Mid.** in comp. ὄμνῦται, δι- Lys. 10, 11, ἐπ- Ar. Plut. 725: imp. ὠμνύμην, κατ- Her. 6, 69, -υτο, δι- Soph. Tr. 378; Aeschin. 3, 150: fut. ἐξ-ομοῦμαι Soph. Ant. 535; Dem. 45, 61, ἀπ- Aeschin. 1, 67, δι- Dem. 23, 67: aor. ὠμοσάμην, δι- Soph. Aj. 1233; Antiph. 5, 90. 96, ἀντ- Isocr. 18, 37, ἐξ- Aeschin. 2, 94, ὑπ- Dem. 48, 25, ἐπ- (Dem.) 18, 137; Luc. Tim. 47. **Vb.** ἀπ-ώμοτος Soph. Ant. 388. 394.

For the *unique* pres. part. ὀμοῦντες Her. 1, 153, Bekker, Dind. Lhardy, Stein read ὀμνύντες perhaps rightly, see ὀμνύντας 2, 118. Imper. ὄμνῦθι Il. 23, 585, Attic ὄμνῦ Soph. Tr. 1185; Eur. I. T. 743, ὄμνῦ before a vowel, Orac. Her. 6, 86. **Fut. act.** ὀμόσω is from ὀμόω, but mid. ὀμοῦμαι, -εῖ, -εῖται seems to be from obs. ὄμω, as νεμοῦμαι, -εῖ, -εῖται from νέμω, not contr. from ὀμόσομαι. ὀμιώμεθα quoted is not subj. but Dor. fut., -ιόμεθα (Elms.), both are legitimate. ὀμόσω fut. act. is late, and never, we think, contr. ὀμῶ, -εῖς, -εῖ; ὀμόσσει was introduced unnecessarily for ὀμόσσῃ Ps. Phocyl. 11, 17 (Bergk), and ἀπ-ομούντων Lys. 16, 6 (Ald. Reisk.) has been displaced by ἀποδημούντων (Mss. Bekk. B. S. Scheib.) The tragedians and Aristophanes seem always to have used the form in -υμι, not -ύω, but in the Com. Fr. and in Ion. and Attic prose both forms occur, -ύμι prevailing. See Her. 2, 118. 4, 68. 1, 212. 5, 106, with 4, 172. 5, 7. Hom. always, we think, augments imp. ὤμν-, but aor. ὤμ-, or ὄμ- as it suits him.

Ὁμοιόω *To make like*, Thuc. 3, 82; Pl. Rep. 393; Ion. pt. -εῦντες ἐξ- Her. 3, 24: imp. ὡμοίουν Pl. Parm. 148: fut. -ώσω v. r. Isocr. 11, 8: aor. ὡμοίωσα, subj. ὁμοιώσωμεν Isocr. 11, 8; -ωσας Eur. Hel. 33; Her. 8, 28: p. p. ὡμοίωμαι Pl. Rep. 431; Isocr. 6, 76: aor. -ώθην Pl. Rep. 510; -ωθῆναι Thuc. 5, 103, Epic -θήμεναι Il. 1, 187. Od. 3, 120: fut. ὁμοιωθήσομαι Pl. Leg. 964; Galen 4, 607: and as pass. fut. mid. ὁμοιώσομαι *shall be like*, Her. 7, 158; Philostr. Apoll. 270. **Mid.** ὁμοιόομαι, Ion. -εύμενος

(Dind. Abicht, -ούμ- Bekk. Stein) as **act.** *liken, compare,* Her. 1, 123: **fut.** -ώσομαι **pass.** see above. The Attics, we think, did not use the **mid.** The **act.** is occasionally used in a seemingly neuter sense, *is like, likens* &c. προσομοιοῦν Dem. 60, 30, where αὐτὸν is Reiske's conject., αὐτοῦ (Bekk.), αὑτοῦ (B. S. Dind.); so ἐξισοῖ Soph. El. 1194; Thuc. 5, 71. 6, 87, *equals* as we say. The *simple* is so used late, Dioscor.

Ὁμοκλέω and -άω *To call to,* Poet. **imp.** unaugm. ὁμοκλέομεν Od. 24, 173, -όκλεον Il. 15, 658; Ap. Rh. 4, 1006, -εεν Orph. Arg. 944, and ὁμόκλα Il. 18, 156. 24, 248; Q. Sm. 3, 166: **aor.** ὁμόκλησα Il. 23, 363. Od. 19, 155; -ήσειε Il. 16, 714; -ήσας Il. 6, 54; Soph. El. 712, iter. ὁμοκλήσασκε Il. 2, 199. This verb is mostly Epic. The **pres.** we have not seen, and **imp.** of the form -άω only in 3 sing. ὁμόκλᾱ. Never augm. either in Hom. or late Epic.

Ὁμολογέω *To agree, confess,* Soph. Ph. 980; Ar. Plut. 94; Her. 8, 94; Antiph. 2, δ, 8; Thuc. 2, 5; Pl. Prot. 317; Isae. 3, 57: **imp.** ὡμολ- Antiph. 5, 39; Lys. 7, 37; Pl. Conv. 173: **fut.** -ήσω Her. 8, 144; Isocr. 14, 10; Isae. 1, 19; Pl. Conv. 174; Xen. Hell. 2, 2, 16: **aor.** ὡμολόγησα Her. 9, 88; Antiph. 5, 14; Thuc. 1, 101; Lys. 12, 9: **p.** ὡμολόγηκα Andoc. 1, 29; Lys. 12, 34; Isae. 3, 11: **plp.** -ήκει Thuc. 2, 95; Dem. 23, 167: **p. p.** -ηται Pl. Phaed. 105; Isae. 4, 15; -ημένα Isocr. 18, 11; Isae. 5, 1: **plp.** -ήμην Xen. An. 1, 9, 14; Dem. 29, 44: **aor.** -ήθην Thuc. 8, 29; Isae. 5, 17: **fut.** -ηθήσεται Hippocr. 6, 6 (Lit.): and as **pass. fut. mid.** ὁμολογήσεται Pl. Theaet. 171; **v. r.** Hippocr. quoted. **Mid.** ὁμολογοῦμαι Pl. Crat. 416; Isocr. 2, 17: **imp.** ὡμολ- Isae. 8, 21: **fut.** -λογήσομαι **pass.** see above, but **mid.** διομολ- Pl. Rep. 392, and late ἐξ- V. T. Ps. 18, 50: **aor.** ὡμολογησάμην, δι- Isae. 3, 28; **subj.** ὁμολογησώμεθα Xen. Conv. 4, 56; Pl. Rep. 436; **opt.** -σαιτο Xen. Mem. 1, 2, 57; -σασθαι Pl. Crat. 439; -σάμενος Rep. 544: and late **p. p.** as **mid.** καθωμολογημένος Plut. Crass. 33. **Vb.** ὁμολογητέον Pl. Leg. 860. Our lexicons are too *sparing* on the **mid. v.**, even the best miss entirely the **fut.** as **pass.**

Ὀμόργνῡμι *To wipe,* Poet. **imp.** ὀμόργνυ in tmesi, Il. 5, 416: **fut.** late in *simple* ὀμόρξω Nic. Ther. 558 (G. Schn.), but ἐξ- Eur. Fr. 781 (Dind.): **aor.** ὤμορξα in tmesi, ἐξ- Eur. Or. 219; ὀμόρξας in tmesi, Nic. Al. 559 (G. Schn.): **p. p.** ὠμοργμένος, ἀπ- Aristot. Physiog. 6, 6: **aor. pass.** ὀμορχθείς, ἀπ- Ar. Vesp. 560, by some needlessly called **act.** **Mid.** ὀμόργνῡμαι *wipe oneself,* Pythag. Diog. Laert. 8, 17: **imp.** ὠμόργνυντο Od. 11, 527: **fut.** ὀμόρξομαι, ἀπ- Eur. Hipp. 653, ἐξ- Ar. Ach. 843: **aor.** ὠμόρξατο Nic. Ther. 859, ἐξ- Pl. Gorg. 525, ὀμόρξατο, ἀπ- Od. 18, 200;

subj. ὀμόρξωμαι, ἐξ- Eur. H. F. 1399; ἀπ-ομορξαι Eur. Fr. 695 (D.); ὀμόρξασθαι, ἐξ- El. 502; in *simple* ὀμορξάμενος Il. 18, 124. Od. 8, 88; Ap. Rh. 2, 242, ἀπ- Ar. Ach. 695. See μόργνυμι.

Ὁμοστῑχάω *To step with, accompany*, Epic and only -στῑχάει Il. 15, 635. ὁμοστιχέων quoted by some from Nonn. Par. 10, 143, as pt. of this verb is gen. pl. of adj. ὁμοστιχής. Hesych. however gives ὁμοστιχεῖ, to explain -στιχάει.

Ὀνειδίζω *To reproach*, Soph. Aj. 1298; Com. Fr. (Alex.) 3, 440; Her. 1, 41; Thuc. 1, 5; Andoc. 2, 5; Isocr. 16, 3; -δίζων Od. 18, 380; Thuc. 1, 5; -δίζειν Andoc. 2, 5: **imp.** ὠνείδιζον Pl. Phaedr. 257: **fut.** Attic -ιῶ Soph. O. R. 1423; Eur. Tr. 430; Pl. Apol. 29, late -ίσω Aristid. 46, 278 (Vulg. -ιῶ Ms. N. Dind.): **aor.** ὠνείδισα Soph. O. R. 412; Com. Fr. (Cratet.) 2, 247; Her. 8, 106; Thuc. 3, 62; Pl. Theaet. 150, ὀνείδ- Il. 9, 34; Theogn. 1115; -δίσαι Aesch. Ch. 917: **p.** ὠνείδικα Lys. 16, 15: **aor. pass.** ὠνειδίσθην late, Polyb. 11, 4 (5) Bekk.: and **fut.** -ισθήσομαι Epist. Phal. 110 (Herch.); Apocr. Syr. 41, 7: classic, **fut. mid.** ὀνειδιοῦμαι, -ιεῖσθε as pass. Soph. O. R. 1500: **pres.** ὀνειδίζομαι Eur. Tr. 936; Thuc. 1, 77; Pl. Tim. 86. **Vb.** ὀνειδιστέον Pl. Leg. 689.

Ὀνεύω *To turn, wind* (ὄνος), -εύοντες Com. Fr. (Stratt.) 2, 772 (Mein.) only **pres.**: and **imp.** ὤνευον Thuc. 7, 25.

Ὀνίνημι *To assist*, (Il.) 24, 45; Hym. 3, 577; Hes. Th. 429; Antiph. 2, β, 1; Isocr. 15, 264, like ἵστημι; part. ὀνῖνάς, -ᾶσα Pl. Phil. 58; inf. ὀνῖνάναι Rep. 600: **imp.** see below: **fut.** ὀνήσω Il. 8, 36; Eur. An. 1004; Com. Fr. (Alex.) 3, 489; Her. 7, 141 (Orac.); Hippocr. 2, 336 (Lit.); Pl. Rep. 426, Dor. -ᾱσῶ Theocr. 7, 36: **aor.** ὤνησα Il. 9, 509; Eur. Tr. 933; Ar. Lys. 1033; Her. 9, 76; Pl. Apol. 27, ὄνησα Il. 1, 503, Dor. ὤνᾱσα Simon. C. 55 (Bergk); Theocr. 16, 57; subj. ὀνάσῃς Theocr. 5, 69 &c.: **p. p.** late, ὤνημαι Liban. Epist. 738 (Wolf); as **mid.** if correct (Hippocr.) Epist. 3, 608 (Erm.), see below: **aor.** ὠνήθην, ὀνηθῆναι Xen. An. 5, 5, 2, Dor. ὠνάθην Theocr. 15, 55. **Mid.** ὀνῖναμαι *benefit oneself, reap benefit*, Pl. Gorg. 525: **imp.** ὠνινάμην Rep. 380: **fut.** ὀνήσομαι Il. 7, 173; Soph. Tr. 570; Eur. Hel. 935; Pl. Apol. 30: **1 aor.** late ὠνησάμην, ὀνήσασθαι Galen 2, 381 (ὠνοσάμην (ὀνόω) Anth. 7, 484, see below): **2 aor.** ὠνάμην *indic.* rare, -ασθε Eur. H. F. 1368 (Vulg. Nauck, -ησθε L. and now W. Dind.): more freq. late, Ael. V. H. 14, 24 (-ήμην Herch.); Luc. D. Mort. 12, 2. Charon 24; Paus. 3, 6, 4; App. Prooem. 11; Dio. Hal. Ant. 1, 23, ὀν- Anth. App. Epigr. 307, ἀπ-ον- Musae. 292; opt. often, ὀναίμην (never ὀνοίμην, Ar. Thesm. 469 &c. have been corrected) Simon. C. 128; Soph. O. R. 644; Eur. Supp.

256; Ar. Plut. 1062; Pl. Theaet. 151; Dem. 28, 20, ἀπ- Il. 24, 556, -ναίατο Soph. El. 211; inf. ὄνασθαι Eur. Hipp. 517; Pl. Rep. 528, ἀπ- Ap. Rh. 2, 196, also ὠνήμην Theogn. 1380; Eur. Alc. 335; Com. Fr. (Men.) 4, 228; rare in prose Pl. Meno 84; Aristot. Rhet. 3, 16, 9; Luc. Prom. 20, ἀπ-ώνητο Her. 1, 168, unaugm. ἀπ-όν- Od. 11, 324. 17, 293; imper. ὄνησο Od. 19, 68; inf. ὀνῆσθαι (Hippocr.) Epist. 9, 392 (Lit. ὠνῆσθαι Erm. 3, 608); ὀνήμενος Od. 2, 33, ἀπ- 24, 30. **Vb.** ἀν-όνητος Soph. Aj. 758, Dor. -ᾱτος Eur. Hipp. 1145 (chor.) The **imp. indic. act.** ὠνίνην is not found, but supplied by ὠφέλουν. The **inf. pres.** ὀνῑνάναι quoted, is Matthiae's emend. approved by Buttm. L. Dind. and Bait. Orell. W. *now* (ed. min. 1847) for ὀνίναι, ὀνῖναι, -εῖναι, -ῆναι, -ῆσαι of the Mss., ὀνῆναι (Bekk. C. Schneidw.), ὀνίναι (B. O. W. ed. maj. 1389); and so quoted by Aristides 47, 328 (v. r. ὀνῆσαι). There are several instances of ὀνινάναι in late authors, Galen de Atr. Bil. 6, 128 &c. Paul. Aeg. 7, 3, p. 230. ὀνῆναι, ὀνίναι, not found elsewhere, point, the first to a **2 aor.** ὤνην, the second to a **1 aor.** ὤνινα from ὀνίνω unused. ὀνεῖται Stob. 68, 36, **pres.** not, as Matthiae says, **fut.** presupposes ὀνέω; ὀνούμενοι (Luc.) Philoptr. 26. A **1 aor.** form ὠνᾰσατο occurs Anth. 7, 484, for which the *v. r.* ὠνόσατο from a Theme (ὀνόω) is approved. ὤνατο Il. 17, 25, belongs to ὄνομαι *I reproach.*

Ὀνομάζω *To name,* Eur. Hel. 1193; C. Fr. (Stratt.) 2, 781; Andoc. 3, 33; Xen. Hell. 2, 3, 1; Pl. Crat. 417; subj. -άζω Pl. Alcib. 1, 135; opt. -άζοι Il. 9, 515; Pl. Rep. 493; -άζων Il. 10, 68; Thuc. 2, 17; Xen. Cyr. 5, 3, 46; Pl. Conv. 212; -άζειν Od. 14, 145; Eur. Bac. 527; Ar. Eccl. 299; Thuc. 8, 92, 11; Pl. Crat. 387, Ion. οὐνομάζω Her. 4, 27. 59: **imp.** ὠνόμ- Aesch. Ag. 681; Aeschin. 2, 38, Hom. of necessity always ὀνόμ- Il. 18, 449. Od. 4, 551: **fut.** -ᾰσω Pl. Rep. 471: and **mid.** Aeol. ὀνυμάξομαι Pind. P. 7, 5: **aor.** ὠνόμασα Od. 24, 339; Pind. P. 12, 23; Aesch. Pr. 597; Ar. Eccl. 190; Thuc. 4, 102; Pl. Prot. 330; Aeschin. 2, 167, οὐνόμ- Her. 4, 6, Aeol. ὀνύμαξε Pind. P. 2, 44. 11, 6: **p.** ὠνόμακα Pl. Soph. 219; Dem. 23, 39: **p. p.** ὠνόμασμαι Soph. O. C. 61; Her. 2, 155 (οὐν- Bekk. Krüg. Abicht); Thuc. 6, 96; Pl. Tim. 65, 3 pl. Ion. ὠνομάδαται Dio Cass. 37, 16 (Bekk.): **aor.** ὠνομάσθην Soph. O. R. 1036; Her. 5, 71 (οὐν- Bekk. Krüg. Abicht); Thuc. 1, 96; Pl. Soph. 262; Isae. 2, 41, Poet. 3 pl. ὀνόμασθεν Pind. Ol. 9, 46; ὀνομασθείς Thuc. 6, 55, Ion. οὐν- Her. 1, 120: **fut.** late, ὀνομασθήσονται Epist. Phal. 103 (Herch.); Galen 3, 488. 7, 367; Joseph. 17, 2, 4. **Mid.** ὀνομάζομαι *call one's own,* **imp.** ὠνομάζετο Soph. O. R. 1021: **fut.** Aeol. and Dor. ὀνυμάξομαι Pind. P. 7, 5: **aor.** late, ὠνομάσαντο, ἐπ- Or. Sib. 3, 141. **Vb.** ὀνομαστέον Pl. Crat. 387. In a Cumaean

Inscr. 3524 (Boeckh) occurs the form προσ-ονυμάσδεσθαι. In Her. Mss. and Editors differ on ὀν- οὐν-, and ὠν- οὐν-.

Ὄνομαι *To insult, think lightly of* (ὄνω, ὀνόω), pres. and imp. like δίδομαι, 2 sing. ὄνοσαι Od. 17, 378, Epic 2 pl. οὔνεσθε Il. 24, 241 (Vulg. Both. Spitzn.), ὄνονται Od. 21, 427; Her. 2, 167; ὄνοιτο Il. 13, 287: **imp.** ὤνοντο, κατ- Her. 2, 172 (Ald. Bekk. Dind.), κατ-όνοντο (Mss. V. S. Gaisf.): **fut.** ὀνόσομαι (σσ) Il. 9, 55; Anth. 7, 398; Ap. Rh. 3, 475; ὀνόσσεσθαι Od. 5, 379; Ap. Rh. 1, 830: **aor.** ὠνοσάμην Il. 14, 95. 17, 173, ὀνόσασθε 24, 241 (Bekk. Dind.); ὀνόσαιτο Il. 17, 399; Theocr. 26, 38; ὀνοσσάμενος Il. 24, 439; ὀνόσασθαι Ap. Rh. 1, 205; Q. Sm. 6, 92, and rare ὤνατο Epic, Il. 17, 25 (Bekk. suggests -οτο): and **aor. pass.** ὠνόσθην, κατ-ονοσθῇς as **mid.** Her. 2, 136. **Vb.** ὀνοστός Il. 9, 164, -στός Pind. I. 4 (3), 50. For the rather singular form οὔνεσθε quoted, Buttm. suggests the reg. οὔνοσθε; Bekk. Dind. La Roche adopt ὀνόσασθε the reading of Aristarchus. Epic and Ionic.

Ὀνομαίνω *To name* (Ion. οὐνομ-), a rather Poet. form of ὀνομάζω, Hom. H. Ven. 290; Luc. Hist. Con. 18 (Dind.), see below: **fut.** Ion. οὐνομᾰνέω Her. 4, 47: **aor.** ὠνόμηνα Isae. 3, 33, in Hom. and Hes. unaugm. ὀνόμ- Il. 16, 491. Od. 24, 341; Hes. Op. 80. Fr. 58; Ap. Rh. 3, 1075; Orph. Arg. 1289; Callim. Jov. 38; -μήνω Il. 9, 121; -ῆναι Hippocr. 3, 503 (Erm.), ἐξ- Od. 6, 66. Aeol. and Dor. ὀνυμαίνω Luc. Hist. Con. 18 (Bekk. Fritzs.); ὀνυμαίνεται, -νονται Tim. Locr. 100; also Aeol. and Boeot. ὀνουμ-, **1 aor.** ὠνούμηνεν Corinn. 4 (Ahrens.) In Epic, excepting H. Ven. 290, the **aor.** alone seems to be used, and, from necessity, always without augm. Never in Attic poetry, and once only in prose, Isae. quoted.

Ὀνοτάζω *To blame,* Poet. Hes. Op. 258; H. Merc. 30. **Mid.** ὀνοταζόμεναι *loathing,* Aesch. Supp. 11.

Ὀξύνω *To sharpen,* Anth. App. Epigr. 304; Theophr. H. P. 4, 3, 4, ἀπ- Od. 6, 269 (Mss. La R. Düntz. Ameis, -ξύουσι Bekk. Buttm. Dind.), παρ- Xen. Mem. 3, 3, 13; Isocr. 12, 37: **imp.** ὤξυνον, παρ- 5, 3: **fut.** ὀξῠνεῖ, παρ- Dem. 2, 11, -υνοῦσι 54, 25: **aor.** ὤξῡνα, -ῦναι Soph. Tr. 1176, ἀπ- Od. 9, 326 (most Mss. La R. ἀπο-ξῦσαι Buttm. Bekk. Dind.); perhaps strengthened by ἐξαπ-οξύνας Eur. Cycl. 456; and ἀπ-οξύνας Luc. D. Mar. 2, 2 (4 Mss. Hemsterh. Fritzsche, Dind.), παρ-ώξυνε Thuc. 6, 88: **p.** ὤξυγκα, παρ- Polyb. 31, 9; Joseph. Ant. 11, 7: **p. p.** ὤξυμμαι, παρ- Lys. 4, 8; Aeschin. 1, 43; Dem. 14, 16; App. Civ. 3, 92. 4, 10 (Bekk.), ἀπ- Polyb. 18, 1, and ὤξυσμαι, ἀπ- Polyb. 1, 22, συν- 6, 22 (Bekk.): **plp.** ὤξυντο, παρ- Dem. 57, 49: **aor.** ὠξύνθην, παρ- Hippocr. 1, 184 (Erm.); Aeschin. 3, 118; Dem. 21, 2; ὀξυνθείῃ, παρ- Isocr. 5, 101; in *simple*, part. ὀξυνθείς Her. 8, 138, παρ- Lycurg. 87: fut. ὀξυνθήσομαι, παρ- Hippocr. 2, 426 (Lit.): pres. ὀξύνονται Aristot. Gen. An. 3, 2, 17. The *simple* form seems not to occur in classic Attic prose.

'Οπᾱδέω *To accompany*, -ηδέω Epic and Ion., only pres. ὀπαδεῖ Simon. C. 15; Pind. P. 4, 287, -ηδεῖ Il. 5, 216; Hes. Th. 80; Theogn. 933; Callim. Del. 19; Theocr. 17, 75 (Mss. Mein. Ahr. -αδεῖ Fritzs. Ziegler): imp. unaugm. ὀπάδει Theocr. 2, 14, -ήδει Il. 2, 184. Od. 19, 398; inf. ὀπηδεῖν Hom. H. 2, 352. **ὀπάζω** Il. 17, 566; Ar. Eq. 200: imp. ὤπαζ- Il. 8, 341, ὄπ- 16, 730: fut. -σω, -άσσω Od. 8, 430; Colluth. 87; -άσσομεν Il. 24, 153; Theocr. 28, 9: aor. ὤπᾰσα Il. 22, 51; Hes. Th. 974; Solon 13, 74; Pind. N. 1, 16; Aesch. Pr. 252, ὄπασσ- Il. 17, 196; Pind. I. 7, 38; Dor. part. -άσαις I. 2, 14, is used by Epic, Lyric, and (in pres. and aor. act.) Attic poets. The mid. seems to be Epic and Lyr. the pass. Epic. We have seen neither verb in prose.

'Οπίζω *To regard, fear*, in act. only part. -ίζων Aristot. Meteor. 4, 7, 9; Anth. App. 223. Mid. ὀπίζομαι as act. Od. 13, 148, classic only pres.: and imp. with and without augm. ὠπίζετο Il. 18, 216, ὀπίζεο 22, 332, -ετο Hes. Sc. 21; Ap. Rh. 2, 181; -όμενος Theogn. 1148; Pind. I. 3, 5: aor. late ὠπίσατο Q. Sm. 2, 618, missed by Lexicogr.—Poet. but in neither Trag. nor Comedy.

'Οπλέω *To (arm) prepare*, Poet. for ὁπλίζω, only imp. ὥπλεον Od. 6, 73, ὅπλ- (La Roche): to which as mid. ὅπλομαι, only inf. -εσθαι Il. 19, 172. 23, 159.

'Οπλίζω *To arm*, Soph. El. 996; Thuc. 3, 27: imp. ὥπλ- Her. 2, 163; Xen. Cyr. 6, 4, 1, iter. ὁπλίζεσκον, ἐφ- Ap. Rh. 3, 843: Epic fut. ὁπλίσσω, ἐφ- Od. 6, 69: aor. ὥπλισα Her. 1, 127; Thuc. 4, 9, ὥπλισσα Il. 11, 641; ὁπλίσας Eur. Ion 980, -ίσσας Callim. Cer. 36: p. ὥπλικε, παρ- Diod. Sic. 4, 10: plp. ὡπλίκει Dio Cass. 78, 6: p. p. ὥπλισμαι Aesch. Sept. 433; Thuc. 4, 94; Xen. Cyr. 6, 4, 16: aor. ὡπλίσθην Thuc. 6, 17; Xen. Eq. 12, 10. Mid. ὁπλίζομαι *arm one's own*, trans. Eur. Or. 926. 1223; Opp. Hal. 4, 364: imp. ὁπλίζοντο Od. 16, 453 (La R. Ameis), ὡπλ- (Bekk. Dind.); Eur. Ion 1124: fut. ὁπλίσομαι Theoph. Epist. 35, ἐφ- Anth. 9, 39: aor. ὡπλισάμην Il. 23, 301. 351, ὡπλισσ- Od. 2, 20. 9, 291. 344. 10, 116; Emped. 316, but ὁπλισάμεσθα Od. 4, 429. 574 (Vulg. Wolf, Dind. La Roche, ὡπλ- Bekk. 2 ed.); Opp. Cyn. 1, 132; subj. ὁπλισόμεσθα for -σώμ- Od. 12, 292, ἐφ- Il. 8, 503; ὁπλισάμενοι Xen. Cyr. 6, 2, 16?: and perhaps p. ὡπλισμένος Eur. Phoen. 267: intrans. -ίζομαι *arm oneself, be in armour*, Eur. Med. 1242; subj. -ώμεθα Od. 24, 495;

-ίζεσθαι Xen. M. Eq. 1, 23: imp. ὥπλιζ- Il. 8, 55. Od. 14, 526 (ὅπλ- Mss. La Roche); Eur. Elec. 627: fut. ὁπλιοῦμαι late, Schol. Il. 13, 20: aor. ὡπλισάμην Xen. Hell. 5, 4, 21: in sense p. p. ὥπλισμαι Eur. Heracl. 672; Her. 7, 79; Thuc. 4, 94; Xen. An. 2, 6, 25: aor. ὡπλίσθην Her. 2, 152; Thuc. 6, 17; Xen. Cyr. 6, 4, 4, Epic 3 pl. ὅπλισθεν Od. 23, 143 (Vulg. Wolf, Dind. La Roche, ὥπλ- Bekk. 2 ed.) Vb. ὁπλιστέον Xen. Hipp. 1, 6. This verb is usually augmented in Hom. but the forms ὁπλισάμεσθα, ὅπλισθεν Od. quoted, have, from tradition, we fancy—the principle we don't see—been left unaugmented. Bekker *now* however uniformly augments it (2 ed.); but La Roche never in the Od.

Ὀπτάω *To roast* &c. Ar. Av. 1691; Her. 9, 120; Xen. Cyr. 8, 2, 6: imp. ὤπτων Od. 3, 33: fut. -ήσω Ar. Ach. 1102: aor. ὤπτησα Il. 7, 318; Hes. Fr. 234; Her. 1, 119, reg. in poetry and prose: pass. -άομαι, -τῷτο Her. 8, 137; Xen. Oec. 16, 14, -έομαι, -εύμενος Theocr. 7, 55: imp. ὠπτᾶτο Com. Fr. (Polioch.) 4, 590: p. ὤπτημαι Callim. Epigr. 44, 5; -ημένος Ar. Plut. 894; Pl. Hipp. maj. 288: aor. -ήθην, -ηθῇ Aristot. Probl. 21, 11; -θῆναι Od. 20, 27; -θείς Com. Fr. (Antiph.) 3, 26: fut. mid. ὀπτήσομαι as pass. (Luc.) Asin. 31, missed by Lexicogr.: and aor. ὀπτησάμενοι *having roasted*, Ar. Av. 532, also missed. Vb. ὀπτός Od. 4, 66.

Ὀπτεύω, see ὑπ-οπτεύω.

Ὀπυίω *To marry*, of the man, -υίεις Hes. Sc. 356, -υίει Pind. I. 4, 59, -υίουσι Aristot. Eth. Nic. 7, 5, 4 (Bekk.); -υίῃ Od. 15, 21; -υίοι Od. 16, 386; -υίειν Theocr. 22, 161, -υιέμεναι Il. 14, 268, -έμεν 13, 379, v. r. ὀπύω (Aristot. Ap. Rh. and Theocr.) which seems to be the Attic form, see fut.: imp. ὤπυιον Il. 18, 383; Hes. Fr. 83; Luc. Alex. 50 (Orac.). Gall. 19 (Bekk. W. Dind.), ὄπυι- Od. 4, 798; Ap. Rh. 1, 46; Orph. Fr. 14, and ὤπυον Luc. Alex. quoted (Jacob. L. Dind.): fut. ὀπύσω Ar. Ach. 255. Pass. ὀπυίομαι *to be married*, usu. of the woman, Il. 8, 304; Anth. 10, 56; Aristot. Eth. Nic. 7, 6, 4; and Plut. Sol. 20 (ὀπυόμ- Bekk. Sint.): p. p. late ὠπυισμένος Dio. Hal. Excerp. 17, 3 (18, 2 Kiessl.), ὠπυσ- (L. Dind.), others pres. ὀπυιόμενος. (ῡ.)

(Ὀπωπέω) *To see*, a new pres. from perf. ὄπωπα imp. ὀπώπεεν Orph. Arg. 184, -πεον 1025. Mid. aor. ὀπωπήσασθαι Euphor. in Schol. Eur. Phoen. 682.

Ὀπωρίζω *To gather fruit*, Pl. Leg. 845: fut. -ιῶ, Ion. part. -ιεῦντες Her. 4, 172. 182. Mid. -ίζομαι Athen. (Theopomp.) 12, 44: aor. Dor. -ιξάμην Stob. (Dius) 65, 16.

Ὁράω *To see* (ὄπω, ἴδω), ὁρῶ Il. 3, 234; Soph. O. C. 29; Ar. Thesm. 19; Antiph. 5, 7; Thuc. 1, 80, ὁρᾷς Aesch. Ag. 1597, ὁράᾳς Il. 21, 108, ὁρᾷ 18, 442, Dor. -ρῇ Epicharm. 117, 3 pl. -ρεῦντι Theocr. 9, 35, Ion. ὁρέω Her. 1, 80, Ep. -όω Il. 11, 651; Epic opt. ὁρόῳτε Il. 4, 347; Dor. imper. ὅρη Theocr. 15, 12: imp. ἑώραον, -ων Thuc. 1, 51; Pl. Rep. 516, Ion. ὥρεον Her. 4, 3 (Gaisf. Dind.), ὥρων (Bekk. Krüg. Stein, 8, 38 Gaisf.), Hom. always unaugm. ὅρα Il. 16, 646: **fut.** ὄψομαι Il. 24, 704; Eur. Tr. 488; Ar. Pax 78; Her. 8, 75; Isocr. 6, 69, 2 sing. in Attic always ὄψει Aesch. Pr. 22; Soph. Tr. 199; Ar. Thesm. 6. Lys. 56; Xen. Athen. 1, 9. Conv. 4, 22; Il. 23, 620. Od. 12, 101, Ion. ὄψεαι Il. 8, 471. 9, 359. Od. 24, 511; Her. 1, 155; Eur. Andr. 1225 chor. (Mss. Vulg. Kirchh. Nauck, ὄψει Herm. Dind. Paley); ὄψοιντο Thuc. 6, 30, -οίατο Soph. O. R. 1274: **1 aor.** see below: **p.** ἑώρᾱκα Lys. 11, 7. 12, 100; Isocr. 15, 38; Pl. Prot. 310; Xen. Cyr. 3, 1, 18; Dem. 17, 20. 21, 65. 25, 77 &c. (Bekk. Popp. B. Saupp.), and ἑόρᾱκα especially in comic Poet. Ar. Thesm. 32. 33 (Ms. R. Bekk. Dind. Bergk, Enger). Av. 1573. Plut. 98. 1045 (Bekk. Dind. Bergk); Com. Fr. (Eup.) 2, 500. (Alex.) 3, 504 &c.; and now L. Dind. in Xen. Hell. 4, 1, 6. 5, 3, 19. Cyr. 3, 1, 18. An. 2, 1, 16 &c.; so W. Dind. in Dem. 18, 190. 17, 20. 19, 157, and always (3 ed.): **plp.** ἑωράκη Pl. Rep. 328 (-ειν Vulg.), ἑωράκεσάν Thuc. 2, 21 (Bekk. Popp. Krüg.), ἑοράκ- (L. Dind. Stahl, Classen): **p. p.** ἑώρᾱμαι Isocr. 15, 110; Dem. 54, 16. 45, 66; Aristot. H. A. 9, 6, 8. 15, προ- Dem. 54, 19, παρ- Aristot. Metaph. 2, 1; Dem. 23, 105, and more Attic ὦμμαι Aesch. Pr. 998; Aristot. Meteor. 1, 6, 8; Dem. 18, 263. 24, 66, κατ- Pl. Rep. 432: **plp.** ἑώρᾱτο Hippocr. 6, 20: **aor.** ὤφθην Soph. Ant. 709; Eur. Hec. 970; Ar. Av. 680; Thuc. 4, 73. 5, 60; subj. ὀφθῶ Xen. Cyr. 4, 1, 17 &c. Ion. -θέω Her. 8, 7, and ἑωράθην perhaps not in classic Attic, Diod. Sic. 20, 6; Jos. c. Ap. 2, 41; ὁραθῇ Aristot. H. A. 9, 37, 6; ὁραθῆναι Aristot. de Mot. 4, 2; (Pl.) Def. 411; Strab. 3, 5, 6. 5, 3, 2; Luc. Jud. v. 6; -θείς Polyb. 3, 58; Plut. Dion. 9; Strab. 15, 1, 2. 17, 1, 34; Anth. 12, 197: **fut.** ὀφθήσομαι Soph. Tr. 452; Eur. H. F. 1155; Andoc. 2, 10; Lys. 3, 34; Isocr. 15, 143, and late ὁραθήσομαι Galen 3, 820. 822: **2 p.** ὄπωπα usu. poet. and Ion. Il. 6, 124. Od. 21, 94; Emped. 333; Aesch. Eum. 57; Soph. Ant. 6; Ar. Lys. 1157. 1225; Her. 3, 37. 63; Hippocr. 4, 78. 8, 606 (Lit.); Aristot. Part. Anim. 3, 1, 18: **plp.** 3 sing. ὀπώπει Od. 21, 123; Theocr. 4, 7, ὀπώπεε Orph. Arg. 184; Her. 5, 92, -πεσαν 7, 125, Dor. ὀπώπη Theocr. quoted (some Mss. and edit.): **2 aor.** εἶδον Aesch. Eum. 50; Soph. El. 62; Thuc. 8, 79; Pl. Rep. 350, see (εἰδέω). **Mid.** ὁράομαι, -ῶμαι as act. and Poet. Il. 13, 99; Soph. Ant. 594; Com. Fr. (Cratin.) 2, 94, 2 sing. Epic ὅρηαι Od. 14, 343, -ᾶται Il. 24, 291; ὁρώμεθα, ἀφ- Ar. Nub. 281, προ- Dem. 18,

281; -ᾶσθαι Il. 3, 306; Eur. Andr. 113, Epic -άασθαι Od. 16, 107. 18, 4; ὁρώμενος Od. 5, 439; Soph. Tr. 306, in prose late in *simple*, ὁρώμενος Plut. Crass. 16; Polyaen. 4, 7, 6, but προ- Thuc. 1, 17. 5, 111; Pl. Tim. 73, Aeschin. 2, 43. 177; Dem. 6, 8. 18, 27. 149. 178. 281. 19, 271. 20, 162, ὑφ- Thuc. 3, 40, Dem. 18, 43; προ-ορᾶσθαι Thuc. 6, 78; Dem. 21, 61, Ion. -ῆσθαι (Hippocr.) Epist. 9, 366 (Lit.): **imp.** unaugm. in Hom. ὁρώμην Il. 1, 56, in prose late in *simple*, ἑωρᾶτο Polyaen. 8, 16, 2, but περι-εώρ- Thuc. 6, 103, προ-εωρ- Xen. Cyr. 4, 3, 21; Dem. 19, 154. 181, late προ-ωρώμην N. T. Act. 2, 25 (Vulg. προ-ορ- Lachm. Tisch.): **fut.** ὄψομαι see above: **aor.** ὠψάμην rare, ὄψαιντο Soph. O. R. 1271 (Herm. but fut. ὄψοιντο Dind. Bergk, Nauck), ἐπ-όψατο Pind. Fr. 65, 6 (Bergk); ὀψώμεθα Menand. Rhet. 68 (ὀψόμ- Spengel), ἐπ-όψωμαι Pl. Leg. 947, ἐπι- (Buttm. Baiter &c.): **2 aor.** εἰδόμην, subj. ἴδωμαι Ar. Vesp. 183 (trimet.), see εἰδέω: and as **mid. p. p.** προ-εωρᾶσθαι Diod. Sic. 20, 102; and δι-ῶμμαι if correct Theogn. 1311 (Herm. Bergk, Ziegl.) **Vb.** ὁρατός Xen. Cyr. 1, 6, 2, ὑφ-ορατέον Plut. Mor. 49, ὀπτέον late, but περι-οπτέον Her. 5, 39; Thuc. 8, 48. See ὄρημι.

Eur. Andr. 1225 (chor.) has the Ion. 2 sing. **fut.** ὄψεαι, which Herm. Dind. and Paley alter to ὄψει, see above. A unique instance of **1 aor.** occurs in opt. ἐσορήσαις Orph. Fr. 2, 16. Homer uses **fut.** ἐπόψομαι and ἐπιόψ-, the former in the sense simply *to look at*, the latter with the accessory notion of *looking at* for selection, *looking out*, in which sense Plato Com. uses the **aor.** ἐπιώψατο Com. Fr. 2, 623. ὄψαιντο Soph. O. R. 1271, is Hermann's emendation for ὄψοιντο (Mss. Dind. Bergk), on the ground of the sense requiring it, and is approved by Lobeck, Wunder &c.; subj. ὀψώμεθα occurs Menand. Rhet. 68 (ὀψόμ- Spengel), -ησθε N. T. Luc. 13, 28 (ὄψεσθε Tisch.), ἐπ-όψωνται Pl. Leg. 947. The **p. p.** form ἑώραμαι we have not seen earlier than Isocrates, nor **aor.** ἑωράθην before Aristotle. Epic form ὁρόω Il. 5, 244. Od. 18, 143 &c. Ion. ὁρέω Her. 7, 236, pl. ὁρέομεν 5, 40 (ὁρέωμεν, ὁρῶμεν perhaps corrupt), ὁρέουσι, ἐπ- 1, 124 (Schaef. Dind. Stein), -έωσι Ms. F. (Bekk. Gaisf.), -ῶσι (Mss. M. K. but φοιτέουσι 2, 66 all the Mss.), 3 sing. ὁρᾷ not ὁρέει, κατ- 2, 38; -έοντες 8, 25; ὁρᾶν Her. 1, 33. 2, 64, ἐν- 1, 170, but -ρῆν Hippocr. 6, 146. 7, 178 (Lit.). 2, 320 (Erm.): **imp.** ὥρεον, pl. -έομεν Her. 2, 131 (Bekk. Dind. Gaisf.) but often in Mss. and edit. ὥρων 4, 3 (Bekk. Stein), ὅρεον 2, 106 (Bekk. Gaisf. ὥρων Stein), ὡρῶμεν, ἐν- 1, 120 (Lhardy, Bekk. Stein), ἑωρῶμεν (Mss.), ὁρέομεν 2, 148 (Bekk. ὡρῶμεν Stein), all which Bredow, Dind. Abicht &c. hold corrupt, and alter to ὥρεον, ὡρέομεν according to *rule* (Pref. to Her. Didot.), 3 sing. ὥρα 1, 11. 3, 72, 2 pl. ὡρᾶτε

7, 8. Lhardy, however, who has examined the subject with an acuteness and care that reminds us of P. Elmsley, is inclined to reduce most of those so-called Ionic forms much nearer the common, thus: ὅρων for ὥρεον, ἑωρ-; ὁρ- and ὡρῶμεν, for ὡρέομεν, ὁρέ-; subj. ὁρῶσι for -έωσι; part. ὁρῶν for ὁρέων, ὁρῶσα for -έουσα, but ὁρέωντα -έωντες for -έοντα, -έοντες (Bekk. Dind.) Uniformity is desirable, but we hold it hazardous to apply a very stringent law in the case. Dindorf says that ἑόρᾱκα, ἑοράκειν is the correct Attic form of **perf.** and **plp.** in poetry and prose. In Comedy, no doubt, this form is sometimes required, perhaps always admissible. But we doubt if this be a safe ground for concluding that it must therefore be the only genuine form in prose. We can see no sound reason, except exigency of metre—and this affects not prose—for exempting the **perf. act.** from double augment, and at the same time holding liable the **imp.** and the **perf. pass.** It is a considerable mistake to confine the **middle** voice to Epic. It is used by Soph. Eur. quoted, Cratin. Com. Fr. 2, 94, and by Attic prose writers in comp. προ- quoted, ὑφ- Xen. Mem. 2, 7, 12; Isae. 2, 7; Dem. 18, 43; Luc. Gall. 3, περι- Thuc. 2, 43. 6, 93, even the *simple* ὁρᾶται seems **mid.** Ael. V. H. 3, 1; ὁρᾶσθαι H. A. 10, 17; certainly ὁρώμενοι Polyaen. 4, 7, 6: **imp.** ἑωρᾶτο Polyaen. 8, 16, quoted, but ἑωρῶντο Plut. Brut. 43, has been altered to ἑώρων (Mss. Sint. Bekk.)

Ὀργάζω *To knead,* Soph. Fr. 432 (D.); Com. Fr. (Eup.) 2, 524; Aristot. Probl. 2, 32: **aor.** imper. ὄργᾰσον Ar. Av. 839; ὀργάσαι, ὑπ- Hipponax 84; ὀργάσας Her. 4, 64: **p. p.** ὠργασμένος Pl. Theaet. 194. **Mid. aor.** ὀργάσασθαι Hippocr. 8, 398. 400 (Lit.); -σάμενος Alciphr. 3, 7, missed by Lexicogr.

Ὀργαίνω *To be angry,* Poet. Soph. Tr. 552; Eur. Alc. 1106: **aor.** (ὤργᾱνα), opt. ὀργάνειας trans. *enrage, irritate,* Soph. O. R. 335. Confined to Trag.

Ὀργίζω *To exasperate,* **act.** rare, Xen. Eq. 9, 2: **fut.** -ιῶ, ἐξ- Aeschin. 1, 192: **aor.** ὤργῐσα Ar. Vesp. 425; -ίσῃ 404; (Pl.) Eryx. 392; inf. -ίσαι Pl. Phaedr. 267; -γίσας Aristot. Eth. Nic. 5, 10, 9. **Pass.** (or **mid.** and **pass.**) ὀργίζομαι *to be enraged,* Eur. Hel. 1646; Thuc. 1, 77; Pl. Apol. 23; Lys. 14, 39; subj. -ίζῃ Soph. O. R. 364; -ιζόμενος Antiph. 5, 72 &c.: **imp.** ὠργιζ- Thuc. 5, 52; Andoc. 1, 24; Lys. 1, 12; Isocr. 16, 14; Lycurg. 111: **p. p.** ὤργισμαι, -μένος Eur. Hipp. 1413; Ar. Vesp. 431; Isocr. 6, 75; Pl. Phaedr. 267; (Dem.) 58, 32: **aor.** ὠργίσθην Com. Fr. (Epicr.) 3, 371; Lys. 22, 2; Dem. 21, 2; subj. -ισθῇ Eur. Med. 129; Pl. Prot. 346; -ισθείη Isocr. 11, 46; -ισθῆναι Thuc. 1, 74; Isocr. 20, 9 &c.: **fut.** ὀργισθήσομαι Lys. 21, 20; Dem. 49, 27. (Dem.) 59, 111, συν- Dem. 21, 100 (Bekk. Dind.): more freq. in same sense **fut. mid.** ὀργιοῦμαι Xen. An. 6, 1, 30; Lys. 15, 9; Isocr. 18, 4; Dem. 9, 46. 14, 41. 36, 28. **Vb.** ὀργιστέον Dem. 21, 123; Aristot. Eth. Nic. 2, 9, 7.

Ὀρέγω *To stretch out*, Il. 15, 371. Od. 12, 257; Eur. Phoen. 1710; Ion. and late prose Her. 2, 2; Aristot. H. An. 2, 1, 6; Plut. Pyr. 17. Arat. 47; Luc. D. Deor. 5, 4, ἀπ- Hippocr. 3, 412 (Lit.), and ὀρέγνῡμι, only part. -γνύς Il. 1, 351. 22, 37: **imp.** ὤρεγον Pind. P. 4, 240; D. Cass. 59, 27; App. Civ. 4, 126; Philostr. Apoll. 54: **fut.** ὀρέξω Il. 13, 327; Eur. Med. 902; Luc. Nav. 21: **aor.** ὤρεξα Il. 23, 406. 24, 102; Pind. N. 7, 58; rare in prose Pl. Phaed. 117; (Hippocr.) Epist. 9, 340 (Lit.), ὄρεξ- Il. 24, 743; subj. -ῃς Il. 22, 57, -ξῃ 5, 33; opt. -ξειαν Od. 17, 407; Luc. Tim. 54; imper. ὄρεξον Soph. O. C. 846. 1130; Ar. Pax 1105 &c.; ὀρέξαι Il. 12, 174; Pind. P. 3, 110; Xen. An. 7, 3, 29; ὀρέξας Eur. Heracl. 844; Luc. Tim. 45: **p. p.** ὤρεγμαι Hippocr. 1, 520 (K. 9, 192 Lit.), redupl. ὀρώρ- see below: **aor.** ὠρέχθην (Hippocr.) Epist. 9, 372 (Lit.); ὀρεχθείη Hippocr. 3, 648 (Vulg. Kühn, 1, 653 (Erm.), but ῥεχθείη Mss. Ald. Lit. 5, 384), see below. **Mid.** ὀρέγομαι *stretch one's own, oneself, desire*, Thuc. 4, 17; Xen. Cyr. 8, 2, 22; Pl. Rep. 439; ὀρέγοιτο Tyrt. 12, 12; ὀρέγεσθαι Il. 24, 506; Pl. Rep. 485; Isocr. 6, 105; -γόμενος Antiph. 2, β, 12, and ὀρέγνῡμαι, -ύμενος Mosch. 2, 112; Anth. 7, 506: **imp.** ὠρέγοντο Thuc. 4, 41; Dem. 16, 22: **fut.** ὀρέξομαι Eur. Hel. 353; Aristot. Eth. Nic. 3, 14 (B.), ἐπ- Emped. 227 (Stein); Pl. Rep. 486: **aor.** ὠρεξάμην Poet. Il. 5, 851. 23, 99; Hes. Th. 178; Ap. Rh. 2, 1111; Eur. H. F. 16. Fr. 242 (D.); Theocr. 21, 44, ὀρέξατο Il. 6, 466. 13, 20; Ap. Rh. 2, 828. 878; imper. ὄρεξαι Eur. Orest. 303, -άσθω Il. 4, 307; -άμενος Il. 23, 805; Hes. Sc. 456, but ἐπ- Hippocr. 9, 194 (Lit.); -ασθαι Od. 11, 392; Theocr. 24, 125; rare in prose, Xen. Mem. 1, 2, 15 (ἐπ- Solon 5, Bergk): and as **mid. aor. pass.** ὠρέχθην (not in Epic) Eur. Hel. 1238; Xen. Mem. 1, 2, 16. Ages. 1, 4; and late Luc. Bis Acc. 29; (Eur.) Epist. 5, ὀρέχθην, ἐπ- Matron, Athen. 4, 136; subj. ὀρεχθῇ Xen. Conv. 8, 35; -θῆναι Eur. Ion 842; -θείς Or. 328; Dio. Hal. 6, 19; D. Sic. 37, 7 (Dind.): **p.** ὀρώρεγμαι, Epic 3 pl. ὀρωρέχαται Il. 16, 834; ὀρωρεγμένος Joseph. Ant. 18, 6, 5: **plp.** ὀρωρέχατο Il. 11, 26. **Vb.** ὀρεκτός Il. 2, 543; Aristot. Metaph. 11, 7, 2. In good Attic prose the active voice is confined to the **aor.** Lexicographers say "the **aor. pass.** is more frequent than the **aor. mid.**" This is true only of Attic prose, in which Xen. alone uses it, and only thrice, the **aor. mid.** once: the Epics use **mid.** only: Eur. both, and each thrice. Collat. form ὀριγνάομαι Eur. Bac. 1255; Themist. 32,

361: **imp.** ὠριγνᾶτο Theocr. 24, 44, -ῶντο Hes. Sc. 190: **fut.** -γνήσομαι late, Dio Cass. 41, 53: **aor.** ὀριγνηθῆναι Antiph. Fr. 109 (B. S.); Isocr. Epist. 6, 9.

'Ορέομαι *To rush*, Epic, -εῖται Epigr. in Paus. 9, 38: **imp.** ὀρέοντο Il. 2, 398. 23, 212. ὀρεῖται in an Epigr. ascribed to Chersias, quoted by Paus. 9, 38, is called **pres.** by Buttmann. We think it may be **fut. mid.** of ὄρνυμι, which see.

'Ορεχθέω *To be stretched* (ὀρέγω), Poet. Nic. Alex. 340; Opp. Hal. 2, 583; Ap. Rh. 1, 275; Aesch. Fr. 155, ἐρεχθ- (Herm. Dind. 2 ed. 'Ερέχθειον 5 ed.); ὀρεχθεῖν Ar. Nub. 1368; Theocr. 11, 43: **imp.** ὀρέχθεον Il. 23, 30; Ap. Rh. 2, 49, ὠρέχ- Athen. (Aristias) 2, 56.

Ὄρημι *To see* (ὁράω), Aeol. and Dor. Sapph. 2, 11 (Ahr. ὄρ- Bergk), ποθ-όρημι Theocr. 6, 25; part. ὀρεὶς Diog. Laert. (Epist. Pittac.) 1, 81. **Mid.** ὄρημαι, 2 sing. ὄρηαι Od. 14, 343, others ὁρῆαι Dor. contr. of ὁράεαι from ὁράομαι.

'Ορθεύω *To set upright* (ὀρθόω), only **imp.** ὤρθευεν Eur. Or. 405. The form ὀρθόω is in general use, **act.** and **pass.** with **mid.** late (unless ὀρθοῦσθαι be mid. intrans. Hippocr. 7, 262) ὠρθώσαντο Q. Sm. 4, 511, but classic in compds. δι-ορθώσομαι Isocr. 4, 181: **aor.** δι-ωρθωσ- Dem. 33, 11, ἐπ- ην- ωρθ- Isocr. 4, 165, see also κατ-ορθόω.

'Οριγνάομαι see collat. form under ὀρέγω.

'Ορίζω *To bound*, Aesch. Supp. 546; Soph. Tr. 754; Thuc. 1, 46; Lycurg. 27, Ion. οὐρ- Her. 4, 42. 56: **imp.** ὥριζ- Thuc. 2, 96: **fut.** -ίσω, Attic -ιῶ Aristot. Categ. 6, 11; Himer. 4, 23, δι- Isocr. 4, 174; Aeschin. 2, 145, Ion. οὐρίσσω, ἀπ- Il. 22, 489 (Bekk. Dind. La Roche): **aor.** ὥρισα Soph. Ant. 452; Eur. Hel. 128; Pl. Leg. 864, δι- Aesch. Pr. 489, Ion. οὔρ- Her. 3, 142 (Bekk. Dind.), οὖρ- (Gaisf.): **p.** ὥρικα Dem. 26, 24; Aristot. Meteor. 4, 4, 6: **p. p.** ὥρισμαι Thuc. 1, 71; Pl. Conv. 182: **plp.** ὥριστο Philostr. Apoll. 3, 110: **aor.** ὡρίσθην Pl. Charm. 171: **fut.** ὁρισθήσομαι Pl. Theaet. 158; Aristot. Metaph. 7, 2, 3: and seemingly as **pass. fut. mid.** ὁριεῖται Aristot. Metaph. 6, 10, 13, δι- Hippocr. 4, 102 (Lit. but **act.** 6, 4.) **Mid. Dep.** ὁρίζομαι *to limit, determine* &c. Aesch. Supp. 256. 394; Soph. Tr. 237; Pl. Rep. 562; Aeschin. 1, 137; Dem. 9, 19, δι- Andoc. 3, 12: **imp.** ὡριζ- Pl. Gorg. 513: **fut.** ὁριοῦμαι Pl. Leg. 737. Theaet. 190, Ion. -ιεῦμαι Hippocr. 9, 264, δι- 6, 4, as **pass.** see above: **aor.** ὡρισάμην Com. Fr. (Epicr.) 3, 370; Pl. Theaet. 148; Lys. 17, 6; Dem. 24, 79: and as **mid. p. p.** ὥρισμαι Eur. Hec. 801; Dem. 31, 5, ἀφ- Pl. Soph. 231, δι- Aristot. Polit. 7, 13, 13; Dem. 24, 192. **Vb.** ὁριστέον Pl. Leg. 632.

'Ορίνω *To raise, rouse*, Epic, Il. 11, 298; Opp. Hal. 2, 511:

aor. ὤρῖνα Il. 19, 272. Od. 7, 273; Hes. Op. 508, ὄρι- Il. 14, 487. Od. 14, 361; subj. ὀρίνω Il. 15, 403; opt. ὀρίναις Il. 11, 792, a rare form in Hom.; Theogn. 1295; part. -ίνας Theocr. 26, 37: aor. pass. ὠρίνθην Il. 16, 509; Opp. Cyn. 1, 491, usu. ὀρίν- Il. 5, 29. 16, 280. 18, 223; Theocr. 22, 89; Ap. Rh. 3, 515; ὀρινθείς Od. 22, 23; Com. Fr. (Epicr.) 3, 371: pres. ὀρίνομαι Il. 11, 525; late prose ὀρίνοιτο Plotin. 26, 28; -ίνεσθαι Aristot. Probl. 27, 3, 2; -ινόμενος Il. 16, 377: imp. ὠρίνετο Il. 9, 595. Od. 18, 75, ὀρίν- Ap. Rh. 2, 971.

Ὁρμάω *To incite, urge, hurry,* trans. and intrans. Eur. Phoen. 259; Ar. Eccl. 6; Xen. Cyr. 8, 8, 25, Epic 3 pl. -ώωσι, ἐφ- Opp. Hal. 2, 94; -ῶντες Aesch. Pers. 394; Soph. Ant. 133: imp. ὥρμα Thuc. 1, 127; Her. 8, 106, -μῶμεν 7, 209 (Bekk.), -μέομεν (Dind.), -εον 7, 188: fut. -ήσω Eur. Hec. 145; Thuc. 2, 20; Xen. Hell. 3, 4, 12, Dor. -άσω Eur. Supp. 1015 (chor.): aor. ὥρμησα Il. 6, 338; Eur. Bac. 435; Her. 4, 159; Thuc. 3, 22; Isocr. 4, 95, Dor. -āσα Soph. Aj. 175 (chor.); opt. -μάσαι Pind. Ol. 10, 21; Dor. imper. ὅρμᾱσον for -ησον, Ar. Lys. 1247 (chor.); inf. -ῆσαι Antiph. 3, δ, 5: p. ὥρμηκα Hippocr. 9, 188; Pl. Polit. 264: plp. ὡρμήκει, ἀφ- Hippocr. 1, 496 (Erm.): p. p. ὥρμημαι Soph. El. 70, usu. mid. see below: so aor. ὡρμήθην Her. 6, 41, but dual ὁρμηθήτην Il. 5, 12. 17, 530 (Dind. La R. Spitzn. ὡρμ- Bekk.), Dor. ὡρμάθη Soph. El. 197 (chor.); subj. -āθῶ Eur. Andr. 859, -āθῇ Med. 189 (Pors. Kirch.), -ηθῇ (Elms. Br. Dind.); ὁρμηθείς Od. 8, 499. 13, 82; Her. 4, 92, -āθείς, ἐφ- Pind. N. 10, 69. Mid. ὁρμάομαι *to set out, rush,* Pind. N. 1, 5; Aesch. Sept. 31; Her. 4, 55; Thuc. 4, 61; Xen. Cyr. 5, 4, 20, Epic 3 pl. -ώωνται Opp. Hal. 1, 598; ὁρμώμενος Thuc. 1, 64, -μεώμ- Her. 4, 57. 6, 137. 7, 30, -μεόμ- (Stein): imp. ὡρμώμην Soph. O. C. 1159, -āτο Il. 3, 142; Thuc. 4, 102, -ώμεθα Ar. Eccl. 490, -ῶντο Thuc. 4, 102, -έοντο Her. 7, 88 (Dind. Stein, Dietsch, ὁρμέωντο Bekk.): fut. ὁρμήσομαι Her. 5, 34; Xen. Cyr. 7, 1, 9: aor. ὡρμησάμην Il. 21, 595, ἐφ- Hes. Sc. 127; Opp. Hal. 3, 397, in prose, only ἐξ- Xen. Hell. 6, 5, 20 (Vulg. Schneid. Breitb. &c. but plp. -μητο Dind. Saupp.): more freq. as mid. aor. pass. ὡρμήθην Il. 5, 12. 10, 359. 13, 182. Od. 10, 214 (ὁρμ- La Roche); Aesch. Pers. 503; Eur. Alc. 1040; Her. 8, 68; Thuc. 3, 98. 4, 73; Xen. Cyr. 5, 1, 25, Dor. -άθην Eur. Tr. 532 (chor.); Theocr. 22, 199 (Vulg. Mein.): fut. late ὁρμηθήσομαι Galen 5, 85: p. ὥρμημαι Xen. Mem. 2, 6, 28; Isocr. 8, 62, -ηνται Thuc. 6, 33, Ion. ὁρμέαται Her. 5, 121 (Bekk. Gaisf. Lhardy, Stein, ὡρμ- Bred. Dind.); ὡρμημένος Eur. Elec. 340; Her. 8, 12 (ὁρμ- Stein): plp. ὡρμήμην, -ητο Her. 5, 50; Thuc. 8, 23, 3 pl. -ηντο Thuc. 2, 65, Ion. ὁρμέατο Her. 1, 83. 158. 7, 215. 8, 25. 35.

109. 9, 61. 102 (Bekk. Stein, so Gaisf. except 7, 215. 9, 61, ὡρμ-), but ὡρμέαται, ὡρμέατο always (Dind. Bred.) Dind. however says "augmentum temporale abjectum videri potest in formis praeteriti passivi pluralis Ionicis in -αται, quales ὁρμέαται, cum plusquamperfecto ὁρμέατο, cujus exempla multa sunt, in libris modo sic, modo per ω scripta." But almost all editors of Her. *now* agree in writing with augment the forms ὥρμηται, ὥρμητο, ὡρμημένος. Of the **act.** Hom. has only 1 **aor.** The **mid. aor.** is rare and Epic in *simple*, never, simple or comp., in Attic poetry, once only in prose ἐξ-ωρμησ- Xen. quoted, but ὁρμησάμ- *v. r.* Dem. 23, 165, -ήσασθαι 35, 28, for -ισάμενος, -ίσασθαι; **aor. pass.** as **mid.** is freq. in every class of writers. Our Lexicographers seem to have overlooked the puzzling form ὅρμᾱον, Dor. imper. for -ᾱσον, -ησον, Ar. Lys. 1247. A poet. collat. form ὁρμαίνω trans. and intrans. Il. 16, 435; Bacchyl. 27, 11 (Bergk); Aesch. Sept. 394. Ag. 1388: **imp.** ὥρμαινον Il. 14, 20; Pind. Ol. 3, 25 (ὥρμα Momms. Christ); Ap. Rh. 3, 452, iter. ὁρμαίνεσκον Q. Sm. 1, 27 (Ms. M. Koechly): **aor.** ὥρμηνα Il. 21, 137. Od. 2, 156. Hom. always augments this verb.

Ὁρμίζω *To bring to anchor, moor,* Thuc. 8, 10: **imp.** ὥρμ- Her. 6, 107, ὅρμ- (Stein): **fut.** -ίσω, -ίσσομεν Il. 14, 77 is perhaps Epic **aor.** subj.: **aor.** ὥρμῐσα Od. 4, 785; Eur. Tr. 1155 (Ald. -ησα Dind. Nauck); Thuc. 7, 30; Epic subj. -ίσσομεν, see **fut.** reg. ὁρμίζομαι *come to, lie at anchor,* Thuc. 1, 46: **fut.** ὁρμιοῦμαι Thuc. 6, 42, προσ- Dem. 4, 44: **aor.** ὡρμισάμην Her. 9, 96; Antiph. 5, 22; Thuc. 1, 51. 2, 86. 8, 92, καθ- 8, 42, and always (except perhaps 6, 49); Xen. An. 6, 1, 15; Dem. 23, 165; Arr. An. 2, 20, 10, see foll.: and less freq. ὡρμίσθην, ὁρμισθῇ Com. Fr. (Phil.) 4, 31; -ισθείς Soph. Ph. 546; Xen. Hell. 1, 4, 18, ἐν-ωρμίσθην Theogn. 1274, ἐφ- Thuc. 6, 49 (Schaef. Popp. Dind. -ήθην Bekk. Krüg.), ἐγκαθ- Arr. An. 2, 20, καθ-ωρμίσθη Polyb. 1, 21. 39. 41 &c.: **p.** ὥρμισμαι Eur. Or. 242. I. T. 1328, καθ- Aristot. Part. An. 3, 9, 7; Plut. Cic. 39. **Vb.** ὁρμιστέον Arr. An. 6, 19, 3.

Ὄρνῡμι *To raise, rouse,* Poet. ὄρνῦθι Il. 19, 139; ὀρνύς Pind. P. 10, 10; ὀρνῦ́μεναι Il. 17, 546, ὀρνύμεν 9, 353, ὀρνύω Pind. Ol. 13, 12; Orph. Lith. 220, and ὄρω 113: **imp.** ὤρνῦον Od. 21, 100 (Bekk. La R.). Il. 12, 142 (ὄρν- La Roche); Pind. P. 4, 170: **fut.** ὄρσω Pind. N. 9, 8; Soph. Ant. 1060; ὄρσουσα Il. 21, 335: **aor.** ὦρσα Il. 5, 8; Hes. Th. 523; Pind. Ol. 10, 24; Ap. Rh. 1, 147; Aesch. Pers. 496; Eur. Andr. 1148, iter. ὄρσασκε Il. 17, 423; ὄρσῃ Il. 9, 703, -σωμεν 7, 38, Ep. -σομεν 4, 16, -ητε 23, 210; ὄρσας 22, 190; ὄρσαι Pind. Ol. 4, 12: **2 aor.** ὤρορον redupl. usually trans. Il. 2, 146. Od. 4, 712 &c., intrans. Il. 13, 78. Od. 19,

201; part. ὀροῦσα, -ούσῃ Hes. Sc. 437 (Goettl.): **2 p.** ὄρωρα intrans. Il. 7, 388; Theogn. 909; Ap. Rh. 3, 59; ὀρώρῃ Il. 9, 610: **2 plp.** ὀρώρειν Il. 2, 810. 8, 59; Hes. Th. 70; Ap. Rh. 3, 457, augm. ὠρώρειν Il. 18, 498; Ap. Rh. 4, 1698; Aesch. Ag. 653; Soph. O. C. 1622. **Mid.** ὄρνῦμαι *to rise, rush,* Il. 4, 423; Aesch. Sept. 90; Soph. O. C. 1320; part. -ύμενος Il. 4, 421; Hes. Th. 843; Pind. Ol. 8, 34; Ar. Ran. 1529 (chor.), Dor. -υμένα Eur. I. T. 1150: **imp.** ὠρνῦμην Il. 16, 635; Hes. Th. 191; Ap. Rh. 2, 122, and ὀρέοντο (ὀρέομαι) Il. 23, 212: **fut.** ὀροῦμαι Il. 20, 140: **p.** ὀρώρεται Od. 19, 377; subj. ὀρώρηται Il. 13, 271: **2 aor.** ὠρόμην, -ρετο Il. 22, 102, ὦρτο 5, 590, see below, unaugm. ὄροντο Od. 3, 471, see ὄρομαι; subj. ὄρηται Od. 20, 267; Hes. Th. 782; ὄροιτο Od. 14, 522; Theogn. 349; ὀρόμενος Aesch. Sept. 87. 115, -μένα Eur. I. A. 186 (chor.), ὄρμενος Il. 11, 572; Aesch. Ag. 1408; Soph. O. R. 177 (chor.), see below. **Vb.** θέ-ορτος Aesch. Pr. 765. ὄρω occurs in **pres. part. act.** ὄροντες Orph. Lith. 113, according to Tyrwhitt's very probable emendation; Epic inf. ὀρνύμεναι Il. 17, 546, ὀρνύμεν 9, 353: ὦρτο 3 sing. **2 aor. mid.** syncop. Il. 5, 590; Hes. Op. 568; Pind. P. 4, 134; Ap. Rh. 1, 708; Aesch. Ag. 987 (chor.); ὄρσο 2 sing. imper. Il. 4, 204; Pind. Ol. 6, 62; Ap. Rh. 1, 703, ὄρσεο Il. 3, 250, contr. ὄρσευ 4, 264; inf. ὄρθαι Il. 8, 474 (Wolf, Bekk. Spitzn. Dind. La R.), ὦρθαι (old edit. Heyn.); part. ὄρμενος Il. 11, 572; Aesch. Ag. 1408 (chor.); Soph. O. R. 177 (chor.)

Ὀροθύνω *To raise, rouse* (ὄρνῡμι), Poet. Od. 18, 407; Eur. Bac. 1169 (Herm. Dind. 5 ed.); Opp. Hal. 2, 330; inf. Epic -θυνέμεν Mosch. 4, 63: **imp.** unaugm. ὀρόθῡνε if not **aor.** Il. 13, 351; Ap. Rh. 1, 1153: **fut.** -ῡνῶ D. Chrys. 2, p. 3, 3, 1: **aor.** ὠρόθῡνα Lycophr. 693; Luc. Char. 7; ὀρόθ- Il. 10, 332; Od. 5, 292; imper. ὀρόθῡνον Il. 21, 312; Ap. Rh. 2, 877. **Pass.** **imp.** ὠροθύνετο Aesch. Pr. 200 (trimet.) This verb is poetic, the **act.** Epic.—For ὀρθοῖς Dind. now 5 ed. edits with Herm. ὀροθύνεις Eur. Bac. 1169 (chor.)

Ὄρομαι *To watch, superintend* (ὄρω, ὄρνυμι, or οὖρος, ὁράω), Epic, in tmesi ἐπὶ—ὄρονται Od. 14, 104: **imp.** ἐπὶ—ὄροντο 3, 471, for ὀρέοντο see ὄρνυμαι: **2 plp.** ἐπὶ—ὀρώρει Il. 23, 112, which favours the first derivation. Passow adopts the second, which seems at least equally easy and suitable. For meaning compare *tueor.*

Ὀρούω *To rush,* Pind. P. 10, 61; Opp. C. 2, 472: **imp.** ὤρουον Eur. H. F. 972: **fut.** ὀρούσω Hom. H. 2, 239: **aor.** ὤρουσα H. Hym. 28, 8; Pind. Ol. 9, 102; Aesch. Eum. 113; Soph. O. R. 877; Eur. Phoen. 1236; Hippocr. 8, 98; and late Plut. Cat. maj. 13, Hom. and Hes. always unaugm. ὄρου- Il. 13, 505; Hes. Sc. 412; ὀρούσας Il. 11, 743, Dor. ὀρούσαισ' Pind. N. 1, 50, ἀν- Ol. 7, 37. This verb is mostly poet. and late prose, ὀρούει Sext. Emp. 346, 20 (B.); ὀρούων Democr. p. 176 (Mull.): aor. ὤρουσα Plut. Brut. 8, 34. Cat. 13 &c. The comp. ἀνορούω seems used only in pres. fut. and aor. ἀνορούει Opp. Hal. 3, 106; -ων Xen. Eq. 8, 5; -ειν 3, 7: fut. -ούσων Orph. Th. 7, 19: and aor. unaugm. ἀνόρουσε Il. 9, 193. Od. 3, 1; -ούσας Il. 10, 519. Our Lexicons wrongly restrict its construction to "absol." Opp. has πέτρην ἀνοροῦσαι Hal. 3, 35.

Ὁρτάζω, see ἑορτ-.

'Ορύσσω *To dig*, Od. 10, 305; Heraclit. 8 (Byw.); Her. 1, 75; Aristot. Pt. An. 3, 1, 16, δι- Thuc. 2, 3, Attic ὀρύττω Ar. Av. 442; Pl. Leg. 844, late ὀρύχω, -χοιεν Arat. 1086: imp. ὤρυσσον Her. 7, 23, -ττον Ar. Eq. 605; Xen. Cyr. 7, 5, 10: fut. ὀρύξω (-ομεν Il. 7, 341 may be a shortened subj. aor.), κατ- Ar. Pax 166; Xen. An. 5, 8, 9: aor. ὤρυξα Her. 3, 39, in Hom. unaugm. ὄρυξα Il. 7, 440. Od. 11, 25; ὀρύξῃ Aristot. Probl. 23, 21, see fut.; ὀρύξας Soph. Aj. 659; Thuc. 2, 76; ὀρύξαι Od. 10, 517; Her. 2, 101, κατ- Xen. Cyr. 3, 3, 3: p. (ὤρυχα late, Phlego) redupl. ὀρώρῦχα, κατ- Com. Fr. (Pher.) 2, 327: plp. ὠρωρύχειν App. Civ. 4, 107 (Bekk.): p. p. ὀρώρυγμαι Her. 3, 60; Xen. Oec. 19, 7, κατ- Pl. Euth. 288. Rep. 533, δι- Dem. 9, 28, and ὤρυγμαι rare in *early authors*, Her. 2, 158 (Gaisf. &c. ὀρώρ- Bekk. Dind. Stein &c.), κατ-ωρύγμεθα Antiph. 3, γ, 12 (Mss. N. A. Maetzn. -ορωρ- Mss. Bekk. B. Saupp. Blass), but ὑποκατ-ώρυκται Sophr. Fr. 33 (Ahr.), and late δι-ώρυκται Luc. Tim. 53; δι-ωρυγμένος Diod. Sic. 4, 43: plp. ὀρωρύγμην Her. 1, 186 (Gaisf. Bekk. Dind. Stein). 1, 185 (Bekk. Dind. Stein &c. ὠρυγ- Vulg. Gaisf.); Pl. Critias 118, also in Attic ὠρωρύγμην, δι- Xen. An. 7, 8, 14 (all Mss.), ἐν- Philostr. 2, 27: 1 aor. ὠρύχθην Her. 2, 158; Pl. Critias 118, κατ- Xen. An. 5, 8, 11: fut. ὀρυχθήσομαι, κατ- Antiph. 3, β, 10; Ar. Av. 394 (Mss. R. V. see below), δι- Luc. Tim. 53: 2 aor. ὠρῦχην?: 2 fut. ὀρυχήσομαι, κατ- Ar. Av. 394 (Elms. Bekk. Dind.): aor. mid. rare in classic authors ὠρύξατο *caused dig*, Her. 1, 186. 3, 9; Ap. Rh. 3, 1032; Num. in Athen. 7, 70; Arat. 1135 (Bekk.); late Attic, Luc. Necyom. 9; Paus. 8, 29, 3; App. Annib. 41. Pun. 134, ἐξ- Dio. Hal. 9, 55. **Vb.** ὀρυκτός Xen. An. 1, 7, 14. A few traces of a form in γ occur, 2 aor. ὤρῦγε Philostr. V. Apol. 1, 25; Phot. (Bekk.); subj. ὀρύγῃ (Solon): 2 aor. pass. late ὠρύγην, -ῆναι Orig. Ref. Haer. 6, 20 (M.), κατ- old reading Xen. An. 5, 8, 11, now κατορυχθ-; ὀρυγείς Geop. 4, 3, ἀν- 5, 7, δι- Heliod. 9, 7: fut. ὀρυγήσομαι, δι- Synes. Epist. 44, ἀν- Geop. 5, 3 (and κατ- Ar. Av. quoted, Dawes, Brunck, now -χήσομαι.)

In obedience to the precept of the old Grammarians, Thom.

Magister &c. "κατώρυκται κοινόν, κατορώρυκται Ἀττικόν" the unreduplicated forms are fast disappearing from *classic* authors. Buttmann hesitated to pronounce ὤρυκτο, ὤρυκται Her. 1, 185. 2, 158, incorrect, but Bekker, Dind. Bredow &c. partly from usage, partly from the analogy of other words, as ἀραίρηκα, ἐλήλακα &c. maintain the redupl. ὀρώρυκται, ὀρώρυκτο (not ὠρωρ-) to be the genuine Herodotean forms.

Ὀρχέω *To make dance, excite*, act. rare, aor. ὤρχησα Trag. Fr. (Ion) 56 (Wagn.): pass. rare, ὀρχοῦνται Athen. 14, 30 (631 C.). **Mid.** ὀρχοῦμαι *to dance*, -εῖται Anacr. 20; Aesch. Ch. 167; Pl. Leg. 654, -οῦνται Com. Fr. (Metag.) 2, 754, Ion. -έονται Her. 2, 60, and -εῦνται Hom. H. 2, 18; Hes. Th. 4; -εόμενος Her. 1, 141: imp. ὠρχείσθην Od. 8, 378, -οῦντο Xen. An. 5, 4, 34, Aeol. -εῦντο Il. 18, 594, -έοντο, κατ- Her. 3, 151 (Gaisf. Bekk. &c.), unaugm. ὀρχέετο 6, 129 (Mss. S V. Schweigh. Gaisf.), but ὠρχ- (Bekk. Bred. Dind. Krüg.): fut. ὀρχήσομαι Com. Fr. (Antiph.) 3, 69; Ar. Thesm. 1178; Luc. Salt. 51: aor. ὠρχησάμην Anacr. 69 (Bergk); Xen. An. 6, 1, 11; Her. 6, 129 (Ms. S. Bekk. Bred. Dind. Krüg.), ὀρχ- (Ms. K. Schweig. Gaisf.), so ὠρχήσαο, ἀπ- ibid. (Bekk. Bred. Dind. &c.), ἀπ-ορχ- (Mss. S V. Gaisf. &c.); ὀρχήσασθαι Od. 8, 371; Aristot. Metaph. 6, 9, 1; -ησάμενος Andoc. 1, 47.

Ὄρω, see ὄρνυμι.

Ὀσμάομαι, see ὀδμ-.

Ὄσσομαι *To see, forebode*, Epic and unaugm. Ap. Rh. 2, 28, προτι- Il. 22, 356; ὀσσόμενος Il. 14, 17. Od. 20, 81: imp. ὄσσετο Od. 18, 154; Hes. Th. 551, -οντο Il. 18, 224. Od. 2, 152.

Ὀσφραίνομαι *To perceive by the smell*, Eur. Cycl. 154; Ar. Lys. 619; Her. 1, 80; Pl. Theaet. 195, rare and perhaps late ὀσφράομαι Luc. Pisc. 48; Paus. 9, 21, 3; Aristid. 25, 315: fut. ὀσφρήσομαι Ar. Pax 152: aor. p. ὠσφράνθην Com. Fr. (Phil.) 4, 27; Athen. (Machon) 13, 577; Hippocr. 1, 468 (K.). 8, 488 (Lit.); Aristot. de Anim. 2, 12, 5: 1 aor. mid. Ion. ὄσφραντο rare, Her. 1, 80 (Mss. R a. Gaisf. Bekk. Lhard. Dind.), ὤσφρ- (Mss. M K S &c. Old ed. Bred. Abicht, Stein), late ὠσφρησάμην Arat. 955; Ael. H. A. 5, 49: 2 aor. ὠσφρόμην Ar. Ach. 179; Com. Fr. (Philon.) 2, 422; Dio Cass. 68, 27; Luc. Jup. Tr. 15; Sext. Emp. 255, 14 (B.) The change of 1 aor. ὄσφραντο or ὤσφρ- Her. quoted, to 2 aor. ὤσφροντο if necessary, is certainly easy, and perhaps some may be inclined to make it. (We now see that Krüger has done so in his edit. of Her.) **Vb.** ὀσφραντός Aristot. de An. 2, 9, 7. 11; Plut. Mor. 969, ὀσφρητός Sext. Emp. 296 (B.) ὀσφρᾶσθαι is the Mss. reading Antiph. Com. Fr. 3, 80, for which Meineke has ὀσφρέσθαι the emendation of

Elmsley. **Act.** ὀσφραίνω gener. *to smell,* is in Galen 10, 595, ἀπ- *make smell,* Anth. 11, 165: **aor.** προσ-οσφράνῃς Geop. 19, 2.

'Οτοβέω *To sound,* Poet. and only **pres.** ὀτοβεῖ Aesch. Pr. 574. Fr. 55 (D.)

'Οτοτύζω *To lament* (ὀτοτοῖ), Poet. Ar. Thesm. 1083; Com. Fr. (Anon.) 4, 629: **imp.** ὠτότυζον, ἐπ- Eur. Phoen. 1038: **fut. mid.** ὀτοτύξομαι Ar. Lys. 520: **aor.** ὠτότυξα, ἀν- Aesch. Ag. 1074; Eur. Hel. 371 chor. (Dind. -οτότυξα Nauck.) **Pass.** ὀτοτύζεται Aesch. Ch. 327.

'Οτρύνω *To rouse, urge on,* Poet. and late prose, Il. 5, 482; Pind. Ol. 3, 38; Aesch. Sept. 726; Soph. El. 28; subj. -ύνωμεν Od. 24, 405, Epic -ύνομεν 1, 85; inf. ὀτρύνειν Aretae. Morb. Ac. 2, 115 (ed. Oxon.), Epic ὀτρυνέμεν Il. 4, 286: **imp.** ὤτρῡνον Il. 5, 520; Hes. Th. 883; Pind. P. 4, 40; Soph. Aj. 60, ὄτρ- Il. 16, 495, iter. ὀτρύνεσκον Il. 24, 24; Ap. Rh. 3, 653: **fut.** ὀτρῡνέω Epic (for ὀτρυνῶ) Il. 10, 55. Od. 2, 253. 15, 3: **aor.** ὤτρῡνα Od. 17, 430 (ὄτρ- Aristarch. La R.); subj. -ύνω Il. 15, 402, -ύνῃσι Od. 14, 374; ὀτρύναιμι Ap. Rh. 1, 701, -ειε Od. 15, 306; Ap. Rh. 1, 382; ὄτρῡνον Il. 19, 69; Pind. Ol. 6, 87; inf. ὀτρῦναι Il. 8, 219: **pass.** ὀτρυνόμενος Aristot. Mund. 6, 24: **aor.** ὠτρύνθη Pseud.-Callisth. 3, 3. **Mid.** ὀτρύνομαι *urge oneself, haste,* Od. 10, 425; -υνώμεθα Il. 14, 369: **imp.** ὠτρύνοντο Od. 17, 183, in which sense the **act.** ὤτρυνον is once used, Il. 7, 420 (Vulg. Wolf, Spitzn.) where however Aristarch. read ὠτρύνοντο, which Heyne, Bekk. Dind. La Roche adopt: **aor.** ὠτρύνατο Androm. Sen. 47; trans. *urge* ὀτρυνώμεθα, ἐπ- Od. 8, 31. This verb seems very much confined to Epic, Pind. and the Traged.: the **mid.** is Epic. ἐποτρύνω is in prose, Thuc. 7, 25, -ώτρυνον 6, 69; -οτρύνας Her. 7, 170. ὀτρυνέουσα with signif. of **pres.** Od. 23, 264 (Vulg.) was read ὀτρύνουσα by Eustath. and this is now the approved reading (Wolf, Bekk. Dind. La R. Ameis.) There thus seems no ground, at most slight, for a **pres.** ὀτρυνέω.

Οὐνομάζω, see ὀνομ-.

Οὐρέω *mingo,* Hes. Op. 758; Ar. Thesm. 615; Her. 2, 35; Hippocr. 1, 78 (Erm.); Aristot. H. An. 6, 20, 1: **imp.** ἐούρεον Luc. Conv. 35, προσ- Dem. 54, 4, Ion. οὔρεον Hippocr. 2, 692 (Lit.), iter. οὔρεσκον late prose, Ant. Lib. 41 (Westerm.): **fut.** οὐρήσω Hippocr. 5, 444. 8, 16 (Lit.): and Attic, **mid.** οὐρήσομαι Ar. Pax 1266: **aor.** ἐούρησα, ἐν- Com. Fr. (Eup.) 2, 444, Ion. οὔρησα Hippocr. 2, 696. 5, 354 (Lit.); also Aristot. H. A. 6, 20, 8 (Bekk.); subj. οὐρήσω Ar. Vesp. 394; -ουρῆσαι Her. 1, 107: **p.** ἐούρηκα, ἐν- Ar. Lys. 402, Ion. οὔρηκα: **plp.** οὐρήκει Hippocr. 5, 354 (Lit.): **aor. pass.** οὐρήθην Hippocr. 5, 534. 716 (Lit.) The Attics seem to have avoided the **fut. act.**: οὐρήσω Ar. Vesp. 394, is subj. 1 aor. in spite of Dawes' and Brunck's canon. This is one of the few verbs which, though beginning with a vowel, take a syllabic augment: so ὠθέω, usu. ἐώθουν; ὠνέομαι, ἐωνούμην &c. and some parts of ἄγνυμι, ἔαξα, ἐάγην, ἔᾱγα; ἁλίσκομαι, ἑάλων, ἑάλωκα; compare ἔοικα, ἔολπα, ἔοργα; ἁνδάνω, ἔᾱδον, ἔᾱδα; ὁράω, ἑώρων, ἑώρᾱκα, ἑόρ-; ἀνοίγω, ἀν-έῳγον, ἀνέῳξα.

Οὐρίζω, see ὀρ-.

Οὐτάω *To wound*, Epic, οὐτᾷ Aesch. Ch. 640 (chor.); imper. οὔτᾰε Od. 22, 356: **imp.** iter. οὔτασκε Il. 15, 745: **fut.** οὐτήσω late Nonn. 21, 37: **aor.** οὔτησα Il. 11, 260, iter. οὐτήσασκε Il. 22, 375; -τήσῃ Opp. Hal. 2, 493; -τῆσαι 2, 474: **aor. pass.** οὐτήθην, -ηθείς Il. 8, 537; Opp. Hal. 2, 468: **2 aor.** (οὔταν for οὔτην?) 3 sing. οὖτᾰ Il. 5, 376. Od. 22, 293. 294, retaining ᾰ from orig. Theme; inf. οὐτᾰ́μεναι Il. 21, 68, and οὐτᾰ́μεν 5, 821; Hes. Sc. 335: **2 aor. mid.** οὐτᾰ́μενος **pass.** Il. 17, 86. Od. 11, 40; Ap. Rh. 3, 1396; Orph. Lith. 452. **Vb.** νε-ούτᾰτος Il. 18, 536, ἀν-ούτατος 4, 540; Aesch. Fr. 126 (D. 5 ed.) Collat. οὐτάζω also Poet. Il. 20, 459; Tyrt. 11, 30; Eur. Fr. 176 (D.): **imp.** οὔταζ- Il. 13, 552: **fut.** -ᾰ́σω Eur. Rhes. 255 (chor.): **aor.** οὔτᾰσα Il. 15, 528; Ap. Rh. 2, 831; -άσας Eur. H. F. 199: **p. p.** οὔτασται Il. 11, 661; Opp. Hal. 4, 553; οὐτασμένος Od. 11, 536; Aesch. Ag. 1344 (chor.): **aor.** late οὐτασθείς Lycophr. 242. **Mid. imp.** οὐτάζετο Opp. C. 4, 278, missed by Lexicogr.

Ὀφείλω *To owe, I ought*, Pind. N. 2, 6; Soph. Ant. 331; Ar. Nub. 117; Her. 1, 41; Thuc. 4, 87; Lys. 9, 9; -είλων Aesch. Pr. 985, Epic ὀφέλλω Il. 19, 200. Od. 8, 332: **imp.** ὤφειλον Hes. Op. 174. Fr. 172; Her. 3, 71. 6, 59 (Gaisf. Bekk. Stein); Lys. 9, 12; Isocr. 5, 36, ὄφειλ- Il. 11, 688 (ὄφελλ- Bekk.), ὤφελλον 7, 390; Hes. quoted (some Mss. Al. Rzach), ὄφελλ- Il. 1, 353: **fut.** ὀφειλήσω, -ήσειν Xen. Cyr. 7, 2, 28; Dem. 30, 9: **aor.** ὠφείλησα Ar. Av. 115, ἐπ- Thuc. 8, 5; ὀφειλῆσαι Dem. 30, 16. 18: **p.** ὠφείληκα: **plp.** -ήκειν (Dem.) 45, 33: **aor. pass.** ὀφειληθείς Thuc. 3, 63: **pres.** ὀφειλόμεθα Simon. C. 122: **imp.** ὀφείλετο Il. 11, 698: **2 aor.** ὤφελον (ὄφελον see below), -ες, -ε *I ought, should have* &c. hence used as expressive of a *wish* only, *O that! utinam!* with or without εἴθε, αἴθε, ὡς, εἰ, γὰρ &c. Il. 3, 428 (ὤφελλον 14, 84. 24, 764); Simon. C. 117; Aesch. Pr. 48; Soph. El. 1022. Ph. 969; Eur. Ion 286. Heracl. 247; Ar. Thesm. 865. Pax 1069; Her. 1, 111. 3, 65 (Bekk. Dind. Stein); Pl. Rep. 432; even 2 pl. -έλετε Il. 24, 254. **2 aor.** is often unaugm. ὄφελον in Epic, Il. 6, 345. 9, 698. Od. 11, 548 (ὄφελλ- Od. 8, 312), in choral odes, and anapaests of the Attic poets, Aesch. Pers. 915; Soph. Aj. 1192; Eur. Med. 1413, and in Ion. and late prose, Her. 1, 111. 3, 65, quoted above (Vulg.

Gaisf. Bred. ὤφ- Bekk. &c.); Luc. Soloec. 1, as a solecism, Epic ὄφελλον, ὤφελλ- Il. and Od. quoted. ὤφειλον Hes. Op. 174. Fr. 172 (Goettl.) seems to be imp. equivalent to aor. ὤφελον. In late Auth. ὤφελον, ὄφελ- is used like a conjunction, Arr. Diss. 218; Callim. Epigr. 18; N. T. 1 Cor. 4, 8.

'Οφέλλω *To increase, assist,* Poet. esp. Epic, Il. 15, 383; Hes. Op. 14; Aesch. Sept. 193 (Vulg. Herm. -λλεται Ms. M. &c. Dind. Weil); inf. -λλειν Pind. P. 4, 260; Aristot. Fr. 539, Epic -λλέμεν Od. 15, 21: imp. ὤφελλον Od. 16, 174, ὄφ- Il. 2, 420; Theocr. 25, 120: aor. (Aeol. ὤφελλα), 3 sing. opt. ὀφέλλειε Il. 16, 651. Od. 2, 334. **Mid.** or **pass.** ὀφέλλεται Od. 3, 367; Aesch. Sept. 193 quoted (Dind. Weil): **imp.** ὀφέλλετο Il. 23, 524. Od. 14, 233. In late authors the opt. form in ει occurs in the pres. also, δείπνειας Athen. 4, 149, ὑποδρήσσειε Nonn. Dion. 15, 125. 43, 116, and ἀλυσκάζειε 42, 135 (Vulg.), but -άσσειε (Rhod. Graef. Koechl.), ἀερτάζειεν 43, 99, -άσσειεν (Rhod. Graef. Koechl.)

'Οφλισκάνω *To owe, incur, be guilty* (ὄφλω), Soph. Ant. 470; Eur. Alc. 1093; Pl. Theaet. 161: **imp.** ὤφλ- Dem. 30, 2: **fut.** ὀφλήσω Soph. O. R. 511; Eur. Hec. 327; Ar. Pax 173; Pl. Phaed. 117; Isocr. 17, 48: **aor.** ὤφλησα rare, Lys. 13, 65; (Hippocr.) Epist. 3, 849 (K.); and late Sopat. Rhet. p. 243, προσ- Alciphr. 3, 26: **p.** ὤφληκα Ar. Nub. 34; Dem. 2, 3. 19, 180; -ήκῃ Ar. Av. 1457; -ήκοι Lys. 23, 3; -ηκώς Antiph. 5, 16; Pl. Apol. 39; -ηκέναι Dem. 19, 280: **plp.** ὠφλήκει Dem. 52, 27: **p. p.** ὤφλημαι, -ημένην Dem. 29, 55: **2 aor.** ὦφλον Com. Fr. (Antiph.) 3, 156; Her. 8, 26; Andoc. 1, 73; Lys. 11, 9; Xen. An. 5, 8, 1; Pl. Apol. 36, -ομεν Isae. 5, 22; subj. ὄφλω Eur. Andr. 188, -λῃ Ar. Eccl. 655; Pl. Leg. 857, -ωμεν Isae. 5, 22, -ωσι Pl. Leg. 856; opt. ὄφλοι Soph. Fr. 470 (D.); Pl. Leg. 778, -οιεν Andoc. 1, 74; ὀφλεῖν Eur. Bac. 854; Thuc. 5, 101; ὀφλών Aesch. Ag. 534; Thuc. 3, 70; Pl. Apol. 39, often with accent of pres. or, as some call it, Attic accent, ὄφλειν, ὄφλων, see Mss. reading and old edit. of Eur. Thuc. and Pl. quoted; Antiph. 5, 13; Dem. 23, 143. 24, 50. 29, 34. 31, 12, where *now* Bekk. &c. always ὀφλεῖν, ὀφλών. But ὄφλω pres. seems certain later, ὄφλουσι Dio Chrys. 31, 642 (L. Dind. Emper.); but for ὄφλων App. B. C. 2, 8, ὀφείλων (Bekk.); and for ὦφλον 5, 77 (Dind.), ὤφειλον (Bekk.); ὤφλεε for ὦφλε in some edit. of Her. 8, 26, seems to be a spurious form. The rarity of aor. ὤφλησα has caused it to be doubted (Lys. 13, 65). Sauppe suggests ὦφλον, Scheibe thinks the passage spurious.

'Οχετεύω *To conduct by a canal, convey, lead,* Pl. Leg. 666: **fut.** -εύσω: **aor.** ὀχέτευσα Emped. 12 (Stein); -εῦσαι Her. 2, 99:

p. ὠχέτευκα Aristot. Part. Anim. 3, 5, 9. **Mid.** as act. **aor.** ὀχετευσάμενος Anth. 9, 162: but **fut.** ὀχετεύσονται seems pass. Com. Fr. (Pher.) 2, 316.

Ὀχέω *To carry, bear,* Od. 7, 211; Ar. Ran. 23; Hippocr. 3, 480; Xen. Cyr. 1, 3, 8; Pl. Crat. 400, Dor. **ὀκχέω,** 3 pl. -χέοντι Pind. Ol. 2, 67: **imp.** ὤχει Eur. Hel. 277 (Musgr. Dind. Paley), iter. ὀχέεσκον Od. 11, 619: **fut.** ὀχήσω Aesch. Pr. 143; Eur. Or. 802; Lycophr. 97; Galen 3, 421: Dor. **aor.** ὤκχησα Callim. Jov. 23. More freq. **pass.** ὀχέομαι *to be carried* &c. Il. 10, 403; Soph. Ph. 190 (Herm. Dind.); Eur. Or. 69; Ar. Ran. 25; Xen. An. 3, 4, 47: **imp.** ὠχέετο Her. 1, 31, -εῖτο Xen. Cyr. 7, 3, 4, ὀχ- H. Ven. 217: with **fut. mid.** ὀχήσομαι Il. 24, 731, ἐπ- 10, 330: and **aor.** ὀχήσατο Od. 5, 54: also **aor. pass.** ὀχηθῆναι Hippocr. 4, 250 (Lit.); ὀχηθείς Luc. Lex. 2: **p. p.** ὀχημένος, ἐπ- Nonn. 8, 229. In good Attic prose, this verb seems to occur in pres. and imp. only. Hom. never augments it. The fut. of the Dor. form ὀκχήσει should perhaps be restored to Lycophr. for ὀγχήσει 64. 1049.

Ὀχθέω *To feel grieved, indignant,* Epic, imper. ὄχθει Theogn. 1032: **fut.** ὀχθήσω late Q. Sm. 3, 451: **aor.** alone classic ὤχθησα, 3 pl. ὤχθησαν Il. 1, 570. 15, 101; and part. ὀχθήσας Il. 1, 517. 16, 48; Hes. Th. 558.

Ὀψείω *To wish to see, long for,* part. ὀψείοντες Il. 14, 37 (Dor. ὀψέω): **imp.** ὤψεον Sophr. 39 (Ahr.) Desider. to ὁράω, ὄψομαι.

Π.

Πᾱδάω, see πηδάω.

Παιδαγωγέω *To lead children, guide, train,* Eur. Heracl. 729; Pl. Leg. 897: **imp.** ἐπαιδ- Rep. 600: **fut.** -γήσω Soph. Fr. 623 (Dind.); (Pl.) Alc. 1, 135: **p.** πεπαιδαγώγηκα Luc. Tim. 13; reg. except **fut. mid.** παιδαγωγήσομαι, -γήσει as pass. (Pl.) Alc. 1, 135.

Παιδεύω *To instruct,* Soph. Tr. 451; Her. 1, 136; Antiph. 3, β, 3; Pl. Rep. 534: **imp.** ἐπαιδ- Pl. Rep. 430; Isae. 1, 12; Lycurg. 101: **fut.** -εύσω Pl. Euth. 272: **aor.** ἐπαίδευσα Pind. Fr. 180; Soph. O. C. 919; Isocr. 8, 77; Aeschin. 1, 140; -ευσον Ar. Ran. 1502: **p.** πεπαίδευκα Pl. Rep. 606; Aeschin. 1, 173: **p. p.** πεπαίδευμαι Com. Fr. (Antiph.) 3, 156; Xen. Cyr. 2, 3, 13: **aor.** ἐπαιδεύθην Soph. O. C. 562; Isocr. 7, 82; Lys. 9, 27; Xen. Cyr. 1, 2, 2: **fut.** παιδευθήσομαι Pl. Rep. 376; Plut. Mor. 212: and as pass. **fut. mid.** παιδεύσομαι Pl. Crito 54; Or. Sib. 9, 165.

Mid. παιδεύομαι *to rear, educate for oneself, get educated,* Com. Fr. (Nausicr.) 4, 575: aor. ἐπαιδευσάμην Pl. Rep. 546, παιδευσ- Theocr. 24, 134: fut. -εύσομαι as pass. see above. **Vb.** παιδευτέος Pl. Rep. 526.

Παιδοποιέω *To beget children* (in act. Poet. and late prose), Soph. El. 589; Eur. Heracl. 524; Ar. Eccl. 615; Luc. D. Deor. 22, 1: aor. -ῆσαι Ael. V. H. 12, 44: p. p. πεπαιδοποίημαι Dem. 25, 80; Plut. Agis 10, also as mid. see below. More freq. mid. -οῦμαι Andoc. 4, 23; Xen. Mem. 4, 4, 23; Pl. Leg. 784: fut. -ήσομαι Pl. Rep. 449: aor. ἐπαιδοποιησάμην Xen. Cyr. 5, 4, 12; imper. -ποίησαι Eur. Or. 1080; -ήσασθαι Pl. Leg. 868: and as mid. p. p. πεπαιδοποιημένος Aeschin. 2, 149; Diod. Sic. 4, 28.

Παίζω *To sport,* Od. 6, 106; Pind. Ol. 1, 16; Soph. El. 567; Eur. H. F. 952; Ar. Ran. 319; Her. 1, 94; Pl. Men. 79, Dor. παίσδω Alcm. 38 (B.); Theocr. 14, 8. 15, 42: imp. ἔπαιζον Od. 6, 100; Pind. Ol. 13, 86; Her. 1, 114; Pl. Lys. 206, παῖζ- H. H. 4, 120, Dor. ἔπαισδ- Theocr. 15, 49: fut. παιξοῦμαι Dor. Xen. Conv. 9, 2, παίξομαι Anth. 12, 46, συμ- Luc. D. Deor. 4, 3: and παίξω Anacreont. 38, 8 (Bergk); Anth. 12, 211: aor. ἔπαισα, προσ- Pl. Phaedr. 265; παίσωμεν Ar. Av. 660. Thesm. 947; imper. παίσατε Od. 8, 251; παίσας Ar. Ran. 392; παῖσαι 388; Pl. Euthyd. 278 (Vulg. Bait. Or. Herm.), perhaps unattic ἔπαιξα Anth. 5, 112; Luc. Prom. 8. D. Deor. 6, 4; Sext. Emp. 108, 8, προσ- Plut. Caes. 63; παίξας Ctes. Fr. Pers. 29, 59; Babr. 32, 9; and παῖξαι Pl. Euthyd. quoted (Mss. A Θ S. Winckl.): p. πέπαικα Com. Fr. (Men.) 4, 237, later πέπαιχα Plut. Demosth. 9: p. p. πέπαισμαι Her. 4, 77; Ar. Thesm. 1227; Pl. Euthyd. 278. Phaedr. 265, later πέπαιγμαι (Pl.) Sisyph. 542; Plut. Mor. 81: aor. ἐπαίχθην Plut. Mor. 123; Heliod. 8, 6. **Vb.** παιστέον Com. Fr. (Plat.) 2, 630. The Traged. seem to use the pres. only. In some edit. of Hes. παίζονται mid. occurs in a suspected line Sc. 299 (Ald. &c.), παίζοντες (Wolf, Goettl.)

Παιφάσσω *To look about fiercely, wildly,* later of any *rapid motion,* only pt. παιφάσσουσα Il. 2, 450; Nic. Ther. 761; -σσοντα Opp. Hal. 2, 288. Cyn. 2, 250: and imp. παίφασσε Ap. Rhod. 4, 1442.

Παίω *To strike,* Aesch. Ag. 1384; Soph. O. R. 807; Ar. Av. 497; Her. 2, 63. 9, 107; Thuc. 7, 36; Xen. An. 6, 1, 5; Dem. 54, 20: imp. ἔπαιον Aesch. Pers. 426; Her. 3, 137; Xen. An. 6, 6, 27: fut. παίσω Eur. El. 688; Xen. An. 3, 2, 19. Cyr. 4, 1, 3, and in Com. Poet. παιήσω Ar. Nub. 1125. Lys. 459: aor. ἔπαισα chiefly Trag. Aesch. Sept. 961; Soph. O. R. 1270. O. C. 544; Eur. El. 841; rare in Comed. Ar. Nub. 549; Com. Fr. (Plat.) 2, 673 (ἐξ- Anaxil. 3, 348); Xen. An. 5, 8, 10. Cyr. 2, 4, 19:

p. πέπαικα *simple* late, V. T. Num. 22, 28, but ὑπερ- Ar. Eccl. 1118; Dem. 50, 34, and late (on the analogy of fut. -ήσω) πεπαίηκα Clem. Alex. Strom. 7, p. 846: p. p. late πέπαισμαι, ἐμ- Athen. 12, 543; Eustath. Od. 1775, 13: aor. ἐπαίσθην Aesch. Ch. 184. Sept. 961: pres. pass. παιόμενος Antiph. 2, δ, 4; Thuc. 4, 47: imp. unaugm. παίοντ' Aesch. Pers. 416 (trimet.) **Mid.** παίομαι *to strike oneself*, imp. ἐπαίοντο Plut. Pomp. 24: fut. παιήσομαι if correct, V. T. Jud. 15, 7 (Paul. Tell.): aor. ἐπαισάμην Xen. Cyr. 7, 3, 6. For perf. and aor. pass. πέπληγμαι, ἐπλήγην were more in use: πληγεὶς ἢ παιόμενος Lys. 4, 6.

Παλαίω *To wrestle*, Hes. Op. 413; Eur. Rhes. 509; Hippocr. 6, 496; -ειν Ar. Pax 896; Pl. Men. 94; pt. -λαίουσα Soph. Fr. 678, Dor. -λαίοισα Pind. P. 9, 27: imp. ἐπάλαιον Il. 23, 733 (Vulg. Dind.), πάλαιον (Bekk. 2 ed. La R.), ἐπάλ- Pseud.-Callisth. 2, 20: fut. παλαίσω Il. 23, 621; late prose Paus. 6, 14, 2. 23, 3, προσ- Pind. I. 4, 53: aor. ἐπάλαισα Od. 4, 343; Xen. Oec. 17, 2; Pl. Men. 94, παλ- Pind. N. 8, 27: p. πεπάλαικα Anth. 12, 90; Philostr. Imag. 846: p. p. πεπάλαισμαι Anth. 9, 411; (Luc.) Asin. 10: aor. ἐπαλαίσθην Eur. El. 686. **Mid.** as act. fut. παλαισόμενοι Plut. Mor. 236, κατα- Pseud.-Callisth. 3, 16 (40), missed by Lexicogr. **Vb.** δυσ-πάλαιστος Aesch. Supp. 468. At Her. 8, 21, the Florent. Ms. has aor. opt. παλαίσειε, which seems to yield not an unsuitable sense, *should struggle, be distressed*, and, as a possible contingency, *fail*, see Eur. Rhes. 509. El. 686; Xen. Oec. 17, 2, but the generally approved reading is παλήσειε which has been referred to an unused pres. form παλέω *to be wrenched, dislocated, disabled* (Hesych.), ἐξ-επάλησεν Hippocr. 3, 552. 4, 240 (Lit.)

Παλάσσω (πάλλω) *To throw, sprinkle, stain*, fut. -άξω, inf. -ξέμεν Od. 13, 395: aor. παλάξαι (Hesych.): p. p. πεπάλαγμαι Il. 6, 268; Callim. Lav. Pal. 7; Ap. Rh. 3, 1046, but as act. *cast lots*, 1, 358; Il. 7, 171. Od. 9, 331, where Bekker, La Roche, Kayser read, with Aristarchus, the ς formation πεπάλασθε, -άσθαι: plp. πεπάλακτο pass. Il. 11, 98; Callim. Del. 78: imp. παλάσσετο Il. 5, 100.

Πάλλω *To shake*, trans. Il. 3, 19; Pind. N. 3, 45; Eur. Bac. 783; Ar. Ach. 965 (δια- Aesch. Fr. 305); rare in prose Pl. Crat. 407; Luc. D. Deor. 8, 1: imp. ἔπαλλον Eur. Ion 1151, πάλλ- Il. 7, 181. Od. 10, 206, and always; Hes. Sc. 321: fut. (πᾰλῶ): 1 aor. ἔπηλα Soph. El. 710, ἀν- Eur. Bac. 1190, πῆλε Il. 6, 474. 16, 117, Dor. ἔπᾱλα Alcm. 69; πήλας, δια- Aesch. Sept. 731: 2 p. πέπηλα, -ηλότι late and rare if correct, Nonn. D. 14, 152 (Scal. Graef. κεκυφότι Koechl.): 2 aor. redupl. (πέπᾰλον) Epic, ἀμ-πεπᾰλών Il. 3, 355: p. p. πέπαλμαι Aesch. Ch. 410, see mid.: 2 aor. late (ἐπάλην), ἀνα-πᾰλείς Strab. 8, 6, 21. Mid. πάλλομαι *shake oneself, quiver* &c. Il. 22, 452; Pind. N. 5, 21; Ar. Ran. 345; Her. 1, 141; Opp. Hal. 1, 166, *shake for oneself, cast lots*, Il. 24, 400: imp. ἐπαλλ- Her. 9, 120, παλλ- Aesch. Supp. 567 (chor.): 1 aor. πήλασθαι Callim. Jov. 64; and perhaps ἀνεπήλατο Mosch. 2, 109: see p. p. πέπαλμαι quoted: 2 aor. sync. ἔπαλτο, ἀν- Il. 8, 85. 23, 694, in tmesi Pind. Ol. 13, 72, πάλτο Il. 15, 645, ἔκ-παλτο 20, 483, but ἐπᾶλτο (ἔπαλτο Bekk. 2 ed.) Il. 13, 643. 21, 140, is sync. aor. of ἐφ-άλλομαι. The act. is sometimes used as mid. πάλλων Soph. O. R. 153: δελφὶς ἔπαλλε Eur. El. 435; Ar. Lys. 1304.

(Πάομαι) *To taste, eat*, for which in pres. πᾰτέομαι Ion. Her. 2, 37. 47. 66; Callim. Fr. 437; Athen. (Agath.) 14, 62: fut. πᾰσομαι Aesch. Sept. 1036 (Vulg. Well. σπάσ- Dind. Herm. *now*): aor. ἐπᾰσάμην Od. 3, 9 (Bekk.); Hes. Th. 642; Ar. Pax 1092; Her. 1, 73, ἐπασσ- Od. 9, 87 (Bekk.), πᾰσάμ- Il. 1, 464. 2, 427. 21, 76 (Bekk.); -σαιτο Ap. Rh. 3, 807; late Attic prose Ael. H. A. 1, 41; πᾰσασθαι Il. 19, 160; Soph. Ant. 202; Ar. Pax 1281; Her. 2, 37, πάσσ- Od. 10, 384; part. Dor. πᾰσαμένα Aesch. Ag. 1408 (chor.), πασσάμενος Od. 1, 124. 4, 61: p. p. (πέπασμαι): plp. πεπάσμην Il. 24, 642. Vb. ἄ-παστος Od. 4, 788. Fut. σπάσομαι seems now to be the best Mss. reading Aesch. Sept. 1036.

(Πάομαι) *To acquire, find*, Poet. fut. πᾱσομαι Aesch. Eum. 177 (Dind. Herm.): aor. Poet. ἐπᾱσάμην Aesch. Fr. 213 (D.); πᾱσάμενος Theogn. 146; Epigr. Athen. 11, 14; Theocr. 15, 90; in prose late and in comp. κατα-πασ- Apocr. 2 Macc. 14, 15: p. πέπᾱμαι Theógn. 663; Pind. P. 8, 73; Eur. Ion 675; Ar. Av. 943; Xen. An. 3, 3, 18; Stob. (Archyt.) 1, 73 (Mein.); πεπᾱμένος Aesch. Ag. 835; Xen. An. 5, 9, 12; -πᾶσθαι Solon 13, 7; Theocr. 10, 33: plp. ἐπεπάμην Anth. 7, 67, but πέπᾱτο Xen. An. 1, 9, 19 (Vulg.), where however the best Mss. point to ἐπέπατο (Krüg. Dind. Saupp. Kühner &c.): 3 fut. πεπάσομαι Stob. (Pempel.) 79, 52. πάσομαι is the preferable reading Aesch. Eum. quoted, both for sense and Ms. authority.

Παραινέω *To exhort*, Pind. I. 6, 68; Aesch. Ch. 903; Soph. Ph. 621; Ar. Thesm. 9; Her. 1, 197; Thuc. 7, 63; Pl. Phaedr. 234: imp. παρῄνουν Soph. O. R. 1512, παρῄνει Thuc. 4, 130, Ion. παραίνεε Her. 8, 19. 9, 17 (Ms. S. Bekk. Dind. Gaisf. Stein): fut. παραινέσω Soph. O. C. 1181; Ar. Pax 1245; Dem. 37, 11. 47, 69; Luc. Char. 20: and mid. παραινέσομαι rare, Pl. Menex. 236: aor. παρῄνεσα Aesch. Pers. 224; Soph. Ph. 1434; Ar. Eq. 660; Isocr. 12, 264, Ion. παραίν- Her. 1, 80: p. παρῄνεκα Isocr. 2, 54. Epist. 2, 1: p. p. παρῄνημαι Hippocr. 3, 484; -ῃνῆσθαι

Thuc. 7, 69: aor. παρηνέθην Hippocr. 3, 446: Thuc. 5, 69. See αἰνέω.

Παραιτέομαι *To solicit from, beg off*, is Dep. Mid., Pind. Nem. 10, 30; Eur. Heracl. 1026; Pl. Criti. 106; -αιτοῦ Aesch. Supp. 521; -εόμενος Her. 1, 24: imp. -ῃτεῖτο Thuc. 5, 63, Ion. -αιτέετο Her. 3, 119. 5, 33: fut. -ήσομαι Pl. Rep. 387; Xen. An. 6, 6, 29: aor. -ῃτησάμην Ar. Vesp. 1257; Pl. Apol. 27, Ion. -αιτησ- Her. 4, 43. 146: p. p. as act. παρῃτῆσθαι D. Laert. 4, 51; Sext. Emp. 193, 21; but pass. ῃτημένος N. T. Luc. 14, 18. 19.

Παρακρούω, see κρούω.

(**Παραμεύω**)=-αμείβω *To surpass*, aor. -αμεῦσαι Hesych.: mid. fut. -μεύσεται Pind. N. 11, 13.

Παρανομέω *To transgress the law*, Antiph. 5, 15; Thuc. 2, 37: imp. (as if from παρ-ανομέω) παρηνόμουν Lys. 3, 17; Aeschin. 3, 77 (Mss. Ald. Vulg.); Plut. Mor. 119; Dio Cass. 63, 13, but παρενόμουν Lys. 3, 17 (Cobet); Aeschin. 3, 77 quoted (Mss. Bekk. Bait. Saupp. Frank.); (Dem.) 17, 22 (Bekk. Dind.); Luc. Apol. 7 (Dind.): fut. -ήσω Luc. Tim. 45 (Jacob.): aor. παρηνόμησα Thuc. 3, 67 (Mss. Bekk. Popp. Krüg.); Plut. Demetr. 37; Dio. Hal. 10, 35; Dio Cass. 46, 13, παρεν- Her. 7, 238; Thuc. quoted (Ms. G. L. Dind. Stahl); (Luc.) Amor. 20: p. παρανενόμηκα Xen. Hell. 2, 3, 36; Dem. 21, 9. 43, 71; Luc. Gall. 4; Diod. Sic. 17, 106 (Bekk. Dind.). 16, 61 (L. Dind.), παρ-ηνόμ- (Vulg. Bekk.): plp. παρανενομήκεσαν Xen. Hell. 2, 1, 31 (Vulg. Breitb. Saupp.), παρενενομ- (Dind. Voemel), παρηνομήκει late Dio Cass. 39, 59: p. p. παρανενομῆσθαι Dem. 44, 31. 54, 2, παρηνομ- Inscr. An. 355 A. Chr.: aor. παρηνομήθην Joseph. Ant. 15, 4, 1; παρανομηθείς Thuc. 5, 16. This verb is prosaic. In the *classic* period Dind. Voemel, and perhaps Krüger &c. prefer the augm. with ε.

Παρασκευάζω, see σκευάζω.

Παρέχω, see ἔχω.

Παρηγορέω *To soothe*, Aesch. Eum. 507; Soph. Fr. 186; Eur. Phoen. 1449; Com. Fr. (Phil.) 4, 53; perhaps late in prose (Dem.) 60, 35; Plut. Pomp. 13. Mor. 156: imp. παρηγόρει Com. Fr. (Phil.) 4, 58, -όρουν Aesch. Pr. 646, -όρεον Her. 9, 54 (Schweigh. Gaisf. Stein, but -ορέοντο Bekk. Dind. Krüg.; so 9, 55 Bekk. Gaisf. Stein &c.), iter. παρηγορέεσκε Ap. Rh. 4, 1740; Musae. 39: fut. -ήσω Plut. Ant. 83: aor. παρηγόρησα Eur. Hec. 288; Hippocr. 1, 320 (Erm.); (Pl.) Ax. 364; Plut. Cat. min. 27: aor. pass. -ηγορηθείς Plut. Caes. 28. T. Gr. 20: fut. -ηθήσεται Brut. Epist. 42, but κατ- Dem. 37, 47: and as pass. fut. mid. παρηγορήσεται Hippocr. 5, 478 (Lit.); Aretae. 130, 29. Mid. παρηγοροῦμαι, Ion. -εύμενος Her. 7, 13: imp. παρηγορέετο Her. 5,

104. 9, 55 (Gaisf. Bekk. Krüg. Dind.), and 9, 54 (Bekk. Dind. Krüg.), Dor. παρᾱγορεῖτο Pind. Ol. 9, 77 : fut. -ήσομαι pass. see above: aor. -ησάμην (Luc.) Amor. 52. Pass. rare and late -οῦνται Athen. 15, 36 ; -εῖσθαι Plut. Mor. 690 : aor. -ηθείς Plut. quoted. The act. form scarcely occurs in *classic* prose: παρηγόρεον Her. 9, 54 (Mss. Gaisf. &c.) has been altered, perhaps rightly, to mid. -έοντο (Bekk. Dind. &c.)

Πᾰροινέω *To behave rudely* (*in wine*), *insult*, Ar. Fr. 243 (D.); Antiph. 4, α, 6. γ, 2 ; Aeschin. 1, 70 (with double augm.): imp. ἐπαρῴνουν Dem. 23, 114. 54, 4 (v. r. ἐπαροίν-); Dio Cass. 45, 28 (Bekk.): fut. -ήσω, ἐμ-παρ- Luc. Tim. 14: aor. ἐπαρῴνησα Xen. An. 5, 8, 4 ; Dem. 22, 62 ; Luc. Conv. 2 ; Dio Cass. 45, 26 (Bekk.), παροίνησα (Tauchn.): p. πεπαρῴνηκα Com. Fr. (Hen.) 3, 563 ; Aeschin. 2, 154 : p. p. πεπαρῴνημαι Luc. Jup. Tr. 14 (Jacob. -ῴδημαι Bekk. Dind.): aor. ἐπαρῳνήθην Dem. 22, 63 (Ms. F. Dind.), παρῳνήθην (Bekk. B. S.) after a vowel. This verb is prosaic, occas. Comic.

Παρ-οίχομαι, see οἴχομαι.

Παρρησιάζομαι *To speak boldly*, Xen. Ages. 11, 5; Pl. Gorg. 491 ; Isocr. Epist. 4, 7 ; Aeschin. 1, 51 : imp. ἐπαρρησ- 1, 172 : fut. -ιάσομαι Pl. Charm. 156 ; Isocr. 15, 43 ; Dem. 11, 17 : aor. ἐπαρρησιασάμην Isocr. 11, 1 ; Aeschin. 1, 80 : p. πεπαρρησίασμαι act. Dem. 4, 51, pass. Isocr. 15, 10. Confined to prose.

Πάσσω *To sprinkle*, Poet. Il. 5, 900, ἐπι- Her. 4, 172, κατα- Hippocr. 6, 448 (Lit.), Attic πάττω Ar. Nub. 912. 1330: imp. ἔπασσον Il. 15, 394, πάσσ- 9, 214 : fut. πᾰσω Com. Fr. (Cratet.) 2, 237, κατα- Ar. Eq. 99 : aor. ἔπᾰσα, ἐπ- Com. Fr. (Men.) 4, 121 ; κατα-πάσας Ar. Nub. 177 ; Aristot. H. A. 9, 40, 59, ὑπο- Her. 1, 132, δια- 6, 125 ; inf. πάσαι, ἐμ- Pl. Lys. 210 : p. p. πεπασμένος Plut. Mor. 505. Sull. 2, δια- Aristot. Hist. An. 4, 3, 7, κατα- Diod. Sic. 1, 72 : plp. ἐπέπαστο Ap. Rh. 1, 729, κατ- (Luc.) Asin. 7, and πέπαστο Long. Past. 1, 12 (Seil.): aor. ἐπάσθην Geop. 19, 9, ἐπι- Pl. Rep. 405 : fut. ἐμ-πασθησόμενος Oribas. 10, 31. Mid. *to sprinkle oneself*, aor. πασάμενος late, Apocr. 3 Macc. 1, 18. Vb. παστέον Ar. Pax 1074. This verb in *simple* is Poet. and late prose.

Πάσχω *To feel, suffer* (παθ- πηθ- πένθω), Il. 20, 297. Od. 16, 189 ; Aesch. Pr. 759 ; Soph. Tr. 535 ; Ar. Pax 696 ; Her. 2, 20 ; Antiph. 2, β, 4 ; Thuc. 6, 78 ; Isocr. 5, 154 ; Poet. inf. πασχέμεν Theogn. 1009 ; Pind. P. 3, 104 : imp. ἔπασχον Il. 17, 375 ; Her. 1, 36 ; Antiph. 4, β, 2 ; Thuc. 2, 21 ; Lys. 7, 12, πάσχ- Od. 24, 27 : fut. πείσομαι Od. 2, 134 ; Aesch. Supp. 777 ; Soph. Ant. 96 ; Ar. Pax 276 ; Lys. 8, 20 ; Pl. Gorg. 513 (the form πήσομαι and aor. ἔπησα see below): 2 p. πέπονθα Od. 13, 6 ;

Solon 11, 1; Soph. Ph. 740; Eur. Or. 1616; Ar. Thesm. 445; Her. 1, 124; Thuc. 6, 11; Andoc. 3, 20; Isocr. 2, 42; πεπόνθῃ Pl. Rep. 376; -πόνθοι Parm. 140; πεπονθώς Pl. Charm. 171, προ- Antiph. 2, α, 5; Epic (πέπηθα), πεπăθυῖα Od. 17, 555; Dor. πέποσχα rare, Epich. Fr. 7 (Ahr.): **2 plp.** ἐπεπόνθειν Od. 13, 92 (Wolf, Dind.); Ar. Eccl. 650; Thuc. 4, 34; Dem. 21, 25. 111, ἐπεπόνθῃ Pl. Conv. 198, -θεε Her. 3, 74, πεπόνθει Od. quoted (Bekk. 2 ed. La R.); Theocr. 10, 1; Thuc. 7, 71 after a vowel (Bekk. Popp. Krüg. ἐπεπόνθ- L. Dind.); Dem. 18, 213; so Aeschin. πεπόνθ- 3, 142, after a conson. (Bekk. B. S. ἐπεπ- Frank. in Praef. Weidner): **2 aor.** ἔπăθον Il. 9, 492; Simon. C. 113; Pind. Ol. 2, 23; Aesch. Eum. 143; Soph. El. 169; Ar. Nub. 408; Her. 1, 197; Antiph. 2, δ, 7; Thuc. 1, 96; Lys. 8, 17; Isocr. 15, 97; Xen. An. 5, 8, 17, ’παθον Soph. Ph. 1012, πάθ- Il. quoted (Bekk. 2 ed. La R.); Pind. P. 3, 20. N. 10, 65; πάθω Il. 11, 404; Pl. Apol. 37, -θῃς Od. 17, 596; Soph. El. 390, -ῃσθα Il. 24, 551; -θοιμι Il. 19, 321; Antiph. 5, 58; παθεῖν Aesch. Pr. 625; Thuc. 5, 103, -θέειν Il. 17, 32; Her. 7, 11 (Bekk. Dind. -θεῖν Bred. Dietsch, Stein, Abicht); παθών Aesch. Sept. 1049; Antiph. 2, γ, 1. **Vb.** παθητός Aristot. ap. Plut. Mor. 887, Plut. Pelop. 16.

The fut. form πήσομαι scarcely occurs *now* except as a v. r. Her. 9, 37; Ar. Nub. 1122; Xen. Cyr. 7, 3, 10; Polyb. 2, 4, 4 &c. probably by an error of the copyist, for the best Mss. generally offer πείσομαι. Heliod. however has πήσομαι 8, 15. 10, 16 (Cor. Bekk.) The aor. (ἔπησα), part. πήσας is the reading of the Mss. and Vict. Aesch. Ag. 1624, and Scholefield adopts it. But scholars generally have not been satisfied either with the form or the meaning which it yields. Butler conjectured πταίσας, and Pors. Blomf. Dind. Weil approved of it; but παίσας, the reading of the Schol. Pind. P. 2, 95, is nearer the draft of the Ms. reading, furnishes an excellent sense, and is approved by Klausen, Franz, and Hermann; Dind. however retains πταίσας (5 edit.) πέποσθε 2 pl. **2 perf.** for πεπόνθατε Il. 3, 99. Od. 23, 53. Part. πεπονθώς, συνευ- Dem. 8, 65, *been benefited.*

Πăτάσσω *To strike,* Il. 13, 282, ἐκ- Eur. H. F. 889 (Steph. Pflugk, Dind. 2 ed.): **imp.** πάτασσε Il. 23, 370, ἐπάτ- (Bekk. 2 ed.): **fut.** -άξω Ar. Lys. 657. Ran. 646; Com. Fr. (Timocl.) 3, 606; prose, Aristot. Meteor. 3, 1, 14; and late Plut. Mor. 185. Them. 11; Luc. Jup. Tr. 53; Heliod. 5, 7: **aor.** ἐπάταξα Theogn. 1199; Ar. Ran. 645; Antiph. 4, δ, 5; Lys. 4, 15; Xen. Hell. 6, 2, 19; Dem. 21, 147. 180; πατάξω, -ῃς 4, 40. 21, 33, -ξῃ Pl. Leg. 879; -άξαιμι Dem. 53, 16; πάταξον Soph. Ph. 748; Ar. Lys. 362; πατάξαι Soph. Ant. 1097; Eur. Phoen.

1463; Ar. Lys. 635; Pl. Leg. 879; -άξας Eur. H. F. 1007; Ar. Ach. 93; Thuc. 8, 92; Antiph. 4, γ, 4; Lys. 1, 25. 13, 71; Dem. 54, 28: (perf.?): p. p. πεπάταγμαι, ἐκ- Od. 18, 327: aor. late ἐπατάχθην Anacreont. 33, 4 (Bergk); Luc. Anach. 40; Achil. Tat. 7, 4, 4. 5: fut. παταχθήσομαι Luc. Fugit. 14: pres. pass. πατασσομένη Orph. H. 22, 3. **Mid.** aor. πατάξασθαι, ἀνα- (Hesych.) The pres. and imp. are Epic (Attic τύπτω, παίω), the fut. and aor. Attic and late prose; in Tragedy and classic prose, the aor. alone is used; for the perf. aor. and fut. pass. the Attics used πέπληγμαι, ἐπλήγην (in comp. ἐπλᾱ́γην), πεπλήξομαι, πληγήσομαι; but for pres., τύπτομαι, or ἐκ-πλήττομαι &c.

Πᾰτέομαι *To taste*, see πᾱ́ομαι. To be distinguished from πατέομαι pass. of πατέω *I tread*. See ἀποπατέω.

Παύω *To repress*, Il. 19, 67; Eur. I. A. 683. Bac. 280; Com. Fr. (Mon.) 156; Xen. Laced. 3, 1; Pl. Phil. 25, ἀμ-παύ- Eur. Hel. 1335; imper. παῦε Il. 1, 282. Od. 24, 543; Soph. Ph. 1275; Ar. Vesp. 37; Pl. Phaedr. 257; παύειν Il. 21, 294; Eur. Med. 197; Xen. Athen. 3, 6, Ep. -έμεναι Od. 10, 22, παυέμεν, κατα- 24, 457: imp. ἔπαυον, ἀν- Xen. Hell. 6, 2, 29, iter. παύεσκον Od. 22, 315; rare in Attic, Soph. Ant. 963 (chor.): fut. παύσω Il. 15, 72 (Vulg. παύω Wolf, Bekk. Spitzn. Dind.); Soph. El. 796; Eur. Hipp. 512; Ar. Eq. 429; Her. 7, 54; Andoc. 1, 136; Pl. Gorg. 481; παύσων Il. 1, 207; Epic inf. παυσέμεν, κατα- Il. 7, 36: aor. ἔπαυσα Il. 15, 15; Pind. N. 3, 39; Aesch. Pr. 248; Soph. O. R. 397; Ar. Eq. 877; Her. 5, 67; Thuc. 6, 103; Xen. Cyr. 8, 6, 7, παῦσα Il. 17, 602; subj. παύσω, -ῃ Od. 4, 35, -ῃσι Il. 4, 191, -ωμεν Il. 7, 29, Epic -ομεν 21, 314; opt. παύσειε Il. 1, 192, παύσαι Thuc. 4, 62; παῦσον Her. 5, 23; παῦσαι Il. 7, 331; Antiph. 2, γ, 3: p. πέπαυκα Dem. 20, 70; Plut. Mor. 402: p. p. as mid. πέπαυμαι Il. 18, 125; Aesch. Pr. 615; Soph. Ph. 1279; Ar. Pax 29; Her. 1, 84. 2, 136; Thuc. 1, 6; Pl. Phaed. 100 (and as a doubtful v. r. πέπαυσμαι Her. 1, 84); Pl. Prot. 328. Euthyd. 278: imper. πέπαυσο Dem. 24, 64, which Franc. Fritzsche had overlooked when he wrote "πέπαυσο seriorum est;" Luc. Herm. 81. Navig. 39: plp. ἐπέπαυτο Her. 1, 83. 7, 9. 191; Thuc. 4, 13: aor. as mid. παύθην Hes. Th. 533, ἐπαυθ- Her. 5, 94. 6, 66 (Bekk. Dind.); Thuc. 2, 77. 5, 91. 100. 6, 59 &c.; Andoc. 2, 8, and as a v. r. at those passages ἐπαύσθην, which however in some editions occurs in text, Her. quoted (Ald. Gaisf. Stein); Thuc. (Vulg.); Paus. 7, 19, 3. 8, 5, 9 (Schub.), but ἐπαύθην 1, 23, 2. 5, 1, 5. 10, 7, 3 (Schub.): **2 aor.** ἐπάην Herm. Past. 1, see below: fut. παυθήσομαι rare, Thuc. 1, 81; Justin. Mart. Apol. 1, 52 (Braun), late παυσθήσ- Schol. Aesch. Pr. 622: **2 fut.** παήσομαι see below: **3 fut.** πεπαύσομαι

Soph. Ant. 91. Tr. 587; Hippocr. 6, 238. 9, 14. 52 (Lit.); and late Alciphr. 1, 36; Ael. Fr. 103; Luc. Pisc. 45; Plut. Crass. 15; (Eur.) Epist. 5. **Mid.** παύομαι *to cease*, Il. 8, 295; Aesch. Supp. 577; Eur. Med. 59; Ar. Pax 327; Antiph. 2, β, 1; Pl. Rep. 531, (ἀνα-) ἀμ-παυ- Her. 1, 181–2: **imp.** ἐπαυ- H. Hym. 3, 97; Com. Fr. (Philem.) 4, 23; Her. 8, 112; Pl. Crat. 396, παυ- Il. 15, 242, iter. παυέσκετο Il. 24, 17: **fut.** παύσομαι Od. 6, 174. Il. 3, 112; Soph. Ph. 1424. O. C. 1040; Eur. Med. 93; Ar. Plut. 23; Her. 1, 56; Thuc. 3, 32; Pl. Euth. 9; Xen. Cyr. 1, 4, 21: **aor.** ἐπαυσάμην Il. 14, 260; Aesch. Pers. 500; Eur. Alc. 938; Ar. Ran. 1188; Her. 8, 93; Antiph. 5, 41; Thuc. 1, 6, παυσ- Il. 11, 267; παύσωμαι Ar. Eq. 579; Xen. Cyr. 5, 1, 17; παυσαίμην Pl. Alc. (1), 104, -αίμαν Eur. Ion 152 (chor.); παύσαιτο Il. 22, 502; Soph. Ant. 884 &c.: and in sense **p.** πέπαυμαι: **aor.** ἐπαύθην: and **fut.** παυθήσομαι: πεπαύσομαι, see above. **Vb.** παυστέον Pl. Rep. 391; Isocr. 15, 175.

With the poets the imper. **pres.** παῦε is used in a middle sense, *cease*, Hes. Sc. 449; Soph. Ph. 1275; Ar. Vesp. 1194. 1208. Ach. 864; and seemingly Pl. Phaedr. 228; Luc. Nigr. 8. D. Mer. 12, 2. Gall. 4. 6. Jup. Tr. 33, but παύε' (-εο) Il. 9, 260, παύου Com. Fr. (Ephipp.) 3, 323; Luc. Imag. 2 (Bekk. Jacob.) Instead of μνηστῆρες—παῦσαν Od. 4, 659, the approved reading now is μνηστῆρας—παῦσαν found in Cod. Vind. and adopted by Buttm. Bekk. Dind. La Roche. The **2 aor. pass.** ἐπάην is given by Choerob. Bekk. Anec. p. 1324, ἀνα- Greg. Nyss. Maii. Coll. 8, p. 9, and Macar. Homil. p. 67: **fut.** ἀνα-παήσονται N. T. Rev. 14, 13 (Mss. A G. Lach. Tisch. 7 edit.) Passow says "the purer Attic writers are reported to have preferred πεπαύσομαι," and refers to Moeris as authority. But the Attic writers uniformly have παύσομαι excepting Sophocles; and even he gives no preference to πεπαύσομαι, for he has it twice, and παύσομαι twice.

Πεδαμείβω, see ἀμείβω.

Πείθω *To persuade*, Od. 23, 230; Aesch. Ag. 1052; Soph. Aj. 150; Ar. Ran. 365; Her. 9, 4; Antiph. 2, δ, 11; Thuc. 1, 58; Xen. Mem. 1, 2, 23; Isae. 5, 13; Poet. inf. πειθέμεν Pind. N. 7, 95: **imp.** ἔπειθον Il. 22, 91; Aesch. Supp. 615; Soph. Tr. 359; Her. 8, 4; Thuc. 3, 3; Lys. 12, 7; Pl. Rep. 367, πεῖθον Il. 16, 842; Hes. Sc. 450, iter. πείθεσκε Or. Sib. 1, 43: **fut.** πείσω Il. 9, 345; Soph. Ph. 1394; Her. 8, 80; Antiph. 5, 56; Thuc. 4, 118; Pl. Leg. 661; πείσειν Il. 22, 357, but -σέμεν 5, 252: **aor.** ἔπεισα Pind. Ol. 2, 80; Aesch. Eum. 84; Soph. Ph. 901; Ar. Plut. 304; Her. 6, 5; Antiph. 6, 47; Thuc. 1, 14; Xen. Hell. 2, 3, 13, παρ- Il. 7, 120; *simple* in Hom. once, πείσειε Od. 14,

123; *now* also Il. 9, 386 (Bekk. Dind.); Ar. Ran. 68; part. Dor. πείσαις Pind. Ol. 3, 16: p. πέπεικα Lys. 26, 7; Isocr. 14, 15; Isae. 8, 24: plp. ἐπεπείκει Aeschin. 1, 57: p. p. πέπεισμαι Eur. El. 578; Thuc. 5, 40; Andoc. 1, 62; Pl. Prot. 328; -σμένος Aesch. Pers. 697; Thuc. 8, 56; -εῖσθαι 5, 40: plp. ἐπεπείσμην Dem. 18, 220. 221, ἀν- Her. 8, 5: aor. ἐπείσθην Aesch. Eum. 593; Ar. Nub. 866; Antiph. 5, 62; Andoc. 3, 31; Isae. 3, 79; Xen. An. 7, 7, 29; -θείη Antiph. 5, 33, -θείησαν Thuc. 3, 42, -θεῖεν Pl. Rep. 415; πεισθείς Soph. O. R. 526; Antiph. 2, δ, 7; Thuc. 3, 97; -σθῆναι Soph. O. C. 1414; Her. 2, 121: fut. πεισθήσομαι Soph. Ph. 624; Xen. Cyr. 5, 1, 8; Pl. Soph. 248; Isocr. 17, 7: 2 aor. (ἔ)πῐθον Poet. Pind. P. 3, 65; πίθοιμι Eur. Hipp. 1062, -θοι Aesch. Supp. 941, -οιμεν Theocr. 22, 64; πιθεῖν Aesch. Pr. 204; -θών Pind. P. 3, 28; Aesch. Pr. 559; Ar. Plut. 949; Ran. 1168, Epic πέπῐθον, -ῐθε Hom. H. 2, 97, -ῐθον Ap. Rh. 1, 964 (*indic.* not in Il. or Od.); πεπίθωμεν Il. 9, 112; πεπίθοιμι 23, 40; Ap. Rh. 3, 14; πεπιθεῖν Il. 9, 184; Ap. Rh. 3, 536; πεπιθοῦσα Il. 15, 26, πεπιθών Pind. I. 4, 90, *trusting*, παρ- *winning over*, Od. 14, 290. Il. 23, 37: 2 p. πέποιθα as pres. mid. *I trust*, Il. 4, 325; Pind. Ol. 1, 103; Aesch. Sept. 37; Soph. El. 323; Ar. Eq. 770; rare in Attic prose, Thuc. 2, 42; Pl. Menex. 248. Epin. 974; freq. late, Luc. Jup. Trag. 18; Plut. Mor. 196. 223. Cic. 9 &c.: plp. ἐπεποίθειν Il. 16, 171; Her. 9, 88; Arr. An. 3, 17, 5, πεποιθ- Theocr. 5, 28, Epic πεποίθεα Od. 8, 181; subj. πεποίθω Od. 24, 329, -θῃς Il. 1, 524, -ομεν, for -ωμεν, Od. 10, 335; opt. πεποιθοίη, for -οίθοι, Ar. Ach. 940. Mid. πείθομαι *to persuade oneself, believe, obey*, Il. 1, 79; Pind. P. 1, 3; Soph. Ph. 1252; Her. 6, 100; Antiph. 5, 79; Pl. Gorg. 513; opt. -οίατο Il. 14, 93: imp. ἐπειθ- Il. 1, 33; Her. 1, 170; Thuc. 1, 91; Lys. 1, 50, πειθ- Il. 2, 834: fut. πείσομαι Il. 20, 127; Solon 22; Soph. Aj. 529; Ar. Pax 276; Her. 2, 146; Thuc. 4, 68; Andoc. 1, 91; Pl. Conv. 193, πείσει Il. 9, 345, Ep. -σεαι 9, 74; -σοιτο Xen. Cyr. 7, 3, 10: 2 aor. Poet. ἐπῐθόμην Il. 3, 260; Ar. Nub. 73, πιθ- Il. 5, 201; πίθωμαι Il. 18, 273; Soph. O. R. 321; Ar. Eq. 962; -οίμην Il. 4, 93; Aesch. Sept. 1065; Soph. O. R. 1065; Eur. Hipp. 950; Ar. Nub. 119, -οίατο Simon. Am. 1, 22; πίθεο Pind. P. 1, 59, πιθοῦ Aesch. Eum. 794; Soph. Ant. 992; rare, if correct, in prose, Pl. Phaed. 117 (Mss. Bekk. Stallb. πείθου Vulg. Bait.); πιθέσθαι Il. 7, 293. Od. 17, 21; Pind. Ol. 13, 79; Soph. El. 429; Ar. Vesp. 573; -όμενος Soph. Phil. 1226, Epic πεπῐθόμην rare, -ίθοντο Orph. Fr. 8, 54; πεπίθωνται Q. Sm. 12, 40; opt. πεπίθοιτο Il. 10, 204; πεπιθέσθαι Anth. 14, 75; Q. Sm. 8, 459. The only trace of 1 aor. mid. we know of is πείσησθε Aristid. 31, 391; πείσασθαι Sopat. Rhet. vol. 8,

p. 150 (Walz). ἐπείσαντο V. T. 3 Reg. 21, 33 (Francf.) is uncertain; and we decline accepting, with Renner, πείσεαι as "conj." Solon 20, 1. The correct reading in 3 Reg. 21, 33 seems to be ἐσπείσαντο (Vat. Tisch. Gaisf.); and subj. πεισώμεθα Dem. 3, 1 (Vulg.) has been altered to fut. πεισόμεθα (Ms. S in corr. Dind. Bekk. B. S.) ἐπέπιθμεν syncop. 2 plp. Epic Il. 2, 341, for ἐπεποίθειμεν; imper. πέπεισθι Aesch. Eum. 599, is a rare form; πέπισθι or πέποισθι would perhaps be more analogical. **Vb.** πιστός *trusty*, Il. 15, 331; πειστέον *must persuade*, Pl. Rep. 421; *must obey*, Soph. Ph. 994; Pl. Apol. 19. The **fut.** πῐθήσω *will obey*, Od. 21, 369, points to (πιθέω) or **aor.** ἔπιθον, but πεπιθήσω (πέπῐθον) *will persuade*, Il. 22, 223; and Hesych. has πεποιθήσω *will trust, be confident:* **aor.** part. πιθήσας *trusting*, Il. 4, 398; Pind. P. 4, 109; Aesch. Ch. 617 (chor.); Lycophr. 735.

Πείκω *To comb, shear* (Epic for πέκω), Od. 18, 316, Attic πεκτέω Ar. Av. 714: **fut.** Dor. πεξῶ Theocr. 5, 98 (Vulg. Ahr. Fritzsch. 1 ed.): **aor.** ἔπεξα Anth. 6, 279; subj. πέξω Theocr. quoted (some Mss. Reisk. Mein. Ziegl. Fritzsch. 2 ed.): **p. p.** πέπεκται, ἀπο- (Hesych.): **aor. pass.** ἐπέχθην Ar. Nub. 1356. **Mid.** *to comb oneself*, **aor.** ἐπέξατο Simon. C. 13 (Bergk); πέξηται Callim. Lav. Pal. 32; πέξαιντο *yield their fleeces*, Theocr. 28, 13; πεξαμένη Il. 14, 176. **Pres. pass.** πεκτούμενος Ar. Lys. 685. This verb is poetic.

Πεινάω *To be hungry*, πεινῶ C. Fr. (Alex.) 3, 444, πεινῇ Ar. Vesp. 1270. Eq. 1271; Pl. Rep. 439, Dor. 1 pl. πεινᾶμες, δια- Ar. Ach. 754, πεινῶσι Ar. Plut. 504; C. Frag. (Antiph.) 3, 66; Xen. Conv. 4, 36, Dor. πεινῶντι Xen. Hell. 1, 1, 23; subj. πεινῇ Pl. Phaed. 85, πεινῶσι C. Fr. (Pher.) 2, 255; πεινάων Il. 3, 25; πεινῶν Soph. Fr. 199 (D.); Eur. Fr. 887; Ar. Av. 787; Her. 1, 133; Pl. Leg. 837; Xen. Cyr. 1, 2, 11, see below: **imp.** ἐπείνων Xen. Hell. 6, 2, 15, 'πείνων Ar. Ach. 535: **fut.** -ήσω Ar. Plut. 539; Her. 2, 13. 14; Xen. Mem. 2, 1, 17 (late -άσω V. T. Esai. 5, 27; N. T. Rev. 7, 16): **aor.** -ησα Xen. Cyr. 8, 3, 39; late -ᾱσα, πεινάσωμεν Pseud.-Callisth. 3, 6; πεινάσαιμι Anth. 11, 402; inf. -ᾶσαι Aesop 62 (Halm): **p.** πεπείνηκα Pl. Rep. 606 &c. reg. except contracting αε into η, αει into ῃ, instead of α, ᾳ, as πεινάει, πεινῇ Ar. Eq. 1270; Hippocr. 6, 488; πεινάειν, πεινῆν Ar. Plut. 595; Pl. Gorg. 496, Epic πεινήμεναι Od. 20, 137. Late writers, however, have πεινᾷ Aristot. H. A. 9, 32, 4 (Vulg.), -νῇ (Ms. C. Bekk.); πεινᾶν Plut. Aristid. 25 (Bekk. Sint.); πεινῶντι Dor. 3 pl. pres. Xen. Hell. 1, 1, 23; part. dat. sing. πεινᾶντι Theocr. 15, 148, Epic acc. πεινώοντα Opp. H. 5, 50, missed by Lexicogr. This verb is scarcely used in Tragedy, πεινῶσα Soph. Fr. 199; πεινῶντι Eur. Fr. incert. 887 (D.)

Πειράζω, see πειράω.

Πειραίνω *To end, complete* (Epic for περαίνω), pres. late -αίνουσι Arat. 24: **imp.** ἐπείραινε Pind. I. 8, 24: **aor.** ἐπείρηνα, πειρήνειας Arat. 289; πειρήνας Od. 22, 175. 192; H. Merc. 3, 48: **p.** 3 sing. πεπείρανται Od. 12, 37; and metri gr. Soph. Tr. 581 (Dind. Nauck, Bergk), where Herm. prefers πεπείρᾶται (Mss. Par. Vat.)

Πειράω *To try, prove*, Il. 8, 8; Pind. P. 10, 67; Soph. O. R. 399; Ar. Lys. 504; Her. 7, 9; Thuc. 6, 38; Isocr. 1, 24: **imp.** ἐπείρων Thuc. 4, 25, -ρα Pind. N. 5, 30: **fut.** πειράσω Thuc. 4, 9. 43, see below: **aor.** ἐπείρᾶσα Soph. O. C. 1276; Thuc. 4, 102; πειράσας Ar. Eq. 517: **p.** πεπείρᾶκα (Luc.) Amor. 26: **p. p.** πεπείρᾶμαι Od. 12, 37; Soph. Tr. 581; -πειράσθω Ar. Vesp. 1129: **aor.** ἐπειράθην Thuc. 6, 54: **fut.** πειραθήσομαι as **mid.** see below. The **perf.** and **aor. pass.** however, are generally **act.** see **mid.** πειράομαι as **act.** *try, attempt*, Il. 2, 193; Soph. El. 83; Her. 1, 193; Isocr. 15, 85; Pl. Conv. 212; opt. -ρῷντο Thuc. 1, 25, -ρῴατο Her. 1, 68; imper. πειρῶ 8, 57, -άσθω Tyrt. 12, 44; -ρώμενος Pl. Leg. 638; Her. 8, 89 (Gaisf. Bekk. Dietsch, -εώμ- Dind. -εόμ- Abicht, Stein); 1, 46 (Stein, -εώμ- Bekk. Gaisf. Dind. -εόμ- Dietsch, Abicht): **imp.** ἐπειρ- Pind. P. 2, 34; Her. 8, 97; Thuc. 2, 65; Lys. 8, 10; Isocr. 5, 93, πειρ- Pind. N. 1, 43: **fut.** πειράσομαι Aesch. Pers. 850; Soph. O. C. 959; Ar. Thesm. 268; Antiph. 2, γ, 1; Thuc. 4, 87; Lys. 3, 21; Isocr. 15, 29, Dor. -ᾱσοῦμαι Ar. Ach. 743; Stob. (Hippod.) 43, 93: **aor.** ἐπειρᾱσάμην Thuc. 2, 44. 85. 4, 60. 114. 117. 5, 69; Pl. Gorg. 474: as **mid. p.** πεπείρᾱμαι Pind. Fr. 87; Soph. Fr. 516 (Dind.); Antiph. 5, 1; Thuc. 5, 111; Lys. 5, 3; Isocr. 16, 45; Dem. 18, 89: and **aor.** ἐπειράθην Hippocr. 5, 336; Isocr. 9, 48; Pl. Phaed. 118; πειρᾱθῶ Thuc. 6, 92; Pl. Leg. 839; -αθείην Xen. Cyr. 5, 3, 26; -άθητι Pl. Soph. 239; -ᾱθείς Soph. El. 1244; Ar. Eq. 506; Thuc. 2, 5. 33, δια- Antiph. 5, 33; -θῆναι Pl. Leg. 892; Xen. Cyr. 6, 3, 6: and late, **fut.** πειρᾱθήσομαι as **mid.** Diod. Sic. 2, 18. 12, 1 (Bekk. -άσομαι L. Dind.); Geop. 12, 13. **Vb.** πειρατέον Isocr. 4, 8. Epic and Ionic forms, **fut.** -ήσω Il. 19, 30: **aor.** πείρησα Ap. Rh. 3, 1249: **p.** πεπείρημαι as **mid.** Od. 3, 23; Her. 9, 46: **plp.** πεπειρέατο Her. 7, 125 (Bekk. Dind. ἐπεπ- Gaisf. Stein &c.) for -ηντο: **aor.** ἐπειρήθην as **mid.** Her. 3, 152. 7, 135, πειρήθ- Il. 19, 384; -ηθῶ 22, 381; -ηθείην 11, 386; Theogn. 126, -ηθεῖμεν Od. 16, 305: **aor. mid.** ἐπειρησάμην (Il. 6, 435) Od. 8, 120; Her. 7, 135. 172; Hippocr. 3, 250 (Lit.), πειρ- Od. 8, 397, ἀπο- Opp. Hal. 2, 214; subj. Epic πειρήσεται for -ήσηται, Od. 21, 159, -ήσωνται Opp. Hal. 4, 512; -ήσαιτο Il. 13, 457; πείρησαι Il. 1, 302: **fut.** -ήσομαι Il. 5, 279; Opp. Hal. 2, 306;

Her. 1, 124. 2, 163. 3, 137; Hippocr. 6, 92 (Lit.)—πειρήσω subj. 1 aor. act. Theogn. 506, has given way to the pass. form πειρηθῶ the reading in *most* Mss.; and πειρηθείης not πειραθ- is the reading of the *best* Ms. at 126. In Attic the aor. mid. is confined to Thuc. and Plato. In Thuc. it is the prevailing form, occurring six times, and aor. pass. thrice: Plato again, has aor. mid. once only, the aor. pass. eleven times. The compounds, except ἀπο- Thuc. 6, 90. 4, 135 &c. and perhaps κατα- Lys. 30, 34, are, in classic authors, not used in the act. and have, we think, always the aor. of the pass. form, ἀπο-πειρηθῇ Her. 2, 73, δι-επειράθην Antiph. 5, 33, ἐξ-επειράθ- Eur. Supp. 1089. Collat. forms πειράζω, -ητίζω scarcely go beyond pres. and imp. πειράζω Od. 23, 114; (Luc.) Tragod. 149: imp. πείραζε Ap. Rh. 3, 10: aor. imper. πείρᾰσον Anth. 11, 183: mid. πειραζόμενος Hippocr. 2, 327 (K.) πειρητίζω Il. 15, 615: imp. πειρήτιζον 12, 257. πειράζω however is complete and reg. in the Septuag. and N. Test.: pres. pass. πειράζεται Plut. Mor. 230. Cleom. 7. In classic Greek it is poetic, except Hippocr. The Attic form is πειράω, for instead of ἐπειράσθην Pl. Lach. 188 (Ast), ἐπειράθην is now adopted by all the editors.

Πείρω *To pierce, traverse,* Ap. Rh. 2, 326; πείρων Od. 13, 91 (Il. 24, 8): imp. ἔπειρον Il. 9, 210. Od. 3, 33; late prose Paus. 4, 17, 1, πεῖρον Od. 2, 434; Ap. Rh. 4, 980: fut. περῶ?: 1 aor. ἔπειρα Il. 1, 465; late prose Strab. 13, 1, 38, πεῖρα Il. 7, 317; δια-πείρας Eur. Phoen. 26, ἀνα-πείρ- Her. 4, 103, Poet. ἀμπείρ- Il. 2, 426: p. p. πέπαρμαι Luc. Tragod. 298, -αρται Opp. H. 4, 554; -μένος Il. 11, 633; Hes. Op. 205; Ap. Rh. 4, 1067; Archil. 84 (Bergk), Poet. ἀμ-πεπαρμ- Ar. Ach. 796: plp. πέπαρτο Hom. H. 1, 92: 2 aor. ἐπᾰρην, περι- Luc. Pisc. 51; subj. ἀνα-πᾰρῶ Athen. (Macho) 8, 41, δια-παρῇ Luc. Pisc. 51; ἀνα-πᾰρείς Her. 4, 94.—περῶ Soph. Aj. 461, is quoted by some as the fut. of this verb, because, say they, "ᾱ in fut. περᾱσω (of περάω) cannot be contracted." But περῶ here may be subj. *pres.* (of περάω) with *future* meaning. No doubt πέλαγος Αἰγαῖον περῶ (from πείρω) is a legitimate expression, but Epic, and besides unnecessary here. This verb in *simple* is Epic, Lyric, and late prose.

Πέκω, see πείκω.

Πελάζω *To bring near,* and intrans. *approach,* Il. 5, 766; Aesch. Supp. 300; Soph. Ph. 301; Ar. Av. 1399; in prose always intrans. Her. 4, 181; Xen. Cyr. 1, 4, 7. 20; Pl. Conv. 195: imp. ἐπέλαζον Xen. Cyr. 7, 1, 48: fut. πελᾰσω intrans. Eur. Elec. 1332 (chor.). I. T. 886 (chor.), ἐμ- Hym. Merc. 523, trans. πελ- Eur. Or. 1684 (chor.), -άσσω Fr. 775, 36 chor. (D.), Attic πελῶ Aesch. Pr. 282 (chor.); Soph. Ph. 1150 (chor.): aor.

ἐπέλασα trans. Eur. Hel. 671. 682, -ασσα Il. 21, 93; Theocr. 25, 212, πέλασα Il. 12, 194, -ασσα 13, 1; Pind. P. 4, 227; πελάσῃς Od. 11, 106, -άσσῃ Il. 13, 180, -άσσομεν for -ωμεν, Od. 10, 424; part. -άσσας Orac. Her. 7, 141, intrans. πέλασεν in Hom. only Il. 12, 112; and subj. -άσῃ 12, 41; Eur. Med. 101; opt. trans. πελάσειε Eur. Med. 760, intrans. Her. 9, 74; πέλᾰσον trans. Pind. Ol. 1, 78, -άσσετον Il. 10, 442, intrans. Soph. Ph. 1162 (chor.); inf. πελάσσαι trans. Il. 23, 719. Od. 10, 440; Eur. Alc. 230 (chor.), -άσαι Od. 22, 176, intrans. Tyrt. 14; Soph. Aj. 889 (chor.); Thuc. 2, 77; Xen. An. 4, 2, 3; πελάσας trans. Aesch. Pr. 155, προσ- Od. 9, 285, intrans. πελ- Hes. Op. 730; Her. 2, 19; Xen. Cyr. 3, 2, 10, -άσσας Opp. Hal. 2, 64, Dor. -άσαις Pind. N. 10, 81: **aor. pass.** ἐπελάσθην *approached*, πελάσθ- Il. 5, 282, 3 pl. Epic πέλασθεν 12, 420; -ασθῆναι Soph. O. R. 213; -ασθείς Ph. 1327. **Mid.** πελάζομαι Poet. *to approach*, Aesch. Sept. 144; Eur. Or. 1279: but aor. ἐπελασάμην trans. -άσσατο Opp. Cyn. 1, 213; opt. 3 pl. Ion. πελασαίατο Il. 17, 341; -άσασθαι Emped. 344. **Vb.** πλαστός Aesch. Eum. 54, προσ- Prom. 716 (Mss. Vulg. πλᾱτός, προσ- Elms. Dind.), ἄ-πλαστος Hes. Th. 151. See πελάω. The prose form πλησιάζω *approach*, is reg. -ᾰ́σω, -ασα, πεπλησίᾰκα Pl. Theaet. 144; (Dem.) 47, 33, rarely trans. *bring near*, Xen. Eq. 2, 5; Gloss. Ar. Ran. 271: hence aor. pass. πλησιασθείην Eur. Elec. 634.

Πελᾰ́ω *To cause to approach*, and intrans. *approach*, Poet. -λᾰ́ει Opp. Cyn. 1, 515; Arat. 74, see inf.; -λῶσι Soph. O. C. 1060 (chor.); imper. πέλα Poet. in Plut. Mor. 457; inf. πελᾶν Soph. Elec. 497 (chor.); in Epic only inf. πελᾰ́αν Hom. H. 7, 44 (except late, πελάει Opp. Cyn. 1, 515; Arat. 74, -άουσι Opp. Hal. 1, 489; πελάειν 5, 496); also πελᾰ́θω *approach*, in Attic poet. and only pres. -ᾰ́θεις Aesch. Fr. 131 (D.); Ar. Ran. 1265. 1271. 1275 &c. (chor.), -ᾰ́θει Eur. Rhes. 556 (chor.); -ᾰ́θειν Elec. 1293 (chor.), and πλάθω Aesch. Ch. 589 (chor.); Soph. Ph. 727 (chor.); Eur. Alc. 119 (chor.): **p. p.** πέπλημαι, -ησαι Anth. 5, 47, 3 pl. πεπλήαται Simon. Am. 36 (Bergk); πεπλημένος Od. 12, 108; Tyrt. 11, 33: **aor.** ἐπλάθην Eur. Rhes. 920, usu. in chor. 347; πλᾱθείην Aesch. Pr. 896 (chor.); -ᾱθείς Eur. Andr. 25. Tr. 203 (chor.): **2 aor. mid.** Epic ἐπλήμην *approached*, -ητο Hes. Th. 193, -ηντο Il. 4, 449. 8, 63, πλῆτο 14, 438, πλῆντο 468. **Pres. mid.** πλάθεται Inscr. Plut. Arat. 14. **Vb.** ἄ-πλᾱτος Soph. Tr. 1093. Elmsley, Wunder, Dind. hold πελῶσι Soph. O. C. 1060, and πελᾶν Elec. 497, **fut.** of πελάζω.

Πελεμίζω *To shake*, Epic, inf. -ιζέμεν Il. 16, 766; -ίζων Pind. Ol. 9, 32 (Bergk, Momms.): **imp.** πελέμιζε Il. 13, 443: **aor.** πελέμιξα Il. 21, 176; Ap. Rh. 2, 92: **aor. pass.** πελεμίχθην *were* *driven back,* Il. 4, 535: pres. πελεμίζεται Hes. Th. 458; Anth. 10, 74; -ιζόμενοι Pind. N. 8, 29: imp. πελεμίζετο Il. 8, 443; Hes. Th. 842; Emped. 142. Never augmented in Hom.

Πέλω *To be,* mostly Poet. Soph. O. R. 245, πέλεις Nonn. D. 44, 193. 197, -λει Il. 9, 134. Od. 5, 186; Solon 13, 16; Pind. P. 4, 145; Aesch. Ch. 534 (Herm.); Soph. Ant. 990; Eur. H. F. 668; Theocr. 4, 43; late Dor. prose, Pempel. Stob. 79, 52, πέλουσι Anth. 7, 56, Dor. -λοντι Pind. Ol. 6, 100; subj. (not in Hom.) πέλω Aesch. Supp. 339, -λῃ Theocr. 28, 22; Ap. Rh. 2, 345; opt. (not in Hom.) πέλοι Pind. P. 1, 56; Aesch. Pers. 526; Soph. Tr. 1161; Eur. Phoen. 1464; Ap. Rh. 4, 1656; Theocr. 21, 54; imper. πέλε Ap. Rh. 1, 304; πέλειν Aesch. Supp. 620. 801; Eur. Rhes. 198; Ap. Rh. 4, 1373, Aeol. πέλην Theocr. 29, 31 (Ziegl. Fritz.); rare in prose, -λειν Pittac. Diog. Laert. 1, 4, 10; late Ion. Aretae. 81, 20, Epic πελέμεν and πελέναι Parmenid. 66. 104; πέλων Aesch. Pr. 895: imp. ἔπελον, -λες Pind. Ol. 1, 46, -λεν Pempel. Stob. 79, 52, -λον Anth. App. Epigr. 170, syncop. ἔπλε Il. 12, 11, usu. unaugm. πέλον, -λες Q. Sm. 3, 564, -λεν Il. 8, 64. 11, 604; Hes. Sc. 164; Theocr. 21, 17; Ar. Pax 1276 (hexam.), Dor. pl. πέλομες Theocr. 29, 27, iter. πελέεσκε Tzetz. Post.-Hom. 348 (Vulg. τελέεσκε Bekk. &c.) **Mid.** πέλομαι as act. more freq. πέλει Aesch. Eum. 199 (trimet.). 149 (chor.), -λεται Il. 14, 345; Simon. Am. 7, 100; Solon 9; Soph. Fr. 583, -λόμεσθα Theocr. 13, 4. 14, 68; Q. Sm. 4, 83, -λεσθε Ap. Rh. 2, 643. 3, 911, -λονται Il. 10, 351; Emped. 102; Pind. I. 5, 6; Soph. Aj. 159 (chor.); rare in prose, Archyt. Stob. 1, 71; subj. πέληται Il. 3, 287, -ώμεθα 6, 358, -ωνται 16, 128; πέλοιτο 22, 443; Aesch. Ag. 255 (chor.), -οιντο Maxim. Ausp. 3; imper. Ion. πέλευ Il. 24, 219, -λέσθω Ap. Rh. 1, 1320. 2, 873; πελόμενος Aesch. Supp. 122. 810 (chor.), syncop. πλόμενος Euphor. Fr. 55, Hom. in comp. ἐπι-πλόμενος Od. 7, 261, περι-πλόμ- Il. 18, 220. 23, 833. Od. 11, 248, *revolving, surrounding*; πέλεσθαι Ap. Rh. 1, 160. 3, 700: imp. ἐπέλοντο Il. 9, 526 (Bekk. 2 ed.); Simon. C. 36 (Bergk), usu. syncop. ἔπλεο Il. 22, 281, contr. ἔπλευ 23, 891; Theogn. 1313, ἔπλετο Il. 22, 116; Hes. Th. 836; Emped. 97; Pind. P. 5, 112, πέλοντο Il. 9, 526 (Vulg. Wolf, Dind. La R. ἐπέλ- Bekk. 2 ed.), iter. πελέσκεο Il. 22, 433, -σκετο Hes. Fr. 44. The augmented and syncop. imp. forms have usually a pres. meaning, ἔπλευ *thou art,* Il. 9, 54 &c. Diog. Laert. Pempel. and Aretaeus quoted, are the only prose instances of act. and Archyt. of mid. we have ever seen. Of πέλω Homer and Hesiod have pres. and imp. *indic.*: the Tragedians have not the imp., Aristoph. has it once in hexam.; inf. and *simple* part. do not occur in Homer and

Hesiod: πέλομαι is more freq. in Homer than πέλω, not so in Attic poetry.

Πέμπω *To send*, Il. 1, 390; Pind. N. 3, 77; Aesch. Pers. 450; Soph. Tr. 55; Ar. Av. 846; Her. 8, 27; Thuc. 1, 91; Xen. Cyr. 2, 4, 22; Dor. part. πέμποισα Pind. Ol. 6, 32; Epic inf. πεμπέμεναι Od. 13, 48, -έμεν 10, 18 (Wolf, Dind. La R.): **imp.** ἔπεμπον Il. 18, 237; Soph. Tr. 35; Her. 7, 32; Antiph. 5, 53. 6, 11; Thuc. 2, 6; Isocr. 7, 29, πέμπ- Il. 23, 137; Hes. Th. 716; Pind. P. 4, 178, iter. πέμπεσκε Her. 7, 106: **fut.** πέμψω rare in Il. 1, 184. often in Od. 1, 93. 15, 34. 18, 84 &c.; Pind. Ol. 9, 25; Aesch. Pers. 1076; Soph. Ph. 1438; Her. 4, 127; Thuc. 6, 91; Xen. Hell. 3, 3, 9; Dor. -ψῶ Theocr. 5, 141; -ψειν Il. 21, 48, -ψέμεναι Od. 10, 484: **aor.** ἔπεμψα Od. 17, 149; Pind. Ol. 4, 2; Aesch. Sept. 37; Soph. O. C. 819; Ar. Ach. 154; Her. 8, 75; Thuc. 6, 75; Dem. 18, 211, πέμψ- Il. 18, 240; Hes. Th. 477; Pind. I. 6, 49; -ψειεν Antiph. 5, 53: **p.** πέπομφα Thuc. 7, 12; Xen. Cyr. 6, 2, 10; Pl. Eryx. 392; Dem. 4, 48. 8, 58. 9, 12 (7, 9): **plp.** ἐπεπόμφει Xen. Cyr. 6, 2, 9; Dem. 23, 164. 50, 5, Ion. ἐπεπόμφεε Her. 1, 85: **p. p.** πέπεμμαι, πέπεμπται Aesch. Sept. 473, προ- Thuc. 7, 77; πεπεμμένος Dem. 23, 159; Luc. Alex. 32; Dio Cass. 50, 13; πεπέμφθαι 41, 46: **plp.** ἐπέπεμπτο Dio Cass. 36, 1 (Bekk.), προυπέπεμπτο Thuc. 8, 79: **aor.** ἐπέμφθην Soph. O. C. 430; Eur. Hec. 772; Thuc. 6, 47; Aeschin. 2, 13; πεμφθῶσι Thuc. 4, 46; -θείην Xen. Hell. 7, 1, 39; πεμφθείς Pind. N. 3, 59; Soph. Ph. 93; Com. Fr. (Alex.) 3, 439; Her. 6, 106; Pl. Leg. 856; -φθῆναι Antiph. 5, 23; Andoc. 3, 33: **fut.** πεμφθήσομαι Plut. Demetr. 27; Dio Cass. 40, 66; Strab. 1, 1, 4, but ἐκ- Pl. Leg. 923. **Mid.** πέμπομαι *send on one's own business*, *send for*, Luc. Tox. 14 (Jacob.), ἀπο- Eur. Hec. 72; Her. 1, 33; Xen. Vect. 1, 7; Pl. Rep. 423: **imp.** ἐπέμποντο Polyb. 32, 5 (Vulg.), μετ- Thuc. 1, 95, ἀπ- Xen. An. 1, 1, 5: **fut.** πέμψομαι Eur. H. F. 1421, μετα- Ar. Plut. 609; Pl. Rep. 567: **aor.** ἐπεμψάμην Eur. Hec. 977, δι- Thuc. 2, 14; opt. πεμψαίατο Soph. O. C. 602 (trimet.); imper. πέμψασθε, ἐκ- Od. 20, 361; πέμψασθαι Soph. O. R. 556 (late prose, Sopat. Rhet. p. 207); πεμψαμένα, προ- Aesch. Pers. 137 (D.), see below. **Vb.** πέμπτος Thuc. 8, 86, -έον Xen. Cyr. 8, 1, 11. The *simple* **pres.** and **imp. Mid.** seem rather doubtful.

In *classic* prose the **mid.** seems not to occur in *simple*, often in comp. ἀπο-πέμπεται Her. 1, 33, προ- Xen. An. 7, 2, 14; -εσθαι Xen. Laced. 13, 10; Pl. Rep. 423: **imp.** μετ-επέμποντο Thuc. 5, 82, προ- Xen. Cyr. 5, 3, 53: **fut.** μετα-πέμψομαι Pl. Rep. 567: **aor.** ἀπ-επεμψάμην Xen. Cyr. 4, 6, 3, δι- Thuc. 2, 14, μετ- Her. 7, 53; Thuc. 7, 31; Isocr. 16, 8; Pl. Conv. 175 &c. &c.

Homer, we think, uses the **mid.** only once, ἐκ-πέμψασθε Od. 20, 361, the **pass.** never. For **imp. mid.** ἐπέμποντο Polyb. 32, 5, 2, Bekker adopts from Reiske ἐποιοῦντο, L. Dind. ἐπήγοντο for which we see not the necessity. πέμψομαι Eur. Or. 111, is very suspicious. Not only have several Mss. the **act.** πέμψομεν, but even the whole verse seems useless where it stands. Matthiae suspected, Hermann, Dindorf, Nauck &c. rejected it. The **aor. mid.** Soph. O. R. 556, is not, as some maintain, used as **act.** Passow has limited far too much the passive voice of this verb. "In the passive," says he, "Pindar and Herodotus have **aor.** 1 part. πεμφθείς, and Photius the part. **perf.** πεπεμμένος. The other tenses are generally supplied by ἀποστέλλω." And other Lexicogr. have prolonged the strain. The **aor.**, so far from being confined to part. and to Pindar and Herodotus, is in frequent use in other parts, and in several of the best *Attic* writers: ἐπέμφθην Soph. O. C. 430; Eur. Hec. 772; Thuc. 5, 54. 6, 47. 7, 11; Xen. Hell. 1, 3, 13; Dem. 18, 244. 19, 5. (49, 31. 57); πεμφθῶσι Thuc. 4, 46; πεμφθείην Xen. Hell. 7, 1, 39; Dem. 18, 45; πεμφθῆναι Antiph. 5, 23; Andoc. 3, 33; Isocr. 5, 23; (Dem.) 49, 58; especially part. πεμφθείς Soph. El. 1163 &c.; Eur. Fr. 908 (D.); Com. Fr. (Alex.) 3, 439; Thuc. 8, 77. 89; Andoc. 3, 34; Lys. 12, 31; Isocr. 4, 85. 177. 12, 174. 195; Pl. Leg. 856 &c.; Xen. Hell. 1, 6, 5. 3, 2, 22. 4, 13. Cyr. 4, 2, 4. 5, 5, 3. 6, 3, 14. An. 2, 1, 17; Dem. 18, 137. 32, 14: and the **perf.** instead of being confined to part. in Photius, is in actual use in *indic.* Aesch. Sept. 473, προ- Thuc. 7, 77; πεπεμμένος Dem. 23, 159; Luc. Alex. 32; Dio Cass. 50, 13. 56, 22; πεπέμφθαι 41, 46: nor are other tenses so very seldom, **pres.** πέμπομαι Eur. Andr. 504, -εται Pl. Leg. 941; -όμενος Eur. Hec. 456; Her. 3, 127; Thuc. 7, 8; Xen. Mem. 3, 3, 12. Hell. 3, 3, 9. Cyr. 4, 5, 13. 8, 2, 4; Dem. 18, 148: **imp.** ἐπεμπόμην Aesch. Ch. 518; Soph. El. 680; Her. 1, 46. 4, 167; Antiph. 5, 23.

Πενθέω *To sorrow*, -θεῖ Aesch. Pers. 579; Her. 6, 58; Pl. Rep. 606, Epic dual πενθείετον Il. 23, 283, for -έετον; πενθῶμεν Ar. Nub. 622; imper. -θει Eur. Alc. 806; πενθεῖν Soph. O. C. 739; Bacchyl. 11 (B.): **imp.** ἐπένθεον Her. 4, 95, -θουν Isocr. 19, 40: **fut.** -ήσω Aesch. Fr. 190 (D. 5 ed.) reg.: **aor.** ἐπένθησα Lys. 2, 66; Aeschin. 3, 211; imper. πενθήσατε Eur. H. F. 1391; -θῆσαι Il. 19, 225; Aesch. Ch. 173; Lys. 2, 60; -ήσας Lycurg. 142: **p.** πεπένθηκα Luc. Demon. 25; Apoll. Tyan. Epist. 58, συμ- (Dem.) 60, 33. Inf. **pres.** Epic πενθήμεναι Od. 19, 120, which some, perhaps wrongly, or needlessly, derive from (πένθημι), others from πενθεέμεναι. **Pass.** very rare, πενθούμενος Isocr.

10, 27. Vb. πενθητέον Apoll. Tyan. Epist. 58, missed by Lexicogr.

Πένομαι *To labour, prepare, be poor*, trans. and intrans. and only **pres.** πένει Aesch. Eum. 431, -εται Ar. Plut. 582, -ονται Solon 15 (Bergk); Theogn. 315; Ap. Rh. 2, 1014; Xen. An. 3, 2, 26; Pl. Rep. 607, ἀμφι- Il. 16, 28; subj. πένηαι Theogn. 929, -ώμεθα Od. 13, 394; opt. -οιτο Eur. Supp. 210; -όμενος Eur. Hec. 1220; Com. Fr. (Herm.) 2, 393. (Mon.) 4, 260; Lys. 8, 7. 24, 16; Isocr. 8, 128. 20, 19; Isae. 5, 35; Xen. Ages. 4, 5; -εσθαι Il. 19, 200. Od. 3, 428. 22, 199 &c.; Hes. Op. 773; Aesch. Ag. 962; Eur. Fr. 284, 7. 364, 16 (D.); Ar. Ran. 1066. Eq. 1271; Com. Fr. (Antiph.) 3, 154; Thuc. 2, 40; Xen. Oec. 2, 2. Conv. 4, 35; Lys. 12, 6: and **imp.** ἐπένοντο Il. 24, 124; late prose Himer. Or. 5, 5, πένοντο Il. 1, 318. 18, 558. Od. 10, 348. 24, 412. The trans. meaning and the **imp.** form seem to be Epic, λοετρὰ πένονται Ap. Rh. 2, 1014; ταῦτα πενώμεθα Od. 13, 394; -εσθαι Il. 19, 200. Od. 16, 319. 24, 407; δαῖτα Od. 3, 428 &c.; ἔργα Hes. Op. 773; πένοντο Il. 18, 558; Callim. Cer. 70; Theocr. 13, 32. The only exception we know is θοίνην πένεσθαι, if correct, Eur. Elec. 785 (Barnes), for θοίνῃ γενέσθαι (Dind. Kirchh. Nauck, Paley &c.) The **fut.** πενεῖ Aesch. Supp. 347 (Herm.) is merely a suggestion of Hermann's supported neither by Mss. nor usage.

Πεπαίνω *To make soft, ripe*, Hippocr. 6, 244; Xen. Oec. 19, 19: **aor.** ἐπέπᾱνα, πεπᾶναι Ar. Vesp. 646; Geop. 5, 2, else reg.: (**perf. act.**?): **p. p.** πεπάνθαι Aristot. Probl. 20, 20: **aor.** ἐπεπάνθην Aristot. Plant. 2, 7, 7; πεπανθῇς Eur. Heracl. 159, -ανθῇ Hippocr. 2, 140 (Lit.); Aristot. Probl. 20, 30; -θείς Paus. 10, 36, 1: **fut.** πεπανθήσομαι Xen. Cyr. 4, 5, 21; Dio Cass. 52, 20.

Πεπαρεῖν, πέπρωται, πεπρωμένη, see (πόρω).

Πέπνῡμαι, see πνέω.

Πέπτω, see πέσσω.

Περαίνω *To end, accomplish*, Pind. P. 10, 28; Aesch. Sept. 1051; Ar. Ran. 401; Hippocr. 2, 458; Pl. Leg. 716; Dem. 4, 28: **imp.** ἐπέραινον Xen. Hell. 6, 2, 30; Dem. 18, 149: **fut.** περᾰνῶ Ar. Plut. 563; Thuc. 6, 86; Pl. Leg. 672, Ion. -ανέω Hippocr. 7, 496 (Lit.); Meliss. Fr. 10 (Mullach): **aor.** ἐπέρᾱνα Pl. Gorg. 522; περάνας Soph. Aj. 22; Pl. Theaet. 207: **p. p.** πεπέρασμαι, -ρανται Pl. Rep. 502, but πεπείρ- for the metre, Soph. Tr. 581; πεπεράνθω Pl. Leg. 736; inf. -ράνθαι Men. 75; -ασμένος Parm. 145. 158; Aristot. Probl. 5, 25; Polyb. 4, 40: **aor.** ἐπεράνθην, περανθῇ Pl. Gorg. 501; -θειεν (Hom.) Epigr. 14, 3; -ανθῆναι Isocr. 5, 40; -ανθείς Xen. Hell. 3, 2, 19. 2, 4, 39 (Wittenb. Dind. Saupp.): **fut.** περανθήσομαι Galen 3, 296. 4, 383,

Dor. περασθήσ- Stob. (Crit.) 3, 74. **Mid.** rare in *simple*, περαίνεσθαι Thuc. 7, 43: **fut.** -ᾰνοῦμαι, δια- Pl. Phil. 53: **aor.** ἐπερᾱνάμην, δι- Leg. 900, συν- Aristot. Soph. 10, 7; -άνασθαι, δια- Eur. Hel. 26; -ανάμενος, δια- Pl. Prot. 314, συν- Dem. 18, 163. **Vb.** ἀ-πέραντος Pl. Critias 119, περαντέον Galen 7, 765, δια- Pl. Leg. 715. See πειραίνω.

Περαιόω *To set over*, Plut. Cat. min. 58. Ant. 7; Polyb. 22, 11 (13), 14 (Dind.): fut. -ώσω Thuc. 2, 67, see below; Plut. Cat. min. 55: **aor.** ἐπεραίωσα Thuc. 4, 121; Plut. Crass. 10; Strab. 16, 4, 24, **pass.** as **mid.** see below. **Mid.** περαιοῦμαι *to go over*, Thuc. 1, 5: **fut.** περαιώσομαι Thuc. 1, 10: **aor.** later and in comp. δια-περαιώσασθαι (Pl.) Ax. 370: with **aor. pass.** ἐπεραιώθην as **mid.** Her. 1, 209; Thuc. 6, 61; Luc. Hist. Con. 31 (but δι-επερ- **pass.** Soph. Aj. 730); περαιωθεὶς Od. 24, 437; Her. 5, 14: **fut.** -ωθήσομαι Ar. Ran. 138: **p.** πεπεραιωμένος Thuc. 3, 26; Polyb. 3, 64; Dio Cass. 50, 24: **plp.** δι-επεπεραίωντο Thuc. 3, 23.—Once in Homer, once in Comedy, never in Tragedy. The **fut.** act. περαιώσειν occurs with sense of **mid.** Thuc. 2, 67, unless ἃ be taken with one Ms. for ᾧ, and ἔμελλε—Poppo's suggestion—for ἔμελλον.

Περᾱ́ω *To go over, cross*, Aesch. Pers. 799; Soph. Ant. 386, Epic 3 sing. ἐκ-περᾴᾳ Od. 9, 323, περ-όωσι 6, 273, ἐκ- 8, 561; περῶν Il. 21, 283; Ar. Av. 1195; Xen. Mem. 2, 1, 31; περᾶν H. Merc. 133; Pind. N. 3, 21; Aesch. Sept. 378; Xen. M. Eq. 6, 5, Epic -ᾰ́αν Il. 12, 63: **imp.** ἐπέρᾰον, ἐπέρα Pind. I. 2, 41, πέρᾰον Il. 16, 367, iter. περάασκε Od. 5, 480; Opp. H. 5, 450: **fut.** περάσω Eur. Bac. 191; Xen. M. Eq. 2, 1, see below: **aor.** ἐπέρᾱσα Theocr. 2, 90; Callim. Cer. 14; περάσῃς Aesch. Pr. 718; Soph. O. R. 674; opt. -άσαι Pind. N. 11, 10 (Vulg.); but inf. -ᾶσαι (Dissen, Bergk, Momms.); Theocr. 15, 44; Dor. part. περάσαις Pind. P. 3, 76 (rare in prose ἐπέρᾱσα App. B. C. 4, 87. Hannib. 2; D. Sic. 23, 11; Plut. Cat. min. 15. Mar. 8. Cam. 25, δι- Pl. Soph. 261. Tim. 85): **p.** πεπέρᾱκα Aesch. Pers. 65; Com. Fr. (Eup.) 2, 499; Xen. Lac. 4, 7. Epic and Ion. forms περόωσι 3 pl. pres. for -άουσι, Od. 4, 709. 6, 272; inf. περᾱ́ᾱν for -άειν, -ᾶν, Il. 2, 613: iter. **imp.** περάασκε Od. 5, 480: **fut.** περήσω Il. 23, 71; Her. 3, 72; Musae. 203; -ήσειν Il. 5, 646; Hom. H. Merc. 158, Epic -ησέμεναι Il. 12, 200. 218: **aor.** ἐπέρησα Il. 5, 291. 21, 594, πέρησ- 4, 502; inf. -ῆσαι 12, 53; Theogn. 427; -ήσας Her. 4, 43: **mid.** περάωντο Opp. C. 2, 623. To be distinguished from the following kindred verb.

(Περάω) *To carry over for sale, sell*, Epic, for which in pres. πέρνημι, Attic πιπράσκω: **fut.** περᾰ́σω, inf. περᾰ́αν for -άσειν, Il. 21, 454: **aor.** πέρᾰσα Od. 15, 428, ἐπέρασσα Il. 21, 40. 78, πέρασσα

21, 102 (Bekk. 2 edit.). Od. 15, 387 (Bekk. 2 edit. La R.); -ἄσητε 15, 453; -ἄσειε 14, 297; -ἄσας Hom. H. Cer. 132: p. πεπέρημαι, -ημένος Il. 21, 58.

Πέρδω *pedo*, ἀπο-πέρδεις Proverb. Plut. 29, the only instance of pres. act. we know: usu. πέρδομαι Ar. Eccl. 78; Com. Fr. (Pher.) 2, 291: imp. ἐπέρδετο Com. Fr. (Cratet.) 2, 241; Ar. Vesp. 1177: fut. παρδήσομαι, ἀπο- Ar. Ran. 10: p. πέπορδα Ar. Nub. 392: plp. ἐπεπόρδειν, 'πεπόρδει Ar. Vesp. 1305, after a long vowel: 2 aor. ἔπαρδον, ἀπ- Ar. Plut. 699, κατ- Pax 547; πάρδω, ἀπο- Ar. Vesp. 394, not -ῶ; πάρδοι, ἀπο- Com. Fr. (Diod.) 3, 545; imper. παρδέτω, προσ- Com. Fr. (Damox.) 4, 531; παρδεῖν, κατα- Ar. Plut. 618, προσ- Ran. 1074; παρδών, ἀπο- Ar. Av. 792. Fut. and aor. seem not to occur in *simple*. This verb with its compounds is considerately confined to Comedy.

Πέρθω *To destroy, sack*, Poet. pres. rare, imper. πέρθε Hom. Epigr. 14, 11; Aesch. Pers. 1057; -θων Il. 18, 342; Eur. Hipp. 542 (chor.): imp. iter. πέρθεσκον Ap. Rh. 1, 800: fut. πέρσω Soph. Ph. 1428; Eur. Bac. 1335; -σοιεν Soph. Ph. 612; -σειν Il. 21, 584, -σέμεν Q. Sm. 12, 20: 1 aor. ἔπερσα Od. 1, 2; Pind. N. 3, 37; Soph. Tr. 467, πέρσα Il. 20, 192; Pind. P. 1, 54; subj. πέρσῃς, ἐκ- Il. 13, 380, -σῃ Pl. Prot. 340, Epic 1 pl. πέρσομεν, δια- Il. 9, 46; πέρσαιμι, -σειεν Soph. Tr. 433, -σειαν Il. 21, 517; πέρσας Od. 14, 241; Soph. Tr. 244; Eur. Hec. 547; πέρσαι Hom. Epigr. 15, 13?; Aesch. Pers. 178; Soph. O. R. 1456: 2 aor. ἔπρᾰθον Epic, Il. 18, 454. Od. 9, 40; Pind. P. 9, 81, δι- Il. 1, 367, πράθεν Pind. N. 7, 35, -θον I. 5, 36; inf. πραθέειν Hes. Sc. 240, δια- Il. 7, 32. 18, 511. Mid. as pass. fut. πέρσεται Il. 24, 729: 2 aor. ἐπρᾰθετο, δι- pass. Od. 15, 384. Pass. πέρθομαι Her. 7, 220 (Orac.): imp. πέρθετο as aor. Il. 12, 15, -θοντο Ap. Rh. 2, 138; part. περθόμενος as aor. Il. 4, 291; Pind. P. 3, 50; πέρθαι Il. 16, 708, is said to be syncop. inf. 2 aor. mid. as pass. Perf. πέπορθα, called "post-Homeric," we have never seen. This verb in the *simple* form seems not to occur in prose. Plato has 1 aor. in comp. ἐκπέρσῃ Prot. 340. In Comedy we have not seen it simple or compound. The prose form is the regular πορθέω, though even it is much more frequent in poetry.

Περιβάλλω *To throw round* &c. as βάλλω, but p. p. περιβέβληται is usu. mid. *put about oneself, surround for oneself* &c. Pl. Conv. 216: plp. περιεβέβληντο Xen. Hell. 7, 4, 22, Ion. -εβεβλήατο Her. 6, 25, -έατο (Stein, Abicht); part. -βεβλημένος Isocr. 4, 184; Pl. Theaet. 174, but pass. Critias 116; Her. 2, 91; Dem. 43, 79: 2 aor. περὶ . . βάλετο in tmesi Od. 5, 231, περιβάλοντο Aesch. Ag. 1147 chor. (Dind. 5 ed. περεβάλ- Herm.)

Περιδῑνέω *To turn, whirl round,* act. rare in classic authors, Soph. Fr. 310 (D.); Aeschin. 3, 167: fut. -ήσω: aor. -εδίνησα Luc. H. V. 1, 9; Alciphr. 1, 39. More freq. mid. -δινοῦμαι *turn oneself round,* -ούμενος Xen. Conv. 7, 3, -εύμενος Tim. Locr. 97: fut. -δινήσομαι Luc. Lex. 2: with aor. pass. -ήθην as mid. Il. 22, 165 (Wolf, Bekk. but πέρι δινήθην Spitzn. Dind. La Roche): aor. mid. περιδινήσασθε trans. Anth. 7, 485, missed by Lexicogr.

Περιέπω, see ἕπω.

Πέρνημι *To sell,* Poet. for πιπράσκω, 3 pl. περνᾶσι Theogn. 1215; Hipponax 46 (Bergk); περνάς Il. 22, 45; Hipponax 52 (Bergk); Eur. Cycl. 271: imp. iter. πέρνασκε Il. 24, 752. Pass. πέρνᾰμαι Ar. Eq. 176; περνάμενος Il. 18, 292: imp. ἐπέρναντο Pind. I. 2, 7. See (περάω).

Πέσσω *To cook,* Il. 4, 513. Od. 7, 119; Hippocr. 7, 516; Aristot. Part. Anim. 3, 5, 15, Attic πέττω Ar. Fr. 267; Com. Fr. (Eup.) 2, 470. (Mnesim.) 3, 570; Aristot. Part. Anim. 4, 5, 60 (B.); Theophr. H. P. 4, 2, 5; Plut. Eum. 11, περι- Ar. Plut. 159; Epic inf. πεσσέμεν Il. 2, 237: imp. ἔπεσσον Her. 8, 137, Attic ἔπεττον Ar. Ran. 505, later πέπτω Dioscor. 3, 33; Theophr. Odor. 50, -ττω Ms. A. Wimmer (but πέπτεσθαι Hippocr. 1, 197; πεπτόμενος Aristot. Ausc. 8, 6, 11) whence: fut. πέψω Com. Fr. (Ar.) 2, 1027 (Fritzsche, Mein. πέμψω Vulg. Dind.); V. T. Lev. 26, 26: aor. ἔπεψα, πέψας Pl. Rep. 372; πέψαι Com. Fr. (Pher.) 2, 345?; Aristot. Eth. Nic. 4, 11, 10 (Bekk.); κατα-πέψῃ Il. 1, 81; κατα-πέψαι Pind. Ol. 1, 55; Hippocr. 2, 490: p. p. πέπεμμαι Ar. Pax 869; Hippocr. 8, 548 (Lit.); Aristot. Gen. An. 2, 7, 17 (B.); Theophr. C. P. 2, 17, 6, περι- Pl. Leg. 886: aor. ἐπέφθην Hippocr. 2, 522 (Lit.); Aristot. Prob. 1, 42; Theophr. C. P. 6, 16, 3, περι- Ar. Vesp. 668: fut. πεφθήσομαι Galen 1, 634. 10, 906; -θησόμενος Aristot. Prob. 21, 8. Mid. πέσσομαι *cook for oneself,* Hegem. Thas. Athen. 15, 55: imp. ἐπέσσετο Her. 1, 160: aor. ἐπεψάμην Hegem. Thas. Athen. 15, 55 (Ms. A, ἐπεμψ- Dind.) Vb. πεπτός Eur. Fr. 470 (Dind.)

Πέτᾰμαι *To fly,* as ἵστᾰμαι, Simon. C. 30; Pind. P. 8, 90. N. 6, 48 (B.); Pseud.-Anacr. 24, 6 (B.); Anth. 11, 208. 12, 105; late prose Aristot. Part. Anim. 4, 14, 1. Incess. An. 9, 13; Ael. H. A. 17, 33 (Schneid. -ομαι Herch.); Plut. Mor. 962; Luc. Pseudol. 29, περι- Aristot. H. A. 9, 1, 15, ἐκ- 9, 40, 23, and πετάομαι Anth. 14, 63 (Aristot. Metaph. 3, 5, 15, has been altered): aor. pass. ἐπετάσθην Pseud.-Anacr. 33, 6 (Bergk), ἐκ- Aristot. H. A. 9, 40, 12, εἰσ- 9, 40, 15, ὑπερ- Luc. Rhet. 6, unless to be referred to πετάννῡμι. The old grammarians, Moeris &c. say that πέταμαι is not Attic: πέτομαι, πέτεται Ἀττικοί, πέταμαι, πέταται

Ἕλληνες. Hence, we presume, Brunck, Musgr. Dind. &c. displaced the Ms. reading πέταται, for πέτεται Eur. Ion 90; Ar. Av. 573. 574; Eubul. Athen. 10, 450. For the established reading πέτονται Xen. An. 1, 5, 3, several Mss. have πέτανται, and for πέτεται Aristot. H. A. 5, 19, 16. 9, 32, 11. 36, 4, πέταται, -ᾶται occur as a v. r. The pres. πετάομαι is perhaps late, and in most cases even doubtful, for καταπετεωμένας Her. 3, 111 (Ms. F. Gaisf.) is supposed by some to be a mistake. Bekker, Krüg. Lhardy, Stein retain the old reading καταπετομένας, Dindorf prefers καταπταμένας offered by two good Mss. πετωμένα Anth. 14, 63 quoted, should, it is supposed, yield to ποτωμένα the poetic and late prose form; and at Aristot. Metaph. 3, 5, 15, and Diod. Sic. 4, 77, it has been changed from Mss. to πετόμενα &c., but προπετώμενος is best supported Arr. An. 3, 3, 6 (Ellendt, Krüg. προπετόμ- Sint.)

Πετάννῡμι *To expand*, imper. πετάννῡ, δια- Ar. Lys. 733, but -ύτωσαν, ἀνα- Luc. Jup. Tr. 33, πεταννύω, ἀνα- πεταννύουσι Xen. An. 7, 1, 17 (Vulg. Popp. Krüg. Saupp. &c. -ύασι Dind. Cob.); -ύουσα, περι- Oec. 19, 18 (Vulg. Breitb. Saupp.); πεταννύειν, ἀνα- Luc. Calumn. 30 (Dind.); later πετάω, ἀνα- Luc. Cal. 21: imp. ἐν-επετάννυς Xen. Cyr. 1, 6, 40 (L. Dind. 4 ed. -άννυες Vulg. Popp. Saupp.): fut. πετάσω Or. Sib. 4, 113 (σσ Nonn. 16, 95), ἐκ- Eur. I. T. 1135 (chor.), Attic πετῶ, ἀνα- Com. Fr. (Men.) 4, 77. 204: aor. ἐπέτᾰσα (κατ- Ar. Plut. 731, περι- Aeschin. 3, 76), Hom. always πέτᾰσα Od. 5, 269. 6, 94, and -ασσα in tmesi Il. 14, 495; πετάσῃς, ἀνα- Luc. Hist. 7; opt. πετάσειε Od. 18, 160; imper. πέτασον Luc. D. Mort. 10, 10; in tmesi Eur. Hel. 1459, ἀμ-πέτασον Eur. Phoen. 297 (chor.); πετάσας (Luc.) Amor. 32, Epic -άσσας Il. 21, 115. Od. 24, 397, ἀνα-πετάσας Her. 3, 146; Pl. Phil. 62, ἀμ- Eur. Phoen. 788 (chor.), κατα- Ar. Vesp. 132: p. πεπέτακα, δια- late Diod. Sic. 17, 115: p. p. πεπέτασμαι Anth. 9, 656; Opp. Hal. 2, 684; App. Pun. 120, ἐκ- Her. 1, 62 (Orac.), παρα- Polyb. 33, 3 (Bekk.), and πέπτᾰμαι Il. 5, 195. Od. 6, 45; Opp. Hal. 2, 173; πεπταμένος Il. 21, 531; always in Attic, Ar. Nub. 343, ἀνα- (Pind. N. 9, 2; Her. 8, 60) Xen. Cyr. 5, 2, 6; Pl. Phaed. 111. Phaedr. 240; Isocr. 15, 126, ἀναπέπταται Xen. Oec. 9, 4, -ανται Conv. 5, 6, Ion. -τέαται Her. 9, 9: plp. ’πέπτατο Ar. Av. 48 (Bekk. Bergk, ’πέπτετο Dawes, Dind. 5 ed.), πέπτ- Il. 17, 371: aor. ἐπετάσθην, πετάσθ- Od. 21, 50; πετασθείς Il. 21, 538, ἐκ- Eur. Cycl. 497 (chor.); Luc. Prom. 1. Mid. aor. πετάσαντο Nonn. D. 2, 704, ἀμ-πετ- Opp. C. 2, 583, missed by Lexicogr. See πέταμαι.

Πέτομαι *To fly*, Il. 2, 89; Soph. O. R. 486, 2 sing. πέτεαι Anacr. 9, πέτει Eur. Bac. 332; Ar. Av. 704; Her. 2, 75; Pl.

Leg. 952; πέτωμαι Ar. Av. 1456; -τοιτο Eccl. 899: **imp.** ἐπετόμην Il. 23, 372. 449 (B.); Ar. Av. 1150, πετόμ- Il. 13, 29 (Bekk. 2 ed.); Hes. Sc. 308, dual πετέσθην Il. 5, 366. Od. 3, 494: **fut.** πετήσομαι Com. Poet. Ar. Pax 77, ἀπο- 1126; and late prose ἐκ- Luc. Ep. Sat. 35, ἐπι- Prom. 20 (in classic prose πτήσομαι, ἐπι- Her. 7, 15, ἀνα- Pl. Leg. 905; Aeschin. 3, 209, see ἵπτημι): **2 aor.** ἐπτόμην, ἀπ- Ar. Av. 90, ἀν- 35, Dor. -όμαν Soph. Aj. 693 (chor. Pors. Ell. Dind. 4 ed., -όμαν Dind. 5 ed. Nauck), ἐπ-έπτου Ar. Av. 118, 'π-έπτετο 48; ἀνά-πτοιτο Pl. Phaed. 109; πτόμενος, ἐπι- Rep. 365; πτέσθαι Soph. O. R. 17 (πτάσθαι Elms.), ἐπι- Il. 4, 126, ἀνα- Pl. Phaedr. 249. The **perf.** πεπότημαι Il. 2, 90; Ar. Nub. 319, Dor. -ᾱμαι Aesch. Eum. 378 (chor.); Eur. Hipp. 564 (chor.): **plp.** πεπότητο Hes. Sc. 148: and **aor.** ποτᾱθείην Ar. Av. 1338 (chor.), are from the poetic and reg. ποτάομαι. **Fut.** πετήσομαι is not in Hom. For πτήσομαι the Attic prose **fut.** form, and aorists ἔπτην, ἐπτάμην, see (ἵπτημι).

Πέττω, see πέσσω.

Πεύθομαι, see πυνθάνομαι.

Πέφνω *To kill*, Poet. and **pres.** late, πέφνουσι Opp. Hal. 2, 133. 5, 390: **2 aor.** ἔπεφνον Il. 10, 478; Hes. Sc. 57; Ap. Rh. 4, 550; Pind. Ol. 2, 42; Soph. O. R. 1497; Eur. Andr. 655, πέφνον Il. 13, 363; Ap. Rh. 1, 1305; Pind. P. 11, 37; subj. πέφνω Od. 11, 135; Opp. Hal. 2, 212; imper. πέφνε Od. 11, 453; Epic inf. πεφνέμεν Il. 6, 180; πεφνόντα Il. 16, 827 (Tyrann. Bekk. La Roche, but with the accent of **pres.** πέφνοντα Aristarch. Spitzn. Dind.), καταπεφνών 17, 539 (Bekk. Bäuml. -πέφνων Dind. La R.): **p.** πέφαται Od. 22, 54, -ανται Il. 5, 531; inf. πεφάσθαι Il. 14, 471: **fut.** πεφήσομαι Il. 15, 140. Grammarians who accent πέφνων on the first, note it as the only barytone **aor.** participle. **Pres.** πέφνω is late in usage; and *may* have been assumed on ἔπεφνον. The root seems to be φεν, whence by reduplication and syncope **aor.** ἔπεφνον: cf. φόνος. See φενω, φάω.

Πέφραδον, see φράζω.

Πεφυζότες, see φεύγω.

Πήγνῡμι *To fix, freeze*, Aesch. Pers. 496; Com. Fr. (Nausicr.) 4, 575; Hippocr. 2, 410; Xen. An. 4, 5, 3; Pl. Tim. 62, -νύω rare in classic Auth. Her. 4, 72 (Vulg. Gaisf. Bekk. Stein, -ῦσι Dind.); Hippocr. 6, 574 (Lit.); Xen. Ven. 6, 7; Aristot. Probl. 26, 27, 5. De Anima 1, 2, 5; Theophr. H. P. 6, 6, 9, κατα- Aristot. Pol. 7, 2, 11, later πήττω Sext. Emp. 441, 1; (Strab. 13, 4, 14), κατα- Dio. Hal. Ant. 3, 22, πήσσω, see foll.: **imp.** πήγνῡον Orph. Lith. 562, περι- 561, ἔπησσον Athen. 12, 534: **fut.** πήξω Il. 22, 283; Aristot. Part. Anim. 2, 7, 19, Dor. πάξω Pind. Ol.

6, 3: aor. ἔπηξα Il. 2, 664; Emped. 240; Soph. Aj. 821; Ar. Ach. 139; Thuc. 6, 66; Andoc. 4, 30, πῆξε Il. 13, 372, Dor. ἔπαξε Pind. N. 7, 26, πᾶξε Theocr. 11, 16; πήξῃ Il. 8, 95; πήξας Il. 3, 217; Hes. Op. 430; Eur. Elec. 898; Pl. Leg. 817, Dor. πάξαις in tmesi Pind. Ol. 11, 45; πῆξαι Il. 18, 177; Soph. El. 420; Hippocr. 8, 594 (as imper. perhaps Od. 5, 163. 11, 77): p. (πέπηχα): late plp. ἐμ-πεπήχεσαν Dio Cass. 40, 40 (Bekk. ἐν-επεπ- Dind.): p. p. πέπηγμαι late, Phil. in Verm. 47, κατα- Dio. Hal. 5, 46, συμ- Arr. An. 2, 21, 1, ξυμ- 5, 12, 4 (Krüg.): plp. πέπηκτο Nonn. 1, 270: 1 aor. Poet. ἐπήχθην, Ep. 3 pl. πῆχθεν Il. 8, 298; Dor. subj. παχθῇ (Theocr.) 23, 31; πηχθείς Eur. Cycl. 302, but late prose κατα- Arr. An. 5, 24, ξυμ- 5, 8. 7, 19: usu. 2 aor. ἐπάγην Il. 10, 374. 22, 276; Theocr. 2, 110; Hippocr. 5, 222; Pl. Tim. 59, πάγη Il. 5, 616, Epic 3 pl. πάγεν 11, 572; Emped. 53; παγείς Aesch. Ag. 1198; Eur. I. A. 395. Fr. 362, 12 (Dind.); Pl. Phaedr. 246; παγῆναι Rep. 530: 2 fut. παγήσομαι Ar. Vesp. 437; Thuc. 4, 92: fut. mid. πήξομαι *shall freeze, be frozen,* Hippocr. 2, 36 (Lit.): 2 p. πέπηγα *am fixed, frozen,* Il. 3, 135; Ibycus 21 (B.); Emped. 217; Aesch. Ch. 67; Soph. Aj. 819; Her. 7, 64; Hippocr. 7, 132 (Lit.); Pl. Tim. 77; Aristot. Mirab. 59; Dem. 4, 8, παρα- Isocr. 1, 46, Dor. πέπᾱγα Alcae. 34 (Bergk); opt. πεπᾱγοίην Eupol. in Schol. Il. 14, 241 (Ahr. D. Dor. p. 330, but Curtius πεπᾰγοίην aor.): plp. ἐπεπήγειν Il. 13, 442; Thuc. 3, 23, πεπήγ- Il. 16, 772 (B.): pres. pass. πήγνυται Il. 22, 453; Pl. Polit. 287: imp. πήγνυτ' Il. 15, 315, ἐπηγνύμην Ar. Eq. 1310. Mid. πήγνῦμαι trans. Hes. Op. 809; Themist. 25, 310: imp. ἐπήγνυτο App. Mithr. 73: fut. πήξομαι trans. Galen 10, 388, as intrans. or pass. see above: aor. ἐπηξάμην Ael. Fr. 75; Plut. Arat. 6; Dio. Hal. Ant. 1, 55; App. Pun. 134, συν- Critias 1, 10 (Bergk), Dor. ἐπαξ- Pind. Fr. 140 (Bergk), 2 sing. ἐπάξα Theocr. 4, 28; πάξαιτο Pind. N. 3, 62; (imper. πῆξαι Od. 5, 163. 11, 77, others inf. 1 aor. act. as imper.); πηξάμενος Anth. 5, 255; Her. 6, 12; Theophr. H. P. 9, 19, 2; Aristid. 2, 14 (Dind.); πήξασθαι Hes. Op. 455; Galen 10, 338, παρα- (Pl.) Ax. 370: 2 aor. ἐν-επήγετο quoted as such by Passow from Aesop 146 (Ernest.), 149 (Schaef.), 234 (Halm) seems to be imp. of ἐνεπάγομαι, but κατ-έπηκτο *stuck*, Il. 11, 378, is called an Epic sync. 2 aor. Vb. πηκτός Eur. Phoen. 489. The mid. seems scarcely to occur either in good Attic poetry or prose. The common reading Her. 4, 72, is πηγνύουσι and retained by Bekk. Gaisf. Krüg. &c., but Dind. decidedly prefers πηγνῦσι (Ms. S.) Hippocr. has both forms πήγνυσι and πηγνύουσι 6, 574 (Lit.) The 2 plp. ἐπεπήγειν, ἐν- is trans. *had fixed in,* Dio Cass. 40, 40 (Tauchn.), unless there should be read 1 plp.

ἐμπεπήχεσαν (which we observe has *now* been edited by Bekker), or σκόλοπας altered to σκόλοπες. πήγνῦτο is opt. Pl. Phaed. 118, -ύοιτο (some Mss.)

Πηδάω *To leap*, Eur. Ion 717; Ar. Vesp. 227; Xen. Ven. 5, 31; Pl. Leg. 672; πηδῶν Soph. Aj. 30; Ion. inf. πηδέειν, ἐκ- Her. 8, 118 (Mss. Bekk. -δᾶν Dind. Stein), see below: **imp.** ἐπήδα Il. 21, 302, -ήδων Eur. Bac. 1094: **fut.** πηδήσομαι Theophr. Char. 5 (21); Luc. de Dom. 24; Ar. Cyn. 15, προ- Aesch. Fr. 22, ἐπι- Pl. Lys. 216, προσ- Com. Fr. (Alex.) 3, 440: perhaps later, act. πηδήσω Anth. Plan. (Incert.) 4, 54. 142; Ach. Tat. 3, 4, ἐκ- App. Hisp. 20: **aor.** ἐπήδησα, πήδησα H. Hym. 7, 52, 'πήδησα Aesch. Sept. 459 (trimet.); Theocr. 25, 251, Epic ἀμ-πήδ- Il. 11, 379, for ἀν-επήδ- Ar. Eccl. 428. Ran. 566; Xen. Hell. 2, 3, 52, εἰσ- Dem. 21, 78; inf. πηδῆσαι Il. 14, 455; Hippocr. 7, 490, ἐμ- Her. 3, 32; -ήσας Soph. O. R. 1300; Eur. Supp. 1039. Andr. 1139: **p.** πεπήδηκα Aesop 203 (Halm), ἀπο- Hippocr. 4, 202 (Lit.), ἐκ- Xen. Hell. 7, 4, 37, ὑπερ- Dem. 23, 73, ἐμ- Polyb. 12, 9: **plp.** ἐπεπηδήκειν, ἐξ- Dem. 54, 20: **p.p.** πεπήδημαι: **plp.** ἐπεπήδητο Hippocr. 7, 490 (Lit.) as **act.** *had leaped*, unless for ἑπταίη (Vulg.), ἑπτά should be read and πηδήματα understood. The Dor. form πᾱδάω occurs in 3 sing. παδῇ Soph. Fr. 46 (Ahr.) παδῆτε, ὑπερ- Theocr. 5, 108; imper. πάδη Ar. Lys. 1317; pt. πᾱδῶν, gen. pl. fem. πᾱδωᾶν Ar. Lys. 1313, Ionic πηδέω, ἐκ- πηδέειν Her. 8, 118 (Bekk. Gaisf. -δᾶν Dind. Dietsch, Stein). For εἰσπεπηδηκόσιν Dem. 57, 49 (Dind.), the best Ms. (S.) has (εἰσεπήδωσιν), εἰσπηδῶσιν (Bekk.)

Πημαίνω *To injure*, Il. 15, 42; Soph. El. 336. O. C. 837 (Vulg. Herm. Bergk); Pl. Leg. 932: **imp.** ἐπήμαινε Her. 9, 13: **fut.** Epic πημᾰνέω, -έει Hom. H. 2, 84, -έειν Il. 24, 781, -ᾰνῶ Soph. Aj. 1314. O. C. 837 (Pors. Dind. Hart. Nauck); Themist. 22, 271; Ar. Ach. 842 (Elms. L. and W. Dind. Bergk) where in other edit. stands **fut. mid.** πημανεῖται, which in the reflexive sense *injure oneself*, is undisputed in Soph. πημανούμενος Aj. 1155: **aor.** ἐπήμηνα, πημήνῃ Pl. Leg. 933; πημήνειαν Il. 3, 299; -ήνας Soph. Tr. 715. O. C. 893; -ῆναι Pl. Rep. 364: **aor. pass.** ἐπημάνθην, πημ- Od. 14, 255; πημανθῇς Aesch. Pr. 334; -ανθῆναι Od. 8, 563; -ανθείς Hes. Cert. 319, 5; Pl. Leg. 933. **Mid. fut.** πημανούμενος reflex or **pass.** *harm oneself, suffer*, Soph. Aj. 1155; but πημανεῖται *will injure*, Ar. Ach. 842 (Vulg. Bekk.), for which Elms. suggested πημανεῖ τις, Dind. &c. -ανεῖ τι, see above: **aor.** as **act.** πημήναντο Q. Sm. 13, 379. The change of πημανεῖται to πημανεῖ τι, seems rather favoured by πημανεῖς τι Soph. Aj. 1314. **Vb.** πημαντέον Theogn. 689. This verb is chiefly poetic, the **mid.** entirely so.

Πήσσω, see *πήγνυμι*.

Πιάζω *To grasp, seize*, called Aeol. and Dor. for *πιέζω*, Alcae. 148: imp. *ἐπίαζεν* Alcm. 44 (Bergk 3 ed.): aor. *ἐπίαξα, πιάξας* Theocr. 4, 35, *ἀμφ-επίαξε* Epigr. 6, *ἐπίασα* N. T. Jo. 8, 20. 21, 3; Hierocl. 28; imper. *πιάσατε* V. T. Cant. 2, 15; *-άσας* N. T. Act. 3, 7 &c.: p. p. *πεπίασμαι* Hippiatr. p. 121, 33: aor. *ἐπιάσθην* N. T. Apoc. 19, 20: fut. *πιασθήσεται* Apocr. Sir. 23, 21. *πιασθέντας* which once stood Her. 4, 11, has been rightly altered to *πιεσθέντας* from Mss. *συμπιασθῆναι* occurs Hippocr. 5, 430 (Lit.). 3, 680 (Kühn), but as he is so clear of Dorisms, it would perhaps be as well to refer, with Littré, this aor. to *συμπιαίνω*. If not, the change is easy from *συμπιασθῆναι* to *-εσθῆναι* (*συμπιέζω*) which Hippocr. uses in *simple*, *πιεσθῇ* 6, 368 (Lit.)

Πιαίνω *To fatten*, Xenophanes 2, 22 (B.); Pind. P. 4, 150; Eur. Cycl. 333; Aristot. Probl. 5, 14, 3: fut. *-ἄνῶ* Aesch. Sept. 587: aor. *ἐπίᾶνα* Ag. 276; Hippocr. 8, 106, *πίᾶνα* Pind. N. 9, 23, later *-ηνα* Diog. Laert. 1, 83: p. p. *πεπίασμαι* Ael. N. A. 13, 14. 25, *κατα-* Pl. Leg. 807: aor. *ἐπιάσθην, συν-* Hippocr. 5, 430? (Lit.), and *ἐπιάνθην* Theocr. 17, 126, *ἀνα-* Hippocr. 7, 242, *κατ-* Ael. H. A. 2, 13. V. H. 9, 13; but early, *πιανθείς* Anan. 5 (Bergk); Opp. Hal. 3, 279: fut. late *πιανθήσεται* V. T. Esai. 58, 11: pres. *πιαίνεται* Simon. Am. 7, 6. This verb is mostly poetic, Ionic and late prose: perhaps not in Comedy, and only once in classic Attic prose, *πιαινόμενος* Pl. Leg. 807?

Πιδύω *To gush forth*, Anth. 9, 322. 10, 13 (*πηδ-* Cod. Pal.), *ἀνα-* Plut. Aemil. P. 14 (Bekk. Sint.): imp. *ἐπίδυον* Hippocr. 5, 214 (L.); Plut. Aemil. P. 14 (v. r. *ἐπήδ-*). **Mid.** *πιδύομαι* Nic. Ther. 302, *ἐκ-πιδύ-* Aesch. Pers. 815 (Pors. Dind. Hart.) Schütz's reading for *ἐκπαιδεύεται* (Vulg. *ἐκμαιεύ-* Herm.) *ῑ, ῡ*, except *πιδύεται* Nic. Ther. quoted, unless *υ* be allowed (contra bonos mores) to swallow *ε*. Akin to *πιδύω* is the trans. *πιδάω*, part. *πιδώσης* Aristot. Meteor. 1, 13, 10, *v. r.* *πιδυούσης*. *πεδύω* is accounted a vicious form.

Πιέζω *To press*, Alcae. 148; Pind. N. 1, 53; Aesch. Ch. 301; Ar. Lys. 416; Hippocr. 3, 334. 504 (Lit.); Xen. Mem. 3, 10, 13; subj. *-έζῃς* Hes. Op. 497; *-έζειν* Od. 4, 419; Pl. Crat. 409: imp. *ἐπίεζε* Il. 16, 510; Her. 5, 35; Thuc. 7, 28, *πίεζ-* Od. 12, 196: fut. *πιέσω* Com. Fr. (Diph.) 4, 383; Geop. 20, 44: aor. *ἐπίεσα* Her. 9, 63; Thuc. 4, 6. 96; Hippocr. 3, 436. 4, 386 (Lit.) and often, but *-εξα, πιέξῃς* 3, 434 (Vulg. *-έζῃς* Lit.); *πιέσας* Pl. Leg. 965, Dor. *-έσαις* Pind. Ol. 6, 37: p. p. *πεπίεσμαι* Aristot. Mund. 3, 4; Hippocr. 5, 196. 7, 520, *ἐκ-* 2, 270 (Lit.), and *πεπίεγμαι* 3, 432; inf. *-έχθαι* 432. 436. 450: aor. *ἐπιέσθην, πιεσθῇ* Solon Fr. 13, 37 (B.); Hippocr. 6, 368; *-εσθείς* Od. 8, 336; Her. 4,

11 *now;* Xen. Hell. 2, 4, 34; Luc. Tox. 58, but ἐπιέχθην Hippocr. 3, 324. 434 &c.: fut. πιεσθήσομαι Oribas. 10, 19, δια- Galen 11, 317: pres. πιέζοιντο Thuc. 1, 49; -όμενος ibid.: imp. ἐπιεζ- 1, 24. 7, 87. Vb. πιεστέον Hippocr. 3, 500 (Lit.) (ῐ) The form πιεζέω, imp. πιέζευν occurs Od. 12, 196 in some editions, in others at 174 also, but Bekker, Dind. Ameis, La Roche read πίεζον at both places. Nor is it certain in Her.; for instead of πιεζεύμενος retained by Bekker, Gaisf. Stein 3, 146. 6, 108. 8, 142, Dind. has restored πιεζόμενος from some of the best Mss.; nor in Aristot. πιεζούμενος Prob. 16, 8, 10 (Mss. Bekk.), -ζόμενος (other Mss.); nor Polyb. πιεζόμενα 3, 74 (Bekk. Dind. Hultsch), ἐπιεζοῦντο 11, 33 (Bekk. Hultsch, -ζοντο Dind.) In Plut. it seems occasionally better supported, πιεζοῦντος, -ούμενος Alcib. 2. Thes. 1 &c. (Bekk. Sint.), and imp. ἐπιέζευν Theocr. 25, 268 (Mein. Fritz.) but -εζον (Ahr. Ziegl.) Hippocr. also has πιεζέουσι 3, 115 (Kühn) but -έζουσι (Mss. Lit. 3, 524), πιεζεῦντα 3, 64 (Kühn); so Littré 3, 334. 450, but πιέζει ibid. (Kühn, Lit.) It would thus appear to be doubtful whether this form is correctly called *Epic* and *Ionic*.

(Πιθέω) Πιθήσω, Πιθήσας, see πείθω.

Πικραίνω *To make bitter, roughen,* act. late, D. Hal. Comp. Verb. 15. de vi Dem. 55: fut. -ανεῖ N. T. Apoc. 10, 9: aor. ἐπίκρᾱνα (V. T.) Apocr. 1 Macc. 3, 7 &c: pass. partially *classic* -αίνεται Hippocr. 2, 288 (Lit.); Com. Fr. (Antiph.) 3, 79; Theocr. 5, 120; -όμενος Pl. Leg. 731; -εσθαι (Dem.) 1464; D. Hal. de vi Dem. 55; Plut. Mor. 1120: aor. ἐπικράνθην V. T. Ruth 1, 13; but πικρανθείη Athen. (Lync.) 6, 40: fut. -ανθήσομαι V. T. Jer. 40, 9: and fut. mid. as pass. πικρανέεσθαι, προσ-εμ- Her. 3, 146: aor. trans. πικράνασθαι Dio Cass. Fr. 81 (Bekk. L. Dind.) missed by Lexicogr.

Πιλνάω *To bring near,* Epic Hes. Op. 510, intrans. *approach,* πιλνᾷς H. Cer. 115 (Mss.), for which editors have given πίλνᾰσαι, and πιλνᾷ. **Mid.** πίλνᾰμαι (πίλνημι) *to approach,* -νᾷ H. Cer. 115, -ναται Il. 19, 94; Ap. Rh. 4, 952, ἐπι- Od. 6, 44: imp. unaugm. πίλνᾰτο Il. 23, 368; Hes. Th. 703, but προσεπίλν- Od. 13, 95.—πίτναντο (πίτνημι), not πίλναντο, seems the preferable reading Il. 22, 402.

(Πιμπλάνω) *To fill,* Epic and only 3 sing. pass. πιμπλᾰ́νεται *is filled,* Il. 9, 679.

Πίμπλημι *To fill* (πλάω), pres. and imp. like ἵστημι, -ησι Hes. Op. 301 (Mss. Vulg. Koechly, -ῇσι Spohn), -ᾶσι Il. 21, 23; Aesch. Fr. 55 (Dind.); Soph. El. 906; Com. Fr. (Xen.) 3, 614; Her. 2, 40; Epic subj. πιμπλῇσι Hes. Op. 301 (Spohn, Goettl. Flach); inf. -πλᾰ́ναι Eur. Fr. 891 (Dind.); Pl. Gorg. 493; -πλάς Pl. Rep.

586, πιμπλάω, -έω rare, see below: **imp.** ἐπίμπλην, -πλᾶσαν Xen. An. 1, 5, 10, but ἐπίμπλων Pind. Fr. 182 (Schneidw.), ἐν-επίμπλα Luc. Calum. 3, pl. -επίμπλων Dio Cass. 68, 31 (Bekk. Dind.): **fut.** πλήσω Eur. Hipp. 691; Anth. 14, 130, ἀνα- Od. 5, 302; Ar. Ach. 847; Dem. 20, 50, ἐμ- Pl. Leg. 875. Alc. (1) 105: **aor.** ἔπλησα Eur. Med. 905. Or. 368; Mosch. 3, 74 (Mein.); Hippocr. 6, 454; (Dem.) Epist. 6; Pseudo-Callisth. 2, 40; in tmesi Her. 2, 87, ἐν- Od. 17, 503; Thuc. 7, 82; Pl. Phaedr. 255, *simple* in Hom. always πλῆσα Il. 13, 60. 14, 35. Od. 17, 411 &c.; πλήσῃ Opp. Hal. 1, 332, ἀνα-πλήσῃς Il. 4, 170; πλήσαιμι Eur. I. A. 234, -σειε Hipp. 1253, -ειαν Il. 16, 72; πλῆσον Eur. Tr. 84; πλήσας, Od. 5, 93. Il. 16, 223; Hes. Fr. 174; Aesch. Ag. 1398; Soph. O. C. 480; Her. 1, 70. 2, 86. 3, 96, ἐμ- Xen. Hell. 7, 1, 20; inf. πλῆσαι Her. 1, 107, ἐμ- Eur. Phoen. 170, ἐπι- Ar. Av. 975 (ἐνι- Cob. Dind.): **p.** πέπληκα, ἐμ- Pl. Apol. 23. Gorg. 519: **p. p.** πέπλησμαι Babr. 60, ἐμ-πέπλησται Pl. Rep. 518, πέπληνται Hippocr. 6, 112 (Lit.), -πλήαται Sim. Am. 36; πεπλησμένος Paus. 6, 26, 1; Galen 5, 213, δια- Andoc. 1, 125: **plp.** ἐν-επέπληντο Lys. 28, 6 (Bekk. B. Saupp.): **1 aor.** ἐπλήσθην Il. 20, 156; Eur. Heracl. 646; Her. 4, 128; Paus. 9, 7, 2 (Schub.), πλήσθησαν Theocr. 25, 98, Epic πλῆσθεν Il. 17, 211; πλησθῇς Eur. Bac. 281; Soph. Ph. 520; Hippocr. 2, 231 (Erm.); -θῆναι Soph. Ant. 122; πλησθείς Eur. Cycl. 409; Her. 3, 16; Thuc. 7, 75; Pl. Phaedr. 248: **fut.** πλησθήσομαι Or. Sib. 3, 311; Himer. Or. 23, 14; Charit. 5, 5; N. T. Luc. 1, 15, ἐμ- Eur. Hipp. 664; Isocr. 6, 69: **3 fut.** late πεπλήσονται Porphyr. Abst. 1, 16: similarly **fut. mid.** ἐμ-πλησόμενος App. Syr. 7; ἐμ-πλήσεσθαι Arat. 1121 (Bekk.), and some unnecessarily ἀνα-πλήσει Ar. Nub. 1023, see below: **imp.** Epic πίμπλαντο Il. 1, 104. Od. 10, 248 (v. r. Il. 22, 402). **Mid.** (πίμπλᾰμαι) *fill oneself*, πιμπλάμενος seems so, Luc. Auct. Vit. 9: **fut.** ἐμπλησόμενος App. Syr. 7; ἐμπλήσεσθαι Arat. 1121, both quoted: **1 aor.** trans. ἐπλησάμην, -ήσω Soph. O. C. 528, -ήσαντο Callim. Dian. 166, πλήσ- Opp. H. 5, 347, ἐμ-πλήσατο Il. 22, 312. Od. 9, 296, ἐν-επλησ- Hermesian. 2, 45 (Schn.); πλήσωνται Her. 2, 87; πλησαίατο Od. 19, 198; πλησάμενος Il. 9, 224; Her. 6, 125; Ach. Tat. 4, 18, ἐμ- Ar. Vesp. 381; Pl. Conv. 214; Luc. Philops. 36; but intrans. Nic. Ther. 176: **2 aor.** Epic ἐπλήμην (πλῆμι) *filled himself, was filled,* unaugm. πλῆτο Il. 14, 438. 21, 16. Od. 17, 436; Hes. Sc. 146, ἐμ- Il. 21, 607 (Dind. La R.), πλῆθ' 21, 300, πλῆντο Od. 8, 57; Hes. Th. 688, ἐμ- Od. 8, 16. Il. 21, 607 (Bekk.); Batr. 167; in Comic Poet. ἐν-έπλητο Ar. Vesp. 911. 1304; opt. ἐμ-πλήμην Ar. Ach. 236, -ῆτο Lys. 235. 236; imper. ἔμ-πλησο Ar. Vesp. 603; ἐμ-πλήμενος 424. 984. Eccl. 56. Eq, 935. **Vb.** ἐμπληστέος Pl. Rep. 373.

In compounds, if μ precede, the pres. and imp. drop the first μ of the *simple*, as ἀμπιπλάντες Pind. N. 10, 57; ἐμπίπλημι, but ἐνεπίμπλην; ἐμπιπλάμενος Com. Fr. (Pher.) 2, 287, ἐμπίμπλαμαι however Eur. Ion 925 (Vulg. Dind. ἐμπίπλ- Kirchh. Nauck); Com. Fr. (Cratin.) 2, 95 &c. πιπλάντων Aesch. Ch. 360 (Herm.), is for πιμπλ- *metri causa* (περαίν- Dind.) πλῆθεν Il. 8, 214, is not for πλήσθησαν, but imp. of πλήθω. ἐμπίπληθι (-πίμπλ- La R.) 2 sing. imper. (for ἐμπίπλἄθι) Il. 21, 311, Dor. and Attic πίμπλη Sophr. 49, ἐμ-πίπλη (-πίμπλ- Dind.) Ar. Av. 1310, as ἵστη (ἵστἄθι). ἐμπιπλείς part. indicating a stem vowel ε not α (ἐμπιπλέω—ἐμπίπλημι) Hippocr. 2, 226 (K.); so πιμπλέω, πιμπλεῦσαι Hes. Th. 880, which in some degree supports ἐμπιπλέει Her. 7, 39, against ἐμπίπλη, ἐμπίπλα &c. ἐπιμπλέετο 3, 108 (Bekk. Krüg. &c.), -πλατο (Schaef. Stein, Dind. Abicht.) ἐμπιπλᾷ again is supported by the analogy of ἱστᾷ 4, 103, and by πιμπλάω part. πιμπλῶσαι Hippocr. 5, 344 (Lit.), late ἐμπιμπλάω, ἐμ-πιπλῶντα Plut. Mor. 994, ἐν-επίμπλα Luc. Calum. 3, -πλων Dio Cass. 68, 31, -πλῶντο D. Sic. Fr. Lib. 35, 29 (Dind.). πίπλω, ἔπιπλον occurs Hes. Sc. 291, in some editions, but ἔπιτνον from πίτνω is better supported. For opt. ἐμπλήμην Ar. Ach. 236, -ῆτο Lys. 235 quoted, Buttmann would write ἐμπλείμην, -εῖτο. For plp. ἐνεπέπληντο Lys. 28, 6 quoted (Mss. Bekk. B. Saupp. &c.) **2 aor.** ἐνέπληντο has been suggested by Cobet, and adopted by Westerm. and Scheibe. We demur to the change on the ground that this aorist is not a prose form. Prose authors said δι-επλήσθη Thuc. 7, 85, περι- Xen. Hell. 3, 2, 28; Pl. Theaet. 156, ἐνεπλήσθη Hippocr. 2, 452; Xen. An. 1, 10, 12; Dem. 54, 27. Nor is it enough that "Aristophanes has used it;" for even in sober trimeters he frequently uses words and forms of words never employed by Attic prose writers: ἀλύει, for instance, Vesp. 111, ἀπύω Eq. 1023, βδέω Plut. 693, βρύκω Av. 26, ἐλινύω Thesm. 598, ἔρδω Vesp. 1431, ἕρπω Lys. 129, θείνω Ach. 564 do not, we think, occur in prose, nor the forms πρίασο Ar. Ach. 870, βαλλήσω Vesp. 222, πετήσομαι Pax 77, ἔθανον *simple* Thesm. 865, nor κατθανεῖν Ran. 1477. Fut. mid. is rare: we have seen only two decided instances, ἐμ-πλησόμενος App. Syr. 7 (Bekk.), and ἐμ-πλήσεσθαι Arat. 1121 (Bekk.) Of ἀνα-πλήσει Ar. Nub. 1024, called by some pass. Hermann says "Dubitari potest activum sit, an passivum."

Πίμπρημι (but ἐμ-πίπρ-, see πίμπλημι) *To blow, burn* (πράω), trans. pres. and imp. like ἵστημι, πίμπρησι Eur. Tr. 893; Aristot. H. An. 3, 21, 4, 3 pl. πιμπρᾶσι Eur. Tr. 299, ἐμ-πιπρᾶσι Thuc. 3, 74; πίμπρησι, ὑπο- Ar. Lys. 348 (chor. -πρῃ Dind.), πιπρῶσι, ἐμ- Pl. Rep. 470; imper. πίμπρη Eur. Ion 974; inf. πιμπράναι Aesch.

Pers. 810; Eur. Tr. 81. 1260; Plut. Alex. 38; πιμπράντες Thuc. 6, 94, ἐμ-πιπράν- Xen. An. 5, 2, 3, and πιμπράω, part. ἐμπιπρῶν Polyb. 1, 53; -πιπρᾶν Plut. Coriol. 26: **imp.** ἐν-επίμπρην Thuc. 6, 94; Xen. Hell. 6, 5, 32; Dem. 18, 169, ἀντ- εν- Her. 5, 102, ἐπίμπρων, -πρας Eur. Ion 1293, ἐν-επίμπρ- Xen. Hell. 6, 5, 22, περι- Cyn. 10, 17, κατ- Dio Cass. 36, 21, rarely πρήθω, **imp.** ἐν-έπρηθον Il. 9, 589: **fut.** πρήσω Aesch. Sept. 434, ἐμ- Il. 9, 242; Thuc. 6, 64; Pl. Rep. 471: **aor.** ἔπρησα Od. 2, 427; Eur. Andr. 390 (-εσα see below); Pseudo-Callisth. 2, 2, ἐν- Il. 22, 374; Ar. Nub. 399; Her. 8, 35; Thuc. 1, 30, πρῆσα Il. 16, 350; πρῆσαι Soph. Ant. 201, ὑπο- Her. 2, 107: **p.** late πέπρηκα, ἐμ- Alciphr. 1, 32, κατα- Dio Cass. 59, 16, ὑπο- (Hippocr.) Epist. 9, 370 (Lit.): **p. p.** πέπρημαι, imper. πέπρησο Com. Fr. (Pher.) 2, 287; πεπρημένης, ἐμ- Ar. Vesp. 36; πεπρῆσθαι, ἐμ- Lys. 322; Her. 5, 105, and πέπρησμαι Ael. H. A. 2, 17; πεπρησμένος, ἐμ- Her. 8, 144; Aristot. Prob. 12, 3, 3; Arr. An. 4, 24, 6; Paus. 2, 5, 4: **aor.** always ἐπρήσθην Com. Fr. (Amph.) 3, 313; Hippocr. 7, 324 (Lit.), ἐν- Her. 5, 102. 6, 25; Xen. Hell. 4, 5, 4; Dem. 24, 136; ἐμ-πρησθείη Pl. Gorg. 469; ἐμ-πρησθῆναι Her. 8, 55; πρησθείς Q. Sm. 14, 416, ἐμ- Thuc. 4, 29; Isocr. 4, 156: **fut.** πρησθήσομαι V. T. Num. 5, 27: **3 fut.** πεπρήσομαι, ἐμ- Her. 6, 9 (Mss. M P K, Gaisf. Bekk. Dind. Stein): and as **pass. fut. mid.** πρήσομαι, ἐμ- Her. 6, 9 quoted (Mss. S c d, Ald. Matth.); Paus. 4, 7, 4, Poet. ἐνι- Q. Sm. 1, 494. **Mid.** πίμπραται Aretae. 61 (ed. Oxon.); Nic. Alex. 345, πιμπρᾷ Theod. Prod. 2, 300: **imp.** ἐπίμπρατο Dio. Hal. C. Verb. 18: **fut.** ἐμπρήσομαι as pass. see above: **aor.** ἐπρήσαντο, ἐμ- Q. Sm. 5, 485, missed by Lexicogr. Mss. and editors are much divided between πέπρησμαι and πέπρημαι. Photius called the latter form Attic; and Bekk. Dind. Bergk edit with Ms. R. ἐμπεπρημένης Ar. Vesp. 36, Brunck, Hirsch. Richter with Ms. N. ἐμπεπρησμ-. Imper. πίμπρη for -πρᾰθι, Eur. Ion 974. Fr. 688 (Dind.) For the subj. form, unusual especially in Attic, ὑποπίμπρησι introduced by Brunck, Ar. Lys. 348, Reisig would read indic. ὑποπίμπρησι, and change the conjunction ἤν into εἰ; but Bekk. Dind. &c. retain ἤν and of course subj. -ησι: see πίπτησι Com. Fr. (Plato) 2, 665. The marvel is lessened by neither being in trimeter. The **aor.** ἔπρεσε Hes. Th. 856, points seemingly to πρέω, so ἔπρεε (some Mss.) which Herm. approves. Goettling says "ἔπρεσε for ἔπρησε in iis Aeolicae dialecti exemplis habendum esse videtur, in quibus η breve est, ut τυπτόμενη." The form πρήθω we have seen only in **imp.** ἐν-έπρηθον Il. 9, 589 quoted. In good prose the *simple* verb scarcely occurs.

Πῑνύσκω *To make wise,* mostly Epic, -ύσκει Callim. Dian. 152; subj. -ύσκῃ Simon. C. 12 (Bergk); imper. πινύσκετε Aesch. Pers.

830, and πινύσσω Stob. (Naumach.) 74, 7, ἀ-πιν- Il. 15, 10: **imp.** ἐπίνυσσεν Il. 14, 249: **p. p.** (πινύω, πνύω) πέπνῡμαι Il. 24, 377 (referred also to πνέω); as also imper. πέπνῠο Theogn. 29 (Bergk), -ῠσο (Vulg.); inf. πεπνῦσθαι Il. 23, 440; πεπνῡμένος 13, 254; Od. 15, 86; Stob. (Naumach.) 74, 7: **plp.** πέπνῦσο Od. 23, 210: **aor.** late ἐπινύσθην Pythag. Procl. in Tim. 5, 291. **Vb.** πῐνῠτός Od. 4, 211.

Πίνω *To drink* (πίω, πόω), Il. 5, 341; Solon 38; Eur. Alc. 757; Ar. Eccl. 135; Her. 2, 78; Thuc. 7, 84; Pl. Conv. 212; imper. πινόντων Od. 1, 340; Epic inf. πινέμεναι Il. 4, 346, -έμεν Od. 7, 220; Hes. Op. 592: **imp.** ἔπῖνον Od. 14, 112; Theogn. 959; Hipponax 39; Aesch. Fr. 123 (D.); Ar. Ach. 141; Her. 2, 173; Antiph. 5, 23. 28; Thuc. 4, 26; Lys. 3, 11, πῖνον Od. 5, 94, iter. πίνεσκον Il. 16, 226: **fut.** πῐομαι Il. 13, 493; Theogn. 962; Pind. Ol. 6, 86; Soph. O. C. 622; Ar. Fr. 294, and πῐομ- Ion 2, 10 (Bergk); Com. Fr. (Plat.) 2, 668, ἐκ-πῐομ- 2, 616. (Amips.) 2, 710 see below, πῐοῦμαι (disapproved by Athen. 10, 446) rare in *classic* authors, Xen. Conv. 4, 7 (Dind. Saupp. -εσθε others); Hippocr. 2, 449 (K.); Aristot. Rhet. 1, 11, 10 (Bekk.); Ael. V. H. 12, 49: **p.** πέπωκα Hipponax 73 (B.); Aesch. Sept. 821; Soph. Tr. 1056; Ar. Eccl. 948; Her. 4, 160; Pl. Phaed. 117: **p. p.** πέπομαι Theogn. 477, ἐκ- Od. 22, 56; Her. 4, 199, προ- Dem. 3, 22: **aor.** ἐπόθην Hippocr. 1, 50. 195 (K.); Plut. Mor. 725, ἐκ- Aesch. Ch. 66, κατα- Pl. Critias 111; Luc. V. H. 1, 33: **fut.** ποθήσομαι, κατα- Ar. Vesp. 1502; Diod. Sic. 16, 81, ἐκ- Plut. Mor. 240: **2 aor. act.** ἔπῐον Od. 15, 373; Soph. O. R. 1401; Com. Fr. (Pher.) 2, 282; Hippocr. 5, 206; Antiph. 6, 15; Xen. Hell. 2, 3, 56, πῐον Il. 9, 177. 22, 2. Od. 3, 342 and always (Bekk.) except Od. 15, 373 quoted; πίω Od. 11, 96, πίῃς Ar. Plut. 645, -ῃσθα Il. 6, 260, πίῃ Od. 10, 328; Aesch. Sept. 736, -ίωσι Pl. Prot. 347; πίοιμι Od. 10, 316; Com. Fr. 3, 11; inf. πῐεῖν (Il. 8, 189). Od. 8, 70; Eur. Cycl. 412; Ar. Eq. 83; Antiph. 6, 15; Thuc. 7, 84; Pl. Rep. 406, Poet. and Ion. πιέειν Il. 7, 481. Od. 11, 232; Hes. Sc. 252; Theocr. 10, 54 (Mein.); Her. 6, 84 (Bekk. Dind. -εῖν Bred. Dietsch, Stein, Abicht, with 4, 172 Bekk. Dind. &c.), Epic πῐέμεν Od. 15, 378; but πῑέμεν in arsi, Il. 16, 825. Od. 16, 143. 18, 3, so ἔπῖον Anacreont. 5, 5 (Vulg. Bergk 2 ed., ἔπῖνον Br. Bergk 3 ed.), πῖεν Stesich. 7 (B. 2 ed. πῖνεν 3 ed.) **Mid.** rare πίνομαι, -ώμεθα Com. Fr. (Herm.) 2, 389; so πίνεο Nic. Ther. 912; δια-πινομένη Hedyl. in Athen. 11, 486: **fut.** πίομαι see above. **Pass.** πίνομαι, Epic part. -ομένοιο Od. 20, 312, Ionic πινεύμενος if correct, Hippocr. 2, 38 (Lit.): **imp.** πίνετο Od. 9, 45. **Vb.** πιστός Aesch. Pr. 480, ποτός Ag. 1408, ποτέος Pl. Leg. 674, μετα- Hippocr. 1, 323 (Erm.)

πίομαι Pind. Ol. 6, 86; Ibyc. 17 (B.); Theogn. 962, is called by some a pres. unnecessarily we think. ι is long in pres. and imp. except late πῐνει Theod. Prodr. 3, 38, long and short in fut. πίομαι Il. Soph. Ar. quoted, πῐομαι Ion 2, 10 (Bergk, πιέτω Mein.); Pl. Com. Fr. &c. quoted; Theocr. 7, 69; Anth. (Meleag.) 5, 137. (Rufin.) 5, 44, called by some pass. ἐμ-πῐομ- Theogn. 1129. ἔπιον has ι long in arsi only, inf. πῑέμεν Il. 6, 825. Od. 18, 3, see above, but πῐέμεν Od. 15, 378, πῐέειν Il. 4, 263 &c. πιέναι Hippocr. 3, 555 (Vulg. Kühn, seems to be a mutilation of ὑπιέναι now the accepted reading 5, 218 Mss. C H K, Lit., Ermerins); πιέουσα 5, 386 (Lit.), but πιοῦσα Il. 24, 102, κατα- Hippocr. 5, 382; imper. πίε (not πῖε) usually Poet. Od. 9, 347; Com. Fr. (Menand.) 4, 113; Luc. D. Mort. 13, 6, ἐκ- Eur. Cycl. 563, for which Attic Poets, especially Comic, have πῖθι Ar. Vesp. 1489; Com. Fr. (Cratin.) 2, 96. (Amips.) 2, 708. (Antiph.) 3, 88. (Men.) 4, 90. (Diph.) 4, 384; also Luc. Lex. 20, ἔκ-πῖθι Eur. Cycl. 570, but ἔκπιε 563; πίῃσθα Epic 2 sing. subj. 2 aor. act. Il. 6, 260; inf. πὶν or πῖν (Mss. πεὶν) for πιεῖν Anth. 11, 140. The fut. form in ου, πιοῦμαι, is not only rare in early writers, but has often, in good recensions of the later, given way to πίομαι, κατα- Luc. Salt. 27. D. Mar. 14; κατα- πιοῦνται Plut. Alcib. 15. πιούμενος Mor. 371, but πιόμ- Mar. 38. The full form πίεσαι 2 sing. of πίομαι, occurs late V. T. Ezec. 23, 34. N. T. Luc. 17, 8. πῶθι, σύμ-πωθι an Aeol. imper. Etym. M. 698, 53 (Ahr. Aeol. Dial. 140.)

Πιπίσκω *To give to drink* (πίω), Hippocr. 7, 382. 8, 128 (Lit.); Luc. Lex. 20: fut. πίσω Pind. I. 6, 74; Com. Fr. (Eup.) 2, 471: aor. ἔπῖσα Hippocr. 8, 118. 182 (Lit.), ἐν- Pind. Fr. 88 (Bergk): aor. pass. ἐμ-πισθέν Nic. Ther. 624. Mid. late, aor. (ἐπῑσάμην), ἐμ-πίσαιο Nic. Ther. 573. 877. Al. 320; imper. ἐμ-πίσεο Nic. Alex. 277, in imitation of the old Epic 1 aor. imper. ὄρσεο &c.

Πίπλημι *To fill*, part. πιπλάς Aesch. Ch. 360, see πίμπλημι.

Πίπλω *To fill*, imp. ἔπιπλον rare, even doubtful Hes. Sc. 291.

Πιπράσκω *To sell* (περάω, πράω), rare and perhaps late in pres. act. (Luc.) Asin. 32; (Hippocr.) Epist. 9, 362 (Vulg. Lit.), but Ionic πιπρήσκω 3, 593 (Mss. Erm.); Callim. Fr. 85 (Maneth. 6, 727): imp. ἐπίπρασκον Plut. Mor. 178: fut. περάσω, and aor. ἐπέρᾱσα are Epic (and referred to περάω, πέρνημι), for which the Attics use ἀποδώσομαι, ἀπεδόμην: p. πέπρᾱκα Pseud.-Anacr. 14, 11 (Bergk); Com. Fr. (Alex.) 3, 450; Isae. 7, 31; Dinarch. 1, 71; Aeschin. 1, 29; Dem. 37, 19, -ακώς 8, 61. 17, 13: plp. ἐπεπρά-κειν 18, 23. 33, 25, and πεπρᾱκὼς ἦν 19, 16: p. p. πέπρᾱμαι Soph. Ph. 978; πεπρᾶσθαι Ar. Ach. 734; Andoc. 1, 73; Lys. 30, 27;

πεπρᾱμένος Aesch. Ch. 132 (Casaub. Dind. Herm.); Isae. 6, 43; Aeschin. 3, 94; (Dem.) 42, 6, Ionic -ημαι, πεπρῆσθαι Her. 2, 56; Buttmann would read part. πεπρημένος Il. 21, 58, for πεπερημ- (Wolf, Bekk. Dind. La R.): **plp.** ἐπέπρᾱτο Ar. Ach. 522; Paus. 2, 8, 3: **aor.** ἐπράθην Solon 4, 25; Aesch. Ch. 915; Thuc. 6, 95; Isae. 6, 34; -ᾱθείη Lys. 4, 13; -αθῆναι Isae. 2, 28; Aristot. Polit. 1, 6, 5; -ᾱθείς Soph. Tr. 252; Pl. Leg. 850; Dem. 38, 7, Ionic ἐπρήθην Her. 2, 56; -θείη 1, 196; πρηθείς 2, 54; πρηθῆναι 1, 156: **fut.** πραθήσομαι rare and unattic, Aristot. Fr. 411; Artemid. Onir. 49, 50; Athen. (Sopat.) 4, 160; Harpocr. Dinarch. Fr. 18, 8; Joseph. Ant. 9, 1, 4: **3 fut.** πεπρᾱ́σομαι Ar. Vesp. 179; Anth. 5, 178; Xen. An. 7, 1, 36. **Vb.** πρατός Soph. Tr. 276, -έος Pl. Leg. 849. The **pres. pass.** is *classical*, πιπρᾱ́σκεται Lys. 18, 20; Pl. Phaed. 69.

Πίπτω *To fall* (πέτω, πτόω), Il. 11, 69; Alcm. 30; Aesch. Supp. 90; Soph. Tr. 62; Ar. Av. 498; Her. 5, 112; Xen. Cyr. 1, 4, 8: **imp.** ἔπιπτον Il. 17, 361; Her. 7, 223; Xen. Hell. 4, 3, 23, πῖπτον Il. 23, 120; Hes. Fr. 4; Aesch. Pers. 506 (trimet.), iter. πίπτεσκον, συμ- Emped. 255 (Stein): **fut.** πεσοῦμαι Aesch. Ch. 971; Soph. El. 399; Com. Fr. (Antiph.) 3, 30; Pl. Euth. 14, προσ- Thuc. 5, 9, ἐμ- Pl. Rep. 616, Ionic πεσέομαι Il. 11, 824; Her. 7, 168, but -εῖται 5, 92 (Orac.), πεσσέομ- Or. Sib. 10, 244, late πέσομαι Or. Sib. 3, 83. 4, 99. 12, 345, πέσσ- 239: **1 aor.** ἔπεσα see below: **p.** πέπτωκα Aesch. Eum. 147; Eur. Or. 88; Ar. Ran. 970; Her. 6, 12; Pl. Phil. 22; πεπτωκώς Soph. O. R. 146; Eur. Hipp. 718; Ar. Pax 904; Thuc. 7, 29; Pl. Rep. 604, πεπτώς Soph. Aj. 828, see below, and later πέπτηκα Anth. (Antip.) 7, 427, for which Epic πεπτηώς Od. 14, 354; Anth. 7, 24, and -εώς Il. 21, 503, see below: **plp.** πεπτώκειν Thuc. 1, 89 (Bekk. Popp. Krüg.), ἐπεπτ- (Vulg. Stahl), ἀνα-πεπτ- Dem. 21, 163 (Bekk. B. Saupp.), ἀνεπεπτ- (Dind.); so Her. ἐπεπτώκεε 9, 62, ἐν- επ- 8, 38: late **1 aor. pass.** πτωθείς Anth. 1, 109: **2 aor.** ἔπεσον Il. 13, 178; Pind. Ol. 12, 10; Soph. Aj. 621; Eur. Hipp. 241; Com. Fr. (Anon.) 4, 688; Her. 5, 64; Thuc. 2, 89; Xen. An. 6, 4, 9, πέσον Il. 14, 460; Hes. Sc. 365; Pind. N. 7, 31; Aesch. Pers. 313 (trimet.); Soph. Ant. 134 (chor.); subj. πέσῃς Ar. Nub. 703, πέσῃ Il. 19, 110; Pl. Phaedr. 248, -ῃσι Il. 15, 624, -ωμεν Pind. I. 8, 7; -σοιμι Soph. Ant. 240, πέσοι Il. 13, 289; πεσών Il. 3, 289; Thuc. 5, 10; πεσεῖν Soph. El. 398, -έειν Il. 6, 82, Aeol. and Dor. ἔπετον Alcae. Fr. 60 (Bergk), πέτον, ἐμ- Pind. P. 8, 81, κάπετον for κατ-έπετ- Ol. 8, 38; Dor. part. πετοῖσαι for πεσοῦσ- Ol. 7, 69: **1 aor.** ἔπεσα perhaps late, Orph. Arg. 523, see below: **1 aor. mid.** late also and rare, διεξ-επέσαντο Polyaen. 4, 2, 14. 7, 48 (Vulg. -επαίσ- Koraës, Woelffl.). The Schol. on Ar. Av.

840, says the 1 aor. was not used; and in reference to *classic* writers he is perhaps right. It occurs however in Orph. ἐν δ' ἔπεσαν Arg. 523, unless a slip for ἔπεσον, and often in writers of the Alexandrine and Byzantine periods, ἔπεσαν V. T. Jud. 12, 6. 2 Reg. 11, 17. N. T. Rev. 1, 17; Phoebam. Rhet. p. 505, ἀντ- Polyb. 3, 19 (Mss. Vulg. Bekk. Hultsch, -εσον v. r. Dind.), ἀν- Apocr. Tob. 2, 1 &c. often doubtful κατ-παρ-επέσαμεν Ach. Tat. 3, 17. 19 (Vulg. -ομεν Mss. V M F. Jacobs); Malalas &c. &c. in which occur also such forms as ἔφυγαν, εὗραν, εἵλατο, ἦλθαν, ἐφάγαμεν &c. In some Mss. and editions of classic authors a trace of ἔπεσα now and then occurs, but so seldom as to induce scholars even on that ground to reject it for the usual form ἔπεσον. For instance, ἐν-επέσαμεν Aeschin. 2, 176 (some Mss.) has been altered from other Mss. to -έσομεν (Bekk. B. Saupp.); πέσειε Eur. Alc. 463, to πέσοι (Mss.), and προσ-έπεσα Tr. 292 (Mss. A B) to προσ-έπεσον Mss. Seidl. Dind. Kirchh. &c. In the latter case the transcriber, though intending -ον, might give it the appearance of -α merely by drawing the ν too near the ο. Buttmann however defends the 1 aor. as a genuine form, and compares it with ἔχεσα, ἔχεσον. Usage, we think, is against this: for Euripides has κατ-έπεσες Cycl. 671, where -έπεσας might have stood, ἐπ-έπεσον Andr. 1042, not -έπεσαν, πέσοιμ' Hec. 927, not πέσαιμ', πέσοι, not -σαι Alc. 1101. Hel. 1082. From πέπτηκα the Epic Poets have, according to Buttmann, part. πεπτηώς Od. 14, 354, -ηυῖα Ap. Rh. 2, 535, ποτι- Od. 13, 98, κατα- Hes. Sc. 265, -ηῶτος Ap. Rh. 3, 321, and -ηότος 4, 1298; Hippocr. 8, 146, and πεπτεώς, -εῶτος Il. 21, 503 (-εότος Vind. Vulg.), and from πεπτωκώς the Attics have πεπτώς, -ῶτος Soph. Aj. 828. Ant. 697. πίπτησι Epic form of subj. Plat. Com. Fr. 2, 665 (anapaest.) πεσέειν Ionic for πεσεῖν Il. 6, 307. πέσεται a late fut. form for πεσεῖται Or. Sib. 4, 82 &c. πετοῖσαι Dor. for πεσοῦσαι Pind. Ol. 7, 69, πετόντεσσι for πεσοῦσι Pyth. 5, 50 (Bergk 3 ed.)

Πιτνέω, see πίτνω.

Πίτνημι *To spread, open,* Epic imper. πίτνᾰτε Anth. 10, 6; part. πιτνάς Od. 11, 392; inf. -νάμεν, ἀνα- Pind. Ol. 6, 27: imp. πίτνᾱ (πιτνάω) Il. 21, 7, πίτναν for ἐπίτνᾰσαν, Pind. N. 5, 11. Mid. πίτνατο Anth. 7, 711, πίτναντο Il. 22, 402, ἐπίτναντο Eur. Elec. 713 (chor.)

Πίτνω, -έω *To fall* (πίπτω), Poet. Eur. Supp. 285, πίτνεις Heracl. 78, -νει Alcm. 6; Aesch. Eum. 515 (Elms. Herm. Dind.); Eur. Hec. 23 (Dind., -νεῖ Herm.), -νεῖ Pind. P. 8, 93; Anth. 10, 6, πίτνομεν, προσ- Soph. O. C. 1754; πίτνων Soph. Aj. 185, -νῶν (Herm.); πίτνειν O. C. 1740, -νεῖν (Herm.): imp. ἔπιτνον perhaps trans. *made fall, smoothed,* ἀλωήν Hes. Sc. 291;

but intrans. as **aor.** *fall*, Soph. O. C. 1732: as **aorist**, ἔπιτνε Soph. O. C. 1732. Thus Schol. Il. 16, 827, Elms. Dind. Ellendt &c., while Etym. Mag. Buttm. Matth. Hermann *formerly* would write πιτνέω, -ῶ as pres. and ἔπιτνον as **2 aorist**, after the analogy of δουπέω, ἔδουπον, στυγέω, ἔστυγον &c. The Mss. vary between πίτνω and πιτνέω: and most editions, especially the older, of the Tragedians have πιτνῶ circumflex. But since Elmsley's able defence of πίτνω Eur. Heracl. 77. Med. 55. Soph. O. C. 1732, several of our best scholars have shewn a decided leaning to his views, and edited πίτνω, πίτνεις, -ει &c. Thus Hermann *now* reads always in Aeschylus πίτνω, -νει, and πίτνων **pres.** pt. for πιτνών **aor.** Sept. 740. Ch. 35; so in Soph. (2. 3 ed.)—Linwood by an oversight gives Hermann's old reading—and πίτνω for -νῶ Eur. Hel. 910, πίτνει for -νεῖ Phoen. 1420. Or. 1542 &c., and Dindorf accents πίτνει, πίτνων Pind. P. 8, 93. N. 5, 42, for πιτνεῖ, πιτνῶν retained by Boeckh, Bergk, and Schneidewin: **imp.** ἔπιτνεν Ol. 2, 23 (Dissen, Christ), -ίτνει (Beck, Bergk). In fact, Dind. in no instance admits πιτνέω -ῶ &c. The supporters of πιτνέω have been challenged to produce a form proving its existence independent of the accent. They can do this, for προσπιτνοῦμεν Soph. O. C. 1754, has Ms. authority. Still this is not decisive, because it is opposed by προσπίτνομεν on at least equal authority, and it is not necessary for the metre; and imper. προσπίτνει, προπιτ- (Elms.), also Ms. reading Eur. Her. 619, is opposed by προσπεσὼν in Ms. Florr., and προσπιτνῶν in the Aldine, which last Elmsley by mere change of accent altered to προσπίτνων, adopted by L. Dind. Pflugk, W. Dind. Nauck &c. After all, there seems to be wisdom in Buttmann's caution in "not rejecting the supposition that πίτνω and πιτνέω may have existed together like βυνέω and βύνω, δυνέω and δύνω, without ἔπιτνον being therefore necessarily an imperfect; ἔκλυον from κλύω is used by the same Tragedians as an aorist." The form πιτνῶντα Pind. I. 2, 26 (Vulg.) has been displaced by πίτνοντα (Bergk, Hart. Momms.), πιτνόντα (Boeckh, Schn.)—Lyric and Tragic.

Πῐφαύσκω *To shew, say* (φάω, φάσκω), Poet. Aesch. Eum. 620; Opp. Hal. 2, 213, -σκει Aretae. 411; -σκων Il. 10, 502; Aesch. Ag. 23; -σκειν Hom. H. Merc. 540, Epic -σκέμεν Od. 11, 442: **imp.** πίφαυσκον Od. 12, 165, -σκε Il. 10, 478, -σκον 10, 202. **Mid.** πιφαύσκομαι Od. 21, 305, -σκεαι Il. 16, 12; Hes. Th. 655, -σκεται Il. 15, 97; imper. -σκεο 21, 99; -σκόμενος 12, 280, and πιφάσκομαι Hes. Th. 655 (Goettl.), which Muetzell and Dindorf think a mistake for πιφαύσκ-: **imp.** πιφαύσκετο Ap. Rh. 3, 606. Nonnus has πιφάσκων 18, 34 (Vulg. Graefe), but -αύσκων (Koechly):

so πιφαύσκω 42, 272 (Vulg. Graefe, Koechly): **imp.** πίφασκε Or. Sib. 1, 6. In the **act.** Homer uses ῑ, Il. 10, 478. 502. Od. 11, 442. 12, 165 &c., in the **mid.** always ῐ; in Aesch. Eum. 620. Ag. 23 &c. and in the later poets, ῐ.

Πίω, see πίνω.

Πλάζω *To cause to wander*, Poet. Il. 2, 132; Anth. 7, 365; but (Hippocr.) Epist. 9, 380 (Lit.); -άζων Il. 17, 751, *simple* unaugm. by Hom.: **imp.** πλάζε Il. 21, 269. Od. 2, 396, προσ-έπλ- 11, 583: **fut.** (πλάγξω): **aor.** πλάγξα Od. 24, 307, but παρ-έπλαγξα 9, 81; Pind. Ol. 7, 31; πλάγξαις in tmesi Opp. Cyn. 1, 511, πλάγξειεν, ἀπο- Ap. Rh. 1, 1220; πλάγξας, περι- Od. 19, 187. **Pass.** πλάζομαι *am driven from the right course, wander*, Il. 10, 91; Emped. 251; Mosch. 2, 148; Ap. Rh. 2, 542; late prose, Plut. Lucull. 24; -ζοιτο Mar. 37; -ζεσθαι Od. 16, 151; Ap. Rh. 3, 1120; Plut. Mor. 896; -ζόμενος Od. 16, 64; Tyrt. 10, 5 (Bergk); Soph. Aj. 886; Ionic and late prose Her. 2, 116; Tim. Locr. 97; Luc. Fugit. 10; Polyb. 34, 10, 3, Dor. πλασδ- Mosch. 3, 24 (Mein.): **imp.** πλάζετο Od. 5, 389, ἐπλάζ- Emped. 245; Her. 2, 117; Plut. Mar. 36: with **fut. mid.** πλάγξομαι Od. 15, 312, ἐπι- Ap. Rh. 3, 1066 (Ms. L. Merkel): **aor.** πλάγξασθαι Ap. Rh. 3, 261 (Mss. L C. Merk.), ἐπι- 3, 1066 (Wellau.), see **fut.**: **aor. pass.** ἐπλάγχθην Aesch. Sept. 784, πλάγχθην Il. 11, 351. Od. 1, 2; Soph. O. C. 1231 (chor.), but ἀπ-επλάγχθην Il. 22, 291. Od. 15, 382; Hom. H. Ven. 254, παρ- Pind. N. 10, 6; Dio. Hal. 11, 13; πλαγχθείς Il. 14, 120; Pind. N. 7, 37. Eur. H. F. 1187. Or. 56. **Vb.** πλαγκτός Od. 21, 363; Aesch. Ag. 593. For **1 aor. mid.** πλάγξασθαι Ap. Rh. 3, 261 quoted, ἐπι- 1066, several Mss. favour the **fut.** -ξεσθαι especially in the latter passage. We should not however feel warranted, with some, to reject the **aorist** simply because "it occurs not in early Epic, nor because it depends on **imp.** ἔμελλον;" for though the **fut.** or **pres.** be the usual construction, Homer has one instance of **aor.** without a various reading, ἔμελλον ἐπαμῦναι Il. 18, 98; so Antiph. ἔμελλε καταστῆσαι 1, 14; Isae. -καταλιπεῖν 9, 13. Homer, we think, never augments the *simple* form. We have not observed this verb simple or comp. in Comedy, nor in classic Attic prose.

Πλάθω, see πελάω.

Πλᾰνάω *To cause to wander*, Aesch. Pr. 573; Soph. O. C. 316; Aristot. Rhet. 3, 14, 6; Dem. 19, 335; -νᾶν Her. 4, 128; Pl. Leg. 655, reg. in **act.**: **imp.** ἐπλᾰνα Com. Fr. (Theogn.) 4, 550; Pl. Prot. 356: **fut.** -ήσω Babr. 1, 14; N. T. Matth. 24, 5: **aor.** ἐπλᾰνησα Pseud.-Callisth. 1, 10; πλανήσῃ Mosch. 1, 25; πλανήσας Batr. 96: **p.** πεπλανηκώς Pl. Leg. 655; Anth. 11, 347.

Mid. and **pass.** πλανάομαι *to wander*, Archil. 56, 5; Aesch. Pr. 473; Ar. Av. 44; Pl. Phaed. 79, -ῶνται Rep. 586, Epic -όωνται Il. 23, 321, Ion. πλανέομαι, -έονται Her. 2, 41 (Bekk. Dind. -ῶνται Stein); opt. πλανῷντο Theocr. 9, 4; -ᾶσθαι Soph. O. C. 304; -ώμενος Simon. Am. 7, 14; Aesch. Pr. 275; Soph. O. C. 347; Ar. Pax 828; Her. 2, 115; Antiph. 2, β, 5; Thuc. 2, 4: **imp.** ἐπλανᾶτο Emped. 246; Thuc. 2, 102: **fut.** πλανήσομαι Pl. Hipp. min. 376; Luc. Peregr. 16: and later in same sense **fut. pass.** πλανηθήσομαι Dio. Hal. in Dem. 9; Luc. V. H. 2, 27: **aor.** rare ἐπλανησάμην, ἐπ- Democr. p. 238 (Mull.): **p.** πεπλάνημαι Aesch. Pr. 565; Pl. Polit. 263; -ημένος Her. 7, 16; Thuc. 8, 105; -ῆσθαι Her. 7, 16: **plp.** ἐπεπλάνητο App. Hannib. 46: **aor.** ἐπλανήθην Thuc. 7, 44; Isocr. 4, 28. 12, 89; πλανηθῇς Com. Fr. (Phil.) 4, 67, Dor. -āθῇς Theocr. 15, 67; -ηθείη Hippocr. 1, 215 (Erm.); -ηθείς Eur. Hel. 598; Hippocr. 2, 286 (Lit.); Lys. 12, 97, Dor. -āθείς Pind. N. 8, 4: **fut.** -ηθήσομαι see above. **Vb.** πλανητός Pl. Rep. 479, -ητέος Xen. Lac. 9, 5.

Πλάσσω *To form*, -σσων Soph. Aj. 148; -σσειν Her. 2, 73, Attic -ττω Pl. Rep. 420; Isae. 11, 22; Dem. 38, 9; Com. Fr. (Men.) 4, 103; -ττειν Isocr. 15, 138: **imp.** ἔπλαττον Ar. Nub. 879; Pl. Rep. 374: **fut.** πλάσω, ἀνα- Hippocr. 4, 346: **aor.** ἔπλασα Com. Fr. (Men.) 4, 231; Aeschin. 2, 153; Aristot. Part. Anim. 2, 12; in tmesi Her. 2, 70, ἔπλασσα Theocr. 24, 107, πλάσσα Hes. Op. 70; πλάσῃ (Poet in) Lycurg. 132; opt. πλάσαι Com. Fr. (Phil.) 4, 22; πλάσας Simon. Am. 7, 21; Her. 2, 47; Pl. Rep. 588; πλάσαι Ar. Vesp. 926: **p.** late πέπλακα Dio. Hal. de Thuc. 41; Dio Cass. 67, 7; Diod. Sic. 15, 11; Christ. Pat. 575: **p. p.** πέπλασμαι Aesch. Pr. 1030; Pratin. 1, 14 (B.); Isae. 7, 2. 8, 13; πεπλάσθω Pl. Leg. 588: **aor.** ἐπλάσθην, -θείς Eur. Fr. inc. 116 (D.); Lys. 12, 48; Pl. Rep. 377: **fut.** πλασθήσεται, δια- Galen 4, 619. **Mid.** πλάττομαι *counterfeit* &c. Aristot. Rhet. 2, 4, 27; Dem. 19, 154. 215: **imp.** ἐπλαττ- Dem. 18, 10. 231: **fut.** πλάσομαι Alciphr. 1, 37, παρα- Sext. Emp. 462, 23: **aor.** ἐπλασάμην Aeschin. 2, 147; in tmesi Her. 2, 85; -σάμενος Thuc. 6, 58; Isocr. 9, 21; Pl. Polit. 297; -άσασθαι Leg. 800; Lys. 8, 13. 19, 60: and as **mid. p.** πέπλασται Dem. 45, 68; Brut. Epist. 32. **Vb.** πλαστός Hes. Th. 513, -έον late, Geop. 6, 2, 4.

Πλείω, see πλέω.

Πλέκω *To plait*, Pind. Ol. 6, 86; Aesch. Ch. 220; Eur. An. 66; Hippocr. 6, 492 (Lit.); Pl. Hipp. Min. 369, 3 pl. Dor. πλέκοντι, ἀνα- Pind. Ol. 2, 74; πλέκῃ Ar. Thesm. 400; -κειν Ar. Vesp. 644; -κων Pl. Conv. 203: **imp.** ἔπλεκε Eur. Ion 826: **fut.** πλέξω Anth. 5, 147. 12, 165: **aor.** ἔπλεξα Il. 14, 176; Eur. Ion 1280, δι- Pl. Tim. 78; inf. πλέξαι Ar. Thesm. 458; Pl.

Hipp. Min. 368; -ξας Pl. Tim. 77, δια- Her. 5, 92, Dor. -πλέξαις Pind. P. 12, 8: p. πέπλεχα, ἐμ- Hippocr. 1, 519, but διαπέπλοχα 518 (K.): p. p. πέπλεγμαι, -εκται Pl. Theaet. 202, συμ- Eur. Bacc. 800; inf. πεπλέχθαι Pl. Soph. 240; πεπλεγμένος Eur. An. 995; Her. 7, 72; Aristot. Pt. An. 4, 9, 9, ἐμ- Soph. O. R. 1264: 1 aor. ἐπλέχθην, πλεχθείς Aesch. Eum. 259; Pl. Polit. 283, Poet. πλέχθην, περι- Od. 23, 33; περι-πλεχθείς 14, 313: fut. πλεχθήσομαι, ἐμ- Aesch. Pr. 1079: 2 aor. ἐπλᾰκην (Schol. Ar. Plut. 1082), κατ- Hippocr. 9, 194; συμ-πλακῇ Dem. 2, 21; συμ-πλᾰκείς Soph. Fr. 548; Ar. Ach. 704; Her. 8. 84; Pl. Theaet. 202, ἐμ- Eur. Hipp. 1236; πλακῆναι, περι- Luc. D. Mer. 4, 2: fut. late πλακήσεται, συμ- Aristot. Topic. 2, 7, 1; Theon. Rhet. 5, 209, περι- Pseudo-Callisth. 3, 21, ἐπι- Galen 6, 873. **Mid.** πλέκονται, συμ- Pl. Conv. 191; Aristot. Topic. 2, 7, 1, περι- Pseudo-Callisth. 3, 21; Cebet. Tab. 6, 2: imp. ἐπλέκετο, συν- Pl. Conv. 191, περι- Pseudo-Callisth. 3, 20. 21: fut. πλέξομαι Stob. (Perict.) 85, 19: aor. ἐπλεξάμην Philostr. Apoll. 333; πλέξηται Opp. Hal. 2, 298, -ωνται Paus. 8, 22, 4; -ξαιο Opp. Hal. 3, 341; -άμενος Od. 10, 168; Ar. Lys. 790 (chor.); Aristot. H. An. 5, 27, 4; Ion. and late prose, Her. 2, 28; Paus. 7, 5, 3; Galen 3, 4; πλέξασθαι Ap. Rh. 3, 47. Vb. πλεκτός Aesch. Pr. 709. πέπλεχα ὁ κοινός, καὶ πέπλοχα ὁ Ἀττικός (old Gramm.) 2 aor. ἐπλάκην has often the *v. r.* ἐπλέκην, and Bekker and Hultsch edit συν-επλέκησαν Polyb. 3, 73 (Ms. A), -άκησαν (Ms. C. Vulg. L. Dind.); ξυμπλεκείς v. r. Pl. Tim. 83. The mid. seems to be mostly poetic, Ion. and late prose.

Πλέω *To sail*, Od. 9, 62; Pind. Fr. 203, Aesch. Pers. 381; Soph. Ph. 383; Ar. Av. 1459; Her. 2, 60; Thuc. 4, 28; Pl. Gorg. 467, Ionic πλείω Od. 15, 34. 16, 368: imp. ἔπλεον Il. 3, 444, πλέον Od. 7, 267, ἔπλεε Il. 14, 251; Her. 4, 43, Attic -λει Aesch. Ag. 841; Soph. Ph. 572; Xen. Hell. 3, 4, 3, συν- Antiph. 5, 20, ἐπλέομεν 5, 20, 3 pl. ἔπλεον Her. 1, 164; Thuc. 6, 50; Isocr. 7, 80, ἀπ-έπλειον Od. 8, 501: fut. πλεύσομαι Od. 12, 25; Anth. 11, 162, 2; Her. 2, 29. 3, 135; Thuc. 6, 104; Xen. An. 5, 7, 8; Dem. 4, 44. 19, 250 (50, 49), ἀνα- Il. 11, 22, συμ- Eur. Hel. 1067, ἐσ- Thuc. 2, 89, ἀπο- 3, 75, ἐκ- 4, 27; Dem. 34, 9, and πλευσοῦμαι Theocr. 14, 55; Thuc. 1, 143. 8, 1; Xen. An. 5, 1, 10 (Popp. Krüg. -ομαι Dind. Saupp.); Dem. 35, 16. 56, 6 (Bekk.), ἐπεσ- Thuc. 4, 13, συμ- Isocr. 17, 19, συνεκ- Lys. 13, 25, κατα- Dem. 32, 11 (Bekk. -ομαι Dind. always); -σοίμην, εἰσ- Isocr. 17, 9: fut. act. πλεύσω (perhaps not Attic) *quoted* by Philem. Com. Fr. 4, 41; Anth. (Nicarch.) 11, 162. (Lucill.) 11, 245; Polyb. 2, 12, ἐκ- Ael. Fr. 87, παρα- D. Sic. 13, 54 (Bekk.), ἐκπερι- Arr. An. 6, 28, 6: aor.

ἔπλευσα Aesch. Ag. 691; Soph. Ph. 1038; Her. 2, 44; Thuc. 6, 90; Lys. 2, 57; Isocr. 15, 39; πλεύσας Pind. P. 4, 69: p. πέπλευκα Soph. Ph. 404; Eur. I. T. 1040; Com. Fr. (Phil.) 4, 60; Thuc. 8, 108; Dem. 56, 34: plp. ἐπεπλεύκειν, περι- Thuc. 6, 99: p. p. πέπλευσμαι, -ευσμένος Xen. Cyr. 6, 1, 16; Dem. 56, 12: aor. late ἐπλεύσθην Babr. 71, 3; Arr. An. 6, 28, 6; Dio Cass. 54, 1: fut. πλευσθήσεται, περι- Arr. An. 5, 26. Vb. πλευστέος Ar. Lys. 411; Dem. 4, 16, -έα Thuc. 6, 25. See πλώω.

Fut. act. πλεύσω seems to be late. ἐκπλεύσεις in some editions of Soph. Ph. 381, is merely an emendation of Brunck for the Mss. reading ἐκπλεύσῃς which is now admitted by scholars to be correct, notwithstanding Dawes' Canon regarding the construction of οὐ μή—an arbitrary canon certainly, and now little regarded; and καταπλεύσειν Dinarch. 3, 2 (Mss.) is, Bekker supposes, a mistake for aor. καταπλεῦσαι which he has accordingly edited, with the approval of our best scholars. Its solitariness creates suspicion; for not only the purer Attics, but the early writers of every class, have so cautiously avoided the use of the active form that, with this exception, we know not an authenticated instance. On the fut. mid. forms πλεύσομαι, -σοῦμαι &c. the best Mss. and editions vary and differ—always -ομαι, however, in Hom. and Her.—: but to what extent, in *Attic* writers, this difference is owing to the copyists, it is difficult to ascertain. Poppo says both forms are Thucydidean: L. Dind. however is expelling the contr. forms -σοῦμαι &c. from Xenophon, and W. Dind. has expelled them from his last edition of Demosthenes: Krüger and Bekker are more conservative. The Attics seem to have contracted only εε, εει of this verb: πλέεις, -εῖς, πλέει, -εῖ, ἔπλεε, -ει, but πλέω, πλέῃς, πλέομεν, ἐπλέομεν &c. πλέει Thuc. 4, 28 (Vulg.) is now corrected from Mss. πλεῖ (Bekk. Popp.), Krüger however still retains πλέει. πλέετε though well supported, Xen. An. 7, 6, 37 (2 Mss. Krüg.) is yielding to πλεῖτε (Dind. Bornem. Cobet, Sauppe), and ἔπλεεν Hell. 6, 2, 27, has been corrected ἔπλει by L. Dind. and Sauppe but retained by Kühner and Breitenbach; πλέων by synizesis Od. 1, 183. The contr. form never takes ν *ephelkust.* thus ἔπλεεν, but ἔπλει, never ἔπλειν. Hom. however has ᾔσκειν for ᾔσκεεν Il. 3, 388.

Πλήγνῡμι, see πλήσσω.

Πληθύω usu. intrans. *To be full, abound,* Aesch. Ch. 1057; Soph. Tr. 54; Her. 2, 20; Pl. Rep. 405; Polyb. 5, 44; D. Sic. 5, 25 (Bekk. -θω L. Dind.); Paus. 6, 25, 5, but if correct, trans. *fills* Soph. Fr. 643, συμ-πληθ- Her. 4, 48. 50: imp. ἐπλήθῡον Aesch. Pers. 421: aor. ἐπλήθυσα, subj. πληθύσῃ Pl. Tim. 83, but trans. in comp. *filled*, συν-επλήθυσε Longin. 23, 3; Dio Cass. 51, 17. **Mid.** πληθύομαι as act. -ύεσθαι Her. 2, 24. 93 (Vulg. Gaisf. Bekk.); and Aesch. Supp. 604 (Mss. Hart. &c.), but πληθύνεται (Wellau. Herm. Dind. *now*), thus avoiding the seemingly questionable **mid.** or **pass.** πληθύεται, and the lengthening of its υ. πληθύει, however, has ῡ in Opp. Cyn. 1, 461, and συμπληθύω is **act.** Her. 4, 48. 50, and thus, if correct, authorizing the **mid.** or **pass.** form; unless here too with Dind. should be substituted πληθύνω, which has sometimes an active meaning, and its penult always long. We say sometimes, for cases occur in which it assumes, in its turn, a neuter or reflex sense, Aristot. Meteor. 1, 14, 4. Gen. An. 2, 4, 12 (*v. r.* πληθύω); Theophr. C. P. 1, 19, 5 (-ύω Wimm.); Plut. Mor. 1005 (Vulg.); N. T. Act. 6, 1. These, to be sure, are easily amended by substituting the *kindred* verb, and in the first passage it is actually a *v. r.* But though uniformity be desirable, it is difficult and rather hazardous to confine words, especially if *akin*, exactly to their own *proper* limits. With them also affinity tends to reciprocity —an occasional interchange of duties. This alternation, therefore, may not always be owing to the mistakes or ignorance of transcribers; and we may be imposing on the Greeks a law which we ourselves do not observe. Examine the usage of our corresponding verb *fill*, and see if we are more uniform than they. The cistern fills sixty gallons, and it *fills* again in forty minutes.

Πλήθω *To be full*, Il. 16, 389. 21, 218; Aesch. Pers. 272, Dor. -ᾱ́θω Ch. 589 (chor.), but see πελάω; πλήθωσι Od. 9, 8; πλήθων Il. 11, 492, -ουσα 18, 484; Pind. P. 4, 85, the only part in *classic* prose Thuc. 8, 92; Xen. An. 1, 8, 1. 2, 1, 7. Mem. 1, 1, 10; Pl. Gorg. 469, but later πλήθει D. Sic. 3, 50, πλήθουσι Dio. Hal. 1, 55; πλήθοντας Plut. Per. et Fab. 1; trans. perhaps later, Anth. (Incert.) 14, 7; Opp. Cyn. 1, 126; Q. Sm. 6, 345; πλήθωσι Pseud.-Phocyl. 166 (Bergk, but suggests βρίθωσι, hence **pass.** πλήθομαι Theophr. Fr. 174, 3, and **imp.** πλήθοντο Ap. Rh. 4, 564; Q. Sm. 11, 302): **imp.** ἔπληθον, πλῆθεν Il. 8, 214: **fut.** πλήσω late and trans. Lycophr. 1115: **2 p.** poet. πέπληθα Com. Fr. (Pher.) 2, 265; Theocr. 22, 38; Arat. 841. 774: **2 plp.** ἐπεπλήθει Ap. Rh. 3, 271. See πίμπλημι. Ahrens and Dindorf refer πλᾱ́θω Aesch. quoted to πελάθω, πλᾱ́θω.

Πληρόω *To fill*, Aesch. Sept. 32; Her. 2, 7; Thuc. 6, 52: **imp.** ἐπλήρουν Her. 1, 171; Thuc. 1, 29; Isocr. 8, 84: **fut.** -ώσω Aesch. Sept. 477; Pl. Polit. 286: **aor.** ἐπλήρωσα Her. 1, 166. 3, 136, poet. πλήρ- Philox. 2, 2 (B.); -ῶσαι Soph. Ph. 324: **p.** -ωκα Aristot. Pol. 2, 6, 3; (Aeschin.) Epist. 2, 5 &c. complete and almost reg.: **p. p.** πεπλήρωμαι Her. 8, 46; Pl. Phil. 35. Leg. 865: **plp.**

ἐπεπλήρωντο Thuc. 1, 29: aor. ἐπληρώθην Eur. Ion 1168; Hippocr. 1, 630 (Lit.); Thuc. 3, 17: fut. πληρωθήσομαι Pl. Conv. 175; Aeschin. 2, 37; and Dem. 17, 28 (B. Saupp.): 3 fut. πεπληρώσομαι Epist. Phal. 19 (Hercher): with fut. mid. πληρώσομαι as pass. Xen. M. Eq. 3, 6; Dem. 17, 28 quoted (Bekk. Dind.); Galen 2, 560. 5, 432, ἀπο- Hippocr. 8, 12 (Lit.) **Mid.** πληροῦμαι *fill oneself, one's own, man* &c. Hippocr. 5, 88. 268, ἀνα- Eur. Hel. 907: **imp.** ἐπληροῦντο Xen. Hell. 6, 2, 14; Dem. 21, 154, συν- Pl. Tim. 36: **fut.** πληρώσομαι *fill oneself* &c. or pass. *be filled*, Xen. Dem. quoted, but trans. *fill, man one's own*, ἐπι-πληρωσόμεθα Thuc. 7, 14: **aor.** ἐπληρωσάμην Xen. Hell. 5, 4, 56. 6, 2, 35; Isae. 11, 48; Pl. Gorg. 493; Dem. 50, 7. **Vb.** πληρωτέον Geop. 6, 2, 4.

Πλησιάζω, see πελάζω.

Πλήσσω, -ττω *To strike*, pres. perhaps late in *simple*, -σσω Batr. 273; Callim. Del. 306; Nic. Al. 456, in tmesi ἐκ . . . πλήσσουσι Od. 18, 231, ἐπι-πλησσ- Il. 12, 211; Her. 7, 136, ἐκ-πλησσ- Thuc. 3, 87, but πλήττω Mosch. Trag. Fr. 9 (Wagn.); Aristot. Nat. Ausc. 5, 1, 2 (-σσω *v. r.*); Paroem. C. 17, 66d; Alciphr. 3, 51; Dio Cass. Fr. 43, 33 (Bekk.); Plut. Mor. 436; Longin. 20, 2; Demetr. Phal. 39; Apollod. 3, 12, 3; Philostr. Imag. 2; Himer. Or. 5, 9. 11, 3; Manass. 1, 17 (Herch.), ἐκ-πληττ- Ar. Ran. 144, ἐπι- Isocr. 15, 65, πλήγνυμι only in **pass.** ἐκπλήγνυσθαι Thuc. 4, 125: **imp.** ἔπληττον Callistr. Discr. 14, ἐπ- Isocr. 11, 30; Dem. 19, 175: **fut.** πλήξω *simple* rare, poet. Aesch. Fr. 270; and late prose Philostr. Ap. 224, but ἐπι- Il. 23, 580, κατα- Xen. Lac. 8, 3, ἐκ- Pl. Rep. 436: **aor.** ἔπληξα Her. 3, 64; so in late Attic, Plut. Mor. 233. Nic. 27; (Luc.) Asin. 10; Aesop 347 (Halm), but ἐξ-έπληξα Eur. Ion 635; Thuc. 4, 36; Xen. Mem. 4, 5, 6, ἐπ- Isocr. 11, 34. 15, 288; Aeschin. 1, 180, κατ- Isae. 8, 42; in Epic always πλῆξα Il. 2, 266. Od. 10, 162; Hes. Th. 855, Dor. πλᾶξα Pind. N. 1, 49. 10, 71; Theocr. 22, 124 (Mein.); subj. πλήξω Od. 18, 57; Her. 3, 78; opt. πλήξειε Il. 10, 489; (Eur.) I. A. 1579; πλῆξαι Her. 5, 111: **2 aor.** redupl. ἐπέπληγον Epic Il. 5, 504, and πέπληγον 23, 363. Od. 8, 264; inf. πεπληγέμεν Il. 16, 728. 23, 660: **p.** (πέπληχα as *v. r.* for): **2 p.** πέπληγα **act.** *have struck*, subj. πεπλήγῃ Ar. Av. 1350; -πληγώς Il. 5, 763. 22, 497. Od. 16, 456; rare in prose πεπληγέναι Xen. An. 6, 1, 5, *been struck*, ἐκπέπληγας Epist. Phal. 144, see below: **plp.** ἐπεπλήγει act. Epic Fr. p. 76 (Kinkel): **p. p.** πέπληγμαι Aesch. Ag. 1343; Soph. El. 1415; Eur. H. F. 1105; Ar. Ran. 1214; Her. 1, 41; Thuc. 8, 38, Dor. -αγμαι Aesch. Sept. 896 (chor.): **plp.** ἐπέπληκτο, κατ- Isae. 8, 27; Dem. 9, 61: **1 aor.** ἐπλήχθην rare, Plut. Mor. 901, ἐκ- Eur. Tr. 183, ἐπ- Plut.

Galb. 17: 3 fut. πεπλήξομαι Eur. Hipp. 894; Ar. Eq. 272; Pl. Theaet. 180; Plut. Mor. 597; Philostr. Apoll. 224. Imag. 830: 2 aor. pass. ἐπλήγην Ar. Ran. 1048; Her. 5, 120; Antiph. 3, β, 8; Xen. An. 5, 8, 12; Dem. 21, 36. 54, 33, κατ- Il. 3, 31, πλήγη in tmesi 16, 403, ἐκ-πλήγ- 18, 225; πλήγῃ Pl. Rep. 462; -γειεν Xen. Cyr. 2, 3, 20; πληγῆναι Soph. O. C. 605; Aristot. Poet. 8; Dem. 21, 36; -γείς Il. 8, 12. 17, 296. Od. 21, 50; Simon. C. 142, 8; Soph. Ant. 172; Eur. H. F. 1393; Ar. Pax 613; Her. 1, 85; Thuc. 5, 14; Lys. 1, 27; Pl. Prot. 329, Dor. πλᾱγείς Epich. 159 (Ahr.); Theocr. 22, 105 (Vulg. Mein. πληγ- Ahr. Fritzs. Ziegl.); Callim. Cer. 40, ἐπλᾰ́γην but only in compounds with the sense *strike with terror* or *amazement*, and post-Homeric, as ἐξ-επλᾰ́γην Com. Fr. (Eup.) 2, 561; Her. 1, 119; Thuc. 5, 66; Pl. Phaedr. 259; Isocr. 5, 22; Dem. 45, 57; ἐκπλᾰγῇς Aesch. Ch. 233, -πλαγῇ Thuc. 6, 33, -πλᾰγῆτε Soph. Ph. 226; ἐκπλᾰγείς Eur. Med. 8; Ar. Eq. 664; Her. 1, 24; Thuc. 3, 113; Pl. Rep. 390; -πλᾰγῆναι Phaedr. 234; κατ-επλᾰ́γην Athen. (Macho) 244; Xen. Hell. 4, 4, 15; -πλαγῆτε Thuc. 6, 76; -πλαγῆναι 1, 81; -πλαγείς 4, 10; Dinarch. 1, 39, but in Hom. ἐκ . . . πλήγην in tmesi Il. 13, 394, κατεπλήγην 3, 31: fut. πληγήσομαι Xen. Cyr. 2, 3, 10; Dem. 18, 263. and πλᾰγήσομαι, ἐκ- Pl. Euthyphr. 360; Plut. Quest. Conv. 706. Aem. Paul. 12. Mid. πλήσσομαι *strike oneself* for grief &c. Epic and Ionic, πλήττομαι, ἀπο- Aristot. Probl. 11, 7: fut. πλήξομαι pass. Or. Sib. 7, 17, κατα- Joseph. Ant. 7, 3, 1, but act. Dio. Hal. Ant. 6, 10. 9, 64; Polyb. 4, 80. 5, 25; Diod. Sic. 2, 16: aor. ἐπλήξατο Her. 3, 14, πλήξατο Hom. H. 5, 245; -άμενος Il. 16, 125 (late Attic prose ἐπλήξατο Jos. 16, 10, 7, κατα- Polyb. 2, 52. 3, 89; Dio. Hal. 1, 82; D. Sic. 11, 20): 2 aor. πεπλήγετο Epic, Il. 12, 162. Od. 13, 198, -γοντο Il. 18, 51. Vb. πληκτέον Hesych., κατα- Dinarch. 1, 108.

The *classic* Attic usage of the *simple* verb seems to have been: in the act. form, fut. πλήξω, p. πέπληγα very rare, aor. ἔπληξα doubtful: in the passive, perf. πέπληγμαι, 2 aor. ἐπλήγην, 3 fut. πεπλήξομαι. The other parts were supplied by τύπτω, παίω (ἐκ-, ἐπι- πλήττω, ἐκ-πατάσσω), fut. παίσω (παιήσω, πατάξω poet.), aor. ἐπάταξα, ἔπαισα: pass. τύπτομαι (ἐκπλήττομαι) rarely παίομαι, never πατάσσομαι—in Hom. however, occurs ἐκ-πεπαταγμένος Od. 18, 327, and in Luc. παταχθείς Gym. 3. Lys. 4, 15, gives us a glimpse of the usage, πότερον ἐπλήγην ἢ ἐπάταξα; and Dem. ὁ πληγείς, κἂν ἑτέρωσε πατάξῃς 4, 40. ἔπληγε Aesop 97 (62. 170) called 2 aor. seems to be a false reading for 1 aor. ἔπληξε, now the approved reading (Halm 347.) πεπλήγοντες Callim. Jov. 53, seems pres. part. as if from a pres. πεπλήγω, see also Nonn. D.

28, 327. The p. πέπληγα is used passively by late writers, Luc. Tragod. 115; Plut. Luc. 31. Nic. 10. Alex. 75; Dio. Hal. 3, 64; Q. Sm. 5, 91; and, according to some, Xen. An. quoted, see Poppo; δια-πεπληχός Hippocr. 2, 838 (Kühn), -ηγός (Lind.), but Littré διαπεπλιχός 8, 346, Erm. 2, 758: plp. κατ-επεπλήγεσαν Luc. D. Mer. 13, 2; App. Hisp. 23.

Πλύνω *To wash*, Ar. Pl. 166; (Theocr.) 27, 7. 8; Hippocr. 6, 492; Aristot. Probl. 23, 40; πλύνων Od. 15, 420; -ειν Xen. Eq. 5, 7; Pl. Charm. 161: imp. ἔπλυνον D. Laert. 2, 68, iter. πλύνεσκον Il. 22, 155: fut. πλυνῶ Ar. Thesm. 248; Com. Fr. (Antiph.) 3, 12; Dem. 39, 11, Epic πλυνέω Od. 6, 31: aor. ἔπλυνα, πλῦναν Od. 6, 93, περιέπλυναν Plut. Mor. 69; ἐκ-πλύνειε Ar. Plut. 1062; πλύνας Od. 24, 148; Com. Fr. (Alex.) 3, 443; Aristot. Mirab. Ausc. 48; Theophr. H. P. 9, 11, 9, περι- Dem. 54, 9: p. p. πέπλυμαι Com. Fr. (Sosip.) 4, 482; Hippocr. 2, 520. 6, 544 (Lit.), κατα- Aeschin. 3, 178; πεπλύσθαι Theocr. 1, 150 (Mss. Ahr. Ziegl. Mein. 3 ed.), -ύνθαι (Ms. Mein. 2 ed. Krüg.): aor. ἐπλύθην Hippocr. 8, 42; Aristot. Mirab. 48, ἐκ- Com. Fr. (Antiph.) 3, 125? κατα- Theophr. C. Pl. 4, 8, 4; Plut. Gen. Socr. 5, late ἐπλύνθην Dioscor. 2, 95: fut. πλυθήσομαι Com. Fr. (Anon.) 4, 647, πλυνθ- Hesych.; late V. T. Lev. 6, 27. 15, 17: and as pass. fut. mid. ἐκ-πλυνεῖται Ar. Plut. 1064. Mid. *to wash one's own, simple* late, fut. πλυνοῦμαι, -εῖσθε V. T. Num. 31, 24, but ἐκ-πλυνεῖται as pass. see above: so aor. πλυνάμενος V. T. Lev. 13, 6. 34, but ἐκ- Her. 4, 73. Vb. πλυτός Hippocr. πλυτέος Com. Fr. (Alex.) 3, 470; Dioscor. 5, 8, 6. The mid. form *simple* and compound has, we think, been entirely missed by our Lexicogr.

Πλώω *To sail*, Poet. and Ionic, Ap. Rh. 4, 525; Opp. Hal. 2, 45; Her. 8, 13, Dor. 3 pl. πλώοντι, ἐπι- Theocr. 17, 91; opt. -οιεν Od. 5, 240; πλώων Hom. H. 22, 7; Her. 8, 10; -ώειν 8, 97, -έμεναι Orac. ap. Luc. Alex. 53: imp. ἔπλωον Her. 8, 23. 66, πλῶον Il. 21, 302, iter. πλώεσκον, ἐπι- Ap. Rh. 1, 549: fut. act. πλώσω late, Lycophr. 1044: classic, mid. πλώσομαι, ἀπο- Her. 8, 5, παρα- Orph. Arg. 1278: aor. ἔπλωσα Her. 4, 148; πλώσῃ, ἀνα- Opp. Hal. 1, 343; πλώσας Her. 7, 128, ἐπι- Il. 3, 47; πλῶσαι Her. 1, 24: p. πέπλωκα Eur. Hel. 532 (Mss. Kirchh. Nauck 2 ed. Paley); Ar. Thesm. 878; Lycophr. 634, παρα- Her. 4, 99, ἐκ- Hippocr. 1, 520: 2 aor. (πλῶμι) ἔπλων, -ως, -ω &c. Poet. Anth. 9, 219. 11, 42, ἐπ-έπλων Hes. Op. 648, -έπλως Od. 3, 15, ἀπ-έπλω 14, 339, παρ- 12, 69; ἐπι-πλώς Il. 6, 291; Her. (Orac.) 2, 116. Vb. πλωτός Od. 10, 3. πεπλωκότα Eur. Hel. 532, is the Mss. reading, and Aristophanes (Thesm. 878) seems to *repeat* it as a jeer on Euripides for using the Ionic form. We therefore do not feel at liberty to substitute πεπλευκότα with Matthiae, Dindorf, and Nauck 3 ed. The collat. form πλωΐζω occurs occasionally, Pl. Rep. 388, in not exactly a verbal quotation from Il. 24, 12, **imp.** ἐπλώιζον Thuc. 1, 13 (Bekk. Popp. Dind. Krüg. ἔπλῳζ- Stahl,), iter. πλωΐζεσκε Hes. Op. 634: later **mid.** πλωΐζομαι as **act.** -όμενος Luc. V. A. 26. Hist. 62.—πλοΐζομαι seems to occur in **mid.** only, and not earlier than Polyb. -όμενος 3, 28. 4, 47; Diod. Sic. 3, 34; Strab. 3, 1, 9. 17, 1, 45. So τελεόω, -ειόω as well as τελέω.

Πνέω *To blow, breathe*, Od. 5, 469; Pind. N. 6, 1; Aesch. Eum. 873; Eur. Alc. 493; Ar. Pax 87; Her. 2, 22; Hippocr. 6, 384; Xen. Oec. 18, 1; Pl. Theaet. 152; Aeol. Dor. fem. pt. πνέοισα Alcae. 66; Pind. Ol. 13, 90, Poet. πνείω Il. 3, 8; Hes. Sc. 24; Her. 1, 67 (Orac.), ἀπο- Tyrtae. 10, 24 (Bergk), κατα- Aesch. Ag. 105 chor. (Dind.), πνεύω, πνεύων, ἐπι- (Hesych.): **imp.** ἔπνει Aesch. Sept. 53; Xen. An. 4, 5, 3; Aristot. Meteor. 2, 6, 10; (Dem.) 25, 57, ἔπνεεν Simon. C. 114 (Bergk), ἀν- Il. 11, 327, πνέον Pind. P. 4, 225, iter. πνείεσκε Anth. 8, 7, -σκον Q. Sm. 8, 349, ἀμ-πνει- Ap. Rh. 3, 231: **fut.** πνεύσω perhaps late, Anth. (Antiph. Thess.) 9, 112; Theophr. Fr. 6, 2, (32); Geop. 1, 12, 34, unless συμ-πνευσόντων be correct, Dem. 18, 168 (Bekk. -σάντων B. S. Dind.), ἀπο- Anth. 3, 6, ἀνα- Q. Sm. 4, 23. 13, 516; Galen. 7, 776; Joseph. Jud. B. 5, 6, 2: πνεύσομαι late in *simple*, Apocr. Sirac. 43, 16, but ἐμ-πνεύσομαι Eur. Andr. 555, ἐκ- H. F. 885, παρα- Hippocr. 8, 284, and πνευσοῦμαι, -εῖται Ar. Ran. 1221, without necessity of metre (Mss. Bekk. Mein. -εται Dind. 5 ed.); Aristot. Meteor. 2, 8, 17 (B.); Theophr. Fr. 6, 2, 34 (Wimm.): **aor.** ἔπνευσα Eur. Andr. 327; Her. 2, 20; Hippocr. 2, 598. 5, 100; Aristot. Meteor. 1, 7, 12, ἐν- Il. 17, 456, ἀν- 11, 382; Soph. Aj. 274; subj. πνεύσω Il. 19, 159; Eur. I. A. 761, ἐπι- Od. 9, 139; opt. πνεύσειε Com. Fr. (Alex.) 3, 403, ἐκ-πνεῦσαι Thuc. 2, 84; πνεύσας Hes. Op. 506; Aesch. Ch. 1067; Soph. Fr. 63 (D.); Hippocr. 5, 100, Dor. -σαις Pind. Ol. 10, 93; πνεῦσαι Eur. I. A. 1324, ἐμ- Pl. Conv. 179, συμ- Leg. 708: **p.** πέπνευκα, ἐπι- Pl. Phaedr. 262, ἐκ- Aristot. Prob. 11, 41; Theophr. Vent. 53, ἀνα- Dio Cass. 52, 16: **p. p.** late πέπνευμαι, ἐμ- Schol. Ap. Rh. 4, 1381, πέπνευσμαι, ἐμ- Justin Mart. 37 (Braun), for the Epic and late form πέπνῦμαι in the sense *I breathe*, Polyb. 6, 47. 53; *am breathed into, inspired, wise*, πέπνῦσαι Il. 24, 377; but πέπνῦσο if sound Theogn. 29 (Vulg. Ziegl. πέπνυο Bergk); πεπνῦμένος Il. 13, 266; πεπνῦσθαι Il. 23, 440. 24, 377. 3, 148 &c.; Theogn. 309; late prose, Plut. Num. 4; Stob. (Perict.) 85, 19, see πινύσκω: **plp.** πέπνῦσο Od. 23, 210: **aor.** late ἐπνεύσθην, δια- Theophr. H. P. 5, 5, 6, ἐπι- Epist. Phal. 19, εἰσ- Galen 4, 478, ἐπνεύθην Philo, Epic ἀμ-πνύνθην

Il. 5, 697; Q. Sm. 9, 430 (Lehrs, Koechly), see ἀμ-πνύω: **fut.** late πνευσθήσομαι, δια- Aretae. P. 77; Oribas. 7, 20, but δια-πνευθήσ- if correct, Galen 11, 588. **Vb.** ἄ-πνευστος Od. 5, 456. See ἀμ-πνύω. For **fut.** συμπνευσόντων Dem. 18, 168 (Ms. S. Bekk.) and so quoted by Dio. Hal. Epist. 1, 11, Elms. and Schaef. suggested **aor.** -σάντων which has been adopted or approved by almost every succeeding editor. Bekker however in his last edition (1854) still retains **fut.** ἐπι-πνεύσουσι is best supported by Ap. Rh. 1, 335, and is perhaps correct, notwithstanding subj. -ωσι (Ms. D. Brunck, Beck.) ἐκ-πεπνευκότας is the Mss. reading Eur. Phoen. 1151, and accepted by Kirchhoff, Klotz, Nauck, and doubtingly by Paley; Valckenaer again, Pors. Dind. Herm. &c. prefer ἐκνενευκότας the suggestion of Markland. πνέω like other dissyllabic verbs in -έω does not contract εη, εο, εω: πνέῃ Xen. Cyn. 6, 2, πνέοι Aesch. Eum. 938, πνέουσι Eur. Elec. 1147. Alc. 493, πνέον Soph. Fr. 147 (D.), -έοντος Xen. Hell. 7, 5, 12; Pl. Theaet. 152, πνέω Aesch. Eum. 840; Eur. H. F. 1092. The only exception we know is ἐκπνέων Aesch. Ag. 1493. 1517, which though not contracted to the eye ἐκπνῶν, is so to the ear, or pronounced a dissyllable. In classic Attic prose the *simple* form of this verb occurs in the **pres.** and **imp. act.** only: later πνεύσας Polyb. 22, 14, but ἀν-έπνευσε Pl. Tim. 91, -πνεῦσαι Dem. 18, 195.

Πνίγω *To strangle,* Sophr. 72 (Ahr.); Com. Fr. (Antiph.) 3, 103; rare in prose Hippocr. 2, 516. 7, 382 (Lit.); Aristot. Gen. An. 1, 11, 6; Luc. Catapl. 12, ἀπο- Her. 4, 60; πνίγωσι Hippocr. 7, 344. 360; Xen. Oec. 17, 14; -γων Antiph. 4, α, 6: **imp.** ἔπνῑγε Hippocr. 5, 230; Babr. 27: **fut.** πνίξω, ἀπο- Com. Fr. (Plat.) 2, 686 (Antiph.) 3, 93; Luc. Char. 23: and **mid.** πνίξομαι, ἀπο- Eunap. p. 24 (Boiss.), Dor. πνιξοῦμαι reflex, Epicharm. 106 (Ahr.): **aor.** ἔπνιξα Hippocr. 6, 212; Apollod. 2, 5, 1, ἀπ- Her. 3, 150; πνίξῃ, ἀπο- Ar. Eq. 893; Her. 4, 72; πνῖξον Com. Fr. (Cratin.) 2, 35; πνίξας Batr. 158; Her. 2, 92, ἀπο- Pl. Gorg. 471: **p. p.** πέπνιγμαι Com. Fr. (Metag.) 2, 753; Ar. Vesp. 511; Aristot. Mirab. 29; Aristid. 24, 305, ἀπο- Her. 4, 72; Aristot. H. A. 7, 4: **1 aor.** late ἐπνίχθην, ἀπ- Aretae. 1, 7, p. 11 (Adams); Babr. 49 (2 pt. Lewis): **2 aor.** ἐπνῐ́γην Batr. 148; Oribas. p. 346; Aretae. p. 73 (Adams), ἀπ-επνῐ́γη Com. Fr. (Pher.) 2, 341, (Alex.) 3, 507; Pl. Gorg. 512; Dem. 32, 6; -πνιγῶ Hippocr. 2, 265 (Erm.); Luc. Luct. 18; ἀπο-πνιγεῖεν Xen. Cyr. 8, 2, 21; πνῐγείς Stob. (Sotad.) 98, 9: **fut.** πνῐγήσομαι Galen 2, 72. 10, 617, but ἀπο- Ar. Nub. 1504; Hippocr. 7, 146 (Lit.); Luc. D. Mar. 6, 3: and late **3 fut.** ἀποπεπνίξεσθαι Eunap. V. Soph. p. 38. **Vb.** πνικτός C. Fr. (Pherecr.) 2, 341.

Πνύω, see ἀμπνύω.

Ποδίζω (πούς) not used *simple* in act. but προ-ποδίζων *footing it, stepping forward*, Il. 13, 158, and better developed in ἐμποδίζω, which see: p. p. πεποδισμένος *foot bound*, Xen. An. 3, 4, 35. Cyr. 3, 3, 27: aor. ποδισθείς Soph. Fr. 60.

Ποέω, see ποιέω.

Ποθέω *to desire, miss*, Od. 1, 343; Emped. 230; Pind. Ol. 6, 16; Aesch. Pr. 785; Soph. El. 1168; Ar. Vesp. 818; Antiph. 5, 64; Pl. Rep. 571; Dor. f. pt. ποθέοισα Theocr. 18, 42, Aeol. -ήω Sapph. 26 (B.); Epic inf. ποθήμεναι Od. 12, 110: imp. ἐπόθουν Xen. An. 6, 4, 8, -εον Her. 4, 95, Dor. -θευν? Ar. Ach. 730 (Bentl. -ουν Dind. Mein.), Poet. 'πόθουν Soph. Aj. 962, in Hom. unaugm. πόθεον Il. 2, 726. 23, 16, iter. ποθέεσκε 1, 492: fut. ποθήσω Xen. Mem. 3, 11, 3. Oec. 8, 10; Luc. D. Deor. 4, 4; ἐπι-ποθήσειν Her. 5, 93: but fut. mid. ποθέσομαι Lys. 8, 18 (Mss. Bekk. B. S. -ήσομαι Mss. D O. Scheib. Westerm.); Pl. Phaed. 97 (2 Mss. Heind. Bekk. Stallb. B. O. W. Herm. Schanz): aor. ἐπόθεσα Her. 9, 22 (Mss. Bekk. Gaisf. Stein, -ησα Dind. Dietsch &c.); Isocr. 19, 7, unaugm. in Hom. πόθ- Il. 15, 219; inf. ποθέσαι Od. 2, 375. 4, 748; Theocr. 10, 8; Isocr. 4, 122, and ἐπόθησα especially in prose, Her. 3, 36; Xen. Ages. 11, 15. Hel. 5, 3, 20; Pl. Men. 84; (Dem.) 25, 42; but in late poet. Coluth. 67; Nonn. 4, 96; Or. Sib. 5, 148. 232: p. πεπόθηκα Anth. (Anon.) 11, 417; Or. Sib. 5, 319; Sext. Emp. 573, 21: p. p. πεπόθημαι, -θημένος Orph. H. 81, 3; Or. Sib. 5, 261. 397. 427. 8, 428: aor. very rare ἐποθήθην, προποθηθείσης Galen 5, 859 missed by all Lexicogr., but ἐποθέσθην *simple* or *compound* we have never found. **Mid.** ποθοῦμαι as act. very rare, Dor. part. ποθουμένᾳ Soph. Tr. 103 (chor.) **Vb.** ποθητός Boeckh Inscr. vol. 1, p. 801; Ael. N. A. 7, 2, τρι-πόθᾱτος Bion 1, 58, ἀ-πόθεστος Od. 17, 296 (Bekk.). ποθήμεναι Od. 12, 110, Epic inf. for ποθεῖν. Hom. does not augm. this verb. Her. has aor. with both ε and η if the Mss. are correct. Eustath. on Od. 2, 375 (p. 1450) quotes, or *accommodates* Pl. Phaed. 97, so: ὡς οὐκέτι ποθέσων &c. a reading offered by no Ms. of Pl. but the only instance we know of fut. act. with ε. The aor. in Isocr. now is not ἐπόθησα, but -εσα (Ms. Urb. Bekk. B. S. Bens. &c.)

Ποιέω *To do, make*, Hes. Op. 751; Aesch. Supp. 911; Soph. O. R. 918; Ar. Ran. 198; Her. 2, 49; Thuc. 7, 4; Xen. Cyr. 2, 2, 7; ποιέοιμι Her. 5, 106, -οίην Ar. V. 348; Isocr. 12, 24, -οίη Her. 6, 35 (Bekk. Krüg. Stein, -έοι Abicht, -έη Dind.); Xen. Oec. 20, 11, ποιοῖ Pl. Rep. 360, -έοιεν Her. 8, 26; imper. ποίει H. Ven. 104: imp. ἐποίουν Ar. Nub. 335, -ευν Her. 8, 64, -εε Her. 4, 78, -ει Od. 19, 34; Thuc. 2, 22; Pl. Rep. 352, ποίεον Il. 20, 147, ποίει 18, 482, iter. ποιέεσκε Her. 4, 78, -έεσκον 1, 36, reg.: fut. -ήσω Il. 13, 120; Soph. Ph. 120; Her. 8, 144; Antiph. 5, 57; Thuc. 1, 40; Pl. Phil. 50; Ep. inf. -ησέμεν Od. 21, 399: aor. ἐποίησα Il. 12, 30; Simon. C. 157; Aesch. Eum. 649; Her. 8, 54; Antiph. 5, 10; Thuc. 6, 2, ποίησ- Il. 20, 12; Hes. Op. 144. Th. 579; Epic subj. -ήσομεν Il. 7, 339: p. πεποίηκα Her. 2, 10; Thuc. 3, 54; Isae. 1, 21; Pl. Conv. 222 &c.: plp. ἐπεποιήκει Thuc. 3, 23, -ήκεε Her. 5, 69: p. p. πεποίημαι Il. 6, 56; Ar. Thesm. 231; Antiph. 5, 77; Thuc. 4, 31; Pl. Gorg. 512: plp. ἐπεποίητο Her. 7, 55: aor. ἐποιήθην Eur. Tr. 988; Her. 2, 159; Thuc. 2, 56: fut. ποιηθήσομαι, μετα- Dem. 23, 62: with fut. mid. ποιήσομαι as pass. Hippocr. 9, 238 (L.); Aristot. Metaph. 4, 15, 7 (B.): and 3 fut. πεποιήσομαι Hippocr. 8, 46. 92 (Lit.). **Mid.** ποιοῦμαι *make for oneself* &c. Od. 2, 126; Soph. Ant. 78; Thuc. 4, 87; Andoc. 1, 6; Xen. Cyr. 5, 3, 19, -εῦνται Her. 1, 193: imp. ἐποιούμην Antiph. 5, 43, -εύμην Her. 1, 118, -έετο 7, 17, -εῖτο Thuc. 8, 41; Isae. 9, 11, -οῦντο Thuc. 1, 5; Lys. 12, 7, -εῦντο Her. 7, 138, ποιεύμην Il. 9, 495, iter. ποιεέσκετο Her. 7, 5. 119 (Gaisf.) ποιέσκ- (Bekk. Dind. Lhard.): fut. ποιήσομαι Il. 9, 397. Od. 10, 433; Her. 8, 4; Antiph. 1, 4; Lys. 3, 43; Pl. Rep. 370; Dem. 23, 109: as 3 fut. and act. ἔσῃ πεποιημένος Luc. Char. 22: aor. ἐποιησάμην Her. 8, 20; Antiph. 1, 14; Andoc. 1, 124; Lys. 12, 19, ποιησ- Il. 8, 2. Od. 5, 251; Hes. Th. 921; subj. -ήσωνται Il. 12, 168, but Epic -ήσεται 3, 409, -ησόμεθα Od. 14, 393: as mid. p. p. πεποίημαι Hippocr. 6, 2; Andoc. 4, 22; Isocr. 1, 48; Isae. 2, 19; Dem. 19, 22. 24, 172; imper. rare πεποίησο Xen. Cyr. 4, 2, 7: plp. ἐπεποίηντο Thuc. 1, 62; Isocr. 9, 54; Dem. 23, 132: aor. ἐποιήθην always pass. in *simple*, but προσ-εποιήθην *pretended*, Polyb. 5, 25. 31, 22; Diod. Sic. 19, 5. 6. 20, 36. Fr. 38, libr. 29 (Bekk. classic -εποιησάμην Thuc. 2, 30; Aeschin. 2, 166), ἀντεποιήθην Luc. D. Mort. 29, 2 (-ησάμην Isae. 8, 4.) **Vb.** ποιητέος Thuc. 4, 99. The form ποῶ occurs often in Inscr. Doric and Attic, in Mss. especially of the Attic poets, and in Bekker's edition of Aristophanes. But though it is pretty clear that this form was in use, it is difficult to determine in what circumstances the form and sound were varied. Editors have, therefore, for the sake of uniformity, generally edited ποιῶ even where the verse requires the first syllable short. So τοιοῦτος, οἷος and others whose first syllable, though often shortened, never loses the ι. See Boeckh's Inscr. Delph. G. 1, 25. Herm. 1193. ποῆ for ποίη, is in Mss. R. Aug. Ar. Lys. 1318 &c. &c., compare the Latin *poëta*.

Ποικίλλω *To variegate, trick out*, Soph. Tr. 1121; Hippocr. 6, 360; Pl. Tim. 87; -κίλλωσι Emped. 119; -κίλλειν Pind. P. 9, 77: imp. ποίκιλλε Il. 18, 590: aor. ποικίλας Soph. Tr. 412; δια-ποικίλαι Isocr. 9, 9: p. p. πεποίκιλται Pl. Rep. 529; -κιλμένη 557, Dor. -μένα Pind. N. 8, 15; but act. -ιλται Eur. Supp. 187. Vb. ποικιλτέον Pl. Rep. 378.

Ποινάω *To punish*, doubtful in act. Theano p. 747; Phot. Lex.: aor. ἐποίνᾱσε Hesych.: aor. pass. ποινᾱθείς Eur. Hel. 1509. Mid. rare, *to exact retribution*, fut. ποινάσομαι Eur. I. T. 1433.

Ποιπνύω *To puff, bustle about* (πνέω, πνύω, others πονέω), Epic Il. 1, 600. 14, 155; Ap. Rh. 4, 1113; Q. Sm. 11, 322: imp. ποίπνῡον Il. 24, 475; Ap. Rh. 4, 1399, but -ῦων Pind. P. 10, 64: also ῠ, ἐποίπνῠον Il. 18, 421. Od. 3, 430; Nonn. D. 5, 57, περι-ποίπνῠον Q. Sm. 9, 530, iter. ποιπνύεσκον, περι- 6, 153: fut. late, ποιπνύσω Or. Sib. Phleg. Trall. c. 4, p. 120: aor. ἐποίπνῡσα, ποιπνύσαντι Il. 8, 219, -ύσασαι Od. 20, 149. Mid. ποιπνύεσθαι Opp. Hal. 2, 615, missed by Lexicogr.

Ποκίζω *To shear* &c. fut. ποκίσω, Att. ποκιῶ, ἐκ- Ar. Thesm. 567, (Dor. -ίξω): aor. mid. ἐποκίξατο Theocr. 5, 26.

Πολεμέω *To wage war*, Eur. Ion 1386; Ar. Lys. 489; Thuc. 5, 76; subj. -μῶμεν Soph. O. C. 191 &c. act. reg.: imp. ἐπολέμουν Thuc. 4, 48; Lys. 12, 57, -εον Her. 5, 94: fut. -ήσω Andoc. 3, 26; Pl. Rep. 373: aor. -ησα Com. Fr. (Antiph.) 3, 25; Her. 5, 67; Thuc. 1, 18: p. πεπολέμηκα Com. Fr. (Ephipp.) 3, 328; Isocr. 4, 140; Dem. 15, 17: p. p. πεπολεμημένος App. Hisp. 48, κατα- Diod. Sic. 15, 80; -ῆσθαι, κατα- Thuc. 6, 16: aor. ἐπολεμήθην Thuc. 5, 26: fut. πολεμηθήσομαι Polyb. 2, 41; Dio Cass. 42, 42: with mid. as pass. πολεμήσομαι Thuc. 1, 68. 8, 43; Dem. 23, 110, see below: and 3 fut. δια-πεπολεμήσεται Thuc. 7, 14; δια-πεπολεμησόμενος 7, 25 (Ms. V. Bekk. Krüg. Dind. and doubtingly Popp.), if correct, the only instance of redupl. fut. *participle* in classic Attic, δια-πολεμησόμενος (most Mss. Vulg. Goell.) Mid. intrans. *war against one's own*, and trans. *war down for oneself, subdue*, fut. late πολεμήσεσθε V. T. 2 Par. 11, 4 (Vat. Gaisf. Tischend.): and aor. πολεμησάμενοι, κατα- missed by all Lexicogr. occur Polyb. 11, 31 (Bekk. L. Dind.); V. T. quoted. Vb. πολεμητέος Thuc. 1, 79. A desiderative form occurs in part. πολεμησείοντας Thuc. 1, 33; Dio Cass. 51, 25.

Bekker has adopted the participle of the reduplicated fut. διαπεπολεμησόμενος Thuc. 7, 25, in preference to the part. fut. mid. as pass. διαπολεμησόμενος. We demur to this as contrary to *classic* usage: αἱρέω, for example, has 3 fut ᾑρήσεται Pl. Prot. 338, never ᾑρησόμενος, but αἱρεθησόμενος Dio. Hal. 8, 75, ἀν- 3, 23 (ἀφ- Joseph. 18, 6, 5): βάλλω, 3 fut. βεβλήσεται Eur. Or. 271, ἐκ- Bac. 1314, δια- Dem. 16, 2, but βληθησόμενος, ἐκ- Pl. Leg. 874: γράφω, 3 fut. γεγράψεται Soph. O. R. 411; Theocr. 18, 48;

Hippocr. 2, 304. 4, 104. 174. 252, ἐγ- Ar. Eq. 1371, but γραφησόμενος Hippocr. 2, 278; Dio. Hal. 1, 1. 6, 78; Aenae. Tact. 31 (Orell.); Joseph. Ant. 1, (11) see below: δικάζω, 3 fut. δεδικάσονται Luc. Bis Acc. 14, but δικασθησόμενος D. Hal. Ant. 5, 61: εἴρω (ῥέω) *say*, 3 fut. εἰρήσεται Eur. Ion 760; Ar. Pl. 114; Thuc. 6, 34; Pl. Theaet. 179; Xen. Cyr. 7, 1, 9 &c. &c., but always ῥηθησόμενος Thuc. 8, 66; Pl. Phaedr. 259; Isocr. 5, 1. 14. 15. 140. 8, 63 &c.: καλέω, 3 fut. κεκλήσομαι Ar. V. 151. Av. 184, -ήσοιτο Pl. Tim. 42, -ήσεσθαι 88, but κληθησόμενος, ἀντι- Xen. Conv. 1, 15: κλάω, 3 fut. κεκλαύσεται Ar. Nub. 1436, but κλαυσόμενος Eur. Cycl. 490: λέγω *say*, 3 fut. λελέξεται Thuc. 3, 53; Pl. Crat. 433. Rep. 457, but λεχθησόμενος Thuc. 5, 86; Isocr. 12, 156. Epist. 9, 2; Pl. Tim. 67. Soph. 251, λεγησόμενος, συλ- Aeschin. 3, 100: λείπω, 3 fut. λελείψεσθαι Thuc. 5, 105, καταλελείψεται 2, 64, but ἀπο-λειψόμενος as pass. Pl. Charm. 176: λύω, 3 fut. λελύσεται Dem. 14, 2, ἀπο- Xen. Cyr. 6, 2, 37, but λυθησόμενος Isocr. 12, 116, κατα- Lys. 13, 16, δια- Dem. 8, 10: μίγνυμι, 3 fut. μεμίξεται (Hes.) Op. 179; Aesch. Pers. 1052 (ἀμ- Dind. Herm.), ἀνα- Hippocr. 7, 498, but μιχθησόμενος Palaeph. Incred. 14: παύω, 3 fut. πεπαύσομαι Soph. Ant. 91. Tr. 587, but παυσόμενος Xen. Cyr. 1, 4, 21, ἀνα- Lys. 13, 12: πλήσσω, 3 fut. πεπλήξεται Eur. Hipp. 894; Pl. Theaet. 180 &c., but πλαγησόμενος, ἐκ- Plut. Aem. Paul. 12: πολεμέω, 3 fut. πεπολεμήσεται, δια- Thuc. 7, 14, but πολεμηθησόμενος Polyb. 2, 41; Strab. 17, 3, 15, and as pass. δια-πολεμησόμενος Thuc. 7, 25 (Vulg.), but—the point in dispute—δια-πεπολεμησόμενος (Bekk. &c.): πράσσω, 3 fut. πεπράξεται Eur. Heracl. 980; Ar. Av. 847; Dem. 19, 74, δια- Pl. Gorg. 510, but πραχθησόμενος Isocr. Epist. 3, 3; Dio Cass. 44, 6: ῥίπτω, 3 fut. ἐρρίψεται Luc. Merc. Con. 17, but ῥιφησόμενος Plut. C. Gracch. 3: τάσσω, 3 fut. τετάξεσθαι Thuc. 5, 71, προστετάξεται Pl. Rep. 465, but ταχθησόμενος, ἐπι- Pl. Leg. 740, προσ- Xen. Mem. 3, 5, 6: τιμάω, 3 fut. τετιμήσεται Lys. 31, 24, but τιμηθησόμενος Aristot. Eth. N. 4, 9 (Bekk.), and τιμησόμενος as pass. Joseph. Ant. 18, 6, 9: τιμωρέω, 3 fut. τετιμωρήσεαι Her. 9, 78 (Süv. Bekk. Dind.), but τιμωρησόμενος Lys. 14, 10; (Dem.) 26, 4: τιτρώσκω, 3 fut. τετρώσῃ Luc. Vot. 37, but τρωθησόμενος Pl. Crito 51: τρίβω, 3 fut. τετρίψεσθε, ἐπι- Ar. Pax 246, but τριφθησόμενος App. Civ. 4, 65, τριβησόμενος Plut. Dion. 25: φαίνω, 3 fut. πεφήσεται Il. 17, 155, but φανησόμενος Dio. Hal. 6, 24, ἀνα- Antiph. 1, 13: φιλέω, 3 fut. πεφιλήσεται Callim. Del. 270, but φιλησομένη Antiph. 1, 19. In the Ionic of Hippocr. and *late* Attic, the repupl. fut. part. occurs occasionally, but always opposed by a *v. r.* γεγραψόμενος Hippocr. 4, 80 (Lit. v. r. γραψόμ-): δεδησόμενος Luc. Tox. 35, v. r. δεθησόμ-: εἰρησόμενος

Hippocr. 3, 516 (Lit. v. r. ῥηθησόμενος strongly supported); so Aelian H. A. 16, 36; Galen 15, 18: δια-βεβλησομένος Philostr. Apoll. 251. We may be told the Greeks were nice in their notation of time; we grant it, and say in turn, examine the previous induction and see if they were always so nice. Do not διαλυθήσεται Dem. 8, 17, πεισθήσεσθε 8, 43, seem to be used as fut. exact? Besides, how did they fare with those verbs that are unsusceptible of a 3 fut. formation?

Πολεμίζω *To war*, Poet. for πολεμέω, Il. 13, 123; Pind. I. 1, 50; Ar. Nub. 419, Epic πτολεμίζω Il. 21, 463; Hes. Sc. 358; πολεμίζῃ Il. 19, 168; -ίζοι Il. 9, 318; imper. -ίζετε 7, 279; -ίζειν 7, 239, Epic -ιζέμεναι 9, 337, -ιζέμεν 16, 220: imp. πολέμιζον Il. 9, 352; Ap. Rh. 1, 43, πτολ- Anth. App. Epigr. 157: fut. πολεμίξω Il. 24, 667, πτολ- 2, 328. 13, 644: aor. πτολέμιξε Ap. Rh. 3, 1234, πολ- (Merk.) **Mid.** πολεμιζόμενοι as act. Pind. N. 8, 29, altered by Wakefield to πελεμ- and adopted by Boeckh, Schneid. and Bergk: fut. late πτολεμίξεται Or. Sib. 5, 382. **Pass.** late, πολεμιζομένῳ Opp. Cyn. 3, 209. Not in Trag. and only once in Comedy.

Πολιορκέω *To besiege*, Ar. Vesp. 685; Her. 8, 28; Thuc. 1, 39; Isocr. 6, 40, act. reg.: imp. ἐπολιόρκουν Thuc. 2, 58, -κεε Her. 1, 17, -κεον 8, 52: fut. -ήσω Xen. Cyr. 7, 5, 12: aor. -ησα Ar. Lys. 281; Her. 5, 65; Thuc. 1, 61: p. p. πεπολιορκημένος, ἐκ- Thuc. 7, 75; Isocr. 14, 26: aor. ἐπολιορκήθην Thuc. 4, 39; Isocr. 6, 57; Pl. Rep. 708: fut. πολιορκηθήσομαι Xen. Hell. 4, 8, 5; D. Sic. 13, 56, 2: and as pass. fut. mid. πολιορκήσομαι Her. 5, 34. 8, 49. 9, 58. 97; Thuc. 3, 109; Xen. Cyr. 6, 1, 15. Hell. 7, 5, 18. **Vb.** πολιορκητέος Xen. Cyr. 7, 5, 7. Excepting Aristoph. quoted, this verb is prosaic.

Πολῑτεύω *To be a citizen, govern &c.* Thuc. 2, 37. 46; Xen. Hell. 1, 4, 13 reg.: fut. -εύσω Thuc. 1, 19; Xen. Hell. 2, 3, 2: aor. ἐπολίτευσα Thuc. 2, 65: p. p. πεπολίτευμαι Isocr. 16, 45; Dem. 18, 11: aor. ἐπολιτεύθην Xen. Mem. 4, 4, 16; Pl. Leg. 693. **Mid.** dep. πολιτεύομαι *discharge the duties, have the privileges, of a citizen &c.* Andoc. 2, 1; Isocr. 5, 140; rare in Trag. opt. -εύοιτο Eur. Fr. 21, 2 (D.): imp. ἐπολιτ- Ar. Lys. 573; Thuc. 2, 15: fut. πολιτεύσομαι Ar. Eq. 1365; Xen. Athen. 3, 9: aor. ἐπολιτευσάμην Andoc. 2, 10; Aeschin. 1, 86; Dem. 18, 207; Ael. V. H. 7, 14; Strab. 12, 4, 3, κατ- Dem. 19, 315, συν- Polyb. 2, 43: with aor. pass. ἐπολιτεύθην Thuc. 6, 92; Lys. 26, 5; Isocr. 7, 15; Aeschin. 2, 176; Aristot. Pol. 2, 12: p. πεπολίτευμαι Pl. Leg. 676; Isocr. 5, 140; Dem. 18, 10. Of classic writers, Thuc. and Xen. alone seem to use the act. voice. Of the poets, Eur. has the verb once only, Ar. twice.

Πονέω *To labour, suffer pain bodily or mental,* Theogn. 919;

Soph. Aj. 38; Her. 2, 14; Pl. Rep. 531, Dor. 1 pl. -εῦμες Bion 7, 11, rarely *to cause pain* Pind. P. 4, 151; subj. πονῇ Thuc. 6, 67; -οίη Hippocr. 5, 374; πόνει Aesch. Pr. 342 &c.: imp. ἐπόνουν Hippocr. 5, 390; Thuc. 4, 96: fut. πονήσω Aesch. Pr. 343; Isocr. 4, 186; Pl. Rep. 410; Hippocr. 1, 598. 8, 16. 30 (Lit.), and πονέσω Hippocr. 4, 512 (Lit.) strongly opposed in the Mss. by πονήσω; Aristot. Mech. 25, 2 (B.); V. T. Esai. 19, 10: aor. ἐπόνησα Eur. Hipp. 1369; Thuc. 6, 104; Isocr. 12, 268; Pl. Rep. 462; Hippocr. 2, 322. 6, 290 (Lit.), πόνησα Pind. N. 7, 36, and ἐπόνεσα Hippocr. 5, 696. 6, 146. 164. 176 (Lit. -ησα Vulg. &c.); and late Polyaen. 3, 10, 6; Themist. 1, 14. 11, 150; V. T. Jerem. 5, 3, Dor. ἐπόνᾱσα Theocr. 15, 80, ἐξ- Pind. P. 4, 236 (B.); Theocr. 7, 51; (Eur.) I. A. 209 (chor.); Dor. pt. πονήσαις Pind. I. 1, 40: p. πεπόνηκα Ar. Pax 820; Hippocr. 6, 584; Xen. Cyr. 4, 5, 22: plp. ἐπεπονήκει Thuc. 7, 38: p. p. πεπόνημαι Soph. Tr. 985; Pl. Phaedr. 232, Dor. -ᾱμαι Pind. P. 9, 93; Theocr. 13, 14: aor. ἐπονήθην in *simple*, poet. and late prose Plut. Themist. 17, but ἐξ- Thuc. 6, 31; Dor. subj. πονᾱθῇ Pind. Ol. 6, 11. **Mid.** πονέομαι dep. *to toil &c.* Theocr. 15, 115; -έωμαι Il. 10, 70; -έοιτο 20, 359; -έεσθαι Il. 10, 116; -ούμενος Ar. Pax 954; Thuc. 4, 59; (Pl.) Ax. 368, Ion. -εύμενος Il. 13, 288: imp. Ion. ἐπονεύμην Orph. Arg. 960, -εῖτο Il. 18, 413. Od. 16, 13, πονεῖτο Il. 9, 12. Od. 15, 222: fut. πονήσομαι Hippocr. 8, 26, trans. ἀμφι- Il. 23, 159, κατα- Diod. Sic. 11, 15 (Bekk.), but πονέσομαι (Luc.) Asin. 9: aor. πονήσατο poet. in *simple*, Il. 9, 348; Simon. Am. 7, 45; Ap. Rh. 4, 718; Epic subj. πονήσομαι Od. 22, 377, δια-πονήσηται Xen. Eq. 5, 10; Pl. Leg. 966; -ήσασθαι Phil. 15; πονησάμενος Od. 9, 250; Hes. Op. 432; Inscr. Paus. 8, 52: and ἐπονήθην Eur. Hel. 1509 (chor. -άθην Herm. Dind. Nauck), ἀμφ- Archil. 12, δια- Isocr. 15, 267; Plut. Pericl. 4: p. πενόνηνται Pl. Phil. 58, Ion. -έαται Her. 2, 63, late Epic -είαται Arat. 82 (B.), -ήαται Anth. 14, 1: plp. πεπόνητο Il. 15, 447, 3 pl. Ion. -ήατο Ap. Rh. 2, 263, and without redupl. πονήατο, or -είατο Orph. Arg. 770. 1160. **Vb.** πονητέον Isocr. 15, 285.

κατα-πονήσεσθαι mid. trans. Diod. Sic. quoted, has been missed by all Lexicogr. The act. form occurs neither in Hom. nor Hes. and rarely in Her. Indeed the early poets seem to have used it as a dep. mid. Some grammarians say that πονέω retains ε, as πονέσω, when it expresses bodily pain. Classic writers however seem constantly to use it with η, as πονήσω &c. Hippocr. and the later writers use it interchangeably with ε and η without any regard to the distinction of grammarians.

Πορεύω *To cause to go, convey*, act. rare in prose, Eur. Or. 949.

Rhes. 350; -εύειν Pind. Ol. 3, 25, intrans. *go*, -εύων Pl. Leg. 893: **imp.** 'πόρευον Soph. Tr. 560: **fut.** πορεύσω Eur. Phoen. 985; Ar. Pax 126; Thuc. 4, 132: **aor.** ἐπόρευσα Eur. Med. 363, πόρευσ- Pind. N. 7, 29; Soph. O. C. 1602 (trimet.); -εῦσαι Pl. Phaed. 107. **Mid.** πορεύομαι *go, march*, in prose and poet. Aesch. Pr. 570; Soph. Tr. 392; Ar. Plut. 1041; Her. 6, 95; Thuc. 1, 133; Pl. Leg. 666: **imp.** ἐπορεύοντο Her. 8, 22; Thuc. 3, 91; Dem. 14, 39: **fut.** -εύσομαι Soph. O. R. 676; Xen. An. 3, 4, 46. Cyr. 7, 5, 20; Pl. Conv. 190: and rare πορευθήσομαι Boeckh's Inscr. 87; V. T. 3 Reg. 14, 2 (Alex.): aor. ἐπορεύθην Thuc. 1, 26; Isocr. 1, 5; Xen. An. 4, 3, 2; πορευθῶ Eur. Hec. 1099; Pl. Tim. 69; -ευθείς Eur. Hel. 51; Her. 7, 196; Xen. Mem. 3, 13, 6; Pl. Phaed. 113; -ευθῆναι Her. 8, 107; Xen. Mem. 3, 13, 5; Pl. Leg. 730: later and in comp. mid. ἐπορευσάμην, ἐν- (Pl.) Epist. 2 (313); Athen. 3, 40; Joseph. Jud. B. 1, 26, προ- Polyb. 2, 27 (Mss. A B D E, -ευόμενος Bekk. Dind. Hultsch): p. πεπόρευμαι Hippocr. 9, 230 (Mss. Lit.); Pl. Polit. 266; Dem. 53, 6. **Vb.** πορευτός Aesch. Ag. 287, -τέος Soph. Aj. 690; Pl. Leg. 968. The **aor. mid.** subj. of the simple form πορευσώμεθα occurs in some Mss. and edit. of the N. T. Jac. 4, 13 (Grsb. Mill, Knapp, Scholz), and, undisputed, earlier in comp. ἐμ-πορευσάμενος (Pl.) Epist. 2 (313), προ- Polyb. 2, 27 (Mss. Vulg.), ἐπι- 3 Macc. 1, 4, ἐμπορεύσαιτο Joseph. Jud. B. 1, 26, παρ-εμ- Luc. Hist. Con. 9.

Πορίζω *To open a way, find* (πόρος), Hom. Epigr. 14, 10; Eur. Med. 879; Ar. Ach. 385; Thuc. 8, 46; Pl. Leg. 631: **imp.** ἐπορ- Thuc. 7, 18: **fut.** -ιῶ Ar. Eq. 1079. 1101; Thuc. 6, 29, late -ίσω Artemid. Onir. 2, 68, reg.: aor. ἐπόρισα Soph. El. 1266 (D.); Isocr. 15, 113; Pl. Leg. 966: **p.** πεπόρικα Pl. Phil. 30: **p. p.** πεπόρισμαι Isocr. 15, 278; Dem. 33, 7. 44, 3: **plp.** ἐπεπόριστο Thuc. 6, 29: **aor.** ἐπορίσθην Xen. Mem. 2, 7, 12; Isocr. 4, 28, Dor. -ίχθην Epist. Pythag. 4 (Orell.): **fut.** πορισθήσομαι Thuc. 6, 37. 94. **Mid.** πορίζομαι *find, provide for oneself*, Pl. Conv. 191; -όμενος Thuc. 1, 142; Lycurg. 131: **imp.** ἐπορίζετο Thuc. 8, 76; Xen. An. 2, 1, 6: **fut.** -ιοῦμαι Thuc. 7, 15; (Pl.) Eryx. 404; Dem. 35, 41, later -ίσομαι Diod. Sc. Fr. Lib. 38–9, 23 (Bekk. -ιοῦμαι Dind. 38, 19): **aor.** ἐπορισάμην Thuc. 2, 38; 7, 58; Isocr. 15, 164; Pl. Tim. 47; πορίσαιντο Isae. 6, 13; Pl. Eryx. 404; -ίσασθαι Ar. Ran. 880; Thuc. 4, 9; Pl. Phaedr. 269; -ισάμενος Pl. Rep. 465; Xen. Mem. 3, 11, 8; Dem. 24, 46, ξυμ- Thuc. 8, 4: and in sense **p.** πεπόρισμαι Hippocr. 9, 220 (Lit.); Lys. 29, 7; Aeschin. 3, 209; Com. Fr. (Phil.) 4, 48: **plp.** ἐπεπόριστο Polyb. 8, 28. **Vb.** ποριστέον Aristot. Rhet. Alex. 37, 2. The Tragedians use only **pres.** Eur. I. A. 745 &c.: and **1 aor. act.** Soph. El. 1266 (D).

Πορπάω *To ring, fetter* (πόρπη), **aor.** ἐπόρπᾱσα, πόρπᾱσον Aesch. Pr. 61: but with η late, **p. p.** πεπορπημένος Schol. Eur. Hec. 915, and in comp. ἐμ-πεπορπημ- as mid. Lycurg. 40, see below. **Vb.** προσ-πορπᾱτός Aesch. Pr. 141. ἐμπορπάω seems not to occur in act. but mid. -άομαι, Ion. -έομαι **aor.** ἐν-επορπήσατο Polyaen. 8, 16; App. Hisp. 43: **p. p.** as mid. ἐμ-πεπορπημένος Lycurg. 40; Luc. D. Mer. 9, 1; Dio. Hal. 2, 70: **plp.** 3 pl. Ion. ἐν-επεπορπέατο Her. 7, 77. A late form is ἐμπορπόομαι, -ποῦσθαι 1 Macc. 14, 44. ἐπιπορπέομαι, -ποῦνται occurs Diod. Sic. 5, 30, but περιπορπάομαι, -ώμενοι App. Hisp. 42.

(Πόρω, πρόω) *To give*, Poet. **2 aor.** ἔπορον Il. 17, 196; Pind. Ol. 10, 93, and πόρον Il. 16, 185; Hes. Th. 412; Pind. Ol. 2, 82; Phryn. 3 (B.); subj. πόρω Il. 23, 893. Od. 22, 7; Soph. O. R. 921; πόροιμι Od. 19, 413; Soph. El. 210; imper. πόρε Il. 9, 513; Pind. I. 7, 49; Aesch. Pr. 631; πορών Il. 16, 178; Pind. P. 11, 58. I. 4, 21; Aesch. Pr. 108. 946; Soph. El. 126; inf. πορεῖν Soph. O. R. 1255; Ap. Rh. 3, 148. 4, 590, redupl. πεπορεῖν *to shew*, Pind. P. 2, 57, edited πεπαρεῖν from several Mss. by Boeckh, Schn. Bergk &c. and seemingly allied to Lat. *pareo*, English *peer*: **p. p.** πέπρωται *it is fated*, Il. 18, 329; Aesch. Pr. 815; Eur. Alc. 21; late prose Dio. Hal. 4, 2; Plut. Nic. 9. C. Gr. 1: ἐπέπρωτο Luc. Jup. conf. 14; Paus. 4, 20, 1, Poet. πέπρωτο Hes. Th. 464; πεπρωμένος Pind. P. 6, 27; Eur. Tr. 340, -ένη Soph. Ant. 1337; Her. 1, 91, -ένον Il. 3, 309; Xen. Hell. 6, 3, 6. Mem. 2, 1, 33. ἡ πεπρωμένη (αἶσα) *fate*, Aesch. Pr. 518, see 103; Isocr. 1, 43. 10, 61, so τὸ πεπρωμένον Pind. Fr. 217 (Bergk); personal μοῖρα πέπρωται and with some appearance of being mid. *has determined*, Aesch. Pr. 512, if so, the only instance we know. The **2 aor.** is entirely poetic. The *indicative* **perf.** and **plp.** occur in poetry and *late* prose, the participle in *early* prose, but rare.

Ποτάομαι *To fly*, Poet. Il. 2, 462, -ᾶται Aesch. Ag. 977; Ar. Av. 251 (Mss. Bekk. Bergk), Aeol. or Dor. -ῆται Alcm. 26; Ar. quoted (Schol. Cob. Dind. Kock), and ποτέομαι but unattic, Od. 24, 7; Alcae. 43 (Bergk); Ap. Rh. 2, 227; Opp. Hal. 1, 430: **imp.** ἐποτᾶτο Hes. Sc. 222, ἀμφ- Il. 2, 315, ποτᾶτο Archil. 125, ποτέοντο Hes. Th. 691: **fut.** ποτήσομαι, -ήσεαι Mosch. 2, 145 (Mein. πετήσ- Ahr.): **p.** πεπότημαι Od. 11, 222; Ar. Nub. 319, 3 pl. Epic -ήαται Il. 2, 90; inf. -ῆσθαι Ar. Av. 1445, Dor. πεπότᾱμαι Aesch. Pers. 669. Eum. 378 (chor.); Eur. Hipp. 564 (chor.), ἐκ- Theocr. 2, 19; also Sapph. 69 (Ahr.): **plp.** πεπότητο Hes. Sc. 148; Ap. Rh. 3, 1151; Nonn. 33, 183: **aor.** ἐποτήθην, ἐξ- Q. Sm. 4, 443, Dor. -άθην, ποτᾱθείην Soph. Fr. 423; Ar. Av. 1338 (chor.) **Vb.** ποτητός Od. 12, 62.—Aeol. 2 sing. **pres.**

πότη from πότηαι, Sapph. 20 (Ahr.), Dor. 3 sing. ποτῆται Alcm. 26 (Bergk); see Ar. Av. 251 chor. (Schol. Cob. Mein. Dind. 5 ed.); part. ποτήμενα Theocr. 29, 30; for subj. -έωνται Arat. 916, Bekker has indic. -έονται.

Πραγμᾰτεύομαι *To endeavour, be engaged in*, Pl. Prot. 361, Ion. πρηγ- Her. see below: **imp.** ἐπραγμ- Ar. Nub. 526; Isocr. 12, 2; Dem. 18, 26: **fut.** late πραγματεύσομαι Joseph. Ant. 11, 7: **aor.** ἐπραγματευσάμην Hippocr. 5, 356 (Lit.); Xen. Oec. 10, 9; (Pl.) Eryx. 398. Epist. 315; (Isocr.) Epist. 6, 5; Plut. Mor. 1061. 1121. 1143, ἐπρηγ- Hippocr. 1, 578 (Lit.): and rarer **aor. pass.** ἐπραγματεύθην as **mid.** Isocr. 12, 249; Aristot. Metaph. 1, 5, 16; Dio. Hal. 6, 91; Strab. 12, 3, 11, Ion. ἐπρηγ- Her. 2, 87: **p.** πεπραγμάτευμαι **act.** Isocr. 11, 1; Pl. Phaed. 100; Dem. 37, 49, but **pass.** Pl. Parm. 129. Apol. 22; Aeschin. 1, 167; Longin. 16, 3. **Vb.** πραγματευτέον Aristot. Pol. 7, 14, 8. This verb is Dep. with **mid.** and **pass. aor.**

Πράσσω *To do*, Batr. 185; Pind. N. 1, 26; Aesch. Eum. 928; Soph. El. 618; Antiph. 2 γ, 5; Thuc. 4, 114, Dor. 1 pl. -σσομες Theocr. 14, 3, 3 pl. -σσοντι Pind. Ol. 3, 7, later Attic -ττω Ar. Av. 800; Antiph. 2, β, 11 (-σσω Blass); Pl. Apol. 28; Isocr. 8, 136; Dem. 19, 77, Ion. πρήσσω which see: **imp.** ἔπρασσον Pind. N. 3, 46; Aesch. Pr. 457; Soph. O. C. 272; Antiph. 3, γ, 3; Thuc. 1, 57, -ττον Ar. Plut. 29; Andoc. 2, 9; Lys. 7, 14; Pl. Lach. 179; Isocr. 17, 46: **fut.** πράξω Pind. P. 8, 52; Aesch. Eum. 896; Ar. Ran. 1414; Antiph. 2, γ, 11; Thuc. 1, 90; Pl. Rep. 366: **aor.** ἔπραξα Pind. P. 2, 40; Aesch. Ag. 1467; Soph. Ph. 1269; Antiph. 2, β, 3; Thuc. 6, 79; Isocr. 5, 61; πράξαιμι Aesch. Supp. 399, -αις Pl. Rep. 353, -ειας Soph. El. 801; Ar. Eq. 498, -ειεν Soph. O. C. 391; πράξας Aesch. Eum. 469; Pl. Gorg. 514, Dor. -ξαις Pind. Ol. 8, 73: **p.** πέπρᾱχα Com. Fr. (Plat.) 2, 669. (Men.) 4, 254; Xen. Cyr. 3, 1, 15; Dinarch. 3, 21; Dem. 19, 17; Aristot. N. Eth. 3, 2 (Bekk.), Ion. -ηχα Her. 5, 106; late intrans. Aristot. Rhet. Alex. 35, 12; Plut. Sert. 3. Cleom. 22. Philop. 16: **plp.** trans. ἐπεπρᾱχει Xen. Hell. 5, 2, 32; D. Cass. 63, 6, 9: **p. p.** πέπραγμαι Aesch. Ag. 551; Soph. Fr. 779; Eur. Hipp. 680; Ar. Eq. 1248; Thuc. 3, 71; Xen. Hell. 1, 4, 1: **plp.** ἐπέπρακτο Thuc. 6, 56; Andoc. 2, 14: **aor.** ἐπράχθην Aesch. Pr. 49; Soph. Tr. 679; Antiph. 2, δ, 1; Thuc. 4, 54; Isocr. 12, 61: **fut.** πραχθήσομαι Lys. 12, 76; Aeschin. 3, 98; Isocr. Epist. 3, 3; Aristot. Rhet. 1, 3, 8 (B.); Luc. Hist. Con. 31: **3 fut.** πεπράξομαι Soph. O. C. 861; Eur. Heracl. 980; Ar. Av. 847; Dem. 19, 74, δια- Pl. Gorg. 510: with **fut. mid.** πράξεται as pass. Pl. Rep. 452 (*v. r.* πεπράξ-); so πράξεσθαι Pind. P. 4, 243 (Herm. Hart. Bergk 3 ed., but πράξασθαι Boeckh,

Schn. Bergk 2 ed. Christ): 2 p. πέπρᾱγα seemingly intrans. *have done, fared* &c. εὖ, καλῶς, κακῶς, ἀγαθά &c. *well*, or *ill*, Pind. P. 2, 73; Eur. H. F. 1375; Pl. Rep. 603: plp. ἐπεπράγειν Thuc. 2, 5; trans. in the sense *do* πέπρᾱγας Ar. Eq. 683, -γᾱσιν Aristot. Oec. 2, 1, 10; πεπραγότες Menand. Fr. 75 (Dind.) written πεπρᾱχ- Com. Fr. quoted above (Mein.), *obtain*, πεπραγότες εἶεν Xen. Hell. 1, 4, 2. **Mid.** πράσσομαι, πράττ- *exact for oneself*, Pind. Ol. 10, 30; Eur. Phoen. 1651; Pl. Prot. 328: **fut.** πράξομαι Xen. Hell. 6, 2, 36: **aor.** ἐπραξάμην Thuc. 4, 65. 8, 3; Pl. Gorg. 511; in the sense of *doing*, Aesch. Ag. 812; Pind. P. 4, 243, where Hermann suggests fut. -ξεσθαι as pass. adopted by Hartung: p. πέπραγμαι, δια- *have obtained*, Xen. Cyr. 7, 2, 12, -πέπρακται *have done*, Hell. 7, 2, 1, δια-πεπραγμένοι εἰσί Dem. 35, 26. 56, 20; Dinarch. 1, 40. 2, 21: plp. ἐπεπράγμην *had exacted*, Dem. 29, 2. **Vb.** πρακτέος Pl. Prot. 356.—α is long, hence πρᾶττε, πρᾶξαι. In Antiphon, Blass always edits -σσω except in the sixth orat. which he thinks a later production. The Ionic form is πρήσσω, Her. 5, 106 &c. πράσσω, -ττω in act. is sometimes used in the sense *exact* Pind. Ol. 3, 7; Aesch. Ch. 311; Her. 1, 106, and also in the seemingly intrans. meaning of πέπρᾱγα, as εὖ πρᾶσσε Eur. Phoen. 403, κακῶς Pl. Prot. 313 &c. but in these formulas the meaning is really trans., the *object* being merely dropped. This appears from fuller expressions, as καλὰ πράσσω Thuc. 6, 16,—τὰ μέγιστα Ar. Eccl. 104, πάντα τἀγαθὰ πεπράγαμεν Ran. 303. Thuc. and the Tragedians use the form πράσσω almost exclusively: πράττω however is the reading of the best Mss. Soph. Tr. 1156. Ph. 1449, ξύμπραττε Aj. 1396, and πράττοντας Eur. Fr. Melan. 13, is still retained (Matth., 20 Wagn., πρασσ- 509 Dind. 5 ed.); Aristoph., Plato, and the Orators, except perhaps Antiphon, πράττω; editors of Xen. vary, Dind. -ττω perhaps uniformly. πεπραξόμενα redupl. fut. part. Joseph. Ant. 18, 6, 6 (Dind. Bekk.) if correct, is unclassic, πραξόμενα, πραχθησόμενα (Mss.) perhaps correctly, see 18, 9, 5. See πολεμέω.

Πρᾱΰνω (ῡ) *To soothe*, Solon. 4, 38; Soph. Ph. 650; Xen. Eq. 9, 6, Ionic πρηΰνω Hes. Th. 254; Opp. Hal. 3, 253: **imp.** ἐπράϋνεν Aesch. Pers. 190; Isocr. 4, 47: **fut.** -ῠνῶ: **aor.** ἐπράϋνα Eur. Fr. 539 (Dind.), Ionic -ήϋνα Hom. H. 3, 417; πράϋνον Aesch. Pers. 837; -ύνας Pl. Rep. 572: **aor. pass.** ἐπραΰνθην, πραϋνθῇ Pl. Rep. 440: but fut. late πραυνθήσομαι Galen 13, 478: and p. πεπραϋσμένος Ael. N. A. 4, 16: **pres.** πραΰνεται Aristot. H. An. 8, 28, 12; πρηϋνόμενος Her. 2, 25. **Mid.** as act. late Epic, aor. πρηΰνατο Nonn. 29, 276, missed by Lexicogr.

Πρέπω *To be conspicuous, becoming, to excel*, Od. 8, 172 in tmesi; Pind. P. 10, 67; Aesch. Supp. 719; Soph. Fr. 62 (D.); Eur. Supp. 1056; Ar. Ran. 371; Pl. Leg. 775, see below: imp. ἔπρεπον Il. 12, 104; Her. 8, 68; Xen. An. 1, 9, 6, πρέπ- Pind. P. 2, 38: fut. πρέψω rare, Aesch. Eum. 995; Pl. Polit. 269. 288; Aristid. 1, 12 (D.): aor. rare, ἔπρεψα Pl. Charm. 158; Ael. V. H. 12, 1; Plut. Phoc. 20, δια- Luc. Salt. 9; πρέψας Anth. App. Epigr. 197. Often impers. πρεπει *it is becoming, fitting, proper*, Pind. P. 5, 43; Aesch. Ag. 941; Ar. Ach. 975; Her. 4, 139; Antiph. 3, γ, 9; Thuc. 7, 68; Pl. Prot. 312.

Πρήθω, see πίμπρημι.

Πρήσσω, never -ττω, *To do*, Ionic for πράσσω, Il. 11, 552. Od. 13, 83; Her. 3, 52. 7, 58; Epic subj. -σσῃσι Od. 3, 476: imp. ἔπρησσον Her. 6, 45, δι- Il. 9, 326, iter. πρήσσεσκον Od. 8, 259: fut. πρήξω Od. 19, 324; Hes. Op. 402; Her. 5, 119: aor. ἔπρηξα Il. 18, 357; Theogn. 953; Her. 1, 87. 3, 25; Hippocr. 2, 318; πρῆξαι Il. 1, 562: p. πέπρηχα *have done*, Her. 5, 106: 2 p. πέπρηγα *have fared*, 2, 172: p. p. πέπρηγμαι Her. 9, 1. 111; Hippocr. 3, 432: aor. ἐπρήχθην Her. 3, 138. 5, 106. Mid. πρήσσομαι *make for oneself* &c., *exact*, Her. 2, 126. 5, 84: fut. πρήξομαι, ἐκ- Her. 7, 158: aor. ἐπρήξαντο, δι- Her. 3, 62, ἐκ- 7, 158, συν- 5, 94, συνεξ- 7, 169. Vb. πρηκτέος Aretae. 94 (ed. Oxon.)

Πρηΰνω, see πρα-.

(Πρίαμαι) *To buy*, only 2 aor. ἐπρῐάμην Com. Fr. (Archip.) 2, 723. (Plat.) 2, 685; Thuc. 6, 98; Andoc. 3, 5; Lys. 19, 21; Lycurg. 23, πρῐάμην Od. 1, 430; Pind. P. 6, 39, 2 pers. ἐπρίω for -ίασο, Ar. Vesp. 1440; late prose Themist. 21, 252, Dor. ἐπρία Dor. Dial. p. 198 (Ahr.); subj. πρῐωμαι Ar. Ach. 812; Dem. 18, 247. 37, 37; Luc. V. Auct. 9; Plut. Mor. 1099, where stands wrongly πριεῖται; opt. πρῐαίμην Soph. Ant. 1171; Com. Fr. (Eup.) 2, 547; Xen. Mem. 2, 5, 3; Dem. 53, 21; imper. πρίᾰσο Ar. Ach. 870, and πρίω ibid. 34, both in trimet., Dor. πρία Epicharm. 93 (Ahr.); πρίασθαι Eur. Med. 233; Ar. V. 253; Lys. 19, 29; Pl. Rep. 333; πρῐάμενος Com. Fr. (Ecph.) 2, 12; Her. 1, 196; Antiph. 5, 47; Thuc. 5, 34; Isae. 11, 48; Pl. Apol. 26. Pres. imp. fut. perf. and aor. pass. supplied by ὠνέομαι, which see.

Πρίω *To saw, grind the teeth*, Hippocr. 6, 480; Opp. Hal. 2, 575; imper. πρῖε Soph. Fr. 777 (D.); Ar. Ran. 927; -ίειν Aristot. Nat. Ausc. 2, 9, 6; Theophr. H. P. 5, 6, 3, and πρίζω later (Pl.) Theag. 124: imp. ἔπριον Luc. Hist. Con. 51, ἐξ- Thuc. 7, 25: fut. (-ίσω): aor. ἔπρισα Thuc. 4, 100; Hippocr. 3, 242 (Lit.), ἀπο- Her. 4, 65, and ἔπρῖσα, ἀπ- Anth. 11, 14 (πρίζω): p. πεπρικώς, ἐμ- Diod. Sic. 17, 92: p. p. πέπρισμαι Hippocr. 3, 242, ἐκ- Ar. Pax 1135, δια- Pl. Conv. 193: **aor.** ἐπρίσθην Soph. Aj. 1030; Hippocr. 5, 214. 226, ἀπ- Archil. 122: **fut.** late πρισθήσεται Aen. Tact. 19. **Mid.** πρίομαι rare, perhaps late, Babr. 28, 8; Luc. D. Mer. 12, 2 (Bekk.); see Menand. Com. Fr. 4, 303; and Dor. part. πρῑομένα Anth. (Antip. Thess.) 9, 77: **fut.** πριεῖται Plut. Mor. 1099 seems a false reading for πρίηται subj. **2 aor.** of (πρίαμαι). **Vb.** πριστός Od. 18, 196.

Προᾰγορεύω *To tell beforehand, proclaim*, Her. 1, 125; Antiph. 5, 10; Thuc. 1, 140: **imp.** προ- ηγ- Her. 1, 22 (Bekk. Krüg. -αγ- Dind. Stein); Thuc. 2, 13: **fut.** -εύσω, for which προ-ερῶ Thuc. 1, 29: **aor.** -ηγόρευσα Her. 1, 74. 125; Com. Fr. (Men.) 4, 247; -ηγόρευκα (Dem.) 11, 20: **p. p.** προηγορευμένος Xen. Mem. 1, 2, 35 (Vulg. Kühn. Breitb. Saupp.): with **fut. mid.** προαγορεύσεται as pass. Xen. M. Eq. 2, 7 (Vulg. Saupp. 1 ed. -εύεται Zeune, Dind. Saupp. 2 ed.) **Vb.** προαγορευτέον Aristot. Sophist. Elench. 17, 19.

Προάγω, see ἄγω.

Προαπορέω, see ἀπορέω.

Προθέω, see τίθημι.

Προθῡμέομαι *To be forward, eager*, Dep. Aesch. Pr. 786; Soph. Tr. 1119; Ar. Vesp. 1173; Her. 1, 206; Thuc. 5, 50; Lys. 9, 19: **imp.** προὐθυμοῦντο Thuc. 4, 12; Pl. Rep. 402, προεθυμεῖτο Crat. 395, -έετο Her. 5, 78. 9, 38: with **fut. mid.** προθυμήσομαι Thuc. 4, 9; Xen. Cyr. 2, 3, 3; Pl. Polit. 262. Men. 74: and pass. as mid. προθυμηθήσομαι Lys. 25, 17; Pl. Phaed. 91. 115 (best Mss. Bekk. B. O. W. Stallb.): (no **mid. aor.**): **aor. p.** προὐθυμήθην as mid. Thuc. 5, 17; Antiph. 1, 6 (προεθ- Vulg.); Xen. An. 4, 1, 22. Our editions present προεθ-, more usually προὐθ-; in the older occur even a few instances of augm. before the prep. as ἐπροθυμεῖτο Xen. Ages. 2, 1, now corrected from Mss. προεθυμ-, so συνεπροθ-, συμπροὐθ- An. 3, 1, 9. The **act.** form is late, συμπροθυμοῦσαν Theodor. Stud. p. 225. **Vb.** προθυμητέον Pl. Phil. 61.

Προΐσσομαι *To beg*, in *simple* only pres. Archil. 130 (Bergk): **fut.** κατα-προΐξομαι Archil. 92 (B.); Her. 3, 36. 156. 5, 105. 7, 17, Attic -οίξομαι Ar. Thesm. 566. Eq. 436. Nub. 1240: **aor.** ἐπροΐξατο, κατ- Plut. Mor. 10, the only instance we know, for Themist. 2, 25, is at least doubtful. Herodian derives this verb from (ἴσσω), Eustath. from (προΐκω). Schneidewin questions its *authenticity*, Beitr. zur Krit. d. Poet. Lyr. 9. If ἴω, ἴσω, ἴσσω be=εἶμι, subj. ἴω, *eo, go, come*, or ἵκω id., the steps in the meanings of the compounds are easy; thus προ-ἰσσ- *I come before*, then the purpose, *to entreat, beg*, κατα-προ-ίσσ- *deprecor, deprecate, succeed in deprecating, beg off*.

Προνοέω, see νοέω.

Προοιμιάζομαι *To make a preface, premise* (προοίμιον), Dep. mid. Pl. Lach. 178: fut. -άσομαι Xen. Mem. 4, 2, 3: aor. unaugm. προοιμιασάμεθα Pl. Leg. 724: but p. πεπροοιμίασται pass. Luc. Nigr. 10, so also in the contr. form πεφροιμιασμένον Aristot. Metaph. 2, 1, 5 (B.) The act. προοιμιάζειν late, Anth. 1, 114 &c.

Προσάγω, see ἄγω.

Προσαυδάω, see αὐδάω.

Προσεμπικραίνω, see πικρ-.

Προσεξανδραποδίζομαι, see ἀνδραπ-.

Προσκαλέω, see καλέω.

Προσκυνέω, see κυνέω.

Προσνέμω, see νέμω.

Προσποιέω, see ποιέω.

Προυσελέω *To insult*, Poet. and only pres. act. προυσελοῦμεν Ar. Ran. 730: and part. pass. προυσελούμενος Aesch. Pr. 438. Derivation various and dark, Fέλος, ἕλος, σφέλας, σφέλλω, σίλλος, with προ-. See Buttm. Lexil.

Προφᾰσίζομαι *To say for oneself, feign an excuse*, Theogn. 941; Ar. Lys. 756; Xen. An. 3, 1, 25; Dem. 48, 38: imp. προὐφασίζετο Thuc. 1, 90; Dem. 48, 20: fut. -ιοῦμαι Aeschin. 3, 24 (-ίσομαι late, Schol. Ar. Eccl. 1019): aor. προεφασισάμην Dio Cass. 59, 26, contr. προὐφ- Thuc. 5, 54; Xen. Cyr. 2, 2, 30; Isae. 3, 45: and aor. pass. προεφασίσθη in pass. sense *was a pretence*, Dio Cass. Fr. 57, 72 (B.); προφασισθέν *being a pretence*, Thuc. 8, 33. **Vb.** προφασιστέον Aristot. Rhet. Alex. 30, 16.

Προφητεύω *To be an interpreter, to prophesy*, Eur. Ion 413; Her. 7, 111; Aristot. Mund. 1, 2: imp. προεφήτευον N. T. Act. 19, 6 (Vulg.), ἐπροφήτ- (Vat. Lach. Tisch.): fut. προφητεύσω Eur. Ion 369, Dor. προφᾱτ- Pind. Fr. 127 (Bergk): aor. προ-εφήτευσα Menand. Rhet. 361 (Walz); N. T. Matth. 7, 22. Marc. 7, 6 (Text. Rec.), ἐπροφήτ- (Vat. Lach. Tisch.): p. p. προπεφητεῦσθαι late, Clem. Alex. p. 604: plp. προ-πεφήτευτο Euseb. adv. Hierocl. 4 (Kayser.) The Text. Recept. of the N. Test. always augments after the preposition, Tisch. always before, so Lachm. except προεφήτευσεν Jude 14; the Septuag. varies, ἐπροφήτευον Jer. 23, 21, προ-εφήτ- 3 Reg. 18, 29: ἐπροφήτευσα Num. 11, 26, προ-εφήτ- 1 Reg. 10, 10 &c. &c.

(**Πταίρω**) in use πτάρω Aristot. Probl. 33, 1, 3 &c. see below, **πτάρνῠμαι** *To sneeze*, Hippocr. 7, 82; Xen. An. 3, 2, 9; Com. Fr. (Philem.) 4, 38; Aristot. Probl. 10, 18, 1. 33, 15; opt.

-νοιντο 10, 18, 2, but -νυντο 33, 10, 2: fut. πτἄρῶ Hippocr. 8, 484: 1 aor. ἔπτᾱρα, πτάραντες Aristot. Probl. 33, 16: usu. 2 aor. ἔπτἄρον Od. 17, 541; Ar. Ran. 647; Com. Fr. (Philem.) 4, 38; Ael. Fr. 74, ἐπ-ἐπτ- Od. 17, 545; Hom. H. 3, 297; Theocr. 7, 96. 18, 16; πτάρῃ Hippocr. 8, 484; Com. Fr. (Men.) 4, 230; πτάρε Pl. Conv. 185; πτἄρεῖν Her. 6, 107: 2 aor. mid. ἐπταρόμην, πταρῆται Hippocr. 1, 466: 2 aor. p. ἐπτἄρην, πταρῇ Anth. 11, 268; Hippocr. 7, 168; πταρείς 5, 214 (Lit.); Aristot. Probl. 8, 8. Dindorf is inclined to write pres. πταίρειν Aristot. Probl. 33, 1, 3. 11, 2. 15, 1, for πτάρειν (Bekk.) The act. form πτάρνυμι is late, Cass. probl. 44.

Πταίω *To stumble*, Thuc. 1, 122; -ωμεν Aristot. Anal. Post. 2, 11, 8; -ων Soph. Ph. 215; Pl. Theaet. 160, προσ- Hipponax 44: imp. ἔπταιεν Hippocr. 5, 414, προσ- Her. 5, 62: fut. πταίσω Dem. 2, 20: aor. ἔπταισα Dem. 18, 286; (Pl.) Epist. 351, προσ- Her. 2, 161. 7, 170; -αίσω Pind. Fr. 205 (Bergk, 4 ed.); Her. 9, 101; Thuc. 2, 43; Pl. Phil. 45; Com. Fr. (Philem.) 4, 24; πταίσας Aesch. Pr. 926; Eur. Fr. 362, 21 (D.); Thuc. 6, 12; Pl. Rep. 553, προσ- Her. 9, 107: p. ἔπταικα Aristot. Rhet. Alex. 3, 33 (Bekk.); Com. Fr. (Men.) 4, 264. (Baton) 4, 499; Dio Cass. 44, 47; Arr. An. 4, 9, προσ- Isocr. 6, 82: p. p. ἔπταισμαι, ἐπταισμένα App. Hisp. 78: aor. ἐπταίσθην Luc. Demon. 7. Vb. εὔ-πταιστος, Hippocr. 1, 78, ἄ-πταιστ- Xen. Eq. 1, 6 (πταῖσμα Dem. 2, 9). The act. alone seems to be classic.

Πτήσσω *To cower*, Ar. Vesp. 1490; Xen. Cyr. 3, 3, 18; Opp. Hal. 1, 152, Aeol. πτάζω: imp. ἔπτησσε Plut. Mor. 529 from Eur. Fr. 311 (but -ηξε 807, so Eur. Fr. Dind.); later Theod. Prodr. Catomyom. 134 (Herch.), Aeol. ἔπταζον Alcae. 27: fut. πτήξω Anth. 12, 141; Or. Sib. 5, 16; Pseudo-Callisth. 1, 35 (Meusel): aor. ἔπτηξα Od. 8, 190; Soph. O. C. 1466; Eur. H. F. 974; Philostr. Apoll. 275, πτῆξα (Il. 14, 40), in tmesi Od. 8, 190 (Bekk.); Ar. Av. 777 (chor.), Dor. ἔπταξα Pind. P. 4, 57; πτήξῃ Pl. Conv. 184, -ωμεν Ar. Thesm. 36; -ειαν Soph. Aj. 171; πτήξας Aesch. Pers. 209; Lycurg. 49; πτῆξαι Theogn. 1015; Eur. Andr. 165; Xen. Cyr. 3, 1, 26: p. ἔπτηχα Isocr. 5, 58, κατ- Lycurg. 40; Dem. 4, 8, late -ηκα Themist. 24, 309: 2 aor. ἔπτἄκον, κατα-πτἄκών Aesch. Eum. 252, also (ἔπτην) Epic, 3 dual πτήτην, κατα- Il. 8, 136: 2 p. πεπτηώς Od. 14, 354, -ῶτες 474, ὑπο- Il. 2, 312, πεπτηυῖα Ap. Rh. 2, 535, ποτι- Od. 13, 98. Pass. rare πτήσσομαι Anth. 7, 626. The part. 2 p. πεπτηώς is apt to be confounded with the corresponding part. of πίπτω. πτῆξε Il. 14, 40, if genuine, has the trans. signification *terrified*, so Theogn. 1015, and ἐξ-έπταξας Eur. Hec. 180 (chor.) In Paul. Sil. Ecphras. 1, 26, πτήσσειν, Passow says, means *to make terrific*. Is this correct? — Collat. forms, generally Epic or Ionic, πτωσκάζω pres. only, Il. 4, 372, πτώσσω Il. 21, 14; Her. 9, 48; Eur. Bacc. 223. Hec. 1065: fut. late πτώξω Maneth. 5, 237: and aor. ἔπτωξα, ὑπ- Aretae. 5, 319.

Πτίσσω, -ττω *To pound*, Com. Fr. (Pher.) 2, 345; Ar. Fr. 267 (D.); Luc. Hermot. 79: fut. -ῐσω: aor. ἔπτῐσα, πτίσας Her. 2, 92: p. p. ἔπτισμαι Hippocr. 1, 600. 6, 536. 8, 102; Aristot. H. A. 8, 7, 1; Plut. Eum. 11, περι- Ar. Ach. 507: aor. ἐπτίσθην, περι-πτισθείς Theophr. H. P. 4, 4, 10. This verb seems not to occur in classic Attic prose.

Πτολεμίζω, see πολεμ-.

Πτύρομαι *To be afraid, fear*, Hippocr. 2, 646 (K.); Plut. Philop. 12; Diod. Sic. 2, 19: **2 aor.** ἐπτῠρην, πτυρείης (Pl.) Ax. 370; -υρείς Plut. Fab. 3. Marc. 6: **fut.** πτυρήσονται Method. Sumpos. 10, 5, 275 (Jahn.) **Act.** late, **aor.** πτύραντες Hom. Clem. 2, 39.

Πτύσσω *To fold, simple* late, Phil. de Eleph. 293, but ἀνα- Soph. Fr. 284: **fut.** πτύξω, ἀνα- Eur. H. F. 1256: **aor.** ἔπτυξα (περι-ἐπτ- Polyb. 13, 7); πτύξειε, δια- Eur. Hipp. 985; πτύξας Od. 1, 439. 6, 252; Soph. O. C. 1611; Com. Fr. (Apoll. Car.) 4, 440; Hippocr. 8, 42, ἀνα- Aesch. Pers. 294; Her. 1, 125, περι- Xen. An. 1, 10, 9; πτύξαι Plut. Rom. 14: **p. p.** ἔπτυγμαι App. Civ. B. 4, 72; Herodn. 1, 17, ἀν- Xen. Hier. 2, 4; ἀν-επτύχθαι Eur. Elec. 357; -επτυγμένος Aristot. Physiog. 3, 1; but πέπτυκται H. A. 4, 9, 10 (Bekk.): **aor.** ἐπτύχθην, ἐπ- Hippocr. 5, 354 (Lit.), δια- Soph. Ant. 709, ἀνα- Hippocr. 1, 151 (K.); Xen. Cyr. 7, 5, 5: **2 aor.** ἐπτῠγην, ἀνα- Hippocr. 7, 284 (Lit.) **Mid.** πτύσσομαι *fold round oneself, bend itself*, Soph. Fr. 791; πτυσσοίμεθα, ποτι-, Od. 2, 77: **imp.** ἐπτύσσοντο Il. 13, 134: **fut.** πτύξομαι, προσ- Od. 11, 451; Eur. Phoen. 1671: **aor.** ἐπτύξατο Ion Chius 1, 5 (Bergk), πτύξατο, προσ- Od. 4, 647; Ap. Rh. 4, 94; Q. Sm. 13, 532; πτύξωνται Ar. Nub. 267, Epic πτύξεται for -ηται, προσ- Od. 3, 22. 8, 478. 15, 509; imper. πρόσ-πτυξαι Theocr. 3, 19; προσ-πτυξάμενος Luc. D. Deor. 7, 3; -πτύξασθαι Eur. Med. 1400: and in comp. **plp.** ἔπτυκτο, προσ- Pind. I. 2, 39. **Vb.** πτυκτός Il. 6, 169. For προσ-πτύσσομαι, an Epic and Doric form is ποτιπτύσσ- Od. 2, 77, see Orph. Lith. 317. In classic Attic prose the *simple* form seems not to occur.

Πτύω *To spit*, Il. 23, 697; Theocr. 15, 133 (ῡ usually in **pres.** Hom. and Theocr. quoted, and ἀπο- Il. 4, 426 &c.; Hes. Op. 726; Aesch. Eum. 303; Theocr. 27, 5); Her. 1, 99; Hippocr. 5, 672. 682. 7, 82 (Lit.); Xen. Cyr. 8, 8, 8; Luc. Nav. 15, κατα- Aeschin. 2, 23. 3, 73, δια- Dem. 18, 258: and **imp.** ἔπτυον Hippocr. 3, 124. 5, 388, ἀν-έπτῡε Soph. Ant. 1009, but ἔπτῠον Nonn. 10, 171, ἐξ-έπτῠον Theocr. 24, 19, ἀν-έπτῠε Ap. Rh. 2, 570. 4, 925: fut. πτῡ́σω Hippocr. 9, 70 (Lit.); Galen 15, 751, ἀνα- 10, 378: and mid. πτῡ́σομαι Hippocr. 2, 396. 6, 198. 8, 98. 100, ἐκ- Anth. 5, 197, προσ- Luc. D. Mort. 20, 2: aor. ἔπτῡσα Hippocr. 4, 218. 5, 406; Ap. Rh. 4, 478; Theocr. 22, 98; Anth. 7, 283, ἐξ- Od. 5, 322, ἀπ- Aesch. Ag. 1192; Eur. H. F. 560. Hec. 1276; Soph. Fr. 616 (D.); Ar. Pax 528, κατ- Luc. Alex. 50; πτύσῃς Apocr. Sir. 28, 12, πτύσῃ Hippocr. 7, 82; πτύσον, κατα- Ar. Ran. 1179; πτύσας Soph. Ant. 653; Luc. Apol. 6; πτῦσαι Com. Fr. (Epicr.) 3, 366; Hippocr. 6, 184; Strab. vol. 3, p. 566 (Kram.): p. late ἔπτῠκα Sext. Emp. 342, 26 (B.); Galen 10, 374: p. p. (ἔπτυσμαι): aor. ἐπτύσθην Hippocr. 6, 194. 198 (Lit.), ἀπ- Long. Past. 3, 90 (Seil.); Alciphr. 1, 10 (Mein.): fut. late πτυσθήσεται, ἀνα- Galen 9, 686; -σόμενος 15, 700; Oribas. 5, 1: 2 aor. ἐπτῠ́ην Hippocr. 5, 106 (Lit.) Vb. κατά-πτυστος Aesch. Eum. 68. Classic writers seem to use the act. only, and rarely in the *simple* form. Hom. and Her. the pres. once, Xen. twice, Soph. and perhaps the comic Poet. Epicrates the aor. once.

Πύθω *To make rot,* Poet. Hes. Op. 626: imp. iter. πύθεσκε Ap. Rh. 4, 1530: fut. πύσω Il. 4, 174; Hom. H. 2, 191: aor. ἔπῡσα, πῦσε Hom. H. 2, 196, κατ-έπῡσε 193, but πῦσε Callim. Fr. 313. Pass. πύθομαι *rot, decay,* Il. 11, 395. Od. 1, 161; Ap. Rh. 4, 1405; late prose, Paus. 10, 6; imper. πύθευ H. H. 2, 185; -όμενος Od. 12, 46: imp. ἐπύθοντο Paus. 10, 6: with perf. κατα-πέπῡθα, κατ- ερρύηκα (Hesych.)

Πῠκάζω *To make thick, cover,* Anacreont. 17, 6 (B.), Dor. -κάσδει Theocr. 3, 14: -κάζοιεν Od. 12, 225; πύκαζε Soph. Aj. 581; Eur. Tr. 353; Dor. inf. -κάσδειν Theocr. 2, 153, -σδεν (Mein.): imp. ἐπύκαζον Theocr. 20, 23; Bion 2, 20: fut. -ᾰ́σω: aor. πύκασε Il. 8, 124. 17, 83, πύκασσε Sapph. 89 (Bergk); πυκᾰ́σας Il. 17, 551, -άσσας Hes. Op. 542; πυκᾰ́σαι Od. 11, 320; Hes. Op. 624: p. p. πεπύκασται Xenophanes 1, 11 (Bergk); Mosch. 1, 15 (Ziegl. Ahr.); -ασμένος Il. 14, 289; Hes. Op. 793; Theocr. 7, 67, Aeol. πεπυκαδμένος Sapph. 56 (Bergk, -κάδμενος Ahr.): aor. ἐπυκάσθην, πυκασθῇ Athen. (Archestr.) 7, 113; Eur. Alc. 796; Her. 7, 197; (Luc.) Amor. 10. Mid. πυκάζομαι *cover, equip oneself with, make ready,* Aesch. Sept. 149 (Vulg.); Eur. Heracl. 725: fut. late -άσσεται Maxim. de Ausp. 513: aor. πυκάσαντο Opp. C. 4, 394; subj. πυκάσωμαι Anth. 11, 19. Not in early Attic prose, rare in Ionic and late.

Πυνθᾰ́νομαι *To hear, inquire,* Od. 2, 315; Aesch. Pr. 744; Soph. O. C. 1155; Ar. Plut. 25; Her. 7, 101; Antiph. 5, 71; Thuc. 7, 12; Xen. Hell. 4, 1, 11, Poet. but not in Comedy, πεύθομαι Od. 3, 87; Mimnerm. 14, 2; Pind. P. 4, 38; Aesch. Ch. 679; Soph. O. R. 604; Eur. I. A. 1138; Theocr. 12, 37; πευθοίατο Od. 4, 70: **imp.** ἐπυνθανόμην *heard*, Her. 9, 18; Lys. 23, 3; Dem. 21, 85, -οντο Her. 2, 160; Thuc. 2, 57, *inquired*, Her. 7, 100; Xen. Cyr. 1, 4, 7, πυνθανόμην Od. 13, 256, ἐπευθόμην Il. 17, 408; Eur. Rhes. 767, πευθ- Il. 11, 21; Hes. Th. 463: **fut.** πεύσομαι Od. 23, 262; Aesch. Ch. 765; Soph. El. 470; Eur. Or. 1368; Ar. Pax 67; Her. 9, 58; Thuc. 3, 26; Lys. 1, 21; Pl. Rep. 530, Ep. 2 sing. -σεαι Il. 18, 19, rarely Dor. πευσοῦμαι Theocr. 3, 51; Aesch. Pr. 988, where Dindorf reads with Ms. N. -σομαι: **p. p.** πέπυσμαι Od. 11, 505; Aesch. Ch. 526; Pl. Charm. 153; Dem. 19, 201. 21, 208, πέπῡσαι Pl. Prot. 310, Epic -υσσαι Od. 11, 494, -υσται Eur. Andr. 70; πεπύσθαι Ar. Av. 957; Thuc. 7, 67; πεπυσμένος Aesch. Ag. 261; Soph. Tr. 292; Her. 2, 91; Antiph. 5, 25; Thuc. 8, 51; Lys. 12, 17; Isocr. 21, 21; Aeschin. 3, 77: **plp.** ἐπεπύσμην (Dem.) 47, 38, -πυστο Il. 13, 674; Hym. Apol. Del. 97, πεπύσμην Ar. Pax 615. Thesm. 596, after a vowel, so πέπυστο Il. 13, 521, dual πεπύσθην Il. 17, 377: **2 aor. mid.** ἐπῡθόμην Il. 18, 530; Ar. Ran. 504; Her. 1, 27; Antiph. 6, 40; Thuc. 4, 6; Lys. 9, 5; Pl. Phaed. 59; Xen. Hell. 1, 1, 14, πυθόμ- Od. 23, 40; -θωμαι Aesch. Pers. 117; Soph. O. C. 11; Her. 1, 32; Pl. Rep. 344; Dem. 19, 341, Ep. 2 sing. -θηαι Il. 5, 351; -θοίμην Il. 19, 322; Soph. Tr. 93; Pl. Rep. 328, Epic πεπυθ- Il. 6, 50; Ap. Rh. 4, 1469, 3 pl. Ion. πυθοίατο Il. 1, 257; in trimeter Soph. O. C. 921; πῡθοῦ Com. Fr. (Menand.) 4, 321, Ionic πύθευ Her. 3, 68 (Gaisf. Bekk. Stein, πυθεῦ Dind.); πυθέσθαι Il. 11, 649; Pind. P. 7, 7; Eur. Hipp. 270; Ar. Av. 47; Thuc. 5, 74; πυθόμενος rare, we think, in Poet. Eur. I. T. 797; Com. Fr. (Alex.) 3, 501. (Timocl.) 3, 598. (Men.) 4, 147; Her. 1, 20. 52 &c.; Thuc. 4, 50; Isocr. 19, 2; Lycurg. 85; Aeschin. 3, 77; Pl. Leg. 917; Xen. Mem. 1, 3, 8 &c. **Vb.** ἀνά-πυστος Od. 11, 274, πυστέος Pl. Soph. 244. No **1 aor. mid.** and no **aor.** or **fut.** of the **pass.** form.

Some assert that this verb in Homer and Herodotus always means *to learn by hearsay* without implying *previous inquiry*. We doubt this. ὅ με προέηκε πυθέσθαι Il. 11, 649, and ἔρχεο πευσόμενος πατρὸς δὴν οἰχομένοιο Od. 1, 281. 15, 270, seem to imply *inquiry*, for besides the *nature* of the errand, Patroclus is enjoined (Il. 11, 611) ἴθι ... ἔρειο, and Telemachus (Od. 1, 284) ἐλθὲ καὶ εἴρεο; and in Her. ἐπυνθάνετο 1, 35. 2, 2. 4, 167. 5, 92, implies direct *inquiry*, and in 7, 100, seems to have as an equivalent, or to be explained by ἐπειρωτέων; so ἄγγελον ἔπεμπον πευσόμενοι Her. 4, 145, see 167. 7, 139; ἐπειρόμενος ἐπύθετο 3, 64 &c. We are inclined to doubt the Dor. fut. form πευσεῖσθε

Aesch. Pr. 988, quoted. It is neither required by the *metre*, nor the *dialect*. Besides, there is not a trace of the Doric form in any other Attic writer, nor even in Aeschylus himself. πεύσομαι stands in all Mss. and edit. Ag. 599, where -οῦμαι is admissible, and for πεύσεσθε Pr. 642, one would as readily expect -εῖσθε as at 988, where in most Mss. and edit. it does stand, nor is there any trace of the Dor. πευσεῖ for πεύσει Pr. 963. Ag. 266. Eum. 415. 419. 454. We are therefore inclined to think that πεύσεται (Mss. Vit. Colb. 1. Par. D. Schütz, Dind.) ought to be preferred to -εῖσθε though supported by (Mss. M. G. Lips. Par. B. old edit. and Blomf. Herm. Well. &c.) Attic prose writers however have both πλεύσομαι and -οῦμαι, and Aristoph. has without necessity of metre at least πνευσεῖται Ran. 1221 (-εται Dind.)

Πῡρέσσω *To have a fever*, Eur. Cycl. 228; Hippocr. 4, 558 (Lit. 1, 437 Erm.), Attic -έττω Ar. Vesp. 813; Pl. Theaet. 178; so Hippocr. 2, 618 (Lit.): but imp. ἐπύρεσσ- 3, 112 (Lit.), -εττε Plut. Alex. 76: fut. πυρέξω Hippocr. 8, 16 (Lit.): aor. ἐπύρεξα Hippocr. 2, 152. 3, 106. 5, 170 (Lit.); Anth. 11, 118; Aristot. Nat. Ausc. 5, 4, 10; Plut. Alex. 76, -εσα see below: p. πεπύρεχα, -ρεχότες Aristot. Probl. 11, 22; -εχέναι Galen 10, 588: p. p. πεπυρέχθαι Galen 4, 447. The aor. form ἐπύρεσε which occurs in Hippocr. 3, 516. 553. 563 (Kühn) appears to be a false reading. In the first instance the Mss. have ἐπηρέτηνεν (C), ἐπύρεσσε (D H K), in the second ἐπύρεσσεν (id.), in the third ἐπύρεσσεν (D Γ G H I). Accordingly Littré reads aor. ἐπυρέτηνεν 5, 150, and imp. ἐπύρεσσε 5, 216. 230, of his edition.

Πῡρῐάω *To put into a vapour bath*, -ιῆν Hippocr. 7, 422, but -ιᾶν 7, 26: fut. -ήσω: aor. -ησα 7, 34. 60 reg.: πεπυριημένος 8, 436: πυριηθῇ 7, 168. 194, and noted here simply because mid. πυριῆσθαι Hippocr. 6, 516. 7, 322: aor. πυριήσηται 7, 322. 422; -ήσασθαι 8, 128, have been missed by all Lexicogr.

Πωλέομαι *To go about*, Epic, Od. 4, 384; Hes. Th. 781, Ionic -εῦμαι Emped. 356; πωλεύμενος Od. 2, 55: imp. πωλεύμην Od. 22, 352, -εῖτο 9, 189, but ἐπ-επωλ- Il. 4, 250, iter. πωλέσκετο Il. 5, 788: fut. πωλήσομαι Hom. H. 2, 151, 2 sing. -ήσεαι Il. 5, 350.—πωλέ' Od. 4, 811, 2 sing. pres. for πωλέεαι, not πώλεο, nor does either it or πωλέσκετο require a form πώλομαι, in an Epic writer.

Πωλέω *To sell*, Eur. Cycl. 260; Ar. Plut. 167; Her. 3, 139; Thuc. 7, 39; Pl. Rep. 260; Aeschin. 1, 119, Dor. 3 pl. -λοῦντι Epich. 120: imp. ἐπώλουν Ar. Eq. 316, -λεε Her. 8, 105, -λει Isae. 2, 28, -λουν Isocr. 13, 4, iter. πωλέεσκε Her. 1, 196: fut. -ήσω Ar. Fr. 460 (D.); Xen. Cyr. 6, 2, 38: aor. ἐπώλησα Plut.

Philop. 16: aor. p. ἐπωλήθην Pl. Polit. 260: 3 fut. πεπωλήσεται late, Aenae. Tact. 10: but classic, fut. mid. πωλήσεται as pass. Com. Fr. (Eubul.) 3, 241: pres. πωλοῖτο Thuc. 2, 60; πωλεόμενος Her. 8, 105, -εύμενος Hom. Epigr. 14, 5, -ούμενος Thuc. 7, 39: imp. ἐπωλ- 8, 95.

Πωτάομαι *To fly*, Epic for ποτ-, H. Hym. 30, 4; Pind. Fr. 109 (Bergk); Theocr. 15, 122; Mosch. 4, 24: imp. πωτῶντο Il. 12, 287; Hom. H. 2, 264; Simon. (C.) 40; Theocr. 7, 142: fut. πωτήσομαι Theogn. 238, for which Ahrens (Dor. Dial. p. 288) says πωτάομαι is Dor. Ar. Lys. 1013, at the same time suggesting πωταίομαι: with aor. p. late ἐπωτήθην Anth. 7, 699, ἐξ- Babr. 12, 1.

Ρ.

Ῥαίνω *To sprinkle*, Pind. P. 8, 57; Com. Fr. (Xenarch.) 3, 621; Aristot. Meteor. 3, 4, 17; Theophr. C. P. 4, 3, 3; Plut. Mor. 614; Philostr. Apoll. 259; Poet. inf. -νέμεν Pind. I. 6, 21: imp. ἔρραινον Com. Fr. (Alex.) 3, 410: fut. ῥᾰνῶ Eur. Fr. 388 (Dind.); Lycophr. 1104: aor. ἔρρᾱνα Eur. Rhes. 73; Com. Fr. (Arched.) 4, 435; Anth. 12, 132; Charit. 1, 3 (D'Orv.); Luc. Scyth. 2, ἐξ- Eur. Cycl. 402, Ionic ἔρρηνα Hippocr. 3, 99, κατα- 2, 160 (K.), Epic ἔρηνα Opp. Hal. 2, 100, and (ῥαδ-) ἔρρασσα, imper. ῥάσσατε Od. 20, 150: p. ἔρραγκα, δι- V. T. Prov. 7, 17: p. p. ἔρρασμαι Schol. Il. 12, 431, ἔρρανται Aesch. Pers. 569 (Herm.), Epic ἐρρᾰ́δᾰται Od. 20, 354: plp. ἐρράδᾰτο Epic 3 pl. Il. 12, 431; late part. ἐρραμένα Athen. (Persae.) 4, 140, -αμμένα (Palat.): aor. ἐρράνθην, ῥανθείς Pind. P. 5, 100; Aristot. Prob. 25, 5 (B.); Dioscor. 4, 15; Geop. 13, 12, but ἐπιρραθ- Dioscor. 3, 45: imp. ῥαίνοντο Il. 11, 282. Mid. late, aor. ῥᾱνάμενος, περι- Plut. Arist. 20; -ράνασθαι Athen. 2, 19; Long. Past. 3, 28. Vb. ῥαντός late. This verb seems not to occur in good Attic prose.

Ῥαίω *To strike, tear in pieces, destroy*, Poet. ῥαίουσι, δια- Od. 12, 290; ῥαίησι Od. 5, 221: imp. ἔρραιε Od. 6, 326: fut. ῥαίσω Orph. L. 598, δια-ρραίσει Il. 9, 78; Q. Sm. 10, 403, ἀπο- Hes. Th. 393; Epic inf. ῥαισέμεναι Od. 8, 569: aor. ἔρραισα Ap. Rh. 1, 617; ῥαίσῃ Od. 23, 235; ῥαῖσαι 13, 151; Opp. H. 4, 686: aor. p. ἐρραίσθην Il. 16, 339; Pind. Fr. 88 (Bergk); ῥαισθῇ Aesch. Pr. 189: with fut. mid. διαρραίσεσθαι as pass. Il. 24, 355 (Schol.), as act. (Damm): pres. pass. ῥαίοιτο Od. 9, 459.

Ῥᾰπίζω *To scourge*, Xenophan. 6, 4 (Bergk); Hipponax 5; Her. 7, 35; Aristot. De Anima 2, 8, 5: imp. ἐρράπιζον Her. 7,

223: fut. ῥαπίσει N. T. Matth. 5, 39 (Vulg. Tisch. 7 edit., -ίζει Vat. Lachm. Tisch. 8 edit.): **aor.** ἐρράπισα Dem. 25, 57; Luc. Herm. 81: **p. p.** redupl. ῥεραπισμένος Anacr. 166 (Bergk): **aor.** ἐρραπίσθην, ῥαπισθείη Hipponax 9; ῥαπισθῆναι Com. Fr. (Timocl.) 3, 607.

Ῥάπτω *To stitch* &c. Od. 16, 422; Com. Fr. (Alex.) 3, 422; ῥάπτειν Ar. Pl. 513: **imp.** ἔραπτον Od. 16, 379, ῥάπτ- 3, 118, iter. ῥάπτεσκε, ποτι-ρρ- Eratosth. 1, 7: **fut.** ῥάψω, ἀπο- Aeschin. 2, 21: **aor.** ἔρραψα Eur. Andr. 911; Her. 9, 17; D. Hal. Ant. 11, 35, Epic ῥάψα Il. 12, 296: **2 aor.** late, ἔρρᾰφον, συν- Nonn. 7, 152: (**perf.**): **plp.** late ἐρρᾰφήκει, συν- Xen. Ephes. 1, 9 (Bast, Passow, συν-ηρμόκει Herch.): **p. p.** ἔρραμμαι, ἔρραπται Dio. Hal. 3, 7; -αμμένος Ar. Eccl. 24; Com. Fr. (Alex.) 3, 423. κατ- Her. 2, 96; ἐρράφθαι Xen. Eq. 12, 9; Dem. 54, 35 (Eur. Bacc. 243 Reisk. Kirchh. Nauck): Epic **plp.** συν-έραπτο Q. Sm. 9, 359: **2 aor.** ἐρρᾰ́φην Eur. Bacc. 243 (Vulg. rejected by Dind.); Hippocr. 3, 524, ἐν- Eur. Bacc. 286 (Vulg. Kirchh. Nauck); ῥαφῆναι Dem. 54, 41: **fut.** late, συρ-ραφήσεται Galen 13, 685. **Mid. aor.** ἐρράψατο, ἐν- Her. 2, 146; ῥάψαιτο Hippocr. 3, 518 (Lit.); -άμενος Ar. Eq. 784; Her. 3, 9; Athen. (Chrysip.) 4, 49; -ασθαι Polyaen. 4, 6, 11. **Vb.** ῥαπτός Od. 24, 228, προσ-ραπτέον Plut. Mor. 190. ἔραψεν Hom. H. Merc. 79, is a conjecture of Matth. (ἔριψεν Mss.), approved by Herm. and Franke, but ἔρριψεν (Schneid. Baumeist.) Dind. rejects the passage where ἐρράφην occurs in Eur. Bacc. 243, ἐν- 286.

Ῥάσσω, -ττω *To throw down*, **pres.** late V. T. Jer. 23, 39, συρ-ράττουσι Dio. Hal. Ant. 8, 18 (allied to ἀράσσω, ῥήσσω, and sometimes interchanged with them): **fut.** ῥάξω V. T. Esai. 9, 11, ξυρ- Thuc. 8, 96: **aor.** ἔρραξα, ῥάξας Dem. 54, 8, ἐπι- Soph. O. C. 1503, συν-έρραξε Xen. Hell. 7, 5, 16, κατ- Ael. N. A. 3, 18: **p. p.** (συν-ερραγμένος Krüg. suggests for συν-ηρραγμ- Dio. Hal. 3, 33): **aor. p.** ἐρράχθην, κατ- Thuc. 7, 6 (some Mss. Haack, κατ-ηράχθην Bekk. Popp. Krüg.); ῥαχθῆναι, ἐπι- Dio. Hal. 8, 18: **fut. mid.** ῥάξεσθαι, καταρρ- as **pass.** Plut. Caes. 44, missed by Lexicogr.

Ῥᾰχίζω *To divide the spine* (ῥάχις), only **pres.** ῥᾰχίζει Dinarch. Fr. 80 (Bait. Saup.); -ίζων Soph. Aj. 56: and **imp.** ἐρράχιζον Aesch. Pers. 426, κἀρράχιζον Soph. Aj. 299.

Ῥέζω *To do* (ἔρδω, ἔργω), Poet. Il. 23, 206; Hes. Op. 685; Pind. N. 4, 32; Mosch. 2, 140; rare in Attic, Com. Fr. (Pher.) 2, 335; Epic subj. ῥέζῃσι Hes. Fr. 185: **imp.** ἔρεζον Il. 2, 400. Od. 23, 56, ῥέζον 3, 5, iter. ῥέζεσκον Il. 8, 250: **fut.** ῥέξω Od. 11, 31; Hym. 2, 213; Aesch. Sept. 105; Soph. O. C. 1724; Eur. Alc. 261: **aor.** ἔρρεξα rare, Il. 9, 536. 10, 49; in prose, only Pl. Leg. 642, usu. poetic ἔρεξα Il. 9, 453. 23, 570. Od. 18, 139;

Hes. Fr. 217; Anacr. 109; Solon 36, 15 (v. r. ἐρρ-); Soph. O. C. 538 (chor.); Eur. Andr. 838. Elec. 1226 (chor.), ῥέξα Il. 9, 535; part. ῥέξας Il. 22, 305; Aesch. Ch. 315, Dor. ῥέξαις Pind. Ol. 9, 94: aor. p. ῥεχθείη Hippocr. 5, 384 (Mss. Lit.); ῥεχθείς Il. 9, 250. 20, 198. Vb. ἄ-ρεκτος Il. 19, 150. The Attic poets seem not to have used the pres. ἀνὴρ τόδε ῥέζει in Pherecr. Com. Fr. 2, 335, is taken, according to Athenaeus, from Hesiod. Epic and Lyric Poets have double or single ρ after the augment; the Tragedians, we think, have single ρ only in chor. Soph. no doubt has ἔρεξα, ἔρεξας in a trimeter O. C. 538, but it is a trimeter in chor. where the poet had the privilege of Epic licence. In 785 of the Rhesus too, where however a case with single ρ would for several reasons be less notable, use to stand ἔρεγκον in the *diverbia*. But now ἔρρεγκον is read by Nauck, Kirchhoff and Dindorf. ἐξ-ερυσάμην Aesch. Pr. 235, seems to be a false reading for ἐξ-ελυσ-.

'Ρέπω *To bend, incline*, Pind. Ol. 8, 23; Aesch. Sept. 21; Eur. Fr. 536 (D.); Ar. Plut. 51; Pl. Rep. 485; ῥέπων Pind. P. 9, 25; Soph. O. R. 847; Isocr. 15, 4; Dem. 18, 298; -πειν Soph. Ant. 722; Xen. Lac. 4, 1: imp. ἔρρεπον Hippocr. 2, 604 (Lit.); Luc. D. Mort. 11, 1, and ἔρεπον Polyb. 29, 9. 33, 15 (Vulg.), ἐρρ- (Bekk. Dind.), Epic ῥέπον Il. 8, 72. 22, 212: fut. ῥέψω Her. 7, 139; Paus. 9, 37: aor. ἔρρεψα Pl. Phil. 46. Epist. 328; Hippocr. 4, 166. 216 (Mss. Lit.); ῥέψω Anth. 12, 86. Pass. ῥεπόμενος Aesch. Supp. 405. Hom. has imp. only, Trag. and Comed. pres. Attic prose pres. and aor.

'Ρέω *To flow* (ῥεύω, ῥύω), ῥέει Il. 22, 149; Mimnerm. 5, 1; Her. 1, 72. 5, 52, ῥεῖ H. Ven. 237; Aesch. Sept. 80; Soph. Tr. 698; Ar. Lys. 1034; Thuc. 2, 96, Dor. 3 pl. ῥέοντι Theocr. 14, 38, occas. ῥείω Hes. Fr. 237 (G.); Anth. 7, 36; Dor. pt. ἀπο-ρρέοισα (Pl.) Tim. Locr. 102: imp. ἔρρει Il. 17, 86; Eur. Ph. 1471; Xen. Hell. 5, 4, 58, ἔρρεε Il. 23, 688; Her. 2, 121 (4), ἔρρεον Hes. Fr. 42; Com. Fr. (Pher.) 2, 299, ῥέε Il. 4, 451, περίρρεε Od. 9, 388, ῥέον Hes. Sc. 267, iter. ῥέεσκε, προ- Ap. Rh. 3, 225: fut. ῥεύσομαι Theogn. 448; Hippocr. 6, 440. 442. 7, 224 &c.; rare in Attic, Eur. Fr. 388 (Dind.); Com. Fr. (Crat.) 2, 238. (Pher.) 2, 316, later -σοῦμαι Aristot. Meteor. 2, 2, 23. 2, 4, 20: and ῥεύσω Anth. 5, 125; Or. Sib. 3, 84; Geop. 9, 12, ἐκ- Aretae. 48 (ed. Oxon.); Hierocl. 182 (Eberh.), see below: aor. ἔρρευσα Mosch. 3, 33; Anth. (Parm.) 5, 33; Hippocr. 7, 612. 6, 296. 302. 308 (Lit.); and late, Paus. 5, 7; Artemidor. 1, 48; Galen 10, 311, ἐπ- Ael. V. H. 12, 60, δι- H. A. 11, 10; ῥεύσῃ Bion 1, 48; rare in Attic, ῥεύσειε (Eur.) Dan. 32; (Alciphr. 3, 64; ῥευσάτω Luc. Bis Acc. 16); ῥεύσας Ar. Eq. 526 (Anapaest.); Himer. Or. 21, 10; ῥεῦσαι

Aristot. Mirab. 87, περι- Lycurg. 96, ῥεῦσαι trans. Themist. 27, 335, late ἔρρῦσα, ὑπεκρύσαντος J. Damasc. T. 1, 126: p. (ῥέρευκα late, Orig. Ref. Haer. p. 136, and ἔρρυκα Galen 5, 398, but) ἐρρύηκα Hippocr. 6, 296; Pl. Rep. 485; Isocr. 8, 5, συν- 8, 44; Isae. 2, 28, παρ- Soph. Ph. 653, ἐξ- Ar. Av. 104, προ- Hippocr. 5, 558: (p. p.): (1 aor.): fut. late ἀπορρυηθήσομαι Barnab. Epist. 11, 19 (Muralto, -ρυήσομαι Tischend.): **2 aor. p.** ἐρρύην as act. Aesch. Fr. 434; Her. 8, 138; Hippocr. 2, 658. 5, 114 (Lit.); Thuc. 3, 116; Xen. Cyr. 8, 3, 30; Dem. 19, 287. Epic ῥύη Od. 3, 455; ῥυῇ Eur. Hipp. 443; Hippocr. 1, 432 (Erm.), καταρρ- Ar. Pax 145; ῥυείς Pl. Tim. 84, ἀπο- Aesch. Ag. 1294; ῥυῆναι Thuc. 3, 116: **2 fut.** ῥυήσομαι Hippocr. 6, 42; Aristid. 1, 7 (Dind.), εἰσ- Isocr. 8, 140. **Mid.** ῥεῖται Anth. 9, 522: **imp.** ἐρρεῖτο Eur. Hel. 1602; Philostr. Apoll. 371, δι- Heliod. 10, 13 (B.); ῥεόμενος Hippocr. 7, 320. 8, 48 (Lit.); Polyaen. 4, 2, 6; Plut. Lucull. 10. Timol. 12; Luc. D. Mort. 14, 5. Tyran. 3. Herm. 5. Salt. 71 &c., Poet. ῥεούμ- Orac. Her. 7, 140 (Gaisf. Bekk.): **fut.** ῥεύσομαι see above: **aor.** late κατερρεύσατο Ann. Comn. 15, p. 475. **Vb.** ῥυτός Eur. Hipp. 123, ῥευστός Plut. Mor. 268.

ῥέει, ἐκ- is trans. *discharges*, Aretae. Morb. Diut. 1, 49 (ed. Oxon.): so **imp.** ἔρρει *poured*, Eur. Hec. 528, αἴρει (Kirchh. Nauck and Dind. 5 ed.); so inf. προρέειν Hom. H. 2, 202 (προχέειν Eust. Wolf); προρέων Orph. Arg. 1137: and **imp.** iter προρέεσκε Ap. Rh. 3, 225 (*v. r.* προχέεσκε &c.); ῥεούμενος in an oracle Her. 7, 140, is not a 'contraction,' but an Epic lengthening for the metre. **Fut. act.** ῥεύσω Hippocr. 1, 432 (Kühn) we suspect for two reasons: *first*, he very frequently uses ῥεύσομαι 6, 440. 442. 7, 224. 256. 556. 588. 8, 100. 124; *second*, in the passage quoted, the reading ῥεύσει τε is so near ῥεύσεται that we believe the former a mistake for the latter. (This emendation is now confirmed: Littré (7, 256) has edited ῥεύσεται from Mss. so Ermerins 2, 365.) The only other instance of **fut. act.** in the *Hippocratic* writings is ῥεύσει τε &c. 8, 596 (Lit.) which, if necessary, may perhaps be treated in the same way, but if thought sound, we should say is a symptom of a late hand. For ῥεύσαντα Pl. Rep. 544, ῥέψαντα has been restored from Mss. ῥύη Epic **2 aor. p.** for ἐρρύη, Od. 3, 455. This verb like other dissyllabic verbs in εω does not contract εη, εο, εω.

(Ῥέω) *To say*, **p.** εἴρηκα Aesch. Pr. 821; Soph. Tr. 456; Ar. Ran. 558. Nub. 910; Thuc. 6, 87: **p. p.** εἴρηται Il. 4, 363; Aesch. Eum. 710; Soph. Ant. 725; Eur. Heracl. 117; Ar. Eccl. 68; Her. 3, 9; Pl. Rep. 468, -ηνται Leg. 804, -έαται Her. 7, 96: **plp.** εἴρητο Thuc. 1, 139: **aor.** ἐρρήθην Eur. I. T. 91; Xen. Cyr. 6, 1, 19; Aeschin. 2, 31; ἐρρέθην perhaps unattic,

Aristot. however, Categ. 9 (Bekk.); Dio Cass. 47, 42 (Bekk.), προ-ερρέθην (*v. r.* -ήθην) Hippocr. 5, 196 (Lit.), genuine Ionic εἰρέθην Her. 4, 77. 156. 6, 15. 7, 184. 8, 119 (Mss. Gaisf. Bekk. Krüg. Dind. Bred.), ἐρρήθ-, εἰρήθ- (some Mss. Wessel. Schaef.); other moods always with η, subj. ῥηθῇ Aeschin. 1, 31, -θῶσι Dinarch. 1, 91; ῥηθείη Aristot. Top. 1, 6; ῥηθείς Od. 18, 414; Pind. P. 4, 74; Soph. El. 668. O. R. 1057; Eur. El. 622; Her. always, 1, 91. 109. 6, 86. 7, 142. 149 &c.; Thuc. 5, 60; Pl. Phil. 48; ῥηθῆναι Her. 3, 9; Isae. 6, 17; Isocr. 12, 192: fut. ῥηθήσομαι, -σεται Hippocr. 2, 362 (Lit.); Thuc. 1, 73; Xen. Hell. 6, 3, 7; Pl. Rep. 473. Leg. 957, προσ- Polit. 259. 301. Rep. 479, ἀναρρηθ- Aeschin. 3, 147, ῥηθήσονται Aristot. Top. 5, 4; Hyperid. Leosth. Col. 2, 13 (B.); Aenae. Tact. 11, the only instances of pl. we know; -ήσεσθαι Isocr. 12, 258. 15, 55. 240 &c.; Aeschin. 1, 192. 3, 8; Pl. Phaed. 88. Critias 107. Leg. 880 &c.; -ησόμενος Thuc. 8, 66; Pl. Critias 107; Isocr. 8, 63; Aeschin. 1, 93; Dem. 22, 4. 24, 194. 27, 53 &c.: **3 fut.** εἰρήσομαι, -σεται always in Hom. Il. 23, 795; Pind. I. 6, 59; always in Trag. Soph. O. R. 365. Ph. 1276; Eur. Hec. 825. Phoen. 928 &c.; Ar. Plut. 114; and Her. 2, 35. 4, 16. 82. 6, 86; Thuc. 6, 34; Pl. Theaet. 179; εἰρήσεσθαι, and εἰρησόμενος are not Attic, see εἴρω. **Vb.** ῥητός Il. 21, 445, -έος Hippocr. 3, 414; Pl. Apol. 22. The strict Attic form of **aor. pass.** seems to be ἐρρήθην, the strict Ionic εἰρέθην. ἐρρέθην has occasionally support in the Mss. and editions of the orators, Aeschin. 2, 31. 118; often in those of Plato, Leg. 664. Theaet. 168. Conv. 193 &c. where late editors have generally substituted ἐρρήθην. Bait. Orell. however still retain ἐρρέθην Theaet. 168. In Her. εἰρήθην is sometimes well supported, 7, 184. At 8, 119, occur as a *v. r.* ἠρέθη, ἐρρέθη. Old editions have often ἐρρήθην, but Gaisf. Bekk. Krüg. Dind. Bred. &c. always, we think, εἰρέθην: ε however is confined to *indic.*, ῥηθείς Her. 1, 109. 6, 86; ῥηθῆναι Her. 3, 9, see above.

Ῥήγνῡμι *To break*, Il. 17, 751; Aesch. Pers. 199; Hippocr. 1, 616. 3, 196. 7, 486, συν- Her. 1, 80, περι- Pl. Critias 113; ῥηγνύς Soph. Fr. 232 (D.), ἀνα- Her. 2, 14, παρα- Thuc. 4, 96, seldom **ῥηγνῠ́ω** Aristot. Mund. 4, 17, ἀναρρηγνῠ́ει Hippocr. 1, 106 (Lit.), κατ- 1, 63 (Erm.), δια- Theophr. C. P. 4, 9, 5, ἀπο- Paus. 5, 27 (see imp.). poetic ῥήσσω *strike*, Il. 18, 571; Hom. H. 2, 338; Ap. Rh. 1, 539; Anth. 7, 485 (Callim. Del. 322); and late prose, Artemid. Onir. 1, 60; Galen 13, 914; Oribas. 15, 1, 18, ῥήττω late prose, Strab. 11, 14, 8; Dioscor. 4, 152, περι-ρρήττω 2, 98. 4, 61: **imp.** ἐρρήγνυ, ἀν- Soph. Aj. 236; Thuc. 7, 40, ἐρρήγνῠε, κατ- Dem. 21, 63; Polyaen. 3, 10, 15, iter. ῥήγνυσκε Il. 7, 141, ῥήσσεσκον, ἐπιρρ-

Il. 24, 454: **fut.** ῥήξω Il. 12, 262; Her. 2, 2, ἐκ- Soph. Aj. 775, ἀνα- Thuc. 7, 36: **aor.** ἔρρηξα Il. 17, 44; Hes. Sc. 140; Aesch. Pers. 468; Soph. Fr. 731 (D.); Com. Fr. (Eup.) 2, 529; Her. 1, 85, ῥῆξα Il. 12, 185; Pind. N. 8, 29; opt. ἀνα-ρρήξειε Il. 20, 63; ῥῆξον Ar. Nub. 960; ῥήξας Il. 12, 241; Ar. Nub. 406, ἀπο- Il. 4, 69; ῥῆξαι 11, 538; Dem. 9, 61: **p.** late, ἔρρηχα, δι- V.T. 2 Reg. 14, 30. 15, 32: **p. p.** ἔρρηγμαι rare, συν- Od. 8, 137, and *now* κατ- Her. 2, 12 (Bekk. Dind.); Arr. An. 2, 23, ἀπ- Socrat. Epist. 7: **plp.** παρ-έρρηκτο Arr. 4, 26: **1 aor.** ἐρρήχθην rare, ῥηχθεῖσα Triphiod. 11; Dioscor. 3, 22; δια-ρρηχθῇ Hippocr. 7, 242: **2 aor.** ἐρράγην Soph. Fr. 507; Ar. Nub. 583; Hippocr. 5, 424. 7, 534; Dem. 56, 40, ὑπ- Il. 16, 300, κατ- Thuc. 4, 115; ῥαγῇ Hippocr. 3, 214; ῥαγείη, ἐκ- Her. 2, 173; ῥαγείς Aesch. Ag. 505; Hippocr. 8, 68; Xen. Cyr. 1, 6, 16, ἀπο- Thuc. 5, 10; ῥαγῆναι Hippocr. 7, 20; Pl. Rep. 359; Dem. 56, 21: fut. ῥαγήσομαι Plut. Quest. Conv. 4, 4, 2; Ael. H. A. 7, 7, ἐκ- Aesch. Pr. 367, δια- Ar. Eq. 340; Com. Fr. (Alex.) 3, 489; Aristot. de Coelo 2, 13, 28, κατα- Hippocr. 5, 732 (Lit.): **2 p.** ἔρρωγα *am broken*, Aesch. Pers. 433; Soph. Tr. 852; Eur. Hipp. 1338; Com. Fr. (Anon.) 4, 665; Hippocr. 2, 30 (Lit.), ἀπ- Archil. 47, 1, δι- Pl. Phaed. 86, ἀν- Aristot. Pt. An. 3, 1, 12, reg. form ἔρρηγα Tab. Heracl. B, ἀν- Philostr. Imag. 2, 26, 851, but -ωγα best supported (Kayser); κατ-ερρηγότες (Hesych.): **plp.** ἐρρώγει Aristid. 13, 125, ξυν- Thuc. 1, 66. **Mid.** ῥήγνυμαι *break for oneself*, or *for one's own*, Il. 12, 440, κατα- Xen. Cyr. 3, 3, 67, ῥήσσομαι, imper. -σσου Anth. 12, 232: **imp.** ῥήγνυντο Il. 13, 718. 20, 55, ἐπ-ερρηγ- App. Lib. 81: **fut.** (ῥήξομαι), but περι-ρρήξεται reflexive *burst* (*itself*) Hippocr. 4, 392: **aor.** ἐρρηξάμην Il. 12, 291; Eur. Heracl. 835; Aretae. 31, 52, κατ- Her. 8, 99; Xen. Cyr. 3, 1, 13, Epic ῥηξ- Il. 11, 90; Epic subj. ῥηξόμεθα Il. 12, 224. **Vb.** ῥηκτός Il. 13, 323.—Perf. p. ἔρρηγμαι is rare, but not so rare as some say. Buttm. Irreg. Verbs, seems to ignore it. ῥηγνύηται usual subj. form, Hippocr. 7, 26 (Lit.), but ῥήγνυνται seems subj. Hes. Sc. 377, so ῥήγνῦται Hipponax 19 (Bergk); and late Themist. Or. 1, 5, ὅταν δείκνυται. See Walz Rhet. vol. 7, p. 1042. διαρρήσσεσθαι *to burst*, intrans. Hippocr. 7, 270 (Lit.), ἀπο- 7, 206 (Lit. 2, 336 Erm.), for which our Lexicons quote Paus. 10, 17, 3.

Ῥῑγέω *To shudder, fear*, mostly Poetic, Hipponax 16. 17 (B.); Pind. N. 5, 50; Hippocr. 1, 58 (Erm.): **imp.** (ἐρρίγει): **fut.** ῥῑγήσω Il. 5, 351: **aor.** ἐρρίγησα Il. 12, 208, ῥίγησα 16, 119 (12, 208 Bekk. La R.); Soph. O. C. 1607 (trim.): **2 p.** as **pres.** ἔρρῑγα Il. 7, 114, 3 pl. ἐρρίγᾱσι Opp. C. 3, 134, Dor. ἐρρίγαντι Theocr. 16, 77 (Mss. Wintert. Ahr.); Epic subj. ἐρρίγῃσι Il. 3,

353; Ap. Rh. 3, 438: **2 plp.** ἐρρίγειν Od. 23, 216; Epic part. ἐρρίγοντι Hes. Sc. 228. For Dor. **perf.** ἐρρίγαντι in several Mss. and edit. Theocr. 16, 77, Meineke, Fritzsche and Ziegler adopt from other Mss. ἐρρίγασι. The only prose instance, if correct, is ἐρριγότες *shivering for cold*, Theophr. Ign. 74, where two Mss. present, perhaps correctly, ἐρριγωκότες. See ῥιγόω, which is now read in the three places of Plut. ῥιγῴη Mor. 233, ῥιγοῦν 157, ῥιγῶσας 132, where ῥιγέω used to stand.

Ῥῖγόω *To shiver with cold*, Pl. Phil. 45; ῥῖγοῦν Her. 5, 92 (7); Xen. Cyr. 5, 1, 11 (Vulg. Popp. Saupp. &c. ῥιγῶν Dind.), see below: **fut.** ῥιγώσω Xen. Mem. 2, 1, 17; Epic inf. -ωσέμεν Od. 14, 481: **aor.** ἐρρίγωσα Hippocr. 3, 50. 5, 168 (Lit.); Plut. Mor. 132, ἐν-ερρίγ- Ar. Plut. 846: **p.** ἐρριγωκότες Theophr. Ign. 74 (2 Mss.); Galen 11, 556. In Attic especially, this verb contracts in ω, ῳ instead of ου, οι; inf. ῥιγῶν for -οῦν, Ar. Ach. 1146. Av. 935. Vesp. 446, but ῥιγοῦν Pl. Rep. 440; Plut. Mor. 157 (Dübn.); Luc. Catapl. 15 (Dind.); Ar. Nub. 441 (Br. Bekk. -γῶν Dind. Bergk); subj. ῥιγῷ for -οῖ, Pl. Gorg. 517, but ῥιγοῖ Phaed. 85 (all Mss.); opt. ῥιγῴη for -γοῖ, Hippocr. 7, 190 (Lit. ῥιγᾷ Erm. 2, 328); Plut. Mor. 233; ῥιγῶσα fem. part. for -οῦσα, Simonid. Amorg. 7, 26 (Bergk).

Ῥιπτέω, see foll.

Ῥίπτω *To throw*, Eur. Hel. 1325; Her. 3, 41. 4, 61; Pl. Phaed. 113; Dem. 32, 6; ῥῖπτε Ar. Pax 962; ῥίπτων Soph. Tr. 790 (Mss. Herm. Ell. Dind. 5 ed.); Thuc. 7, 44, ἐκ- Aesch. Pr. 932; -τειν Thuc. 2, 49; Eur. Tr. 729. Hel. 1595 (D.), ἀνα- Od. 7, 328: **imp.** ἔρριπτον Eur. Bacc. 1097; Her. 5, 92 (6); Xen. An. 4, 8, 3, iter. ῥίπτασκον Il. 15, 23; Hes. Sc. 256; Orph. Fr. 16, 3, -τεσκε Nic. Fr. 26; Orph. quoted (Gesn.); and, in **pres.** and **imp.** only, ῥιπτέω, -εῖ Soph. Aj. 239. Ant. 131. Tr. 780 (Mss. Ellendt, Dind. -ει Erf. Herm. Nauck &c.); -έουσι Her. 4, 188, -εῦσι 4, 94 (Bekk. Dind.), -οῦσι Xen. Ven. 9, 20, ἀνα- Thuc. 5, 103, -οῦμεν 4, 95; imper. -τεῖτε Ar. Eccl. 507 (Dind.); -οῦνθ' Eur. Hel. 1096 (Mss. Herm. -ουθ' Elms. Dind. Kirchh. 2 ed.), -οῦντες Xen. Cyr. 3, 1, 25 (Pl. Tim. 80); ῥιπτεῖν Conv. 2, 8: **imp.** ἐρρίπτεον Her. 8, 53, -ουν Xen. Cyr. 4, 2, 33; App. Hisp. 82. Lib. 49, ἀν- Od. 13, 78, δι- Aeschin. 1, 59: **fut.** ῥίψω Il. 24, 735; Eur. H. F. 562; Hippocr. 8, 16; Xen. An. 4, 7, 13: **aor.** ἔρριψα Il. 23, 845; Hes. Th. 181; Pind. I. 7, 44; Aesch. Pr. 748; Soph. Ph. 265; Ar. Eccl. 66; Thuc. 2, 4; Lys. 13, 82; Pl. Leg. 944, Poet. ἔριψα Arion 18 (B.); Mosch. 3, 32, ἀπ- Pind. P. 6, 37, ῥῖψε Il. 3, 378; Hes. Th. 868; Dor. pt. ῥίψαις Pind. P. 1, 45; ῥῖψαι Eur. Tr. 729; Her. 1, 24. 2, 100: (**2 aor.** ἔρρῐφον see below): **p.** ἔρρῖφα Lys. 10, 9. 21: **p. p.** ἔρριμμαι Eur. Med.

1404; Ar. Eccl. 850; Her. 1, 62; Xen. Mem. 3, 1, 7, Poet. ῥέριμμ- Pind. Fr. 314 (Bergk): **plp.** ἔρριπτο Luc. Nec. 17: **1 aor.** ἐρρίφθην, ῥιφθῶ Soph. Aj. 830; Eur. Hec. 335. Andr. 10 (D.); Pl. Leg. 944; Polyb. 8, 8; Plut. Luc. 42, ἀπ- Aesch. Supp. 484, ἐκ- Soph. El. 512: **fut.** ῥιφθήσομαι, ἀπο-ρρ- Soph. Aj. 1019, κατα- Joseph. Jud. B. 3, 7, 20: **2 aor.** ἐρρῐ́φην Eur. Fr. 486 (D.). Andr. 10 quoted (most Mss. Kirchh. Nauck); Pl. Leg. 944. Phil. 16; Dio Cass. 79, 20; (Luc.) Amor. 33; ῥιφείς Opp. Cyn. 1, 500; Polyb. 4, 71; D. Sic. 13, 73; Plut. Rom. 7; Ael. H. A. 14, 8, ἐξ- Aeschin. 2, 153, Poet. ἐρῐ́φη Anth. 12, 234: **2 fut.** ῥιφήσομαι perhaps later, Plut. C. Gr. 3; E. T. Esai. 34, 3; Joseph. Ant. 7, 11, ἀπο- *v. r.* Soph. Aj. 1019 quoted, and adopted by Wunder: **3 fut.** ἐρρίψεται Luc. Merc. Cond. 17. **Mid.** late, ἀπορριπτόμενος Theodor. Stud. p. 194: **aor.** ῥίψαντο Maneth. 6, 10; ῥίψασθαι, ἀπο- Galen 16, 146, both missed by Lexicogr.: **Vb.** ῥιπτός Soph. Tr. 357. Oppian Cyn. 4, 350, has **2 aor. act.** ἔρρῐφε a dactyle. Does this point to *theme* ῥίφω? or may it be for ἔρρῐπε? or is it the **perf.** with ῐ, though it be *naturally* long, ῥῖπτε, ῥῖψαι, ῥιπή? Elms. Eur. Heracl. 150, wished to banish the form ῥιπτέω from the Tragedians, and Nauck and Kirchhoff, we think, sympathise with him. Ellendt, again, and Paley vary with the Mss. In Soph. however Dind. *now* always edits the pure form (-έω, -ῶ) -εῖ; but pt. ῥίπτων with Elms. Herm. held, with the old Grammarians, ῥιπτέω to be a strengthened form of ῥίπτω, as *jacto* of *jacio*, and was inclined to think that the form should be determined by the *meaning*. We doubt if the Greeks *always* observed this distinction. Ar. uses ῥιπτεῖτε χλαίνας Eccl. 507, where the form ῥίπτετε is inadmissible, but its meaning required —a simple throw, no *repetition* of the act. At Pax 962, again, τοῖς θεαταῖς ῥῖπτε τῶν κριθῶν savours more of *repetition*, and yet ῥιπτεῖτε could not stand; so ἔρριπτε Her. 5, 92 (6) decidedly of repetition.

Ῥοιβδέω *To suck in, shake,* Poet. and only **pres.** ῥοιβδοῦσα Aesch. Eum. 404; ἀνα-ρροιβδεῖ Od. 12, 104; Aesch. Fr. 217; Soph. Fr. 390, Poet. ἀνα-ροιβ- Od. 12, 105: and **aor.** ῥοίβδησε Orph. Arg. 1260, ἀν-εῤῥοίβ- Od. 12, 236, 431; -ήσῃ Lycophr. 247; -ήσειε Od. 12, 106; ῥοιβδήσας Anth. 7, 636.

Ῥοιζέω *To whiz,* Aristot. H. A. 4, 9, 7; (Luc.) Amor. 22: **imp.** Epic ῥοίζει Ap. Rh. 4, 129, iter. ῥοίζασκε Hes. Th. 835, -εσκε (Ms. m. Goettl. Flach): **aor.** ἐρροίζησα Opp. Hal. 1, 563, δι- Soph. Tr. 568, ῥοίζησα Il. 10, 502: **plp. p.** as act. ἐρροίζητο Anth. 11, 106: and **pres.** ῥοιζούμενος Lycophr. 1426.

Ῥοφέω *To sup up,* Soph. Tr. 1055; Ar. Vesp. 906; Hippocr.

2, 456; Xen. An. 4, 5, 32; ῥοφεῖν Aesch. Eum. 264; ῥυφέων Hippocr. 5, 370 (Lit. 1, 643 Erm.): **imp.** ἐρρόφεον Hippocr. 2, 306: **fut.** ῥοφήσω, -ήσεις Ar. Ach. 278. Pax 716, ἐκ- Eq. 360 (Bekk. Bergk) see below, certain late ῥοφήσω Eustath. Phil. 4, 25, ἐκ- 3, 4, 3: but **fut. mid.** ῥοφήσομαι Ar. Vesp. 814: **aor.** ἐρρόφησα Hippocr. 7, 60 (Lit.); Ar. Eq. 51; Aristot. Meteor. 2, 3, 2, ἐκ- Ar. Eq. 701, ἀπ- Xen. Cyr. 1, 3, 10, Ion. ἐρρύφ- Hippocr. 5, 374: **aor. p.** ῥοφηθείς Nic. Al. 389: **aor. mid.** Ion. ῥυφήσασθαι Hippocr. 5, 386 (Lit.) missed by Lexicogr.—For **fut. act.** ῥοφήσεις Ar. Ach. 278. Pax 716. Eq. 360, Elms. and Dind. read **fut. mid.** ῥοφήσει as the *legitimate* Attic form, and refer to ῥοφήσομαι Vesp. 814. This assumes however that Aristoph. would in no case use the **act.** and **mid. fut.** in the same sense. We think this rather stringent, for with **fut. mid.** καύσεται Plut. 1054, he has κατα-καύσω Lys. 1218, which, we think, both would allow to be **fut. act.** not aor. subj., and τέξομαι Lys. 744, but **fut. act.** τέξει Eq. 1037, -ειν Thesm. 509, πατήσεις Eq. 166, but ἀπο-πατησόμενοι Plut. 1184. Unfortunately, in this and several other verbs similarly circumstanced the **fut.** occurs most frequently in 2 sing. where the difference between **act.** and **mid.** is so small —only ς—as to raise doubt and provoke change.

'Ρύομαι *To draw to oneself, defend*, Il. 10, 259; Aesch. Sept. 824; Eur. H. F. 197; Her. 4, 187; Hippocr. 5, 288. 304 (Lit.); opt. Ion. 3 pl. -οίατο Her. 4, 135: **imp.** ἐρρύετο Eur. Alc. 770; Her. 5, 100; Nonn. 41, 281, ῥύ- Il. 16, 799; Pind. I. 8, 53; Ap. Rh. 4, 1397, 3 pl. ῥύατο for -οντο Il. 18, 515. Od. 17, 201, iter. ῥύσκευ Il. 24, 730: **fut.** ῥύσομαι Hes. Th. 662; Solon 13, 56; Aesch. Sept. 92; Eur. Bacc. 1338; Her. 1, 86; Thuc. 5, 63, Dor. ῥυσεῦνται Callim. Lav. Pal. 112: **aor.** ἐρρῡσάμην Il. 20, 194. Od. 1, 6; Pind. P. 12, 19; Soph. Aj. 1276; Eur. Ion 1298; Ar. Lys. 342; Her. 3, 132. 7, 154; Hippocr. 2, 630 (Lit.); rare in Attic prose, Hyperid. Fr. 80; Dio. Hal. 4, 68. 10, 25; Ael. V. H. 4, 5; Luc. Alex. 45. Asin. 33; Paus. 10, 26; Herodn. 1, 15, 6, ἐρῡσ- Od. 14, 279 (Dind. Bekk. La R.), ἐξ- we hold incorrect, Aesch. Pr. 235, ῥύσατο Od. 23, 244, ῥῡσάσθην Il. 14, 406, ῠ once, ῥῠσάμην (ἐρύω?) 15, 29; ῥύσηται Theocr. 7, 56 (Ahr. Ziegl.); -σαιτο Od. 12, 107; Aesch. Eum. 300; -σάμενος Anacr. 107; Her. 3, 138: **aor. p.** late ἐρρύσθη Diod. Sic. 21, 6 (Bekk.); Malal. p. 141; ῥυσθῇ Orig. Ref. Haer. 10, 15; Malal. 3, p. 65; ῥυσθῆναι Heliod. 10, 7 (Cor. Bekk.). **Vb.** ῥῡτός Od. 6, 267. This verb occurs once only in early Attic prose, Thuc. quoted.

ῥῦσθαι syncop. inf. for ῥύεσθ- Il. 15, 141; so **imp.** ἔρρῡτο as aor. Soph. O. R. 1352 (chor. ἔρυ- Dind.), 3 pl. ῥύατο for -οντο,

Il. 18, 515, ῥύσκευ Ionic for -εο, Il. quoted, may belong to a form (ῥύσκομαι). In the pres. and imp. υ is variable with Epic writers, ῥῠεται Il. 10, 259; Hes. Sc. 105, ῥῡονται Il. 9, 396; Opp. Hal. 4, 40, but ῥύομαι Il. 15, 257; Opp. Hal. 2, 486, ῥῡόμεθα Theocr. 25, 25; subj. ῥύηται Theocr. 7, 56 (Fritzs. ῥῡσ- others); opt. ῥύοιτο Il. 12, 8. 17, 224: imp. ῥῠετο Il. 16, 799, ῥῡοντο Q. Sm. 11, 344, Ionic ῥῡατο Il. 18, 515, always long in Attic, except ῥῠεσθε Aesch. Sept. 303. 824 (chor.); in fut. long; so in aor. except ῥῠσάμην in *thesi* Il. quoted. For ἐξ-ερυσάμην Aesch. Pr. 235 (Mss. G. &c. Ald. Vulg.), Herm. and Dind. read, perhaps correctly, ἐξελυσ- with Mss. Med. Lips. 1, 2, &c. See ἐρύω.

Ῥῠπαίνω *To make foul, insult*, Com. Fr. (Pher.) 2, 352; Aristot. Eth. N. 1, 9, 16 (B.); Themist. 1, 8, καταρρῠπ- Pl. Leg. 937: fut. ῥῠπᾰνῶ, καταρρ- Isocr. 12, 63: aor. p. late ἐρρυπάνθην Plut. Mor. 434: pres. p. ῥυπαίνομαι Xen. Lac. 11, 3.

Ῥῠπάω *To be foul*, Ar. Plut. 266; Luc. Nec. 4, Epic ῥῠπόω, Od. 19, 72. 23, 115; -όωντα 6, 87: imp. ἐρρῠπων Ar. Av. 1282: also *make foul*, hence p. p. redupl. ῥερῠπωμένος Od. 6, 59; Hippocr. 4, 374. 8, 140. 236. 368 (Lit.); Themist. 7, 93 (Dind.), ἐρρυπωμ- Schol. Ar. Ach. 425.

Ῥυφάω, see ῥοφ-.

Ῥώννῡμι *To strengthen*, Hippocr. 9, 98 (Lit.); (Pl.) Locr. 103, and -ννῠω (Pl.) Locr. 103; Oribas. 1, 42: imp. ἐρρώννῡν Philostr. Apoll. 5, 218. 7, 285, and ἐρρώννῠον Imag. 31, 395, ἐπ- Apoll. 4, 145: fut. ῥώσω, ἐπι- Plut. Mor. 9, ἀνα- Aretae. 136 (ed. Oxon.): aor. ἔρρωσα Plut. Pericl. 19, ἐπ- Her. 8, 14; Thuc. 4, 36; (Dem.) 10, 36: p. p. ἔρρωμαι Pl. Conv. 176, -ωσαι Dem. 22, 26, -ωται Hippocr. 1, 616, -ώμεθα Eur. Heracl. 636, -ωνται Thuc. 6, 17; -ῶσθαι Com. Fr. (Crat.) 2, 214; Pl. Phaed. 61; -ωμένος Pl. Phil. 49; Isocr. 15, 115: plp. ἐρρώμην Thuc. 7, 15, -ρωτο Her. 6, 111; Thuc. 2, 8; Lys. 13, 31, -ρωντο Thuc. 8, 78: aor. ἐρρώσθην Thuc. 4, 72; Pl. Phaedr. 238, ἐπ- Soph. O. C. 661: ῥωσθήσομαι Apollod. 1, 6, 10, ἐπι- Luc. Som. 18: pres. p. rare ῥώννῠται Hippocr. 2, 400 (Erm.); ῥωννύμενος Plut. Mor. 130. Dion. 25. Vb. ἄ-ρρωστος Xen. Apol. 30. ἔρρωσο *vale, farewell*, imper. p. p. Xen. Cyr. 4, 5, 33, 2 pl. ἔρρωσθε (Hippocr.) Epist. 3, 781 (K.): inf. ἐρρῶσθαι Pl. Phaed. 61; Com. Fr. (Antiph.) 3, 48.

Ῥώομαι *To move quickly, hasten*, Epic, pres. late if correct, Orph. Lith. 701, ῥώονθ' Dio. Per. 518 (Mss. ὁρμῶνθ' in text): imp. ἐρρώοντο Il. 23, 368; Hes. Sc. 230, ῥώοντο Il. 18, 411; Ap. Rh. 4, 942, ῥώετο late, Nic. Ther. 351: fut. ῥώσονται? Callim. Del. 175 (Mss. Ernest. Brunck, subj. -σωνται Blomf. Mein.): aor. ἐρρώσαντο Il. 24, 616. Od. 24, 69; H. Merc. 505, ἐπ- Il. 1, 529; Hes. Th. 8; subj. ῥώσωνται Callim. Del. 175 quoted (Blomf. Mein.), see fut.

Σ.

Σαίνω *To fawn upon*, Hes. Th. 771; Soph. O. C. 320; Opp. Hal. 1, 36, περι- Od. 16, 10; σαίωσι Od. 10, 217; σαίνοιμεν Aesch. Sept. 704; -ων Od. 16, 6; Pind. P. 2, 82; Aesch. Ag. 726 (perhaps not in *classic* prose, Aristot. Metaph. 13, 3, 5; Luc. D. Deor. 12, 2 &c.; Plut. Rom. 7 &c.): **imp.** ἔσαινον Soph. Fr. 508 (D.); Babr. 87, σαῖνον Od. 10, 219: **fut.** σᾰνῶ: **aor.** ἔσηνα Od. 17, 302; Com. Fr. (Apoll.) 4, 455 (Mein. -ᾱνα Mss.), Dor. ἔσᾱνα Pind. Ol. 4, 4. P. 1, 52; Lycophr. 1444; and in Mss. Apollod. Com. Fr. quoted. **Pass.** σαίνομαι Aesch. Ch. 194; -όμενοι D. Laert. 8, 21, 41.

Σαίρω *To sweep*, Eur. Ion 115; Plut. Mor. 362; Luc. D. Deor. 24, 1: **fut.** σᾰρῶ N. T. Luc. 15, 8: **aor.** ἔσηρα, σήρας Soph. Ant. 409: **2 p.** σέσηρα as **pres.** *grin*, Com. Fr. (Alex.) 3, 423; Plut. Mor. 13. 223; σεσηρέναι Ael. V. H. 3, 40; chiefly part. σεσηρώς Ar. Pax 620. Vesp. 901; Hippocr. 3, 532. 8, 568 (Lit.); Aristot. Physiog. 3, 10; Luc. Philopatr. 26, Dor. σεσᾱρώς Theocr. 7, 19. 20, 14, Epic fem. σεσᾰρυῖα for σεσηρ- Hes. Sc. 268: **plp.** ἐσεσήρει Themist. 22, 282. A late form is σαρόω, -ούμενος Lycophr. 389.

Σᾰλεύω *To shake*, trans. and intrans. Soph. O. R. 23; Eur. Cycl. 434 (Musgr. Dind. 2 ed. ἀλύει Herm. Nauck, Dind. 5 ed.). Rhes. 249; Pl. Leg. 923: **fut.** -εύσω Or. Sib. 3, 177: **aor.** ἐσάλευσα Anth. 11, 83; Isocr. 8, 95; Themist. 24, 308, ἀν- Alciphr. 1, 39, ἀπο-σαλεύσας Thuc. 1, 137: **p. p.** σεσάλευμαι Aesch. Pr. 1081; Anth. 12, 31, δια- Luc. Merc. Cond. 33: **aor.** ἐσαλεύθην Pseudo-Callisth. 3, 29; N. T. Act. 4, 31 (v. r. Isocr. 8, 95): **fut.** -ευθήσομαι N. T. Luc. 21, 26: **fut. mid.** σαλεύσεται as **pass.** Or. Sib. 3, 675. 714. 751, missed, we think, by Lexicogr.: **pres. pass.** σαλευμένη Archil. 102.

Σαλπίζω *To sound a trumpet*, Anth. App. Epigr. 30; Xen. An. 7, 3, 32: **imp.** σάλπιζε Nonn. 2, 365: **aor.** ἐσάλπιγξα Batr. 200; Com. Fr. (Archipp.) 2, 722; Xen. An. 1, 2, 17 (-ιξα Cobet), σάλπιγξα Il. 21, 388; Opp. Cyn. 2, 59. Late **fut.** σαλπίσω, N. T. 1 Cor. 15, 52, -ιῶ V. T. Num. 10, 3; Jud. 7, 18 &c.: **aor.** ἐσάλπισα Dio Cass. 57, 19; (Luc.) Ocyp. 114; Athen. 10, 7; Pseud.-Callisth. 3, 3; V. T. Jos. 6, 16; Niceph. 3, 1: (**perf.**?): **p. p.** σεσάλπισται, περι- Plut. Mor. 192. 220, -πιγκται Eudaim. Stob. 54, 65. Lud. Dindorf is inclined to write ἐσάλπιξε without γ, as Cobet does.

Σᾰόω -ώω *To preserve* (σάω), Epic, σαοῖ Theogn. 868 (Bergk &c.); Callim. Del. 22, σαοῦσι Tyrt. 11, 13: imp. ἐσάω Il. 21, 238 (Vulg.), σάω (Wolf, Bekk. Dind. La R.). 16, 363: fut. σᾱώσω Il. 1, 83; Hes. Fr. 139; Her. 7, 148 (Orac.); Epic inf. -ωσέμεν Il. 19, 401, -ωσέμεναι 13, 96; Ap. Rh. 4, 837: aor. ἐσάωσα Il. 8, 500; Pind. Fr. 216. Dem. (Epigr.) 18, 289, σάωσ- Il. 5, 23. Od. 4, 364. 513 (Bekk. 2 ed.); -ώσειας Il. 17, 149, -ειαν 12, 123: aor. pass. ἐσαώθην, Epic 3 pl. -ωθεν Od. 3, 185, σαώθη Pind. P. 4, 161; σαωθῆναι Il. 15, 503; -ωθείς Ap. Rh. 3, 786: fut. mid. reflex σαώσομαι, Epic 2 sing. -ώσεαι *save yourself*, Od. 21, 309. (See σάω, σόω).—σάω 2 sing. imperat. for σάου (σάοε) Epic, Od. 13, 230. 17, 595; Anth. 8, 37. 13, 2; but σάω (ἐσάω some ed.) Il. 16, 363. 21, 238, is 3 sing. imperf.; σαῷς or σάῳς Aristarchus' reading Il. 9, 681, σόῳς Bekker, for σόῃς, is subj. of σαόω, the *first* for σαοῖς, like ῥιγῷ for ῥιγοῖ, the *second* with a double contraction, thus σαόῃς, σαοῖς, σῷς, then σόῳς not -ῷς; so 3 sing. σόῳ in Ms. Ven. also adopted by Bekker for σόῃ Il. 9, 424, and 3 pl. σόωσι 9, 393, not -ῶσι which would require σοέω. An Aeol. form σάωμι, 2 pers. σάως occurs Alcae. 92 (Ahr. 73 Bergk).

Σάττω *To equip, furnish*, Aristot. Probl. 21, 14, 2; -ττοιμι Xen. Oec. 19, 11, and σάσσω Hippocr. 2, 226 (K.): imp. ἔσαττον Com. Fr. (Pher.) 2, 286: fut. (σάξω), and σάσω, ἐσ- Hippocr. 2, 345: aor. ἔσαξα Her. 3, 7; Xen. Oec. 19, 11; Com. Fr. (Alex.) 3, 443, and ἔσασα, ἐσ- Hippocr. 2, 330. 345: p. p. σέσακται Aristot. Probl. 21, 21; Stob. (Cercid.) 4, 43; σεσάχθω Com. Fr. (Antiph.) 3, 130; -αγμένος Aesch. Ag. 644; Xen. Conv. 4, 64. Oec. 19, 11: plp. 3 pl. Ionic ἐσεσάχατο Her. 7, 62. 70. 73. **Mid.** aor. σαξάμενος Orac. Luc. Peregr. 30. ἐσάσει fut. and ἐσάσειεν aor. opt. Hippocr. quoted, seem to be mistakes for ἐσ-σάσει ἐσ-σάσειεν. σάσσω is found in Hippocr. 2, 226 (Kühn)=7, 26 (Lit.)

Σᾱ́ω *To save*, Poet. and only 3 pl. σᾱ́ουσι Tyrtae. 8, 13 (Schneidew.), but -οῦσι (Buttm. Bergk 11, 13); and 3 sing. opt. σᾱ́οι Anth. 7, 109. A mere change of accent however as σαοῦσι, σαοῖ would refer those to σαόω and preclude the necessity of σάω. This Bergk has done in his 2 ed. σάοι is in some editions of Theogn. 868, but σαοῖ is best supported.

Σάω *To sift*, 3 pl. σῶσι (σάουσι) Her. 1, 200, late σήθω Galen 13, 244. 342, ἀπο- Herodic. Athen. 13, 60: aor. ἔσησα, part. σήσας Hippocr. 8, 132 (Lit.); Geop. 2, 32: inf. σῆσαι Hippocr. 8, 132: p. p. σεσημένος Hippocr. 2, 569 (K.); Dioscor. 1, 83, and σεσησμένος Hippocr. 7, 132. 176 (Lit.); Dioscor. 4, 155; Geop. 10, 22: aor. ἐσήσθην Aretae. 92 (ed. Oxon.); Dioscor. 2,

208, ἀπο- 5, 103, and -ήθην 2, 118. **Vb.** σηστέον Dioscor. 5, 103. ἐττημένα for ἐσσημ- perhaps as ἔσσῦμαι or ἔσσευμ- from σεύω, occurs Com. Fr. (Pher.) 2, 351. Meineke now thinks ἡττημένα should be read, or that ἐττημ- if correct, is taken from some Ionic writer.

Σβέννῦμι *To extinguish*, Her. 2, 66; Hippocr. 7, 474; Pl. Leg. 835; Aristot. Probl. 23, 7; Com. Fr. (Ephipp.) 3, 323, κατα- Xen. Conv. 7, 4, and σβεννύω Pind. P. 1, 5; Heraclit. 103 (Byw.); Hippocr. 2, 342 (Lit. -υσι Galen); Aristot. Probl. 22, 8, 2; Theophr. Ign. 19. 58; Aen. Tact. 28. 34; Diog. Laert. 9, 1, 2; Geop. 7, 12: **imp.** ἐσβέννῦεν Paus. 4, 21, 3, κατ- Polyaen. 6, 3: **fut.** σβέσω App. Civ. 2, 68, σβέσσ- Orac. Her. 8, 77; Theocr. 23, 26, κατα- Aesch. Ag. 958; Sept. 584 (Dind.); Eur. I. T. 633; Ar. Lys. 376: **aor.** ἔσβεσα in tmesi Il. 16, 293 (σβέσ- Bekk.); Simon. C. 132 (Bergk); Soph. Aj. 1057; Ar. Av. 779; Her. (Orac.) 5, 77; Pl. Leg. 888; σβέσον Luc. D. Deor. 10, 1, -σατε Anth. 12, 81, in tmesi Il. 23, 237; inf. σβέσαι Thuc. 2, 77, Epic σβέσσαι Il. 16, 621: **p.** ἔσβηκα, κατ- intrans. Aesch. Ag. 888, ἀπ- Xen. Cyr. 8, 8, 13: **plp.** ἐσβήκει, ἀπ- Pl. Conv. 218: **p. p.** ἔσβεσμαι Ael. H. A. 9, 54; Galen 16, 604; Or. Sib. 5, 397; Geop. 16, 17, ἀπ- Hippocr. 7, 274 (Lit.); Aristot. Meteor. 2, 3, 39: **plp.** ἔσβεστο App. Syr. 33: **aor.** ἐσβέσθην Anth. 7, 20. 12, 39; Hippocr. 2, 446 (Lit.); App. Civ. 2, 68; Philostr. Apoll. 277, κατ- Xen. Conv. 6, 10. Hell. 5, 3, 8; σβεσθείς Aristot. Prob. 3, 5, 3, ἀπο- Ar. Lys. 294; Pl. Crit. 112. Tim. 58: **fut.** σβεσθήσομαι Oribas. 8, 2; Galen 7, 17: **2 aor.** ἔσβην intrans. Il. 9, 471, ἀπ- Eur. Med. 1218. Fr. 961 (Dind.), κατ- Hippocr. 2, 600, Dor. ἔσβᾱν, ἀπ- Theocr. 4, 39; inf. σβῆναι, κατα- Her. 4, 5, ἀπο- Xen. Cyr. 5, 4, 30; σβείς, ἀπο- Hippocr. 5, 176 (Lit.) **Mid.** σβέννῦμαι *extinguish oneself, go out, die*, Epic pt. σβεννυμενάων Hes. Op. 590; but ἀπο-σβέννυται Hippocr. 2, 22 (Lit.); Pl. Rep. 498, and (σβεννύομαι) in subj. κατα-σβεννύηται Pl. Tim. 57: **imp.** σβέννυντο Anth. 9, 128: **fut.** σβήσομαι, ἀπο- Pl. Leg. 805: **aor.** ἐσβέσατο Anth. (Alpheus Mit.) 9, 104 (Jacobs), σβέσσ- Q. Sm. 1, 795: **2 aor.** (ἐσβέμην), ἔσβετο Theodr. Prodr. 1, 408, συν- Opp. Hal. 2, 477, or plp. for ἔσβεστο? **Vb.** σβεστός late, Nonn. 28, 189, but ἄ-σβεστος Il. 22, 96. The form -ύω seems late in Attic prose, but Hippocr. 2, 342, ἐναπο- 8, 162 &c.

Σεβάζομαι *To stand in awe, fear*, Orac. Euseb. praep. 9, p. 413: **aor. mid.** Epic σεβάσσατο Il. 6, 167; subj. σεβάσησθε Orph. Arg. 554: with **aor. pass.** ἐσεβάσθην act. Anth. 7, 122 (Epigr. Diog. Laert. 8, 1, 45); Or. Sib. 4, 405. 8, 46, **pass.** 8, 477; σεβασθείς act. Theophylact. Hist. 7, 3, p. 169: **fut.** σεβασθήσομαι act. Niceph. Rhet. 7, 13. **Act.** form late σεβάζοντες

Clem. Alex. Protr. p. 33. **Vb.** σεβαστέον Philostr. Epist. 58 (402).

Σεβίζω *To reverence*, Poet, Pind. P. 5, 80; Aesch. Eum. 12; Soph. O. C. 1007; Eur. Elec. 994; Ar. Thesm. 674: **fut.** σεβιῶ late prose, Dio Cass. 52, 40: **aor.** ἐσέβισα Soph. Ant. 942; Ar. Thesm. 106. **Mid.** σεβίζομαι as act. Aesch. Supp. 922; Callim. Del. 247; and late prose (Luc.) Astrol. 7: with **aor. pass.** σεβισθείς as act. Soph. O. C. 636. **Pass.** σεβίζομαι Emped. 359; Pind. I. 5, 29.

Σέβω *To revere*, only **pres.** Aesch. Eum. 22; Soph. Ant. 745; Ar. Nub. 600 (chor.); Pl. Leg. 647, Dor. 3 pl. σέβοντι Pind. Ol. 14, 12; σέβωμεν Aesch. Supp. 1025; -βοι Aesch. Eum. 525, -οιεν Xen. Ages. 1, 27; σέβειν Soph. El. 981; Thuc. 2, 53; Xen. Mem. 4, 4, 19; σέβων Archil. 120; Soph. Aj. 712; Pl. Leg. 777: and **imp.** ἔσεβον late, Luc. pro Imag. 7; Malal. p. 432. **Mid.** σέβομαι as act. Il. 4, 242; Pind. P. 6, 25; Aesch. Pers. 693; Eur. Bacc. 566; Ar. Nub. 293; Her. 1, 66. 138; Antiph. 2, δ, 12; Pl. Leg. 798: **imp.** ἐσεβόμην Her. 2, 172. 7, 197; Xen. Cyr. 8, 8, 1; Pl. Rep. 393: with **aor. pass.** ἐσέφθην Soph. Fr. 175 (D.); σεφθῆναι (Hesych.); σεφθεῖσα *awestricken*, Pl. Phaedr. 254: **2 fut.** late, σεβήσεσθαι Diog. Laert. 7, 120. **Vb.** σεπτός Aesch. Pr. 812. **Act.** σέβω is post-Homeric. σέβομαι occurs once passively σέβοιτ' Soph. O. C. 760. σέψασθαι **aor. mid.** (Hesych.) This is perhaps the only instance of a verb in -έβω going beyond the **imperf.**

Σείω *To shake*, Aesch. Sept. 385; Ar. Av. 1751; Xen. Cyn. 3, 4, ὑπο-σσ- Od. 9, 385; σείειν Her. 7, 129; σείων Il. 5, 563; Soph. Ant. 291; Pl. Tim. 88, Poet. σἴω Anacr. 50 (Bergk): **imp.** ἔσειον Antiph. 6, 43, σεῖον Od. 3, 486, iter. σείασκε, ἀνα-σσ- H. H. 2, 225: **fut.** σείσω V. T. Esai. 10, 14, but ἐπι- Eur. Or. 613, δια- Her. 6, 109: **aor.** ἔσεισα Soph. El. 713; Eur. Ion 1204; Ar. Ach. 12; Thuc. 4, 52, σεῖσα Il. 15, 321; σεῖσαι Pind. P. 4, 272; Eur. Bacc. 185: **p.** σέσεικα, κατα- Com. Fr. (Phil.) 4, 29, ἐν- Luc. Merc. Con. 30: **p. p.** σέσεισμαι Pind. P. 8, 94; Ar. Nub. 1276, ἐκ- Ach. 344: **aor.** ἐσείσθην Soph. Ant. 584; Her. 6, 98; Thuc. 2, 8, προεπαν- 5, 17: **pres.** σειόμενος Il. 13, 135: **imp.** ἐσσείοντο 20, 59 (σεί- Bekk.), σείετο 13, 805. 14, 285. **Mid.** σείομαι *to move oneself, shake*, intrans. Hes. Sc. 298, trans. Anth. 5, 273, ἀπο- Ar. Ran. 346; Her. 9, 22; Xen. Cyr. 7, 1, 37: **fut.** σείσεται, δια- Arr. Cyn. 10, ἀπο- Themist. 19, 229: **aor.** ἐσείσατο Callim. Apoll. 1, σείσ- Il. 8, 199, but trans. ἀπ-εσείσ- Her. 7, 88; App. Lib. 26; Herodn. 7, 1, 3; Themist. 19, 229; σεισάμενος Ap. Rh. 4, 1367; Theocr. 13, 13, ἀπο- Theogn. 348; Ar. Nub. 287; Pl. Gorg. 484; and late Luc. Gall. 23;

Galen 9, 295, δια- Dio. Hal. Ant. 1, 56. Vb. σειστός Ar. Ach. 346.—ἀνα-σσείασκε Hom. H. Apol. P. 225, iter. imp. Epic.

Σεύω *To move, urge,* Poet. Opp. Hal. 2, 445; Epic inf. σευέμεναι Orph. Lith. 723 (after augm. generally σσ, always in Hom. except ἐξ-εσύθη Il. 5, 293): imp. ἔσσευεν, ἐπ- Od. 18, 256, σεῦε Il. 6, 133, iter. σεύεσκε Q. Sm. 2, 353: aor. ἔσσευα Il. 5, 208. 14, 413, ἔσσευσα, ἐπι-σσεύσας Anth. 7, 439, ἔσευα, συν- H. Merc. 94, σεῦα Il. 20, 189: p.p. ἔσσυμαι as pres. mid. Il. 13, 79. Od. 10, 484; Pind. I. 8, 61, ἐπ- Il. 6, 361; ἐσσύμενος Il. 13, 142. Od. 4, 733: plp. ἐσσύμην (which may be also syncop. 2 aor. mid.), ἔσσυο for -υσο, Il. 16, 585. Od. 9, 447 &c., ἔσσυτο Il. 14, 519; Hes. Sc. 458; Ar. Thesm. 126 (chor.), and ἔσυτο Eur. H. F. 919. Hel. 1133 (chor.), σύτο Il. 21, 167; Pind. Ol. 1, 20: 1 aor. ἐσσύθην Soph. Aj. 294 (Aretae. 43 ed. Oxon., the only instance of the *simple* verb in prose), Epic 3 pl. ἔσσυθεν, ἀπ- Hes. Th. 183, and ἐσύθην Eur. Hel. 1302 (chor.), ἐξ- Il. 5, 293 (Zenod. Wolf, Dind. La R. -ελύθη Aristarch. Bekk. 2 ed.), σύθην Aesch. Pr. 135 (chor.); συθῶμεν Soph. O. C. 1725; σύθεις Aesch. Sept. 942, ἀπο- Hippocr. 2, 450 (Lit.): 2 aor. ἐσσύην, Lacon. ἔσσυα, ἀπ- Xen. Hell. 1, 1, 23 (Ms. B. Dind. Sauppe, -ύα Breitb. -ουα others) *he is gone, is dead,* see below. **Mid.** σεύομαι *to hasten after, pursue,* syncop. σεῦται Soph. Tr. 645, σεύονται Opp. Hal. 3, 643; σεύωνται Il. 11, 415: imp. ἐσσεύοντο Il. 2, 808: 1 aor. ἐσσεύαντο Il. 11, 549. 15, 272 (Bekk.), σεύατο Il. 6, 505. 7, 208; opt. σεύαιτο 23, 198, and *now* 17, 463; Mimnerm. 14, 7; -άμενος Orph. Lith. 12: 2 aor. syncop. (say some) ἐσσύμην, -υο, -υτο Il. 16, 585. Od. 14, 34, ἔσυτο Eur. Hel. 1133 (chor.), ἐπ- 1162. Phoen. 1065 (chor.); Ar. Fr. 582 (557 5 ed.), σύτο Il. 21, 167; Pind. Ol. 1, 20; part. σύμενοι Aesch. Eum. 1007 (chor.), Dor. συμένα Ag. 746, ἐπι-σύμενος Eum. 786. 816. See plp. and σοῦμαι. **Vb.** ἐπίσσυτος Aesch. Eum. 924. See σόομαι.

σεῦται Soph. quoted, is 3 sing. pres. for σεύεται. σύμενος accented as pres. Aesch. Ag. 747. Eum. 1007, is part. of syncop. aor. ἐσύμην; others refer it to pres. (σύμι). Opt. with augm. ἐσσεύαιτο is in the Mss. Il. 17, 463, and used so to be edited before Wolf; so subj. 1 aor. pass. ἐσσυθῇ Hippocr. 1, 394, but grammarians and late editors hold these to be vicious forms, and have substituted σεύαιτο in Hom., and suggested or adopted ἐκσιθῇ in Hippocr. ἀπέσσυα, -ουα given above as 2 aor. pass. Laconic for ἀπεσσύη seems to some rather doubtful. The reading is not certain; for both at Xen. Hell. 1, 1, 23, and Plut. Alcib. 28, it is opposed by ἀπέσσυται &c. Besides, say they, in genuine Doric, η of the aor. pass. was not changed; nor does ου seem to have been used for υ when this letter was written. Both of these assertions however Bergk denies (Zeitschr. für Altert., Erstes Heft. 1852). Ahrens (Dial. Dor. p. 147) thinks that Hippocr. wrote ἀπέσστα=ἀπέστη, which is certainly very near Hesychius's gloss ἀπεσία (cod. ἀπεσσία), ἀπέδρα. We hesitate however to condemn with Ahrens ἐσσύην as not Greek. If the Greeks could form ἐδύην from δύω, διεκδυῆναι Hippocr. 1, 601 (K.), ἐπτύην from πτύω, 5, 106 (Lit.), ἐρρύην from ῥέω, Thuc. 3, 116, ἐφύην from φύω, if sound Eur. Fr. 378; Hippocr. 1, 404 &c. we do not see why they might not form ἐσσύην from σεύω or σύω.

Σήθω, see σάω, *to sift.*

Σηκάζω *To enclose*, is confined, we think, to **aor. pass.** ἐσηκάσθην, Epic 3 pl. σήκασθεν Il. 8, 131; and pt. σηκασθέντες Xen. Hell. 3, 2, 4.

Σημαίνω *To shew*, Il. 10, 58; Aesch. Ag. 293; Soph. O. C. 320; Her. 1, 34; Antiph. 3, γ, 1. 4, γ, 3; Thuc. 2, 43, Dor. σάμ- Theocr. 17, 89: **imp.** ἐσήμαινον Her. 4, 79; Thuc. 8, 102; Pl. Polit. 275, σήμ- Od. 22, 450; Simon. C. 112, iter. σημαίνεσκεν Q. Sm. 4, 193: **fut.** -ᾰνῶ Aesch. Ag. 497; Thuc. 6, 20, Ionic -ᾰνέω Od. 12, 26; Her. 1, 75: **aor.** ἐσήμηνα Aesch. Ch. 667; Eur. Heracl. 830; Her. 1, 43. 2, 2. 3, 72. 106, and always (Gaisf. Bekk.); Thuc. 5, 71; Xen. Cyr. 2, 3, 18. An. 3, 4, 4. Hell. 2, 1, 22 &c.; Aristot. Metaph. 3, 4, 20, σήμηνα Il. 23, 358, and less freq. if correct, in Attic, ἐσήμᾱνα Xen. Hell. 1, 1, 2. 2, 1, 5. 28 (Mss. Vulg. Breitb. -ηνα always *now* Dind. Saupp.); Polyaen. 1, 41; Arr. An. 1, 6, 2 (Mss. Ellendt, but -ηνα 1, 8, 3. 20, 1, Ellendt, and always Krüg.); V. T. Jud. 7, 21 &c.; N. T. Rev. 1, 1; Hierocl. p. 28, 8 (Mullach), προ- Plut. Arist. 19; subj. σημᾱ́νῃ Xen. Cyr. 4, 5, 36 (Poppo, Born. Hertl. -ήνῃ Dind. Saupp. Hertl. 3 ed.); Luc. Vot. 36 (Jacobitz, Bekk. -ήνῃ Dind.): **p.** σεσήμαγκα late, Epict. Diss. 3, 26, 29: **p. p.** σεσήμασμαι, 3 sing. -μανται Her. 2, 125; σεσημασμένος Her. 2, 39; Pl. Leg. 954; Isocr. 17, 34; Dem. 39, 17; σεσημάνθαι Ar. Lys. 1198: **aor.** ἐσημάνθην Xen. Hell. 6, 2, 34; Dem. 47, 16: **fut.** σημανθήσομαι Polyaen. 8, 21; Sext. Emp. 345 (B.), ἐπι- Eur. Ion 1593; and seemingly as **pass. fut. mid.** σημᾰνέεται Hippocr. 7, 276 (Lit.), see below. **Mid.** σημαίνομαι *to mark for oneself, infer* &c. Soph. Aj. 32; Her. 2, 38: **fut.** σημᾰνοῦμαι Hippocr. 2, 228 (Lit.), ἐν- Isocr. 20, 22, but σημανέεται Hippocr. 7, 276, seems **pass.** or as we say *will shew a mark:* **aor.** ἐσημηνάμην Il. 7, 175; Xen. Cyr. 8, 2, 17; Isae. 7, 2; Dem. 28, 6, σημην- Opp. Cyn. 1, 454; ἀπο-σημήνασθαι Her. 9, 71. **Vb.** σημαντέος Aretae. 16 (ed. Oxon.), ἐπι- Aristot. Top. 8, 7, 2. ἀ-σήμαντος Il. 10, 485. **Aor.** always ἐσήμηνα in

Her. *now*, even 3, 106 (Mss. S V F. Gaisf. Bekk. Dind. Stein, -ανα Vulg.), and always, we think, in Attic except Xen. Hell. quoted, where however Dind. and Saupp. adopt it even against the Mss. as decidedly the prevailing form. Even in late writers, baiting the Septuag. and N. Test., -ανα is, we think, less frequent than is commonly supposed.

Σήπω *To corrupt, rot*, trans. Aesch. Ch. 995; Hippocr. 6, 196; Pl. Tim. 84. Theaet. 153, κατα- Xen. Cyr. 8, 2, 21: **fut.** σήψω Aesch. Fr. 270 (D.): **aor.** ἔσηψα, κατ- Ael. H. A. 9, 62 (Schneid. δι- Herch.): **2 p.** σέσηπα as **pass.** *am rotten*, Il. 2, 135; Eur. Elec. 319; Luc. Philops. 11, κατα- Ar. Plut. 1035, συν- Hippocr. 6, 192, ἀπο- Xen. An. 4, 5, 12: **p. p.** σέσημμαι Aristot. H. A. 10, 1, 10 (B.); Luc. Philop. 20: **1 aor.** late ἐσήφθην Apollinar. Ps. 37, 10: **2 aor.** ἐσάπην Her. 3, 66; σαπῇ 2, 41; Pl. Phaed. 80; Aristot. Mirab. 86, Epic σαπήῃ Il. 19, 27; σαπείς Hes. Sc. 152; Emped. 221; Ar. Eq. 1308; Her. 6, 136; Pl. Phaed. 87: **fut.** σαπήσομαι Galen 7, 397, ἀπο- Hippocr. 9, 6 (Lit.), κατα- Pl. Phaed. 86: σήπεται Il. 24, 414.

Σθένω *To be strong, be able*, mostly in Trag. and only **pres.** Aesch. Ag. 938; Soph. O. C. 846; Eur. Alc. 267; subj. σθένω Soph. Ant. 91; Ar. Plut. 912; opt. σθένοιμι, -νοι Soph. O. C. 501; Eur. Fr. 454 (Dind.), -οιμεν Soph. O. C. 256; σθένειν Aesch. Eum. 896; Eur. Supp. 216; σθένων Aesch. Ag. 296; Soph. Aj. 488; Eur. H. F. 312; Luc. Ocyp. 120: and **imp.** ἔσθενον Soph. Tr. 927; Ap. Rh. 3, 965; Anth. 6, 93; Orph. Lith. 435; Q. Sm. 8, 447; late prose Ael. H. A. 11, 31, Poet. σθένον Ap. Rh. 1, 62. Aelian 11, 31. Fr. 98 (Herch.) quoted, are the only prose instances we have met.

Σῑγάω *To be silent, pass over in silence*, Simon. C. 66; Pind. N. 10, 29; Aesch. Sept. 263; Ar. Lys. 70; Pl. Apol. 24, Dor. 3 sing. σιγῇ, 3 pl. σιγῶντι Theocr. 2, 38; opt. σιγῷμι Pind. Fr. 58, Attic σιγῴη Thuc. 8, 66; Hom. only imper. σίγα Il. 14, 90, -άτω Pind. I. 2, 44; σιγᾶν H. Merc. 93; Pind. N. 5, 18; Aesch. Pr. 106; Soph. O. R. 569; Her. 1, 88. 7, 104; Aeschin. 1, 107, Dor. σιγῆν Epich. 130; σιγῶν Solon 4, 15; Her. 8, 26, -έων (Stein, Abicht): **imp.** ἐσίγων Com. Fr. (Cratin.) 2, 155; Pl. Prot. 360; Aeschin. 2, 163; Ar. Lys. 515, 'σίγων 515, 'σίγας 516: **fut.** σιγήσομαι mostly Poet. Soph. O. C. 113. 980; Eur. Bacc. 801. Hipp. 604; Ar. Nub. 1088. Lys. 515 &c.; Hippocr. 4, 630; late Attic prose, Alciphr. 3, 62: and late σιγήσω Anth. 8, 25. 9, 27; Or. Sib. 3, 473. 5, 59; Charit. 1, 10 (Herch.): **aor.** ἐσίγησα Xen. Cyr. 4, 5, 19; Pl. Euth. 286, σίγησα Eur. Bacc. 1084 (trimet.); Dor. subj. σιγάσω Eur. Ion 859 (chor.); σίγησον Aesch. Sept. 262; Soph. Aj. 975, -ήσατε Eur. Hipp. 565; -ήσας

Soph. Fr. 696 (D.); Pl. Rep. 616: p. σεσίγηκα Aeschin. 3, 218; p. p. σεσίγημαι Eur. Alc. 78; Aeschin. 3, 4, Dor. σεσίγᾱμαι Pind. Ol. 9, 103: aor. ἐσιγήθην Eur. Supp. 298; Her. 5, 21; Aeschin. 2, 86, Dor. -ᾱ́θην Eur. Phoen. 349 (chor.); Theocr. 16, 54: fut. σιγηθήσομαι Eur. I. T. 1076; (Pl.) Epist. 310: 3 fut. σεσιγήσομαι (Pl.) Epist. 311. Vb. σιγητέος Eur. Hel. 1387. σιγάσω Eur. Ion 859, is not fut. but subj. aor., see 860; and σιγήσομεν Ar. Ran. 253 (Ms. A. Brunck) is held an interpolation, and has been rejected by all subsequent editors. It occurs however certainly later, see above, and Dio Chrysost. Cor. p. 305 (Dind.), κατα- Orat. 13 (227), ὑπο- 20 (264). διασιγάσομαι is in some inferior Mss. and common text, Pind. Ol. 13, 91, for which Boeckh restored διασωπάσομαι (best Mss. Schneidew. Bergk. -σιωπ- Herm. Momms.) The collat. form σῑγάζω *bid be silent*, is rare and defective, -άζει Opp. Cyn. 3, 286; *classic* only pres. part. σῑγάζοντος Xen. An. 6, 1, 32: late 1 aor. part. σιγάσας Dio Cass. (Xiphil.) 64, 14: late p. p. σεσιγασμένος, κατα- Athen. 1, 4: and late, aor. p. σιγασθῇ Dio Cass. 39, 34 (Bekk.) missed or denied by all Lexicogr.

Σίνομαι *To injure*, Il. 24, 45; Hes. Op. 318; Sapph. 12; Her. 2, 68; Xen. Cyr. 3, 3, 15 -έομαι see below; Epic subj. σίνηαι Od. 12, 139, -ηται Pl. Leg. 936; opt. -οιτο Od. 12, 114, Ion. 3 pl. -οίατο Her. 9, 51; -εσθαι Theocr. 24, 87; Her. 6, 97; Xen. Lac. 12, 5, in Hom. and Attic, only pres.: and imp. ἐσίνοντο Her. 5, 74; Xen. An. 3, 4, 16, iter. σινέσκετο Hes. Fr. 221, -έσκοντο Od. 6, 6: fut. σινήσομαι so, with Ms. C, reads Lud. Dind. Hippocr. 8, 112, ἰνήσ- Lit. and Erm. 2, 582, εἰνήσ- Vulg. Foes 610, 10; Kühn 2, 676: aor. ἐσινάμην, -αντο Her. 8, 31, but -έατο 7, 147; -ασθαι Hippocr. 3, 236 (Lit.): p. p. σεσιμμένος pass. Inscr. Chish. p. 130: so pres. σίνεται Hippocr. 7, 232: and imp. σίνετο Orph. Arg. 212. The form σινέομαι, -έεσθαι occurs in Ms. S. Her. 4, 123, -εόμενος 9, 73, and imp. ἐσινέετο 9, 13, -έοντο 9, 49, and is adopted by Gaisf., but Bekker reads σίνομαι, ἐσινόμην always, we think, except 5, 81, where he retains with the Mss. the vulg. ἐσινέοντο, Dind. ἐσίνοντο, Stein ἐσικνέοντο. The same variation occurs in Hippocr. σινεόμενος 7, 562. 592, σίνομ- 7, 592 &c. (Lit.) But as σίνομαι alone occurs in Hom. and the earlier writers, and often in Her. without a variation, 1, 17. 5, 27. 6, 97, σινοίατο 9, 51, ἐσίνοντο 5, 74, one feels rather inclined to believe it the genuine form. "Recta haec est verbi forma" (Dind. Dial. Her. p. 42); so Bredow p. 363. Act. σίνω late, ἔσινον Palaeph. 1 (Vulg. *now* ἐσίνοντο Mss. Westerm.); Aeol. σίννομαι Sapph. 72 (Ahr.) A late form is σινόω Maneth. 6, 608: fut. -ώσω 552.

Σῑτέω *To feed,* rare and late if correct in act. -εόντων Galen 15, 118, from Hippocr. 6, 54 (Lit.) where now stands σιτευμένων, but παρα-σιτέω Pl. Lach. 179, more freq. συσ-σιτέω Pl. Lach. 179: imp. συν-εσίτ- Pl. Conv. 219; Aeschin. 2, 126: fut. συσσιτήσω Philostr. Apoll. 252: aor. συσσιτήσας Lys. 13, 79: p. -σεσιτηκώς Dem. 19, 191. Usu. σῑτέομαι *to eat,* in classic prose and poetry, Ar. Eccl. 665; Her. 1, 200; Xen. Cyr. 1, 2, 8; -εόμενος Her. 6, 57, -ούμενος Aesch. Ag. 1668; -έεσθαι Her. 1, 94, -εῖσθαι Pl. Leg. 942: imp. ἐσῑτεῖτο Isae. 6, 21, -έοντο Her. 8, 115. 9, 118, iter. σῑτέσκοντο Od. 24, 209; with fut. mid. σιτήσομαι Ar. Nub. 491. Pax 724; Aristot. Mund. 6, 34; and aor. p. σῑτήθην *ate,* Theocr. 9, 26: but aor. mid. σιτήσασθαι, κατα- Strab. 15, 727 (Kram.), missed by Lexicogr. The collat. σιτεύω is rare, partially used and prosaic, but not in classic Attic, Plut. Mor. 661: imp. iter. σιτεύεσκον Her. 7, 119. Mid. σιτεύομαι *to eat, live on,* Polyb. 12, 2; σιτευομένην Plut. Lucull. 40, seems pass.

Σῑτίζω *To feed,* Ar. Eq. 716; Her. 6, 52; Isocr. 1, 29: fut. -ίσω, -ιῶ: aor. ἐσίτισα Xen. Conv. 4, 9. Mid. σῑτίζομαι *to eat,* Theocr. 4, 16: fut. -ίσομαι, ἐπι- Arr. An. 3, 20, 4 (Kr.), Attic -ιοῦμαι, ἐπι- Com. Fr. (Pher.) 2, 266; Philostr. Apoll. 252, Ionic -ιεῦμαι, ἐπι- Her. 9, 50: aor. ἐσιτισάμην, ἐπ- Thuc. 6, 94. 8, 101; Dem. 50, 53: with p. p. σεσίτισμαι as mid. Pyth. in Dio. Hal. de Isae. 4.

Σῑωπάω *To be silent, pass over in silence,* Ion Chius 1, 8; Soph. Ph. 951; Com. Fr. (Pher.) 2, 275; Andoc. 1, 26; Xen. Conv. 6, 10; σῑωπᾶν Il. 2, 280; Isocr. 12, 110: imp. ἐσιώπων Eur. Alc. 93; Lys. 1, 14; Xen. Cyr. 3, 1, 13; Isocr. 12, 265: fut. σιωπήσομαι Soph. O. R. 233; Ar. Av. 226. Lys. 364; Pl. Phaedr. 234; Isocr. 17, 19; Dem. 18, 112. 24, 62. 45, 83; Luc. Demon. 14, Dor. σωπάσομαι, δια- Pind. Ol. 13, 91, -σιωπ- (Herm. Momms.): and later σιωπήσω (Aeschin.) Epist. 10, 1; Dio. Hal. 11, 6; Plut. Mor. 240. Phoc. 21; Longin. Rhet. p. 593 (Walz); Geop. 13, 18: aor. ἐσιώπησα Hippocr. 5, 396; Isocr. 21, 3; Plut. Mor. 184; -ήσῃ Luc. Nigr. 35; σιωπήσαιμι Soph. Ant. 185; Ar. Pax 378, -αιμεν Eur. Phoen. 926, -ειαν Od. 17, 513; σιωπῆσαι Il. 23, 568; Ar. Lys. 713; Xen. Cyr. 3, 1, 13; -ήσας Soph. O. R. 1146; Andoc. 1, 58: p. σεσιώπηκα Ar. Vesp. 944; Dem. 6, 34, ἀπο- Isocr. 6, 2: p. p. σεσιώπηται late Stob. 403 (Gaisf.); -ημένος Dio. Hal. 1, 76 (Vulg. σιωπώμ- Kiessl.), but Dor. σεσωπāμένος Pind. I. 1, 63 (B.): aor. ἐσιωπήθην (Dem.) Prooem. 21, 12, κατα- Isocr. 4, 27: fut. σιωπηθήσομαι Aeschin. 3, 155; Himer. 5, 24: pres. σιωπᾶσθαι Eur. Ion 432; Isocr. 1, 22. Mid. σιωπῶμαι *to silence,* aor. σιωπησάμενος Polyb. 18, 29 (Bekk. κατα- Lobeck, Dind. Hultsch); intrans. *be silent,* -ήσωμαι Procop. Epist.

46. **Vb.** σιωπητέον Luc. Hist. Con. 6, κατα- Isocr. 12, 96. διασωπάσομαι Dor. fut. quoted, has been restored from the best Mss. to Pind. Ol. 13, 91, for διασιγάσομαι. Lexicons generally err, some by giving no **fut. act.** at all, some by ranking it with **fut. mid.** and some by placing it too late. Even in late Greek, fut. mid. is, we think, the prevailing form. In Luc. for example, always; in Septuag. always, except σιωπήσω Esai. 65, 6 (Vat. Tisch. &c.), -ήσομαι (Alex.)

Σκάζω *To halt*, Epic and late prose, scarcely goes beyond part. σκάζων Il. 11, 811. 19, 17; Plut. Mor. 317; Luc. Merc. Cond. 39; and inf. -ζειν Anth. 6, 54.

Σκαίρω *To leap, frisk, dance*, is usu. Epic, and gets the length of the **imp.** σκαίρει Theocr. 4, 19, -ουσι Od. 10, 412 (-ωσι Bekk. 2 ed.); Opp. Hal. 1, 656; Aristot. Probl. 2, 31, 2. Fr. 313; -οντες Il. 18, 572; Ap. Rh. 1, 1135: **imp.** iter. σκαίρεσκε Ap. Rh. 4, 1402, ἀνα- Q. Sm. 8, 321.

Σκάλλω, see σκέλλω.

Σκάπτω *To dig*, Hom. H. Merc. 90; Eur. H. F. 999; -τειν Hipponax 35; Ar. Plut. 525; (Pl.) de Just. 375; Aristot. Mirab. Ausc. 91; Luc. Tim. 31; -των Xen. Oec. 16, 15; Aeschin. 2, 156: **imp.** ἔσκαπτον H. Merc. 207; Thuc. 4, 90; App. Lib. 15: **fut.** σκάψω Pl. Leg. 778, κατα- Eur. H. F. 566: **aor.** ἔσκαψα Hippocr. 4, 116 (Lit.), κατ- Her. 7, 156; Thuc. 4, 109: **p.** ἔσκăφα, κατ- Isocr. 14, 7. 35: **p. p.** ἔσκαμμαι Pl. Crat. 413; Luc. Gall. 6: **1 aor.** late ἐσκάφθην Tzetz. Hes. Op. 569, κατ- *v. r.* Diod. Sic. 13, 57: **2 aor.** ἐσκᾰ́φην Geop. 12, 5, κατ- Soph. O. C. 1318; Eur. Hec. 22; Her. 6, 72; Lys. 13, 34; Isocr. 15, 319; Diod. Sic. 13, 57: fut. σκăφήσομαι, ἀπο- Polyaen. 5, 10, 3, κατα- Joseph. Ant. 20, 6, 1. **Mid.** σκάπτομαι, -τοιτο Pseud.-Phocyl. 146 (Bergk).

Σκεδάω, -δάννῡμι *To scatter*, σκεδάων Nic. Al. 596, σκεδδαννῡ́ναι Theophr. C. P. 3, 6, 4; -ύντος Luc. Dem. Enc. 7 (-ννυνται Xen. Mag. Eq. 7, 9), and **σκεδάζω** see below, **σκεδαννύω** see foll.: **imp.** ἐσκεδάννῠσαν Dio Cass. 40, 22, κατ- Herodn. 8, 4, 9, and ἐσκεδάννῠον, κατ- Dem. 54, 4, -υσαν (Bekk.): **fut.** σκεδάσω Theogn. 883; Orac. Sib. 1, 188; Plut. Coriol. 12; Joseph. Jud. B. 4, 9, 6, δια- Luc. D. Mer. 9, 5; Arr. An. 1, 1, 7; Plut. Pericl. 32. Syll. 28; Geop. 5, 31, Attic σκεδῶ, -ᾷς, ᾷ &c. Aesch. Pr. 925, ἀπο- Soph. O. R. 138, δια- Ar. Av. 1053. Vesp. 229; Her. 8, 68; inf. συ-σκεδᾶν Ar. Ran. 903 (chor.): **aor.** ἐσκέδᾰσα Il. 7, 330; Hes. Op. 95; Sapph. 95 (Bergk); Soph. Tr. 989; Com. Fr. (Diph.) 4, 383; late prose, Polyaen. 5, 14, but δι- Thuc. 1, 54, κατα- Pl. Apol. 18; Dem. 18, 50, σκέδ- Il. 20, 341: **p. p.** ἐσκέδασται Aristot. Prob. 6, 4; -ασμένος Her. 4, 14; Hippocr. 6, 152 (Lit.); Thuc.

4, 56. 6, 52; Pl. Conv. 221: aor. ἐσκεδάσθην Aesch. Pers. 502; Her. 5, 102; Thuc. 1, 74; Pl. Leg. 699, δι- Thuc. 3, 98: fut. late σκεδασθήσεται Marc. Aur. 6, 4; Galen 6, 6, δια- Dio Cass. 47, 38. **Mid.** as act. aor. σκεδάσαντο in tmesi Q. Sm. 14, 596, κατ- Xen. An. 7, 3, 32 (Dind. Krüg. Cobet), ἀπο- (Pl.) Ax. 365. **Vb.** σκεδαστός Pl. Tim. 37. See κεδάννυμι, κίδνημι, σκίδνημι. σκεδάω, σκεδάννυμι *simple* seem late in pres. and the form σκεδάζω still later, σκεδάζων Theodor. Stud. p. 139, κατα- Athenag. p. 280, δια-σκεδάζεις Theodor. Stud. p. 609. διασκεδάννῡσι Pl. Phaed. 77, is subj. pres. for -ννύησι, and διασκεδάννῡται subj. pres. pass. for -ννύηται ibid.

Σκέλλω (-άλλω) *To dry up*, late -λλοντες Galen 6, 558, σκελέω, -λοῦντες, if not fut. of σκέλλω, Galen de Alim. fac. 2, 2, and σκάλλω *to hoe* &c. -λλουσι Hippocr. 1, 337 (Erm. 2, 426 Lit.); Aristot. Mirab. Ausc. 91: aor. ἔσκηλα Epic, σκήλειε Il. 23, 191; subj. ἐνι-σκήλῃ Nic. Ther. 694: p. ἔσκληκα as mid. *am dried up*, rare in *simple*, Choeril. Fr. 4; Anth. Pl. 4, 111; Nic. Ther. 718. 789, ἐξ- Epicharm. 106 (Ahr.), ἐν- Hippocr. 6, 196 (Lit.), κατ- Theophr. C. P. 6, 14, 11; Luc. Gall. 29; syncop. part. ἐσκληῶτες Ap. Rh. 2, 53: plp. ἐσκλήκει Ap. Rh. 2, 201: 2 aor. ἔσκλην, σκλαίη, ἀπο- Hesych.; inf. ἀπο-σκλῆναι as mid. Ar. Vesp. 160, κατα- Alciphr. 3, 3, 4: fut. σκλήσομαι, ἀπο- Anth. 11, 37. **Mid.** σκέλλομαι *to be dried up, wither*, Hesych.: imp. κατ-εσκέλλοντο Aesch. Pr. 481: fut. σκελοῦμαι Hesych. The 3 pl. perf. is shortened by Nicand. ἐσκλήκᾰσι Ther. 789. The Epic formation seems to point to σκάλλω.

Σκέπτομαι *To view*, Dep. Il. 17, 652; Theogn. 1095; Theocr. 25, 234; Her. 3, 37. 4, 196; Hippocr. 2, 112. 132. 4, 474. 6, 440 &c. (Lit.); rare in Attic, Pl. Lach. 185. Alcib. (2), 140; Aristot. Eth. Nic. 2, 2, 1; Menand. Fr. incert. 28; Luc. Herm. 50; Plut. Mor. 187, ἐπι- Menand. Fr. incert. 162: imp. ἐσκεπτόμην, σκεπτ- Il. 16, 361; late and rare in Attic, Luc. V. Hist. Con. 2, 10: fut. σκέψομαι Ar. Pax 29; Thuc. 6, 40; Pl. Rep. 458. Conv. 175; Xen. Cyr. 8, 3, 30: aor. ἐσκεψάμην Hom. H. Merc. 360; Eur. Or. 494; Thuc. 6, 82; Lys. 15, 10; Pl. Theaet. 196, σκεψ- H. Cer. 245; Hippocr. 7, 546; -ψηται Lys. 12, 12; -ψαιτο Isocr. 5, 43; σκέψαι Aesch. Ch. 229; Soph. El. 442; Antiph. 1, 21; Isocr. 5, 68; -ασθαι Thuc. 6, 9; -άμενος Od. 12, 247; Her. 1, 30; Pl. Leg. 854: p. p. ἔσκεμμαι act. Eur. Heracl. 147; Hippocr. 1, 634 (Lit.); Pl. Gorg. 501. Crat. 428; Xen. Mem. 3, 6, 5; Dem. 15, 25. 21, 192. 24, 158, but pass. Thuc. 7, 62; Xen. Hell. 3, 3, 8; Pl. Rep. 369; Dem. 20, 54. 21, 191: plp. ἔσκεπτο Hippocr. 1, 570 (Lit.), προύσκεπτο Thuc. 8, 66: 1 aor. ἐσκέφθην pass. and rare, σκεφθῆναι Hippocr. 6, 18

(Lit.); σκεφθέν late Zosim. 1, 60: 2 aor. late ἐσκέπην, ἐπ- V. T. Num. 1, 19. 47. Esdr. 6, 20: fut. σκεπήσομαι, ἐπι- 1 Reg. 20, 18: 3 fut. ἐσκέψομαι pass. Pl. Rep. 392; Aristid. 37 (471). **Vb.** σκεπτέος Antiph. 3, δ, 2; Thuc. 1, 72; Xen. Cyr. 1, 3, 17. For pres. and imp. σκέπτομαι, ἐσκεπτόμην, the older Attics generally used σκοπῶ, ἐσκοποῦν, σκοποῦμαι, ἐσκοπούμην; but though rare in Attic, the instances quoted will prove that they are not quite unattic, as Elmsley maintained (Eur. Her. 148). **Imp.** προυσκέπτετο Thuc. 8, 66 (Vulg.) is now read plp. προύσκεπτο (Bau. Bekk. Popp. Krüg.)

Σκευάζω *To prepare*, Pl. Crat. 424; -άζων H. Merc. 285; -άζειν Her. 1, 73: fut. -ᾰ́σω Ar. Eq. 372, Dor. -άξω: aor. ἐσκεύασα Ar. Thesm. 591; Her. 1, 73; Thuc. 2, 15; Pl. Parm. 127, Dor. -αξα, κατ- (Pl.) Locr. 99 &c.: p. p. ἐσκεύασμαι Thuc. 4, 33; Xen. Cyr. 6, 2, 28, 3 pl. Ionic ἐσκευάδᾰται Her. 4, 58: plp. ἐσκεύαστο App. Lib. 78, Ionic 3 pl. ἐσκευάδατο Her. 7, 62, and ἐσκευασμένοι ἦσαν 7, 68: aor. ἐσκευάσθην Galen 13, 180. 250. 341, παρ- Thuc. 4, 78: fut. σκευασθήσομαι Oribas. 4, 1, κατα- Dem. 19, 219. **Mid.** -άζομαι *to prepare for oneself*, Eur. H. F. 956. 969; Pl. Rep. 372: imp. ἐσκευάζ- Her. 6, 100, παρ- Thuc. 5, 6: fut. -άσομαι, παρα- Xen. Mem. 3, 4, 11; Dem. 13, 2: aor. -ασάμενος Dinarch. Fr. 89, 31 (B. Saupp.); Plut. Sol. 8; παρ-εσκευάσαντο Thuc. 1, 18: with p. p. as mid. ἐσκεύασμαι Eur. Supp. 1057; Lys. Fr. 54 (Scheibe), παρ- Pl. Menex. 234; Dem. 29, 28, δι- 13, 8, κατ- 3, 29. **Vb.** σκευαστός Pl. Rep. 510, -έος Ar. Pax 855; Galen 13, 649. 814, κατα- Pl. Leg. 964.

Σκευωρέω *To watch the baggage, examine, contrive*, act. late, Philo vol. 2, p. 569, δια- (Ph.) Epist. 3, 316: aor. ἐσκευώρησα Hesych. **Mid.** σκευωρέομαι Aristot. H. An. 9, 32, 8; Dem. 9, 17: fut. -ωρήσομαι: aor. -ήσατο 45, 47; -ήσασθαι, μετα- Pl. Politic. 276: p. ἐσκευώρηται act. 32, 11; -ημένος 32, 9, but pass. 45, 5.

Σκήπτω *To prop* &c. Poet. in act. Aesch. Ag. 310, ἐπι- Her. 3, 65; Thuc. 3, 59; Aeschin. 1, 146: imp. ἔσκηπτον, ἐπ- Pl. Menex. 246: fut. -ψω, ἐπι- Pl. Theaet. 145: aor. ἔσκηψα Aesch. Ag. 302; Eur. Med. 1333, ἐν- Her. 1, 105; σκήψειεν Aesch. Ag. 366; σκήψας Aesch. Pr. 749; Soph. O. R. 28; Eur. Hel. 834, ἐπι- Antiph. 1, 1: p. ἔσκηφα, ἐπ- Diog. Laert. 1, 118: p. p. ἔσκημμαι, ἐπ- Isae. 3, 12. 66: aor. ἐσκήφθην, σκηφθεῖσα Inscr. (Boeckh, Urk. p. 214); ἐπι-σκηφθῇ Pl. Leg. 937. **Mid.** σκήπτομαι *to prop oneself, pretend, defend*, prose and poet. Il. 14, 457; Ar. Plut. 904; Her. 5, 102; Thuc. 6, 18; Dem. 34, 28: imp. ἐσκηπτ- Lys. 4, 14: fut. σκήψομαι Ar. Eccl. 1027; Her. 7, 28; Aeschin. 3, 242: aor. ἐσκηψάμην Dem. 33, 18; Plut. Sol. 8; -ψησθε Aesch. Eum. 801; -ψαιτο Dem. 6, 13; -ψάμενος Isae. 6, 13.

Σκιάζω *To shade* (σκιά), Soph. Fr. 348; Her. 6, 117; Xen. Oec. 19, 18: **imp.** ἐσκίαζον Eur. I. T. 1152, κατ- Archil. 29: **fut.** σκιᾶῶ, κατα- Soph. O. C. 406: **aor.** ἐσκίασα Hes. Th. 716; Simon. C. 148, 4; Callim. Epigr. 49, 4; σκιάσῃ Il. 21, 232; -άσας Opp. Hal. 4, 165; inf. σκιάσαι Luc. Zeux. 5: **p. p.** ἐσκιασμένη Simon. Am. 7, 66; Hippocr. 2, 210 (Erm.), ἐπ- Soph. Tr. 914; Dio. Hal. Rhet. 8, 8: **aor.** ἐσκιάσθην perhaps rather late in *simple*, Aristot. De Color. 2, 4; Dio Cass. 65, 8; unless σκιασθείς be correct Eur. Andr. 1115 (Mss. Kirchh. Nauck, Dind. 5 ed. πυκασθείς Mss. Br. Herm.), but συσκιασθείς Pl. Tim. 75. σκιάω *to overshadow*, only **pres. act.** and late in this form, -άει Ap. Rh. 1, 604; Nic. Ther. 30, -άουσι Opp. Hal. 1, 625; -ιόων Nonn. 1, 292. 44, 127: and **imp.** in comp. κατεσκίαον Od. 12, 436, but iter. σκιάασκε Tzetz. P. H. 248: **pass.** σκιόωνται Epic for -άονται, Arat. 600: **imp.** σκιόωντο Od. 3, 487. 11, 12, ἐσκιόωντο, ἐπ- Q. Sm. 5, 346.—So κομόω for -άω, Il. 2, 542. 8, 42 &c.

Σκίδνημι *To scatter*, rare in *simple*, Heraclit. 40 (Byw.); and late Plut. Mor. 933. 939; Aretae. 36 (ed. Oxon.), but δια-σκιδνᾶσι Il. 5, 526; Hes. Th. 875; -σκιδνάς Her. 2, 25: **imp.** ἐσκίδνη, δι- App. Lib. 12. Civ. 2, 81: **aor. pass.** ἐσκιδνάσθην, subj. σκιδνασθῇ Hippocr. 6, 374 (Lit.) **Mid.** σκίδνᾰμαι Il. 11, 308. Od. 7, 130; Her. 9, 80; Hippocr. 6, 178. 372 (Lit.): **imp.** ἐσκίδναντο Il. 24, 2, σκίδ- Il. 1, 487. 23, 3. Od. 2, 258, and always *now*, except Il. 24, 2 (Bekk. 2 ed. ἐσκίδ- La R.); imper. σκίδνασθε Od. 2, 252; inf. σκίδνασθαι Od. 1, 274; Plut. Crass. 24, ἀπο- Thuc. 6, 98; σκιδνάμενος Hes. Th. 42; Sapph. 28 (Bergk); Her. 8, 23; Luc. Nigr. 37; Plut. Mor. 647. Galb. 26. See κίδνημι. The **act.** in *simple* is rare and confined to late prose, Plut. and Aretae. quoted. The **mid.** occurs chiefly in Epic, and in Ionic and late prose. In classic Attic prose we have never seen the verb in any shape except ἀπο-σκίδνασθαι Thuc. 6, 98. σκεδάννυμι is the Attic form.

Σκοπέω *To view, consider* (in the earlier and purer writers, only **pres.** and **imp. act.** and **mid.**) Pind. Ol. 1, 5; Aesch. Supp. 232; Soph. Phil. 589; Eur. Elec. 427; Ar. Nub. 1097; Antiph. 2, δ, 6. 6, 16; Thuc. 2, 43; Pl. Euth. 9; Isae. 10, 2; σκοπεῖν Isocr. 4, 188, -πέειν Her. 1, 32: **imp.** ἐσκόπουν Ar. Nub. 231; Thuc. 6, 44; Isocr. 4, 78; Isae. 2, 18; Xen. Mem. 1, 1, 12; Pl. Gorg. 514: **fut.** -ήσω: **aor.** -ησα &c. see below: **pass.** indic. late σκοπεῖται Herophil. ap. Ideler. 1, 410. **Mid.** σκοποῦμαι as **act.** Eur. I. T. 68; Ar. Thesm. 396; Andoc. 2, 19; Isocr. 12, 175; Pl. Leg. 627; -πῆται Theaet. 196; Isocr. 12, 41; -ποῖτο Soph. O. R. 964; Isocr. 12, 84. 19, 48; -εῖσθε

Andoc. 1, 54; Isocr. 17, 25; Dem. 2, 12; -έεσθαι Hippocr. 7, 146, -εῖσθαι Thuc. 8, 48; -ούμενος Soph. Tr. 296; Pl. Phaed. 100; Isocr. 5, 29; but by some held passive Pl. Leg. 772; Dem. 20, 54: **imp.** ἐσκοπούμην Ar. Eccl. 193; Xen. An. 5, 2, 8; Lys. 9, 7; Dem. 33, 10: **fut.** in early writers, σκέψομαι: **aor.** ἐσκεψάμην: **p.** ἔσκεμμαι, from σκέπτομαι, which see. From Aristotle however onward, occurs the regular formation, fut. σκοπήσω, -ήσετε Rhet. vol. 1, p. 615 (Walz); -ήσειν Galen 3, 236; -ήσων Anna Comn. p. 186, ἐπι- Babr. 103, 8, κατα- Heliod. 5, 4: **aor.** ἐσκόπησα Liban. Or. 1; subj. σκοπήσωμεν Aristot. Plant. 1, 7, 10 (B.); Sext. Emp. 119, 17, ἐπι- Luc. Herm. 59. Catapl. 24; imper. σκόπησον Babr. 98, 10; Heliod. 3, 7, ἐπι- Luc. Herm. 44; part. σκοπήσας Heliod. 8, 16, προ- Theophr. Fr. 6, 1; Dio Cass. 52, 14, περι- Polyb. Fr. incert. 90 (Bekk.), δια- Ach. Tat. 7, 12, ἐπι- Themist. 21, 248; inf. κατα-σκοπῆσαι Pseud.-Callisth. 2, 24; V. T. 2 Sam. 10, 3; N. T. Gal. 2, 4. **Mid. aor.** περι-σκοπήσασθαι Luc. H. V. 1, 32, κατα- V. T. Ezec. 21, 21 (Vat.): with **p. p.** προ-αν-εσκοπημένοι Joseph. Ant. 17, 5, 6. 17, 6, 3. **Vb.** σκοπητέον Geop. 7, 15. We have been the more particular with the parts of the regular formation, because in Grammars, Lexicons, and various philological works they are usually either ignored or expressly denied.

Σκύζομαι *To be angry*, Epic, and in *simple*, only **pres.** imper. σκύζευ Od. 23, 209; inf. -εσθαι Il. 24, 113; pt. -όμενος Il. 4, 23; Theocr. 16, 8; ἐπι-σκύζωνται Il. 9, 370: and late **imp.** ἐσκύζοντο Q. Sm. 3, 133, σκύζ- 5, 338: **aor.** in comp. ἐπι-σκύσσαιτο Od. 7, 306.

Σκώπτω *To jeer*, Ar. Plut. 973; Com. Fr. (Cephis.) 2, 883; Pl. Rep. 487; Isocr. 15, 284; Dem. 18, 262; σκώπτων 18, 245, παρα- H. Cer. 203: **imp.** ἔσκωπτον Xen. Cyr. 1, 5, 1; Aeschin. 2, 41, κατ- Her. 2, 173: **fut.** σκώψομαι Ar. Ach. 854: but σκώψω, -εις Nub. 296 (Br. Bekk. σκώψει **mid.** Elms. Dind.), late ἀπο-σκώψω Nicet. Annal. p. 81: **aor.** ἔσκωψα Ar. Nub. 540; Her. 2, 121 (4); Xen. Conv. 4, 28; Pl. Men. 80: **p. p.** ἔσκωμμαι, ἀπ-εσκώφθω Luc. Bacch. 8: **aor.** ἐσκώφθην Xen. Cyr. 5, 2, 18. **Mid. aor.** ἐσκωψάμην Alciphr. 3, 57, missed by Lexicogr.

Σμάω *To anoint*, (in Attic contracts in η) 3 sing. σμῇ, ἐπι- Com. Fr. (Cratin.) 2, 71; Ar. Thesm. 389; inf. σμῆν Luc. Lex. 3, Ionic σμέω, δια-σμέωντες Her. 2, 37 (Mss. R V F &c. Bekk. Gaisf. -έοντ- Dietsch, Abicht) but διασμῶντες (Mss. M K. Lhardy, Dind. Stein), and σμήχω Hippocr. 2, 366. 8, 162 (Lit.); Babr. 76; Lycophr. 876; Luc. Indoct. 28: **imp.** ἔσμων, ἐξ- Her. 3, 148, ἔσμηχον Od. 6, 226: **aor.** ἔσμησα, σμήσας Com. Fr. (Alex.) 3, 471, unattic ἔσμηξα Nonn. 25, 331. 37, 462; Pseud.-Callisth. 3, 29;

Aretae. 90, 37; Geop. 16, 6, ἀπο- Hippocr. 7, 24 (Lit.); Charit. 2, 2 (Herch.): p. p. ἐσμηγμένος Dioscor. 5, 95: aor. ἐσμήχθην, δια-σμηχθεὶς Ar. Nub. 1237; Geop. 16, 15. **Mid.** σμάομαι, -ῆται Com. Fr. (Antiph.) 3, 81, Ionic -ᾶται Her. 9, 110, σμήχομαι Hippocr. 2, 364 (Lit.); Strab. 3, p. 469 (Kram.); σμωμένης Ar. Fr. 326 (D.), σμηχομένα Anth. (Antip.) 6, 276: aor. ἐσμησάμην Her. 4, 73, ἐσμηξ- Hippocr. 8, 424. 488 (Lit.), ἀπ- Nonn. 32, 289, Dor. ἐσμᾶσ-, σμᾱσαμένα Callim. Lav. Pall. 32 (Vulg. σμαξ- Mein.). **Vb.** νεό-σμηκτος Il. 13, 342, ἄ-σμηκτ- Com. Fr. (Pher.) 2, 355. In **act.** and **mid.** σμῶ, σμῶμαι, is the Attic form, but in **pass.** Aristoph. has from σμήχω, aor. δια-σμηχθεὶς Nub. 1237, the only instance, we think, in Attic. In Ionic and late Attic this verb contracts in α, σμᾶται Her. quoted, ἀπο-σμᾷ Luc. Gymn. 29, though in Lex. 3, quoted, he writes σμῆν in imitation of the old Attic.

Σμύχω *To burn*, -ύχων Ap. Rh. 3, 762, κατα- Theocr. 3, 17, ἀνα- Aretae. 32 (ed. Oxon.): **aor.** ἔσμυξα, σμῦξαι in tmesi Il. 9, 653; κατα-σμύξῃ Anth. 5, 254: **p. p.** late ἐσμυγμένος, κατ- Heliod. 7, 21: **1 aor.** ἐσμύχθην, κατ- Theocr. 8, 89: **2 aor.** ἐσμύγην, ἀπο- Luc. D. Mort. 6, 3: **pres.** σμύχεται Aretae. 62 (ed. Oxon.); σμύχοιτο Il. 22, 411: **imp.** ἐσμύχετο Mosch. 6, 4.

Σόομαι *To hasten* (σεύομαι), σοῦσθε Ar. Vesp. 458, σοῦνται Aesch. Pers. 25, Dor. σῶμαι Com. Fr. (Epilyc.) 2, 887; imper. σοῦ Ar. Vesp. 209, σούσθω Soph. Aj. 1414, σοῦσθε Aesch. Sept. 31; Callim. Lav. Pall. 4; σοῦσθαι Plut. Mor. 362: **imp.** ἐσοῦτο, δι- (Hesych.). For σοῦται Aesch. Ch. 640 (Mss. and old edit.) οὐτᾷ, Hermann's emendation, has been universally adopted. σεῦται, see σεύω.

Σοφίζω *To make wise, instruct*, late in **act.** App. Mithr. 15 (B.); V. T. Ps. 18 (19), 8: **aor.** ἐσόφισα Ps. 118 (119), 98; σοφίσαι N. T. 2 Tim. 3, 15: **p. p.** σεσόφισμαι Hes. Op. 649 (Lenn.); (Phocyl.) 130, and as **mid.** see below: **aor.** ἐσοφίσθην Soph. Ph. 77 (as **mid.** Schol.): **fut.** late σοφισθήσομαι Apocr. Sir. 50, 28. **Mid.** σοφίζομαι *deal cleverly, devise, trick* &c. Eur. I. A. 744; Her. 8, 27; Pl. Gorg. 497: **fut.** -ίσομαι late Theoph. Epist. 80: **aor.** ἐσοφισάμην Ar. Av. 1401; Ael. Fr. 112; Polyb. 6, 58; Luc. Herm. 79; Strab. 10, 2, 25: and as **mid.** **p. p.** σεσοφισμένος Dem. 29, 28: **plp.** ἐσεσόφιστο Her. 1, 80. **Vb.** σοφιστέον Aristot. Polit. 6, 4, 19.

Σόω *To save*, Epic subj. σόῃς Il. 9, 681, σόῃ 424, σόωσι 393 (Spitzn.), but σόῳς, σόῳ, σόωσι (Bekk. Dind. La R.), see σαόω. σόωσι may however be referred to σάω, 3 pl. σάουσι contr. σῶσι, Epic σόωσι.

Σπᾰδίζω *To draw off* (σπάω), **aor.** σπαδίξας Her. 5, 25.

Σπᾰράσσω, **-ττω** *To tear*, Ar. Ach. 688; Pl. Rep. 539: **fut.**

-άξω Aesch. Pr. 1018: aor. ἐσπάραξα Pind. Fr. 88; Babr. 95, 40, κατ- Ar. Eq. 729: p. p. δι-εσπάρακται Com. Fr. (Eubul.) 3, 211: aor. σπαραχθῆναι Luc. Indoct. 19: fut. mid. σπαραξόμενος as pass. Theophylact. Epist. 65; σπαράξεσθαι is uncertain Eur. I. A. 1459 (Mss. Herm. Kirchh. 1 edit. -άσσεσθαι Elms. Dind. Nauck, Paley); it is trans. Andr. 1211.

(Σπάργω) *To roll, wrap*, Epic and only aor. σπάρξαν Hom. H. 1, 121. For σπάραξαν (σπαράσσω) says Doederlein, σπάρξαι—σπαράξαι (Hesych.)

Σπάω *To draw*, Pl. Leg. 644; imper. σπᾶτε Ar. Pax 498; σπῶν Soph. Ant. 1003; Eur. Cycl. 571: imp. ἔσπων Com. Fr. 4, 615: fut. σπᾰ́σω Lycophr. 484, ἐπι- Soph. Aj. 769, δια- Her. 7, 236, ἀνα- Luc. Hist. Con. 40: aor. ἔσπᾰσα Il. 13, 178 (Dind. La R.); Aesch. Ag. 333; Ar. Vesp. 175; Ap. Rh. 1, 1239; Pl. Phaedr. 254, σπάσεν in tmesi Il. 5, 859. 13, 178, and always (Bekk.); σπάσῃ Hippocr. 2, 276 (Erm.); σπάσας Soph. Ant. 258; Pl. Leg. 666, Poet. ἀν-σπασσ- Pind. P. 4, 27; σπάσαι Aesch. Ch. 533, -ῆσαι if correct, Aretae. 46 (ed. Oxon.): p. ἔσπᾰκα Aristot. Prob. 22, 2; Heliod. 10, 14; Sext. Emp. 396, 11, ἀν- Ar. Ach. 1069; Hippocr. 8, 488 (Lit.); Dem. 19, 314: p. p. ἔσπασμαι Hippocr. 6, 178; Plut. Cleom. 8. Caes. 66, δι- Emped. 270; Thuc. 6, 98. 8, 104; Xen. An. 1, 5, 9. 4, 8, 10, as mid. see below: aor. ἐσπάσθην Eur. Cycl. 639. 640, ἀπ- Thuc. 7, 80, κατ- 1, 63; Xen. An. 1, 9, 6; σπασθῇ Hippocr. 7, 172; σπασθείς Il. 11, 458; Soph. Fr. 587; Hippocr. 1, 77 (Erm.); σπασθῆναι Her. 6, 134: fut. σπασθήσομαι Galen 9, 186, δια- Xen. An. 4, 8, 10; Aristot. De An. 2, 4, 11, ἀπο- Luc. Char. 17. Mid. σπάομαι *draw one's own*, or *for oneself*, Her. 9, 107, ἐπι- Hippocr. 2, 406 (Lit.); Xen. An. 4, 7, 14: imp. ἐσπᾶτο Ar. Ran. 564: fut. σπᾰ́σομαι Aesch. Sept. 1036 (Mss. Blomf. Dind. Herm.); Hippocr. 6, 534 (Lit.), δια- Ar. Ran. 477; Dio. Hal. 16, 5; (Luc.) Asin. 25: aor. ἐσπασάμην Il. 19, 387; Philostr. Apoll. 320, ἐπ- Thuc. 5, 111, σπασ- Od. 10, 166, σπασσ- Il. 11, 240; subj. σπάσῃ Eur. Cycl. 573, παρα- Dem. 1, 3; σπάσαιτο, ἐπι- Thuc. 3, 44; imper. Epic σπάσσασθε Od. 22, 74; σπασάμενος Her. 3, 29; Lycurg. 87; Xen. Hell. 4, 4, 3, σπασσ- Il. 16, 473. Od. 11, 231 (Bekk.); Pind. P. 4, 234: and as mid. p. ἔσπασμαι Xen. An. 7, 4, 16. Cyr. 7, 5, 29. Vb. ἀντίσπαστος Soph. Tr. 770, -έον Hippocr. 6, 654. Homer has of the *simple* form only aor. mid. and once aor. pass. σπάσατ' Od. 2, 321, is for ἐσπάσατο.

Σπείρω *To scatter*, Hes. Fr. 217. Sc. 399; Aesch. Fr. 155 (D. 5 ed.); Ar. Av. 1697; Her. 2, 37; σπείρῃ Xen. Oec. 17, 5; σπεῖρε Pind. N. 1, 13; Soph. Fr. 585 (D.); σπείρων Od. 6, 179; Soph. Tr. 33; Pl. Leg. 838; -ρειν Hes. Op. 463; Pl. Leg. 841:

imp. ἔσπειρον Her. 9, 116, δια- Plut. Pomp. 18, iter. σπείρεσκον Her. 4, 42: **fut.** σπερῶ Eur. Elec. 79; Pl. Phaedr. 276 (Aeol. σπέρσω Schol. Eur Hec. 198): **aor.** ἔσπειρα Soph. El. 533; Eur. Phoen. 22; Her. 7, 107; Pl. Phaedr. 260. 276; σπείρας Aesch. Sept. 754; Pl. Tim. 41: **p.** late ἔσπαρκα Polyaen. 2, 1, 1; V. T. Esai. 37, 30; Schol. Eur. Phoen. 670: **p. p.** ἔσπαρμαι Eur. H. F. 1098; Ar. Ran. 1207; Her. 5, 92 (6); Xen. Ages. 1, 30; Pl. Leg. 693, δι- Thuc. 3, 30: **1 aor.** (ἐσπάρθην see below): **1 fut.** late if sound διασπαρθήσομαι V. T. Zach. 14, 2 (Schleusn. διαρπαγήσ- Vat. Alex. Gaisf. &c.): **2 aor.** ἐσπάρην Soph. O. R. 1498; Thuc. 2, 27: **2 fut.** late σπᾰρήσομαι V. T. Deut. 29, 23, δια- Diod. Sic. 17, 69; Galen 3, 637. **Mid.** aor. σπείρασθαι trans. Ap. Rh. 3, 1028: **2 aor.** σπᾰρέσθαι, if correct, intrans. *yield fruit*, Polyaen. 8, 26 (Mss. P D Vulg.) missed by Lexicogr., but σπείρεσθαι (Koraës, Woelff.) **Vb.** σπαρτός Soph. O. C. 1534, -τέον late Geop. 2, 20. 39. 14, 23. We have seen no sure instance of **1 aor. pass.** ἐσπάρθην; δι-εσπάρθησαν Xen. An. 4, 8, 17 (some Mss. Zeune) has been altered to δι-εσπάσθησαν (Popp. Krüg. Dind. Saupp. &c.); nor of **2 p.** ἔσπορα, but noun σπορά Soph. Tr. 316, which, however, could be formed *analogically* without the *actual use* of ἔσπορα; fut. δια-σπαρθήσομαι V. T. quoted we are inclined to doubt.

Σπένδω *To pour, offer a libation to the gods*, Hom. H. 29, 6; Terpand. 1 (B.); Ar. Eccl. 140; Thuc. 4, 98; σπένδησθα Od. 4, 591, -δῃ 8, 432; σπένδε Eur. Bac. 313; -δων Il. 11, 775; Soph. El. 270; Her. 7, 54; Pl. Leg. 799; Aeschin. 2, 84; -ειν Pind. I. 6, 9; Soph. Ph. 1033; Ar. Thesm. 793; Her. 2, 151: **imp.** ἔσπενδον Ar. Pax 1093; Her. 2, 151; Xen. An. 4, 3, 13; Dem. 19, 130, iter. σπένδεσκον Il. 16, 227. Od. 7, 138: **fut.** σπείσω perhaps late in *simple*, Or. Sib. 7, 81; Nonn. 19, 194; Nicol. Rhet. 11, 14; Himer. Or. 23, 18; V. T. Numb. 28, 7, but κατα- Eur. Or. 1187; Her. 2, 151: aor. ἔσπεισα Od. 13, 55; Soph. Fr. 49 (D.); Eur. Ion 1202; Philostr. Apoll. 55, ἀπ- Antiph. 1, 20, σπεῖσ- Il. 9, 177. Od. 7, 228, iter. σπείσασκε Od. 8, 89; -σω Il. 6, 259; Theocr. 1, 144, Epic 1 pl. -σομεν Od. 7, 165. 181; -αιμι Ar. Nub. 426; σπεῖσον Il. 24, 287; Ar. Eq. 106; σπείσας Il. 16, 253; Her. 4, 187; Xen. Hell. 7, 2, 23. An. 4, 3, 13; Pl. Leg. 806; σπεῖσαι Od. 3, 47; H. Hym. 2, 320; Anth. 9, 422, ἀπο- Pl. Phaed. 117: **p.** ἔσπεικα later, κατ-εσπεικώς Plut. Sert. 14: **p. p.** ἔσπεισμαι Thuc. 3, 111. 4, 16, see below: **plp.** ἔσπειστο Thuc. 3, 111: **aor.** ἐσπείσθην later, Plut. Rom. 19, ἀπ- Anth. (Dioscor.) 5, 55, κατ- (Antip. Sid.), 7, 27. **Mid.** σπένδομαι *to pour mutual libations, make a treaty*, (not in Hom.) Eur. Bac. 284; Ar. Ach. 199; Thuc. 5, 14. 60: **imp.** ἐσπένδ- Thuc.

4, 99: fut. σπείσομαι Dem. 19, 163; -σεσθαι Xen. An. 7, 4, 23 (Popp. Dind. -σασθαι Born. Krüg. Cob. Sauppe, Hug): aor. ἐσπεισάμην Eur. Phoen. 1240; Ar. Ach. 727; Thuc. 2, 73. 5, 5; Xen. An. 4, 4, 6; -σάμενος Her. 3, 144. 7, 148; Isocr. 4, 43: as mid. p. p. ἔσπεισμαι Eur. Med. 1140. Vb. ἄ-σπειστος Dem. 25, 52.—Epic forms σπένδησθα subj. 2 pres. Od. 4, 591, σπένδεσκε iter. imp. Il. 16, 227, -εσκον Od. 7, 138, aor. σπείσασκε Od. 8, 89, subj. σπείσομεν for -σωμεν, Od. 7, 165. 181.

Σπέρχω *To urge, drive*, Orph. Arg. 1169, ἐπι- Od. 5, 304; and Attic, Aesch. Sept. 689; subj. σπέρχωσι Il. 13, 334; Hom. H. 33, 7; -οιεν Od. 3, 283 (Bekk. La R.); κατα-σπέρχων Ar. Ach. 1188; Thuc. 4, 126, but περι-σπερχέω *to be greatly moved, indignant*, -εόντων Her. 7, 207 (Mss. Gaisf. Bekk. Stein, -ερχθέντων Valken. Dind. Abicht): imp. ἔσπερχε Luc. Tragod. 236, Attic ἐπ- Thuc. 4, 12: aor. ἔσπερξα, ἐπ- Hesych. σπέρχομαι *to haste, be angry*, Nic. Ther. 417. 814; σπερχοίατο Il. 19, 317. Od. 13, 22; σπέρχου Eur. Med. 1133; -χόμενος Il. 23, 870; Eur. Alc. 256; Her. 3, 72: imp. ἐσπέρχετο Her. 5, 33: fut. m. σπέρξομαι (Hesych.): aor. ἐσπερξάμην (Hesych.): pass. σπερχθείς Pind. N. 1, 40; Her. 1, 32. The *simple* form seems confined to poetry and Ionic prose.

Σπεύδω *To urge on, speed*, trans. and intrans. Od. 19, 137; Solon 13, 43; Pind. Ol. 4, 13; Soph. O. C. 1017; Ar. Plut. 1167; Her. 1, 42; Thuc. 6, 10; Pl. Crito 45, Dor. 3 pl. -δοντι Theocr. 16, 15; σπεύδῃ Aesch. Pers. 743, Dor. 1 pl. σπεύδωμες Theocr. 15, 59; σπεύδειν Il. 13, 236, Epic -δέμεν Od. 24, 324: imp. ἔσπευδον Soph. El. 935; Her. 9, 101; Isocr. 5, 23, σπεῦδ- Pind. N. 9, 21: fut. σπεύσω Eur. Hec. 66; Ar. Eq. 926; Xen. Cyr. 5, 3, 27: aor. ἔσπευσα Soph. Aj. 1223; Eur. H. F. 1133; Her. 8, 41; Pl. Crit. 45, σπεῦσα Od. 9, 250; subj. σπεύσωμεν Ar. Lys. 266, Epic -ομεν Il. 17, 121; σπεῦσαι Aesch. Supp. 599: p. later ἔσπευκα Plut. Mor. 582: -κότι Paus. 7, 15, 5: and p. p. ἔσπευσμαι (Luc.) Amor. 33; Dion. descrip. Graec. 20, p. 138 (Mein.), ἔσπευμαι if correct, Galen 13, 487. Mid. σπεύδομαι as act. poet. Aesch. Ag. 151: fut. σπεύσομαι Il. 15, 402. Vb. σπευστέον Ar. Lys. 320.

Σπουδάζω *To make haste, be eager*, Soph. O. C. 1143; Ar. Pax 471; Isocr. 3, 25; Xen. Cyr. 1, 3, 11: imp. ἐσπ- Xen. Oec. 9, 1; Isocr. 12, 188; Isae. 8, 16: fut. σπουδάσω late, Polyb. 3, 5; Diod. Sic. 1, 58; Dio Cass. 44, 36. 45, 6; Dio Chrys. Or. 3 (45); Joseph. Ant. 13, 9, 2: classic fut. m. σπουδάσομαι Pl. Euth. 3; Dem. 21, 213; Luc. Salt. 25: aor. ἐσπούδασα Eur. H. F. 507; Isocr. 2, 44; Pl. Phaed. 114: p. ἐσπούδακα Ar. Vesp. 694; Com. Fr. (Antiph.) 3, 101; Xen. Conv. 2, 17; Pl. Phaedr.

236: **plp.** -δάκεσαν App. Hisp. 94; **p. p.** ἐσπούδασμαι Simon. C. 223; Xen. Cyr. 4, 2, 38; Pl. Leg. 722, κατ- Her. 2, 173, δι- Dem. 20, 157, but **act.** 23, 182: **aor.** later, ἐσπουδάσθην Plut. Per. 24; Strab. 17, 3, 15: and **fut.** σπουδασθήσομαι Ael. H. A. 4, 13 (Schneid.) **Vb.** σπουδαστός Pl. Hipp. maj. 297, -τέος Eur. I. A. 902; Pl. Rep. 608. δια-σπουδάζω in **act.** is rare and late, **aor.** διασπουδάσαντες Dio Cass. 36, 38 (21): **p.** διεσπουδακώς Dio. Hal. de Lys. 14: **p. p.** διεσπούδασται Dem. 20, 157. 23, 79. **Mid.** as **act.** διασπουδάζομαι: **imp.** διεσπουδάζετο Arr. An. 7, 23, 8: **fut.** διασπουδάσομαι Dio Cass. 52, 20: as **mid.** **p. p.** δι-εσπούδασται Dem. 23, 182.

Στάζω *To drop*, Hipponax 57 (B.); Aesch. Ch. 1058; Soph. El. 1423; Her. 6, 74; Hippocr. 8, 278; Pl. Tim. 82: **imp.** ἔσταζον Eur. Bacc. 711; Hippocr. 3, 82 (Lit.); Babr. 72, 5; Ael. V. H. 3, 42: **fut.** στάξω V. T. Jer. 49 (42), 18, κατα- Luc. Luct. 19, Dor. 1 pl. σταξεῦμες Theocr. 18, 46, 3 pl. στάξοισι Pind. P. 9, 63: **aor.** ἔσταξα Batr. 229; Eur. H. F. 1355; Hippocr. 2, 654 (Lit.), στάξε Il. 19, 39. 354; Pind. N. 10, 82: **p. p.** ἔστακται, ἐν- Od. 2, 271: **plp.** ἐν-έστακτο Her. 9, 3: **1 aor.** ἐστάχθην, ἐπι-σταχθέν Hippocr. 6, 424 (Lit.), ἐν- Dioscor. 2, 210: **2 aor.** ἐστᾰ́γην, ἐπιστᾰγῇ Dioscor. 2, 75; ἐπι-στᾰγείς 1, 18, ἐν- 2, 37. στακτός Ar. Plut. 529; Pl. Critias 115. στάζω is rare in prose.

(**Σταθμάω**) *To measure, estimate*, rare in **act.**: **fut.** (-ήσω): **aor.** ἐστάθμησα, σταθμήσας Eur. Ion 1137; late prose, Athen. 2, 18: **p. p.** ἐστάθμηται Arat. 234 (Bekk.): as **pass. fut. mid.** σταθμήσομαι Ar. Ran. 797. Usu. Dep. mid. σταθμάομαι Pl. Lys. 205; -μᾶσθαι Soph. O. R. 1111; Pl. Leg. 643; -μώμενος Her. 7, 237, Ionic σταθμέομαι, -εόμενοι Her. 2, 150, or -όομαι, -εύμενοι 8, 130: **imp.** σταθμᾶτο Pind. Ol. 10, 45: **fut.** σταθμήσομαι Luc. Hist. Con. 63, but **pass.** Ar. Ran. 797, quoted: **aor.** ἐσταθμησάμην, -ησάμενος Her. 2, 2. 9, 37; Ionic -μώσασθαι 3, 15. 38. 4, 58. 7, 10. 11, 214: **pres. pt.** σταθμεόμενα Hippocr. 7, 532 (Lit.) is **pass.** **Vb.** σταθμητός Pl. Charm. 154. Lhardy and W. Dind. are inclined to think σταθμόομαι the true Herodotean form, and accordingly would inflect it uniformly in his writings, σταθμούμενος (or -ευμ-), σταθμώσασθαι, σταθμωσάμενος. They are both good judges, but dialects are freakish.

(**Στᾰχῡ́ω** -ῠόω) *To shoot up, sprout, grow* (στάχυς), of the **act.** we have seen only σταχύῃ, ἀπο- Geop. 2, 24, 3. 3, 3, 13: iter. **imp.** σταχύεσκον, ἐπι- Ap. Rh. 1, 972, ἀνα- 3, 1354. **Pass.** ὑπο-σταχύοιτο Od. 20, 212: **p.** late ἐσταχυωμένος Diosc. 4, 11 (Spengel).

Στέγω *To cover, defend*, in pure Attic perhaps only **pres.** Aesch. Sept. 797; Soph. O. C. 15; Eur. Hipp. 843; Hippocr.

7, 610; Pl. Tim. 78; subj. στέγω Soph. O. R. 341; στέγειν Aesch. Sept. 216; Ar. Vesp. 1295; Pl. Gorg. 493; στέγων Soph. El. 1118; Thuc. 2, 94: and imp. ἔστεγον Thuc. 4, 34: later, fut. στέξω Diod. Sic. 11, 29: aor. ἔστεξα Polyb. 8, 14; Plut. Alex. 35: aor. p. ἐστέχθην Simplic.: pres. pass. στεγοίμεθα Soph. Tr. 596; στέγεσθαι Thuc. 6, 72. **Mid.** στέγομαι *to keep off from oneself*, imp. στέγετο Pind. P. 4, 81: aor. ἐστέξατο Anth. (Phalaec.) 13, 27 (Jacobs.) στέξαντες is in some Mss. and old edit. Soph. O. R. 11, for the better supported στέρξαντες; and στέξαιμι, Brunck's reading Tr. 993, is a mere conjecture of Valckenaer for στέρξαιμι.

Στείβω *To tread*, usu. only pres. H. Hym. 19, 4; Eur. Ion 495; στείβων Il. 11, 534: and imp. ἔστειβον, στεῖβ- Il. 20, 499. Od. 6, 92, iter. στείβεσκον Q. Sm. 1, 352: fut. late, στείψει Apollinar. Ps. 138, 19: aor. ἔστειψα, κατ- Soph. O. C. 467: p. p. (στῐβέω) ἐστίβηται Soph. Aj. 874. **Vb.** στειπτός Soph. Ph. 33, στιπτ- (Dind.); so Ar. Ach. 180. **Pres. pass.** στειβόμενος not στιβόμ- as if from a form στίβω, is the approved reading Xen. An. 1, 9, 13 (L. Dind. Popp. Krüg. Cobet, Saupp.), στιβόμ- still however (Kühner). στειβόμενος Theocr. 17, 122, is mid. but στειβομένα is perhaps the best reading, and joined with κονία requires a passive sense: imp. ἐστείβετο Q. Sm. 10, 452. We have never seen 2 aor. act. ἔστῐβον, nor pass. ἐστῐ́βην.

Στείνω *To make strait*, Poet. (Attic στένω) στείνοντες Nonn. D. 23, 5 (Rhod. Graefe, Koechly, στίζ- Vulg.): imp. στεῖνον Orph. Arg. 115 (Schneid. Ruhnk.). **Pass.** στείνομαι *to become straitened, crowded, distressed*, Ap. Rh. 2, 128; Opp. Hal. 4, 398; στείνοιτο Od. 18, 386; -νόμενος Il. 21, 220. Od. 9, 445; Hes. Th. 160; Ap. Rh. 4, 335: imp. στείνοντο Il. 14, 34. Od. 9, 219; Theocr. 25, 97, later ἐστείν- Q. Sm. 6, 642. 7, 100. The form στεινόω we have seen only in comp. ἀπ-εστείνωτο Theocr. 22, 101. See στένω.

Στείχω *To go*, Poet. Ionic and late Attic prose, Alcae. 19; Aesch. Sept. 467; Soph. Ant. 1129 (στίχ- Dind.); Opp. Hal. 1, 675; subj. στείχω Soph. Ph. 1402, -χῃ Her. 1, 9, Epic -ῃσι Od. 7, 72; στείχοιμι Aesch. Supp. 500; Soph. Ant. 1108; στεῖχε Pind. N. 5, 3; Soph. Ant. 98; Com. Fr. (Mnesim.) 3, 568; στείχειν Il. 11, 331; Eur. Or. 97; -χων Il. 2, 287; Pind. N. 1, 65; Ar. Av. 1398; Her. 3, 76, -ουσα Soph. Ant. 186; which Dem. (19, 248) rather quotes than uses; but late, Plut. Mor. 901; Philostr. Apoll. 2, 33: imp. ἔστειχον Od. 9, 444; Hes. Fr. 174; Soph. Tr. 47; Philostr. Apoll. 2, 32, δι- Pind. I. 3, 17, στεῖχ- Il. 9, 86; Hes. Th. 10: fut. (στείξω): 1 aor. Epic ἔστειξα, περί-στειξας Od. 4, 277, -στιξας (Aristarch.): 2 aor. Epic ἔστῐχον Il. 16, 258;

Callim. Del. 153; Ap. Rh. 3, 1212; Theocr. 25, 223; στίχωμεν, βαδίσωμεν (Hesych.) The aorists are Epic. For δι-έστιχον Pind. I. 3, 17 (Vulg.), Herm. Boeckh, Bergk &c. διέστειχον. Hesychius presents a pres. form στίχουσι, and Dind. Bergk &c. so edit Soph. Ant. 1129 (chor.): aor. περι-στίξαι (Hesych.) Schmidt thinks spurious, see above.

Στέλλω *To send, send for, equip*, Aesch. Pr. 387; Eur. Tr. 168; Luc. Herm. 27, ἀπο- Thuc. 4, 50; -λοιμι Il. 12, 325; -λειν Aesch. Fr. 82; Her. 5, 125; -λων Il. 4, 294: imp. ἔστελλον Soph. Ph. 571; Her. 3, 141, ἀπ- Thuc. 8, 64: fut. στελῶ Soph. Ph. 983; Eur. Bac. 827, Epic στελέω Od. 2, 287: aor. ἔστειλα Aesch. Pers. 609; Soph. Ant. 165; Thuc. 2, 69. 3, 86, στεῖλ- Od. 14, 248; στείλας Od. 14, 247; Her. 3, 14, περι- Od. 24, 293, Aeol. ἔστελσε Hesych.: p. ἔσταλκα Arr. An. 2, 11, 9, ἐπ- Eur. Phoen. 863; Xen. Hell. 1, 5, 3, ἀπ- Isocr. 1, 2; (Dem.) 12, 6: plp. ἐστάλκει Arr. An. 3, 16, 6; Ind. 42, ἐπ- Thuc. 5, 37: p. p. ἔσταλμαι, -αλται Her. 4, 189; App. Lib. 66; -μένος Aesch. Ch. 766; Soph. Tr. 776; Her. 1, 80; Pl. Leg. 833: plp. ἐστάλμην, ἔσταλτο Philostr. Apoll. 3, 116, 3 pl. ἐστάλατο Hes. Sc. 288 (Goettl.); Her. 7, 89 (Dobr. Bekk. Dind. Stein), -λάδατο (Vulg. Gaisf.), see below: 1 aor. very rare, ἐστάλθην, ἀποσταλθέντες Inscr. 3053 (Boeckh); ἀπο-σταλθῇ Schol. Od. 8, 21: 2 aor. ἐστᾰλην usu. as mid. Pind. Ol. 13, 49; Soph. Aj. 328; Her. 4, 159. 5, 126; Aristot. Fr. 560; Dio. Hal. Ant. 18, 5 (Kiessl.); Luc. Nigr. 2; Arr. An. 2, 13, 5, ἐπ- Thuc. 1, 91; Xen. Cyr. 5, 3, 15: 2 fut. στᾰλήσομαι, ἀπο- Aeschin. 3, 114; Dem. 24, 93; Polyb. 3, 17, κατα- Com. Fr. (Apoll.) 4, 457: 2 p. (ἔστολα Cram. Anecd.) Mid. στέλλομαι *to equip oneself, go, set out, send for* &c. Il. 23, 285; Aesch. Pr. 392; Soph. Ph. 466; Her. 3, 102; Xen. An. 5, 6, 5: imp. ἐστέλλετο Her. 3, 53; App. Syr. 44: fut. στελοῦμαι Lycophr. 604, ὑπο- V. T. Haggae. 1, 10: aor. ἐστειλάμην Hermes. 2, 2; Soph. O. R. 434; Eur. Bac. 821; Dio. Hal. 13, 15; Luc. Philops. 32 &c., ὑπο- Hippocr. 1, 580 (Lit.); Isocr. 6, 89. 8, 41; Dem. 1, 16, στειλ- *furled*, Il. 1, 433: see p. p. ἔσταλμαι Her. 7, 62; Xen. An. 3, 2, 7; Pl. Leg. 833: plp. ἐστάλατο Hes. and Her. quoted: and 2 aor. ἐστάλην, ἐξ- Ar. Vesp. 487, see above.

ἐσταλάδατο Her. 7, 89 (Vulg. Gaisf.) is said to be Ionic plp. 3 pl. for ἐστάλατο, and it appears to have some support from such Homeric forms as ἐληλάδατο &c. and, besides, is noted without disapproval, both by Hesych. and Eustath. Buttmann however is inclined to think it a mistake; Goettling, Hes. Sc. 288, pronounces it monstrous; and Bekker has restored ἐστάλατο which Bredow approves, and which now seems the undoubted reading also in Hes. Sc. quoted, where, by the bye, a 2 aor. act.

ἔσταλον occurs in some editions, without however any Ms. authority; it is a mere conjecture of Schmidt. The 1 aor. pass. ἐστάλθην, which Buttm. says is used by the poets, we have never seen *early* or *late* except in the instance quoted.

Στενάζω *To groan, sigh*, Aesch. Pr. 696; Soph. Ant. 882; Eur. H. F. 1065; Hippocr. 7, 36; -άζειν Soph. Aj. 982; Ar. Vesp. 316 (chor.): **imp.** ἐστεν- Eur. Ph. 1035, ἀν- Soph. Aj. 930 (chor.): **fut.** στενάξω Eur. H. F. 248 (Heath, Dind. Kirchh. -αζ- Mss.); Aeschin. 3, 259 (Ms. Z. Bekk. Franke, -νάξαι Bait. Saupp.); Lycophr. 973; late prose Himer. Or. 23, 21; V. T. Esai. 24, 7; Joseph. Jud. B. 1, 32, 2, ἀνα- Eur. I. T. 656: **aor.** ἐστέναξα Eur. I. T. 550; Com. Fr. (Diph.) 4, 390; Dem. 23, 210. 27, 69; Plut. Mor. 171. 202. 204 &c. Cat. min. 70. Mar. 6. Feb. 12 &c.; Luc. Cal. 14, ἀνα- Her. 1, 86; Xen. Conv. 1, 15: **p. p.** ἐστέναγμαι, -μένος late Lycophr. 412, κατ- Alciphr. 1, 36. **Vb.** στενακτός Eur. H. F. 914, -τέος Supp. 291. In classic Attic prose, this verb in the *simple* form is used by Aeschin. and Dem. alone, and only in **aor.**

Στενᾰχέω *To groan*, **aor.** στεναχῆσαι Il. 18, 124 (old edit.), rejected from Hom. by Wolf, Bekker &c. for στονᾰχέω, which see.

Στενᾰχίζω *To sigh, lament*, Epic, Od. 1, 243; subj. -ίζω 9, 13; -ίζων Il. 19, 304. Od. 24, 317 (Bekk. Dind. La R.): **imp.** στενᾰχιζε Hes. Th. 858, ἀν-εστ- Il. 10, 9. **Mid.** στεναχίζομαι as **act.**, περι- Od. 10, 10: **imp.** στεναχίζετο Il. 7, 95; Hes. Th. 159 (some Mss. Lennep), others στονᾰχίζετο, a form which Wolf banished from Homer, but which Buttm. defends. Wolf with Ms. Ven. gives the *mute* form with ε, στεναχίζω, but the *pure* form with ο, στοναχέω; Ms. Vindob. and old edit. vary between ε and ο. In Hes. however, Sc. 92. 344, Wolf approved μετεστοναχίζετο, περι-στονάχιζε, which other editors have adopted. In Hom. Bekker edits στεναχ-, Spitzner leans to it (Excurs. 3.)

Στενᾰχω *To groan, bewail*, Poet. Il. 16, 391. 24, 639; Callin. 1, 17; Aesch. Pr. 99 (chor.); -ᾰχῃ Eur. Fr. 265 (D.); -ᾰχειν Soph. El. 133 (chor.) 1076. (Elms. and *now* Dind.); Eur. Tr. 106 (ch.); -χων Il. 18, 318, -χουσα Soph. El. 141 (chor.); Ar. Ach. 548 (trimet.); Opp. Hal. 4, 200: **imp.** iter. στενᾰχεσκε Il. 19, 132. **Mid.** as **act.** **imp.** στενάχοντο Il. 23, 1. Od. 9, 467; Ap. Rh. 1, 388; Q. Sm. 3, 388, but ἐπ-εστεν- Il. 4, 154; Q. Sm. 10, 368. This verb in **act.** is chiefly Epic—the Traged. use it simple and comp. only, we think, in chor.—the **mid.** always Epic. Some read στοναχεῖν Soph. El. 133 quoted (Br. Bergk), ἐπιστοναχοῦσιν O. R. 185 (Bergk &c.), Elms. Dind. and Nauck always στενάχειν &c.

Στένω Epic στείνω (στενός) properly *To make narrow, to sigh,* *lament* only pres. στένει Il. 20, 169; Aesch. Sept. 967; Soph. Ph. 338; Ar. Ach. 30; Hippocr. 7, 384. 8, 328 (Lit.); Aristot. H. An. 8, 2, 6; Dem. 18, 244. 323. Epist. 3 (1485); Phal. Epist. 54 (Herch.): and imp. ἔστενον Il. Od. (Wolf, Dind. La R.), see below; Simon. C. 142, 7; Aesch. Ag. 408; Eur. Ion 944; Theocr. 7, 141; D. Sic. 13, 16; Luc. D. Deor. 6, 2. Mort. 27, 2, στένε Il. 10, 16. 23, 230. Od. 21, 247, and always (Bekk. 2 ed.), στεῖν- Orph. Arg. 115 (Schneid. Ruhnk.) **Mid.** στένομαι trans. Eur. Bac. 1371, intrans. Aesch. Sept. 872. Pers. 62 (chor.); Opp. Hal. 3, 390, περι- Il. 16, 163; Dor. part. στενομένα Eur. Ion 721 chor. (πενομ- Herm. Dind. 5 ed.), στείνονται *crowd* Ap. Rh. 2, 128; Opp. C. 2, 436: imp. ἐστείνετο *crowded, thronged,* Q. Sm. 5, 651. **Pass.** στείνομαι, -νοιτο Od. 18, 386, -νόμενος Od. 9, 445: imp. ἐστείνοντο *were narrow,* Tryphiod. 336, στείν- Il. 14, 34; Theocr. 25, 97. The primary meaning *straiten* seems confined to the Epic form στείνω, the secondary *sigh* to the Attic στένω. In Hom. Wolf, Dind. &c. always augment imp. ἔστενε, Bekker always στένε, but μετ-έστ- Od. 4, 261. This verb is very rare in prose, the mid. and pass. never.

Στέργω *To love,* Aesch. Eum. 911; Soph. Tr. 280; Ar. Eq. 769; Isocr. 3, 40; Pl. Leg. 908; -οιμι Eur. Hec. 779; στέργε Theogn. 87; Isocr. 1, 15; -γειν Aesch. Ag. 1570; Her. 7, 104; Dor. pt. στέργοισα Theocr. 17, 130: imp. ἔστεργον Soph. Fr. 709 (D. 2 ed.); Eur. Ion 817; Her. 3, 85. 9, 117; Alciphr. 3, 32; Plut. Ant. 31: fut. στέρξω Soph. Ph. 458; Eur. Or. 1023; Pl. Hipp. Maj. 295; Dem. 18, 112: aor. ἔστερξα Simon. Am. 7, 45; Soph. O. R. 1023; Ar. Ran. 229; Her. 2, 181. 7, 69; Isocr. 12, 45; Pl. Leg. 907: 2 p. ἔστοργα Her. 7, 104: p. p. ἔστεργμαι Emped. 190 (Stein); Anth. 6, 120: aor. ἐστέρχθην Lycophr. 1190; Plut. Ant. 31; Stob. (Pomp. Macr.) 78, 7; Nicol. Dam. 56 (L. Dind.): fut. mid. as pass. στέρξομαι, -ξῃ Or. Sib. 3, 437: pres. στέργομαι Thuc. 1, 38. **Vb.** στερκτός Soph. O. R. 1338, -τέος Dinarch. 1, 91.

Στερέω *To deprive,* pres. rare στερεῖ Aesch. Pr. 862? see fut., ἀπο- Ar. Vesp. 509; Pl. Prot. 353; imper. στερείτω Pl. Leg. 958, and **στερίσκω** rare and pres. only, Thuc. 2, 43; Artemid. Onir. 1, 44. 2, 3, ἀπο- Soph. O. C. 376: fut. στερήσω Soph. Ant. 574; Thuc. 4, 64, and perhaps (στερέσω) -ρῶ, -ρεῖ Aesch. Pr. 862, unless pres. as fut.: aor. ἐστέρησα Eur. Andr. 1213; Her. 9, 93; Pl. Leg. 873, ἀπ- Lys. 24, 22, Epic ἐστέρεσα Anth. 11, 124; inf. στερέσαι Od. 13, 262; Orph. Arg. 1330; -έσας Anth. 9, 174: p. ἐστέρηκα Polyb. 31, 19, ἀπ- Thuc. 7, 6; Pl. Leg. 868: p. p. ἐστέρημαι Eur. Fr. 456 (Dind.); Her. 3, 65; Lys. 2,

72. 19, 7; -ῆσθαι Her. 8, 29; Thuc. 2, 62; Pl. Tim. 77; -ημένος Aesch. Eum. 755; Soph. O. C. 857; Eur. Med. 286. 1023; Her. 3, 137; Xen. Hell. 3, 5, 12 (ἐστέρεσμαι Cram. Anecd.): **plp.** ἐστέρητο Thuc. 2, 65: **1 aor.** ἐστερήθην Soph. Ant. 13; Eur. Alc. 200; Her. 8, 142; Antiph. 4, δ, 1; Thuc. 1, 24; Pl. Phaed. 99; Isocr. 16, 40; -ηθῶ Soph. O. R. 771; Dem. 28, 17; στερηθείς Pind. N. 8, 27; Aesch. Pers. 579: **fut.** στερηθήσομαι Dio Cass. 41, 7; Diod. Sic. 4, 23 (Bekk. στερήσ- L. Dind.); Apollod. 1, 3, 2; Babr. 72 (Isocr. 6, 28 Vulg.), ἀπο- Lys. 12, 70; Dem. 1, 22; and Isocr. 7, 34 (Ms. U. Bekk. B. S. but -ρήσομαι Vulg. Bens.): **2 aor.** poet. ἐστέρην, στερείς Eur. Alc. 622. Hec. 623 &c.: **2 fut.** στερήσομαι which may also be **fut. mid.** as **pass.** Soph. El. 1210; Thuc. 3, 2. 39; Xen. Cyr. 4, 2, 32 (Popp. Dind.); Lys. 19, 1; Isocr. 6, 28. 16, 49 (Ms. U. Bekk. B. S. Bens.); Pl. Phil. 66; Dem. 20, 40, ἀπο- Eur. H. F. 137; Thuc. 6, 91; Dem. 24, 210. 39, 11. 40, 10: (3 **fut.** ἐστερήσομαι Eur. I. A. 1203, is a suggestion of Reiske and Porson, and adopted by Bothe, Nauck, Dind. 5 ed. for ὑστερήσ- Vulg., ἀπ-εστ- H. Fur. 137 Dind. for ἀπο-στ-.) **Pass.** (and **Mid.**?) στερέομαι very rare, -εῖσθαι Eur. Supp. 793 (Ms. C. Ald. Nauck, -εῖσα Markl. Dind.): στερῶνται, ἀπο- Aesch. 1, 195; στεροῖτο Xen. An. 7, 6, 16 (Vulg. Kühner, στέροιτο Popp. Krüg. Dind.); στερούμενος Xen. An. 1, 9, 13 (Krüg. -όμενος Dind. Saupp.); more freq. στερίσκομαι only **pres.** Eur. Supp. 1093; Her. 4, 159; Thuc. 1, 73; Xen. Ages. 11, 5; Pl. Rep. 413, and στέρομαι *am deprived of, want,* Hes. Op. 211; Dem. 20, 51; -ρεσθαι Soph. Tr. 136; Her. 8, 140; Antiph. 5, 13; Thuc. 3, 46; Andoc. 3, 20; Xen. Conv. 4, 31. An. 3, 2, 2; Isocr. 19, 23. 47; -ρόμενος Antiph. 4, α, 2: **imp.** ἐστερούμην Antiph. 2, β, 9, ἐστερόμην rare, Xen. Hell. 2, 2, 9: **fut.** late (στεροῦμαι), στεροῖτο Liban. V. 1, 683, unless ἀποστερεῖσθε Andoc. 1, 149, and στερήσομαι see above, be held **fut. mid.** as **pass.**—the former may be **pres.** (Krüg.)

The **pres.** of ἀπο-στερέω **act.** and **pass.** is more frequently used, especially in prose. An **act.** form στέρω, ἀποστέρω has some Ms. support Isocr. 12, 243, opposed by ἀποστερῶ, to which it is possible to refer as **fut.** στερεῖ Aesch. quoted, and **mid.** ἀποστερεῖσθε as **pass.** Andoc. quoted, which however may be **pres.** compare στέρομαι Eur. Elec. 1309. στέρομαι is perhaps always used with the force of a **perf.** *have been deprived, am without,* and on this ground Buttmann would substitute στερομένους for στερουμ- Xen. An. 1, 9, 13 (Krüg.) &c. We rather demur to this, because στεροῦμαι also has sometimes decidedly the force of a **perf.** ζῆν ἀποστερούμενος τῆς πατρίδος Isocr. 6, 25. 14, 17, ἀποστεροῦμαι χρημάτων 17, 2; Dem. 30, 15, and the *simple,* though later, στερούμενος τέκνων Dio. Hal. 8, 30. 41 (-ομ- Kiessl.); Diod. Sic. 1, 84 (-ομ- L. Dind.); Luc. Char. 1 (Jacob.) L. Dindorf in Steph. Thesaur. (στερῶ) agrees with Buttm. in confining the *perf. meaning* to the barytone form στέρομαι, and accordingly would substitute it for στεροῦμαι wherever this occurs with the sense of the perf. We think his remarks too unqualified.

Στερίσκω, στέρω, στέρομαι, see στερέω.

Στεῦμαι properly *To stand, pledge oneself, affirm,* &c. Epic def. Dep. Orph. Lith. 82 (Herm.), στεῦται Il. 3, 83. Od. 17, 525; Ap. Rh. 3, 337; Aesch. Pers. 49 chor. (Herm. Dind.), -εῦνται (Blomf. Hart. &c.): **imp.** στεῦτο Il. 18, 191. Od. 11, 584; Ap. Rh. 3, 579. **1 pers.** στεῦμαι Orph. L. 82, is Herm. emendation for ὑπισχνοῦμαι (Vulg.) This verb seems connected with ἵστημι. Eustath. says it arose from a contraction of the form στέομαι into στεῦμαι, the diphthong remaining in the other persons στεῦνται, στεῦτο.

Στέφω *To encircle, crown,* Od. 8, 170; Soph. Ant. 431; Aristot. Fr. 108; Hyperid. Fr. 120; Luc. Nigr. 30: **imp.** ἔστεφον Il. 18, 205; Aesch. Sept. 50, στέφ- Hes. Op. 75: **fut.** στέψω Soph. Aj. 93; Eur. Tr. 576: **aor.** ἔστεψα Eur. Alc. 1015; Com. Fr. (Alex.) 3, 435; Her. 2, 45; Pl. Phaed. 58. Rep. 398; στέψον Theocr. 2, 2; στέψας Pind. Fr. 145 (B.): (**p. act.**?): **p. p.** ἔστεμμαι Aesch. Supp. 344; Xen. Cyr. 8, 3, 12; Pl. Phaed. 58: **aor.** ἐστέφθην Eur. Hel. 1360: **fut.** late, στεφθήσομαι Galen 1, 36. 10, 19. **Mid.** στέφομαι *crown oneself,* Eur. Bac. 313; Luc. Nigr. 32: **fut.** late στέψομαι Athen. 15, 18: **aor.** ἐστεψάμην Anth. (Meleag.) 9, 363; Orph. Arg. 327; Coluth. 83; Opp. C. 4, 245; late prose Plut. Rom. 16; Dio. Hal. Rhet. 1, 6, but ἐπ- Il. 1, 470; Simon. C. 174. **Vb.** στεπτός Anth. Plan. 306 (Jacobs.) In comedy and classic prose this verb is very rare, and only in **pres.** and **aor. act.** and **p. pass.** στεφανόω is much more freq. in every class of writers, **act. mid.** and **pass.** with **fut.** -ωθήσεται Aeschin. 3, 20. 147. 244. 259: and **fut. mid.** as **pass.** -ώσεται Aristid. 39 (496), but **act.** Philostr. T. Apoll. 7, 294, both missed by Lexicogr.

Στήκω late, see ἑστήκω.

Στηρίζω *To support,* Hippocr. 5, 340; -ίζῃ 7, 592; -ίζων Eur. Hipp. 1207; -ίζειν Aristot. Nat. Ausc. 3, 5, 17: **imp.** ἐστήριζε Eur. Bac. 1083 (Mss. Dind. Kirch. Nauck): **fut.** στηρίξω (Hippocr. 1, 541 Erm. 7, 590, some Mss. Ald. -ίζω Lit.) Nonn. 1, 449; N. T. 1 Pet. 5, 10, and -ίσω V. T. Jer. 17, 5, -ιῶ 24, 6: **aor.** ἐστήριξα Il. 4, 443; Opp. Hal. 2, 464 (Eur. Bacc. 1083 Ald. Herm. Christ. pat. 2259, -ιζε Mss. Dind. Nauck, Kirchh.); rare in prose, Hippocr. 3, 208, στήριξε Il. 11, 28; Hes. Th.

498; στηρίξῃ Hippocr. 2, 456. 7, 212; στηρίξαι Od. 12, 434; Thuc. 2, 49; -ίξας Hippocr. 7, 592; Luc. D. Mar. 10, 1; inf. -ίξαι Od. 12, 434, late ἐστήρισα Anth. 14, 72; App. Civ. 1, 98: p. p. ἐστήριγμαι Hes. Th. 779; -ιγμένος Hippocr. 7, 122 (Lit.); Aristot. Prob. 5, 20, κατ- Eur. Fr. 385 (Dind.): plp. ἐστήρικτο Il. 16, 111; Hes. Sc. 218: aor. ἐστηρίχθην, στηριχθείς Tyrtae. 11, 22 (Bergk); Hippocr. 3, 194 (Lit.): fut. late στηριχθήσομαι Galen 3, 749. **Mid.** στηρίζομαι *to support oneself, stand firmly,* Soph. Aj. 195, ἀπο- Aristot. Prob. 5, 19; Anth. Plan. 265: fut. στηρίξεται Philostr. Apoll. 218: aor. ἐστηριξάμην Hippocr. 3, 452. 4, 324. 372 (Lit.); στηρίξασθαι Il. 21, 242, later ἐστηρισάμην Plut. Eum. 11; V. T. Esai. 59, 16. Editors are divided between aor. ἐστήριξε Eur. Bac. 1083 (Ald. Christ. Pat. Herm.) and imp. ἐστήριζε (Mss. Valcken. Elms. Matth. Dind. Nauck.) Paley also adopts imp. swayed, it would appear, by some scruple about admitting "the form in ξ into a senarius." But we think the examples given above shew that the early inflection of this verb was with γ, not with ς, and that the Attics followed it. If therefore a fut. aor. &c. were required, a form in ξ was the only one their usage afforded. So στίζω always with ξ, aor. στίξας Ar. Ran. 1511 (chor.), but fut. στίξω Eup. Com. Fr. 2, 530 (senar.) συρίζω, -ττω, aor. συρίξας Ar. Plut. 689 (senar.)

(Στιβέω) *To tread,* p. p. ἐστίβημαι Soph. Aj. 874. See στείβω.

Στίζω *To prick,* Simon. C. 78 (Bergk): imp. ἔστιζον Her. 7, 233; Plut. Per. 26: fut. στίξω Com. Fr. (Eup.) 2, 530; Her. 7, 35: aor. ἔστιξα Her. 5, 35: (p. act.?): p. p. ἔστιγμαι, -μένος Ar. Av. 760; Xen. An. 5, 4, 32; Aeschin. 2, 79; Her. 5, 35; inf. ἐστίχθαι 5, 6; Sext. Emp. 168, 33: aor. ἐστίχθην, στιχθείς Porph. V. Pythag. 15 (Nauck). **Mid.** late στίζομαι *to tattoo oneself,* Luc. D. Syr. 59; Herodn. 3, 14, 7: aor. ἐστίξατο Nonn. 43, 232. **Vb.** στικτός Soph. Ph. 184, -τέος Schol. Ar. Plut. 220.

Στίλβω *To shine,* -βει Eur. Hipp. 195, -βουσι Hom. H. 31, 11; Eur. Rhes. 618; Maneth. 4, 426; -βοιεν Opp. Cyn. 1, 403; στίλβων Il. 3, 392; Com. Fr. (Eup.) 2, 561; Ar. Av. 697; Theocr. 2, 79; rare in prose, -βουσι Aristot. Anal. Post. 1, 13, 2; -βων Pl. Phaed. 110. Tim. 59; στίλβειν Aristot. de coelo 2, 8, 10: imp. ἔστιλβον Philox. Athen. 4, 28: aor. late ἔστιλψα Charit. 2, 2; στίλψασα Aristaen. 1, 25.

Στιχάομαι *To advance in line, march,* only Epic 3 pl. imp. ἐστιχόωντο Il. 2, 92; Theocr. 25, 126. Late Epic writers use the act. intrans. στιχόωσι Ap. Rh. 1, 30; Orph. L. 269; Mosch. 2, 142, so Hom. in comp. ὁμοστιχάει Il. 15, 635; trans. στιχόωσι Arat. 191.

Στονᾰχέω *To sigh, lament* (στονᾰχή), Poet. -χεῖ Orph. H. 38, 17,

Dor. 3 pl. -χεῦντι Mosch. 3, 28; Anth. 7, 10; imper. -χεῖτε Mosch. 3, 1; στοναχεῖν Soph. El. 133 chor. (Vulg. Bergk, Ellendt. στενάχειν Elms. Dind. Nauck): **fut. mid.** στοναχήσεται Hom. H. 4, 252 (Vulg.); Or. Sib. 9, 297: and late **fut. act.** στοναχήσει Or. Sib. 10, 297: **aor.** στονάχησε Q. Sm. 1, 573, ἐπ-εστ- Il. 24, 79; στοναχῆσαι 18, 124. For **fut. mid.** στοναχήσεται Hom. H. 4, 252 quoted, Martin and Baumeister read στόμα χείσεται. This verb seems Epic. At Soph. El. quoted, the Mss. give στοναχεῖν, στεναχεῖν, and at O. R. 185 occurs the compound ἐπιστενάχουσι; hence Elmsley suggested στενάχειν, which is now approved by Dindorf &c. Ellendt and Bergk, however, retain στοναχεῖν.

Στονᾰχίζω *To groan, sigh,* Epic, but in Hom. v. r. only for στενάχ- Il. 23, 225: **imp.** ἐστονάχιζε Musae. 115, στονάχ- Q. Sm. 7, 393, περι- Hes. Sc. 344. **Mid.** as act. στοναχίζεται, ἐπι- Q. Sm. 7, 532: **imp.** στοναχίζετο Hes. Th. 159, μετ-εστοναχ- Scu. 92. See στεναχίζω.

(**Στορέννῡμι**) *To spread, lay out* (**pass.** στορέννυται late, Schol. Theocr. 7, 59) syncop. στόρνῡμι Eur. Her. 702; Theocr. 17, 133; -ύναι Aesch. Ag. 909 (Elms. Dind.); -νύς Soph. Tr. 902; Her. 7, 54 (κατα-) κα-στ Od. 17, 32: **imp.** ἐστόρνυ- ὑπ- Philostr. Apoll. 3, 118: **fut.** στορέσω Nonn. 16, 95, -έσει Or. Sib. 8, 273, ἐπι- Hippocr. 3, 201 (Vulg. Kühn, but -έσαι Mss. Lit. 4, 204), Dor. 3 pl. -σεῦντι Theocr. 7, 57; -έσοιμι Nonn. 42, 395; -εσεῖν Theocr. 6, 33, Attic στορῶ, παρα- Ar. Eq. 481, ὑπο- Com. Fr. (Eub.) 3, 247: **aor.** ἐστόρεσα Od. 3, 158. 14, 50; Hom. H. 33, 15; Epigr. Lycurg. 109; Her. 8, 99; Alciphr. 1, 1, κατ- Her. 9, 69, στόρ- Il. 9, 660. 24, 648. Od. 20, 2. 13, 73 (Bekk. Dind.); -έσω Thuc. 6, 18; στόρεσον Od. 23, 177; -έσας Il. 9, 213; Aesch. Pr. 190 (chor.); -έσαιμι H. Cer. 143; -έσαι Il. 9, 659; Plut. Mor. 856, κατα- Plut. Nic. 9: **p. p.** late ἐστορεσμένος Theodr. Prodr. 6, 259 (Herch.), but as **mid.** ὑπ-εστορ- Philostr. Apoll. 238: **plp.** late ἐστόρεστο Dio Cass. 74, 13 (B.); Himer. 13, 2: **aor.** late in *simple,* ἐστορέσθη Dio Cass. 39, 42. 67, 14 (Bekk.); but κατα-στορεσθῇ Hippocr. 1, 618 (Lit.); στορεσθείς Plut. Mor. 787; Ael. H. A. 13, 2 (ἐστορήθην Hesych.) **Mid.** (στορρέννῦμαι) στόρνῦμαι Ap. Rh. 1, 1184, trans. ὑπο- Xen. Cyr. 8, 8, 16: **imp.** ἐστόρνυντο Theocr. 22, 33: **aor.** ἐστορεσάμην in tmesi Orph. Arg. 1343, στορεσ- Theocr. 13, 33; Ap. Rh. 1, 375; imper. ὑπο-στόρεσαι Ar. Eccl. 1030: as **mid. p. p.** ὑπ-εστορεσμένος missed by Lexicogr. see above. Rare in Attic prose; we have met with **aor.** only. See στρώννυμι. στόρνῡ 2 sing. imper. for -ῦθι, Ar. Pax 844. καστορνῦσα for κατα-στορν- Od. 17, 32. στορέσας **aor. act.** as **mid.** Anacreont. 30, 3 (Bergk).

Στοχάζομαι *To aim, guess,* Dep. mid. Soph. Ant. 241; Antiph.

2, α, 4; Pl. Gorg. 465; Aeschin. 2, 103: imp. ἐστοχ- Pl. Euthyd. 277: fut. -άσομαι Isocr. Epist. 6, 10; Aristot. Eth. N. 4, 12; Aristid. 45, 46: aor. ἐστοχασάμην Pl. Gorg. 465; Hippocr. 1, 588. 4, 86 (Lit.); Isocr. 1, 50: with p. p. ἐστόχασμαι as mid. Pl. Leg. 635; Aristot. H. A. 6, 17, 15 (B.); Luc. Salt. 74; Galen 13, 136. 216. 476, but pass. 10, 885. 11, 35: aor. ἐστοχάσθη seems late and pass. Galen 13, 713; Babr. 10 (2 pt. Lewis); στοχασθείη Oribas. 7, 26; -ασθέν 10, 5; but -ασθείς act. Pseud.-Callisth. 1, 3. Vb. στοχαστέον Aristot. Polit. 2, 7, 7. Our Lexicons have missed the aor. pass. and, if we are right, the perf. with pass. sense.

Στρᾰτεύω *To do military service, take the field*, &c. Her. 1, 77; Thuc. 1, 26; Lycurg. 84: imp. ἐστράτ- Her. 6, 7: fut. -εύσω: p. -ευκα reg. Mid. -εύομαι Her. 2, 29; Thuc. 8, 22; Isae. 4, 27; -εύοισθε Aesch. Pers. 790: imp. ἐστρατ- Her. 8, 10; Lys. 14, 14: fut. -εύσομαι Her. 7, 11; Thuc. 5, 54; Dem. 8, 23: aor. -ευσάμην Soph. Aj. 1111; Her. 1, 156; Thuc. 5, 63; Isocr. 5, 144: with p. ἐστράτευμαι Lys. 9, 4; Isae. 2, 42. 4, 29. 7, 41; Dinarch. 2, 17, ἐξ- Thuc. 2, 12. 5, 55: and rare aor. ἐστρατεύθην Pind. P. 1, 51; late prose Apollod. 1, 9, 13 (Bekk.), which some may think a defence of συν-εστρατεύθησαν Diod. Sic. 8, 1, against Bekker's and L. Dindorf's alteration συν-εστράτευσαν. A Boeotic form of this aor. ἐστροτευάθη occurs in Ussing's Inscr. Gr. ined. p. 41, n. 52. We may mention here an oversight of one of our best Lexicons regarding the compound συ- or ξυ-στρατεύω, that "Thuc. always uses it as act." We are certain of four or five instances of mid. ξυνεστρατεύοντο 2, 56. 80; -όμενος 5, 60. 7, 42. 61; -εσθαι 7, 20. The remark would apply better to Thucydides' use of ἐπιστρατεύω. The form στρατόομαι is Epic and Lyric, and confined to imp. ἐστρατόωντο Il. 3, 187. 4, 378, στρατ- Ap. Ph. 2, 387: and aor. στρατωθέν Aesch. Ag. 133 (chor.)

Στρεβλόω *To twist, rack*, Ar. Nub. 620; Her. 3, 129; Antiph. 5, 32; Isocr. 17, 15: fut. -ώσω Plut. Phoc. 35: aor. -ωσα Dinarch. 1, 63: p. p. ἐστρεβλῶσθαι Polyb. 7, 7, 4: aor. στρεβλωθῆναι Andoc. 1, 44; -ωθείς Lys. 13, 54: fut. mid. as pass. στρεβλώσεται Pl. Rep. 361. 613; Philostr. Apoll. 5, 207.

Στρεφεδῑνέω *To turn round*, rare and Epic, imp. (ἐ)στρεφεδίνεον Q. Sm. 13, 7: 1 aor. pass. στρεφεδῑνήθην, Epic 3 pl. -δίνηθεν Il. 16, 792. Aeschylus has a mid. form with ο, στροφοδινοῦνται *wheel*, Ag. 51 (chor.): act. late, στροφοδινεῖν Schol. Il. 21, 269. One is apt to think that Aeschylus would have used the Homeric form, but he has followed the same analogy in τροχοδινεῖται Pr. 882 (chor.)

Στρέφω *To turn*, Il. 23, 323; Eur. Supp. 413; Hippocr. 2, 353 (Erm.); Pl. Rep. 330; στρέφοι Pind. N. 4, 93; στρέφων Aesch. Eum. 651; Soph. Aj. 575; Her. 5, 12; στρέφειν Ar. Ran. 957: imp. ἔστρεφον Il. 17, 699. 5, 505 (στρ- Bekk.); Pl. Euthyd. 276, στρέφε, περι- H. Merc. 409: fut. στρέψω Eur. Med. 415. 1152 (Elms. Dind. Nauck); Anth. 9, 27; Aristot. Eth. Eud. 7, 13, 7. 8; Ael. V. H. 14, 15 (-ειεν Herch.), μετα- Il. 15, 203, ἀπο- Soph. O. R. 1154; Xen. M. Eq. 1, 12, ἀνα- Eur. Bac. 793, δια- Aesch. Supp. 1017; Dem. 18, 140: aor. ἔστρεψα Eur. Tr. 1243, στρέψ- Od. 4, 518; στρέψῃς, κατα- Xen. Oec. 17, 10, στρέψωσι, ὑπο- Il. 12, 71; στρέψειας, ὑπο- Il. 3, 407; στρέψον Theogn. 1324; Eur. H. F. 1406; στρέψαι Il. 13, 396; Pl. Tim. 43; στρέψας Il. 18, 544; Aesch. Pr. 708; Soph. Ant. 717; Ar. Nub. 1455; Xen. Hell. 4, 3, 5, iter. στρέψασκον 3 pl. Il. 18, 546: p. ἔστροφα, ἀν- Com. Fr. (Theognet.) 4, 549 (quoted in Athen. 15, 11); Stob. (Corisc.) 7, 53, ἐπ- Polyb. 5, 110, μετ- Aristid. 34, 436 (D.): p. p. ἔστραμμαι Hom. H. 3, 411; Com. Fr. (Antiph.) 3, 140; Hippocr. 1, 248 (Erm.); Xen. An. 4, 7, 15, κατ- Thuc. 1, 75, ἀν- Her. 6, 47; Isocr. 15, 283, see mid.: plp. ἐστράμμην, κατ-έστραπτο Thuc. 5, 29, Ionic 3 pl. -εστράφατο Her. 1, 27: 1 aor. rare ἐστρέφθην, στρεφθῶ Ar. Thesm. 1128; στρεφθείς Il. 5, 40. 16, 308. 598; Anth. 12, 128; Ap. Rh. 3, 650 (μετα- Mosch. 2, 111); Attic prose, only Pl. Polit. 273, ἀπο- Aristot. Xenoph. 2, 30, Ionic and Dor. ἐστράφθην Sophr. 78 (Ahr.), κατ- Her. 1, 130; στραφθείς Theocr. 7, 132: 2 aor. ἐστράφην Solon 37, 6 (Bergk); Her. 3, 129, ἐπ- Soph. Ant. 1111, ἀπ- Ar. Plut. 702; στραφῇ Aristot. H. An. 6, 22, 7; στραφείη Soph. Tr. 1134, μετα- Ar. Ach. 537; στραφείς Soph. Ant. 315; Com. Fr. (Antiph.) 3, 125; Xen. An. 3, 5, 1; Pl. Tim. 77. Polit. 282; στραφῆναι Her. 3, 129, ἀπο- Ar. Pax 279, κατα- Thuc. 5, 97: fut. στραφήσομαι *simple* late, V. T. 1 Reg. 10, 6, Apocr. Sir. 6, 28; Orig. Ref. Haer. p. 170, but δια- Ar. Eq. 175. Av. 177, συσ- Hippocr. 7, 516 (Lit.), ἀνα- Isocr. 5, 64, μετα- Pl. Rep. 518. **Mid.** στρέφομαι *to turn oneself, turn to flee*, Il. 18, 488; Soph. El. 516; Xen. Cyr. 6, 3, 27; Pl. Theaet. 181, trans. Rep. 405, κατα- Her. 6, 94; intrans. Epic subj. στρέφεται Il. 12, 42: imp. ἐστρεφ- intrans. Il. 24, 5, trans. Pl. Euthyd. 302, κατ- Her. 4, 144; Thuc. 1, 15; Dem. 18, 244: fut. στρέψομαι Il. 6, 516, ὑπο- Od. 18, 23, ἀπο- Xen. Cyr. 5, 5, 36, but κατα- trans. Her. 7, 209. 9, 2; Thuc. 3, 13: aor. ἐστρεψάμην trans. *turn for, with oneself*, στρέψαι Soph. O. C. 1416, κατ- Her. 1, 30; Thuc. 1, 94; Xen. Cyr. 1, 1, 4: and as mid. p. p. κατ-έστραπται *has subdued*, Isocr. 5, 21; Dem. 4, 6, -εστράμμεθα Xen. Cyr. 7, 5, 53; -αμμένος Her. 1, 171; Xen. Hell. 5, 2, 38: and often 1 and 2 aor. pass. intrans. ἐστρέφθην

Il. 15, 645 &c.: **2 aor.** ἐστράφην Xen. Cyr. 7, 1, 25; -φείς An. 1, 10, 6 &c. Pl. Tim. 77: even **act. pres.** στρέφων Soph. Fr. 771: and **aor.** στρέψαντες Xen. An. 4, 3, 32. **Vb.** στρεπτός Il. 5, 113. 15, 203. The Epics always use **1 aor.** ἐστρέφθην simple and compd.: the Tragedians, again, though said to be fond of "strong aspirated forms," seem never to use the **1 aor. pass.** simple or compd., often the **2 aor.** In Attic poetry and prose, in fact, there is in each only one instance of **1 aor.** στρεφθῶ Ar. Thesm. 1128, and στρεφθείς Pl. Polit. 273; and in Ionic, only one of ἐστράφθην, κατ- Her. 1, 130, *v. r.* -άφην. In the compds. except κατα- the **mid. fut.** and **aor.** are very rare, ἀποστρέψομαι intrans. Xen. Cyr. 5, 5, 36; Plut. Mor. 387: **aor.** ἀπ-εστρέψατο trans. (late, unless sound Hermesianax 83, Athen. 598) V. T. Hosea 8, 3, -αυτο 3 Macc. 3, 23, missed by Lexicogr.: as **mid. p. p.** ἀπ-έστραπται Euenus 2, 5 (Bergk). ἀνα-στρέφω has, we think, contrary to our Lexicons, never **fut. mid.** ἀναστρέψομαι, but **fut. pass.** as **mid.** -στραφήσομαι Isocr. quoted; Apocr. Sir. 39, 3.

Στροβέω *To turn, roll,* Aesch. Ag. 1216; Ar. Vesp. 1528: classic **fut.** στροβήσομαι Ar. Ran. 817: later στροβήσω Lycophr. 756: **aor.** ἐστρόβησα late prose, Plut. Num. 13, δια- Alciphr. 3, 9: **p. p.** ἐστροβημένος Lycophr. 172. **Pass.** στροβοῦμαι Aesch. Ch. 203: **imp.** ἐστροβούμην Polyb. 24, 8, 13.

Στρώννῡμι *To spread,* Aesch. Ag. 909 (Blomf. Herm. -στόρν- Elms. Dind.); C. Fr. (Anon.) 4, 605; Xen. Cyr. 8, 2, 6, late and rare στρωννύω Gl. Aesch. Ag. 909; Aristid. 14, 216 (D.); Geop. 19, 2, ὑπο- Athen. 2, 31; Geop. 2, 27: **imp.** ἐστρώννῠον N.T. Matt. 21, 8: **fut.** στρώσω late in *simple* V. T. Esai. 14, 11, but ὑπο- Eur. Hel. 59; Com. Fr. (Amph.) 3, 319, and στρωννύσω, ἐπι- (Luc.) Philop. 24: **aor.** ἔστρωσα Aesch. Ag. 921; Eur. Supp. 766; Her. 6, 139: **p.** ἔστρωκα: **plp.** ἐστρώκει late Heliod. 4, 16, ὑπ- Babr. 34: **p. p.** ἔστρωμαι Hom. H. Ven. 158; Eur. Med. 380; Com. Fr. (Diod.) 3, 544; Theocr. 15, 157; Her. 6, 58. 9, 82; Thuc. 2, 34, ὑπ- Her. 1, 47 (Orac.): **plp.** ἐστρώμην Il. 10, 155; Her. 7, 193: **aor.** ἐστρώθην, κατ- Diod. Sic. 14, 114; but στρωθείς Soph. Tr. 653 (Musgr. Dind. 5 ed.): **fut.** late στρωθήσομαι Orac. Sib. 5, 438. **Mid.** στρώννῠμαι *spread on,* or *for oneself,* **fut.** στρώσομαι late V. T. Ezec. 27, 30: **aor.** στρωσάμενοι (Theocr.) 21, 7, ὑπο- Paus. 1, 34, missed by Lexicogr. **Vb.** στρωτός Hes. Th. 798; Eur. Or. 313. στρώννῡ imper. for -ῠθι Com. Fr. (Anax.) 4, 605.

Στῠγέω *To hate, dread* (στύγω, στύζω), Il. 7, 112; Hes. Th. 739; Emped. 232; Aesch. Pr. 46; Soph. Tr. 583; Ar. Ach. 33; Her. 7, 236; and late Alciphr. 3, 28, Dor. 3 pl. στυγέοισι Pind. Fr. 186; subj. -γέῃ Il. 1, 186, Epic -γέῃσι 8, 515: **imp.**

ἐστύγουν late Babr. 27, 11 (2 pt. Bergk), but ἀπ-ἐστύγεον Melanip. 4 (B.), iter. στῠγέεσκον late Nonn. Joh. 15, 72: fut. στυγήσω Hesych.: aor. ἐστύγησα Eur. Tr. 705; Aesch. Supp. 528 (late prose Heliod. 8, 10; Ptol. N. Hist. 3), ἀπ- Soph. O. C. 692; Dio Cass. Fr. 40, 44, and ἔστυξα *made terrible*, στύξαιμι Od. 11, 502; but στύξαν *hated*, Ap. Rh. 4, 512; στύξον Anth. 7, 430; στύξας 9, 186: p. ἐστύγηκα late in *simple*, Joseph. Ant. 16, 7, 3. contra App. 2, 24, but ἀπ- as pres. Her. 2, 47: p. p. ἐστύγημαι late, Lycophr. 421, κατ- Phil. in Verm. 9 (ἔστυγμαι Hesych.): aor. ἐστυγήθην, -ηθείς Aesch. Sept. 691; Eur. Alc. 465: (2 aor. ἐστύγην?): fut. mid. στυγήσομαι pass. Soph. O. R. 672: 2 aor. act. ἔστῐγον Simon. C. 59; Ap. Rh. 2, 1196; Anth. 7, 596, in tmesi Od. 10, 113, κατ- Il. 17, 694, ἀπ- Callim. Del. 223. Vb. στυγητός Aesch. Pr. 592. (ῠ). This verb *simple* or compound seems not to occur in early Attic prose: in Hom. Hesiod, Theogn. Ap. Rh. it is always open στυγέει, -έουσι.

Στῠφελίζω *To dash*, Poet. imper. -ίζετε Od. 18, 416; -ίζειν Il. 21, 380; -ίζων Soph. Ant. 139 (chor.); in prose, only Hippocr. 3, 524 (Lit.): imp. στύφ- Musae. 296: aor. ἐστυφέλιξα Il. 5, 437; Pind. Fr. 210 (Bergk); Anth. 7, 297. 665, στυφ- Il. 12, 405: aor. pass. ἐστυφελίχθην Nic. Eug. 5, 286: pres. στυφελιζόμενος Od. 16, 108: imp. στυφελίζετο Coluth. 26 (Dübn.)

Στύω *To make erect*, fut. στύσω Anth. 10, 100: aor. ἔστῡσα, στῦσαι Ar. Lys. 598: p. ἔστῡκα intrans. Ar. Pax 728. Av. 557. Lys. 989, Lacon. 3 pl. ἐστῑ́καντι Lys. 996. Pass. στύομαι *to be erect*, Ar. Ach. 1220. Av. 1256; late prose -ύεσθαι Luc. Alex. 11: in sense p. ἔστῡκα. ῡ always.

Σῡλάω *To spoil, rob*, Eur. Hel. 669; subj. συλᾷ Aeschin. 2, 115; συλῶν Aesch. Pr. 83; Soph. O. C. 922; Pl. Leg. 942; Isocr. 10, 33; -λᾶν Aesch. Pers. 810; Pl. Rep. 469: imp. ἐσύλα Il. 6, 28, σύλα 4, 116, Aeol. dual συλήτην 13, 202, iter. σύλασκε Hes. Sc. 480: fut. -ήσω Il. 6, 71; Her. 5, 36; Pl. Leg. 854: 1 aor. ἐσύλησα Her. 1, 105; App. Hannib. 55; συλήσω Il. 22, 258 &c.; -ήσας 7, 82; Her. 8, 33; Pl. Leg. 869; Dem. 19, 313, Dor. συλάσαις Pind. P. 12, 16: p. σεσύληκα Dem. 22, 74. 24, 120. 182: plp. ἐσεσυλήκειν App. Hisp. 57: p. p. σεσύλημαι Her. 6, 118; Dem. 35, 26: plp. ἐσεσύλητο 18, 139: aor. ἐσυλήθην Soph. Ph. 413; -ηθείς Her. 6, 19; Isocr. 6, 19, Dor. -āθείς Pind. Ol. 9, 89; Eur. Ion 917 (chor.): fut. -ηθήσεται Aesch. Pr. 761: and as pass. fut. mid. συλήσεσθαι late, Paus. 4, 7, 4 (Schub.), the only instance of the mid. form we have ever met: Lexicogr. seem to have missed it. The collat. σῡλεύω is Epic, and confined to pres. Il. 24, 436; Anth. 5, 231: and imp. ἐσύλευον Il. 5, 48. συλέω to pres. -οῦσι Xanth. Fr. 1 (Müll.); part. -έων

Inscr. Delph. vol. 1, 1699, 11. 1704, 13λ &c.: **imp.** ἐσύλεον Q. Sm. 2, 547; and **mid.** συλεύμενος (Theocr.) 19, 2. **Pass.** very late.

Συλλέγω *To gather, collect,* Eur. Fr. 510 (Dind.); Her. 1, 93; Dem. 21, 184, ξυλ- Thuc. 3, 111: **imp.** συν-έλεγον Soph. Fr. 218 (D.), ξυν- Thuc. 7, 36: **fut.** συλλέξω Xen. Cyr. 1, 3, 14, ξυλ- Thuc. 7, 7: **aor.** συν-έλεξα Ar. Ran. 1297; Her. 7, 8; Antiph. 6, 11, ξυν- Thuc. 6, 71; pt. συλ-λέξας Il. 18, 301: **p.** συνείλοχα Dem. 18, 308 (-λεχ- Bekk.). 21, 23: **p. p.** συνείλεγμαι Ar. Av. 294; Lycurg. 82; Dem. 18, 312, ξυν- Thuc. 3, 94; Xen. Hell. 4, 2, 10 (Dind.); Pl. Rep. 574; Arr. An. 1, 3, 5. 4, 2, 2, also συλ-λέλεγμαι Ar. Eccl. 58; Her. 7, 26. 9, 41; Arr. An. 2, 21. 6, 22. 26 (not in good Attic prose, but ἐκ-λέλεγμαι Xen. Hell. 1, 6, 16, ἐπι-λέλεγ- Cyr. 3, 3, 41): **plp.** εἴλεκτο, ξυν- Arr. An. 3, 19, 2: **1 aor.** συνελέχθην rare in Attic, Ar. Lys. 526; Xen. Cyr. 4, 6, 12; Pl. Leg. 784 (Epist. 348); Aristot. Meteor. 1, 13, 5; freq. in Ionic, Her. 1, 97. 2, 62. 3, 130. 4, 87. 159. 5, 118 &c.: usu. **2 aor.** in Attic συνελέγην Xen. An. 4, 1, 11. Cyr. 5, 3, 24 (Dind.); Pl. Phaed. 59: Isocr. 9, 56; Aeschin. 3, 128, ξυν- Ar. Eccl. 116. Fr. 244 (Dind.); Thuc. 6, 9. 98. 7, 59 &c., rare in Ionic, Her. 7, 173. 9, 27. 29. 32: **fut.** συλλεγησόμενος Aeschin. 3, 100. **Mid.** συλλέγομαι *to gather for oneself, collect oneself,* Her. 3, 105; Pl. Rep. 553: **imp.** ξυνελέγοντο Ar. Ach. 184: **fut.** συλλέξομαι Od. 2, 292; Xen. Hell. 4, 1, 33: **aor.** συν-ελεξάμην Xen. An. 7, 4, 8, Epic ξυλλέξατο Il. 18, 413 (Bekk. συλλ- Dind. La R.); subj. ξυλλέξωνται Her. 2, 94; Thuc. 6, 71; imper. σύλλεξαι Eur. Phoen. 850; -ξάμενος Isocr. 15, 155; -ξασθαι Dem. 21, 101: with **p. p.** συνείλεγμαι (Pl.) Ax. 370, -είλεκται Hyperid. Eux. p. 14 (Sch.); -εγμένος Xen. Mem. 4, 2, 1; (Dem.) 59, 18.

Συμβολέω *To meet,* ξυμβολεῖ Aesch. Sept. 352 (chor.), **pres.** only classic: **fut.** late -ήσω App. Civ. 4, 85: and **aor.** -ησα 4, 65.

Συναντάω, Ion. -έω *To meet, happen,* Ar. Ach. 1187; Xen. An. 7, 2, 5: **imp.** συνήντα Herodn. 1, 17, 4 (Bekk.) -ήντεον Ap. Rh. 4, 1485, Epic 3 dual συναντήτην Od. 16, 333: **fut.** late -ήσω V. T. Esai. 34, 14; Maneth. 4, 554; N. T. Act. 20, 22: **aor.** συνήντησα Eur. Ion 534; Ar. Plut. 41; Xen. An. 1, 8, 15: **p.** συνήντηκα late, Polyb. 4, 61; Luc. Philop. 1. συναντάομαι Dep. **mid.** (v. r. Hes. Th. 877) Chishull. Inscr. p. 103; Polyb. 22, 7; Aristenaet. 1, 12: **fut.** late συναντήσομαι V. T. Deut. 31, 29. Job 5, 14. Esai. 64, 5 (formerly Il. 17, 134 Eustath. and old edit., and so quoted Plut. Mor. 494): now **aor.** subj. συναντήσωνται Il. 17, 134 (Mss. Ven. Vind. Wolf, Bekk. Dind. Spitzn. La R.):

as mid. p. συνήντηται late, Herodn. 1, 17, 4 (Vulg. -ήντα Bekk. quoted). συναντήτην has been called 2 aor. from a form (ἄντημι); it is not however *necessarily* 2 aor. for αε, εε are often contracted by the Epics into η, as dual προσαυδήτην (-αυδάω), φοιτήτην (φοιτάω), ἀπειλήτην (ἀπειλέω), ὁμαρτήτην (ὁμαρτέω), ὁρῆαι (ὁράεαι) &c. The collat. συναντιάζω is poetic, and occurs in imp. only, ξυνηντίαζον Soph. O. R. 804. συνάντομαι in *classic* authors is also poetic, and confined to pres. Od. 15, 538; Hes. Th. 877; Pind. Ol. 2, 96: and imp. συνήντετο Il. 21, 34; Archil. 89; Eur. Ion 831; Theocr. 8, 1, but dual unaugm. συναντέσθην Il. 7, 22.

Συνίημι *To know, understand*, Pl. Gorg. 453, ξυν- Soph. El. 131; Ar. Av. 946; Pl. Theaet. 208, -ίῃς Soph. El. 1347; Pl. Soph. 238, -ιεῖς v. r., -ίησι Theaet. 147, late -ιεῖ, and 3 pl. -ιοῦσι; imper. ξυνίει Od. 8, 241 &c. and ξύνιε Theogn. 1240 (Bergk); inf. ξυνιέναι Pl. Prot. 339, Epic -ιέμεν Hes. Th. 831, -ιεῖν Theogn. 565: imp. (ξυνίην) and συνίειν Luc. Philops. 39. D. Deor. 6, 2 (Dind.), -ίει Xen. An. 7, 6, 8, -ίη Ceb. Tab. 3, 2, 3 pl. ξυνίεσαν Thuc. 1, 3, Epic -ιεν Il. 1, 273 (Bekk. Spitz. Dind. La R.), -ιον (Vulg.): fut. always συνήσω Her. 9, 98; Pl. Prot. 325; Dem. 23, 21, ξυν- Pl. Tim. 71, never συνήσομαι, Eur. Ion 694, and Dem. 33, 14, have been corrected: aor. συνῆκα, ξυν- Aesch. Ch. 887; Soph. Aj. 99; Eur. An. 919 (D.); Ar. Ach. 101; Pl. Rep. 347, συν- Parm. 128, ἐσυν- Alcae. 132 (Bergk), ἐξυν- Anacr. 146 (Bergk), Epic ξυνέηκα Il. 2, 182. Od. 18, 34, Dor. 1 pl. συν-ήκαμες Plut. Mor. 232, -ήκατε Ar. Ach. 101: p. later, συνεῖκα, -εικέναι Polyb. 5, 101 (Bekk.): 2 aor. ξύνην, dual -έτην Luc. D. Deor. 26, 2; opt. συν-είης Xen. Cyr. 1, 6, 2, -είη Pl. Ion 530, -είητε Dem. 6, 3; imper. ξύνες, Il. 2, 26; Pind. Fr. 82 (Bergk); Soph. Tr. 868; Ar. Av. 945; Pl. Phaedr. 236; inf. -εῖναι Crat. 414, Ep. συνέμεν Pind. P. 3, 80; ξυν-είς Aesch. Pers. 361: 2 aor. mid. σύνετο Od. 4, 76 (Bekk. ξυν- Vulg. Dind. La R.); συνώμεθα Il. 13, 381. See ἵημι. This verb has a few peculiarities; but our chief aim in introducing it is to correct a mistaken notion regarding the fut. συνήσομαι. Instead of being "more freq. than act. -ήσω," it seems not to rise above a v. r. for ξυνοίσεται Eur. Ion 694, and συνείσονται Dem. 33, 14.

Σύνοχωκώς *Held together, contracted, curved* (ἔχω, p. ὄχα, ὦχα, Attic redupl. ὄκωχα, ὄχωκα) an Epic p. part. Il. 2, 218; Q. Sm. 7, 502.

Σῦρίζω *To play on the pipe, whistle* &c. Aesch. Sept. 463; Eur. Ion 501; Hippocr. 7, 190 (Lit.), ἀπο- H. Merc. 280, συρίττω Pl. Theaet. 203; Aristot. H. An. 9, 5, 10; Plut. Mor. 230, Dor. -ίσδω, 2 sing. -ίσδες Theocr. 1, 3; so inf. -ίσδεν 1, 14. 16: imp. ἐσύριττον Dem. 18, 265. 21, 226; Plut. Mor. 230, late σύριζον

Nonn. 2, 181, but ὑπ-εσύρ- Hippocr. 5, 378 (Lit.), Dor. σύρισδ- Theocr. 6, 44: fut. late, σῡρίσω Longus 2, 23; Mechan. Vet. p. 194, -ιῶ V. T. Job 27, 23, and -ίξω Or. Sib. 5, 253: and mid. συρίξομαι Luc. Bis Acc. 12. Nigr. 10: aor. ἐσύριξα Ar. Plut. 689, σύρ- Orph. Arg. 998, later ἐσύρῐσα Babr. 114; Ael. H. A. 6, 63; Luc. Harm. 2; Longus 2, 37, σύρισα Nonn. 43, 235. **Pass.** συριττόμενος *hissed*, (Pl.) Ax. 368; -ίττεσθαι Aeschin. 3, 76. 231. (ῡ). In Longus, Seiler edits from Mss. -ίζω and -ίττω, 1, 23. 2, 36. 37. 38. 3, 23. 24 &c. Hercher always -ίττω.

Σύρω *To draw*, Opp. Hal. 4, 303; Plut. Mor. 5. 977; Luc. Herod. 5. Asin. 56; σύρων Batr. 75; Aristot. Incess. Anim. 10, 10, παρα- Ar. Eq. 527, Dor. fem. σύροισα Theocr. 2, 73: **imp.** ἔσῡρον Anth. 7, 105, ἀπ- Thuc. 7, 43, δι- Dem. 18, 299; Luc. Pisc. 4: **fut.** σῡρῶ late, V. T. 2 Reg. 17, 13, ἐπι- Ach. Tat. 4, 13: **aor.** ἔσῡρα Anth. 7, 216; D. Laert. 6, 2, 35; in tmesi Her. 5, 81, παρ- Aesch. Pr. 1065, δια- Dem. 19, 313: **p.** σέσυρκα, δια- Com. Fr. (Diph.) 4, 412 (Ms. B. Pors. Mein. -ηκα Vulg.), ὑπο- Dio. Hal. 1, 7 (Vulg. ἐπι- Kiessl.): **p. p.** σέσυρμαι, δια- (Aristot.) Rhet. Alex. 19, 12, ἐπι- Polyb. 12, 4 b (Bekk.); Luc. D. Mer. 10, 3. Nav. 2: **2 aor.** ἐσύρην Dio Cass. 79, 20; Paus. 2, 32, 1; Herodn. 5, 8, 9, ἐξ- Anth. 9, 56, ἀπο- Luc. Nav. 9: **fut.** συρήσομαι, περι- Greg. Naz. **Mid.** σύρομαι *simple* late, *to draw oneself, creep*, Joseph. Ant. 1, 4; Schol. Od. 11, 270, but ἀνα- Her. 2, 60, ἐπι- Xen. Cyn. 5, 13, and *draw to, after oneself*, Luc. V. H. 2, 46: **aor.** ἐσύρατο, ἀν- Orph. Fr. 16; App. Civ. 2, 146, περι-εσύραντο Hyperid. Fr. 292 (B. S.); App. Hisp. 65; συράμεναι, ἀνα- Diod. Sic. 1, 85; Polyaen. 7, 45, 2. **Vb.** συρτέον, δια- Aristot. Rhet. Alex. 37, 17. ῡ, except fut. and aor. pass.

Σφᾰγῐάζω *To slay a victim*, act. rare, espec. in classic Auth. Ar. Av. 569; Plut. Mor. 221; Polyaen. 3, 9, 40: **aor.** ἐσφαγίασα Diod. Sic. 13, 86: (**p.**: **p. p.**): **aor.** ἐσφαγιάσθην Her. 7, 180; Heliod. 10, 10. 20. 22. 28: **fut.** -ασθήσομαι 10, 18. Generally σφαγιάζομαι as Dep. **mid.** Xen. An. 6, 5, 8: **imp.** ἐσφαγιαζόμην Her. 6, 76. 9, 72: **aor.** ἐσφαγιασάμην Her. 6, 76; Xen. An. 6, 4, 25. σφαγιάζομαι is pass. Ar. Av. 570; Xen. Lac. 13, 8.

Σφάζω *To slay*, Od. 4, 320; Eur. Tr. 134; Her. 2, 39; Aristot. H. An. 9, 6, 9, in Comedy, and usu. in Attic prose σφάττω Com. Fr. (Cratin.) 2, 224. (Theop.) 2, 810; Xen. Cyr. 7, 3, 14; Pl. Gorg. 468; Isocr. 6, 68; Aristot. Eth. Nic. 5, 15, 2: **imp.** ἔσφαζον Il. 9, 467; Soph. Aj. 299; Her. 3, 11; Thuc. 7, 84, -φαττον Pl. Critias 119: **fut.** σφάξω Eur. Heracl. 493; Ar. Pax 1018, ἐπι- Eur. H. F. 602. 995, ἀπο- Luc. Jup. Trag. 52; Dio Cass. 78, 7: **aor.** ἔσφαξα Il. 2, 422; Aesch. Ag. 1433; Her. 7, 180; Thuc. 2, 92; Xen. Cyr. 8, 3, 24, σφάξα Od. 3, 454:

(p. ἔσφᾰκα: plp. ἐσφάκει Dio Cass. (Xiphil.) 73, 6, ἀπ- Dio Cass. 78, 7, see below): p. p. ἔσφαγμαι Od. 10, 532. 11, 45; Dem. 23, 68, ἐπ- Aristot. de Color. 5, 19: 1 aor. ἐσφάχθην rare, Pind. P. 11, 23; Eur. I. T. 177 (chor.); Her. 5, 5, perhaps never in Attic prose: more freq. 2 aor. ἐσφᾰ́γην mostly poetic in *simple*, Aesch. Eum. 305; Eur. Phoen. 933. I. T. 598 &c.; late prose Dio Cass. 40, 27. 42, 5; App. de Reg. Rom. 2; Plut. Publ. 4; Strab. 12, 3, 6; Pseudo-Callisth. 2, 20, but ἀπο- Her. 4, 62; (Dem.) 59, 103, κατ- Xen. An. 4, 1, 23: fut. σφᾰγήσομαι Eur. Andr. 315. Heracl. 583; Plut. Mor. 259; Dio Cass. 46, 53 (B), ἀπο- Ar. Thesm. 750–3; -σφαγήσοιντο Xen. Hell. 3, 1, 27: pres. p. σφάζεται Her. 5, 5; σφαττόμενος Antiph. 2, β, 8. Mid. in comp. σφάττομαι, ἀπο- Xen. Cyr. 3, 1, 25: aor. σφάξασθαι, ἐπι- Xen. An. 1, 8, 29 (some Mss. Dind. Krüg. Kühn. Saupp. -σφάξαι act. others). Vb. σφακτός Eur. Hec. 1077. The plp. ἐσφάκει would seem to show that this verb had, in the later stage of the language, been inflected also with ς, σφάζω, -ττω, -άσω, ἔσφᾰκα. The Tragedians, though alleged to be fond of "strong rough forms" as ἐσφάχθην, have, actually of choice, taken the smoother ἐσφάγην, see Eur. Hec. 24. Phoen. 933. Tr. 619 (D).

Σφάλλω *To trip up, deceive*, Soph. Fr. 204; Eur. Med. 198; Her. 7, 16; Thuc. 3, 37; Xen. Lac. 5, 4, Dor. 3 pl. -λοντι Theocr. 24, 110: imp. ἔσφ- Her. 7, 142: fut. σφᾰλῶ Thuc. 7, 67; Pl. Euth. 296: aor. ἔσφηλα Soph. El. 416; Eur. Phoen. 1419; Thuc. 6, 15; Aeschin. 3, 125, σφῆλ- Od. 17, 464, Dor. ἔσφᾱλα Pind. Ol. 2, 81. P. 8, 15. I. 4, 35 (B.), παρ- N. 11, 31: p. ἔσφαλκα Polyb. 8, 11: p. p. ἔσφαλμαι Eur. Andr. 897; Pl. Crat. 436: plp. ἔσφαλτο Thuc. 7, 47: 1 aor. ἐσφάλθην late, Galen 5, 62 the only instance we know: 2 aor. ἐσφᾰ́λην Soph. Aj. 1136; Eur. Supp. 337; Her. 4, 140; Thuc. 8, 24, 'σφάλην Eur. Supp. 156, δι- Aeschin. 2, 35; subj. σφαλῶ Soph. Tr. 621; Ar. Plut. 351; Her. 7, 168; Thuc. 4, 18 &c.; -είην 2, 43; Antiph. 5, 75; -λείς Soph. Tr. 727; Eur. Hipp. 671; Ar. Pax 146; Thuc. 6, 33, ἀπο- Aesch. Pr. 472; σφᾰλῆναι Xen. M. Eq. 8, 9, δια- Aeschin. 3, 91: 2 fut. σφᾰλήσομαι Soph. Tr. 719. 1113; Thuc. 5, 113. 6, 80 &c.: less freq. fut. mid. σφᾰλοῦμαι reflex. *fall, fail*, Soph. Fr. 513 (D); Xen. Conv. 2, 26; but Eur. Supp. 303 has been altered to pres. σφάλλει (compare imp. ἐσφάλλοντο . . . δέμας *dropped*, Eur. Bacc. 744): pres. σφάλλεται Aesch. Eum. 717.

There seems to be no undoubted classical instance of either the 2 aor. act. ἔσφᾰλον, or mid. ἐσφαλόμην. ἔσφαλε certainly occurs in Pind. Ol. quoted, Pyth. 8, 15, and Nem. 11, 31, but it is the Dor. form of the 1 aor. ἔσφᾱλε. At Pl. Euthyd. 296, σφῆλῃ subj. is better supported than σφάλῃ, now written σφαλεῖ fut. since Heindorf. ἔσφᾰλε Ap. Rh. 3, 1310 (Brunck) has been altered to σφῆλε from ἔσφηλε of the Mss. &c. &c. and σφάλωνται Thuc. 1, 140. 6, 23. 75 (Vulg.) has been corrected from Mss. to pres. σφάλλωνται (Elms. Bekk. Popp. Krüg. Dind.); and διασφάλοιτο Polyb. 6, 9 (Vulg.) is now διασφάλλοιτο (Bekk. Dind.) &c. A few instances, if correct, occur in late authors, ἀνέσφᾰλε Ann. Comm. 6, 133, σφαλόμενος Galen 16, 213, Julian, see Lobeck Soph. Aj. p. 225.

Σφᾰρᾰγέω *To swell, sound, hiss,* Epic and only **mid. imp.** σφᾰρᾰγεῦντο Od. 9, 390. 440.

Σφετερίζω *To appropriate,* Pl. Leg. 843: **fut.** -ιῶ: **aor.** ἐσφετέρισα Pl. Leg. 715: **p. p.** late ἐσφετερισμένος App. Hannib. 45. σφετερίζομαι Dep. mid. Xen. Hell. 5, 1, 36; Dem. 7, 41. 18, 71: **imp.** ἐσφετερ- App. Hisp. 60: **fut.** -ιεῖσθαι Dio Cass. 40, 50: **aor.** ἐσφετερισάμην Dem. 32, 2; (Pl.) Epist. 7, 333; Polyb. 4, 50; Dio Cass. 37, 8, Dor. -ιξάμην Aesch. Supp. 39 (chor.): as mid. **p. p.** ἐσφετερίσθαι Dio Cass. Fr. 97, 2 (Bekk.); -ισμένος Dio. Hal. 10, 32: **plp.** ἐσφετέριστο Dio Cass. 50, 1.

Σφίγγω *To bind, fasten,* Pl. Tim. 58; σφίγγε Aesch. Pr. 58, -γγετε Theocr. 10, 45: **imp.** ἔσφιγγον Batr. 71; Com. Fr. (Pher.) 2, 265: **fut.** late σφίγξω Anth. 12, 208; *v. r.* V. T. Exod. 28, 28: **aor.** ἔσφιγξα Com. Fr. (Alex.) 3, 398; Anth. 5, 294; Musae. 252; (Luc.) Asin. 24, ἀπο- Hippocr. 7, 40: **p. act.** ? **p. p.** ἔσφιγμαι, -ιγμένοι Dio. Hal. 7, 72; Luc. Musc. enc. 3, but 3 pers. ἔσφιγκται, Galen 1, 615; ἐσφίχθαι Philostr. V. Ap. 2, 63, but -ίγχθαι (Ms. p. Kaiser): **aor.** ἐσφίγχθην Anth. 6, 331, ἀπο- Hippocr. 4, 376 (Lit.): **imp.** ἐσφίγγετο Theocr. 7, 17. **Mid.** σφίγγομαι *to bind one's own,* **imp.** ἐσφίγγετο may be pass. Anth. (Christod.) 2, 273: but **aor.** ἐσφίγξατο Hermes. 81 (Schneid.); and late Nonn. D. 15, 246; -ξάμενος Opp. C. 4, 155.

Σφύζω, Dor. -σδω, late -ττω, *To throb,* Hippocr. 7, 16 (Lit.); Aristot. H. A. 3, 19, 7; -οντα- Pl. Phaedr. 251; -ύσδειν Theocr. 11, 71, σφύττει Dio Chrys. 4, 116: **imp.** ἔσφυζε Hippocr. 5, 94: **fut.** σφύξω late, Galen 10, 387: **aor.** ἔσφυξα Galen.

Σχάζω *To cut open, let go,* Hippocr. 5, 320. 6, 212; Xen. Hell. 5, 4, 58, and σχάω, σχᾷ Hesych.; κατα-σχᾶν Hippocr. 5, 434 (Lit.): **imp.** ἔσχαζον Phrynich. p. 219, ἔσχων Ar. Nub. 409: **fut.** σχᾰ́σω Hesych., ἀπο- Com. Fr. (Cratet.) 2, 249: **aor.** ἔσχᾰσα Eur. Tr. 810; σχάσῃ Aristot. H. An. 8, 21, 3; σχάσον Pind. P. 10, 51; Eur. Ph. 454; σχάσας 960; Ar. Nub. 740; Xen. Ven. 3, 5, Dor. -άσαις Pind. N. 4, 64; -άσαι Hippocr. 6, 210: **p. p.** ἔσχασμαι, ἐσχασμένη Dioscor. 3, 160: **plp.** ἔσχαστο Heliod. 4, 3: **aor.** ἐσχάσθην Hippocr. 6, 428; Stob. (Antisth.) 18, 27; Plut.

Mor. 567; Joseph. Jud. B. 5, 6, 3; fut. late, σχασθήσεται V. T. Amos 3, 5, ἀπο- Oribas. 7, 17. **Mid.** aor. ἐσχασάμην *cut, gave up*, Ar. Nub. 107; Com. Fr. (Plat.) 2, 626; Synes. Epist. 129. **Vb.** σχαστέον, κατα- Dioscor. Ther. 424.

Lycophr. 21, has ἐσχάζοσαν an Alexandrine form of the 3 pl. imp. for ἔσχαζον. σχᾶσαντες Callim. Fr. 104, 1, seems to be a false reading. Blomf. in loc. says "σχάσαντες *demittentes*, uti vertit Bentleius, stare nequit, cum penultimam corripiat. Corrige σχήσαντες, *inhibentes*, cujus quidem aoristi aliud exemplum non habeo." An example of this aor. occurs in Nonnus, σχήσειε 17, 177, and σχήσησθα in H. Hym. Cer. 366, but seemingly a mistake for fut. σχήσεισθα; but it might, perhaps, be as easy to read in Callim. σχάσσαντες which seems to satisfy both the sense and metre. See Pind. P. 10, 51; Eur. Tr. 810.

Σχέθω, see ἔχω.

Σχημᾰτίζω *To fashion, dress*, Ar. Pax 324; Pl. Rep. 526: fut. -ιῶ Philostr. Epist. 1 (Boiss.) reg.: p. ἐσχημάτικα Dio. Hal. de Thuc. 26: p. p. -ισμαι Aesch. Sept. 465; Hippocr. 4, 228. 320; Aristot. Nat. Ausc. 1, 5, 5; Luc. Jup. Trag. 8: aor. -ίσθην Hippocr. 5, 688 (Lit.); Aristot. Gen. An. 1, 18, 33. **Mid.** -ίζομαι *to dress oneself, pretend*, Eur. Med. 1161; Pl. Prot. 342: aor. late -ισάμην Niceph. Rhet. 2, 4: p. p. as mid. ἐσχημάτισται Pl. Soph. 268; -ισμένη Gorg. 511; see Hippocr. 4, 228.

Σώζω *To save*, Od. 5, 490 (Vulg. Wolf, Dind. La Roche, σώων Bekk. 2 ed.); Aesch. Pers. 349; Soph. El. 768; Ar. Av. 1062; Antiph. 5, 73. 85; Thuc. 6, 38: imp. ἔσωζον Her. 8, 34; Andoc. 1, 59; Pl. Prot. 356: fut. σώσω Soph. Ph. 1391; Eur. Cycl. 202; Her. 3, 122; Thuc. 1, 137; Lys. 12, 10. 11: aor. ἔσωσα Aesch. Eum. 661; Soph. El. 321; Ar. Pax 867; Her. 8, 8; Thuc. 1, 129; Xen. An. 1, 10, 3; opt. σώσαις Eur. I. T. 1184, -σαιεν Andoc. 1, 137: p. σέσωκα Pl. Leg. 776; Isocr. 7, 52. Epist. 2, 19; Dem. 57, 60: p. p. σέσωμαι, -ωται Pl. Critias 109 (v. r. Eur. I. T. 607), δια- Pl. Critias 110; -ωμένος Leg. 848 (Bekk. Herm. B. O. W.), usu. σέσωσμαι Eur. I. A. 1441; Xen. Cyr. 5, 4, 11, -ωσται Aesch. Sept. 280; Eur. I. T. 607; Com. Fr. (Men.) 4, 88; Xen. An. 7, 7, 56; Dem. 56, 33. 37, -ώσμεθα Soph. Tr. 84; Eur. Hel. 1032; σεσῶσθαι Aesch. Pers. 737; Andoc. 1, 113; Dem. 18, 218. 56, 22; Com. Fr. (Men.) 4, 174; -σωσμένος Aesch. Ag. 618; Soph. Ant. 314; Eur. Or. 473; Com. Fr. (Herm.) 2, 383; Xen. Cyr. 3, 2, 15. An. 5, 5, 8; Pl. Leg. 645; Dem. 16, 31. (Dem.) 10, 73: aor. always ἐσώθην Simon. C. 165; Soph. O. R. 1457; Antiph. 5, 3; Thuc. 3, 24; Xen. Hell. 1, 1, 36; Lys. 13, 58; Isae. 1, 10; Pl. Charm. 153; σωθῇ Eur. Hel. 292; Xen. An. 5, 3, 6, σωθῶσι Dem. 16, 31; σωθείην Andoc. 1, 54;

σωθείημεν Com. Fr. (Menand.) 4, 295, -εῖμεν Eur. Hel. 815, σωθεῖεν Pl. Phaed. 58; σώθητι Crit. 44; σωθῆναι Her. 7, 230. 8, 92; Antiph. 5, 2; σωθείς Simon. C. 165; Aesch. Pers. 214; Soph. Ant. 331; Her. 4, 97. 9, 71; Isocr. 9, 27; ἐσώσθην?: fut. σωθήσομαι Eur. Or. 309; Ar. N. 77; Hippocr. 2, 112 (Lit.); Thuc. 5, 111; Pl. Apol. 31; Dem. 5, 3. **Mid.** σώζομαι, usu. trans. *to save for oneself, preserve,* Soph. El. 994; Pl. Theaet. 153; σώζοιτο Xen. Hell. 4, 5, 1; Pl. Rep. 455, 3 pl. σωζοίατο, ἐκ- Aesch. Pers. 451: **imp.** ἐσωζ- Soph. Tr. 682: **fut.** σώσομαι Eur. Bacc. 793; σωσοίατο, δια- Aesch. Pers. 360; σωσόμενοι, δια- Xen. Cyr. 4, 2, 28: **aor.** ἐσωσάμην Ar. Eccl. 402, ἀν- Her. 1, 106, δι- Xen. An. 5, 5, 13; opt. ἀνα- σωσαίμεθα Ar. Lys. 141; σώσασθαι (Eur. Alc. 147 Monk), ἀνα- Soph. El. 1133, δια- Thuc. 7, 63. So **act.** ἔσωζον Eur. Hel. 266. **Vb.** σωστέος Eur. H. F. 1385; Ar. Lys. 501, σωτέος (Hesych.) Epic σαόω, σώω.

The form σώζω is rare in Epic: Hom. only once, σώζων Od. quoted (Mss. Wolf, Dind. La R.) which Bekk. however writes *now* with Buttm. σώων; Hes. once as a *v. r.* σώζοι Opp. 376; Theogn. thrice, 68. 235. 675; Callim. thrice, Del. 150. 151. Epigr. 50, 4; Orph. thrice, Hym. 9, 12. 75, 5. 85, 10 (δια- 85, 7); Mosch. once, 4, 3; Maneth. once, 1, 325; Ap. Rh. never; Nicand. never, &c. Dor. σῴζω, **fut.** σῴξω, aor. ἔσῳξα, κατ- Inscr. Tab. Heracl. 2, 30, but κατ-έσῳσα B. 47, 1, 3, and σῶσαι Sophr. 26 (Ahr.) which however may be referred to **pres.** σωννύω (Dinol. Siculus); Lacon. σωάδδει (Hesych.) We know no instance of **fut. mid.** σώσεσθαι being **passive**; for **pres.** σώζεσθαι, not **fut.** σώσεσθαι, is the approved reading Dem. 19, 44 (Bekk. B. S. Dind.) σέσωμαι, though less frequent, is by some accounted more Attic than σέσωσμαι. Photius says οἱ παλαιοὶ ἄνευ τοῦ s, and Buttm. and L. Dind. approve. Accordingly, in his last edit. of Xen. An. Dind. edits σέσωται 7, 7, 56 (-ωσται Saupp.), σεσωμένος 5, 5, 8 (so Saupp.): in the Cyr. however he still retains—why we see not—σέσωσμαι 5, 4, 11, σεσωσμένος 3, 2, 15 (so Saupp.) We think it likely that both forms were in use. Buttm. notices a form found in Inscr. (600) σώω which he calls an *old* **fut.** like the Epic **fut.** ἐρύουσι &c. L. Dind. writes it σωῶ, and says that σωεῖ is the reading of Ms. Med. Aesch. Ch. 1059, and W. Dind. has so edited (3 edit.) If this be correct, it is a striking peculiarity in Attic usage—so striking as to rouse demur. In the ed. of 1865, he recalled σώσει, for which he now (5 ed.) reads εἴς σοι with Erfurdt.

Σωπάω, see σιωπ-.

Σώω *To save*, Epic, imper. σώετε Ap. Rh. 4, 197; σώων Od. 5, 490 (Bekk. -ζων Vulg.), σώοντες 9, 430: **imp.** iter. σώεσκον Il. 8,

363. Pass. σώεσθαι Ap. Rh. 2, 610; σωόμενος 3, 307: imp. σώοντο Ap. Rh. 2, 1010, σώετο Anth. 9, 53 mid.? See σώζω.

T.

Τᾰγέω *To be commander of* (τᾱγός), only inf. ταγεῖν Aesch. Pers. 764. The prose form is τᾱγεύω Inscr.: fut. -εύσω: aor. ἐτάγευσα Xen. Hell. 6, 1, 19. Pass. ταγεύηται 6, 1, 8. Mid. Poet. aor. τάγευσαι Aesch. Sept. 58.

(Τάγω or Τήγω) *To seize*, only redupl. 2 aor. part. Epic τετᾰγών Il. 1, 591. 15, 23, ἀν- Ap. Rh. 2, 119 (Sanctam. Well. Merkel.)

Τᾰλαιπωρέω *To endure, suffer*, intrans. and trans. *wear out*, Eur. Or. 672; Hippocr. 7, 582; Antiph. 5, 93; Thuc. 1, 134 &c.: p. τεταλαιπώρηκα Isocr. 8, 19 &c.: with fut. mid. late -ήσομαι as pass. Aristid. 34, 438: aor. -ησάμενος also late Clem. Al. Protr. p. 28, both missed by Lexicogr.: classic, pres. pass. -πωρεῖται Thuc. 4, 27, imp. ἐταλαιπ- 7, 28, perf. τεταλαιπώρημαι 3, 3; Isocr. 5, 38, and 1 aor. ταλαιπωρηθείς Isocr. 3, 64.

(Ταλάω) sync. τλάω *To bear, dare*, Poet. and pres. rare and late, τλῶσα Tzetz. Hist. 9, 132: fut. usu. τλήσομαι Il. 11, 317; Aesch. Ag. 1542; Soph. Aj. 463; Eur. I. T. 617; late prose Plut. Mor. 253, ἀνα- Mar. 39, Aeol. and Dor. τλᾱσομαι Sapph. 75; Pind. P. 3, 41: late τλήσω, -ήσοι Babr. 91 (Lewis 2 pt.), and ταλάσσω Lycophr. 746: 1 aor. Epic ἐτάλασσα Il. 17, 166; Anth. 9, 152; ταλάσσῃς Il. 13, 829, -σσῃ 15, 164; ταλάσσας Anth. 5, 246, late ἔτλησα Christ. Pat. 22; δια-τλήσας Epigr. Diog. L. 9, 3, 4, ἀνα- Clement. Epist. 26 (Muralt.): p. τέτληκα usu. as pres. Il. 1, 228. Od. 19, 347; Theogn. 825; Eur. Fr. 701 (Dind.); as perf. Ar. Thesm. 544. Plut. 280, syncop. 1 pl. τέτλᾰμεν Od. 20, 311; H. Cer. 148, τετλᾶσι Opp. C. 3, 132; (subj. τετλῶ?); opt. τετλαίην Il. 9, 373; Tyrtae. 12, 11 (Bergk); imper. τέτλᾰθι Il. 5, 382; Hes. Op. 718; Ap. Rh. 4, 64, τετλᾰ́τω Od. 16, 275; inf. τετλάναι Athen. (Metag.?) 271, Epic τετλάμεναι Od. 13, 307, and τετλάμεν 6, 190; part. (τετληώς), -υῖα Od. 20, 23, -ότος Il. 5, 873. Od. 11, 181, -ῶτος Orph. Arg. 1358. Lith. 375, -ηότι Od. 4, 447. 16, 37; Her. (Orac.) 5, 56 (τετληκώς we have not seen): plp. ἐτέτλᾰμεν Ap. Rh. 1, 807: 2 aor. ἔτλην Il. 22, 251. Od. 17, 104; Simon. C. 94; Aesch. Pr. 657; Soph. Tr. 71; Eur. Alc. 1; Ar. Nub. 1387; rare in Attic prose, Xen. Cyr. 3, 1, 2; Isocr. 4, 96 (Bait. Saupp. Bens. and so quoted by Aristot. Rhet. 3, 7, 11; and D. Hal. de vi Dem. 40); Luc. Pseudol.

21, without syllab. augm. τλῆ Il. 5, 385, Dor. ἔτλᾱν Simon. C. 107, 7; Pind. I. 7, 37; Aesch. Ch. 433 (chor.); Soph. Ph. 1201 (chor.); Eur. Andr. 1045 (chor.). Alc. 462 (chor.) &c., ἔτλημεν, ἀν- Od. 3, 104, τλῆμεν Il. 5, 383, ἔτλητε Il. 24, 35; Aesch. Supp. 240. 326, Dor. ἔτλᾱτε, ἀν- Soph. O.C. 239 (chor.), ἔτλησαν Att. poet. Eur. Supp. 171; and if correct Isocr. 4, 96 quoted, Dor. -ᾱσαν Soph. Ph. 1201 (chor.), Epic ἔτλαν Il. 21, 608; subj. rare, and perhaps 2 sing. only, τλῇς Aesch. Supp. 429; Soph. Aj. 1333; Eur. Alc. 275. Cycl. 288; opt. τλαίην Il. 4, 94; Soph. O. R. 602; Eur. Phoen. 192; Ar. Nub. 119; imper. τλῆθι Theogn. 1237; Simon. C. 85, 14; Her. (Orac.) 5, 56; Soph. Ph. 475; Eur. Hec. 1251; Ap. Rh. 1, 300, Dor. τλᾶθι Pind. P. 4, 276, τλήτω Od. 11, 350, ἐπι- Il. 19, 220, τλῆτε Il. 2, 299; Archil. 9, 10; τλῆναι Aesch. Ag. 1041; Soph. Ph. 870; Eur. Hel. 603, τλήμεναι Theocr. 25, 174; Q. Sm. 3, 8; τλάς Soph. O. C. 1076; Eur. Phoen. 1726, ἀνα- Ar. Pax 1035, τλᾶσα Aesch. Ag. 408. 895, ἀνα- 716. Soph. Eur. **Mid.** later, **aor.** as **act.** ταλάσσατο Opp. Cyn. 3, 155. **Vb.** τλητός Il. 24, 49; Soph. Aj. 466, ἄ-τλητος Her. (Orac.) 5, 56. ἔτλᾰν Epic 3 pl. **2 aor.** for ἔτλησαν, Il. 21, 608; subj. (τλῶ), τλῇς is rare. Buttmann omits, he does not deny it; τλαῖεν 3 pl. opt. for τλαίησαν, 17, 490. The Tragedians often use the Doric forms, **2 aor.** ἔτλᾱ Aesch. Ag. 224. Sept. 757 (Herm. Blomf. Dind.), ἔτλᾱσαν Soph. Ph. 1201; τλᾶθι Eur. Alc. 892 &c. all in chor.

Τᾰμῐεύω *To be a manager*, and trans. *to dispense* &c. Pl. Rep. 465: **imp.** iter. ταμιεύεσκε rare in Attic poetry, Soph. Ant. 950 (chor.): **fut.** -εύσω Ar. Eq. 948; Isae. 6, 61 &c.: **p. p.** -ευμαι Plut. Mor. 157: **aor.** -εύθην very late, Greg. Naz.: **pres.** -ευομέναν Pind. Ol. 8, 30, -ένην Pl. Rep. 508. **Mid.** -εύομαι Ar. Eccl. 600; Thuc. 6, 18; Xen. Conv. 4, 41: **fut.** -εύσομαι Dio. Hal. 1, 82; Ach. Tat. 8, 8 (Vulg.): **aor.** -ευσάμην Luc. Imag. 21; Diod. Sic. 4, 12: with **p. p.** τεταμίευμαι Lys. 30, 3; Hyperid. Fr. 1, 4.

Τάμνω, see τέμνω.

Τᾰνῡ́ω *To stretch*, Epic lengthened form of τείνω, Il. 17, 391. Od. 21, 152, ἐν- Her. 2, 173, ἐκ- Hippocr. 4, 244 (Lit.): **imp.** τάνῡεν Pind. P. 4, 129: **fut.** τανῡ́σω *simple* late, Orac. Sib. 10, 82; Anth. (Paul. Sil.) 5, 262, ἐν- Od. 21, 127, Epic -ύσσω Orph. L. 179; Nonn. 2, 234, and some say (σ elided) τανῡ́ω Od. 21, 174: **aor.** ἐτάνῡσα- τάνυ- Il. 16, 567. Od. 21, 409, and ἐτάνυσσα Il. 16, 662. Od. 21, 407, τάνῡσα Il. 16, 567, ἐκ- Pind. P. 4, 242, τάνυσσα Il. 9, 213; τανύσῃ Il. 23, 324, -ύσσῃ 17, 547. 23, 761; -ύσσειε Od. 18, 92; τανύσσας Il. 23, 25, -ύσας Ap. Rh. 4, 890; rare in prose, Hippocr. 3, 39 (Kühn), ἐν- Her. 5, 25, Dor. τανύσαις Pind.

Ol. 2, 91; -ύσσαι Od. 21, 171: p. p. τετάνυσται Od. 9, 116; Ap. Rh. 4, 1583; Opp. Hal. 2, 113, and late prose τετάνῦται, -υμένα Galen 13, 991; -ύσθαι Aretae. S. Ac. Morb. 1, 2 (ed. Oxon.): plp. τετάνυστο Il. 10, 156. Od. 5, 68; Ap. Rh. 4, 161; Theocr. 25, 157: aor. ἐτανύσθην Hes. Th. 177, ἐξ- Il. 7, 271, Epic 3 pl. τάνυσθεν Il. 16, 475; -υσθείς 16, 485; Theocr. 25, 148: 3 fut. τετανύσσεται Orph. Lith. 319: and as pass. fut. mid. τανύσσεται in tmesi Archil. 4 (Bergk). **Mid.** τανύομαι *to stretch oneself, one's own*, or *for oneself*, reflex. and trans. imp. τανύοντο Il. 16, 375. Od. 6, 83: fut. τανύσσεται as pass. see above: aor. ἐτανυσσάμην Hym. Merc. 51; Callim. Dian. 27, τανύσσ- Ap. Rh. 2, 91, τανύσα- Opp. C. 4, 61; τανύσασθαι, ἐν- Od. 21, 403; τανυσσάμενος Il. 4, 112. Od. 9, 298. ῠ always, except once late ἐκτανΰειν Anacreont. 35, 5 (Bergk). τάνῠται 3 sing. pres. pass. as from (τάνῡμι, τάνῦμαι) Il. 17, 393. τάνυσθεν 3 pl. Epic for -ύσθησαν, Il. 16, 475. Od. 16, 175. τανύσαις Doric part. 1 aor. Pind. Ol. 2, 91, συν- P. 1, 81. This verb, though mostly Epic, occurs in Ionic prose, and in some Mss. and edit. with double ν, ἐκταννύω &c. Hippocr. 3, 226 (Kühn.) This, however, would seem to be a mistake, for though ἐνταννύειν has the best Mss. support in the second, seventh, eighteenth and twentieth lines of the section (57th Littré, vol. 4, 244), ἐκτανύουσι, ξυνεκτανυ- with single ν, have the best in lines fourth and eighth; and ἐκτανύειν 4, 254 (Lit.) has far better support than ἐκτανν- (Vulg.); so παρατανύσαντα without *v. r.* 4, 188 (Lit.), τανύσας 3, 39 (Kühn) &c. &c.; Littré uniformly, we think, edits with single ν.

Τᾰράσσω *To disturb*, Pind. Ol. 2, 63; Aesch. Ch. 289; Soph. O. R. 483; Her. 9, 51, new Attic -ττω Ar. Eq. 902; Pl. Phaed. 103; Xen. Mem. 2, 6, 17 (Mss. Saupp. Kühn., θράττ- Dind. Cob.); ταράττῃ 2, 4, 6 (Dind. Saupp.); Ep. inf. -ασσέμεν Pind. P. 11, 42: imp. ἐτάρασσον Her. 4, 129. 8, 12; Theocr. 22, 102, -αττον Dem. 18, 19: fut. -άξω Eur. Tr. 88; Ar. Eq. 358: aor. ἐτάραξα Od. 5, 291; Her. 4, 125; Lys. 6, 36; subj. -άξῃς Eur. H. F. 605, -άξῃ in tmesi Il. 1, 579; -άξειε Pl. Rep. 381; -άξας Solon 36, 21; Xen. An. 6, 2, 9; Dem. 18, 154: p. (τετάραχα): plp. ἐτεταράχει, συν- Dio Cass. 42, 36: Epic p. τέτρηχα *am in commotion*, Philet. Fr. 2, 7 (Schn.); Opp. H. 5, 244; -ηχώς Il. 7, 346; Anth. 7, 283: plp. τετρήχει Il. 2, 95: p. p. τετάραγμαι Ar. Nub. 388; Hippocr. 7, 572 (Lit.); -αγμένος Her. 4, 125; Thuc. 4, 25; Xen. Cyr. 3, 1, 30: plp. ἐτεταράγμην Pl. Phaed. 59, -ακτο Thuc. 7, 44: aor. ἐταράχθην Ar. Nub. 386; Hippocr. 1, 208 (Erm.); Thuc. 2, 65; Aeschin. 2, 35; -αχθείς Aesch. Ch. 331; Eur. Tr. 687; Her. 4, 125; Pl. Leg. 797: fut. ταραχθήσομαι Com. Fr. (Menand.) 4,

288 ?; and late Epict. Ench. 3; Marc. Ant. 7, 27; Sext. Emp. 569 (B.): and as pass. fut. mid. ταράξομαι Thuc. 7, 36. 67; Xen. Cyr. 6, 1, 43: pres. -άσσεται Solon 12 (B.); Thuc. 7, 84: imp. ἐταρασσ- 2, 84.—Pind. the Traged. and Thuc. -σσω, the Comed. Xen. and Orators -ττω. Buttmann would form the perf. directly from θράσσω, which he says is formed on ταράσσω by transposing the first α, τραάσσω, then contracting the two into one long, and asperating the τ before ρ, θράσσω, -άξω, τέτρᾱχα, Ionic -ηχα, the θ before ρ again becoming τ for euphony. The Scholiast on Il. 7, 346, has simply and briefly said "τετάραχα συνκόπῃ καὶ τροπῇ ἰωνικῇ τέτρηχα."

Ταρχύω *To bury*, Poet. shortened form for ταριχεύω, Ap. Rh. 3, 208: fut. -ύσω Il. 16, 456: aor. τάρχῡσα Q. Sm. 1, 801. 8, 482; subj. -ύσωσι Il. 7, 85: p. τετάρχῡμαι Epigr. Gr. p. 69 (Welck.): aor. ταρχύθην Anth. 7, 176. App. Epigr. 166; Lycophr. 369. Mid. aor. ἐταρχῡσαντο Nonn. D. 37, 96, ταρχύσ- Ap. Rh. 1, 83; Lycophr. 882. ῡ throughout. τᾰρῑχεύω seems confined to prose.

Τάσσω *To arrange, order*, Aesch. Ag. 332; Soph. El. 1495; Eur. Hec. 223, -ττω Com. Fr. (Antiph.) 3, 108; Xen. Mem. 2, 1, 9; Isocr. 5, 151; Pl. Rep. 371: imp. ἔτασσον Thuc. 4, 93, δι- Her. 5, 110, ἔταττ- Pl. Apol. 28; Dem. 18, 221: fut. τάξω Aesch. Sept. 284; Soph. O. C. 639; Xen. Mem. 2, 1, 7, Dor. -ξῶ, κατα- Theocr. Epigr. 6: aor. ἔταξα Aesch. Supp. 986; Eur. Hel. 1390; Her. 3, 25; Thuc. 6, 67; Lys. 1, 29: p. τέτᾰχα Xen. Oec. 4, 5, συν- Pl. Leg. 625; Dem. 32, 24: plp. ἐτετάχει, παρ- App. Syr. 36: p. p. τέταγμαι Pind. Ol. 2, 30; Aesch. Sept. 448; Soph. Ph. 1180; Eur. Alc. 49; Her. 9, 15; Andoc. 4, 18; Isocr. 6, 76: plp. τετάγμην Eur. Fr. 566, ἐτέτακτο Her. 1, 84, 3 pl. -τάχατο 1, 191. 8, 85; Thuc. 5, 6: 1 aor. ἐτάχθην Aesch. Eum. 279; Soph. O. C. 851; Her. 5, 109; Pl. Leg. 728: fut. ταχθήσομαι D. Sic. 11, 41, ἐπι- Thuc. 1, 140, ὑπο- Pseud.-Callisth. 2, 40; -ησόμενον Pl. Leg. 740: 2 aor. ἐτᾰγην rare, Eur. Fr. 979 (Dind.); Stob. 79, 50, ἐπι- Apollod. 1, 9, 23, κατα- Herodn. 6, 8, 1, ὑπο- Com. Fr. 2, 603; D. Sic. 4, 19: 2 fut. rare and late, τᾰγήσομαι, ὑπο- N. T. 1 Cor. 15, 28, ἐν- Oribas. 8, 1: 3 fut. τετάξομαι Eur. I. T. 1046; Ar. Av. 637; Thuc. 5, 71; Luc. Navig. 31. D. Deor. 4, 4: and seemingly as pass. fut. mid. ἐπι-τάξομαι Eur. Supp. 521, see below. **Mid.** τάσσομαι, -ττομαι *to arrange, post oneself*, or *for oneself*, reflex. and intrans. Aesch. Supp. 977; Eur. Heracl. 664: imp. ἐτάσσοντο Thuc. 3, 107, ἐτάττετο, συν- Xen. An. 1, 8, 14: aor. ἐταξάμην Eur. An. 1099; Her. 3, 13; Thuc. 4, 93. intrans. 4, 11. 5, 67: fut. *simple* late, τάξομαι *place myself, meet*, V. T. Exod. 29, 43, so ἀντι- *meet, oppose*, Eur. Phoen. 622; Paus. 9,

17, 2, παρα- Dem. 15, 24, ἐπι- *place myself next, behind, take orders from*, Eur. Supp. 521, called by some pass.: p. τετάχθαι, παρα- Pl. Prot. 333: with plp. δι-ετέτακτο late as act. *had ordered*, Joseph. Ant. 12, 5, 4. Vb. τακτός Pl. Leg. 632, -τέος 631. τετάχᾰται Ionic 3 pl. p. p. occas. Attic, Thuc. 3, 13, ἀντι- Xen. An. 4, 8, 5: plp. ἐτετάχατο Her. 6, 113; Thuc. 5, 6. 7, 4, δι- 4, 31. -σσω Traged. and Thuc., -ττω Comed. Xen. Pl. and Orators.

(Τάω) *To take*, Epic, and only imper. 2 sing. τῆ (contr. from τάε as ζῆ from ζάε) *take, there*, Il. 14, 219. 23, 618. Od. 10, 287, and 2 pl. τῆτε Sophr. 100 (Ahr.)

Τέγγω *To wet*, Aesch. Pers. 540; Soph. Ant. 831; Eur. Hel. 456; Aristot. Probl. 2, 32, 1; τέγγοι Anth. 7, 24; τέγγε Alcae. 39; -γων Pind. N. 10, 75; Pl. Rep. 866; -γειν Hippocr. 4, 280: imp. ἔτεγγον Aesch. Pers. 317; Soph. O. R. 1277: fut. τέγξω Pind. Ol. 4, 19; Eur. Supp. 979 (chor.): aor. ἔτεγξα Aesch. Pr. 401 (chor.); Hippocr. 7, 378 (Lit.): (perf.?): aor. pass. ἐτέγχθην Soph. Ph. 1456 (chor.); Pl. Leg. 880. Mid. τέγγομαι rare, *to weep*, Aesch. Pers. 1065; later trans. *to moisten*, Eratosth. Macrob. Sat. 7, 15, 23. Vb. τεγκτός Aristot. Meteor. 4, 9, 3, ἄ-τεγκτος Eur. H. F. 833. Rare in Attic prose, only once in Comedy, τέγγεσθε Ar. Lys. 550.

Τέθηπα, see (θάπω).

Τείνω *To stretch*, trans. and intrans. Il. 16, 365 (Vulg.); Aesch. Sept. 763; Her. 2, 6; Pl. Conv. 186; τείνῃ Il. 16, 365 (Bekk. &c.); Ar. Ran. 1101 &c.; τείνοι Xen. Oec. 7, 39, -νειεν Il. 20, 101; τεῖνε Soph. Aj. 1040; -νων Pind. Ol. 13, 85: imp. ἔτεινον Eur. Or. 1494; Xen. An. 4, 3, 21, iter. τείνεσκε, ἐπι- Her. 1, 186: fut. τενῶ Ar. Thesm. 1205, ἐκ- Eur. Med. 585, ἀπο- Pl. Gorg. 458: aor. ἔτεινα Il. 4, 124; Aesch. Ch. 510; Theocr. 21, 51, τεῖν- in tmesi Il. 3, 261, παρ-έτ- Thuc. 8, 104, ἀπ- Pl. Prot. 361; τεῖνον Pind. N. 5, 51: p. τέτᾰκα Dio. Hal. Excerp. 18, 2; V. T. Prov. 7, 16, ἐκ- Orph. Fr. 1, 20, ἀπο- Pl. Gorg. 465: p. p. τέταμαι Od. 11, 19; Emped. 288; Pind. P. 11, 54; Her. 2, 8; Soph. Ph. 831; Pl. Rep. 432: plp. ἐτέτατο Hippocr. 5, 94, τετ- Od. 11, 11; Hes. Th. 638; Soph. Ant. 600, dual τετάσθην Il. 4, 536, pl. -αντο Il. 4, 544: aor. ἐτάθην Soph. Ant. 124; Hippocr. 5, 204 (Lit.); Ael. Fr. 12, ἐξ- Xen. Hell. 7, 5, 22, τάθ- Il. 23, 375; ταθῇ Aesch. Pers. 708, ἐπι- Pl. Phaed. 86; ταθείς Il. 13, 655, ἐκ- Eur. Or. 302; Pl. Leg. 887: f. ταθήσομαι Galen 9, 411, ἐκ- Eur. Alc. 349, παρα- Pl. Lys. 204. Mid. τείνομαι *to stretch one's own, exert oneself* &c. Anth. P. 9, 220. 12, 232; Theocr. 21, 48, προ- Her. 5, 24: imp. τείνετο Ap. Rh. 4, 127, δι-ετειν- Her. 9, 18: fut. τενοῦμαι, παρα- Thuc. 3, 46, προ- Dem. 14, 5: aor. (ἐ)τείνατο

Ap. Rh. 2, 1043, προ- Her. 9, 34, δι- Antiph. 5, 46; Pl. Tim. 78; τεινάμενος Ap. Rh. 4, 705; Opp. Cyn. 1, 121, κατα- Hippocr. 3, 434; τείνασθαι, ἀνα- Dem. 19, 153, ἐν- Aeschin. 2, 157; Pl. Rep. 536. **Vb.** τατός Aristot. H. An. 3, 13, τατέος, προ- Aristot. Top. 8, 11, 2, ξυν- (Pl.) Epist. 7, 340. Except κρίνω, τίνω, τείνω, verbs in νω seldom have the 1 perf. in good Attic writers. κλίνω, κρίνω, τείνω, πλύνω generally drop ν before a consonant, or are inflected from a simpler theme. Φαίνω, however, has πέφαγκα, ἀπο- Dinarch. 1, 54 &c.

Τείρω *To rub, gall,* Poet. and only **pres.** and **imp.** Il. 4, 315; Mimnerm. 1, 7; Aesch. Pr. 348; Eur. Hel. 420: **imp.** τεῖρον Il. 16, 510, ἔτειρον 5, 796; H. Merc. 131; Telest. 1, 8 (B.): (fut. τέρσω belongs not here): **p.** τέτορεν Hesych.; τετόρῃ ibid. **Pass.** τείρομαι Ar. Lys. 960 (chor.); -όμενος Il. 8, 363; Soph. Ph. 203; τείρεσθαι Il. 6, 387: **imp.** ἐτειρόμην Il. 22, 242; Eur. Alc. 421, τειρ- Il. 5, 797. Od. 10, 78, see τέρσω. The only instance of this verb in classic prose is τειρομένους Lys. 12, 35, Canter's emend. for τηρομ- of the Mss. and adopted by Bekk. Markland suggested τιμωρουμένους which Bait. Saupp. and Scheibe have received, and L. Dind. approved. Canter's reading is easier, and we think Lys. may be indulged in a poetical expression. It occurs in later prose, τείρεται Ael. N. A. 14, 11, -ομένην Galen 8, 840.

Τειχίζω *To build a wall,* &c. Pind. Fr. 176; Thuc. 1, 90; Dem. 1, 22: **imp.** ἐτείχ- Thuc. 5, 82: **fut.** τειχιῶ Thuc. 6, 97; Dem. 6, 14: **aor.** ἐτείχισα Thuc. 6, 98; Andoc. 3, 5. 38, τείχ- Anth. Ap. Epigr. 147; -ίσαντες Her. 1, 175: **p.** τετείχικα Dem. 19, 112 &c. reg.: **plp.** τετείχιστο Her. 1, 181, ἐτετεί- (Dind. Stein). **Mid.** -ίζομαι Thuc. 4, 3: **fut.** τειχιεῖσθαι Xen. Cyr. 6, 1, 19 (Vulg. and *now* Dind. Saupp. -ίσασθαι Popp.): **aor.** ἐτειχίσαντο Thuc. 1, 11, Epic -ίσσαντο Il. 7, 449; -ισάμενος Thuc. 3, 105; -ίσασθαι Xen. Cyr. 6, 1, 19 (Popp. Breitb. τειχιεῖσθαι Vulg. Dind. Saupp.): and **p. p.** as **mid.** τετειχισμένος ἀντ-επι- Thuc. 1, 142. The purely Ionic form τειχέω occurs in **pres.** part. only, τειχέοντες Her. 5, 23. 8, 40, and **imp.** ἐτείχεον Her. 1, 99. 4, 124. 9, 7. 8.

Τεκμαίρομαι *To ordain, infer,* Dep. mid. Il. 7, 70; Aesch. Pr. 336; Soph. O. R. 916; Ar. Vesp. 76; Her. 1, 57. 7, 234; Thuc. 4, 123; Pl. Rep. 368: **imp.** ἐτεκμ- Xen. Cyr. 8, 1, 28: **fut.** τεκμαροῦμαι Hippocr. 6, 24; Xen. Cyr. 4, 3, 21: **aor.** ἐτεκμηράμην, τεκμηρ- Il. 6, 349; -ήραιο Xen. Mem. 3, 5, 6, -αιτο Isae. 7, 8; -ήρασθαι Pl. Phaedr. 230; Dem. 16, 4; -ηράμενος Antiph. 5, 81, ξυν- Thuc. 2, 76. The **act.** form τεκμαίρω is poet. and occurs not before Pind. Ol. 6, 73, N. 6, 8, *to put a mark, to* *limit, shew*: aor. ἐτέκμηρα, imper. τέκμηρον Aesch. Pr. 605, -ήρατε Q. Sm. 12, 221; Arat. 18 (Bekk.) Vb. τεκμαρτός C. Fr. (Cratin.) 2, 164, τεκμαρτέον Hippocr. 3, 318 (Lit.)

Τελέθω *To arise, become, be* (τέλλω), Poet. -έθεις Anth. 7, 531, -έθει Il. 7, 293; Pind. P. 2, 78; Aesch. Supp. 1040; Eur. And. 783; Hippocr. 7, 12. 34. 112 (Lit.), Dor. 1 pl. -έθομες Epich. 94 (Ahr.), -έθουσι Il. 12, 347; Eur. Med. 1996, Dor. -έθοντι Pind. P. 2, 31 (late trans. τελέθει *makes rise, yields*, Orac. Sib. 3, 263); subj. τελέθωσι Hes. Op. 181; Opp. Hal. 3, 365; opt. -έθοι Aesch. Supp. 691, -οιτε Theocr. 24, 99, -οιεν 5, 18; -έθειν Theogn. 770; Her. 7, 141 (Orac.); -έθοντος Aesch. Ag. 466, -οντες Od. 17, 486: **imp.** iter. τελέθεσκε H. Hym. Cer. 241, -εσκον Callim. Lav. Pal. 67. **Pass.** τελέθονται Pseudo-Phocyl. 104 (Bergk): **imp.** τελέθοντο Orac. Sib. 3, 264. Hippocr. quoted is the only prose instance we have met, except Diotog. Stob. 43, 130; Tab. Heracl. 1, 63. In Traged. always in chor. Our Lexicons give this verb scrimp justice.

Τελείω, see τελέω.

Τελευτάω *To end, finish*, Il. 18, 328; Soph. Tr. 1252; Her. 1, 25; Thuc. 1, 138; Pl. Leg. 630; opt. -ῴην Gorg. 522; -ευτῶν Ar. Eq. 524, Ion. -έων Her. 3, 38: **imp.** ἐτελεύτα Thuc. 2, 47, τελεύ- Od. 3, 62: **fut.** -ήσω Il. 13, 375; Aesch. Supp. 210; Her. 1, 32; Pl. Euth. 285, Dor. -άσω Pind. Ol. 2, 33: **aor.** ἐτελεύτησα Her. 6, 24; Thuc. 2, 41, τελεύτ- Od. 12, 304, Dor. -ᾶσεν Pind. P. 1, 54; Aesch. Sept. 931 (chor.); -τήσῃς Od. 1, 293, -τήσῃ Soph. Fr. 572 (D.); -τήσειας Od. 21, 200, -σειεν 7, 331; Isae. 1, 10; -ήσας Od. 4, 585; Aj. 496 &c.: **p.** τετελεύτηκα Her. 8, 71; Lys. 2, 74; Pl. Menex. 246: **plp.** ἐτετελ- Dem. 36, 8: (**p. p.**?): **aor.** ἐτελευτήθην, τελευτηθῇ Eur. Or. 1218; -τηθῆναι Il. 15, 74. Od. 2, 171: as pass. fut. mid. τελευτήσομαι seemingly always, Il. 13, 100. Od. 8, 510. 9, 511; Orph. Arg. 1338; Galen 16, 617, Dor. -άσομαι Eur. Hipp. 370 (chor.) The part. τελευτῶν with another verb, even another participle, is often used adverbially, *as a finish, to finish, at last*, τελευτῶν εἶπε Xen. Cyr. 1, 4, 9, -ῶντες ἀπέστησαν Thuc. 2, 47; τελευτῶν δήσας Lys. 14, 26. **Vb.** ἀ-τελεύτητος Il. 4, 175; Soph. O. R. 336; Aristot. Metaph. 10, 10, 1.

Τελέω *To bring to an end, accomplish*, Il. 23, 180; Her. 2, 51, Epic -είω Od. 6, 234, Attic -λῶ Soph. O. R. 222; Thuc. 2, 97, Ion. 3 pl. τελεῦσι Hes. Th. 89, Dor. -εῦντι Theocr. 7, 32; imper. -λεῖτε Aesch. Sept. 627: **imp.** ἐτέλουν Dem. 18, 265, τέλεον Il. 23, 768, ἐτέλειον Il. 15, 593, iter. τέλεσκον Callim. Dian. 123. Frag. 434, -λέεσκον Q. Sm. 8, 213: **fut.** τελέσω Pind. N. 4, 43; Xen. Cyr. 8, 6, 3 (Vulg. Born. Popp. -λῶ Saupp. Dind. 4 ed.), δια Pl.

Rep. 425; Dem. 21, 66, ἐκ- Theocr. 28, 10; Luc. Fug. 23, συν- Plut. Ant. 23, Epic -έσσω Il. 23, 559, Attic τελῶ Aesch. Sept. 35; Soph. El. 1435; Ar. Ran. 173; Pl. Prot. 311, δια- Isocr. 6, 87 (Bekk. B. Saupp. -έσω Bens.), Ionic τελέω Il. 8, 415. 9, 156: aor. ἐτέλεσα Aesch. Sept. 782; Soph. Tr. 917; Thuc. 4, 78, Epic -εσσα Il. 12, 222; Pind. P. 2, 13, τέλεσ- Hes. Sc. 36, Pind. P. 4, 246, τέλεσσ- Od. 7, 325; Pind. Ol. 2, 40; subj. rare, τελέσω Od. 11, 352, -έσσω Il. 1, 523, -έσῃ 14, 44, -έσσῃ 23, 543; -σειας Od. 15, 195, -σειε Il. 10, 303; Dor. pt. τελέσαις Pind. P. 1, 79: p. τετέλεκα Pl. Apol. 20, δια- Dinarch. 1, 65: plp. ἐτετελέκει, προσ- Thuc. 6, 31: p. p. τετέλεσμαι Il. 18, 74. Od. 13, 40; Aesch. Supp. 19; Her. 7, 118; Pl. Euth. 277: plp. τετέλεστο Il. 19, 242; Mosch. 2, 162, ἐπ-ετετ- Thuc. 7, 2: aor. ἐτελέσθην Od. 4, 663. Il. 15, 228 (Wolf, Dind. La R. τελ- Bekk.); Aesch. Ch. 1067; Ar. Ran. 357; Her. 4, 79; Thuc. 1, 93; τελεσθῇ Xen. Lac. 13, 5 &c.: fut. τελεσθήσομαι Theophr. Char. 16 (Foss); Heliod. 10, 41, ἀπο- Aristot. Polit. 1, 4, 1; Luc. Rhet. 24, ἐπι- Dio. Hal. Ant. 4, 19: and as pass. fut. mid. τελέομαι, -έεσθαι Il. 2, 36 (ἐπι- Her. 6, 140), -εῖσθαι Od. 23, 284, so perhaps τελεῖται Aesch. Ag. 68. Pr. 929: pres. τελεῖται Il. 14, 48. Od. 13, 178; Aesch. Ag. 1487; Pl. Politic. 288, -είεται Od. 14, 160. 19, 161; Bion 3, 3: imp. ἐτελοῦντο Pl. Phaedr. 250, -είετο Il. 1, 5. Od. 11, 297. Mid. τελεῖσθαι, ἐπι- trans. Xen. Mem. 4, 8, 8: fut. -οῦμαι as pass. see above: aor. rare, ἐτελεσάμην trans. -έσσατο Opp. Cyn. 2, 205; τελέσαισθε Dem. 38, 18, ἐπι- Pl. Phil. 27; τελέσασθαι Dem. 18, 150. 39, 38, ἐπι- Hippocr. 3, 420 (Lit.), συν- Inscr. p. 5 (Urlich): and later p. p. as mid. συν-τετελεσμένος Polyb. 5, 100 (B. Dind.) Vb. ἐπιτελεστέος Isocr. 12, 37.

Hom. has also the Attic fut. τελῶ Il. 4, 161. Perf. with long vowel τετέληκα occurs C. Inscr. 2885, 7: and aor. mid. τελήσασθαι Aristid. vol. 2, p. 153 (Jebb, -έσασθαι Dind.) Buttm. says τελεύμενα Her. 3, 134, is a fut. and so, we suppose, 1, 206. Is this necessary? At Il. 15, 228, Bekk. now reads γε τελέσθη for γ' ἐτελ- but holds it spurious. τέλεσκε Callim. Fr. 434, and, as it ought to be, τέλεσκον Dian. 123, not ἐτελ- (Blomf. &c.) are for -έεσκε &c. Some think τελέσκων Nicand. Fr. 2, 10 (74, 10 Otto Schn.), a false form for τελίσκων, as εὑρίσκω &c. and which Nic. uses Alex. 583 (Gottlob Schn.); but τελέσκω may be formed from τελέω, as κορέσκω from κορέω, Alex. 225. 360 &c. &c. and Otto Schneid. actually reads τέλεσκε Alex. 583 (Ms. P.) for τελίσκει (Vulg.) The forms τελειόω, -εόω are reg. and used indiscriminately in Poet. and Prose. Her. however always -εόω, 1, 120. 160. 3, 86. 5, 11.

Τέλλω *To perform, raise, complete*, and intrans. *rise* (in *simple*, **pres.** and **aor.** only), τέλλει Pind. Ol. 13, 83 (Herm. Schn. see fut.); Nicand. Fr. 2, 32; -λοντος Soph. El. 699, ἐπαν- Pind. Ol. 8, 28: **imp.** ἔτελλεν in tmesi Il. 1, 25. 16, 199. Od. 23, 349: **fut.** τελῶ Pind. Ol. 13, 83 quoted (Bergk, Christ, Momms.): **aor.** ἔτειλα Pind. Ol. 2, 70, ἄν-τειλας I. 7, 5: τέλλεται *exists, is*, Pind. Ol. 11 (10), 6: τέλλετο Pyth. 4, 257: **plp.** ἐτέταλτο in tmesi Il. 2, 643.—More usual, and better developed in comp. ἀνα-, ἐν-, ἐπι- &c. as follows: ἀνα-τέλλω *make rise*, and intrans. *rise*, Aesch. Sept. 535; Soph. Ph. 1138; Her. 2, 142; Pl. Polit. 269, poetic ἀντέλλ- Ap. Rh. 3, 959; Aesch. Sept. 535, Dor. 3 pl. -λλοντι Theocr. 13, 25; pt. -λλοισα 18, 26: **imp.** ἀνέτελλον Pl. Polit. 269; Ap. Rh. 2, 1247 (1, 601, -τειλε Et. M. Gaisf. Merk.); Coluth. 219, ἐπ-αν- Her. 7, 54: **fut.** ἀνα-τελεῖ V. T. Job 11, 17, Poet., ἀν-τελέουσι Nic. Fr. 74, 25 (Otto Schn.): **aor.** ἀνέτειλα Il. 5, 777; Pind. I. 6, 75, ἄντειλ- I. 7, 5; -τείλῃ Pl. Crat. 409; -τεῖλαι Her. 2, 142; Dio. Hal. 2, 38; -τείλας Her. 7, 223: **p.** ἀνατεταλκός Polyb. 9, 15 (Bekk.). **Mid.** ἀνατέλλομαι *rise*, Dor. part. -λλομένα Pind. I. 4, 65 (Bergk). ἐντέλλω *enjoin*, rare in **act.** Soph. Fr. 252 (D): **aor.** ἔντειλα Pind. Ol. 7, 40: **p. p.** ἐντέταλμαι Soph. Fr. 411 (D); Eur. Phoen. 1648; Her. 1, 60; Xen. Cyr. 5, 5, 3, see below. Usu. **mid.** ἐντέλλομαι as act. Her. 4, 94. 9, 98; Pl. Prot. 325: **imp.** ἐνετελλ- Her. 1, 90: **fut.** ἐντελοῦμαι late, Schol. Il. 24, 117; V. T. Ps. 90, 11. N. T. Mat. 4, 6: **aor.** ἐνετειλάμην Her. 1, 90. 9, 18; Xen. An. 5, 1, 13: **p.** ἐντέταλμαι usu. **pass.** see above, but as **act.** ἐντεταλμένοι ἦσαν Polyb. 17, 2 (Bekk.): **aor.** ἐνταλθέντα (Hesych.) ἐπιτέλλω *enjoin*, Poet. Il. 9, 369; Ar. Av. 977; intrans. subj. -τέλλῃ Hippocr. 7, 260 (Lit.): **imp.** ἐπέτελλε Il. 4, 229: **aor.** ἐπέτειλα Il. 5, 818; Pind. N. 10, 77, intrans. *rose*, Aesch. Pr. 100: **plp.** in tmesi ἐπὶ . . . ἐτέταλτο Il. 2, 643. **Mid.** ἐπιτέλλομαι as act. Il. 19, 192; Pind. P. 1, 70, intrans. *rise*, Hes. Op. 567: **imp.** ἐπετέλλετο Od. 11, 622; Hes. Scut. 94: **aor.** ἐπετείλατο Od. 1, 327. ἐπανατέλλω Her. 3, 84, Poet. ἐπαντέλ- Pind. Ol. 8, 28; Aesch. Ch. 282; Eur. H. F. 1053. Phoen. 104: has **aor.** inf. ἐπανατεῖλαι Her. 2, 142; poet. part. ἐπαντείλας Aesch. Ag. 27: **p.** ἐπανατεταλκέτω Aristot. Meteor. 3, 5, 17 (Bekk.), but no **mid.** or **pass.**

Τέμνω *To cut*, Pind. Ol. 13, 57 (ταμ- Momms.); Aesch. Supp. 807; Soph. Aj. 1179; Thuc. 3, 26; Pl. Tim. 61, Epic, Ionic and Dor. τάμνω Il. 3, 105; Her. 2, 65; Hippocr. 8, 146; once Pind. Ol. 12, 6 (best Mss. Bergk, Momms.), δια- (Tab. Heracl.), rare τέμω Il. 13, 707; Epic inf. ταμνέμεν Hes. Op. 791: **imp.** ἔτεμνον Thuc. 2, 19; Pl. Conv. 190, τέμν- H. Cer. 383, ἔταμν- Il. 4, 155; Her. 2, 125. 9, 86, τάμν- Il. 21, 38, iter. τέμνεσκε Ap.

Rh. 1215; Q. Sm. 6, 217: **fut.** τεμῶ Eur. Bacc. 493; Thuc. 1, 82; Pl. Conv. 190, Ionic τεμέω rare Hippocr. 4, 630 Lit.); Q. Sm. 6, 48: (no **1 aor.**): **p.** τέτμηκα Aristot. Soph. 22, 3; Dio. Hal. 8, 31, ἀπο- Pl. Meno 85, ἀνα- Aeschin. 3, 166; Epic part. τετμηώς as **pass.** Ap. Rh. 4, 156: **p. p.** τέτμημαι Od. 17, 195; Pind. I. 5, 22; Aesch. Ch. 198; Soph. El. 901; Ar. Ach. 183; Her. 4, 136; Thuc. 3, 26; Pl. Tim. 80: **plp.** ἐτέτμητο, ἐν- Her. 5, 49: **aor.** ἐτμήθην Eur. Tr. 480; Hippocr. 5, 94; Pl. Conv. 191, κατ- Her. 2, 108; τμηθείς Eur. Med. 4; Thuc. 2, 18; -θῆναι Andoc. 3, 8; Thuc. 2, 20; Xen. Ath. 2, 14, Dor. -θῆμεν Stob. (Diotog.) 43, 95: **fut.** τμηθήσομαι Aristot. Lin. insec. 9, 30. 31. 49; Sext. Emp. 448, ἀπο- (Lys.) 6, 26: **3 fut.** *simple* late τετμήσομαι Philostr. Apoll. 162, but ἐκ- Pl. Rep. 564 (Mss. B. O. W.), ἀπο- Luc. Tox. 62: **2 aor. act.** ἔτᾰμον, Hom. always τάμον in *simple* Il. 6, 194. 20, 184 &c.; and Pind. Ol. 1, 49 &c., ἔταμον Her. 7, 132; and old Attic Eur. Hel. 1224 (Mss. Vulg. Kirchh. Nauck, ἔτεμ- Dind. *now*); Theocr. 18, 34, ἐξ- Il. 1, 460. Od. 12, 360, ἀπ- Aesch. Ag. 1410 (Vulg. -εμ- Dind.); τάμησι Od. 18, 339, τάμωμεν Il. 3, 94; Thuc. 1, 81; ταμών Pind. N. 3, 33; Her. 4, 201; ταμέειν Il. 19, 197, ταμεῖν Hes. Op. 807, περι- Her. 2, 162, δια- 7, 39 and always; usu. ἔτεμον Eur. Hel. 231; Thuc. 6, 7 &c.; Pl. Tim. 70. 77; Isocr. 8, 100; τέμω Soph. Ph. 1208; τεμών Aesch. Eum. 592; Soph. El. 449; Ar. Av. 1560; τεμεῖν Pl. Leg. 944: **2 aor. mid.** ἐταμόμην Eur. Hec. 634 (chor.); Theocr. 13, 35; τάμοιο Hes. Op. 425, ταμοίμην, προ- Od. 18, 375; ταμόμενος Her. 1, 194; ταμέσθαι Il. 9, 580; Her. 5, 82, and ἐτεμόμην Luc. pro Imag. 24, ἀπ- Pl. Polit. 280; τεμοίμεθα, ἐν- Ar. Lys. 192; τεμόμενος Pl. Leg. 695, ἀπο- Thuc. 8, 46; -τεμέσθαι Isocr. 8, 24. **Mid.** τάμνομαι *cut for oneself*, ἀπο- Her. 4, 71, τέμνωμαι, ἀπο- Isocr. 6, 88; ταμνόμενος Od. 24, 364; Her. 4, 70, so τεμνόμενος Pl. Phaedr. 266; τέμνεσθαι Andoc. 2, 11: **imp.** ἐταμνόμην Her. 1, 186, ταμν- Od. 5, 243: **fut.** τεμοῦμαι, ὑπο- Xen. Cyr. 1, 4, 19; Ar. Eq. 291, ἐπι- Luc. pro Imag. 16, ἀπο- Paus. 3, 7, 3: and as **mid. p. p.** τέτμημαι, ὑπο- Polyb. 5, 107 (pass. Aeschin. 3, 166): **2 aor.** ἐταμόμην, ἐτεμ- see above. **Vb.** τμητός Soph. El. 747; Aristot. Metaph. 4, 15, 1, -έος Pl. Rep. 510. See τμήγω.

Τέμει Il. 13, 707, is retained as pres. by Bekk. Spitzner and La Roche; Wolf and Dind. read fut. τεμεῖ. Hom. always uses τάμνω except once τέμνειν Od. 3, 175 (Mss. Vulg. Dind. La Roche &c.), τάμν- Dünster, so Bekk. (2 ed.), and never augments the **2 aor.** τάμον, τάμε &c.; inf. Epic τομέειν Il. 19, 197; so Hippocr. 7, 70. 152 (Lit.), but Her. ταμεῖν, see above. Her. besides ἔταμον has once ἔτεμον, ἀπ- 3, 69 (Vulg. Gaisf. Bekk.

Krüg. &c.), but ἀπ- έταμον (Dind. Dietsch, Stein). In Attic *prose*, this tense with α (ἔταμον) seems to occur once only before Aristotle, Thuc. 1, 81: ἐτέτμετο syncop. and redupl. for ἐτέμετο, Orph. Arg. 366, has been displaced by ἐτέμνετο a conject. of Ruhnken's, and adopted by Hermann. Q. Sm. has a form in μι, ἐκ-τάμνησι 3, 224 (Koechly.)

Τέρπω *To gladden, amuse*, Hes. Op. 487; Eur. An. 208; Com. Fr. (Alex.) 3, 454; Hippocr. 6, 492; Thuc. 2, 44; Pl. Leg. 658; Epic subj. τέρπησι Od. 17, 385; τέρπειν Od. 1, 347: **imp.** ἔτερπον Il. 9, 189; Mosch. 2, 64, τερπ- H. Merc. 565, iter. τέρπεσκεν Anth. 9, 136; Q. Sm. 7, 378: **fut.** τέρψω Soph. Tr. 1246; Thuc. 2, 41: **aor.** ἔτερψα Hom. H. 19, 47; Eur. Her. 433; Her. 8, 99; τέρψῃ Pl. Leg. 658; τέρψον Theocr. 27, 13: **1 aor. pass.** ἐτέρφθην Od. 8, 131. 17, 174 &c. (Vulg. Wolf, Dind. La R. ἐτάρφθ- Bekk. 2 ed.); Soph. O. C. 1140; Eur. Ion 541; rare in prose Xen. Mem. 2, 1, 24; and late V. T. Ps. 118, 14, Epic 3 pl. ἔτερφθεν H. Hym. 19, 45; Epic and unaugm. τάρφθην Od. 19, 213. 251. 21, 57 La R. Bekker (and now 5, 74, ἐτ- 8, 131. 17, 174, and always Bekk. 2 edit. τέρφ- La R.), Epic 3 pl. τάρφθεν 6, 99: **fut.** late τερφθήσομαι Scymn. Per. 92 (Mein.); V. T. Ps. 34, 9, συν- Schol. Ar. Lys. 227: **2 aor.** ἐτάρπην Epic, Od. 23, 300, τάρπ- Il. 11, 780. Od. 4, 47; subj. Epic τρᾰπείω, hence τραπείομεν for τραπῶμεν, Il. 3, 441. 14, 314; inf. ταρπήμεναι Il. 24, 3, and ταρπῆναι Od. 23, 212. **Mid.** τέρπομαι *to satisfy oneself, feel delight*, Il. 5, 760; Pind. P. 2, 74; Ar. Plut. 288; Pl. Phil. 47, Epic 2 sing. τέρπεαι Od. 4, 372; imper. τέρπεο Od. 13, 61, Ion. τέρπευ Her. 2, 78: imp. τέρποντο Hes. Op. 115, ἐτερπ- Archil. 29 (B.); Her. 8, 69: fut. τέρψομαι Il. 20, 23; Archil. 9 (Bergk); Soph. Ant. 691; Eur. An. 1180; Theocr. 28, 6, but as **act.** *gladden*, Q. Sm. 5, 551: **1 aor.** (ἐτερψάμην) rare, subj. τέρψομαι for -ωμαι intrans. Od. 16, 26; τέρψαιτο trans. H. H. Apol. 153; -άμενος intrans. Od. 12, 188: **2 aor.** (ἐταρπόμην), ταρπώμεθα Il. 24, 636. Od. 4, 295. 23, 255, but indic. redupl. τετάρπετο Il. 19, 19. 24, 513; so throughout, τεταρπώμεσθα Il. 23, 98; τεταρπόμενος Od. 1, 310. Buttmann says the change of vowel in the **1 aor. pass.** ἐτέρφθην, ἐτάρφθην is not supported by sufficient analogy. It may be so, but is the analogy stronger for the change of ἐστρέφθην to ἐστράφθην Her. 1, 130; or for τρεφθέντες (Hom.) Epigr. 14, 7, τραφθῆναι Od. 15, 80? **p.** τέτραμμαι, **p. act.** τέτροφα Ar. Nub. 858, τέτραφα Dinarch. 1, 108, ἀνα- Dem. 18, 296 (Ms. S.) Compare τρέφω, τέθραμμαι Eur. Her. 578, ἐθρέφθην Hec. 351. The **fut. mid.** we have not seen in prose, the **aorists mid.** and **pass.** with α are Epic.

Τερσαίνω *To dry*, Epic, **pres.** late Lycophr. 390; Nic. Al. 551:

aor. τέρσηνα Il. 16, 529. Pass. τερσαίνονται Ap. Rh. 4, 607: imp. τερσαίνοντο 4, 1405. See foll.

Τέρσω or **-ρρω** *To dry*, pres. not found, except τέρσει, ξηραίνει (Hesych.): fut. τέρσω Theocr. 22, 63: aor. ἔτερσα late Epic, subj. τέρσῃ Q. Sm. 9, 386; imper. τέρσον Nic. Ther. 693 (Vulg.) τέρσομαι *become dry*, Epic and Ionic, Od. 7, 124; subj. τέρσηται (if not aor.) Hippocr. 8, 42; -σομένης Anth. 5, 225: imp. ἐτέρσετο Il. 11, 848, τέρσ- Od. 5, 152: 2 aor. pass. ἐτέρσην, inf. τερσῆναι Il. 16, 519, Epic τερσήμεναι Od. 6, 98: aor. mid. ἐτερσάμην, opt. τέρσαιο Nic. Ther. 709; τέρσαι 96. 693 quoted (Otto Schneid.), ἐτέρρατο (Hesych.) which points to Aeol. τέρρω, like θέρρω. As the legitimate form of the 2 aor. would be ἐτάρσην or ἐτράσην, a doubt may arise whether τερσήμεναι, -σῆναι may not possibly belong to aor. act. of τερσαίνω with neuter sense, as γλυκαίνω, ἀλεαίνω &c.

Τετεύχημαι, see (τευχέω). Τετίημαι, see (τιέω).

(**Τέτμω**) *To find*, only 2 aor. Epic ἔτετμον Il. 4, 293. Od. 1, 218, and τέτμον Il. 6, 374; Ap. Rh. 4, 537; subj. τέτμῃς Od. 15, 15, τέτμῃ Hes. Th. 610; Ap. Rh. 1, 908; opt. τέτμοιμεν Theocr. 25, 61. Hither some refer ἐτέτμετο *was cut*, Orph. Arg. 366. See τέμνω.

Τετραίνω *To bore*, pres. in comp. συν- Her. 2, 11; Aesch. Ch. 451: fut. (τετρᾰνῶ) Ionic -ανέω, δια- Her. 3, 12: aor. τέτρηνα Il. 22, 396. Od. 23, 198, ἐτέτρ- Aretae. 77 (ed. Oxon.); -τρήνας Hipponax 56; Aretae. 58 (ed. Oxon.), later ἐτέτρᾱνα, subj. τετράνωσι Theophr. H. P. 2, 7, 6: aor. pass. τετρανθείς Lycophr. 781; Anth. 6, 296. Mid. aor. ἐτετρηνάμην, δι- trans. Ar. Thesm. 18; late prose Galen 3, 687. Other parts supplied by τιτράω. Buttmann thinks the form τιτραίνω a mistake for τετραίνω. Wimmer however edits with Cod. Urb. τιτραίνεται Theophr. H. P. 5, 4, 5, δια- C. P. 1, 17, 9. Τετρήνεται called Ionic, Hippocr. 7, 498 (Lit.), imp. τετρήνοντο Callim. Dian. 244 (Vulg. -αντο aor. Mein.), are from a form (τετρήνω) or *perhaps* corruptions for τετραίνεται, -αίνοντο.

Τέτρηχα *Am tumultuous*, Epic, p. τέτρηχεν Opp. Hal. 5, 244; -ηχυῖα Il. 7, 346: plp. τετρήχει Il. 2, 95; later, *to be rough, uneven*, τετρηχότα Ap. Rh. 3, 1393, -ηχυῖα Anth. 7, 283. See ταράσσω.

Τετῠκεῖν *To get prepared*, Epic 2 aor. of τεύχω, with redupl. and change of aspirate, in act. only inf. Od. 15, 77; usu. mid. τετῠκοντο Il. 7, 319; Callim. Dian. 50; τετυκοίμεθα Od. 12, 283; τετυκέσθαι 21, 428. See τεύχω.

(**Τευχέω**) *To arm*, Epic, and only p. p. τετευχῆσθαι Od. 22, 104.

Τεύχω *To prepare, make*, Poet. Il. 1, 110; Pind. Ol. 1, 30;

Eur. Her. 614; τεύχῃ Aesch. Ag. 970; -χειν Aesch. Pers. 189; Soph. Tr. 756; Dor. pt. τύχοισα Theocr. 1, 50 (Vulg. Mein. Paley): **imp.** ἔτευχον Il. 18, 373; Theocr. 7, 3, τεῦχον Il. 1, 4; Theocr. 22, 192: **fut.** τεύξω Il. 14, 240; Soph. Ph. 1189: **aor.** ἔτευξα Il. 14, 338. Od. 4, 174; Hes. Fr. 110; Pind. P. 7, 11; Aesch. Supp. 306; Soph. Fr. 379 (D.); Com. Fr. (Eub.) 3, 226, τεῦξ- Il. 18, 609. Od. 8, 276; Hes. Th. 162; Pind. Ol. 7, 48: **p.** τέτευχα, -ευχώς as **pass.** Od. 12, 423; late prose (Hippocr.) Epist. 9, 382 (Lit.), but **act.** τετεύχατον Anth. 6, 40. 9, 202; and Il. 13, 346 (Old Edit.), see below: **p. p.** τέτυγμαι Il. 16, 622. 24, 317; Aesch. Ag. 751 (chor.); Eur. El. 457 (chor.); Theocr. 2, 20; τετυγμένος Il. 14, 9; Alcm. 33; Alcae. 85; Simon. C. 5, 2 (B.); Aesch. Sept. 388 (trim.), Epic and Ionic τέτευγμ-, 3 pl. -εύχἄται Il. 13, 22; late prose τετευγμένος, ἀπο- Dioscor. 5, 92: **plp.** ἐτετύγμην Il. 15, 337; Theocr. 25, 141, τετύγμ- Il. 6, 7. Od. 14, 234; Hes. Sc. 154, and ἐτετεύγμ-, ἐτέτευξο Q. Sm. 5, 558 (Vulg. -τυξο Spitzn. Koechly), 3 pl. ἐτετεύχἄτο Il. 11, 808, τετεύχ- 18, 574; Hes. Th. 581; Mosch. 2, 43: **aor.** ἐτύχθην indic. only, Il. 4, 470; Aesch. Eum. 353 (chor.); Theocr. 22, 83. 24, 22, Ionic ἐτεύχθην, τευχθέν Hippocr. 9, 242 (Lit.); Anth. 6, 207; Anacreont. 10, 5 (Vulg. but τυχθ- ex margine cod. Melhorn, Bergk): **3 fut.** τετεύξομαι Il. 21, 322. 585: **2 aor. act. redupl.** τετὔκεῖν Epic and Ion. Od. 15, 94, see separately. **Mid.** *to prepare for oneself*, **imp.** τεύχοντο Od. 10, 182: **fut.** τεύξομαι Il. 19, 208; Aesch. Ag. 1230, but **pass.** Il. 5, 653?: **aor.** τεύξασθαι trans. Hom. H. 2, 43. 67: **2 aor.** τετύκοιτο Il. 1, 467. Od. 8, 61; -κοίμεθα 12, 283; -υκέσθαι 21, 428. See τετυκεῖν. **Vb.** τυκτός Il. 12, 105. For τετεύχατον act. Il. 13, 346 quoted above, Wolf with some Mss. edited τετεύχετον, Buttm. Bekk. Spitzn. Dind. La Roche ἐτεύχετον, with Schol. Ven. from old Mss. The quotations from the Anthology however shew that Buttm. was mistaken in asserting that "there is no genuine instance of the **perf.** of τεύχω being used actively." This verb seems never to occur in Attic prose, perhaps only once in comedy.

Τεχνάω *To form with art* &c. doubtful in **act.**, **aor. inf.** τεχνῆσαι Od. 7, 110 (Vulg. but Bekk. Faesi, and *now* Dind. τεχνήσσαι adject.) **Dep. mid.** τεχνάομαι Soph. Aj. 86; Ar. V. 176; Bion 13, 3; Thuc. 1, 122; Xen. Ages. 9, 3, Ion. -έομαι Hippocr. 6, 360: **imp.** ἐτεχν- Thuc. 4, 26: **fut.** τεχνήσομαι Il. 23, 415; H. Apol. P. 148: **aor.** ἐτεχνησάμην Soph. Tr. 534, ἐξ- Thuc. 6, 46, τεχνήσ- Od. 5, 259, Dor. τεχνᾱσ- Anth. Pl. 161; -ήσαιτο Od. 11, 613; -ησάμενος Hippocr. 6, 358; Thuc. 4, 47; -ήσασθαι (Luc.) Hipp. 2: late as **mid. p. p.** τετεχνημένος Galen 11, 570. **Pass.** τεχνάομαι, opt. -ῷτο Xen. Cyr. 8, 6, 23; -ώμενος Eur. Her.

1003; Ar. V. 176: p. τετέχνημαι, Ionic 3 pl. -έαται Hippocr. 1, 628; -ημένος 2, 66 (Lit.)

Τῆ, see τάω.

Τήκω *To melt, make liquid,* Aesch. Fr. 304 (D.); Eur. Med. 141 (Dind.); Her. 2, 25; Pl. Rep. 609, Dor. τάκω Soph. El. 123 (chor.); Theocr. 2, 28; imper. τῆκε Od. 19, 264: fut. τήξω Anth. 5, 278; in tmesi Eur. Or. 1047, συν- Eur. I. A. 398, ἐκ- Eur. Cycl. 459, Dor. ταξῶ, κατα- Theocr. Epigr. 6, 1: aor. ἔτηξα Anth. 4, 1, 10. 9, 292; Her. 3, 96; Hippocr. 7, 366. 8, 190 (Lit.); App. Hannib. 7, κατ- Od. 19, 206, δια- Ar. Nub. 149, ἐκ- Pl. Rep. 411: p. see below: p. p. τέτηγμαι Plut. Mor. 106; Anth. 5, 273; Galen 10, 405: plp. ἐτέτηκτο Polyaen. 1, 6, κατ- Paus. 4, 3, 5: 1 aor. ἐτήχθην rare, Pl. Tim. 61; Hippocr. 7, 612 (Lit.); Galen 13, 380, συν- Eur. Supp. 1029: usu. **2 aor.** ἐτᾰκην Anth. Epigr. 349; Eur. Fr. 230 (D.); Pl. Phaedr. 251; Galen 13, 383, ἐκ- Aesch. Pr. 535, ἐν- Soph. Tr. 463, συν- Pl. Conv. 192. Tim. 83: **fut.** τᾰκήσομαι Anacreont. 10, 16 (Bergk), ἀπο- Hippocr. 299, 55 (Foes, 2, 135 Erm., see **fut. mid.**), συν- Plut. Mor. 752: so **fut. mid.** τηξόμεναι Hippocr. 6, 110 (Ms. A. Lit. ἀπο-τακησ- Vulg.): **pres. pass.** τήκομαι Ar. Vesp. 317, τᾰκομαι Pind. Fr. 100, 9; Eur. Andr. 116 (Eleg.), τάκεαι Theocr. 1, 82, τᾱκῇ Mosch. 3, 75, -εται Theocr. 1, 88; -κοιτο 2, 29; τηκόμενος Od. 5, 396. 19, 207, Dor. τᾱκόμεναι Aesch. Eum. 374 (chor.): **imp.** τήκετο Od. 8, 522; Hes. Th. 867, ἐτᾰκευ Theocr. 5, 12, -κετο 2, 83; Callim. Cer. 93: and **2 p.** τέτηκα *am melted,* Il. 3, 176; Soph. El. 283; Hippocr. 5, 728; Xen. An. 4, 5, 15; Pl. Tim. 85, Dor. τέτᾱκα Eur. Supp. 1141 (chor.), προσ- Soph. Tr. 836 (chor.): **plp.** ἐτετήκειν Xen. An. 4, 5, 15 (Vulg. Krüg. Dind. Cob., τετήκ- Mss. A B. Popp. Kühner). **Mid.** rare, **fut.** τήξεται trans. Hippocr. 1, 378 (Kühn) has been altered to opt. **aor. act.** τήξειε 7, 478 (Ms. C. Lit.), as **pass.** or intrans. see above: but **aor.** late τήξαιο Nic. Al. 164; -άμενος 63. 350. **Vb.** τηκτός Pl. Soph. 265, -έος late, Galen. 13, 523. 667. Our Lexicons have, we think, missed the **mid.** form.

Τηλεθάω *To bloom, flourish* (prob. for θηλετάω from τέθηλα), Epic only **pres.** and indic. rare, -θᾰει Theocr. Epigr. 4, 6; Anth. 9, 663, -θάουσι Q. Sm. 6, 344; Dion. Per. 1079, Epic -θόωσι 836. 1127; part. freq. -θάων Hom. H. 7, 41, -θάον Il. 17, 55, -θόωσα 6, 148, -θόωσαι Od. 11, 590, -θάοντας Il. 22, 423; Mosch. 4, 97, -θόωντα Od. 13, 196; Emped. 358. (ᾰ.)

Τηρέω *To guard, watch,* Eur. Fr. 597 (D.); Antiph. 2, β, 8; Thuc. 4, 60; Pl. Theaet. 169; subj. Dor. 3 pl. -έωντι Pind. P. 2, 88; -ροίης Hippocr. 1, 634: **imp.** ἐτήρουν Thuc. 7, 80; Isocr. 7, 30: **fut.** -ήσω Pl. Rep. 442: **aor.** ἐτήρησα Soph. O. R. 808; Thuc.

3, 22; Lys. 3, 34, ἐπι- Hym. Cer. 244: p. τετήρηκα Aristot. de Cael. 2, 12, 3 (Bekk.); Polyb. 5, 77; Luc. Abd. 32: p. p. τετήρημαι Dem. 21, 3. 23, 181: aor. ἐτηρήθην Hippocr. 9, 254; Lys. 12, 71: fut. τηρηθήσομαι D. Sic. 13, 96; Dio Cass. 69, 8; Marc. Ant. 11, 10: for which early Attic writers use fut. mid. τηρήσομαι as pass. Thuc. 4, 30. **Mid.** τηρέομαι *to guard oneself, be on one's guard*, Ar. Vesp. 372: fut. late, τηρήσομαι, παρα- V. T. Ps. 36, 12; Joseph. Ant. 11, 6, 13 (Bekk.); as pass. see above. **Vb.** τηρητέος Pl. Rep. 412.

Τητάομαι *To want, be deprived of*, only pres. Hes. Op. 408; Eur. Or. 1084; τητώμενος Soph. El. 1326; Eur. Her. 24; rare in prose, Pl. Leg. 810; Xen. Cyr. 8, 4, 33 (*now* L. Dind. Saupp.); Aristot. Eth. Nic. 1, 8 (9), 16, Dor. τᾱτώμ- Pind. N. 10, 78; τητᾶσθαι Soph. El. 265.

(**Τιέω** an obsolete Theme akin to τίω) *To trouble, afflict*, Epic, hence syncop. p. part. τετιηώς as pass. *troubled, vexed*, Il. 11, 555. 9, 13: p. p. τετίημαι, 2 dual τετίησθον Il. 8, 447; τετιημένος 8, 437; Hes. Th. 163.

Τῐθέω *To put, place* (θέω), *classic* only sing. pres. and imp. 1 pers. τιθῶ late (Luc.) Ocyp. 43. 81, τιθεῖς Pind. P. 8, 11, τίθεισθα v. r. Od. 9, 404 (Ahr.), -θεῖ Il. 13, 731; Mimn. 1, 6. 5, 7 (Bergk); Her. 1, 113, προ- 133, παρ- Od. 1, 192, παρα- Her. 4, 73, ἐπι- 5, 95. 7, 35, 3 pl. late -θοῦσι Ephr. Vit. Caes. 8708, ἐν- 8204; imper. τίθει Il. 1, 509; Archil. 56; Aesch. Sept. 201; Eur. Hel. 346; Ar. Lys. 243; Pl. Phil. 43. Rep. 510, προσ- Hippocr. 8, 380 (Lit.); Thuc. 6, 14, δια- Xen. Cyr. 5, 3, 21; inf. τιθεῖν Theogn. 286, τιθέμεν Hes. Op. 744: imp. ἐτίθουν 1 pers. perhaps late Procop. Epist. 140 (v. r. Pl. Gorg. 500), ἐν- Sever. Rhet. p. 547 (Walz), ἐτίθεις Pl. Rep. 497; Dem. 24, 60. 31, 6, ἐν- Ar. Nub. 59, ἐτίθει Il. 18, 561. Od. 6, 76 (Vulg. Wolf, Dind. La R. -ίθη Bekk. always 2 ed.); Andoc. 1, 117; Dem. 24, 135. 159, προσ- Ar. Nub. 63, κατ- Antiph. 5, 77, ἀντεπ- Thuc. 1, 129, περι- Her. 6, 69, προ- Dem. 18, 273, -ετίθεε Her. 1, 206, τίθει Il. 1, 441. 446. 18, 412. 20, 95 (Vulg. Dind. Ameis, La R. -θη Bekk.), 3 pl. ἐτίθουν late N. T. Act. 4, 35, ἀπ- Malal. p. 469, 11, iter. τίθεσκε Hes. Fr. 96: 1 aor. late ἐτίθησα, τιθήσας Or. Sib. 4, 122: fut. mid. τιθήσεσθαι (Hippocr.) Epist. 9, 424 (Lit.) The Attics seem rarely, perhaps never, to have used the pure form τιθέω, -εῖς, -εῖ in the pres. but τίθημι, -ης, -ησι. In the very few instances where it does occur, editors generally, especially since Porson, have altered it: thus ἐντιθεῖς Ar. Eq. 717 (Br. Bekk. Mein.) has been changed to ἐντίθης (Dind. Bergk, Kock), τιθεῖς Soph. Ph. 992 (Br.), τίθης (Pors. Erf. Herm. Ell. Dind. Bergk), τιθεῖς Eur. Cycl. 545 (Mss. B. Kirchh. 1 ed.), τίθης

(Ms. C. ex corr. Pors. Matth. Herm. Dind. Nauck, Paley, Kirchh. 2 ed.). "Nec me fugit," says Porson, "Brunckium pluribus in locis Sophoclis et Aristophanis τιθεῖς- et similes barbarismos aut reliquisse aut intulisse. Attici dicebant τίθημι, τίθης, τίθησι. Ubicunque τιθεῖς legitur, legitur ex errore scribarum ει et η permutantium." See note, Eur. Or. 141.

Τίθημι *To put, place* (θέω, τιθέω), Aesch. Ch. 145; Soph. El. 1270; Ar. Thesm. 1100; Her. 7, 8 (4); Isocr. 4, 145; Pl. Phil. 51; Dem. 23, 148, -θης Soph. Ph. 992; Pl. Rep. 348, -θησθα Od. 9, 404, -θησι Il. 4, 83; Hes. Op. 518; Solon 13, 62; Pind. P. 2, 10; Soph. Ant. 674; Ar. Plut. 451; Andoc. 1, 121; Pl. Crat. 389, Dor. τίθητι Theocr. 3, 48, τίθεμεν Pl. Polit. 306, -ετε, προ- (Dem.) 25, 9, τιθέᾱσι Com. Fr. (Alex.) 3, 437; Thuc. 5, 96; Pl. Rep. 339, προ- Her. 3, 53. 5, 8 (Stob. Bekk. Dind.), συν- 4, 23 (Bekk. Dind. -εῖσι Bred. Stein, Abicht), Ionic τιθεῖσι Il. 16, 262; Hes. Th. 597; Her. 2, 91. 4, 34; so Aesch. Ag. 465 (chor.); τιθῶ Aesch. Supp. 518; Pl. Leg. 801; -θείης Rep. 543, -είη Hes. Op. 470; Pl. Rep. 477; Dem. 22, 30, -θεῖμεν Pl. Rep. 605; inf. τιθέναι Thuc. 3, 58, Epic τιθήμεναι Il. 23, 83, and Epic τιθέμεν Hes. Op. 744; Pind. P. 1, 40: **imp.** ἐτίθην Lys. 30, 17; Pl. Gorg. 500, -ίθης rare, Rep. 528, -ίθη in Il. and Od. Bekk. always *now*, Il. 18, 541. Od. 6, 76 &c. (2 edit. -ίθει Dind. La R.); rare in Attic, Pl. Leg. 630 (Bekk. B. O. W.), usu. -ίθεις Pl. Rep. 497; Dem. 31, 6, ἐν- Ar. Nub. 59, ἐτίθει Ar. Ach. 532; Andoc. 1, 117; Dem. 22, 30, κατ- Antiph. 5, 77, ἐτίθεμεν Pl. Rep. 507, -θετε, ἐτίθεσαν Her. 1, 144; Xen. Mem. 3, 14, 1, τίθ- Od. 22, 456, τίθεν Pind. P. 3, 65, προ- Od. 1, 112 (Bekk. Dind. -τίθεντο La R.): **fut.** θήσω Il. 16, 673; Pind. Ol. 13, 98; Aesch. Eum. 484; Soph. O. C. 859; Her. 7, 8; Thuc. 1, 40; Xen. Mem. 4, 2, 17, Dor. θησῶ Theocr. 8, 14, 3 pl. θησεῦντι Bion 7, 3 (Ms. Reg. Br. Ziegl. -σοντι Vulg. Ahr.); Poet. inf. θησέμεν Pind. P. 10, 58, -σέμεναι Il. 12, 35: **aor.** ἔθηκα only *indic. classic* Il. 9, 485; Solon 36, 13; Aesch. Pr. 444; Soph. Tr. 691; Andoc. 1, 114; Dem. 14, 37. 18, 102, -ηκας Il. 17, 37; Aesch. Eum. 458; Soph. O. C. 1357; Eur. Med. 510; Pl. Conv. 222; Dem. 24, 195, προσ- 23, 75, συν- Isocr. 12, 249, ἔθηκε Il. 1, 2; Solon. 13, 22; Pind. N. 3, 22; Soph. Ph. 632; Ar. Vesp. 467; Her. 1, 113; Xen. Lac. 6, 4; Dem. 18, 107, θῆκε Il. 8, 324; Theogn. 196; Pind. Ol. 13, 39, dual rare and late ἐθηκάτην, περι- Polyaen. 2, 31, 4, 1 and 2 pl. rare ἐθήκαμεν Xen. Mem. 4, 2, 15; Aristot. Nat. Ausc. 8, 4, 6, ἐπ- Dem. 34, 28; Aristid. 47, 330, ἐξ- Long. P. 4, 36, δι- App. Civ. 4, 95, ἐθήκατε doubtful Aeschin. 1, 33 (some Mss. Bekk.), but ἀν- Hyperid. Eux. 24 (Lind.), προσ- Dio. Hal. Ant. 2, 3, δι- Aristid. 41, 512, often ἔθηκαν Il. 6, 300; Hes.

Op. 289; Eur. H. F. 590. Or. 1166; Her. 4, 196; Aeschin. 1, 13; Dem. 24, 211, ἀν- Simon. C.? 139 (Bergk); Com. Fr. (Men.) 4, 225; (Dem.) 59, 97, ἐπ- Her. 1, 144; (Dem.) 60, 11, ξυν- Xen. Hell. 2, 3, 20, δι- Dem. 19, 88. 54, 8, κατ- Her. 8, 28; Dem. 24, 16. 59, 96, περι- Hyperid. 4, 17, 7, θῆκαν Il. 24, 795. Od. 1, 223; Simon. C. 148, 12; Eur. Bac. 129 (chor.); opt. late θήκαιμι, ἀνα- Theoph. Epist. 29 (Hercher): **p.** τέθεικα Eur. El. 7; Com. Fr. (Alex.) 3, 389; Xen. Mem. 4, 4, 19; Dem. 20, 55. 22, 16, Dor. τέθεκα, ἀνα- Inscr. Ross. 1, 10: **p. p.** τέθειμαι, τέθειται V. T. 1 Reg. 9, 24. N. T. Marc. 15, 47, προσ- Aristot. Mechan. 18, 1, ἀνα- D. Hal. Ant. 1, 76, δια- 4, 80 (Kiesl.), rare in Classic Auth. τεθεῖσθαι (if not mid.) Ar. Fr. 304 (Dind.); and late τεθειμένος (Demad.) 12 (Bekk.); τεθεῖσθαι Argum. Dem. 39, but προ- Xen. Hier. 9, 11 (L. Dind. Saupp.), δια- Com. Fr. (Men.) 4, 252; Luc. Imag. 10. Nigr. 24, ἐκ- Catapl. 5, συν- Alex. 22, Dor. τέθεμαι, ἀνα- Inscr. Ross. 1, 14, as mid. see below: **aor.** ἐτέθην Eur. H. F. 1245; Her. 2, 42. 4, 45; Antiph. 6, 50; Thuc. 6, 4. 38; Pl. Tim. 62; τεθῇ Eur. H. F. 1245; Pl. Hipp. Maj. 284; Dem. 24, 44; τεθείη Dem. 24, 28; τεθήτω Pl. Leg. 689; τεθῆναι Ar. Nub. 1425; Pl. Leg. 721. Phaedr. 264; τεθείς Eur. Elec. 1266; Pl. Leg. 957, ἀμφι- Il. 10, 271: **fut.** τεθήσομαι Eur. El. 1268; Thuc. 4, 120; Pl. Leg. 730; Dem. 24, 17: and as pass. **fut. mid.** θήσομαι? Emped. in Aristot. de Xenoph. 2, 6 (στήσ- Emped. 50 (Stein), περι- Theon. Rhet. 5, p. 216 (Walz): **2 aor. act.** (ἔθην), indic. *sing.* not used, pl. ἔθεμεν Od. 3, 179; Eur. Tr. 6; Andoc. 4, 18; Pl. Rep. 492; in tmesi Od. 3, 179, ἔθετε Eur. An. 1020; Andoc. 2, 28, ἔθεσαν Il. 1, 290; Hes. Op. 74; Archil. 9, 6; Pind. Ol. 1, 64; Aesch. Pers. 283 (chor.); Eur. I. A. 1078 (chor.); Hippocr. 6, 486; Pl. Tim. 21, θέσαν Il. 12, 29. 24, 49. Od. 23, 11; Pind. P. 2, 39; subj. θέω Od. 24, 485; Her. 4, 71, θῶ Soph. O. C. 480; Antiph. 2, γ, 6; Isocr. 15, 158; Aeschin. 3, 163; Dem. 14, 27, Epic θείω see below; opt. θείην Il. 5, 215; Andoc. 1, 115; Isocr. 5, 82, θείημεν Pl. Prot. 343; Dem. 23, 128, θεῖμεν Od. 12, 347, προσ- Pl. Meno 84, θείητε, ἐν- Dem. 18, 324, θεῖτε, ἐπι- Il. 24, 264. Od. 22, 62, κατα- Dem. 14, 27 (Mss. Bekk. Dind.), but -θοιτε (Mss. Bait. Saupp. &c.) if correct, the only instance of **act.** in this form, 3 pl. θεῖεν Il. 4, 363; Soph. O.C. 865, προσ- Pl. Leg. 742; θές Il. 6, 273; Theocr. 8, 14; Pl. Rep. 424, 3 pl. θέντων Od. 19, 599; θεῖναι Il. 4, 26; Hes. Op. 815; Soph. Ant. 8; Her. 4, 179; Pl. Leg. 719, Ep. θέμεναι Il. 4, 57; Theogn. 152, θέμεν Od. 21, 3; Theogn. 846; Pind. Ol. 2, 97; θείς Il. 23, 254. Od. 21, 55; Ar. Ach. 365; Her. 2, 52; Thuc. 5, 105. **Mid.** τίθεμαι *to put, make &c. for oneself*, Soph. Phil. 1448; Dem. 23, 24, 2 sing. τίθεσαι Pl. Phil.

47, late τίθῃ Anth. (Pallad.) 11, 300, -θεται Her. 2, 46; Pl. Rep. 338, -ενται Od. 17, 269; Thuc. 1, 41, -θέαται, προ- Her. 1, 133; τιθῶμαι Pl. Phil. 32; τιθείμην Tyrt. 12, 1; Pl. Leg. 674; τίθεσθε Od. 19, 406; Isae. 7, 45; τιθέμενος Thuc. 5, 80; -θεσθαι 2, 2; imper. τίθεσο Theogn. 1096; Ar. Pax 1039; Pl. Soph. 237, -εσσο Anth. 9, 564, τίθου Aesch. Eum. 226; Eur. Fr. 343, κατα- Monost. 154: imp. ἐτιθ- Her. 8, 108, τιθ- Il. 9, 88, ἐτίθεσο Pl. Rep. 352, ἐτίθετο 340; Aristot. Metaph. 11, 8, 11, παρ- Thuc. 1, 130: fut. θήσομαι Il. 24, 402; Pind. P. 9, 63; Aesch. Ag. 32; Soph. Ph. 590; Ar. Av. 817; Her. 3, 29; Thuc. 6, 11; Pl. Crat. 390 (Dor. θησεύμεσθα Theocr. 8, 13); as pass. if sound, Emped. in Aristot. de Xenoph. 2, 6 (στήσονται Emped. 50 Stein), περι- Theon. Rhet. 5, p. 216 (Walz), which he would alter to περιτεθήσ-: and as mid. p. τέθειμαι Ar. Fr. 304? Dem. 21, 49. 39, 40; Luc. Somn. 9, ἐν- Dem. 34, 16. 34: 1 aor. ἐθηκάμην unattic, and chiefly *indic.* ἐθήκαο Theocr. 29, 18, ὑπ- Her. 7, 15, ἐθήκατο Opp. Cyn. 1, 355; Anth. 11, 187, θήκατο Il. 10, 31; Hes. Sc. 128, ἀπ- εθήκ- Pind. Ol. 8, 68, ἐπ- Her. 1, 26, προσ- 5, 69; Plut. Lys. 21, ὑπ- Hes. Th. 175; Plut. Mor. 839, ἐθήκαντο, προσ- Her. 4, 65. 6, 21, συν- 9, 53, ὑπ- 2, 160; but part. θηκάμενος Pind. P. 4, 29. 113; Theogn. 1150 (Bergk), -αμένη Philet. Fr. 16 (Schneid.): 2 aor. ἐθέμην Eur. Ph. 858; Ar. Eccl. 658, ἔθου Aesch. Sept. 107; Soph. Aj. 13; Pl. Leg. 626, Ion. ἔθευ Her. 7, 209, ἔθετο &c. Il. 2, 750; Hes. Sc. 261; Pind. Ol. 9, 44; Her. 1, 107; Thuc. 4, 44; Andoc. 1, 85; Pl. Phaed. 91; Isocr. 15, 254, θέτο Il. 10, 149; Hes. Th. 886; Pind. N. 10, 89; θῶμαι Eur. H. F. 486; Thuc. 8, 84; Pl. Rep. 339, Ion. θέωμαι, ὑπερ- Her. 5, 24; Epic 2 sing., θῆαι Od. 19, 403 (Bekk. Dind.), κατα- Hes. Op. 601, θῆται Pl. Crat. 384; so Her. 1, 29; θείμην Soph. Ant. 188; Plut. Phoc. 17, παρα- Od. 15, 506, θεῖο Od. 19, 403 quoted (Faesi, Ameis), θεῖτο Od. 17, 225; Aesch. Pr. 527; Pl. Theaet. 195, προσ- Dem. 6, 12 (Bekk. Dind.), -θοιτο (Voem.), θοίμεθα, ἐπι- Thuc. 6, 34 (Mss. Popp. Krüg. Stahl &c.), -θείμεθα (Mss. Bekk.), θεῖσθε, προσ- Dem. 21, 188 (Bekk.), -θοισθε (B. S. Dind. Voem.), θεῖντο, ἐπι- Thuc. 6, 11 (Bekk.), -θοιντο (Popp. Krüg Stahl), θείατο Aesch. Supp. 695 (Herm. Dind.); imper. (θέσο) θέο Od. 10, 333, ἐν- Theogn. 1321, θοῦ Soph. O. C. 466, θεῦ, ὑπο- Od. 15, 310, θέσθε Il. 13, 121; Lys. 24, 26; θέσθαι Il. 12, 418; Her. 4, 202; Andoc. 1, 128; Pl. Leg. 929; θέμενος Od. 9, 171; Soph. El. 1434; Her. 2, 43; Thuc. 4, 90. Vb. θετέος Pl. Rep. 413.

Τίθησθα 2 sing. pres. indic. Od. 24, 476, and always in Hom. 3 pl. in the contracted form τιθεῖσιν is rare in Attic, Aesch. Ag. 465 (chor.); usual in Her. but τιθέασι, προ- 3, 53. 5, 8, συν- 4,

23 (Gaisf. Bekk. Dind. Dietsch, -θεῖσι Bred. Stein); τέθετι reg. imper. rare and late, ἐπι- τίθετι Galen 14, 417 (Kühn, 10, 611 Chart.) Τιθήμεναι, τιθέμεν Epic inf. for τιθέναι, Il. 23, 83; Hes. Op. 744; part. τιθήμενος for τιθέμ- Il. 10, 34: Ionic imp. ἐτίθεα, ὑπερ- Her. 3, 155 for -ίθην, ἐτίθεε, προ- 8, 49, Poet. 3 pl. τίθεν Pind. P. 3, 65, iter. τίθεσκεν Hes. Fr. 96: θησέμεναι Epic inf. fut. for θήσειν, Il. 12, 35, θησέμεν Pind. P. 10, 58. The reg. **1 aor.** ἔθησα is very late, θήσας Malal. 247, 3. 276, 3 &c.: **2 aor.** 3 pl. ἔθεν Epigr. Paus. 5, 23, 7, rather doubtful, but ἀν-έθεν Simon. C. 134 (Bergk 3 ed.); subj. Ionic θέω Sapph. 12, προσ- Her. 1, 108, pl. θέωμεν dissyll. Od. 24, 485, περι- Her. 3, 81, θέωσι 4, 71, and θείω Il. 16, 83, 2 sing. θῇης Il. 16, 96, but θείῃς Hes. Op. 556; Od. 10, 341, θείῃ 301 (Wolf, Dind.), but θήῃς, θήῃ (Bekker 2 edit. La R.), pl. with ω shortened, θείομεν for θείωμεν, θῶμεν, Il. 23, 244. Od. 13, 364; imper. Lacon. σέτω for θέτω, Ar. Lys. 1081; inf. Epic θέμεναι Il. 2, 285, and in Od. θέμεν 21, 3; so Hes. Op. 61; Pind. Ol. 6, 4: ἔθευ Ionic 2 sing. **2 aor. mid.** Her. 7, 209, συν- Pind. P. 11, 41; θείομαι subj. for θῶμαι, ἀπο-θείομαι Il. 18, 409, κατα- 22, 111. Od. 19, 17; opt. σύν-θοιτο, others -θοῖτο for -θεῖτο, Xen. An. 1, 9, 7, πρόθοιτο or -οῖτο Thuc. 8, 85 (best Mss. Popp. Krüg. Stahl), -θεῖτο (Mss. Bekk.), πρόσ-θοιτο (Dem.) 11, 6 (B. Saupp. Dind.), -θεῖτο (Bekk.), πρόσ-θοισθε 21, 188 (B. Saupp. Dind.), -θεῖσθε (Bekk.), Ion. προσ-θέοιτο Her. 1, 53, ὑπο- 7, 237, προ- 3, 148 (Krüg. Abicht), -θεῖτο (Mss. Bekk. Dind. Stein). The radical θέω occurs in comp. 3 pl. pres. προ-θέουσι Il. 1, 291, unless this be from προ-θέω *rush forth.*

Τίκτω *To bring forth, beget* (τέκω), Od. 4, 86; Hes. Op. 235; Emped. 64; Aesch. Eum. 660; Soph. Tr. 94; Ar. Av. 695; Her. 6, 131; Pl. Conv. 206: imp. ἔτικτον Il. 22, 421; Pind. Ol. 6, 85; Aesch. Eum. 321; Soph. O. C. 982; Her. 9, 93; Pl. Conv. 191, ἔτιχθ' ὁ- Eur. H. F. 3, ἄτικτον=ἃ ἔτ- 281, τίκτ- Il. 16, 34; Hes. Th. 346; Pind. P. 3, 101: fut. τέξω Poet. Od. 11, 249 (Mss. Vulg. Kaiser, La R.) but see mid.; H. Merc. 493; Aesch. Pr. 851. 869; Eur. Tr. 742; Ar. Eq. 1037. Thesm. 509; Her. 5, 92 (Orac.); but late prose, Pseud.-Callisth. 1, 12: rather more freq. τέξομαι Il. 19, 99. Od. 11, 249 (Bekk. Dind.); H. Apol. 101; Hes. Th. 469. 898; Pind. P. 9, 59; Aesch. Pr. 768; (Eur.) Fr. Dan. 1117 (D.); Ar. Lys. 744; Her. 7, 49; Hippocr. 7, 538. 8, 322 (Lit.); Xen. Cyr. 7, 5, 23; Ael. V. H. 14, 22, poet. and rare τεκοῦμαι, τεκεῖσθαι H. Ven. 127, so τεξείεσθε late, Arat. 124: **1 aor.** ἔτεξα rare, τέξασα Orph. H. 41, 8; subj. ἐν-τέξῃ Ar. Lys. 553 (Vulg. -τήξῃ Bergk, -στάξῃ Hirsch. Dind. 5 ed.): **2 p.** τέτοκα Hes. Op. 591; Ar. Pax 757; Com. Fr. (Plat.) 2, 637; Her. 1, 112; Hippocr. 8, 126; Xen. Ven. 5, 13; Luc.

D. Deor. 9, 1, ἐκ- Pl. Theaet. 210, but ἐν- pass. Ar. Vesp. 651: p. p. τέτεγμαι perhaps late, -εκται Ael. H. A. 2, 12; τετέχθαι Paus. 3, 7, 7; Heliod. 9, 25, and late τέτογμαι Synes. Epist. 141, but τέτεγμ- (Dind. Herch.), and τέτυγμαι Alcae. 85 (Bergk. Ahr.), τέτογ- (Seidl.) approved by Schneidewin, condemned by Dind.: aor. ἐτέχθην rare (Eur.) Fr. Dan. 1117, 44 (Dind.); Anacreont. 36, 8. 38, 1 (Bergk); Hippocr. 8, 486; Alciphr. 1, 4; Ael. H. A. 10, 26; Plut. Dion 24. Cic. 2; Luc. D. Mort. 13, 1. D. Mer. 2, 1. D. Deor. 10, 1: fut. late τεχθήσομαι Maneth. 4, 459; Geop. 17, 6. 18, 3; Joseph. Ant. 2, 9, 2; V. T. Ps. 21, 32: 2 aor. act. ἔτεκον freq. Il. 1, 352. 20, 225; Pind. Ol. 7, 74; Soph. Tr. 893; Eur. Hipp. 1145; Ar. Eccl. 549; Her. 5, 41; Pl. Leg. 673; Xen. Hell. 4, 4, 19, τέκ- Il. 5, 875; Hes. Th. 53; Theogn. 5; Pind. I. 1, 12; subj. τέκῃ Od. 19, 266; Soph. El. 771; Pl. Rep. 467; τέκοι Il. 13, 826; Soph. O. R. 1250; τεκεῖν Pind. Ol. 2, 93; Ar. Thesm. 741; Her. 6, 131; Pl. Rep. 574, -έειν Il. 24, 608, -έμεν Pind. Ol. 6, 30; τεκών Il. 1, 414; Isae. 3, 15; Pl. Menex. 237. Mid. τίκτομαι as Dep. poet. Aesch. Ch. 127. Fr. 41 (D.): fut. (τέξομαι, see above): 2 fut. τεκοῦμαι, -εῖσθαι rare, H. Ven. 127: 1 aor. ἐτεξάμην, -ασθαι v. r. Hes. Th. 889: usu. 2 aor. Poet. ἐτεκόμην, Dor. -μαν Eur. Tr. 265 (chor.), ἐτέκετο Ar. Av. 1191, τέκετο Il. 4, 59; Hes. Th. 308; Pind. Fr. 11; Soph. Tr. 834 chor. (Lob. Dind.), τεκόμεσθα Od. 23, 61; τέκωμαι, -ηαι Ap. Rh. 1, 905, -ωνται Pind. P. 4, 52; Opp. Hal. 1, 599; opt. τέκοιτο Theocr. 18, 21; τεκόμενος Aesch. Ch. 419; τεκέσθαι Il. 22, 481; Hes. Th. 478.

Od. 11, 249, fut. act. τέξεις seems to have been the reading of Aristarchus, mid. τέξεαι of Zenodotus, which has been adopted by Porson, Bekker, Foesi, and now Dindorf (4 ed.). The mid. is rather the more freq. form in classic authors, decidedly so in late. The rare fut. form τεξείεσθε Aratus 124 (Bekk.) seems to resemble (θερείομαι) θερειόμενος Nic. Ther. 124. Alex. 567. Τέτεγμαι, τέτογμαι, ἐτέχθην rare, and in *classic Attic* rather doubtful. Buttm. doubts the fut. form τεκεῖσθαι H. Ven. 127, and suggests aor. τεκέσθαι.

Τίλλω *To pluck*, Il. 22, 78; Anacr. Fr. 37 (Bergk); Aesch. Pers. 209; Aristot. H. A. 9, 1, 15; -λων Her. 3, 76, Dor. fem. -λοισα Theocr. 2, 54; -λειν, ἀπο- Her. 3, 16: imp. ἔτιλλε Hippocr. 3, 142 (Lit.); Anth. 5, 275; Nic. Damasc. 67, τίλλε Il. 22, 406: fut. τῐλῶ, ἀπο- Com. Fr. (Cratin.) 2, 89: aor. ἔτῑλα, ἐξ- Aristot. H. A. 9, 6, 7; Geop. 2, 22, ἀπ- Luc. Gall. 28; τῖλαι Theocr. 3, 21, ἀπο- Ar. Lys. 578; ἀπο- τίλας Her. 1, 123, reg.: (perf.?): p. p. τέτιλμαι *simple* late, Athen. (Artemidor.) 14, 84; Demetr. Cynosoph. 28, p. 369 (Herch.), ἐκ- Anacr. 21, 11, δια-

Soph. Fr. 588 (D.), παρα- Ar. Ran. 516, ἀπο- Com. Fr. (Anaxil.) 3, 348, περι- Luc. Merc. Cond. 33 : **aor.** ἐτίλθην, τιλθῇ Ar. Nub. 1083; Dioscor. 4, 108, ἐκ- Aristot. H. A. 6, 2, 23. **Mid.** τίλλομαι *to pluck, tear one's own hair*, τιλλέσθην Il. 24, 711, τίλλοντο Od. 10, 567, ἐτίλλ- Hippocr. 5, 420; Luc. Fug. 28; App. Hannib. 18. Lib. 91 : **fut.** τιλοῦμαι, παρα- Com. Fr. (Men.) 4, 178. This verb is poetic, but occas. in Ionic and late Attic prose.

Τιμάω *To value, honour*, Il. 23, 788 ; Solon 13, 11 ; Pind. Ol. 6, 80 ; Aesch. Supp. 116 ; Soph. Ant. 514 ; Her. 2, 29 ; Thuc. 1, 38 ; Pl. Conv. 212, Ion. -έω Her. 5, 67, προ- Heraclit. 13 (Byw.): **imp.** τίμα Il. 15, 612 ; Hes. Th. 532, ἐτίμ- Od. 14, 203 ; Aesch. Ag. 246 ; Her. 7, 107 ; Thuc. 3, 58 ; Isae. 7, 38, Ion. -εον Her. 5, 67 (Dind. Stein, Abicht, -ῶν Bekk. Bred.) : **fut.** τιμήσω Il. 9, 155 ; Aesch. Sept. 1046 ; Thuc. 4, 20 ; Lys. 8, 1, Dor. -ᾱσῶ, 3 pl. -ασεῦντι (Theocr.) Epigr. 15 : **aor.** ἐτίμησα Her. 8, 124 ; Thuc. 1, 74 ; Aeschin. 1, 113, τίμησα Il. 16, 237, 'τίμησα Hes. Th. 399 ; Soph. Ant. 904, Dor. -ᾱσα Pind. N. 6, 41 ; Dor. pt. -ᾱσαις Pind. Ol. 7, 5 ; Epic subj. -ήσομεν Il. 16, 271, reg.: **p.** τετίμηκα Lys. 26, 17 ; Pl. Rep. 548, Dor. -ᾱκα Pind. I. 4, 37 : **plp.** ἐτετιμήκει, ἀπ- Dem. 41, 28 (Schaef. Dind.) : **p. p.** τετίμημαι Il. 12, 310 ; Soph. O. C. 1304 ; Her. 2, 75. 8, 69 ; Thuc. 4, 26, Dor. -ᾱμαι Pind. I. 4, 59 : **plp.** ἐτετίμητο Her. 2, 179, 3 pl. -έατο 6, 124 : **aor.** ἐτιμήθην Her. 7, 213 ; Antiph. 6, 38 ; Thuc. 3, 56 ; Pl. Menex. 242, Dor. -ᾱθην Soph. O. R. 1203 (chor.) : **fut.** τιμηθήσομαι rare in classic authors, Thuc. 6, 80 ; Dem. 19, 223 ; Aristot. Eth. N. 4, 9 ; Plut. Mor. 112 ; Dio Cass. 37, 56. 59, 16, and often : usu. **fut. mid.** τιμήσομαι almost always **pass.** H. Apoll. 307 ; Aesch. Ag. 581 ; Soph. Ant. 210 ; Eur. Fr. 362, 49 (Dind. 5 ed.) ; Thuc. 2, 87 ; Pl. Rep. 426. Hipp. maj. 284 ; Xen. Hier. 9, 9. Cyr. 8, 7, 15 ; Dem. 19, 100 (104 Bekk.), προ- Xen. An. 1, 4, 14, ἀντι- Oec. 9, 11 : **3 fut.** τετιμήσομαι rare, Lys. 31, 24. **Mid.** τιμάομαι *to prize, estimate, lay a punishment &c.* Her. 3, 154 ; Pl. Conv. 175 : **imp.** ἐτιμῶντο Dem. 53, 18 : **fut.** τιμήσομαι Pl. Apol. 37 ; (Xen. Cyr. 8, 7, 15?) see below : **aor.** ἐτιμησάμην Od. 20, 129 ; Theocr. 12, 29 ; Thuc. 3, 40. 6, 10 ; Lys. 19, 48, τιμήσ- Od. 23, 339 ; -ησαίμην Dem. 18, 214 ; -ήσασθαι Il. 22, 235 (Bekk.) ; Pl. Crit. 52 : as **mid. p.** τετίμηται Dem. 53, 1 ; τετιμημένος Dinarch. 1, 1. **Vb.** τιμητέος Xen. Mem. 1, 4, 10. (ῑ.)

In *classic* Greek, **fut. mid.** τιμήσομαι in **act.** sense, seems doubtful, except as a law term. At Xen. Cyr. 8, 7, 15, with the usual reading τίς τιμήσεται δὴ ἄνδρα it is certainly **active**, but with Dindorf's emendation δι' ἄνδρα approved by Bornemann, Jacobitz, Hertlein and Sauppe it is **pass.**: so for τιμήσεσθαι Il. 22, 235 (Vulg.) τιμήσασθαι has, for good reasons, been substituted (Wolf,

Spitzn. Bekk. Dind.); and τιμήσεται Eur. Fr. 362, 49, quoted Lycurg. 161, 27, we think decidedly passive. At Pl. Apol. 37, it seems to have a mid. sense, τιμήσεσθαι τοιούτου τινὸς ἐμαυτῷ *rate my punishment* at some such, *pronounce some such punishment on myself:* but see τιμήσεται Aristid. 42, 524, and τιμήσονται Aene. Tact. 29; for the last however Hercher edits aor. opt. τιμήσαιντο.

Τῑμωρέω *To help, succour,* &c. Eur. Phoen. 935; Her. 7, 157; Hyperid. 2, 17, 22; -ρῶν Eur. Elec. 974; Antiph. 2, β, 2; Thuc. 1, 127; Lys. 13, 51, -έων Her. 7, 155; -ρεῖν Soph. O. R. 107; Eur. Or. 924; Thuc. 3, 92. 4, 15; Lys. 13, 1; Pl. Apol. 28, -έειν Her. 4, 118. 7, 157: imp. ἐτιμώρουν, -ρεον Her. 1, 18: fut. -ήσω Her. 4, 119; Antiph. 5, 87; Thuc. 1, 40; Pl. Apol. 28: aor. ἐτιμώρησα Thuc. 4, 85; Pl. Conv. 179: p. -ηκα Lys. 13, 97: p. p. τετιμώρημαι Thuc. 7, 77; -ῆσθαι Her. 9, 79; -ημένος Lys. 25, 15, as mid. see below: plp. ἐτετιμώρητο Thuc. 6, 60, see mid.: aor. always pass. ἐτιμωρήθην Andoc. 1, 29; -ηθείς Xen. An. 2, 6, 29; Pl. Leg. 867; Plut. Mor. 117; -ηθῆναι Xen. An. 2, 5, 27: fut. τιμωρηθήσεται Lys. 13, 1. 31, 24. 26: **3 fut.** as mid. τετιμωρήσεαι see below. **Mid.** τιμοροῦμαι *to avenge oneself,* Eur. Bacc. 1081; Lys. 6, 3. 10, 30. 11, 6; -ούμενος Soph. El. 349. 399; Com. Fr. (Men.) 4, 177: imp. ἐτιμωρέετο Her. 3, 53. 7, 20, -εῖσθε Lys. 27, 15, -οῦντο Thuc. 1, 132: fut. τιμωρήσομαι Soph. Ph. 1258; Eur. Alc. 733; Ar. Ach. 303. Eccl. 1044; Her. 3, 145. 6, 87. 7, 9; Thuc. 3, 58; Aeschin. 1, 185: aor. -ησάμην Eur. Cycl. 695; Pl. Rep. 377; Lys. 9, 14; Isocr. 9, 32; Aeschin. 1, 112: p. p. as mid. τετιμώρημαι Antiph. 3, β, 8. γ, 10; Xen. Hell. 3, 4, 26; Dem. 58, 63; -ῆσθαι Lys. 9, 17; -ημένος Antiph. 3, β, 8; Lys. 7, 20; Thuc. 3, 67?: plp. ἐτετιμώρητο Plut. Ages. 10, τετιμωρημένος ἦσθα Lys. 7, 20: as mid. **3** fut. τετιμωρήσεαι Her. 9, 78 (Süvern, Bekk. &c.) for p. τετιμώρησαι (Mss. Gaisf.). We doubt the necessity for change, see Aesch. Ag. 866-8; Soph. Phil. 76; Luc. D. Deor. 2, 1; at least Xen. has preferred τετιμωρηκότας ἔσεσθαι Hell. 7, 3, 11; so Lys. 13, 97. **Vb.** τιμωρητέον Her. 7, 168; Isocr. 15, 174, -τέα Thuc. 1, 86.

Τινάσσω *To shake,* mostly Poet. see διατινάσσω.

Τίνῠμαι, see foll.

Τίνω *To pay, expiate,* Il. 18, 407; Solon 13, 31; Aesch. Pr. 112; Soph. O. C. 635; Pl. Theaet. 177, ἐκ- Her. 3, 47; Epic inf. τινέμεν, ἀπο- Il. 3, 459: imp. iter. τίνεσκεν Ap. Rh. 2, 475: fut. τίσω Il. 17, 34; Pind. Ol. 10, 12; Aesch. Ch. 435; Her. 3, 14; Pl. Leg. 905, ἐκ- Thuc. 5, 49, ἀπο- Dem. 40, 56: aor. ἔτῑσα Od. 24, 352; Pind. Ol. 2, 58; Aesch. Ag. 537; Soph. O. R. 810; Pl. Leg. 873, ἀπ- Antiph. 5, 63: p. τέτῑκα Lycophr.

765; Dio. Hal. Ant. 6, 18, ἐκ- Isae. 10, 15; Dinarch. 2, 18; Dem. 21, 89. 40, 52: p. p. τέτισμαι, ἐκ- Pl. Phaedr. 257; Dem. 24, 187: plp. ἐξ-ετέτιστο (Dem.) 47, 65: aor. ἐτίσθην, ἐξ- Dem. 28, 2 (ἀπ- 49, 63.) Mid. τίνομαι *to take payment, avenge, punish,* Theogn. 204; Ar. Thesm. 686 (Bekk. Dind.), Ionic τίνῡμαι Il. 3, 279. 19, 260; opt. τίνοι' Soph. O. C. 994. 996; τίνεσθαι Pind. P. 2, 24; Her. 9, 120 (Wessl. Gaisf. Stein, σίν- Bekk. Dind.), τίνυσθαι Hes. Op. 711; Her. 5, 77 (Bekk. Dind., τίνν- Gaisf.); τινύμενος Od. 24, 326; Eur. Or. 323 (chor.), ἀπο- Theogn. 362 (B.); Her. 6, 101, late τιννύμενος App. Syr. 65. Civ. 2, 110 (v. r. Hes. Op. 804): imp. ἐτίνῡτο App. Samn. 12, but ἐτῑνῠτο, ἀπ- Il. 16, 398: fut. τίσομαι Od. 15, 177; Theogn. 1248; Eur. Hel. 1624; Her. 1, 10; -σεσθαι Il. 3, 366 (Vulg. Spitzn. Dind. -σασθαι Bekk. Ameis, La R.): aor. ἐτῑσάμην Il. 2, 743; Soph. Aj. 181; Eur. I. T. 78; Her. 1, 190, τισ- Od. 9, 479; τίσωμαι Her. 1, 27, Epic τίσεαι, ἀπο- Od. 16, 255; τίσαιτ' Soph. Tr. 809, -αίατο Her. 3, 75, ἐκ- Eur. H. F. 547; τῖσαι Her. 1, 124; -σάμενος 2, 108; -σασθαι Il. 15, 116; Aesch. Ch. 18; Her. 3, 120; rare in Attic prose Xen. Cyr. 1, 6, 11. Vb. τῑτός Il. 24, 213, ἄ-τῑτος 13, 414, ἄ-τῑτος 14, 484, ἀπο-τιστέον Xen. Lac. 9, 5.

In the pres. and imp. ι is long in Epic, short in Attic and Solon's Fr. 13, 31 (Bergk); Pind. P. 2, 24; in Theogn. short and long, ἀντιτῐ́νειν 740, but in arsi τῑ́νονται 204; so Anth. τῑ́νεις 9, 286, but τῑ́νοιτε 7, 657 &c.; in the other tenses it is *always long* with poets of every description. ἐκτίνομεν Eur. Hipp. 626 (Vulg.) with ι long, is a false reading, as is clear from its giving no suitable meaning. Kirchhoff has restored ἐκτείνομεν from the best Mss. but suggests ἐκτήκομεν: Monk *now* reads ἐκτείνομεν: Pierson suggested ἐκπίνομεν, and this Dind. adopted; Seidler ἐτίνυμεν, which, if correct, is we think the only *classic* instance of the act. form. Now however Kirch. 2 ed. and Dind. 5 ed. reject, with Nauck, 625-6 as spurious. τῑ́νυμαι from τίνω, as ἄνυμαι from ἄνω, not τίνν-, the ι is always long. Bekker in Hom. and Her. always writes it with single ν, so Dind. τινύμεναι Eur. Or. 323 (chor.) where alone it occurs in Attic, and apparently with ῐ; Buttm. however τίννυμαι, and in *late* Greek, Bekker. The act. form τίνυμι, -ύω, or τινν- is late and rare, τιννύοντες Plut. Brut. 33 (Bekk), ἐκ- τινύς Diod. Sic. 16, 29, τινῦσα, ἀπο- Pseud.-Callisth. 3, 11.

Τῐταίνω *To stretch, draw* (τείνω), Epic, Il. 2, 390; Opp. Hal. 5, 257: imp. ἐτῐ́ταινον Il. 22, 209; Q. Sm. 3, 332: aor. ἐτίτηνα, τιτήνας Il. 13, 534; Opp. Hal. 2, 324. Mid. τῐταίνομαι *to stretch oneself, exert,* intrans. Il. 22, 23. Od. 2, 149; -ταίνοιτο 21, 259; -ταινόμενος Il. 22, 23: imp. ἐτῐταίνετο trans.—*for oneself,* Il.

5, 97: **aor.** τιτηνάμενος Orph. Arg. 253. **Act.** as **mid.** intrans. τῐταίνετον Il. 23, 403; so Hes. τιταίνοντας Th. 209, but with ῑ, either from arsis, or as a play on the word τῑτάν.

Τιτράω *To bore*, see Dioscor. 5, 77; τιτρῶν, ἀνα- App. Mithr. 25 (τράω obsol.), τίτρημι, -τρησι, κατα- Galen 13, 937 (Kühn); τιτράναι 13, 616; τιτράς 16, 683, δια- D. Cass. 69, 12: **imp.** ἐτίτρη, δι- App. Lib. 122, ἐτίτρων, δι- App. Iber. 77: **fut.** τρήσω late, Lycophr. 655: **aor.** ἔτρησα Hippocr. 7, 46. 8, 148 (Lit.); Polyb. 10, 44; Polyaen. 6, 17; Strab. 16, 4, 18, συν- Pl. Tim. 91; Dem. 37, 38: (**p.** τέτρηκα?): **p. p.** τέτρημαι Emped. 289 (Stein); Ar. Pax 21; Her. 4, 158; Xen. Oec. 7, 40; Aristot. Polit. 6, 5, 7, κατα- Pl. Tim. 70: **plp.** ἐτέτρητο, συν- Pl. Criti. 115: **aor.** late, τρηθῇ, κατα- Galen 13, 938; τρηθείη Geop. 12, 18; τρηθεῖσα Geop. 5, 33; -θῆναι, ἀνα- Athen. 4, 80. **Mid. aor.** τρήσαιο, δια- Galen 4, 708, missed by all Lexicogr. **Vb.** τρητός Aristot. H. An. 3, 7, 5. See τετραίνω. **Perf.** τέτρηκα given by Kühner and Jelf, we have never seen.

Τιτρώσκω *To wound*, rare and Epic τρώω Od. 21, 293; Callim. Dian. 133, τιτρώσκει Hippocr. 3, 218; Xen. Cyr. 5, 4, 5; Pl. Phil. 13; rare in poet. Com. Fr. (Mon.) 393; Mosch. 1, 21: **imp.** ἐτιτρ- Xen. An. 3, 4, 26: **fut.** τρώσω Theogn. 1287; Eur. Cycl. 422; Hippocr. 8, 290; Dio Cass. 47, 44; App. Mithr. 57; Orac. Sib. 4, 106, κατα- Xen. Hell. 2, 4, 15: **aor.** ἔτρωσα Pind. N. 10, 60; Eur. Hipp. 392; Antiph. 3, β, 4; Thuc. 4, 14, τρῶσ- Pind. I. 5, 42; subj. τρώσῃς Il. 23, 341; τρῶσαι Aesch. Fr. 41 (D.): **p.** later, τέτρωκε (Hippocr.) Epist. 9, 312 (Lit.); τετρωκώς Ach. Tat. 2, 22: **plp.** late ἐτετρώκει Philostr. Her. 690: **p. p.** τέτρωμαι Pind. P. 3, 48; Aesch. Ag. 868; Her. 8, 18; Thuc. 4, 57; Pl. Conv. 219: **plp.** ἐτέτρωσο Philostr. Apoll. 73, -ωντο App. Lib. 23: **aor.** ἐτρώθην Eur. An. 616; Hippocr. 3, 238; Xen. Cyr. 4, 1, 4; τρωθῇ Batr. 194; Hippocr. 1, 102 (Erm.): **fut.** τρωθησόμενος Pl. Crit. 51; -σεσθαι Dio Cass. Fr. 111, 49 (Bekk.); Luc. Herm. 28: **3 fut.** τετρώσομαι Luc. Vot. 37: and **mid.** τρώσομαι as pass. or *will get oneself wounded*, Il. 12, 66. **Vb.** τρωτός Il. 21, 568. In some editions of Hippocr. the subj. **1 aor. pass.** occurs redupl. τιτρωθῶσιν 1, 320 (Kühn), but τρωθῶσι (Opsopae. Litt. 5, 698), so ἀποτιτρωθῇ Dioscor. 4, 138.

Τῐτύσκω *To prepare, aim* (a redupl. form of τεύχω, τύχω), Poet. combining the meanings of τεύχω and τυγχάνω, only **pres.** and **imp.** and late in **act.** (unless Ruhnken's conjecture τιτύσκῃ for πινύσκῃ, Simon. 18, 2 (Gaisf.) be correct, and τιτύσκει Antim. Fr. 9 Bergk 3 ed., Schol. Nic. Ther. 472, see **imp.**) τῐτύσκει Arat. 418; τιτύσκων Lycophr. 1403; Opp. Hal. 2, 99: **imp.** τί̆τυσκε Antim. Fr. 9 (Bergk 2 ed). **Mid.** as **act.** τῐτύσκομαι

Anth. 5, 221; τῑτυσκόμενος Il. 3, 80; Theocr. 22, 88: imp. τῑτύσκετο Il. 13, 159. 21, 342; Ap. Rh. 4, 248. Bergk retains πινύσκῃ Simon. 12, Gaisf. τιτύσκῃ (Ruhnken's conject.)

Τίω *To value at, honour* (ῐ, but ῑ before σ), Poet. Il. 9, 238; Aesch. Sept. 77; Eur. Her. 1013; Epic inf. τιέμεν Od. 15, 543: imp. ἔτῑον Il. 15, 439. Od. 22, 370, τῖον Il. 18, 81, τῐ́ον 8, 161; Hes. Sc. 85; Aesch. Sept. 775 (chor.), τῖες Od. 24, 78, τῖε Il. 16, 146, τῖ' 24, 575, iter. τῐ́εσκεν Il. 13, 461, τίεσκον Od. 23, 65; Hes. Sc. 9; Mosch. 4, 9: fut. τίσω Il. 9, 284. Od. 14, 166: aor. ἔτῑσα Il. 1, 412. 16, 274; very rare in Attic προ-τίσας Soph. Ant. 22: p. p. τέτῑμαι, τετῑμένος Il. 20, 426. Od. 13, 28; Hes. Th. 415; Emped. 356: pres. p. τῐ́εται Aesch. Supp. 1037 (chor.): imp. τίετο Il. 10, 33, iter. τῑέσκετο Il. 4, 46, but τῑεσκόμενοι Welcker Syll. Epigr. p. 229, 183. **Mid.** as act. τῖεται rare Hes. Th. 428 (τίεν Schoem.) **Vb.** ἄτῐτος Il. 13, 414. ἄτῑτος 14, 484. Aesch. has pres. pass. τίεται Supp. quoted; but p. part τετιμέναι Ch. 399 (Vulg.) is held by some a false reading for τε τιμαί (Ahr. Franz, τιτῆναι *now* Dind.) written τετιμαι in the Med. Ms. corr. τετιμέναι; Herm. *now* πρότιμα. See Franz in loc. In Epic, ι in pres. and imp. is long in arsi, Il. 5, 467 &c. short in thesi, 4, 257. 9, 378. 13, 176. Od. 20, 132, &c. though sometimes even there long when a long succeeds, Od. 14, 84. 22, 414; short in Attic, Aesch. Ag. 259. 531; Eur. Her. 1013; Ar. Ran. 1266: always long in fut. aor. &c. Meineke may be right in preferring ἐκτίνει to ἐκτίει Com. Fr. 4, 33, but we are not sure what he exactly means by saying in his index "τίειν non Atticum."

Τλάω *To bear* (see ταλάω) pres. rare and late, τλῶσα Tzetz. Hist. 9, 132: imp. ἔτλων Babr. 16, 7 (2 pt. Bergk): 2 aor. ἔτλην, subj. τλῇς, opt. τλαίην, imper. τλῆθι, part. τλάς, τλᾶσα: fut. τλήσοι Babr. 91 (Lewis. 2 pt.): fut. mid. τλήσομαι: p. τέτληκα. **Vb.** τλητός Aesch. Pr. 1065. In Attic prose this verb is rather rare. See ταλάω.

Τμήγω *To cut*, a Poet. collateral form of τέμνω, Euthydem. Athen. 3, 116; Dion. Per. 1043; Maneth. 2, 75, ἀπο- Il. 16, 390: fut. τμήξω Parmen. 90; Orac. Sib. 5, 32, ἀπο- Ap. Rh. 4, 1120: 1 aor. ἔτμηξα Ap. Rh. 2, 481; τμήξειε, ἀπο- Il. 18, 34 (Vulg. Spitzn. Dind.); τμήξας Il. 11, 146 (Spitzn. Dind. La R. πλήξας Bekk.), ἀπο- 10, 364. 11, 468; Hes. Th. 188, Dor. ἔτμαξα, δι- Theocr. 8, 24: 2 aor. ἔτμᾰγον Opp. Hal. 3, 333, δι- Od. 7, 276: 2 aor. pass. ἐτμᾰ́γην, Epic 3 pl. τμάγεν Il. 16, 374, δι-έτμαγεν 7, 302, late ἐτμήγην Anth. 9, 661; Callim. Fr. 300; ἀπο-τμηγείς Ap. Rh. 4, 1052. **Mid.** aor. ἐτμηξάμην trans. Anth. 7, 480; Nic. Alex. 68, ὑπ- Ap. Rh. 4, 328.—Fut. τμήξεις Nic. Ther. 886, has been altered from Mss. to aor. opt. τμήξαις. τμάγεν Epic 3 pl. 2 aor. for ἐτμάγησαν, Il. 16, 374, δι- 16, 354. 7, 302. For τμήξας Il. 11, 146, and ἀπο-τμήξειε 18, 34, Bekker reads πλήξας, and ἀπ-αμήσειε with Aristarch. A form τμήσσω sometimes occurs: *e.g.* in some edit. of Athen. 3, 116 quoted, and Mosch. 2, 81 (Junt.). Schweigh. however, Meineke, Lobeck &c. reject it for τμήγω; and fut. τμήσω, δια- Nonn. Par. 15, 2, which also Lobeck would correct: aor. mid. τμήσαιο Androm. Sen. 89.

Τόζω, see τόσσω.

Τοξεύω *To shoot*, Soph. Ant. 1034; Her. 4, 114; -εύειν Il. 23, 855; Xen. Cyr. 1, 6, 29: imp. ἐτοξ- Pind. I. 2, 3; Her. 8, 128; Thuc. 4, 48; Xen. Hell. 2, 4, 33: aor. ἐτόξευσα Aesch. Supp. 446; Her. 3, 36; Xen. Cyr. 1, 2, 10, reg.: p. p. τετόξευται Aesch. Eum. 676 &c. **Mid.** τοξευόμενος Heliodor. 9, 5; -εύεσθαι Opp. C. 3, 403: τοξεύοντο Hesych.: fut. τοξεύσομαι, δια- Xen. Cyr. 1, 4, 4: and as mid. p. p. τετόξευται, ἀπο- Luc. Prom. 2, missed by Lexicographers.

(Τορέω) *To bore, pierce*, pres. *simple* unused, but ἀντι-τορεῦντα H. Merc. 283: fut. τορήσω, ἀντι-τορήσων H. Merc. 178, irreg. *simple* fut. τετορήσω Ar. Pax 381: 1 aor. ἐτόρησα Opp. Cyn. 3, 321, ἀντ- Il. 5, 337; τορήσας H. Merc. 119; Opp. Cyn. 1, 59, ἀντι- Il. 10, 267: p. p. τετορημένος late, Nonn. 5, 26. 13, 493: 2 aor. ἔτορον Il. 11, 236, redupl. τέτορεν; τετόρῃ; but τορεῖν (Hesych.) Ar. uses τετορήσω in the sense *utter in a piercing tone;* and Hesych. explains τέτορεν, τετρόρῃ by ἔτρωσε, τρώσῃ (*pierced so as*) *to wound*, but inf. τορεῖν by τορῆσαι, τεμεῖν.

Τορνόω *To make round, round off*, (Hesych.) **Mid.** τορνοῦμαι Hesych.: aor. Epic only τορνώσαντο Il. 23, 255; Tryph. 64; Dion. Per. 1170; subj. Epic -ώσεται Od. 5, 249.

(Τόσσω or -ζω) *To hit, find* (as τυχεῖν), occurring only in aor. inf. τόσσαι Pind. Fr. 22 (Bergk 4 ed.); Dor. part. τόσσαις P. 3, 27, ἐπι- 10, 33; and indic. ἐπ-έτοσσε 4, 25.

Τρᾰπέω *To turn, tread grapes*, Epic Od. 7, 125, ἐπι- Il. 10, 421; subj. -έωσι Anan. Athen. 282: imp. ἐτρᾰπεον Hes. Sc. 301.

Τράφω, see τρέφω.

Τρᾱχύνω *To make rough*, Aesch. Sept. 1045; Pl. Tim. 65, Ion. τρηχ- Ap. Rh. 768: imp. τρήχῡνε Nonn. 2, 198: fut. -ῠνῶ: aor. ἐτράχῡνα, -ήχυνα Hippocr. 5, 276: p. τετράχυκε, ἀπο- Dio. Hal. C. Verb. 22: p. p. τετράχυσμαι Aristot. H. A. 4, 9, 20 (Bekk.); Galen 13, 59. 16, 713, ἐκ- Luc. Pisc. 51 (-χυμμ- Dind.), -τράχυνται Aristot. Prob. 11, 22; inf. τετραχύνθαι Pl. Prot. 333; also -τράχῡμαι Plut. Num. 8; *v. r.* Aristot. H. A. 4, 9, 20, and -υμμαι Luc. Pisc. 51 quoted (Dind.); Galen 13, 20; Schol. Ap.

Rh. 3, 276: aor. ἐτραχύνθην, subj. Ion. τρηχυνθῇ Hippocr. 8, 450, τραχ- Aristot. de Color. 1, 5; τραχυνθείς Pl. Tim. 66; Isae. 8, 37, τρηχ- Hippocr. 1, 69 (Erm.) **Mid.** late, aor. τρηχύνατο Paul. Sil. Amb. 217.

Τράω, see τιτράω.

Τρέμω *To tremble*, Aesch. Sept. 419; Soph. O. C. 129; Eur. Ion 1452; Ar. Ach. 493; Hippocr. 7, 276. 8, 354; Xen. Ven. 3, 6 (Vulg. Saupp.); Aristot. Probl. 27, 6, 2; Luc. D. Mer. 9, 3; τρέμειν Pl. Phaed. 81; -μων Soph. O. R. 947; Ar. Lys. 385; Antiph. 2, γ, 8; Pl. Rep. 554; Dem. 18, 263: **imp.** ἔτρεμον Il. 10, 390; Theocr. 27, 51; Pseud.-Callisth. 3, 22, τρέμε Il. 13, 18, τρέμον Od. 11, 527. **Imp.** seems not in use with classic prose writers.

Τρέπω *To turn*, Her. 1, 63 (Bekk., τράπ- Dind. Stein); Thuc. 3, 90, Ion. τράπω, Her. 2, 92 (Bekk. Dind.): imper. τρέπε Il. 8, 399; Soph. Ant. 1107; -πων Aesch. Fr. 321 (D.): **imp.** ἔτρεπον Thuc. 6, 35, ἐπ- Il. 10, 79, iter. τρέπεσκε Her. 4, 128 (Bekk.), τράπ- (Dind. Bred.): **fut.** τρέψω Il. 15, 261; Ar. Eccl. 681; Pl. Parm. 135, so in Ionic, ἀπο- Her. 8, 29, ἀνα- 62, Dor. 3 pl. τρέψοντι, ἐπι- Pind. Ol. 6, 21, τραψῶ, ἐπι- Cret. Inscr. 2555: **aor.** ἔτρεψα Il. 18, 469; Aesch. Sept. 255; Her. 7, 100. 105; Thuc. 5, 72; Xen. An. 1, 8, 24, τρέψε Il. 16, 645, Ion. ἔτραψα, ἐπ- Her. 4, 202 (Vulg. Bekk.), but -έτρεψ- (Gaisf. Dind. Bred. Stein &c. Mss. S P F a b); Dor. pt. τρέψαις Pind. P. 3, 35: **p.** τέτροφα Ar. Nub. 858; Com. Fr. (Anax.) 3, 194, ἀνα- Soph. Tr. 1008; Andoc. 1, 131; Aeschin. 1, 190. 3, 158 (B. Saupp. Franke, -τέτραφα Bekk.), and τέτρăφα Dinarch. 1, 108, ἀνα- 30; τετραφώς 3, 4 (Bekk. B. S. Maetzn. -οφώς v. r.); Dem. 18, 296 (Bekk. B. Saupp. -οφώς Dind.), ἐπι-τετραφ- Polyb. 30, 6, 6: **p. p.** τέτραμμαι Il. 17, 227; Pind. I. 5, 22; Eur. Hipp. 246; Ar. Ach. 207; Her. 7, 16; Pl. Rep. 519, τετράφαται Theogn. 42; τετράφθω Il. 12, 273; -αμμένος Il. 17, 227; Aesch. Sept. 955; Her. 9, 34; Thuc. 5, 9; Isae. 6, 41; τετράφθαι Thuc. 7, 73, see **mid.**: **plp.** ἐτέτραπτο Pl. Crit. 118, τέτραπτο Il. 14, 403, 3 pl. τετράφαθ' for -φατο, -φυτο Il. 10, 189: **1 aor.** ἐτρέφθην Eur. El. 1046; Xen. Hell. 3, 4, 14. 5, 20. An. 5, 4, 23 (Popp. Dind.); τρεφθῇ Theogn. 379; τρεφθῆναι, ἐπι- Antiph. 4, γ, 5. δ, 3; τρεφθείς (Hom.) Epigr. 14, 7, ἐπι- Antiph. 4, β, 4, Epic and Ionic ἐτράφθην, -θῆναι Od. 15, 80 *now* (Wolf, Bekk. Dind. La R.); τραφθείς always Her. 4, 12. 9, 56, ἐπι- 1, 7: **2 aor.** ἐτράπην usu. as **mid.** intrans. Aesch. Pers. 1027; Soph. O. C. 1537; Ar. Eccl. 416; Pl. Lys. 213; Xen. Hell. 5, 1, 12. An. 5, 4, 23 (Vulg.); for Epic subj. τραπείομεν, see τέρπω: fut. late τραπήσομαι Plut. Nic. 21; Paus. 5, 21, 1, ἀνα- Dio Cass. 56, 25, ἐκ- Luc.

Herm. 86: **3 fut.** τετράψομαι Hesych., ἐπι- Pisistr. in Diog. Laert. 1, 2, 6: **2 aor. act.** ἔτρἄπον Poet. Il. 20, 439; Hes. Sc. 456; Pind. P. 9, 43; Theocr. 25, 85, τράπ- Il. 12, 24; Pind. Ol. 10, 15, intrans. ἔτραπ- Hes. Th. 58, τράπ- Il. 16, 657. **Mid.** τρέπομαι *to turn oneself, flee*, Thuc. 1, 20; Pl. Prot. 339. Leg. 680, μετα- Il. 9, 630, Ionic τράπ- Her. 4, 60, also trans. *put to flight*, Xen. An. 6, 3, 5. 5, 26 &c.: **imp.** ἐτρεπ- trans. App. Syr. 42, intrans. Thuc. 7, 71, προ-τρεπ- Il. 5, 700: **fut.** τρέψομαι Eur. Hipp. 1066; Her. 1, 97. 8, 57; Hippocr. 2, 170. 8, 100; Thuc. 5, 111; Xen. An. 3, 5, 13; Lys. 10, 30, trans. Ar. Eq. 276, Ionic? τράψομαι, ἐπι- Her. 3, 155 (Vulg. Gaisf. Bekk. Lhard.), but -τρέψομαι (Dind. Bred. Stein with Mss. S. V.), see below: **1 aor.** ἐτρεψάμην usu. trans. Hym. Cer. 203; Eur. Heracl. 842; Her. 7, 225; Thuc. 6, 98; Xen. Ages. 2, 11; but intrans. τρεψάμενος Od. 1, 422. 18, 305: **2 aor.** ἐτραπόμην perhaps always intrans. or reflex. Il. 16, 594; Archil. 9; Aesch. Ag. 1532; Ar. Ran. 1025; Her. 1, 80. 3, 13; Thuc. 4, 44; Isocr. 14, 46; it seems a mistake to call it **act.** Pl. Euthyd. 303, τραπ- Il. 18, 138; rarely **pass.** ἀν-ετράπετο Pl. Crat. 395; Theocr. 8, 90: and sometimes as **mid.** intrans. **p. p.** τέτραμμαι Il. 12, 273; Ar. Ach. 207; Her. 7, 16; Thuc. 7, 73; Pl. Rep. 533, see **pass.**: **2 aor.** ἐτράπην Soph. Aj. 743. **Vb.** τρεπτός Aristot. Mund. 2, 10, τρεπτέος Pl. Leg. 747, τραπητέον Luc. Rhet. prec. 8. For ἐτρέψατο Her. 7, 105 (Schw. &c.) Gaisf. Bekk. Dind. read ἔτρεψε with Mss. M P K F, and ἀποτετραμμένοι **act.** Polyb. 10, 14, 1 (Vulg.) is now -τετριμμ-.

Her. seems to have used both τρέπω and τράπω, but always ἐτράφθην, and perhaps always τρέψω, ἔτρεψα, τρέψομαι, ἐτρέψατο. ἀπο-τρέψω occurs twice 8, 29. 62, no *v. r.*; the **aor.** ἔτρεψα and compds. twenty-six times with only one *v. r.* ἐπ-έτραψε 4, 202 (Vulg. Bekk.), which however is strongly opposed by -τρεψε (Mss. S P F a b. Gaisf. Dind. Bred.); τρέψομαι thrice without *v. r.*, τράψομαι, ἐπι- once only 3, 155 (Vulg. Bekk. Gaisf.), but τρέψ- (Mss. S V); and ἐτρέψατο once 7, 225, without *v. r.* Usage therefore being so decidedly in favour of the **fut.** and **aor.** forms with ε, ἐπι-τράψονται 3, 155 (Vulg. Bekk. Gaisf. Lhard.) should, perhaps, be altered with Mss. S V to ἐπι-τρέψ-, which we observe has been recommended by Bredow, and actually adopted by Dietsch, Dind. Stein and Abicht. **Iter. imp.** τρέπεσκε Her. 4, 128 (Bekk. τράπ- Dind.) τετράφαται Ion. 3 pl. **p. p.** Theogn. 42; even Pl. Rep. 533. τρέπομαι **mid.** *to turn oneself, flee*, has for **aor.** ἐτραπόμην; τρέπομαι *turn from oneself, put to flight*, has for **aor.** ἐτρεψάμην, which though once or twice reflexive in Hom. is perhaps never so in Attic. A **pres.** τραπέω, τραπέουσι occurs Od. 7, 125, ἐπι- Il. 10, 421, and τροπέω, imp. τρόπεον Il. 18, 224. τρέπω has its full complement of aorists, ἔτρεψα, ἔτραπον: ἐτρεψάμην, ἐτραπόμην: ἐτρέφθην -άφθην, ἐτράπην, and is one of the very few verbs that have both 2 aor. act. and pass. in actual use—so τύπτω &c.

Τρέφω *To make thick, nourish* (θρέφω), Il. 5, 52; Pind. Ol. 1, 112; Aesch. Ag. 880; Soph. Ant. 897; Her. 8, 115; Thuc. 1, 81, Dor. τράφ- Pind. I. 8, 40; Ar. Ach. 787, Dor. 3 pl. τρέφοντι Pind. Ol. 10, 95; opt. 1 pers. τρέφοιν rare Eur. Fr. 895, τρέφοι Aesch. Eum. 946, see below: imp. ἔτρεφον Il. 22, 421; Her. 7, 119; Andoc. 1, 131; Thuc. 3, 52; Isae. 6, 19; Pl. Rep. 414, τρέφ- Il. 1, 414 (Bekk.), Dor. ἔτραφ- Theocr. 3, 16. 9, 23 (Ahr. Mein. &c.): fut. θρέψω Hym. Ven. 257; Pind. Ol. 9, 106; Soph. Ant. 660; Her. 1, 82; Thuc. 2, 46: aor. ἔθρεψα Il. 13, 466; Pind. Fr. 133; Aesch. Ch. 908; Ar. Nub. 986; Isae. 6, 20; Pl. Tim. 23, θρέψ- Il. 2, 548; Hes. Th. 314; Pind. P. 1, 17; Dor. pt. θρέψαις P. 8, 26: p. (τέθρεφε only as *v. r.* Com. Fr. (Crobyl.) 4, 566) τέτροφα intrans. Od. 23, 237, συν- Hippocr. 6, 380 (Mss. Lit. -έτροφε Vulg.), trans. Soph. O. C. 186; Anth. App. Epigr. 111, ἀνα- Luc. Abd. 10, and τέτρᾰφα intrans. Simmias, Tzetz. Chil. 7, 705; trans. Polyb. 12, 25^{h} (Bekk. -οφα Hey, Dind. Hultsch): plp. late ἐτετρόφει trans. Polyb. 5, 74, and ἐτετράφη intrans. Babr. 7, 5 (Lewis 2 pt.): p. p. τέθραμμαι Eur. Heracl. 578; Ar. Eq. 293. Fr. 179 (Dind.); Hippocr. 6, 44; Isocr. 6, 102; Aeschin. 1, 121, τέθραφθε Pl. Leg. 625, but συν-τέτραφθε Xen. Cyr. 6, 4, 14 (Dind. Popp. Schneid. Saupp. τέθραφ- Krüg.); τεθράφθαι Pl. Gorg. 525; Xen. Hell. 2, 3, 24 (Dind. Saupp.), τετράφ- (Schneid.); and *v. r.* Pl. quoted; -αμμένος Aesch. Eum. 665; Thuc. 2, 61; Isae. 9, 29: plp. ἐτέθραπτο App. Lib. 10: 1 aor. ἐθρέφθην Hes. Th. 192; Emped. 139; Eur. Hec. 351, προσ- Aesch. Ag. 735; θρέφ- Hes. Th. 198; θρεφθῆναι Eur. Hec. 600; -φθείς Emped. 65; in Attic prose, only Pl. Polit. 310: oftener 2 aor. ἐτρᾰ́φην Il. 23, 84; Aesch. Sept. 754; Ar. Av. 335; Her. 3, 111; Xen. Cyr. 2, 1, 15; Aeschin. 1, 146; Dem. 40, 2, 'τράφης Soph. Aj. 557, τράφη Il. 3, 201 (Bekk.); Soph. Ant. 984 (chor.), Epic 3 pl. τράφεν Il. 1, 251. Od. 10, 417 (Bekk.); τραφῆναι Eur. Bacc. 295; Ar. Eq. 334; Her. 1, 122; Isocr. 16, 28; Aeschin. 1, 7; τραφείς Pind. Ol. 6, 35; Her. 1, 130; Thuc. 2, 44: fut. τρᾰφήσομαι perhaps late (Dem. ?) 60, 32; Alciphr. 3, 71; Dio. Hal. Ant. 8, 41; Plut. Mor. 315; Dio Cass. 43, 18; Paus. 1, 22, 2. 3, 18, 7; Maneth. 4, 596 &c.: classic, fut. mid. θρέψομαι as pass. Hippocr. 7, 482. 518 (Lit.); Thuc. 7, 49; Xen. An. 6, 5, 20; Pl. Rep. 372. 568; Aristot. de Anim. 3, 12, 3, see mid.:

2 aor. act. Epic ἔτρᾰφον as **pass.** Il. 5, 555. 21, 279 (inf. τραφέμεν 7, 199. 18, 436. Od. 3, 28) Callim. Jov. 55; Opp. Hal. 1, 774 (Orph. Arg. 382 old reading), ἀν- Anth. 5, 157, τράφε Il. 2, 661 (Bekk. La R.); trans. Pind. N. 3, 53, ἔτραφε Opp. Cyn. 2, 176; Hom. only Il. 23, 90 (Wolf, Bekk. Dind. La R.), where however Spitzn. with some Mss. reads ἔτρεφε, so quoted, Aeschin. 1, 149 (Bekk.); and Luc. Paras. 47. **Mid.** τρέφομαι reflex or **pass.** *to nourish oneself, be supported,* see Xen. Hell. 4, 5, 1: so **fut.** θρέψομαι Xen. Cyr. 3, 3, 16; Luc. Somn. 7; Opp. Hal. 1, 637, trans. Pl. Rep. 541 (some Mss. old edit., θρέψωνται Bekk. Schneid. B. O. W.): **aor.** trans. ἐθρεψάμην *nourished for oneself,* Pind. Ol. 6, 46; Aesch. Ch. 928; Eur. H. F. 458; Pl. Leg. 695, θρεψ- Pind. P. 9, 88; θρεψαίμην Soph. O. R. 1143, -ψαιο Od. 19, 368; Theogn. 275; -ψάμενος Lycurg. 85. **Vb.** θρεπτέος Pl. Rep. 403.

Dor. forms, τρέφοντι 3 pl. for -ουσι, Pind. Ol. 10, 95; τράφεν inf. pres. Pind. P. 4, 115; Ar. Ach. 787, for τράφειν which occurs Pind. I. 8, 40, Epic τραφέμεν Hes. Th. 480; part. τράφοισα Pind. P. 2, 44; **1 aor.** part. θρέψαισα Pind. P. 8, 26. **2 aor.** ἔτραφον *trans.* seems exceedingly rare, if not rather doubtful; for though it be coupled with an **aor.** in Pind. N. 3, 53, and Il. 23, 90, it may notwithstanding, perhaps, be an imperfect. Hes. uses **imperf.** ἔτρεφε Fr. 78, apparently in the same sense as **aor.** θρέψεν Fr. 111 (Goettl.) Buttm. maintains that **2 aor. pass.** ἐτράφην is not Homeric, and that the forms ἐτραφέτην, Il. 5, 555 (ἐτράφεμεν as quoted in Aeschin. 1, 149, from Il. 23, 84 ἐτράφημ-), τραφέμεν for -έειν, Il. 7, 199 &c., ἔτραφε Il. 21, 279, are forms of the **2 aor. act.** with intrans. signification. Thiersch, Boeckh &c. suppose an Epic shortening for ἐτραφήτην (ἐτράφημεν), τραφῆναι, ἐτράφη, and thus accent ἐτράφ' not ἔτραφ' Il. 21, 279. The assertion of Buttm. that ἔτραφον became obsolete is rather strong: see late Auth. quoted above. With regard to the laws which regulate the Greek aspirates, he says, "where two successive syllables begin each with an aspirate, one of the aspirates, generally the first, is changed to the tenuis of the same organ; and when by any formation the second disappears, the first is restored. Thus, the root of this verb is θρεφ-, whence τρέφω, and again θρέψω." This law, though general, is limited in several cases, as composition ὀρνιθο-θήρας, λιθω-θῆναι, ἀμφι-φόβηθεν Il. 16, 290 &c.; synaloephe ἔφθιθ' οὗτος (ἔφθιτο) Aesch. Eum. 458; intervention of a consonant ἐθρέφθην, ἐθραύσθην (but τέθραυμαι), ἐθέλχθην &c. &c. Editors however are not always consistent; see above.

Τρέχω *To run,* Il. 23, 520; Simon. Am. 5; Aesch. Eum. 37;

Ar. Av. 79; Her. 7, 57; Hippocr. 6, 496 (Lit.); Pl. Soph. 262, Dor. τράχ- Pind. P. 8, 32: **imp.** ἔτρεχον Ar. Thesm. 510; Xen. An. 1, 5, 2, ἐπ- Il. 23, 504, Dor. ἔτρᾶχ- Theocr. 2, 147: **fut.** θρέξω late, Lycophr. 108, earlier in comp. ἀπο- Com. Fr. (Plat.) 2, 695: and **mid.** only in comp. and only in Comedy, ἀπο-θρέξομαι Ar. Nub. 1005; except Luc. Lex. 3, μετα- Ar. Pax 261, περι- Ran. 193, usu. δρᾰμοῦμαι (from obsol. δρέμω) Alcm. p. 835 (Bergk); Eur. I. T. 1424. Or. 878; Xen. An. 7, 3, 45. Eq. 8, 6, ἐπι- (Dem.) 17, 19, Ionic -έομαι Her. 8, 102, ἐπι- Ap. Rh. 1, 373, περι-δραμεῖται Ar. Vesp. 138, ἐκ- Com. Fr. (Diph.) 4, 384, ἀπο- Xen. An. 7, 6, 5, συν- 7, 6, 6; rare δρᾰμῶ Asclep. or Dioscor. p. 132 (Didot); V. T. Cant. 1, 4, ὑπερ- Com. Fr. (Philetaer.) 3, 292, see below: and δράμομαι, ἀνα- Anth. 9, 575: **aor.** ἔθρεξα rare and poet. Eur. I. A. 1569; θρέξας Epigr. Plut. Aristid. 20, ἐπι- Il. 13, 409, δια- Callim. Pal. 23; θρέξαι, περι- Ar. Thesm. 657, iter. θρέξασκον Il. 18, 599: **p.** δεδράμηκα, ἀνα- Her. 8, 55, κατα- Xen. Hell. 4, 7, 6, ξυν- Hippocr. 3, 538; Pl. Polit. 266, συν- Dem. 17, 9, περι- (Pl.) Clit. 410: **plp.** κατα-δεδραμήκεσαν Thuc. 8, 92 (Bekk. Krüg. Popp.), κατ-εδεδρ- (L. Dind.); Xen. Cyr. 7, 2, 5 (Dind. Saupp.): **p. p.** δεδράμημαι, ἐπι- Xen. Oec. 15, 1: **2 aor.** ἔδρᾰμον Il. 18, 30; Pind. N. 1, 51; Aesch. Ag. 1121; Eur. Hel. 1118; Ar. Vesp. 1204; Anth. 12, 202; Her. 9, 33; Xen. An. 4, 5, 18, ἐπ- Thuc. 4, 32, δραμ- Od. 23, 207, dual δραμάτην Il. 23, 393, παρα- 22, 157; δράμοι Xen. An. 1, 5, 8, παρα- H. Hym. 19, 16; δραμών Batr. 101; Soph. Aj. 731. 1083; Pl. Rep. 327: **2 p.** poet. δέδρομα, ἀνα- Od. 5, 412, ἀμφι- Simon. Am. 7, 89 (Bergk.), ἐπι- Od. 20, 357; Com. Fr. (Hermip.) 2, 410 (Hexam.) **Vb.** περι-θρεκτέον Pl. Theaet. 160; and late δραμητέον Sext. Emp. 346, 22 (B.), ἀνα- Procl. in Tim. 1, 32. See δρομάω. The **fut. mid.** ἀναδράμομαι Anth. 9, 575 quoted, seems analogous to the **fut.** ἔδομαι, φάγομαι &c. **Fut. act.** ὑπερδραμῶ also quoted, is the only instance we know in *classic* Greek: the *simple* δραμοῦμεν occurs late, V. T. Cant. 1, 4; see 2 Reg. 18, 19. The Greeks would seem to have said θεῖν δρόμῳ Thuc. 3, 111; Xen. An. 1, 8, 18; Ar. Av. 205, perhaps never τρέχειν or δραμεῖν δρόμῳ, like the Latin curriculo currere. A present form τρήχω occurs late Nic. Ther. 521, and perhaps 72, where τετρήχοντα is, we think, a false reading for αὔτως τε τρήχοντα, and not a **perf.** with form of **pres.** Otto Schneider, we observe, has lately edited δὲ τρήχ-.

Τρέω *To tremble*, Aesch. Sept. 790 (chor.), τρεῖ Il. 11, 554; imper. τρέε Il. 21, 288; τρέων Aesch. Eum. 426: **imp.** ἔτρεον, ἔτρεις Aesch. Ag. 549, τρεέτην Hes. Sc. 171, τρέον 213: **fut.** (τρέσω): **aor.** ἔτρεσα Il. 11, 745; Xen. An. 1, 9, 6; Luc. D.

Mort. 27, 7, τρέσ- Il. 15, 586, τρέσσ- 17, 603 (Bekk.); Hes. Th. 850, παρ-ετρεσσ- Il. 5, 295; subj. τρέσῃς Eur. Alc. 328. Or. 1104, τρέσητε Aesch. Supp. 729; -σαιμι Aesch. Sept. 397; τρέσας Soph. Ant. 1042; Her. 7, 231; Pl. Phaed. 117, Poet. τρέσσ- Il. 14, 522; Tyrtae. 11, 14 (Bergk); τρέσαι Soph. El. 1240, τρέσσαι Il. 13, 515. **Vb.** ἄ-τρεστος Aesch. Pr. 416. This verb is rare in classic prose. An Epic form τρείω occurs in Opp. Cyn. 1, 417. 4, 117, ὑπο- Tim. Phlias, Plut. Mor. 705: **imp.** iter. τρείεσκον Tzetz. Antehom. 315. τρέω *extended*, says one of *our* Lexicons, from τρέμω!! The extension seems to be centripetal.

Τρίβω *To rub*, Hes. Op. 251; Soph. El. 602; Her. 2, 37; Pl. Phaedr. 117, δια- Od. 20, 341; subj. Dor. 1 pl. τρίβωμες Theocr. 7, 123; τρίβειν Aesch. Ag. 1056; Thuc. 7, 49, Ep. -βέμεναι Il. 20, 496: **imp.** ἔτριβον Com. Fr. (Eup.) 2, 440; Hippocr. 5, 216, δια- Od. 2, 265, συν- Aeschin. 1, 59, iter. τρίβεσκε Ap. Rh. 2, 480: **fut.** τρίψω Soph. Fr. 429 (D); Ar. Plut. 526. Av. 636, ἀπο- Od. 17, 232, δια- Xen. An. 4, 6, 9, Dor. 3 pl. τρίψοντι, κατα- Theocr. 24, 77 (Ahr. Ziegl. Fritz.): **aor.** ἔτριψα Com. Fr. (Plat.) 3, 84; Pl. Phaed. 60 (Bekk.); inf. τρῖψαι Od. 9, 333; Hippocr. 8, 380; τρίψας Ar. Pax 27; Hippocr. 6, 412; Pl. Euthyd. 299, δια- Il. 11, 847: **p.** τέτρῐφα, συν- Com. Fr. (Eubul.) 3, 235, ἐπι- Ar. Lys. 952, δια- Isocr. 4, 141; Pl. Theaet. 143: **p. p.** τέτριμμαι Pl. Phaed. 116, Ion. 3 pl. τετρίφᾰται Her. 2, 93; -ιμμένος Her. ibid.; Ar. Ran. 123: **1 aor.** ἐτρίφθην, App. Syr. 51; τριφθῇ Aristot. Probl. 21, 8, 2, τριφθῶσι, δια- Dio Cass. 47, 38; τριφθείη Hippocr. 5, 206; τριφθῆναι Com. Fr. (Antiph.) 3, 54, δια- Dem. 19, 164; τριφθείς Thuc. 2, 77; Hippocr. 8, 380 (Lit.), δια- Isocr. 4, 14. 5, 84: more freq. **2 aor.** ἐτρῐ́βην Anth. 6, 24; Aristot. Prob. 10, 27; Luc. Paras. 52, ἐπι- Ar. Thesm. 557. Nub. 1407. Eccl. 1068, συν- Pax 71; Andoc. 1, 61; Dem. 18, 194, δι- Her. 7, 120; Thuc. 1, 125. 8, 78, κατα- Xen. Oec. 15, 10; Pl. Leg. 678: **1 fut.** τριφθήσομαι App. Civ. 4, 65; Aristid. 17, 249: **2 fut.** τρῐβήσομαι Plut. Dion 25, ἐκ- Soph. O. R. 428; τριβήσοιντο, κατα- Xen. Hell. 5, 4, 60: **3 fut.** τετρίψομαι Agath. 1, 10, ἐπι- Ar. Pax 246 (Elms. Dind. Bergk, Richter, ἐπιτρίψ- Vulg. Bekk.): and as pass. **fut. mid.** τρίψομαι Thuc. 6, 18. 7, 42, ἐπι- Ar. Pax 246 (Vulg. Bekk.), see preceding, and as act. see below. **Mid.** τρίβομαι *to rub oneself on*, Aesch. Eum. 195; subj. κατα-τρίβηται Pl. Rep. 405: **fut.** τρίψομαι, προσ- *will rub on, inflict*, Antiph. 4, β, 8, ἀπο- Dio Cass. 62, 23, as pass. see above: **aor.** ἐτριψάμην Callim. Pall. L. 25; Galen 6, 370, ἀνα- Hippocr. 6, 634 (Lit.), ἀπο- Aeschin. 1, 120. 179; Dem. 1, 11, προσ- 22, 75. 25, 52: and as mid. **p. p.** τετριμμένος, ἀπο- Polyb. 10, 14, 1 (Scal. Bekk. Dind. Hultsch, -τετραμμ- Vulg.); τετρῖφθαι, προσ- Plut. Sol. 3 (προστετρίφ-?) **Vb.** ἄ-τριπτος Od. 21, 151, late τριπτέον Geop. 17, 5. ῑ, except in perf. and 2 aor. pass. (and pres. late συν-τρῐ̄βειν, in 4 foot, Theod. Prod. 2, 276.)

Τρίζω *To chirp, squeak, mourn* &c. Od. 24, 5; Hippocr. 7, 86 (Lit.); Aristot. H. A. 2, 12, 6: imp. ἔτριζον Pseud-Callisth. 3, 22, κατ- Batr. 85 (Franke, -τρυζον Baum.): fut. (τρίξω): aor. late ἔτριξα Nilus, Octo vit. 6: **2 p.** τέτρῑγα as pres. Epich. 9, 3 (Ahr.); Her. 3, 110; Hippocr. 7, 28: plp. τετρίγει as imp. Il. 23, 714, ἐτετρῑ́γει Babr. 52; Synes. Epist. 4 (Herch.); τετρῑγώς, -υῖα Il. 23, 101; Plut. Mar. 19, -ῑγότες Com. Fr. 2, 469; Arat. 1132; Luc. Tim. 21, Epic -ιγῶτες Il. 2, 314. In the *classic* period, this verb is poetic and Ionic.

Τρομέω *To tremble, dread,* Poet. and *classic* only pres. and imp. Il. 17, 203; Hippocr. 6, 100 (Lit.), Dor. 3 pl. -έοντι Theocr. 2, 12; τρομέων Aesch. Pr. 542 (chor.); -έειν Simon C. 130 (Bergk): imp. ἐτρόμεον H. Apoll. 47; Il. 7, 151 (Vulg. La R.), τρόμ- (Bekk. 2 ed.); Pind. Ol. 13, 60, iter. τρομέεσκον Q. Sm. 3, 180, ὑπο- Il. 20, 28: aor. late ἐτρόμησα 1 Macc. 2, 24. **Mid.** as act. τρομέονται Aesch. Pers. 64 (chor.); opt. 3 pl. Ionic -εοίατο Il. 10, 492; τρομέεσθαι Od. 16, 446; always, we think, uncontr. except part. τρομεύμενος Solon 36, 12 (Bergk): imp. τρομέοντο Il. 10, 10.

Τροπέω *To turn* (τρέπω), Epic and only imp. τρόπεον Il. 18, 224: **Mid.** τροπέοντο, ἐπάτουν (Hesych.) The collat. τρωπάω has in act. only pt. τρωπῶσα Od. 19, 521: mid. τρωπᾶσθε Il. 15, 666; -ᾶσθαι 16, 95: imp. τρωπῶντο Od. 24, 536, iter. syncop. τρωπάσκετο Il. 11, 568, or from a form τρωπάσκομαι, of which Hesych. has imper. τρωπασκέσθω, ἐπιστρεφέσθω.

Τρύζω *To mourn, murmur,* Anth. 5, 292; Opp. C. 3, 125; Hippocr. 8, 358; subj. -ητε Il. 9, 311; -ζειν Hippocr. 2, 134 (Lit.); -ζουσα Arr. An. 1, 25, 6: imp. ἔτρυζεν, κατ- Batr. 88, iter. τρύζεσκεν Theocr. 7, 140: fut. (-ξω): aor. ἔτρυξα Athen. (Sopat.) 14, 74; ἐπι-τρύξας Babr. 112. Lexicons confine this verb to "pres. and imp."

(Τρῡχόω) *To waste, afflict,* fut. in comp. τρῡχώσω, ἐκ- Thuc. 7, 48: aor. *simple* late ἐτρῡ́χωσα Herodn. 3, 2, 8, ἐξ- Thuc. 3, 93: p. p. τετρῡχωμένος Thuc. 4, 60. 7, 28; Pl. Leg. 807: plp. late ἐτετρύχωντο Herodn. 6, 6, 5: aor. τρυχωθῆναι Hippocr. 8, 28 (Lit.); -ωθείς 8, 30: pres. pass. τρῡχοῦται Mimnerm. 2, 12; Maneth. 1, 160 (Axt. Rig.) The pure form τρυχόω seems never to occur in the pres. simple or compd. except in Galen's Lex. Hippocr. τρυχοῦν (Ald.)

Τρύχω *To waste, exhaust,* Od. 16, 125; Soph. O. R. 666 (chor.); Eur. Hel. 1286 (Dind. Herm. Paley); Xen. Hell. 5, 2, 4; subj. τρύχω Theogn. 913, κατα- Od. 15, 309: imp. iter. τρύχεσκεν Ap. Rh. 2, 473: fut. τρύξω Od. 17, 387: p. p. (from τρυχόω) τετρυχωμένος Thuc. 4, 60; Plut. Pomp. 10, ἐκ- Luc. Tox. 30: pres. pass. τρύχομαι Solon 4, 22 (Bergk); Ar. Pax 989; Hippocr. 6, 624 (Lit.); subj. -ώμεθα Od. 10, 177; Theogn. 752 (Bekk. Ziegl.); -όμενος Od. 1, 288; Soph. Aj. 605 (chor.); Thuc. 1, 126; -χεσθαι Soph. Tr. 110 (chor.): imp. ἐτρυχόμην Ar. Ach. 68. For τρύχουσα σαυτήν Eur. Hel. 1286 (Mss. Herm. Dind. Paley &c.), some read τρύχου mid. trans. τρύχου σὺ σαυτήν Musur. (Kirchh. Nauck.) See (τρυχόω.)

Τρύω *To rub, distress,* Orph. Fr. 31, 5, ἀπο- Soph. Tr. 124: fut. τρύσω Aesch. Pr. 27, ἐκ- App. Civ. 4, 108: p. p. τέτρυμαι Simon. C. 144, 3 (Bergk); Anth. 9, 549; τετρῦσθαι Her. 1, 22, κατα- Xen. Cyr. 5, 4, 6; espec. part. τετρυμένος Callim. Epigr. 69; Her. 2, 129. 6, 12; Pl. Leg. 761. Mid. late, aor. τρύσαιο, κατα- Nic. Al. 593. Vb. ἄ-τρυτος Soph. Aj. 788; Her. 9, 52.

Τρώγω *To eat,* Od. 6, 90; Hipponax 35, 5; Solon 38; Com. Fr. (Theop.) 2, 817; Her. 2, 37; Dem. 19, 197, Dor. 3 pl. -γοντι Theocr. 4, 45; -γοίσας 9, 11: imp. ἔτρωγον Ar. Fr. 76 (Dind.); Hierocl. 44 (Eberh.): fut. mid. τρώξομαι Ar. Ach. 806; Xen. Conv. 4, 8, ἐκ- Ar. Vesp. 155, κατα- Com. Fr. (Cratin.) 2, 95, περι- Luc. Gall. 28: 1 aor. perhaps in comp. only, κατ-έτρωξαν Batr. 182; subj. κατα-τρώξῃ Hippocr. 7, 322 (Lit.); -ξαντες Timon. Fr. 7: p. p. τέτρωγμαι, δια- Ar. Vesp. 371, παρεν- Com. Fr. (Eubul.) 3, 212, παρα- Plut. Mor. 665: 2 aor. ἔτρᾰγον Com. Fr. (Pher.) 2, 280; Theophr. H. P. 2, 7, 6, κατ- Ar. Ach. 809, παρ- Ran. 988; Hippocr. 5, 252 (Lit.), ἐν- Com. Fr. (Timocl.) 3, 603; Luc. Conv. 38. Vb. τρωκτός Xen. An. 5, 3, 12.

Τρωπάω, see τροπέω.

Τρωχάω *To run* (τρέχω), Epic and only pres. τρωχῶσι Il. 22, 163; -ῶντα Od. 15, 451 (Schol. Bekk. La R. Düntzer, τροχόωντα Vulg. Ameis, Dind. Baüml.): and imp. τρώχων Od. 6, 318; Ap. Rh. 3, 874. τροχάω seems to be late, unless sound Od. 15, 451 quoted. Had this form been current in Homer's time, we think he would have given for *graphic effect* τροχόων for τρώχων Od. 6, 318.

Τρώω, see τιτρώσκω.

Τυγχᾰ́νω *To hit, obtain, chance,* Theogn. 253; Aesch. Supp. 384; Soph. El. 31; Ar. Ran. 598; Her. 1, 38; Andoc. 2, 26; Thuc. 2, 74; Pl. Prot. 313; -άνειν Antiph. 2, β, 11, Epic -ανέμεν Pind. Ol. 2, 47: imp. ἐτύγχᾰνον Aesch. Ag. 866; Soph. Aj. 748; Her. 1, 29; Antiph. 6, 12; Thuc. 3, 98; Lys. 12,

15, τύγχαν- Od. 14, 231: **fut. mid.** τεύξομαι Soph. Ph. 1090; Eur. Tr. 499; Ar. Eq. 112; Isocr. 15, 32; Xen. Mem. 4, 8, 10; Dem. 37, 60, τεύξει Ar. Nub. 436, Epic and Ion. -ξεαι Od. 19, 314; Hes. Op. 401; Her. 1, 90, -εται &c. Aesch. Ag. 175; Thuc. 6, 13; Lys. 18, 23; Isocr. 15, 309; -ξεσθαι Il. 16, 609; Her. 3, 155; Aeschin. 2, 30; Dem. 37, 60. 51, 11 &c.: **1 aor.** ἐτύχησα Epic Il. 15, 581. 23, 466; Hes. Fr. 45, τύχ- Od. 14, 334; subj. τυχήσω Anth. 5, 278. 294: **p.** τετύχηκα Hom. intrans. Il. 17, 748. Od. 10, 88; Hippocr. 3, 434 (Lit.); Thuc. 1, 32; (Pl.) Eryx. 396; Luc. Jud. V. 4; trans. Xen. Cyr. 4, 1, 2; Isocr. 3, 59; Dem. 18, 128. 19, 39. 27, 175: less freq. τέτευχα trans. Aristot. Part. An. 2, 2, 1; Dem. 21, 150 (Bekk. Dind.); Com. Fr. (Mon.) 44; Macho, Athen. 13, 44; Polyb. 4, 77; D. Sic. 1, 57. 2, 22. 3, 9. 6, 2. 12, 17; Geop. 2, 14 (Bas. but τετυχηκ- Mss. Niclas); τετυχέναι Aesop. 88 (Schaef. but τετυχηκέναι in vocab. so Halm 363); τέτυχε N. T. Hebr. 8, 6 (Sinait. Alex. Tisch. Lachm. τέτευχε Vat. Vulg.); D. Sic. 2, 22. 3, 9. 6, 1, 11. 12, 17, now τέτευχ- (Bekk. L. Dind.), late if correct τέτυχα, -υχυῖαν Joseph. Jud. B. 7, 5, 4: **plp.** ἐτετύχηκειν App. Lib. 79, ἐτετεύχεε Ionic, intrans. Her. 3, 14: **p.p.** late, ἐπιτετευγμένος Polyb. 6, 53: so aor. ἐν-τευχθείς 35, 6: **2 aor. act.** ἔτῠχον Il. 5, 287; Aesch. Pers. 508; Eur. Hel. 180. Tr. 499; Ar. Vesp. 462; Her. 1, 176; Antiph. 1, 16; Thuc. 2, 31; Xen. Cyr. 8, 4, 3; Pl. Phaedr. 232; Lys. 13, 53; Isocr. 12, 265, τύχε Il. 11, 684; Pind. N. 1, 49; subj. τύχω Aesch. Ch. 14; Isocr. 7, 71, Epic τύχωμι Il. 7, 243. Od. 22, 7, τύχῃ Soph. O. C. 482, Epic -ῃσι Il. 11, 116 (late Epic τετύχῃσι Maxim. κατ- 577); τύχοιμι Soph. Ph. 223, τύχοι Antiph. 5, 65; Pl. Conv. 193, τύχοιμεν Pind. I. 4, 43 (61), τύχοιεν Thuc. 5, 56 (late Epic τετύχοιεν Maneth. 3, 299); τυχεῖν Pind. P. 2, 92; Soph. Ant. 465; Antiph. 3, β, 4; τυχών Il. 13, 371; Thuc. 3, 42; -οῦσα Aesch. Eum. 719; Pl. Gorg. 504, Dor. τυχοῖσα Pind. I. 8, 37. **Mid.** late, aor. τεύξασθαι Themist. 13, 161; Apocr. 2 Macc. 15, 7, ἐπι- Theoph. Epist. 49. 78, the only instances we ever met. Dindorf is inclined to read with Harduin, εὔξασθαι for τεύξ- Themist. quoted, on the ground that it is not in use, and unsuited to the sense. The second reason is the stronger, but it does not affect the instance in Maccabees. In the sense *to happen, chance*, this verb has τυγχάνω Soph. O. R. 757: ἐτύγχανον Pl. Conv. 172, τύγχ- Od. 14, 231: τύχησα Od. 14, 334: τετύχηκα Od. 10, 88; elsewhere rare, Thuc. 1, 32; (Pl.) Eryx. 396: **plp.** ἐτετεύχεε Ionic, Her. 3, 14: ἔτῠχον Il. 11, 116; Pind. N. 1, 49; Soph. Aj. 742; Pl. Euthyd. 272; Xen. Mem. 3, 9, 13. **Vb.** τευκτός C. Fr. (Antiph.) 3, 26.

Τύπτω *To strike*, Il. 11, 561; Aesch. Ag. 1128; Ar. Nub. 1331; Her. 2, 70; Antiph. 4, α, 6; Pl. Gorg. 476; Isocr. 3, 4; Aeschin. 1, 183: **imp.** ἔτυπτον Antiph. 4, β, 6; Thuc. 6, 57; Lys. 3, 45. 10, 8; Isocr. 20, 1, τύπτον Il. 21 20: **fut.** τύψω late, Hierocl. 200 (Eberh.); Nonn. D. 44, 160; *v. r.* Q. Sm. 11, 209 (Ms. H.), Attic τυπτήσω Ar. Nub. 1444. Plut. 21; Pl. Gorg. 527. Hipp. Maj. 292; Dem. 21, 204. 221; Artstot. Soph. 5, 13: **aor.** ἔτυψα Il. 13, 529. 21, 180 (Bekk. τύψα Dind. La R.); Theocr. 10, 4; Ap. Rh. 4, 866; Her. 3, 64; rare in Attic, Aesch. Eum. 156 (chor.); late, Prolegom. τῶν στάσ- Rhet. Graec. V. 7, pt. 1, p. 15 (Walz), τύψ- Il. 4, 531. 17, 313; Ap. Rh. 2, 20; Theocr. 22, 88; inf. τύψαι Her. 3, 29; Hippocr. 7, 352, ἀπο- 7, 86 (Lit.); τύψας Her. 4, 70, ὑπο- 6, 119; and late, Athen. 3, 94. 6, 100; see Argum. Dem. 21, 107, and ἐτύπτησα not *classic* Attic, Aristot. Polit. 2, 12, 13 (Bekk.); Philostr. Soph. 555; Hierocl. 86 (Eberh.); Aesop 66 (Halm); Galen. 5, 17: **p.** (τέτυφα Cherobosc. in Theodos. p. 564, 20) τετύπτηκα perhaps late, Pollux 9, 129; Philostr. V. Soph. 588; Sopat. Rhet. p. 381; Argum. Dem. Orat. 21, 24: **p. p.** τέτυμμαι, -ένος Il. 13, 782; Aesch. Sept. 888 (chor.). Eum. 509 (chor.); τετύφθαι Her. 3, 64, and late τετύπτημαι Luc. Demon. 16; Ach. Tat. 5, 26; Argum. to Dem. 21 (26); -τῆσθαι 54 (3): **1 aor.** late, ἐτυπτήθην Sopat. Rhet. p. 38; Philo Leg. Spec. 2, 799, and ἐτύφθην Paroem. Zenob. Cent. 2, 68; τυφθῇ Geop. 18, 17; τυφθείς Plut. Galb. 26 (Ms. A. Bekk. Sint.); Orac. Sib. 11, 20. 101; Anth. 9, 140 (Lemm); τυφθῆναι Hierocl. 138 (Eberh.): **2 aor.** ἐτύπην poet. Il. 24, 421; Theocr. 4, 53; τυπείης Il. 13, 288; τυπείς Il. 15, 495; Pind. N. 1, 53; Aesch. Pr. 361; Soph. O. R. 811; Eur. Andr. 1150; Ar. Ach. 1194; late prose, Alciphr. 3, 57; Luc. Calumn. 14: as **pass. fut. mid.** τυπτήσομαι Ar. Nub. 1379 (Ms. Bekk. Bergk): for which **fut. p.** τυπήσομαι (Buttm. Dind. Mein.): **2 aor. act.** ἔτυπον rare, Eur. Ion 767; τυπεῖν Ach. Tat. 7, 15 (Vulg. but τύπτειν Jacobs, Herch.); part. redupl. τετύποντες Callim. Dian. 61: **pres. p.** τύπτομαι Ar. Eq. 257. 266. 730. Nub. 494, -τεται Com. Fr. 3, 235; -τόμενος Eur. Cycl. 645; Ar. Nub. 972. Pax 743; Antiph. 4, β, 2; Xen. Hell. 4, 2, 12. 4, 3; -τεσθαι Ar. N. 1341; Xen. Athen. 1, 10; Aeschin. 1, 139; Dem. 21, 72: **imp.** ἐτυπτόμην rare, Ar. Plut. 1015. **Mid.** τύπτομαι *to strike oneself, bewail*, Her. 2, 61. 132; Plut. Alex. 3; Luc. D. Syr. 6, κατ- Sapph. 62: **imp.** ἐτύπτετο Luc. D. Mer. 9, 2, -τοντο App. Lib. 91 (Ms. A, Mendels.): (**fut.** τυπτήσομαι **pass.** see above): **aor.** ἐτυψάμην *simple* late, (Luc.) Asin. 14, ὑπ- Nic. Alex. 163; ἀποτύψωνται *ceased beating themselves, mourning*, Her. 2, 40; Luc. D. Syr. 6; ἀνα-τυψάμενος Joseph. Ant. 17, 6, 7. **Vb.** τυπτητέος Dem. 54, 44.

For the **aorists** ἔτυψα, ἔτυπον the Attics used ἐπάταξα, ἔπαισα: τύπτει τὸν φρύνικον καὶ καταβάλλει πατάξας Lys. 13, 71. The **pres.** seems to have had three forms, τύπω, -πτω, -πτέω, and each with only partial development, at least in *written classic* speech. **1 fut.** τύψω we have not seen earlier than Hierocles and Nonnus, but there it stands without a *v. r.*; the **aor.** ἔτυψα however of the same formation, is both early and frequent. Buttmann seems inclined to doubt τυπτήσομαι Ar. quoted, on what grounds we see not, and Dindorf follows him, and reads **2 fut. p.** τυπήσομαι instead. τύπτω is one of the very few verbs that have **2 aor. act.** and **pass.** in actual use. **1 perf.** τέτυφα, **2 p.** τέτυπα, **1 fut. p.** τυφθήσομαι, and, unless correct Ar. quoted, τυπήσομαι we have never seen except in grammars.

Τῠραννέω *To be sovereign, to rule*, Soph. O. R. 408; Eur. Med. 967; Ar. Thesm. 338; Thuc. 1, 13; Xen. Cyr. 1, 1, 1; Isocr. 16, 38; Pl. Leg. 693; Dem. 9, 62, and -ννεύω always Her. 1. 15. 59 &c.; Soph. O. C. 449; Eur. Hel. 786; Xen. Hell. 4, 4, 6; Pl. Men. 76; Isocr. 2, 4. Epist. 7, 3: **imp.** ἐτυράννουν Ar. Av. 483; Thuc. 2, 30; Dem. 17, 7, and -ννευον Ar. Fr. 324 (D.); Her. 1, 23. 73: **fut.** -ήσω perhaps late, App. Civ. 2, 139; Plut. Mor. 403; Luc. Gall. 22 (Jacob. Dind.), but -εύσω Eur. Elec. 877; Ar. Lys. 632: **aor.** -ησα rather rare, Eur. H. F. 29; Xen. Hell. 2, 2, 24; Dem. 17, 7, freq. -ευσα Solon 33, 6 (B.); always Her. 1, 163. 7, 155; Thuc. 6, 55. 59 &c.; and Pl. Rep. 576. 579. Gorg. 473 &c.; Isocr. 9, 39: **p.** -ηκα late, Polyb. 2, 59, but -ευκα Isocr. 8, 113: **p. p.** τετυράννηται late, Greg. Naz. Orat. de Filio, -νευμαι?: **aor.** -ήθην late, Dio. Hal. Ant. 4, 82; Strabo 8, 6, 25; Epist. Phal. 2, but -εύθην Thuc. 1, 18; Pl. Rep. 574; Plut. Mor. 240: **fut.** perhaps late -νηθήσομαι (Dem. 20, 161 Vulg.); Sopat. Rhet. p. 335: and as **pass. fut. mid.** τυραννήσομαι Dem. 20, 161 quoted (Mss. S. ω &c. Bekk. B. Saupp. Dind.) **Vb.** τυραννητέον (Solon) Diog. Laert. 1, 2, 17. Desider. τυραννησείω, and -νιάω (Solon) Diog. Laert. 1, 2, 18. 3, 1, 14, and -αννίζω Dem. 17, 7.

Τύφω *To raise smoke, smoke, burn*, Her. 4, 196; -τύφῃ Dem. 37, 36; imper. τῦφε Ar. Vesp. 457: **imp.** ἔτῡφον Soph. Ant. 1009: **fut.** (θύψω): **aor.** θῦψαι Suid. Hesych.: **p.** τέθῡφα if correct, Com. Fr. (Crob.) 4, 566 (Mein.): **p. p.** τέθυμμαι, -ένος Aesch. Supp. 186, ἐπι- Pl. Phaedr. 230: **2 aor.** ἐτῠ́φην, ἐπι-τῠφῇ Ar. Lys. 221. 222: **fut.** τῠφήσομαι, ἐκ- Com. Fr. (Men.) 4, 220: **pres.** τύφεσθαι Aristot. Meteor. 2, 5, 6. The simple form very rare in Attic prose.

Τωθάζω *To taunt*, Her. 2. 60; Dor. part. -άζοισαι Theocr. 16, 9: **imp.** ἐτώθ- Dio Cass. Fr. 39, 7 (Bekk. Dind.): **fut. mid.** τωθᾰ́-

σομαι Pl. Hipp. Maj. 290: aor. ἐτώθᾰσα late, Jul. Imp. p. 159, ἐπ- (Hippocr.) Epist. 9, 356 (Lit.); App. Civ. 2, 153; but subj. τωθάσω Ar. Vesp. 1362; inf. τωθάσαι Aristot. Rhet. 2, 4, 13, ἐπι- App. Civ. 2, 153; but -άξαντες Tzetz. Epist. 38, p. 32.

Υ.

Ὑβρίζω *To abuse, insult,* Od. 18, 381; Soph. El. 790; Ar. Ach. 1117; Antiph. 4, δ, 2; Xen. Cyr. 5, 2, 28; Isae. 6, 48; Dor. -ίσδω Theocr. 14, 9; imper. ὕβριζε Aesch. Pr. 82; -ίζων Il. 11, 695; Pind. P. 4, 284; Aesch. Supp. 879; Thuc. 8, 45: imp. ὕβριζον Aesch. Fr. 178; Eur. Tr. 1020; Ar. Nub. 1506; Lys. 14, 26; Isocr. 8, 99: fut. ὑβρῐσω, -ίσει Soph. Aj. 560 (Br. but aor. -ίσῃ Elms. Herm. Dind. &c.), ἐν-υβρίσεις Ar. Thesm. 719 (Mss. Bekk.), ἐν-υβριεῖς (Reisig, Dobr. Herm. Dind. &c.), ὑβριεῖν Dem. 21, 221, but later ἐξ-υβρῐσειν App. Mithr. 79 (Bekk. -ιεῖν Mendels.): and mid. ὑβριεῖται as act. Ar. Eccl. 666; pass. Polemon Declam. 2, 2 (Hinck): aor. ὕβρῐσα Soph. El. 613; Eur. An. 995; Her. 6, 87; Pl. Conv. 222; Dem. 21, 18; -ίσας Thuc. 4, 18; Isocr. 20, 4: p. ὕβρῐκα Ar. Lys. 400; Dem. 21, 128: plp. ὑβρίκειν 3, 14: p. p. ὕβρισμαι Eur. Cycl. 665; Ar. Thesm. 903; Thuc. 6, 57; Xen. Cyr. 2, 4, 5; Dem. 21, 7, περι- Her. 1, 114. 5, 74: plp. ὑβρίσμην Dem. 54, 28, ὕβριστο Poet in Plut. Mor. 993: aor. ὑβρίσθην Soph. Aj. 367; Isae. 12, 12; Pl. Leg. 885: fut. ὑβρισθήσομαι Dem. 21, 222. Vb. ὑβριστος Com. Fr. (Pher.) 2, 347, -τέος Dem. 54, 44. Futures mid. in -ιοῦμαι are rarely passive. Among these Krüger ranks ὑβριεῖται, we doubt if rightly. See ἀνασκολοπίζω, ὁμαλίζω, ὀνειδίζω.

Ὑγῐαίνω *To be in,* or *recover health,* Theogn. 255; Her. 3, 33; Pl. Gorg. 495; subj. -αίνω Her. 1, 153; -αίνων Thuc. 2, 58: fut. ὑγιᾰνῶ Hippocr. 6, 662 (Lit.); Xen. Mem. 2, 2, 10 (Schn. Dind. Saupp.); Aristot. Metaph. 6, 7, 7. Eth. N. 3, 4, 9 (Bekk.): aor. ὑγίᾱνα Aristot. Interp. 3, 3; Dem. 54, 1, Ionic -ίηνα Hippocr. 5, 86. 7, 508 (Lit.): aor. pass. ὑγιάνθην Hippocr. 5, 174. 6, 8 &c., but ὑγιάσθην Hippocr. 5, 678. 6, 8 (Lit.); Aristot. Rhet. 2, 19: and fut. -ασθήσομαι Dio. Hal. 9, 53; Galen 9, 741, are from ὑγιάζω (Aristot. Prob. 1, 2) which is not used by the earlier Attic writers. Vb. ὑγιαντόν Aristot. Nat. Ausc. 5, 1, 2. At Xen. Mem. 2, 2, 10, Schneider altered, perhaps unnecessarily, the received reading ὑγιαίνῃς to fut. ὑγιανεῖς. The *ratio* of the sentence seems analogous to 2, 4, 2. An. 4, 6, 10. Ages. 7, 7 &c. This verb is trans. *make whole,* Dicaearch. descript. Pelii, p. 30 (Huds.); and perhaps Hippocr. from his using the passive voice ἐξ-υγιαίνονται 6, 6, ὑγιάνθην 5, 174. 6, 8. 8, 410 (Lit.) Imper. ὑγίαινε like χαῖρε, *vale*, is used as a form of salutation verbal or written, usually on taking leave, *farewell*, Ar. Eccl. 477. Ran. 165; Luc. Laps. 8.

Ὑλάσκω *To bark*, late -άσσω, only pres. ὑλάσκοι Aesch. Supp. 877 (-κων Weil, so Dind. 5 ed.); ὑλάσσων Charit. 6, 4 (Herch.): and **aor.** late ὕλαξε Dio Cass. 63, 28; ὑλάξῃ Dio Chrys. 9, 290. (ῠ.)

Ὑλάω *To howl, bark at*, Epic and only **pres.** ὑλάει Od. 20, 15; Opp. Cyn. 4, 219, -άουσι Od. 16, 9; Opp. Cyn. 3, 281; -άων Anth. 6, 175, -άοντες Theocr. 25, 70; ὑλάειν Opp. Cyn. 1, 449 (Vulg.), -άαν perhaps wrongly (Ms. A. Schneid.): and **imp.** ὕλᾰον Od. 16, 5. **Mid. imp.** ὑλάοντο Od. 16, 162. With ῠ ᾰ, and always *open*, which throws a doubt on Schneider's reading ὑλάαν for -άειν. ὑλακτέω also is mostly in **pres.** and **imp.** only, but not confined to poetry, Od. 20, 13; Soph. El. 299; Eur. Alc. 760; Ar. Vesp. 904; Theocr. 8, 27; Xen. Ven. 3, 5. 10, 7; Isocr. 1, 29; Plut. Mor. 734; Luc. Pisc. 36: **imp.** ὕλάκτεον Il. 18, 586, ὕλάκτει Ar. Vesp. 1402; Polyb. 16, 24; Pseudo-Callisth. 2, 33: **aor.** ὑλάκτησα Luc. Nec. 10. (ῠ, ῡ by augm.)

(**Ὑπανιάω**) *To annoy*, Poet. and only **opt. pres. pass.** ὑπάνιῷντο Ar. Nub. 1195.

Ὑπεικάθω *To yield*, Poet. ὑποεικ- (a lengthened form for ὑπείκω), **opt.** -άθοιμι Soph. El. 361; Pl. Apol. 32; Ar. An. 7, 3, 2; ὑπεικαθέων Opp. Hal. 5, 500: **imp.** ὑποείκᾰθε Epic, Orph. Arg. 709. All these parts are assigned by some to the **2 aor.**

Ὑπείκω *To yield*, Soph. Ant. 713; Hippocr. 1, 632; Thuc. 1, 127. 3, 39; Pl. Tim. 62, Epic ὑποείκ- Il. 20, 266: **imp.** ὑπεῖκον Pl. Tim. 56; Xen. Ages. 11, 10, ὑπόεικ- Il. 16, 305; Ap. Rh. 2, 1266: **fut.** ὑπείξω Aesch. Ag. 1362; Soph. O. R. 625; Her. 7, 160; Dem. 15, 24; Ap. Rh. 2, 23, ὑποείξ- Il. 15, 211. 4, 62, if not aor. subj.: and **mid.** as act. ὑπείξομαι Il. 1, 294. Od. 12, 117; Opp. Hal. 3, 331, ὑποείξ- Il. 23, 602: **1 aor.** ὑπεῖξα Hippocr. 1, 632; Xen. An. 7, 7, 31; Pl. Tim. 56 (Steph.), ὑπόειξα Il. 15, 227; Epic subj. ὑποείξομεν Il. 4, 62 quoted: **2 aor.** ὑπείκᾰθον according to some, see ὑπεικάθω. **Mid. aor.** ὑπείξωμαι Ap. Rh. 4, 408 (Vulg.) has been altered to ὑπείξω μή (Gerh. Well. Merk.) **Vb.** ὑπεικτέον Pl. Crit. 51.

Ὑπεμνήμῡκε *Is bent down*, Il. 22, 491, **perf. act.** of ὑπημύω (Coluth. 331), thus -ημύω, -ήμῡκα, redupl. -εμήμυκα, strengthened for the metre -εμνήμυκα (Vulg. Wolf, Bekk. Dind. &c.), -εμμήμυκα (Toup. Heyn. Bothe.)

(**Ὑπερηνορέω**) *To excel in manliness, be overweening, overbearing,* only pt. -ορέων Il. 13, 258, usu. pl. -έοντες Il. 4, 176. Od. 2, 266. 4, 766; Ar. Pax 53.

Ὑπισχνέομαι *To hold oneself under, to promise* (a strengthened form of ὑπέχομαι), Thuc. 1, 129; Andoc. 1, 136; Pl. Phaedr. 235. Gorg. 449; Isocr. 13, 4; imper. -ισχνοῦ Ar. Vesp. 750, see below; -ισχνούμενος Thuc. 3, 73; Xen. Cyr. 2, 2, 12, Ionic -ισχνεύμενος Her. 2, 152. 8, 106 &c.: **imp.** ὑπισχνεῖτο Thuc. 1, 132; Isocr. 5, 63; Dem. 19, 47, Ionic -χνέετο Her. 9, 109, -χνοῦντο Xen. Hell. 2, 3, 13, Poet. and Ionic ὑπίσχομαι only **pres.** Il. 23, 209. Od. 8, 347; Aesch. Eum. 804; Ar. Fr. 516; Her. 7, 104. 158. 5, 30: and **imp.** ὑπίσχεο Il. 20, 84 (Bekk. La R.), ὑπίσχοντο Her. 7, 168: **fut.** ὑποσχήσομαι Dem. 19, 324: **p.** ὑπέσχημαι Xen. Oec. 3, 1; -εσχῆσθαι Thuc. 8, 48; -ημένος Dem. 23, 18 (later **pass.** ὑπεσχημένα App. Civ. 2, 102. 4, 99. 5, 129, προϋπεσχ- 3, 74): **plp.** ὑπέσχητο **act.** Dem. 23, 167; Dio Cass. Fr. 102 (Bekk.): **1 aor.** ὑπεσχέθην, -σχέθητι Pl. Phaedr. 235? see below: **2 aor. mid.** ὑπεσχόμην Solon 36, 15; Dem. 19, 178, -έσχεο Il. 15, 374. -έσχετο Il. 13, 366; Soph. O. C. 1490; Eur. An. 969; Her. 1, 208. 5, 107. 9, 6; Antiph. 6, 16; Thuc. 6, 46; Xen. Cyr. 3, 1, 31; Lys. 12, 14; Pl. Euth. 278; subj. -σχωμαι Il. 22, 114,- σχηται 10, 39; Ar. Thesm. 344; -σχόμενος Ar. Plut. 865; Thuc. 2, 101.

With the Poets the **pres.** ὑπισχνοῦμαι is rare, imper. ὑπισχνοῦ Ar. Vesp. 750, quoted says the Schol. from Eur. Fr. Hipp. 19 (Wagn.): with this exception, they use **2 aor.** only. Her. has both forms, ὑπίσχομαι, ὑπισχνέομ-, the former more freq. but ὑπισχνεύμενος 2, 152. 3, 74. 5, 51, -εόμ- 8, 106, ὑπισχνέετο 9, 109, in the best Mss. and in all edit. we have seen. The **1 aor. pass.** ὑποσχέθητι is so rare that the instance quoted above is perhaps the only one in classic Attic; and though it has Ms. authority, its rarity as well as other reasons have rendered it suspicious. Bekker accordingly has displaced it by the kindred noun ὑποσχέσει offered by some good Mss. This **aor.** however certainly occurs later in other combinations, ἐπεσχέθην Callisth. Stob. 7, 65, κατα- (Eur.) Fr. Dan. 1117, 27 (Dind.); Arr. An. 5, 2, 7 (Krüg.), also the *simple* ἐσχέθην 5, 7, 4, σχεθῆναι 6, 11, 2. An **act. pres.** form ὑπισχνῶν occurs late, Aesop 205 (Halm.) Hom. has κατ-ίσχω, and once κατ-ισχάνω. It would seem that ἴσχομαι is exclusively Poet. and Ionic only in combination with ὑπό: προσ-ίσχομαι Ar. Plut. 1096; Plut. Mor. 699, προϊσχόμενος Thuc. 3, 58. 66. 4, 87, ἐπισχ- Pl. Conv. 216, ἀμπίσχομαι Eur. Hel. 422, ἀμπίσχοιο Pl. Alc. (1), 113. The Tragedians seem not to use the **mid.** form except with ὑπ-, and ἀμπ-.

Ὑπνόω (*To cause to sleep*), *to sleep*, Aristot. De Somno 1, 3. Fr.

12; Luc. Ocyp. 107; Dor. inf. ὑπνῶν Ar. Lys. 143: fut. ὑπνώσω late, Orac. Sib. 7, 45; Geop. 18, 14; (Nic. Ther. 127 Vulg.): aor. ὕπνωσα Hippocr. 3, 64. 134; Plut. Alex. 76, κατ- Her. 7, 12; -ώσῃ Eur. Cycl. 454 (Mss. Dind. 2 ed., -ώσσῃ Herm. Paley, Dind. 5 ed. &c.); inf. -ῶσαι Hippocr. 8, 416; Polyb. 3, 81; Luc. V. H. 1, 29, κατ- Her. 4, 8; -ώσας Anth. 7, 305, Dor. -ώσαις Callim. Epigr. 73: p. -ωκέναι Plut. Mor. 236: p. p. ὑπνωμένος *asleep*, Her. 1, 11. 3, 69: pres. ὑπνοῦται Plut. Mor. 383. **Mid.** intrans. fut. ὑπνωσομένη Joseph. Ant. 5, 9, 3, missed by all Lexicogr. We have not found the act. in the trans. sense *cause to sleep*; see however Dioscor. 4, 64. The Epic form is ὑπνώω Anth. 11, 25; Opp. C. 3, 51; Coluth. 349; -ώοντας Il. 24, 344. Od. 5, 48; Mosch. 2, 24; Op. Hal. 2, 657: imp. iter. ὑπνώεσκον Q. Sm. 8, 503, ὑπνώεσκεν 10, 191. ὑπνώσσω, -ώττω is Attic, and confined to pres. -σσεις Aesch. Eum. 121. 124, -σσει Sept. 287; Eur. Or. 173; Hippocr. 6, 634. 7, 56 (Lit.); -σσῃ 8, 436; -σσειν 2, 462; -σσοντες Aristot. Pt. An. 2, 7, 14, -ττοντα Pl. Rep. 534. ὑπνάω we have never seen in any Greek writer; nor does ὑπνέω seem to exist, for part. ὑπνοῦντα Aesop 346 (Halm), and -νοῦντες V. T. 1 Reg. 26, 12, belong to ὑπνόω, and the verbal ὑπνητικός in some edit. of Athen. 1, 31, is -νωτικός in Theophr. H. P. 9, 18, 11, from whom it is quoted.

Ὑπογλαύσσω *To glance stealthily*, Poetic and only pt. -σσων Callim. Dian. 54: and iter. imp. ὑπ-εγλαύσσεσκε Mosch. 2, 86. The comp. with δια- has only 3 pl. δια-γλαύσσουσι Ap. Rh. 1, 1281. γλαύσσω *simple*, not in use, but Hesych. has γλαύσσει, λάμπει.

Ὑποκορίζομαι *To speak coaxingly, gloss* &c. Pl. Rep. 400, Ion. ὑποκουρ- Pind. P. 3, 19: imp. ὑπ-εκορίζετο Ar. Plut. 1010: aor. -ίσαιτο Aristid. 39, 493; -ισάμενος Charit. 3, 7, missed or denied by Lexicogr.

Ὑποκρίνομαι *To answer*, Il. 7, 407; Theocr. 9, 6. 24, 67 (Ar. Ach. 401; Xen. Mem. 1, 3, 1; Thuc. 7, 44, some edit.); Aristot. Rhet. Alex. 37, 40; in Attic, usu. *to play a part, act* &c. Dem. 18, 15: imp. ὑπ-εκριν- *answered* Her. 3, 31; *acted* Aristot. Rhet. 3, 1, 3: fut. -νοῦμαι Luc. Salt. 66, Ionic -έομαι Her. 1, 164: aor. ὑπ-εκρῑνάμην Her. 1, 2. 78. 91; Dem. 19, 246; -κρῖναιτο Od. 15, 170; -κριναι 19, 535; -κρίνασθαι 19. 555; Her. 9, 16; Arr. An. 7, 1, 5. 2, 3. 26, 3 (Sint. ἀποκριν- Ell. Krüg.): as mid. p. p. ὑποκέκρῖται Dem. 19, 246: and aor. ὑπεκρῖθην Ctes. Pers. 29, 41 (Müll.); and late App. Syr. 24. Civ. 4, 46; Polyb. 5, 25. (ῑ in pres. and aor. mid.)

Ὑπ-οπτεύω *To suspect*, reg. except that in Her. Mss. and editors divide on the augm. Dind. and Stein always -ώπτευον 3, 44. 70; 6, 129; -ώπτευσα 3, 68, Bekker and Bredow always

-όπτευον, -όπτευσα, so Krüg. and Abicht except -ώπτευον 6, 129: with aor. mid. -ευσάμενος D. Sic. 4, 31, missed by Lexicogr. The *simple* verb is very rare but not "obsolete," ὀπτεύω Ar. Av. 1061 without *v. r.*

Ὑποτέμνω, see τέμνω.

Ὑποτοπέω *To surmise, suspect* (as ὑποπτεύω), rare in act. imp. ὑπετόπει Dio Cass. 57, 3. 6: **aor.** -πήσας Thuc. 1, 20. 2, 13; -πῆσαι 3, 24: **p.** -τετόπηκε Dio Cass. 38, 42. **Mid.** dep. ὑποτοποῦμαι, subj. -τοπῆται Ar. Thesm. 496; -τοπεῖσθαι Ran. 958: **imp.** ὑπετοπούμην Lys. 9, 4: with **aor. pass.** ὑποτοπηθέντες trans. Her. 6, 70. 9, 116; Dio. Hal. 1, 81.

Ὑστερέω *To be later, too late, lose,* Pl. Gorg. 447: **fut.** -ήσω late, V. T. Ps. 22, 1 &c.; Synes. Epist. 141: **mid.** ὑστερήσομαι Eur. I. A. 1203 (Vulg. Dind. Kirchh. 1 ed., ἐστερήσ- Reisk. Pors. Nauck, Kirchh. 2 ed., Dind. 5 ed., στερήσ- Herm.): **aor.** ὑστέρησα Her. 1, 70; Thuc. 1, 134; Xen. An. 1, 7, 12; -ήσῃς Eur. Phoen. 976; -ήσειε Xen. Hell. 3, 5, 25; -ήσας Thuc. 7, 29: **p.** ὑστέρηκα Dio. Sic. 15, 47; N. T. Hebr. 4, 1: but **plp.** ὑστερήκει Thuc. 3, 31: **aor.** ὑστερήθην late, N. T. 2 Cor. 11, 8; Joseph. 15, 6, 7. The **fut. mid.** has been suspected by several able scholars. Reiske and Porson conjectured ἐστερήσομαι, Herm. ἧς στερήσομαι, Matthiae defends the reading of the Mss., but Dind. and Kirchh. have now dropt it. We doubt Hermann's grounds of preference, see Eur. use of ἀμπλακίσκω Alc. 418. 824 &c.

Ὑφαίνω *To weave* (ὑφάω), Od. 15, 517; Pind. Fr. 160; Ar. Eccl. 556; Her. 2, 35; Pl. Lys. 208, late -ανάω, -όωντας Maneth. 6, 433: **imp.** ὕφαινον Il. 6, 187. Od. 4, 678; Hes. Sc. 28; Theocr. 7, 8; Pl. Critias 116, iter. -νεσκον Od. 19, 149: **fut.** ὑφᾰνῶ Ar. Eccl. 654: **aor.** ὕφηνα Eur. I. T. 817. Ion 1417; Ar. Lys. 630, later -ᾱνα Batr. 186; Anth. 6, 265; subj. -ήνω Od. 13, 303; inf. -ῆναι Ar. Lys. 586; Pl. Hipp. Min. 368; Aristot. H. An. 5, 19, 11; -ήνας Od. 4, 739; Eur. I. T. 814; Com. Fr. (Anon.) 4, 701, ἐξ- Her. 2, 122: **p.** ὕφαγκα late, συν- Dio. Hal. C. Verb. 18, ἐξ- Artemid. 4, 40, ὕφαγκα (Ms. V.): **p. p.** ὕφασμαι Com. Fr. (Antiph.) 3, 52; Luc. V. H. 1, 18; Stob. (Phintys) 74, 61, ἐν- Her. 3, 47; Aristot. Mirab. 96, παρ- Xen. Cyr. 5, 4, 48: **aor.** ὑφάνθην Pl. Tim. 72, ἐν- Her. 1, 203, συν- 5, 105. **Mid.** ὑφαίνομαι trans. Soph. Fr. 604 (D.): **aor.** ὑφηνάμην Anth. 6, 287; -ηνάμενος Xen. Mem. 3, 11, 6; Pl. Phaed. 87; -ήνασθαι Xen. Mem. 3, 11, 7, late ὑφᾱνάμ-, ἐξ- Themist. 21, 250. **Vb.** ὑφαντός Od. 13, 136; Thuc. 2, 97. ῠ, occas. ῡ in augm. tenses, but never, we think, in Hom. ῡ̔φᾱνα Batr. 186, ῡ̔φ- Anth. (Nossis), 6, 265, ἐξῡ́φ- Batr. 182. Such forms as ὑφήφανται, ὑφύφασμαι seem to occur in the old Grammarians only, B. A. 20, 3. Suid. Etym. Mag.

Ὑφάω *To weave*, Epic and only 3 pl. ὑφόωσι for ὑφῶσι contr. from ὑφάουσι, Od. 7, 105.

Ὕω *To rain* (ῡ), Hes. Op. 552; Alcae. 34, 1 (Bergk); Ar. Nub. 368; Her. 4, 28; Xen. Hell. 1, 1, 16: **imp.** ὗον Il. 12, 25; Her. 4, 151: **fut.** ὕσω Com. Fr. (Cratin.) 2, 92; Ar. Nub. 1118. 1129; late prose Ael. H. A. 7, 8 (Schn. ὕειν Herch.); Aristid. 48, 338: **aor.** ὗσα Pind. Ol. 7, 50; Her. 2, 22; Aristot. H. An. 1, 1, 22. Soph. El. 5, 8; and later Attic prose, Theophr. C. P. 4, 14, 3; Luc. Hes. 7: **p. p.** ὕσμαι, ἐφ-υσμένος Xen. Ven. 9, 5: **aor.** ὕσθην Her. 3, 10; late Attic, Theophr. H. P. 8, 11, 4; Plut. Rom. 24; Strab. Fr. 655, p. 439 (Kram.): **fut.** ὑσθήσεται late, Themist. Paraphr. 2, 8 (Spengel): and **fut. mid.** ὕσεται **pass.** Her. 2, 14: **pres.** ὕεται Her. 4, 50; ὑόμενος Od. 6, 131; Aristot. Meteor. 2, 4, 5.

Φ.

(**Φάγω**), see ἐσθίω.

Φαέθω *To shine*, Poet. and only part. φᾰέθων Il. 11, 735; Hes. Th. 760; Soph. El. 824 (chor.); Eur. El. 464 (chor.); Epigr. D. Laert. 8, 78 (fem. φᾰέθουσα *sister of the sun*, Od. 12, 132).

Φαείνω, see foll.

Φαίνω *To show* (φάω), Od. 20, 114; Aesch. Ch. 326; Soph. El. 24; Xen. Cyr. 6, 4, 13; φαίνειν Her. 3, 75, Ep. -νέμεν Od. 8, 237; Pind. P. 4, 171; -νων Il. 2, 353; Her. 3, 36, Dor. fem. -νοισα Pind. N. 5, 17 (and sometimes in **pres. imp.** and **fut.** intrans. *to shine*, Pl. Tim. 39; Theocr. 2, 11; Ar. Nub. 586), Poet. φᾰείνω **pres.** only, and intrans. Hes. Th. 372; trans. late, Nic. Ther. 390; subj. intrans. φᾰείνω Od. 12, 383: **imp.** ἔφαινον Od. 19, 25; Hes. Th. 677; Soph. El. 1359; Her. 1, 116; Xen. Hell. 6, 5, 10, φαῖν- Od. 18, 67; Hes. Th. 689, iter. φαίνεσκε in παμφαίν- Eratosth. 1, 37: **fut.** φᾰνῶ Aesch. Ch. 815; Soph. O. R. 710. Aj. 1362; Eur. I. T. 898; Ar. Ach. 914; Pl. Leg. 745, ἐκ- Il. 19, 104 (φᾰνῶ see below), Ion. φανέω, ἀπο- Hippocr. 7, 542. 8, 408 (Lit.); Epic ἀμ-φανέειν H. Merc. 16: **aor.** ἔφηνα Il. 2, 318; Soph. Ph. 297; Her. 2, 49; Xen. Hell. 3, 2, 23; Isocr. 17, 42, Dor. -ᾶνα Pind. I. 4, 2, δι- Theocr. 18, 26, and late prose ἐξ- Ael. V. H. 12, 33, ἐπι- N. T. Luc. 1, 79; φήνωσι Od. 15, 26; -νειε 12, 334; φήνας Ar. Ach. 542; Xen. Hell. 5, 1, 36; Isocr. 18, 20; φῆναι Od. 3, 173; Her. 1, 95; Antiph. 4, δ, 11, ἀνα- intrans. if sound, Her. 1, 165 (Gaisf. Bekk. Dind. -φανῆναι Reiske, Stein, Abicht, -πεφηνέναι Krüg.), Dor. φᾶναι, ἐκ- Plut. Mor. 214: **p.** πέφαγκα Pseud.-Callisth. 2, 10? ἀπο- Dinarch. 1, 15. 54. 59 &c. 2, 17. 19. 3, 18: **p. p.** πέφασμαι **pass.** and **mid.** Soph. O. C. 1543, (-ανσαι), -ανται Il. 2, 122; Pind. N. 6, 14;

Aesch. Ag. 374; Eur. Med. 769; Pl. Soph. 231, for which πέφαται Stob. (Perict.) 85, 19; πεφασμένος Solon 13, 71; Soph. O. C. 1122; Pl. Phaedr. 245, ἀπο- Dinarch. 1, 89; πεφάνθαι Pl. Euthyd. 294: plp. ἐπέφαντο Hes. Sc. 166: aor. ἐφάνθην (ἐφαάνθ- see below) pass. and mid. Aesch. Pers. 263; Soph. O. R. 525. Ant. 103, φάνθ- Eur. H. F. 804 (chor.); rare in prose, Hippocr. 8, 50; Xen. Hell. 6, 4, 11; (Dem.) 58, 13, ἀπο- Lys. 19, 41, 44; Dem. 5, 9. (Epist. 3, p. 1485), Epic φαάνθην in tmesi Il. 17, 650, 3 pl. φάανθεν 1, 200; Mosch. 2, 33, ἐξ-εφαάνθην Il. 4, 468. 13, 278; Hes. Th. 200: fut. πεφήσεται Epic, Il. 17, 155: 2 aor. ἐφᾰνην as mid. Il. 15, 275; Aesch. Eum. 320; Soph. Aj. 739; Ar. Eq. 790; Her. 3, 82; Antiph. 5, 27; Thuc. 5, 68; Xen. Lac. 1, 1; Pl. Phaed. 76; Lys. 19, 45; Isae. 5, 14, φάν- Pind. Ol. 1, 74. 9, 96, Ep. 3 pl. φάνεν Od. 18, 68; Pind. Ol. 10, 85; φᾰνῶ Anth. App. Epigr. 236; Antiph. 2, δ, 8; Isocr. 9, 48, φανῇ Il. 9, 707; Her. 3, 27, Ep. -ήῃ Il. 19, 375, -είῃ Hes. Op. 680 (Goettl. Schoem.) -ῶμεν Dem. 1, 15; opt. -είην Il. 20, 64. Od. 13, 402; Soph. Aj. 170; Her. 3, 82; Isocr. 5, 35, -είημεν Dem. 14, 2, -εῖμεν Aesch. Pers. 786; Isocr. 8, 89, -είητε (Dem.) 51, 9, -είησαν Xen. Hell. 6, 5, 42, -εῖεν Isocr. 12, 99; φάνηθι Il. 18, 198; -ῆναι Od. 18, 160; Aesch. Ch. 143; Her. 6, 135; Thuc. 1, 91; Dem. 19, 116, -ήμεναι Il. 9, 240; φανείς Od. 9, 230; Her. 3, 27: fut. φανήσομαι Aesch. Fr. 315 (D.); Soph. Tr. 666. O. R. 457. O. C. 662 &c.; Eur. Hipp. 479. Supp. 605. Hel. 1001 &c.; Ar. Vesp. 528. Thesm. 1 &c.; Com. Fr. (Alex.) 3, 453; Her. 4, 97. 8, 108 &c.; Thuc. 4, 27; Pl. Rep. 351; Lys. 7, 27. 13, 79; Isocr. 3, 45. 5, 70. 6, 93 &c.; Aeschin. 1, 3; Dem. 2, 13. 5, 10. 7, 35 &c., ἀνα- Antiph. 1, 13; Xen. Hell. 3, 5, 11: 2 aor. act. ἔφᾰνον seems not to occur at least in classic Greek, except in the Epic iter. form φάνεσκε intrans. *showed*, *appeared*, Il. 11, 64. Od. 11, 587; Hes. Fr. 44, 3, assigned however by some to a shortened 2 aor. pass.: 2 p. πέφηνα intrans. Aesch. Pr. 111; Eur. I. A. 973; Soph. O. C. 329. El. 646; rare in prose, Her. 9, 120; Dem. 3, 22. 19, 294; late, Aristid. 46, 148, ἀνα- Her. 2, 15; Xen. Cyr. 3, 2, 16. Hell. 3, 5, 12, Dor. 3 pl. πεφάναντι, ἐκ- Sophr. 75 (Ahr.): plp. ἐπεφήνεις Dio Cass. 46, 10 (Bekk.) **Mid.** φαίνομαι *show oneself*, *appear*, Od. 7, 201; Her. 8, 142; Antiph. 5, 22; Thuc. 3, 88, ἀπο-φαίν- trans. Her. 5, 45; Xen. Mem. 4, 4, 9 &c., Epic φᾰείνομαι Callim. Apol. 9; Ap. Rh. 4, 1362: imp. ἐφαίνεο Theogn. 455, ἐφαίνετο Her. 7, 173. 8, 10; Antiph. 5, 24. 77; Thuc. 2, 21, προυφ- Od. 9, 143, trans. ἀπ- Her. 9, 5, iter. φαινέσκετο Od. 13, 194: fut. φᾰνοῦμαι Od. 12, 230; Aesch. Supp. 54; Soph. Ant. 1195; Eur. Med. 302. 600. Hipp. 332 &c.; Ar. Av. 765. Plut. 923; Antiph. 2, β, 4; Thuc.

1, 22. 3, 56; Pl. Apol. 33; Isocr. 9, 65. 12, 237; Lycurg. 78; Aeschin. 1, 4; Dem. 20, 46. 21, 41 &c., Ionic -έομαι Her. 3, 35, but -εύμεθα (Hippocr.) Epist. 9, 424: **aor.** ἐφηνάμην trans. *showed*, rare and Poet., Soph. Ph. 944, but ἀπ- Her. 7, 52; Xen. Oec. 2, 5; Pl. Leg. 776; Dem. 33, 20, Dor. ἀν-εφᾶν- Pind. I. 4, 71, ἀπ- N. 6, 25: **2 aor.** (ἐφανόμην), subj. dual φανῆσθον Pl. Eryx. 399 (Mss. φαίνησθον Bekk. B. O. W.); but imper. Dor. φάνευ Stob. (Teles) 108, 83, see below: in a **mid.** sense intrans. are used also πέφασμαι, ἐφάνην (and ἐφάνθην Traged. -αάνθ- Hom.), φανήσομαι, πέφηνα. **Vb.** ἄ-φαντος Il. 6, 60. The Attic poets have, each, **fut. mid.** -οῦμαι more freq. than **fut. pass.** -ήσομαι; united, double the times. In the Attic Historians also, -οῦμαι is quite the prevailing form; indeed we know only two instances of -ήσομαι, Thuc. and Xen. quoted: but in Her. and the Orators -ήσομαι exceeds -οῦμαι by 5 to 1. In Isocr. and Dem. the disproportion is very great; in the former 40 to 5, in the latter 58 or 60 to 16. Over all, then, in classic prose -ήσομαι is far the more frequent. This will serve to limit properly Buttmann's statement "the **fut. mid.** is the more common, the **fut. pass.** more frequent in verse." On both points he is wrong.

The **2 aor. act.** and **mid.** have been entirely or almost banished from classic Greek, since for ἔφᾰνε Eur. H. F. 794, with **pass.** signif. ἐφάνη has been substituted; for subj. μὴ φᾰνῃς Com. Fr. (Philem.) 4, 53, which Lobeck calls a *neoteric* form of the **1 aor.**, Meineke suggests μὴ 'κφήνῃς; is not μὴ φήνῃς easier? 'κφᾰνῃς also, Mon. 418, admits, *if necessary*, of the same emendation; φάνεν δέ ἑ *and showed herself*, Q. Sm. 9, 484, has been altered by Lobeck to φάνεσκε, and by Koechly to φάνη δ'; Lehrs however retains the old reading, &c. &c.; opt. φανοίην Soph. Aj. 313, belongs to **fut.** φᾰνῶ; and φανοίμην opt. **2 aor. mid.** which used to stand Xen. Cyr. 3, 1, 34, and retained by Poppo, has been altered for the *v. r.* φαινοίμην by Bornem. Dind. Saupp. &c., in which Poppo would probably now acquiesce; φανοίμεθα formerly Isocr. 18, 30, now φαινοίμ-; but Dor. φᾰνευ still, Stob. (Teles) 108, 83. In Attic prose, the **1 aor. pass.** ἐφάνθην seems to be strictly **pass.**, *was shown*, *made known*, Dem. 5, 9 &c.; in Hom. however perhaps always, and occasionally in the Traged. it takes the **mid.** or intrans. meaning, *appear*, which **2 aor.** ἐφάνην uniformly has, Il. 1, 200; Soph. Ant. 103. At Archimed. Aren. p. 331, occurs the Dor. **fut.** φανήσειν, which Lobeck (Buttm. Gramm. V. 2, p. 311), thinks corrupted from φανήσομαι. Epic forms: ἐφαάνθην for ἐφάνθ- Ap. Rh. 2, 449, in tmesi Il. 17, 650, ἐξ- Hes. Th. 200, φάανθεν 3 pl. for ἐφάνθησαν, Il. 1, 200: so φᾰνεν **2 aor. pass.** for ἐφᾰνησαν, Od. 18, 68; subj. φανήῃ for φανῇ

Il. 22, 73; inf. φανήμεναι for φανῆναι, 9, 240. **Fut.** φανῶ, contrary to its usual quantity, has ᾰ Ar. Eq. 300 (Bekk. Dind. 2 ed.), so ἀναφᾰνῶ Eur. Bac. 527 (Dind.), for which however Herm. Kirchh. Nauck read **pres.** ἀναφαίνω, and Aristoph. admits of the same emendation—and Burges, Bergk, Meineke, Dind. 5 ed. adopt it; an easy emendation certainly, if the anomaly cannot be satisfactorily explained, and this seems difficult to do. Some say it is from φαείνω, fut. φαένω contr. φανῶ? This is at least intelligible; but Aristophanes' own usage rather inclines us to the change. He uses ἀποφᾰνῶ Nub. 1331, but shirks ἀποφᾱνῶ 1334, and escapes on ἀποδείξω—unless, which some may think more probable, he here selects the latter as a stronger term. See Lys. 13, 51. Isae. 5, 35.

Φαντάζομαι *To appear*, Her. 7, 15; Aesch. Ag. 1500; Eur. Ion 1444; Pl. Rep. 572: **imp.** ἐφαντ- Her. 4, 124: **fut.** -ασθήσομαι Pl. Conv. 211: **aor.** ἐφαντάσθην (Hippocr.) Epist. 9, 338; Dio Cass. 65, 8; -τασθείη Aristot. Nat. Ausc. 1, 9, 3; -θέντα Pl. Phil. 38. This is the classic usage; but late, **act.** φαντάζω *make appear*, Callisth. 13 &c. and **mid.** trans. φαντάζεται Longin. 15, 8: with **aor. pass.** ἐφαντάσθη as **mid.** Longin. 15, 4. **Vb.** φανταστός Aristot. Memor. 1, 9.

Φάσκω *To say, affirm* (φημί), indic. rare φάσκεις Philostr. Apoll. 315, φάσκει Isae. 6, 16; Aristot. Rhet. Alex. 9, 3; Babr. 22, 14 (Lach.) 18, 31 (Lewis 2 pt.), φάσκομεν if correct, Com. Fr. (Alex.) 3, 450, κατα- Theon Rhet. vol. 2, p. 90 (Spengel), φάσκουσι Aristid. 45, 39; (Aeschin.) Epist. 11, 11; Plut. Anton. 86. Mor. 856. 1124; Luc. Pisc. 37. Herm. 38; Athen. 10, 34; Tzetz. Antehom. 144. 148. Hom. 251 (*v. r.* Pl. Phaed. 113, Steph.); subj. φάσκω Aesch. Ch. 93; Ar. Vesp. 561, -κῃ Ar. Ran. 1007; Hippocr. 7, 172; Antiph. 3, δ, 3; Dem. 40, 30. 48, 55, -κωσι Lys. 1, 36; Isae. 10, 11; opt. φάσκοιμι Soph. Aj. 1037, -κοι Dem. 30, 27, -κοιεν Lys. 7, 12 &c.; φάσκε Eur. Hel. 1077; Aristot. Rhet. Alex. 8, 14; φάσκειν Soph. O. R. 462; Ar. Ran. 695; Antiph. 5, 51; Lys. 1, 36; Isocr. 8, 1; φάσκων Soph. El. 319; Ar. Nub. 895; Antiph. 2, γ, 8; Thuc. 3, 70; Isocr. 18, 7; Pl. Theaet. 169, -κουσα Ar. Ran. 1082; Pl. Theaet. 190: **imp.** ἔφασκον Il. 13, 100; Ar. Nub. 55, -κες Il. 19, 297; Soph. O. R. 842; Ar. Vesp. 602. Ran. 742, -κε Od. 13, 173; Aesch. Ch. 276; Ar. Eccl. 410; Her. 2, 33; Pl. Leg. 901; Dem. 34, 16, Poet. φάσκε Od. 24, 75; Hes. Th. 209; Mosch. 2, 12, 'φασκ' Com. Fr. (Cratin.) 2, 166, pl. rare ἐφάσκετε Od. 22, 35; Lys. 8, 5. 14, ἔφασκον Soph. Tr. 425; Ar. Eccl. 194. Lys. 703; Dem. 59, 72: **imp. pass.** ἐφάσκετο Soph. Ph. 114. Hom. has **imp.** only. The **pres.** *indic.* is rare; φάσκουσι Pl. Phaed. 113

(Steph.) has been altered to λέγουσι (Mss. Heind. Bekk. B. O. W.); but the instances quoted above from other writers prove that it was a mistake in Elmsley to say "presens non est in usu."

Φᾰτίζω *To say, name* (φάτις), Poet. and Ion. prose, Stob. (Dius) 65, 17: **fut.** (-ίσω), Dor. -ίξω Parmen. 119: **aor.** ἐφᾰτισα Her. 5, 58; -ίσαιμι Soph. Aj. 715 (-ίξαιμι Mss.); -ίσας Eur. I. A. 135: **p. p.** πεφάτισμαι Ap. Rh. 4, 658; Parmen. 94: **aor.** ἐφατίσθην, -τισθεῖσα Eur. I. A. 936: **pres.** φατίζεται Ap. Rh. 1, 24. For φατίζω Stob. quoted, Meineke reads φατίξω.

Φάω *To shine*, Epic, **pres.** late, subj. φάησι, προ- Maxim. Auspic. 280; opt. φάοι 22; part. φᾰουσι Arat. 607: **imp.** φᾰε as **aor.** Od. 14, 502: **p. p.** πέφᾰται Stob. (Perict.) 85, 19: **3 fut.** πεφήσομαι Il. 17, 155, see φαίνω. To be distinguished from

(**Φάω**) *To kill*, (see φένω), and (φάω) stem of φημί *to say*.

Φέβομαι *To fear for oneself, flee*, defect. Dep. only **pres.** and **imp.** (a poetic collat. form of φοβέομαι), subj. φέβωμαι Il. 11, 404, -ώμεθα 5, 232; Q. Sm. 1, 419; φέβεσθαι Il. 8, 107; Ap. Rh. 4, 22; Opp. Hal. 2, 82: **imp.** ἐφέβοντο Il. 15, 345. Od. 22, 299 (Bekk.), φέβ- Il. 5, 527. 8, 342. 11, 121. 178 &c. (Bekk.); Ap. Rh. 2, 1056.

Φείδομαι *To spare*, Dep. mid. Anacr. 101; Eur. H. F. 1146; Ar. Ach. 319; Lys. 21, 16; imper. φείδου Soph. Aj. 115; Ar. Av. 987, Ion. -δεο Od. 22, 54; Her. 8, 68, -δευ Theocr. 8, 63; -δόμενος Il. 5, 202; Her. 9, 39; Thuc. 3, 74: **imp.** ἐφειδόμην Theogn. 915; Xen. Ages. 7, 1, φειδ- Soph. El. 716 (Trim.): **fut.** φείσομαι Ar. Ach. 312; Xen. Hell. 7, 1, 24; Pl. Apol. 31, Epic πεφῐδήσομαι Il. 15, 215: **aor.** ἐφεισάμην Solon 32; Aesch. Sept. 412; Andoc. 2, 11; Pl. Menex. 242, φεισ- Il. 24, 236; Pind. I. 6, 33; subj. φείσῃ Soph. Ph. 749; Lys. 30, 27; -σαιτο Pl. Phil. 16; -σασθαι Pind. N. 9, 20; Thuc. 3, 59; -σάμενος Ar. Plut. 556: **p. p.** πεφεισμένος **pass.** *spared, spare*, Luc. Hist. 59; **act.** Dio Cass. 50, 20 (Bekk.); Aristid. 47, 325 (Jebb, but adv. πεφεισμένως Dind. see Hippocr. 5, 464 Lit.); πεφεῖσθαι Luc. Salt. 76, late Epic πεφῐδημένος Nonn. 11, 417. 12, 392. 17, 369: **2 aor. mid.** redupl. (πεφῐδόμην) Epic, opt. πεφιδοίμην Od. 9, 277, -οιτο Il. 20, 464; -έσθαι 21, 101. **Vb.** φειστέον Isocr. 14, 15. A collat. form φειδέομαι, part. -εύμενοι occurs late, Stob. (Euseb.) 10, 33 (Mein.), but "**fut.** φειδήσομαι" given in our Lexicons, we have never seen except in Phot. and Suid. p. 1454. φίδοντο Anth. 15, 25, some think a false reading for φείδ-.

(**Φένω, Φάω**) *To kill*, neither in use, but whence (late **aor.** φάσαι Schol. Pind. N. 1, 70) **p. p.** πέφᾰται Epic, Il. 17, 164. Od. 22, 54, 3 pl. πέφανται Il. 5, 531; inf. πεφάσθαι Il. 13, 447; πεφασμένος Lycophr. 269. 1374; Opp. Hal. 5, 122: **3 fut.** πεφήσομαι, -ήσεαι

Od. 22, 217, -ήσεται Il. 15, 140: **2 aor.** ἔπεφνον Il. 21, 55, πέφν- 13, 363; subj. πέφνῃ Il. 20, 172; inf. πεφνέμεν 6, 180; πέφνοντα accented as a pres. Aristarch. Spitzn. Dind. &c., but Bekker, La R. with Tyrann. &c. πεφνόντα Il. 16, 827, so καταπέφνων 17, 539 (Spitzn. Dind.) -πεφνών (Bekk.), see πέφνω. **Pres.** φάω, φῶ, seems never, and **aor.** φάσαι scarcely, used even by late writers unless *etymologically*. See Schol. Il. 1, 190, Apollon. Lex. Hom.

Φέρβω *To feed*, chiefly Poet. Hom. H. 30, 2; Pind. Ol. 2, 73; φέρβε Callim. Cer. 138; φέρβειν Eur. Hipp. 75, Epic, -βέμεν Hes. Op. 377: **imp.** ἔφερβον Eur. Or. 869; Opp. Hal. 1, 271; Pl. Criti. 115, the only instance in classic Attic prose; later, App. Syr. 62; Philostr. Apoll. 3, 20, 111, φέρβον Theocr. 7, 80: **2 p.** (πέφορβα): **plp.** ἐπεφόρβει H. Merc. 105. **Mid.** φέρβομαι *to feed oneself, maintain, live on*, Pind. P. 5, 110; Hippocr. 5, 314 (Lit.); Opp. Hal. 1, 64, ἀπο- Eur. Med. 827: **pass.** φέρβομαι *to be fed, live*, Hom. H. 30, 4; Ap. Rh. 2, 393; (Hippocr.) Epist. 9, 366 (Lit.): **imp.** ἐφερβόμην Soph. Ph. 957.

Φέρω *To bear, bring* (οἴω, ἐνέκω, ἐνέγκω), Il. 21, 458; Pind. N. 9, 34; Aesch. Ch. 659; Soph. O. C. 420; Ar. Ran. 28; Her. 1, 155; Antiph. 3, δ, 8; Thuc. 6, 16; Pl. Phaed. 63, Dor. 3 pl. φέροντι Pind. P. 10, 70, and φέροισι Fr. 205; Ep. subj. -ρῃσι Od. 10, 507; Dor. pt. -ροισα Pind. P. 3, 15; Theocr. 2, 148; Epic inf. φερέμεν Il. 9, 411; Hes. Op. 215: **imp.** ἔφερον Il. 17, 458; Simon. C. 163; Pind. Ol. 10, 67; Her. 8, 60; Thuc. 7, 57; Isocr. 9, 54, φέρον Il. 3, 245; Hes. Fr. 174, iter. φέρεσκεν Od. 9, 429, -σκον 10, 108: **fut.** οἴσω Il. 7, 82; Pind. P. 9, 61; Aesch. Ch. 487; Soph. Tr. 123. 1183; Eur. Alc. 336; Ar. Pax 18; Her. 2, 91; Thuc. 6, 41; Andoc. 1, 2. 31; Isocr. 15, 52; Pl. Rep. 477, Dor. οἰσῶ Theocr. 3, 11, 1 pl. -σεῦμες 15, 133: **1 aor.** ἤνεγκα Soph. El. 13; Eur. Ion 38; Isocr. 15, 5 (Bait. -αμεν Vulg. Bens.); Aeschin. 2, 4; Luc. Pisc. 32. 33. D. Mort. 12, 3 &c., -κας Eur. Hel. 1250; Ar. Av. 540; Dem. 19, 250; Luc. Laps. 1; Himer. Or. 23, 7, -κε freq. see below, dual. ἠνεγκάτην, δι- Pl. Leg. 723, ἠνέγκαμεν Dem. 19, 40, ἀν- Andoc. 3, 7, ἠνέγκατε Dem. 23, 167. 44, 43, -καν Theogn. 880; Eur. I. A. 800; Isae. 11, 18, ἔνεγκαν Q. Sm. 6, 595, Epic and Ion. ἔνεικα Orph. Arg. 312, ἀν- Od. 11, 625, ἔνεικας, ἀπ- Il. 14, 255, ἤνεικεν Od. 18, 300; Theocr. 23, 16; Her. 2, 146. 3, 155, ἔνεικ- Pind. Ol. 2, 79. P. 9, 6, ἐνείκαμεν Od. 24, 43, ἔνεικαν Od. 4, 784 (Bekk. ἤνεικ- Dind. La R.), ἀπ-έν- 16, 326. 360, ἤνεικ- Her. 3, 30, ὑπ- Il. 5, 885, also (ᾦσα) rare, opt. late οἴσαιμι Christ. Pat. 990; inf. ἀνα-οῖσαι, ἀνῷσαι Her. 1, 157 (Mss. Gaisf. Bekk. Dind. Dietsch), ἀνοῖσαι (Bred. Stein, Abicht); Poet. imper. **act.** οἶσε for -σον, see below: **p.** ἐνήνοχα Isocr. 6, 60; Dem. 21, 108, 22, 62, εἰσ- Andoc. 3, 20, συν- Dem. 18, 198 (Xen. Mem.

3, 5, 22 Vulg.): **plp.** ἐνηνόχει, ἀπ- (Dem.) 49, 62: **p. p.** ἐνήνεγμαι, -εξαι, -εκται Pl. Rep. 584, εἰσ- Eur. Ion 1340, and -εγξαι, -εγται, ἀν- Inscr. 1, 67, 4 (Boeckh), Ionic ἐνήνειγμαι, ἐξ- Her. 8, 37, rarely (οἶσμαι) προ-οῖσται late, Luc. Paras. 2 (Vulg. Bekk. Jacobitz, for which Dind. reads προῶσται, with Jacobs, from προωθέω): **plp.** ἐνήνεκτο, προσ- Xen. Hell. 4, 3, 20: **aor.** ἠνέχθην Xen. An. 4, 7, 12; Pl. Leg. 756. Tim. 63; Dem. 18, 134, κατ- Thuc. 3, 69, Ion. ἠνείχθην, ἀπ- Her. 1, 66. 2, 116, περι- 1, 84, ἀν- 2, 121 &c.: **fut.** ἐνεχθήσομαι Aristot. Nat. Ausc. 3, 5, 18 (Bekk.); Marc. Ant. 4, 43. 10, 33; Galen 3, 71, ἐπ- Thuc. 7, 56, κατ- Isocr. 13, 19, and οἰσθήσομαι Aristot. Nat. Ausc. 3, 5, 13. Probl. 16, 3; Dem. 44, 45, ἐξ- Eur. Supp. 561: and as pass. **fut. mid.** οἴσομαι Eur. Or. 440; Xen. Oec. 18, 6, ἐξ- Her. 8, 49. 76, περι- Hippocr. 7, 580 (more freq. as mid. see below): **2 aor. act.** ἤνεγκον perhaps only 1 sing. Soph. O. C. 521. 964; Ar. Ran. 1299. Lys. 944, δι- Isocr. 18, 59, the only prose instance, and perhaps to avoid *hiatus*, except 3 pl. προσήνεγκον if correct Hippocr. 1, 655 (Erm. -ήνεγκαν Lit. 5, 388); Ionic (ἤνεικον), opt. ἐνείκοι Od. 21, 196 (Vulg. -είκαι Bekk. Dind.); Epic inf. ἐνεικέμεν Il. 19, 194; imper. οἶσε &c. belongs perhaps to **1 aor.** see below. **Mid.** φέρομαι *to bear, carry for oneself*, &c. Soph. Ph. 117; Her. 7, 50; Thuc. 1, 69; Pl. Phaed. 113, rare and Epic ἐνείκεται, συν- Hes. Sc. 440; φέρωμαι Il. 23, 413; Eur. Hec. 308; Pl. Rep. 584; Dor. opt. -οίμαν Aesch. Eum. 266: **imp.** ἐφερ- Xen. An. 7, 4, 3: **fut.** οἴσομαι Il. 22, 217. 23, 663. 858; Soph. El. 969; Eur. An. 1282. Ph. 1546; Ar. Pax 1032; Her. 6, 100. 132; Thuc. 2, 11; Pl. Rep. 537; Isocr. 8, 33, as pass. see above: **p. p.** εἰσ-ενηνεγμένη as mid. Dem. 27, 4: **1 aor.** ἠνεγκάμην Soph. Tr. 462; Eur. Supp. 583; Pl. Rep. 406; Dem. 40, 26, ἐξ- Ar. Eccl. 76, Ionic ἠνεικ- Il. 9, 127; Her. 1, 57. 2, 180, ἐσ- 7, 152, ἐνεικ-, ἀν- Theocr. 23, 18; Mosch. 2, 20. 134; subj. common to both, ἐνέγκωμαι, ἐξ- Soph. El. 60; Eur. El. 871, ἐνέγκηται, ἐξ- Hippocr. 4, 640, εἰσενέγκησθε Dem. 19, 220, ἐνέγκωνται, προσ- Hippocr. 1, 582. 592 (Lit.), Ion. ἐνείκωνται Her. 4, 67; opt. ἐνεγκαίμην, -καιτο Luc. D. Mort. 12, 2, προσ- Oribas. 1, 46, ἐνεγκαίμεθα, εἰσ- Dem. 10, 36; imper. ἔνεγκαι, ἀπ- Luc. Icar. 20 (Vulg. Bekk. Jacob. -εγκε Dind.); so in some edit. of Eur. I. A. 724 (but συν-ενέγκαι opt. act. Musgr. Herm. Kirchh. Paley, -ενέγκοι L. Dind. W. Dind. 5 ed.); ἐνεγκάμενος Aeschin. 1, 131; Dem. 40, 59, ἐσ- Thuc. 5, 115, Ionic ἐνεικάμενος, ἀν- Her. 1, 86; ἐνέγκασθαι App. Civ. 2, 11. 3, 6, ἀπ- Isocr. 6, 74, Ionic ἐνείκασθαι, ἐξ- Her. 6, 103, ἐσ- 2, 23; late and rare if correct, οἴσασθαι, ἀπ- (Hippocr.) Epist. 9, 418 (Lit.); Aspin. Rhet. p. 482 (Walz, *v. r.* ἀπ-οίσεσθαι): **2 aor.** (ἠνεγκόμην), ἐνέγκοιτο, προσ-

Theophr. H. P. 8, 4, 5 (Ms. P. 2. Ald. Wimm. -αιτο Schneid.); Galen 5, 276, εἰσ- Epist. Phal. 103 (Herch.); imper. ἐνέγκου Soph. O. C. 470 (Mss. Ellendt &c.), ἐνεγκοῦ (Elms. Herm. Dind. Bergk); ἐνεγκέσθαι, προσ- Galen 15, 204. **Vb.** οἰστός Thuc. 7, 75, ἀν- Her. 6, 66 (Bred. Stein, Abicht, -ώϊστος Bekk. Dind. Aretae. 2, 11), οἰστέος Soph. Ant. 310; Isocr. 14, 10, ἐνεκτέον συμπερι- Stob. 79, 42, φερτός Eur. Hec. 158, συμ- Il. 13, 237.

Attic writers use both **aorists act.** ἤνεγκα, ἤνεγκον, but partially. In *simple*, ἤνεγκον is more frequent than ἤνεγκα, but *Poetic*, and perhaps in 1 sing. only, Soph. O. C. 521. 964. Fr. 592; Ar. Ran. 1299. Thesm. 743. Lys. 944, δι- Isocr. 18, 59, ἤνεγκα however is neither unattic, nor so rare as some affirm, Soph. El. 13; Eur. Ion 38; Isocr. 15, 5 (Bait. -αμεν Vulg. Bekk. Bens.); Luc. Pisc. 33; Aeschin. 2, 4, ἀπ- 3, 217. 227; Dem. 52, 30, μετ- 18, 108, παρ- 18, 232, δι- Eur. Ion 15, εἰσ- Isocr. 17, 41; Com. Fr. (Dion.) 3, 547. (Demetr.) 4, 539, προεισ- Dem. 50, 8, ἐπ- Isae. 8, 39; 2 pers. ἤνεγκες I have not seen, but ἤνεγκας Eur. Hel. 1250; Ar. Thesm. 743. Av. 540; Dem. 19, 250; Luc. Laps. 1, ἐξ- Soph. Tr. 741; Aeschin. 2, 165, εἰσ- Dem. 45, 69, δι- 61, 19. 27; 3 pers. ἤνεγκε freq. but common to both aor.; dual of ἤνεγκον I have not seen, but δι-ηνεγκάτην Pl. Leg. 723; 1 pl. ἠνέγκαμεν Isocr. 15, 5 (Vulg. Bekk. see above); Dem. 19, 40, ἀν- Andoc. 3, 7. 8; Aeschin. 2, 174. 175, ἐξ- 2, 176, δι- Isocr. 4, 48. 12, 53. 19, 17; Xen. Oec. 9, 8 (Vulg. Dind. -ομεν some Mss. Breitb. Saupp.), ἐπ- Pl. Polit. 275. Rep. 612; ἠνέγκετε I have not seen, but ἠνέγκατε Dem. 23, 167. 44, 43 (B. Saupp.). 55, 7 (Dind.), ἐξ- Ar. Vesp. 815, παρ- (Dem.) 21, 53, nor 3 pers. ἤνεγκον (except προσ- if correct, Dio Cass. Fr. 7, 3 (Bekk. Dind.), but ἤνεγκαν Eur. I. A. 800; Xen. Hell. 4, 1, 27; Isae. 11, 18; Aeschin. 2, 87. 3, 104; (Dem.) 11, 16. 49, 52; Dio Cass. Fr. 12, 9 (Bekk.) 54, 16 &c. ἀπ- Thuc. 5, 10, δι- Isocr. 4, 83. 92. 12, 55; Lycurg. 108; Aeschin. 2, 9; (Dem.) 60, 17, εἰσ- Xen. Hell. 2, 1, 5. 5, 1, 21; Isocr. 19, 36; Isae. 5, 38. 41, ἐξ- Isocr. 5, 54, ἐπ- Xen. Hell. 6, 5, 36, προσ- Aesch. Ch. 76, ξυνδι- Ar. Eq. 597, ἀν- Dem. 24, 120. It would thus appear that the **1 aor.** is more complete and less confined in usage, and that its parts with α, excepting 1 sing., are more frequent than the corresponding parts with ο and ε of the **2 aor.**

3 sing. ἤνεγκε seems referrible to both, but as the form in ον is confined, or almost confined, to Poetry, a doubt may arise whether ἤνεγκε in prose may not properly belong to the form in α, and whether Breitenbach, Sauppe, Shenkl have done well in disturbing the received reading διηνέγκαμεν Xen. Oec. 9, 8, for -ομεν of some Mss. No doubt Xen. is not shy of a Poetic

form, but in this very treatise he uses διήνεγκαν 20, 18, so ἤνεγκαν Hell. 4, 1, 27, εἰσ- 2, 1, 5. 5, 1, 21, ἐπ- 6, 5, 36, προσ- 7, 2, 5. Cyr. 7, 1, 1: and Isocr. though using 1 pers. διήνεγκον 18, 59 —the only certain instance of 2 aor. we know in *classic* prose —seems to do so merely to avoid *hiatus* -εγκον, ὅτι, for before a consonant he has εἰσήνεγκα τῶν 17, 41, and 1 pl. ἠνέγκαμεν 15, 5, δι- 12, 53. 19, 17, διήνεγκαν 8, 85. 104. 12, 55. 123. 189. 15, 207. 208, εἰσ- 19, 36, ἐξ- 5, 54 &c. Nay, even in Poetry ἤνεγκα has perhaps the best claims to ἤνεγκε. Facts seem to confirm this, at least to point this way: Aesch. has ἤνεγκε Ch. 992, but προσ-ήνεγκαν 76; Soph. has 1 pers. ἤνεγκα Elec. 13, and ἤνεγκον O. C. 521. 964 &c., but ἐξήνεγκας Tr. 741; Eur. has ἤνεγκε Heracl. 332, but ἤνεγκαν I. A. 800, δι- Bac. 1087; Ar. has ἤνεγκον Lys. 944. Ran. 1299 (both for the metre?), but ἤνεγκας Av. 540, ἐξ-ηνέγκατε Vesp. 815, and, what we think a stronger case, in Thesm. 743, one of the women says ἐγὼ ἤνεγκον, Mnesilochus sharply asks ἤνεγκας σύ? evidently shying ἤνεγκες, and by implication showing, one is apt to surmise, no favour for its *lineal descendant* ἤνεγκε. Since then the Attic Poets use, beyond the 1 pers. no form which must *necessarily* be referred to the formation in ο, and since they seem to have even avoided *proceeding* on this formation, the natural inference appears to be that *Indic.* ἤνεγκον was limited in usage to the 1 sing.

The oblique moods are also *partially* used: subj. common to both, ἐνέγκω Ar. Vesp. 848, -κῃς Com. Fr. (Philem.) 4, 56, -κῃ Xen. Conv. 4, 7, -κητε Isae. 8, 4 (Dem. 44, 43 Bekk.), -κωσι Pl. Leg. 946; opt. 1 aor. ἐνέγκαιμι Eur. Hipp. 393 (-οιμι Dind. 5 ed.); Pl. Crit. 43, ἀπ- Com. Fr. (Alex.) 3, 428, συν- Eur. H. F. 488 (-οιμι Dind. 5 ed.), ἐνέγκαι Xen. Conv. 2, 3 (-οι Saupp.), εἰσ- Dem. 14, 26, δι- 25, 20, -καιμεν, ὑπ- Xen. Mem. 4, 3, 9 (-οιμεν Dind. Saupp.), ἐνέγκαιτε Eur. Heracl. 751 (Herm. Nauck, Dind. 2 ed., -οιτε 5 ed. &c.), ἐνέγκαιεν, εἰσ- Dem. 14, 25; imper. ἔνεγκον rare Com. Fr. (Anax.) 4, 466 (Pors.), ἀπ- Ar. Pax 1109 (R. Bekk. Dind. Bergk, Mein. -εγκε V. Vulg. Richter), late prose ἀπ- Luc. D. Mort. 1, 4, προσ- N. T. Matt. 8, 4 (Vat.), but always ἐνεγκάτω Ar. Thesm. 238; Com. Fr. (Cratin.) 2, 165; Pl. Phaed. 116, προσ- Xen. Conv. 5, 2, and pl. ἐνέγκατε Eur. Heracl. 751 (Vulg. Kirchh. see opt.); Luc. Bis Acc. 32. 34, ἐξ- Ar. Ran. 847, ἀν- Dem. 20, 118; inf. ἐνέγκαι seems not to occur in *classic* Attic, but Aristot. Oec. 2, 26; Sopat. Rhet. vol. 8. p. 4. 20 &c.; V. T. Neh. 12, 27, εἰσ- Aristot. Oec. 2, 21. 26, δι- Diod. Sic. 5, 71, ὑπ- 15, 55, προσ- Hippocr. 6, 210; Polyb. 32, 7, δι- Hippocr. 7, 340 (Lit.), Epic and Ion. ἐνεῖκαι, see below; part. ἐνέγκας Aristot. Oec. 2, 26 (Bekk.); (Dem.) 49, 51; Plut. Mor.

233. 308. 350, δι- Xen. Mem. 3, 6, 18, ἐξ- 1, 2, 53 (-ων Dind.), (Dem.) 49, 43, περι- Aeschin. 1, 131, εἰσ- Com. Fr. (Demetr.) 4, 539; Aristot. Polit. 3, 9, 5, ἐπ- (Dem.) 59, 9; Strab. 2, 1, 35, μετ- 7, 3, 6: 2 aor. ἐνέγκοιμι (Dind. reading Eur. Hipp. 393, -αιμι Vulg. &c.), ἐνέγκοις, μετ- Xen. Cyr. 1, 6, 39, ἐνέγκοι Soph. Tr. 774. Fr. 105; Eur. Rhes. 260; Pl. Rep. 330; Dem. 21, 28, εἰσ- Ar. Eccl. 807, συν- Thuc. 6, 20; Isocr. 15, 10; Dem. 9, 76, ἐνέγκοιμεν, ἐπ- Isocr. 12, 138, -κοιτε Eur. Heracl. 751 (Dind. 5 ed.), ἐνέγκοιεν, δι- Xen. Mem. 3, 3, 14 (-κεῖν Dind. Saupp.); Pl. Rep. 501 (Bekk.); Isocr. 12, 121; imper. only 2 sing. ἔνεγκε Eur. Heracl. 699; Ar. Eq. 98. 110. Pax 1219; Xen. Mem. 3, 6, 9, προσ- Luc. D. Mar. 4, 2, other parts supplied by 1 aor. ἐνεγκάτω, -έγκατε; part. ἐνεγκών (Pind. I. 8, 21) Soph. El. 692; Eur. Supp. 920; Thuc. 6, 56; Dem. 6, 28. 24, 141; Luc. Laps. 11, ἐξ- Ar. Ach. 359; inf. ἐνεγκεῖν Aesch. Supp. 766; Soph. Ph. 873; Eur. Ion 424; Com. Fr. (Antiph.) 3, 34; Thuc. 7, 56; Pl. Apol. 37; Dem. 27, 2, προσ- Pind. P. 9, 36, ἐξ- Ar. Nub. 634, εἰσ- Dem. 24, 141 &c. (Epic ἐνεικ- see below.) Of a pres. ἐνείκω called Boeotic (Etym. Magn.), there occurs a trace in συνενείκεται Hes. Sc. 440, approved by Goettling, Schoem. Flach, but altered by Herm. to plp. συνενήνεκτο from the *v. r.* συνενήνεκται.

I have confined these observations to Attic Greek, but from considerable investigation I am satisfied they will apply equally to Epic and Ionic: ἔνεικα Orph. Arg. 312, ἀν- Od. 11, 625, ἔνεικας, ἀπ- Il. 14, 255, ἔνεικεν 15, 705; Pind. Ol. 3, 14, ἤνεικ- Od. 18, 300; Her. 3, 155, pl. ἐνείκαμεν Od. 24, 43, ἔνεικαν Il. 13, 213; Tyrt. 4, ἤνεικ- Her. 3, 30, ἐσ- 9, 70, ὑπ- Il. 5, 885; subj. ἐνείκω Il. 6, 258, -είκῃ Od. 2, 329; opt. ἐνείκαι Il. 18, 147. Od. 21, 196; Theocr. 5, 125, -κειε Her. 6, 61, ἐνείκαιεν, συν- Her. 7, 152; imper. ἔνεικον Anacr. 63 (Bergk), -είκατε Od. 8, 393; inf. ἐνεῖκαι Il. 18, 334; Hes. Th. 784; Pind. P. 9, 53; Her. 1, 32; part. ἐνείκας Il. 17, 39; Her. 4, 64: passing sparingly into the ο formation of 2 aor. ἐνείκοι Od. 21, 196 (Vulg. Wolf, -είκαι Bekk. Dind. La R.); imper. ἔνεικε Od. 21, 178; inf. ἐνεικέμεν Il. 19, 194.

The *indic.* aor. mid. is *uniformly* of the α formation, ἠνεγκάμην, ἐξ- Ar. Eccl. 76, ἠνέγκω Eur. Supp. 583; Xen. Oec. 7, 13, ἠνέγκατο Soph. Tr. 462; Pl. Tim. 21; Dem. 40, 26, Ion. ἠνείκ- Her. 5, 47, Epic ἐνείκ-, ἀν- Il. 19, 314, ἠνεγκάμεθα Pl. Ion 530, ἠνέγκαντο Plut. Mor. 407, Ion. ἠνείκ- Il. 9, 127; Her. 1, 57. 173. 2, 180; subj. ἐνέγκωμαι, εἰσ- Soph. El. 60; Eur. El. 871, -ενέγκησθε Dem. 19, 220, ἐνέγκωνται, προσ- Hippocr. 1, 582 (Lit.), Ion. ἐνείκ- Her. 4, 67; opt. ἐνέγκαιτο Luc. D. Mort. 12, 2, ἐνεγκαίμεθα, εἰσ- Dem. 10, 36; imper. ἔνεγκαι, ἀπ- Luc. Icar. 20 (Vulg. Bekk. Jacob. -κε Dind. Cob.), and συν- in some edit. of Eur. I. A. 724; ἐνεγκάμενος Aeschin. 1, 131; Dem. 40, 59, ἐσ- Thuc. 5, 115, ἐνεικάμ- Alcae. 35 (Bergk); ἐνέγκασθαι App. Civ. 2, 11. 3, 6, εἰσ- Isocr. 15, 188, ἀπ- 6, 74; Dem. 23, 68, προσ- Aeschin. 1, 145, Ion. ἐνείκ- ἐξ- Her. 2, 121. 6, 103. 125: 2 aor. (ἠνεγκόμην) only in oblique moods, and rare, ἐνέγκοιτο, προσ- Theophr. H. P. 8, 4, 5 (Ms. Pr. Ald. Wimm. -αιτο Schn.); Galen 4, 584. 5, 276, εἰσ- Epist. Phal. 97; imper. ἐνεγκοῦ Soph. O. C. 470; προσ-ενεγκέσθαι Galen 15, 204.

If then these data be correct, and the induction just, there appear grounds for supposing *first*, that 2 aor. ἤνεγκον is not, or scarcely, a prose form; *second*, that it is *probably* confined to the 1 pers. sing.; *third*, that it is more frequent than ἤνεγκα in the *simple* only, not in the *compound* form, ἀπ-ήνεγκα, εἰσ-, ἐξ-, ἐπ-, μετ- &c. A few exceptions, if correct, occur as *v. r.* and occasionally in text, ἐπ-ήνεγκες late, Sopat. Rhet. vol. 8, p. 40 (Walz), δι- Epist. Socrat. 8 (L. Allat.) seemingly a false reading, -ενέγκαις (Olear. Herch.), διηνέγκομεν Xen. Oec. 9, 8 (Breitb. Saupp. -αμεν Schn. Dind.), προσήνεγκον Dio Cass. Fr. 7, 3 (Bekk. Dind.). The usage of the *later* writers is, I think, still more exclusively in favour of *Indic.* 1 aor. We submit for the consideration of Scholars whether ἤνεγκα, imper. ἔνεγκε were not used *of choice*, Isocr. 17, 41; Com. Fr. (Dionys.) 3, 547. Ar. Eq. 95. 110 &c. and ἤνεγκον, imper. ἔνεγκον for the metre, or to avoid hiatus? Ar. Ran. 1299; Isocr. 18, 59; Ar. Pax 1109. α seems to have been rarely elided, εἰσ-ήνεγκ' once Com. Fr. (Demetr.) 4, 539, perhaps never by prose writers, ἤνεγκα, ὅθ'- Aeschin. 2, 4; ἐπ-ήνεγκα, ὡς Isae. 8, 39; later ἤνεγκα ὅρων Luc. Pisc. 33, ἤνεγκα ἄν 37, ἤνεγκα, ἐπι- Himer. 10, 4.

φέρησι 2 sing. pres. indic. as from φέρημι, Od. 19, 111 (Wolf, &c.), but subj. φέρῃσι (Bekk. Dind. La R.); φέρτε 2 pl. imper. for φέρετε, Il. 9, 171. οἶσε imper. 1 aor. from obsol. (οἴω), with the inflexion of 2 aor. Poet. Od. 22, 106; Ar. Ran. 482, οἰσέτω Il. 19, 173, but οἴσετε Od. 20, 154 may be future, 3 pl. οἰσόντων Antim. Fr. 10; inf. οἶσειν Pind. P. 4, 102, Epic οἰσέμεναι Il. 3, 120, -έμεν Od. 3, 429.

Φεύγω *To flee*, Il. 21, 472; Pind. Ol. 6, 90; Aesch. Supp. 5; Soph. O. R. 1010; Ar. Ach. 22; Her. 2, 65; Antiph. 2, δ, 5. 5, 9; Thuc. 7, 70; Lys. 12, 34; Pl. Phaed. 65, Dor. 3 pl. -γοντι Pind. N. 9, 27, ὑπ- εκ- Bion 6, 4; 3 pl. imper. φευγόντων Il. 9, 47; Ep. inf. φευγέμεναι Il. 21, 13, φευγέμεν 10, 147: imp. ἔφευγον Il. 22, 158; Soph. O. R. 796; Her. 8, 38; Antiph. 6, 27; Thuc. 3, 98; Lys. 12, 16, φεῦγον Il. 9, 478; Hes. Fr. 82; Tyrt. 5, 8; Pind. N. 9, 13, iter. φεύγεσκε Il. 17, 461, -εσκον Her. 4, 43: **fut.** φεύξομαι Il. 18, 307; Aesch. Supp. 456; Soph. Ph. 1404; Eur. Her. 506. El. 975; Ar. Ach. 203. Eccl. 625; Her. 1, 207; Pl. Apol. 29. Theaet. 168. 181; Lys. 6, 15. 34, 11; Dem. 19, 88. 20, 138. 21, 32 &c., ἀπο- Thuc. 3, 13; Antiph. 6, 35. 36; Andoc. 1, 123; Aeschin. 1, 85. 90, κατα- Isocr. 8, 138; φεύξοιτο Thuc. 6, 74, 3 pl. -ξοίαθ' Aesch. Pers. 369 (Trimet.); -ξόμενοι Xen. Hell. 4, 4, 5, and φευξοῦμαι Eur. Med. 338. 341. Hel. 500. 1041 &c.; Ar. Plut. 447. Ach. 1129 (οῦ- required for the metre); Eur. Med. 604. Hipp. 1093. Bac. 797 (not required, Vulg. Kirchh. Nauck, -ομαι Elms. Dind.); Pl. Leg. 635; -ξεῖσθαι Dem. 38, 19 (Bekk. B. S. -εσθαι Dind.), ἀπο- Pl. Leg. 762, ἐκ- Rep. 432, κατα- Polyb. 18, 35 (Bekk. 49 Hultsch): (**act.** form φεύξω late, Orac. Sib. 9, 283, ἐκ- 3, 566, ὑπεκ- 567, see Aesop 349 Halm, 187 Tauchn.): **1 aor.** ἔφευξα given by Matthiae and others from Aesch. Ag. 1281 (1308 D.) is aor. of φεύζω: but late, ἐκφεύξας Or. Sib. 6, 6; and Hesych. explains ἔφευξα by ἔφυγον: **2 p.** πέφευγα Aesch. Ag. 268; Soph. O. R. 356; Eur. Hec. 345; Ar. Av. 954; Her. 7, 154; Pl. Alcib. (1) 103; Dem. 18, 233, περι- Pind. Ol. 2, 98, δια- Isocr. 4, 187; opt. πεφεύγοιμι, -γοι Il. 21, 609 (Vulg. Dind. La R. -γειν Bekk.), πεφευγοίην, ἐκ- Soph. O. R. 840; πεφευγώς Od. 1, 12; Pind. Fr. 120; Soph. Ant. 412; Her. 1, 65; Thuc. 1, 122; Pl. Prot. 318; Isae. 8, 29; Dem. 23, 42, κατα- Antiph. 3, β, 2; πεφευγέναι Soph. Ant. 437; Lys. 19, 58, ἐκ- Xen. Cyr. 6, 1, 40: **plp.** ἐπεφεύγει Thuc. 4, 133; D. Sic. 11, 14, πεφ- Il. 21, 609 (Bekk.), see **perf.**: **p. p.** (πέφυγμαι), Epic πεφυγμένος act. *having escaped*, Il. 6, 488. Od. 9, 455 (also Epic πεφυζότες act. Il. 21, 6. 532): **aor.** late (ἐφεύχθην), φευχθῆναι Joseph. Ant. 19, 1, 17; δι- εφεύχθη 18, 9, 1. 17, 3, 1, the only instances we know: **2 aor.** ἔφῠγον Il. 11, 362; (Attic Poets?); Her. 4, 127; Antiph. 5, 38; Thuc. 2, 42; Lys. 12, 4; Pl. Apol. 26; Isocr. 6, 100, ἀπ- Soph. O. C. 1739, δι- Eur. Hel. 794, ἐξ- Ar. Ach. 217, φύγον Il. 3, 4; Pind. P. 5, 58; iter. φύγεσκε Od. 17, 316; φύγω Aesch. Ch. 925; Soph. O. C. 828; Eur. Hec. 1249; Ar. Av. 354, φύγῃ Il. 21, 103, -γῃσι 5, 258, -γέῃσι, ἐκ- Opp. Hal. 3, 131, -γωσι Pl. Leg. 855; φύγοιμι Od. 14, 312; Soph. Aj. 456; C. Fr. (Eup.) 2, 526; Pl. Lach. 184 &c., Epic 2 sing. φύγοισθα, προ- Od. 22, 325; -γών Il. 21, 57; Aesch. Sept. 208; Com. Fr. 3, 270; Thuc. 2, 61; φυγεῖν Il. 12, 327; Soph. O. R. 823; Her. 6, 103; Pl. Leg. 833, -έειν Il. 14, 80; Her. 8, 76. **Mid. 1 aor.** φεύξασθαι preferred, perhaps wrongly, by Wellauer Ap. Rh. 2, 172 (some Mss.) to φεύξεσθαι (best Mss. Vulg. Lobeck, Merkel), but δια-φεύξασθαι (Hippocr.) Epist. 9, 400 (Lit.). Desider. φευξείω Eur. H. F. 628.

Vb. φυκτός Il. 16, 128, φευκτός Soph. Aj. 222; Aristot. Eth. Nic. 7, 6, 5 (Bekk.), -τέος Xen. Mem. 2, 6, 4.

A 2 fut. seems to occur late, φυγεῖς Praecept. Salubr. l. 42, p. 133 (Didots), ἐκ- ibid. favouring φυγεῖ (=φεύξεται) a gloss in Cod. Paris. Ar. Plut. 496, for which Dind. suggests, perhaps needlessly, subj. φύγῃ: and mid. φῠγοῦμαι, -γεῖται Orac. Sib. 12, 109, -γοῦνται 9, 45. 239 (also, if correct, φύγεται 10, 93. 253, -γονται 3, 265.) πεφυζότες is perhaps syncopated for πεφυζηκότες from φυζάω, whence aor. pass. φυζηθείς Nic. Ther. 825, as μεμυδότες for μεμυδηκότες Antim. (Lob. Techn. p. 81). The Attic Poets use the Dor. fut. form. -οῦμαι, at least when the metre requires, -ούμεθα Eur. Med. 341. 346. Bac. 658. Hel. 500. 1041; -ούμενον Ar. Ach. 1129. Plut. 447, ἀπο- Av. 932; anapaestic -εῖται Ar. Plut. 496, διαφευξοῦμαι Nub. 443. Several cases however occur "praeter *necessitatem*," -οῦμαι Eur. Med. 604; Ar. Ach. 203, -ούμεσθα Eur. Hipp. 1093, -εῖσθε Bac. 797 (Vulg. Kirchh. Nauck, Bergk)—these Elms. suspected, Dind. repudiates, and now edits -ξομαι, -ξόμεσθα, -ξεσθε, which Paley adopts. Hom. Hes. Her. and, we think, Aesch. Soph. Thuc. Xen. have always -ξομαι: so likewise the Orators except Dem. once only -ξεῖσθαι 38, 19 (Ms. S. Bekk. B. S. -ξεσθαι Dind.): in Plato also -ξομαι is quite the prevailing form; indeed, Dind. asserts that the Dor. -εῖται occurs only Leg. 635. B. C. We think he has overlooked ἀπο-φευξεῖσθαι 762, and ἐκ- Rep. 432. Was this fut. then admitted only in *hard* cases? or was it generally *just tolerated*, or was it in all cases so familiar as to mix in good society without offending the scrupulous, or fear of *the shell?* οἱ Δωριεῖς . . κλασοῦμαι, φευξοῦμαι &c. καὶ παρὰ Ἀττικοῖς δὲ ταῦτα οὕτως ἐπεκράτησαν λέγεσθαι (Cramer. An. 4, 198.)

Φεύζω *To cry* φεῦ, *lament*, whence aor. ἔφευξας Aesch. Ag. 1308.

Φημί *To say* (φάω), Il. 5, 103; Aesch. Ag. 831; Soph. Ant. 443; Ar. Ach. 187; Her. 2, 49; Hippocr. 6, 44; Antiph. 3, δ, 4; Thuc. 6, 10; Pl. Phaedr. 270, φῄς Il. 4, 351; Her. 1, 39; Pl. Prot. 312, φῆσθα Il. 21, 186. Od. 14. 149, φησί Il. 15, 181; Andoc. 1, 22, φῄ Anacr. 41; Lys. 31, 13 (pres. and imp. like ἵστημι), Dor. φᾱμί Pind. P. 2, 64; Aesch. Eum. 553; Soph. Tr. 125 (chor.); Theocr. 8, 7, 3 sing. φατί Ar. Ach. 771; Theocr. 1, 51, Aeol. φαῖσι Sapph. 66 (B.), pl. φᾰμέν Il. 15, 735; Pind. P. 12, 17; Soph. Ph. 1073; Her. 6, 86; Thuc. 3, 54; Isae. 1, 21, φᾰτέ Od. 16, 93; Ar. Plut. 200; Thuc. 3, 63; Aeschin. 3, 232; Pl. Rep. 366. Euthyd. 296, φᾱσί Il. 11, 831; Soph. Ph. 89; Her. 8, 88; Antiph. 6, 43; Thuc. 1, 37, Dor. φαντί Pind. P. 1, 52; Theocr. 2, 45; subj. φῶ Aesch. Ch. 91; Pl.

Euthyd. 296; Dem. 9, 18, φῇ Od. 19, 122; Dem. 22, 23, Epic φήῃ Od. 11, 128, and φῆσιν 1, 168, φᾶσι Her. 4, 68; Isae. 4, 5; opt. φαίην Il. 6, 283; Pind. Ol. 13, 103; Antiph. 6, 30; Pl. Prot. 330, 1 pl. φαίημεν Eur. Ion 943; Xen. An. 3, 2, 23 (Krüg. Saupp. and L. Dind. though he would always -αῖμεν); Pl. Alc. (2) 139, contr. φαῖμεν Il. 2, 81; Pind. N. 7, 87; Pl. Phil. 63, φαίητε Xen. Hell. 2, 4, 41. An. 7, 6, 23, φαίησαν Thuc. 8, 53, but φαῖεν 3, 68; Pl. Phil. 63, συμ- Xen. Mem. 3, 8, 9; imper. φάθι or φăθί Ar. Eq. 23; Pl. Prot. 349. Rep. 475, φάτω Hippocr. 3, 322. 436 (Lit.); Pl. Leg. 902; inf. φάναι Her. 1, 27. 39. 7, 151; Hippocr. 7, 222; Xen. Oec. 7, 18; Pl. Crat. 429, Poet. φάμεν Pind. N. 8, 19; φάς Il. 9, 35. 3, 44; Her. 1, 111. 117. 122. 2, 18. 5, 39. 50. 6, 65; Hippocr. 4, 78; in Attic prose perhaps only (Pl.) Alc. (2) 139. 146; Aristot. Soph. 22, 7. 30, 4; later, Strab. 14, 1, 25; Galen 6, 349; in Attic poetry, perhaps only Com. Fr. (Dioxip.) 4, 541; and *now* Aesch. Ch. 418 chor. (Both. Bamb. Dind. Herm.): imp. ἔφην often as aor. Soph. O. R. 349; Ar. Nub. 70; Lys. 1, 18; Pl. Prot. 317, 2 sing. ἔφης Il. 22, 280; rare if correct in Attic, Xen. Cyr. 4, 1, 23; Pl. Gorg. 466. 496. Euthyd. 293 (Vulg. Stallb. -ησθα Bait.); Aeschin. 2, 86 (Vulg. Bekk. B. Saupp. -ησθα Franke *now*, Weidner); Aesch. Ag. 1613 (Vulg. Wellau. φῄς Dind. Herm. &c.); Plut. Mor. 123; Luc. Imag. 10. D. Mer. 13, 5. Soloec. 2. Rhet. 21 (Vulg. Dind. invitus), usu. ἔφησθα Il. 1, 397. 16, 830. Od. 23, 71; Ar. Lys. 132; Xen. An. 1, 6, 7. 7, 2, 27. 7, 7, 9. Cyr. 1, 6, 3. 6 &c.; Pl. Crat. 438. Rep. 501; Aeschin. 3, 164. 224; Dem. 18, 70. 36, 43; Luc. Gall. 24. 25. Herm. 3. 6. 9. Auct. V. 27. Fugit. 5. Pro Im. 8 &c. (Dind.), ἔφη Il. 5, 111; Her. 8, 65; Antiph. 2, α, 9, unaugm. φῆν Il. 18, 326, φῆς 5, 473, φῆσθα 21, 186. Od. 14, 149, φῆ Il. 2, 37. Od. 17, 142; Hes. Th. 550, Dor. ἔφα Timocr. 6 (B.); Pind. P. 4, 278; Aesch. Ag. 369 (chor.); Theocr. 7, 43, φᾶ Pind. I. 2, 11; Theocr. 24, 100, dual ἐφάτην Eur. Hec. 130; Pl. Euth. 278. 294, pl. ἔφăμεν Isocr. 3, 26; Pl. Rep. 459, φάμεν Od. 9, 496, ἔφăτε Andoc. 2, 25; Dem. 7, 23, ἔφασαν Od. 10, 46; Hes. Th. 29; Her. 8, 2; Antiph. 5, 29; Thuc. 5, 35; Isocr. 17, 16, φάσαν Od. 10, 67, ἔφαν Il. 13, 89. Od. 18, 75, φάν Il. 6, 108. Od. 18, 342; Pind. Fr. 228: fut. φήσω Il. 8, 148; Soph. Ant. 535; Eur. H. F. 578; Ar. Eccl. 590; Her. 2, 49; Pl. Gorg. 449, φήσομεν Ar. Av. 397; Her. 4, 45; Isocr. 1, 49, φήσετε Thuc. 4, 87; Dem. 9, 17. 24, 205, -σουσι Ar. Eccl. 774; Isocr. 15, 62, Dor. φᾱσῶ Ar. Ach. 739; Theocr. 11, 70, -σεῖς 15, 79, φάσω, -σει Pind. N. 7, 102, φάσουσι Anth. Pl. 4, 182; opt. φήσοιμι rare indeed -σοιτε Aristid. 39, 501 (Vulg. but -σαιτε Ms. θ, Dind.); Agath. p. 317;

φήσων Dinarch. 1, 43; Dem. 24, 111; φήσειν 24, 144: **aor.** ἔφησα Her. 3, 153. 6, 137; Antiph. 5, 51; Xen. An. 5, 8, 5; Pl. Polit. 297; Isocr. 5, 119, Dor. ἔφᾱσα, φᾶσε Pind. N. 1, 66; subj. φήσω Hippocr. 6, 36; Pl. Prot. 349; opt. φήσαιμι Dem. 18, 293, -σειας 36, 31, -σειεν Aesch. Pr. 503; Isocr. 7, 2, -σαιτε Lys. 11, 8; Dem. 15, 16, -σαιεν 38, 25; imper. φῆσον? (for which φράσον Aesch. Pers. 333, -άτω Dem. 16, 8 &c.); φῆσαι (Pl.) Demod. 382; Dem. 4, 46. 16, 20; φήσας Xen. Cyr. 4, 1, 22; Isocr. 12, 239: **p. p.** πεφασμένος Il. 14, 127; Aesch. Pr. 843; imper. πεφάσθω Pl. Tim. 72; late Epic, indic. 3 sing. πέφᾰται Ap. Rh. 2, 500: **aor.** ἐφάθην, ἀπο- Aristot. Interp. 9, 9, κατα- ibid.

Mid. (φάμαι) as **act.** 2 pl. φάσθε Od. 6, 200. 10, 562; φαῖο Mosch. 2, 97; imper. φάο Od. 18, 171, φάσθω 20, 100, φάσθε, ἀπο- Il. 9, 422; inf. φάσθαι Il. 9, 100; Pind. N. 4, 92; Xenophan. 6, 3 (Bergk); rare in Attic, Aesch. Pers. 700 (chor.); φάμενος Il. 5, 290. 22, 247; Pind. I. 6, 49; Her. 2, 18. 22. 28. 6, 69; Hippocr. 6, 342; occas. in Attic, Aesch. Ch. 316 (chor.); Xen. Hell. 1, 6, 3; (Pl.) Alc. (2) 142; Aristot. Nat. Ausc. 4, 8, 3. Metaph. 13, 3, 8; later, Plut. Crass. 28. Philop. 3; Luc. Demon. 66; App. Annib. 10. Mithr. 59; Paus. 9, 41: **imp.** ἐφᾰ́μην Il. 5, 190. 12, 165; Her. 6, 69, Dor. -φάμαν Theocr. 2, 102, φάμην Od. 13, 131 (Bekk. ἐφάμ- Dind.), ἔφατο Il. 1, 43. Od. 21, 248; Hes. Op. 69 (formerly Xen. Cyr. 6, 1, 21, now ἔφη); but late, Ael. V. H. 1, 21. 2, 2. 4, 8. 6, 11 &c.; Parthen. 4, Poet. φάτο Il. 20, 262; Hes. Th. 173; Pind. P. 4, 33; Simon. C. 5, 9 (Bergk), ἔφαντο Il. 17, 379; Theocr. 25, 187; rare if correct in Attic, Lys. Fr. 5, 1 (Bait. Saupp., 4 Scheibe), φάντο Od. 24, 460: **fut.** (φήσομαι), Dor. φᾱσομαι Pind. N. 9, 43. **Vb.** φατός Pind. Ol. 6, 37, φατέος Pl. Phil. 56. See ἠμί. ᾰ, except 3 pl. **pres.** φᾱσί, and part. φάς, φᾶσα; φάναι however Eubul. Com. Fr. 3, 362, probably corrupt. Porson transposed φάναι and inserted δέ, φᾱ́ναι δ'; Meineke suggests φῆσαι.

φημί in indic. is enclitic, except the 2 pers. sing. φής others φῄς; φαμέν 1 pl. **pres.** *we say*, Il. 15, 735; Thuc. 1, 38, but φάμεν inf. for φάναι, Pind. Ol. 1, 35. N. 8, 19. In classic Attic the form ἔφης is *now* scarcely to be found: φῄς instead is now read Isocr. 11, 7 (Ms. Bekk. B. S. Bens.); Pl. Gorg. and Euthyd. quoted (Bait.), and ἔφησθ' Aeschin. 2, 86 (Frank. Bait.) in accordance with 3, 164. L. Dind. has still left, reluctantly, one instance in Xen., and W. Dind. as reluctantly a few even in Lucian. Though φῶ, oftener φαίην, φάναι be used of past time, they are not for that reason to be called aoristic, since this use admits of explanation on syntactical grounds; nor are we sure that it is correct to say that ἔφην is always **aor.** any more than ἔλεγεν, ἐκέλευεν which are often used when we should expect ἔλεξεν, ἐκέλευσεν; and we are still more doubtful of the correctness of assigning the more decided meanings *affirm*, *grant* &c. to the fut. and aor. only, and denying them to the pres. and imp. See Krüg. Gr. Gram. p. 140.

Φημίζω *To say, tell* (φήμη), pres. late, Callim. Fr. 276 (Dor. φαμ-): fut. (-ίσω, -ιῶ) Epic -ίξω Or. Sib. 3, 406. 9, 316: aor. ἐφήμισα Aesch. Ch. 558; Eur. I. A. 1356; late Epic, Opp. Hal. 1, 158. 4, 659. 5, 70. 632, -ιξα Hes. Op. 764 (Dem. 19, 243); Q. Sm. 13, 538, φήμ- Opp. Hal. 5, 476, Dor. ἐφάμιξε, κατ- Pind. Ol. 6, 56; late prose, φημίσαι Arr. An. 5, 3: and p. p. πεφημισμένος Strabo 1, 2, 12 (Kram.): aor. also late, ἐφημίσθην Plut. Mor. 264; Theon. Rhet. p. 222 (Spengel), and -ίχθην, φημιχθείς Or. Sib. 5, 7. 10, 7: fut. φημισθήσεται Lycophr. 1082. Mid. aor. ἐφημισάμην Aesch. Ag. 629. 1173, -ιξάμην Dion. Per. 90; Nonn. 40, 233, δι- Arat. 442 (Bekk.); Dion. Per. 50. Our Lexicons ignore the pass. v. and the mid. with ξ.

Φθάνω *To get before, anticipate* (φθάω), -ά̆νει Il. 9, 506, -ά̄νει Eur. Med. 1169. H. F. 996; Her. 3, 78; Thuc. 5, 3; Xen. An. 5, 7, 16; φθάνωσι Antiph. 1, 29; φθά̄νοις Ar. Eccl. 118, -ά̄νοι Eur. Or. 941: imp. rare ἔφθᾰνε Anth. 9, 272; Xen. Hell. 6, 2, 30: fut. φθά̄σω Hippocr. 7, 134 (Lit.); Xen. Cyr. 5, 4, 38. 7, 1, 19; and late, Pseud.-Callisth. 1, 8; Plut. Mor. 211; Luc. Conv. 4; App. Lyb. 20. 24, ὑπο- Arr. An. 1, 13, 3: and mid. φθήσομαι Il. 23, 444; Thuc. 5, 10. 8, 12; Pl. Rep. 375; Isocr. 4, 79: 1 aor. ἔφθᾰσα Hippocr. 5, 152; Thuc. 3, 49. 112. 7, 42; Xen. Cyr. 4, 1, 3; Isocr. 5, 53. 8, 98. 9, 53; Lycurg. 128; Aeschin. 2, 16; subj. φθάσω Eur. Phoen. 975. 1280; Thuc. 5, 3; Xen. Cyr. 3, 2, 4; Dem. 6, 18; opt. φθάσαιμι, -σειε Ar. Plut. 685; Isocr. 8, 120, -σαιεν Thuc. 3, 49 (Bekk. Popp. Krüg.), -σειαν Xen. Hell. 7, 2, 14; Thuc. quoted (Classen, Stahl); imper. φθάσον (Hippocr. 9, 332; Joseph. Ant. 6, 11, 7, προ- V. T. Ps. 16, 13; inf. φθάσαι Thuc. 1, 33. 3, 5. 4, 67. 5, 72; Xen. Cyr. 1, 3, 12. 3, 1, 19. 4, 3, 16. 5, 4, 38. An. 2, 5, 5. 4, 1, 4 &c. Mem. 2, 1, 23; Dem. 21, 38; φθάσας Aesch. Pers. 752; Ar. Plut. 1103; Her. 6, 65. 7, 161; Thuc. 2, 91. 4. 127. 5, 9; Xen. An. 4, 6, 11; Dem. 15, 8. 21, 41, Dor. ἔφθαξα Theocr. 2, 115 (Vulg.), but -θασσα (Ahr. Mein. &c.): p. ἔφθᾰκα (Dem.) 18, 39; App. Celt. 21; Epist. Phal. 138 (Herch.); Oribas. 8, 2, πέφθᾰκα Christ. Pat. 2077; Pseud.-Callisth. 2, 10: plp. ἐφθάκει Plut. Galb. 17; Luc. Philops. 6; Arr. An. 3, 20, 2: 1 aor. pass. ἐφθάσθην late, Dio. Hal. 6, 25; Galen 4, 560; Joseph. Ant. 8, 4. Jud. B. 6, 7, 3: 2 aor. act. ἔφθην like ἔστην, 1 pers. rare Theogn. 969; Luc. Paras. 3; Plut. Mor. 774, ἔφθης

Od. 11, 58; Eur. Heracl. 121. I. T. 669; Ar. Eccl. 596, -θῃ Il. 16, 322; Her. 6, 70 &c.; Xen. Hell. 1, 6, 17. 7, 5, 10; Isocr. 17, 23; Dem. 43, 69. 57, 65, -θημεν Eur. Phoen. 1468; Isocr. 19, 22, -θητε 5, 7, -θησαν Her. 4, 136. 6, 91. 9, 70; Antiph. 2, β, 5; Isocr. 4, 86. 16, 37 (Bekk. B. S.), φθῆ Il. 11, 451, 3 pl. φθάν Il. 11, 51; subj. φθῶ, φθῇς Pl. Polit. 266, φθῇ Eur. Or. 1220. Andr. 991; Hippocr. 6, 232; Pl. Euthyd. 275, Epic φθῇσι Il. 23, 805, φθήῃ 16, 861, φθέωμεν Od. 16, 383, φθέωσι 24, 437; opt. φθαίην, -αίης Ar. Eq. 935. Av. 1018, -αίη Il. 13, 815, -αίησι, παρα- 10, 346 (Bekk.), -αίητε Her. 6, 108, φθαῖεν Plut. Marcel. 6; Joseph. Ant. 18, 6, 5; (φθῆθι?); φθῆναι Her. 6, 115; Thuc. 3, 89. 4, 4. 5, 72. 8, 92; Isocr. 4, 87. 165, προ- Eur. Phoen. 1385; φθάς Ionic, Her. 3, 71. 9, 46, and Epic in comp. ὑπο- Il. 7, 144, παρα- 22, 197: **2 aor. mid.** only part. φθάμενος as **act.** and Epic, Il. 13, 387; Hes. Op. 554. **Vb.** φθαστέον Oribas. 7, 8. φθανόμενος late, Joseph. 3, 7, 20; -εσθαι 4, 7, 2: **imp.** ἐφθάνοντο Jud. B. 5, 2, 4.

φθάνω has ᾱ Epic, ᾰ Attic. φθάν Epic 3 pl. for ἔφθησαν, Il. 11, 51, φθήῃ, φθῇσιν Epic 3 subj. for φθῇ, Il. 16, 861. 23, 805, also φθήῃσι, παρα- rare, Il. 10, 346 (Spitzn. Dind. La R.), but opt. παραφθαίησι (Bäuml. and now Bekk.) if correct, the only case of opt. with -σι, 1 pl. Epic φθέωμεν Od. 16, 383, φθέωσι 24, 437. The Epics have only **2 aor.**: Her. has both, but the 1st perhaps only twice φθάσας 6, 65. 7, 161. The Attics use both, excepting φθάς pt. of the 2: Aesch. only 1st, Eur. both, but 2d usually; and so Aristophanes: Thuc. Xen. and Dem. both, but 1st far more freq. Isocr. nearly alike, Antiph. 2d, Lycurg. 1st only. Thomas Magist. says the inf. "φθῆναι κάλλιον ἢ φθάσαι," and some able scholars have approved. We don't see the grounds of preference—if Thuc. and Dem. did, they disregarded them.

Φθέγγομαι *To utter, speak*, Dep. **mid.** Soph. O. C. 987; Eur. Hec. 192; Mosch. 1, 9; Dem. 37, 52; -γώμεθα Od. 10, 228; Pl. Leg. 664; -γοιντο Thuc. 7, 70; φθέγγου Aesch. Ch. 109, Ion. -γεο Il. 10, 67; -γεσθαι Her. 2, 57; Thuc. 7, 71; -όμενος Il. 10, 457; Heraclit. 12 (Byw.); Her. (Orac.) 1, 85. 8, 65; Xen. An. 6, 1, 23; Pl. Leg. 817; Crat. 435; Dem. 19, 337: **imp.** ἐφθεγγ- Ar. Eccl. 391; Hippocr. 5, 214; Pl. Phil. 25; Dem. 21, 79; Od. 10, 229. 255 (Wolf, Dind. La R.), φθεγγ- (Bekk.); so 12, 249 (Wolf, Bekk. Dind. La R.); Hes. Th. 831; Theogn. 266: **fut.** φθέγξομαι Pind. Ol. 1, 36; Aesch. Pr. 34; Ar. Ran. 242; Pl. Phil. 49 (Il. 21, 341 seems subj. aor.), Dor. -γξεῖται Theocr. 15, 99: **aor.** ἐφθεγξάμην Isocr. 12, 265, -έγξω Eur. Med. 1307; Pl. Phil. 24, Ion. -ξαο Her. 7, 103, -ξατο Batr. 271; Pind. P. 8, 56; Eur. Ion 729; Her. 1, 85; Xen. Cyr. 7, 1, 3; Dem. 34, 14, -ξάμεθα Pl.

Crat. 399, -άμεσθα Ar. Ran. 248 (chor.), φθεγξ- Il. 18, 218; Hes. Th. 168; Pind. Ol. 6, 14; -ξηται Her. 3, 84; -ξαιο Pind. P. 1, 81, -ξαιτο Her. 2, 57; Dem. 21, 79; -ασθαι 21, 95: **p.** ἔφθεγμαι -θέγμεθα (Pl.) Epist. 342, 2 sing. ἔφθεγξαι Pl. Leg. 830, -θεγκται Aristot. Anal. Post. 1, 10, 8; Aristid. 38 (488); but **pass.** Aristot. de Coelo 1, 9, 15, overlooked by Lexicogr. **Vb.** φθεγκτός Plut. Mor. 1017. Where three consonants occur difficult to be sounded together, the law of euphony requires the middle one to be thrown out: thus γγ before μαι in the **perf. pass.** (ἔφθεγχμαι) ἔφθεγγμαι, ἔφθεγμαι, but again ἔφθεγξαι; so μμ (κέκαμπμαι, κέκαμμμαι) κέκαμμαι. The **act.** form occurs in **aor.** φθέγξαι Babr. 27, 5 (2 pt. Bergk.)

Φθείρω *To corrupt, destroy*, Od. 17, 246; Simon. Am. 1, 13; Aesch. Ag. 949; Soph. Tr. 716; Ar. Av. 1068; Thuc. 4, 92; Pl. Leg. 906: **imp.** ἔφθειρον Thuc. 3, 85, iter. φθείρεσκε, δια- Her. 1, 36: **fut.** φθερῶ Xen. Hell. 7, 2, 11, δια- Aesch. Ag. 1266; Soph. Phil. 1069; Pl. Prot. 360, Ion. φθερέω, δια- Her. 5, 51, Epic φθέρσω, δια- Il. 13, 625: **aor.** ἔφθειρα Thuc. 2, 91; opt. φθείρειαν Soph. Aj. 1391; inf. φθεῖραι Aesch. Pers. 244; φθείραντες Xen. Hell. 7, 2, 4, late ἔφθερσα Lycophr. 1402: **p.** ἔφθαρκα Dinarch. 1, 64, δι- Eur. Med. 226; Pl. Leg. 659; Lys. 1, 16; Aeschin. 1, 158: **plp.** ἐφθάρκει, δι- Dem. 45, 27: **p. p.** ἔφθαρμαι Soph. El. 765; Thuc. 7, 12, 3 pl. -θάραται 3, 13; inf. ἐφθάρθαι Aristot. Met. 4, 16, δι- Isae. 9, 37; ἐφθαρμένος Aesch. Pers. 272: **plp.** ἐφθάρμην Ionic 3 pl. ἐφθάρᾰτο, δι- Her. 8, 90: **2 aor.** ἐφθάρην Her. 7, 10; Thuc. 7, 13; Pl. Leg. 708, 3 pl. ἔφθαρεν for -ησαν, Pind. P. 3, 36; φθαρείς Aesch. Pers. 283; φθαρῆναι Soph. O. R. 1502: **fut.** φθᾰρήσομαι Hippocr. 1, 598 (Lit.); Aristot. Met. 10, 10, 7; Plut. Mor. 374; Dio Cass. 50, 8, δια- Eur. Hec. 802; Thuc. 8, 75; Isocr. 4, 124; Pl. Apol. 29, Dor. φθαρησοῦμαι (Pl.) Tim. Locr. 94 (-σομαι Steph.): and as **pass. fut. mid.** φθεροῦμαι Soph. O. R. 272; Eur. Andr. 708; Thuc. 7, 48, and with change of vowel as **2 fut.**? φθαροῦμαι Oribas. 8, 23, Ionic διαφθαρέονται Her. 9, 42 (Mss. P F Bekk. Dind. -φθερέονται Gaisf. Stein) -φθαρέεται 8, 108 (Mss. M P K F S b Bekk. Gaisf. Dind. διαφθερ- Mss. a c Vulg. Stein): as **3 fut.** διεφθαρμέναι ἔσονται Xen. Cyr. 7, 2, 13: **pres.** φθείρεσθε Il. 21, 128: **2 perf.** ἔφθορα *simple* late, Galen 13, 343. 743, but δι- intrans. *am ruined*, Il. 15, 128; Hippocr. 8, 246 (Lit.); Plut. Lucull. 7; Luc. Soloec. 3; Philostr. Apoll. 123 (Kayser), and generally in late authors; but in the older Attic poets especially, **act.** *have destroyed*, Soph. El. 306; Eur. Hipp. 1014. I. T. 719. Med. 349; C. Fr. (Cratin.) 2, 226. (Eup.) 2, 565; Ar. Fr. 418. 479. **Mid.** φθείρομαι, δια- *to destroy, lose one's own*, Hippocr. 8, 60 (Lit.): **fut.** φθεροῦμαι as

pass. see above: **2 aor.** ? Ion. 3 pl. διεφθαρέατο **pass.** Her. 8, 90 (Gaisf. &c.), but **plp.** διεφθάρατο (Herm. Bekk. Dind. Bredow, Stein) perhaps correctly; though we do not with some think it a valid reason for rejecting the **aorist** simply because it is found nowhere else. The **plp.** certainly expresses the time more exactly, but we are not fond of saying that Her. could not in the circumstances express his meaning with sufficient precision by the **aorist.** In our language, at least, *were destroyed* would convey the meaning nearly as well as *had been destroyed* —διεφθειρέετο **imp.** in Ms. a c, is evidently wrong. **Vb.** φθαρτός Aristot. Met. 9, 10. A Dor. form of **fut. act.** καταφθαρεῖ occurs Plut. Mor. 240 (Vulg.), but -φθερεῖ (Dübn.); and διαφθαρέει *v. r.* for -φθερέει Her. 5, 51. φθαρησούμενος (Pl.) Tim. Locr. 94, has better support than -σόμενος, but in Plato's genuine writings, Eur. &c. the approved form is φθαρησόμ-. 3 pl. **p. p.** occurs in the Ionic form ἐφθάραται Thuc. 3, 13—a rare form this in Attic prose, occurring only, we think, in τάσσω, τρέφω, φθείρω, and only in Thuc. 3, 13. 4, 31. 5, 6. 7, 4; Xen. An. 4, 8, 5; and Pl. Rep. 533.

Φθινύθω *To consume, destroy, waste away* (φθίνω), trans. and intrans. Poet. and only **pres.** Il. 6, 327. Od. 1, 250, κατα- Emped. 27, ἀπο- Eur. Fr. 908; subj. -ύθωσι, ἀπο- Ap. Rh. 1, 683; φθινύθειν Il. 2, 346; Galen 10, 426; -ύθων Ap. Rh. 4, 902, -θουσα Opp. Hall. 1, 587, κατα- Hym. Cer. 353: and **imp.** unaugm. φθῐνῠθον Il. 17, 364, iter. φθινύθεσκε Il. 1, 491: except late if correct, **fut.** φθινύσω intrans. Geop. 1, 12, which Dind. would alter to φθινήσω. (ῐ ῠ.)

Φθίνω *To waste, decay* (φθίω), usu. intrans. Od. 11, 183; Pind. P. 1, 94; Soph. Aj. 1005; Com. Fr. (Xen.) 3, 614; Hippocr. 6, 314; Pl. Tim. 81; -ίνων Thuc. 5, 54; Aeschin. 2, 90, Ion. Dat. pl. -ινεῦσι Hippocr. 2, 674; -νειν Com. Fr. (Alex.) 3, 493: **imp.** ἔφθινον Her. 3, 29; Pl. Tim. 77, κατ- Pind. I. 8, 46: **fut.** φθινήσω Geop. 1, 12, 34, suggested by Dind. for φθινύσω (Vulg.), as if from a form (φθινέω): and **aor.** ἐφθίνησα, φθινήσας Hippocr. 5, 468 (Lit.); Luc. Paras. 57, κατα- Plut. Mor. 117, and late ἔφθῖνα, φθῖναι Nicol. Rhet. 9, 3 (Walz): **p.** (ἔφθῐκα, see φθίω) ἐφθινηκότες, κατ- Plut. Cic. 14: as **2 aor.** might be reckoned ἔφθῐθον, ἀπ- (from a form in -θω) which used to stand Od. 5, 110. 133. 7, 251, but is now altered from the v. r. to ἀπέφθιθεν for -θησαν, which occurs in tmesi 23, 331 (Bekk.) See φθίω. ῑ Epic, ῐ Attic, and Pind. φθίνει P. 1, 94, κατέφθῐνε I. 8, 46. φθίνει is trans. Soph. El. 1414 (Nauck), and is the reading of the Mss. Herm. however contrives to make it intrans. by altering it to inf. φθίνειν and making σε the subject, instead of the object.

φθίνων act. Chariton 1, 1, 8, he would change to fut. φθίσων, which Matthiae and Wunder approve: Hercher reads σώματος αὐτῷ φθίνοντος intrans. καταφθίνουσι also is a well-supported reading, and trans. Theocr. 25, 122 (Fritzsche, and Ziegl. 1 ed.) Meineke from some misgiving about its being act. in the pres. recalls the old reading καταφθιίρουσι (so Ziegl. 2 ed.), but suggests καταφθινύθουσι. The emendation suggested is not violent, and it satisfies the sense and metre; but καταφθινύθω is notoriously intrans. as well as trans. and we really do not see why φθίνω should not be allowed to be so too: ἥλιος πάντα βλαστάνει καὶ φθίνει Trag. Fr. adesp. 376 (Nauck). Kühner and Jelf say "φθίνω is found intrans. in prose also, but only in the pres." This we think is a mistake, ἔφθινε Her. 3, 29; Pl. Tim. 77.

Φθίω *To waste, consume*, Poet. indic. not found except in the form φθείει, θνήσκει Hesych; subj. φθίῃς Od. 2, 368; imp. ἔφθιον Il. 18, 446 (pres. and imp. in Hom. only, and intrans. except perhaps Il. 18, 446 quoted, fut. and aor. trans.): fut. φθίσω Il. 22, 61. 16, 461, ἀπο- Soph. Aj. 1027 (Dind. *now*): aor. ἔφθισα, Epic φθῖσα Od. 20, 67, but ἀπ-έφθισα Aesch. Ag. 1454; subj. φθίσωμεν Od. 16, 369; φθίσειεν Ap. Rh. 3, 460; φθίσον Soph. O. R. 202; φθῖσαι Od. 4, 741; φθίσας Aesch. Eum. 172; Soph. Tr. 1043: p. ἔφθῖκα intrans. and late, Dioscor. Praef. 1, 2, p. 6, ἀπο- Themist. 28, 341: p. p. ἔφθῖμαι Od. 20, 340; Theogn. 1141 (Schaef. Bergk, Ziegl.), ἐξ- Aesch. Pers. 927, see aor.: plp. ἐφθίμην, -θῖσο Aesch. Sept. 970, -θῖτο Theogn. 1141 (Vulg.); Soph. O. R. 962; Eur. Alc. 414, ὑπερ- Pind. P. 6, 30, 3 pl. ἐφθίατο Il. 1, 251, see 2 aor. mid.: aor. pass. ἐφθίθην, 3 pl. -θιθεν for -θησαν, in tmesi Od. 23, 331. **Mid.** intrans. *to perish*, fut. φθίσομαι Il. 11, 821. Od. 13, 384; Ap. Rh. 3, 465: 1 aor. φθίσασθαι, ἀπο- Q. Sm. 14, 545: and as 2 aor. syncop. ἐφθίμην Il. 18, 100? Soph. O. R. 962, ἐξ- εφθ- Od. 9, 163; subj. Epic φθίεται for -ηται, Il. 20, 173, φθιόμεσθα for -ώμεσθα 14, 87; opt. φθίμην, ἀπο- Od. 10, 51, (φθῖο), φθῖτο Od. 11, 330; imper. 3 sing. φθίσθω Ap. Rh. 3, 778, ἀπο- Il. 8, 429; inf. φθῖσθαι Il. 9, 246; φθίμενος Il. 8, 359; Pind. P. 4, 112; Aesch. Ch. 364; Soph. Tr. 1161; Eur. Tr. 1083, -ένη Alc. 80; rare in prose -μενοι Xen. Cyr. 8, 7, 18. The ι of φθίω is short in Hom. except φθίῃς Od. 2, 368, ἔφθῖεν Il. 18, 446, φθῖεται 20, 173; in φθίσω long in Epic, Il. 6, 407, φθίσονται 11, 821.; Ap. Rh. 3, 465, φθίσειεν 3, 460, ἀπο- 4, 1292, but ἔφθῖσαν Opp. H. 5, 577, ἀπέφθῖσεν Ap. Rh. 4, 1440; short in Attic, ἀποφθίσειν Soph. Aj. 1027, -φθίσας Aesch. Eum. 73, κατα- 727, ἀποφθῖσαι Soph. Tr. 709, always in ἔφθῖμαι, ἐφθίμην (plp. or syncop. aor. except opt. ἀποφθίμην, φθῖτο for -φθιίμην &c.), and ἐφθἴθην. So Vb. φθῖτός Aesch. Pers. 523; Aristot. Nat. Ausc. 3, 1, 5, ἄ-φθῖτος Il. 2, 186.

φθείσθω, φθεῖσθαι which used to stand Ap. Rh. 3, 778. 754, have been altered from Mss. to φθίσθω, φθῖσθαι, but φθεῖσθαι still Q. Sm. 3, 17. 12, 351. 13, 230 (Koechl.), and φθεῖται Or. Sib. 3, 400, for φθίεται; or, as some think, for fut. φθίσεται, -ίεται, contr. -ῖται, and to represent ῑ, -εῖται. The fut. and aor. of this verb are always act. but the pres. and imp. according to Buttm. and others, neuter. We think φρένας ἔφθιεν Il. 18, 446, at least doubtful, see φθινύθω κῆρ Od. 10, 485, αἰῶνα 18, 204.

Φθονέω *To envy*, Il. 4, 55; Od. 18, 16; Pind. I. 5, 24; Aesch. Sept. 236; Soph. Ant. 553; Ar. Thesm. 252; Her. 7, 237; Thuc. 6, 78; Lys. 24, 2; Xen. Conv. 4, 43; -έοιμι Od. 11, 381, -οῖμι Pl. Rep. 528; -νῶν Thuc. 2, 35; -έειν Od. 18, 18, -εῖν Thuc. 3, 84: imp. ἐφθόνουν Lys. 2, 67; Isocr. 18, 51: fut. -ήσω Thuc. 2, 64; Pl. Prot. 320; Isocr. 5, 131: aor. ἐφθόνησα Eur. Fr. 347 (D.); Her. 8, 109; Pl. Apol. 33; Isocr. 4, 29; subj. -ήσω Aesch. Pr. 584; Ar. Ach. 497; Pl. Prot. 320; -ήσας Soph. O. R. 310; Thuc. 3, 43 &c., and -νεσα, -νέσῃς Anth. 5, 304; -νέσειε Nonn. Dion. 3, 159; -νέσας Anth. 7, 607 (Pseud.-Phocyl. 70, now corrected from -νέσῃς to φθονέοις Mss. Bergk): (perf.?): p. p. late ἐφθονημένος Joseph. Ant. 6, 11, 10: aor. ἐφθονήθην Plut. Mor. 772; -ηθείη Eur. Elec. 30; (Hippocr.) 9, 320; D. Hal. Ant. 5, 66; -ηθείς Xen. Mem. 4, 2, 33: fut. φθονηθήσομαι Xen. Hier. 11, 15: and as pass. fut. mid. φθονήσομαι Aristot. Rhet. Alex. 37, 47; (Dem.) 47, 70: pres. φθονεῖται Thuc. 6, 16. Mid. only fut. φθονήσει, -σονται as pass. *will incur envy* Aristot. and (Dem.) quoted.

Φῐλέω *To love*, Il. 10, 552; Aesch. Ch. 894; Soph. Ant. 1056; Ar. Eq. 732; Her. 3, 82; Thuc. 4, 28; Pl. Phaedr. 228, Aeol. φίλημι Sapph. 79 (Bergk), -ληισθα 22, 3 pl. -έοισι Pind. P. 3, 18, Dor. -λεῦντι Theocr. 5, 80; Epic subj. φιλέῃσι Od. 15, 70; φιλέοι 15, 305, and -λοίη 4, 692; imper. φίλει Pind. P. 5, 26; Soph. Ant. 524; Dor. pt. φιλέοισα Theocr. 16, 105, -λεῦσα 27, 2, φιλεῦντας Od. 3, 221: imp. ἐφίλει Il. 14, 491; Pl. Leg. 680, -ουν Lycurg. 71, -ευν Theogn. 786, φίλεον Il. 9, 343. Od. 5, 135, iter. φιλέεσκον Il. 3, 388. 9, 450; Anth. 5, 285: fut. φιλήσω Aesch. Ag. 1559; Soph. O. C. 1131; Xen. Conv. 8, 21, Dor. -άσω Theocr. 23, 33: aor. ἐφίλησα Pind. P. 2, 16. 9, 18 (most or best Mss. Ahr. Schneidw. Momms. Christ, -ᾱσα Boeckh, Dissen); Soph. El. 1363; Xen. Cyr. 7, 3, 9, φίλησα Il. 3, 207; Pind. N. 5, 44, Dor. ἐφίλᾱσα Theocr. 20, 31. 42 (Pind. P. 2, 16 &c. quoted, Boeckh, Bergk), φιλᾱσ- Theocr. 20, 36. 38 (Pind. N. 5, 44 quoted, Boeckh); subj. -ήσω

Il. 9, 117; Ar. Lys. 1036, Dor. -ἁσω Theocr. 3, 19; opt. -ήσειε Her. 2, 41; φίλησον Ar. Thesm. 1191, Dor. -ᾶσον Theocr. 23, 40; -ῆσαι Od. 14, 322; Ar. Av. 671; Pl. Rep. 468, Dor. -ᾶσαι Theocr. 20, 1; -ήσας Pind. N. 7, 88 (all Mss. Bergk, Momms.); Com. Fr. (Men.) 4, 232, Dor. -άσας Theocr. 23, 42 (Pind. N. 7, 88 quoted, Boeckh); p. πεφίληκα Pind. P. 1, 13: p. p. πεφίλημαι Pind. N. 4, 46; Xen. An. 1, 9, 28; -ᾱμένος Theocr. 3, 3. 11, 6 (Vulg. Fritz. -ημ- Ahrens, Ziegl.): aor. ἐφιλήθην Eur. Hec. 1000; Pl. Phaedr. 253, Epic 3 pl. ἐφίληθεν Il. 2, 668 (φίλ- Bekk.), -λᾶθεν Theocr. 7, 60 (Vulg. Fritz. -ληθ- Ahr. Ziegl.); -ηθείς Her. 4, 176: fut. φιληθήσομαι Stob. (Epictet.) 46, 88: as pass. fut. mid. φιλήσομαι Od. 1, 123. 15, 281; Antiph. 1, 19, ἀντι- Theocr. 28, 6 (some edit.): 3 fut. πεφιλήσομαι Callim. Del. 270. **Mid.** from (φίλλω), aor. ἐφῑλάμην as act. and Epic, ἐφίλαο Anth. 5, 289, -ίλατο Il. 5, 61, φίλατο 20, 304; subj. φίλωμαι H. Cer. 117; Hes. Th. 97; imper. φῖλαι Il. 5, 117 (pass. φίλᾰτο Ap. Rh. 3, 66; φῑλάμενος Anth. App. 317): to this form belongs p. p. πέφιλμαι late, Ephraem. Caes. v. 35 (Maii nov. Collect. T. 3); Tzetz. Exeg. Il. p. 21, 15; Prol. Christ. Pat. 7.—φῑλήμεναι Epic inf. pres. Il. 22, 265; inf. fut. φῑλησέμεν Od. 4, 171. φίλησθα Aeol. 2 pres. Sappho 22 (Bergk *now*), -εισθα (Ahr.), -ῆσθα (Vulg.) Vb. φιλητός Aristot. Eth. Nic. 8 (2), 1, -τέος Soph. Ant. 524; Aristot. Eth. Nic. 9, 3, 3.

Φῑλοτῑμέομαι *To love honour, be jealous, feel piqued,* Pl. Rep. 336; Lys. 14, 2; Isocr. 8, 41 (Dep. with aor. pass. and later mid.): imp. ἐφιλοτ- Lycurg. 98; D. Sic. 4, 28: fut. -τιμήσομαι Pl. Phaedr. 234; Lys. 29, 14; Dem. 20, 103; later as mid. fut. pass. -τιμηθήσομαι Diod. Sic. 11, 18 (Bekk. -τιμήσ- Dind.): aor. ἐφιλοτιμησάμην Ael. V. H. 3, 1. 9, 29; Polyb. 20, 8; Herodn. 1, 13, 6; Ach. Tat. 7, 11; Joseph. Ant. 3, 6, 1: *classic*, aor. pass. as mid. ἐφιλοτιμήθην Xen. Mem. 2, 9, 3; Pl. Lach. 182; Isocr. 4, 44; Isae. 2, 42: p. p. πεφιλοτίμημαι as mid. Dem. 28, 22 (42, 24); Diod. Sic. 5, 49; Aristaen, 1, 1, but pass. Aristid. 34, 446: plp. ἐπεφιλοτίμητο Joseph. Genes. 47. The act. form we have not seen, except aor. pt. φιλοτιμήσας late, Pseud.-Callisth. 3, 3 (Meusel), missed by Lexicogr.

Φῐλοφρονέομαι *To be well disposed, receive kindly,* Pl. Leg. 738, Dep. (with aor. mid. and pass.): imp. ἐφῐλοφρονέετο Her. 3, 50, -νοῦντο Pl. Leg. 678: fut. -νήσομαι Luc. Tim. 48. Nav. 22: aor. ἐφῐλοφρονησάμην Xen. An. 4, 5, 34. Cyr. 3, 1, 8; Plut. Pyrrh. 34. Pomp. 3: aor. pass. as mid. ἐφιλοφρονήθην, -ηθείς Xen. Cyr. 3, 1, 40; Plut. Alcib. 5. Cat. Min. 68. Marcell. 10; Dio. Hal. 3, 7. Vb. φῐλοφρονητέον Theod. Prod. 9, 378 (Herch.) In late authors the aor. pass. is the more frequent. The act. form is denied, but if the reading be sound Plut. Mor. 750, there stands φιλοφρονοῦσι; so 2 Macc. 2, 25; φιλοφρονεῖν Stob. (Nicostr.) 70, 12.

Φιτύω *To sow* &c. Aesch. Supp. 312; Soph. Ant. 645; Pl. Rep. 461, usu. Poet. for φυτεύω: **fut.** φῑτύσω Eur. Alc. 294: **aor.** ἐφίτῡσα Soph. Aj. 1296; Eur. Alc. 1137; Pl. Critias. 116, -ῦσαι Aesch. Pr. 233; Pl. Leg. 879. **Mid. fut.** φῑτύσομαι, -ύσεαι Mosch. 2, 160: **aor.** φιτύσατο Hes. Th. 986; Opp. Cyn. 1, 4; opt. -ύσαιο Ap. Rh. 4, 807. (φῑτύω, but φῑτύσ-.) Of prose writers, Plato alone seems to use this verb.

(Φλάζω) *To burst*, intrans. and only **2 aor.** ἔφλᾰδον Aesch. Ch. 28 (chor.) So φράζω, πέφρᾰδον.

Φλάω *To bruise*, a collateral form of θλάω, Ar. Plut. 784; Hippocr. 3, 218. 220 (Lit.): **imp.** ἔφλα Ar. Nub. 1376: **fut.** φλᾱσω, Dor. -ασσῶ Theocr. 5, 148 (Mss. Ziegl. Ahr. and *now* Mein.), -ᾱσῶ (Vulg.): **aor.** ἔφλᾰσα, φλᾱσα Pind. N. 10, 68; φλάσειε Hippocr. 3, 218 (Lit.), -άσσαιμι Theocr. 5, 150 (Mss. Ziegl. Ahr. Mein. -ᾱσαιμι Vulg.); -άσας Hippocr. 7, 160: **p. p.** πέφλασμαι Hippocr. 3, 202. 232 (Lit.): **aor.** ἐφλάσθην Hippocr. 6, 402; φλασθῇ 6, 306; -θείη 3, 200; -θῆναι 3, 218; -θείς 3, 220 (Lit.) In Kühn's edit. σ is sometimes dropped, φλαθῆναι. **Fut.** φλάσει Hippocr. 3, 358 (Kühn), has been altered to **pres.** φλᾷ (Lit.) In Theocr. the **fut.** and **aor.** forms -ᾱσῶ, -αξῶ; -ᾱσαιμι, -άξαιμι have been withdrawn for -ασσῶ, -άσσαιμι. There is also φλάω *to eat greedily, swallow*, only **pres.** and **imp.** and confined to Comedy, Ar. Pax 1306. Plut. 718.

Φλεγέθω *To burn*, Poet. trans. and intrans. only **pres. act.** -έθει Il. 17, 738; Aesch. Supp. 87 (chor.), -έθουσιν Il. 18, 211; -έθων Il. 21, 358; Hes. Th. 846; Soph. Tr. 99 (chor.); Eur. Phoen. 169 (chor.): and **pass.** φλεγεθοίατο for -οιντο, Il. 23, 197.

Φλέγω *To burn*, trans. and intrans. Il. 21, 13; Pind. Ol. 2, 72; Aesch. Sept. 433; Soph. O. R. 191; Eur. Tr. 308, Dor. 3 pl. -γοντι Pind. P. 5, 45; -γων Aesch. Sept. 52; Ar. Thesm. 680; -γειν Soph. Aj. 673: **imp.** ἔφλεγον Anth. 5, 123; Opp. Hal. 2, 669, φλέγον Pind. N. 6, 38; Mosch. 6, 3: **fut.** φλέξω Trag. Fr. (Incert.) 268 (Wagn.); Anth. 5, 179; Ap. Rh. 3, 582, κατα- Il. 22, 512: **aor.** ἔφλεξα in tmesi Pind. Ol. 10, 74; φλέξον Aesch. Pr. 582, in comp. ἀντ-έφλεξε Pind. Ol. 3, 20, ἐξ- Ar. Pax 608; inf. ἐπιφλέξαι Thuc. 2, 77: (**perf.** ?): **p. p.** πέφλεγμαι late, Lycophr. 806, συμ- Plut. Mor. 770: **1 aor.** ἐφλέχθην Hom. Epigr. 14, 23; Heracl. Incred. 26, κατ- Thuc. 4, 133, ἀν- (Pl.) Epist. 349: **2 aor.** late, ἐφλέγην, ἀν- Luc. D. Deor. 9, 2; Ach. Tat. 6, 18, ἐξ- Anth. 12, 178, κατα- Dio Chrys. 46, 1, συγκατα- Plut. Mor. 499; Dio. Hal. 14, 2 (4) Kiessl.: **fut.** late συμ-φλεγησόμενος Joseph. Jud. B.

7, 8, 5; -γήσεσθαι Themist. Paraphr. 3, 5: and mid. as pass. κατα-φλέξεσθαι Joseph. Jud. B. 4, 6, 3, missed by Lexicographers: pres. p. φλέγονται Aesch. Ag. 91; Bacchyl. 14, 12 (B.): imp. φλέγετο Il. 21, 365. Vb. ἄ-φλεκτος Eur. Hel. 1334. This verb is very rare in prose. The act. *simple* form we have not seen before Plutarch, part. φλέγουσι Rom. 28, -γοντα Mor. 646; φλέγεται however is used by Pl. Leg. 716, -γεσθαι Tim. 85, and ἐφλεγόμην Charm. 155: rare even in comp. ἐπέφλεγον Her. 8, 32, ἐπιφλέξαι Thuc. 2, 77, ἀνεφλέχθη (Pl.) Epist. 349, κατα-φλεχθείς Thuc. 4, 133.

Φλέω *To flow, abound*, only part. φλέων Aesch. Ag. 377. 1416.

Φλίβω *To squeeze*, Aeol. and Ion. for θλίβω (Theocr. pres. pass. φλίβεται 15, 76); Hippocr. φλιβόμενος 6, 300 (Lit.): fut. mid. φλίψεται formerly Od. 17, 221, now θλίψεται: aor. ἔφλιψα Hesych.; ἐκ-φλίψας Hippocr. 6, 292 (Lit.): 2 aor. pass. ἐφλίβην, ἐκ-φλιβῇ Hippocr. 6, 292 (Lit.).

Φλύω *To boil up, over, bubble*, Aesch. Sept. 661, ἐπι- Ap. Rh. 1, 481: imp. ἔφλυε in tmesi, Il. 21, 361 (ῠ in Hom. ῡ in Ap. Rh.): aor. ἔφλῠσα Anth. 7, 351, ἀπ- Archil. 35 (Lob. Schneid. -έφλοσα Vulg. Bergk, so Gaisf. 104); φλύξωσι, ἀπο- Ap. Rh. 3, 583; inf. φλύσαι Aesch. Pr. 504, also φλύξαι, ἐκ- Ap. Rh. 1, 275, perhaps from φλύζω Nic. Al. 214. The reading Archil. Fr. 35, used to be ἀπέφλοσαν (Gaisf. 104, so Bergk *now*). φλῡων Athen. (Alex. Aetol.) 15, 56, is a conjecture of Schweigh. for φλοίων. There seems to be no decisive instance of ῡ in the fut. and aor. φλῡω in the sense *burn, scorch*, with ῡ, περι-φλῡω should, perhaps, be written περι-φλεύω, to which belongs περι-πεφλευσμένος Her. 5, 77.

Φοβέω *To terrify* (φόβος), in Hom. always with the accessory idea of *flight, make flee*, Il. 17, 177; Soph. O. R. 296; Hippocr. 6, 660; Antiph. 4, γ, 2; Thuc. 7, 77; Pl. Theag. 121; imper. φόβει Aesch. Sept. 262, 3 pl. φοβεόντων for -βείτωσαν, Her. 7, 235: imp. ἐφόβουν Thuc. 5, 45, iter. φοβέεσκον Hes. Sc. 162: fut. φοβήσω rare, Eur. Heracl. 357, ἐκ- Thuc. 4, 126: aor. ἐφόβησα, Il. 15, 15; Thuc. 2, 76. 4, 115, φοβ- Il. 20, 90; φοβῆσαι 20, 187; Xen. Cyr. 5, 3, 47; φοβήσας Pl. Rep. 551: p. p. πεφόβημαι and other pass. forms as mid. see below. Mid. φοβέομαι *to fear for oneself, dread, flee*, espec. in Hom. Il. 12, 46; Aesch. Ch. 46; Soph. Aj. 228; Ar. Nub. 1178; Thuc. 3, 31; Isocr. 5, 84, -βεῦμαι Bion 3, 14, Ion. 2 sing. -βέαι Her. 1, 39; -βέηται 7, 36; imper. -βοῦ Ar. Plut. 1091, Ion. φοβέο Her. 7, 52, -βεῦ 1, 9; φοβούμενος Antiph. 2, γ, 7, -εύμ- Il. 8, 149, -εόμ- Her. 7, 235: imp. ἐφοβούμην Soph. O. R. 722; Thuc. 4, 108; Andoc. 3, 2; Lys. 14, 15; Pl. Conv. 198, φοβέοντο Il. 16, 304: fut. φοβήσομαι Il.

22, 250; Xen. Cyr. 1, 4, 19. 3, 3, 18. 8, 7, 15; Pl. Leg. 649; Isocr. 15, 121; Aeschin. 3, 212; Dem. 15, 23 (B. S. Dind. and *now* Bekk.); -βήσοιντο Xen. Hell. 2, 3, 39: **aor.** late, ἐφυβησάμην, imper. φόβησαι Anacreont. 31, 11 (Bergk): as **mid. p. p.** πεφόβημαι Il. 10, 510: Soph. Aj. 139; Ar. Nub. 294; Her. 9, 70; Antiph. 5, 45; Thuc. 1, 144. 2, 89; Pl. Euthyphr. 12: **plp.** ἐπεφοβήμην, -ησθε Andoc. 2, 8, -ηντο Thuc. 5, 50, πεφοβήατο Il. 21, 206: **aor.** ἐφοβήθην Eur. Rhes. 47; Her. 8, 27; Thuc. 1, 51; Pl. Polit. 268, Hom. always 3 pl. ἐφόβηθεν Il. 15, 326. 637, and φόβηθεν 5, 498 (Bekk. La R.). 16, 294. 659 &c. (Bekk.); subj. φοβηθῶ, -θῇς Aesch. Pr. 128; Eur. Andr. 994; Ar. Av. 654; Isocr. 12, 180, Dor. -āθῇς Theocr. 23, 41; -βηθείς Il. 22, 137; Aesch. Sept. 476; Antiph. 2, β, 5. 4, δ, 1; Thuc. 6, 21 &c.: **fut.** φοβηθήσομαι Xen. Cyr. 3, 3, 30 (Vulg. Popp. Saupp. -βήσομαι Dind.); Plut. Brut. 40; Luc. Zeux. 9. **Vb.** φοβητός Soph. Phil. 1154, φοβητέος Pl. Rep. 452. **Fut. pass.** φοβηθήσομαι is losing ground in classic authors. Lud. Dind. admits only **mid.** φοβήσομαι in Xen. *now*, and Bekk. &c. in Dem.; so in Plato φοβηθησόμεθα Rep. 470 (Vulg.), -βησόμεθα (best Mss. Bait. O. W. F. Herm.), so -βηθήσομαι Apol. 29 (some Mss. Bekk. Stallb.), -βήσομαι (best Mss. Bait. O. W. Herm.)

Φοιτάω *To go to and fro*, has some dialectic peculiarities, φοιτῶσι Od. 2, 182; Eur. Ion 154, Ionic -τέουσι Her. 2, 66; φοιτᾶν Pl. Phaed. 59, Dor. -τῆν Bion 13; φοιτῶντες Thuc. 1, 139, -τέοντες Her. 6, 49, φοιτῶσα Eur. H. F. 846, -τέουσα Her. 3, 119: **imp.** ἐφοίτων Thuc. 6, 104, -τεον Her. 6, 126. 9, 25, ἐφοίτα Thuc. 8, 18, φοίτα Il. 9, 10, ἐφοίτεε, ἐπ- Nonn. 1, 321, ἐφοίτη Theocr. 2, 155, Dual ἐφοιτάτην C. Fr. 4, 615, φοιτήτην Il. 12, 266, φοίτεσκον Asii Fr. 13 (Markscheff.): **fut.** -ήσω, Aeol. and Dor. -άσω Sapph. 68 (B.), -āσῶ Callim. L. Pal. 130.

Φορέω *To carry* (φέρω), Il. 5, 499; Soph. Tr. 965; Ar. Thesm. 148; Her. 1, 135; Xen. An. 7, 4, 4; Isae. 5, 11, Aeol. 3 pl. -έοισι Theocr. 28, 11; Epic subj. φορέῃσι Od. 5, 328. 9, 10; φορέοις Il. 6, 457, φοροῖ Pl. Theaet. 197, and φοροίης Eur. Hel. 619, -ροίη Od. 9, 320; φόρει Soph. Ant. 705; -ρῶν Thuc. 1, 6, Dor. -εῦντος Theocr. 13, 7, -εῦσαι 15, 105; Epic inf. φορήμεναι Il. 15, 310, -ρῆναι 2, 107. Od. 17, 224: **imp.** ἐφόρουν Thuc. 2, 75, 'φόρουν Ar. Eccl. 341, ἐφόρει Il. 4, 137; Archil. 93, ἐφόρεον trisyll. Od. 22, 456; Her. 1, 171, φόρεον Od. 22, 448, ἐφόρευν Hes. Sc. 293, iter. φορέεσκε Il. 13, 372, -έεσκον 2, 770: **fut.** -ρήσω Ar. Lys. 632; Xen. Vect. 4, 32, and late -ρέσω V. T. Prov. 16, 23; Orac. Sib. 8, 294, reg.: **aor.** ἐφόρησα Isae. 4, 7 (B. S. Scheibe); Callim. Dian. 213, φόρησ- Il. 19, 11; δια-φορήσας Isae. 6, 43. 61, ἐκ- 6, 42; δια-φορῆσαι 6, 39; (Dem.) 47, 65, and ἐφόρεσα perhaps later, for though it is the Mss. reading Isae. 4, 7 (Vulg. Bekk.), yet in every other instance he uses the formation in η, see passages quoted, and 11, 31: Bait. Saupp. have edited uniformly -ησα. The formation in ε, -ρεσα seems certain in later Auth. Aristid. 545; Palaeph. 52; V. T. Apocr. Sir. 11, 5; Clemens. Epist. 5 (Muralto); Herm. Past. p. 94; D. Sic. 16, 64 (Bekk. -ησα L. Dind.): p. late πεφορηκότες Herm. Past. p. 97, but κατα-πεφόρηκας Pl. Rep. 5, 87, ἐκ- Dem. 42, 30: p. p. πεφόρηται Opp. C. 4, 407; πεφορημένος Her. 2, 91; Pl. Tim. 52: plp. πεφόρητο Orph. Arg. 819: aor. φορηθείς Simon. C. 148, 10 (B.); but ἐφορήθην, ἐξ- Her. 2, 150; -ηθῶ, δια- Ar. Av. 355: as pass. fut. mid. φορήσομαι Plut. Mor. 398. **Mid.** φορέυμαι *to carry, take to oneself*, -ουμένη Eur. El. 309, -εύμενος Ap. Rh. 2, 192: fut. φορήσομαι Hesych.; but pass. Plut. Mor. (Serap.) 398: aor. ἐφορησάμην, ἐξ- Isae. 6, 39; (Dem.) 47, 53, παρα- Pl. Leg. 858, ἐν- Alciphr. 1, 35; D. Sic. 4, 4; Epist. Phal. 5: and as mid. aor. pass. ἐν-εφορήθης (Isocr.) Epist. 10 (Bens.); Plut. Mor. 703. 871 &c.; Paus. 10, 23, 8. **Vb.** φορητός Pind. Fr. 65 (Bergk); Aesch. Pr. 979; Aristot. Nat. Ausc. 3, 1, 5. φορέησι Bion 1, 83 (Vulg. Mein. 1 ed., now variously -έουσι, -έοισι, ἐφέρησε) seems to be a false form. It has been called and accepted as Doric for φορέει. Doric it is not; for in the concourse έει indic. sing. the Dorians invariably either left the ε open φιλέεις, -έει, or absorbed it φιλεῖς, -λεῖ, never -λῇς, -λῇ: only in the inf. does -έειν become -ῆν, and rarely if at all now in the later Doric, except in the old recensions.

Φορύνω *To mix, soil, spoil*, Hesych. Suid. (imp. pass. φορύνετο Od. 22, 21, ἐφορύν- Q. Sm. 2, 356): 1 aor. (from φορύσσω) φορύξας Od. 18, 336; Hippocr. 1, 576. 8, 174 (Lit.): p. p. πεφορυγμένος late, Nic. Ther. 302; Opp. Cyn. 1, 381; Q. Sm. 12, 550: pres. pass. φορύσσεται Opp. Hal. 5, 269. **Mid.** aor. ἐφορύξατο Nic. Ther. 203.

Φράγνυμι *To break*, rare in *simple*, and only pres. φράγνυτε Anth. 7, 391; φραγνύντες Anon. in Suid.; Jos. Ant. 18, 9, 1: imp. ἐφράγνυσαν, ἀπ- Thuc. 7, 74. **Mid.** φράγνυται Plut. Caes. 24, φράγνυσαι, ἀπο- Soph. Ant. 241, φράγνυνται Ar. Fr. 336 (D.): imp. ἐφράγνυντο Plut. Phoc. 11. **Vb.** ἄ-φρακτος Thuc. 1, 6. See φράσσω.

(**Φραδάζω** or **φραδάω**) *To tell, make known*, only aor. φρᾰδᾰσε Pind. N. 3, 26 (Mss. Bergk), -ασσε (Vulg. Momms. Bergk 4 ed.), collat. form of φράζω.

Φράζω *To show, tell* (φράδω), Soph. Ph. 25; Ar. Av. 50; Her. 1, 119; Thuc. 5, 66; Lys. 1, 23; Isocr. 7, 36; Isae. 11, 3; late Epic Opp. Cyn. 1, 306, Dor. -άσδω Theocr. 20, 7; φράζοι Antiph. 6, 13; φράζε Aesch. Ag. 1061 &c.; -άζων Pind. I. 6, 68:

imp. ἔφραζον Ar. Eq. 1048; Her. 4, 113; Antiph. 6, 23; Thuc. 7, 43; Dem. 27, 55. 50, 27, φράζον Pind. N. 1, 61: fut. φρᾰ́σω Aesch. Pr. 844; Her. 3, 6; Pl. Phil. 25; Andoc. 3, 4; Lycurg. 32; Aeschin. 3, 171: aor. ἔφρᾰσα, -ασεν Hom. H. Ven. 128. Merc. 442; Pind. I. 4, 38; Her. 7, 213. 219; Hippocr. 8, 98, Hom. only φράσε Od. 11, 22; Aesch. Ag. 231 (chor.), φράσσεν Hes. Fr. 125, φρασάτην Hes. Th. 892, ἔφρασαν Her. 2, 150. 8, 55, in Attic ἔφρασα Ar. Eq. 647, ἔφρασας Soph. El. 1265; Pl. Men. 92, ἔφρασεν Thuc. 1, 145; Xen. An. 2, 3, 3. 4, 5, 29. Hell. 1, 6, 38; Isae. 3, 31, φράσεν Aesch. Ag. 231 (chor.), ἔφρασαν Thuc. 3, 33; subj. φράσω Pl. Charm. 167; Com. Fr. (Philyll.) 2, 859, -άσῃς (Mon.) 516, -σωσιν Thuc. 7, 25; φράσαιμι Soph. Ph. 551. Ar. Av. 1544, -σειας Soph. Ph. 1222; Ar. Ran. 110, φράσαις Luc. Halc. 4, φράσειε Soph. O. C. 1657; Ar. Fr. 187 (D), and φράσαι Com. Fr. (Antiph.) 3, 61; φράσον Aesch. Pers. 333; Ar. Nub. 314; Isae. 11, 5, -σάτω Ar. Fr. 1 (D); Lys. 4, 5; Dem. 1, 12. 16, 8, φράσατε Ar. Eccl. 1125, -άσσατε Pind. P. 4, 117; inf. φράσαι Pind. Ol. 2, 100; Soph. Ant. 1060; Thuc. 3, 42; Com. Fr. (Pher.) 2, 346 &c.; Pl. Phaedr. 255; Andoc. 2, 21; Isocr. 15, 100. 117; Aeschin. 3, 229 &c.; φράσας Soph. O. C. 1274; Ar. Eccl. 552; Her. 2, 86; Thuc. 5, 60. 6, 58; Pl. Men. 92; Andoc. 1, 65; Dem. 8, 76 &c., Dor. φράσαις Pind. Ol. 2, 60: p. πέφρᾰκα Isocr. 5, 93: p. p. πέφρασμαι Aesch. Supp. 438; Hippocr. 3, 208. 6, 54 (Lit.); Isocr. 15, 195. 16, 39; Aristot. Mirab. 109; Epic part. πεφραδμένος, προ- Hes. Op. 655: aor. ἐφράσθην as mid. see below: 2 aor. act. ἔφρᾰδον Hesych., Epic. ἐπέφραδον Il. 10, 127. 16, 51. Od. 8, 68; Hes. Th. 74; Ap. Rh. 2, 959 (from ἐπιφράζω? Thiersch), and πέφρᾰδον Il. 14, 500. Od. 1, 444; Ap. Rh. 4, 260, -δέτην Hes. Th. 475; πεφράδοι Il. 14, 335; imper. πέφραδε Od. 1, 273; inf. πεφραδέμεν Od. 7, 49; Hes. Op. 766, and πεφραδέειν Od. 19, 477. Mid. φράζομαι *to show, say to oneself, consider, observe*, Il. 2, 14; Pind. I. 1, 68; Soph. Ant. 1048, Dor. φράσδ- Theocr. 1, 102; -άζεο Theogn. 100; Il. 14, 3, -άζευ 9, 251, -άζου Aesch. Eum. 130: imp. ἐφράζετο H. Apol. 210; Her. 3, 154, φράζ- Od. 11, 624, iter. φραζέσκετο H. Apol. 168: fut. φράσομαι Epic, Il. 15, 234 &c., oftener -σσομαι Il. 9, 619. Od. 23, 140 &c.: aor. ἐφρασάμην Il. 23, 450. Od. 17, 161; Solon 5, 4; Archil. 94 (Bergk), ἐπ- Il. 5, 665, ἐφρασσ- Il. 9, 426 &c., φρασάμην Il. 10, 339, φρασσ- 23, 126. Od. 24, 391 &c. Dor. ἐφρασάμαν Theocr. 2, 84; Epic subj. φράσσεται Od. 24, 217, -σσωνται Opp. Hal. 1, 204; -σαιντο C. 4, 66, -σσαίατο, ἐπι- Il. 2, 282; φράσαι Il. 1. 83; Aesch. Ch. 113; φράσασθαι Eur. Med. 653; Hippocr. 3, 222. 224, ἐπι- Her. 1, 48. 5, 9, φράσσ- 3, 57 (Orac.); Ar. Eq. 1058.

1067 (hexam.): as **mid. aor. pass.** ἐφράσθην Od. 19, 485. 23, 260; Pind. N. 5, 34; Eur. Hec. 546; Her. 1, 84. 7, 46, ἐπ- Od. 5. 183; Her. 4, 200; and late, Arr. An. 3, 2, 4, 8. Ind. 5, 11: with **p. p.** πέφρασμαι Aesch. Supp. 438, ξυμ- Soph. Ant. 364. **Vb.** φραστέος (Pl.) Epist. 312, ἄ-φραστος Aesch. Supp. 94. The **Mid.** seems not to occur in Comedy, except in hexameters, Ar. Eq. 1015. 1030. 1058; nor Attic prose; it does however in Ionic, ἐφράζετο Her. 3, 154, φραζόμενοι, ἐπι- 6, 133: **aor.** φράσασθαι Hippocr. 3, 226. 228. 5, 252 (Lit.), ἐπι- Her. 1, 48. 5, 9, so that the assertions "the middle occurs only in the Epic poets, and in one Oracle in Her. 3, 57," and "ἐφρασάμην is Epic only" are rather too unqualified; the more so as Solon has ἐφρασάμην 5, 4, -άσαντο 34, 1 (Bergk), Archil. ἐφράσω Fr. 94 (Bergk); Aesch. imper. φράσαι Ch. 113 (trimet.). 592 (chor.); and Eur. inf. φράσασθαι Med. 653 (chor.) ἐπέφραδον, πέφραδον seems to have analogy in πέφνον, ἔπεφνον &c. sufficient to prevent the necessity of having recourse, with Thiersch, to ἐπιφράζω; though we cannot allow with some, that the mere fact of the non-occurrence of the moods in the compound form *proves* his view to be incorrect: it may be a *presumption* against it. By the way, ἐπιφράζω in the act. form seems rather doubtful; ἐπιφράσαι Her. 1, 179 (Vulg.) is now read ἔτι φράσαι (Matth. Bekk. Dind. Gaisf.) We have been the more particular with this verb because we have seen statements regarding its *usage* tending to mislead.

Φράσσω *To stop up, fence,* Hippocr. 6, 608 (Lit.); Herodn. 3, 4, 8 (Bekk.), ἀπο- Hippocr. 2, 410 (Lit.), Attic -ττω Xen. Ven. 2, 9; Dem. 21, 17. 55, 30; Athen. 4, 157, ἀπο- Pl. Tim. 91 (φράγνυμι, see mid.): **fut.** -ξω: **aor.** ἔφραξα, φράξε Od. 5, 256, ἐν-έφραξαν Lycurg. 124; φράξω Ar. Av. 183 (Vulg.), φάρξ- (Dind.); φράξειεν Aesch. Ag. 1376, φάρξ- (Dind.); φράξας Il. 13, 130; Aesch. Pers. 456 (φάρξ- Dind.); Her. 8, 7, ἐμ- Thuc. 7, 34; φράξαι Pind. I. 1, 66; Thuc. 4, 13: **p.** late πέφρᾰγα, περιπεφραγυῖαι Schol. Hes. Sc. 298: but **plp.** ἐπεφράκεσαν Jos. Ant. 12, 8, 5: **p. p.** πέφραγμαι Eur. Ph. 733; -φραγμένος Soph. Fr. 376 (-φαργ- Dind.); Her. 5, 34; Thuc. 1, 82; Xen. Cyr. 2, 4, 25: **plp.** ἐπεφράγμην Luc. Cron. 11, -ακτο Her. 7, 142: **1 aor.** ἐφράχθην Il. 17, 268; Pl. Leg. 779, συν- Hippocr. 8, 96, κατα- 6, 484 (Lit.): **2 aor.** late ἐφρᾰ́γην N. T. Rom. 3, 19, ἀπ- Luc. D. Mort. 28, 2, ἐμ- Plut. Mor. 521; Aretae. 7 (ed. Oxon.): **1 fut.** late, ἐμ- φραχθήσομαι Galen 5, 616: and late, **2 fut.** φραγήσομαι N. T. 2 Cor. 11, 10, ἐμ- Galen 5, 3. 10, 314. **Mid.** φράγνῡμαι Ar. Fr. 336, ἀπο- Soph. Ant. 241: **fut.** φράξεται, ἐμ- Luc. Tim. 19 (Bekk. Dind.): **aor.** ἐφραξάμην Her. 9, 70; Themist. 23, 294; Aesch. Sept. 798, ἐφαρξ- (Dind.), φραξ- Il. 15, 566;

imper. φράξαι Aesch. Sept. 63, φάρξ- (Dind.); φραξάμενος Batr. 166; Thuc. 8, 35. Hom. uses only the aorists of this verb. Lehrs (Quest. Ep. p. 306) says that Oppian uses the aor. mid. in a pass. sense, Hal. 1, 260. 2, 363. Cyn. 4, 7. These instances are not quite decisive, inasmuch as they seem to admit of a middle sense.

(**Φρέω, φρα-, φρῆμι, πίφρημι**) *To let pass in, out, through*, in comp. inf. ἐσ-πιφράναι Aristot. Hist. An. 5, 6, 3: imp. εἰσέφρουν Dem. 20, 53, 1 pl. ἐξ-εφρείομεν for the metre Ar. Vesp. 125 (Dind. 2 ed. -φρίεμεν Nauck, Dind. 5 ed.): fut. φρήσω, ἐκ- Ar. Vesp. 156, ἐσ- 892, δια- Av. 193; Thuc. 7, 32 (Bekk. Dobr. Dind.): aor. ἔφρησα, εἰσ- Heliod. 9, 11; Hesych.; Schol. Ar. Eq. 4, ἐπ-εισ-έφρησα Eur. H. F. 1267, ἀπ- Com. Fr. (Cratin.) 2, 66, ἐξ- Luc. Lex. 9; φρήσωσι, εἰσ- Aristot. Mirab. 14: p. ἔφρηκε, ἐξ- (Hesych.), ἐπ-εισ- Eur. Elec. 1033 (Dind. Kirchh. Nauck). H. F. 1267 quoted (Nauck, Cobet): 1 aor. pass. ἐκ-φρησθείς Ael. Fr. 39; -σθῆναι 89: 2 aor. act. (φρῆμι), imper. φρές C. Fr. (Anon.) 4, 651 (Mein. εἴσ-φρες Dind. Lehrs), ἐκ- Ar. Vesp. 162; subj. ἐπ-εσ-φρῶ Eur. Alc. 1056, ἐκ-φρῶσι Phoen. 264 (Dind. Kirchh. Nauck); ἐπ-εισ-φρείς Eur. Fr. 781, 46; φρῆναι, εἰσ- (Hesych. if not for -ῆσαι). Mid. *to let in to myself*, imp. εἰσ-εφρούμην Eur. Tr. 647: fut. εἰσ-φρήσεσθαι Dem. 8, 15; Aristid. 39, 496 (Mss. Dind.): aor. εἰσ-φρήσασθαι (Hesych.). The form ἐξεφρίομεν Ar. Vesp. 125 (Bekk.) is said to be in the best Mss. Dind. however recalled ἐξεφρείομεν (Vulg.), and Bergk adopts it; now, with Nauck, Dind. reads -φρίεμεν: Buttm. calls it an extraordinary form. In Epic, at least, occur τελέω and -λείω

Φρίσσω *To shudder, be rough* (φρίκω), Il. 13, 473; Aesch. Pr. 540; Soph. Ant. 997; Eur. Hipp. 855; Hippocr. 6, 100. 634; Aristot. Physiog. 6, 41, Attic -ττω Pl. Rep. 387; Aristot. H. An. 6, 2, 20; (Dem.) 51, 9: imp. φρῖσσον Hes. Sc. 171, ἔφριττον Himer. 36, 13: fut. φρίξω Or. Sib. 3, 679. 9, 83; Galen 13, 365: aor. ἔφριξα Il. 13, 339; Pind. Ol. 7, 38; Aesch. Sept. 490; Soph. Tr. 1044; Hippocr. 5, 448. 8, 610 (Lit.); Pl. Phaedr. 251; Dem. 21, 135, φρίξ- Pind. I. 1, 13; φρίξας Od. 19, 446; Ar. Ran. 822: p. πέφρῑκα as pres. Il. 11, 383. 24, 775; Aesch. Ag. 1243; Ar. Nub. 1133; Hippocr. 7, 122 (Lit.); Ael. Epist. 16, late 3 pl. πέφρικαν Lycophr. 252; πεφρῑκώς Il. 7, 62; Pind. I. 6, 40; Eur. Ph. 1121; Dem. 18, 323; Luc. Tim. 23, Aeol. or Boeot. πεφρίκοντας Pind. P. 4, 183: plp. ἐπεφρίκει Plut. Mor. 781. Mid. late, aor. φριξάμενος Polyaen. 4, 6, 7, missed by Lexicogr., φριμαξ- (Ms. P. Woelffl.) Vb. φρικτός Anth. 1, 120; Plut. C. M. Coriol. 18.

Φροιμῐάζομαι *To prelude, preface* (φροίμιον), Aesch. Eum. 20.

Ag. 1354; Eur. I. T. 1162; Plut. Mor. 224; -άζηται Luc. Hist. 53; -αζόμενος Aristot. Rhet. Alex. 35, 5; Themist. Or. 13, 173: **imp.** ἐφροιμ- Themist. 19, 229: **fut.** -ιάσομαι: **aor.** ἐφροιμιασάμην, φροιμιασάμενος Aristot. Poet. 24, 14. Rhet. ad Alex. 38, 4: but **pass. p.** πεφροιμίασται Aristot. Pol. 7, 4, 1 &c. **Vb.** φροιμιαστέον Aristot. Rhet. ad Alex. 36. Our youths are taught to believe in "*no fut. or other tense.*" The classic prose form is προοιμιάζ-.

Φρονέω *To think* (φρήν), Il. 9, 608; Emped. 337; Pind. Fr. 19; Aesch. Ch. 774; Soph. O. R. 550; Her. 6, 97; Antiph. 2, 1; Thuc. 5, 89; Isocr. 10, 1; Epic subj. φρονέῃσι Od. 7, 75, reg.: **imp.** ἐφρόνουν Lys. 2, 15; Pl. Conv. 217, Ion. ἐφρόνεον Syniz. Archil. 112; Her. 2, 162, φρόνεον Il. 17, 286, iter. φρονέεσκε Ap. Rh. 4, 1164: **fut.** -ήσω Ar. Eccl. 630; Xen. Cyr. 8, 7, 23; Isocr. 15, 317: **aor.** ἐφρόνησα Isocr. 11, 10. 16, 29; Dem. 24, 199; φρόνησον Aesch. Eum. 115; Soph. Ant. 49; -ήσας 1031; Her. 1, 60. 5, 72. 117. 7, 145; Isocr. 8, 141; -ῆσαι Thuc. 6, 36: **p.** πεφρόνηκα Emped. 195; Isocr. 5, 124; Dio. Sic. 18, 66; Phal. Epist. 4: no **mid.**: **pass.** late if correct, and in **pres.** only, imper. φρονείσθω N. T. Philip. 2, 5 (Vulg. Tisch.); φρονεῖσθαι; -ούμενος Aristot. Gorg. 6, 10 (Bekk.). See κατα-φρον-. Benseler in Rost and Palm's Gr. Lex. errs by confining this verb "in Herodotus" to **pres.** and **imp.**

Φροντίζω *To think, consider,* Theogn. 912; Aesch. Pr. 1034; Eur. Heracl. 680; Ar. Nub. 723; Her. 1, 155; Andoc. 4, 27. 39; Pl. Gorg. 502; Aeol. inf. φροντίσδην Sapph. 41: **imp.** ἐφρ- Her. 8, 36; Lys. 3, 16; Pl. Lys. 223; Dem. 50, 27: **fut.** φροντιῶ Eur. Tr. 1234; Ar. Nub. 735; Xen. Mem. 2, 1, 24: and rare **mid.** -ιοῦμαι Eur. I. T. 343, -ιοῦμεν (Badh. Koechl.): **aor.** ἐφρόντισα Eur. Tr. 1046; Lys. 14, 9; Pl. Apol. 25; Aeschin. 1, 165; -τίσῃς Soph. Ph. 1404; -τισον Aesch. Supp. 419: **p.** πεφρόντικα Eur. Alc. 773; Ar. Eccl. 263; Xen. Mem. 3, 3, 8: **plp.** ἐπεφροντίκει App. Mithr. 7: **p. p.** late πεφροντισμένος Ael. H. A. 7, 9; Plut. Aemil. P. 28: **pres. pass.** φροντιζόμενος Xen. Hier. 7, 10. **Vb.** φροντιστέον Pl. Crito 48. Eur. I. T. quoted, if sound, seems to be the only instance of the **mid.** form.

Φρουρέω *To watch, guard,* Simon. C. 110; Aesch. Eum. 1024; Soph. Fr. 35; Ar. Ran. 472; Her. 2, 30; Pl. Rep. 420: **imp.** ἐφρούρουν Thuc. 4, 1, -ρεε Her. 1, 165, -εον 4, 128, 'φρούρουν Soph. Tr. 915: **fut.** -ρήσω Aesch. Pr. 31; Soph. El. 1402; Xen. Cyr. 6, 1, 17: **aor.** ἐφρούρησα Soph. El. 74; Her. 2, 30; Xen. Cyr. 1, 2, 12; (**perf.**?): **p. p.** πεφρούρημαι (Hippocr.) Epist. 3, 825 (Kühn), δια- Aesch. Fr. 263 (D): **aor.** ἐφρουρήθην Eur. Ion 1390, ἐν- Phal. Epist. 5: as **pass. fut. mid.** φρουρήσομαι Eur.

Ion 603; Plut. Caes. 27. **Mid.** φρουροῦμαι *to guard oneself, guard off*, Eur. An. 1135: fut. -ρήσομαι as pass. see above. **Pass.** rather rare, φρουροῦμαι Soph. O. C. 1013; -ούμενος Eur. Hec. 995; Pl. Rep. 579, -εομένη Her. 7, 203: imp. ἐφρουρεῖτο Eur. Supp. 1041; Thuc. 1, 107; Isocr. 19, 19. **Imp. act.** ἐφρούρει Eur. Supp. 900, seems used as mid.

Φρύγω *To roast, bake*, Ar. Eccl. 221; Theocr. 6, 16. 12, 9 (Mss. Mein. Ahr. Ziegl. φρύττ- Vulg.); Alciphr. 3, 27: imp. ἔφρῡγον Ar. Ran. 511: fut. φρύξω Her. 8, 96 (Orac.), Dor. -ξῶ Theocr. 7, 66: aor. ἔφρυξα Com. Fr. (Cratin.) 2, 95; Her. 2, 94; Hippocr. 6, 410. 412 (Lit.): p. p. πέφρυγμαι Com. Fr. (Pher.) 2, 341; Hippocr. 2, 486. 8, 100; Thuc. 6, 22: 1 aor. ἐφρύχθην Hom. Epigr. 14, 4; Orac. Sib. 8, 237; Geop. 12, 22; Galen 6, 289; Oribas. 1, 31 (Bussem.): 2 aor. ἐφρύγην Anth. 7, 293; φρυγῇ Hippocr. 6, 414 (Lit.); φρυγείς Dioscor. 4, 52: fut. φρυγήσεται, κατα- Hesych. Vb. φρυκτός Ar. Vesp. 1331; Thuc. 2, 94. The form φρίγω is still in Hippocr. 2, 876 (Vulg. Kühn), but φρύγω (Mss. Lit.), and fut. φρίξουσι Her. 8, 96 (Vulg. Schweigh. Gaisf. &c.) has been altered to φρύξουσι (Schaef. Bekk. Krüg. Dind.) φρύττω, -σσω seem late forms, Galen 6, 550; Schol. Od. 18, 27; Eustath. 1547.

Φυγγάνω *To flee* (a collat. form of φεύγω), only pres. Aesch. Pr. 513; Soph. El. 132; Hippocr. 7, 194, δία- Heraclit. 116 (Bywater): and imp. ἐφύγγᾰνον late, Greg. Naz. T. 2, p. 241, 235, but δι-εφύγγ- Thuc. 7, 44; Aeschin. 3, 10. So ἐκ-φυγγάνω Aesch. Pr. 525; Com. Fr. (Diph.) 4, 378; Hippocr. 7, 330 (Lit.), κατα- Her. 6, 16; Aeschin. 3, 208, ἀπο- Dem. 23, 74. Alcaeus has πεφύγγω 147 (Bergk).

Φύζω, see φεύγω.

Φῠλάσσω *To guard*, Il. 5, 809; Aesch. Ag. 8; Soph. Ph. 1328; Eur. Ion 736; Her. 3, 107; Antiph. 2, δ, 9; Thuc. 7, 17, -άττω Ar. Thesm. 976; Xen. Cyr. 8, 2, 23; Isocr. 8, 112; Pl. Theaet. 203, Dor. 3 pl. -άσσοισι Pind. N. 11, 5; Ep. inf. φυλασσέμεναι Il. 10, 419: imp. ἐφύλασσον Od. 2, 346; Her. 8, 46; Thuc. 3, 17, φύλασσ- Il. 15, 461 (Bekk.), ἐφύλαττ- Ar. Vesp. 358; Lys. 1, 6; Isae. 6, 39; Pl. Men. 89: fut. φυλάξω Od. 22, 195; Eur. Bac. 497; Ar. Eq. 434; Her. 1, 210; Thuc. 4, 43; Pl. Rep. 530, Dor. -αξῶ Theocr. 1, 63: aor. ἐφύλαξα Callim. Del. 204; Her. 5, 41, 'φύλαξα Soph. Aj. 535, φύλαξα Il. 16, 686; φυλάξῃ Pl. Rep. 415, -ξωμεν Leg. 783, Epic -ξομεν Il. 8, 529; φύλαξον Thuc. 7, 77; φυλάξαι Pind. P. 4, 41; Aesch. Supp. 179; Soph. El. 1504; Her. 9, 38; Pl. Rep. 484; -ύξας Eur. Or. 57; Her. 8, 9: p. πεφύλαχα, παρα- Pl. Leg. 632, δια- Dinarch. 1, 9; Xen. Cyr. 8, 6, 3 (Buttm. Bornem. Dind. Saupp.), -ακα

(Vulg. Poppo) which occurs late in *simple* V. T. 1 Reg. 25, 21; πεφυλακέναι Argum. Eur. Med. (Mss. Dind. -λαχέναι Nauck): p. p. πεφύλαγμαι Theocr. 15, 113; Nonnus 41, 363 (Vulg.), but as mid. see below: aor. ἐφυλάχθην Dem. 21, 3; Plut. Tit. Flamin. 7; Luc. Pisc. 15; Heliod. 10, 29, δι- Xen. Cyr. 8, 1, 2: fut. late, φυλαχθήσομαι Geop. 2, 18; Galen 1, 426; D. Hal. Rhet. 5, 6; Epist. Phal. 12 (Herch.), δια- Ant. 10, 50: classic, fut. mid. as pass. φυλάξομαι Soph. Ph. 48; Xen. Oec. 4, 9, as mid. see below. **Mid.** φυλάσσομαι, -άττομαι *to keep for, with oneself, guard oneself, to beware,* Hes. Op. 491; Solon 4, 14; Eur. I. T. 67; Her. 1, 108, φυλάττ- Pl. Phaedr. 232; -άσσου Aesch. Pr. 390; -ασσόμενος Il. 10, 188: **imp.** ἐφυλαττ- Lys. 3, 13, -ασσ- Thuc. 4, 48: **fut.** φυλάξομαι Aesch. Supp. 205; Soph. El. 1012; Eur. Med. 289; Ar. Eccl. 831; Thuc. 5, 103; Isocr. 4, 165: **aor.** ἐφυλαξάμην Her. 7, 130; Antiph. 3, δ, 7; Xen. Ages. 8, 5; subj. -ξώμεθα Thuc. 6, 11; imper. φύλαξαι H. H. Apol. 366; Aesch. Ch. 924; Her. 7, 157; Pl. Polit. 263; φυλάξασθαι Pind. Ol. 7, 40; Aesch. Pr. 715; Antiph. 2, β, 8; Isocr. 4, 47: **p. p.** as mid. πεφύλαγμαι *guarded, on one's guard* &c. Eur. Fr. 475 a, 19 (Dind.); imper. πεφύλαξο Hes. Op. 797; Her. 7, 148 (Orac.); -λαχθαι Sapph. 27, δια- Hippocr. 2, 504; -αγμένος Il. 23, 343; Hes. Op. 765; Solon 42 (Bergk); Her. 7, 148 (Orac.); Theocr. 16, 95; Xen. Hell. 7, 5, 9. **Vb.** φυλακτέον Eur. An. 63; Pl. Rep. 416. Epic inf. pres. φυλασσέμεναι Il. 10, 419. The anomalous form προφύλαχθε Hom. H. 2, 360, is considered by Buttm. to be a syncopated pres. for προφυλάσσετε, formed from the root φυλακ- with termination -χθε for -κτε, like ἄνωχθε. Schneidewin's suggestion πεφύλαχθε seems easy and apposite, and would, if necessary, at least remove the anomaly. προφύλαχθε, if sound, is certainly not "the only irregularity connected with this verb."

Φύρω *To mix, moisten, knead,* Hes. Op. 61; Pl. Phaed. 97: **imp.** ἔφῡρον Il. 24, 162; Aesch. Pr. 450: **fut.** (φύρσω): **aor.** ἔφυρσα, subj. φύρσω Od. 18, 21; φῦρσον Nic. Ther. 693; φύρσας 593; φῦρσαι Ap. Rh. 2, 59 (late ἔφῦρα, φύρας Luc. Prom. 13; φῦραι Eustath. Opusc. 279. 80): **p. p.** πέφυρμαι Od. 9, 397; Eur. El. 1173; Xen. Ages. 2, 14, ἀνα- Her. 3, 157: **plp.** ἐπέφυρτο Aristid. 24, 305: **1 aor.** ἐφύρθην Aesch. Ag. 732: **2 aor.** late, ἐφῠρην Aretae. 104 (ed. Oxon.), συνανα- Luc. Ep. Sat. 28: **fut.** late, φυρήσομαι, συμ- Schol. Pind. N. 1, 68: **3 fut.** πεφύρσομαι Pind. N. 1, 68. **Mid.** φύρομαι Pl. Phaed. 101: **aor.** φυρσάμενος Nic. Ther. 507. **Vb.** φυρτός Hesych., συμ- Eur. Hipp. 1234. The forms with σ seem to be poetic. φῡράω is reg. Her. 2, 36: **fut.** -ᾱσω Aesch. Sept. 48, Ion. -ήσω: **aor.** ἐφύρᾱσα Pl. Tim. 73, -ησα Hippocr. 6, 460. 538. 8, 244 (Lit.): **p. p.** -ρᾶμαι Thuc. 3,

49; Dioscor. 5, 85; Geop. 14, 11, προ- Ar. Av. 462, πεφύρημαι Philet. 7 (Schn.); Hippocr. 6, 540 (Lit.): aor. ἐφυράθην Anth. Pl. (Nicaen.) 191; Pl. Theaet. 147, -ήθην Anth. 7, 748, προ- Hippocr. 6, 536. 538 (Lit.) **Mid.** aor. ἐφυρᾱσάμην Ar. Nub. 979, ἐφυρησ- Opp. Hal. 3, 485, and φυρησ- 4, 660; Nic. Ther. 932. **Vb.** φυρατέον Dioscor. 5, 103.

Φῡσῐάω *To breathe, pant,* only pres. ind. φυσιᾷ Aesch. Eum. 248; and pt. φυσιῶν Soph. Ant. 1238, Epic φυσιόων Il. 4, 227; Ap. Rh. 3, 410, ἀνα- Hes. Sc. 211; Ap. Rh. 2, 431. The collat. form φῡσιόω *to blow, puff up, make proud,* is late φυσιοῖ N. T. 1 Cor. 8, 1: pass. pres. perf. and aor. N. T. and later.

Φῠτεύω *To plant,* Od. 5, 340; Pind. I. 6, 12; Soph. Aj. 953; Thuc. 1, 2; Pl. Tim. 77; Epic inf. -ευέμεν Hes. Op. 812: imp. ἐφύτ-, φύτ- Od. 17, 27; Pind. N. 4, 59, Ar. Pax 558: fut. -εύσω Xen. Oec. 19, 13: aor. ἐφύτευσα Il. 6, 419; Pl. Tim. 80; Isae. 9, 28, 'φύτευσα Soph. O. R. 1504; -τεύσω Od. 17, 82; -τεῦσαι Il. 15, 134; Pind. N. 7, 84; Her. 4, 145: p. late, πεφύτευκα, 3 pl. -τευκαν for -τεύκασιν, V. T. Ezech. 19, 13: p. p. πεφύτευμαι Her. 2, 138; Xen. Hell. 3, 2, 10: aor. ἐφυτεύθην Xen. An. 5, 3, 12, Epic 3 pl. φύτευθεν Pind. P. 4, 69; -ευθείς Pind. P. 4, 256; Soph. O. C. 1324; Pl. Rep. 492: fut. late, φυτευθήσομαι Geop. 5, 19, 1. **Mid.** φυτεύομαι *to plant for oneself,* fut. -εύσεσθαι Pind. P. 4, 15: aor. ἐφυτευσάμην Luc. Catapl. 20; -σάμενος Xen. Mem. 1, 1, 8. This verb is often confounded with φῑτύω. It has not, as some have supposed, the irregularity of fut. mid. as fut. act.

Φύω *To produce* (Aeol. φυίω), usu. trans. Il. 6, 148; Soph. Aj. 647; Eur. Bac. 651; Ar. Pax 1164; Her. 8, 104; Pl. Rep. 621, rarely intrans. *grow, spring,* Il. 6, 149; Mimnerm. 2, 1; Alcae. 97 (Bergk), ἐκ- Aristot. Prob. 5, 27, 3 pl. Dor. φύοντι Theocr. 4, 24. 7, 75; Mosch. 3, 103: imp. ἔφῠε Pl. Menex. 237, φῦεν Il. 14, 347; Athen. (Pancrat.) 677: fut. φύσω Il. 1, 235; Soph. O. R. 438: aor. ἔφῡσα Od. 10, 393; Aesch. Fr. 302; Soph. O. R. 436; Eur. Ion 547; Ar. Ran. 418; Her. 2, 68; Antiph. 4, α, 2; Pl. Tim. 44: p. πέφῡκα intrans. *to be naturally, to be* &c. Od. 7, 114 (Herodn. Bekk. Ameis); Theogn. 801; Aesch. Pr. 27; Soph. El. 608; Eur. Hec. 743; Her. 2, 8; Antiph. 2, 1; Thuc. 4, 61; Lys. 7, 35; Pl. Leg. 649; -φυκώς Soph. O. C. 1294; Eur. Ph. 908; Xen. Ages. 10, 4, -κυῖα Isocr. 15, 210, -κυίη Her. 2, 56 &c., Epic πεφύᾱσι Il. 4, 484. Od. 7, 128; Hes. Th. 728; πεφύῃ, ἐμ- Theogn. 396 (Bergk); πεφῠῶτας Od. 5, 477, ἐμ-πεφυυῖα Il. 1, 513: plp. ἐπεφύκειν Xen. Cyr. 5, 1, 9, πεφύκει Il. 4, 109; Theocr. 5, 33; so Pl. Tim. 69. Crat. 389 (Bekk. *v. r.* ἐπεφ- and p. πέφυκε Stallb. &c.);

Hes. has ἐπέφῦκον for -ύκεσαν, Th. 152. Op. 149. Sc. 76: **2 aor. act.** ἔφῡν intrans. *to be, be born*, Od. 10, 397. 23, 190; Aesch. Pers. 157; Soph. Ant. 79. O. R. 822; Eur. Ph. 538; Ar. Nub. 1414. Av. 471; Xen. Cyr. 5, 4, 12; Pl. Leg. 746; Dem. 36, 44, φῦ Il. 6, 253. 14, 232 (Bekk.); ἔφῡτον Soph. O. C. 1379 (-ύτην Elms. Dind. Nauck), ἔφῡμεν Soph. Ant. 62; Eur. Fr. 362, 8; Isocr. 4, 24. 48; Aeschin. 3, 132, ἔφῡτε Xen. Cyr. 2, 1, 15, ἔφῡσαν H. Hym. Ven. 265; C. Fr. (Anon.) 4, 62; Theocr. 13, 47; Isocr. 12, 125, poet. ἔφῡν Od. 5, 481, but ἔφῠν Pind. P. 1, 42; subj. φύω, φύῃ Eur. Fr. 378 (Cob. Dind. Nauck), ἐμ- φύῃ Xen. Hier. 7, 3 (Dind. Saupp.), -ύωσι *v. r.* Pl. Phaedr. 251; opt. φύην, -ύη Theocr. 15, 94 (Mein. Ziegl.), φυίη (Herm.); φῦναι Soph. Ant. 721; Her. 1, 108; Isocr. 11, 41; Pl. Rep. 489, περι- Od. 24, 236, Epic φύμεναι Theocr. 25, 39; φύς Od. 18, 410; Pind. Ol. 11, 20; Soph. O. R. 1184; Isocr. 12, 126; Pl. Rep. 461; Aeschin. 1, 178: **1 aor. pass.** φυθείς, συμ- Galen 7, 725, the only instance we ever met: **2 aor.** ἐφύην Joseph. Ant. 18, 1, 1, ἀν- Theophr. H. P. 4, 16, 2; subj. φυῶ, -ῇ Eur. Fr. 377 (Wagn. φύῃ Dind. Nauck); so Pl. Rep. 494, συμ- Hippocr. 6, 182 (Lit.), φυῶσι Pl. Rep. 597. Phaedr. 251 (*v. r.* φύωσι); φυείς Hippocr. 7, 514 (Lit.); Com. Fr. (Men.) 4, 257; φυῆναι Dioscor. 2, 8, ἀνα- Dio. Sic. 1, 7 (Bekk. -φῦναι L. Dind.), ἐκ- Hippocr. 3, 51, διεκ- 1, 601 (Vulg. Kühn), altered to εὐφυΐα, and διεκδῦναι from Mss. by Lit. 3, 286. 6, 374, but still συμ-φυῆναι 6, 182 (Lit.): **fut.** φυήσομαι late, Themist. 21, 248; Geop. 2, 37; Aesop 105 (Halm, ἐκ- *v. r.* Hippocr. 7, 508), προσ- Geop. 5, 6, 4, συμ- Oribas. 7, 14, ἀνα- Galen 5, 813 (*v. r.* Luc. Jup. Trag. 19). **Pass.** or **mid.** intrans. φύομαι *to be produced, grow*, Od. 9, 109; Soph. Fr. 109, 4 (D); Her. 8, 138; Xen. Cyr. 4, 2, 44; Pl. Theaet. 144; -ύηται Hippocr. 7, 186 (Lit.); Pl. Rep. 565; Theocr. 8, 68: **imp.** ἐφυόμην Pl. Euth. 296; (Dem.) 60, 18, φυομ- Od. 24, 410: **fut.** φύσομαι Aesch. Pr. 871; Pl. Leg. 831; Hippocr. 4, 392 (Lit.), and ἐκ-φύσεται trans. *produce*, 1, 399 (Vulg. Kühn), but *now* ἐκφύσει 7, 508 (Mss. C. ξ. Lit.) which, if correct, destroys the only instance we know of **mid.** *trans.*: and as **mid.** intrans. πέφῡκα, ἐπεφύκειν, πέφῠα, ἔφυν, rarely φύω. **Vb.** φυτός late, V. T. Ezech. 17, 5, but ἔμ-φῠτος Soph. O. C. 1671; Pl. Rep. 610.

ἔφῡσαν 3 pl. **1 aor.** *they produced*, Soph. O. R. 436 &c. to be distinguished from ἔφῡσαν 3 pl. **2 aor.** *they grew*, Hom. H. Ven. 265; Theocr. 22, 213, syncop. ἔφῡν in *arsi*, Od. 5, 481, -ῠν in *thesi* Pind. P. 1, 42; Aeol. part. **2 aor.** φοῦσα for φῦσα, Corinn. 21 (Bergk). φύς in late auth. is occas. trans. ὁ φύς, οἱ φύντες *the parent, parents*, Heliod. 2, 16. 7, 7. 9, 11 (Bekk.) **A fut. act.**

form in -ήσω occurs late, ἀναφυήσει V. T. Esai. 34, 13 (Vat.), -φύσει (Alex.) In Hom. ῠ before a vowel, φύω, φύομαι &c. πέφυα; in Attic ῡ, φύει Soph. Fr. 757; φύεται Fr. 109, 4, φύομεν Ar. Av. 106; before a consonant ῡ always, -ῡσω, -ῡσα, -ῡκα. Late Poets too have the pres. and imp. sometimes long, φύουσι Nic. Al. 14; even in thesis, προσφύ- 506, αἱ φύ- Dion. Per. 1031. πεφύκᾰσι is now read by Ameis, Kayser, La R. Od. 7, 114; so Bekk. 2 ed. but in Monatsber. 1864, 4, he recalls πεφύκει.

Φώγω *To roast, toast*, Epicharm. 102 (Ahr.), φώζω Hippocr. 6, 566, φώγνυμι late: **aor.** ἔφωξα Hippocr. 6, 460. 8, 196, and -ωσα 8, 244. 276: **p. p.** πέφωγμαι Com. Fr. (Pher.) 2, 281, and -ωσμαι Hippocr. 5, 436. 6, 454. 7, 98. 416 (Lit.); Geop. 20, 2: **aor.** φωχθείς Aretae. 104 (Ed. Oxon.); Dioscor. 2, 119, προ- 2, 112. **Pres. pass.** φώγνῠται. Dioscor. 1, 80.

X.

(Χάζω) *To make retire, force back*, and intrans. *give way, retreat, simple* act. form unused, but χάζει, χάζειν (Hesych.); and in comp. imper. ἄγ-χαζε intrans. Soph. Fr. 800; ἀνα-χάζοντες Xen. An. 4, 1, 16: **imp.** ἔχαζον, ἀν- Hesych.; Eunap. 174 (112 Boisson.): **1 aor.** ἀν-έχασσαν Pind. N. 10, 69: **aor. pass.** ἐχάσθην, χασθῇ, ἀπο- Hesych.: **2 aor.** κέκᾰδον (*caused to retire from*) *deprived of*, -αδών Il. 11, 334: **fut.** κεκαδήσω *will deprive*, Od. 21, 153. 170: **1 aor.** κεκαδῆσαι, βλάψαι Hesych. **Mid.** χάζομαι *to give way, retire*, Epic Ap. Rh. 1, 841; Opp. Hal. 3, 571; -ωμαι Il. 5, 34; χάζεο 5, 440: **imp.** ἐχάζετο Il. 3, 32; Nonn. 48, 618, ἀν- Xen. An. 4, 7, 10. Cyr. 7, 1, 34, χάζ- Il. 11, 539: **fut.** χᾰσομαι, Epic χάσσ- Il. 13, 153: **aor.** ἐχᾰσάμην, ἐχασσ- Q. Sm. 2, 338, χασσ- Il. 13, 193; -ηται Opp. Hal. 1, 755; χασσάμενος Il. 4, 535, ἀνα- 13, 740; χάσσασθαι 12, 173, δια-χάσασθαι Xen. Cyr. 7, 1, 31: **2 aor.** κεκᾰδόμην -δοντο Il. 4, 497. α is short, hence the doubling of σ. This verb is Poet. especially Epic, rare if at all in Attic poetry; for in the solitary instance Eur. Or. 1116, οὐ χάζομαι is opposed in the Mss. by οὐχ ἅζομαι, which is approved by Elms. Monk, Herm. Dind. Kirchh. Paley; χάζομαι however is the reading of Br. Pors. Matth. In Attic prose, Xen. has **pres. act. imp.** and **1 aor. mid.** in comp. For διαχάσασθαι Cyr. 7, 1, 31 (Dind. Popp. Saupp.) some good Mss. and edit. have διαχωρῆσαι; but the fact of Xen. using ἀνα-χάζω, -άζετο, and his fondness for poetic words, favour the received reading.

Besides, we quite agree with Poppo "verbum (διαχάσασθαι) non videtur a librariis aut grammaticis confingi potuisse."

Χαίνω *To gape*, see χάσκω.

Χαίρω *To rejoice, be glad*, Il. 7, 191; Simon. Am. 7, 111; Pind. N. 8, 48; Aesch. Ag. 539; Soph. O. R. 596; Her. 3, 80; Xen. Mem. 2, 6, 35; Isocr. 9, 78; imper. 3 pl. χαιρόντων Eur. H. F. 575; Dor. pt. χαίροισα Theocr. 2, 163; Bion 6, 11; Aeol. inf. χαίρην Sapph. 86: imp. ἔχαιρον Il. 11, 73; Pind. Ol. 2, 66; Ar. Av. 116; Lys. 18, 9; Pl. Rep. 450, χαῖρε Il. 14, 156; Pind. I. 4, 29, iter. χαίρεσκον Il. 18, 259: fut. χαιρήσω Il. 20, 363; Theogn. 992; Simon. C. 122; Ar. Plut. 64; Her. 1, 128; Andoc. 1, 101; Pl. Phil. 21 (late χαρῶ if correct, N. T. Rev. 11, 10 Vulg. Mai): and χᾰρήσομαι late, Orac. Sib. 6, 20; (Luc.) Philop. 24, συγ- Polyb. 30, 10; Diod. Sic. Fr. Lib. 31, 9 (B), Dor. χαρησοῦμαι Pythag. Epist. 4: also late χαροῦμαι, κατα- V. T. Prov. 1, 26; Clement. Epist. 57 (Muralt.): Epic κεχᾰρήσω, inf. -ησέμεν Il. 15, 98: and κεχᾰρήσομαι Od. 23, 266; Theocr. 16, 73 (Bergk, and formerly Mein.): aor. ἐχαίρησα late, Plut. Lucull. 25: p. κεχᾰρηκα Ar. Vesp. 764; -ηκώς Her. 3, 27. 42, Epic κεχαρηότα Il. 7, 312; Hes. Fr. 223: p. p. Poet. κεχάρημαι as act. -χάρησαι Ar. V. 389; -ημένος Hom. H. 7, 10; Eur. I. A. 200 (chor.); Theocr. 27, 70, and κέχαρμαι Poet. -μένος Eur. Cycl. 368. Elec. 1077. Or. 1122; Orph. Hym. 51, 5: plp. κεχάρητο Hes. Sc. 65, -ηντο Hym. Cer. 458: **2 aor.** as **act.** ἐχᾰρην Il. 7, 54. Od. 10, 419; Ar. Av. 1743 (chor.) Ran. 1028 (anapaest.); Her. 8, 101; Xen. Ven. 1, 2; Arr. An. 2, 27, 2, χαρ- Il. 5, 682; χαρῇς Pl. Rep. 606; χαρείη Il. 6, 481; χᾰρῆναι Simon. C. 164 (Bergk); χᾰρείς Il. 10, 541; Pind. I. 6, 10; Ar. Thesm. 981, -εῖσα Sapph. 118; Eur. I. A. 1525; Ar. Nub. 274; Anth. 6, 269. **Mid.** as **act.** (χαίρομαι Ar. Pax 291, accounted barbarous for χαίρω, see Schol.): fut. χαιρήσομαι *v. r.* (Luc.) Philop. 24, χαρήσ-, κεχαρήσ- see above: **1 aor.** Epic, χήρατο Il. 14, 270, ἐχήρ- Opp. Cyn. 1, 509. 534, ἐπ- Ap. Rh. 4, 55; χηρᾰμένη Anth. 7, 198: **2 aor.** mostly Epic, χᾰροντο rare Q. Sm. 6, 315, redupl. κεχάροντο Il. 16, 600; Ap. Rh. 4, 998; opt. κεχαροίμεθα Philox. 1, 24 (Bergk), κεχάροιτο Od. 2, 249; Ap. Rh. 1, 920, 3 pl. -οίατο Il. 1, 256: also p. κεχάρημαι, and κέχαρμαι, see above. **Vb.** χαρτός Soph. El. 1457; Pl. Prot. 358.

The Scholiast remarks on χαίρομαι Ar. Pax 291, "Δᾶτις σατράπης Περσῶν εἶπεν ἥδομαι καὶ χαίρομαι, καὶ ἐβαρβάρισεν· ἔδει γὰρ εἰπεῖν χαίρω." It may have been *duty* to say χαίρω, but we would rather put the *obligation* on *usage* than on the *reason* or *principle* assigned, "αὐτὸ γὰρ τὸ χαίρω αὐτοπαθὲς ὂν προυφήρπασεν αὐτοῦ τὸ σημαινόμενον." This is not confined in its scope to the present;

and so should *barbarise* κεχαρήσεται in the Odyssee, because κεχαρησέμεν occurs in the Iliad.

Χᾰλάω *To loosen*, Aesch. Eum. 219; Soph. O. R. 1266; Hippocr. 7, 472. 494; Xen. Eq. 5, 4, Epic 3 pl. -λόωσι Opp. Hal. 2, 451; subj. χαλῶσι Ar. Lys. 310: imp. ἐχάλα Hippocr. 3, 438. 5, 398: fut. χαλάσω Hippocr. 2, 36. 5, 436 (Lit.); Plut. Mor. 321: aor. ἐχάλᾰσα Hippocr. 5, 258. 390; Pl. Soph. 242, -ασσα Hom. H. 1, 6; Opp. C. 3, 124, χάλασσ- Orph. Arg. 376, Dor. ἐχάλαξα Theocr. 21, 51; subj. -άσῃ Aesch. Pr. 176, -άσωσι Pl. Rep. 329; χάλασον Eur. Cycl. 55; Ar. Lys. 419. Thesm. 1003; Pl. Men. 86; Ael. Epist. 15; χαλάσας Hom. H. 27, 12; (Pl.) Locr. 104, Dor. -άξαις Pind. P. 1, 6: p. κεχάλᾰκα Hippocr. 5, 394 (Lit.): p. p. κεχάλασμαι Anth. 9, 297; Arat. 351; App. Mithr. 74; Herodn. 1, 14, 1: plp. ἐκεχάλαστο Aristid. 25, 315, κεχάλ- Ap. Rh. 1, 744; Nonn. 42, 5: aor. ἐχαλάσθην, -λασθῇ Aesch. Pr. 991; Pl. Phaed. 86. **Mid.** *to loosen for oneself*, or *one's own*, aor. χαλάσαντο Ap. Rh. 2, 1264, perhaps unnoticed by our Lexicogr.

Χᾰλεπαίνω *To be offended* (χαλεπός), Od. 16, 114; Ar. Ran. 1020; Thuc. 2, 22; Xen. Mem. 2, 2, 9; Epic inf. -παινέμεν Theocr. 25, 81: imp. ἐχαλέπαινε Her. 1, 189; Thuc. 1, 26, χαλέπ- Il. 14, 256; Theogn. 897: fut. -ᾰνῶ Pl. Phaed. 116 (Bekk. Stallb.); Luc. Tim. 37: aor. ἐχαλέπηνα Dio Cass. 44, 9; χαλεπήνῃ Il. 16, 386; -πήνας Isocr. 4, 102; Aristot. Polit. 5, 42; -πῆναι Il. 18, 108: (perf.?): aor. pass. ἐχαλεπάνθη Xen. An. 4, 6, 2; subj. -πανθῇς Cyr. 3, 1, 38: pres. pass. χαλεπαίνεσθαι Xen. Cyr. 5, 2, 18; Pl. Rep. 337. This verb seems not to occur in Tragedy, and once only in Comedy.

Χανδάνω *To contain* (χάω, χέω, χάδω), Ar. Ran. 260 (chor.); Hippocr. 8, 182 (Lit.): imp. ἐχάνδᾰνον Od. 17, 344; Theocr. 13, 57, χάνδ- Il. 23, 742: fut. χείσομαι Od. 18, 17; H. Ven. 252: p. κέχανδα as pres. -χανδώς Il. 23, 268. Od. 4, 96: plp. κεχάνδει Il. 24, 192: 2 aor. ἔχᾰδον Il. 4, 24, χάδε 11, 462; Anth. 7, 4; χαδέειν Il. 14, 34; Hippocr. 7, 482 (Lit.) Poetic, especially Epic, occasionally Ionic prose.

Χᾰρίζομαι *To gratify* (Dep. mid.), Il. 13, 633; Archil. 75; Simon. Am. 7, 92; Eur. Fr. 31 (Dind.); Her. 6, 130; Thuc. 3, 37; Pl. Rep. 351; -ίζεσθαι Soph. El. 331; Com. Fr. (Theop.) 2, 803; Antiph. 4, γ, 2; -όμενος Lys. 20, 31: imp. ἐχᾰριζόμην Her. 1, 33; Pl. Tim. 20, χαριζ- Od. 1, 61: fut. χαρῐοῦμαι Ar. Thesm. 756; Her. 1, 90; Thuc. 3, 40; Xen. An. 7, 6, 2; -ιοίμην Ar. Eq. 776; -ιεῖσθαι Her. 1, 158. 3, 39; Antiph. 5, 32; Thuc. 8, 65; -ιούμενος Isocr. 8, 15, late -ίσομαι Sopat. Rhet. p. 332; Diod. Sic. Fr. p. 179 (Bekk. -ιοῦμαι Dind. p. 157);

Pseud.-Callisth. 2, 19; Galen 15, 13; N. T. Rom. 8, 32, Dor. -ιξῇ Archyt. Epist. 2, -ιξιόμεθα Cret. Tit. 3048: aor. ἐχαρισάμην Ar. Eq. 1368; Her. 1, 91; Dem. 21, 91; -ίσωμαι Ar. Thesm. 939; Pl. Men. 75; Xen. An. 2, 1, 10, Dor. χαρίξ Theocr. 5, 71; -ισαίμην Il. 6, 49. 11, 134; Pl. Menex. 236; χάρισαι Eur. Elec. 192 if sound (Vulg. Kirchh. Paley); Ar. Thesm. 938; Pl. Rep. 457; -ίσασθαι Od. 13, 15; Aesch. Pers. 700; Xen. Cyr. 3, 3, 1. 6, 1, 38; -ισάμενος Thuc. 4, 20: p. κεχάρισμαι, -ισαι Ar. Eccl. 1045, -ισται Eq. 54; imper. κεχαρίσθω called pass. Pl. Phaedr. 250; κεχαρίσθαι Xen. Mem. 3, 11, 10; Isocr. 19, 38; κεχαρισμένος, η, ον, usu. as adjective, *pleasing*, *acceptable*, Il. 5, 243. Od. 2, 54; Eur. H. F. 892 (chor.); Ar. Pax 386 (chor.); Her. 3, 119; Isocr. 2, 48; Pl. Soph. 218: plp. κεχάριστο Od. 6, 23, ἐκεχάριστο impers. and called pass. Her. 8, 5: aor. late, χαρισθῆναι N. T. Act. 3, 14; -ισθείς 1 Cor. 2, 12: late also fut. χαρισθήσομαι N. T. Philem. 22. Vb. χαριστέον Pl. Phaedr. 227.

Χάσκω *To gape*, Anacr. 14, 8 (Bergk); Hipponax 8; Ar. Vesp. 1493; Aristot. H. An. 4, 8, 32; χάσκῃς Ar. Eq. 1032; χάσκειν Xen. Eq. 10, 7, ἐγ- Ar. Vesp. 721; χάσκων Solon 13, 36 (Bergk); Hippocr. 4, 144, ἀνα- Ar. Av. 502, and χαίνω late in pres. Anth. 9, 797. 11, 242; Dioscor. 3, 127; Geop. 10, 30, περι- Ael. H. A. 3, 20, ἐπι- Luc. D. Mort. 6, 3 (Bekk. Dind. -χειρῶ Ms. A. Fritz.): imp. ἔχασκ- Hippocr. 5, 194, ἀμφ- Aesch. Ch. 545: fut. mid. χανοῦμαι, ἐγ- Ar. Lys. 271. Eq. 1313 &c., ἀνα- Hippocr. 8, 422. 498: (1 p. κέχαγκα Bekk. Anecd. 611): 2 p. κέχηνα Ar. Av. 264. 308. Eq. 755. 1119; Hippocr. 8, 64; Luc. Icar. 3; Philostr. Apoll. 61, Dor. 3 pl. κεχάναντι Sophr. 51 (Ahr.); κεχήνῃ Ar. Eq. 804; imper. κεχήνετε Ach. 133 (Dind. -ατε Mein.); -χηνέναι Hippocr. 5, 694; -χηνώς Il. 16, 409; Simon. Am. 7, 110; Ar. Vesp. 617; Pl. Rep. 529: plp. ἐκεχήνειν Luc. Merc. Con. 3, Dor. and old Attic 'κεχήνη Ar. Ach. 10: 2 aor. ἔχᾰνον Ar. Fr. 319 (D); Hippocr. 7, 534, ἀμφ- Il. 23, 79, χάνον H. Cer. 16; χάνῃ Her. 2, 68; Hippocr. 7, 330 (Lit.), ἐγ- Ar. Ach. 221; χάνοι Il. 4, 182. 8, 150; Hippocr. 1, 70 (Erm.); χανών Il. 16, 350. Od. 12, 350; Soph. Fr. 449 (Suid.); Com. Fr. (Eub.) 3, 212; Hippocr. 4, 142 (Lit.); Aristot. Probl. 26, 48, 2; Luc. Peregr. 21; χανεῖν Soph. Aj. 1227; Ar. Vesp. 342; Luc. Sump. 28, -έειν Hippocr. 4, 142. This verb is scarcely used in *classic* prose; often in *late*, especially 2 p. and 2 aor. Alciphr. 1, 8; Plut. Mor. 48. 967; Luc. Icar. 3. Pisc. 34. V. H. 2, 1; Strab. 14, 2, 5. For στοναχήσεται H. Ven. 252, Buttm. would read στόμα χήσεται, and assign χήσεται to this verb as another form of the fut.; and for subj. aor.

ἀναχάνηται Hippocr. 1, 475. 3, 12 (Kühn), Lobeck would substitute fut. -χανεῖται, and Littré adopts it (8, 498.)

Χατέω *To wish, want,* Poet. and confined by Lexicons to **pres.** κατέεις Anth. 7, 583, -έουσι Od. 15, 376; Ap. Rh. 4, 1557; -έωσι 2, 316; -έων Il. 15, 399; Ap. Rh. 3, 584; Mosch. 3, 114; Anth. 7, 585: but **imp.** iter. χατέεσκε Nonn. 4, 56. The collat. χατίζω is confined to **pres.** and chiefly Epic, -τίζεις Il. 2, 225, -τίζει 18, 392; Pind. Ol. 2, 86; -τίζων Il. 17, 221. Od. 22, 50; Hes. Op. 21; Eur. Heracl. 465 (trimet.) **Pass.** χατίζεσθαι Aesch. Ag. 304, is a suggestion of Heath and Porson, and adopted by Hermann, Enger, Paley, doubtingly by Blomf. for χαρίζεσθαι (Mss. Vulg.), ῥαχίζεσθαι (Dind. 5 ed.) This verb is not as Lexicons say "nur dichterich," for χατίζει is in Hippocr. 7, 558 (Lit. 2, 445 Erm.) without v. r.

Χέζω *Alvum exonero* (χέδ-), Com. Poet. Ar. Eq. 70; but Artemidor. Onir. 4, 33; Hierocl. 250 (Eberh.): **fut.** (χέσω, -σειν Anth. 7, 683?): χέσομαι, κατα- rare Ar. Fr. 207, usu. χεσοῦμαι Ar. Pax 1235. Vesp. 941, ἐπι- Lys. 440. 441: **1 aor.** ἔχεσα, κατ- Ar. Nub. 174; χέσαιμι, ἐγ- Eccl. 347; χέσας 320; χέσαι 808; Com. Fr. (Stratt.) 2, 783: **2 aor.** ἔχεσον, κατ- Com. Fr. (Alc.) 2, 826; subj. χέσω Com. Fr. (Eup.) 2, 519 may belong to either **aor.**, probably to the 1st; χεσεῖν Ar. Thesm. 570: **p. p.** κεχεσμένος Ar. Ach. 1170: **2 p.** κέχοδα, ἐγ- Ar. Ran. 479; ἐπι-κεχοδώς Av. 68. **Mid. aor.** ἐχεσάμην, χέσαιτο *defile oneself,* Ar. Eq. 1057. Late in prose; **1 aor. act.** χεσάντων Plut. Mor. 232. The **2 aor.** is certainly rare, but κατ-έχεσον occurs in Alcae. Comic. quoted; and Ar. has χεσεῖν Thesm. 570, where, if he chose, he might have used χέσαι. Besides, Lobeck says the **fut.** χέσειν Anth. quoted, should be **2 aor.** χεσεῖν—we think him right: and for καταπεσών Ar. Av. 89, Bergk would read καταχεσών (Act. Soc. Graec. 1, 201). χέσαιτο Ar. Eq. 1057 quoted, is a solitary instance of the **mid.** form, and is supposed by some to have been used merely for a play on words, to chime with μαχέσαιτο.

Χειρίζω, see μεταχειρίζω.

Χειρόω *To handle, treat* (χείρ), rare in **act.** Ar. Vesp. 443; Ael. H. A. 17, 32 (old edit.) Usu. **mid.** χειροῦμαι *to get into, under one's hand, subdue,* Aesch. Ch. 694; Soph. Tr. 279; Her. 2, 70; Xen. Ages. 2, 31; Pl. Soph. 219, sometimes passively *to be subdued,* Aesch. Pr. 353; Eur. Elec. 1168; Ar. Vesp. 439 &c.: **imp.** ἐχειρούμην Soph. O. C. 950, -οῦντο Xen. Hell. 2, 4, 26, but **pass.** Diod. Sic. 16, 20: **fut.** χειρώσομαι Soph. Tr. 1109; Eur. H. F. 570; Thuc. 1, 122; Pl. Soph. 222; Dio. Hal. Ant. 1, 47: **aor.** ἐχειρωσάμην Her. 1, 169; Thuc. 3, 11; Pl. Menex.

240; -ώσωμαι Her. 4, 103; Thuc. 3, 46; -ώσασθαι Her. 5, 31; Thuc. 4, 24 &c.: as mid. p. p. κεχείρωμαι Dio Cass. 50, 24; Plut. Timol. 19; Luc. Salt. 79, but in the *classic* period, passive Aesch. Sept. 326; Thuc. 5, 96; Pl. Leg. 919: **aor.** always **pass.** ἐχειρώθην Her. 5, 16; Thuc. 3, 39; -ωθεῖεν 4, 19; -ωθείς Soph. O. C. 903; Her. 5, 17; -ωθῆναι Her. 3, 120; Thuc. 8, 71: **fut.** χειρωθήσεται (Dem.) 11, 5.

Χερνίπτομαι *To wash one's hands* before a sacred duty, *dedicate* &c. Ar. Pax 961: **fut.** χερνίψομαι Eur. I. T. 622: **aor.** ἐχερνίψατο Lys. 6, 52, χερνίψ- Il. 1, 449: **pass. aor.** χερνιφθείς Anth. 6, 156. **Act.** late (χερνίπτω) *I offer*, fut. -νίψουσι Lycophr. 184.

Χέω *To pour* (χύω, χύνω, see below), mostly Poetic in *simple*, Il. 16, 385; Hes. Op. 421; Aesch. Supp. 1026; Soph. El. 84; Eur. Cycl. 405; late prose, Apocr. Sir. 43, 19, but κατα- Her. 3, 96, ἐσ- 4, 195, ἐγ- Xen. Cyr. 1, 3, 8; Epic χείω Hes. Th. 83, ἐγ- Od. 9, 10, and perhaps late χεύω, -εις Nonn. 18, 344, -ει Q. Sm. 1, 301; but imper. ἔγ-χευε if correct, Alcae. 33 (Ahr. -χεε 41 Bergk), χεέτω Simon. C. 168; χεύων Q. Sm. 3, 491; Opp. Cyn. 2, 127, see χεύομαι below: **imp.** χέον Il. 7, 480; Theocr. 7, 82, ἔχεεν, κατ- Ar. Nub. 74, συν- Pl. Rep. 379, χεῦον Q. Sm. 7, 385; Tzetz. Homer. 18, δι-έχευον Q. Sm. 16, 504 (Vulg.), iter. χέεσκον Or. Sib. 1, 111: **fut.** Attic χέω, εῖς, εῖ, like **pres.**, συγ-χέω Eur. Fr. 388 (Dind.), ἐκ-χέω Supp. 773 (Nauck, Kirchh. -χεῶ Dind. by oversight), ἐπι-χεῖς Ar. Pax 169, ἐγ- Dem. 19, 213; παρα-χέωσι Com. Fr. (Plat.) 2, 637; late as some call it, χεῶ, ἐκ- V. T. Joel 2, 28, χεεῖ Malach. 3, 3, Epic χεύω Od. 2, 222, -ομεν Il. 7, 336, if not aor. subj.: **aor.** ἔχεα Il. 18, 347; Pind. I. 8, 59 (Schmid, Bergk), ἐν- Com. Fr. (Pher.) 2, 282, ἐξ- Ar. Thesm. 554; Arr. An. 2, 19; subj. χέω Soph. O. C. 478? Eur. Cycl. 329, ἐγ- Ar. Ach. 1068; χέαιμι, ἐγ- 1055; χέον, ἐγ- Eur. Cycl. 568; Com. Fr. (Pher.) 2, 282, ἀπο- Hippocr. 2, 518 (Lit.), ἐγ-χεάτω Com. Fr. (Philem.) 4, 6; Xen. Conv. 2, 23; ἐγ-χέας Epicharm. 61; Com. Fr. (Amips.) 2, 701; Xen. Cyr. 1, 3, 9; Pl. Conv. 214, παρα- Hippocr. 7, 238; χέαι, ἀμφι- Hes. Opp. 65, συγ- Eur. Hipp. 813; Isae. 5, 18, δια- Her. 8, 57, ἐγ- Dem. 43, 8, Epic ἔχευα Il. 3, 270. 4, 269; Archil. 103; Timoth. 5 (B.), χεῦα Il. 14, 436. Od. 24, 81; subj. χεύῃ Il. 14. 165, χεύωσιν Il. 7, 86; χεῦον Alcae. 42, -άτω 36, χευάντων Od. 4, 214; χεύας Il. 23, 257. Od. 12, 14; inf. χεῦαι Il. 23, 45. Od. 11, 75 &c., late ἔχευσα, χεύσας Anth. 14, 124, περι- Diod. Sic. 2, 15 (Vulg. but -χέας Bekk. Dind.): **p.** κέχῠκα, ἐκ- Anth. Plan. 242, συγ- Com. Fr. (Men.) 4, 294, προσυγ- Polyb. 5, 84: **p. p.** κέχῠμαι Il. 5, 141; Simon. C. 89; Pind. I. 1, 4; Soph. Tr. 853; Her. 1, 22. 4, 7; Pl. Tim. 66; Arist. Probl. 4, 32, ἐκ- Pl. Crito 49, συγ- (Dem.) 25, 25 (κέχῡται in arsi, Or. Sib. 1, 139, -υνται Mein.), Ionic 3 pl. κεχύαται, κατα- Her. 2, 75: **plp.** ἐκέχυντο Com. Fr. (Pher.) 2, 299; Theocr. 7, 145, κέχυ- Il. 20, 421. Od. 19, 539; Theocr. 20, 23: **aor.** ἐχῠ́θην Ap. Rh. 3, 1009; in tmesi Emped. 273; Theocr. 22, 125, ἀμφ- Od. 4, 716, ἐξ- Ar. Vesp. 1469, κατ- Pl. Soph. 264; χῠθῇ Eur. Or. 1398; Hippocr. 2, 386 (Erm.); χῠθείη Od. 19, 590; χῠθείς Soph. Ph. 293; Eur. Elec. 486. 514, ἀμφι- Il. 23, 63; (Hippocr.) Epist. 9, 366, ἐπι- Her. 2, 141, ἐκ- 3, 13, περι- Pl. Tim. 60: **fut.** χυθήσομαι Joseph. Ant. 8, 8, 5, συγ- Dem. 23, 62, ἐκ- Luc. Tim. 18: (**2 aor.** ἐχύη, ἐχύθη Hesych.) **Mid.** χέομαι trans. *to pour for oneself*, and intrans. *pour oneself, stream*, Od. 10, 518; Eur. Or. 472; Pl. Tim. 83, Epic χεύομαι (περι- Od. 6, 232, is by most referred to subj. **aor.**) Opp. Hal. 2, 280, κατα- Hes. Op. 583, ἀπο- Eur. Ion 148 (chor.), μετα- Opp. Hal. 1, 572; opt. χέοιτο, δια- Thuc. 2, 75; χευόμενος Q. Sm. 2, 222: **imp.** ἐχέοντο, Il. 16, 267; Mosch. 4, 57, ἀμφ- Od. 22, 498, ἐπ- Theocr. 2, 152, χέοντο Il. 8, 159, προ-χε- Il. 2, 465: **fut.** Attic (χέομαι) χεόμενον Isae. 6, 51: **1 aor.** ἐχεάμην rare in prose, Her. 7, 43, ἐπ- Com. Fr. (Antiph.) 3, 45; χεώμεθα, ἐγ- Xen. Conv. 2, 26; χέασθαι Aesch. Pers. 220; Soph. O. C. 477; Ar. Vesp. 1020; late prose Plut. Mor. 579; χεάμενος Plut. Mor. 388. Aristid. 21, ἐγ- Ar. Vesp. 906; Xen. Cyr. 1, 3, 9, κατα- Her. 1, 50; Dio. Hal. 9, 28, προσ- Hippocr. 8, 442, ἐπι- Plut. Mor. 318, χειάμ- Opp. C. 3, 172, Epic ἐχευάμην Il. 5, 314. 7, 63, χευ- 18, 24; περι-χεύεται called by some subj. for -ηται, Od. 6, 232; χευάμενος accommodated from Il. 18, 24, by Pl. Rep. 388; Orph. Arg. 729; Anth. 6, 173 &c.: **2 aor.** syncop. (ἐχῠ́μην) ἔχῠτο Od. 22, 88, ἐξ- 19, 470, χῠ́το Il. 23, 385. Od. 7, 143, ἔχυντο Od. 10, 415, χύντο Il. 4, 526; χυμένη Il. 19, 284. Od. 8, 527; occas. in Trag. Aesch. Ch. 401 (chor.), χύμενον Eum. 263 (chor.); Eur. Heracl. 75 (chor.): so (κέχῠμαι), κέχυτο *spread* &c. Il. 5, 696. 16, 344; κεχυμένος Eur. Bac. 456. Desider. χεσείω Ar. Nub. 296. **Vb.** χυτός Il. 6, 464; Pl. Tim. 59, ἐγ-χυτέον Dioscor. 5, 103; Geop. 6, 7.

In late recensions of the Iliad and Od. the fut. and aor. with σ, χεύσω, ἔχευσα have disappeared. In Alcae. Fr. 34, Schneidewin reads χεῦσον; but strangely enough, χευάτω not χευσ- 29, 3; Ahrens, and *now* Bergk χεῖον, χευάτω. χύω, χύνω are late forms, χύον Aretae. Cur. Diut. 130 (ed. Oxon.), but χέον (Cod. Par.); ἐπίχυε Alex. Trall. 1, 3, 8, ἐπίχυνε (Dind.); ἐκ-χύνειν see Luc.-Pseudol. 29; διασυγχύνω Apollon. de Pron. p. 616, συγχύνεσθαι 132: **imp.** συν-έχυνε N. T. Act. 9, 22: **fut.** κατα-χύσει Geop. 3, 10, δια- 7, 8, ἐκ-χῠ́σει Nicet. Eug. 4, 123: **aor.** κατα-χύσας Alex. Trall. 1, 9, 16; χῦσαι Tryphiod. 205 (Vulg. λῦσαι Lehrs), δια-χῦσαι Xen. Mem. 4, 3, 8, but the passage occurs in one Ms. only, and is supposed to be an interpolation; and for χῦσον Ar. Av. 210 (Vulg.), λῦσον has been substituted from Ms. V (Bekk. Dind. Bergk); so also ἀπο-χύσαντα Hippocr. 8, 200 (Vulg.) has given way to ἀπό-χεαι (Mss. C θ, Lit.); and ἐγ-χυνόμενον Luc. pro Imag. 29 (Solan.) is now ἐκ-κεχυμένον (Ms. A. Jacob. ἐγ- Dind.) Buttm. says a pres. χεύω does not occur in Epic diction, as χείω satisfies the metre. It certainly occurs in late Epic, χεύεις Nonn. D. 18, 344, χεύων Opp. Cyn. 2, 127, ἐκ-χεύετον Nicand. Fr. 74, 34 &c. χεύω Eur. Elec. 181 chor. (Mss. Vulg.) has been altered to χορεύω (Pors. Dind.), νυχεύω (Herm. Kirchh. Nauck.) **Mid.** καταχεύεται Hes. Op. 583, ἀπο- Eur. Ion. 148 (chor.) **1 aor.** and **fut. pass.** regularly formed from χέω, -έσω, occur late, χεθείς Galen 1, 433; Phil. de Plant. 254, even Aristot. παρα-χεθῇ if correct, Probl. 20, 35 (Bekk.): χεθήσεται Galen 7, 317, ἐκ- Arr. Epict. 4, 10, 26, δια- Themist. Paraphr. 4, 9 (Spengel.)

The Epics seem not to have contracted εει of this verb, χέει Il. 9, 15. Od. 19, 521; Hes. Sc. 396. Op. 421, προ-χέειν Il. 21, 219; the Attics always, ἐκ-χεῖ Soph. El. 1291, συγ- Eur I. A. 37, κατα-χεῖν Ar. Eq. 1091; both varied in εε, χεῖτε Theocr. 1, 118, and imper. σύγ-χει Il. 9, 612, ἔγ-χει Callim. Epigr. 30, κατά-χει Ar. Ach. 1040. 1130, ἐκ-χεῖτε Eur. H. F. 941, but **imp.** ἔχεε Callim. Jov. 32, χέε Il. 20, 321. 23, 220 &c. and σύγ-χει (συν-έχεε) Il. 13, 808, so Attic ἐν-έχεε Com. Fr. (Pher.) 2, 282; Ar. Fr. 209 (D), κατ-έχεε Ar. Nub. 74; Com. Fr. (Xen.) 3, 621; (Dem.) 45, 74, συν-έχεε Pl. Rep. 379, and ἐν-έχεις Ar. Plut. 1021, ἐν-έχει Antiph. 1, 19, ἐξ-έχει Aesch. Ag. 1029; Ar. Ach. 987, ἐπ-έχει Com. Fr. (Drom.) 3, 541, χέεσθαι Ap. Rh. 3, 205, χεῖσθαι Od. 10, 518, κατα- Ar. Av. 463, κακ-χέεται Sapph. 2, 13 (Bergk), χεῖται Pl. Tim. 83, κατα- Ar. Vesp. 713; neither seems to have contracted εη, εω, ἐπι-χέῃς Com. Fr. (Magn.) 2, 10, χέῃ Eur. Cycl. 329, ἐκ- 323; Ar. Ran. 855, δια- Pl. Phil. 46, χέω Soph. O. C. 478, χέων Eur. Cycl. 405, ἐγ-χέω Eur. Cycl. 568; Ar. Ach. 1068, ἐκ- Soph. Ph. 13, nor εο (except ἐγ-χεῦντα Theocr. 10, 54) χέον Il. 7, 480, παρ-έχεον Com. Fr. (Alex.) 3, 445, ἔγ-χεον Eur. Cycl. 568; Com. Fr. (Pher.) 2, 282; Ar. Eq. 122, χέοντα Od. 4, 556, Il. 7, 426; Soph. El. 84, ἐκ- Ar. Ach. 616, ἐπι- Pl. Rep. 407, ἐπι-χέοι Xen. An. 4, 5, 27, χέουσα Il. 3, 142; Eur. Tr. 38, ἐγ- Antiph. 1, 19, χέουσι Aesch. Supp. 1028, ἐγ-χέουσι Xen. Cyr. 1, 3, 8, κατα-χέουσι Pl. Leg. 800. We feel therefore some misgivings about admitting Cobet's emendation ἐγχοῦ Com. Fr. (Menand.) 4, 153, for εὔχου (Vulg. ἔγχει Piers. Meinek.) It would appear from σύγ-χει Il. 9, 612. 13, 808, that χεῖσθαι Od. 10, 518, is not "the only instance of this verb being contracted in Hom."

(**Χλάδω**) *To sound, ring, swell,* Dor. Poet. and only **2 perf.**

κεχλαδώς Pind. Ol. 9, 1; -άδοντας P. 4, 179; inf. κεχλάδειν Fr. 57 (Bergk) for -αδέναι, Hesych. has κεχληδέναι, ψοφεῖν.

Χλῐαίνω *To warm,* Soph. Epigr. 4 (Bergk); Hippocr. 7, 180. 238 (Lit.); Plut. Mor. 952: fut. χλιᾰνῶ Ar. Lys. 386: aor. ἔχλίηνε Hermesianax Col. 89; Hippocr. 7, 388, and -ᾶνα 2, 265 (Erm.): aor. pass. χλιανθῇ Hippocr. 2, 354 (Erm.); χλιανθείς Plut. Mor. 725; Luc. Lex. 14. Amor. 40, ἀνα- Aristot. Probl. 22, 7. (ῑ Hermes. 89; Ar. Lys. 386; Alex. Com. Fr. 3, 452; Anth. 9, 244, ῐ Ar. Eccl. 64; Soph. Epigr. 4; Meleag. 13. 24. 81. 93. 102.)

Χολόω *To enrage* (χόλος), -λῶν late prose, Stob. (Nicostr.) 70, 12: fut. -ώσω, Epic inf. -ωσέμεν Il. 1, 78: aor. ἐχόλωσα Il. 18, 111; Soph. Tr. 1035 reg. Mid. and pass. χολοῦμαι *to be enraged,* Il. 8, 407; Plut. Mor. 461, late Epic χολώεται Nonn. 5, 447; opt. χολῷτο for -όοιτο, Theogn. 325 (Bergk); -ούμενος Archil. 95, late Epic χολωόμ- Nonn. 4, 169. 5, 437; Anth. Plan. 4, 128: fut. χολώσομαι Eur. Tr. 730; hither some refer χολώσεαι Il. 14, 310, others to subj. aor.: in Hom. redupl. κεχολώσομαι as mid. Il. 1, 139. 5, 421. Od. 15, 214: aor. ἐχολωσάμην Il. 15, 155, χολωσ- 21, 136; Epic subj. χολώσεαι, for -ηαι, Il. 14, 310; Ap. Rh. 1, 1332, see fut.; χολώσαιτο Od. 6, 147; -σάμενος Il. 23, 482; Callim. Pall. 79; Ap. Rh. 4, 1138: aor. pass. as mid. ἐχολώθην Il. 13, 206; χολώθ- 13, 660; Callim. Del. 86; -ωθῇς Il. 9, 33; -θῆναι Hippocr. 7, 494 (Lit. 2, 495 Erm.); χολωθείς Il. 23, 23; Pind. Ol. 7, 30; Soph. Ph. 374; Eur. Alc. 5 (late prose Diod. Sic. 3, 67): p. p. κεχόλωμαι as mid. Od. 1, 69; -ωμένος Il. 13, 203; Her. 8, 31; Plut. Mor. 195. Fab. M. 22. Marcell. 21: plp. κεχολώμην Il. 16, 585, 3 pl. -ώατο Od. 14, 282. Vb. χολωτός Il. 4, 241; Luc. Lex. 20 (Jacob.) This verb is Poet. (Attic, only aor. act. and pass. and fut. mid.) and occas. in Ionic and late prose. The redupl. fut. κεχολώσομαι is freq., some say the only form in Hom. Il. 23, 543, -ώσεαι 5, 421. 762, -ώσεται 1, 139. Od. 15, 214, with μή πως Il. 20, 301. Od. 24, 544. But χολώσεαι also Il. 14, 310, is fut. in *form,* and under the influence of the *same words* (μή πως), is it therefore under exactly the *same influence?* Or is the latter a softer touch, shading off into the milder subjunctive? If so, χολώσεαι in Hom. is a shortened form for -ώσηαι.

Χορεύω *To dance, celebrate, honour with dancing,* Soph. Ant. 1154; Ar. Pax 325; Her. 1, 191; Pl. Leg. 665: imp. ἐχόρ- Xen. An. 4, 7, 16: fut. χορεύσω Eur. H. F. 871; Ar. Ran. 326; Dem. 39, 23: and -εύσομαι see mid.: aor. ἐχόρευσα Eur. H. F. 686; Ar. Ran. 356, χόρευσ- Eur. Alc. 582 (chor.): p. κεχόρευκα Pl. Leg. 654: p. p. κεχόρευται impers. Ar. Nub. 1510; Plut. Mor.

792: aor. ἐχορεύθην Eur. H. F. 879; Pl. Leg. 655. **Mid.** χορευόμεναι as act. Eur. Ion 1084: fut. χορεύσομαι Aesch. Ag. 31 (Theophr. Fr. 83 Wimm.): aor. ἐχορευσάμην Ar. Thesm. 103, ἐξ- Eur. Hel. 381. **Vb.** χορευτέον Eur. Bac. 324. The mid. seems to be almost confined to Attic poetry.

Χόω *To heap up*, Her. 4, 71; inf. χοῦν Her. 2, 137; Thuc. 2, 76; Pl. Leg. 958 (Mss. Bekk. &c. χωννύναι Vulg.); χῶν Her. 1, 162, also χωννύω late Polyb. 1, 47. 10, 28; Geop. 5, 44, προσ- Theophr. H. P. 2, 5, 5, and χώννυμι Arr. An. 2, 18, 3. 2, 18, 6; Nic. Damasc. 52 (L. Dind.); Galen 16, 507: imp. ἔχουν Thuc. 2, 75, ἐχώννυε Ctes. Fr. 29, 26 (Müll.); App. Mithr. 78; Arr. An. 1, 20, 8. 4, 29, 7; Diod. Sic. 14, 49, ἐπ- 13, 107, but ἐχώννυσαν Dio Cass. 66, 4, ἀπ- Plut. Phoc. 11: fut. χώσω Ar. Ach. 295; Xen. Cyr. 7, 3, 11; -σουσα Soph. Ant. 81: aor. ἔχωσα (Dem.) 25, 84; Arr. 4, 30, 1; χώσω Eur. Or. 1585; χῶσον I. T. 702; χῶσαι Her. 9, 85; χώσας 2, 140; Soph. Ant. 1204; Pl. Leg. 947: p. κέχωκα, προ-κεχωκέναι Aristot. Mirab. 81; ἀνα-κεχωκότες Dem. 55, 28, προσ- Strab. 6, 2, 10: p. p. κέχωσμαι Com. Fr. (Plat.) 2, 679; Thuc. 2, 102; Xen. Cyr. 7, 3, 16, ἐκ- Her. 2, 138, συγ- 8, 144: aor. ἐχώσθην Emped. 303; Her. 2, 137; Xen. Cyr. 7, 3, 16: fut. χωσθήσομαι Eur. I. A. 1443; Polyb. 4, 42. **Mid.** late, aor. ἐχωσάμην Luc. D. Deor. 14; χώσασθαι Philostr. Apoll. 4, 147; χωσαμένη Or. Sib. 5, 320, missed by Lexicogr. **Vb.** χωστός Eur. Rhes. 414. The forms -υμι, -ύω seem to be late, see above; and App. Mithr. 78; Joseph. Jud. B. 3, 7, 8; χώννυσθαι Polyb. 4, 40, 4; χωννυμένης, ἐγ-, Strab. 7, 5, 8; ἐχώννυτο Arr. An. 2, 18, 4.

Χραισμέω *To help, ward off*, Epic, pres. late and rare, Nic. Ther. 914: fut. χραισμήσω Il. 20, 296; Epic inf. -ησέμεν Il. 21, 316: 1 aor. χραίσμησεν Il. 16, 837; inf. χραισμῆσαι Il. 18, 62: 2 aor. ἔχραισμον Il. 14, 66, χραῖσμ- 7, 144; subj. χραίσμῃ 15, 32, -ησι 11, 387; opt. -μοι 3, 54 (Bekk. Doederl. -μῃ Vulg. Spitzn. Dind. Ameis); χραίσμετε Ap. Rh. 2, 218; χραισμεῖν Il. 21, 193; Ap. Rh. 2, 249. 3, 643.

Χράομαι *To use*, -ῶμαι Ar. Eq. 889; Isocr. 4, 143; Isae. 6, 1, Ion. -έομαι? χρῇ Com. Fr. (Alexand.) 4, 553; Pl. Hipp. min. 369, -ῆται Aesch. Ag. 953; Ar. Vesp. 1028; Andoc. 4, 27; Xen. Conv. 2, 5, Ion. -ᾶται Her. 1, 132. 2, 95 &c. (Bekk. Gaisf. Stein), and if correct, -έεται 4, 50, δια- 1, 58 (Gaisf. Bekk. Dind. -ᾶται Lhard. Bred. Stein), χρῆσθε Pl. Lach. 194 &c., -ῶνται Antiph. 5, 17; Thuc. 1, 70, Ion. -έονται Her. 1, 34 (Bekk. Gaisf. Dind.), -έωνται 1, 173. 4, 108 (Bekk. Gaisf. Stein); opt. χρῷο Isocr. 5, 68; imper. χρῶ Ar. Thesm. 212; Isocr. 1, 34, Ion. χρέω Her. 1, 155, χρέο (Schaef. Stein, -έεο Dietsch, Abicht); Hippocr. 2, 516, -ῆσθε Andoc. 1, 11; inf. χρῆσθαι Soph. Ant. 213; Ar. Av.

1040; Antiph. 4, γ, 5. 5, 64; Andoc. 3, 2; Isae. 3, 22, Ion. -ᾶσθαι Her. 2, 15. 3, 20. 4, 76. 5, 36 &c. (Bekk. Gaisf. Stein); and late, Plut. Mor. 149; Paus. 2, 28, 3, and -έεσθαι Hippocr. 1, 253 (Erm.); Her. 1, 21. 187 (Bekk. Gaisf.), still occas. -ῆσθαι 1, 47 (Bekk. Gaisf.). 7, 10. 16. 18 (Bekk. Gaisf. Dind. -ᾶσθαι Stein); χρώμενος Simon. C. 95; Aesch. Eum. 655; Antiph. 4, δ, 2; Thuc. 1, 132, Ion. -εόμενος Her. 2, 108 (Bekk. Gaisf.), -εώμενος (Lhard. Stein &c.); rare in Hom. Il. 23, 834, see perf.: imp. ἐχρώμην Isocr. 15, 96, ἐχρῶ Andoc. 1, 49, ἐχρῆτο Antiph. 5, 33; Isae. 1, 30; Pl. Prot. 315, Ion. -ᾶτο Her. 3, 3. 4, 44 &c., -ῶντο Antiph. 6, 28; Pl. Rep. 406, -έοντο Her. 2, 108. 6, 46 (Bekk. Gaisf. Dind.), and -έωντο 3, 57. 5, 68 (Bekk. Gaisf. Stein): fut. χρήσομαι Soph. Ph. 1133; Eur. Ion 444; Ar. Pax 230; Her. 8, 85; Antiph. 5, 36; Lys. 14, 4; Pl. Rep. 451, Dor. χρησεῖται, δια- Theocr. 15, 54: aor. ἐχρησάμην Soph. O. R. 117; Ar. Nub. 22; Her. 8, 112; Antiph. 5, 83; Thuc. 5, 7; Lys. 13, 44; Isocr. 16, 12; -σάμενος Pind. N. 4, 58; Antiph. 4, γ, 4: p. p. κέχρημαι usu. trans. Od. 3, 266; Eur. Med. 347; Her. 1, 42; Antiph. 3, β, 8; Pl. Men. 72; Isocr. 11, 33; Dem. 22, 54, κατα- Pl. Crat. 426 (Epist. 8, 353 C); Dem. 35, 44; but pass. Com. Fr. (Amph.) 3, 306; Isocr. 4, 74, προκατα- Dem. 19, 154, in poetry, also *to need, long for,* κέχρησαι Eur. I. A. 382, -ήμεθα Med. 334, -ησθε Theocr. 26, 18; κεχρῆσθαι Lys. 25, 15; κεχρημένος Il. 19, 262. Od. 1, 13; Emped. 361 (Stein); Soph. Ph. 1264; Eur. Ion 1199; *needy, poor,* Od. 14, 155; Hes. Op. 317: plp. ἐκεχρήμην, Dem. 19, 225, -χρητο Lycurg. 42, κέχρητο Od. 3, 266: aor. ἐχρήσθην pass. Her. 7, 144; χρησθῇ Dem. 21, 16; κατα-χρησθῆναι Her. 9, 120: act. χρησθείς if sound, Soph. Ant. 24 (Vulg. Bergk), rejected by (Wund. Dind. Hart. &c.); συγ-χρησθῆναι Polyb. 2, 32 (Mss. D E, Vulg. but συγχρῆσθαι Bekk. Dind.): 3 fut. κεχρήσομαι act. *will want, wish,* Theocr. 16, 73 (Vulg. Ahr. and *now* Meinek.) Vb. χρηστός *good,* Soph. Tr. 3, -έος Hippocr. 1, 319 (Erm.); Xen. Mem. 3, 1, 11.

In Attic, this verb with some others contracts in η instead of α, χρῇ, χρῆται, χρῆσθε, χρῆσθαι, ἐχρῆτο, Pl. Hipp. min. 369; Soph. O. R. 878. Tr. 906; Eur. Hipp. 107; Ar. Eq. 124; Thuc. 1, 68. 6, 92; Pl. Lach. 194, but ἐχρᾶτο Anaxipp. Com. Fr. 4, 459; so late, Paus. &c., and usu. in Ion. χρᾶται, χρᾶσθαι, χράσθω, ἐχρᾶτο &c. Her. 1, 132. 3, 20. 2, 123. 3, 3 &c. &c., rarely χρῆσθαι 7, 18, κατα- 3, 36 (Bekk. Gaisf. Dind. -ᾶσθαι Lhard. Bred. Stein), ἐχρῆτο 3, 41. 129 (Bekk. Gaisf.), -ᾶτο (Lhard. Bred. Stein.) Indeed Lhardy and Bredow would write uniformly with α as the true Ionic form; and Mss. as well as analogy seem to favour them, see ὁρμᾶται Her. 2, 33, σπᾶται 9, 107, κατ-ορᾶται 2, 138 &c. &c. Buttmann's assertion that Her. contracts αε into η if ι precede, is rather strong, for θυμιῆται 4, 75, quoted as an instance, is opposed by θυμιᾶται (Mss. S V), and βιᾶται 3, 80 without *v. r.*, ἐπαιτιᾶται 2, 121, *v. r.* -ᾶσθαι, -ᾶσαι, not ῆσ-. From the formation in -έομαι, χρέεται Her. 4, 50, δια- 1, 58, -έονται 1, 34, -έεσθαι 1, 21, ἀπεχρέετο 8, 14, ἐχρέοντο 2, 108; so Hippocr. -εόμεθα 7, 224 (Lit.); imper. χρέο 2, 520, *v. r.* -έω (Mss. A G), -εέσθω 7, 246. 288, -έεσθαι 7, 168. 176 &c.; -εόμενος 2, 108 (Bekk.), see below: for εο often -εω, as χρέωνται Her. 1, 94. 132. 2, 86 &c. (Vulg. Bekk. Gaisf. -έονται Schaef. Dind. Bred.), ἐχρέωντο 1, 53. 3, 57. 5, 114 &c. (Vulg. Bekk. Gaisf. Stein, -έοντο Schaef. Dind. Bred.), especially part. χρεώμενος 1, 203. 2, 15. 3, 77. 4, 96. 5, 9 &c. (Schaef. Bekk. Gaisf. Dind. Stein, -εόμενος Bred. Abicht); so Hom. χρέωμ- Il. 23, 834, imper. χρέω Her. 1, 155 (χρέο Schaef. Stein; so Hippocr. 2, 520 Lit., *v. r.* -έω Mss. A G). In this verb Lhardy condemns the forms in εε, εο, and maintains those in ᾶ, εω, to be genuine Ionic.

(Χραύω) *To scratch, graze* (prop. χράϝω Aeol. for χράω), imp. ἔχραυε, ἐν- Her. 6, 75: in *simple* only subj. 1 aor. χραύσῃ Il. 5, 138; and part. χραύσαντα Q. Sm. 11, 76.

Χράω *To give what is asked for, utter an oracle*, χρᾷς Her. 4, 155, Attic χρῇς Soph. Aj. 1373 (Dind.), see Com. Fr. (Cratin.) 2, 87, χρᾷ Her. 1, 62. 5, 43; Luc. D. Mort. 3, 2, Attic χρῇ Soph. El. 35 (D.) &c.; χρᾶν Her. 8, 135; Luc. Alex. 19; Ionic part. χρέων H. Hym. 2, 75, -έουσα Her. 7, 111, Epic χρείων Od. 8, 79; H. Hym. 2, 215: imp. ἔχρᾰον Pind. Ol. 7, 92, -εον (Momms.); Ap. Rh. 2, 454, ἔχρα Luc. Alex. 22, ἔχρη Tyrtae. 3, 3; Hermes. 2, 89 (Schn.); Ap. Rh. 1, 302, ἐξ- Soph. O. C. 87: fut. χρήσω Hom. H. 1, 132; Aesch. Ag. 1083; Her. 1, 19: aor. ἔχρησα Aesch. Eum. 203; Eur. Ion 682; Ar. Vesp. 159; Her. 4, 156; Thuc. 1, 134, χρῆσε Pind. P. 4, 6: p. κέχρηκα Com. Fr. (Men.) 4, 205; Theoph. Epist. 35: plp. κεχρήκει App. Civ. 2, 29: p. p. κέχρησμαι, -ησμένος Her. 4, 164. 7, 141 (Bekk. Bred. Dind. Stein), -χρημένος (Schweigh. &c.); Antisth. Fr. 2, 21 (Bekk.): plp. ἐκεχρήσμην Her. 2, 147. 151. 3, 64. 7, 220 (Bekk. Bred. Dind. Stein), ἐκεχρήμ- (Schaef. Gaisf. &c.): aor. ἐχρήσθην Soph. O. C. 355; Eur. Ion 792; Her. 6, 19. 7, 178. 9, 94; χρησθείς Pind. Ol. 2, 39; Soph. O. R. 604; Thuc. 3, 96. Mid. χράομαι, Ionic -έομαι *to consult an oracle*, χρώμενος Thuc. 1, 126, Ion. χρεώμ- Her. 4, 151; -έεσθαι 1, 157, -ᾶσθαι (Lhardy, Stein, 7, 141 Bekk. Gaisf. Stein, Abicht): imp. ἐχρέοντο Her. 4, 157. 5, 82. 7, 141 (Dind. Bred.), -έωντο (Bekk. Gaisf. Lhard. Stein): fut. χρήσομαι Od. 10, 492. 11, 165; Her. 1, 46. 4, 155: aor. ἐχρησάμην Her. 8, 134: p. κέχρημαι *have consulted, been warned*, Aristot. Rhet. 2, 23, 12; hither some refer Aesch. Pers. 829.

In Attic, χράω contracts in η, χρῇ Soph. El. 35, ἔχρη Hermes. 2, 89 (Schn.), ἐξ- Soph. O. C. 87; Ionic in α, χρᾷς Her. 4, 155, χρᾷ 1, 55, χρᾶν 8, 135, but χρῆσθαι 1, 47 (Mss. Bekk.), -έεσθαι (Dind.), -ᾶσθαι (Lhard. Stein, Gaisf. in note.)

(Χράω) *To press, attack*, Epic, and only **imp.** or perhaps **aor.** ἔχρᾰε Il. 21, 369. Od. 5, 396; Anth. 5, 297, ἐχρᾰετ' Od. 21, 69, ἔχραον, ἐπ- Il. 16, 352. 356. Od. 2, 50: unless p. p. ἐγκεχρημένος Her. 7, 145 belong to this, for which Bredow (p. 343) would read ἐγκεχριμένος.

Χράω *To lend*, see κίχρημι.

Χρεμέθω *To neigh* (χρέμω unused), only -έθουσι Opp. Cyn. 1, 224; subj. -έθωσι 1, 163; and part. -έθων 1, 234, -έθοντα Anth. 9, 295.

Χρεμετάω *To neigh*, -ετᾷ Callim. Fr. 352, and χρεμετίζω Pl. Phaedr. 254: **imp.** χρεμέτιζον Il. 12, 51: **aor.** ἐχρεμέτισα Her. 3, 86; -ισαι 3, 87; χρεμετίσας Ael. V. H. 12, 46; but from (χρεμίζω obs.) χρέμισαν Hes. Sc. 348.

Χρέω, -είω, see χράω.

Χρή *It is necessary* (χράω), impers. (unless be referred hither χρῆσθα Ar. Ach. 778, χρῆμεν Theogn. 806 (Bergk 3 ed. χρή 4 ed.), Il. 1, 216; Aesch. Pr. 721; Soph. O. R. 235; Ar. Eq. 16; Her. 1, 32; Thuc. 1, 10; Pl. Conv. 190, Ion. χρᾷ, ἀπο- Her. 9, 79, κατα- 1, 164: **imp.** ἐχρῆν Pind. N. 7, 44; Aesch. Ch. 907; Soph. Fr. 94 (D); Ar. Ran. 152; Antiph. 1, 1; Thuc. 6, 57; Pl. Prot. 335. Leg. 631; Xen. Cyr. 8, 1, 1, Ion ἔχρα, ἀπ- Her. 1, 66, κατ- 7, 70, oftener χρῆν Pind. Fr. 100, 1; Soph. El. 529. 579. Tr. 1133; Ar. Ach. 540. Eq. 535. N. 371. 1359; Thuc. 3, 63; Pl. Conv. 181. Apol. 17; Isocr. 4, 176 (not ἔχρη nor ἔχρην, except in comp.); subj. χρῇ Soph. Ph. 999; opt. χρείη Aesch. Pr. 213; Soph. Tr. 162; Pl. Rep. 394; inf. χρῆναι Ar. Eccl. 210; Antiph. 5, 84; Thuc. 8, 78; Xen. Athen. 3, 6, and poetic τὸ χρῆν Eur. Hec. 260 (Pors. Herm. Dind. Nauck). H. F. 828 (Dind. Paley, τὸ χρεών Matth. Pflugk, τὸ χρή Nauck), Ion. χρᾶν, ἀπο- Her. 6, 137. 9, 94; part. χρεών indecl. Aesch. Pr. 772; Ar. Eq. 138; Thuc. 6, 18, τοῦ χρεών Eur. Hipp. 1256. H. F. 21, τῷ χρεὼν πόσει Eur. Fr. 503, 2 (Dind.), εἰς τὸ μὴ χρεὼν 494, 3: **fut.** χρήσει: **aor.** ἔχρησε, see ἀπόχρη.

2 sing. χρῇς or -ῆς Com. Fr. (Cratin.) 2, 87; Soph. Aj. 1373 (D), χρῆσθα Ar. Ach. 778, χρῇ Soph. Ant. 887 (D) some think better referred to χράω equivalent to χρῄζω *to wish, want*, or to χρῄζω itself, as shortened forms. With regard to the accentuation -ῆν, Goettling says "ἐχρῆν has no augment, but merely a prefix of ε for the sake of euphony, as in ἐχθές and χθές; otherwise it must have been ἔχρην. Even then," he adds, "there

would have been no reason for the paragogic ν; ἐχρῆν is an old infinitive used as an adverb." The Schol. however on Eur. Hec. 257, writes ἔχρη, and Hippocr. 1, 489 (Kühn); 9, 86 (Littré.) τὸ χρῆν, τὸ χρεών are used as nouns, see above—the latter even in the dat. In the three dependent moods, subj. opt. and inf. this verb follows the formation of verbs in μι, retaining however η in the inf. and taking ει instead of αι in the opt.; part. (χρᾶον) χρεών, in Her. some edit. have χρέον 5, 49. 109 (Gaisf. Stein), -εών always (Bekk. Dind. &c.)

Χρήζω *To want, wish, ask*, Aesch. Pr. 374; Soph. O. C. 574. O. R. 91; Ar. Nub. 891; Xen. Cyr. 4, 5, 22; -ζων Thuc. 3, 109, Ion. χρηίζω Od. 17, 558; Her. 1, 41. 5, 19; -ίζων Il. 11, 835. Od. 17, 121; Phocyl. 7; Aesch. Ch. 815 (chor.), Dor. χρῄσδω Theocr. 8, 11. 12, 3 pl. -σδοντι 15, 28 (Kiesl. Mein.), Megar. χρῄδδω Ar. Ach. 734, in Attic only pres.: and imp. ἔχρῃζον Aesch. Pr. 245; Soph. O. R. 1439, Ion. -ῄιζον Her. 1, 112. 4, 83: fut. χρῄσω (Pl.) Tim. Locr. 99; Her. 7, 38 (Bekk. Dind. Krüg.), -ηίσω (Schaef. Gaisf. Dietsch, Stein): aor. χρῆσαι Her. 5, 65 (Gaisf.), -ηίσαι (Bekk. Dind. Krüg. Stein); χρήσας 5, 20 (Gaisf.), -ηίσας (Bekk. Krüg. Dind. Stein); so 7, 38 (Bekk. Krüg. Stein), where however Dind. perhaps by oversight reads χρήσας (Gaisf.) Bekker seems to have restored the Ionic form everywhere in Her. except fut. χρῄσειν 7, 38. χρήσουσι Hippocr. 2, 814 (Kühn) seems a mistake for pres. χρῄζουσι 8, 310 (Lit.) This verb has occasionally the signif. of χράω *to give an oracular response*, Eur. Hel. 516. W. Dind. says that χρῄζεις, χρῄζει are sometimes shortened to χρῇς, χρῇ Soph. Aj. 1373. Ant. 887, see χρή. A collat. form χρηίσκοντο occurs Her. 3, 117 (Bekk. -ονται Port. Stein.)

Χρίω *To anoint, sting*, χρίει Aesch. Pr. 567; Soph. Tr. 832; Hippocr. 8, 368; Luc. Anach. 24, ἐπι-χρίων Od. 21, 179, but χρίει Anth. (Nossis) 6, 275: imp. ἔχριον Soph. Tr. 675, χρῖον Il. 23, 186; Bion 11, 3, iter. χρίεσκε Ap. Rh. 4, 871: fut. χρίσω Eur. Med. 789; Trag. Fr. (Achae.) 16; Geop. 5, 38, ἐγ- Hippocr. 8, 606: aor. ἔχρῖσα Od. 10, 364; Soph. Tr. 689, χρῖσ- Il. 16, 680. Od. 4, 49; D. Sic. 4, 38; -ίσας Hippocr. 3, 430 (Lit.); Aristot. Mirab. Ausc. 6; χρῖσαι Apollod. 1, 9, 23: p. κέχρικα V. T. 1 Reg. 10, 1: p. p. κέχρισμαι Ar. Fr. 231 (Dind. 2 ed.); Hippocr. 3, 430 (Lit.); Xen. Cyr. 7, 5, 22 (Vulg. Popp. -ιμαι L. Dind. Saupp.); Plut. Artax. 19; Luc. Trag. 296; Diod. Sic. 4, 38 (Bekk. -ιμαι Dind.), and κέχρῖμαι Ar. Fr. 231 quoted (Dind. 5 ed.); Com. Fr. (Magn.) 2, 10. (Eub.) 3, 250; Callim. Dian. 69; Her. 4, 189. 195 (Xen. Cyr. quoted): plp. ἐκέχριστο Xen. Cyr. 7, 1, 2 (Vulg. Popp.), -χριτο (Dind. Saupp.): aor. ἐχρίσθην Aesch. Pr. 675; Trag. Fr. (Achae.) 10;

Apollod. 1, 9, 23: fut. χρισθήσομαι V. T. Exod. 30, 32. **Mid.** χρίομαι *to anoint oneself*, or *for oneself*, Od. 1, 262. 18, 194; Pind. P. 4, 222; Her. 4, 191; Xen. Hier. 1, 24: **imp.** ἐχρ- Xen. An. 4, 4, 12; Ael. V. H. 9, 9: **fut.** χρίσομαι Od. 6, 220; Geop. 15, 7: **aor.** ἐχρῖσάμην, χρισάμενος Od. 6, 96; Hes. Op. 523; Anacr. 9 (Bergk); Hippocr. 6, 634; Xen. Conv. 1, 7. **Vb.** χριστός Aesch. Pr. 480, ἐπι-χριστέον Geop. 16, 18. The **aor. pass.** always with σ, χρισθείς; but the **perf.** and **plp. pass.** some able scholars would, in Attic, always write without, κεχριμένος, ἐκέχρῖτο. Even in Lucian, W. Dindorf edits κεχριμένος for -ισμένος Saturn. 2 (Mss. Vulg. Fritzsche), ἐγ- Peregr. 45 (Mss. Vulg. Fritzsche); and L. Dind. in Diod. Sic. 4, 38. ῐ usu. in **pres.** and **imp.**, always in the derivative tenses ἔχρῖσα, χρῖσαι, κεχρῖσθαι; for Buttmann's remark that "in the sense *to sting*, the ι is short, ἔχρῐσα, χρίσαι, κέχρισθαι," is not borne out by the usage of the poets, nor perhaps a fair inference from Phrynichus, κεχρεῖσθαι τὸ ὑπὸ ἐλαίου διὰ διφθόγγου, τὸ δὲ πεπλῆχθαι διὰ τοῦ ι πανταχοῦ.

Χροΐζω *To touch, colour, stain* (χρόα), Poet. Eur. Heracl. 915. **Mid.** χροΐζομαι Theocr. 10, 18 (Vulg. Ahr. Fritzsche 2 ed.): others **fut.** χροϊξεῖται Theocr. quoted (Mein. Ziegl. Fritzsche 1 ed.): **aor. pass.** (χρωΐζω) χρωισθεῖσαι Nicand. Fr. 74, 26 (Otto Schn.)

Χρώζω *To touch, colour, stain* (χρώς), Eur. Ph. 1625; Com. Fr. (Alex.) 3, 447; Aristot. Mirab. Ausc. 50, later χρώννῦμι Luc. Hist. 48, -ύω Liban.: **fut.** χρώσω Hesych.: **aor.** ἔχρωσα Anth. Plan. 138; Aristot. Meteor. 3, 1, 10; Luc. Imag. 7: **p.** κέχρωκα, ἐπι- Plut. Mor. 395: **p. p.** κέχρωσμαι Eur. Med. 497; Hippocr. 5, 390 (Lit.); Aristot. Meteor. 3, 4, 25; Theophr. H. P. 7, 9, 2; (Pl.) Tim. Locr. 101; Luc. Anach. 25, ἐπι- (Pl.) Epist. 340: **aor.** χρωσθῇ Aristot. de Color. 3, 12; χρωσθῆναι Pl. Theaet. 156; χρωσθείς Com. Fr. (Antiph.) 3, 125: **fut.** χρωσθήσεται Galen 1, 278. 9, 394.

Χύνω, χύω, see χέω.

Χώννυμι, -ύω, see χόω.

Χώομαι *To be enraged, grieved*, Epic, dep. mid. Il. 20, 29; imper. χώεο Od. 5, 215; -όμενος Il. 14, 260; Hes. Th. 561; Ap. Rh. 4, 616, -ομένη Il. 21, 413; Callim. Dian. 31 &c.: **imp.** χώετο Il. 21, 306; Ap. Rh. 1, 492: **fut.** χώσομαι Lycophr. 362 (-σεται Il. 1, 80, seems aor. subj.): **aor.** ἐχώσατο Il. 1, 64; Bion 2, 11, χώσ- Il. 8, 397; Hes. Th. 554; subj. χώσεται for -ηται Il. 1, 80; χωσάμενος 21, 212, -αμένη 9, 534, Dor. -μένα Callim. Cer. 42. Not contracted.

Χωρέω *To give place, go, contain* (χῶρος), Anacr. 108; Aesch. Sept. 60; Soph. Aj. 116; Ar. Pax 472; Her. 1, 192; Thuc.

1, 69, ἀνα- Il. 11, 189: **imp.** ἐχώρουν Aesch. Pers. 379; Soph. Ph. 397; Ar. Av. 496; Her. 1, 10; Thuc. 3, 83, ὑπ- Il. 22, 96: **fut.** χωρήσω Il. 16, 629; Her. 5, 89. 8, 68; Hippocr. 7, 502. 522. 8, 20. 72 (Lit.); *simple* rare in *classic* Attic, perhaps only Thuc. 1, 82 (but often late, Dio Cass. 38, 46; Luc. D. D. 20, 15; Alciphr. 3, 58; Dio. Hal. Ant. 4, 9. 6, 5; Paus. 1, 12, 1; App. Civ. 5, 142; Charit. 6, 8), freq. in comp. ἀνα- Thuc. 7, 73, ἀπο- Xen. M. Eq. 6, 2; Aristot. Plant. 2, 6, 1, ἐγ- Pl. Rep. 536; Isae. 3, 34 (ἐκ- Her. 2, 139; Hippocr. 8, 368; Dio Cass. 39, 46, δια- 52, 33, μετα- Arr. An. 2, 17, 3; Luc. Herm. 84), προ- Thuc. 3, 4, προσ- (Her. 7, 235), Thuc. 2, 2. 79 &c., συγ- (Her. 7, 161); Thuc. 1, 140; Xen. Hell. 3, 2, 12; Isocr. 6, 13 &c.; Aeschin. 2, 126; Dem. 7, 4. 17, 18. 39, 32. 56, 22, ὑπεκ- Pl. Phaed. 103, παρα- late D. Sic. 38, 3; Aristid. 35, 456; Heliod. 9, 6 (Bekk.); Jos. Ant. 3, 14, 1; Dio Chrys. Or. 72 (629), and usu. ὑπο- Hippocr. 7, 234 (Lit.); Plut. Ant. 62: more freq. in *simple*, **fut. mid.** χωρήσομαι (but never in Hom. Her. nor Hippocr.) Aesch. Sept. 476; Soph. El. 404; Eur. Supp. 588. Hec. 52. An. 1067. El. 875. Hipp. 941; Ar. Nub. 1238; Thuc. 2, 20. 5, 57; (Pl.) Eryx. 398, so in comp. ἀπο- Thuc. 3, 13; (Dem.) 25, 78, παρα- Dem. 23, 105, προσ- Thuc. 3, 13. 8, 48; Xen. Hell. 7, 4, 16, συγ- Eur. I. T. 741; Thuc. 4, 64; Pl. Tim. 53. Theaet. 191 &c.; Dem. 20, 143; Com. Fr. (Men.) 4, 129, ὑπο- later Luc. Tox. 11 (but ἀνα-, δια-, ἐγ-, ἐκ-, μετα-, προ- we have not seen in the **mid.** form except ἐγ- Dem. 20, 143 Ms. Laur. S, for συγ-): **aor.** ἐχώρησα Il. 15, 655; Soph. Tr. 304; Her. 7, 10; Thuc. 4, 120; Pl. Leg. 684, χώρ- Il. 12, 406; Pind. N. 10, 73: **p.** κεχώρηκα Her. 1, 120. 122; Hippocr. 2, 264 (Lit.); Thuc. 1, 122. 7, 81; Pl. Soph. 253: **plp.** ἐκεχωρήκει, ἐξ- Dem. 41, 5: **p. p.** συγ-κεχώρηται Pl. Phil. 15, παρα- Dio. Hal. 11, 52: **aor.** συγ-χωρηθείς Xen. Hell. 3, 2, 31; Dem. 38, 4: **fut.** συγ-χωρηθήσομαι Polyb. 15, 17; Sext. Emp. 273, 6. **Vb.** χωρητέον Dio. Hal. 1, 56, ἀνα- Pl. Crito 51.

Hom. has of the *simple* form only fut. and aor. The Attic poets seem not to have used the active fut. form simple or comp. συγχωρήσει Eur. I. T. 874, is now read συγκυρήσει. The *simple* fut. active is of more freq. use in late prose, Dio. Hal. Ant. 3, 2. 26. 6, 5. 38. 7, 16. 17. 8, 8. 9, 1; Dio Cass. 76, 15 &c., and always, simple and comp.; Luc. D. Deor. 20, 15; Socrat. Epist. 5 (Orell.); Orac. Sib. 3, 18, ἀνα- Dio. Hal. 11, 26, ἀπο- Dio Cass. 49, 6; Diod. Sic. 19, 26, δια- Dio Cass. 52, 33, ἐκ- 39, 46, παρα- Dio. Hal. 7, 16. 14, 21; Diod. Sic. 18, 52, περι- Dio Cass. 40, 49, προσ- 41, 25. 63, 8, συγ- Dio. Hal. 6, 61. 7, 32; Diod. Sic. 1, 40. 20, 40 &c.

Ψ.

Ψαίρω *To graze, skim, flutter,* seems to occur only in pres. ψαίρει Aesch. Pr. 394; Luc. Tragod. 315; ψαίρειν Hippocr. 8, 316 (Lit.) We have not seen this verb in Attic prose.

Ψαύω *To touch,* Il. 23, 519; Soph. Tr. 565. 1020; Com. Fr. (Mon.) 214; Her. 2, 93; Hippocr. 6, 640; Xen. Mem. 1, 4, 12: **imp.** ἔψαυον Ap. Rh. 2, 266, ψαῦον Il. 13, 132, iter. ψαύεσκεν, ἐπι- Orph. Lith. 126: **fut.** ψαύσω Aesch. Ch. 182; Soph. O. C. 863 (D.); Eur. Med. 1320; Hippocr. 8, 144 (Lit.); Philostr. Apoll. 53: **aor.** ἔψαυσα Pind. N. 5, 42; Aesch. Pers. 202; Soph. Ant. 857; Hippocr. 2, 411 (Erm.); ψαύσῃ Il. 23, 806; Her. 2, 47; ψαύσαιμι Luc. D. Mer. 11, 1, -σειε Simon. Am. 7, 59; Her. 3, 30; Hippocr. 8, 356 (L.); ψαῦσαι Her. 2, 90; Mosch. 2, 91; ψαύσας Antiph. 3, γ, 5; Luc. Bis Acc. 8 &c.: **p.** late, ἐψαυκέναι, παρ- Sext. Emp. 215, 27: **p. p.** ἔψαυσμαι, παρ- Hippocr. 7, 556 (Lit.): **aor.** ἐψαύσθην late, Dioscor. Mat. 2, 16. **Mid.** ψαύομαι Dioscor. 5, 27.

Ψάω *To rub,* contracts in η, ψῇ Soph. Tr. 678; usu. in comp. inf. περι-ψῆν Ar. Eq. 909; κατα-ψῶν Pax 75: **imp.** ἀπ-έψη Eur. I. T. 311 (Elms. Herm. Dind. Nauck, Paley, Kirchh. 2 ed.), ἀπέψα (Mss. Matth. Kirchh. 1 ed.), and so quoted by (Luc.) Amor. 47: **fut.** ἀπο-ψήσω Ar. Lys. 1035: **aor.** ἔψησα Ap. Rh. 3, 831, περι- Ar. Plut. 730, συμ- Her. 1, 189, κατα- Pl. Phaed. 89: **p. p.** (instead of late ἔψησμαι or -ημαι Pollux 4, 152, *v. r.* παρέψησμ-: and **aor.** ἐψήσθην or -ήθην, συν- V. T. Jer. 22, 19. 31, 33) the Attics used ἔψηγμαι, κατ- Soph. Tr. 698: **aor.** ἐψήχθην however, late, κατα-ψηχθείς Nicand. Al. 265 (Gottl. Schn.), -θεῖσα Ther. 53, from the derivative ψήχω Xen. Eq. 6, 1, -ήξω 4, 4. **Mid.** ψάομαι *to rub, wipe oneself,* ἀπο-ψώμεσθα Ar. Plut. 817; imper. ἀποψῶ Eq. 910; -ψώμενος Xen. Cyr. 1, 3, 5: **fut.** ἀπο-ψήσομαι Ar. Pax 1231: **aor.** ἀπ-εψησάμην Ar. Ran. 490, -σαντο Eq. 572; late ψήξασθαι, ἀπο- Clem. Al. Paed. p. 100, 11. **Vb.** ἀπο-ψηκτέον Geop. 17, 20. Late, this verb contracts in α, ἀπο-ψᾶν, ψᾶσθαι Dioscor. 4, 65.

Ψέγω *To blame,* Soph. O. R. 338; Ar. Nub. 1045; Hippocr. 6, 2; Pl. Crat. 417; Xen. Hell. 6, 5, 51; Isocr. 3, 1; Aeschin. 1, 136; ψέγων Aesch. Ag. 185; Andoc. 3, 34; -γειν Aesch. Ag. 1403; Isocr. 12, 223: **imp.** ἔψεγον Xen. Hell. 6, 5, 49: **fut.** ψέξω Pl. Gorg. 518: **aor.** ἔψεξε Pl. Leg. 629; Aeschin. 1, 156; ψέξαιμι Soph. Aj. 1130, -ξειεν Pl. Phaedr. 240; ψέξαι Theogn. 611: (**perf.**?): **p. p.** ἔψεκται Hippocr. 2, 334 (Lit.): but **2 aor.**

ἐψέγην given by Buttm.: and **2 p.** ἔψογα by Passow, we have never seen: **pres.** ψέγεται Hippocr. 6, 6; Thuc. 5, 86. **Vb.** ψεκτός Pl. Crat. 416, -τέος Plut. Mor. 27.

Ψεύδω *To deceive*, **act.** not in Epic, rare in Comic, and prose, Soph. Ant. 389; Eur. Fr. 652 (Dind.): **fut.** ψεύσω Soph. O. C. 628; Xen. Hell. 4, 4, 10. Cyr. 1, 5, 13: **aor.** ἔψευσα Aesch. Pers. 472; Soph. Aj. 1382; ψεύσῃ Eur. Heracl. 384; ψεῦσον Ar. Thesm. 870; ψεῦσαι Polyb. 17, 11, 11: (**perf.**?): **p. p.** ἔψευσμαι Her. 2, 22. 8, 40; Antiph. 3, β, 1; Thuc. 4, 108; Lys. 2, 27; *falsely reported* Dem. 52, 23: **aor.** ἐψεύσθην Her. 9, 61; Antiph. 5, 46; Thuc. 8, 103; Pl. Apol. 22; Ar. Nub. 618: **fut.** ψευσθήσομαι Soph. Tr. 712; Galen 15, 143: and as **pass. fut. mid.** ψεύσομαι rare, Pl. Soph. 240; *falsely reported* Eur. An. 346 (Mss. Vulg. Nauck 2 ed. Kirchh. 1 ed.): for which, **3 fut.** ἐψεύσεται if correct, Eur. An. 346, first suggested in the Quart. Review, vol. 5, 396, and adopted by Herm. Dind. *now*, Nauck 1 ed. Paley, Kirchh. 2 ed. for ψεύσεται (Mss. Vulg. Kirchh. 1 ed. Nauck 2 ed.), see below. Dep. **mid.** ψεύδομαι *to lie, report falsely, belie*, Od. 14, 125; Solon 29; Soph. Tr. 450; Eur. Cycl. 261; Ar. Plut. 571; Her. 1, 138; Antiph. 5, 37; Isocr. 18, 57; Pl. Euthyd. 284; imper. ψεύδε' Il. 4, 404: **imp.** ἐψευδ- Her. 1, 117; Antiph. 5, 37, ψευδ- Theocr. 21, 22: **fut.** ψεύσομαι Il. 10, 534; Pind. Ol. 13, 52; Aesch. Eum. 615; Eur. Hel. 1626. Rhes. 189; Ar. Eccl. 568; Andoc. 1, 123; Isae. 10, 9. 11; Dem. 38, 25: **aor.** ἐψευσάμην Aesch. Ag. 1208; Soph. O. C. 1145; Eur. Bac. 31; Ar. Eccl. 445; Her. 6, 32; Antiph. 5, 3; Pl. Leg. 663, ψευσ- Anacr. 116; -σάμενος Il. 7, 352; Thuc. 3, 43: and as **mid. p. p.** ἔψευσμαι Soph. O. R. 461; Thuc. 6, 17; Xen. An. 1, 3, 10; Lys. 3, 21: **plp.** ἔψευστο Thuc. 5, 83: and **aor.** ἐψεύσθην Soph. Ph. 1342?

Pass. in the sense *falsely reported, untruly said*, **p.** ἔψευσται Dem. 52, 23: **fut. mid.** ψεύσεται rare if correct, Eur. An. 346 (Mss. Vulg. Kirchh.) indicated by Porson as faulty on metrical grounds, Pref. Hec. p. 40, and rejected by Herm. because "nemini non active dictum videretur" for ἐψεύσεται because "hoc passiva significatione dici non mirum"—and Paley approves. We think the objections of neither decisive. The only other instance of ἐψεύσεται we ever met is Galen 15, 137 (Kühn) where it is used in a **mid.** sense *state incorrectly*, exactly as ψεύσεται a few lines below—proving, if correct, that the later writers at least, and we are inclined to include the earlier, did not always use the fut. forms in exactly the senses assigned to them by Grammarians.

Ψηφίζω *To reckon with* (ψῆφοι) *pebbles* or *counters, count*, Anth.

(Antiph.) 11, 168; Polyb. 5, 26; (Hippocr.) Epist. 3, 811 (Kühn); ἐπι-ψήφιζε Thuc. 6, 14, *put to the vote;* ψηφίζων Anth. 11, 290; but (Aeschin.) 1, 35, seems a false reading for -ομένων (Reisk. Bekk. B. S. Franke &c.): imp. ἐψήφιζε, ἐπ- Thuc. 1, 87 *put to the vote:* fut. ψηφἴεῖν, ἐπι- Aeschin. 2, 84: aor. rare, ἐψήφισα Plut. Mor. 141; as mid. *voted (with a pebble)*, Soph. Aj. 449, ἐπι- *put to the vote,* Thuc. 2, 24: p. ἐψηφικώς, ἐπ- Xen. An. 5, 6, 35, κατ- D. Hal. Ant. 5, 8: p. p. ἐψήφισμαι Eur. Heracl. 141; Ar. Eccl. 706; Thuc. 6, 15; Aeschin. 2, 37, as mid. see below: plp. ἐψήφιστο Dem. 19, 157: aor. ἐψηφίσθην always pass. Antiph. 6, 6; Thuc. 6, 8; Lys. 13, 23; Isocr. 8, 52 &c.: fut. ψηφισθήσομαι Isocr. 6, 92. **Mid.** ψηφίζομαι *to vote, decree,* Aesch. Ag. 1353; Ar. Av. 1626; Her. 9, 55; Antiph. 5, 81; Thuc. 1, 86. 7, 48; Lycurg. 113: imp. ἐψηφίζετο Her. 7, 207, -οντο Thuc. 6, 31: fut. ψηφίσεσθε faultily Lys. 12, 44 (some Mss. -σαισθε Bekk. B. S.), -ίσονται 14, 47 (Ms. X.), -ιοῦνται (Ms. C. Bekk. B. S. Scheib.), so κατα-ψηφίσεσθε Antiph. 1, 12, ἀπο- 6, 10 (Mss. A N. Maetzn. -σησθε Vulg. -σαισθε Bekk. B. S.), correctly ψηφιοῦμαι Ar. Lys. 951; Thuc. 7, 48; Pl. Conv. 177; Andoc. 1, 31; Lys. 14, 47; Isae. 6, 2; Lycurg. 54; Aristot. Probl. 29, 3: aor. ἐψηφισάμην Ar. Eccl. 816; Her. 5, 97; Antiph. 3, 1; Thuc. 1, 88. 6, 73; Pl. Gorg. 516; Isocr. 8, 82; Isae. 11, 14; Lycurg. 114, Dor. ψᾱφίξασθαι Cret. Tit. 3050: with p. p. as mid. ἐψήφισμαι Ar. Vesp. 591; Thuc. 1, 120; Xen. Hell. 2, 1, 31; Isocr. 15, 17; Lycurg. 14; Dem. 2, 11, but pass. Eur. &c., see above: as 3 fut. ἐψηφισμένοι, ἔσεσθε Dem. 35, 56. 45, 88. **Vb.** κατα-ψηφιστέος Xen. Hell. 2, 4, 9. ἐπιψηφίζω *to put to the vote,* Thuc. 6, 14 &c.: aor. ἐπ-εψήφισα Thuc. 2, 24; Xen. Mem. 1, 1, 18; Aeschin. 2, 68: p. ἐπ-εψηφικώς Xen. Ant. 5, 6, 35 &c. **Mid.** ἐπιψηφίζομαι *to vote,* Xen. An. 7, 3, 14 (Küst. Krüg.): -εψηφίζετο Aeschin. 2, 67: fut. -ιοῦμαι &c.; but κατα-ψηφίζω *to vote against,* is late and partial in act. -εψήφικα Dio. Hal. 4, 58. **Mid.** καταψηφίζομαι, -ιοῦμαι, -ισάμην, and p. -εψήφισμαι Xen. Hell. 1, 5, 19; Lycurg. 10, but pass. Xen. Apol. 27; Thuc. 2, 53: plp. -ιστο Ael. V. H. 13, 1: aor. -εψηφίσθην always pass. Pl. Rep. 299.

Ψήχω, see ψάω.

Ψύχω *To breathe, cool, dry,* Her. 3, 104; Isocr. 15, 287; ψύχειν Aesch. Pr. 692 (ψήξειν Mein. Dind.); ψύχουσα Soph. Fr. 400 (D): imp. ἔψῡχον Aesop 401 (Halm), ἀν- Il. 13, 84; Her. 7, 59, iter. ψύχεσκε, ἀνα- Orph. Lith. 556: fut. ψύξω Com. Fr. (Alex.) 3, 395; Aristot. Part. Anim. 2, 7, 19 (B): aor. ἔψυξα Hippocr. 1, 612. 6, 100 (Lit.), ἀν- Theogn. 1273, ἀπ- Soph. Aj. 1031; ψῦξον Com. Fr. (Diph.) 4, 402, ἀνά-ψυξον Eur. Hel. 1094; ψύξας

Il. 20, 440; Hippocr. 6, 102; ψῦξαι, δια- Thuc. 7, 12: p. p. ἔψυγμαι, -υκται Hippocr. 6, 512 (L.); -υγμένος 7, 14; Pl. Critias 120; Com. Fr. (Alex.) 3, 440; ἐψῦχθαι Hippocr. 7, 16 (Lit.): 1 aor. ἐψύχθην Theocr. 2, 106; Hippocr. 5, 218; Xen. Ven. 5, 3; Pl. Tim. 60. 76; Aristot. Gen. An. 4, 3, 19, ἀν- Xen. Hell. 7, 1, 19, Epic 3 pl. -έψυχθεν Il. 10, 575: fut. ψυχθήσομαι Hippocr. 2, 424 (Lit.), ἐμ- Galen 1, 678: 2 aor. ἐψῦχην, ἀπ- Aesch. Fr. 102; Pl. Phaedr. 242, ἀν- C. Fr. 2, 706; ψυχείς Ar. Nub. 151 (Dind. Mein. -γείς Vulg.), and ἐψῦγην Galen 7, 748; φυγῇ Dioscor. 1, 65, περι- Arr. Epict. 3, 22, 460; ψῦγείς Ar. Nub. 151 (Mss. Bekk. Bergk, -χείς Dind.); Geop. 5, 38; Pseud.-Callisth. 1, 41 (Meusel), ἀπο- Heliod. 2, 3; ψῦγῆναι Dioscor. 3, 3; Galen 13, 249, κατα- Aristot. Probl. 10, 54, 4 (*v. r.* -υχθ-): fut. ψυγήσομαι Galen 11, 388; N. T. Matth. 24, 12, -χήσομαι (Ms. K.) **Mid.** in comp. intrans. ψυχόμενος, ὑπο- Athen. (Nicand.) 7, 48: **imp.** trans. ἐψύχοντο, ἀπ- Il. 11, 621, παρ- Theocr. 13, 54: but aor. ψύξασθαι (Hesych.) **Vb.** ψυκτός Hesych., -τέος Hippocr. 6, 126 (Lit.) An aor. form ἐξ-εψύξησε occurs late, Pseud.-Callisth. 3, 33, see 2, 25.

Ω.

Ὠδίνω *To be in travail*, classic in, perhaps, pres. only, Il. 11, 269; Soph. Aj. 794; Eur. I. A. 1234. Hipp. 258; Ar. Thesm. 502; Hippocr. 5, 224 (Lit.); Pl. Theaet. 148. 151. 210. Rep. 395: **imp.** ὤδῖνον V. T. Esai. 23, 4: **fut.** ὠδινήσω V. T. Hab. 3, 9, *v. r.* ὠδῖνῶ: **aor.** ὤδῖνα, -ίνᾱσα Anth. 7, 561; Opp. Cyn. 1, 5, and ὠδίνησα V. T. Ps. 7, 15. Apocr. Sir. 48, 19, though no pres. form -νάω seems to occur: **aor. pass.** -ήθην Aquil. Prov. 8, 25. **Mid. aor.** ὠδινησάμην Aquil. Ps. 113, 7.

Ὠθέω *To push* (ὤθω), Od. 3, 295; Soph. Aj. 1307; Ar. Thesm. 643; Her. 3, 81; Pl. Leg. 899; Aeschin. 2, 86; Aeol. imper. ὠθήτω Alcae. 41, 6; -θεῖν Aesch. Pr. 665: **imp.** in Epic and Ionic, ὤθεον Pind. Fr. 143 (B.), ὦθει Il. 21, 241; rare in Attic, Eur. I. T. 1395; Pl. Charm. 155, -θουν Trag. Fr. p. 51 (Wagn.) (ὠθέετο, δι- Her. 6, 86, -οῦντο Thuc. 2, 84), usu. with syllab. augm. ἐώθουν H. Merc. 305; Ar. Pax 637; Xen. Cyr. 7, 1, 33; Dem. 9, 66. 53, 17, ἐξ- Thuc. 7, 52: **fut.** ὠθήσω Poet. Eur. Cycl. 592; Ar. Eccl. 300 (chor.), ἐξ- Soph. Aj. 1248, and ὤσω Eur. Andr. 344 (Hel. 1564 Vulg. Kirchh. 1 ed. ὠθεῖ 2 ed. ὤθει Duport. Dind.); Pl. Rep. 415 and perhaps always in Attic prose, ἀπ- Od. 15, 280; Soph. O. R. 234; Eur. Heracl. 183, ἐξ- Xen.

Cyr. 6, 4, 18; Epic inf. ὠσέμεν, ἀπ- Il. 13, 367: aor. ἔωσα Pl. Tim. 60, 92; Lys. 1, 24, ἐξ- Soph. O. C. 1296. 1330; Thuc. 2, 90. 5, 72. 8, 105; rare in Epic, ἔωσαν Ap. Rh. 4, 104, ἔωσε in tmesi Il. 16, 410, ἀπ- Od. 9, 81, and ὦσα usu. Epic and Ionic, Il. 5, 19. 8, 336; Anth. 12, 131; Theocr. 22, 201. 25, 147; Her. 3, 78. 7, 167, but ἀπ-ῶσε Soph. Fr. 380; Ep. subj. ἀπ-ώσομεν Il. 8, 96; πρώσας Luc. Asin. 9, late ὤθησα Dio Cass. Fr. Vat. 207 (vol. 5, p. 190 Dind.); Ael. H. A. 13, 17; Charit. 2, 7, 7, ἀπ- D. Cass. 38, 28 (Bekk. -ῶσα L. Dind.): p. ἔωκα, ἐξ- Plut. Mor. 48: plp. ἐξ-εώκει Plut. Brut. 42: p. p. ἔωσμαι Emped. 164; Xen. Cyr. 7, 1, 36, ἀπ- Thuc. 2, 39, περι- 3, 57, ξυν- Pl. Tim. 59, Ionic ὦσμαι, *simple* late ὠσμένος V. T. Ps. 61, 4, ἀπ-ωσμένος Her. 5, 69; so Diod. Sic. 18, 66 (Vulg. -εωσμ- Bekk. L. Dind.): aor. in early Attic always with syllab. augm. ἐώσθην Aristot. Mechan. 24, 12, ἐξ- Xen. Hell. 2, 4, 34. 4, 3, 12, but ὤσθην, ἐξ- Arr. An. 4, 25. 5, 23; subj. ἀπ-ωσθῇ Thuc. 5, 45; ὠσθείς Pl. Tim. 60: fut. ὠσθήσομαι Eur. Med. 335, ἐξ- Dem. 24, 61. **Mid.** ὠθοῦμαι *to push from oneself, repel,* Xen. An. 3, 4, 48, Dor. 3 pl. -θεῦνται Theocr. 15, 73: imp. ἐωθοῦντο, ἀπ- Thuc, 2, 4, but δι-ωθ- 2, 84 (Mss. Bekk. Krüg. Poppo, δι-εωθ- Boehme, Stahl): fut. ὤσομαι, ἀπ- Il. 8, 533; Simon. Am. 7, 101; Soph. El. 944; Pl. Rep. 366, δι- Aesch. Fr. 196 (D); Eur. Andr. 869; Democr. Fr. 20 (Mull.): late ὠθήσομαι as pass. Galen 3, 400, δι- Eunap. 74, 29, if not fut. pass. for ὠσθήσ-: aor. ἐωσάμην Attic, Thuc. 4, 43; Ar. Vesp. 1085 (Bergk, Dind. 5 ed., ἀπεωσ- Bekk., ἀπωσ- Dind. 2 ed.), δι- Dem. 21, 124; ὠσάμενος Thuc. 6, 70, παρ- Pl. Rep. 471, late ἐωσάμενος, παρ- Epist. Pythag. 4 (Mss. Orell. παρ-ωσ- Hercher), Epic and Ionic ὠσάμην Il. 16, 592; Her. 9, 25; App. Civ. 1, 64. 120, ἀπ- Ar. Vesp. 1085 quoted (Dind. 2 ed., ἀπεωσ- Bekk.); Com. Fr. (Incert.) 4, 628, and late ὠθήσατο, δι- Dio Cass. Fr. 18 (Bekk., δι-εώσ- Dind.); ὠθησάμενος, ἐξ- Sever. Rhet. p. 541. **Vb.** ὠστέος Dio Chrys., ἀπ- Eur. H. F. 294, ἀπ-ωστός Soph. Aj. 1019.

ὤθεσκε imp. iter. Od. 11, 596: aor. ὤσασκε 599; part. πρώσας for προ-ώσας Hippocr. 7, 314 (Lit.); (Luc.) Asin. 9; Anth. 12, 206: ἀπ-εώθησαν if correct, for -εώσθησαν, Hippocr. 1, 75 (Kühn), and late ὠθηθείς (ὠθέω) Apollinar. Ps. 117, 25. Her. always, Hom. usually neglects the syllab. augm. but ἔωσε Il. 16, 410, ἀπ- Od. 9, 81, ἐώθει H. Merc. 305; the Attics almost always use it, but ὦθει Eur. I. A. 1395; Pl. Charm. 155; so Pind. ὤθεον Fr. 143 (Bergk), δι-ωθοῦντο Thuc. 2, 84; and late authors from Polyb. onward often neglect it, προώθουν 15, 33, συνωθοῦντο 3, 74 (Bekk. Hultsch, -εωθ- Lud. Dind.), ὠθεῖτο Plut. Sull. 21, ὠθοῦντο Luc. Bis Acc. 21; on the other hand ἐξ-εώσεις

Theodr. Prodr. 1, 156, παρ-εωσάμενος Epist. Pythag. 4 (Mss. Orell. παρ-ωσ- Hercher).

Ὠνέομαι *To buy*, Hes. Op. 341; Eur. I. A. 1170; Ar. Av. 530; Her. 8, 105; Antiph. 6, 13; Xen. An. 5, 3, 7; -νοῖτο Aesch. Supp. 336: imp. Attic usu. ἐωνούμην Com. Fr. (Eup.) 2, 505; Andoc. 1, 134; Lys. 7, 4 (Scheibe); Dem. 38, 8, pass. Xen. Eq. 8, 2, Ionic act. ὠνεόμην Her. 1, 69. 3, 139, occas. Attic ὠνούμ- if correct, Lys. 7, 4 (Mss. Bekk. B. Saupp.); Luc. Navig. 13 (Mss. Bekk. Fritzs.); Palaeph. 46, see below: fut. ὠνήσομαι Eur. Hec. 360; Xen. Cyr. 4, 5, 41; Lys. 22, 22, Dor. ὠνᾱσεῖται Sophr. 89 (Ahr.): aor. scarcely classic Attic, ὠνησάμην Com. Fr. (Eupol.) 2, 533 if correct, the only instance; but Anth. 11, 249; Plut. Nic. 10; Luc. Herm. 81. D. Mort. 4, 1. Nav. 20; Paus. 3, 4, 4. 5, 21, 5, and ἐωνησ-, Plut. Mor. 176. Cic. 3; Athen. (Caryst.) 12, 60; ὠνησάμενος Anth. 11, 177; (Hippocr.) Epist. 9, 362 (Lit.); Polyb. 4, 50; Dio. Hal. 7, 20; Xen. Ephes. 4, 3. 5, 9; -ήσασθαι 5, 9; Luc. Herm. 61 (for which, in Attic, ἐπριάμην): p. p. ἐώνημαι act. Ar. Plut. 7; Lys. 7, 2; Isae. 8, 23; Dem. 32, 18. 37, 31 &c., pass. Ar. Pax 1182; Pl. Rep. 563; Isae. 11, 42; Dem. 19, 209; Lys. 32, 21, συν- 22, 12: plp. ἐώνητο act. Dem. 37, 5: aor. ἐωνήθην pass. Xen. Mem. 2, 7, 12. Vect. 4, 35; Pl. Leg. 850; Isae. 6, 19; Dem. 45, 81: fut. ὠνηθήσεται, ἀπ- Com. Fr. 2, 823. Vb. ὠνητός Od. 14, 202; Thuc. 3, 40, ὠνητέος Pl. Leg. 849. The act. form ὠνέω seems to have been in use, ὠνεῖν, πωλεῖν (Hesych.): perf. ἐωνηκώς Bekk. Anecd. 95, 25, from Lys. κατὰ Καλλίου ἐνδειξ-: aor. ἐξ-ωνήσαντες in Schol. Aphthon. Rhet. V. 2, 17 (Walz), hence the occasional passive use of ὠνέομαι Pl. Phaed. 69: imp. ἐωνεῖτο Xen. Eq. 8, 2.

The Attics generally used the syllab. augm. the Ionics and occas. the Attics neglected it, ὠνούμην Lys. 7, 4 (Bekk. B. Saupp. ἐων- Scheib.), ὠνέετο Her. 3, 139, -έοντο 1, 69, ὠνοῦντο Aristot. Oec, 2, 5, ἀντ-ωνεῖτο Andoc. 1, 134; Dio Cass. 59, 14 (Bekk., -εων- Dind.), ἐξ-ωνεῖτο Aeschin. 3, 91 (Bekk. B. S., ἐξεων- Franke). The Attics, with one exception, seem to have avoided the aor. mid. Athenaeus assigns to Eupolis quoted, χῖος δεσπότην ὠνήσατο, but Meineke questions the authorship, and thinks that if Eupolis did use the expression, he quoted an *Ionic* proverb, in which dialect the aor. would be no offence. He is correct at least in the last assertion, for Hippocr. (if the Epistles are his) has ὠνησάμενος 9, 362 (Lit.) In *classic* Attic, the syllabic augm. seems to be dropped in compds. only: Andoc. has ἐωνοῦντο along with ἀντωνεῖτο 1, 134, Xen. ἀντ-εων- Oec. 20, 26. ὠνούμην Lys. quoted, should perhaps be ἐωνούμην (Scheibe), see συν-εωνοῦντο 22, 11.

'Ωρύω *To howl*, in act. only part. ὠρύουσα Or. Sib. 8, 240, ὠρῦον Anth. 11, 31. ὠρύομαι Dep. mid. Ap. Rh. 4, 1339; Callim. Fr. 423; Theocr. 2, 35; Bion 1, 18; Her. 4, 75; -όμενος 3, 117; Theophr. Sign. 3, 46; Luc. D. Mort. 10, 13, ὠρῦ- only Com. Fr. (Plat.) 2, 659; Dion. Per. 83: imp. ὠρύετο Philostr. Apoll. 278, ὠρύοντο Coluth. 116: aor. ὠρυσάμην Theocr. 1, 71; Q. Sm. 12, 518; imper. ὤρυσαι Pind. Ol. 9, 109; ὠρύσασθαι Plut. Mor. 973. This verb is not in good Attic prose. Rhedantz however has lately edited ὠρυομένας for ὀρωμ- Lycurg. 40.

'Ωστίζομαι *To be pushed, jostled about, press, squeeze* (freq. from ὠθέω), pass. and mid. Com. Fr. (Telecl.) 2, 362; Ar. Ach. 42. Plut. 330; Luc. Lexiph. 4: fut. ὠστιοῦμαι Ar. Ach. 24. 844.

'Ωφελέω *To aid* (ὄφελος), Simon. Am. 7, 97; Aesch. Pers. 842; Soph. O. R. 141; Ar. Eq. 94; Her. 2, 95; Antiph. 5, 51; Thuc. 2, 87; Isocr. 12, 223: imp. ὠφέλουν Eur. Ph. 402; Ar. Vesp. 445; Thuc. 2, 77, -λεε Her. 3, 126: fut. -λήσω Eur. Suppl. 1107; Ar. Av. 358; Hippocr. 2, 476; Thuc. 6, 15; Isocr. 6, 5; Pl. Leg. 820: aor. ὠφέλησα Eur. Andr. 681; Her. 3, 127; Antiph. 5, 2; Thuc. 2, 42; Lys. 12, 26; -ήσαις Ar. Plut. 1134, but -ήσειε Nub. 753; Isocr. 5, 76; Hyperid. 4, 27, 6: p. ὠφέληκα Hippocr. 2, 318; Isae. 5, 45; Pl. Gorg. 511: plp. ὠφελήκη for -ειν, Apol. 31: p. p. -ημαι Lys. 21, 18; Pl. Gorg. 512; Dem. 24, 162; -ημένος Aesch. Pr. 222: plp. -ητο Thuc. 6, 60: aor. -ήθην Hippocr. 5, 114; Pl. Epist. 360; -ηθῶ Thuc. 6, 12; Pl. Rep. 526; -θείην Thuc. 2, 39; Pl. Leg. 913; -ηθῆναι Thuc. 5, 90; Lys. 31, 3; -θείς Thuc. 1, 43: fut. ὠφεληθήσομαι Hippocr. 7, 256; Andoc. 2, 22; Lys. 18, 20. 29, 4; Pl. Theag. 128; Isae. 10, 16; Xen. Mem. 2, 7, 8 (Kühner, Saupp. Breitb.). 3, 3, 15. Cyr. 3, 2, 20 (Kühner, Popp. -λήσομαι Dind. Saupp.): more freq. as pass. fut. mid. ὠφελήσομαι Thuc. 6, 18. 7, 67; Xen. Mem. 1, 6, 14. 3, 7, 9. 3, 11, 3. Oec. 2, 8; Pl. Rep. 343; Lys. 19, 61 (Ms. C. Bekk. B. Saupp. Scheibe, -ηθήσομαι Ms. X. Westerm. Rauch. Frohberg); Dem. 18, 144: pres. ὠφελοῦμαι Thuc. 3, 42; imper. ὠφελείσθωσαν 3, 67 (-είσθων Stahl). Vb. ὠφελητέος Xen. Mem. 2, 1, 28.

FINIS.

C
Pr
BV be obtained at www.ICGtesting.com
413

5B/57/P